University Casebook Series

ACCOUNTING AND THE LAW, Third Edition (1964), with Problem Pamphlet

The late James L. Dohr, Director, Institute of Accounting, Columbia University,

Ellis L. Phillips, Jr., Professor of Law, Columbia University.

George C. Thompson, Professor, Columbia University Graduate School of Business, and

William C. Warren, Professor of Law, Columbia University.

ACCOUNTING, LAW AND (1949)

Donald Schapiro, Instructor in Law, Yale University, and

Ralph Wienshienk, Visiting Lecturer in Law, Yale University.

ACCOUNTING, MATERIALS ON, (1959), with 1968 Supplement

Robert Amory, Jr., Esq.,

W. Covington Hardee, Esq., Third Edition by

David R. Herwitz, Professor of Law, Harvard University, and

Donald T. Trautman, Professor of Law, Harvard University.

ADMINISTRATIVE LAW, Fifth Edition (1970), with 1973 Problems Supplement

Walter Gellhorn, Professor of Law, Columbia University, and

Clark Byse, Professor of Law, Harvard University.

ADMIRALTY (1969) with 1972 Supplement

Jo Desha Lucas, Professor of Law, University of Chicago.

ADMIRALTY (1954)

The late Stanley Morrison, Professor of Law, Stanford University, and

The late George W. Stumberg, Professor of Law, University of Texas.

ADVOCACY, INTRODUCTION TO (1970) with Supplementary Cases Pamphlet

Board of Student Advisers, Harvard Law School.

AGENCY–ASSOCIATIONS–EMPLOYMENT–PARTNERSHIPS (1972)

Reprinted from Conard, Knauss & Siegel's Enterprise Organization

AGENCY, see also Enterprise Organization

ANTITRUST LAW (1967), with 1969 Supplement

Harlan M. Blake, Professor of Law, Columbia University.

Robert Pitofsky, Professor of Law, Georgetown University.

ARBITRATION (1968)

The late Shelden D. Elliott, Professor of Law, New York University.

BANKRUPTCY ACT (Annotated) 1967 Edition

The late James Angell MacLachlan, Professor of Law Emeritus, Harvard University.

BIOGRAPHY OF A LEGAL DISPUTE, THE: An Introduction to American Civil Procedure (1968)

Marc A. Franklin, Professor of Law, Stanford University.

UNIVERSITY CASEBOOK SERIES — Continued

BUSINESS ORGANIZATION, see also Enterprise Organization

BUSINESS PLANNING (1966) with 1973 Problem Supplement
David R. Herwitz, Professor of Law, Harvard University.

BUSINESS TORTS (1972)
Milton Handler, Professor of Law, Columbia University.

CIVIL PROCEDURE, see Procedure

COMMERCIAL AND CONSUMER TRANSACTIONS (1972) with 1973 Supplement
William E. Hogan, Professor of Law, Cornell University.
William D. Warren, Professor of Law, Stanford University.

COMMERCIAL AND INVESTMENT PAPER, Third Edition (1964) with Statutory Materials
Roscoe T. Steffen, Professor of Law, University of California, Hastings College of the Law.

COMMERCIAL LAW, CASES & MATERIALS ON, Second Edition (1968) with Statutory Supplement
E. Allan Farnsworth, Professor of Law, Columbia University.
John Honnold, Professor of Law, University of Pennsylvania.

COMMERCIAL PAPER (1968), with Statutory Supplement
E. Allan Farnsworth, Professor of Law, Columbia University.

COMMERCIAL PAPER AND BANK DEPOSITS AND COLLECTIONS (1967) with Statutory Supplement
William D. Hawkland, Professor of Law, University of Illinois.

COMMERCIAL TRANSACTIONS—Text, Cases and Problems, Fourth Edition (1968)
Robert Braucher, Professor of Law, Harvard University, and
The late Arthur E. Sutherland, Jr., Professor of Law, Harvard University.

COMPARATIVE LAW, Third Edition (1970)
Rudolf B. Schlesinger, Professor of Law, Cornell University.

COMPETITIVE PROCESS, LEGAL REGULATION OF THE (1972) with Statutory Supplement
Edmund W. Kitch, Professor of Law, University of Chicago.
Harvey S. Perlman, Professor of Law, University of Nebraska.

CONFLICT OF LAWS, Sixth Edition (1971)
Willis L. M. Reese, Professor of Law, Columbia University, and
Maurice Rosenberg, Professor of Law, Columbia University.

CONSTITUTIONAL LAW, Fourth Edition (1973)
Edward L. Barrett, Jr., Professor of Law, University of California, Davis.
Paul W. Bruton, Professor of Law, University of Pennsylvania.

CONSTITUTIONAL LAW, Eighth Edition (1970) with 1973 Supplement
Gerald Gunther, Professor of Law, Stanford University.
Noel T. Dowling, late Professor of Law, Columbia University.

CONSTITUTIONAL LAW, INDIVIDUAL RIGHTS IN (1970) with 1973 Supplement

Gerald Gunther, Professor of Law, Stanford University.
Noel T. Dowling, late Professor of Law, Columbia University.

CONTRACT LAW AND ITS APPLICATION (1971)

Addison Mueller, Professor of Law, University of California, Los Angeles.
Arthur I. Rosett, Professor of Law, University of California, Los Angeles.

CONTRACT LAW, STUDIES IN (1970)

Edward J. Murphy, Professor of Law, University of Notre Dame.
Richard E. Speidel, Professor of Law, University of Virginia.

CONTRACTS AND CONTRACT REMEDIES, Fourth Edition (1957)

The late Harold Shepherd, Professor of Law Emeritus, Stanford University, and
Harry H. Wellington, Professor of Law, Yale University.

CONTRACTS AND CONTRACT REMEDIES, Second Edition (1969)

John P. Dawson, Professor of Law, Harvard University, and
Wm. Burnett Harvey, Professor of Law, Indiana University.

CONTRACTS, Second Edition (1972) with Statutory Supplement

E. Allan Farnsworth, Professor of Law, Columbia University.
William F. Young, Jr., Professor of Law, Columbia University.
Harry W. Jones, Professor of Law, Columbia University.

CONTRACTS (1971) with Statutory and Administrative Law Supplement

Ian R. Macneil, Professor of Law, University of Virginia.

CONVEYANCES, Second Edition (1941)

Marion R. Kirkwood, Professor of Law Emeritus, Stanford University.

COPYRIGHT, Unfair Competition, and Other Topics Bearing on the Protection of Literary, Musical, and Artistic Works (1960)

Benjamin Kaplan, Professor of Law, Harvard University, and
Ralph S. Brown, Jr., Professor of Law, Yale University.

CORPORATE FINANCE (1972)

Victor Brudney, Professor of Law, Harvard University.
Marvin A. Chirelstein, Professor of Law, Yale University.

CORPORATION LAW, with Statutory Supplement (1973)

Detlev F. Vagts, Professor of Law, Harvard University.

CORPORATIONS, Fourth Edition—Unabridged (1969) with Case Supplement and Special Supplement

William L. Cary, Professor of Law, Columbia University.

CORPORATIONS, Fourth Edition—Abridged (1970) with Case Supplement and Special Supplement

William L. Cary, Professor of Law, Columbia University.

CORPORATIONS (1972)

Reprinted from Conard, Knauss & Siegels' Enterprise Organization

CORPORATIONS, see also Enterprise Organization

CORRECTIONAL PROCESS (1971) (Pamphlet)

Reprinted from Miller, Dawson, Dix and Parnas's Criminal Justice Administration & Related Processes

CREDITORS' RIGHTS, Fifth Edition (1957)

The late John Hanna, Professor of Law Emeritus, Columbia University, and The late James Angell MacLachlan, Professor of Law Emeritus, Harvard University.

CREDITORS' RIGHTS AND CORPORATE REORGANIZATION, Fifth Edition (1957)

The late John Hanna, Professor of Law Emeritus, Columbia University, and The late James Angell MacLachlan, Professor of Law Emeritus, Harvard University.

CREDITORS' RIGHTS AND SECURED TRANSACTIONS, 1967

William E. Hogan, Professor of Law, Cornell University.
William D. Warren, Professor of Law, Stanford University.

CRIMINAL JUSTICE, THE ADMINISTRATION OF, CASES AND MATERIALS ON, Second Edition (1969)

Francis C. Sullivan, Professor of Law, Louisiana State University.
Paul Hardin III, Professor of Law, Duke University.
John Huston, Professor of Law, University of Washington.
Frank R. Lacy, Professor of Law, University of Oregon.
Daniel E. Murray, Professor of Law, University of Miami.
George W. Pugh, Professor of Law, Louisiana State University.

CRIMINAL JUSTICE, Third Edition, 1968, two volumes: I. Criminal Law, II. Criminal Law Administration, with 1971 Supplement

Fred E. Inbau, Professor of Law, Northwestern University.
James R. Thompson, Professor of Law, Northwestern University, and Claude R. Sowle, President, Ohio University.

CRIMINAL JUSTICE ADMINISTRATION AND RELATED PROCESSES (1971) with Supplement

Frank W. Miller, Professor of Law, Washington University.
Robert O. Dawson, Professor of Law, University of Texas.
George E. Dix, Professor of Law, University of Texas.
Raymond I. Parnas, Professor of Law, University of California, Davis.

CRIMINAL LAW (1969)

Lloyd L. Weinreb, Professor of Law, Harvard University.

CRIMINAL LAW AND ITS ADMINISTRATION (1940), with 1956 Supplement

The late Jerome Michael, Professor of Law, Columbia University, and Herbert Wechsler, Professor of Law, Columbia University.

CRIMINAL LAW AND PROCEDURE, Fourth Edition (1972)

Rollin M. Perkins, Professor of Law, University of California, Hastings College of the Law.

CRIMINAL PROCESS (1969)

Lloyd L. Weinreb, Professor of Law, Harvard University.

DAMAGES, Second Edition (1952)

The late Charles T. McCormick, Professor of Law, University of Texas, and The late William F. Fritz, Professor of Law, University of Texas.

DECEDENTS' ESTATES (1971)

Max Rheinstein, Professor of Law Emeritus, University of Chicago.
Mary Ann Glendon, Professor of Law, Boston College Law School.

DECEDENTS' ESTATES AND TRUSTS, Fourth Edition (1971)

John Ritchie III, Professor of Law, University of Virginia,
Neill H. Alford, Jr., Professor of Law, University of Virginia, and
Richard W. Effland, Professor of Law, Arizona State University.

DECEDENTS' ESTATES AND TRUSTS (1968)

Howard R. Williams, Professor of Law, Stanford University.

DOMESTIC RELATIONS (1970), with Statutory Supplement

Monrad G. Paulsen, Dean of the Law School, University of Virginia.
Walter Wadlington, Professor of Law, University of Virginia.
Julius Goebel, Jr., Professor of Law Emeritus, Columbia University.

DOMESTIC RELATIONS: STATUTORY MATERIALS

Monrad G. Paulsen, Dean of the Law School, University of Virginia.
Walter Wadlington, Professor of Law, University of Virginia.

DOMESTIC RELATIONS—Civil and Canon Law (1963)

Philip A. Ryan, Professor of Law, Georgetown University, and
Dom David Granfield, Associate Professor, Catholic University of America.

DYNAMICS OF AMERICAN LAW, THE: Courts, the Legal Process and Freedom of Expression (1968)

Marc A. Franklin, Professor of Law, Stanford University.

ENTERPRISE ORGANIZATION (1972)

Alfred F. Conard, Professor of Law, University of Michigan.
Robert L. Knauss, Dean of the School of Law, Vanderbilt University.
Stanley Siegel, Professor of Law, University of Michigan.

ENVIRONMENTAL PROTECTION, SELECTED LEGAL AND ECONOMIC ASPECTS OF (1971)

Charles J. Meyers, Professor of Law, Stanford University.
A. Dan Tarlock, Professor of Law, Indiana University.

EQUITY, Fifth Edition (1967)

The late Zechariah Chafee, Jr., Professor of Law, Harvard University, and
Edward D. Re, Professor of Law, St. John's University.

EQUITY, RESTITUTION AND DAMAGES (1969)

Robert Childres, Professor of Law, Northwestern University.

ESTATE PLANNING PROBLEMS (1973)

David Westfall, Professor of Law, Harvard University.

ETHICS, see Legal Profession

EVIDENCE, Second Edition (1972)

David W. Louisell, Professor of Law, University of California, Berkeley,
John Kaplan, Professor of Law, Stanford University,
Jon R. Waltz, Professor of Law, Northwestern University.

EVIDENCE, Sixth Edition (1973) with Statutory Supplement

John M. Maguire, Professor of Law Emeritus, Harvard University.
Jack B. Weinstein, Professor of Law, Columbia University.
James H. Chadbourn, Professor of Law, Harvard University.
John H. Mansfield, Professor of Law, Harvard University.

EVIDENCE (1968)

Francis C. Sullivan, Professor of Law, Louisiana State University,
Paul Hardin, III, Professor of Law, Duke University.

FEDERAL COURTS, Fifth Edition (1970) with 1973 Supplement

The late Charles T. McCormick, Professor of Law, University of Texas, James H. Chadbourn, Professor of Law, Harvard University, and Charles Alan Wright, Professor of Law, University of Texas.

FEDERAL COURTS AND THE FEDERAL SYSTEM, Second Edition (1973)

The late Henry M. Hart, Jr., Professor of Law, Harvard University.
Herbert Wechsler, Professor of Law, Columbia University.
Paul M. Bator, Professor of Law, Harvard University.
Paul J. Mishkin, Professor of Law, University of California, Berkeley.
David L. Shapiro, Professor of Law, Harvard University.

FEDERAL RULES OF CIVIL PROCEDURE, 1973 Edition

FEDERAL TAXATION, see Taxation

FREE ENTERPRISE AND ECONOMIC ORGANIZATION, Fourth Edition (1972)

Louis B. Schwartz, Professor of Law, University of Pennsylvania.

FUTURE INTERESTS AND ESTATE PLANNING (1961) with 1962 Supplement

The late W. Barton Leach, Profesesor of Law, Harvard University, and James K. Logan, Dean of the Law School, University of Kansas.

FUTURE INTERESTS (1958)

The late Philip Mechem, Professor of Law Emeritus, University of Pennsylvania.

FUTURE INTERESTS (1970)

Howard R. Williams, Professor of Law, Stanford University.

HOUSING (THE ILL-HOUSED) (1971)

Peter W. Martin, Professor of Law, Cornell University.

INJUNCTIONS (1972)

Owen M. Fiss, Professor of Law, University of Chicago.

INSURANCE (1971)

William F. Young, Professor of Law, Columbia University.

INTELLECTUAL PROPERTY (1960–71) (Prepared for use as a supplement to Kaplan & Brown: Copyright, Unfair Competition and Other Topics (1972)

Albert P. Blaustein, Professor of Law, Rutgers University, Camden.
Robert A. Gorman, Professor of Law, University of Pennsylvania.

INTERNATIONAL LAW, See also Transnational Legal Problems and United Nations Law

INTERNATIONAL LEGAL SYSTEM (1973) with Documentary Supplement

Noyes E. Leech, Professor of Law, University of Pennsylvania.
Covey T. Oliver, Professor of Law, University of Pennsylvania.
Joseph Modeste Sweeney, Dean of the School of Law, Tulane University.

INTERNATIONAL TRADE AND INVESTMENT, REGULATION OF (1970)

Carl H. Fulda, Professor of Law, University of Texas,
Warren F. Schwartz, Professor of Law, University of Virginia.

INTERNATIONAL TRANSACTIONS AND RELATIONS (1960)

Milton Katz, Professor of Law, Harvard University, and
Kingman Brewster, Jr., President, Yale University.

INTRODUCTION TO THE STUDY OF LAW (1970)

E. Wayne Thode, Professor of Law, University of Utah.
J. Leon Lebowitz, Professor of Law, University of Texas.
Lester J. Mazor, Professor of Law, University of Utah.

INTRODUCTION TO LAW, see also Legal Method, also On Law In Courts, also Dynamics of American Law

JUDICIAL CODE: Rules of Procedure in the Federal Courts with Excerpts from the Criminal Code, 1973 Edition

The late Henry M. Hart, Jr., Professor of Law, Harvard University, and Herbert Wechsler, Professor of Law, Columbia University.

JURISPRUDENCE (Temporary Edition Hard Bound) (1949)

Lon L. Fuller, Professor of Law, Harvard University.

JUVENILE COURTS (1967)

Hon. Orman W. Ketcham, Juvenile Court of the District of Columbia.
Monrad G. Paulsen, Dean of the Law School, University of Virginia.

JUVENILE JUSTICE PROCESS (1971) (Pamphlet)

Reprinted from Miller, Dawson, Dix & Parnas's Criminal Justice Administration & Related Processes

LABOR LAW, Seventh Edition (1969) with Statutory Supplement and 1973 Case Supplement

Archibald Cox, Professor of Law, Harvard University, and Derek C. Bok, President, Harvard University.

LABOR LAW (1968) with Statutory Supplement

Clyde W. Summers, Professor of Law, Yale University.
Harry H. Wellington, Professor of Law, Yale University.

LABOR RELATIONS (1949)

The late Harry Shulman, Dean of the Law School, Yale University, and Neil Chamberlain, Professor of Economics, Columbia University.

LAND FINANCING (1970)

Norman Penney, Professor of Law, Cornell University.
Richard F. Broude, Professor of Law, Georgetown University.

LAW, LANGUAGE AND ETHICS (1972)

William R. Bishin, Professor of Law, University of Southern California.
Christopher D. Stone, Professor of Law, University of Southern California.

LEGAL DRAFTING (1951)

Robert N. Cook, Professor of Law, University of Cincinnati.

LEGAL METHOD, Second Edition (1952)

Noel T. Dowling, late Professor of Law, Columbia University,
The late Edwin W. Patterson, Professor of Law, Columbia University, and
Richard R. B. Powell, Professor of Law, University of California, Hastings College of the Law.
Second Edition by Harry W. Jones, Professor of Law, Columbia University.

LEGAL METHODS (1969)

Robert N. Covington, Professor of Law, Vanderbilt University,
E. Blythe Stason, Professor of Law, Vanderbilt University,
John W. Wade, Professor of Law, Vanderbilt University,
The late Elliott E. Cheatham, Professor of Law, Vanderbilt University,
Theodore A. Smedley, Professor of Law, Vanderbilt University.

LEGAL PROFESSION (1970)

Samuel D. Thurman, Dean of the College of Law, University of Utah.
Ellis L. Phillips, Jr., Professor of Law, Columbia University.
The late Elliott E. Cheatham, Professor of Law, Vanderbilt University.

LEGISLATION, Third Edition (1973)

Horace E. Read, Vice President, Dalhousie University.
John W. MacDonald, Professor of Law, Cornell Law School,
Jefferson B. Fordham, Professor of Law, University of Utah, and
William J. Pierce, Professor of Law, University of Michigan.

LOCAL GOVERNMENT LAW (1949)

Jefferson B. Fordham, Professor of Law, University of Utah.

MENTAL HEALTH PROCESS (1971) (Pamphlet)

Reprinted from Miller, Dawson, Dix & Parnas's Criminal Justice Administration & Related Processes

MODERN REAL ESTATE TRANSACTIONS, Second Edition (1958)

Allison Dunham, Professor of Law, University of Chicago.

MUNICIPAL CORPORATIONS, see Local Government Law

NEGOTIABLE INSTRUMENTS, see Commercial Paper

NEW YORK PRACTICE, Second Edition (1968)

Herbert Peterfreund, Professor of Law, New York University,
Joseph M. McLaughlin, Dean of the Law School, Fordham University.

OIL AND GAS, Second Edition (1964)

Howard R. Williams, Professor of Law, Stanford University,
Richard C. Maxwell, Professor of Law, University of California, Los Angeles, and
Charles J. Meyers, Professor of Law, Stanford University.

ON LAW IN COURTS (1965)

Paul J. Mishkin, Professor of Law, University of California, Berkeley.
Clarence Morris, Professor of Law, University of Pennsylvania.

OWNERSHIP AND DEVELOPMENT OF LAND (1965)

Jan Krasnowiecki, Professor of Law, University of Pennsylvania.

PARTNERSHIP PLANNING (1970) (Pamphlet)

William L. Cary, Professor of Law, Columbia University.

PATENT, TRADEMARK AND COPYRIGHT LAW (1959)

E. Ernest Goldstein, Professor of Law, University of Texas.

PLEADING & PROCEDURE: STATE AND FEDERAL, Third Edition (1973)

David W. Louisell, Professor of Law, University of California, Berkeley, and
Geoffrey C. Hazard, Jr., Professor of Law, Yale University.

POLICE FUNCTION (1971) (Pamphlet)

Reprinted from Miller, Dawson, Dix & Parnas's Criminal Justice Administration and Related Processes

PROCEDURE—Biography of a Legal Dispute (1968)

Marc A. Franklin, Professor of Law, Stanford University.

PROCEDURE—CIVIL PROCEDURE (1961)

James H. Chadbourn, Professor of Law, Harvard University, and
A. Leo Levin, Professor of Law, University of Pennsylvania.

PROCEDURE—CIVIL PROCEDURE, Third Edition (1973)

Richard H. Field, Professor of Law, Harvard University, and
Benjamin Kaplan, Professor of Law, Harvard University.

PROCEDURE—CIVIL PROCEDURE, Second Edition (1970)

Maurice Rosenberg, Professor of Law, Columbia University,
Jack B. Weinstein, Professor of Law, Columbia University.
Hans Smit, Professor of Law, Columbia University.

PROCEDURE—FEDERAL RULES OF CIVIL PROCEDURE, 1971 Edition

PROCEDURE PORTFOLIO (1962)

James H. Chadbourn, Professor of Law, Harvard University, and
A. Leo Levin, Professor of Law, University of Pennsylvania.

PRODUCTS AND THE CONSUMER: DECEPTIVE PRACTICES (1972)

W. Page Keeton, Dean of the School of Law, University of Texas,
Marshall S. Shapo, Professor of Law, University of Virginia.

PRODUCTS AND THE CONSUMER: DEFECTIVE AND DANGEROUS PRODUCTS (1970)

W. Page Keeton, Dean of the School of Law, University of Texas,
Marshall S. Shapo, Professor of Law, University of Virginia.

PROPERTY, Third Edition (1972)

John E. Cribbet, Dean of the Law School, University of Illinois,
The late William F. Fritz, Professor of Law, University of Texas, and
Corwin W. Johnson, Professor of Law, University of Texas.

PROPERTY—PERSONAL (1953)

The late S. Kenneth Skolfield, Professor of Law Emeritus, Boston University.

PROPERTY—PERSONAL, Third Edition (1954)

The late Everett Fraser, Dean of the Law School Emeritus, University of Minnesota—Third Edition by
Charles W. Taintor II, late Professor of Law, University of Pittsburgh.

PROPERTY—REAL—INTRODUCTION, Third Edition (1954)

The late Everett Fraser, Dean of the Law School Emeritus, University of Minnesota.

PROPERTY—REAL PROPERTY AND CONVEYANCING (1954)

Edward E. Bade, late Professor of Law, University of Minnesota.

PROPERTY, REAL, PROBLEMS IN (Pamphlet) (1969)

Edward H. Rabin, Professor of Law, University of California, Davis.

PUBLIC UTILITY LAW, see Free Enterprise, also Regulated Industries

RECEIVERSHIP AND CORPORATE REORGANIZATION, see Creditors' Rights

REGULATED INDUSTRIES (1967) with Statutory Supplement

William K. Jones, Professor of Law, Columbia University.

RESTITUTION, Second Edition (1966)

John W. Wade, Professor of Law, Vanderbilt University.

SALES AND SECURITY, Fourth Edition (1962), with Statutory Supplement

George G. Bogert, James Parker Hall Professor of Law Emeritus, University of Chicago.
The late William E. Britton, Professor of Law, University of California, Hastings College of the Law, and
William D. Hawkland, Professor of Law, University of Illinois.

SALES AND SALES FINANCING, Third Edition (1968) with Statutory Supplement

John Honnold, Professor of Law, University of Pennsylvania.

SECURITY, Third Edition (1959)

The late John Hanna, Professor of Law Emeritus, Columbia University

SECURITIES REGULATION, Third Edition (1972) with 1973 Statutory and Case Supplement

Richard W. Jennings, Professor of Law, University of California, Berkeley.
Harold Marsh, Jr., Professor of Law, University of California, Los Angeles.

SOCIAL WELFARE AND THE INDIVIDUAL (1971)

Robert J. Levy, Professor of Law, University of Minnesota.
Thomas P. Lewis, Professor of Law, Boston University.
Peter W. Martin, Professor of Law, Cornell University.

TAXATION, FEDERAL, Sixth Edition (1966) with 1972 Supplement

Erwin N. Griswold, Solicitor General of the United States.

TAXATION, FEDERAL ESTATE AND GIFT, 1961 Edition with 1973 Supplement

William C. Warren, Professor of Law, Columbia University, and
Stanley S. Surrey, Professor of Law, Harvard University.

TAXATION, FEDERAL INCOME (1972)

James J. Freeland, Professor of Law, University of Florida.
Richard B. Stephens, Professor of Law, University of Florida.

TAXATION, FEDERAL INCOME, Volume I, Personal Tax (1972); Volume II, Corporate and Partnership Taxation (1973)

Stanley S. Surrey, Professor of Law, Harvard University.
William C. Warren, Professor of Law, Columbia University.
Paul R. McDaniel, Professor of Law, Boston College Law School.
Hugh J. Ault, Professor of Law, Boston College Law School.

TORT LAW AND ALTERNATIVES: INJURIES AND REMEDIES (1971)

    Marc A. Franklin, Professor of Law, Stanford University.

TORTS, Second Edition (1952)

    The late Harry Shulman, Dean of the Law School, Yale University, and Fleming James, Jr., Professor of Law, Yale University.

TORTS, Fifth Edition (1971)

    The late William L. Prosser, Professor of Law, University of California, Hastings College of the Law.

    John W. Wade, Professor of Law, Vanderbilt University.

TRADE REGULATION, Fourth Edition (1967) with 1970 Supplement

    Milton Handler, Professor of Law, Columbia University.

TRADE REGULATION, see Free Enterprise

TRANSNATIONAL LEGAL PROBLEMS (1968) with Documentary Supplement

    Henry J. Steiner, Professor of Law, Harvard University,

    Detlev F. Vagts, Professor of Law, Harvard University.

TRIAL ADVOCACY (1968)

    A. Leo Levin, Professor of Law, University of Pennsylvania,

    Harold Cramer, Esq., Member of the Philadelphia Bar, (Maurice Rosenberg, Professor of Law, Columbia University, as consultant).

TRUSTS, Fourth Edition (1967)

    George G. Bogert, James Parker Hall Professor of Law Emeritus, University of Chicago.

    Dallin H. Oaks, President, Brigham Young University.

TRUSTS AND SUCCESSION, Second Edition (1968)

    George E. Palmer, Professor of Law, University of Michigan.

UNFAIR COMPETITION, see Competitive Process and Business Torts

UNITED NATIONS IN ACTION (1968)

    Louis B. Sohn, Professor of Law, Harvard University.

UNITED NATIONS LAW, Second Edition (1967) with Documentary Supplement (1968)

    Louis B. Sohn, Professor of Law, Harvard University.

WATER RESOURCE MANAGEMENT (1971) with 1973 Supplement

    Charles J. Meyers, Professor of Law, Stanford University.

    A. Dan Tarlock, Professor of Law, Indiana University.

WILLS AND ADMINISTRATION, 5th Edition (1961)

    The late Philip Mechem, Professor of Law, University of Pennsylvania, and

    The late Thomas E. Atkinson, Professor of Law, New York University.

WORLD LAW, see United Nations Law

University Casebook Series

EDITORIAL BOARD

CASES AND MATERIALS

ON

THE INTERNATIONAL LEGAL SYSTEM

By

NOYES E. LEECH
Professor of Law, University of Pennsylvania

COVEY T. OLIVER
Ferdinand Wakeman Hubbell, Professor of Law,
University of Pennsylvania

JOSEPH MODESTE SWEENEY
Dean and Professor of Law, Tulane University

Mineola, New York
THE FOUNDATION PRESS, INC.
1973

PREFACE

We have done our best to make this book a teaching tool. It may be useful also to practitioners and even to scholars—at least at some points. But what we have wanted most to do is to get the attention of today's law students, those men and women who, for better or worse, will have so much influence on how the world will go. We, like our brother and sister teachers in international legal studies, covet the attention of these students, largely because we know how much there is still to be done and how much new, trained minds are needed for operations—for actual decision-making in and about the system we call the "international legal system."

We try through the materials chosen and through the arrangement of them in the book to give to students bases for coming to perceive—with the guidance of their instructors—how the stuff that lawyers use (concepts, principles, norms, values, and interests) work, or are treated as if they worked. And beyond this understanding, we hope that individualized impressions will be formed as to how much is worthy of survival, how much ought to be pared away, what new applications are desirable for old principles, and how to formulate new rules within a paradigm of what is needed and what may be attainable. In a field that, for American lawyers at least, has seemed to be more than usually doctrinal and conceptualistic, we have tried to suggest functional ways of looking at problems and building new generalizations.

This book is intended for use in a core course in the international legal studies sector of a modern law school curriculum. The material does not slight the policy fundamentals of international public law in favor of bread and butter "international lawyering." But the book builds trails toward the various advanced courses in international transactions. It is also background for the further study of international organizations law and of transnational human rights law. With rearrangements that we shall suggest the book can be used outside law schools. For law schools that can include only one course in the sector, the coverage offered along specialty lines serves also the function of basic familiarization with them.

We have not wished to enlist in the old or current guerres des savants. These enliven but also often obfuscate the field. Nor do we see any point in beginning with the usual philosophic questions. We think that students ought to experience right from the start the reality that there are enough law-like materials and operations involved here to keep them occupied and concerned in professional ways. Our treatment of theory about international law, therefore, comes toward the end, when, we expect, students will be able to savor the implications and influences of legal philosophy in the context of the system they have observed in action. Some teachers may, of course, wish to alter our order of presentation, as to this or any other sequence.

We were all involved in the preparation of the Restatement of the Foreign Relations Law of the United States (1965), two of us as co-authors, the other as a substantive editor. We hope users and other readers will agree that we have achieved our objective not to make this a studybook companion to the Restatement. The Restatement was, as restatements are supposed to be, an evaluative and analytical presentation of lex lata, in this instance in a United States cross-section that included some (but not all) of the fundamentals of inter-national public law, national law related to foreign affairs operations, and transnational conflict of laws. Here our task is a different one. The Restatement sometimes helps us, as when it seems to have helped the courts in this country. But, to use a phrase remembered with affection from the chief Reporter, Dean Adrian S. Fisher, "We are not fanatics about it."

We have been enthusiastic—if not fanatical—anti-parochialists in our selections of materials for this book. Wherever the same point could be made as well or better by a more recent decision, we have eliminated the old war-horses, but we have kept an "oldie" where our analysis showed that—to vary the metaphor—it is the only piano player the system has on the particular point. Wherever interna-tional law norms must be communicated through national decisions and other actions, we have tried to break away from Anglo-American sources into those of other legal systems. To us it seems that realis-tic conditioning to the international legal system requires this. And we have not forgotten the pioneering earlier efforts in this regard of, inter alia, Manley O. Hudson, Ernest G. Lorenzen, George W. Stum-berg, and Hessel E. Yntema.

Recognizing that, unfortunately, the ratio of dross to pure gold is rather high in this field, we have pared sharply a lot of what we have included. We hope, however, that we know gold when we find it. The book should be comfortable to cover in a 60 classroom hour (3000 minute) course; manageable—with some variations in em-phasis—in a 45 hour course; and impossibly tight in a 30 hour course. We should be happy to make individualized suggestions to such of our brethren and potential users who might have—but not for long, we hope—to suffer such a curricular indignity as 30 hours for interna-tional law.

This book comes on the scene at a time when the actual interna-tional legal system is very different from the projections that many of us and our colleagues in casebook architecture and in teaching had made, roughly from 1946 on. We have tried to grasp the differences. We cheerfully and unstintingly admit our ineluctable indebtednesses to our admired friends who have published studybooks since World

War II, particularly to that grand master and friend of us all, Professor William W. Bishop, Jr. The editions of Bishop, from the earliest mimeograph which one of us used first in 1949 on coming fresh to this field from government, to the latest edition, are quite literally parts of our professional beings. So is what we learned from Hudson's and Dickinson's casebooks as students. And from great and scholarly teachers, such as Philip C. Jessup.

––––––

Small type footnotes are minimal herein. If we bother to write a note, we want it to be perceived psychologically by students as being as important for development of analysis as the cases and other third source items we have selected for insertion. The footnotes we have included are of two varieties. Numbered footnotes are those we have retained from cases and other quoted material. We have eliminated most of such footnotes but have kept the original numbering of those we have retained. **Our** own footnotes are indicated alphabetically.

We have selected two closing dates, one for cases, the other for treaties. Cases have been Shepardized through October 1, 1972. In general, treaty information is given as of January 1, 1972, largely because we have relied on the United States Department of State publication (as of that date), Treaties in Force, for dates of entry into force for the United States and for lists of parties. We have not been rigid about this and thus have included treaty information as of later dates when it has come to our attention, such as a treaty's recent entry into force for the United States.

Aside from these two formal closing dates, the informational flow in this book is cut off at approximately March 1, 1973.

We have prepared a companion volume of primary source materials, a Documentary Supplement, referred to frequently throughout the book. It contains most of the multilateral conventions and United Nations declarations that comprise the modern body of "international legislation" in the general fields of public international law and international organizations.

––––––

This book has taken us a long time, largely because we have not been sufficiently free of other duties to do it quickly. We hope this has helped to make the result reasonably well-joined, but we know that a lot more sanding and polishing must come in later editions. We shall be most grateful for users' suggestions, whether from teachers, students, or others—including reviewers.

NOYES E. LEECH
COVEY T. OLIVER
JOSEPH MODESTE SWEENEY

June 1, 1973

SUMMARY OF CONTENTS

SUMMARY OF CONTENTS

PART I. ALLOCATION OF COMPETENCE IN THE INTERNATIONAL SYSTEM

SUMMARY OF CONTENTS

PART V. METHODS OF OPERATION IN THE INTERNATIONAL SYSTEM

PART VI. THEORIES ABOUT THE INTERNATIONAL LEGAL SYSTEM

*

TABLE OF CONTENTS

CHAPTER 1

APPLICATION OF THE LAW OF THE INTERNATIONAL SYSTEM

TABLE OF CONTENTS

NOTE TO PARTS I, II AND III

PART I

ALLOCATION OF COMPETENCE IN THE INTERNATIONAL SYSTEM

CHAPTER 2

BASES OF JURISDICTION

CHAPTER 3

CONTROL AND USE OF THE SEA

TABLE OF CONTENTS

CHAPTER 4

CONTROL OF AIRSPACE, SPACE AND CELESTIAL BODIES

SECTION A.   ACTIVITIES IN AIRSPACE—Continued

PART II

LIMITATIONS ON THE EXERCISE OF JURISDICTION

CHAPTER 5

THE IMMUNITY OF STATES

CHAPTER 6

THE ACT OF STATE DOCTRINE

CHAPTER 7

RESOLUTION OF JURISDICTIONAL CONFLICTS

PART III

THE INDIVIDUAL IN THE INTERNATIONAL LEGAL SYSTEM

CHAPTER 8

PROTECTION AND ALLEGIANCE

CHAPTER 9

THE GROWTH OF STATE RESPONSIBILITY TO INDIVIDUALS

TABLE OF CONTENTS

CHAPTER 10

THE GROWTH OF INDIVIDUAL RESPONSIBILITY

PART IV

THE STRUCTURE OF THE INTERNATIONAL SYSTEM

CHAPTER 11

STATEHOOD: ANALYSIS OF THE CONCEPT

CHAPTER 12

RECOGNITION OF STATES AND GOVERNMENTS

TABLE OF CONTENTS

CHAPTER 13

DIPLOMATIC AND CONSULAR PROTECTION AND IMMUNITY

xlvii

CHAPTER 14

INTERNATIONAL ORGANIZATIONS

PART V

METHODS OF OPERATION IN THE INTERNATIONAL SYSTEM

CHAPTER 15

INTERNATIONAL AGREEMENTS: THE INTERNATIONAL LAW

CHAPTER 16

INTERNATIONAL AGREEMENTS: THE LAW OF THE UNITED STATES

CHAPTER 17

THE REGULATION OF ECONOMIC ACTIVITY WITHIN THE INTERNATIONAL SYSTEM

SECTION B. ECONOMIC INTERESTS OF ALIENS WITHIN
A STATE—Continued
3. The Fundamentals of International Claims—Continued

PART VI

THEORIES ABOUT THE INTERNATIONAL LEGAL SYSTEM

CHAPTER 18

THE INFLUENCE OF LEGAL PHILOSOPHY

PART VII

THE USE OF FORCE IN THE INTERNATIONAL SYSTEM

TABLE OF CONTENTS

A BIBLIOGRAPHY FOR COLLATERAL STUDY

The student who wishes to supplement his reading of the materials in this book will find this selected bibliography useful. We have not attempted to be comprehensive, finding that that task has been admirably performed by Jacob Robinson in his one volume work, International Law and Organization (A. W. Sijthoff-Leyden, 1967), a world-wide ranging bibliography, subtitled "General Sources of Information."

Some of the works cited below are the sources of materials reproduced in this casebook; many are not.

General Texts on International Law

American Law Institute, Restatement of the Law, Second, Foreign Relations Law of the United States (1965)

J. Brierly, The Law of Nations (6th ed. 1963)

I. Brownlie, Principles of Public International Law (2d ed. 1972)

C. Fenwick, International Law (4th ed. 1965)

W. Friedmann, The Changing Structure of International Law (1964)

C. Hyde, International Law (2d rev. ed. 1945) (3 vols.)

H. Kelsen, Principles of International Law (R. Tucker, 2d ed. 1966)

D. O'Connell, International Law (2d ed. 1970) (2 vols.)

L. Oppenheim, International Law (H. Lauterpacht, Vol. I, 8th ed. 1955; Vol. II, 7th ed. 1952)

C. Rousseau, Droit International Public (1970) (Tome I)

M. Sørensen, ed., Manual of Public International Law (1968)

J. Starke, An Introduction to International Law (7th ed. 1972)

A. Verdross, Völkerrecht (5th ed. 1964)

C. De Visscher, Theory and Reality in Public International Law (Corbett trans., rev. ed., 1968)

Texts on a Variety of Aspects of International Law and Organization

D. Bowett, Self-Defense in International Law (1958)

G. Clark and L. Sohn, World Peace Through World Law (3d ed. 1966)

A. Ehrenzweig, Private International Law (1967)

W. Friedmann and R. Pugh, eds., Legal Aspects of Foreign Investment (1959)

R. Falk, ed., The Vietnam War and International Law (3 vols. 1968–72)

R. Falk and S. Mendlovitz, eds., The Strategy of World Order (1966) (4 vols.)

L. Gross, ed., International Law in the Twentieth Century (1969)

K. Grzybowski, The Socialist Commonwealth of Nations (1964)

L. Henkin, Foreign Affairs and the Constitution (1972)

L. Henkin, How Nations Behave (1968)

M. Hudson, The Permanent Court of International Justice, 1920–1942 (1943)

M. Kaplan and N. Katzenbach, The Political Foundations of International Law (1961)

P. Jessup, A Modern Law of Nations (1948)

P. Jessup, Transnational Law (1956)

P. Jessup, The Use of International Law (1959)

J. Kunz, The Changing Law of Nations (1968)

O. Lissitzyn, International Law Today and Tomorrow (1965)

S. Metzger, International Law, Trade and Finance (1962)

M. McDougal and F. Feliciano, Law and Minimum World Public Order (1961)

M. McDougal, H. Lasswell, and J. Miller, The Interpretation of Agreements and World Public Order (1967)

Lord McNair, The Law of Treaties (1961)

H. Morgenthau, Politics Among Nations (4th ed. 1967)

D. O'Connell, State Succession in Municipal Law and International Law (1967) (2 vols.)

S. Rosenne, The Law and Practice of the International Court (1965) (2 vols.)

J. Stone, Aggression and World Order (1958)

J. Stone, Legal Controls of International Conflict (1954) [2d imp. rev'd w/supp. 1953–58 (1959)]

Texts on the United Nations

S. Bailey, The United Nations (1963)

I. Claude, Jr., The Changing United Nations (1967)

D. Coyle, The United Nations and How It Works (new ed. 1966)

L. Goodrich, E. Hambro and A. Simons, Charter of the United Nations (3d ed. 1969)

R. Higgins, The Development of International Law Through the Political Organs of the United Nations (1963)

P. Jacob and A. Atherton, The Dynamics of International Organization (1965)

H. Kelsen, The Law of the United Nations (1950)

H. Nicholas, The United Nations as a Political Institution (4th ed. 1971)

F. Seyersted, United Nations Forces in the Law of Peace and War (1966)

Digests

G. Hackworth, Digest of International Law (1940–1944) (8 vols.)

A. Kiss, Répertoire de la Pratique Française en Matière de Droit International Public (1962–1972) (7 vols.)

J. Moore, Digest of International Law (1906) (8 vols.)

C. Parry, A British Digest of International Law (1965 on) (multivolumed)

United Nations, Repertory of Practice of United Nations Organs (5 vols. and Table of Contents and Subject Index, 1955–57), with Supplement no. 1 (2 vols. 1958) and Supplement no. 2 (3 vols. 1963–64)

M. Whiteman, Digest of International Law (15 vols. 1963–73)

Coursebooks and Case Collections

W. Bishop, Jr., International Law: Cases and Materials (3d ed. 1971)

H. Briggs, The Law of Nations (2d ed. 1952)

A. Chayes, T. Ehrlich and A. Lowenfeld, International Legal Process (1968) (with Documents Supplement)

F. Deak, American International Law Cases (1971 on) (multivolumed)

E. Dickinson, Cases and Materials on International Law (1950)

W. Friedmann, O. Lissitzyn and R. Pugh, Cases and Materials on International Law (1969)

C. Fulda and W. Schwartz, Cases and Materials on the Regulation of International Trade and Investment (1970)

L. Green, International Law Through the Cases (3d ed. 1970)

R. Higgins, United Nations Peacekeeping 1946–1967 (1969) (2 vols.)

M. Hudson, Cases and Other Materials on International Law (3d ed. 1951)

L. Orfield and E. Re, Cases and Materials on International Law (rev. ed. 1965)

C. Parry, British International Law Cases (1964–1973) (9 vols.)

L. Sohn, Cases on United Nations Law (2d ed., rev. 1967) (with Basic Documents Supplement)

H. Steiner and D. Vagts, Transnational Legal Problems (1968) (with Documentary Supplement)

*

TABLE OF ABBREVIATIONS

The following are abbreviations that have been used by the editors in their citations to principal cases and major materials and in their notes.

A.B.A.J.	American Bar Association Journal
A.2d	Atlantic Reporter, Second Series
A.C.	Law Report series [British], House of Lords
A.D.2d	Appellate Division Reports, New York Supreme Court, Second Series
ADIZ	Air Defense Identification Zone
ALL E.R.	All England Law Reports [1936–date]
Am.J.Int'l L.	American Journal of International Law
Am.Soc.Int'l L.	American Society of International Law
ANCOM	Andean Common Market
Ann.Dig.	Annual Digest and Reports of International Law Cases [title of Int'l Law Reports prior to 1953]
Brit.Yr.B.Int'l Law	British Yearbook of International Law
C.A.	Law Report series, Court of Appeal
CACM	Central American Common Market
C.F.R.	Code of Federal Regulations
Cal.2d	California Supreme Court Reports, Second Series
Cal.L.Rev.	California Law Review
CCH Trade Cases	Trade Regulation Reporter [Commerce Clearing House]
Ch.	Law Report series, Chancery [1891–date]
Cong.Rec.	Congressional Record, United States
Cr.Cas.Res.	Law Report series, Crown Cases Reserved [1865–1875]
Dalloz Rec.Heb.	Dalloz, Recueil Hebdomadaire de Jurisprudence en matière civile, etc. [France]
DEWIZ	Distant Early Warning Identification Zone
ECOSOC Off.Rec.	United Nations Economic and Social Council, Official Records
EEC	European Economic Community
EFTA	European Free Trade Association
F.2d	Federal Reporter, Second Series [1924–date]
F.Supp.	Federal Supplement
Fed.Reg.	Federal Register
FCN	Friendship, Commerce and Navigation Treaties
FM	Department of the Army Field Manual
G.A.Res.	General Assembly Resolution
GATT	General Agreement on Tariffs and Trade
GNP	Gross national product
Harv.L.Rev.	Harvard Law Review
IATA	International Air Transport Association
ICI	Imperial Chemical Industries, Ltd.

I.C.A.O.	International Civil Aviation Organization
I.C.J.Rep.	International Court of Justice Reports
I.C.J.Y.B.	International Court of Justice Yearbook
Ill.Rev.Stat.	Illinois Revised Statutes
I.L.C.	International Law Commission
I.L.O.Off.Bull.	International Labour Office, Official Bulletin
Int'l & Comp.L.	International and Comparative Law Quarterly
Int'l L.Rep.	International Law Reports
IMT	International Military Tribunal
IRA	Irish Republican Army
ITT	International Telephone and Telegraph Corp.
K.B.	Law Report series, Kings Bench
LAFTA	Latin American Free Trade Association
L.N.T.S.	League of Nations Treaty Series
MFN	Most favored nation
Misc.	New York Miscellaneous [1892–1955]
Misc.2d	New York Miscellaneous, Second Series [1955–date]
MNEs	Multinational enterprises
NATO	North Atlantic Treaty Organization
N.E.	North Eastern Reporter [1885–1936]
N.J.Super.	New Jersey Superior Court Reports
N.Y.	New York Reports
N.Y.S.	New York Supplement [1888–1937]
N.Y.S.2d	New York Supplement, Second Series [1937–date]
OPIC	Overseas Private Investment Corporation
P.	Law Report series, Probate, Divorce and Admiralty
P.2d	Pacific Reporter, Second Series
P.C.I.J.	Permanent Court of International Justice
Pa.	Pennsylvania State Reports [1845–date]
Pub.L.	Public Law Number
S.Ct.	Supreme Court Reporter [U. S., 1882–date]
Sirey	Sirey, Recueil Général des Lois et des Arréts [France]
So.2d	Southern Reporter, Second Series [1941–date]
So.African L.Rep.	South African Law Reports
Stat.	Statutes at Large, United States
T.I.A.S.	Treaties and Other International Acts Series
T.L.R.	Times Law Reports [England, 1884–1952]
U.N.Conf.Int'l Org.	United Nations Conference on International Organization [San Francisco Conference]
UNCTAD	United Nations Conference on Trade and Development
U.N.Doc.	United Nations Document
U.N.Gen.Ass.Off.Rec.	United Nations General Assembly, Official Records
U.N.Gen.Ass.Off.Rec.Supp.	United Nations General Assembly Official Records, Supplement
U.N.Rep.Int'l Arb.Awards	United Nations Reports of International Arbitration Awards

TABLE OF ABBREVIATIONS

U.N.T.S.	United Nations Treaty Series
U.Pa.L.Rev.	University of Pennsylvania Law Review
U.S.	United States Supreme Court Reports
U.S.A.I.D.	United States Foreign Assistance Administration
U.S.App.D.C.	United States Court of Appeals, District of Columbia Circuit Reports
U.S.C.	United States Code
U.S.C.A.	United States Code Annotated
U.S.Dep't State Bull.	United States Department of State Bulletin
U.S.T.	U. S. Treaties and Other International Agreements
Vand.L.Rev.	Vanderbilt Law Review
W.L.R.	Weekly Law Reports [England, 1953–date]
Western Weekly Rep.	Western Weekly Reports, New Series [Canada]
Yale L.J.	Yale Law Journal

*

TABLE OF SECONDARY SOURCES

We have listed below the major secondary sources from which we have excerpted material that appears in this book, as well as certain of those sources to which passing reference has been made or which have been briefly quoted.

*

ACKNOWLEDGMENTS

Although many individuals have assisted us in our editorial tasks, we wish to express our appreciation especially to Margaret E. Gates and Wilhelm E. A. Wulf of Tulane University for their preparation of the index.

We wish gratefully to acknowledge permission extended by the following authors, publishers and organizations to reprint excerpts from the books, periodicals and other documents indicated in parentheses:

Almquist & Wiksell, Stockholm (excerpts from Scandinavian Studies in Law: Smith, International Law in Norwegian Courts); *American Bar Association* (excerpt from the American Bar Association Journal: Lippert, The Eichmann Case and the Nuremberg Trials); *American Bar Association, Section on International and Comparative Law* (excerpts from the Proceedings: Cisneros, The 200 Mile Limit in the South Pacific: A New Position in International Law with a Human and Juridical Content); *American Jewish Committee* (excerpts from Commentary Magazine: Bishop, The Question of War Crimes); *American Law Institute* (excerpts from Restatement of Foreign Relations Law of the United States); *American Society of International Law* (excerpts from American Journal of International Law, Proceedings of the American Society of International Law, International Journal: Lippert, The Eichmann Case and the Nuremberg Manley O. Hudson, International Tribunals, Past and Present); *Burroughs & Co., Ltd.*, Calgary, Alberta, Canada (excerpts from Western Weekly Reports); *Butterworth & Co., Ltd.*, London (excerpts from Annual Digest and International Law Reports); *Carnegie Endowment for International Peace* (excerpts from Phillipson, Introduction to 2 Gentili, Classics of International Law Carnegie Endowment, Section 5, and Wolff, Classics of International Law Carnegie Endowment); *The University of Chicago Press* (excerpts from Lay and Taubenfeld, The Law Relating to Activities of Man in Space); *The Christian Science Publishing Society* (excerpts from The Christian Science Monitor); *Editions du Centre National de la Recherche Scientifique* (excerpts from Kiss, Répertoire de la Pratique Francaise en Matière de Droit International Public); *Clarendon Press*, Oxford (excerpts from Brownlie, Principles of Public International Law); *Columbia Journal of Transnational Law* (excerpts from the Journal: Wolfgang G. Friedmann, The Reality of International Law—A Reappraisal); *Columbia University Press* (excerpts from Friedmann and Beguin, Joint International Business Ventures in Developing Countries; and Carlston, The Process of International Arbitration); *Commerce Clearing House, Inc.* (excerpts from CCH Common Market Reports and CCH Trade Cases); *Dalloz*, Paris (excerpts from Rousseau, Droit International

Public); *Department of the Army* (excerpts from Army Field Manual FM 27–10, The Law of Land Warfare, available from the Superintendent of Documents, U. S. Government Printing Office, Washington, D. C. 20402); *The Dorsey Press, Inc.* (excerpts from Jacob and Atherton, The Dynamics of International Organization); *Dow Jones & Co., Inc.* (excerpts from the Wall Street Journal); *Georgetown University* (excerpts from Metzger, International Law, Trade and Finance: Realities and Prospects); *The Hague Academy of International Law* (excerpts from Tunkin, Co-Existence and International Law; Recueil des Cours: Oliver, Contemporary Problems of Treaty Law, and McDougal, International Law, Power and Policy: A Contemporary Conception); *Harvard Law Review and A. J. Chayes* (excerpts from Chayes, A Common Lawyer Looks at International Law, Harvard Law Review); *Holt, Rinehart & Winston, Inc.* (excerpts from Stone [ed.], Wilson and The League of Nations; Kelsen, Principles of International Law; Kelsen and Tucker, Principles of International Law); *Incorporated Council of Law Reporting for England and Wales* and *Eastern Press, Ltd.*, London (excerpts from Weekly Law Reports); *International Bureau of Fiscal Documentation*, Amsterdam (excerpts from European Taxation and Supplementary Service to European Taxation); *Journal of Air Law & Commerce* (excerpts from the Journal: Lissitzyn, Bilateral Agreements on Air Transport); *Longman Group Ltd.*, London, and *David McKay Company, Inc.* (excerpts from L. Oppenheim, International Law, 8th Edition); *Macmillan Publishing Co., Inc.* (excerpts from The Guns of August by Barbara W. Tuchman; A Commentary on the Constitution of the United States by Bernard Schwartz; and Nuremberg by Calvocaressi); *Martinus Nijhoff*, The Hague (excerpts from Peaslee, Constitutions of Nations); *Michigan Law Review* (excerpts from the Review: Bilder, The Canadian Arctic Waters Pollution Prevention Act: New Stresses on the Law of the Sea; and Note, Punishment for War Crimes: Duty or Discretion?); *J. Murray*, London (excerpts from Austin, Jurisprudence); *The New York Times Company* (excerpts from the New York Times); *W. W. Norton & Company, Inc.* (excerpts from Robert F. Kennedy, Thirteen Days, A Memoir of the Cuban Missile Crisis); *OECD Publications Center* (excerpts); *Oxford University Press, Inc.* (excerpts from The Development of International Law Through the Political Organs of the United Nations by Rosalyn Higgins); *The Pall Mall Press*, London (Henkin, How Nations Behave); *Editions A. Pedone*, Paris, and *Rousseau* (excerpts from Revue Générale de Droit International Public); *University of Pennsylvania Law Review* and *Fred B. Rothman & Co.* (excerpts from the Review: Dickinson, The Law of Nations as Part of the Law of the United States); *The Philadelphia Inquirer* (excerpts); *Editions Polygraphiques*, Zurich (excerpts from Annuaire Suisse de Droit International); *Frederick A. Praeger, Inc.* (excerpts from Henkin, How Nations Behave; Lauterpacht, The Development of International Law by the International Court; Schwarzenberger, A Manual of International Law; Luard [ed.], The International Protection of Human Rights); *Princeton University Press* (excerpts from Charles de Visscher, translated by P. E. Corbett, Theory and Reality in Public International Law; and Gardner Patterson, Discrimination in International Trade, The Policy Issues: 1945–1965); *Quadrangle Books, Inc.* (excerpts from Taylor, Nuremberg and Vietnam); *Random House, Inc.* (excerpts from Hans J. Morgenthau, Politics Among Nations, Fourth Edition); *Russell & Volkening, Inc.* (excerpts from The Guns of August by Barbara W. Tuchman); *A. W. Sijthoff,* Leiden, Netherlands (excerpts from Nederlands Tijdschrift Voor International Recht [Netherlands International Law Review]; Rosenne, The Law and Practice of the International Court; Seyersted, United Nations Forces in the Law of Peace and War); *Stevens & Sons, Ltd.* (excerpts from Lauterpacht, The Development of International Law by the International Court; McNair, The Law of the Air; O'Connell, International Law; Schwarzenberger, A Manual of International Law; and the Law Quarterly Review); *Julius Stone* and *Wm. W. Gaunt & Sons, Inc.* (excerpts from Stone, Legal Controls of International Conflict); *Editions Techniques, S.A.,* Paris (excerpts from Journal du Droit International); *The Times-Picayune Publishing Company,* New Orleans (excerpts from The Times-Picayune); *Tulane Law Review* (excerpts from the Review); *U. S. News & World Report* (excerpts); *The Washington Post* (excerpts from Henkin, Sea Bed Pact Would Help U. S., and Schwebel, "Cognition" and the Peking Visit, Is the Recognition of Governments Obsolete?); *Wayne Law Review* (excerpts from the Review: Wilkes, The Use of World Resources without Conflict: Myths about the Territorial Sea); *John Wiley & Sons, Inc.* (excerpts from Kaplan and Katzenbach, The Political Foundations of International Law); *The Yale Law Journal Company* and *Fred B. Rothman & Company* (excerpts from The Yale Law Journal: McDougal and Schiel, The Hydrogen Bomb Tests in Perspective: Lawful Measures for Security).

*

TABLE OF CASES

The principal cases are in italic type. Cases cited or discussed are in roman type. References are to Pages.

TABLE OF CASES

TABLE OF CASES

†

THE INTERNATIONAL LEGAL SYSTEM

CASES AND MATERIALS

Chapter 1

APPLICATION OF THE LAW OF THE INTERNATIONAL SYSTEM

This book begins with a sketch of the structure of the present legal order of the planet. Along with many others, we think there is one, albeit less intricate and possibly less assuredly applicable than internal law in those modern states where there is a reasonably high correlation between the rules and what happens.

We could have begun with such classic introductory devices as: (1) Is "international law" law? (2) What is "law" anyway? (3) Can there be "law" if there is no supranational authority to impose it? We believe, however, that the student will be better able to deal with these questions after some exposure to the subject matter that is the corpus juris of what is called "international public law," "transnational law," and "foreign affairs law" and dealt with as such by lawyers all over the world, whether in advocacy, consultative or decision-making roles.

The more "jurisprudential" materials are in our Chapter 18. Some may prefer to take them earlier than this order suggests. Even so, we think Chapter 1 should be taken first.

The law we study is not adequate to the management of planetary affairs even now. A major purpose of a law school course in this area is to draw attention to the urgent need for the growth of order beyond the rules that have developed in the West, along with the national state system, over the past half millenium. In any case, it is imperative that men do the best they can with what is currently available.

Chapter 1 is analytically descriptive of the system. At the same time, it introduces some of the major operational challenges, viz: (1)

universality, (2) effectiveness, (3) state dissent from binding effect, (4) limitations of the arbitral-adjudicatory process as a means of resolving conflicts.

SECTION A. APPLICATION WITHIN NATIONAL LEGAL SYSTEMS

YES — *The Supreme Court of the United States: A municipal court?* A former Legal Adviser to the Department of State was discussing with the late Mr. Justice Frankfurter the position of national courts in the international legal system and said: "Mr. Justice, with all due deference, I would say that from the standpoint of international law, your court is but another municipal court and a decision of your court does not have any more effect internationally than a decision by a bureaucrat."

---

1. RULES OF CUSTOMARY INTERNATIONAL LAW NOT IN CONFLICT WITH DOMESTIC LAW

WEST RAND CENTRAL GOLD MINING CO. v. THE KING

England, King's Bench, 1905.
[1905] 2 K.B. 391.

The judgment of the Court (Lord Alverstone C. J., Wills and Kennedy JJ.) was read by

LORD ALVERSTONE C. J. In this case the Attorney-General, on behalf of the Crown, demurred to a petition of right presented in the month of June, 1904, by the West Rand Central Gold Mining Company, Limited. The petition of right alleged that two parcels of gold, amounting in all to the value of 3804£, had been seized by officials of the South African Republic—1104£ on October 2 in course of transit from Johannesburg to Cape Town, and 2700£ on October 9, taken from the bank premises of the petitioners. No further statement was made in the petition of the circumstances under which, or the right by which, the Government of the Transvaal Republic claimed to seize the gold; * * * The petition then alleged that a state of war commenced at 5 P.M. on October 11, 1899, that the forces of the late Queen conquered the Republic, and that by a Proclamation of September 1, 1900, the whole of the territories of the Republic were annexed to, and became part of, Her Majesty's dominions, and that the Government of the Republic ceased to exist. The petition then averred that by reason of the conquest and annexation Her Majesty succeeded to the sovereignty of the Transvaal Republic, and became entitled to its property; and that the obligation which vested in the Government was binding upon His present Majesty the King.

* * *

* * * His main proposition was divided into three heads. First, that, by international law, the Sovereign of a conquering State is liable for the obligations of the conquered; secondly, that international law forms part of the law of England; and, thirdly, that rights and obligations, which were binding upon the conquered State, must be protected and can be enforced by the municipal Courts of the conquering State.

In support of his first proposition Lord Robert Cecil cited passages from various writers on international law. In regard to this class of authority it is important to remember certain necessary limitations to its value. There is an essential difference, as to certainty and definiteness, between municipal law and a system or body of rules in regard to international conduct, which, so far as it exists at all (and its existence is assumed by the phrase "international law"), rests upon a consensus of civilized States, not expressed in any code or pact, nor possessing, in case of dispute, any authorized or authoritative interpreter; and capable, indeed, of proof, in the absence of some express international agreement, only by evidence of usage to be obtained from the action of nations in similar cases in the course of their history. It is obvious that, in respect of many questions that may arise, there will be room for difference of opinion as to whether such a consensus could be shewn to exist. * * * The views expressed by learned writers on international law have done in the past, and will do in the future, valuable service in helping to create the opinion by which the range of the consensus of civilized nations is enlarged. But in many instances their pronouncements must be regarded rather as the embodiments of their views as to what ought to be, from an ethical standpoint, the conduct of nations inter se, than the enunciation of a rule or practice so universally approved or assented to as to be fairly termed, even in the qualified sense in which that word can be understood in reference to the relations between independent political communities, "law." * * *

[margin note: WRITERS ENLARGE CONSENSUS AMONG NATIONS... BUT NOT ABSOLUTE RULE... NORMATIVE ONLY ∧ STATEMENTS]

Before, however, dealing with the specific passages in the writings of jurists upon which the suppliants rely, we desire to consider the proposition, that by international law the conquering country is bound to fulfil the obligations of the conquered, upon principle; and upon principle we think it cannot be sustained. When making peace the conquering Sovereign can make any conditions he thinks fit respecting the financial obligations of the conquered country, and it is entirely at his option to what extent he will adopt them. It is a case in which the only law is that of military force. This, indeed, was not disputed by counsel for the suppliants; but it was suggested that

[margin note: CONQUEROR NOT BOUND TO OLD DEBTS...]

although the Sovereign when making peace may limit the obligations to be taken over, if he does not do so they are all taken over, and no subsequent limitation can be put upon them. What possible reason can be assigned for such a distinction? * * * We can see no reason at all why silence should be supposed to be equivalent to a promise of universal novation of existing contracts with the Government of the conquered State. It was suggested that a distinction might be drawn between obligations incurred for the purpose of waging war with the conquering country and those incurred for general State expenditure. What municipal tribunal could determine, according to the laws of evidence to be observed by that tribunal, how particular sums had been expended, whether borrowed before or during the war? It was this and cognate difficulties which compelled Lord Robert Cecil ultimately to concede that he must contend that the obligation was absolute to take over all debts and contractual obligations incurred before war had been actually declared.

Turning now to the text-writers, we may observe that the proposition we have put forward that the conqueror may impose what terms he thinks fit in respect of the obligations of the conquered territory, and that he alone must be the judge in such a matter, is clearly recognised by Grotius: see "War and Peace," book iii. chap. 8, s. 4, and the Notes to Barbeyrac's edition of 1724, vol. ii. p. 632. For the assertion that a line is to be drawn at the moment of annexation, and that the conquering Sovereign has no right at any later stage to say what obligations he will or will not assume, we venture to think that there is no authority whatever. A doctrine was at one time urged by some of the older writers that to the extent of the assets taken over by the conqueror he ought to satisfy the debts of the conquered State. It is, in our opinion, a mere expression of the ethical views of the writers; but the proposition now contended for is a vast extension even of that doctrine. * * * But whatever may be the view taken of the opinions of these writers, they are, in our judgment, inconsistent with the law as recognised for many years in the English Courts; * * *

The second proposition urged by Lord Robert Cecil, that international law forms part of the law of England, requires a word of explanation and comment. It is quite true that whatever has received the common consent of civilized nations must have received the assent of our country, and that to which we have assented along with other nations in general may properly be called international law, and as such will be acknowledged and applied by our municipal tribunals when legitimate occasion arises for those tribunals to decide questions to which doctrines of international law may be relevant. But any doctrine so invoked must be one really accepted as binding between nations, and the international law sought to be applied must, like anything else, be proved by satisfactory evidence, which must shew either that the particular proposition put forward has been recognised

CT: Cardozo — if nations accept it

TEST:

and acted upon by our own country, or that it is of such a nature, and has been so widely and generally accepted, that it can hardly be supposed that any civilized State would repudiate it. The mere opinions of jurists, however eminent or learned, that it ought to be so recognised, are not in themselves sufficient. They must have received the express sanction of international agreement, or gradually have grown to be part of international law by their frequent practical recognition in dealings between various nations. We adopt the language used by Lord Russell of Killowen in his address at Saratoga in 1896 on the subject of international law and arbitration: "What, then, is international law? I know no better definition of it than that it is the sum of the rules or usages which civilized States have agreed shall be binding upon them in their dealings with one another." In our judgment, the second proposition for which Lord Robert Cecil contended in his argument before us ought to be treated as correct only if the term "international law" is understood in the sense, and subject to the limitations of application, which we have explained. * * * [T]he expressions used by Lord Mansfield when dealing with the particular and recognised rule of international law on this subject, that the law of nations forms part of the law of England, ought not to be construed so as to include as part of the law of England opinions of text-writers upon a question as to which there is no evidence that Great Britain has ever assented, and a fortiori if they are contrary to the principles of her laws as declared by her Courts. * * *

We pass now to consider the third proposition upon which the success of the suppliants in this case must depend—namely, that the claims of the suppliants based upon the alleged principle that the conquering State is bound by the obligations of the conquered can be enforced by petition of right. * * * Upon this part of the case there is a series of authorities from the year 1793 down to the present time holding that matters which fall properly to be determined by the Crown by treaty or as an act of State are not subject to the jurisdiction of the municipal Courts, and that rights supposed to be acquired thereunder cannot be enforced by such Courts. * * * We are of opinion, for the reasons given, that no right on the part of the suppliants is disclosed by the petition which can be enforced as against His Majesty in this or in any municipal Court; and we therefore allow the demurrer, with costs.

Judgment for the Crown.

THE PAQUETE HABANA
THE LOLA

United States Supreme Court, 1900.
175 U.S. 677, 20 S.Ct. 290.

MR. JUSTICE GRAY delivered the opinion of the court.

These are two appeals from decrees of the District Court of the United States for the Southern District of Florida, condemning two fishing vessels and their cargoes as prize of war.

Each vessel was a fishing smack, running in and out of Havana, and regularly engaged in fishing on the coast of Cuba; sailed under the Spanish flag; was owned by a Spanish subject of Cuban birth, living in the city of Havana; was commanded by a subject of Spain, also residing in Havana; and her master and crew had no interest in the vessel, but were entitled to shares, amounting in all to two thirds, of her catch, the other third belonging to her owner. Her cargo consisted of fresh fish, caught by her crew from the sea, put on board as they were caught, and kept and sold alive. Until stopped by the blockading squadron, she had no knowledge of the existence of the war, or of any blockade. She had no arms or ammunition on board, and made no attempt to run the blockade after she knew of its existence, nor any resistance at the time of the capture.

     * * *

Both the fishing vessels were brought by their captors into Key West. A libel for the condemnation of each vessel and her cargo as prize of war was there filed on April 27, 1898; a claim was interposed by her master, on behalf of himself and the other members of the crew, and of her owner; evidence was taken, showing the facts above stated; and on May 30, 1898, a final decree of condemnation and sale was entered, "the court not being satisfied that as a matter of law, without any ordinance, treaty or proclamation, fishing vessels of this class are exempt from seizure."

Each vessel was thereupon sold by auction; the Paquete Habana for the sum of $490; and the Lola for the sum of $800. * * *

     * * *

We are then brought to the consideration of the question whether, upon the facts appearing in these records, the fishing smacks were subject to capture by the armed vessels of the United States during the recent war with Spain.

By an ancient usage among civilized nations, beginning centuries ago, and gradually ripening into a rule of international law, coast fishing vessels, pursuing their vocation of catching and bringing in fresh fish, have been recognized as exempt, with their cargoes and crews, from capture as prize of war.

This doctrine, however, has been earnestly contested at the bar; and no complete collection of the instances illustrating it is to be found, so far as we are aware, in a single published work, although many are referred to and discussed by the writers on international law, notably in 2 Ortolan, Règles Internationales et Diplomatie de la Mer, (4th ed.) lib. 3, c. 2, pp. 51–56; in 4 Calvo, Droit International, (5th ed.) §§ 2367–2373; in De Boeck, Propriété Privée Ennemie sous Pavillon Ennemi, §§ 191–196; and in Hall, International Law, (4th ed.) § 148. It is therefore worth the while to trace the history of the rule, from the earliest accessible sources, through the increasing recognition of it, with occasional setbacks, to what we may now justly consider as its final establishment in our own country and generally throughout the civilized world.

[The Court then proceeds to "trace the history of the rule" through an extensive examination of state practice, beginning with the issuance of orders by Henry IV to his admirals in 1403 and 1406.]

Since the English orders in council of 1806 and 1810, before quoted, in favor of fishing vessels employed in catching and bringing to market fresh fish, no instance has been found in which the exemption from capture of private coast fishing vessels, honestly pursuing their peaceful industry, has been denied by England, or by any other nation. And the Empire of Japan, (the last State admitted into the rank of civilized nations,) by an ordinance promulgated at the beginning of its war with China in August, 1894, established prize courts, and ordained that "the following enemy's vessels are exempt from detention"—including in the exemption "boats engaged in coast fisheries," as well as "ships engaged exclusively on a voyage of scientific discovery, philanthropy or religious mission." Takahashi, International Law, 11, 178.

International law is part of our law, and must be ascertained and administered by the courts of justice of appropriate jurisdiction, as often as questions of right depending upon it are duly presented for their determination. For this purpose, where there is no treaty, and no controlling executive or legislative act or judicial decision, resort must be had to the customs and usages of civilized nations; and, as evidence of these, to the works of jurists and commentators, who by years of labor, research and experience, have made themselves peculiarly well acquainted with the subjects of which they treat. Such works are resorted to by judicial tribunals, not for the speculations of their authors concerning what the law ought to be, but for trustworthy evidence of what the law really is. Hilton v. Guyot, 159 U.S. 113, 163, 164, 214, 215.

* * *

This review of the precedents and authorities on the subject appears to us abundantly to demonstrate that at the present day, by the general consent of the civilized nations of the world, and inde-

HOLDING:

pendently of any express treaty or other public act, it is an established rule of international law, founded on considerations of humanity to a poor and industrious order of men, and of the mutual convenience of belligerent States, that coast fishing vessels, with their implements and supplies, cargoes and crews, unarmed, and honestly pursuing their peaceful calling of catching and bringing in fresh fish, are exempt from capture as prize of war.

EXCEPTIONS:

The exemption, of course, does not apply to coast fishermen or their vessels, if employed for a warlike purpose, or in such a way as to give aid or information to the enemy; nor when military or naval operations create a necessity to which all private interests must give way.

Nor has the exemption been extended to ships or vessels employed on the high sea in taking whales or seals, or cod or other fish which are not brought fresh to market, but are salted or otherwise cured and made a regular article of commerce.

This rule of international law is one which prize courts, administering the law of nations, are bound to take judicial notice of, and to give effect to, in the absence of any treaty or other public act of their own government in relation to the matter.

* * *

The position taken by the United States during the recent war with Spain was quite in accord with the rule of international law, now generally recognized by civilized nations, in regard to coast fishing vessels.

On April 21, 1898, the Secretary of the Navy gave instructions to Admiral Sampson commanding the North Atlantic Squadron, to "immediately institute a blockade of the north coast of Cuba, extending from Cardenas on the east to Bahia Honda on the west." Bureau of Navigation Report of 1898, appx. 175. The blockade was immediately instituted accordingly. On April 22, the President issued a proclamation, declaring that the United States had instituted and would maintain that blockade, "in pursuance of the laws of the United States, and the law of nations applicable to such cases." 30 Stat. 1769. And by the act of Congress of April 25, 1898, c. 189, it was declared that the war between the United States and Spain existed on that day, and had existed since and including April 21. 30 Stat. 364.

On April 26, 1898, the President issued another proclamation, which, after reciting the existence of the war, as declared by Congress, contained this further recital: "It being desirable that such war should be conducted upon principles in harmony with the present views of nations and sanctioned by their recent practice." This recital was followed by specific declarations of certain rules for the conduct of the war by sea, making no mention of fishing vessels. 30 Stat. 1770. But the proclamation clearly manifests the general policy of the

Government to conduct the war in accordance with the principles of international law sanctioned by the recent practice of nations.

*   *   *

Upon the facts proved in either case, it is the duty of this court, sitting as the highest prize court of the United States, and administering the law of nations, to declare and adjudge that the capture was unlawful, and without probable cause; and it is therefore, in each case,

Ordered, that the decree of the District Court be reversed, and the proceeds of the sale of the vessel, together with the proceeds of any sale of her cargo, be restored to the claimant, with damages and costs.

[Dissenting opinion of Mr. Chief Justice Fuller, with whom concurred Mr. Justice Harlan and Mr. Justice McKenna, omitted.]

PRACTICES OF NATIONAL COURTS

It would be difficult, perhaps impossible, to find a national legal system the courts of which arbitrarily refused to apply rules of customary international law not in conflict with domestic law, and the two cases above are illustrative of the general practice of national courts. The main point at issue in this Section is not whether courts in national legal systems give effect to such rules, but rather how they go about it.

1. *Where there is no constitutional or other legislative provision directing courts to apply rules of customary international law.* In states where the common law prevails, courts usually justify their application of such rules by stating that international law is part of the law of the land. The simplicity of the proposition is deceptive, however, for if it were accepted as literally true, courts would need only determine whether there was an applicable rule of customary international law and, so long as they found an applicable rule not in conflict with domestic law, apply it. Yet this is not quite the way the courts proceeded in the cases set forth above.

Even after determining there was no rule of customary international law applicable to the facts in issue, the English court went on to decide that in any event there was no applicable rule of domestic law under which the plaintiff could recover. In the American case, the court proceeded to determine there was an applicable rule of customary international law only after ascertaining there was no applicable rule of domestic law already established by previous executive or legislative act or judicial decision. If international law is part of the law of the land, why should it be necessary to determine whether there is an applicable rule of domestic law? Consider in this connection the following case.

In Triquet v. Bath, 3 Burr. 1478 (K.B.1764), Lord Mansfield delivered the opinion and in the course of it made the statements to which reference was made in the West Rand Central Gold Mining Company case. The defendant, an Englishman, was secretary to an ambassador from a foreign state. The issue was whether he was immune from arrest. Holding that he was, Lord Mansfield said:

> * * * This privilege of foreign ministers and their domestic servants depends upon the law of nations. The Act of Parliament of 7 Ann. c. 12, is declaratory of it. * * *
>
> * * *
>
> But the Act was not occasioned by any doubt "whether the law of nations, particularly the part relative to public ministers, was not part of the law of England; * * * nor intended to vary, an iota from it."
>
> I remember in a case before Lord Talbot, * * * the matter was very elaborately argued at the Bar; and a solemn deliberate opinion given by the Court. These questions arose and were discussed. * * * "What was the rule of decision: the Act of Parliament; or, the law of nations." Lord Talbot declared a clear opinion—"That the law of nations, in its full extent was part of the law of England."—"That the Act of Parliament was declaratory; and occasioned by a particular incident."—"That the law of nations was to be collected from the practice of different nations, and the authority of writers." Accordingly, he argued and determined from such instances, and the authority of Grotius, Barbeyrac, Binkershoek, Wiquefort, &c. there being no English writer of eminence, upon the subject.

In states where the civil law or some other legal system prevails and there is no constitutional or other legislative provision directing them to apply rules of customary international law, the courts, just as those in states where the common law prevails, feel compelled to justify their application of such rules in some way. They do not necessarily resort to the proposition that international law is part of the law of the land, but in whatever way they determine a rule of customary international law is applicable, they often show the same proclivity as common law courts to find that there is in any event an applicable rule of domestic law. The following case is illustrative.

Immunity Case, Yugoslavia, Supreme Court of the People's Republic of Croatia, No. Gz–766–56 (1956), 86 Journal du Droit International 525 (1959). The plaintiff was injured by an automobile belonging to the military mission of a foreign embassy in Belgrade and sued the embassy for damages. The court held that the embassy could not be sued but ruled that the suit could be treated as one in effect against the state represented by the foreign embassy. In considering whether, and to what extent, the foreign state could be sued in the courts of Yugoslavia, the court said: [a]

> A practice exists in international relations under which a State enjoys before the Courts of another State a right which is known as "immunity from jurisdiction". This immunity means ✓ that the State which enjoys it cannot, without its own consent, be brought before the Courts of another State. This is considered to be a customary rule of public international law which ought to be respected.
>
> But there is also an internal legal provision on this subject. This is Article 19(2) of the Statute introducing the old Yugoslav Code of Criminal Procedure. This provision is still applicable under the terms of Article 4 of the Statute of 1946 * * * (see Official Gazette of the P.F.R. of Yugoslavia, No. 86/46). Under the terms of this provision the jurisdiction of the Yugoslav tribunals extends to all persons who, under the principles of international law, enjoy extra-territorial rights, on the condition always that they agree to submit to such jurisdiction, or that the case in which they are involved concerns their immovable property situated in Yugoslavia or a right in rem which they exercise over immovable property belonging to another person, but also situated in Yugoslavia. Although this provision is only designed to cover natural persons in their capacity as diplomatic representatives of a foreign State, it is beyond doubt that the foreign State itself cannot enjoy a lesser degree of immunity from jurisdiction * * * In consequence it may be said that the immunity from jurisdiction enjoyed by foreign States before Yugoslav tribunals is a rule of Yugoslav positive law.
>
> * * *
>
> In the light of the reasons just set out, the court of first instance acted in conformity with the law in rejecting the Plaintiff's action and asserting that the normal legal course was not open to him in this case. * * *

Suppose that in the West Rand Central Gold Mining Company case, the court had found there was a rule of customary international law applicable to the facts in issue, though there was no applicable rule of domestic law. Would it have applied the rule of customary international law as the rule of decision? Did the Supreme Court of the United States apply a rule of customary international law as the rule of decision in The Paquete Habana? In the Yugoslav case, suppose the court had found there was no applicable rule of domestic law, though there was an applicable rule of customary international law. What would it have done? In those three cases, did the English, the American and the Yugoslav courts follow identical theories concerning the relationship of customary international law to domestic

---

a. English text in the Journal. Reprinted by permission of Editions Techniques, S.A., Paris.

law? In what way do their theories in the matter differ from the theory implicit in the opinion of Lord Mansfield in Triquet v. Bath?

2. *Provisions in constitutions.* In national legal systems, constitutional provisions may provide a legal basis for the application by the courts of rules of customary international law. Provisions expressing in broad terms the acceptance by the state of rules of international law are found in some national legal systems.

For example, Article 29(3) of the Constitution of Ireland provides: "Ireland accepts the generally recognized principles of international law as its rule of conduct in its relations with other states." III (1) Peaslee, Constitutions of Nations 482 (3d ed. 1968). Article 211 of the Constitution of Burma declares: "The Union of Burma * * * accepts the generally recognized principles of international law as its rule of conduct in its relations with foreign states." II (1) Peaslee, Constitutions of Nations 109 (3d ed. 1966). And Article 25 of the Constitution of the German Democratic Republic states: "The generally accepted rules of international law are binding upon the state power and upon every citizen." III (1) Peaslee, Constitutions of Nations 386 (3d ed. 1968).

Whether a broadly worded constitutional provision is helpful to courts in justifying their application of customary international law may depend on their past practice. The French courts have traditionally given effect to such rules and for this reason some argue that the preamble to the French Constitution of 1946 merely acknowledged the fact in stating: "The French Republic, faithful to its tradition, abides by the rules of international law." II Peaslee, Constitutions of Nations 7 (2d ed. 1956). The provision was incorporated by reference in the 1958 Constitution of the Fifth French Republic but it has been contended by a French author that the provision is not only unnecessary but also dangerous, because it might put into question the inherent power of French courts to apply rules of international law. Rousseau, Droit International Public 14 (Precis Dalloz, 5th ed. 1970).

Some constitutions provide courts with a basis for applying rules of customary international law by declaring specifically that international law is part of the law of the land. Thus Article 2(3) of the Constitution of the Philippines states: "The Philippines * * * adopts the generally accepted principles of international law as part of the law of the Nation." II (2) Peaslee, Constitutions of Nations 1068 (3d ed. 1966). The Austrian Constitution states in Article 9: "The generally recognized rules of international law shall be considered as component parts of the Federal Law." III (1) Peaslee, Constitutions of Nations 25 (3d ed. 1968). And Article 25 of the Constitution of the German Federal Republic provides: "The general rules of public international law are an integral part of federal law." III (1) Peaslee, Constitutions of Nations 366 (3d ed. 1968).

A very few constitutions go further and contemplate not only the application of rules of customary international law by the courts but also the possibility of conflict between such rules and rules of domestic law and indicate the manner in which the conflict should be resolved. For the text of constitutional provisions of this type, see p. 23.

see p. 23.

---

2. RULES OF DOMESTIC LAW IN CONFLICT WITH CUSTOMARY INTERNATIONAL LAW

THE OVER THE TOP
SCHROEDER v. BISSELL

United States District Court, D.Conn., 1925.
5 F.2d 838.

Three libels by the United States, one against the schooner Over the Top, and two against its cargo, with application by A. L. Schroeder, owner of the cargo, against Harvey Bissell, Collector, for return of cargo. Libels dismissed.

THOMAS, DISTRICT JUDGE.   *   *   *

From the evidence I find the following facts established: On August 27, 1924, the schooner Over the Top, carrying a cargo of whisky and operating under the British flag and under British registry, cleared for Cuba from St. Johns, New Brunswick. It arrived at a point off the coast of Block Island several weeks prior to October 19, 1924. * * *

On the 19th of October, 1924, at about 10 o'clock in the evening, the supercargo on board the schooner sold 25 cases of whisky for $550 to a special agent of the Internal Revenue Department. The sale was made in the presence of the captain, and thereupon the crew of the vessel, in the presence and under the direction of the captain, unloaded these cases of whisky and transferred the same to a sea sled employed in the government service. Both captain and supercargo knew that the whisky so transferred was to be transported to a point on the adjacent coast, but neither one of them knew that the sea sled or the men on it were in the government service. The transaction occurred at a point approximately 19 miles distant from the shore, or 115 degrees true from the southeast light of Block Island, * * *

On the following day, Over the Top was seized by officers of the United States coast guard, and the captain and crew were placed under arrest, and the ship and her cargo were towed into the Port of New London and turned over to the collector of customs and are now in his custody.

I further find that the schooner had been hovering for some time off the coast of the United States at the point where she was seized, and that those in command were engaged during that period in selling liquor and delivering the same to boats proceeding from the coast of the United States and returning thereto. The testimony seems to support the conclusion that business was slow.

Upon these facts, the United States demands judgment decreeing the forfeiture and sale of the ship and cargo. The owner of the ship and the owner of the cargo have appeared separately, but the trial of the three actions was consolidated, and, as will be seen in the sequel, the principles of law governing are applicable alike to both the schooner and cargo.

The government bases its claim of forfeiture upon the alleged violation of sections 447, 448, 450, 453, 585, 586, 593, and 594 of the Tariff Act of 1922 * * * as well as upon the provisions of the American-British Treaty which became effective May 22, 1924. The above sections of the Tariff Act provide as follows:

> Sec. 447. *Unlading—Place.*—It shall be unlawful to make entry of any vessel or to unlade the cargo or any part thereof of any vessel elsewhere than at a port of entry * * *.
>
> *   *   *

> Sec. 586. *Unlawful Unlading—Exception.*—The master of any vessel from a foreign port or place who allows any merchandise (including sea stores) to be unladen from such vessel at any time after its arrival within four leagues of the coast of the United States and before such vessel has come to the proper place for the discharge of such merchandise, and before he has received a permit to unlade, shall be liable to a penalty equal to twice the value of the merchandise but not less than $1,000, and such vessel and the merchandise shall be subject to seizure and forfeiture:
>
> *   *   *

But before we proceed to discuss the above-quoted sections of the Tariff Act as well as the treaty, it may be well to dispose of one of the contentions made by counsel in behalf of the cargo and the schooner.

The proposition is advanced that, regardless of our municipal legislation, the acts complained of could not constitute offenses against the United States when committed by foreign nationals, on foreign bottoms, on the high seas at a point beyond the territorial jurisdiction of the country. Well-known principles of international practice are invoked in support of this contention accompanied with the citation of authority. Upon careful consideration, however, I am led to conclude that a misconception exists here as to the status, in a federal forum, of so-called international law when that law encounters a municipal enactment.

If we assume for the present that the national legislation has, by its terms, made the acts complained of a crime against the United States even when committed on the high seas by foreign nationals upon a ship of foreign registry, then there is no discretion vested in the federal court, once it obtains jurisdiction, to decline enforcement. International practice is law only in so far as we adopt it, and like all common or statute law it bends to the will of the Congress. It is not the function of courts to annul legislation; it is their duty to interpret and by their judicial decrees to enforce it—and even when an act of Congress is declared invalid, it is only because the basic law is being enforced in that declaration. There is one ground only upon which a federal court may refuse to enforce an act of Congress and that is when the act is held to be unconstitutional. The act may contravene recognized principles of international comity, but that affords no more basis for judicial disregard of it than it does for executive disregard of it. These libels, therefore, cannot be attacked upon the ground that the territorial jurisdiction of the United States cannot be extended beyond the three-mile sea zone under international law.

If, however, the court has no option to refuse the enforcement of legislation in contravention of principles of international law, it does not follow that in construing the terms and provisions of a statute it may not assume that such principles were on the national conscience and that the congressional act did not deliberately intend to infringe them. In other words, unless it unmistakably appears that a congressional act was intended to be in disregard of a principle of international comity, the presumption is that it was intended to be in conformity with it. It is with such a principle in mind that we now proceed to an examination of the legislation upon which the government relies.

Section 447 of the Tariff Act of 1922, quoted supra, makes it unlawful for the vessel to make entry of or to unlade any part of its cargo elsewhere than at a port of entry. Part of the cargo of Over the Top was unloaded on the high seas, and the government contends that the statute was thereby violated. To me it seems that the statute was intended to prevent entry or unlading at a port or place in the country other than a port of entry. It had no reference to unlading on the seas even when done within the three-mile zone. But waiving that question, it is to be noted that the act is phrased in general language and that it bespeaks no suggestion of territorial limitation. The proposition has not heretofore been advanced that for that reason the act has attempted to extend the territorial jurisdiction of the United States over the whole earth. Almost all criminal statutes, or statutes prohibiting defined conduct, are phrased in general language without mention of territorial limitation. But they are all to be read in the light of the principle that jurisdiction is not extraterritorial and that the municipal legislation is not attempting to regulate or to punish conduct performed outside of the national domain. For example, the statutes of Connecticut do not forbid larceny in Connecticut—they forbid larceny. The statutes of the United States do not forbid counterfeiting in the United States—they forbid counterfeiting. That the

Congress may, in disregard of the law of nations, prohibit acts by foreign nationals not committed within our domain, has already been conceded; but unless such intent clearly appears from the language of the statute such intent is not to be presumed.

* * *

The same considerations apply with equal force to the provisions of sections 448, 450, 453, 585, 593, and 594 of the Tariff Act of 1922. These enactments of the Congress are implicit with the proviso that the acts therein denounced be accomplished within the territory of the United States. No attempt is there discernible to extend the legislative jurisdiction of the United States beyond its boundaries. Of utmost significance, therefore, is the language of section 586 of the act providing that the master of any vessel from a foreign port, who allows any merchandise to be unladen from such vessel at any time after its arrival within four leagues of the coast of the United States, and before such vessel has come to the proper place for the discharge of such merchandise, and before permission has been given to unlade, shall be liable to a penalty, and the vessel and the merchandise shall be subject to seizure and forfeiture. It appears to me that this section has a most important, if not a determinative, bearing upon the point under discussion. This enactment has been part of our legislation for over a hundred years. Here we have a distinct extension of our sea jurisdiction to a point 12 miles from the coast—an assertion of authority which may perhaps clash with international practice, but which, whether challenged or not, is unmistakable, and which, therefore, it is the business of our courts to enforce. Had the master and super cargo of Over the Top been guilty of unlading the liquor at a point within this 12-mile zone, it may be that we would have had no difficulty in sustaining the libels.

* * *

My conclusion, then, is that as no statute embracing the subject-matter of sections 447, 448, 450, 453, 585, 586, 593, and 594 of the Tariff Act of 1922 has extended our territorial jurisdiction to a point on the high seas distant 19 miles from our coast, conduct which would have been in violation of these sections if performed within our territory cannot constitute an offense against the United States when performed at such a distance by foreign nationals on ships of foreign registry. If, for the purpose of our treasury, we can extend our sea jurisdiction to a point four leagues from the coast, I see no reason why we cannot extend it four leagues more. I merely observe that we have not done so yet.

I now come to the provisions of the American-British Treaty, which was obviously contracted for the purpose of preventing hovering ships from supplying intoxicating liquor to carriers running between the ships and the shore. * * *

* * *

Whether therefore the Senate and the Executive may constitutionally enact criminal legislation by the device of a mere treaty is a question which fortunately we need not discuss. It is sufficient to conclude that the American-British Treaty did not in fact enact new criminal legislation.

* * *

The considerations as above expressed therefore impel the conclusion that there is no legal basis for these libels, and it follows that they must be and the same are dismissed. * * *

UNITED STATES v. BERRIGAN

United States District Court, D.Md., 1968.
283 F.Supp. 336.a

NORTHROP, DISTRICT JUDGE. The defendants before this court are charged in three counts that they did willfully

1. injure property of the United States;

2. mutilate records filed in a public office of the United States; and

3. hinder the administration of the Military Selective Service Act.

Defendants wish to proffer an opening statement to the jury as to what they would present for their defense. Specifically, they contend that, by virtue of what they have read, heard, and seen, the war in Vietnam is immoral and illegal; and that the United States, in carrying on the war in Vietnam, is violating certain precepts of international law, constitutional law, and judgments which were handed down at Nurnberg.

To serve as a foundation and a basis for their beliefs, defendants wish to produce in court, among other evidence, "the outstanding experts" on international law who would testify that the acts of the United States government in Vietnam are illegal. Their conduct, they say, was prompted by their belief that the United States is acting illegally and was intended to prevent criminal acts from being committed. Because this belief prompted their acts, they argue that the necessary *mens rea* is lacking.

Initially, it must be pointed out that in law once the commission of a crime is established—the doing of a prohibited act with the necessary intent—proof of a good motive will not save the accused from conviction. * * *

MOTIVE NOT SUFFICIENT TO OFFSET CONVICTION

* * *

Counsel also contends that the defendants' acts are symbolic expressions of speech which are protected by the First Amendment of

a. Cert. denied 397 U.S. 909, 90 S.Ct. 907 (1970).

the United States Constitution and thus he is entitled to offer this defense before the jury. * * *

* * *

This court finds that under the circumstances of this case the conduct which is charged in the indictment is not afforded the protections of the First Amendment and a conviction under these criminal statutes would not deny to these defendants any of the guarantees of that Amendment.

Finally, counsel contends that these defendants should be allowed to present to the jury what is popularly known as the "Nurnberg Defense." The trial of the Nazi war criminals at Nurnberg was premised on the generally accepted view that there are, as a part of international law, certain crimes against peace and humanity which are punishable. The Nurnberg Trial, 6 F.R.D. 69 (1946). It is urged here that the belief of these defendants that the United States was waging a war of aggression, and thus committing a crime against peace, justified the acts charged.

It is not clear what standing these defendants have to raise the legality of this country's involvement in Vietnam when they have not been called to serve in the armed forces, are not directly affected by our government's actions in that country, and are not even directly affected by the Selective Service apparatus. As pointed out by Judge Charles E. Wyzanski in an article in the February 1968 issue of the Atlantic Monthly:

> As the Nuremberg verdicts show, merely to fight in an aggressive war is no crime. What is a crime is *personally* to fight by foul means. [Emphasis supplied.]

The important element in this defense, assuming its applicability in an American court, is the individual responsibility which is necessary before it can be raised. These defendants do not have standing to raise the validity of governmental actions, either under international law or constitutional law, on the grounds that the rights of parties not before this court are violated. Courts "must deal with the case in hand, and not with imaginary ones." Yazoo & M. V. R. Co. v. Jackson Vinegar Co., 226 U.S. 217, 218, 33 S.Ct. 40, 41, 57 L.Ed. 193 (1912).

I refer again to the opinions expressed by Judge Wyzanski because they are timely articulations of ancient principles found in scores of cases. In our disturbed times, modern expressions seem to have more persuasion than the authority of antiquity.

> For men of conscience there remains a less risky but not a less worthy moral choice. Each of us may bide his time until he personally is faced with an order requiring him as an individual to do a wrongful act. Such patience, fortitude, and resolution find illustration in the career of Sir Thomas More. He did not rush in to protest the Act of Henry VIII's Parliament re-

quiring Englishmen to take an oath of supremacy attesting to the King's instead of the Pope's headship of the English Church. Only when attempt was made to force him to subscribe to the oath did he resist. * * *

This waiting until an issue is squarely presented to an individual and cannot further be avoided will not be a course appealing to those who have a burning desire to intervene affirmatively to save his nation's honor and the lives of its citizens and citizens of other lands. It seems at first blush a not very heroic attitude. But heroism sometimes lies in withholding action until it is compelled, and using the interval to discern competing interests, to ascertain their values, and to seek to strike a balance that marshals the claims not only of the accountant and of others in his society, but of men of distant lands and times.

But irrespective of the lack of standing of these defendants to raise the issue of the legality of the government's actions as they relate to the Vietnam situation, the proffered defense suffers from a more fundamental bar. It is clear that there are certain questions of substantive law, that is, "political questions", which are not cognizable in our courts because of the nature of our governmental system which is based upon a separation of functions among different branches of the government. The doctrine

> is one of "political questions," not one of "political cases." The courts cannot reject as "no law suit" a bona fide controversy as to whether some action denominated "political" exceeds constitutional authority. Baker v. Carr, 369 U.S. 186, 217, 82 S.Ct. 691, 710, 7 L.Ed.2d 663 (1962).

Certain clearly defined areas have traditionally and necessarily been left to other departments of the government, free from interference by the judiciary. One such area is foreign relations. Baker v. Carr, supra, at 211, 82 S.Ct. at 691.

It is true that not every case which touches the foreign-relations power of the country is necessarily a "political question." Courts have usually decided the constitutional questions concerning international agreements, Reid v. Covert, 354 U.S. 1, 77 S.Ct. 1222, 1 L.Ed.2d 1148 (1957), but the corresponding question of international law has been treated as a "political question."

The activities of these defendants were directed towards the Selective Service System, which system counsel has admitted is not criminal or illegal in and of itself. What is called into question here is the utilization of the armed forces by the executive and legislative branches. It cannot be disputed that the recognition of belligerency abroad, and the measures necessary to meet a crisis to preserve the peace and safety of this country, is uniquely an executive and a legislative responsibility. Whether the actions by the executive and the legislative branches in utilizing our armed forces are in accord with international law is a question which necessarily must be left to the elected representatives of the people and not to the judiciary. This is so even if the government's actions are contrary to valid treaties to which the government is a signatory. And the Supreme Court has held that Congress may constitutionally override treaties by later enactment of an inconsistent statute, even though the subsequent statute is in violation of international law.

The categorization of this defense as a "political question" is not an abdication of responsibility by the judiciary. Rather, it is a recognition that the responsibility is assumed by that level of government which under the Constitution and international law is authorized to commit the nation.

The "Nurnberg Defense" is premised on a finding that the government is acting in violation of international law in waging an agressive war, and, as such, cannot be raised here because the question of violations of international law by the government is uniquely a "political" question.

Counsel will govern themselves accordingly, and the court's instructions to the jury will reflect this decision if any transgression makes it necessary.

ATTORNEY–GENERAL OF ISRAEL v. EICHMANN

Israel, District Court of Jerusalem, 1961.
36 Int'l L.Rep. 5, 24 (1968).

[Adolf Eichmann was tried in Israel under a law punishing Nazis and Nazi collaborators for crimes against the Jewish people committed in Germany in World War II.]

The first argument of counsel, that Israel law is in conflict with international law and that it therefore cannot vest jurisdiction in this Court, raises the preliminary question of the validity of international law in Israel and whether, in the event of conflict, it is to be preferred to the law of the land. The law in force in Israel resembles that in force in England in this regard. * * *

As regards Israel, the Deputy President, Justice Cheshin, said in Criminal Appeal 174/54 (10 Piske Din 5, 17) :

As to the question of the incorporation of the principles of international law in the national law, we rely on Blackstone, Commentaries on the Laws of England (Book IV, Chap. 5) :

"In England * * * the law of nations * * * is * * * adopted in its full extent by the common law, and it is held to be a part of the law of the land * * * without which it must cease to be a part of the civilized world."

The same applies to other countries, such as the United States of America, France, Belgium and Switzerland, where the usages of international law have been recognized as part of the national law. * * *

With respect to statutory law, Justice Agranat said in High Court Case No. 279/51 (6 Piske Din 945, 966):

> B. It is a well-known maxim that a municipal statute should —except where its contents require a different interpretation— be interpreted in accordance with the rules of public international law.

And in Criminal Appeal No. 5/51 (5 Piske Din 1061) Mr. Justice Sussman said (p. 1065):

> It is a well-known rule that in interpreting a statute the Court will as far as possible try to avoid a conflict between the municipal law and the obligations incumbent on the State by virtue of international law. But this is only one of the canons of interpretation. That is to say, where we are dealing not with the Common Law but with a written statute which expresses the will of the legislator, then the Court must carry out the will of the legislator without considering if there exists a contradiction between the statute and international law * * * Furthermore, the Courts here derive their jurisdiction from municipal law and not from international law.

Our jurisdiction to try this case is based on the Nazi and Nazi Collaborators (Punishment) Law, *an enacted Law the provisions of which are unequivocal.* The Court has to give effect to a law of the Knesset, and we cannot entertain the contention that this Law conflicts with the principles of international law. For this reason alone counsel's first submission must be rejected.

We have, however, also considered the sources of international law, including the numerous authorities cited by learned defence counsel in his basic written brief upon which he based his oral pleadings, and by the learned Attorney-General in his comprehensive oral pleadings, and have failed to find any foundation for the contention that Israel law is in conflict with the principles of international law. On the contrary, we have reached the conclusion that the Law in question conforms to the best traditions of the law of nations.[a]

* * *

a. For a discussion of this case as it relates to individual responsibility for war crimes, see Chapter 10.

THE NYUGAT
SWISS CORPORATION SOCIETE ANONYME MARITIME ET COMMERCIALE v. STATE OF THE NETHERLANDS

Netherlands, Supreme Court, 1959.
10 Nederlands Tijdschrift Voor International Recht 82 (1963).a

[The owners of The Nyugat, a merchant ship, sued the state of the Netherlands for damages suffered as a result of its capture by a Dutch warship in April 1941 and its eventual loss while it was under the control of the Dutch Government in exile in London.

At the time of its capture, The Nyugat flew the Hungarian flag and since the Netherlands was not at war with Hungary, it would not have been subject to capture as a merchant ship flying an "enemy flag" under the Prize Rules for the Kingdom of the Netherlands in effect until 1941. Shortly before the capture, however, the Dutch Government in exile had modified the Prize Rules by a series of decrees and under their provisions a ship sailing under the flag of a state not at war with the Netherlands would, under certain conditions, be treated as an enemy ship. In a previous ruling, the Supreme Court of the Netherlands had held that these conditions had been satisfied in the case of The Nyugat because, prior to the capture, the Dutch Government in exile had broken diplomatic relations with Hungary and Hungary had attacked Yugoslavia as an ally of Germany. Hence the capture was valid under the prize law of the Netherlands and the shipowners were not entitled to damages.

On rehearing, the owners contended, inter alia, that the provisions for capture introduced by the decrees of 1941 were contrary to customary international law and argued the court had power to decide whether it was so by virtue of Article 66 of the Constitution of the Netherlands. The article empowered the Dutch courts to declare domestic legislation inapplicable if it were in conflict with certain international agreements entered into by the Netherlands. The plaintiffs argued that the court was implicitly empowered by the article to declare domestic legislation inapplicable if it were in conflict with customary international law.

While not conceding there was a conflict in the case, the court rejected the argument. A portion of its opinion appears below.]

It has been alleged that the régime as laid down by the Decrees * * * is contrary to customary and written international law and, for this reason, should not be applied. The Supreme Court desires to give prominence to the fact that the first judgment * * * left aside the question whether the Decrees enacted by the Netherlands Government at London * * * could be judged by customary in-

a. English text in the Tijdschrift. Reprinted from Netherlands International   Law Review with the permission of W. A. Sijhoff, Leiden.

ternational law * * * [The] shipowners now allege that, following the first judgment, the Constitution * * * was changed * * * [and now provides for] judicial review of the relations between international law and municipal public law. According to the new Article 66 of the Constitution, legislation in force within the Kingdom shall, under certain circumstances, not apply if this application would be incompatible with provisions of [international] agreements * * * which have been entered into either before or after the enactment of such legislation. [The] shipowners are of the opinion that a principle of wider scope has been enunciated here. This principle would, in a case of clear conflict * * * allow the national courts to review municipal law by rules of customary international law * * * As appears from the history of the new Article 66, this provision specifically aimed to settle the difference of opinion as to how far a Netherlands court is entitled to judge Netherlands law by the standards of international law. The provision expressly * * * [intended] to restrict this review to the cases * * * of agreements mentioned by it. The Netherlands courts which until then were free to solve this question as they deemed fit, were, after its entry into force, bound by this provision of the Constitution, even where the facts of the case or the judgment challenged antedated the enactment of the new rule. The Supreme Court, therefore, is not entitled to enter into the question raised by [the] shipowners whether the Decrees are in conflict with customary international law * * *

---

1. *Publicists' reaction to the Nyugat decision.* The decision of the Supreme Court of the Netherlands in The Nyugat was severely criticized. In the "Notes" which follow the report of the case set forth above, Erades contends the courts of The Netherlands had previously given effect to rules of customary international law which deviated from domestic law and also maintains the Supreme Court of the Netherlands misconstrued the legislative history and meaning of the constitutional provision involved. Another author labels the decision "wrong in almost all respects." Verzijl, I International Law in Historical Perspective 97 (1968).

2. *Treatment of the problem in other national legal systems.* Article 10 of the Italian Constitution states: "Italy's legal system conforms with the generally recognized principles of international law." III (1) Peaslee, Constitutions of Nations 501 (3d ed. 1968). Conformity between the two means, according to the Supreme Court of Italy, that rules of municipal law which are contrary to customary international law "must be eliminated." Re Martinez, Italy, Court of Cassation, 1959, 28 Int'l L.Rep. 170 (1963), the text of which appears at p. 184. Article 25 of the Constitution of the Federal Republic of

Germany not only states that the general rules of public international law are an integral part of federal law, but goes on to provide: "They shall take precedence over the laws and shall directly create rights and duties for the inhabitants of the territory." III (1) Peaslee, Constitutions of Nations 366 (3d ed. 1968).

Absent such types of constitutional provisions, the courts of national legal systems frequently assert they would give effect to their domestic law if it were in clear conflict with customary international law. Yet should a national court resolve the conflict in such manner, the state to which it belongs would be in violation of international law. The rule on this point is clear and is stated in Section 3(2) of The Restatement of the Foreign Relations Law of the United States (1965) as follows: "The domestic law of a state is not a defense to a violation by the state of international law." Comment *i* to the section states: " * * * Thus a state cannot justify its violation of international law by invoking its own contrary domestic law even if embodied in its constitution."

Courts in national legal systems, however, are not often confronted with the necessity of resolving the conflict by giving precedence to their domestic law and their proclivity to say they would if necessary is seldom put to the test. For example, English courts usually make a point of stating that they would give effect to the will of the parliament if its legislation were in clear conflict with customary international law. But this is no more than "a deferential nod to Cerberus before by-passing him," according to an observer of English judicial practice. 1 O'Connell, International Law 57 (2d ed. 1970). He goes on to state that the "collision between international law and the will of Parliament is abstract and only on the rare occasion of the Second World War did it become actual." (at 57)

Smith, International Law in Norwegian Courts, 12 Scandinavian Studies in Law 1968, at 153 (1968), discusses the question of conflict between domestic law and international law, whether customary or otherwise, and states:

> Legal writers have been especially concerned with the areas of conflict between international and national law. This is not, in my opinion, the most interesting aspect. In spite of everything the conflicts are the pathological cases. Besides, clear conflict situations are rare. Significantly enough, scarcely one has been brought before the Norwegian Supreme Court, and probably such cases will not be frequent in the future either. One will also acquire a somewhat distorted and a too negative view of the significance of international law in the municipal sphere by concentrating upon those situations.

> During the proceedings of the French-Norwegian gold clause case before the International Court of Justice at The Hague in 1957, Maurice Bourquin, the Belgian professor who represented

[Handwritten margin note: STATE CANNOT INVOKE CONTRARY DOMESTIC LAW TO JUSTIFY VIOLATION OF INT'L. LAW]

[Handwritten margin note: PROBLEM DOES NOT ARISE OFTEN HOWEVER]

the Norwegian Government, stated in the course of his oral argument that all the lacunae, all the obscurities, and all the uncertainties in the municipal law afford the Norwegian courts the opportunity to apply international law. It is here that one arrives at the more practically important fields. This statement may perhaps contain a certain element of over-emphasis. But our courts have gone a long way in the direction of creating a harmonious relationship with international law. (at 160).

TUNKIN, CO–EXISTENCE AND INTERNATIONAL LAW

[1958] III Académie De Droit International, Recueil des Cours 1, 23 [a]

The concept that international custom constitutes a primary and the most important means of creating norms of international law was certainly correct for the 19th century, but * * * it no longer reflects the present day situation in international law. In contemporary conditions the principal means of creating norms of international law is a treaty. This is the point of view held by the great majority, if not by all, of the Soviet authors who have treated this subject.

[margin note: TREATY NOT CUSTOM IS BASIS OF IL —]

[margin note: WHOM DOES THIS BENEFIT?]

LUKASHUK, SOURCES OF PRESENT–DAY INTERNATIONAL LAW

Contemporary International Law 164, 174 (Moscow 1969).

For historical reasons, custom predominated in the past. In the last century the situation has changed and it has been relegated to second place by the treaty. However, the rules of customary law continue to play a very big role in the practice of international law.

3. RULES OF DOMESTIC LAW IN CONFLICT WITH INTERNATIONAL AGREEMENTS

A conflict between domestic law and an international agreement may arise in either of two ways. First, the agreement may be in conflict with a rule of domestic law already in effect at the time the international agreement becomes binding. Second, a rule of domestic law may come into effect after the agreement has become binding and be in conflict with it. In either case, a state would be in violation of international law if it gave effect to the conflicting rule of domestic law, for it cannot invoke its contrary domestic law as justification for its failure to abide by the agreement any more than it can invoke it as a defense for its failure to abide by a rule of customary international law.

[margin note: (1) conflict with existing law]

[margin note: (2) conflict w/ new law]

a. English text in the Recueil.

1. *International agreement in conflict with constitutional provision.* Should the provisions of an international agreement be in conflict with the constitution of the national legal system, and the constitution not expressly specify that it can be modified by an international agreement, such provisions usually would not become operative as domestic law. They would not be valid as the law of the United States. See Chapter 16. Neither would they be internally operative in Mexico. In re Vera, Supreme Court, 1948, [1948] Ann. Dig. 328 (No. 114). The Court of Appeal for East Africa at Nairobi takes the same position. Criminal Appeal No. 156 of 1969, IX International Legal Materials 561 (1970). Article 324 of the Constitution of Nicaragua expressly provides that an international agreement in conflict with the constitution has no validity. IV(2) Peaslee, Constitutions of Nations 1006 (2d ed. 1970).

In recent years, however, the constitutions of some national systems have made provision for resolving conflicts between the constitution and an international agreement. Thus the Constitution of The Netherlands of 1815 was amended in 1953 to provide in Article 63: "If the development of the international legal order requires this, the contents of an agreement may deviate from certain provisions of the Constitution." The article goes on to provide that in such cases, the agreement must receive the approval of the legislature by a two-thirds majority of the votes cast. III (2) Peaslee, Constitutions of Nations 660 (3d ed. 1968).

In France Article 54 of the Constitution of 1958 provides that if the Constitutional Council should declare that an international agreement contains a clause contrary to the constitution, the authorization of the legislature "to ratify or approve this commitment may be given only after amendment of the Constitution." III (1) Peaslee, Constitutions of Nations 323 (3d ed. 1968).

Upon becoming independent, former French overseas territories adopted similar provisions in their constitutions. Gabon, Article 53; Ivory Coast, Article 55; Mali, Article 39; Mauritania, Article 45; Senegal, Article 78; Togo, Article 68; Upper Volta, Article 55. A similar provision also appears in Article 11 of the Constitution of Congo-Kinshasa (now Zaire). I Peaslee, Constitutions of Nations 205, 249, 542, 555, 709, 901, 1019, 105 (3d ed. 1965).

2. *International agreement in conflict with legislation.* Where the conflict is between an international agreement and anterior legislation, courts have usually not found it difficult to resolve a conflict in favor of the international agreement but in doing so, courts usually do not take the position that the agreement is intrinsically superior to existing legislation. Instead, they treat it as equal in rank with the legislation and apply the rule of construction that as between anterior and posterior laws in conflict, the one later in time prevails.

In the United States, the equality in rank of treaties and acts of Congress is provided by Article VI, Clause 2 of the Constitution. Since neither is superior to the other, the one later in time is held to prevail. Hence a self-executing treaty, i. e. one whose provisions are directly applicable as rules of domestic law without the need of implementation by an act of Congress, supersedes the provisions of prior and inconsistent federal legislation. Should the treaty not be self-executing, its provisions, once enacted into rules of domestic law by act of congress, also supersede, because they are later in time, the provisions of prior and inconsistent federal legislation. On these and other aspects of the internal effect of international agreements of the United States, see Chapter 16.

Article 133 of the Constitution of Mexico of January 31, 1917, is very similar to Article VI, Clause 2, of the Constitution of the United States and gives equal rank to a treaty and federal law. IV (2) Peaslee, Constitutions of Nations 951 (3d ed. 1970). So does Article 31 of the Constitution of Argentina of May 1, 1853. IV (1) Peaslee, Constitutions of Nations 12 (3d ed. 1970). The Supreme Court of Argentina has stated that since the article does not give precedence to either the treaty or federal law, a conflict between the two is resolved by giving effect to the one later in time. S. A. Martin & Cia. v. Nacion, 257 Fallos de la Corta Suprema 99 (1963).

National courts are presented with a more difficult issue when, absent an applicable constitutional provision, they must resolve a conflict between an international agreement and domestic legislation that becomes effective at a later date. The rule of construction that the law later in time prevails operates to deprive of internal effect the conflicting provisions of the prior agreement.

The position of the Supreme Court of the United States on the point is illustrative: "This Court has also repeatedly taken the position that an Act of Congress * * * is on a full parity with a treaty, and that when a statute which is subsequent in time is inconsistent with a treaty, the statute to the extent of conflict renders the treaty null." Reid v. Covert, 354 U.S. 1, 18, 77 S.Ct. 1222, 1231 (1957). The courts of many national legal systems frequently state they would apply the rule of construction should a conflict between an international agreement and subsequent domestic law arise and occasionally find themselves compelled to do just that. The Supreme Court of the United States in fact has given effect to a subsequent act of Congress in conflict with a prior treaty.

In recent years, however, the courts of some other national legal systems have shown a willingness to give more weight to international agreements in conflict with subsequent domestic law than might be expected under the doctrine of precedence for the one later in time. What rules for the resolution of this conflict are being applied by the courts in the next three cases?

LIBRAIRIE HACHETTE S.A. v. SOCIETE COOPERATIVE

Switzerland, Federal Tribunal, 1st Civil Court, 1967.
XXV Annuaire Suisse de Droit
International 239 (1968).a

A suit [for damages], brought before the Civil Court of Geneva and based on the law of cartels [of 1962], involved two Swiss corporations, as plaintiffs, and four other corporations [as defendants] of which two were French [and two were Swiss]. The two French corporations [relying on the Franco-Swiss Convention of 1869] pleaded that the court had no jurisdiction. The court stated that the two [French] defendants, since they had no [business] establishment * * * in Switzerland, could in principle rely on the Franco-Swiss Convention on Jurisdiction and Execution of Judgments of June 15, 1869 * * * The first article of that convention provides:

In disputes involving claims in personam, whether civil or commercial, arising either between Swiss and French [nationals], or between French and Swiss [nationals], the plaintiff shall be required to bring his action before the natural judge [i. e. the courts in the state of nationality] of the defendant.

Holding however that the [Swiss] federal law on cartels and analogous arrangements of December 20, 1962 * * * was applicable to the case * * * and was not governed by the convention, the Civil Court of Geneva held it had jurisdiction. The two French corporations then appealed to the Federal Tribunal * * * [A portion of the opinion by the Federal Tribunal appears below.]

That the convention controls as against [jurisdictional] rules of domestic law cannot be a matter of any doubt * * *. The case involves * * * a litigation between Swiss [nationals], domiciled in Switzerland and French [nationals], domiciled in France. The natural judge of the latter is the French judge * * *. [T]he French defendants are entitled to the benefit of the convention even though they are legal entities [rather than natural persons] * * *. The first article of the convention shall therefore be applicable if the claim asserted in the present case involves a claim in personam within the meaning of the article.

[The court went on to determine it did and hence the action would have to be brought in the courts of France.]

Background in aid of analysis. Though the Swiss court chose to give a broad construction to Article 1 of the 1869 Convention, there

a. Translation by the editors.

were weighty arguments for giving a strict construction to the article, declaring it inapplicable, and applying the Swiss law on cartels of 1962.

First, the reference of certain types of cases to the courts of the nationality of the defendant, though not unusual in some of the international agreements concluded in the 19th century, would be highly unusual today.   National legal systems do not now normally relinquish the jurisdiction which is lawfully theirs under international law and there was no question in the case at hand that, aside from the convention, the Swiss courts had every right to proceed with the suit.

Second, national courts usually construe strictly rather than liberally derogations from rules of international law.   French courts had held several times that Article 1 of the Convention of 1869, because it derogated from international law rules of jurisdiction, must be given a strict construction.   In particular, they had held that since the article did not say anything about a plurality of defendants of different nationalities, some of them French and others Swiss, it was not applicable to that type of case.

Third, it was open to question whether a suit for damages arising from acts in restraint of trade should be assimilated to an ordinary suit in tort such as was contemplated by the convention.   Though the Swiss law on cartels of 1962 was designed to protect both private economic interests and the public interest of Switzerland in its economy, there was no guarantee that the French courts would be willing to apply the law of cartels of Switzerland when the suit was brought before them.

Some of these arguments were made, but dismissed by the Swiss court, as explained in the comment on the decision by Lalive in Chronique de Jurisprudence Suisse, 97 Journal du Droit International 408, 434 (1970).

ASSOCIATION OF NORWEGIAN DENTISTS v. NORWEGIAN GOVERNMENT

Norway, Supreme Court, 1966.
96 Journal du Droit International 419 (1969).[a]

The Facts.   Upon the creation in 1949 of a public service of dentistry, there developed a shortage of trained personnel.   For several years, all future dentists, when registering as students, were required to commit themselves to serve for a period of two years following the termination of their studies, in such posts as might be open in this public service.   Thereafter a temporary law [in date] of 1956 made it mandatory to serve [the two years period] and supplanted the indi-

a. Translation by the editors. The text in the Journal is an account of the case, consisting of a summary of the facts, a summary of the decision, and a "note," i. e., a comment by the author. Reprinted by permission of Editions Techniques, S.A., Paris.

vidual commitments, * * *. That law was re-enacted * * * in 1962 and 1965. * * *

In the case, the Association of Dentists argued that the laws could not bind its members * * * [because]: it amounted to an unconstitutional "expropriation of labor;" discriminated against dentists * * *; [and] violated the constitutional principles of equality and freedom of choice of profession and residence. The last, but not least, argument was that the law violated the prohibition against forced or compulsory labor [in the European Convention for the Protection of Human Rights and Fundamental Freedoms which had gone into effect on September 3, 1953, and to which Norway was a party].

* * *

The Decision. The attacks on the law [as re-enacted in 1965] were rejected

The decision follows a previous decision [of 1961] * * * which concerned another and older side of the same conflict. The earlier judgment was rendered in a case where a dentist had been prosecuted [and] sentenced for having quit his post * * * [during the period he was required to serve in the public service of dentistry]. Thereupon he filed a complaint with the European Commission on Human Rights * * * alleging that his service constituted "forced or compulsory labor" prohibited by Article 4 of the European Convention on Human Rights * * *. [The commission rejected the complaint.]

* * *

In the present case, the Supreme Court expounded [in detail] the reasons for its view that the compulsory service of dentists does not violate the convention. * * * [I]t relied on the reasoning followed by the four members of the European Commission who had given an interpretation of the term "forced or compulsory labor" * * * [and discussed] the factors which, according to the members of the commission, characterize by implication the concept of forced labor [prohibited by the convention].

[The court then ruled that under this interpretation of forced labor, the law of 1965 providing for the mandatory service of dentists did not violate either the convention or the constitution.]

Note. So far as concerns principles, it must be noted that once more, as in the decision of 1961 * * *, the Supreme Court refrained from relying on the old and well established doctrine according to which, in Norwegian courts, any Norwegian law prevails over an international agreement. This doctrine has been the object of strong attacks by Hambro, Angdahl, Wold and others. * * *

So far as concerns more particularly the European Convention on Human Rights, Wold has maintained in Legal Essais, Festskrift til Frede Castberg (1963) p. 358 and following, that it must be applied as against legislative provisions to the contrary. He is President of the

Supreme Court of Norway and [also] a judge on the European Court for Human Rights; he took part in [the decision of the case here reported] and joined in the unanimous opinion [of the Supreme Court]. Nevertheless, the court held the law did not violate the convention; in the name of the court, accordingly, Justice Heiberg said there was no reason "to examine the question whether the convention would have prevailed over the law in the event of conflict between the two."

However, if the court had meant to reassert the old doctrine, it was superfluous for it to discuss in detail the interpretation of the law. Therefore, we may consider the decision as another illustration of what may be called the indirect application of the convention. It is of particular interest that in discussing the constitutional aspects of the case here reported the Supreme Court should have gone so far as to adopt expressly the interpretation of the convention for point of departure in interpreting [Norwegian] constitutional principles of much older origin which protect the rights of the individual.

* * *

S. A. v. CLERK OF THE TRIBUNAL OF COMMERCE

Belgium, Civil Tribunal of Brussels, 1966.
[1967] Pasicrisie Belge, III, 50.[a]

[A law of 1963 on the use of the Flemish and French languages directed all business associations * * * to use in their official documents and communications to their employees the language of the region where they had their headquarters or their place of business.

A company whose place of business and headquarters were in the Flemish speaking part of the country decided to open an office in Brussels, where French is the controlling language, and for this purpose it filed with the Clerk of the Tribunal of Commerce certain documents so he could register them and give them publication, as required by law. The documents were in the French language. The clerk refused to accept them on the ground that the place of business of the company was in the Flemish speaking part of the country and hence the documents should be in that language. The company declined to put them in Flemish. The clerk secured a court order for the appointment of a translator who would put the documents into Flemish.

The company sued the clerk in the Tribunal Civil for symbolic damages in the amount of one franc, on each of two counts, and an order directing the clerk to accept the documents and secure their

a. Translation by the editors. The decision is in the form of a series of clauses, each of which begins with the term "attendu que," or "whereas." The term, wherever it appears, has been omitted in this translation, as indicated by asterisks, and the punctuation has been modified to conform more substantially to English usage.

publication in French. The company contended that the law of 1963 on the use of the Flemish and French languages was contrary to Articles 10(1) and 14 of the European Convention for the Protection of Human Rights and Fundamental Freedoms which had gone into effect in September 3, 1953, and to which Belgium had become a party on May 13, 1955.

Article 10(1) of the convention provides: "Every person has the right to freedom of expression. This right shall include freedom to hold opinions and to receive and impart information and ideas without interference by public authority and regardless of frontiers * * *."

Article 14 of the convention provides: "The enjoyment of rights and freedoms set forth in this Convention shall be secured without any discrimination on any grounds such as sex, race, color, language, religion, political or other opinion, national or social origin, association with a national minority, property, birth or other status."

A portion of the opinion of the Tribunal Civil appears below.]

* * * [T]he defendant contends he has [only] abided by the provisions of Article 41 of the law of August 2, 1963, concerning the use of the [Flemish and French languages].

* * * [I]t is essential to note that these provisions are in conflict with Articles 10(1) and 14 on the Convention for the Protection of Human Rights * * *.

* * * [U]nless we are going to deny any useful effect to international rules which constitute a supranational law endowed * * * with obligatory force, we are bound to hold that in case of conflict between domestic law and international law, hierarchic superiority must be given to international agreements so long as * * * they have been ratified by a Belgian law.

* * * [O]n the basis of writings and case law * * *, we must recognize that international agreements can confer private rights upon the nationals of a state party to the convention, and we [must] insure their exercise beyond and against contrary rules established even at a posterior date by domestic legislation * * * [the court here gave citations to a Mercuriale [b] by the Procureur General of Belgium, some writings, and a decision by the Court of Justice of the European Communities].

* * * [I]t follows that Article 41(1) of the Belgian law of August 2, 1963, is not applicable to the extent that, in violation of Articles 10(1) and 14 of the Convention * * *, it may dictate the use of a particular language in records and documents of industrial, commercial or financial establishments.

* * * [A]ccordingly, it is no defense for the defendant to plead the provisions of the domestic law [of August 2, 1963].

b. The controlling importance of the Mercuriale is explained on p. 33.

* * *   [Though] the law of August 2, 1963, has given rise to many difficulties [in its application] and human understanding makes us perceive that the defendant, as a civil servant, may have been intimidated by the article   * * *   in the law which provides disciplinary sanctions for   * * *   civil servants who by their orders or actions avoid or try to nullify its mandate, it must be noted he was aware that   * * *   the plaintiff had opened a place of business in Brussels but nevertheless resorted to the procedure [for compelling a translation in Flemish].

* * *   [I]n refusing to believe the plaintiff's explanations and contending, as he still does in the pleadings, that the [subsequent] transfer of the headquarters of the company to [the office in] Brussels was done to the end of avoiding the provisions of the law of August 2, 1963   * * *   he behaved in a manner which was prejudicial to the plaintiff.

* * *   [K]nowing as early as 1963 the existence of the place of business of the plaintiff in Brussels, nothing justified his waiting till September 1964 to proceed with the [registration] and publication of the documents in controversy.

* * *

For these reasons, [the court]   * * *   holds the plaintiff was entitled to use the French language in the documents   * * * ; holds nevertheless there is no need to order the publication of the documents, this having been done already ; holds the defendant must pay the plaintiff one franc in damages for the delay in publication of [the first document] and one franc in damages for the delay in publication of [the second] ;   * * *   holds the defendant liable for costs.

––––––

1. *Background of the Belgian decision.* The key factor in this decision is the matter of fact citation by the court to a Mercuriale by the Procureur General of Belgium. The organization of the legal system of Belgium is somewhat different from that in the United States. Magistrates are civil servants under the control of a Ministry of Justice. Some of them are assigned to the bench while others are assigned to represent the Belgian state in civil and criminal cases in each of the courts in the system. At the apex of the pyramid of those assigned to represent the interests of the state is the procureur general, who is attached to the Supreme Court of Belgium.

A Mercuriale by the procureur general of Belgium is an address he usually delivers on the occasion of the opening of courts. It is more than a perfunctory speech. Rather it is a review of the state of the law in a particular field and contains recommendations as to the course the law should take in the future. There is no guarantee that what the procureur general recommends will be acted upon by the courts. Still, when the procureur general, on the occasion of the ceremonial opening of the Supreme Court of Belgium, takes the position that prior international agreements should prevail over subsequent and conflicting domestic law, all magistrates are likely to give great weight to his views.

That is why the decision is significant, even though it comes from a lower court—equivalent to a district court in the federal judiciary of the United States—and is not based on any constitutional provision whatever. The Mercuriale the procureur general delivered before the Supreme Court of Belgium on September 2, 1963, is published in 78 Journal des Tribunaux 481 (1963) and is entitled "Le Conflict Traité-Loi Interne". After a thorough review of authorities in point and analysis of the issue, it concludes (at 486) that, short of a constitutional or other legislative mandate expressly ordering the courts to give subsequent legislation prevalence over an anterior and conflicting international agreement, the courts should give prevalence to the agreement and indeed must do so, so far as concerns agreements establishing the European Communities.

Whether the Supreme Court of Belgium will eventually uphold the position adopted by the procureur general and the Tribunal Civil of Brussels remains, of course, to be seen. Several proposals for amendment of the Constitution of Belgium are under consideration which would, inter alia, provide for the prevalence of international agreements over anterior or posterior domestic law. They are discussed in van der Meersch, Reflexions sur le Droit International et la Revision de la Constitution Belge, [1969] Revue Belge de Droit International 1.

2. *A similar view.* The Council of State of Luxembourg—the highest administrative court—has held that the provisions of an international agreement "preclude the application of provisions to the contrary of a municipal law, even if the latter have been enacted subsequently." Dieudonné v. Administration des Contributions, 1951, 18 Int'l L.Rep. 11, 12 (1957). The High Court of Justice has held the same way in Public Prosecuteur v. Brasseur, 1951, 18 Int'l L.Rep. 396 (1957).

REMARKS OF PROFESSOR LOUIS B. SOHN

1969 Proceedings of the American Society of International Law 180.

Professor Louis B. Sohn addressed the question of the status of international law in the domestic law of the United States. The obsolete doctrine that international law is not controlling in United States courts when confronted with a later statute is a product of the jurisprudence of a period when international law was quite different from what it is today. The earlier cases concerned mostly problems relating to tariffs, customs, and property rights under treaties with France and Spain. Therefore, it was not difficult to say that a later United States statute would be of greater dignity.

The treaties in that period were bilateral treaties in the main. There was no conception of multilateral treaties applying to subjects of universal concern. In this regard, the United Nations Charter is completely different; it has a special, almost constitutional character. To an international instrument of this stature, the "later in time" overruling canon should not apply. It should be possible for the Supreme Court to say that the rules derived from the Charter prevail not only over earlier law but also over later statutes.

Question: What do you think now of the dictum in Reid v. Covert, p. 27?

INTERNAL EFFECT OF INTERNATIONAL AGREEMENTS IN FRANCE

Rousseau, Droit International Public 60,
(Precis Dalloz, 5th ed. 1970).[a]

Until recently * * * French courts started from the principle that international agreements properly ratified and promulgated had the force of law and, by application of the rule lex posterior derogat priori, made international agreements prevail over anterior domestic law when their provisions were in conflict. On the other hand, if the conflict arose between an international agreement and a posterior law, the recent case law showed an accommodating attitude; relying on the concept that it would not be proper to presume on the part of the legislature an intention to avoid the international obligations [of France], the courts [usually] found there was not truly a conflict between the provisions alleged to be inconsistent * * * [citations to cases]. This technique of conciliation was nonetheless unfortunate inasmuch as it could lead, in the case of a clear conflict, to setting aside the international agreement and thereby denying its binding effect.

But this case law belongs to the past since the text of Article 26 of the Constitution of October 27, 1946, specifies, without any equivocation, that "diplomatic treaties duly ratified and published shall have the force of law even when they are contrary to internal French legislation * * *." Ever since, the case law * * * [citations to cases] has made international agreements, including those which became binding before 1946, prevail over conflicting domestic law.

a. Translation by the editors.

The preceding text has been somewhat modified by Article 55 of the Constitution of 1958, according to which "treaties or agreements duly ratified or approved shall, upon their publication, have an authority superior to that of laws, subject, for each agreement and treaty, to its application by the other party." Quite aside from the fact that this provision requires a French court to proceed with laborious research into the practice of a state party to an agreement with France, it runs the risk of creating insoluble difficulties in the case of multilateral agreements.

Time sequence immaterial. Article 55 of the French Constitution of 1958 does not specify that the term "laws" includes both anterior and posterior laws. The specification, however, would have been superfluous and French courts as well as writers have never had any doubts about it. For once the international agreement is declared— not equal in rank with domestic laws—but to have an "authority superior to laws," it makes no difference whether the laws are anterior or posterior to the agreement. The international agreement, in a literal sense, is supreme.

Upon becoming independent, former French overseas territories adopted in their constitutions provisions similar to Article 55 in the French Constitution of 1958. Central African Republic, Article 35; Congo (Brazzaville), Article 62; Gabon, Article 54; Ivory Coast, Article 56; Mauritania, Article 46; Senegal, Article 79; Togo, Article 69; Upper Volta, Article 56. A similar provision also appears in Article 10 of the Constitution of Congo-Kinshasa (now Zaire) of May 30, 1964. I Peaslee, Constitutions of Nations 59, 93, 206, 249, 555, 709, 901, 1019, 105 (3d ed. 1965).

In 1953, the Constitution of the Netherlands of 1815, was amended in order to provide in Article 66: "Legal regulations in force within the Kingdom shall not apply if this application should be incompatible with provisions * * * of agreements entered into either before or after the enactment of the regulations." III (2) Peaslee, Constitutions of Nations 660 (3d ed. 1968). In 1954 the Supreme Court of the Netherlands relied on this article in holding that provisions of a law of 1943 were inapplicable because they were in conflict with the 1868 Convention of Manheim on the Navigation of the Rhine. Public Prosecutor v. J. de B., 21 Int'l L.Rep. 3 (1957). In a "note" following the report the editor points out that before the constitutional enactment, the court had always found there was no conflict and reached the result by "interpreting either the law or the agreement in such a way as to obviate a conflict." (at 8)

4. DOMESTIC ARRANGEMENTS FOR INSURING NATIONAL ACTION IN CONFORMITY WITH INTERNATIONAL LAW

CREATION OF DEPARTMENT OF FOREIGN AFFAIRS

A first order of business for a new state is to create a department to conduct its foreign relations. In the case of the United States, it was created by the Act of July 27, 1789 for Establishing an Executive Department to be Denominated the Department of Foreign Affairs, 1 Stat. 28. The Act of September 15, 1789, 1 Stat. 68, directed that it be denominated the "Department of State." This early legislation was brief and general, consisting essentially of a broad delegation of powers from the President to the Secretary of State for conducting the foreign affairs of the United States. Since then, legislation concerning the "Foreign Relations and Intercourse" of the United States has grown voluminous and is collected in Title 22 of the United States Code.

During the early days, the legal work of the Department of State was often conducted personally by the Secretaries of State, who proved to be able lawyers. Eventually, the handling of legal affairs in the department became a specialized function and is now vested in the Office of the Legal Adviser, as explained in the material which follows.

LEGAL ADVISER TO DEPARTMENT OF FOREIGN AFFAIRS

BILDER, THE OFFICE OF THE LEGAL ADVISER: THE STATE DEPARTMENT LAWYER AND FOREIGN AFFAIRS

56 American Journal of International Law 633 (1962).

As "house counsel" to the Department of State, the Office of the Legal Adviser exerts a major influence on the views and policies of the United States Government concerning matters of international law. It plays a significant role as well with respect to a broad range of domestic law matters related to the international dealings of the United States and its citizens. * * *

* * * [A] discussion of the Office's work may be of interest to persons generally concerned with international law by providing some insight into the way foreign offices such as the State Department actually develop and implement international law.

* * *

General Functions and a Bit of History

The Office of the Legal Adviser furnishes legal advice to the Secretary of State and the Department of State, including the Foreign Service and diplomatic and consular posts abroad, with respect to all legal problems involving either domestic or international law which arise in the course of the Department's work. Its task thus generally corresponds to that of the various Offices of General Counsel of other Executive branch agencies. Since the Department of State has primary responsibility for carrying out the foreign policy and conducting the international relations of the United States, the bulk of the Office's work relates in some way to international matters.

While the Department of State was established in 1789, the Office of the Legal Adviser has a much briefer history. In the early days of the Republic, the legal work of the Department was often handled personally by such Secretaries of State as Jefferson, Monroe and Madison, who were able lawyers. The particular duty of processing and handling international claims, however, soon became quite burdensome, and in 1848 Congress authorized the appointment of a clerk within the Department with the exclusive function of dealing with such claims. The number of such clerks was gradually increased * * *. With the establishment of the Department of Justice in 1870, the Attorney General assumed principal responsibility for the legal work of the Department of State * * *.

In 1891, the Office of Solicitor of the Department of State was established. * * *

In 1909, Congress created the high-level position of Counselor of the Department, whose functions were to include the study of international law questions. John Bassett Moore at one time filled this post. However, the Counselor's political responsibilities soon came to dominate his legal ones, and the Solicitor remained the official primarily responsible for legal matters.

In 1931, the Office of the Solicitor was abolished and the position of The Legal Adviser was established by statute. Since that time this position has been held by eight Legal Advisers.

* * *

The Work of the Office

In carrying out its job of furnishing legal assistance to the Department, the Office is called upon to perform a number of related but analytically distinct functions. Some of these are similar to the functions of any private lawyer or "house counsel" to a large corporation. Others are peculiar to the Office's special rôle as counsel for a Government agency.

These various functions might be outlined as follows:

a. The Office as Counselor. The Office, through its various branches, works closely with the policy desks of the Department in every aspect of their daily work, and is continually available for consultation as to any legal problems which might arise in the course of Departmental operations. It gives formal and informal legal opinions as required on questions of international and domestic law, including the interpretation of international agreements, statutes, and various legal documents. * * *

b. The Office as Draftsman. The Office's particular expertise as draftsman is in the area of the preparation of treaties and other international agreements. But its responsibilities frequently involve it also in the drafting of legislation, executive orders, proclamations, and Departmental regulations. Thus, it has played a major part in the drafting of the various foreign aid and trade agreements acts, and regularly drafts executive proclamations implementing trade agreements.

c. The Office as Advocate and Negotiator. The Office is responsible for the actual litigation of any case in which the United States is involved before the International Court of Justice. It has not, however, in recent years represented either the Department of State or the U. S. Government in domestic or foreign national courts, this function being reserved by statute and tradition to the Department of Justice.

However, despite the fact that the Office does not often appear in court to actually litigate cases, its rôle as advocate and negotiator remains an important one; for the Office is frequently called upon to urge or argue the position of a desk, the Department, or the Government itself in the various intra-government and international fora where much of the actual business of government and international relations is carried on. * * *

d. The Office as Judge. In performing its function of giving opinions on legal questions, particularly those involving international law, which arise in the course of the Department's work, the Office inevitably acts to some degree as judge. In many cases, its opinion may determine the question, either because other agencies and the courts typically defer to its decisions in such matters, or simply because there is in practice no appeal to the courts or other agencies from its decisions. * * *

e. The Office as International Law Expert. Because of the Office's special expertise in international law, it is frequently called upon by other governments, other U. S. Government agencies, Congress, the courts, State officials, and private companies and individuals for information or its views concerning questions of international law. Thus, the Office is frequently asked by Federal and State courts for an interpretation of particular treaties or its views on particular questions of customary international law, and it has been asked by a State Attorney General whether his State may discriminate against foreign producers or products in its public purchases without being in violation of U. S. international agreements. As will be later discussed, while the Office's views as "expert" generally are not binding, at least as regards addressees of its opinions outside of the Executive branch, these views will usually have great influence with respect to the determination of the matter.

                    *   *   *

The problems in which the Office becomes involved are almost unlimited in variety. They may concern such diverse areas as atomic energy and airplane hijacking; foreign bases and agricultural surplus disposal; satellites and shrimp fishing; the legal status of Okinawa and rights of performing artists to protection from unauthorized exploitation of their performances; arms shipments to the Congo and pollution of the sea by oil. These problems tend, however, to fall into the following principal categories:

a.   Does the United States have a valid complaint against a foreign government under international law by reason of particular action or prospective action by that government? The alleged violation may principally affect the United States Government itself, as in the case of Soviet action in Berlin; or it may principally affect private United States citizens, as in the case of Cuban expropriation of American property, or allegedly discriminatory taxation of an American firm in a foreign country contrary to the provisions of a commercial treaty.

b.   Does a foreign government have a valid complaint against the United States under international law by reason of particular action or prospective action by the United States? Again, the alleged violation may principally affect the foreign government itself, as in the case of the U–2 reconnaissance flights over the U.S.S.R.; or it may principally affect private citizens of the foreign government, as in the case of the wartime seizure by the United States under the Trading With the Enemy Act of the assets of the Swiss-owned but allegedly German-controlled General Aniline and Film Company (the Interhandel Case), or the denial of social security benefits earned in the United States to a citizen of a foreign country with which the United States has a commercial treaty containing provisions relating to social security.

c.   May the Department or the United States Government take a particular course of action consistently with domestic and international law? The Department or the United States Government may contemplate taking some action having a bearing on foreign relations which raises legal questions. The proposed measure may pose solely questions of international law, as in the case of the proposed orbiting of a reconnaissance satellite; solely domestic law questions, as in the case of the proposed denial of a passport to a newspaper reporter intending to go to Communist China; or both, as in the case of the possible denial by the Civil Aeronautics Board on economic grounds of permission to a foreign air carrier to operate a particular route allegedly covered by a bilateral air transport agreement, despite a provision of U. S. law requiring the Civil Aeronautics Board to exercise its powers consistently with international agreements.

d. How may a general policy objective be achieved consistently with domestic and international law? In connection with the making of policy decisions by the Department, the Office becomes involved in the examination of various legal means of reaching the desired result, including the possibility of new or amended legislation or international agreements. Thus, such legal instruments as the Foreign Assistance Act of 1961 and the Convention establishing the Organization for Economic Co-operation and Development, in the preparation of both of which the Office played a considerable part, were essentially legal means of implementing certain foreign policy objectives. Similarly, implementation of foreign policy objectives regarding Cuba and the Dominican Republic was a factor in the preparation of various amendments to the Sugar Act; and the United States commitment pursuant to a U. N. resolution to prevent Americans from participating in arms shipments to the Congo led to an amendment of Department of Commerce Export Control Regulations and Transportation Orders to prohibit such shipments.

* * *

The Office and the Courts

The function of interpreting and applying international law and agreements is, of course, performed not only by foreign offices such as the Department of State, but also by both international and national courts. In United States international law practice, the Office of the Legal Adviser shares its functions in this regard with Federal and State courts, and occasionally with certain Federal administrative agencies which perform quasi-judicial functions, such as the Civil Aeronautics Board and the National Labor Relations Board.

It is not always appreciated, however, that the over-all influence of adjudicative agencies on international law is in general considerably less important than that exercised by foreign offices. The number of international law questions passed on by international or United States tribunals is probably no more than a fraction of the number of such questions passed on by the Office of the Legal Adviser in any equivalent period, and the types of such questions considered by courts are generally of comparatively minor significance in the broad context of international regulation. Moreover, the nature of adjudicative techniques, which are restricted to disputes which have already arisen and which can deal only with such questions as the litigants choose to bring before tribunals, inherently limits their capacity to establish broad and flexible means of regulation for complex and changing international situations. Finally, even in this area of supposedly independent judicial influence with respect to international law, the opinions and policies of the Office frequently exert considerable weight on decisions reached by courts. Thus, despite the important rôle played by judicial agencies in certain areas of international law, the Department of State and its Office of Legal Adviser in practice tend to carry the main burden of vindicating the international rights and obligations of the United States and its citizens, and play the principal creative rôle in this country in implementing and developing international law.

* * *

EXPRESS LEGISLATIVE DIRECTIVE

RESTATEMENT OF THE FOREIGN RELATIONS LAW OF THE UNITED STATES

Reporters' Notes to Section 145 (1965).*

2. The Internal Revenue Code. Section 7852(d) of the Revenue Code of 1954 provides that "No provision of this title shall apply in any case where its application would be contrary to any treaty obligation of the United States in effect on the date of enactment of this title." Section 31 of the Revenue Act of 1962 provides that Section 7852(d) does not apply to the provisions of the 1962 Act.

The Treasury Department informed the Congress that in its view there would be no conflict between the Revenue Act of 1962 and provisions of tax treaties of the United States—"with one minor exception relating to the real estate clause of the Greek Estate Tax Treaty which the Treasury will seek to have renegotiated before July 1, 1964," the date upon which the conflicting provisions in the Revenue Act would become effective. H.R.Rep.No.2508, 87th Cong., 2d Sess. 48. The treaty with Greece was renegotiated by protocol signed February 12, 1964. See S.Ex.A, 88th Cong., 2d Sess. (1964); Department of State Press Release No. 60, Feb. 13, 1964.

INFERRED LEGISLATIVE DIRECTIVE

JESSUP, THE ANTI–SMUGGLING ACT OF 1935

31 American Journal of International Law 101 (1937).

The "Anti-Smuggling Act" was passed on August 5, 1935. Its principal purpose was to facilitate the more adequate enforcement of the revenue laws of the United States, particularly against vessels smuggling liquor from the sea into the United States. Extensive hearings were held on the bill before the Committee on Ways and Means of the House. The bill was sponsored by the Treasury Department, and despite repeated efforts on the part of the House Committee to obtain a statement of the views of the Department of State, no statement was made on behalf of that Department. A letter to the Chairman of the Committee from Secretary of State Hull was read into the record. This letter declared that "Such communications as this Department has seen fit to make regarding the bill have been brought to the attention of the Secretary of the Treasury, who is charged with the duty of enforcing anti-smuggling legislation, and I assume that such of those comments as may be deemed pertinent to you here will be brought to the attention of the Committee by officials of the Treasury Department." Although the representative of the Treasury who appeared in defense of the bill before the Committee was asked to obtain from the Secretary of the Treasury authorization to communicate to the Committee the comments which had been made by the State Department, the Treasury representative reported that he was authorized to state only "that the State Department has advised the Treasury Department that it will not oppose the enactment of this bill." There seems to be considerable justification for the view of several members of the Committee who read between the lines of Secretary Hull's letter a desire to avoid becoming involved in the matter in any way. There is an inescapable implication that the State Department had some reservations regarding the legislation.

Whether or not the Anti-Smuggling Act will result in diplomatic controversies will probably depend upon the way in which it is enforced. There are provisions in the Act which are open to grave question and which may cause serious international complications, but, as the Government of the United States learned in the course of a long series of negotiations with the Mexican Government, it is usually futile to enter into a controversy with a foreign government regarding the terms of legislation before the legislation is applied in any particular case. It is understood that one foreign government, however, has indicated that it questions whether this legislation is in accord with recognized principles of international law.

Only certain provisions of the Act can be treated within the scope of this comment; attention will be called to aspects which are of particular interest from the international standpoint.

The Act contemplates the existence of four different zones in the water adjacent to the coasts of the United States * * * The fourth zone is entirely new. It is called a "customs-enforcement area." The extent of this zone varies from time to time and from place to place. Customs-enforcement areas are fixed by the President upon the basis of information supplied to him by the Coast Guard to the effect that a smuggling vessel or vessels are hovering or are being kept near the coasts of the United States for the purpose of unlawfully introducing merchandise into the United States. * * *

*   *   *

To illustrate: if the Coast Guard informs the President that a foreign vessel suspected of intending to smuggle goods into the United States is hovering forty-five miles off the northerly tip of Long Island, the President may proclaim a customs-enforcement area extending one hundred nautical miles north and south from that point and including all of the waters sixty-two miles from the coast within that stretch of two hundred miles. * * * The presence of a particular suspected vessel is necessary in order to have an area declared, but once it is declared, *any vessel* may be boarded in that area. It should be made clear, however, that the Act is scrupulously careful to respect the treaty obligations of the United States, and in no case may a vessel be boarded or seized in contravention of a treaty, notwithstanding any proclamation of a customs-enforcement area. * * *

The Act contains detailed provisions describing the circumstances under which vessels may be boarded and seized. Briefly, it may be said that these provisions are far reaching, apparently allowing the customs officers to act upon the basis of any suspicion as to the character and intentions of the vessel. Under the broad terms of Sec. 3(a), for example, a foreign vessel which had been fitted out or "held" for the purpose of being employed to smuggle goods into the United States, may be seized and forfeited with its cargo if found later in a customs-enforcement area. Under Sec. 203(a) of the Act (amending Sec. 581 of the Tariff Act of 1930) boarding officers may use "all necessary force to compel compliance." One may also note in the same section this further provision suggesting a broadened base for the right of hot pursuit. * * * But this provision is also specifically made subject to compliance with the liquor treaties except as foreign governments agree to special rules. Note also that under Sec. 207, the testimony of a boarding customs officer is made "prima facie evidence of the place where the act in question occurred."

In the hearings before the House Committee a great deal of time was devoted to examining the question whether, under international law, the United States had a right to assert such jurisdiction at such distances from the coast. It was on this point particularly that the Committee desired but failed to secure the views of the Department of State. The case of the Treasury Department was ably supported before the Committee by Professor H. E. Yntema, of the University of Michigan Law School. * * *

* * *

If the courts have occasion to interpret this Act, they will undoubtedly take cognizance of the fact that both the Hearings and the Committee Report lay great stress upon the intent that no jurisdiction should be asserted outside the limits authorized by international law.

STANDING INSTRUCTIONS TO SERVICES

In the services of the Government of the United States such as the Armed Forces, the Coast Guard and the Foreign Service, standing instructions are issued to officers who, because of their position or mission, may have to handle situations susceptible of creating serious international repercussions for the United States.

The instructions may anticipate some specific situations and spell out procedures for meeting them which are in conformity with international law. For a flawless execution of procedures in a case of this type, see below the boarding and inspection by a U. S. naval vessel of a Soviet trawler suspected of damaging submarine cables. With respect to situations which cannot be specifically anticipated, the instructions provide for reference through channels to higher authority and eventually to the Department of State. For a situation where the system of reference broke down through human error, see below the case of the Soviet sailor who sought refuge aboard a Coast Guard vessel.

Of course, the issuance of standing instructions to services for insuring national action in conformity with international law is a practice followed in many national legal systems.

BOARDING AND INSPECTION BY UNITED STATES NAVAL VESSEL OF SOVIET TRAWLER SUSPECTED OF DAMAGING SUBMARINE CABLES: EXCHANGE OF NOTES BETWEEN THE UNITED STATES AND THE UNION OF SOVIET SOCIALIST REPUBLICS

53 United States Naval War College, International Law Studies
1959–1960, at 159 (1961).

[The boarding and inspection of the Soviet trawler were carried out on February 26, 1959. By an aide memoire dated February 28, 1959, the embassy of the United States in Moscow informed the Minister of Foreign Affairs of the Soviet Union of the boarding and inspection. On March 4, 1959, the Minister of Foreign Affairs of the Soviet Union sent a note to the embassy in which it protested the "detention and inspection" of the Soviet fishing trawler. In a note dated March 23, 1959, the embassy of the United States conveyed the reply of the government of the United States. A portion of that note appears below.]

The Embassy of the United States of America refers to the Ministry's note No. 17/OSA, dated March 4, 1959 concerning recent breaks in certain transatlantic submarine tele-communication cables and the consequent visit to the Soviet trawler Novorossiisk by a boarding party of the U.S.S. Roy O. Hale, which was the subject of the Embassy's aide memoire of February 28, 1959.

* * *

For the reasons set out hereinafter the United States Government considers there is no basis for a protest in this case and the Soviet protest is therefore rejected. * * *

* * *

The Government of the United States, acting under the provisions of Article X of the Convention for the Protection of Submarine Cables, of 1884, to which both the United States and the Union of Soviet Socialist Republics adhere, and also in conformity with United States law (47 United States Code, Section 26), implementing the convention, on February 25, 1959, dispatched the United States radar picket escort U.S.S. Roy O. Hale to the area to investigate the reported breaks in the submarine cables. On February 26, 1959, about 11:55 a. m., eastern standard time, the Commander of the U.S.S. Roy O. Hale sent a party consisting of one officer and four enlisted men, without arms, aboard the Soviet trawler Novorossiisk. At the time of the visit the trawler was in position latitude 48°26′ N., longitude 49°10′W. There were no other ships in the immediate vicinity.

* * *

The boarding officer, communicating by means of French through an interpreter, duly informed and explained to the master of the trawler Novorossiisk the purpose of his visit and his authority to do so under the provisions of the convention of 1884. He examined, with the consent and acquiescence of the master, the papers of the trawler which appeared to be in order.

The boarding officer found that the latitude and longitude which the trawler Novorossiisk recorded in her journal for the previous days' positions also showed her to have been in the immediate vicinity of all five cable breaks. * * * On the basis of the foregoing evidence, the boarding officer concluded that an examination of the fishing gear and equipment was justified to determine whether the trawler was capable of causing the cable breaks.

The unarmed boarding officer, with the consent of the master of the trawler, observed without deep examination, on the upper deck of the trawler only, the trawling equipment and fishing gear. The boarding officer noted that the trawling equipment was of the type for deep sea fishing, and was in general fairly new, with the exception of the otter boards and net discs which were well worn and in poor condition. The trawling cable was estimated to be about 300 fathoms in length, sufficiently long enough to drag the gear on the bottom at the depth in the area—about 180 fathoms. Two broken sections of trawling cable each about 60 feet in length were observed wrapped around the hatch on deck. The four ends of these cables were shredded and frayed and appeared to have parted as a result of a sudden strain such as could have been caused by snagging the gear. These sections are identical in type, age, and condition with the trawling cable. Some of the fish observed lying frozen on deck were of the bottom type.

The visit on board the trawler lasted about 70 minutes, and was completed at 1:05 p. m., eastern standard time. * * *

A preliminary report emanating from the cable repair ship Lord Kelvin which has since repaired the first broken cable states that the eastern portion of the damaged cable had been badly scraped and scuffed for about a mile east of the break. The cable had been severed by cutting. The technical opinion is that such evidence indicates that a trawler had picked up the cable with its drag, then having pulled it on deck, had cut it to release the nets.

The protection of submarine telecommunications cables on the high seas constitutes an international obligation. The locations and presence of the transatlantic submarine cables that have been cut are widely known among world fishing and maritime circles. They are shown and marked on United States admiralty and navigation maps which are available to the general public.

The above-stated record of events shows that, contrary to the assertions and charges made in the above-mentioned note of the Union of Soviet Socialist Republics, the visit to the Soviet trawler Novorossiisk under the circumstances shown was entirely justified and was in every respect in accordance with international law and applicable treaty provisions.

* * *

SOVIET SAILOR SEEKS U. S. HAVEN, BUT LOSES

U. S. News & World Report
December 14, 1970, at 30.*

An international controversy has boiled up around the case of a Soviet sailor who sought refuge in the U. S. and was turned back.[a]

* * * The incident that set off all this uproar took place at sea off Martha's Vineyard, Mass., on November 23. The command ship for a Soviet fishing fleet and the U. S. Coast Guard cutter Vigilant were moored side by side while authorities discussed a new fishing agreement.

During the day, there were visits back and forth by crewmen of the two ships. One Soviet sailor, identified as a Lithuanian named Simas Kudirka, told U. S. sailors that he wished to defect and

---

* Copyright, 1970, U. S. News & World Report.

a. The international law concerning asylum and refuge is treated in Chapter 9.

would leap into the water when the ships separated. The State Department and Coast Guard headquarters in Washington were notified.

Later, Mr. Kudirka leaped directly onto the Vigilant. Russian crewmen were permitted to return him to the Soviet ship. Witnesses said they used force and the refugee was beaten.

Adm. Chester A. Bender, Coast Guard Commandant, said the decision to deny Mr. Kudirka sanctuary was that of the commander in the Boston area.

Said Admiral Bender:

> While it is not yet clearly established whether or not he took the proper action, I believe it to be understood how he would make this decision on the existing circumstances.

> I do not approve of the use of force on a Coast Guard ship by personnel of another nation, but do recognize that considerable force was required as the defector was resisting strongly.

Washington, the Admiral said, had not provided "specific advice * * * as to what action to take."

Well-founded fear. The U. N. agreement on defectors, which the U. S. has signed but Russia has not, defines a refugee this way:

> Any person who, owing to well-founded fear of being persecuted for reasons of race, religion, nationality, membership of a particular social group, or political opinion, is outside the country of his nationality and is unable or, owing to such fear, is unwilling to avail himself of the protection of that country.

The obligation of a country which has signed the refugee agreement is also spelled out:

> No contracting state shall expel or return a refugee in any manner whatsoever to the frontiers of territory where his life or freedom would be threatened on account of race, religion, nationality, membership of a particular social group, or political opinion.

Fugitives from criminal proceedings are not protected by the agreement. The Russians claimed Mr. Kudirka had stolen $2,000 from the ship's safe. The State Department later said the seaman's case "should have been handled through the U. S. judicial system."

Since 1945, nearly 1.5 million refugees have been admitted to the U. S. for political reasons. Cubans—totaling 538,000—make up the largest single nationality. East Europeans and ethnic Germans displaced from East Europe constitute the largest regional group.

White House action. In the wake of the incident, Mr. Nixon ordered a report from the State Department and the Department of Transportation, which controls the Coast Guard. After studying the report, said the White House, the President ordered "immediate remedial action to insure that there will never be a recurrence of a shocking incident of this kind."

Among actions taken:

The White House promulgated interim rules setting forth more-specific policies on how to deal with would-be defectors and refugees.

Direct communication links were ordered between the Coast Guard and the State Department and White House.

Strict instructions were issued that the White House be immediately advised of similar incidents.

In Cambridge, Mass., the Coast Guard began a formal inquiry to determine if a court-martial is warranted.

The Voice of America told the world in 23 languages—including Lithuanian—that the denial of asylum was a bureaucratic bungle and that the United States had not changed its policy on refugees.

INTERVENTION BY HIGHEST AUTHORITY

NORWEGIAN STATE v. CARLILE

Norway, Supreme Court (Appeals Division), 1964.
96 Journal du Droit International 438 (1969).[a]

[Carlile, a British subject, was arrested and indicted for swindling. On several occasions, he had gone to hotels in Norway and simulated stumbling, falling and suffering injuries, and collected damages. He had done the same thing several times in Denmark and Sweden. The governments of Denmark and Sweden requested the Norwegian authorities also to indict Carlile for his acts in Denmark and Sweden. They did. Thereupon Carlile objected on the ground that Norway had no jurisdiction under international law to indict him for acts done in Denmark and Sweden.

On appeal, the Supreme Court held that even if international law prohibited the application of Norwegian penal law to acts committed in Denmark and Sweden, the prohibition did not apply at the stage of indictment for infractions punishable under the law of all three countries. Hence, it said, the objection was premature and would have to be ruled upon at trial. The British Embassy in Oslo took up the matter with the Norwegian Ministry of Foreign Affairs and questioned the basis of jurisdiction of Norway with respect to the acts committed by Carlile in Denmark and Sweden. The outcome is explained in a "note" which follows the report of the case. A portion of the note appears below.]

* * * At the request of the Public Prosecutor, the Ministry of Foreign Affairs requested an opinion from its Legal Adviser, Pro-

a. Translation by the editors. Reprinted by permission of Editions Techniques, S.A., Paris.

fessor Castberg. He took the position that the grounds [relied upon by the Supreme Court] were highly questionable, despite the requests for prosecution made by Denmark and Sweden, so long as the United Kingdom did not consent to the exercise of jurisdiction over its national.

By decision of the Cabinet, a royal decree of April 17, 1964, voided the indictment to the extent it covered acts done in Denmark and Sweden.

* * *

NATIONAL APOLOGY

AFFAIRE MANTOVANI, ITALY–SWITZERLAND, 1965

Rousseau, Chronique des Faits Internationaux,
69 Revue Générale de Droit International Public 761, 834 (1965)a

On the 7th of March, at about one o'clock in the morning, three inspectors of the Italian police in civilian clothes and attached to the police of Milan, arrested an Italian national, a resident of Como already sentenced twice in Italy for contraband, one Bruno Giuseppe Mantovani, age thirty-five, when he was coming out of a restaurant in Lugano. After handcuffing him, they took him away in an Italian car which reached the Italian territory of Campione. Alerted by a passerby who had witnessed the scene, the * * * [local Swiss] police went into action immediately and the same day at about noontime Mantovani was brought back to Swiss territory. He said to the Swiss authorities that the Italian policemen had tried, while he was being interrogated at Campione, to make him sign a declaration to the effect that he had been arrested, not on Swiss territory, but on Italian territory, on the right bank of Lake Lugano. Again according to the * * * [local Swiss] police, Mantovani was being sought by the Italian police for contraband; but * * * the offense would not have been by itself a sufficient basis for a request of extradition to the Swiss authorities.

The 9th of March, the Federal Department of Justice and Police published a communique on the incident. [Its text follows.]

On Monday afternoon, the Attorney General of the Confederation granted audience at Berne, at their request, to * * * [high officials of the Italian Police from Milan and Rome], who came accompanied by the chief of the * * * [local Swiss] police. * * * According to the Italian officials, Mantovani was being sought in Italy to make him serve certain prison terms to which he had been sentenced, not only for acts of contraband, but also for * * * other crimes.

On the basis of the statements by the * * * [local Swiss] police and of the complementary explanations given by the two high

---

a. Translation by the editors. Reprinted with permission of Charles Rousseau and Editions A. Pedone, Paris.

officials from Italy, it became clear that the frontier incident must be attributed to the excess of zeal of a sergeant of the Italian police, who was in charge of a patrol with the assignment of arresting Mantovani at Campione (Italy) where he was expected to arrive.

The two high officials of the Italian police presented official apologies for the violation of the territorial sovereignty of Switzerland by their subordinates and gave assurances that everything would be done to avoid a repetition of such an incident, while measures against the guilty subordinates, who acted without the knowledge of their superiors, were being considered.

The federal authorities consider the case closed.

SECTION B. APPLICATION IN DIPLOMATIC PRACTICE

CHARTER OF THE UNITED NATIONS

Article 33

1. The parties to any dispute, the continuance of which is likely to endanger the maintenance of international peace and security, shall, first of all, seek a solution by negotiation, enquiry, mediation, conciliation, arbitration, judicial settlement, resort to regional agencies or arrangements, or other peaceful means of their own choice.

2. The Security Council shall, when it deems necessary, call upon the parties to settle their dispute by such means.

ATTORNEY–GENERAL OF ISRAEL v. EICHMANN

Israel, District Court of Jerusalem, 1961.
36 Int'l L.Rep. 5 (1968).

SUMMARY—On May 11, 1960, Adolph Eichmann was abducted from Buenos Aires, Argentina, where he had been living since 1950 under the assumed name of Ricardo Klement. After signing a letter purporting to consent to trial in Israel, he was removed to Israel by members of the Israel Secret Service. On May 23, the Prime Minister of Israel announced that Eichmann had been found and would be put on trial for his part in the "Final Solution". The Government of Argentina protested that the capture was a violation of Argentine territorial sovereignty, for which it alleged that the State of Israel was responsible by reason of its express approval of the action, and asked for Eichmann's return and the punishment of those responsible for the violation of Argentine law. In a Note of June 3, the Government of Israel attributed the capture to a "volunteer group" and expressed its regret if it had "violated Argentine law and interfered with matters within the sovereignty of Argentina". Similar expressions of regret, and references also to the lofty motives and the historical and ethical factors involved, were made in a personal letter from Mr. Ben Gurion, the Israel Prime Minister, to Mr. Frondizi, President of Argentina.

The dispute, however, failed to be resolved through normal diplomatic channels, and Argentina presented a complaint to the Security Council of the United Nations requesting an urgent meeting to consider the violation of its sovereign rights. At the meeting of the Security Council held on June 22, 1960, the Argentine representative emphasized that Argentina had protested against a violation of its sovereignty by the unlawful exercise of foreign authority within its territory—to which it was irrelevant that Eichmann had been living there under an assumed name and in breach of its national laws—rather than against a violation of the general rules governing territorial asylum or political refugees. He submitted a draft resolution (subsequently approved—with minor amendments—by eight votes to nil, with two abstentions) which, while disclaiming any condonation of the crimes of which Eichmann was accused, declared that "acts such as that under consideration, which affect the sovereignty of a Member State and therefore cause international friction, may, if repeated, endanger international peace and security", and requested the Government of Israel "to make appropriate reparation in accordance with the Charter of the United Nations and the rules of international law". The Argentine representative declined to specify what form of reparation would be "appropriate", and it appeared to be the view of most representatives that the resolution itself and the expressions of regret by the Government of Israel constituted, in the special circumstances, "appropriate reparation". In the resolution as finally adopted, the hope was expressed that "the traditionally friendly relations between Argentina and Israel will be advanced". (The full text of the resolution appears in paragraph 40 of the judgment of the District Court.)

The dispute was finally closed by a joint communiqué issued on August 3, 1960, by the Argentine and Israel Governments:

> The Governments of Argentina and Israel, animated by a desire to give effect to the resolution of the Security Council of June 23, 1960, in so far as the hope was expressed that the traditionally friendly relations between the two countries will be advanced, resolve to regard as closed the incident which arose out of the action taken by citizens of Israel, which infringed the fundamental rights of the State of Argentina.[a]

a. For a discussion of this case as it relates to individual responsibility for war crimes, see Chapter 10.

Diplomatic practice. The primary means of resolving claims asserted under international law by one state against another is diplomatic correspondence. It is the everyday working method of the international system for settling legal disputes and its effectiveness is attested to by centuries of practice. Hence correspondence recording the diplomatic negotiations of states in settling their legal claims is a vast and valuable repository of information on the application of the law of the international system.

A note of caution is in order, however, concerning the use of this correspondence.

The assertion of a claim under international law by one state against another is a contentious statement and in the diplomatic presentation of its claim a state is often stating a partisan position, a one-sided view of the facts and the law applicable to them. In some cases, of course, the claim may be exactly stated and incontrovertible on both facts and law, and hence may be accepted as valid by the other. In many more cases, however, the defending state questions either or both. Not until they have achieved mutual agreement as to both can it be said they have recognized a particular rule of international law as applicable to the particular case.

Thus the totality of the relevant diplomatic exchanges has to be considered before any conclusion can be reached regarding the rule of international law applied to the resolution of a claim. Moreover, it must be kept in mind that the resolution of a claim by diplomatic negotiation may turn in the end, not solely on considerations of international law, but partly on political, economic, and other empirical factors.

"Digests of International Law" published by governments contain, inter alia, a great deal of diplomatic correspondence on issues of international law. In the United States, the digest of Moore of 1906 was followed by that of Hackworth in 1940, and since 1963 fifteen volumes of Whiteman's Digest of International Law have been published. In the United Kingdom, Parry began to publish in 1965 A British Digest of International Law which is compiled principally from the archives of the Foreign Office of the United Kingdom. An increasing number of other states are also making this kind of information available to the public.

The volumes of the Foreign Relations of the United States, usually published from 20 to 25 years after the events, frequently throw light on legal issues involved in originally highly classified documents.

THE RED CRUSADER

Commission of Enquiry, (Denmark-United Kingdom), 1962.
35 Int'l L.Rep. 485 (1967).

* * * On May 29, 1961, the British trawler Red Crusader was arrested by the Danish authorities off the coast of the Faroe Islands. A Commission of Enquiry was set up by an Exchange of Notes of November 15, 1961, between the Governments of Denmark and the United Kingdom to investigate certain incidents relating to this arrest and to subsequent events.

The Exchange of Notes requested the Commission to investigate and report to the two Governments:

(1) the facts leading up to the arrest of the British trawler, Red Crusader, on the night of the 29th of May, 1961, including the question whether the Red Crusader was fishing, or with her fishing gear not stowed, inside the blue line on the map annexed to the Agreement between the two Governments concerning the Regulation of Fishing around the Faroe Islands constituted by the Exchange of Notes of the 27th of April, 1959;

(2) the circumstances of the arrest; and

(3) the facts and incidents that occurred thereafter before the Red Crusader reached Aberdeen.

The Commission was constituted on November 21, 1961, in The Hague, with Professor Charles De Visscher as President, and Professor André Gros and Captain C. Moolenburgh as Members.
* * *

The Commission heard the Danish witnesses and experts at the meetings held on March 5-9. After examination by the Danish Agent the witnesses were cross-examined by British Counsel and, in some cases, re-examined. From March 10, the British witnesses and one expert were heard by the Commission. After examination by the British Counsel the witnesses and the expert were cross-examined by the Danish Agent and, in some cases, re-examined. From March 14-16 the Commission heard the oral statements and replies.

[There follows the text of the commission's report with findings concerning the facts leading up to the arrest of the Red Crusader, the circumstances of the arrest, the attempted escape of the Red Crusader after the arrest, the use of gunfire by the Danish naval vessel to stop the escape, and the actions of British naval vessels which had come on the scene.]

* * * On April 4, 1962, the Lord Privy Seal, a Minister in the British Government, said in the House of Commons:

In accordance with the Agreement for reference to the Commission, Her Majesty's Government accept its findings as final. House of Commons Debates, Vol. 657, Written Answers, col. 43.

On January 23, 1963, the Joint Under-Secretary of State for Foreign Affairs made the following statement in the House of Commons:

> Her Majesty's Government and the Danish Government have now completed their consultation about the Report of the Commission of Enquiry into the incidents affecting the Scottish trawler Red Crusader at the end of May 1961. In their desire to remove a source of disagreement between them, the two Governments have decided that the incident should be settled by a mutual waiver of all claims and charges arising out of the incident. These waivers enter into effect forthwith. The owners of the trawler have concurred in this settlement.

> As a result Skipper Wood and the Red Crusader are free to enter Danish waters without fear of arrest in relation to the events of May 1961, and the owners' claim for compensation has been dropped. The two Governments consider that the incident can now be considered closed, though without prejudice to the view on points of law maintained by each Government. House of Commons Debates, Vol. 670, Written Answers, cols. 77–78.

COMMISSIONS OF INQUIRY OF THE UNITED NATIONS

Whiteman, 12 Digest of International Law 946, 950 (1970).

Referring to "enquiry" as a means mentioned in article 33 of the Charter of the United Nations for the peaceful settlement of international disputes, the United Kingdom Representative to the United Nations (Gutteridge) made the following statement in the Sixth Committee during its discussion of peaceful settlement of international disputes:

> The method of enquiry is, as Goodrich and Hambro rightly state, strictly not a means of settlement at all but rather an effort to find a basis for settlement. This is not to belittle the significance of enquiry since it can often happen that a disagreement or difference can be more easily eliminated when once the facts have been clearly established. Thus, it was on the basis of the facts as established by the Commission of Enquiry set up in 1962 by the United Kingdom and Danish Governments to investigate the circumstances of the incident involving a British trawler the "Red Crusader" off the Faroe Islands that it was possible for the two governments amicably to compose their differences.

> Many international agreements (both bilateral and multilateral) embody provisions enabling specific organs or bodies to carry out defined tasks of inspection, investigation and fact-find-

ing. A number of European conventions are particularly illustrative in this respect—I need only mention the European Convention on Human Rights, the treaties establishing the three European Communities and the revised Brussels Treaty which established an Agency for the Control of Armaments under the auspices of the Western European Union. * * *

Mr. Chairman, I cannot leave the topic of enquiry without referring, however, briefly, to the experience of the United Nations in this field. This experience is vast, extensive and not very clearly charted. * * * Although the efforts of the United Nations in this field have not always been uniformly successful, we must not assume that the method of enquiry itself is at fault. It is a method which can achieve limited results in a given situation, or in relation to specific matters. Provided these limitations are recognised, the method of enquiry can, in certain cases, lead to useful results.

* * *

With regard to the development of the institution of international inquiry since the establishment of the United Nations, the Secretary-General's report states:

The period prior to the establishment of the United Nations was characterized by the large number of treaties which were concluded providing for inquiry or conciliation and by the relatively small number of cases of inquiries which were held, whether within the framework of the League of Nations or outside it. The period following the creation of the United Nations has witnessed a reverse trend. Only a few treaties have been concluded in the matter. On the other hand, a considerable number of cases of inquiry or conciliation have been conducted through the agency of the United Nations. A further point distinguishing the two periods lies in the fact that, whereas in the earlier period, commissions of inquiry evolved in such a manner as to increase in competence and to assume conciliatory functions, since the establishment of the United Nations such bodies have tended to be reduced to their initial fact-finding role. This tendency on the part of United Nations bodies has not, however, been a uniform one and a significant number of exceptions may be found.

As regards the practice developed by the United Nations, the fact-finding bodies established by the United Nations have formed a part of the general machinery—in a very broad sense—of the peace-keeping system created under the Charter. The fact that the body set up by the United Nations has been called upon to report to a permanent United Nations organ, usually the Security Council or the General Assembly, has at once avoided the need for the fact-finding, or fact-observing, mission itself to undertake diplomatic or political efforts, even assuming that it was empowered to do so, and has enabled the permanent United Nations organ to decide what course of action should be followed in the light of prevailing circumstances. While United Nations bodies have been most clearly successful when charged with a specific task relating, for example, to the investigation of a given range of incidents or to observing the implementation of the terms of a Security Council or General Assembly resolution, their role as a stabilizing factor in themselves, in situations potentially endangering the maintenance of international peace and security, should not be overlooked, nor the part which they have on occasions played in providing a means of liaison and communication between conflicting parties.

SECTION C. APPLICATION IN INTERNATIONAL TRIBUNALS

1. THE INTERNATIONAL COURT OF JUSTICE

THE "WORLD COURT"

International Court of Justice, Yearbook
1971–1972, at 1, 15, 16, 17, 36, 39–40, 41 (1972).

The International Court of Justice, which has its seat in The Hague, is the principal judicial organ of the United Nations.

It had as its predecessor the Permanent Court of International Justice, which was instituted by the League of Nations in 1920 and was dissolved in 1946.

* * *

The constitutional texts of the Court are the Charter of the United Nations and the Statute of the Court. A third basic text is the Rules of Court.

* * *

The International Court of Justice was brought into being by the Charter of the United Nations, signed at San Francisco on 26 June 1945. The Charter deals with the Court in Article 7, paragraph 1, Article 36, paragraph 3, and Articles 92–96, which form Chapter XIV.

* * *

By virtue of Article 92 of the Charter of the United Nations, the Statute of the Court is annexed to the Charter, of which it forms an integral part. * * *

The above-mentioned Article indicates that the Statute is based upon that of the Permanent Court of International Justice. The modi-

fications are few in number, most of them being formal adaptations designed to take account of the replacement of the League of Nations by the United Nations.　*　*　*
*　*　*

Article 93 of the Charter provides:

"1.　All Members of the United Nations are ipso facto parties to the Statute of the International Court of Justice.

2.　A State which is not a Member of the United Nations may become a party to the Statute of the International Court of Justice on conditions to be determined in each case by the General Assembly upon the recommendation of the Security Council." (at 1)
*　*　*

The Court consists of 15 members (Statute, Art. 3, para. 1).

On 31 July 1972 the composition of the Court was as follows:

Order of precedence	Country	Date of expiry of term of office
President Sir Muhammad Zafrulla Khan	Pakistan	5 February 1973
Vice-President F. Ammoun	Lebanon	5 February 1976
Judges Sir Gerald Fitzmaurice	United Kingdom	5 February 1973
L. Padilla Nervo	Mexico	5 February 1973
I. Forster	Senegal	5 February 1973
A. Gros	France	5 February 1973
C. Bengzon	Philippines	5 February 1976
S. Petrén	Sweden	5 February 1976
M. Lachs	Poland	5 February 1976
C. D. Onyeama	Nigeria	5 February 1976
H. C. Dillard	United States	5 February 1979
L. Ignacio-Pinto	Dahomey	5 February 1979
F. de Castro	Spain	5 February 1979
P. D. Morozov	USSR	5 February 1979
E. Jiménez de Aréchaga	Uruguay	5 February 1979

The Members of the Court are elected for nine years, one-third of the total number of judges being elected every three years; they may be re-elected (Statute, Art. 13).　In the event of a vacancy, a supplementary election is held and the new judge holds office for the remainder of his predecessor's term (Statute, Arts. 14 and 15).　(at 15)

As required by Article 7 of the Statute, the Secretary-General of the United Nations prepares for each election a list of the persons nominated in accordance with Articles 5 and 6.　The election is held by the General Assembly and the Security Council of the United Nations, proceeding independently of each other and simultaneously (Statute, Arts. 8–12).　The States parties to the Statute of the Court

which are not members of the United Nations take part in the election by the General Assembly in the same manner as Members of the United Nations * * *. (at 16)
* * *

If in a case the Court includes upon the Bench a judge of the nationality of one of the parties, any other party may choose a person to sit as judge. Similarly, if the Court includes upon the Bench no judge of the nationality of the parties, each of these parties may choose a judge (Statute, Art. 31. * * *). Should there be several parties in the same interest they are reckoned for this purpose as one party only (ibid.). (at 17)
* * *

Article 34, paragraph 1, of the Statute provides that "Only States may be parties in cases before the Court". Private persons are therefore not entitled to institute proceedings before the Court.

States entitled to appear before the Court fall into three categories:
(a) States Members of the United Nations

Article 35, paragraph 1, of the Statute provides that the Court shall be open to the States parties to the Statute, and Article 93, paragraph 1, of the Charter of the United Nations provides that all Members of the United Nations are ipso facto parties to the Statute.

On 31 July 1972 * * * 132 States were Members of the United Nations. (at 36)
* * *

(b) States, not Members of the United Nations, Parties to the Statute

Article 93, paragraph 2, of the Charter of the United Nations provides that States which are not members of the United Nations may become parties to the Statute of the Court on conditions to be determined in each case by the General Assembly upon the recommendation of the Security Council.

The conditions laid down have hitherto been the same in each case. They were laid down for the first time as a result of a request by the Swiss Federal Council; on that occasion the General Assembly, on 11 December 1946, adopted resolution 91 (I) which prescribed the following conditions:

(a) Acceptance of the provisions of the Statute of the International Court of Justice;

(b) Acceptance of all the obligations of a Member of the United Nations under Article 94 of the Charter;

(c) An undertaking to contribute to the expenses of the Court such equitable amount as the General Assembly shall assess from time to time after consultation with the Swiss Government. (at 39–40)
* * *

The following States not members of the United Nations are at present parties to the Statute:

State	Resolution of the General Assembly	Deposit of the instrument of acceptance
Liechtenstein	363 (IV), 1 December 1949	29 March 1950
San Marino	806 (VIII), 9 December 1953	18 February 1954
Switzerland	91 (I), 11 December 1946	28 July 1948

(c) States not Parties to the Statute to which the Court is Open

The Court, which is open to States parties to the Statute, is also open to other States, in accordance with Article 35, paragraph 2, of the Statute. This Article provides that the conditions upon which the Court shall be open to such States shall, subject to the special provisions contained in treaties in force, be laid down by the Security Council, but in no case shall such conditions place the parties in a position of inequality before the Court.

On 15 October 1946, the Security Council adopted resolution 9 (1946) which reads as follows:

The Security Council

In virtue of the powers conferred upon it by Article 35, paragraph 2, of the Statute of the International Court of Justice and subject to the provisions of that Article,

Resolves that:

1. The International Court of Justice shall be open to a State which is not a party to the Statute of the International Court of Justice, upon the following condition, namely, that such State shall previously have deposited with the Registrar of the Court a declaration by which it accepts the jurisdiction of the Court, in accordance with the Charter of the United Nations and with the terms and subject to the conditions of the Statute and Rules of the Court, and undertakes to comply in good faith with the decision or decisions of the Court and to accept all the obligations of a Member of the United Nations under Article 94 of the Charter [a] * * *. (at 41)

* * *

---

1. *The advisory jurisdiction of the court.* Under the provisions of Article 96 of the Charter of the United Nations and Article 65 of the Statute of the International Court of Justice, the court is em-

---

[a]. General declarations have been filed by the Federal Republic of Germany and the Republic of Vietnam.

powered to give an advisory opinion on "any legal question." The Charter provides that the request for an advisory opinion may be made by the General Assembly, the Security Council and such other organs of the United Nations and specialized agencies as may be authorized by the General Assembly. Among the organs and agencies authorized to request advisory opinions are the Economic and Social Council, the Trusteeship Council, the Committee on Applications for Review of Judgments of the United Nations Administrative Tribunal, the International Labor Organization, the United Nations Educational, Scientific and Cultural Organization, the International Bank for Reconstruction and Development, the World Health Organization and the International Atomic Energy Agency. See the ICJ Yearbook 1971–1972, at 49 (1972), for a detailed list of documents confirming such authority. States are not authorized to request an advisory opinion.

Although, without more, an advisory opinion is not considered legally "binding", see Section 30 of the Convention on the Privileges and Immunities of the United Nations, 21 U.S.T. 1418, 1 U.N.T.S. 15, which provides:

> All differences arising out of the interpretation or application of the present convention shall be referred to the International Court of Justice, unless in any case it is agreed by the parties to have recourse to another mode of settlement. If a difference arises between the United Nations on the one hand and a Member on the other hand, a request shall be made for an advisory opinion on any legal question involved in accordance with Article 96 of the Charter and Article 65 of the Statute of the Court. The opinion given by the Court shall be accepted as decisive by the parties.

2. *The jurisdiction of the court in "contentious cases".* Article 36 of the Statute of the International Court of Justice provides:

> 1. The jurisdiction of the Court comprises all cases which the parties refer to it and all matters specially provided for in the Charter of the United Nations or in treaties and conventions in force.

> 2. The states parties to the present Statute may at any time declare that they recognize as compulsory ipso facto and without special agreement, in relation to any other state accepting the same obligation, the jurisdiction of the Court in all legal disputes concerning:
>
> a. the interpretation of a treaty;
>
> b. any question of international law;
>
> c. the existence of any fact which, if established, would constitute a breach of an international obligation;
>
> d. the nature or extent of the reparation to be made for the breach of an international obligation.

3.   The declarations referred to above may be made unconditionally or on condition of reciprocity on the part of several or certain states, or for a certain time.

4.   Such declarations shall be deposited with the Secretary-General of the United Nations, who shall transmit copies thereof to the parties to the Statute and to the Registrar of the Court.

5.   Declarations made under Article 36 of the Statute of the Permanent Court of International Justice and which are still in force shall be deemed, as between the parties to the present Statute, to be acceptances of the compulsory jurisdiction of the International Court of Justice for the period which they still have to run and in accordance with their terms.

6.   In the event of a dispute as to whether the Court has jurisdiction, the matter shall be settled by the decision of the Court.

EXAMPLES OF PROVISIONS IN INTERNATIONAL AGREEMENTS MAKING REFERENCE TO SETTLEMENT OF DISPUTES BY THE INTERNATIONAL COURT OF JUSTICE

Treaty of Friendship, Commerce and Navigation between the United States and the Federal Republic of Germany of October 29, 1954, 7 U.S.T. 1839, 273 U.N.T.S. 3.

Article XXVII

1.   Each Party shall accord sympathetic consideration to, and shall afford adequate opportunity for consultation regarding, such representations as the other Party may make with respect to any matter affecting the operation of the present Treaty.

2.   Any dispute between the Parties as to the interpretation or the application of the present Treaty which the Parties do not satisfactorily adjust by diplomacy or some other agreed means shall be submitted to arbitration or, upon agreement of the Parties, to the International Court of Justice.

Convention of Establishment Between the United States and France of November 25, 1959, 11 U.S.T. 2398, 401 U.N.T.S. 75.

Article XVI

1.   Each High Contracting Party shall accord sympathetic consideration to such representations as the other High Contracting Party may make with respect to any question affecting the application of the present Convention, and shall afford opportunity for an exchange of views relative thereto.

2.   Any dispute between the High Contracting Parties as to the interpretation or application of the present Convention, not satisfactorily adjusted by diplomacy, shall be submitted to the International

Court of Justice, unless the High Contracting Parties agree to settlement by some other pacific means.

EXAMPLES OF DECLARATIONS UNDER ARTICLE 36(2) OF THE STATUTE OF THE INTERNATIONAL COURT OF JUSTICE.

International Court of Justice, Yearbook 1971–1972, at 63 (1972).

FINLAND

[Translation from the French]

On behalf of the Finnish Government, I hereby declare that I recognize as compulsory ipso facto and without special agreement, in relation to any other State accepting the same obligation, that is to say, on condition of reciprocity, the jurisdiction of the International Court of Justice, in accordance with Article 36, paragraph 2, of the Statute of the Court, for a period of five years from 25 June 1958. This declaration shall be renewed by tacit agreement for further periods of the same duration, unless it is denounced not later than six months before the expiry of any such period. This declaration shall apply only to disputes arising in regard to situations or facts subsequent to 25 June 1958.

New York, 25 June 1958.

(Signed) G. A. GRIPENBERG,
Permanent Representative of Finland
to the United Nations.

NICARAGUA

[Translation from the French]

On behalf of the Republic of Nicaragua I recognize as compulsory unconditionally the jurisdiction of the Permanent Court of International Justice.[a]

Geneva, 24 September 1929.

(Signed) T. F. MEDINA.

SWITZERLAND

[Translation from the French]

The Swiss Federal Council, duly authorized for that purpose by a Federal decree which was adopted on 12 March 1948 by the Federal

---

a. Under Article 36(5) of the Statute of the International Court of Justice, declarations of states accepting the jurisdiction of the Permanent Court of International Justice, which have not lapsed or been withdrawn, are deemed to be acceptances of the compulsory jurisdiction of the present court. "There are now nine such declarations." International Court of Justice, Yearbook 1971–1972, at 55 (1972).

Assembly of the Swiss Confederation and became operative on 17 June 1948,

Hereby declares that the Swiss Confederation recognizes as compulsory ipso facto and without special agreement, in relation to any other State accepting the same obligation, the jurisdiction of the International Court of Justice in all legal disputes concerning:

(a) the interpretation of a treaty;

(b) any question of international law;

(c) the existence of any fact which, if established, would constitute a breach of an international obligation;

(d) the nature or extent of the reparation to be made for the breach of an international obligation.

This declaration, which is made under Article 36 of the Statute of the International Court of Justice, shall take effect from the date on which the Swiss Confederation becomes a party to that Statute and shall have effect as long as it has not been abrogated subject to one year's notice.

Done at Berne, 6 July 1948.

On behalf of the Swiss Federal Council:
(Signed) CELIO,
The President of the Confederation.
(Signed) LEIMGRUBER,
The Chancellor of the Confederation.

UNITED STATES OF AMERICA

I, Harry S. Truman, President of the United States of America, declare on behalf of the United States of America, under Article 36, paragraph 2, of the Statute of the International Court of Justice, and in accordance with the Resolution of 2 August 1946 of the Senate of the United States of America (two-thirds of the Senators present concurring therein), that the United States of America recognizes as compulsory ipso facto and without special agreement, in relation to any other State accepting the same obligation, the jurisdiction of the International Court of Justice in all legal disputes hereafter arising concerning

(a) the interpretation of a treaty;

(b) any question of international law;

(c) the existence of any fact which, if established, would constitute a breach of an international obligation;

(d) the nature or extent of the reparation to be made for the breach of an international obligation;

Provided, that this declaration shall not apply to

(a) disputes the solution of which the parties shall entrust to other tribunals by virtue of agreements already in existence or which may be concluded in the future; or

(b) disputes with regard to matters which are essentially within the domestic jurisdiction of the United States of America as determined by the United States of America; or

(c) disputes arising under a multilateral treaty, unless (1) all parties to the treaty affected by the decision are also parties to the case before the Court, or (2) the United States of America specially agrees to jurisdiction; and

Provided further, that this declaration shall remain in force for a period of five years and thereafter until the expiration of six months after notice may be given to terminate this declaration.

Done at Washington this fourteenth day of August 1946.

(Signed) HARRY S. TRUMAN.

---

1. *States accepting compulsory jurisdiction.* As of July 31, 1972, declarations accepting the jurisdiction of the court in some form similar to those set forth above were in effect with respect to the following 46 states:

Australia	Malawi
Austria	Malta
Belgium	Mauritius
Botswana	Mexico
Canada	Netherlands
China	New Zealand
Colombia	Nicaragua
Denmark	Nigeria
Dominican Republic	Norway
Egypt	Pakistan
El Salvador	Panama
Finland	Philippines
France	Portugal
Gambia	Somalia
Haiti	Sudan
Honduras	Swaziland
India	Sweden
Israel	Switzerland
Japan	Uganda
Kenya	United Kingdom
Khmer Republic	United States of America
Liberia	Uruguay
Liechtenstein	
Luxembourg	

2. *The work-load of the court.* It is reported in the ICJ Yearbook 1971–1972 that, between May 22, 1947 (when its first case was submitted) and August 18, 1972 "the Court has had a total of 56 cases to deal with * * *. In those cases it gave 32 judgments and 14 advisory opinions." (at 12)

That a world court which has been in existence for over 25 years has rendered only 32 judgments is a fact worth examining. One begins by observing that its jurisdiction depends upon the willingness of states to submit to that jurisdiction. But why are states so reluctant? And why are the organs and agencies of the United Nations so reluctant to request advisory opinions?

I ROSENNE, THE LAW AND PRACTICE OF THE INTERNATIONAL COURT 15 (1965)

The reasons for this state of affairs are undoubtedly many and complex, but the impression is inescapable that their origin lies in the relentless quest after security which is the major preoccupation of all responsible statesmen and of all peoples, and the lack of general intellectual calmness engendered by it. The lawyer may regret that more use is not made of legal and judicial techniques in contemporary international affairs (although the unwary may fall into the trap of too readily assuming that too little use is made of those techniques). But he should not permit himself to be blinded into the mistaken belief that legal and judicial techniques by themselves are inherently superior or more effective in keeping international situations of tension under control than others which modern political and diplomatic experience has evolved. An assertion of that kind, unsupported by the evidence of history, runs the risk of assuming that which has to be proved and would be a petitio principii.

 * * * It is significant that the present Court, after a hesitant start which was not particularly successful, has not been asked by interested States to deal with disputes relating even marginally to the major international tension which has emerged since the end of the Second World War. The Court is not now being invoked to deal with problems of East-West relations, and when attempts have been made to invoke it, these have for the most part been completely inconclusive. This fact, on the one hand, has naturally reduced the amount of business brought before the Court. On the other hand, this is not necessarily without advantage, for it has freed the Court from what might be misdirected efforts to find legal solutions for problems which are not in reality legal problems at all.

On the other hand * * * the present Court has been asked to decide the central issues of several major international disputes which were not directly connected with the major international situation. Some of these, being in reality conflicts of interest and of national aspirations, even contained a sufficient number of elements to give rise to concern that they might constitute a threat to international peace, if not on a universal scale then at least on a regional scale. The International Court has shown that when States are agreed that the time has come for a final settlement of a given dispute of this character, it is perfectly capable of assisting them, if they so desire, to reach their objective.   *   *   *

      *   *   *

On the negative side of the Court's work to date, noticeable is the fact that, albeit on technical grounds of lack of jurisdiction or inadmissibility, the Court has not found it possible to decide on the substance of any dispute relating to events occurring during the Second World War, whether or not that dispute ended up also by being a dispute involving East-West relations   *   *   *. But this negative conclusion too requires further examination, for it is possibly not accidental, since Article 107 of the Charter can be interpreted as excluding actions taken during the Second World War against enemy States from the normal competence of the United Nations and its different organs. Although the Court has never directly referred to this Article, its action in declining to decide the merits of this type of case cannot necessarily be regarded as being contrary to the spirit of the Charter.

It is usual today to say that the expectations generated by the decision of the San Francisco Conference to make the Court a principal organ of the United Nations, and which led to the assumption that the new Court would be able to play a major role in the pacific settlement of international disputes, have not been fully realized. The reason for this state of affairs are many and complex, and are only partly due to the general attitude of reserve towards the Court manifested by some of the major contemporary world Powers. There is prevalent in the world today a widespread questioning of the contemporary international law. This feeling is based on the view that for the greater part international law is the product of European imperialism and colonialism and does not take sufficient account of the completely changed pattern of international relations which now exists. This feeling has been very marked in the prolonged discussions in the United Nations on questions of the codification of different aspects of international law. Its existence is not conducive to recourse to the Court. Whereas before the Second World War it was on the whole the small Powers which were inclined to look to international law and its organs as a means to protect themselves against the rapacity of the Great Powers, paradoxically enough the situation today is changing rapidly, and it is the Great Powers who are inclined to take refuge behind a formal position based on traditional international law when faced with claims by small and new States who object to the traditional position. This is particularly evident in the sphere of international economic relations.

What is perhaps not sufficiently known is that in this type of case the International Court has shown itself sympathetic towards the psychological attitudes of the new and of the small States, and considerable awareness of the need to refurbish the rules of international law. Careful scrutiny of the record of the Court may lead to the conclusion that it has been remarkably perceptive of the changing currents of internationalist thought. In this respect it has performed a major service to the international community as a whole, because the need to bring international law into line with present-day requirements and conditions is real and urgent. * * *

Above all, in considering the work of the Court and the role which it has been called upon to play, it has to be remembered that, unlike the situation after the First World War, when, after a few years, the illusion of general pacification and relaxation of tension became commonplace, the period since the Second World War has been marked by a high degree of suspicion and by unceasing international tension and unrelieved anxiety on the part of all statesmen and on the part of the public at large over what the future might bring. The international situation has lacked any element of relaxation and tranquility. The development of this situation has been stamped by continuous weakening of the authority of all the international institutions established to deal with the intercourse of States in time of peace. At the same time, the increasing politicization of all aspects of international organization is itself but a reflection of the widespread view that in general the political factors predominate in most international activities. This has led to the view that judicial settlement of a dispute composed primarily of political facets may not contribute to a solution of the underlying problem, and that it is much more realistic to allow political considerations full sway. This general atmosphere is not propitious for any extended use of international judicial techniques. In the light of the general international situation, the wonder perhaps is not so much what the Court has been able to do, as that in fact States continue to show willingness to refer a number of major disputes to its decision, and great interest in all that pertains to the Court. This is the encouraging feature of the experience of the International Court, for it shows that even if its jurisdiction is not compulsory, its permanency as an international organ enables it to play its own constructive role in the pacific settlement of international disputes despite the constantly disintegrating international situation.

CHAYES, A COMMON LAWYER LOOKS AT INTERNATIONAL LAW

78 Harvard Law Review 1396 (1965).*

Common law is case law. So a common lawyer approaching international law—where courts and cases are few—may begin to worry whether what he is involved in is law at all. It is true that in our own system if judicial decision ever was the sole or even the primary source of law it is so no longer. The practicing lawyer typically finds his law in codes, statutes, and rule books. He goes to the reports for exegesis rather than statement of basic rules. But, if we no longer look to the judge as the source of law, we still tend to think of him as the one who enforces the law and, in this, vindicates it. So we hear a plaintive lament, not only from laymen, but from distinguished members of the international law profession: why is it that sovereign states refuse to submit their disputes and their sovereign wills to the arbitrament of a judicial tribunal? Until they do, it is said, we will not have very much in the way of international law.

I think this court-centered view, in which the health of international law is measured by the congestion of the World Court's docket, is misguided. It creates the wrong kind of expectations about international law, expectations that are bound to be disappointed. Meanwhile, attention is diverted from the ways in which international law really operates and how these may be strengthened.

The burden of my argument is that we are myopic about international law when we focus too narrowly on the linkage between law and courts. Law as regulator of private relations and private rights is intimately related to courts and perhaps in some sense depends on a system of adjudication. But law as a system allocating public powers is by no means so clearly a creature of courts and judges. In this aspect it betrays more clearly its origins in politics.

AERIAL INCIDENT OF OCTOBER 7th, 1952 (UNITED STATES v. UNION OF SOVIET SOCIALIST REPUBLICS)

International Court of Justice, 1956.
[1956] I.C.J.Rep. 9.

Order

* * *

Whereas on June 2nd, 1955, the Ambassador of the United States of America to the Netherlands filed in the Registry an Application dated May 26th, 1955, and signed by the Agent of the Government of the United States of America instituting proceedings before the Court against the Government of the Union of Soviet Socialist Republics on account of "certain willful acts committed by fighter aircraft of the Soviet Government against a United States Air Force B–29 aircraft and its crew off Hokkaido, Japan, on October 7th, 1952";

Whereas the Application was duly communicated by the Registry on June 4th, 1955, to the Ambassador of the Union of Soviet Socialist Republics to the Netherlands;

Whereas the Application was also duly communicated by the Registry to the Members of the United Nations, through the Secretary-General of the United Nations, and to the other States entitled to appear before the Court;

Whereas the Application contains the following paragraphs:

The United States Government, in filing this application with the Court, submits to the Court's jurisdiction for the purposes of this case. The Soviet Government appears not to have filed any declaration with the Court thus far, although it was invited to do so by the United States Government in the note annexed hereto. The Soviet Government is, however, qualified to submit to the jurisdiction of the Court in this matter and may upon notification of this application by the Registrar, in accordance with the Rules of the Court, take the necessary steps to enable the Court's jurisdiction over both parties to the dispute to be confirmed.

The United States Government thus founds the jurisdiction of this Court on the foregoing considerations and on Article 36(1) of the Statute.

Whereas the note annexed to the Application, which was addressed on September 25th, 1954, by the Government of the United States of America to the Government of the Union of Soviet Socialist Republics, ends with the following passage:

Since it appears that the Soviet Government has thus far not filed with that Court any declaration of acceptance of the compulsory jurisdiction of the Court, the United States Government invites the Soviet Government to file an appropriate declaration with the Court, or to enter into a Special Agreement, by which the Court may be empowered in accordance with its Statute and Rules to determine the issues of fact and law which have been set forth herein; and the Soviet Government is requested to inform the United States Government in its reply to the present note of its intentions with respect to such a declaration or Special Agreement.

Whereas in a letter dated August 26th, 1955, from the Chargé d'affaires of the Union of Soviet Socialist Republics in the Netherlands to the Registry it was stated that:

In its last note on this question, dated December 30th, 1954, addressed to the Government of the United States of America, the Government of the U.S.S.R. indicated that since the American military aircraft violated the frontier of the U.S.S.R. and opened fire without any reason upon Soviet fighter aircraft, responsibility for the incident which occurred and for its consequences rests entirely upon the American side; in these circumstances the Soviet Government cannot take into consideration the claim set forth in the note of the Government of the United States of America of September 25th, 1954, and considers that the proposal that this case should be referred for consideration to the International Court of Justice is totally unfounded.

Having regard to the foregoing, the Soviet Government considers that no question arises in this case which calls for a decision of the International Court of Justice and it sees no reason why the question should be dealt with by the International Court of Justice.

Whereas a certified true copy of the above-mentioned letter was communicated to the Agent of the Government of the United States of America on August 29th, 1955;

Whereas the said letter of August 26th, 1955, does not constitute on the part of the Government of the Union of Soviet Socialist Republics either the appropriate declaration or consent to conclude a Special Agreement;

Whereas, in these circumstances, the Court finds that it has not before it any acceptance by the Government of the Union of Soviet Socialist Republics of the jurisdiction of the Court to deal with the dispute which is the subject of the Application submitted to it by the Government of the United States of America and that therefore it can take no further steps upon this Application;

THE COURT orders that the case shall be removed from the list.

* * *

CASE OF CERTAIN NORWEGIAN LOANS
(FRANCE v. NORWAY)

International Court of Justice, 1957.
[1957] I.C.J.Rep. 9.

* * *

The facts which led the French Government to institute the present proceedings before the Court are as follows:

Between 1896 and 1905, the Norwegian Government floated six public loans on the French market and on other foreign markets. From 1885 to 1909, various loans were floated on foreign markets, including the French market, by the Mortgage Bank of the Kingdom of Norway, an establishment created by the State and whose capital

belongs to the State. Finally, in 1904, the Norwegian Small Holding and Workers' Housing Bank floated a loan on the French market and on other foreign markets. The French Government contends that the bonds contain a gold clause which varies in form from bond to bond, but which that Government regards as sufficient in the case of each bond, this being disputed by the Norwegian Government.
* * *

[Legislation in Norway permitted payment of the foregoing loans in Bank of Norway notes instead of gold. The French Government espoused the claims of French nationals who held the Norwegian bonds and desired payment in gold. The French Government asserted to the Norwegian Government "that it would not seem that a unilateral decision can be relied upon as against foreign creditors." The Norwegian Government rejected French proposals to submit the matter to a mixed commission of economic and financial experts, to arbitration or to the International Court of Justice, maintaining that the claims of bondholders involved solely the interpretation and application of Norwegian law and that the bondholders should sue in the Norwegian courts.

The French Government referred the matter to the International Court of Justice.]

In its Application, the French Government requests the Court to adjudge and declare that the international loans issued by the Kingdom of Norway, by the Mortgage Bank of the Kingdom of Norway and by the Small Holding and Workers' Housing Bank, which are listed in the Application, stipulate in gold the amount of the borrower's obligation for the service of coupons and the redemption of bonds; and that the borrower can only discharge the substance of his debt by the payment of the gold value of the coupons on the date of payment and of the gold value of the redeemed bonds on the date of repayment.
* * *

The Application expressly refers to Article 36, paragraph 2, of the Statute of the Court and to the acceptance of the compulsory jurisdiction of the Court by Norway on November 16th, 1946, and by France on March 1st, 1949. The Norwegian Declaration reads:

I declare on behalf of the Norwegian Government that Norway recognizes as compulsory ipso facto and without special agreement, in relation to any other State accepting the same obligation, that is to say, on condition of reciprocity, the jurisdiction of the International Court of Justice in conformity with Article 36, paragraph 2, of the Statute of the Court, for a period of ten years as from 3rd October 1946.

The French Declaration reads:

On behalf of the Government of the French Republic, and subject to ratification, I declare that I recognize as compulsory ipso facto and without special agreement, in relation to any other

State accepting the same obligation, that is on condition of reciprocity, the jurisdiction of the International Court of Justice, in conformity with Article 36, paragraph 2, of the Statute of the said Court, for all disputes which may arise in respect of facts or situations subsequent to the ratification of the present declaration, with the exception of those with regard to which the parties may have agreed or may agree to have recourse to another method of peaceful settlement.

This declaration does not apply to differences relating to matters which are essentially within the national jurisdiction as understood by the Government of the French Republic.

* * *

On April 20th, 1956, the Norwegian Government filed four Preliminary Objections. The first Objection consisted of two parts. In the first part the Norwegian Government maintained that the subject of the dispute was within the exclusive domain of the municipal law of Norway, and that it did not fall within any of the categories of disputes enumerated in Article 36, paragraph 2, of the Statute, by reference to which both Parties had by their Declarations accepted the compulsory jurisdiction of the Court. In the second part of that Objection the Norwegian Government relied upon the reservation in the French Declaration with regard to differences relating to matters which are essentially within the national jurisdiction as understood by the French Government. It challenged the jurisdiction of the Court on both grounds.

* * *

After presenting the first ground of its first Preliminary Objection on the basis that the loan contracts are governed by municipal law, the Norwegian Government continues in its Preliminary Objections:

There can be no possible doubt on this point. If, however, there should still be some doubt, the Norwegian Government would rely upon the reservations made by the French Government in its Declaration of March 1st, 1949. By virtue of the principle of reciprocity, which is embodied in Article 36, paragraph 2, of the Statute of the Court and which has been clearly expressed in the Norwegian Declaration of November 16th, 1946, the Norwegian Government cannot be bound, vis-à-vis the French Government, by undertakings which are either broader or stricter than those given by the latter Government.

* * *

It will be recalled that the French Declaration accepting the compulsory jurisdiction of the Court contains the following reservation:

This declaration does not apply to differences relating to matters which are essentially within the national jurisdiction as understood by the Government of the French Republic.

In the Preliminary Objections filed by the Norwegian Government it is stated:

> The Norwegian Government did not insert any such reservation in its own Declaration. But it has the right to rely upon the restrictions placed by France upon her own undertakings.

> Convinced that the dispute which has been brought before the Court by the Application of July 6th, 1955, is within the domestic jurisdiction, the Norwegian Government considers itself fully entitled to rely on this right. Accordingly, it requests the Court to decline, on grounds that it lacks jurisdiction, the function which the French Government would have it assume.

In considering this ground of the Objection the Court notes in the first place that the present case has been brought before it on the basis of Article 36, paragraph 2, of the Statute and of the corresponding Declarations of acceptance of compulsory jurisdiction; that in the present case the jurisdiction of the Court depends upon the Declarations made by the Parties in accordance with Article 36, paragraph 2, of the Statute on condition of reciprocity; and that, since two unilateral declarations are involved, such jurisdiction is conferred upon the Court only to the extent to which the Declarations coincide in conferring it. A comparison between the two Declarations shows that the French Declaration accepts the Court's jurisdiction within narrower limits than the Norwegian Declaration; consequently, the common will of the Parties, which is the basis of the Court's jurisdiction, exists within these narrower limits indicated by the French reservation. Following in this connection the jurisprudence of the Permanent Court of International Justice (Phosphates in Morocco case, Judgment of June 14th, 1938, P.C.I.J., Series A/B, No. 74, p. 22; Electricity Company of Sofia and Bulgaria case, Judgment of April 4th, 1939, P.C.I.J., Series A/B, No. 77, p. 81) the Court has reaffirmed this method of defining the limits of its jurisdiction. Thus the judgment of the Court in the Anglo-Iranian Oil Company case states:

> As the Iranian Declaration is more limited in scope than the United Kingdom Declaration, it is the Iranian Declaration on which the Court must base itself. (I.C.J. Reports 1952, p. 103.)

France has limited her acceptance of the compulsory jurisdiction of the Court by excluding beforehand disputes "relating to matters which are essentially within the national jurisdiction as understood by the Government of the French Republic". In accordance with the condition of reciprocity to which acceptance of the compulsory jurisdiction is made subject in both Declarations and which is provided for in Article 36, paragraph 3, of the Statute, Norway, equally with France, is entitled to except from the compulsory jurisdiction of the Court disputes understood by Norway to be essentially within its national jurisdiction.

*   *   *

The Court does not consider that it should examine whether the French reservation is consistent with the undertaking of a legal obligation and is compatible with Article 36, paragraph 6, of the Statute which provides:

> In the event of a dispute as to whether the Court has jurisdiction, the matter shall be settled by the decision of the Court.

The validity of the reservation has not been questioned by the Parties. It is clear that France fully maintains its Declaration, including the reservation, and that Norway relies upon the reservation.

In consequence the Court has before it a provision which both Parties to the dispute regard as constituting an expression of their common will relating to the competence of the Court. The Court does not therefore consider that it is called upon to enter into an examination of the reservation in the light of considerations which are not presented by the issues in the proceedings. The Court, without prejudging the question, gives effect to the reservation as it stands and as the Parties recognize it.

     * * *

The Court considers that the Norwegian Government is entitled by virtue of the condition of reciprocity, to invoke the reservation contained in the French Declaration of March 1st, 1949; that this reservation excludes from the jurisdiction of the Court the dispute which has been referred to it by the Application of the French Government; that consequently the Court is without jurisdiction to entertain the Application.

     * * *

For these reasons,

THE COURT, by twelve votes to three, finds that it is without jurisdiction to adjudicate upon the dispute which has been brought before it by the Application of the Government of the French Republic of July 6th, 1955.

     * * *

Separate Opinion of JUDGE SIR HERSCH LAUTERPACHT

     * * * I consider that as the French Declaration of Acceptance excludes from the jurisdiction of the Court "matters which are essentially within the national jurisdiction as understood by the Government of the French Republic"—the emphasis being here on the words "as understood by the Government of the French Republic"—it is for the reason of that latter qualification an instrument incapable of producing legal effects before this Court and of establishing its jurisdiction. This is so for the double reason that: (a) it is contrary to the Statute of the Court; (b) the existence of the obligation being dependent upon the determination by the Government accepting the Optional Clause, the Acceptance does not constitute a legal obligation. That Declaration of Acceptance cannot, accordingly, provide a basis

for the jurisdiction of the Court. Norway has not accepted the jurisdiction of the Court on any other basis. The Court therefore has no jurisdiction.

As stated, the first reason for that view is that that particular part of the acceptance of the Optional Clause on the part of the French Republic is contrary to the Statute of the Court. In the reservation in question the Government of France says in effect: If a Government brings an application before the Court in reliance on the French acceptance of the jurisdiction of the Court and if the Government of France maintains that the Court has no jurisdiction on the ground that the subject-matter of the dispute is essentially within the domestic jurisdiction of France, then the Court has no power to decide upon that particular allegation; it must accept as binding the French understanding of the legal position on the subject.

If that type of reservation is valid, then the Court is not in the position to exercise the power conferred upon it—in fact, the duty imposed upon it—under paragraph 6 of Article 36 of its Statute. That paragraph provides that "in the event of a dispute as to whether the Court has jurisdiction, the matter shall be settled by a decision of the Court". The French reservation lays down that if, with regard to that particular question, there is a dispute between the Parties as to whether the Court has jurisdiction, the matter shall be settled by a decision of the French Government. The French reservation is thus not only contrary to one of the most fundamental principles of international—and national—jurisprudence according to which it is within the inherent power of a tribunal to interpret the text establishing its jurisdiction. It is also contrary to a clear specific provision of the Statute of the Court as well as to the general Articles 1 and 92 of the Statute and of the Charter, respectively, which require the Court to function in accordance with its Statute.

Now what is the result of the fact that a reservation or part of it is contrary to the provisions of the Statute of the Court? The result is that that reservation or that part of it is invalid.　*　*　*

*　*　*

My conclusion is therefore that, having regard to the reservation relating to matters which are essentially within domestic jurisdiction as understood by the French Republic, the French Declaration of Acceptance is invalid for the reason:

(1) That it is contrary to the Statute of the Court;

(2) That it is incapable of giving rise to a legal obligation inasmuch as it claims, and effectively secures, the right of unilateral determination of the extent and of the existence of the obligation of judicial settlement with regard to a comprehensive and indefinite category of disputes covering potentially most disputes which may come before the Court;

(3) That the particular qualification of the reservation in question forms an essential part of the Acceptance and that it is not possible to treat it as invalid and at the same time to maintain the validity of the reservation to which it is attached or of the Acceptance as a whole.

Accordingly, in my view the entire French Declaration of Acceptance must be treated as devoid of legal effect and as incapable of providing a basis for the jurisdiction of the Court. It is for that reason that, in my view, the Court has no jurisdiction over the dispute. The majority of the Court has reached the same result by acting upon the "automatic reservation" and the French Declaration of Acceptance —both of which I consider to be invalid. However, as the Court has expressly stated that, having regard to the circumstances before it, its Judgment does not pre-judge the major issue involved, I feel that a Separate Opinion—as distinguished from a Dissenting Opinion— meets the requirement of the case.

[A declaration, a separate opinion and dissenting opinions omitted.]

---

1. *Problems.*

a. Suppose the Norwegian declaration had been cast in the words of the Nicaraguan declaration, p. 63 (i. e., "unconditionally", rather than in terms of "reciprocity"). Would the court have reached a different result? Consider paragraph (3) of Article 36 of the statute of the court and the following commentary in Waldock, Decline of the Optional Clause, 32 Brit.Y.B. Int'l L.1955–6, at 244, 255 (1957):

"Paragraph 3 of Article 36 * * * provides that a declaration may be made 'unconditionally or on condition of reciprocity on the part of several or certain States or for a certain time'. This paragraph does not relate to 'reciprocity'. It simply authorizes States to accept compulsory jurisdiction under the Optional Clause for limited periods, and to make their liability to jurisdiction conditional on compulsory jurisdiction having been also accepted by a particular number of other States or by particular named States. The reference in paragraph 3 to a 'condition of reciprocity on the part of several or certain States' is, indeed, a legacy from a special preoccupation of the Brazilian delegate, M. Fernandez, in the 1920 Committee of Jurists. Brazil considered it impolitic to venture on a unilateral acceptance of compulsory jurisdiction unless some at least of the Great Powers did likewise. Accordingly, M. Fernandez proposed the following formula for the Optional Clause:

They may adhere unconditionally or conditionally to the Article providing for compulsory jurisdiction *a possible condi-*

tion being reciprocity on the part of a certain number of Members or, again, of a number of Members including such and such specified Members.

Although M. Fernandez's version of the Optional Clause itself was dropped in favour of the one which now appears in the Statute, the 'condition of reciprocity' on the part of several or certain States was included in paragraph 3 in order to satisfy him. Afterwards Brazil did in fact make her declaration subject to a condition of reciprocity on the part of two, at least, of the Great Powers, but she is the only State to have resorted to this form of condition. Such a condition, as will be appreciated, is not really a 'condition of reciprocity' but rather a condition that the declaration is not to be in force unless and until a certain number of States or certain named States have accepted compulsory jurisdiction under the Optional Clause."

b. If France were a respondent and pleaded its reservation in an effort to oust the court of jurisdiction, what result? What if the matter before the court involved a question of treaty interpretation and the applicant state (plaintiff) argued that the French Government could not lawfully understand the matter to be "essentially within the national jurisdiction" of France? (What was the position of the parties in the Norwegian Loans case as to the validity of the French reservation?)

c. The so-called Nuclear Test Ban Treaty and the Treaty on the Non-Proliferation of Nuclear Weapons both contain the following provision:

> Each Party shall in exercising its national sovereignty have the right to withdraw from the Treaty if it decides that extraordinary events, related to the subject matter of this Treaty, have jeopardized the supreme interests of its country.

What effect does this clause have on the jurisdiction of the International Court of Justice to decide what is meant by the words "extraordinary event?" The text of these treaties appears in the Documentary Supplement.

2. *The United States reservation in the International Court.* In the Interhandel case (Switzerland v. United States), [1959] I.C.J. Rep. 6, Switzerland asked the Court to declare that the United States was under an obligation to restore assets of the Interhandel Company, a Swiss company. Interhandel owned most of the shares of General Aniline and Film Corporation (GAF); almost all of these shares had been vested by the United States during World War II under the Trading With the Enemy Act, on the ground that General Aniline's shares in reality belonged to I. G. Farben, a German company, or that GAF was controlled by that company. Among the preliminary objections raised by the United States was that the court was "without jurisdiction to entertain the Application of the Swiss Government, for that reason that the sale or disposition by the Gov-

ernment of the United States of the shares of the GAF which have been vested as enemy property 'has been determined by the United States of America, pursuant to paragraph (b) of the Conditions attached to this country's acceptance of this Court's jurisiction, to be a matter essentially within the domestic jurisdiction of this country.' " (at 25)

The court did not rule upon this objection, but upheld a different preliminary objection and thereby held that the Application of the Swiss Government was inadmissible because Switzerland had not exhausted the local remedies available to it in the United States courts.

3.   *Other international courts.*

a.   The function of the Court of Justice of the European Communities is to serve, not world-wide, but the special purposes of the Communities (i. e., the European Economic Community, the European Coal and Steel Community, and the European Atomic Energy Community), the members of which are Belgium, Denmark, France, Ireland, Italy, Luxembourg, the Netherlands, the United Kingdom and West Germany.   Whereas parties to cases before the International Court of Justice are limited to states, parties before the court of the communities, in proper cases, can consist of individuals and firms as well as member states or institutions of the communities. For a brief description of the jurisdiction of the court, see Marsh, Foreword to 1 Common Market Law Reports (1962).   An analysis of the structure of the European Communities (commonly referred to in the singular as the European Community) is made in Chapter 14.

b.   Another international court serving the purposes of a regional group of states (the Council of Europe) is the European Court of Human Rights, established by the European Convention for the Protection of Human Rights and Fundamental Freedoms.   Its jurisdiction is limited to cases referred to it by the European Commission of Human Rights or by a state party to the convention (i. e., not by individuals).   See Chapter 9 for a fuller description of the work of the court.

c.   See Hudson, The Central American Court of Justice, 26 Am. J. Int'l L. 759 (1932), for an account of the creation, jurisprudence and demise of "the first international court in modern history to be endowed with continuing functions."   The court sat from 1908 to 1918; its jurisdiction included cases between individuals and governments other than those of the individuals' own country.

2. INTERNATIONAL ARBITRATION

The failure of the International Court of Justice to attract litigation does not mean that there is no third party settlement of international disputes.   Indeed, international arbitration has antedated international adjudication by a number of years.

2 O'CONNELL, INTERNATIONAL LAW 1068 (2d ed. 1970)

[T]he Alabama claims in 1871   *   *   *   arose out of the alleged default of Great Britain in her duties as a neutral during the American Civil War.   The Heads of State of Italy, Brazil and Switzerland each appointed a member of the tribunal to sit with a representative each of Great Britain and the United States.   Each was entitled to write a separate (and dissenting) judgment.   Certain private claims were at the same time referred to a Mixed Claims Commission of two commissioners each appointed by the United States and Great Britain jointly and by Italy.   Thereafter the Mixed Commission, with or without an umpire, became the ordinary method of arbitral settlement, though where reference to Head of State was made it was usual for one or more jurists to be appointed by the nominated sovereign.

A distinction had thus emerged during the nineteenth century between major litigation and minor.   The Alabama case illustrated the form of tribunal suitable for the major, the reference to Mixed Commission or to Head of State was found suitable for minor   *   *   *.

The pattern was now set for a permanent body, and the Hague Peace Conference of 1899 directed itself substantially to this end.   A Convention for the Pacific Settlement of International Disputes was adopted and provided for a Permanent Court of Arbitration.   It was a court only in name, since it consisted of little more than a panel from which arbitrators could be selected and a Bureau to provide the machinery.   The Convention was amended in 1907 and is still in force.   The arbitrators are appointed for terms of six years by the parties to the Convention to the number of not more than four each.   Two of them, only one of whom is a national, are selected by each litigant when a case is referred to the Court, and the four selected then choose an umpire.   When the arbitrators are evenly divided in their choice a third Power performs this office, the Power in question being selected according to a complex procedure.   There is a detailed scheme of procedural rules.   If the parties agree the Court may settle the compromis, although this has never been done   *   *   *.

The deficiencies of the Permanent Court of Arbitration are substantial.   It operates only at the instance of parties to a dispute, its judges are no more than names on a panel, and it has no machinery for compulsory jurisdiction, even when provision exists in treaties for reference to it.   The references that had actually been made to arbitration before 1899 were entirely ad hoc, and only in 1903 was the first agreement arrived at for anticipatory reference of disputes to arbitration. This was the Treaty between Great Britain and France which sealed the Entente Cordiale. It contained, however, a reservation which was severely restrictive of the obligation to submit. This was the reservation that the "vital interests," "independence" or "honour" of the contracting parties must not be "affected." This or a similar formulation became common in the many similar bilateral treaties on the subject between 1903 and 1914.

In fact the Permanent Court of Arbitration did not decide many questions before the Permanent Court of International Justice was set up in 1920 and substantially usurped its functions. This Court survived until replaced by the International Court of Justice in 1946. The new tribunal had the advantage of institutional permanence, and also of some measure of compulsory jurisdiction when this was recognised in advance by declaration of States members to the Statute of the Court. The practice of delivering reasoned judgments or opinions stimulated enormously the formulation of customary international law, and before its expiry the old Permanent Court of International Justice delivered seventy-seven judgments and advisory opinions. * * *

The foundation of the Court did not mean the end of arbitration by mixed commission. The Peace Treaties of 1919 made provision for various tribunals to handle the numerous claims which would follow the boundary adjustments of Europe, and which arose out of exceptional war measures. Each tribunal consisted of one member appointed by each government and a president appointed by the two governments jointly, or in the absence of agreement by the Council of the League. In 1922 a Mixed Claims Commission was set up between the United States and Germany to deal with claims of American citizens in respect of German war measures. In 1928 an effort was made to secure more compulsive jurisdiction both for the International Court and for prospective arbitral tribunals, and the General Act for the Pacific Settlement of International Disputes was the result. All disputes as to rights were to be referred to the Court or, if the parties agreed, to arbitration. Arbitration of non-legal questions was also provided for, and the tribunal was empowered in the absence of an applicable rule (which by definition of non-legal question would seem to be the ordinary situation) to decide ex aequo et bono. Reservations were allowed in respect of disputes arising prior to accession, or concerning questions which, by international law, are solely within the domestic jurisdiction, and concerning particular cases such as territorial status, or disputes falling within clearly defined categories. The United Kingdom subjected its acceptance to the reservation that preliminary reference must be made to the Council of the League of Nations. The General Act was revised in 1949, but has not substantially added to the obligation to submit to judicial settlement.

In 1949 the International Law Commission was entrusted with the task of proposing a draft code on arbitral procedure. This was presented in the Report to the General Assembly of 1958. It was decided that a code to oblige all would not commend itself to acceptance, and hence instead a "model" was produced to guide the draftsmen of bilateral or regional arbitration treaties.

The arbitral tribunal seems in recent years to have been a more popular instrumentality of judicial settlement than the International Court. The Peace Treaties after the Second World War set up conciliation commissions, usually consisting of one representative of each of the litigants with provision for the addition of an umpire by the Secretary-General of the United Nations. The Agreement on German External Debts provided for two tribunals, an arbitral tribunal of three members appointed by Germany and of one each appointed by the United Kingdom, the United States and France, and two appointed jointly by the four governments, and a Mixed Commission of the same eight arbitrators with original jurisdiction with respect to the interpretation of Annex IV, relating to a miscellany of claims. The Bonn Conventions of 1954 relating to the Termination of the Occupation Régime in Germany also provided for arbitral machinery. In addition to these relatively permanent bodies there have been several ad hoc tribunals, notably that between Greece and the United Kingdom of 1955 referring to the Ambatielos claim, and that which dealt with the Buraimi Oasis question in the same year. These were mixed commissions. The submission to Head of State is not an obsolescent procedure. The Luxembourg Agreement of 1952 between Germany and Israel provides for appointment of a mediator by the King of either Denmark or Sweden.

Arbitration of disputes between states and persons. For a recent development in the field of "international" arbitration, see the discussion of the International Centre for Investment Disputes in Chapter 17. This new institution provides for access to an arbitral board by individuals and firms who have certain disputes with states other than those of their own nationality.

3. RULES OF DECISION IN INTERNATIONAL TRIBUNALS

a. *The International Court of Justice.* Article 38 of the statute of the court provides:

1. The Court, whose function is to decide in accordance with international law such disputes as are submitted to it, shall apply:

a. international conventions, whether general or particular, establishing rules expressly recognized by the contesting states;

b. international custom, as evidence of a general practice accepted as law;

c. the general principles of law recognized by civilized nations;

d. subject to the provisions of Article 59, judicial decisions and the teachings of the most highly qualified publicists of the various nations, as subsidiary means for the determination of rules of law.

2. This provision shall not prejudice the power of the Court to decide a case ex aequo et bono, if the parties agree thereto.

b. *International arbitral tribunals.* Cases are referred to arbitral tribunals on an ad hoc basis; the states referring a dispute to a tribunal frequently specify in the compromis (the agreement to submit to arbitration) the governing rules to be applied. In drafting the compromis there is first the question whether the tribunal shall be instructed to decide in accordance with rules of international law or to be accorded a wider discretion to decide according to "justice", "equity", or "ex aequo et bono" without regard to technical legal rights. At times the decision to direct one basis for decision rather than another has been thought by the states agreeing to arbitration to depend upon whether the dispute is of a non-legal nature. For a useful extensive analysis of international practice, see Sohn, The Function of International Arbitration Today, [1963] I Académie De Droit International, Recueil des Cours 1, 41.

Upon occasion the matter may be left in doubt by the parties, in which case the tribunal will have to make its own determination.

RANN OF KUTCH ARBITRATION (INDIA AND PAKISTAN)

The Indo-Pakistan Western Boundary Case Tribunal, 1968.
VII International Legal Materials 633 (1968).

[In April 1965, hostilities broke out between Pakistan and India in an area known as the Rann of Kutch as a result of tension over the question of the border between the two states. On June 30, 1965, the two states concluded an agreement providing for a cease-fire and, in the event of their failing to agree on the border matter, for reference to an arbitral tribunal "for determination of the border in the light of their respective claims and evidence produced before it * * *." Since agreement was not reached by the states on the border question, the matter was submitted to the tribunal. Before considering the merits, the tribunal dealt with a preliminary question concerning its power to adjudicate ex aequo et bono and made the statement which follows.]

During the Meetings of the Tribunal in February 1966, the question arose whether the Tribunal was invested with power to adjudicate ex aequo et bono. On this issue, after hearing the Parties, the Tribunal, on 23 February 1966, rendered the following decision:

The question submitted to the Tribunal is whether or not the Agreement of 30 June 1965 confers upon it the power to decide the case ex aequo et bono.

India moves that this Agreement does not authorise the Tribunal to decide the present case ex aequo et bono, while Pakistan submits that the said Agreement gives the Tribunal such power.

India requests the Tribunal to decide this issue during the present Session. Pakistan moves that the issue should not be decided until after the closure of the written proceedings.

Having regard to the circumstances of the case, the Tribunal deems it appropriate to resolve the issue at this stage of the proceedings.

As both Parties have pointed out, equity forms part of International Law; therefore, the Parties are free to present and develop their cases with reliance on principles of equity.

An international Tribunal will have the wider power to adjudicate a case ex aequo et bono, and thus to go outside the bounds of law, only if such power has been conferred on it by mutual agreement between the Parties.

The Tribunal cannot find that the Agreement of 30 June 1965 does authorise it clearly and beyond doubt to adjudicate ex aequo et bono.

Therefore, and as the Parties have not by any subsequent agreement consented to confer the power upon the Tribunal to adjudicate ex aequo et bono, the Tribunal resolves that it has no such power. (at 642)

4. COMPLIANCE WITH DECISIONS OF INTERNATIONAL TRIBUNALS

a. *Judgments of the International Court of Justice.* Article 94 of the United Nations Charter provides:

> 1. Each Member of the United Nations undertakes to comply with the decision of the International Court of Justice in any case to which it is a party.

> 2. If any party to a case fails to perform the obligations incumbent upon it under a judgment rendered by the Court, the other party may have recourse to the Security Council, which may, if it deems necessary, make recommendations or decide upon measures to be taken to give effect to the judgment.

On the whole, judgments of the court have been complied with. The outstanding exception is the court's judgment in the Corfu Channel Case, [1949] I.C.J.Rep. 4. In I Rosenne, The Law and Practice of the International Court 143 (1965) it is pointed out that although Albania had contested the court's jurisdiction to award damages, it nevertheless, after judgment, offered Britain the sum of £40,000 in final settlement of the British claim. The judgment had been for £843,947 and Britain rejected the offer.

No case has arisen in which recourse has been made to the Security Council of the United Nations to decide upon measures to be taken "to give effect to the judgment." Questions as yet undecided include the following: Does the Security Council have power under the Charter to order a state to comply with a judgment? Can the Security Council direct or authorize the use of force to enforce such an order? Is the council limited, in its use of force to "enforce" a judgment of the court, to those situations in which non-performance of an order of the court can be considered a threat to the peace, breach of the peace, or act of aggression under Article 39 of the Charter of the United Nations?

b. *Awards of arbitral tribunals.* The effectiveness of the awards of international arbitral tribunals depends upon the willingness of states to abide by their agreements to be bound by such awards. "It is a striking fact that states have seldom refused to carry out or abide by the decisions of international tribunals. * * * In the vast majority of instances in which positive action has been required, execution has followed as a matter of course." Hudson, International Tribunals 129 (1944).

In some instances, however, disputes over the award have delayed final compliance or settlement for years.

THE CHAMIZAL BOUNDARY DISPUTE

49 United States Department of State Bulletin 199 (1963).

Department Statement, July 18

The Presidents of the United States and Mexico announced to-day their agreement to conclude a convention for the settlement of the Chamizal boundary dispute. The recommended terms of settlement which the Presidents have approved were submitted to them in identical memoranda by the Department of State and the Mexican Ministry of Foreign Relations. According to the terms of the recommended settlement, the United States would transfer to Mexico 437 acres in the vicinity of El Paso, Texas. Conclusion of the convention will be a final step in the resolution of this controversy, which has been earnestly sought by every United States administration since 1910.

An international arbitral commission awarded to Mexico in 1911 an undeterminable part of the Chamizal zone in El Paso, Texas. The area of the zone then totaled approximately 598 acres. The Mexican claim was based on a shift in the channel of the Rio Grande. The United States Government, which had disputed the claim, rejected the award on several grounds,[a] but in the understanding that the Governments of the two countries could proceed at once to settle their differences through diplomatic channels. Since 1911 the controversy has been a major problem in relations between the two countries. Every United States administration beginning with that of President Taft has attempted to resolve it in a mutually satisfactory manner. Proposals for a settlement have varied, and every practical means of settling the matter is believed to have been explored by the Governments at one time or another. In June 1962 President López Mateos

---

a. Carlston, The Process of International Arbitration 153 (1946):

The validity of the award in attempting to divide the Chamizal tract was vigorously attacked by the American commissioner in a dissenting opinion upon the following bases: (1) It clearly departed from the terms of reference in deciding a question not submitted by the parties. Article I of the convention of 1910 bounded the tract with technical accuracy; Article III provided that the commission was to decide solely whether the title to the tract was in the United States or in Mexico. Neither government, in its diplomatic correspondence or in its arguments before the tribunal, took any other position than that the question was as to the ownership of the tract in its entirety. (2) It departed from the terms of submission by fail-

ing to apply the rules of the convention of 1884. In the language of the Hague Court in the Orinoco Steamship Company Case, " 'excessive exercise of power may consist * * * in misinterpreting the express provisions of the agreement in respect of the way in which they are to reach their decisions, notably with regard to the legislation or the principles of law to be applied.' " That convention classed all changes either as slow and gradual erosion and accretion or the cutting of a new bed. The decision imported into the treaty a rule unknown to it as well as to international law—rapid and violent erosion. (3) It was "equivocal and uncertain in its terms and impossible of accomplishment." It would be impossible to locate the channel of 1864.

urged that a further attempt be made, and President Kennedy agreed. The two Presidents instructed their respective executive agencies to recommend a complete solution which, without prejudice to the juridical positions of the two Governments, would take into account the entire history of the tract. They recognized that any mutually acceptable settlement would affect many people in the city of El Paso and agreed that respect for the rights and interests of the people affected on both sides of the border should be a principal consideration in reaching a solution. The recommended settlement follows generally the solution set forth in the international arbitral award of 1911.

* * *

5. CONCILIATION

A marked feature of recently proposed international conventions (not all of which are in force) has been the provision of procedures for conciliation to which parties can resort for an "amicable solution" of their disputes, either in place of or prior to submission of the dispute to arbitration or to adjudication. Among the conventions in the Documentary Supplement see, e. g., the following: Art. 42 of the International Covenant on Civil and Political Rights, Art. 12 of the International Convention on the Elimination of all Forms of Racial Discrimination, Art. 66 of the Vienna Convention on the Law of Treaties, Art. III of the Optional Protocol to the Vienna Convention on Diplomatic Relations, Art. IV of the Optional Protocol to the Conventions on the Law of the Sea.

SECTION D.   APPLICATION IN THE UNITED NATIONS

THE CASE OF AN ATTACK ON A SENEGALESE POST BY PORTUGAL

IX U.N. Monthly Chronicle, Nov. 1972, p. 3.

The Security Council met on 19, 20 and 23 October [1972] at the request of Senegal. The request was contained in a letter dated 16 October, addressed to the President. In its letter, Senegal stated that on 12 October at about 5 p. m., a unit of the regular Portuguese army, including five armoured cars, had attacked a Senegalese post in the department of Velingara, in the region of Casamance. One Senegalese soldier was killed, another wounded and a civilian working in his fields was killed by a Portuguese tank. The letter said the

Senegalese army had intervened and forced the enemy troops to withdraw to their base at Pirada, three kilometres from the Senegalese border.

The letter further recalled that the Council had adopted several resolutions condemning Portugal for systematic acts of aggression and provocation against Senegal, but that the latest incident, although not the first that had occurred on the border between Senegal and Guinea (Bissau), must be considered the most serious and significant, because a deliberately planned act of war had been involved. Senegal said that Portugal's main aim in its constant aggressive conduct towards various African countries was to show that the United Nations was powerless and to make its highest decision-making body appear ridiculous.

* * *

In a letter dated 18 October, addressed to the President of the Council, Portugal replied to the aforementioned letter from Senegal. In its letter Portugal said, referring to the incident of 12 October, that the Commander Headquarters of the Portuguese armed forces in Portuguese Guinea had published a communiqué, on 13 October, stating:

"On the 12th of the current month, at about 1800 hours, a unit of the Portuguese army, composed of three armoured cars, violated the frontier of Senegal in the region of Pirada, causing one dead and one wounded in a detachment of the Senegalese army, and also one civilian dead of Portuguese nationality. The Command-in-Chief laments deeply this occurrence and has ordered that criminal proceedings be begun against the commander of the unit in question, so that he may be submitted to trial by court martial. It is presumed that this was a case of mental agitation on the part of the unit commander, seeing that he operated outside the zone to which he was assigned and in violation of all superior orders.

"This Commander Headquarters immediately entered into contact with the Senegalese authorities in order to present to them its apologies and to express its readiness immediately to pay all the compensation that justice should dictate."

The Portuguese letter further stated that the Portuguese Government in Lisbon had summoned the Ambassador of Switzerland, whose country represented Portuguese interests in Senegal, to inform him of the details of the incident and to request that he transmit to the Government of Dakar the willingness of the Portuguese Government to pay compensation and to give all necessary guarantees to the Senegalese Government.

The Portuguese letter said that Portugal was unable to understand the purpose of the meeting of the Council convened at the request of Senegal, since no other conclusions could be drawn from the facts of the incident in question beyond those detailed in the communiqué of the Commander Headquarters of the Portuguese armed forces in Portuguese Guinea and transmitted to the Senegalese Government through the Swiss Ambassador. In those circumstances the Council meetings were one more step in the campaign against Portugal being carried on by certain interests hostile to it in the United Nations, with a view to serving predetermined policies to which those interests were dedicated.

With the consent of the Council, the President invited the representatives of Algeria, Mali, Mauritania and Senegal to participate in the discussion without the right to vote.

    *   *   *

[Members of the Security Council debated whether to adopt a draft resolution sponsored by Guinea, Somalia and the Sudan. Among the arguments presented in this debate were the following:]

Coumba N'Doffene Diouf, Minister for Foreign Affairs (Senegal), said that on 12 October at about 1700 hours, Portuguese military forces, including five armoured cars, attacked the Senegalese post of Nianao in the district of Kourane. The attack caused the death of a Senegalese lieutenant and a civilian worker in the fields, and seriously wounded a peaceful farmer. It was not the first time the Council had had to be seized of such provocations committed by Portuguese troops in violation of the sovereignty and territorial integrity of Senegal.

Since the first month of its independence Senegal had had to confront on its southern frontier acts of deliberate aggression by Portugal, which maintained in Guinea (Bissau) an unfortunate African Territory, and a colonial war which the Council had unequivocally condemned. In resolution 178 (1963) the Council had requested "the Government of Portugal, in accordance with its declared intentions, to take whatever action may be necessary to prevent any violation of Senegal's sovereignty and territorial integrity". That resolution had never been complied with.

Incursions into Senegal's territory by Portugal had been frequent, and while Senegal maintained its faith in the Security Council, the time had come for Senegal to defend by all measures within its means its population and territory against repeated actions of the Portuguese troops. At the same time, it was for the Council to take up the challenge Portugal had launched against the world community and prevent it from pursuing with impunity an anachronistic colonial war in Africa.

Portugal had made a public declaration concerning its most recent incursion, which recognized physical facts, and even offered apologies to the Senegalese Government and compensation for the victims of the attack. Portugal announced that the chief of the military district responsible for the horrible crime would eventually be court-martialled. Senegal wished to protest against such a subtle and immoral manoeuvre which suggested there might be justice with regard to what had happened at Pirada. It was inaccurate for Portugal to say its military commander had at any time lost his mental faculties. He knew exactly what he was doing. He was able to travel in his car with the lights off and to slow down in order to carry out his surprise attack. Senegal categorically rejected the proposal for compensation which Portugal hastened to present.

By what means had a country with such limited material and technical capacity as Portugal, not only faced the restraints imposed on it because of 10 years of colonial wars, but even thought unceasingly of enlarging the circle of its enemies? It was because of the impunity guaranteed by countries that had withdrawn from all open colonial actions—members of NATO, which at the time of certain votes did not hesitate practically to approve the attitude of defiance permanently observed by Portugal for the international community.

Imperialism and colonialism were doomed. Portugal must realize that. It must create immediate conditions of peace in Guinea (Bissau) by negotiating with PAIGC on the basis of the three-stage peace plan presented by Senegal in March 1969. The first phase would consist of a cease-fire followed by negotiations without any pre-condition. The second phase would start, as a result of the negotiation, by a period of internal autonomy for Guinea (Bissau). The modalities and time-limits would be discussed freely between the representatives of the Portuguese Government and the representatives of the various political movements of Guinea (Bissau). In the last stage, independence would be granted after negotiations, within the framework of a Portuguese-African community, which was not to be excluded a priori.

* * *

Lazar Mojsov (Yugoslavia) said it was in the context of Portugal's long-established, systematic and carefully planned policy of aggression against African States, and of its unremitting colonial wars, that the Council must consider and finally reject the Portuguese apology and explanation for its most recent incursion into Senegalese territory. That act was not, as Portugal maintained, the result of the madness of one man but of a policy that thought it could stop the winds of change in what it called "its corner of Africa". The Portuguese "apology" was an apology until the next aggression.

The Portuguese policy of trying to keep its colonial possessions and of attacking and threatening the sovereignty and territorial integrity of African States was all part of the same policy. One needed the other, one fed the other, and without the removal of both, both would persist. Without the removal of major political, economic and military assistance and support by the allies of Portugal and South Africa, those two colonial and racist régimes, together with the illegal régime of Ian Smith in Southern Rhodesia, would not cease to conduct co-ordinated and mutually essential policies of subjugating southern Africa and threatening the rest of it.   Juxtaposed with those grave realities, bland apologies could not be seriously considered.

* * *

Edouard Longerstaey (Belgium) said the text of the revised draft resolution was out of proportion to its object.   However regrettable the incursion into Senegalese territory on 12 October by a detachment of the Portuguese army, it was not comparable to the acts of violence and destruction that had been going on since 1963.   Instead of the condemnation that appeared in operative paragraph 2, the Council should have merely deplored the recent incident, as well as the resulting threats to the territorial integrity and sovereignty of Senegal and the loss of human lives entailed.

The revised draft should not have missed the opportunity, however tenuous and fragile, to lessen tension in the area by taking note of the assurances Portugal was prepared to give to Senegal and by requesting it to take appropriate measures to prevent the repetition of frontier incidents with Senegal.   Belgium would abstain from voting.   Portugal should not be condemned on the basis of background alone, without taking into account its intentions, regrets and promises to pay compensation.

* * *

Christopher Phillips (United States) said the United States retained its conviction that the people of Portuguese Guinea had an inalienable right to self-determination.   The United States had abstained because of the one-sided nature of the resolution.   That resolution, while taking note of the letter from the representative of Portugal, did not reflect adequately its contents as they bore on the complaint before the Council.   The Foreign Minister of Senegal had emphasized the need to look for some form of peaceful settlement by the parties concerned in the conflict.   Regrettably, nothing of that spirit of conciliation had been included in the resolution.

Last November the United States had suggested establishing a commission "acceptable to all parties, which might be in a position to investigate border incidents, and to report periodically to the Security Council on such questions as progress towards self-determination in Guinea (Bissau) and other elements which could lead to a satisfactory settlement in the region".   The Council should point its activities in that direction in dealing with the difficult problem before it.

* * *

[The following] resolution was adopted by a vote of 12 in favour (Argentina, China, France, Guinea, India, Italy, Japan, Panama, Somalia, Sudan, USSR, Yugoslavia) to none against, with 3 abstentions (Belgium, United Kingdom, United States).

* * *

Text of Resolution 321 (1972)

THE SECURITY COUNCIL,

Considering the complaint of the Republic of Senegal against Portugal contained in document S/10807,

Having heard the Minister for Foreign Affairs of Senegal,

Taking note of the letter of the representative of Portugal contained in document S/10810,

Considering its resolutions 178 (1963) of 24 April 1963, 204 (1965) of 19 May 1965, 273 (1969) of 9 December 1969, 302 (1971) of 24 November 1971 and the report of 2 February 1971 (E/CN.-4/1050) of the Working Group of Experts of the Commission on Human Rights concerning Portuguese acts of violence in Senegalese territory,

Deeply disturbed by the attitude of Portugal, which persistently refuses to comply with the relevant Security Council resolutions,

Deeply concerned about the multiplication of incidents which entail the risk of a threat to international peace and security,

Reaffirming that only complete respect for the sovereignty and territorial integrity of Senegal and all the African States bordering the territories of Guinea (Bissau), Angola and Mozambique, and for the principle of self-determination and independence defined in particular in General Assembly resolution 1514 (XV), will make it possible to eliminate the causes of tension in those regions of the African continent and create a climate of confidence, peace and security,

1. Condemns the frontier violation and attack on the Senegalese post at Nianao committed by regular forces of the Portuguese army on 12 October 1972;

2. Recalls its resolution 294 (1971) condemning the acts of violence and destruction committed by the Portuguese forces against the people and villages of Senegal since 1963;

3. Demands that the Government of Portugal should stop immediately and definitively any acts of violence and destruction directed against Senegalese territory and scrupulously respect the sovereignty, territorial integrity and security of that State and all other independent African States;

4. Calls upon the Government of Portugal to respect the principle of self-determination and independence defined in particular in General Assembly resolution 1514 (XV) and to take immediately all necessary steps to apply that principle;

5. Declares that if Portugal does not comply with the provisions of the present resolution the Security Council will meet to consider other steps;

6. Decides to remain seized of the question.

SCHACHTER, THE QUASI–JUDICIAL ROLE OF THE SECURITY COUNCIL AND THE GENERAL ASSEMBLY

58 American Journal of International Law 960 (1964).

* * * [G]overnments have repeatedly called upon the political organs to pass judgments on whether states have observed their obligations, and in several cases the organs have in fact done so, either explicitly or by clear implication. True, these cases are few in number, compared to the multitude of questions dealt with by the United Nations, but they are regarded as among the "leading" cases because of their legal implications and political repercussions. Examples which come to mind are the cases relating to Suez, Hungary, Korea, Congo, South Africa, and the Portuguese territories.[1]

It may be said that none of these cases is a shining example of United Nations achievement; nearly all have left deep scars and a sense of frustration. Is this because they have been dealt with in terms of the Charter obligations (rather than through negotiation) or is it the other way around—that the legal prescriptions were invoked because the problems could not be settled merely through compromise and adjustment? There is, of course, no ready answer for all cases, but they suggest that the intractability of the problems tends to bring about a focusing on legal principles and a recourse to normative judgments by the political bodies. This is so, in spite of both the general predisposition to favor compromise and the recognized limits on United Nations authority. Certainly almost everyone would prefer settlements that did not place in issue the authority of the United Nations—an almost inevitable result of its judgments attributing "guilt" to a state. It is not surprising that these cases involve the burning issues of our day rather than the lesser disputes (such as boundary quarrels) which are usually considered as more suitable for legal adjudication. These lesser disputes can be side-stepped; the others cannot: they either involve violence with its threat of global conflagration or the insistent demands to eliminate colonialism and stigma of racial discrimination, both equally incendiary issues.

It would perhaps be stretching a point to conclude from this that when the chips are down, law becomes necessary. The cases do, however, indicate how difficult it can be to ignore the problem of legal responsibility when disputes are brought to the United Nations political organs and the Charter principles are invoked as a basis for de-

1. In all of these cases, resolutions were adopted at one stage or another which explicitly or by unmistakable implication declared state conduct to be contrary to the Charter. There was, of course, a much larger number of cases in which charges of illegality were extensively debated without the adoption by the organs of decisions confirming such charges. However, in some of these cases, the proceedings may be said to exhibit a broad consensus on the characterization of certain conduct as legally impermissible.

cision. True, governments do not have to assert non-compliance with a Charter obligation as a basis of competence, since both the General Assembly and the Security Council have ample authority to consider disputes and situations on other grounds. Yet, in most cases affecting peace and security or questions of colonialism or acute matters of human rights, charges will be made by the complaining states that Charter obligations have been violated. The evident reason for this is that the behavior of a state cannot easily be challenged solely on grounds of "policy." For, unless it can be shown that a course of conduct involves a departure from legal obligations, the matter will normally be regarded as within the discretion of the state or, in Charter language, within its "sovereign" rights or domestic jurisdiction. The question of responsibility may be, of course, ultimately avoided if a settlement should be achieved, but when a solution is not obtained and the pressures continue, the issue of Charter compliance is likely to become the focus of the debate.

It can hardly be claimed that, in considering such charges of violations, the members of the organs observe judicial standards of impartiality. They will, of course, exhibit partisanship and interest in varying degree. Governments are expected to take positions in the political organs in accordance with their conceptions of national interest and it is apparent that these conceptions will embrace considerations based on ties of alliance, friendship or political bargaining. However, it is not sufficient for Member states to argue their case on grounds of national interest alone, since the organs contain varied and conflicting ideas of national interest. Whatever the actual motives for a state's position, its justification in the international forum must include grounds that will be acceptable to other states, a requirement which is not simply a matter of logic but the consequence of the political necessity of achieving the widest possible support. The decision that emerges, as shown by the cases mentioned above, will be supported (one might even say "necessarily" supported) by Member states having divergent interests and ideologies and their agreed evaluation of the specific facts in Charter terms will be accorded weight precisely because of their diverse and representative composition. It does not seem far-fetched to characterize such decisions in conventional legal terms as a contemporaneous construction by the parties of their treaty obligations expressed through formal decisions of a competent organ.

It may be asked whether such judgments can be considered authoritative unless it is shown that they have an effect on state conduct and are not merely verbal admonitions. To respond that they have moral weight and influence public opinion seems too vague and uncertain to carry conviction, especially in the face of a determined stand by the "target" governments. On the other hand, one can hardly disregard the evidence that resolutions of United Nations organs critical of state behavior as contrary to the peremptory principles of the Charter have played a rôle in both domestic and external criticism of the government concerned. Thus, in regard to Suez and the Congo, it was apparent that, in the countries directly concerned, important political groups and personalities were influenced by the positions of United Nations organs in relation to the commitments of their governments and that their criticism had an impact on governmental policy. Nor can one overlook the consequences of a resolution on the officialdom of a government. Just as a superior official will rarely direct a subordinate to disobey a rule, officials in most governments would probably be reluctant (except under great pressure) to disregard an authoritative decision of a United Nations organ which asserts a legal requirement based on the Charter. Even if we recognize that these are points on which verifiable data are fragmentary, it is difficult to deny that influential groups within national states generally believe that the self-interest of their states not only extends to immediate gains and losses but also includes the factor of reciprocity and a long-term interest in order and stability. Rarely will responsible national officials lose sight of the possibility that a failure on their part to observe the rules can be used "against" them in the future and thereby weaken the basis for their own reliance on commonly accepted restraints.

This is, of course, far from saying that all United Nations decisions are given effect or are enforced; it is merely pointing out that judgments by United Nations organs asserting legal requirements possess a degree of authority that generates pressures—internal or external—in favor of compliance. Perhaps that is all that can be said, short of plunging into the details of each historical situation. One other point might be noted: the test of "effectiveness" is not only measured by compliance; for a government may flout a United Nations decision and then pay a price for it. This price may take various forms; for example, defections from political parties ideologically disposed to support of the recalcitrant state or a weakening of confidence in internal order which reduces the flow of investment to the non-complying country. It is not inconceivable that the governments affected will modify their position in future situations or that others in similar circumstances will profit by the example.

* * *

1. *Questions.* Did the Security Council of the United Nations apply any rules of law in the case of the attack on a Senegalese post by Portugal? Did it find Portugal in violation of Article 2(4) of the Charter? Could it have so found? What "constitutional" basis did the Security Council have for its adoption of the resolution? Did it act under Article VI of the Charter, or under Article VII? Or did it act unlawfully?

Suppose that Portugal does not comply with the provisions of the resolution. In paragraph 5 of the resolution, the council declares that it will meet to consider other steps. What steps can it take to bring Portugal into compliance with its legal obligations? Further attention is given to these problems in Chapter 20.

2. *Law-making by the political organs of the United Nations.* In its resolution in the Senegalese case the Security Council refers to General Assembly resolution 1514 (XV). That resolution is entitled "Declaration on the granting of independence to colonial countries and peoples." (Its text is set forth in the Documentary Supplement). Does the council imply that Portugal is legally bound by the terms of that resolution? By what process, if any, can a resolution of the General Assembly become law so that its provisions can subsequently be applied by other organs of the United Nations?

HIGGINS, THE DEVELOPMENT OF INTERNATIONAL LAW THROUGH THE POLITICAL ORGANS OF THE UNITED NATIONS 4 (1963) *

It is necessary at this point to ask ourselves if political organs do in fact have the authority to prescribe rules of law, or may they only recommend solutions? That they have authority for internal prescription is not in doubt; * * * Similarly, it may be observed that political organs sometimes make declarations of consciously legal content—the Declaration on the Nuremberg principles and the resolutions on sovereignty over natural resources may both be cited as examples.

However, the Assembly certainly has no right to legislate in the commonly understood sense of the term. Resolutions of the Assembly are not per se binding: though those rules of general international law which they may embody are binding on member states, with or without the help of the resolution. But the body of resolutions as a whole, taken as indications of a general customary law, undoubtedly provide a rich source of evidence. Those resolutions of the Assembly which deliberately—rather than incidentally—provide declarations on international law are invariably based on other quasi-judicial forms of support. Thus the Nuremberg principles were adopted on the recommendation of the International Law Commission, and pronouncements on the status of prisoners of war have been based on the work of commissions set up specifically to study these aspects of the problem.

In the case of the Security Council—and to a lesser extent, the Assembly—the reference to specific legal authority is muted, in the sense that decisions are often demanded with some urgency. The

* FROM THE DEVELOPMENT OF IN-
TERNATIONAL LAW THROUGH
THE POLITICAL ORGANS OF THE
UNITED NATIONS by Rosalyn Hig-
gins. Published by Oxford University
Press under the auspices of the Royal
Institute of International Affairs.

prescription of law, rather than its application, thus becomes involved. This is especially true of decisions made concerning peace and security, where the feeling may well be that, quite apart from traditional law on the subject concerned, it is essential to pacify the situation. Although, in such a situation, the Security Council is likely to state that it is basing itself on the law as it conceives it to be, the line between applying law and legislating it becomes thin: certainly a question of developing law becomes involved.

SECTION E. WHEN "SUPREME INTERESTS" ARE "JEOPARDIZED"

HENKIN, HOW NATIONS BEHAVE 216 (1968) *

THE CUBAN QUARANTINE [a]

The Cuban missile crisis of 1962 saw the world's superpowers in deadly confrontation in circumstances involving their security, their global interests, and the peace and survival of international society. Since it ended successfully for the United States, it has become a highlight of American foreign policy after the Second World War. Friend and enemy have expressed deepest respect for President Kennedy's policy and diplomacy during those fateful days; it has become a standard by which American actions since then have been measured (and sometimes found inadequate).

To explore the influence of law on the political actions that comprised the "missile crisis," we should look for law in the decisions of many governments: what was said about law in the Kremlin, in Havana, in the foreign offices of naval powers whose vessels were interdicted by the blockade, in the councils of governments instructing their delegates to the United Nations or the Organization of American States, in the meetings—and in the corridors—of those organizations, in the office of Secretary General U Thant. Hopefully, scholars may someday shed light on the different influences of law in different places. I, of necessity, limit myself to the decisions and deliberations of the government of the United States.

International law, I believe, influenced the policies of the United States, the decision to do what was done and to say what was said. The processes of decision are not available for public scrutiny, but fortunately our speculations need be less than wholly speculative: American society is open, and adroit journalists have again succeeded in pulling apart the curtains of policymaking. In the decision taken, we

---

* Reprinted by permission of Frederick A. Praeger, New York, and the Pall Mall Press, London.

a. See also Chapter 19 for exposition of certain legal questions involved in the Cuban quarantine.

know, lawyers were present at virtually all the deliberations. The Attorney General of the United States was the President's brother and enjoyed a special working relation with him. George Ball, a lawyer, was Under Secretary of State. The legal advisers of the State Department took part at all stages. Adlai Stevenson, the United States representative to the United Nations, also a lawyer, was consulted.

On October 22, 1962, President Kennedy addressed the people of the United States by television in an atmosphere of crisis. He announced that the United States had clear evidence that the Soviet Union was in the process of installing in Cuba "large, long-range, and clearly offensive weapons of sudden mass destruction." These weapons constituted "an explicit threat to the peace and security of all the Americas," and their introduction was "a deliberately provocative and unjustified change in the status quo which cannot be accepted by this country." The President announced that the United States would impose a defensive maritime quarantine to prevent the further introduction into Cuba of offensive missiles, and to induce the Soviet Union to withdraw the missiles already there.

On the same day, the United States placed the Cuban situation before the United Nations Security Council and asked for an urgent meeting of the Council. The Council met on the following day, October 23, and discussed the crisis and the proposed quarantine but took no action. On that day, the Organization of American States, acting under the Rio Treaty of 1947, adopted a resolution recommending that the members

> take all measures, individually and collectively, including the use of armed force, which they may deem necessary to ensure that the Government of Cuba cannot continue to receive from the Sino-Soviet powers military material and related supplies which may threaten the peace and security of the Continent and to prevent the missiles in Cuba with offensive capability from ever becoming an active threat to the peace and security of the Continent.

In the evening of October 23, after the action of the OAS, President Kennedy proclaimed the quarantine to take effect on the following day. Under the quarantine all vessels, of whatever nationality, in defined zones would be intercepted but would be allowed to continue to Cuba if they were not carrying prohibited materials.

Pursuant to the quarantine, vessels of the Soviet Union and of other nations were trailed, boarded, inspected. Soviet submarines were located, tracked, surfaced, and photographed. Other vessels apparently destined for Cuba changed course and proceeded elsewhere. No vessels were forcefully seized or diverted, and military force was not actually used.

The outcome is well known. The Soviet Union agreed to discontinue bringing missiles into Cuba; it agreed to discontinue building its missile bases in Cuba and to dismantle and remove missiles that had already been installed. The United States agreed to end the quarantine and gave assurances against an invasion of Cuba. When Premier Castro refused to agree to United Nations inspection in Cuba to monitor Soviet compliance with its undertakings, the Soviet Union permitted its vessels going to and from Cuba to be inspected (from alongside) by American officials. The United States also maintained surveillance of Cuba from the air.

Context for Policy

What happened in and about Cuba in October-November 1962 can be understood only in a complex context that includes the basic confrontation between East and West, the strategic import of the new military technology, the significance for both the Soviet Union and the United States of Castro's alignment with the Communist powers, the history and politics of the Western Hemisphere, domestic politics in the United States, and much more. None of these can be ignored in any examination of the effect of law on American decisions, particularly in an attempt to assess cost and advantage of compliance with or violation of international law as seen by American policy-makers at the time.

Let me assert some over-simple propositions. The United States has been deeply disturbed by Castro's Cuba as a foothold for Soviet communism in the Western Hemisphere. A Soviet satellite in Cuba is inconsistent with the policy of the United States, dating from the Monroe Doctrine of 1823, to exclude new European penetrations of the Western Hemisphere. An aggressive Soviet satellite in Cuba not only sets a bad example, but also is dangerous as a base for propaganda and subversion in Latin America. The people of the United States and congressional leaders were also disturbed by the presence of a Soviet military base in the Caribbean, so close to the shores of the United States.

In an earlier day the United States might have dealt with this disturbing occurrence by using military means to replace Premier Castro by Cuban leadership with a friendly orientation. But by 1962, in Latin America surely, the day of unilateral intervention by the United States seemed over, replaced by collective judgment if not by truly collective action. Military and geographic realities have compelled the governments of the area to accept United States protection for the Western Hemisphere against external attack, as well as its power and influence to maintain peace within the hemisphere, but they have insisted that action must be based on collective judgment and have been vehement against unilateral intervention in the affairs of any state in the region. The Cuban revolution, moreover, stirred sympathetic echoes in various Latin American countries; it was only Castro's alignment with the Soviet Union that led to collective adverse judgments and actions, but even that alignment would not bring support or tolerance for unilateral use of force by the United States against Cuba.

The United States, then, aware of its obligations under the United Nations Charter and the Charter of the OAS and of the new postwar attitudes against force, and concerned both to avoid antagonizing the nations of Latin America and to obtain their support for anti-Castro measures, had been deterred from military action against Cuba. Involvement in the Bay of Pigs incident in 1961 only underscored the limitations on action by the United States; it had promoted and supported action by Cubans in rebellion, but its support was ambivalent and on a small scale. Even that action was admittedly a mistake, and apparently no other military action against Castro was contemplated.

October 1962 was different. Observers are not agreed as to the motives and significance of the Soviet attempt to emplace missiles in Cuba, but in retrospect, at least, most of them see it as a challenge and a threat which the United States could not tolerate. Many see the Soviet action as primarily of psychological-political significance: particularly since the United States had just proclaimed that the "missile gap" was in its favor, the Soviet Union sought to dramatize and flaunt its strategic "parity" with the United States for the sake of its prestige at home and influence abroad. It would permit Khrushchev to reopen the Berlin issue from a new strategic posture. From the point of view of the United States, Soviet intrusion into its "sphere" and unilateral disturbance in the array of strategic forces were a gauntlet that had to be taken up. The United States also feared the political and psychological impact of this sudden, dramatic move on Latin America. Other observers see the Soviet action as having important implications for hemispheric security and U. S. strategic policy. The security of the Western world and its global political alignments depended on deterrence—a state of mind reflecting a perception of the balance of nuclear power. The new Soviet program in Cuba might disturb the balance of forces, or, at least the perception of those forces on which the policies of nations were built. A missile base in Cuba, even if control of the missiles remained firmly in Soviet hands, threatened to disturb the delicate strategic balance between East and West. Soviet missiles could reach anywhere in the hemisphere and could circumvent the defense-warning system of the United States, depriving it of most of the critical minutes of notice that an attack was on the way. Within the hemisphere, Cuban missiles could be used for political blackmail and in support of subversion. They might sufficiently offset American military power so as to create questions as to whether the United States would act in defense of the hemisphere. With no danger to itself, the Soviet Union could hide behind Cuba, letting Cuba be the counterpoise to United States power.

On the global scene, too, Cuban bases would have immeasurable effect on the delicate balance of power and terror. Until the Cuban crisis, it was believed that Soviet missiles could not reach the United States in sufficient numbers to destroy it, while the United States, with more, longer-range missiles, could largely destroy the Soviet Union. On the other hand, the Soviet Union had plenty of medium-range delivery vehicles and could destroy Western Europe. As hostage for the West, Western Europe found its security in the promise that if it was subjected to a Soviet attack, the United States would retaliate against the U.S.S.R., risking whatever further "strike" the Soviet Union might still be able to launch. This had been, and promised to be for some time, the basis for security and peace between the East and West. Cuban missile bases threatened this balance, by putting the United States itself within reach of Soviet medium-range weapons. In sufficient numbers, some argued, they would have neutralized United States weapons enough to distract or deter them from coming to the aid of Western Europe.

Such appeared to be the significance of Cuban missile bases in the logic of the deterrent and its political role in international relations. Within the United States, moreover, it would be difficult to exaggerate how deeply troubling was the new presence, at its doorstep, of Soviet missile bases with the capacity of destroying the United States. Were they to remain there, the shock would severely shake the country, with far-reaching consequences for the administration and for political parties and institutions. Determined to eliminate this threat, President Kennedy and other American policy-makers prepared to face a major political and military confrontation that carried the risk of total war. In the calculus of cost and advantage the United States found the price of inaction very high, and may well have been prepared to violate international law and face the substantial costs of violation.

Choice Among Alternatives

What were the possible courses of action open to the United States? First, the evidence could be presented to the Soviet Union with a demand that the missiles be removed. Instead, or in addition, the matter might be brought to the United Nations as a threat to the peace, and the world organization asked to take measures to have the missiles removed and to see that no new ones were introduced. Either of these moves, without more, would have raised no questions under international law. But, it is clear, American policy-makers had little faith that these steps would succeed, and their failure might make other measures more difficult. Bilateral talks might have led only to Soviet denials. The U.N. Security Council would have been frustrated by veto. The General Assembly would have debated at length, and it was not sure that a majority would have been prepared to act in a global confrontation between the two giants. There would have been delay, confusion, and obfuscation rather than the firm action needed to impress the Soviet Union—during which time the Soviet Union would have been warned, might have expedited construction of the bases to achieve a fait accompli, or taken other measures to frustrate further reactions by the United States.

It was early decided that the United States would act directly to meet the Soviet threat. Three main lines of action seemed open. The most serious would be an invasion of Cuba, which would not only dispose of the missile problem but would also topple the Castro regime. Short of invasion, the United States could move in one of two ways: either destroy existing bases by bombing, and deter future installations by threat of further bombing or prevent them by blockade; or, begin by blockade to prevent completion of the installations; then, with that show of strength, demand the removal of existing missiles; held in reserve would be the threat and possibility of bombing.

No one can say exactly what factors, in what degree, weighed in the decision among these alternatives. Even the versions of the deliberations which have been published to date do not tell exactly the same story, and much remains untold. From all available sources I conclude that legal considerations were not insignificant. While law was not expressly stressed, it lay, I am satisfied, behind much of what was said. Arguments in terms of "morality," "moderateness," "responsibility," "low-key response" in effect subsumed legal considerations.[1] Discussion of the possible costs of the various alternatives included those reactions and consequences reflecting, among other things, views as to the lawfulness or unlawfulness of proposed U. S. action.[2]

An immediate invasion of Cuba, it appears, was an alternative soon discarded. Unlike the earlier Bay of Pigs mishap, this would presumably have meant not support of Cuban rebels but a direct attack with American forces. Although the purpose of the attack would not have been conquest, it would clearly be a violation of the most important norm of international law—Article 2(4) of the United Nations Charter.[3] Of course, one might guess, it was not only the wish to obey the law that deterred the United States. Such an attack could not afford to fail, and adequate preparation might have taken some time. The ever-present possibility of a Soviet military response

1. Attorney General Robert F. Kennedy, for example, argued that a bombing attack, especially without warning, would be another "Pearl Harbor" and would blacken the name of the United States. * * * "In retrospect most participants regarded Robert Kennedy's speech as the turning point."

2. In an address on December 9, 1964, Dean Acheson said: "Those involved in the Cuban crisis of October 1962 will remember the irrelevance of the supposed moral considerations brought out in the discussions." N.Y. Times, Dec. 10, 1964, p. 16. On the basis of other sources, I do not share his conclusion that these considerations were irrelevant. In fact, Mr. Acheson admitted that there were in the balance of decision considerations of "prudence," and the consequences of "doing too much."

3. The United States would have been compelled to argue "anticipatory self-defense," an argument hardly likely to have been accepted. * * * Even those sympathetic to such argument might have agreed that the United States response was out of all proportion to the threat.

could not be totally discounted: Soviet weapons would be destroyed and Soviet personnel probably killed; and the loss of Cuba might have seemed to the Russians a serious blow which they would seek to prevent, as in Hungary in 1956. The United States would have faced a storm of adverse world opinion from allies and others both within and without the United Nations. Its influence for order and against force, nurtured in Korea and at Suez, would have been gravely damaged. Latin American approval for this action would have been difficult to obtain and would have jeopardized the essential surprise; if done without such approval, it would have revived the specter of "Yankee intervention" and destroyed the delicate balance of trust and mistrust which supports United States relations with Latin America. But these political reasons merely vindicate the international norm and reflect the interests that lead nations to accept it. In our world, international law is observed because of political reasons—the fear of political sanctions, of responses and consequences.

The remaining two alternatives differed in the likelihood of their effectiveness as well as in their legal and political import. Bombing would more likely achieve the military objective even if at some cost in casualties. The deed would be done quickly and irrevocably. It would not depend for its success on Soviet compliance and the acquiescence of other nations. But bombing the missile sites would probably have killed Soviet personnel in charge of the missiles, increasing the likelihood of a Soviet military reaction. Despite the photographic evidence which the United States was able to spread before the world, it might have been easier, after the sites were destroyed, for the Soviet Union to deny the evidence as fabricated. Even if the evidence were believed, a bombing attack by the United States in violation of Cuban territory, causing loss of lives and the danger of world conflagration, would have been deplored if not condemned. Again, legal justifications for such bombing would be questionable and would have received little hearing. The desire for surprise would have made it difficult to seek the authorization of the OAS; if sought, it is not clear that it would have been obtained.

The quarantine, on the other hand, might be less effective. Even if successful, it was inherently only a partial measure. It might prevent the introduction of additional equipment; it would not by itself eliminate from Cuba what was already there. The quarantine, moreover, depended for its success on Soviet acquiescence if not submission. It would affect the shipping of third nations. Being an action which might continue for some time (unlike the fait accompli of a bombing), it might cause festering disputes both with the Soviet Union and with others. But the quarantine also had important political advantage. The United States would show itself determined, but moderate and responsible, aware of the stakes for the whole world. There would be no invasion of Cuban territory, no loss of lives, no irreversible course of action. Arguments for its legality might be heard with some sympathy. Being a continuing action involving no irrevocable consequences, it could be taken to the United Nations in accordance with the Charter; hopefully, it might lead the Soviet Union to negotiate instead of reacting by force; it would also permit time for mediation after the flow of missiles halted. The same factors would make it easier for Latin America to support, and even for the Soviet Union to swallow the quarantine.

On balance, the immediate military objective could better be assured by bombing; the political factors seemed to weigh on the side of the quarantine. There are reports that lawyers helped carry the day for the quarantine. In that decision, clearly, legal and political considerations were deeply entangled; but for some of the lawyers, at least, it mattered that bombing would be a serious breach in the fabric of law, a damaging blow to the efforts of the Charter to establish order by outlawing the unilateral use of force. A bombing attack, even one strictly limited in purpose and effect, would probably be deemed a use of force against the territorial integrity (and perhaps the political independence) of Cuba. The quarantine would be less difficult to defend as a modest extension of law to a new situation. The quarantine could also be more readily combined with initiatives in the Organization of American States and in the United Nations— measures which would strengthen the legal foundations for the proposed action and thereby also political support or acceptance of it. Of course, it should be clear, there were risks in these steps too: if the OAS refused to act, the major legal foundation on which the United States wished to base its action would vanish, and it would be even more difficult for the United States to act than if it had not sought OAS authorization. But law and politics impelled that the risk be taken. Building the best legal case, making the action of the United States as legal and reasonable as possible, would help persuade other nations to cooperate or comply, perhaps also help persuade the Soviet Union to a moderate reaction, even to acquiescence.

If this informed speculation is correct, concern for maximum legality and maximum appearance of legality, and fear of the political reactions to violation of the most political norm of international law, helped persuade the United States government to adopt the more moderate quarantine.[4]

4. At least in the first instance. No doubt, some who concurred in this decision did so on the understanding that if the quarantine failed, bombing would be available as a later resort. * * * We cannot know, of course, whether, had the quarantine failed, the United States would have proceeded, after all, to commit serious violations of law and to court their cost and consequences.

REMARKS BY THE HONORABLE DEAN ACHESON

1963 Proceedings of the American Society of International Law 13.

To talk of the legal aspects of the Cuban incident reminds me of the story of the women discussing the Quiz Program scandals. One said that she felt the scandals presented serious moral issues. The other answered, "And I always say that moral issues are more important than real issues." Mr. Chayes has cited legal principles to justify the actions taken by our Government in October of 1962, observing in passing that "law was not wholly irrelevant."

Today, in the analyses presented, several legal theories to justify the Cuban quarantine have appeared. Professor Hart has been quoted to the effect that a legal system is all-pervasive, and that an all-pervasive system will necessarily provide an answer for all problems which arise within it. Others found justification within treaties or agreements; still others within the realm of "generally accepted" ideas. What can one expect to find? Clearly, a simple answer that the action was lawful or unlawful will not be found.

In my estimation, however, the quarantine is not a legal issue or an issue of international law as these terms should be understood. Much of what is called international law is a body of ethical distillation, and one must take care not to confuse this distillation with law. We should not rationalize general legal policy restricting sovereignty from international documents composed for specific purposes.

Further, the law through its long history has been respectful of power, especially that power which is close to the sanctions of law. This point is exemplified in the history of English law during the era of Richard II. The Court of the King's Bench was asked to pass on the validity of the Duke of York's claim to the English Crown. The Court refused to consider the question, since it "concerned the king's own estate & regalie." The Court indeed assumed a respectful attitude toward power.

There are indications in our country today which suggest that some segments of our sovereign people resist judicial entry into the inner sanctuary of power. In the field of labor-management relations, where law had once entered boldly, it has withdrawn before power. The same court that was willing to apply a yet-to-be announced doctrine of law to apportionment of legislative representatives has left the issue of featherbedding, where no rules were applicable, to power. Again in the steel price controversy, law has left the arbitrament to other principles.

I must conclude that the propriety of the Cuban quarantine is not a legal issue. The power, position and prestige of the United States had been challenged by another state; and law simply does not deal with such questions of ultimate pwer—power that comes close to the sources of sovereignty. I cannot believe that there are principles of law that say we must accept destruction of our way of life. One would be surprised if practical men, trained in legal history and thought, had devised and brought to a state of general acceptance a principle condemnatory of an action so essential to the continuation of pre-eminent power as that taken by the United States last October. Such a principle would be as harmful to the development of restraining procedures as it would be futile. No law can destroy the state creating the law. The survival of states is not a matter of law.

However, in the action taken in the Cuban quarantine, one can see the influence of accepted legal principles. These principles are procedural devices designed to reduce the severity of a possible clash. Those devices cause wise delay before drastic action, create a "cooling off" period, permit the consideration of others' views. The importance of the Organization of American States was also procedural, and emphasized the desirability of collective action, thus creating a common denominator of action. Some of these desirable consequences are familiar to us in the domestic industrial area.

In October the United States was faced with grave problems of policy and procedure in relation to its own and outside interests. The action taken was the right action. "Right" means more than legally justifiable, or even successful. The United States resolved very grave issues of policy in a way consonant with ethical restraint.

The most perplexing aspect of the decision was the difficulty of comparing, of weighing, competing considerations. How could one weigh the desirability of less drastic action at the outset against the undesirability of losing sight of the missiles, or having them used against us, which might be avoided by more drastic action from the onset, such as destroying the weapons. The President had no scales in which to test these weights, no policy litmus paper. Wisdom for the decision was not to be found in law, but in judgment. Principles, certainly legal principles, do not decide concrete cases.

TUCHMAN, THE GUNS OF AUGUST 127 (1962)*

Berlin, August 4, 1914:

At three o'clock members reconvened in the Reichstag to hear an address by the Chancellor and to perform the remainder of their duty which consisted first of voting war credits and then adjournment. The Social Democrats agreed to make the vote unanimous, and spent their last hours of parliamentary responsibility in anxious consultation whether to join in a "Hoch!" for the Kaiser which they satisfactorily resolved by making it a Hoch for "Kaiser, People, and Country."

Everyone, as Bethmann rose to speak, waited in painful expectancy for what he had to say about Belgium. A year ago Foreign Minister Jagow had assured a secret session of the Reichstag steering committee that Germany would never violate Belgium, and General von Heeringen, then War Minister, had promised that the Supreme Com-

* © Barbara W. Tuchman 1962. Reprinted by permission of the publish-   er, The Macmillan Company, New York.

mand in the event of war would respect Belgium's neutrality as long as Germany's enemies did. On August 4 deputies did not know that their armies had invaded Belgium that morning. They knew of the ultimatum but nothing of the Belgian reply because the German government, wishing to give the impression that Belgium had acquiesced and that her armed resistance was therefore illegal, never published it.

"Our troops," Bethmann informed the tense audience, "have occupied Luxembourg and perhaps"—the "perhaps" was posthumous by eight hours—"are already in Belgium." (Great commotion.) True, France had given Belgium a pledge to respect her neutrality, but "We knew that France was standing ready to invade Belgium" and "we could not wait." It was, he said inevitably, a case of military necessity, and "necessity knows no law."

So far he had his hearers, both the right which despised him and the left which mistrusted him, in thrall. His next sentence created a sensation. "Our invasion of Belgium is contrary to international law but the wrong—I speak openly—that we are committing we will make good as soon as our military goal has been reached." Admiral Tirpitz considered this the greatest blunder ever spoken by a German statesman; Conrad Haussman, a leader of the Liberal party, considered it the finest part of the speech. The act having been confessed in a public mea culpa, he and his fellow deputies of the left felt purged of guilt and saluted the Chancellor with a loud "Sehr richtig!" In a final striking phrase—and before his day of memorable maxims was over he was to add one more that would make him immortal—Bethmann said that whoever was as badly threatened as were the Germans could think only of how to "hack his way through."

A war credit of five billion marks was voted unanimously, after which the Reichstag voted itself out of session for four months or for what was generally expected to be the duration. Bethmann closed the proceedings with an assurance that carried overtones of the gladiators' salute: "Whatever our lot may be, August 4, 1914, will remain for all eternity one of Germany's greatest days!"

NOTE TO PARTS I, II AND III

Every state in the international system has capacity to administer a national legal system. In one way or another, all the rules in the system serve to regulate the conduct of people. An obvious illustration is supplied by rules of criminal law. But the regulation of the conduct of people by rules of domestic law goes far beyond the regulation of criminal activity. It embraces the totality of their lives and actions. Rules of domestic law determine, for example, the status of a person—i.e., whether he is married or a minor and so on—as well as the kind of interest—i.e., ownership, possession and the like—he may have in a thing such as a piece of land. But the freedom of a state to administer a national legal system is restricted by rules of international law.

It is restricted, in the first place, by international law rules of jurisdiction which determine the categories of persons, events and places that a state may subject to rules of domestic law. Thus a state may not regulate everyday affairs within the territory of another.

In the second place, there are rules of international law which determine whether or not a state—even though it has capacity to subject persons, events and places to its rules of domestic law—may exercise such capacity. Thus a state may not apply its rules of domestic law to certain persons such as diplomatic representatives.

In the third place, rules of international law regulate the manner in which a state may exercise its capacity to subject persons, events and places to its domestic law. They require a state to administer its rules of domestic law in accordance with international standards of fairness and justice, which may be different from domestic standards of fairness and justice.

Whenever a state violates any of these three sets of international law rules, it gives another state a basis for claim to redress. Conceivably a state might violate more than one of the sets of international law rules involved and thus give another state several bases for claims to redress. Whichever the case, the claim or claims would require settlement through one or more of the international procedures covered in the Introductory Chapter.

Part I of this book deals with the restrictions imposed by international law upon the capacity of a state to subject persons, events and places to its rules of domestic law. Part II deals with the limitations imposed by international law upon the exercise of this capacity. Part III deals, inter alia, with the standards of fairness and justice a state must observe when it is using its capacity to administer a national legal system.

Part I

ALLOCATION OF COMPETENCE IN THE INTERNATIONAL SYSTEM

Chapter 2

BASES OF JURISDICTION

1. *Meaning of jurisdiction in national legal systems.* The term "jurisdiction," or its equivalent in other languages, expresses a concept which is common to national legal systems.

In the United States, for example, we speak of "federal jurisdiction" as opposed to the jurisdiction of the states of the Union. We do so because under our domestic law—the Constitution in this instance—certain categories of persons, events or places are subject to federal law and others to the law of the several states. Whenever we say a matter is one of "federal jurisdiction," we mean that the federal government is empowered under the domestic law of the United States to act—by way of legislation, judicial decision or executive action—with respect to the particular category of persons, events or places involved in the matter at hand. And we have the same concept in mind when we speak of the jurisdiction of the states.

The concept of jurisdiction is also commonly used in national legal systems to allocate the judicial function to different courts. In many states of the world, domestic law places limits upon the categories of persons, events or places with which particular courts may deal. Thus we may find certain courts have jurisdiction over civil matters and others over criminal matters. In certain states the civil courts are specialized, each having jurisdiction over certain civil matters but not others. In some, the jurisdiction of different criminal courts is determined by the level of gravity of the offense. There are states where jurisdiction over litigation between individuals and the government is vested in a system of administrative courts, separate and distinct from the other civil courts.

2. *Meaning of jurisdiction in the international legal system.* In the international legal system, the term "jurisdiction" expresses a concept similar to the concept it expresses in national legal systems. When we speak of the "jurisdiction" of a state in the international system, we mean the state is entitled under international law to sub-

109

ject certain categories of persons, events or places to its rules of law. It does not follow, however, that the rules of international law determining whether a state has jurisdiction over a particular person, event or place, are the same as those used in a national legal system in determining, for example, whether this court or that court has jurisdiction over a particular person, event or place.

In the international legal system, jurisdiction refers to the jurisdiction of the state as a whole and not of its constituent units or political subdivisions. The United States is a federation and France, for example, is not. Whether in the United States an alien is tried by a court of New York State or a federal court, or whether in France he is tried by a court in Paris or Marseilles, does not create an international issue of jurisdiction. The jurisdictional question in the international system is whether the United States in the one case, or France in the other, is entitled to try the alien, and not where or by what court in the United States or France he is being tried.

Furthermore, the international legal system is not concerned with the allocation by a state of its jurisdiction among its branches of government. In a national legal system, the making of legal rules might be vested in a legislature and their enforcement vested in the executive or judicial branch. But this division of functions is not always so clear cut. The House of Lords in the United Kingdom has legislative functions and also functions as a law court. In turn a court of law in a national legal system may not have been instructed by its legislature to apply a particular rule and may have to articulate one of its own devising before it can proceed to give it effect. Or the executive may be empowered to make legal rules. International law does not determine which branch of government should do what.

Accordingly it is advisable, if not indeed necessary, to discuss the jurisdiction of states under international law in terms which are neutral so far as the organs of government exercising the jurisdiction are concerned.

3. *Jurisdiction to prescribe and jurisdiction to enforce.* The term jurisdiction is all too often used imprecisely. A sharp distinction between rule-making and rule-enforcing jurisdiction is essential to effective analysis. First, the state "prescribes" a rule, which is to say that either by act of the legislature, decree of the executive or decision of a court, it declares a generalized principle or legal norm. Second, the state "enforces" the rule. That is, it arrests, subpoenas witnesses and documents, tries and punishes for violation of the rule, or decides civil suits in vindication of the rule. Any one of these actions—and of course all of them together—is enforcement. Hence we discuss jurisdiction in terms of the "jurisdiction of a state to prescribe" rules of domestic law and its "jurisdiction to enforce" them.

A state normally has jurisdiction to prescribe rules of domestic law governing conduct taking place physically within its territory. At the other extreme no state has jurisdiction to prescribe rules of domestic law governing the conduct of everyone everywhere in the world. A state normally also has jurisdiction to enforce within its own territory the rules of law it has properly prescribed. Yet at the other extreme, a state may not normally send its police and courts outside ✓ its borders to arrest and punish people even for murders committed within its territory.

Between these extremes lies the international law of jurisdiction. This chapter examines some of the factual bases which are accepted in the international legal system as adequate foundations for a state's prescription and enforcement of rules of domestic law. The materials in this chapter are introductory only; jurisdictional issues will be presented in greater complexity in subsequent chapters.

4. *The legal consequences of lack of jurisdiction.* Under the domestic law of states these consequences are frequently different from those in the international legal system. Thus, should a court purport to convict an alien of a crime when it lacks jurisdiction to do so under the domestic law of a state, the consequence usually will be the release of that person from imprisonment. Yet should the trial be in violation of international law rules of jurisdiction, there may be no legal consequence under the domestic law of the state involved, i.e. the person may remain in prison. The legal consequence under international law, however, would be the accrual to the state of nationality of the alien of a claim against the offending state.

5. *Jurisdiction, vel non, not always dispositive.* One must be careful not to read too much into the term jurisdiction. To say that a state has acted outside its jurisdiction suggests an immediate legal consequence. But to say that it has acted within its jurisdiction may be only the first step in analysis. As will be seen, a state is considered to owe special obligations of fair treatment to aliens who are within the state. For example, the United States is required by international law to give a fair trial to an alien arrested here for a murder committed here. If the United States tries the man unfairly, the state of his nationality has a claim against the United States, even though the United States, in trying the man at all, acted within its rights under international rules of jurisdiction.

SECTION A.   JURISDICTION TO PRESCRIBE
RULES OF LAW

1.   CONDUCT WITHIN THE TERRITORY

J. H. G. v. PUBLIC PROSECUTOR

Netherlands, Court of Appeal of Arnhem, 1958.
26 Int'l L.Rep. 158 (1963).

THE FACTS.—The driving licence of J. H. G. had been withdrawn by an order of a Netherlands Court.   According to Article 32, paragraph I, of the Netherlands Road Traffic Act, it is an offence to drive a car when one's driving licence has been withdrawn by a court.   J. H. G., who had been a passenger in a car while it was being driven in the Netherlands, took over the driving after the car had passed the Netherlands-German frontier and drove the car further into Germany.   Subsequently, he was charged with an offence under Article 32, paragraph I, and the lower Court imposed a fine.

Held: that the prosecutor's case should be dismissed.   [A portion of the opinion of the court appears below.]

*   *   *   One of the elements of the offence defined by Article 32, paragraph I, of the Act on Road Traffic is the driving of a car on a road.   Article I of this Act defines "road" as a road open to public traffic, whether motorized or otherwise.   According to the preamble of this Act, it purports to lay down rules for traffic on the roads.   As a rule, the Netherlands Legislature can only legislate for its own territory, i.e., the territory of the Realm in Europe.   This is quite certainly the case when the matter involved is of such a typically territorial character as road traffic.   A "road" as mentioned in Article 32, paragraph I, can only be understood to mean a road in that territory.   This provision is not applicable to roads outside the Realm in Europe.   The appellant, therefore, did not commit an offence.

[handwritten margin note: CANNOT GO OUTSIDE TERRITORY]

RE PENATI

Italy, Court of Cassation, 1946.
[1946] Ann.Dig. 74 (No. 30).

THE FACTS.—The appellant, a Swiss subject resident in Italy, was convicted on the ground that he had given aid to the enemy, namely, the German occupation authorities in Italy.   Upon appeal, he contended that, being an alien, he was not subject to the Italian rules of criminal law relating to treason and similar crimes.

[handwritten margin note: ABETTING ENEMY—BUT ALIEN ∴ NOT SUBJECT TO DOMESTIC LAW]

Article 3 of the Italian Penal Code of 1930 provided:

(1) Italian criminal law binds all those who, whether nationals or aliens, reside in Italian territory, subject to the exceptions provided by Italian public law or by international law.

(2) Italian criminal law binds, in addition, all those who, whether nationals or aliens, reside abroad, but only in those cases which are expressly provided for by the Penal Code or by international law.

Held: that the appeal must be dismissed. Aliens are subject to the criminal law of the country where they reside, even in respect of political crimes, such as treason. [A portion of the opinion of the court appears below.]

Contrary to the contention of the appellant, the crime of favouring the political designs of the enemy can also be committed by an alien. According to Article 3 of the Penal Code, Italian criminal law binds all those who, whether they are Italian nationals or aliens, reside in Italy, subject to the exceptions provided by Italian public law or by international law. There is no rule of Italian public law or of international law which exempts from punishment an alien who commits an act in Italy which constitutes a crime against the existence of the State, against its military defence, and against the duty of loyalty of the citizens towards the State which he attempts to undermine. Not only does no rule of this kind exist, but it is legally inconceivable, for no State can allow aliens who enjoy its hospitality to carry out activities which are contrary to its vital interests in the military and political sphere. The prohibition of such activities does not only exist, but it must be enforced with special rigour in time of war. The possibility that aliens can commit crimes against the existence of the State is clearly assumed by Article 312 of the Penal Code, according to which an alien must be expelled if he has been sentenced to imprisonment for one of the crimes envisaged in title I of Book 2 of the Penal Code [i. e., against the existence of the State] * * *. Aiding the political designs of the enemy in time of war is a crime according to Article 265 of the Penal Code, which punishes the exercise, in time of war, of any activity which harms national interests. The crime of which the appellant has been found guilty, is not less a crime because the appellant is a Swiss national * * *.

---

1. *Conduct having effect outside the territory.* In many instances conduct within the territory has its effect exclusively therein. This is not always the case, however, and there are situations where the effect of conduct within the territory takes place outside of it. Whether the effect be within or without the territory, the state where

the conduct occurs has jurisdiction to prescribe rules of law dealing with it. It is true that if the effect is outside the territory, the state in whose territory it takes place also has jurisdiction to prescribe rules of law dealing with the conduct. The jurisdiction of that state is considered at p. 116, but does not affect the jurisdiction of the state where the conduct occurs. The following case is illustrative.

Public Prosecutor v. D. S., Netherlands, Supreme Court, 1958, 26 Int'l L.Rep. 209 (1963). A Dutch merchant sent a defamatory letter from the Netherlands to an acquaintance in London where the letter was received and read by the addressee. He contended that the offense had taken place in England. The court said:

> The contention of the accused that if a person is insulted by another person by means of a letter sent to him by post, the offence is committed exclusively at the place where the letter reaches, and is read by, the person insulted, is incorrect. The offence, in such circumstances, is committed at the place where the offender posted the letter. It is therefore unnecessary to decide whether the place where the letter came into the hands of the addressee can likewise be considered as the locus delicti. (at 209)

2. *Conduct partly within and partly without the territory.* In some situations, the conduct may consist of a series of acts, some taking place within the territory and some outside of it. This was the case in Denunciation to the Enemy, Netherlands, Court of Cassation, 1958, 88 Journal du Droit International 893 (1961).[a] The reporter summarized the case as follows:

> Benders, an employee of the Twentsche Bank, revealed to the German authorities in 1936 that the Spier brothers, Jews of German nationality, had, contrary to the legislation then in force in Germany, placed a considerable fortune in safety in the Twentsche Bank in the Netherlands. By * * * imprisoning one of the Spier brothers and the wife of the other the German authorities were able to constrain them to return the fortune to Germany, after which, naturally under a cloak of legitimacy, it it was almost entirely confiscated. The heirs now sued Benders and the Bank.

> What is the law governing Benders' unlawful act? In order to carry out his * * * design, he went just beyond the Netherlands frontier, to make contact in Germany with Oberzollrat Kinzel of Dusseldorf. The interview consummating this betrayal, which netted 10,000 deniers for Benders, therefore took place in Germany. Was Germany therefore the locus delicti and German law for that reason applicable? The Court of Appeal of Amsterdam rightly thought that this was a little too easy. The execution of the design, the Court said, began by the compilation of documents in the offices of the Bank in the Netherlands; the

a. English text in the Journal. Reprinted by permission of Editions Techniques, S.A., Paris.

infamous act was directed against a fortune in the Netherlands, while it was at the same time calculated to injure the Bank in the Netherlands. "In the light of all these facts" goes on the Court, "Benders' act took place to such an extent in the Netherlands that the Tribunal was fully justified in subjecting it to Netherlands law".

      *   *   *   [The decision below was upheld by the supreme court.]

3. *Conduct in the territory involving events outside of it.* Even though the conduct takes place entirely in the territory, it may be made criminal because of prior events which took place outside of it. This was the situation in R. v. Nel, South Africa, Supreme Court, Appellate Division, 1953, 20 Int'l L.Rep. 192 (1957), which is reported in part as follows:

The facts. Nel was convicted in a South African Magistrate's Court on nine counts of contravening s. 2 of the Stock Theft Act. The relevant provisions read:

A person who in any manner, otherwise than at a public sale, acquires or receives into his possession from any other person stolen stock or stolen produce without having reasonable cause, proof of which shall be on such first mentioned person, for believing at the time of such acquisition or receipt, that such stock or produce was the property of the person from whom he received it or that such person was duly authorised by the owner thereof to deal with or dispose of it shall be guilty of an offence.

He appealed against his conviction to the Transvaal Provincial Division of the Supreme Court on the ground, inter alia, that the cattle had been stolen in Rhodesia, beyond the borders of the Union, and therefore the Act invoked had no application to the present circumstances, as the criminal jurisdiction of a State is strictly territorial in its operation. The appeal was dismissed, but leave was granted to take the case to the Appellate Division of the Supreme Court. Nel again put forward the same argument. [A portion of the opinion of the court appears below].

It was clear from the evidence and was admitted by the appellant that in each of the counts (a) the cattle concerned were acquired by him otherwise than at a public sale, (b) that these cattle had been stolen. This cast on the appellant the onus referred to in the section (supra) and it was rightly admitted by his counsel that the magistrate had correctly held that, on a balance of probabilities, the onus had not been discharged. But counsel contended that the Act applied only to stock stolen in the Union, that consequently the words 'stolen stock' in the section meant stock so stolen and that the appellant's acts, therefore, did not fall within the section because the evidence showed it had been stolen in Rhodesia. The argument was based on the general submission that, at any rate in the absence of express provision, the Courts of any State have no jurisdiction in regard to crimes committed outside the borders of such State and that the provisions of the Stock Theft Act showed that it was not intended to apply in any respect to stock stolen outside the Union. Counsel conceded that if stock is so stolen by an accused person and brought into the Union by that person, he falls within the provisions of the Act because theft is a continuous offence (R. v. von Elling, 1945, A.D. 234) and the accused in such a case would be stealing within the Union; but counsel contended that this doctrine would not apply in this case where the only transaction proved against the appellant was that he had bought the cattle in the Union. I am prepared to assume that the general submission put forward by counsel is well-founded, but this in itself would not avail the appellant as the act, viz., the purchase of the cattle, on which his conviction was founded, took place within the Union   *   *   *   There is no warrant for holding that the words 'stolen stock' mean stock stolen in the Union or that they mean anything more than stock which, according to our law, is stolen stock   *   *   *   The appellant   *   *   *   was therefore rightly convicted." (at 193).

4. *Problem.* Suppose something more complicated than cattle theft had been involved, say, securities fraud, with different standards of fraud in the two states. Would the result be the same, (a) in a criminal case, (b) in a civil case?

---

2. CONDUCT OUTSIDE THE TERRITORY CAUSING EFFECT WITHIN

THE CUTTING CASE
LETTER, SECRETARY OF STATE TO UNITED STATES AMBASSADOR TO MEXICO

[1887] Foreign Relations of the United States 751 (1888).

DEPARTMENT OF STATE.
Washington, November 1, 1887.

SIR: On the 19th of July, 1886, the minister of the United States at the City of Mexico was instructed to demand of the Mexican Government the release of A. K. Cutting, a citizen of the United States, then imprisoned at Paso del Norte, where he had been incarcerated since the 23d of the preceding month on a charge of libel alleged to have been published by him in Texas.

The case was first brought to the notice of the Department by Mr. Brigham, consul of the United States at Paso del Norte, who, in a dispatch dated the 1st July, 1886, reported that Mr. Cutting had been arrested and imprisoned for the publication in Texas, in the United States, of an alleged libel against a citizen of Mexico. Accompanying the consul's dispatch were affidavits substantiating his statements. * * *

* * * It is sufficient here to state, as was set forth at the time of the demand, that the ground upon which Mr. Cutting's release was demanded was that the judicial tribunals of Mexico were not competent under the rules of international law to try a citizen of the United States for an offense committed and consummated in his own country, merely because the person offended happened to be a Mexican.

* * *

* * * Not only was this claim, which is defined in Article 186 of the Mexican penal code, defended and enforced by Judge Zubia, before whom the case of Mr. Cutting was tried, and whose decision was affirmed by the supreme court of Chihuahua * * *, but the claim was defended and justified by the Mexican Government in communications to this Department, emanating both from the Mexican minister at this capital and from the department of foreign affairs in the City of Mexico.

The statement of the consul at Paso del Norte that Mr. Cutting was arrested on the charge of the publication in Texas of an alleged libel against a Mexican is fully sustained by the opinion of Judge Zubia. Under the head of "It appears 6," in that decision, it is stated that on the 22d of June, 1886, "the plaintiff enlarged the accusation, stating that although the newspaper, the El Paso Sunday Herald, is published in Texas, Mr. Cutting had had circulated a great number in this town (Paso del Norte) and in the interior of the Republic, it having been read by more than three persons, for which reason an order had been issued to seize the copies which were still in the office of the said Cutting." The conclusive inference from this statement is that the charge upon which the warrant of arrest was issued was the publication of the alleged libel in Texas. * * * It appears, however, under "Considering 6," in Judge Zubia's decision, that the claim made in Article 186 of the Mexican penal code was actually enforced in the case in question as a distinct and original ground of prosecution. The decision of Judge Zubia was framed in the alternative, and it was held that, even supposing the defamation arose solely from the publication of the alleged libel in the El Paso (Texas) Sunday Herald, Article 186 of the Mexican penal code provided for punishment in that case; Judge Zubia saying that it did not belong to the judge to examine the principle laid down in that article but to apply it fully, it being the law in force in the State of Chihuahua. It nowhere appears that the Texas publication was ever circulated in Mexico so as to constitute the crime of defamation under the Mexican law. As has been seen, this was not a part of the original charge on which the warrant for Mr. Cutting's arrest was issued; and while it is stated in Judge Zubia's decision that an order was issued for the seizure of copies of the Texas paper which might be found in the office of Mr. Cutting in Paso del Norte, it nowhere appears from that decision that any copies were actually found in that place or elsewhere in Mexico.

But, however this may be, this Government is still compelled to deny what it denied on the 19th of July, 1886, and what the Mexican Government has since executively and judicially maintained, that a citizen of the United States can be held under the rules of international law to answer in Mexico for an offense committed in the United States, simply because the object of that offense happens to be a citizen of Mexico.   *   *   *

*   *   *

As to the question of international law, I am unable to discover any principle upon which the assumption of jurisdiction made in Article 186 of the Mexican penal code can be justified. There is no principle better settled than that the penal laws of a country have no extraterritorial force. Each state may, it is true, provide for the punishment of its own citizens for acts committed by them outside of its territory; but this makes the penal law a personal statute, and while it may give rise to inconvenience and injustice in many cases, it is a matter in which no other Government has the right to interfere. To say, however, that the penal laws of a country can bind foreigners and regulate their conduct, either in their own or any other foreign country, is to assert a jurisdiction over such countries and to impair their independence. Such is the consensus of opinion of the leading authorities on international law at the present day, *   *   *. There being then no principle of international law which justifies such a pretension, any assertion of it must rest, as an exception to the rule, either upon the general concurrence of nations or upon express conventions. Such a concurrence in respect to the claim made in Article 186 of the Mexican penal code can not be found in the legislation of the present day. Though formerly asserted by a number of minor states, it has now been generally abandoned, and may be regarded as almost obsolete.

The only assertion I have found in the legislation of Europe of a general jurisdiction by one state of offenses committed abroad by foreigners against subjects is in the cases of Greece and Russia.
*   *   *

*   *   *

It has constantly been laid down in the United States as a rule of action, that citizens of the United States can not be held answerable in foreign countries for offenses which were wholly committed and consummated either in their own country or in other countries not subject to the jurisdiction of the punishing state. When a citizen of the United States commits in his own country a violation of its laws, it is his right to be tried under and in accordance with those laws, and in accordance with the fundamental guaranties of the Federal Constitution in respect to criminal trials in every part of the United States.

To say that he may be tried in another country for his offense, simply because its object happens to be a citizen of that country, would be to assert that foreigners coming to the United States bring hither the penal laws of the country from which they come, and thus subject citizens of the United States in their own country to an indefinite criminal responsibility. Such a pretension can never be admitted by this Government.

*   *   *

You are therefore instructed to say to the Mexican Government, not only that an indemnity should be paid to Mr. Cutting for his arrest and detention in Mexico on the charge of publishing a libel in the United States against a Mexican, but also, in the interests of good neighborhood and future amity, that the statute proposing to confer such extraterritorial jurisdiction should, as containing a claim invasive of the independent sovereignty of a neighboring and friendly state, be repealed.   *   *   *

*   *   *

I am, etc.

T. F. BAYARD.

THE S. S. "LOTUS" (FRANCE v. TURKEY)

Permanent Court of International Justice, 1927.
P.C.I.J., Ser. A, No. 10.

*   *   *

By a special agreement signed at Geneva on October 12th, 1926, between the Governments of the French and Turkish Republics *   *   *,   [France and Turkey] have submitted to the Permanent Court of International Justice the question of jurisdiction which has arisen between them following upon the collision which occurred on August 2nd, 1926, between the steamships Boz-Kourt and Lotus.

According to the special agreement, the Court has to decide the following questions:

(1) Has Turkey, contrary to Article 15 of the Convention of Lausanne of July 24th, 1923, respecting conditions of residence and business and jurisdiction, acted in conflict with the principles of international law—and if so, what principles—by instituting, following the collision which occurred on August 2nd, 1926, on the high seas between the French steamer Lotus

and the Turkish steamer Boz-Kourt and upon the arrival of the French steamer at Constantinople—as well as against the captain of the Turkish steamship—joint criminal proceedings in pursuance of Turkish law against M. Demons, officer of the watch on board the Lotus at the time of the collision, in consequence of the loss of the Boz-Kourt having involved the death of eight Turkish sailors and passengers?

(2) Should the reply be in the affirmative, what pecuniary reparation is due to M. Demons, provided, according to the principles of international law, reparation should be made in similar cases?

* * *

On August 2nd, 1926, just before midnight, a collision occurred between the French mail steamer Lotus, proceeding to Constantinople, and the Turkish collier Boz-Kourt, between five and six nautical miles to the north of Cape Sigri (Mitylene). The Boz-Kourt, which was cut in two, sank, and eight Turkish nationals who were on board perished. After having done everything possible to succour the shipwrecked persons, of whom ten were able to be saved, the Lotus continued on its course to Constantinople, where it arrived on August 3rd.

At the time of the collision, the officer of the watch on board the Lotus was Monsieur Demons, a French citizen, lieutenant in the merchant service and first officer of the ship, whilst the movements of the Boz-Kourt were directed by its captain, Hassan Bey, who was one of those saved from the wreck.

* * *

On August 5th, Lieutenant Demons was requested by the Turkish authorities to go ashore to give evidence. The examination, the length of which incidentally resulted in delaying the departure of the Lotus, led to the placing under arrest of Lieutenant Demons—without previous notice being given to the French Consul-General—and Hassan Bey, amongst others. This arrest, which has been characterized by the Turkish Agent as arrest pending trial (arrestation préventive), was effected in order to ensure that the criminal prosecution instituted against the two officers, on a charge of manslaughter, by the Public Prosecutor of Stamboul, on the complaint of the families of the victims of the collision, should follow its normal course.

The case was first heard by the Criminal Court of Stamboul on August 28th. On that occasion, Lieutenant Demons submitted that the Turkish Courts had no jurisdiction; the Court, however, overruled his objection. When the proceedings were resumed on September 11th, Lieutenant Demons demanded his release on bail: this request was complied with * * *.

On September 15th, the Criminal Court delivered its judgment, the terms of which have not been communicated to the Court by the Parties. It is, however, common ground, that it sentenced Lieutenant Demons to eighty days' imprisonment and a fine of twenty-two pounds, Hassan Bey being sentenced to a slightly more severe penalty.

* * *

The action of the Turkish judicial authorities with regard to Lieutenant Demons at once gave rise to many diplomatic representations and other steps on the part of the French Government or its representatives in Turkey, either protesting against the arrest of Lieutenant Demons or demanding his release, or with a view to obtaining the transfer of the case from the Turkish Courts to the French Courts.

As a result of these representations, the Government of the Turkish Republic declared on September 2nd, 1926, that "it would have no objection to the reference of the conflict of jurisdiction to the Court at The Hague". The French Government having, on the 6th of the same month, given "its full consent to the proposed solution", the two Governments appointed their plenipotentiaries with a view to the drawing up of the special agreement to be submitted to the Court; this special agreement was signed at Geneva on October 12th, 1926, * * * and the ratifications were deposited on December 27th, 1926.

* * *

I

Before approaching the consideration of the principles of international law contrary to which Turkey is alleged to have acted—thereby infringing the terms of Article 15 of the Convention of Lausanne of July 24th, 1923, respecting conditions of residence and business and jurisdiction—, it is necessary to define, in the light of the written and oral proceedings, the position resulting from the special agreement. * * *

1. The collision which occurred on August 2nd, 1926, between the S.S. Lotus, flying the French flag, and the S.S. Boz-Kourt, flying the Turkish flag, took place on the high seas; the territorial jurisdiction of any State other than France and Turkey therefore does not enter into account.

2. The violation, if any, of the principles of international law would have consisted in the taking of criminal proceedings against Lieutenant Demons. It is not therefore a question relating to any particular step in these proceedings—such as his being put to trial, his arrest, his detention pending trial or the judgment given by the Criminal Court of Stamboul—but of the very fact of the Turkish Courts exercising criminal jurisdiction. That is why the arguments

put forward by the Parties in both phases of the proceedings relate exclusively to the question whether Turkey has or has not, according to the principles of international law, jurisdiction to prosecute in this case.

The Parties agree that the Court has not to consider whether the prosecution was in conformity with Turkish law; it need not therefore consider whether, apart from the actual question of jurisdiction, the provisions of Turkish law cited by Turkish authorities were really applicable in this case, or whether the manner in which the proceedings against Lieutenant Demons were conducted might constitute a denial of justice, and accordingly, a violation of international law. The discussions have borne exclusively upon the question whether criminal jurisdiction does or does not exist in this case.

3. The prosecution was instituted because the loss of the Boz-Kourt involved the death of eight Turkish sailors and passengers. * * * [N]o criminal intention has been imputed to either of the officers responsible for navigating the two vessels; it is therefore a case of prosecution for involuntary manslaughter. * * * Moreover, the exact conditions in which these persons perished do not appear from the documents submitted to the Court; nevertheless, there is no doubt that their death may be regarded as the direct outcome of the collision, and the French Government has not contended that this relation of cause and effect cannot exist.

* * *

5. The prosecution was instituted in pursuance of Turkish legislation. The special agreement does not indicate what clause or clauses of that legislation apply. No document has been submitted to the Court indicating on what article of the Turkish Penal Code the prosecution was based; the French Government however declares that the Criminal Court claimed jurisdiction under Article 6 of the Turkish Penal Code, and far from denying this statement, Turkey, in the submissions of her Counter-Case, contends that that article is in conformity with the principles of international law. It does not appear from the proceedings whether the prosecution was instituted solely on the basis of that article.

Article 6 of the Turkish Penal Code, * * * runs as follows:

[Translation] Any foreigner who, apart from the cases contemplated by Article 4, commits an offence abroad to the prejudice of Turkey or of a Turkish subject, for which offence Turkish law prescribes a penalty involving loss of freedom for a minimum period of not less than one year, shall be punished in accordance with the Turkish Penal Code provided that he is arrested in Turkey. * * *

* * *

Even if the Court must hold that the Turkish authorities had seen fit to base the prosecution of Lieutenant Demons upon the above-mentioned Article 6, the question submitted to the Court is not whether that article is compatible with the principles of international law; it is more general. The Court is asked to state whether or not the principles of international law prevent Turkey from instituting criminal proceedings against Lieutenant Demons under Turkish law. Neither the conformity of Article 6 in itself with the principles of international law nor the application of that article by the Turkish authorities constitutes the point at issue; it is the very fact of the institution of proceedings which is held by France to be contrary to those principles.   *   *   *

II

Having determined the position resulting from the terms of the special agreement, the Court must now ascertain which were the principles of international law that the prosecution of Lieutenant Demons could conceivably be said to contravene.

It is Article 15 of the Convention of Lausanne of July 24th, 1923, respecting conditions of residence and business and jurisdiction, which refers the contracting Parties to the principles of international law as regards the delimitation of their respective jurisdiction.

This clause is as follows:

> Subject to the provisions of Article 16, all questions of jurisdiction shall, as between Turkey and the other contracting Powers, be decided in accordance with the principles of international law.

*   *   *   In these circumstances it is impossible—except in pursuance of a definite stipulation—to construe the expression "principles of international law" otherwise than as meaning the principles which are in force between all independent nations and which therefore apply equally to all the contracting Parties.

*   *   *

III

*   *   *   The French Government contends that the Turkish Courts, in order to have jurisdiction, should be able to point to some title to jurisdiction recognized by international law in favour of Turkey. On the other hand, the Turkish Government takes the view that Article 15 allows Turkey jurisdiction whenever such jurisdiction does not come into conflict with a principle of international law.

*   *   *

International law governs relations between independent States. The rules of law binding upon States therefore emanate from their own free will as expressed in conventions or by usages generally accepted as expressing principles of law and established in order to regulate the relations between these co-existing independent communities or with a view to the achievement of common aims. Restrictions upon the independence of States cannot therefore be presumed.

Now the first and foremost restriction imposed by international law upon a State is that—failing the existence of a permissive rule to the contrary—it may not exercise its power in any form in the territory of another State. In this sense jurisdiction is certainly territorial; it cannot be exercised by a State outside its territory except by virtue of a permissive rule derived from international custom or from a convention.

It does not, however, follow that international law prohibits a State from exercising jurisdiction in its own territory, in respect of any case which relates to acts which have taken place abroad, and in which it cannot rely on some permissive rule of international law. Such a view would only be tenable if international law contained a general prohibition to States to extend the application of their laws and the jurisdiction of their courts to persons, property and acts outside their territory, and if, as an exception to this general prohibition, it allowed States to do so in certain specific cases. But this is certainly not the case under international law as it stands at present. Far from laying down a general prohibition to the effect that States may not extend the application of their laws and the jurisdiction of their courts to persons, property and acts outside their territory, it leaves them in this respect a wide measure of discretion which is only limited in certain cases by prohibitive rules; as regards other cases, every State remains free to adopt the principles which it regards as best and most suitable.

This discretion left to States by international law explains the great variety of rules which they have been able to adopt without objections or complaints on the part of other States; it is in order to remedy the difficulties resulting from such variety that efforts have been made for many years past, both in Europe and America, to prepare conventions the effect of which would be precisely to limit the discretion at present left to States in this respect by international law, thus making good the existing lacunæ in respect of jurisdiction or removing the conflicting jurisdictions arising from the diversity of the principles adopted by the various States.

In these circumstances, all that can be required of a State is that it should not overstep the limits which international law places upon its jurisdiction; within these limits, its title to exercise jurisdiction rests in its sovereignty.

It follows from the foregoing that the contention of the French Government to the effect that Turkey must in each case be able to cite a rule of international law authorizing her to exercise jurisdic-

[handwritten: FRENCH CLAIM NOT STRONG ENOUGH]

tion, is opposed to the generally accepted international law to which Article 15 of the Convention of Lausanne refers. * * *

* * *

The Court therefore must, in any event, ascertain whether or not there exists a rule of international law limiting the freedom of States to extend the criminal jurisdiction of their courts to a situation uniting the circumstances of the present case.

IV

The Court will now proceed to ascertain whether general international law, to which Article 15 of the Convention of Lausanne refers, contains a rule prohibiting Turkey from prosecuting Lieutenant Demons.

For this purpose, it will in the first place examine the value of the arguments advanced by the French Government, without however omitting to take into account other possible aspects of the problem, which might show the existence of a restrictive rule applicable in this case.

The arguments advanced by the French Government [include the following] :

(1) International law does not allow a State to take proceedings with regard to offences committed by foreigners abroad, simply by reason of the nationality of the victim; and such is the situation in the present case because the offence must be regarded as having been committed on board the French vessel.

[handwritten: OFFENSE ON FRENCH VESSEL —]

* * *

As regards the first argument, the Court feels obliged in the first place to recall that its examination is strictly confined to the specific situation in the present case, for it is only in regard to this situation that its decision is asked for.

As has already been observed, the characteristic features of the situation of fact are as follows: there has been a collision on the high seas between two vessels flying different flags, on one of which was one of the persons alleged to be guilty of the offence, whilst the victims were on board the other.

This being so, the Court does not think it necessary to consider the contention that a State cannot punish offences committed abroad by a foreigner simply by reason of the nationality of the victim. For this contention only relates to the case where the nationality of the victim is the only criterion on which the criminal jurisdiction of the State is based. Even if that argument were correct generally speaking—and in regard to this the Court reserves its opinion—it could only be used in the present case if international law forbade Turkey to take into consideration the fact that the offence produced its effects on the Turkish vessel and consequently in a place assimilated to

Turkish territory in which the application of Turkish criminal law cannot be challenged, even in regard to offences committed there by foreigners. But no such rule of international law exists. No argument has come to the knowledge of the Court from which it could be deduced that States recognize themselves to be under an obligation towards each other only to have regard to the place where the author of the offence happens to be at the time of the offence. On the contrary, it is certain that the courts of many countries, even of countries which have given their criminal legislation a strictly territorial character, interpret criminal law in the sense that offences, the authors of which at the moment of commission are in the territory of another State, are nevertheless to be regarded as having been committed in the national territory, if one of the constituent elements of the offence, and more especially its effects, have taken place there. French courts have, in regard to a variety of situations, given decisions sanctioning this way of interpreting the territorial principle. Again, the Court does not know of any cases in which governments have protested against the fact that the criminal law of some country contained a rule to this effect or that the courts of a country construed their criminal law in this sense. Consequently, once it is admitted that the effects of the offence were produced on the Turkish vessel, it becomes impossible to hold that there is a rule of international law which prohibits Turkey from prosecuting Lieutenant Demons because of the fact that the author of the offence was on board the French ship. Since, as has already been observed, the special agreement does not deal with the provision of Turkish law under which the prosecution was instituted, but only with the question whether the prosecution should be regarded as contrary to the principles of international law, there is no reason preventing the Court from confining itself to observing that, in this case, a prosecution may also be justified from the point of view of the so-called territorial principle.

   *   *   *   The fact that the judicial authorities may have committed an error in their choice of the legal provision applicable to the particular case and compatible with international law only concerns municipal law and can only affect international law in so far as a treaty provision enters into account, or the possibility of a denial of justice arises.

   *   *   *

   The offence for which Lieutenant Demons appears to have been prosecuted was an act—of negligence or imprudence—having its origin on board the Lotus, whilst its effects made themselves felt on board the Boz-Kourt. These two elements are, legally, entirely inseparable, so much so that their separation renders the offence nonexistent. Neither the exclusive jurisdiction of either State, nor the limitations of the jurisdiction of each to the occurrences which took place on the respective ships would appear calculated to satisfy the requirements of justice and effectively to protect the interests of the two States. It is only natural that each should be able to exercise jurisdiction and to do so in respect of the incident as a whole. It is therefore a case of concurrent jurisdiction.

*   *   *

FOR THESE REASONS, the Court, having heard both Parties, gives, by the President's casting vote ᵃ—the votes being equally divided—, judgment to the effect

(1) that, following the collision which occurred on August 2nd, 1926, on the high seas between the French steamship Lotus and the Turkish steamship Boz-Kourt, and upon the arrival of the French ship at Stamboul, and in consequence of the loss of the Boz-Kourt having involved the death of eight Turkish nationals, Turkey, by instituting criminal proceedings in pursuance of Turkish law against Lieutenant Demons, officer of the watch on board the Lotus at the time of the collision, has not acted in conflict with the principles of international law, contrary to Article 15 of the Convention of Lausanne of July 24th, 1923, respecting conditions of residence and business and jurisdiction;

(2) that, consequently, there is no occasion to give judgment on the question of the pecuniary reparation which might have been due to Lieutenant Demons if Turkey, by prosecuting him as above stated, had acted in a manner contrary to the principles of international law.

*   *   *

[Separate and dissenting opinions omitted.]

---

1. *Question.* Does the decision in the Lotus case state (a) a rule of jurisdiction in international law or (b) the legal consequences of the lack of a rule of international law on the issue?

2. *Present rule as to prosecution for high seas collision.* The Convention on the High Seas,ᵇ the text of which appears in the Documentary Supplement, provides in Article 11:

In the event of a collision or of any other incident of navigation concerning a ship on the high seas, involving the penal or disciplinary responsibility of the master or of any person in the service of the ship, no penal or disciplinary proceedings may

a. Article 55 of the Statute of the International Court of Justice provides: "1. All questions shall be decided by a majority of the judges present. 2. In the event of an equality of votes, the President or the judge who sits in his place shall have a casting vote." The text of the statute is in the Documentary Supplement.

b. 49 states were parties to this convention on January 1, 1972.

be instituted against such persons except before the judicial or administrative authorities either of the flag state or of the state of which such person is a national.

In view of this provision, consider whether Italy violated international law if its judicial authorities proceeded as stated in a newsreport taken from The Philadelphia Inquirer of August 30, 1971:

Greek Ferry Captain Arrested, Accused of Homicide in Italy. Brindisi, Italy.—Italian police arrested the captain of the Greek ferry Heleanna Sunday night on a charge of multiple homicide as he sought to leave Italy on another Greek ferryboat.

Authorities had ordered Captain Demetrios Antipas to remain in Italy pending further investigation of the disaster which cost at least 26 lives when fire swept the ship from stem to stern Saturday in the Adriatic Sea. More than 1,000 persons were aboard.

An officer patrolling the docks recognized Antipas on board the ferry Egnatia as it was preparing to leave for Corfu, Igoumenitsa and Patras, Greece, an overnight cruise taking 19 hours.

Police said they had planned to deliver a summons to Antipas Monday morning, but when he tried to leave Italy a magistrate issued the murder warrant.

Antipas defended himself and the crew of the Heleanna, and rejected as "absolutely not true" allegations by some passengers that he was among the first to abandon ship. He said he was the last.

He denied that the giant ferry, which carried more than 1,000 persons, was overcrowded.

   *   *   *   (at 2, col. 7).

RIVARD v. UNITED STATES

United States Court of Appeals, Fifth Circuit, 1967.
375 F.2d 882.[a]

[Four Canadian nationals were indicted for conspiracy to smuggle heroin into the United States. They were extradited from Canada, tried and convicted in a United States District Court in Texas. The defendants were at all times prior to their extradition outside of the United States.]

   *   *   *

Under international law a state does not have jurisdiction to enforce a rule of law prescribed by it, unless it had jurisdiction to

---

a. Cert. denied 389 U.S. 884, 88 S.Ct. 151 (1967).

prescribe the rule. Restatement, Second, Foreign Relations Law of the United States § 7(2).

It is for this reason that the mere physical presence of the four alien appellants before the court did not give the District Court jurisdiction. The question remains whether their conduct without the United States had such a deleterious effect within the United States to justify this country in prohibiting the conduct. Restatement, Second, supra § 18.

The law of nations permits the exercise of criminal jurisdiction by a nation under five general principles. They are the territorial,[5] national,[6] protective,[7] universality,[8] and passive personality [9] principles. * * * All nations utilize the territorial principle, and it is under this principle that the District Court had jurisdiction over appellants. There are, however, two views as to the scope of the territorial principle. Under the subjective view, jurisdiction extends over all persons in the state and there violating its laws. Under the objective view, jurisdiction extends over all acts which take effect within the sovereign even though the author is elsewhere. * * *

     *   *   *

The first question we are called upon to decide is whether the District Court had jurisdiction to try an alien for a conspiracy to commit a crime against the United States, formed without the United States, several of the overt acts having been committed in furtherance of the conspiracy within the United States by a co-conspirator.

     *   *   *

* * * Rivard twice sent co-conspirator Caron across the Canadian border to deliver caches of heroin brought back from Europe by Massey and Jones to another co-conspirator, Miller, in Connecticut. Caron also travelled by automobile from Quebec to Mexico through the United States and was on his way back through the United States with yet another load of heroin to be delivered in Connecticut when he was apprehended in Texas. There is thus no doubt that the object of the conspiracy was to violate the narcotics laws of the United States; that the conspiracy was carried on partly in and partly out of this country; and that overt acts were committed within the United States by co-conspirators. * * *

---

5. Jurisdiction is based on the place where the offense is committed.

6. Jurisdiction is based on the nationality or national character of the offender.

7. Jurisdiction is based on whether the national interest is injured.

8. Custody of the offender gives jurisdiction under this principle.

9. Jurisdiction is based on the nationality or national character of the victim.

Conduct outside the territory producing intangible effects within the territory. Under customary international law are the following cases distinguishable as to the legitimacy of the application of its law by State B?

1.   In State A, X and Y conspire to and do send poisoned chocolates into State B with the intention that Z, the addressee, eat them and die. This happens. State B has X and Y before its courts on indictment for murder. X and Y are nationals of State A, and State A objects on the ground that international law does not authorize State B to apply its law.

2.   The same states and the same parties, except that in State A, X and Y conspire to and do perpetrate a stock fraud by mail on Z in State B. State B has X and Y before its courts on indictment for embezzlement. X and Y are nationals of State A. State A objects on the ground that international law does not authorize State B to apply its law of fraudulent stock offers to X and Y.

3.   The same states and the same parties, except that in State A, X and Y agree to divide world markets, allocate and restrict production, and fix prices for commodities as to which, between them, they have a dominant world position. In State B this agreement is assumed to have the effect of reducing State B's exports of the commodity and of increasing its imports, at higher prices, thus reducing its favorable balance of trade. State B has X and Y before its courts on indictment under its antitrust law. State A objects on these grounds: (a) same as in cases 1 and 2; (b) that "economic effects" cannot be "likened to shooting bullets or sending poisoned chocolates across frontiers"; (c) that no measurement of adverse effect is possible; (d) that A and B did not "intend" any injury to State B or its nationals but only to achieve their profit maximization objectives.

4.   Would it make any difference as to any of State A's arguments if the suit in State B had been private litigation by B nationals in the same commodity trade who claim injury and seek recovery under a treble damages provision in the antitrust law of State B?

The above hypothetical cases pose the major variables in a continuing debate on the role and rule of customary international law as to the extent to which a state may prescribe the legal consequences of economic conduct outside the territory by non-nationals that is objectionable to the state. Detailed consideration of the reach of antitrust laws of the United States is in Chapter 7.

The following materials illustrate the attitude of various states as to the effects doctrine.

1.   German cartel law. On July 27, 1957, the Federal Republic of Germany enacted an Act against Restraints of Competition, Gesetz gegen Wettbewerbsbeschränkungen, usually cited as GWB. An English translation of it appears in 1 Guide to Legislation on Restrictive Business Practices, Germany 1.0, 1 (1964), published by the Organi-

zation for Economic Cooperation and Development (OECD). As translated, Section 98(2) of the cartel law provides:

> This Act shall apply to all restraints of competition which have effect in the area in which this Act applies, even if they result from acts done outside such area. (at 42)

2.　Ali Ahmed v. The State of Bombay, India, Supreme Court, 24 Int'l L.Rep. 156 (1961). The defendant, a Pakistani, is before the courts of India, and is convicted of "cheating", an offense under § 420 of the Indian Penal Code. The accused, while in Karachi, Pakistan, fraudulently induced an Indian in Bombay to part with a substantial sum of money. The supreme court affirmed the conviction, as against the defendant's contention that he " *　*　* is a Pakistani national who during the entire period of the [alleged] commission of the offense never stepped into India 　*　*　* and cannot be tried by an Indian Court." The supreme court cited the Lotus in support of the objective territorial principle.

3.　Brown v. Old England Ship and Wagner, France, Court of Cassation, 38 Journal de Droit International Privé 1192 (1911). A British manufacturer of "Meltonian Cream," a leather polish, sues the French seller of a confusingly similar "Melton" for fraudulent imitation of trademark. The French defendant defends that Wagner, a German, supplied the product that he sold in France, and Wagner, served in France and before the courts there, contends that the sale was made in Germany and hence the French courts have no jurisdiction. The court below upheld his contention. The Court of Cassation reversed and upheld French jurisdiction not only because Wagner showed samples in France but also because Wagner, though he was not the owner of the infringing product when it was introduced in the French territory, cooperated in having it introduced and was indeed the principal actor in causing its introduction.

4.　EEC Commission Decision of December 13, 1971, CCH, Common Market Reporter par. 9481 (1971). "Article 1.　Continental Can Company, Inc., of New York, N. Y., which holds, through its [German] subsidiary 　*　*　* a dominant position in a substantial part of the Common Market on the market for light containers for the packaging of meats, meat products, fish and shell fish, as well as on the market for metal lids for glass jars, is found to have abused that dominant position through the purchase in April, 1970, by its subsidiary Europemballage Corporation, of approximately 80% of the stock and convertible bonds of the Dutch enterprise Thomassen en Drijver, N. V. * * *. Article 2.　Continental Can Company, Inc., must terminate the violation of Article 86 of the Treaty [of Rome]. To this end, it must submit proposals to the Commission before July 1, 1972."

Continental Can has appealed to the Court of the European Communities.

5. Decisions of the Court of the European Communities. In several important antitrust decisions in 1972, the Court of the European Communities upheld the application by the commission of Article 85 (restrictive trade practices) of the Treaty of Rome to corporations registered outside the community (in the United Kingdom and Switzerland, for example). Imperial Chemical Industries Ltd. v. E. C. Commission, [1972] Common Market Law Reports 557. In these "dyestuffs cartel" cases the Advocate General assigned to advise the court had no difficulty with the application of the treaty to corporate actors outside the European Community on the basis of economic effects within the Community. He referred specifically to the German law on cartels and to the United States decisions on "extraterritoriality" (at 593–608). The court, however, chose to uphold the commission's fines on the out-of-area parties on the ground that they controlled subsidiary corporations within the European Community that had violated Article 85 by engaging in concerted practices to fix prices, allocate production, etc.

Why, do you suppose, did the court not base its holding on the ground suggested to it by its own high-ranking "legal adviser"? Is there, in practical terms, any substantial difference in results as between the course suggested by the Advocate General and the one followed by the court?

Very recently there have been press accounts that the court has upheld fines on an American chemical company under Article 85, because of the actions of its wholly controlled Italian subsidiary.

AMERICAN GETS STIFF SENTENCE IN CZECHOSLOVAKIA

The Times-Picayune of New Orleans, Louisiana.
December 19, 1970, at 5, col. 1.*

Prague, Czechoslovakia (AP)—A young American who once worked as a researcher and broadcast monitor for Radio Free Europe in West Germany in order to finance his college studies was convicted Friday of subversion against Czechoslovakia and sentenced to four years in prison.

Fred H. Eidlin, 28, of Rochester, N. Y., had eight days to appeal the sentence, and he is expected to do so.

A U. S. Embassy spokesman said the embassy was "surprised at the severity of the sentence but is withholding any further comment until we know the nature of any further legal steps planned on Eidlin's behalf."

Eidlin's Czech lawyer, Waclav Petracek, argued for an acquittal, reminding the five-man panel of municipal court judges that all his

* Reprinted by permission of The Times-
Picayune Publishing Company, New
Orleans, Louisiana.

client had done was to work "as an American in an American agency in the territory of a state where this is not prohibited."

He described Eidlin as "a progressive boy who has his own ideas and who did not come with hostile attitudes to our country." But the court found in its verdict delivered after a seven-hour trial, that Eidlin's job with the U. S.—financed anti-Communist station was in itself subversion against Czechoslovakia.

Eidlin, who learned Czech before going to work for Radio Free Europe, made an eloquent personal defense.

"I am not a Communist," he told the court. "I don't agree with many things that are done in your country. But this is not my home so I never intervened in your affairs."

Eidlin said he had always tried to convince his friends that they should visit Communist nations for themselves because "if tension is to be relaxed there must be travel without fear." That is why he never dreamed he would be arrested on the two occasions he traveled into Czechoslovakia, he added. He was arrested in Prague last July 26 and has been in prison since.

Eidlin testified he worked as a "policy assistant" for RFE from August 1968 until November 1969. He said his work was about 95 per cent research and scientific and 5 per cent listening to Czech language broadcasts over the propaganda station to make sure they were not too rabidly anti-communist. He said he helped in "slowing down the immigrants * * * When I heard negative polemics or cold war criticism, I would report it to the director." Eidlin said he worked at the station so he could resume his studies at the University of Toronto, in Canada.

---

3.   CONDUCT AFFECTING GOVERNMENTAL INTERESTS

UNITED STATES v. PIZZARUSSO

United States Court of Appeals, Second Circuit, 1968.
388 F.2d 8 [a].

MEDINA, CIRCUIT JUDGE. This case is of interest because it brings before this Court for the first time the question of the jurisdiction of the District Court to indict and convict a foreign citizen of the crime of knowingly making a false statement under oath in a visa application to an American consular official located in a foreign country, in violation of 18 U.S.C. Section 1546.[1] Supreme Court cases

a.   Cert. denied 392 U.S. 936, 88 S.Ct. 2306 (1968).

1.   Fraud and misuse of visas, permits and other entry documents. * * * Whoever knowingly makes under oath any false statement with respect to a material fact in any application, affidavit, or other document required by the immigration laws or regulations prescribed thereunder, or knowingly presents any such application, affidavit, or other document containing any such false statement—

give some guidance but none of them passes on this question directly.[2] A Ninth Circuit decision, Rocha v. United States, 288 F.2d 545 (9th Cir.), cert. denied 366 U.S. 948, 81 S.Ct. 1902, 6 L.Ed.2d 1241 (1961), is in point but we sustain jurisdiction on the basis of somewhat different reasons.

The indictment charges that on March 4, 1965 Jean Philomena Pizzarusso wilfully made under oath a number of false statements in her "Application for Immigrant Visa And Alien Registration" at the American Consulate, Montreal, Canada. Each of these false statements was patently material to the matter in hand. For example: she falsely swore that since her sixteenth birthday her only places of residence for six months or more had been London, England and Montreal, Canada; she falsely swore that she had been in the United States only for short visits for pleasure; she falsely swore that she had never been arrested, and so on. Although at all times pertinent to this case she was a citizen of Canada, she was taken into custody in the Southern District of New York on April 18, 1966.

Upon the issuance of the visa and by its use Mrs. Pizzarusso immediately entered the territory of the United States, but this fact is not alleged in the indictment nor required by the terms of the statute, nor is it material, as we find the crime was complete when the false statements were made to an American consular official in Montreal. We shall return later to this feature of the case.

The evidence to sustain the charge is so overwhelming that we shall not pause to discuss it. Indeed, the only contention made on this appeal is that the District Court lacked jurisdiction to indict appellant and convict her of the crime alleged.[3] As we find no lack of jurisdiction, we affirm the judgment. Our reasons follow.

    *   *   *

International law has recognized, in varying degrees, five bases of jurisdiction with respect to the enforcement of the criminal law. See Harvard Research In International Law, Jurisdiction with Respect to Crime, 29 Am.J.Int'l L.Spec.Supp. 435, 445 (1935) (hereinafter cited as Harvard Research). Thus both the territoriality and nationality principles, under which jurisdiction is determined by either the situs of the crime or the nationality of the accused, are universally accepted. The third basis, the protective principle, covers the instant case. By virtue of this theory a state "has jurisdiction to prescribe a rule of law attaching legal consequences to conduct outside its territory that threatens its security as a state or the operation of its

Shall be fined not more than $2,000 or imprisoned not more than five years, or both.

2. United States v. Bowman, 260 U.S. 94, 43 S.Ct. 39, 67 L.Ed. 149 (1922) cited by appellee as authority for upholding jurisdiction in the instant case

is distinguishable as that case involved imposition of criminal liability on United States citizens for acts committed abroad.

3. Appellant received a one-year suspended sentence and was placed on probation for two years.

governmental functions, provided the conduct is generally recognized as a crime under the law of states that have reasonably developed legal systems." Restatement (Second), Foreign Relations, Section 33 (1965). See also Harvard Research Section 7.[5]

Traditionally, the United States has relied primarily upon the territoriality and nationality principles, Harvard Research at p. 543, and judges have often been reluctant to ascribe extraterritorial effect to statutes. See, e. g., American Banana Co. v. United Fruit Co., 213 U.S. 347, 29 S.Ct. 511, 53 L.Ed. 826 (1909). Nonetheless, our courts have developed what has come to be termed the objective territorial principle as a means of expanding the power to control activities detrimental to the state. This principle has been aptly defined by Mr. Justice Holmes in Strassheim v. Daily, 221 U.S. 280, 285, 31 S.Ct. 558, 560, 55 L.Ed. 735 (1911). "Acts done outside a jurisdiction, but intended to produce and producing detrimental effects within it, justify a state in punishing the cause of the harm as if he had been present at the effect * * *." See also Judge Learned Hand's opinion in United States v. Aluminum Co. of America, 148 F.2d 416 (2d Cir. 1945). Underlying this principle is the theory that the "detrimental effects" constitute an element of the offense and since they occur within the country, jurisdiction is properly invoked under the territorial principle. See also Restatement (Second), Foreign Relations Law Section 18.

[handwritten margin note: DETRI-MENTAL EFFECTS]

However, the objective territorial principle is quite distinct from the protective theory. Under the latter, all the elements of the crime occur in the foreign country and jurisdiction exists because these actions have a "potentially adverse effect" upon security or governmental functions, Restatement (Second) Foreign Relations Law, Comment to Section 33 at p. 93, and there need not be any actual effect in the country as would be required under the objective territorial principle. Courts have often failed to perceive this distinction. Thus, the Ninth Circuit,[6] in upholding a conviction under a factual situation similar to the one in the instant case, relied on the protective theory, but still felt constrained to say that jurisdiction rested partially on the adverse effect produced as a result of the alien's entry into the United States. The Ninth Circuit also cited Strassheim and Aluminum Company of America as support for its decision. With all due deference to our brothers of the Ninth Circuit, however, we think this reliance is unwarranted. A violation of 18 U.S.C.A. Section 1546 is complete at the time the alien perjures himself in the foreign country. It may be possible that the particular criminal sanctions of Section 1546 will never be enforced unless the defendant enters the country, but entry

[handwritten margin note: PROT- ALL CRIME OCCURS W/IN STATE (UNLIKE ABOVE)]

5. The other two principles are universality, where jurisdiction is determined by the custody of the person committing the offense and passive personality where jurisdiction is determined by reference to the nationality of the person injured. Harvard Research at p. 445.

6. Rocha v. United States, 288 F.2d 545 (9th Cir.), cert. denied 366 U.S. 948, 81 S.Ct. 1902, 6 L.Ed.2d 1241 (1961).

is not an element of the statutory offense. Were the statute re-drafted and entry made a part of the crime we would then be presented with a clear case of jurisdiction under the objective territorial principle.

Statutes imposing criminal liability on aliens for committing perjury in United States Consulates in foreign countries have been in existence for over one hundred years, see, e. g., 22 U.S.C. Section 1203, which was derived from an act of 1856, and oftentimes courts have routinely sustained convictions without even considering the jurisdictional question. See, e. g., United States v. Flores-Rodriguez, 237 F.2d 405 (2d Cir. 1956).[7] Only one court has ever held that the United States did not have jurisdiction to proceed against an alien under the legislation governing this case. United States v. Baker, 136 F.Supp. 546 (S.D.N.Y.1955). In Baker it was conceded that there was authority for deporting an alien for making perjurious statements to a United States Consul, United States ex rel. Majka v. Palmer, 67 F.2d 146 (7th Cir. 1933), but the court thought the imposition of criminal sanctions was "far different" from deportation and dismissed the indictment. We would have sustained jurisdiction in Baker had the case been before us, and in this view we are apparently joined by the judge who decided Baker, since he presided over the instant case in the court below.

Affirmed.

————————

1. *Distinction between the territorial and protective principles.* In United States v. Rodriguez, 182 F.Supp. 479 (S.D.Cal.1960),[a] the defendant aliens were charged with making false statements in immigration applications while they were outside the United States. The court discussed the territorial and the protective principles in the following terms:

> Acts committed outside the territorial limits of the State but intended to produce, or producing, effects within the boundaries of the State are subject to penal sanctions; * * * Where the effect is felt by private persons within the State, penal sanctions rest on the "objective," or "subjective," territorial principle * * *. Where the effect of the acts committed outside the

7. One other court has upheld jurisdiction under a statute comparable to 18 U.S.C. Section 1546 on an alternative ground. The District Court for the Southern District of California, relying in part on the territorial principle, sustained the conviction of an alien for false swearing in a visa application, on the somewhat novel theory that the United States Consulate was part of United States territory. United States v. Archer, 51 F.Supp. 708 (S.D.Cal.1943).

a. Affirmed sub nom. Rocha v. United States, 288 F.2d 545 (9th Cir. 1961), with respect to the substantive counts of the indictment, reversed as to conspiracy counts not at issue in Rodriguez; cert. denied 366 U.S. 948, 81 S.Ct. 1902 (1961).

United States is felt by the government, the protective theory affords the basis by which the state is empowered to punish all those offenses which impinge upon its sovereignty, wherever these actions take place and by whomever they may be committed. The results of such a theory are, in many ways, similar to those reached in the Strassheim case * * * where the court directed its attention to the objective results of the criminal act and the location of its effect. Any act which would offend the sovereignty of a nation must, of necessity, have some effect within the territorial limits of that state or there would be no adverse effect upon the government justifying a penal sanction. (at 488–489)

2. *Expansion of protective principle in the United States.* Both the Court of Appeals for the second circuit in Pizzarusso and the District Court in Rodriguez predicate the jurisdiction of the United States on the protective principle. It is true they phrase it somewhat differently. The court in Pizzarusso holds the principle to be applicable because the conduct of the aliens abroad had a "potentially adverse effect" upon the governmental function. The court in Rodriguez holds the principle applicable because the conduct of the aliens abroad of necessity had "some effect" upon the governmental function in the United States. It may be that the difference between the two formulations is metaphysical. What is important, however, is the willingness of both courts to use the protective principle.

The alternative in both cases would have been to hold that an effect in the territory had taken place when the aliens entered the United States. Had the courts involved adopted this position, they would have reflected a traditional attitude towards the protective principle, for little use has been made of it in the United States in the past. A manifestation of this traditional attitude can be found in legislation concerning counterfeiting: it is a federal offense to counterfeit foreign currency in the United States, but not a federal offense to counterfeit United States currency abroad.

The wider use of the protective principle reflected in the two cases is consistent with an international practice of long standing. The Restatement of the Foreign Relations Law of the United States (1965) reflects this international practice in its formulation of the protective principle. Section 33 provides: "A state has jurisdiction to prescribe a rule of law attaching legal consequences to conduct outside its territory that threatens its security as a state or the operation of its governmental functions * * *." The section adds the qualification that the conduct must be generally recognized as a crime.

3. *Dangers inherent in the protective principle.* It is beyond doubt that the protective principle applies to crimes such as the counterfeiting of state seals, currency, stamps, passports or other public documents. Most states punish these offenses wheresoever and by whomever committed. The danger, however, is that the principle

can be abused because it is susceptible of practically unlimited expansion. The danger is particularly great when the principle is formulated in broad terms, as it often is, and made to cover any crime against the security, territorial integrity or political independence of the state. But even under the restrained formulation in Section 33 of the Restatement, what conduct is included in addition to counterfeiting of seals, currency and public documents?

Consider, for example, the decision in Public Prosecutor v. L., Netherlands, Supreme Court, 1951, 18 Int'l L.Rep. 206 (1951):

> The Facts. The defendant, a woman of Belgian nationality and domiciled in Belgium, was prosecuted in the Special Police Court of Breda on November 2, 1950, for having acted in Belgium as an accessory to offences committed by Netherlands subjects against the Dutch Currency Decree (Deviezenbesluit) of October 10, 1945 (Staatsblad, No. F 222), by giving them an opportunity and means to commit the said offences. Under Article 31(5) of the Decree the acts therein defined as offences were made punishable if committed in a foreign country. The defendant's contention that she was not subject to Dutch criminal law was not accepted, and she was convicted. The conviction was upheld by the Court of Appeal at 's'Hertogenbosch on March 7, 1951.
>
> The defendant appealed further.
>
> Held (by the Supreme Court): that the accused was rightly convicted. The acts committed by the accused did not come under any of the general principles of applicability of Netherlands criminal law as laid down in Book I, Section I, of the Netherlands Penal Code. These acts could therefore only fall under the scope of Dutch criminal law in virtue of the special provisions contained in Article 31 of the Emergency Decree of 1945 on Currency Restrictions. Those provisions were directed not only against Netherlands subjects who committed currency offences in a foreign country, but also to foreign nationals abroad who were accessories to such offences.

Does the decision mean that in order to protect its currency, a state has jurisdiction to make it a crime for an alien to sell or buy its currency, outside the territory, from one of its nationals? What if the transaction was between two aliens?

SECTION B. JURISDICTION TO ENFORCE RULES OF LAW

1. DEPENDENCE OF JURISDICTION TO ENFORCE UPON JURISDICTION TO PRESCRIBE

ARRET FORNAGE

France, Court of Cassation, 1873.
84 Journal du Palais 229 (1873).[a]

[The accused was prosecuted for grand larceny committed in Switzerland. In accordance with French procedure, the indictment was presented to a court whose function was to decide whether the evidence was sufficient to support prosecution and which criminal court had jurisdiction to try the case. It found sufficient evidence for prosecution and decided the case should be tried by the Court of Assizes. From this decision, the accused could have appealed to the Court of Cassation, i. e., the supreme court, but failed to do so.

At trial, he objected he could not be prosecuted in the French courts for a crime committed in a foreign country. Previously, the supreme court had held several times that decisions of the indicting court as to which criminal court had jurisdiction to try a case must be appealed directly and the Court of Assizes, once seized of the case, could not entertain jurisdictional attacks. Accordingly, the Court of Assizes ruled it could not hear the objection. From the ruling, the accused appealed to the Court of Cassation.

The appeal was heard by the Criminal Section of the Court of Cassation and decided in accord with the arguments presented by a "conseiller rapporteur," i. e. a member of the court appointed to make recommendations, and those presented by the "avocat general," i. e. simultaneously the prosecutor for the state and representative of the general public interest.

The conseiller rapporteur conceded the ruling of the Court of Assizes was in accord with the precedents established by the Court of Cassation, but went on to make the argument which appears below.]

Is it not possible also to say that, in the case presented to you, there are considerations of a superior nature justifying an exception to the general rule? The only basis for the right to punish is sovereignty, which dies at the border. If French law allows the prosecution of French nationals for crimes or offenses committed in a foreign country, it is because criminal law applies both on a territorial and personal basis. A French national, even abroad, still remains a citizen of his country and as such remains subject to French law, which has power over him as soon as he comes back to France. But the law

---

a. Translation by the editors. The same comments apply to this transla-   tion as those set forth in note a) on p. 31.

itself cannot give French courts the power to try foreign nationals for crimes or offenses committed outside French territory; such exorbitant jurisdiction, whose basis could neither be territorial nor personal, would constitute a violation of international law, a breach of the sovereignty of other states. There is only one exception to this rule of international law. When a foreign national has committed, even abroad, a crime against the security of the state, he can be prosecuted, tried and punished in France. But apart from this exception, which is based on the right of self-defense, foreign nationals can only be prosecuted by the courts of their own country for acts committed outside the territory. * * * The Court of Assizes, by punishing this act, would commit an abuse of power; it would usurp a right of sovereignty belonging to a foreign power. Would it not be contrary to all principles of justice to force the judges into knowingly becoming guilty of an arbitrary act, a violation of international law? * * * [The Court of Assizes] must examine the evidence presented by the accused in support of his claims and declare itself without jurisdiction if it finds that he is an alien and the act of which he is accused has been committed outside French territory.

[The avocat general argued the precedents did not control the case and could be distinguished because of the nature of the objection raised. His conclusion appears immediately below.]

Indeed, French justice has jurisdiction only to try French nationals for crimes committed by them outside the territory * * *; it has no jurisdiction over aliens; so the question of nationality must be decided beforehand; for the right of jurisdiction depends upon the resolution of the question. The ruling which is challenged appears to me to have overlooked those fundamental principles.

[The opinion of the court appears below].

[Held:] * * * [I]t is a general principle that if the judgment * * * which sends an accused to the Court of Assizes is not appealed within the time provided by Art. 296 of the Code of Criminal Instruction, the court may not declare itself without jurisdiction * * *; the rule is based on the fact that Courts of Assizes have general jurisdiction in criminal matters and can, without exceeding their power or exceeding their jurisdiction, hear all cases punishable by French law; but this jurisdiction, however broad it may be, cannot extend to crimes committed outside the territory by aliens who, in respect to those acts, are not punishable in French courts. * * * [T]his lack of jurisdiction in this regard is absolute, permanent; it can be cured neither by the silence nor by the consent of the accused; it continues to exist at all levels * * * [and the indicting court] cannot give the Court of Assizes a right it does not itself possess, to try acts which do not come under the jurisdiction of French law. * * * [R]aymond Fornage was sent to the Court of Assizes of Haute-Savoie and accused of having committed grand larceny in the

Canton of Valais (Switzerland) ; before the trial began, he presented arguments to the effect that the court was without jurisdiction, because he was born in France of foreign parents, did not claim French nationality and consequently did not come under the jurisdiction of French courts for an act committed in a foreign country. * * * [T]he claim, which challenged the very legality of the prosecution and the jurisdiction of the Court of Assizes * * * had to be decided by the court before hearing the merits; * * * the accused could not be deprived of the right to present this peremptory argument either by his silence during the investigation or by his failure to appeal the judgment of * * * [the indicting court]. * * * [I]n ruling the accused could not present his motion for lack of jurisdiction * * * the Court of Assizes wrongly applied * * * [the law] ; and by ordering the trial to proceed without deciding the motion based on nationality * * * disregarded the rights of the defendant.

---

1. *Enforcement of rules prescribed on the basis of nationality of the individual.*   A state has jurisdiction to prescribe rules governing the conduct of its nationals outside its territory. As a result, it may use its enforcement jurisdiction to give effect to such rules by action taken against its nationals if they are found in the territory or, if they are not, by action taken against their property in the territory. But it may not enforce them by taking action in the territory of another state. See p. 144. Hence the limitations on the scope of its enforcement jurisdiction restrict the usefulness of its broad jurisdiction to prescribe rules governing the conduct of its nationals wherever it occurs.

[handwritten margin note: NO ENFORCE- MENT BY ACTING IN ANOTHER STATE TERRITORY —]

States exercise their jurisdiction to prescribe rules governing the conduct of their nationals in various degrees. They often exercise it to punish treasonable acts by their nationals wherever committed. The United States does. 18 U.S.C. § 2381. It does not use extensively its prescriptive jurisdiction based on nationality, however. More generally, the use of this prescriptive jurisdiction is the exception rather than the rule in common law states. Civil law states usually make more use of it, sometimes going so far as to provide that all, or nearly all, offenses committed by their nationals abroad are punishable if they are found in the national territory, but in some cases conditioning the application of national law upon certain restrictive factors. Some illustrative cases follow.

In the case of In Re Guttierez, the defendant was a Mexican national charged with stealing a truck in Texas. The Mexican court dismissed his challenge to its jurisdiction on the broad ground, apparently, that a crime committed abroad by a Mexican national is punishable in Mexico. Supreme Court, 1957, 24 Int'l L.Rep. 265 (1961). A Dutch national "is liable to prosecution in Holland for an offense committed abroad, which is punishable under Netherlands law and which is also punishable under the law of the country where the offense was committed." Public Prosecutor v. Y., Supreme Court, 1957, 24 Int'l L. Rep. 264, 265 (1961).

In the case of In Re Roquain, Belgium, Court of Cassation, 1958, 26 Int'l L.Rep. 209 (1963), the defendant, while lawfully married, committed adultery in Paris. The court held the defendant could not be prosecuted because under "the law governing criminal proceedings in respect of offenses committed outside Belgian territory," the offense of adultery may be prosecuted only if it was committed against a Belgian national. As to offenses generally, Spain apparently will not prosecute a Spanish national for an offense committed abroad unless the victim is also of Spanish nationality. Forgery Committed in Venezuela by a Spaniard, Supreme Court, 1960, 89 Journal du Droit International 189 (1962).

In X. v. Prosecutor, Netherlands, District Court of Middleburg, 1952, Court of Appeal of the Hague, 1952, 19 Int'l L.Rep. 226 (1957), the defendant was a national of the Netherlands. She lost her nationality by marriage, then committed outside the Netherlands a criminal offense for which she was prosecuted and convicted in the state where it was committed. Upon the dissolution of her marriage, she recovered her former Dutch nationality. She was then prosecuted for the same offense in the Netherlands. It was held that the previous prosecution abroad did not preclude a new prosecution in Holland, though it might mitigate the punishment, and moreover she could not object to the prosecution on the ground that she had lost her nationality at the time the offense was committed. Any alien committing an offense abroad could be prosecuted if and when such person subsequently became a citizen of the Netherlands.

The Supreme Court of India, on the other hand, takes the view that a person cannot be prosecuted in India for an offense committed abroad if he was not a national of India at the time of commission of the offense. Central Bank of India v. Ram Narain, 1954, 21 Int'l L. Rep. 95 (1957). Moreover, a number of states will not prosecute their nationals again if they were previously prosecuted for an offense committed outside the territory. Harvard Research in International Law, Jurisdiction with Respect to Crime, 29 Am.J.Int'l L. Supp. 435, 606 (1935).

Prescriptive jurisdiction based on the nationality of individuals is also applicable to corporations or other legal entities which are nationals of the state. Suppose a corporation in a foreign state and doing all its business there is owned by United States nationals. May the United States use its prescriptive jurisdiction to compel its nationals to conduct the business of the corporation in violation of the law of the foreign state?

2. *Enforcement of rules prescribed on the basis of the national-ity of vessels, aircraft and military services.* Whereas the prescrip-tive jurisdiction of a state based upon the nationality of individuals is limited in its effectiveness because the rules prescribed on this basis can be enforced only by action taken in the territory, prescriptive ju-risdiction based on the nationality of vessels, aircraft and military services does not suffer from the same limitation. Jurisdiction to en-force rules prescribed on this basis accompanies the vessels, aircraft or military services wherever they go, although the exercise of the enforcement jurisdiction is limited by rules of international law when the vessels, aircraft or military services are in the territory of an-other state. See Chapters 3, 4 and 7.

Jurisdiction based on the nationality of vessels, aircraft and mili-tary services extends, moreover, to persons aboard the vessels or air-craft, as well as to members of the military services, regardless of the nationality of the individuals involved. In The Queen v. Anderson, [1868] L.R. 1 Cr.Cas.Res. 161, an American seaman was convicted of manslaughter on a British vessel which was in the Garonne river in France, some 45 miles upstream from the sea. While France had concurrent jurisdiction on the basis of territory, it did not claim to exercise it. The court held that the defendant was subject to British law and hence the conviction was valid.

3. *Enforcement of rules prescribed on other bases.* In the chap-ters which follow, other bases of jurisdiction to prescribe are consid-ered as well as the scope of enforcement jurisdiction of rules prescribed on such bases.

As to prescriptive and enforcement jurisdiction based on prox-imity to territory (contiguous zone, hot pursuit and continental shelf), see Chapter 3.

As to prescriptive and enforcement jurisdiction based on the pro-tection of universal interests (piracy, collision and salvage on the high seas, and fisheries conservation), see Chapter 3.

4. *Enforcement of rules of conflict of laws: problem.* Suppose that in a state of the United States a "long-arm statute" gives the courts jurisdiction over any person who "transacts any business with-in the state." The plaintiff sues a European airline for injuries suf-fered in Paris, France, as a result of the alleged negligence of the air-line. In the state of the United States involved, the airline does not provide passenger or cargo service of any kind and does not sell any tickets. Its only activities in the state, or in the United States gen-erally, consist of making reservations for travel in Europe and adver-tising its services there.

Suppose the court takes jurisdiction on the ground that the airline is doing business in the state, even though the airline defends that its activities in the state are unrelated to the cause of action of the plain-tiff. Suppose further that in determining the liability of the airline, the court decides to apply its own rules of negligence, which happen to be much more favorable to the plaintiff than those of French law, even though the airline contends the applicable rules of negligence are those of the place where the injury was suffered.

Are the actions of the court consistent with international law? Does the court have under international law—not domestic law—a basis of jurisdiction to prescribe rules attaching legal consequences to the conduct of the airline in France? Does the state of the nationality of the airline have a valid claim against the United States under international law if it should contend the court had no jurisdiction to enforce rules of negligence it had no jurisdiction to prescribe?

2. TERRITORIAL CHARACTER OF JURISDICTION TO ENFORCE

THE SCHOONER EXCHANGE v. McFADDON

United States Supreme Court, 1812.
7 Cranch 116, 136.

MARSHALL, C. J. * * *

* * *

The jurisdiction of the nation within its own territory is necessarily exclusive and absolute. It is susceptible of no limitation not imposed by itself. Any restriction upon it, deriving validity from an external source, would imply a diminution of its sovereignty to the extent of the restriction, and an investment of that sovereignty to the same extent in that power which could impose such restriction.

* * *

THE HIGGS CASE

Rousseau, Chronique des Faits Internationaux.
69 Revue Générale de Droit International Public, 101, 105 (1964).[a]

* * * Mr. Dennis Higgs, a British national, former professor of mathematics at the University of Witwatersrand, former member of the liberal party of South Africa and opponent of the apartheid policy, was found during the night of the 29th of August 1969, his hands tied and blindfolded, in a car in Johannesburg, in a park known as Zoo Lake, after being kidnapped the day before by unknown agents, 1600 kilometers away, at his home in Lusaka, Northern Rhodesia. From Mrs. Higgs' statement, it appears that the professor was at home on the evening of August 28 when three men came inside the

a. Translation by the editors. Reprinted with permission of Charles Rousseau and Editions A. Pedone, Paris.

house, asked Mr. Higgs for his identification papers, beat him and forced him to get in a car that disappeared immediately.

The news of this kidnapping brought about a strong reaction in Lusaka, where it was openly suspected that the secret police of South Africa had organized Mr. Higgs' kidnapping. The Prime Minister of Northern Rhodesia, Mr. Kenneth Kaunda, lodged a protest with the British Government—still responsible for the security in Northern Rhodesia at the time   *   *   *—and asked it to intervene with the government of South Africa and obtain the return of Mr. Higgs to Lusaka.

On the 31st of August, the Minister of Justice of South Africa, Mr. Vorster, published an official statement relating the incident. After indicating that Mr. Higgs was heavily involved with an organization that had committed numerous   *   *   * acts of sabotage and [was responsible] in particular for an explosion on the previous 24th of July in the Johannesburg station which had caused the death of a seventy-seven-year-old woman, Mrs. Ethel Rhys, and wounded twenty-two persons, the statement ended with the following words:

> If the information given by the newspapers is correct, neither the Government nor the police want any part in an action [i. e. kidnapping] which is contrary to international law and international practice. The British Government will be notified of the charges against Higgs and his extradition will be asked on the ground that he was an accessory to the murder of Mrs. Rhys.
>
> Until the difficulties concerning the matter are cleared up, Higgs will remain in the hands of the South African police and an inquiry will be made to check if he was actually kidnapped.
>   *   *   *

But the incident was solved in an unexpected manner. During the night of the 31st of August   *   *   *, after a talk between Dr. Kilgen Muller, South African Minister of Foreign Affairs, and Sir Hugh Stephenson, Ambassador of Great Britain, the Government of Pretoria declared that Mr. Higgs would be handed over to the British authorities. Doctor Muller stated that his government had no knowledge of the kidnapping of Professor Higgs and was in no way involved in the affair.   *   *   * The Government in Pretoria [stated it] had no desire to participate in any way in an act contrary to international practice.

   *   *   * Mr. Higgs was transferred by plane to Northern Rhodesia on the 2d of September   *   *   *.

Standing to object to unlawful arrest. In the case of In Re Jolis, France, Tribunal Correctionnel d'Avesnes, 1933 [1933–1934] Ann. Dig. 191 (No. 77), a Belgian national had crossed over the border to visit in a cafe in France, and gone back to Belgium. Suspecting him of theft, the proprietor of the cafe called two French policemen who crossed over into Belgium, arrested him and brought him back to France where he was indicted. The Belgian government lodged an official protest with the French government through diplomatic channels. The court ordered the release of the defendant.

On the other hand, the Supreme Court of France ruled differently in a celebrated case in that country. Colonel Argoud, a French national notorious for his opposition to General de Gaulle's policies of independence for Algeria, was being sought for prosecution by the French authorities but found refuge in Western Germany. He was kidnapped there by persons unknown and found tied up in a truck in Paris after an anonymous phone call. The court ruled that in the absence of an objection by the Federal Republic of Germany, no international law issue was before it. Argoud Case, Court of Cassation, 1964, 38 Semaine Juridique 1964, II, No. 13886. In argument before the court, much was made by the prosecution of applicable precedents in "Anglo-Saxon" law.

In Ker v. Illinois, 119 U.S. 436, 7 S.Ct. 225 (1886), the defendant had been kidnapped in Peru by officials from Illinois, but the court held the mode of his arrest was not valid ground for objection to his trial. In Frisbie v. Collins, 342 U.S. 519, 72 S.Ct. 509 (1952), the court relied on its decision in Ker v. Illinois in holding that a defendant arrested in Illinois by officers from Michigan had no ground for objecting to his trial. In Ker v. Illinois the defendant appeared to be a national of the United States, but the court did not discuss the bearing, if any, of the nationality of the defendant in holding he had no standing to object to his unlawful arrest.

SERVICE OF SUMMONS IN CRIMINAL PROCEEDINGS CASE

Austria, Supreme Court, 1961.
38 Int'l L.Rep. 133 (1969).

THE FACTS.—A German citizen was tried in Austria in absentia and convicted of a criminal offence. The question arose whether the trial and the subsequent verdict were valid, having regard to the fact that the summons to attend the trial was served by the Austrian trial court on the accused in Germany by ordinary post. It was contended before the Supreme Court that an Austrian court was not entitled to serve a summons by post on a foreign citizen in a foreign country, and that proceedings before an Austrian court in pursuance of a summons so served were null and void.

Held: (i) that a summons in criminal proceedings can be served abroad only in accordance with the procedure laid down in treaties between Austria and the foreign country concerned; (ii) that as the relevant provisions of the treaty between Austria and the Federal Republic of Germany did not provide for service of a summons by post, the summons in the present case had not been validly served. The proceedings and the subsequent verdict were therefore null and void and must be set aside. [A portion of the opinion of the court appears below.]

* * * A foreign citizen who commits a criminal offence in Austria is subject to punishment under Austrian law, in accordance with the rule of territoriality. This rule is an emanation of territorial sovereignty, and its application therefore causes no difficulty if the foreign citizen is in Austria and thus within the jurisdiction of the Austrian courts. Where, as in the present case, a foreign offender is not in Austria but in his home State at the time of the prosecution, he is removed from the direct influence of the Austrian courts because the power of the courts, which depends on the jurisdictional authority of the State, ends at the boundary of the State, and the exercise of that power on the other side of the State boundary must, as a general rule be considered an interference with the sovereign authority of a foreign State.

As every act performed by a criminal court—and this includes not only judgments but also interim orders and orders of any other kind—constitutes an act performed by the State in the exercise of its sovereign jurisdiction, service of such acts constitutes an exercise of sovereign authority, at any rate where such service is not so-called "simple service" but service which for the recipient produces a legally relevant effect which on occasion may be detrimental to him.

According to the generally recognized rules of international law, which by Article 9 of the Constitution form part of Austrian federal law, the exercise of sovereign authority in foreign territory is permissible in Continental Europe only in so far as it has been generally recognized in international law (as, e. g., the performance of official duties by foreign diplomats) or is in accordance with general international usage (as, e. g., where customs control posts have been established beyond the frontier of a State) or, as the case may be, has been expressly provided for in treaties (as, e. g., in Article 2 of the Additional Protocol to the Austro-Belgian Extradition Treaty of 12 January 1881, which provides that, so far as concerns non-political criminal offences, documents issued in the course of proceedings or judgments may be served on persons resident in the territory of the other Contracting Party not only through diplomatic channels or by the authorities of the represented State but by post addressed to the recipient himself). Where these conditions are not present and where the conduct of criminal proceedings in individual cases requires the performance of official acts of a sovereign character in the territory of a foreign State—even though it may only be service of a document —the court conducting the proceedings must invoke the assistance of the competent foreign authority for the purpose. The assistance which is feasible and required in individual cases is laid down in treaties and in municipal statutes enacted in pursuance of such treaties.

* * *

All relevant questions relating to these matters were settled, as between Austria and Germany, by the Treaties of 22 September 1958. The Treaties did not come into force until 8 October 1960. * * * It follows that the Court must proceed on the basis that according to the general rules of international law applicable in Continental Europe such service, as a general rule, is not permitted, and that accordingly service by post was not permissible even before the entry into force of the Treaty of 22 September 1958 for Judicial Assistance in Criminal Matters. This view is also confirmed by the view that, according to the Decree of the Ministry of Justice of 23 December 1960, service of official court documents by post is not even permitted in civil proceedings, as between Austria and Germany.

It follows that in the present case the District Court of R. was not entitled to summon the accused, who was then in his home State, i. e. the Federal Republic of Germany, to attend the trial, by sending the summons to him through the post and enclosing an international reply coupon. The District Court should have summoned the accused in accordance with the Decree for Judicial Assistance in Criminal Matters (of 13 July 1959) by invoking the assistance of the competent court of the Federal Republic of Germany. In accordance with this Decree it could have entered into direct contact with the competent German court, but on no account was it permitted to effect postal service on the accused who was in a foreign country. * * *

Accordingly, there has been no "proper" summons within the meaning of section 459 of the Code of Criminal Procedure because a proper summons is one served in accordance with the procedural provisions laid down by law. Thus the primary prerequisite of the proceedings and the subsequent verdict against the accused in his absence was lacking, and there has been a violation of the provisions of section 459 of the Code of Criminal Procedure. The direct service of the judgment and the dispatch of an international reply coupon were in violation of the law, and service so effected could not produce any legal effect. Accordingly there was no basis for the request to pay the fine and the costs of the proceedings, nor was there any basis for the threat to impose imprisonment in lieu of a fine or any of the other orders of the District Court of R., which all rested on the assumption that a judgment in absentia had been validly given.

SECURITIES AND EXCHANGE COMMISSION v. BRIGGS

United States District Court, N.D.Ohio, 1964.
234 F.Supp. 618.

[The S.E.C. sought to enjoin defendant from violating the anti-fraud provisions of the Securities Act of 1933. The defendant was physically located in Canada at the time of suit.]

On the filing of the complaint a temporary restraining order was granted, and an order was entered pursuant to Rule 4(i) of the Federal Rules of Civil Procedure providing for service upon the defendant Briggs by any one or more of four methods: Service by registered mail, personal service by the sheriff of Vancouver County, British Columbia or any of his designated agents, service by said sheriff in accordance with the local rules of British Columbia, or service upon her by the United States Marshal. Pursuant to that order the defendant Briggs was served by registered mail on September 10, 1964. (Cf. Affidavit of Harry M. Jones) On September 17, 1964 the defendant Briggs was personally served by a Deputy Sheriff of British Columbia, Canada. (Cf. Affidavit of Alfred J. Tuttle) On September 18, 1964 counsel for the defendant Jessie Briggs appeared specially in open court and, by oral motion under Rule 12(b) of the Federal Rules of Civil Procedure, objected to this Court's assertion of jurisdiction over the defendant Briggs and moved to dismiss the complaint.

* * *

The defendant next contends that we cannot exercise that power lest we offend the sovereignty of our neighbor Canada, where the defendant was found and served. The defendant suggests that our right to exercise jurisdiction must be conditioned upon approval by Canada through a treaty. We seriously doubt that the defendant, admittedly a citizen of the United States, has standing to complain of an affront to a sovereign which is foreign to her. We need not reach that issue, however, because we perceive of no such invasion of Canada's sovereignty. In Blackmer v. United States, 284 U.S. 421, 52 S.Ct. 252 * * * the Supreme Court stated:

> * * * The mere giving of such a notice to the citizen in the foreign country of the requirement of his government that he shall return is in no sense an invasion of any right of the foreign government * * *.

Therefore, we find no principle of comity between nations which precludes this Court from the exercise of jurisdiction over Mrs. Briggs.

UNITED STATES, FEDERAL RULES OF CIVIL PROCEDURE, PROCESS

28 U.S.C., App., Rule 4.

(i) Alternative Provisions for Service in a Foreign Country.

(1) Manner. When the federal or state law referred to in subdivision (e) of this rule authorizes service upon a party not an inhabitant of or found within the state in which the district court is held, and service is to be effected upon the party in a foreign country, it is also sufficient if service of the summons and complaint is made: (A) in the manner prescribed by the law of the foreign country for service in that country in an action in any of its courts of general jurisdiction; or (B) as directed by the foreign authority in response to a letter rogatory, when service in either case is reasonably calculated to give actual notice; or (C) upon an individual, by delivery to him personally, and upon a corporation or partnership or association, by delivery to an officer, a managing or general agent; or (D) by any form of mail, requiring a signed receipt, to be addressed and dispatched by the clerk of the court to the party to be served; or (E) as directed by order of the court. Service under (C) or (E) above may be made by any person who is not a party and is not less than 18 years of age or who is designated by order of the district court or by the foreign court. On request, the clerk shall deliver the summons to the plaintiff for transmission to the person or the foreign court or officer who will make the service.

---

1. *Problem.* Suppose that the Briggs case had been a suit for damages for securities fraud and the defendant had not appeared. Would a default judgment for the plaintiff give Canada a claim against the United States under international law: (a) if the defendant was a citizen of the United States; (b) if he were a Canadian?

Suppose the defendant were French and the Canadian government did not complain. Would France have a claim against the United States?

2. *Position of the Department of State.* In 56 Am.J.Int'l L. 794 (1962), the following statement appears:

In an aide-memoire delivered to the Department of State on November 16, 1961, the Embassy of Switzerland noted that an agency of the United States Government had, on several occasions, served documents through the mail on a Swiss corporation in Basle. The aide-memoire pointed out that "the service of judicial documents on persons residing in Switzerland is, under Swiss law, a governmental function to be exercised exclusively by the appropriate Swiss authorities," and that "service of such documents by mail constitutes an infringement of Switzerland's sovereign powers, which is incompatible with international law." The aide-memoire added that "documents destined for Switzerland should be transmitted by the U. S. Embassy in Berne to the Federal Division of Police."

In an aide-memoire to the Embassy of Switzerland, dated November 28, 1961, the Department of State replied:

> The Department of State has informed the competent United States authorities of the Swiss law referred to in the aide-memoire. The Department believes that this action will avoid any future transmittals of such documents in a manner inconsistent with Swiss law. The inadvertent violation of applicable Swiss law by United States authorities is regretted.

Chapter 3

CONTROL AND USE OF THE SEA

1. *The struggle over control and use of the sea.* Navigation, fishing and extraction of minerals take place on or under the sea. There is an ongoing struggle over whether these activities can be engaged in freely by all almost anywhere in the sea or whether states can each carve out areas of the sea for their exclusive use and control.

There is agreement that a state has jurisdiction over its "internal waters" and an area of the sea adjoining the coastline, the "territorial sea." There is not agreement as to how wide an area of the sea may be lawfully claimed as territorial sea. The various positions on this question will be examined later in this chapter. The United States claims a territorial sea three miles wide though it has indicated it might accept a 12 miles limit. The claims of most states do not exceed 12 miles. A few states claim as much as 200 miles.

Beyond the territorial sea, there are claims to more limited use of the sea, with respect to so-called contiguous zones, and beyond these zones, with respect to portions of the sea-bed such as the so-called continental shelf. An older body of law governs many of the uses of the high seas, but new law is in the making with respect to the bed of the deep sea.

2. *The 1958 Geneva Conference on the Law of the Sea.* It had an important influence on the development of the law. The conventions emanating from that conference variously codified portions of the customary law or created new law in other cases.[a] Not all of the problems that were then perceived were solved by the conventions e.g., the conference was unable to agree on the breadth of the territorial sea. Further, technological developments have created new problems about the exploitation of the sea-bed. Three of the four conventions are set forth in the Documentary Supplement. They are:

1. Convention on the Territorial Sea and the Contiguous Zone, which entered into force on September 10, 1964; as of Jan. 1, 1972, 41 states were parties to this convention;

a. In the North Sea Continental Shelf Cases [1969] I.C.J.Rep. 3, the issue was whether Article 6 of the 1958 Convention on the Continental Shelf reflected or crystallized a rule of customary international law. Denmark and the Netherlands contended it did. Hence, they argued, the equidistance method of delimiting the continental shelf of adjacent states incorporated in Article 6 was binding upon the Federal Republic of Germany even though it was not a party to the convention as Denmark and the Netherlands were. After an extensive review of the history of the equidistance method of delimitation, the International Court of Justice concluded it was not a rule of customary international law and hence was binding only on parties to the convention.

2.   Convention on the High Seas, which entered into force on September 30, 1962; as of Jan. 1, 1972, 49 states were parties to this convention; and

3.   Convention on the Continental Shelf, which entered into force on June 10, 1964; as of Jan. 1, 1972, 49 states were parties to this convention.

A fourth, Convention on Fishing and Conservation of the Living Resources of the High Seas, is not included.   The text of this convention is in 17 U.S.T. 138, 559 U.N.T.S. 285.

3.   *New conference on the law of the sea scheduled for 1974.* A second conference on the law of the sea was convened in 1960 essentially to seek agreement on the breadth of the territorial sea, but none was reached.

In 1970, the General Assembly of the United Nations decided to convene a third conference on the law of the sea in 1973.   The assembly assigned the task of preparing draft articles to its Committee on the Peaceful Uses of the Seabed and the Ocean Floor Beyond the Limits of National Jurisdiction.   The committee held meetings in 1971 and 1972.   It produced some draft articles on seabed principles. As to all other aspects of the law of the sea, it reached agreement only on an agenda of 107 issues, and did not begin the drafting of articles. In 1972, the assembly rescheduled the conference on the law of the sea to take place in Santiago, Chile, April–May 1974.

SECTION A.   WATERS WITHIN THE TERRITORY

1.   BASELINE SEPARATING INTERNAL WATERS FROM TERRITORIAL SEA

Significance of baseline. The baseline separates internal waters from the territorial sea; the breadth of the territorial sea is measured from that line.   The manner in which the baseline is drawn is important because this can be done in such a way as to thrust it far away from the coast with two resulting consequences: first, expansion of the area of inland waters lying between the coast and the baseline; second, placing the outer limit of the territorial sea, which is measured from the baseline, at great distances from the coast.

Suppose, by way of exaggerated example, that the baseline on the eastern coast of the United States were drawn by means of a straight line running from Maine to the tip of Florida.   A huge area of the sea inside the baseline would become internal waters, i.e. assimilated to land territory so far as concerns the jurisdiction of the United States. Moreover the outer limit of the territorial sea of the United States would at some points be so many miles from the coast as to make arguments about the breadth of the territorial sea—3 miles, 12 miles, and the like—entirely meaningless.

FISHERIES CASE (UNITED KINGDOM v. NORWAY)

International Court of Justice, 1951.
[1951] I.C.J.Rep. 116.

* * *

On September 28th, 1949, the Government of the United Kingdom of Great Britain and Northern Ireland filed in the Registry an Application instituting proceedings before the Court against the Kingdom of Norway, the subject of the proceedings being the validity or otherwise, under international law, of the lines of delimitation of the Norwegian fisheries zone laid down by the Royal Decree of July 12th, 1935, as amended by a Decree of December 10th, 1937, for that part of Norway which is situated northward of 66° 28.8′ (or 66° 28′ 48″) N. latitude. The Application refers to the Declarations by which the United Kingdom and Norway have accepted the compulsory jurisdiction of the Court in accordance with Article 36, paragraph 2, of the Statute.

* * *

The facts which led the United Kingdom to bring the case before the Court are briefly as follows.

The historical facts laid before the Court establish that as the result of complaints from the King of Denmark and of Norway, at the beginning of the seventeenth century, British fishermen refrained from fishing in Norwegian coastal waters for a long period, from 1616–1618 until 1906.

In 1906 a few British fishing vessels appeared off the coasts of Eastern Finnmark. From 1908 onwards they returned in greater numbers. These were trawlers equipped with improved and powerful gear. The local population became perturbed, and measures were taken by the Norwegian Government with a view to specifying the limits within which fishing was prohibited to foreigners.

The first incident occurred in 1911 when a British trawler was seized and condemned for having violated these measures. Negotiations ensued between the two Governments. These were interrupted by the war in 1914. From 1922 onwards incidents recurred. Further conversations were initiated in 1924. In 1932, British trawlers, extending the range of their activities, appeared in the sectors off the Norwegian coast west of the North Cape, and the number of warnings and arrests increased. On July 27th, 1933, the United Kingdom Government sent a memorandum to the Norwegian Government complaining that in delimiting the territorial sea the Norwegian authorities had made use of unjustifiable base-lines. On July 12th, 1935, a Norwegian Royal Decree was enacted delimiting the Norwegian fisheries zone north of 66° 28.8′ North latitude.

* * *

The Norwegian Royal Decree of July 12th, 1935, concerning the delimitation of the Norwegian fisheries zone sets out in the preamble the considerations on which its provisions are based. In this connection it refers to "well-established national titles of right", "the geographical conditions prevailing on the Norwegian coasts", "the safeguard of the vital interests of the inhabitants of the northernmost parts of the country"; it further relies on the Royal Decrees of February 22nd, 1812, October 16th, 1869, January 5th, 1881, and September 9th, 1889.

The Decree provides that "lines of delimitation towards the high sea of the Norwegian fisheries zone as regards that part of Norway which is situated northward of 66° 28.8′ North latitude * * * shall run parallel with straight base-lines drawn between fixed points on the mainland, on islands or rocks, starting from the final point of the boundary line of the Realm in the easternmost part of the Varangerfjord and going as far as Træna in the County of Nordland". An appended schedule indicates the fixed points between which the base-lines are drawn.

* * *

Although the Decree of July 12th, 1935, refers to the Norwegian fisheries zone and does not specifically mention the territorial sea, there can be no doubt that the zone delimited by this Decree is none other than the sea area which Norway considers to be her territorial sea. That is how the Parties argued the question and that is the way in which they submitted it to the Court for decision.

* * *

The claim of the United Kingdom Government is founded on what it regards as the general international law applicable to the delimitation of the Norwegian fisheries zone.

The Norwegian Government does not deny that there exist rules of international law to which this delimitation must conform. It contends that the propositions formulated by the United Kingdom Government in its "Conclusions" do not possess the character attributed to them by that Government. It further relies on its own system of delimitation which it asserts to be in every respect in conformity with the requirements of international law.

The Court will examine in turn these various aspects of the claim of the United Kingdom and of the defence of the Norwegian Government.

The coastal zone concerned in the dispute is of considerable length. It lies north of latitude 66° 28.8′ N., that is to say, north of the Arctic Circle, and it includes the coast of the mainland of Norway and all the islands, islets, rocks and reefs, known by the name of the "skjær-gaard" (literally, rock rampart), together with all Norwegian internal and territorial waters. The coast of the mainland, which, without taking any account of fjords, bays and minor indentations, is over 1,500 kilometres in length, is of a very distinctive configuration. Very broken along its whole length, it constantly opens out into indentations often penetrating for great distances inland: the Porsanger-fjord, for instance, penetrates 75 sea miles inland. To the west, the land configuration stretches out into the sea: the large and small islands, mountainous in character, the islets, rocks and reefs, some always above water, others emerging only at low tide, are in truth but an extension of the Norwegian mainland. The number of insular formations, large and small, which make up the "skjærgaard", is estimated by the Norwegian Government to be one hundred and twenty thousand. From the southern extremity of the disputed area to the North Cape, the "skjærgaard" lies along the whole of the coast of the mainland; east of the North Cape, the "skjærgaard" ends, but the coast line continues to be broken by large and deeply indented fjords.

Within the "skjærgaard", almost every island has its large and its small bays; countless arms of the sea, straits, channels and mere waterways serve as a means of communication for the local population which inhabits the islands as it does the mainland. The coast of the mainland does not constitute, as it does in practically all other countries, a clear dividing line between land and sea. What matters, what really constitutes the Norwegian coast line, is the outer line of the "skjærgaard".

The whole of this region is mountainous. The North Cape, a sheer rock little more than 300 metres high, can be seen from a considerable distance; there are other summits rising to over a thousand metres, so that the Norwegian coast, mainland and "skjærgaard", is visible from far off.

Along the coast are situated comparatively shallow banks, veritable under-water terraces which constitute fishing grounds where fish are particularly abundant; these grounds were known to Norwegian fishermen and exploited by them from time immemorial. Since these banks lay within the range of vision, the most desirable fishing grounds were always located and identified by means of the method of alignments ("meds"), at points where two lines drawn between points selected on the coast or on islands intersected.

In these barren regions the inhabitants of the coastal zone derive their livelihood essentially from fishing.

Such are the realities which must be borne in mind in appraising the validity of the United Kingdom contention that the limits of the Norwegian fisheries zone laid down in the 1935 Decree are contrary to international law.

The Parties being in agreement on the figure of 4 miles for the breadth of the territorial sea, the problem which arises is from what base-line this breadth is to be reckoned. The Conclusions of the United Kingdom are explicit on this point: the base-line must be low-water mark on permanently dry land which is a part of Norwegian territory, or the proper closing line of Norwegian internal waters.

The Court has no difficulty in finding that, for the purpose of measuring the breadth of the territorial sea, it is the low-water mark as opposed to the high-water mark, or the mean between the two tides, which has generally been adopted in the practice of States. This criterion is the most favourable to the coastal State and clearly shows the character of territorial waters as appurtenant to the land territory. The Court notes that the Parties agree as to this criterion, but that they differ as to its application.

* * *

The Court finds itself obliged to decide whether the relevant low-water mark is that of the mainland or of the "skjærgaard". Since the mainland is bordered in its western sector by the "skjærgaard", which constitutes a whole with the mainland, it is the outer line of the "skjærgaard" which must be taken into account in delimiting the belt of Norwegian territorial waters. This solution is dictated by geographic realities.

Three methods have been contemplated to effect the application of the low-water mark rule. The simplest would appear to be the method of the *tracé parallèle*, which consists of drawing the outer limit of the belt of territorial waters by following the coast in all its sinuosities. This method may be applied without difficulty to an ordinary coast, which is not too broken. Where a coast is deeply indented and cut into, as is that of Eastern Finnmark, or where it is bordered by an archipelago such as the "skjærgaard" along the western sector of the coast here in question, the base-line becomes independent of the low-water mark, and can only be determined by means of a geometrical construction. In such circumstances the line of the low-water mark can no longer be put forward as a rule requiring the coastline to be followed in all its sinuosities. Nor can one characterize as exceptions to the rule the very many derogations which would be necessitated by such a rugged coast: the rule would disappear under the exceptions. Such a coast, viewed as a whole, calls for the application of a different method; that is, the method of base-lines which, within reasonable limits, may depart from the physical line of the coast.

[The court determined it need not deal with the other methods]

The principle that the belt of territorial waters must follow the general direction of the coast makes it possible to fix certain criteria valid for any delimitation of the territorial sea; these criteria will be elucidated later. The Court will confine itself at this stage to noting that, in order to apply this principle, several States have deemed it necessary to follow the straight base-lines method and that they have not encountered objections of principle by other States. This method consists of selecting appropriate points on the low-water mark and drawing straight lines between them. This has been done, not only in the case of well-defined bays, but also in cases of minor curvatures of the coast line where it was solely a question of giving a simpler form to the belt of territorial waters.

It has been contended, on behalf of the United Kingdom, that Norway may draw straight lines only across bays. The Court is unable to share this view. If the belt of territorial waters must follow the outer line of the "skjærgaard", and if the method of straight base-lines must be admitted in certain cases, there is no valid reason to draw them only across bays, as in Eastern Finnmark, and not also to draw them between islands, islets and rocks, across the sea areas separating them, even when such areas do not fall within the conception of a bay. It is sufficient that they should be situated between the island formations of the "skjærgaard", *inter fauces terrarum*.

* * *

* * * [T]he United Kingdom Government concedes that Norway is entitled to claim as internal waters all the waters of fjords and sunds which fall within the conception of a bay as defined in international law whether the closing line of the indentation is more or less than ten sea miles long. But the United Kingdom Government concedes this only on the basis of historic title; it must therefore be taken that that Government has not abandoned its contention that the ten-mile rule is to be regarded as a rule of international law.

In these circumstances the Court deems it necessary to point out that although the ten-mile rule has been adopted by certain States both in their national law and in their treaties and conventions, and although certain arbitral decisions have applied it as between these States, other States have adopted a different limit. Consequently, the ten-mile rule has not acquired the authority of a general rule of international law.

In any event the ten-mile rule would appear to be inapplicable as against Norway inasmuch as she has always opposed any attempt to apply it to the Norwegian coast.

The Court now comes to the question of the length of the baselines drawn across the waters lying between the various formations of the "skjærgaard". Basing itself on the analogy with the alleged general rule of ten miles relating to bays, the United Kingdom Government still maintains on this point that the length of straight lines must not exceed ten miles.

In this connection, the practice of States does not justify the formulation of any general rule of law. The attempts that have been made to subject groups of islands or coastal archipelagoes to conditions analogous to the limitations concerning bays (distance between the islands not exceeding twice the breadth of the territorial waters, or ten or twelve sea miles), have not got beyond the stage of proposals.

Furthermore, apart from any question of limiting the lines to ten miles, it may be that several lines can be envisaged. In such cases the coastal State would seem to be in the best position to appraise the local conditions dictating the selection.

Consequently, the Court is unable to share the view of the United Kingdom Government, that "Norway, in the matter of base-lines, now claims recognition of an exceptional system". As will be shown later, all that the Court can see therein is the application of general international law to a specific case.

*   *   *

It does not at all follow that, in the absence of rules having the technically precise character alleged by the United Kingdom Government, the delimitation undertaken by the Norwegian Government in 1935 is not subject to certain principles which make it possible to judge as to its validity under international law. The delimitation of sea areas has always an international aspect; it cannot be dependent merely upon the will of the coastal State as expressed in its municipal law. Although it is true that the act of delimitation is necessarily a unilateral act, because only the coastal State is competent to undertake it, the validity of the delimitation with regard to other States depends upon international law.

In this connection, certain basic considerations inherent in the nature of the territorial sea, bring to light certain criteria which, though not entirely precise, can provide courts with an adequate basis for their decisions, which can be adapted to the diverse facts in question.

Among these considerations, some reference must be made to the close dependence of the territorial sea upon the land domain. It is the land which confers upon the coastal State a right to the waters off its coasts. It follows that while such a State must be allowed the latitude necessary in order to be able to adapt its delimitation to practical needs and local requirements, the drawing of base-lines must not depart to any appreciable extent from the general direction of the coast.

Another fundamental consideration, of particular importance in this case, is the more or less close relationship existing between certain sea areas and the land formations which divide or surround them.

✱ The real question raised in the choice of base-lines is in effect whether certain sea areas lying within these lines are sufficiently closely linked to the land domain to be subject to the regime of internal waters. This idea, which is at the basis of the determination of the rules relating to bays, should be liberally applied in the case of a coast, the geographical configuration of which is as unusual as that of Norway.

Finally, there is one consideration not to be overlooked, the scope of which extends beyond purely geographical factors: that of certain economic interests peculiar to a region, the reality and importance of which are clearly evidenced by a long usage.

Norway puts forward the 1935 Decree as the application of a traditional system of delimitation, a system which she claims to be in complete conformity with international law. The Norwegian Government has referred in this connection to an historic title, the meaning of which was made clear by Counsel for Norway at the sitting on October 12th, 1951: "The Norwegian Government does not rely upon history to justify exceptional rights, to claim areas of sea which the general law would deny; it invokes history, together with other factors, to justify the way in which it applies the general law." This conception of an historic title is in consonance with the Norwegian Government's understanding of the general rules of international law. In its view, these rules of international law take into account the diversity of facts and, therefore, concede that the drawing of base-lines must be adapted to the special conditions obtaining in different regions. In its view, the system of delimitation applied in 1935, a system characterized by the use of straight lines, does not therefore infringe the general law; it is an adaptation rendered necessary by local conditions.

The Court must ascertain precisely what this alleged system of delimitation consists of, what is its effect in law as against the United Kingdom, and whether it was applied by the 1935 Decree in a manner which conformed to international law.

[The court reviewed the historical development of the Norwegian legislation establishing the baselines method].

In the light of these considerations, and in the absence of convincing evidence to the contrary, the Court is bound to hold that the Norwegian authorities applied their system of delimitation consistently and uninterruptedly from 1869 until the time when the dispute arose.

From the standpoint of international law, it is now necessary to consider whether the application of the Norwegian system encountered any opposition from foreign States.

Norway has been in a position to argue without any contradiction that neither the promulgation of her delimitation Decrees in 1869 and in 1889, nor their application, gave rise to any opposition on the part of foreign States. Since, moreover, these Decrees constitute, as has been shown above, the application of a well-defined and uniform system, it is indeed this system itself which would reap the benefit of general toleration, the basis of an historical consolidation which would make it enforceable as against all States.

The general toleration of foreign States with regard to the Norwegian practice is an unchallenged fact. For a period of more than sixty years the United Kingdom Government itself in no way contested it. One cannot indeed consider as raising objections the discussions to which the Lord Roberts incident gave rise in 1911, for the controversy which arose in this connection related to two questions, that of the four-mile limit, and that of Norwegian sovereignty over the Varangerfjord, both of which were unconnected with the position of base-lines. It would appear that it was only in its Memorandum of July 27th, 1933, that the United Kingdom made a formal and definite protest on this point.

* * *

The Court is thus led to conclude that the method of straight lines, established in the Norwegian system, was imposed by the peculiar geography of the Norwegian coast; that even before the dispute arose, this method had been consolidated by a constant and sufficiently long practice, in the face of which the attitude of governments bears witness to the fact that they did not consider it to be contrary to international law.

The question now arises whether the Decree of July 12th, 1935, which in its preamble is expressed to be an application of this method, conforms to it in its drawing of the base-lines, or whether, at certain points, it departs from this method to any considerable extent.

[The court reviewed the arguments and concluded that Norway had properly applied the straight baselines method].

For these reasons,

THE COURT, rejecting all submissions to the contrary, Finds by ten votes to two, that the method employed for the delimitation of the fisheries zone by the Royal Norwegian Decree of July 12th, 1935, is not contrary to international law; and by eight votes to four, that the base-lines fixed by the said Decree in application of this method are not contrary to international law.

* * *

[A declaration, individual and dissenting opinions omitted].

Convention on the Territorial Sea and the Contiguous Zone. The convention deals in detail with the drawing of the baseline. See Articles 3 through 13, Documentary Supplement.

Article 4 deals specifically with the use of the "straight baselines method." Compare the provision of this article with the terms of the decision in the Fisheries Case upholding the validity of the straight baseline method and its application by Norway. Are the two entirely consistent or does the convention go further than the decision?

Article 5 of the convention makes provision for a right of innocent passage, under certain conditions, through inland waters created by the use of the straight baselines method. Why?

Article 6 provides that the outer limit of the territorial sea "is the line every point of which is at a distance from the nearest point on the baseline equal to the breadth of the territorial sea." But the convention does not establish the number of miles which constitute the "breadth of the territorial sea."

---

2.   FOREIGN VESSELS IN INTERNAL WATERS

Consent to entry into internal waters. Foreign vessels enter the internal waters of a coastal state only with its consent.

As to merchant vessels, the consent is usually implied. Prohibiting the entry of foreign merchant vessels is the exception rather than the rule in practice. The United States prohibits Soviet vessels from bunkering in its ports if they have called or will call at Cuban, North Vietnamese or North Korean ports. In addition, the United States and the Soviet Union each conditions the entry into its ports of merchant vessels of the other upon a 14 day advance request. They signed on October 14, 1972 an Agreement Regarding Certain Maritime Matters which lowers the requirement to a 4 day advance notice so far as concerns 40 designated ports in the United States and 40 in the Soviet Union. For a press release discussing the maritime relations of the two states and for the text of the agreement, see 67 U. S. Dep't State Bull. 661 (1972).

As to naval vessels, formal notification of their intended visit is customary. Unless the coastal state expressly prohibits the visit, naval vessels are deemed to have received the necessary consent.

WILDENHUS'S CASE

United States Supreme Court, 1887.
120 U.S. 1, 7 S.Ct. 385.

This appeal brought up an application made to the Circuit Court of the United States for the District of New Jersey, by Charles Mali, the "Consul of His Majesty the King of the Belgians, for the States of New York and New Jersey, in the United States," for himself as such consul, "and in behalf of one Joseph Wildenhus, one Gionviennie Gobnbosich, and one John J. Ostenmeyer," for the release, upon a writ of habeas corpus, of Wildenhus, Gobnbosich, and Ostenmeyer from the custody of the keeper of the common jail of Hudson County, New Jersey, and their delivery to the consul, "to be dealt with according to the law of Belgium." The facts on which the application rested were thus stated in the petition for the writ:

Second.   That on or about the sixth day of October, 1886, on board the Belgian steamship Noordland, there occurred an affray between the said Joseph Wildenhus and one Fijens, wherein and whereby it is charged that the said Wildenhus stabbed with a knife and inflicted upon the said Fijens a mortal wound, of which he afterwards died.   W. KILLS

FIJENS

Third.   That the said Wildenhus is a subject of the Kingdom of Belgium and has his domicil therein, and is one of the crew of the said steamship Noordland, and was such when the said affray occurred.

Fourth.   That the said Fijens was also a subject of Belgium and had his domicil and residence therein, and at the time of the said affray, as well as at the time of his subsequent death, was one of the crew of the said steamship.

Fifth.   That at the time said affray occurred the said steamship Noordland was lying moored at the dock of the port of Jersey City, in said state of New Jersey.

Sixth.   That the said affray occurred and ended wholly below the deck of the said steamship, and that the tranquillity of the said port of Jersey City was in nowise disturbed or endangered thereby.

Seventh.   That said affray occurred in the presence of several witnesses all of whom were and still are of the crew of the said vessel, and that no other person or persons except those of the crew of said vessel were present or near by.

Eighth.   Your petitioner therefore respectfully shows unto this honorable court that the said affray occurred outside of the jurisdiction of the said state of New Jersey.

Ninth.   But, notwithstanding the foregoing facts, your petitioner respectfully further shows that the police authorities of Jersey City, in said state of New Jersey, have arrested the said Joseph Wildenhus, and also the said Gionviennie Gobnbosich and John J. Ostenmeyer, of the crew of the said vessel (one of whom is a quartermaster thereof), and that said Joseph Wildenhus has been committed by a police magistrate, acting under the authority of the said state, to the common jail of the county of Hudson, on a charge of an indictable offence under the laws of the said state of New Jersey, and is now held in confinement by the keeper of the said jail, and that the others of the said crew arrested as aforesaid are also detained in custody and confinement as witnesses to testify in such proceedings as may hereafter be had against the said Wildenhus.

* * *

Article XI of a Convention between the United States and Belgium "concerning the rights, privileges, and immunities of consular officers," concluded March 9, 1880, and proclaimed by the President of the United States, March 1, 1881, 21 Stat. 776, 781, is as follows:

The respective consuls-general, consuls, vice-consuls, and consular agents shall have exclusive charge of the internal order of the merchant vessels of their nation, and shall alone take cognizance of all differences which may arise, either at sea or in port, between the captains, officers, and crews, without exception, particularly with reference to the adjustment of wages and the execution of contracts. The local authorities shall not interfere, except when the disorder that has arisen is of such a nature as to disturb tranquillity and public order on shore, or in the port, or when a person of the country or not belonging to the crew, shall be concerned therein.

In all other cases, the aforesaid authorities shall confine themselves to lending aid to the consuls and vice-consuls or consular agents, if they are requested by them to do so, in causing the arrest and imprisonment of any person whose name is inscribed on the crew list, whenever, for any cause, the said officers shall think proper.

The claim of the consul was, that, by the law of nations, and the provisions of this treaty, the offence with which Wildenhus was charged is "solely cognizable by the authority of the laws of the Kingdom of Belgium," and that the State of New Jersey was without jurisdiction in the premises. The Circuit Court refused to deliver the prisoners to the consul and remanded them to the custody of the jailer. 28 Fed.Rep. 924. To reverse that decision this appeal was taken.

* * *

MR. CHIEF JUSTICE WAITE, after stating the case as above reported, delivered the opinion of the court.

By §§ 751 and 753 of the Revised Statutes the courts of the United States have power to issue writs of habeas corpus which shall extend to prisoners in jail when they are in "custody in violation of the Constitution or a law or treaty of the United States," and the question we have to consider is, whether these prisoners are held in violation of the provisions of the existing treaty between the United States and Belgium.

It is part of the law of civilized nations that when a merchant vessel of one country enters the ports of another for the purposes of trade, it subjects itself to the law of the place to which it goes, unless by treaty or otherwise the two countries have come to some different understanding or agreement; for, as was said by Chief Justice

Marshall in The Exchange, 7 Cranch, 116, 144, "it would be obviously inconvenient and dangerous to society, and would subject the laws to continual infraction, and the government to degradation, if such . . . merchants did not owe temporary and local allegiance, and were not amenable to the jurisdiction of the country." * * * And the English judges have uniformly recognized the rights of the courts of the country of which the port is part to punish crimes committed by one foreigner on another in a foreign merchant ship. * * * As the owner has voluntarily taken his vessel for his own private purposes to a place within the dominion of a government other than his own, and from which he seeks protection during his stay, he owes that government such allegiance for the time being as is due for the protection to which he becomes entitled.

From experience, however, it was found long ago that it would be beneficial to commerce if the local government would abstain from interfering with the internal discipline of the ship, and the general regulation of the rights and duties of the officers and crew towards the vessel or among themselves. And so by comity it came to be generally understood among civilized nations that all matters of discipline and all things done on board which affected only the vessel or those belonging to her, and did not involve the peace or dignity of the country, or the tranquillity of the port, should be left by the local government to be dealt with by the authorities of the nation to which the vessel belonged as the laws of that nation or the interests of its commerce should require. But if crimes are committed on board of a character to disturb the peace and tranquillity of the country to which the vessel has been brought, the offenders have never by comity or usage been entitled to any exemption from the operation of the local laws for their punishment, if the local tribunals see fit to assert their authority. Such being the general public law on this subject, treaties and conventions have been entered into by nations having commercial intercourse, the purpose of which was to settle and define the rights and duties of the contracting parties with respect to each other in these particulars, and thus prevent the inconvenience that might arise from attempts to exercise conflicting jurisdictions.

* * *

Next came a form of convention which in terms gave the consuls authority to cause proper order to be maintained on board and to decide disputes between the officers and crew, but allowed the local authorities to interfere if the disorders taking place on board were of such a nature as to disturb the public tranquillity, and that is substantially all there is in the convention with Belgium which we have now to consider. This treaty is the law which now governs the conduct of the United States and Belgium towards each other in this particular. Each nation has granted to the other such local jurisdiction within its own dominion as may be necessary to maintain order on board a merchant vessel, but has reserved to itself the right to interfere if the disorder on board is of a nature to disturb the public tranquillity.

The treaty is part of the supreme law of the United States, and has the same force and effect in New Jersey that it is entitled to elsewhere. If it gives the consul of Belgium exclusive jurisdiction over the offence which it is alleged has been committed within the territory of New Jersey, we see no reason why he may not enforce his rights under the treaty by writ of habeas corpus in any proper court of the United States. This being the case, the only important question left for our determination is whether the thing which has been done—the disorder that has arisen—on board this vessel is of a nature to disturb the public peace, or, as some writers term it, the "public repose" of the people who look to the state of New Jersey for their protection. If the thing done—"the disorder," as it is called in the treaty—is of a character to affect those on shore or in the port when it becomes known, the fact that only those on the ship saw it when it was done is a matter of no moment. Those who are not on the vessel pay no special attention to the mere disputes or quarrels of the seamen while on board, whether they occur under deck or above. Neither do they as a rule care for anything done on board which relates only to the discipline of the ship, or to the preservation of order and authority. Not so, however, with crimes which from their gravity awaken a public interest as soon as they become known, and especially those of a character which every civilized nation considers itself bound to provide a severe punishment for when committed within its own jurisdiction. In such cases inquiry is certain to be instituted at once to ascertain how or why the thing was done, and the popular excitement rises or falls as the news spreads and the facts become known. It is not alone the publicity of the act, or the noise and clamor which attends it, that fixes the nature of the crime, but the act itself. If that is of a character to awaken public interest when it becomes known, it is a "disorder" the nature of which is to affect the community at large, and consequently to invoke the power of the local government whose people have been disturbed by what was done. The very nature of such an act is to disturb the quiet of a peaceful community, and to create, in the language of the treaty, a "disorder" which will "disturb tranquillity and public order on shore or in the port." The principle which governs the whole matter is this: Disorders which disturb only the peace of the ship or those on board are to be dealt with exclusively by the sovereignty of the home of the ship, but those which disturb the public peace may be suppressed, and, if need be, the offenders punished by the proper authorities of the local jurisdiction. It may not be easy at all times to determine to which of the two jurisdictions a particular act of disorder belongs. Much will undoubtedly depend on the attending circumstances of the particular case, but all must concede that felonious homicide is a subject for the local jurisdiction, and that if the proper authorities are proceeding with the case in a regular way, the consul has no right to interfere to prevent it.   That, according to the petition for the habeas corpus, is this case.

* * *

The judgment of the Circuit Court is affirmed.

---

1. *Questions.*   Is a treaty necessary for the application of the principle enunciated by the court?   Would an accused be able to defend on the ground that the crime of which he is charged did not disturb the peace of the port?

2. *Convention on the Territorial Sea and Contiguous Zone.*   The convention provides in Article 19 that criminal jurisdiction should not be exercised on board a foreign vessel passing through the territorial sea to arrest a person in connection with any crime committed on board during passage except in specific instances, including among them: "If the crime is of a kind to disturb the peace of the country or the good order of the territorial sea."   The convention does not speak to the question of crimes committed while a foreign vessel is in port.

3. *Foreign naval vessels in port.*   In The Schooner Exchange v. McFaddon, 7 Cranch 116 (U.S.1812), Chief Justice Marshall said: " * * *   [T]he Exchange being a public armed ship, in the service of a foreign sovereign, with whom the government of the United States is at peace, and having entered an American port open for her reception, on the terms on which ships of war are generally permitted to enter the ports of a friendly power, must be considered as having come into the American territory, under an implied promise that * * *   she should be exempt from the jurisdiction of the country." (at 147)

The question whether a person can seek asylum aboard a foreign naval vessel in port is raised in Chapter 9.

HOFF, ADMINISTRATRIX
(UNITED STATES v. UNITED
MEXICAN STATES)

General Claims Commission, 1929.
IV U.N.Rep. Int'l Arb. Awards 444.

COMMISSIONER NIELSEN, FOR THE COMMISSION:

Claim in the amount of $10,000.00 with interest is made in this case by the United States of America in behalf of Kate Allison Hoff, Administratrix of the estate of Samuel B. Allison.   The latter was the owner of a small American schooner called the Rebecca, which together with its cargo was seized by Mexican authorities at Tampico in 1884. Allegations with respect to the occurrences on which the claim is predicated are made in the Memorial in substance as follows:

The Rebecca was built in the United States and registered at Galveston, Texas. Its approximate value was $5,000.00. In the month of January, 1884, Gilbert F. Dujay, the master of the vessel, loaded it at a small port called Patersonville, nine miles above Morgan City, in the State of Louisiana, with a cargo consisting of six cases of merchandise destined for Brazos Santiago, Texas, and of a consignment of lumber for Tampico, Mexico. The vessel cleared at Brashear City, now known as Morgan City, on the 30th day of January, 1884, bound for Santiago, Texas. When it reached a point off this port the wind and the tide were so high that it was unsafe to enter. While lying off Brazos Santiago, on the 13th of February, waiting for a favorable opportunity to enter the port, an adverse wind from the north became so strong and the sea so rough, that the vessel was driven to the southward before a furious wind and sea, and when the wind abated it was found that the vessel was in a disabled and unsafe condition off the port of Tampico. The master, realizing the dangerous condition of his vessel, entered the port of Tampico as the nearest place of safety for the vessel, cargo and crew. The crew concurred in and advised such action. When the Rebecca entered the port she was leaking badly. Her standing rigging had been torn away. The cabin windows were broken. The cooking stove was so badly broken it could not be used. While at sea the vessel began to leak so that the water reached the cases of merchandise, and the crew was compelled to break open the packages and store them so that they would not be ruined by the water.

When the Rebecca entered the port the master presented to the Mexican customs official a manifest for the goods destined for Tampico and a so-called "master's manifest" for the consignment for Brazos Santiago, Texas, which met the requirements of the law of the United States. As soon as the vessel reached Tampico, which was on Sunday afternoon, February 17th, it was anchored off the custom house and a protest of distress was immediately entered with A. J. Cassard, the American Consul at that port.

On the day following the arrival at Tampico, February 18, 1884, the Mexican custom house officials demanded from the master of the Rebecca the packages of merchandise on board the vessel. The demand was refused and thereupon the packages were taken by force and no receipt or other evidence of possession by the custom house authorities was given.

On the 21st of February the master was arrested on a charge of attempt to smuggle, was placed in the barracks with armed soldiers guarding him, was not permitted to speak to anyone, and was kept in close confinement until the day following, a period of 28 hours, when he was brought before the Judge of the District Court at Tampico, and without the privilege of having counsel, was tried and was acquitted and released. On the 23rd of February the master was again arrested by the Mexican authorities and was required to give bond for his appearance before the Criminal Court at Tampico to answer a charge of bringing goods into a Mexican port without proper papers. While awaiting trial he remained under bond, but without permission to leave Mexico, until the 24th day of April, a period of over two months. On that date a decree was entered by the court which released the master from bail but assessed treble damages against the merchandise seized, and charged the master with the cost of revenue stamps used in the proceedings. Because of the refusal and inability of the master to pay the penalties thus assessed, the Rebecca and its cargo were sold by order of court, and the proceeds were applied to the Federal Treasury, a balance being distributed among certain customs employees.

* * *

It is of course well established that, when a merchant vessel belonging to one nation enters the territorial waters of another nation, it becomes amenable to the jurisdiction of the latter and is subject to its laws, except in so far as treaty stipulations may relieve the vessel from the operation of local laws. On the other hand, there appears to be general recognition among the nations of the world of what may doubtless be considered to be an exception, or perhaps it may be said two exceptions, to this general, fundamental rule of subjection to local jurisdiction over vessels in foreign ports.

Recognition has been given to the so-called right of "innocent passage" for vessels through the maritime belt in so far as it forms a part of the high seas for international traffic. Similarly, recognition has also been given—perhaps it may be said in a more concrete and emphatic manner—to the immunity of a ship whose presence in territorial waters is due to a superior force. The principles with respect to the status of a vessel in "distress" find recognition both in domestic laws and in international law. * * *

* * *

While recognizing the general principle of immunity of vessels in distress, domestic courts and international courts have frequently given consideration to the question as to the degree of necessity prompting vessels to seek refuge. It has been said that the necessity must be urgent. It seems possible to formulate certain reasonably concrete criteria applicable and controlling in the instant case. Assuredly a ship floundering in distress, resulting either from the weather or from other causes affecting management of the vessel, need not be in such a condition that it is dashed helplessly on the shore or against rocks before a claim of distress can properly be invoked in its behalf. The fact that it may be able to come into port under its own power can obviously not be cited as conclusive evidence that the plea is unjustifiable. If a captain delayed seeking refuge until his ship was wrecked, obviously he would not be using his best judgment with a view to the preservation of the ship, the cargo and the lives of people on board. Clearly an important consideration may be the determination of the question whether there is any evidence in a given case of a fraudulent attempt to circumvent local laws. And even in the absence of any such attempt, it can probably be correctly said that a mere matter of convenience in making repairs or in avoiding a measure of difficulty in navigation can not justify a disregard of local laws.

The Rebecca did sail into Tampico, as observed by the judge who condemned the vessel, under its own power. However, it did not enter the port until after it had for three days, in a crippled condition, been contending with a storm in an attempt to enter the port at Brazos Santiago, Texas. It is therefore certain that the vessel did not by choice abandon its attempt to make port at that place, but only because according to the best judgment of the captain and his crew absolute necessity so required. In such a case a captain's judgment would scarcely seem subject to question. It may also be concluded from the evidence in the case that a well grounded apprehension of the loss of the vessel and cargo and persons on board prompted the captain to turn south towards Tampico. It was argued in behalf of the United States that under the conditions of the weather it could be assumed that no other port of refuge was available. And even if such were not the case, there would seem to be no reason why refuge should not have been sought at Tampico. The fact that the ship had cargo for that place in addition to that consigned to Brazos Santiago, did not make the former any less available as the port of refuge. It may be concluded from the evidence that the captain had no intent to perpetrate a fraud on Mexican customs laws. Indeed his acquittal on the criminal charge preferred against him appears to be conclusive on that point, even if there were no other evidence bearing on the matter which there is. It may also be concluded that the captain had no intent merely as a matter of convenience to flout Mexican laws. This very small vessel had been driven before a strong north wind; its cabin had been damaged; its pumps had been broken and repaired; the cooking stove on the vessel had been rendered useless; there were one and a half to two feet of water in the vessel; and it had been leaking.

*   *   *   The ship entered the port of Tampico in distress, and the seizure of both the vessel and cargo was wrongful.

*   *   *

Decision

The United Mexican States shall pay to the United States of America on behalf of Kate A. Hoff the sum of $5,000.00, with interest at the rate of six per centum per annum from April 24, 1884, to the date on which the last award is rendered by the Commission.

---

1. *Basis of decision.* The compromis establishing the USA/Mexican General Claims Commission provided that the claims to be submitted to the commission should be decided "in accordance with the principles of international law, justice and equity." IV U.N.Rep. Int'l Arb.Awards 11, 12.

2. *Nuclear vessels.* A Convention on the Liability of Operators of Nuclear Ships was signed at Brussels, May 25, 1962. Its text appears at 57 Am.J.Int'l L. 268 (1963). Article 17 provides:

> Nothing in this Convention shall affect any right which a Contracting State may have under international law to deny access to its waters and harbours to nuclear ships licensed by another Contracting State, even when it has formally complied with all the provisions of this Convention.

Does a contracting state have a right under international law to deny access to a nuclear ship entering in distress? What if the distress is a leaking nuclear reactor? See the Restatement of the Foreign Relations Law of the United States, Reporters' Note to Section 48 (1965).

---

3. FOREIGN VESSELS IN THE TERRITORIAL SEA

CORFU CHANNEL CASE (UNITED KINGDOM v. ALBANIA)

International Court of Justice, 1949.
[1949] I.C.J.Rep. 4.

* * *

By the first part of the Special Agreement, the following question is submitted to the Court:

> (1) Is Albania responsible under international law for the explosions which occurred on the 22nd October 1946 in Albanian waters and for the damage and loss of human life which resulted from them and is there any duty to pay compensation?

On October 22nd, 1946, a squadron of British warships, the cruisers Mauritius and Leander and the destroyers Saumarez and Volage, left the port of Corfu and proceeded northward through a channel previously swept for mines in the North Corfu Strait. The cruiser Mauritius was leading, followed by the destroyer Saumarez; at a certain distance thereafter came the cruiser Leander followed by the destroyer Volage. Outside the Bay of Saranda, Saumarez struck a mine and was heavily damaged. Volage was ordered to give her assistance and to take her in tow. Whilst towing the damaged ship, Volage struck a mine and was much damaged. Nevertheless, she succeeded in towing the other ship back to Corfu.

Three weeks later, on November 13th, the North Corfu Channel was swept by British minesweepers and twenty-two moored mines were cut. Two mines were taken to Malta for expert examination. During the minesweeping operation it was thought that the mines were of the German GR type, but it was subsequently established that they were of the German GY type.

The Court will consider first whether the two explosions that occurred on October 22nd, 1946, were caused by mines belonging to the minefield discovered on November 13th.

* * *

The Court * * * finds that the following facts are established. The two ships were mined in Albanian territorial waters in a previously swept and check-swept channel just at the place where a newly laid minefield consisting of moored contact German GY mines was discovered three weeks later. The damage sustained by the ships was inconsistent with damage which could have been caused by floating mines, magnetic ground mines, magnetic moored mines, or German GR mines, but its nature and extent were such as would be caused by mines of the type found in the minefield. In such circumstances the Court arrives at the conclusion that the explosions were due to mines belonging to that minefield.

* * *

To begin with, the foundation for Albania's responsibility, as alleged by the United Kingdom, must be considered. On this subject, the main position of the United Kingdom is to be found in its submission No. 2: that the minefield which caused the explosions was laid between May 15th, 1946, and October 22nd, 1946, by or with the connivance or knowledge of the Albanian Government.

* * *

From all the facts and observations mentioned above, the Court draws the conclusion that the laying of the minefield which caused the explosions on October 22nd, 1946, could not have been accomplished without the knowledge of the Albanian Government.

The obligations resulting for Albania from this knowledge are not disputed between the Parties. Counsel for the Albanian Government expressly recognized that [translation] "if Albania had been informed of the operation before the incidents of October 22nd, and in time to warn the British vessels and shipping in general of the existence of mines in the Corfu Channel, her responsibility would be involved * * *."

The obligations incumbent upon the Albanian authorities consisted in notifying, for the benefit of shipping in general, the exist-

ence of a minefield in Albanian territorial waters and in warning
the approaching British warships of the imminent danger to which
the minefield exposed them. Such obligations are based, not on the
Hague Convention of 1907, No. VIII, which is applicable in time of
war, but on certain general and well-recognized principles, namely:
elementary considerations of humanity, even more exacting in peace
than in war; the principle of the freedom of maritime communication; and every State's obligation not to allow knowingly its territory
to be used for acts contrary to the rights of other States.

OBLIGATORY GROUNDS

In fact, Albania neither notified the existence of the minefield,
nor warned the British warships of the danger they were approaching.

But Albania's obligation to notify shipping of the existence of
mines in her waters depends on her having obtained knowledge of
that fact in sufficient time before October 22nd; and the duty of
the Albanian coastal authorities to warn the British ships depends on
the time that elapsed between the moment that these ships were reported and the moment of the first explosion.

On this subject, the Court makes the following observations.
As has already been stated, the Parties agree that the mines were
recently laid. It must be concluded that the minelaying, whatever
may have been its exact date, was done at a time when there was a
close Albanian surveillance over the Strait. If it be supposed that it
took place at the last possible moment, i. e., in the night of October
21st-22nd, the only conclusion to be drawn would be that a general
notification to the shipping of all States before the time of the explosions would have been difficult, perhaps even impossible. But this
would certainly not have prevented the Albanian authorities from
taking, as they should have done, all necessary steps immediately to
warn ships near the danger zone, more especially those that were
approaching that zone. When on October 22nd about 13.00 hours
the British warships were reported by the look-out post at St.
George's Monastery to the Commander of the Coastal Defences as
approaching Cape Long, it was perfectly possible for the Albanian
authorities to use the interval of almost two hours that elapsed before the explosion affecting Saumarez (14.53 hours or 14.55 hours)
to warn the vessels of the danger into which they were running.

In fact, nothing was attempted by the Albanian authorities to
prevent the disaster. These grave omissions involve the international responsibility of Albania.

The Court therefore reaches the conclusion that Albania is responsible under international law for the explosions which occurred
on October 22nd, 1946, in Albanian waters, and for the damage and
loss of human life which resulted from them, and that there is a
duty upon Albania to pay compensation to the United Kingdom.

* * *

In the second part of the Special Agreement, the following question is submitted to the Court:

(2) Has the United Kingdom under international law violated the sovereignty of the Albanian People's Republic by reason of the acts of the Royal Navy in Albanian waters on the 22nd October and on the 12th and 13th November 1946 and is there any duty to give satisfaction?

The Court will first consider whether the sovereignty of Albania was violated by reason of the acts of the British Navy in Albanian waters on October 22nd, 1946.

On May 15th, 1946, the British cruisers Orion and Superb, while passing southward through the North Corfu Channel, were fired at by an Albanian battery in the vicinity of Saranda. It appears from the report of the commanding naval officer dated May 29th, 1946, that the firing started when the ships had already passed the battery and were moving away from it; that from 12 to 20 rounds were fired; that the firing lasted 12 minutes and ceased only when the ships were out of range; but that the ships were not hit although there were a number of "shorts" and of "overs". An Albanian note of May 21st states that the Coastal Commander ordered a few shots to be fired in the direction of the ships "in accordance with a General Order founded on international law".

The United Kingdom Government at once protested to the Albanian Government, stating that innocent passage through straits is a right recognized by international law. There ensued a diplomatic correspondence in which the Albanian Government asserted that foreign warships and merchant vessels had no right to pass through Albanian territorial waters without prior notification to, and the permission of, the Albanian authorities. This view was put into effect by a communication of the Albanian Chief of Staff, dated May 17th, 1946, which purported to subject the passage of foreign warships and merchant vessels in Albanian territorial waters to previous notification to and authorization by the Albanian Government. The diplomatic correspondence continued, and culminated in a United Kingdom note of August 2nd, 1946, in which the United Kingdom Government maintained its view with regard to the right of innocent passage through straits forming routes for international maritime traffic between two parts of the high seas. The note ended with the warning that if Albanian coastal batteries in the future opened fire on any British warship passing through the Corfu Channel, the fire would be returned.

The contents of this note were, on August 1st, communicated by the British Admiralty to the Commander-in-Chief, Mediterranean, with the instruction that he should refrain from using the Channel until the note had been presented to the Albanian Government. On August 10th, he received from the Admiralty the following telegram: "The Albanians have now received the note. North Corfu Strait may now be used by ships of your fleet, but only when essential and with armament in fore and aft position. If coastal guns fire at ships passing through the Strait, ships should fire back." On September 21st, the following telegram was sent by the Admiralty to the Commander-in-Chief, Mediterranean: "Establishment of diplomatic relations with Albania is again under consideration by His Majesty's Government who wish to know whether the Albanian Government have learnt to behave themselves. Information is requested whether any ships under your command have passed through the North Corfu Strait since August and, if not, whether you intend them to do so shortly." The Commander-in-Chief answered the next day that his ships had not done so yet, but that it was his intention that Mauritius and Leander and two destroyers should do so when they departed from Corfu on October 22nd.

It was in such circumstances that these two cruisers together with the destroyers Saumarez and Volage were sent through the North Corfu Strait on that date.

The Court will now consider the Albanian contention that the United Kingdom Government violated Albanian sovereignty by sending the warships through this Strait without the previous authorization of the Albanian Government.

It is, in the opinion of the Court, generally recognized and in accordance with international custom that States in time of peace have a right to send their warships through straits used for international navigation between two parts of the high seas without the previous authorization of a coastal State, provided that the passage is innocent. Unless otherwise prescribed in an international convention, there is no right for a coastal State to prohibit such passage through straits in time of peace.

The Albanian Government does not dispute that the North Corfu Channel is a strait in the geographical sense; but it denies that this Channel belongs to the class of international highways through which a right of passage exists, on the grounds that it is only of secondary importance and not even a necessary route between two parts of the high seas, and that it is used almost exclusively for local traffic to and from the ports of Corfu and Saranda.

It may be asked whether the test is to be found in the volume of traffic passing through the Strait or in its greater or lesser importance for international navigation. But in the opinion of the Court the decisive criterion is rather its geographical situation as connecting two parts of the high seas and the fact of its being used for international navigation. Nor can it be decisive that this Strait is not a necessary route between two parts of the high seas, but only an alternative passage between the Ægean and the Adriatic Seas. It has nevertheless been a useful route for international maritime traffic. * * *

* * *

Having regard to these various considerations, the Court has arrived at the conclusion that the North Corfu Channel should be considered as belonging to the class of international highways through which passage cannot be prohibited by a coastal State in time of peace.

On the other hand, it is a fact that the two coastal States did not maintain normal relations, that Greece had made territorial claims precisely with regard to a part of Albanian territory bordering on the Channel, that Greece had declared that she considered herself technically in a state of war with Albania, and that Albania, invoking the danger of Greek incursions, had considered it necessary to take certain measures of vigilance in this region. The Court is of opinion that Albania, in view of these exceptional circumstances, would have been justified in issuing regulations in respect of the passage of warships through the Strait, but not in prohibiting such passage or in subjecting it to the requirement of special authorization.

For these reasons the Court is unable to accept the Albanian contention that the Government of the United Kingdom has violated Albanian sovereignty by sending the warships through the Strait without having obtained the previous authorization of the Albanian Government.

In these circumstances, it is unnecessary to consider the more general question, much debated by the Parties, whether States under international law have a right to send warships in time of peace through territorial waters not included in a strait.

The Albanian Government has further contended that the sovereignty of Albania was violated because the passage of the British warships on October 22nd, 1946, was not an *innocent passage.* * * *

* * *

Having thus examined the various contentions of the Albanian Government in so far as they appear to be relevant, the Court has arrived at the conclusion that the United Kingdom did not violate the sovereignty of Albania by reason of the acts of the British Navy in Albanian waters on October 22nd, 1946.

* * *

For These Reasons,

The Court, on the first question put by the Special Agreement of March 25th, 1948, by eleven votes to five,

Gives judgment that the People's Republic of Albania is responsible under international law for the explosions which occurred on October 22nd, 1946, in Albanian waters, and for the damage and loss of human life that resulted therefrom; and

by ten votes to six,

Reserves for further consideration the assessment of the amount of compensation and regulates the procedure on this subject by an Order dated this day;

on the second question put by the Special Agreement of March 25th, 1948,

by fourteen votes to two,

Gives judgment that the United Kingdom did not violate the sovereignty of the People's Republic of Albania by reason of the acts of the British Navy in Albanian waters on October 22nd, 1946 * * *.

* * *

[A statement, a declaration, an individual opinion and dissenting opinions omitted.]

Straits of Tiran and Gulf of Aqaba. The gulf opens onto the Red Sea. It is elongated and deep, with Saudi Arabia on its east coast, Egypt on its west coast, and, at the northern end, short pieces of the coast belonging to Israel and Jordan. The straits of Tiran, at its opening on the Red Sea on the south, consist of two passages separated by an island. One of the passages is not navigable. The other, the one lying between the island and the Egyptian coast, is navigable and is about three miles wide.

Prior to 1967, Egypt claimed it had the right to control the straits and denied that Israel had a right of innocent passage through them. Consider the validity of Egypt's claim at that time in view of the following provisions of the Convention on the Territorial Sea and the Contiguous Zone (to which neither Egypt nor Israel was a party):

Article 7(1) (relating to the closing of bays): "This article relates only to bays the coasts of which belong to a single State."

Article 14(2) (relating to innocent passage): "Passage means navigation through the territorial sea for the purpose either of traversing that sea without entering internal waters, or of proceeding to internal waters, or of making for the high seas from internal waters."

Article 16(4) (relating to innocent passage): "There shall be no suspension of the innocent passage of foreign ships through straits which are used for international navigation between one part of the high seas and another part of the high seas or the territorial sea of a foreign State."

THE DAVID, PANAMA v. UNITED STATES

United States—Panama Claims Commission, 1933.
[1933–1934] Ann.Dig. 137 (No. 52).

THE FACTS. On May 11, 1923, the steamer Yorba Linda, belonging to the General Petroleum Corporation, an American corporation, collided with the steamer David, belonging to the Compañía de Navegación Nacional, of Panama. The latter Company started an action in the Court of Panama in respect of the alleged negligence of The Yorba Linda and obtained judgment for 27,103.50 balboas. This action was not begun by personal service but by service through publication, as permitted by Articles 470–473 of the Judicial Code of Panama. The Petroleum Company never appeared, but was represented by an attorney designated by the Court who offered no evidence. The judgment remained unsatisfied. Fifteen days after its confirmation by the Supreme Court of Panama the Petroleum Company issued a writ in rem of the United States District Court of the Canal Zone against The David and her owners, alleging that the collision had taken place in territorial waters of the United States and that it had been caused by the negligence of The David. The Marshal of the District Court thereupon arrested The David within a few hundred yards of Flamenco Island, and between that island and the San José Rock, which lies off the Pacific entrance to the Panama Canal. The judge of the District Court held the arrest to be valid, and the parties promptly settled the action. The terms of the settlement were that the Petroleum Company should pay to the Navegación Company the sum of $16,250, that the writ against The David should be discharged, and that the Panamanian judgment be cancelled.

Before the Commission it was alleged that the arrest of The David had been illegal as, first, it had taken place outside the territorial waters of the Canal Zone and, secondly, the vessel had been in innocent passage at the time and therefore immune from arrest even if within territorial waters. Damages were claimed in respect of the loss occasioned by the settlement and for the injury to the standing of the Navegación Company which the proceedings in the District Court had occasioned.

Held (by the majority): that the claim must be disallowed as the arrest had been made within territorial waters. The fact that the vessel had been in innocent passage did not confer on her any immunity.

I. Jurisdiction over Ships in Innocent Passage. The question whether or not the arrest was lawful even if within the territorial waters of the Canal Zone was argued at great length by the parties. Upon this question the Commission said:

> The general rule of the extension of sovereignty over the three-mile zone is clearly established. Exceptions to the completeness of this sovereignty should be supported by clear authority. There is a clear preponderance of authority to the effect that this sovereignty is qualified by what is known as the right of innocent passage, and that this qualification forbids the sovereign actually to prohibit the innocent passage of alien merchant vessels through its territorial waters.
>
> There is no clear preponderance of authority to the effect that such vessels when passing through territorial waters are ex-

empt from civil arrest: In the absence of such authority, the Commission cannot say that a country may not, under the rules of international law, assert the right to arrest on civil process merchant ships passing through its territorial waters.

Incidentally it may be said that the evidence and maps submitted to the Commission raise a real question as to whether the point at which The David was arrested was not in fact a roadstead subject to the rules which pertain to harbours rather than those which pertain to ordinary coastal waters within the three-mile zone.

II.   Breadth of the Maritime Belt.   In holding that, according to the ordinary rules for measuring territorial waters, both the island of Flamenco and the place at which The David was arrested fell within the sovereignty which the United States had in the Canal Zone, the Commission raised the interesting question of "whether the Island of Flamenco, which appears to be a fortified point guarding the entrance of the Canal, would not itself carry its own three-mile zone clearly including the situs of the arrest."   But the point was not decided.

Convention on the Territorial Sea and the Contiguous Zone. Compare Article 20 of the convention with the opinion of the commission in the above case.

PUBLIC PROSECUTOR v. KAIRISMAA

Sweden, Court of Appeal of Svea, 1960.
Supreme Court, 1960.
32 Int'l L.Rep. 117 (1966).

THE FACTS.   Kairismaa, a Finnish citizen, was charged before the City Court of Stockholm with, inter alia, obtaining a loan of 1,000 Swedish crowns from another Finnish citizen, Stjernvall, superintendent on the Finnish ship the Bore II, by fraudulently alleging that he needed the money immediately for a business transaction concerning an automobile and that he would repay it later the same day.   The Public Prosecutor alleged that the crime had been committed within Swedish territorial waters.   The City Court having found the defendant guilty, he appealed.   Referring to the fact that the ship was Finnish, that both he himself and Stjernvall were Finnish citizens, and claiming that the transaction had taken place while the Bore II was outside Swedish territorial waters, the defendant urged the Appeal Court to reject the present part of the charge.

Held (by the Court of Appeal of Svea) : that the appeal must fail and the judgment of the Court below must be confirmed.   [The Court said:]

* * *   It has been made clear [however], chiefly by the evidence given by Stjernvall before the City Court, that the transaction had taken place after the ship's entry into the Stockholm

archipelago. As the Bore II—which plies in regular passenger traffic between Stockholm and Helsinki—thus at the time when the act was committed was in Swedish territorial waters, the Court of Appeal finds that the act shall be deemed to have taken place within the country. Under Chapter 1, Article 2, paragraph 1, of the Penal Code, a Swedish Court is consequently competent to consider the present part of the charge.

Kairismaa applied for permission to appeal to the Supreme Court and urged that Court to reject the charge. * * *

* * *

Kairismaa also contended that it was not clear from the reasons given by the Court of Appeal for its judgment whether the present charge could be brought in Sweden on the sole ground that, at the time when the crime was committed, the ship was in Swedish territorial waters, or whether a second condition was required, namely, that the ship be plying in regular traffic between a Swedish and a foreign port. * * * It was true that the principle applied by the Court of Appeal had been expressed earlier, in cases concerning crimes by Swedish citizens. * * * It was much more natural, however, to consider a crime committed against an alien on a foreign ship within Swedish territorial waters as a matter of Swedish concern when committed by a Swede than when it was committed by an alien. * * *

Held (by the Supreme Court): that the application for permission to appeal must be rejected.

The Court found no reason to alter the decision of the City Court. Accordingly, the judgment of the Court of Appeal must be affirmed.

----

1. *Amendment of Swedish law subsequent to decision.* The decision appears to have been the cause of an amendment to the Swedish code of criminal law which went into effect on January 1, 1965. Under this amendment, special permission from the executive is required before prosecution is initiated for an offense committed by an alien aboard a foreign vessel in Swedish territory and affecting another alien or alien interests. The amendment is reported in a note at the end of a comment on the case by Eek, Chronique de Jurisprudence Suédoise Relative au Droit International Privé 1960–1964, 93 Journal du Droit International 410 (1965–1966).

2. *Question.* Can a state lawfully prohibit foreign aircraft from flying over its territorial sea? See Article 2 of the Convention on the Territorial Sea and the Contiguous Zone, Documentary Supplement.

SECTION B.   WATERS BEYOND THE TERRITORIAL SEA

---

1.   EXERCISE OF AUTHORITY BEYOND THE TERRITORIAL SEA

EUROPEAN AGREEMENT FOR THE PREVENTION OF BROADCASTS TRANSMITTED FROM STATIONS OUTSIDE NATIONAL TERRITORIES OF JANUARY 22, 1965 [a]

634 U.N.T.S. 239.

The member states of the Council of Europe signatory hereto,

Considering that the aim of the Council of Europe is to achieve a greater unity between its Members;

Considering that the Radio Regulations annexed to the International Telecommunication Convention prohibit the establishment and use of broadcasting stations on board ships, aircraft or any other floating or airborne objects outside national territories;

Considering also the desirability of providing for the possibility of preventing the establishment and use of broadcasting stations on objects affixed to or supported by the bed of the sea outside national territories;

Considering the desirability of European collaboration in this matter,

Have agreed as follows:

Article 1

This Agreement is concerned with broadcasting stations which are installed or maintained on board ships, aircraft, or any other floating or airborne objects and which, outside national territories, transmit broadcasts intended for reception or capable of being received, wholly or in part, within the territory of any Contracting Party, or which cause harmful interference to any radio-communication service operating under the authority of a Contracting Party in accordance with the Radio Regulations.

Article 2

1.   Each Contracting Party undertakes to take appropriate steps to make punishable as offences, in accordance with its domestic law, the establishment or operation of broadcasting stations referred to in Article 1, as well as acts of collaboration knowingly performed.

2.   The following shall, in relation to broadcasting stations referred to in Article 1, be acts of collaboration:

(a) the provision, maintenance or repairing of equipment;

---

a.   Entered into force Oct. 19, 1967.

(b) the provision of supplies;

(c) the provision of transport for, or the transporting of, persons, equipment or supplies;

(d) the ordering or production of material of any kind, including advertisements, to be broadcast;

(e) the provision of services concerning advertising for the benefit of the stations.

Article 3

Each Contracting Party shall, in accordance with its domestic law, apply the provisions of this Agreement in regard to:

(a) its nationals who have committed any act referred to in Article 2 on its territory, ships, or aircraft, or outside national territories on any ships, aircraft or any other floating or airborne object;

(b) non-nationals who, on its territory, ships or aircraft, or on board any floating or airborne object under its jurisdiction have committed any act referred to in Article 2.

Article 4

Nothing in this Agreement shall be deemed to prevent a Contracting Party:

(a) from also treating as punishable offences acts other than those referred to in Article 2 and also applying the provisions concerned to persons other than those referred to in Article 3;

(b) from also applying the provisions of this Agreement to broadcasting stations installed or maintained on objects affixed to or supported by the bed of the sea.

Article 5

The Contracting Parties may elect not to apply the provisions of this Agreement in respect of the services of performers which have been provided elsewhere than on the stations referred to in Article 1.

Article 6

The provisions of Article 2 shall not apply to any acts performed for the purpose of giving assistance to a ship or aircraft or any other floating or airborne object in distress or of protecting human life.

Article 7

No reservation may be made to the provisions of this Agreement.

* * *

Pirate broadcasting off the coast of The Netherlands.   The facts of the situation are reported in Rousseau, Chronique des Faits Internationaux, 69 Revue Générale de Droit International Public 436, 517 (1965).

Under Dutch law, radio (and television) broadcasting in the territory is a state monopoly and no privately owned radio station may be built and operated without the prior authorization of the government. A radio broadcasting station was established on a tower outside the territorial sea of The Netherlands. The builders did not seek authorization from the Dutch government. The tower was built in an Irish factory belonging to a Dutch financier. The broadcasting equipment was purchased in the United States, despite attempts by the Dutch government to prevent the sale. The tower and the broadcasting equipment were owned by persons who were not Dutch nationals.

The station was operated by a Dutch corporation and began broadcasting in July of 1964. Its income came from advertising and it is probable—though Rousseau does not say so in his report—that the owners of the station escaped such taxation as the Dutch government would levy if the station were located in its territory. On December 11, 1964, Dutch legislation was enacted which authorized the government to take action against broadcasting stations outside the territorial sea of The Netherlands, even if owned by aliens. The day the legislation became effective, ownership of the station was transferred to a Panamanian corporation and the operation of the facilities was contracted to an English corporation.

On December 17, 1964, police brought in by helicopters of the Dutch navy took possession of the platform, without resistance from the personnel of the station, and closed down the facilities. Was the action of the Dutch government valid under international law? Under the European Agreement for the Prevention of Broadcasts Transmitted from Stations Outside National Territories?

Is the situation different if the broadcasting facilities are aboard a vessel anchored outside the territorial sea? In 1965, a station aboard a vessel owned by an American national began operating outside the territorial sea of Great Britain. Rousseau, Chronique des Faits Internationaux, 70 Revue Générale de Droit International Public 481, 483 (1966). What action could Great Britain take, under international law, to terminate its activities?

Does Article 24 of the Convention on the Territorial Sea and the Contiguous Zone contribute to the solution of the problem of "pirate" broadcasting? Does Article 24 describe the exclusive powers which a state has in a zone contiguous to the territorial sea?

RE MARTINEZ

Italy, Court of Cassation, 1959.
28 Int'l L.Rep. 170 (1963).

THE FACTS.   Article 2 of the Italian Maritime Code fixes the limit of territorial waters at six miles from the coast.   Article 33 of the Customs Law of September 25, 1940, on the other hand, provides that Italy shall be entitled to exercise jurisdiction over a further six-mile zone for the purpose of preventing and punishing smuggling along the Italian coast.   This latter zone is referred to as the "zone of vigilance" (contiguous zone).   The appellants, who were foreign nationals, were convicted of smuggling in the following circumstances: while their vessel was at a distance of nine miles from the coast, warning shots were fired, and upon these shots being ignored the vessel was pursued and ultimately captured at a distance of 54 miles from the coast.   The appellants appealed against their conviction and contended that Article 24 of the Geneva Convention of 1958 on the Territorial Sea and the Contiguous Zone was declaratory of existing customary international law and accordingly a coastal State, while entitled to prevent customs offences from being committed in the contiguous zone, was not entitled to exercise jurisdiction and inflict punishment in respect of such offences; that jurisdiction could only be exercised if an offence had actually been committed within the territorial sea, and therefore Article 33 of the Customs Law was contrary to Article 10 of the Italian Constitution, which provided that Italian law must be consistent with international law.   They therefore contended that their conviction should be quashed.

Held: that the appeal must be dismissed.   (i) Article 24 of the Convention was not declaratory of existing customary international law, and there was no rule of international law which precluded a coastal State from exercising jurisdiction over offences by foreign nationals which were committed in the contiguous zone of between six and twelve miles from the coast.   (ii) Accordingly, Article 33 of the Customs Law was not contrary to Article 10 of the Constitution (or international law), and as the offence had been committed at a distance of nine miles from the coast when the pursuit of the vessel began, the Italian courts were entitled to exercise jurisdiction.   [A portion of the opinion of the court appears below.]

*   *   *   It is contended that Article 33 of the Customs Law, which extends the territorial sea beyond the limit of six nautical miles laid down in Article 2 of the Maritime Code, and confers on the coastal State sovereignty and jurisdiction over a stretch of sea between six and twelve miles, is contrary to Article 10 of the Italian Constitution which provides that Italian law shall be in conformity with the generally recognized rules of international law.   By a rule

of customary international law recognized and laid down in Article 24 of the "Convention on the Territorial Sea and the Contiguous Zone", which was adopted at the Geneva Conference on February 24 and April 27, 1958, the sovereignty and jurisdiction of the coastal State—it is said—cannot extend beyond six miles, and sovereignty and jurisdiction over a belt extending between six and twelve miles from the coast, this belt being defined as the contiguous zone, are not recognized except in specially defined cases. According to the argument put forward on behalf of the appellants, the coastal State can exercise the requisite control for the purpose of preventing and punishing offences against its customs, tax and sanitary laws over a portion of the high seas contiguous to the territorial sea, on condition only that the offences have been committed in the territorial sea within six miles from the coast. It follows—so it is said—that the coastal State can exercise its jurisdiction over the contiguous zone only in respect of offences committed in its territorial sea, the contiguous zone being the intermediate zone between the territorial sea and the high seas. This, it is said, would be contrary to Article 33 of the Customs Law which, in delimiting the zone of customs vigilance as being twelve miles from the coast, includes in the latter the territorial sea as laid down in Article 2 of the Maritime Code and the zone of vigilance, which latter it makes coincide with the territorial sea.

The contention that Article 33 of the Customs Law is contrary to the Constitution is misconceived and has been rejected by the judgment under appeal. It is undoubtedly true that the rule laid down in Article 10 of the Constitution, according to which Italian law must comply with generally recognized rules of international law, ensures the compatibility of Italian municipal law with international law, viz., with the duties imposed upon the State by international law, so that rules of municipal law which are contrary to international law must be eliminated. However, in order for this to be so, it is necessary for the rules of international law to be generally recognized, and it is admitted on behalf of the defendants that the Geneva Convention, which has been signed by Italy, is not yet in force.

It is not true that Article 24 of the Convention constitutes a customary rule of international law governing the delimitation of the territorial sea in the sense that the sovereignty of the coastal State is limited to the territorial sea itself, without being capable of being extended over the contiguous zone when smuggling has occurred in the latter and not in the territorial sea. No such rule can be said to have been generally accepted in international law. In substance custom is a manifestation of social life which hardens by means of constant and uniform repetition of certain acts on the part of States or individuals, extending over a period of time, to which municipal law attributes legal relevance. In the international field this presupposes the existence of a substantive element, namely, the constant repetition of certain rules of conduct between States, and a psychological element, namely, the conviction that such conduct is obligatory for everybody, so that others can insist upon it, and which does not depend on purely subjective judgment. Only then can custom be a source of law equal to municipal law.

As far as the present case is concerned, not all maritime States have accepted such a rule in practice. The International Law Commission, in its draft code prepared at the session held between April and July 1956, recognized (in Article 3) "that international practice is not uniform as far as the delimitation of the territorial sea is concerned". The comment on Article 66 of the draft code relating to the contiguous zone states that smuggling could not be dealt with adequately, having regard to the fact that Article 66 provided only for offences committed "within the territory or in the territorial sea". The Italian delegation [sic.] observed that "having regard to the geographical position of the country and the configuration of its coasts, the limitation of the powers conferred on the coastal State in the contiguous zone would render preventive and punitive measures against smuggling ineffective, especially in parts of the sea adjacent to the Italian coast where smuggling was particularly active and aggressive".

At the Geneva Conference, which opened on February 24, 1958, there was no change. The Italian delegation proposed an amendment aiming at the omission of the words "in the territorial sea", in order to be able to prevent and punish offences committed in the contiguous zone and not only on State territory and in the territorial sea. This proposal was not accepted in plenary session, nor was any other put forward by way of compromise by other delegations, on the extension of the territorial sea. A solution of the problem could not be found.

It is contended on behalf of the defendants that the [International Law] Commission was set up for the progressive development and codification of international law, and that when preparing the report on which the Convention is based it investigated substantially the rules of customary international law. This, it is argued, shows that these rules existed prior to codification, which was merely intended to lay down in codified form what was already custom. Hence the wording of the rule contained in Article 24 of the Convention, which is said to be a faithful reproduction of a pre-existing customary rule which as such is generally recognized and must be considered, by virtue of Article 10 of the Constitution, as having been automatically incorporated in Italian law, and which must not be contrary to the rule laid down in that article.

It must be remembered, however, that this rule cannot be said to be a generally recognized rule of customary international law

because the rule relating to the width of the territorial sea is still ✓
under discussion between States. States apply different rules according to their respective municipal laws, which fact in itself precludes recognition of any pre-existing custom in the matter. In fact,
although the Conference on the Law of the Sea was successful in
defining a number of rules governing the matter under discussion,
it left unsolved the problem of the width of the territorial sea, as can
be seen from the preparatory work of the Conference. The disagreement was due to different contrasting views put forward by participating States, one group being in favour of the three-mile limit for
territorial waters, as in the past, another holding the opposite view
and applying various criteria to the actual width of the territorial
sea, without affirming a right to twelve miles. Although various
proposals were put forward to reconcile the opposing wishes of
States, no positive solution was found. Accordingly, it cannot be
said that the rule contained in Article 24 of the Convention existed
previously as a generally recognized customary rule when the conditions surrounding the delimitation of the territorial sea and the contiguous zone were very different from those contained in that article
and when agreement could not be reached. * * *

     In fact, not all States have accepted the three-mile limit, which
in the past represented a compromise between States: Norway and
Sweden have fixed the limit of their territorial sea at four miles;
Spain, Portugal, Yugoslavia, Italy and other countries at six, while
Bulgaria, the Soviet Union, Communist China, Egypt, Ethiopia, Rumania and Guatemala have fixed it at twelve miles, and Chile and
other countries at two hundred. Italy, on the other hand, as we have
already stated, has not accepted the limit of the contiguous zone in
the form in which it is expressed in Article 24. The rules of municipal law of coastal States have therefore remained in force. In Italy
it is the rule laid down in Article 33 of the Customs Law, which cannot be said to be contrary to Article 10 of the Constitution. It follows that the offence of smuggling committed in the zone of vigilance, the so-called contiguous zone, is punishable in Italy, and that
the arrest of a foreign national is lawful by Article 137 of the Customs Law. Equally lawful is the pursuit of a foreign vessel, which
is recognized by customary international law except with regard to
the limit of the territorial sea and the contiguous zone.

     We now come to the second and third grounds of appeal. The
rule laid down in Article 33 of the Customs Law, which, as we have
said, puts the zone of vigilance—the contiguous zone—on the same
legal basis as the territorial sea for the purpose of customs offences,
is well established so far as concerns the right of pursuit. By virtue
of this right a foreign vessel can be pursued if the competent authorities of a coastal State have good reason to suspect that the vessel
has violated the law of that State, provided that the pursuit begins
while the foreign vessel or one of its auxiliary craft is in internal

waters, in the territorial sea or in the contiguous zone of the pursuing State; the pursuit can be extended beyond the limits of the territorial sea if it has not been interrupted. It follows that it is lawful to capture the crew and seize the vessel with its cargo of contraband.

The appellants contend that as Article 2 of the Maritime Code fixes the limit of the territorial sea at six miles from the coast and provides that this is without prejudice to various legal provisions which are to apply in specific cases, the only purpose of the Code was to lay down a six-mile limit for the territorial sea, reserving the right to extend the limit for specific purposes other than sovereignty, and less extensive than the latter. Accordingly, the zone of vigilance provided for by Article 33 of the Customs Law as being between six and twelve miles is not the territorial sea but merely an area of the sea which is subject to control for the purpose of prevention only and not punishment. Although in theory it may seem as if in the contiguous zone only police and preventive measures may be taken, because this zone forms part of the open sea rather than the territorial sea, a different view must be taken when one considers that the draft code of the Institute of International Law on the contiguous zone clearly recognizes the right to exercise jurisdiction. The International Law Commission, in its report on the session held in 1953, was decidedly in favour of acknowledging the right to exercise jurisdiction, while in its 1951 draft it merely referred to preventive measures.

(The Court then pointed out that Article 33 of the Customs Law was designed to give the widest possible powers to the Italian courts and not merely to enable the police to prevent smuggling in the vicinity of the Italian coast. It then considered the facts and found that warning shots had been fired at the foreign vessel concerned when the latter was at a distance of nine miles from the coast, and that upon the shots being ignored the vessel was pursued until it was captured at a distance of 54 miles from the coast. The appeal was accordingly dismissed.)

Contraband outside the customs zone. A British vessel transferred contraband goods to an Italian vessel outside the 12 miles customs zone of Italy. An Italian coastguard cutter boarded the British vessel and arrested its crew while it was still on the high seas. The Supreme Court of Italy ordered the release of the crew on the ground that a state cannot exercise its jurisdiction over foreign vessels on the high seas, save in the exceptional case of hot pursuit. Re McSporran et al.; s.s. Sito, Court of Cassation, 1957, 89 Journal du Droit International 229 (1962).

BILDER, THE CANADIAN ARCTIC WATERS POLLUTION PREVENTION ACT: NEW STRESSES ON THE LAW OF THE SEA

69 Michigan Law Review 1 (1970).*

On June 17, 1970, the Canadian Parliament approved the Arctic Waters Pollution Prevention Act, which asserts Canada's jurisdiction to regulate all shipping in zones up to 100 nautical miles off its Arctic coasts in order to guard against pollution of the region's coastal and marine resources. Related legislation extends Canada's territorial sea from three miles to twelve miles and authorizes the Government to establish exclusive Canadian fishing zones in marine areas adjacent to the coasts of Canada but beyond the new twelve-mile territorial sea. At the same time that this legislation was introduced into the Canadian Parliament, the Government took steps to remove the possibility of a challenge in the International Court of Justice to its establishment of such contiguous pollution and fishery zones by adding a reservation to that effect to its long-standing acceptance of the Court's compulsory jurisdiction.

The Canadian Pollution Prevention Act is of interest in several respects. It opens a new round in the historic and multifaceted struggle over freedom of the seas. It raises complex questions of international law and policy regarding the legal regime of Arctic waters, the concept of contiguous zones, the status of waters within archipelagoes, and the doctrines of innocent passage and international straits. It illustrates both the perception of an increasing number of coastal states that existing international law and international arrangements are inadequate to protect their legitimate interests, and the strong pressures within such states for unilateral action to remedy these perceived deficiencies. It suggests, in particular, the type of stress that the growing concern on the part of coastal states regarding ocean pollution is likely to exert on traditional law-of-the-sea doctrines, and it also suggests the complex issues which may be involved in attempting to achieve international agreement on a regulatory regime adequate to prevent such pollution. Finally, the Act offers an instructive study of the international legal process in action.

The immediate stimulus for the Canadian legislation was the historic voyage in the summer of 1969 of the United States tanker S. S. Manhattan through the waters and ice of the Northwest Passage, north of the Canadian mainland. The voyage was designed to demonstrate the feasibility of utilizing ice-breaking supertankers on this route for the large-scale transportation of oil from the developing oil fields of Alaska's North Slope to the markets of the Eastern Seaboard of the United States. Previously, the 1967 Torrey Canyon incident, the 1968 Santa Barbara oil spill, and a succession of similar incidents

* Reprinted by permission of the Michigan Law Review.

had dramatically highlighted the environmental hazards posed by the possibility of maritime-tanker and oil-drilling accidents. The Manhattan's feat gave warning that Canada's Arctic environment might soon be subjected to similar threats. The immediacy of the potential problem was further underlined in Canadian public consciousness by the grounding of the Liberian tanker Arrow in February 1970 in Chadabucto Bay off Nova Scotia, which caused oil pollution of the waters and adjacent coast.

                    *   *   *

Uncontested Canadian sovereignty over key straits, coupled perhaps with Canada's claim over all archipelagic waters, might have provided a feasible basis for an assertion of Canadian jurisdiction over the Northwest Passage. However, the Arctic Waters Pollution Prevention Act appears to be based on a separate and more far-reaching contiguous-zone theory. A brief summary of the Act should make this theory clear.

The Arctic Waters Pollution Prevention Act deals with pollution arising from shipping, from land-based installations, and from commercial activities, such as oil drilling, carried out on the Canadian Continental Shelf. The Act's provisions apply to "arctic waters" which are defined as waters in both a liquid and a frozen state "adjacent to the mainland and islands of the Canadian arctic within the area enclosed by the sixtieth parallel of north latitude, the one hundred and forty-first meridian of longitude *and a line measured seaward from the nearest Canadian land a distance of one hundred nautical miles * * *"*. In addition, "arctic waters" include waters adjacent to those in the area described above to the extent that such adjacent waters overlie "submarine areas [that] Her Majesty in right of Canada has the right to dispose of or exploit" insofar as the Act applies to persons exploring for, developing, or exploiting natural resources in such submarine areas.

The Act prohibits, and prescribes penalties for, the deposit of "waste" in Arctic waters or on the islands or mainland under conditions which may cause such waste to enter the Arctic waters, and further requires that any deposit of waste or danger thereof be reported. Exceptions to these requirements may be authorized by the Governor in Council. The Governor in Council may also order the destruction or removal of ships in distress which are depositing waste or which are likely to deposit waste in Arctic waters. The definition of "waste" is comprehensive and covers, among other things, "any substance that, if added to any waters, would degrade or alter . . . those waters to any extent that is detrimental to their use by man or by any animal, fish or plant that is useful to man * * *."

The Governor in Council may, by order, prescribe as a "shipping safety control zone" any area of the Arctic waters. He may then make regulations relating to navigation in such zones and prohibit any ship from entering any zone unless it meets the prescribed regulations. Such regulations may relate to hull and fuel tank construction, navigational aids, safety equipment, qualification of personnel, time and route of passage, pilotage, icebreaker escort, and so forth. At certain times of the year, or when certain ice conditions prevail, ships may be completely banned from entering any given zone. Finally, the Governor in Council may exempt from the application of such regulations any ship or class of ships that is owned or operated by a sovereign power other than Canada when he is satisfied that such ships comply with standards substantially equivalent to those prescribed by Canadian regulations and that all reasonable precautions will be taken by those ships to reduce the danger of any deposit of waste.

The Act further provides for the appointment of "pollution prevention officers" having broad powers, including authority both to board ships within a shipping safety control zone for inspection purposes, and to order ships in or near a safety control zone to remain outside it if the ofifcers suspect that the ships do not comply with the standards applicable within the zone.

*   *   *

The Canadian Government was well aware that the Pollution Prevention Act might raise foreign-relations problems, particularly with the United States, and its expectations were realized. The American response was prompt and legalistic. On April 9, 1970, a State Department spokesman stated that:

> We regret the introduction of this legislation by the Canadian Government which, in our view, constitutes a unilateral approach to a problem which we believe should be resolved by cooperative international action.

> The United States does not recognize any exercise of coastal state jurisdiction over our vessels in the high seas and thus does not recognize the right of any state unilaterally to establish a territorial sea of more than three miles or exercise more limited jurisdiction in any area beyond 12 miles.

He added, however, that the United States "is prepared promptly to seek either bilateral or multilateral solutions to these problems in the framework of international law."

In a further statement on April 15, reflecting an official note to the Canadian Government, the Department of State developed its position more fully:

> International law provides no basis for these proposed unilateral extensions of jurisdiction on the high seas, and the United States can neither accept nor acquiesce in the assertion of such jurisdiction.

> We are concerned that this action by Canada if not opposed by us, would be taken as a precedent in other parts of the world for other unilateral infringements of the freedom of the seas.

If Canada had the right to claim and exercise exclusive pollution and resource jurisdiction on the high seas, other countries could assert the right to exercise jurisdiction for other purposes, some reasonable and some not, but all equally invalid according to international law.

The State Department asked the Canadian Government to defer making its proposed legislation effective until an international agreement was reached. However, in the event that the Canadian Government was unwilling to make this concession, the State Department urged that the issue be voluntarily submitted to the International Court of Justice.

The Canadian Government, in turn, promptly rejected the American position and suggestions. In a note delivered to the United States Government on April 16, 1970, the Ministry of External Affairs stated that the Pollution Prevention Bill was justified since it was "based on the overriding right of self-defence of coastal states to protect themselves against grave threats to their environment"; that such extensions of jurisdiction for limited protective purposes outside the territorial seas had ample precedent, particularly in American practice; and that, while the Canadian Government was prepared to participate in international efforts to deal with the problem, it was not prepared to await the development of international rules as the solution. Indeed, the Canadian Government viewed its own unilateral action as a positive contribution to the development of such rules since it is a well-established principle that customary international law is developed by state practice. Moreover, the Canadian Government refused to accept the American suggestion that the Northwest Passage constituted high seas, that it was an international strait, or that the waters of the Arctic Archipelago were other than Canadian. Finally, Canada would not agree to submit the dispute to the International Court. Canada then proceeded to enact the new legislation and the United States in turn proceeded with plans to convene an international conference on Arctic pollution problems　＊　＊　＊.

RIGHT OF APPROACH

4 Whiteman, Digest of International Law 667 (1965).

The right of any ship to fly a particular flag must obviously be subject to verification by proper authority, and from this it follows that warships have a general right to verify the nationality of any merchant ship which they may meet on the high seas. This "right of approach" (*vérification du pavillon* or *reconnaissance*) is the only qualification under customary law of the general principle which forbids any interference in time of peace with ships of another nationality upon the high seas. Any other act of interference (apart from the repression of piracy) must be justified under powers conferred by treaty. Provided that the ✓ merchant vessel responds by showing her flag the captain of the warship is not justified in boarding her or taking any further action, unless there is reasonable ground for suspecting that she is engaged in piracy or some other improper activity. In the absence of good cause for suspicion his government may have to accept substantial responsibility for any interference. If the vessel approached shows a foreign flag even suspicious conduct will not justify active interference except in those cases, such as slave trading, where it is authorized by treaty. Otherwise the captain should merely report the incident to superior authority so that further action, if deemed necessary, may be taken through diplomatic channels.

In the past the question of the right of approach has been the subject of some controversy and has occasionally given rise to friction. Under modern conditions the general use of wireless and other developments have made the matter one of very small importance. Smith, The Law and Custom of the Sea (1959) 64–65.

On December 20, 1960, the Soviet Ministry of Foreign Affairs addressed the following note to the American Embassy at Moscow:

[The note alleged that an American destroyer had engaged in provocative and dangerous maneuvers toward a Soviet merchant vessel in the Mediterranean Sea.]

After a careful investigation of the facts concerning the alleged incident, the Department of State, on January 4, 1961, addressed the following reply to the Soviet Government:

The Department of State refers the Embassy of the Union of Soviet Socialist Republics to the note 138/OSA of December 20, 1960 from the Ministry of Foreign Affairs of the Union of Soviet Socialist Republics to the Embassy of the United States of America in Moscow alleging that an American destroyer carried out maneuvers in the Mediterranean Sea on November 4, 1960 which seriously endangered the Soviet ship *Faleshty*, and wishes to state the following.

A careful investigation of the facts has clearly established that the American ship which passed the *Faleshty* on November 4 did not carry out any provocative maneuvers. No alerts were sounded for a mock attack, as alleged in the Ministry's note, nor did the American ship ever approach the *Faleshty* in such a way as to endanger the Soviet ship.

It is common practice for ships moving in international waters to establish mutual identification. This, the investigation clearly showed, was the full extent of the American vessel's action.

Under the circumstances, the Government of the United States rejects the Soviet Government's charges.

* * *

1. *Right of visit under the Convention on the High Seas.* See Article 22 of the convention, Documentary Supplement.

2. *Right of visit under an international agreement.* See Chapter 1, p. 45, for a case of boarding by a U. S. naval vessel of a Soviet trawler suspected of damaging submarine cables, pursuant to the Convention for the Protection of Submarine Cables of March 14, 1884. Both the Soviet Union and the United States are parties to the convention.

PIRACY

6 Whiteman, Digest of International Law 348 (1968).

[The author quotes from Smith, The End of the Consular Courts, 37 Foreign Service Journal (Jan. 1960) 44, 47–48.]

* * * In November 1952 there occurred on the high seas between Tangier and Malaga, Spain, one of the most audacious crimes in modern legal history. Two American citizens, Elliot Forrest and Sidney Paley, were suspected of highjacking a Dutch ship, the Combinatie, and relieving it of its cargo of American cigarettes, valued at more than $100,000, under circumstances reminiscent of the days of Captain Kidd. Men wearing hoods, and armed with machine guns, were alleged to have boarded the Combinatie on the High Seas, in the early morning hours, and to have handcuffed the Master and members of the crew and locked them in their quarters. The piratical crew was said to have sailed the Combinatie to a point off Marseille, where they unloaded part of the cargo onto small fishing boats and then proceeded to Corsica to unload the remainder of the cargo before returning the vessel to its rightful masters. Paley was arrested in Madrid and returned to the Consular Court at Tangier for trial. * * *

Paley was not present at the actual robbery and was charged with aiding and abetting robbery on the high seas and with conspiring to commit the crime of robbery on the high seas. The judge of the United States Consular Court [a] at Tangier found him guilty on both counts

---

a. On the basis of treaties concluded with Morocco as early as 1787, the United States, like a number of other states, had rights of "extraterritorial jurisdiction" in Moroccan territory.

By virtue of this jurisdiction, American nationals who committed crimes in Morocco were tried, not by the Moroccan courts and under Moroccan law, but rather by the consul of the "and sentenced him to three years imprisonment on both counts, the sentences to run concurrently. The judge's associates [assessors] in the case, however, found Paley not guilty and, in accordance with the existing laws, the case was referred to the Ministerial Court for final decision."

" *   *   * Forrest, the other American involved, later was arrested and tried in France, where he was found guilty and given a very heavy fine in addition to a five-year sentence." Forrest had participated in the actual robbery.

*   *   *

After [a] rehearing, the Ministerial Court again sustained "the conviction as found by the Consul on both Counts of the Information". The Court, however, was of the opinion that "under the power of adjudication conferred by Section 152, Title 22, United States Code, this Court is not bound by the judgment and sentence of the Consular Court and that in the present case the ends of justice would be best served by the imposition of less rigorous punishment". The case was, therefore, remanded to the Consular Court with instructions to affirm the finding of guilty on the first count and the sentence of imprisonment but to suspend such sentence on condition that the appellant be placed on probation in the United States for 3 years. The finding of guilty and the sentence of imprisonment on the second count were also to be affirmed but the sentence was suspended on condition that the appellant pay a fine of $6,500.

1. *Piracy under international law.* In a British case, In re Piracy Jure Gentium, [1934] A.C. 586, His Majesty in Council referred to the Judicial Committee a question concerning piracy under international law. The answer stated in part:

With regard to crimes as defined by international law, that law has no means of trying or punishing them. The recognition of them as constituting crimes, and the trial and punishment of the criminals, are left to the municipal law of each country. But whereas according to international law the criminal jurisdiction of municipal law is ordinarily restricted to crimes committed on its terra firma or territorial waters or its own ships, and to crimes by its own nationals wherever committed, it is also recognized as extending to piracy committed on the high seas by any nationals on any ship, because a person guilty of such piracy has placed

United States and under American law. Appeals from the consular court were taken to the court of the American minister in Tangier. The United States exercised this jurisdiction until 1956, when the protectorate of France over Morocco was terminated.

himself beyond the protection of any state. He is no longer a national, but hostis humani generis and as such he is justiciable by any state anywhere: Grotius (1583–1645) De Jure Belli ac Pacis, vol. 2, cap. 20, § 40. * * *

2. *Definition of piracy in the Convention on the High Seas.* See Article 15, Documentary Supplement.

3. *Problem.* Suppose that a group of political dissidents in a small motor launch board a cruise vessel flying their country's flag and sailing on the high seas. They seize control of the ship, confine the officers and set sail for a foreign port. They broadcast their exploit, explaining that it is to publicize to the world the "intolerable state of affairs in our beloved homeland and the ruthless and oppressive nature of the illegitimate regime that governs her." Are they pirates under Article 15 of the convention?

4. *Other crimes of universal interest.* Piracy is not the only crime of universal interest. Rather it is the most ancient. Since its development, and particularly of late, several other crimes have become recognized as being of universal interest. Such recognition may have begun in customary international law for some of these crimes, but is now usually embodied in international agreements. These agreements must be consulted to determine under what circumstances and to what extent a state may participate in the repression of the particular crime involved even though it was not committed in its territory, was not committed by one of its nationals or was not otherwise within its jurisdiction to prescribe and enforce. Some of the crimes involved are:

Slave trade; see Articles 13 and 22 of the Convention on the High Seas, Documentary Supplement.

War crimes; see Chapter 10.

Genocide; see Chapter 10.

Hijacking; see Chapter 4.

Sabotage of civil aircraft; see Chapter 4.

Acts of violence against diplomats; see Chapter 13.

The last three of the categories of crimes listed are discussed in Stevenson, International Law and the Export of Terrorism, 67 U. S. Dep't State Bull. 645 (1972). As to traffic in narcotics, see the voluminous Study of International Control of Narcotics and Dangerous Drugs published by the Bureau of Narcotics and Dangerous Drugs of the Department of Justice (Washington, 1972). The last of its four volumes includes the texts of some 12 international agreements dealing with narcotics control from 1909 to 1971.

2. BREADTH OF THE TERRITORIAL SEA

Freedom of the Seas: 3, 4, 6, 12.

WILKES, THE USE OF WORLD RESOURCES WITHOUT CONFLICT: MYTHS ABOUT THE TERRITORIAL SEA

14 Wayne Law Review 441 (1968).*

MYTH #1

"The concept of the territorial sea originated from the distance a cannon could shoot from land. Thus, with increased capabilities of military control, we should have an increased territorial sea."

FACT

The concept of a narrow belt of territorial sea beyond which the seas would be open to vessels of all nations did not originate with late eighteenth century references to a "cannon shot." This concept may be traced to Hugo de Groot's Mare Liberum, first published in 1609, when he excepted the belt of sea "visible from shore" from the compelling arguments by which he established the doctrine of "Freedom of the Seas."

It is true that de Groot based this doctrine on the two-pronged argument that (1) the sea was not reducible to possession because of its limitlessness, and (2) the sea must remain free and open to all for navigation, trade and fishing because it is self-evidently adapted for the use of all. Yet he never limited his concept of the territorial belt to any supposed "zone of effective control," nor did he ever permit the "use" argument to become dependent on the "possession" argument. Indeed, in something akin to a prevision of the approach which was to be taken with regard to "Texas towers" under the Convention on the Continental Shelf, Hugo de Groot dealt with the question of attempts to appropriate the sea through piles that could be driven into it. He recognized that piles could be driven into the sea, and that the man who drove them would own them. Nevertheless, the freedom of the seas was paramount and could neither be diminished nor interfered with by this type of possession.

It is vital to appreciate the context in which de Groot's doctrine contested Spanish, Portuguese and Venetian claims to be able to appropriate the seas by establishing effective military control over them, a contest that was not fully won until the nineteenth century. After the Treaty of Tordesillas of 1494, Spain and Portugal set about establishing dominion over the seas and lands divided between them along

---

a line close to that assigned them by Pope Pius VI. By the time of de Groot's Mare Liberum, Spain had been enforcing "control by arms" over the Pacific Ocean and the Gulf of Mexico while Portugal had dominated the whole Atlantic south of Morocco and the Indian Ocean.

Over the next two centuries, these claims were disputed and were finally laid to rest in favor of a narrow belt of territorial sea beyond which all was open and free. The way in which the doctrine of this narrow belt was described differed from country to country and from time to time. For instance, the eighteenth century Dutch writer Bynkershoek, in a dissertation reaffirming the freedom of the seas doctrine in 1702, said that the power of the coastal state went only so far as the reach of its arms. In fact, for a very brief period a few nations actually made agreements between themselves to recognize sovereignty within cannon shot range of the coastal state.

However, it was not the "cannon shot" rule that gained the widest acceptance. The marine league, which had the virtues of being fixed and of guaranteeing the narrowness of the coastal state's encroachment on the free seas, became the most widely accepted. It is true that some early writers referred to the new three-mile rule as also matching the farthest range of a cannonball. However, it is not because British and American cannon shot three miles, Norwegian, Swedish and Danish cannon shot four miles and Spanish cannon shot nine miles that different rules emerged. The fact is that the British, American and continental marine league was three miles, the Scandinavian marine league was four miles, and the old Spanish marine league was nine miles. Indeed, six years after Jefferson obtained English agreement on a three-mile limit, the British rejected an American proposal to make the limit two leagues instead of one on the ground of increased ability of shore batteries to effect control. The rejection, accepted by the United States, was based in part on the British Law Officer's concern that "[i]f the right of territory is to extend to two Leagues, may not demand be set up to extend it to twenty or two hundred?"

We have lived to see such a 200-mile claim made in the Santiago Declaration on the Maritime Zone by Chile, Ecuador and Peru. The claim for such increased extension was made solely on the ground of fish and marine conservation. Ecuador, on the other hand, had just raised its territorial sea claim some twenty-one months before to a twelve-mile limit on the ground that military considerations had led nations to extend their territorial waters.

In each case of a claimed extension by Chile, Ecuador and Peru, we have seen reasons advanced for an assertion of total sovereignty that went beyond the circumstance upon which it was grounded. An attempt has been made to enlarge the small intrusion originally made into the open seas. In each case, there were two tacit assumptions made by the claimants: (1) that the self-interest of the coastal state overrides the interests of the 100-odd other nations of the planet;

and (2) that this self-interest is served, not by preserving freedom of the seas, but by narrowing the open area in some way.

The basic fallacy in both of these assumptions is that, with increased mobility, each nation will often be "the other nation" in someone else's claimed private preserve carved from the open seas. Any fair examination of the first assumption—that of the overriding interest—reveals that this rule is more likely to increase potential conflict rather than reduce it. Further, precisely because the chance of conflict is raised, the second assumption—that extension serves national interests—proves false as well.

The freedom of the seas doctrine is in every nation's self-interest for two reasons. First, it preserves access to seas away from its shore. Second, it reduces the possibility of military conflict with its risks of escalation. Thus the military necessity arguments advanced by Ecuador and some other Latin American states to justify initial extensions from the three-mile limit prove ill-conceived. One's real military necessity in this enlightened age is to foster climates that reduce conflict and pave the way for cooperation.

NATIONAL RESOURCES: 200

THE OLYMPIC VICTOR

Peru, Judgment of the Port Officer of Paita, 1954.
22 Int'l L.Rep. 278 (1958).

THE FACTS (as stated in the Judgment [1]). "On information received by the Government that a whaling fleet under the orders of Captain Wilhelm Reichert of the Olympic Challenger [which appeared to have been the mother ship] was whaling in Peruvian territorial waters without first having obtained permission, and killing whales in breach of the international and national regulations made for the preservation of these marine resources, ships of the Peruvian Navy intercepted and arrested the two whalers Olympic Victor and Olympic Lightning; nine other whalers made off, and the Olympic Fighter, Olympic Conqueror and Olympic Challenger were arrested later. These facts have been fully proved by the report and maps, exhibited to the Court, giving the positions and sightings and movements of

---

1. The Olympic Victor and the four other vessels were whaling vessels owned by A. S. Onassis and flying the Panamanian flag. In November 1954 they were seized by Peruvian naval and air units. Two were captured 160 miles off the Peruvian coast, two were attacked 300 miles off the coast, and the fifth, a factory vessel, was attacked 364 miles off the coast. Panama (whose flag the vessels flew), the United States of America and the United Kingdom protested against the seizure and against the Judgment reported above.

the ships of the Peruvian Navy." The other relevant facts, as ascertained by the Port Officer, are stated in the Judgment below.

Held: (1) that Captains Sofus Sauger, Willi Schlatermunel, Juel Eugbretsen, Bjarne Anderson and Wilhelm Reichert, masters respectively of the ships Olympic Victor, Olympic Lightning, Olympic Fighter, Olympic Conqueror and Olympic Challenger, and the owners or proprietors of the arrested ships, whose agents at law the said masters are, shall pay jointly and in common a fine of three million dollars or its equivalent in the national currency, within five days reckoned from the date of notification of this judgment, into the Deposit Accounts Fund, Revenue Department, Lima.

(2) The ships Olympic Victor, Olympic Lightning, Olympic Fighter, Olympic Conqueror and Olympic Challenger shall remain impounded as security for the payment of the aforesaid, and shall be released on its payment in full. [A portion of the opinion of the court appears below.]

* * * 1. In this case none of the masters responsible for the offence the subject of these proceedings asked permission of the Supreme Government to hunt either in coastal or in deep waters.

* * *

3. It has been proved that the position of 11 whalers—that is, practically the whole whaling fleet—was ascertained by the ships of the Peruvian Navy, which detected and sighted them in a position exactly 110 miles from the Peruvian coast. The ships Olympic Victor and Olympic Lightning were captured at a distance of exactly 126 miles from the Peruvian coast, and the ships Olympic Fighter, Olympic Conqueror and Olympic Challenger were intercepted later when they took to flight.

* * *

5. It has also been proved that the arrested ships and those which made off had operated within Peruvian territorial waters and had taken between 2,500 and 3,000 whales. This was admitted in the depositions put in evidence, starting at page 3. It was necessary for the required manoeuvre that the Olympic Challenger should be close to the catchers. This was corroborated by the depositions of the members of the crew. The fact that the Olympic Challenger was captured outside the 200-mile limit does not weaken that evidence in any way, for those depositions show that when the mother-ship received word of the capture of the first two of the ships just mentioned she proceeded continuously for 24 hours at high speed with special precautions, so that she was able to leave the zone and reach the point from which she was obliged to return and be impounded in this port. The Olympic Challenger was the ship which directed the catchers and gave them their bearings, and received and processed the catch taken within the 200-mile limit: about 6,800 tons of whale oil was found in her tanks.

6.   Hunting and fishing in territorial waters is permitted only to Peruvian nationals and to aliens domiciled in the Republic, by Article 731 of the Port Authorities Regulations. Foreign vessels are not permitted to fish in territorial waters.   *   *   *

7.   The Supreme Decree of 1 August 1947, considering that it is necessary that the State protect, maintain and establish a control of fisheries and other natural resources found in the continental waters which cover the submarine shelf and the adjacent continental seas in order that these resources, which are so essential to our national life, may continue to be exploited now and in the future in such a way as to cause no detriment to the country's economy or to its food production, lays down that national sovereignty and jurisdiction are ✓ to be extended over the sea adjoining the shores of the national territory, whatever its depth and to the extent necessary to preserve, protect, maintain and utilize natural resources and wealth of any kind which may be found in or below those waters. These provisions are in harmony with those of the Declaration of the Maritime Zone signed SANTIAGO by Peru, Chile and Ecuador on 18 August 1952, to ensure the conserva- DECLARATION tion and protection of their natural resources and to regulate the use thereof to the greatest possible advantage of each country; hence it is likewise the duty of each Government to prevent the said resources from being used outside the area of its jurisdiction so as to endanger their existence, integrity and conservation to the prejudice of peoples so situated geographically that their seas are irreplaceable sources of essential economic materials.

*   *   *

10.   In this case not only has a breach of the Port Authorities Regulations been committed, but there has also been evasion of payment of dues and the provocative attitude of the masters and of the persons who have instructed them to trespass in territorial waters. They were debarred from entering these because it was common knowledge that they had had notice of the prohibition by Peru of encroachment on her waters. Although these circumstances have not been a subject of examination in these proceedings, they constitute circumstances aggravating the offence charged.

*   *   *

CISNEROS, THE 200 MILE LIMIT IN THE SOUTH PACIFIC: A NEW POSITION IN INTERNATIONAL LAW WITH A HUMAN AND JURIDICAL CONTENT

1964 Proceedings of the American Bar Association Section of International and Comparative Law 56.

*   *   *

Peru's position about the Law of the Sea was established by a Supreme Decree issued on August 1, 1947 by the then President of the

Republic, doctor Jose Luis Bustamante y Rivero, an eminent jurist who is now a member of the International Court of Justice, and doctor Enrique Garcia Sayan, then Minister of Foreign Affairs, a very well known specialist in International Law.

Peru proclaimed in this Supreme Decree its national sovereignty and jurisdiction with regard to the continental shelf, the waters that cover it and an adjoining zone of the ocean up to a distance of 200 sea miles, for purposes of reserving, protecting, conserving and using the natural resources and wealth found in or under said sea. The same Decree specified that this declaration "does not affect the free navigation rights of ships of all nations in accordance with International Law."

Afterwards, in 1952, the plenipotentiaries of Chile, Ecuador and Peru met in Santiago and signed on August 18th of that year, a three party pact known as the "Santiago Declaration" pursuant to which the three Governments state that they believe in the obligation of insuring the necessary subsistence conditions for their people as well as the means for economic development, and believe that they have the duty of preventing the exploitation of natural resources, outside of their own jurisdiction, when it endangers the existence, integrity and conservation of this wealth and injures their people who, due to their geographical position, possess in their seas, vital and irreplaceable sources of subsistence and economic resources. The Governments of Chile, Ecuador and Peru proclaimed as a rule of their international maritime policy, their exclusive and absolute jurisdiction on the seas that adjoin the coasts of their respective countries, up to a minimum distance of 200 sea miles from said coasts and added that this declaration did not imply a refusal to recognize the necessary limitations to the exercise of sovereignty and jurisdiction established by international law in favor of innocent and inoffensive passage through said zone of ships of all nations.

This is the juridical position internationally known under the denomination of "the 200 mile limit in the South Pacific"—and attacked by commentators of International Law as well as officially by several Governments, including the United States of America. These opponents consider it inapplicable because it violates the universal principle of Freedom of the Sea.

Of course as a new juridical position and insofar as it shows a materialization of an evaluation of the Law, its meaning is arguable, but I believe it has a background of facts as well as a human and juridical aspect, that produce an unquestionable and endurable position due to its intrinsic justice and morality.

*   *   *

Grotius literally says in his work:

"Because everybody admits that if a great number of people hunt on land or fish in a river, the forest can be easily depopulated of wild animals and the river of fish, *but this contingency is impossible in the case of the sea."*   (Emphasis added)

It is obvious then that Grotius based his idea of Freedom of Fishing as a part of the Freedom of the Sea, on the premise, then apparently true and now evidently false, of the inexhaustibility of the resources and species of the sea.

In another paragraph of his work he says:

"Besides, even in the case that a man could claim dominion over the sea, he could still not deny things of common use   .   .   .   And if it were possible to forbid, for example, fishing, because it is, *in a way, possible to maintain that fish are exhaustible,* it would still be impossible to forbid navigation, *because the sea cannot be used up."* ═══ (Emphasis added)

OPEN SEAS ═══ UNLESS SEAS USED UP

It is clear, then, that the Freedom of the Sea, defended by Grotius, is based on its inexhaustibility by use, and it is evident that the writer himself conceived the possibility of forbidding fishing if the possibility were proved, however improbable it may have seemed at the time, that fish were exhaustible.

The Freedom of the Sea was therefore always essentially the freedom of navigation and trade and this essential position was respected by the "200 mile limit in the South Pacific," that expressly refers to their intangibility.

The Freedom of Fishing was an easily derived consequence of juridical logic applied to this opportunity and to geography. Because it was believed that the sea was free, its riches could be used by all. But as we have seen, the basis of that juridical conception consisted in the belief in the inexhaustibility of marine resources and this belief was in accordance with the knowledge of that time.

*   *   *

But this Humboldt current, which is a factor that provides our icthyological wealth, also causes the variations in our climatological conditions that make all the Peruvian coast, which by its geographic situation should be tropical, a sandy desert as completely desert as the Sahara in Africa, only interrupted by a few valleys formed by rivers flowing into the sea from the Andes. Only 4% of the total extent of the coast is cultivated and this by means of expensive artificial irrigation, since we completely lack rain. Nothing, absolutely nothing is cultivated with rainfall, with which generous nature aids men of other regions or countries.

This geographic irregularity forces the inhabitant of the Peruvian coast to live, whether he wants to or not, from fishing, because he has no other means of subsistence.

Our Government thus fulfilled its duty of supervising the subsistence of its people by its Supreme Decree of August 1, 1947. The great fertility of our sea, offered by nature as compensation for the desert provided by climatological conditions on the coast, has forced Peruvians since Prehistoric times, to look to the sea for the food denied to them by the land, and today, for the same reason, the modern State searches for a source of wealth to complement its poor economy.

The Peruvian jurists, who like myself, have contributed in some way to create our international maritime policy, feel pride in our mission and our consciences are clear.

We do not believe we are attacking International Law, when we promote new legal concepts in line with the reality of our times. * * *

ORGANIZATION OF AMERICAN STATES: FOREIGN MINISTERS DISCUSS COASTAL STATE FISHERIES QUESTION

64 United States Department of State Bulletin 245 (1971).

[In the Permanent Council of the Organization of American States, Ambassador Jova, U. S. representative to the OAS, made on January 27, 1971, the statement which appears in part below.]

The United States delegation wishes to take this opportunity to state again the reasons for opposing the resolution proposed by the delegation of Ecuador to convoke a Meeting of Consultation of Ministers of Foreign Affairs. This meeting is proposed, as provided in article 59 of the Charter of the Organization of American States, in order to consider problems of an urgent nature and of common interest to the American states.

This difference with Ecuador arises from varying interpretations as to territorial waters or jurisdiction over adjacent waters. The United States, and most of the countries of the world, believe that exclusive coastal state fisheries jurisdiction over adjacent waters extends no further than 12 miles and anything beyond that is international waters. Certain other nations, including Ecuador, maintain that their jurisdiction extends for 200 miles. The root of the dispute, I am sure, will not be solved until the nations of the world agree on a common standard for the law of the sea. In the meantime, however, we have long maintained that it should be possible to work out by common agreement some sort of arrangements which would provide for an orderly setting for the carrying out of international commerce and fisheries with due respect for the position of each state concerned. (This, of course, must be a two-way street.) We have been willing to attempt to work out such a modus vivendi through negotiation and, together with the Governments of Chile, Ecuador, and Peru, have for some 2½ years been engaged in slow but progressively useful negotiations in the forum of the so-called quadripartite talks.

Our mutual dilemma lies in the fact that Ecuadorean law apparently requires that any ship fishing within 200 miles of its coast purchase fishing licenses. We consider these to be international waters, open to fishing without licenses by vessels of any nationality. Our Government is obliged by law to furnish protection to the interests of its fishermen. A recent law enacted by the Congress of the United States specifically provides for the suspension of sales of military equipment to a Government which seizes (in our view illegally) United States fishing vessels in waters beyond 12 miles. As you see, the laws of the sovereign nation of Ecuador seem to be in conflict with the laws of the sovereign nation of the United States. In a situation such as this, particularly one existing between old friends and traditional allies, the only route is to seek an amicable solution through negotiation. It was for this reason that the quadripartite talks were considered so important by my Government. (at 245–246)

[The 14th Meeting of Consultation of Foreign Affairs of the OAS approved on January 31, 1971, by a vote of 19 (including the United States and Ecuador) to 0, with 4 abstentions, a resolution the text of which appears below.]

WHEREAS:

Article 3.b of the Charter of the Organization of American States establishes that:

"International order consists essentially of respect for the personality, sovereignty, and independence of States, and the faithful fulfillment of obligations derived from treaties and other sources of international law";

Article 19 of the Charter states that:

"No State may use or encourage the use of coercive measures of an economic or political character in order to force the sovereign will of another State and obtain from it advantages of any kind";

The position of Ecuador is that without violating any rule whatsoever of international law, and in the exercise of its sovereignty, it has fixed the extent of its territorial sea at 200 nautical miles and therefore, according to Ecuadorian law, foreign boats may not fish within those 200 nautical miles without a license or registration issued by the Ecuadorian Government;

The position of the United States of America is that under international law coastal states' exclusive fishing jurisdiction may not extend more than 12 miles off their coast;

There has arisen a state of uneasiness with respect to this matter,

THE FOURTEENTH MEETING OF CONSULTATION OF MINISTERS OF FOREIGN AFFAIRS

RESOLVES:

1.   To urge the Parties to avoid the aggravation of their differences.

2.   To urge the Parties to use the negotiations in which they have shown special interest.

3.   To urge the Member States that in their reciprocal relations they observe strictly the principles of the Charter of the Organization of American States and abstain from the use of any kind of measure that may affect the sovereignty of the States and the tranquility of the Hemisphere.   (at 250)

BRAZIL STANDS FIRM ON 200–MILE SEA LIMIT AND JOINS FIVE OTHER LATIN NATIONS IN CONFLICT WITH THE UNITED STATES

The New York Times, June 6, 1971, Sec. 1, at 12, col. 1.*

Rio De Janeiro, June 5—Brazil has joined five other South American countries that are apparently frozen into a diplomatic confrontation with the United States over control of coastal waters in general and over fishing rights in particular.

The events that made Brazil part of the seeming deadlock began last year, when Brazil joined Ecuador, Peru, Chile, Argentina and Uruguay in claiming control over 200 nautical miles measured seaward from the coastline.   The United States Government, for almost 20 years, has insisted that such unilateral claims are not founded in international law and that it would not recognize them.

Two months ago Brazil established by decree the rules for fishing within her territorial waters, going beyond her neighbors in apparent toughness.   But, unlike her neighbors, she left the door open for the negotiation of bilateral fishing agreements.

After a 60-day grace period, the Brazilian Navy began patrolling coastal waters this week, searching for offenders against the new rules.

On Wednesday in Washington, a State Department spokesman answered a reporter's question by saying that American fishermen had been told they were not obliged under international law to purchase licenses and that vessels flying the United States flag would not be advised to buy licenses.   His statement was the lead article in all major Brazilian newspapers on Thursday, and, in the opinion of diplomatic observers here, the stage was set for conflict, not negotiations.

*   *   *

According to information available here, as many as 500 foreign shrimp trawlers operate, depending on the season, within 50 miles of the Brazilian coast from the mouth of the Amazon northward. Most of them are reported to be American-owned and to be fishing for the United States market.

Brazilian officials have reported vessels flying the Japanese and South Korean flag among the fleet, as well as American-flag shrimpers operating with mother ships out of Gulf Coast ports. The other boats operate from ports in Trinidad-Tobago, Guyana, Surinam and French Guiana.

* * *

In Washington, fishing sources report, the Defense Department has carried the day with the argument that any such agreements would recognize a claim to sovereignty 200 miles out to sea, with drastic consequences for free navigation and research for the United States Navy and, thus, for national security of the United States as a sea power.

Rationale of claims by states on west coast. Are their claims justified on the ground that the continental shelf off the west coast of South America is so narrow it can provide them with little if any mineral resources, and hence they must appropriate the only resource available off their coast, i. e. fish? If so, what of the fishing claims up to 200 miles made by states on the east coast of South America, such as Brazil, where the continental shelf is very broad?

LETTER FROM THE SECRETARY OF STATE OF THE UNITED STATES SUBMITTING TO THE PRESIDENT, FOR TRANSMISSION TO THE SENATE, THE AGREEMENT BETWEEN THE UNITED STATES AND BRAZIL CONCERNING SHRIMP SIGNED MAY 9, 1972

United States Senate, Executive P, 92d Congress, 2d Session (1972).

DEPARTMENT OF STATE,
Washington, June 23, 1972.

THE PRESIDENT,
The White House:

* * *

The necessity for this Agreement arose when Brazil, in 1970, asserted a claim to a territorial sea extending 200 miles from its coast and subsequently promulgated regulations purporting to control fishing by foreign flag vessels within the claimed territorial sea. This jurisdictional claim, which was not recognized by the United States, encompassed important shrimp resources that had been exploited for several years by a large number of United States flag vessels in waters lying entirely beyond 12 nautical miles from the coast and therefore, in the view of the United States, not subject to the exclusive fishery jurisdiction of Brazil.

The Agreement provides for the conservation of shrimp resources in which the United States and Brazil have a mutual interest and is also designed to forestall problems which might arise because of the difference in the views of the Governments concerning jurisdiction over those resources. The Agreement seeks to accomplish this objective without prejudice to the legal position maintained by either Government with respect to the breadth of the territorial sea or fisheries jurisdiction under international law.

The major provisions of the Agreement are as follows. The United States, in recognition of the lack of adequate information concerning the potential productivity of shrimp resources off the coast of northeastern Brazil, agrees to limit the number of its vessels participating in the exploitation of those resources to 325. The area within which this limitation will apply is defined as delimited by the 30-meter isobath, the latitude of 1 degree north and the meridian of 47 degrees 30 minutes west longitude. The United States will limit fishing for shrimp by its vessels within the area of the Agreement to the period from March 1 through November 30. In the most southern part of the area, southeast of a bearing of 240 degrees to the Ponta do Ceu radiobeacon, United States vessels will fish for shrimp during the period March 1 to July 1. Not more than 160 of the vessels authorized by the United States to fish under the Agreement will operate within the area at any one time. Vessels fishing under the Agreement will keep records of their operations, and the Parties will exchange information concerning conditions in the fishery. The vessels to be authorized by the United States, and the fishing gear and methods which they will use, will be essentially the same as those commonly employed in the fishery hitherto. Under the Agreement, Brazilian shrimp fishermen will also be under certain specified limitations of types appropriate to the stage of development of the Brazilian shrimp industry.

The Agreement assigns responsibility for enforcement of its terms to the Government of Brazil, for reasons of convenience and economy, and provides that the United States shall pay Brazil $200,-000 annually for the expenses resulting from enforcement functions, as well as a specified fee for any unusual expenses which Brazil might incur in carrying out these functions. United States vessels which may be apprehended by Brazilian authorities in violation of any provision of the Agreement are to be turned over promptly to United States authorities for investigation and for punishment if found guilty.

The Agreement will terminate on January 1, 1974, unless extended by the Parties.

* * *

WILLIAM P. ROGERS.

Interim order by the International Court of Justice in fisheries case. In proceedings instituted on April 14, 1972, the United Kingdom asked the court to declare invalid under international law the claim of Iceland to extend as of September 1, 1972, its exclusive jurisdiction over fisheries around Iceland to a distance of 50 nautical miles from the coast. The United Kingdom then moved for the issuance of interim measures of protection. On August 17, 1972, the court issued an order which states that, pending final decision, Iceland "should not" enforce its fisheries regulation against vessels of the United Kingdom outside the 12 mile limit and the United Kingdom "should" ensure its vessels do not take a catch of more than 170,000 metric tons in designated sea areas around Iceland. The text of the order is in 11 International Legal Materials 1069 (1972). The editors of the publication indicate in a footnote that a similar order of interim measures of protection was issued by the court in the fisheries case between the Federal Republic of Germany and Iceland.

TRADE-OFF

UNION OF SOVIET SOCIALIST REPUBLICS, MINISTRY OF FISHERIES ARTICLE ON FREEDOM OF HIGH SEAS [1]

VIII International Legal Materials 896 (1969).

Violations of Freedom of the High Seas—A Generally Recognized Principle of International Law—Are Inadmissible

Recognition of freedom of the high seas is one of the most important principles of the international law of the sea. This principle was strengthened, in particular, in the 1958 Geneva Convention on the High Seas, which was signed by fifty-seven states. It is proclaimed in the Convention that the high seas are open to all nations, and no state may validly purport to subject any part of them to its sovereignty. Freedom of the high seas comprises, especially, freedom of fishing, which all countries exercise reasonably, taking into account the interest of other states.

* * *

[1]. Translated for International Legal Materials by William E. Butler, Research Associate, Harvard Law School. The Russian text was the lead editorial in the March 1967 issue of Rybnoe khoziaistvo, the organ of the Ministry of Fisheries of the U.S.S.R.

After the Second World War, some capitalist countries began to attempt to extend in a unilateral manner their jurisdiction to areas of high seas.

These claims were not recognized by the overwhelming majority of other states and, in many instances, brought forth strong protests on their part. Regrettably, this practice has not ceased up to the present time. We recall that in 1958 Argentina signed all four Geneva Conventions on the Law of the Sea, but then departed from its previous position.

On December 29, 1966, the President of Argentina sanctioned the entry into force of a law in which the sovereignty of the country "to the seas contiguous to its territory out to a distance of 200-nautical miles from the lowest watermark" is proclaimed. * * *

The Minister of Foreign Affairs and Worship of Argentina, in explaining the reasons for issuing the new law, pointed to the exceptional importance of a precise delimitation of national territory, since legislation in force is not sufficiently concrete, and "sovereignty must be one and indivisible". He also declared it was the intention of the Executive Power "to continue in an ever broadening form the investigative work in all areas affecting the exploitation of mineral, vegetable, and animal resources for the purpose of intensively using the sea".

* * *

And what is the crux of the new legislative act of Argentina? One is struck in examining it that many provisions of the new law, as well as the decree on provisional rules for its application, are, first, an infringement of the principle of freedom of the high seas and, second, that they not only contravene international legal norms, but each other as well.

Thus, for example, it is indicated in the law that the 200-mile zone mentioned therein is considered to be territorial waters. It specifies in the law (Article 3) that freedom of navigation and of air navigation in the 200-mile zone shall not be affected by its provisions. We recall that according to Article 2 of the 1958 Geneva Convention on the Territorial Sea, over which there is the signature of Argentina, the sovereignty of a coastal state extends to the air space over its territorial sea. Consequently, strictly following the wording of the law, the 200-mile zone of Argentina, over which foreign aircraft may fly freely, is not considered by its President as being territorial waters. It would appear that the law refers only to establishment of an excessively broad fishing zone on the high seas. However, this is not so.

In Article 1 of the decree it is said that the Command of Naval Operations has been authorized to issue to vessels under foreign flag which apply, on condition that they are obliged to notify their location daily, "permits to continue fishing in the Argentine territorial sea [!] at a distance of not less than 12-miles from shore".

This means, in contrast to the President of Argentina, that the Command of the Navy will consider the 200-mile zone to be territorial waters. These obvious contradictions between the law and the decree are difficult to explain.

* * *

The content of Article 4 of the decree, according to which the Command of Naval Operations will exact from foreign fishing vessels a charge of 10,000 pesos * * * for the "right of inspection"[?], also arouses perplexity. Logic and legal practice suggest that those who perform and not those who are the object of such activities should pay for the right of carrying out any actions (if payment may be established at all for this right), all the more so since the Government of Argentina grants the "right of inspection" to its own naval forces.

As it later turned out unofficially, the decree contemplated the exaction of a charge for the maintenance of inspection vessels.

The Government of Argentina, in adopting the new law, is essentially attempting to place under its sovereignty broad areas of the high seas to the prejudice of the rights and interests of other states. These actions of the Government of Argentina are fraught with dangerous consequences, and they are in obvious contravention of the principles of contemporary international law.

EVOLUTION OF THE POSITION OF THE UNITED STATES

Until recently, the United States supported a three-mile limit as the appropriate breadth of the territorial waters. At the First Geneva Conference on the Law of the Sea in 1958, the United States first maintained its support of the three-mile limit, but eventually shifted its support to a compromise proposal providing for a six-mile limit of territorial sea and, subject to certain qualifications, a six-mile fishing zone beyond it. The proposal was not adopted. It supported a similar proposal at the Second Geneva Conference on the Law of the Sea in 1960 and again the proposal failed. Since then the position of the United States has evolved some more, as shown by the materials which follow.

AN ACT TO ESTABLISH A CONTIGUOUS FISHERY ZONE BEYOND THE TERRITORIAL SEA OF THE UNITED STATES

80 Stat. 908.

Be it enacted by the Senate and House of Representatives of the United States of America in Congress assembled, That there is established a fisheries zone contiguous to the territorial sea of the United States. The United States will exercise the same exclusive rights in respect to fisheries in the zone as it has in its territorial sea, subject to the continuation of traditional fishing by foreign states within this zone as may be recognized by the United States.

SEC. 2.   The fisheries zone has as its inner boundary the outer limits of the territorial sea and as its seaward boundary a line drawn so that each point on the line is nine nautical miles from the nearest point in the inner boundary.

SEC. 3.   Whenever the President determines that a portion of the fisheries zone conflicts with the territorial waters or fisheries zone of another country, he may establish a seaward boundary for such portion of the zone in substitution for the seaward boundary described in section 2.

SEC. 4.   Nothing in this Act shall be construed as extending the jurisdiction of the States to the natural resources beneath and in the waters within the fisheries zone established by this Act or as diminishing their jurisdiction to such resources beneath and in the waters of the territorial seas of the United States.

Approved October 14, 1966.

UNITED STATES STATEMENT ON CANADIAN FISHERIES CLOSING LINES ANNOUNCEMENT, DEC. 18, 1970.

65 American Journal of International Law 388 (1971).

On December 18, 1970, the Department of State released the following statement:

Today, the Government of Canada announced the establishment of fisheries closing lines which purport to extend unilaterally Canadian jurisdiction over areas which are traditionally regarded as the high seas.   The areas affected are: Strait of Belle Isle, Cabot Strait, Bay of Fundy, Queen Charlotte Sound, and Dixon Entrance.

The United States deeply regrets this action.   The United States regards this unilateral act as totally without foundation in international law.   The United States firmly opposes such unilateral extensions of jurisdiction and believes that outstanding issues concerning the oceans can only be resolved by effective international action.

*   *   *

STATEMENT BY THE LEGAL ADVISER OF THE DEPARTMENT OF STATE OF THE UNITED STATES CONCERNING THE BREADTH OF THE TERRITORIAL SEA, AUGUST 27, 1971.

66 American Journal of International Law 133 (1972).

[The U.N. Committee on the Peaceful Uses of the Seabed and the Ocean Floor Beyond the Limits of National Jurisdiction met at Geneva

July 19 to August 27, 1971. Following are excerpts from a statement by John R. Stevenson, Legal Adviser of the Department of State and U.S. Representative to the Committee, made in Subcommittee II on August 3, 1971, (referring to the) text of draft articles on the breadth of the territorial sea, straits, and fisheries which were submitted to the subcommittee the same day by the U.S. Delegation.]

The first article presented by my Government would establish a maximum breadth of 12 miles for the territorial sea. The prime distinguishing characteristic of the territorial sea is that the coastal state exercises jurisdiction over navigation and overflight, subject to a limited right of innocent passage for vessels. We believe agreement must be reached on a narrow territorial sea. While my Government adheres to the traditional 3-mile limit, it is prepared to take into account the views of others and to agree to a treaty fixing the maximum breadth of the territorial sea at 12 nautical miles, if there is an adequate agreement concerning international straits—to which I shall refer shortly. We use the 12-mile figure because it represents the best—probably the only—possibility for reaching agreement. It is apparent that the overwhelming majority of states are prepared to accept the 12-mile limit. In most cases where broader jurisdictional claims have been made, the reasons for those claims were resource-oriented. We believe that the real concerns of those few states that have claimed broader limits for the territorial sea can be accommodated in the course of the work of this and the other subcommittees.

However, interests in international navigation and overflight are not adequately accommodated with a 12-mile territorial sea alone. By agreeing to extend the territorial sea from 3 to 12 miles, we would place many important straits totally within the territorial sea of riparian states, thus subjecting movements through such straits to the limitations of innocent passage. The doctrine of innocent passage is not adequate when applied to international straits. For example, some states consider "innocence" to be a subjective criterion to be left to the discretion of the coastal state. Some argue that passage of certain types of vessels is inherently non-innocent, or that innocence may depend on the flag, cargo, or destination of a vessel. Under the Territorial Sea Convention, neither aircraft nor submerged submarines have a right of innocent passage.

We believe the right to transit straits should be regarded in law for what it is in fact: an inherent and inseparable adjunct of the freedoms of navigation and overflight on the high seas themselves. Without such a right of transit, these high seas freedoms would lose much of their meaning if an expansion of the territorial sea to 12 miles is to be recognized and agreed.

We do not know whether most states that already claim or recognize territorial seas of more than 3 miles thereby intended to relinquish their own rights of transit in important international straits overlapped by territorial seas of more than 3 miles. Neither history nor logic compels any state to concede that an extension of territorial seas has the same effects upon the rights of the international community in straits as it has in other coastal areas. The balance of international and coastal interests is quite different in these two situations.

The second article we are presenting recognizes this distinction by providing for a right of free transit for vessels and aircraft through and over all international straits overlapped by territorial seas. Coastal states would have the right to designate corridors suitable for transit but they would not be obliged to do so. For our part, we are prepared to consider whether coastal and international interests could be similarly reconciled in the case of island nations * * *

* * * [T]he United States believes that straits wider than 6 miles currently have high seas within them, where states may exercise the freedoms of the high seas. In short, the present rule of international law in virtually all of the straits of concern is freedom of the seas. To achieve widespread international agreement we are prepared to give up high seas freedoms in these international straits in exchange for a limited but vital right. Subject only to the right of free transit, territorial waters in international straits would retain their national character in each and every respect. The new right of free transit would only apply in international straits, using the definition that was adopted at the 1958 Law of the Sea Conference; it would not apply to other territorial or internal waters. Moreover, the right is a narrow one—merely one of transiting the strait, not of conducting any other activities. Should a vessel conduct any other activities that are in violation of coastal state laws and regulations, it would be exceeding the scope of its right, and would be subject to appropriate enforcement action by the coastal state.

When we refer to enforcement of coastal state laws and regulations, we intend to include reasonable traffic safety regulations both for vessels and aircraft. We will, of course, want to approach this question cautiously in order to preserve the basic right of free transit and avoid a situation in which the coastal state has a legal basis for using safety regulations as a way of impairing the right of free transit.

We recognize the concern of many states bordering straits regarding the need to prevent pollution. Pollution control problems, however, are not unique in straits. For example, the same problems pertain in heavily traveled shipping routes. The doctrine of innocent passage is not adequate to protect both coastal and maritime interests in international straits. It applies only in territorial seas and, as I have mentioned, it is subject to varying interpretations by different coastal states. Specific international agreements are required to insure appropriate protection from the hazards of pollution.

* * *

SECTION C. ALLOCATION OF THE RESOURCES OF THE SEABED

1. *Evolution of the doctrine of the continental shelf.* President Truman proclaimed on September 28, 1945 that "the natural resources of the subsoil and sea bed of the continental shelf beneath the high seas but contiguous to the coast of the United States" were regarded by the United States as appertaining to it and "subject to its jurisdiction and control." Presidential Proclamation No. 2667, 59 Stat. 884. It was the first time anywhere in the world that such a claim had been made. Thereafter, claims to the resources of the continental shelf were made by a large number of other states.

Only thirteen years after the presidential proclamation, the Convention on the Continental Shelf was signed. As of January 1, 1972, 49 states were parties to it. The ready acceptance of the new basis of jurisdiction illustrates the capacity of international law to adapt and change very rapidly when the international community so demands.

2. *Division of the resources of the continental shelf between the States and the federal government.* In the Submerged Lands Act of May 22, 1953, 67 Stat. 29, the States of the United States were granted rights to the lands which are part of the continental shelf of the United States up to three nautical miles from the coast on the Atlantic and Pacific Oceans, and up to nine nautical miles in the Gulf of Mexico if the states involved could establish an historical claim to such distance. Beyond those limits, the federal government controls the resources of the continental shelf. Outer Continental Shelf Lands Act of August 7, 1953, 67 Stat. 462. The division of the resources does not create an issue of international law, however. The issue is one of domestic law. The Outer Continental Shelf Lands Act conforms to the Convention on the Continental Shelf.

CONVENTION ON THE CONTINENTAL SHELF OF APRIL 29, 1958

15 U.S.T. 471, 499 U.N.T.S. 311.

Article 1

For the purpose of these articles, the term "continental shelf" is used as referring (a) to the seabed and subsoil of the submarine areas adjacent to the coast but outside the area of the territorial sea, to a depth of 200 metres or, beyond that limit, to where the depth of the superjacent waters admits of the exploitation of the natural resources of the said areas; (b) to the seabed and subsoil of similar submarine areas adjacent to the coasts of islands.

UNITED STATES v. RAY

United States Court of Appeals, Fifth Circuit, 1970.
423 F.2d 16.

AINSWORTH, CIRCUIT JUDGE. Triumph and Long Reefs are two coral reefs which lie in international waters about four and one-half miles off the southeast coast of Florida, near Miami, and are the subject of this interesting and fantastic controversy between two rival private claimants and the United States. To the District Court (Judge Charles B. Fulton), the case was reminiscent of a fairy tale.[1] To the defendants, the reefs were to become an island nation to be known as Grand Capri Republic; to intervenor, a new sovereign country would be established on the reefs, to be named Atlantis, Isle of Gold. Defendants would organize some semblance of a defense but have no intention of attacking the Coast Guard or Navy. Intervenor envisioned the reefs as a property worth one billion dollars, where a post office, building offices, stamp department and foreign office would be built, as well as a government palace and congress.

The fairy tale has an unhappy ending, with the granting by the District Court of the petition of the United States for a permanent injunction against the activities of defendants and intervenor on these reefs, and by the action which we take here in affirming in part and reversing in part the judgment of the trial court. The dreams of the separate groups for a new nation must perish, like the lost continent "Atlantis," beneath the waves and waters of the sea which constantly submerge the reefs.

The United States brought this action for injunctive relief against Louis M. Ray and Acme General Contractors, Inc. alleging interference with the rights of the United States on coral reefs located on its Continental Shelf on two grounds. In the first count the Government alleged that the activities of these defendants in building caissons on the reefs, dredging material from the seabed and depositing that material within the caissons was causing irreparable injury to the reefs which are subject to the control of the United States, and that these activities constituted trespass. The second count alleged that these activities were being unlawfully conducted without the required authorization of the Secretary of the Army. See 33 U.S.C.A. § 403; 43 U.S.C.A. § 1333(f). A preliminary injunction was granted against defendants. Thereafter Atlantis Development Corporation, Ltd., which was also contemplating commercial development of the reefs, was allowed by

---

1. Judge Fulton quoted the following as appropriate to his remark:

   "They thought I was crazy when I bought the island. I said it was a bargain * * *.

   They thought it was anarchy to fly my own personal flag * * *."

   Donleavy, J. P.; "At Longitude and Latitude," in Meet My Maker the Mad Molecule, pp. 26–28; Delacorte Press, N. Y. (1960); United States v. Ray, S.D.Fla., 1969, 294 F.Supp. 532.

this Court to intervene in the proceedings. Intervenor filed a cross claim, alleging its <u>superior title to the property by virtue of discovery</u> of the reefs by its predecessor. After an extensive nonjury trial, at which numerous witnesses, lay and expert, testified and at which voluminous exhibits were introduced, the District Court adopted all of the facts stipulated by the parties and further found:

1. Triumph and Long Reefs are a part of the Continental Shelf ✓ extending seaward from the East Coast of Florida, and all waters overlying the reefs do not exceed one hundred fathoms in depth.

2. Triumph and Long Reefs are completely submerged at all times, except when their highest projections are fleetingly visible while awash at mean low water. Accordingly, Triumph and Long Reefs are part of the "seabed" and "subsoil" of the ✓ Outer Continental Shelf within the Outer Continental Shelf Lands Act of 1953, 43 U.S.C. § 1331, et seq.

3. These reefs, together with the organisms attached thereto, are "natural resources" within the Outer Continental Shelf ✓ Lands Act, and the Geneva Convention on the Continental Shelf.

4. The caissons positioned by Ray and the jack platform construction or "boathouses" built on pilings proposed by Atlantis constitute "artificial islands and fixed structures * * * erected * * * for the purpose of * * * developing" the reefs, within the Outer Continental Shelf Lands Act.

The District Court denied all claims of defendants and intervenor, granted the claim of the Government under its second count, <u>but denied the Government's claim of trespass under the first</u> count. In so doing, the District Court recognized the sovereign rights of the United States, but concluded that those rights are limited as the claimed interest of the United States is something less than a property right, consisting of neither ownership nor possession, and consequently not supporting a common law action for trespass quare clausum fregit.

All parties have appealed. The Government's appeal is limited to the Court's denial of an injunction on count one of the amended complaint. We affirm the District Court's factual findings and its grant of injunctive relief under the Government's second count. However, we reverse the Court's denial of injunctive relief on the first count of the Government's amended complaint.

LACK OF STATUTORY PERMIT ISSUE:

The District Court correctly concluded that the past and proposed activities of defendants and intervenor were unlawful in the absence ✓ of a statutory permit from the Secretary of the Army. Section 10 of the Rivers and Harbors Act, 33 U.S.C. § 403, prohibits construction in navigable waters of the United States unless the work has been "recommended by the Chief of Engineers and authorized by the Secretary of the Army." The authority of the Secretary of the Army is extended to the Outer Continental Shelf by Section 1333(f) of the Outer Continental Shelf Lands Act, 43 U.S.C. § 1331 et seq.:

> The authority of the Secretary of the Army to prevent obstruction to navigation in the navigable waters of the United States is extended to artificial islands and fixed structures located on the outer Continental Shelf.

It is undisputed that defendants and intervenor did not obtain permission or authority for their activities on the reefs. The argument is made that the area is not navigable and therefore not governed by Section 1333(f) of the Outer Continental Shelf Lands Act. Apparently the Court did not, nor do we, deem it necessary to predicate the injunction on navigability of waters covering the reefs, although a specific finding of navigability was made. The quoted section extends the authority of the Secretary to "fixed structures located on the outer Continental Shelf" without regard to the navigability of the particular area involved. If it were necessary to find navigability, however, the evidence amply supports such a finding, and fully establishes that the structures herein involved interfere with the exclusive rights of the United States under the Convention to explore the Continental Shelf and exploit its natural resources. Under the circumstances we do not decide what the result would be if the structures did not interfere with the rights of the United States as recognized by the Convention, our decision being limited to the particular facts of this case.

THE TRESPASS ISSUE:

It is clear that the reefs in question are within the area designated as the Continental Shelf by both national (Outer Continental Shelf Lands Act, supra) and international (Geneva Convention on the Continental Shelf, 15 U.S.T. 473, executed in 1958 and effective in 1964) law.

The Outer Continental Shelf Lands Act, 43 U.S.C.A. § 1331(a), in pertinent part provides:

> The term "outer Continental Shelf" means all submerged lands lying seaward and outside of the area of lands beneath navigable waters as defined in section 1301 of this title, and of which the subsoil and seabed appertain to the United States and are subject to its jurisdiction and control.

Article 1 of the international Convention on the Continental Shelf similarly reads:

> For the purpose of these articles, the term "continental shelf" is used as referring (a) to the seabed and subsoil of the submarine areas adjacent to the coast but outside the area of the territorial sea, to a depth of 200 metres or, beyond that limit, to where the

depth of the superjacent waters admits of the exploitation of the natural resources of the said areas; * * * 15 U.S.T. 473.

The evidence shows that the reefs are completely submerged at mean high water, and as the Court specifically found, "at all times, except when their highest projections are fleetingly visible while awash at mean low water." Thus the reefs are contemplated within the definition of the Outer Continental Shelf Lands Act and the Geneva Convention on the Continental Shelf, if they meet the definition of "seabed" or "subsoil" contained therein. Webster defines "seabed" as "lands underlying the sea." The evidence establishes that the term "seabed" is commonly understood to be any terrain below the high water line. The federal and common law comports with this understanding in defining the "bed" of a body of water as lands below the ordinary high water mark. * * * The record shows that on the death of the coral, which has a natural predilection for cementing itself onto preexisting rocky structures, its skeletal remains become part of the seabed of the Continental Shelf. The District Court's finding that the reefs are part of the "seabed" of the Shelf is fully supported by substantial evidence of record.

The same national and international laws (The Outer Continental Shelf Lands Act and the Geneva Convention on the Continental Shelf) explicitly recognize the sovereign rights of the United States and the exclusiveness of those rights to explore the Shelf and exploit its natural resources.

The Outer Continental Shelf Lands Act (43 U.S.C.A. § 1332(a)) states:

> It is declared to be the policy of the United States that the subsoil and seabed of the outer Continental Shelf appertain to the United States and are subject to its jurisdiction, control, and power of disposition as provided in this subchapter.

To the extent that any of the terms of the Act are inconsistent with the later adopted Geneva Convention on the Continental Shelf they should be considered superseded. See Cook v. United States, 288 U.S. 102, 118–119, 53 S.Ct. 305, 77 L.Ed. 641 (1933). But there is nothing in the pertinent language of the Geneva Convention on the Continental Shelf which detracts from or is inconsistent with the Outer Continental Shelf Lands Act. To the contrary, the Geneva Convention confirms and crystallizes the exclusiveness of those rights, particularly with reference to the natural resources of the Shelf.

Article 2 of the Geneva Convention on the Continental Shelf provides:

1. The coastal State exercises over the continental shelf sovereign rights for the purpose of exploring it and exploiting its natural resources.

2. The rights referred to in paragraph 1 of this article are exclusive in the sense that if the coastal State does not explore

the continental shelf or exploit its natural resources, no one
may undertake these activities, or make a claim to the continental shelf, without the express consent of the coastal
State.

3. The rights of the coastal State over the continental shelf do
not depend on occupation, effective or notional, or on any
express proclamation.

4. The natural resources referred to in these articles consist of
the mineral and other non-living resources of the seabed and
subsoil together with living organisms belonging to sedentary
species, that is to say, organisms which, at the harvestable
stage, either are immobile on or under the seabed or are unable to move except in constant physical contact with the seabed or the subsoil.

It is unnecessary for us to decide whether the Outer Continental
Shelf Lands Act, Section 1332(a), supra (which does not limit the nation's "jurisdiction, control, and power of disposition" to the natural
resources of the Shelf), alone confers rights sufficient to authorize the
injunctive relief sought. The right of the United States to control
those resources is implicit in Article 2, paragraphs 1, 2 and 3, supra, of
the Geneva Convention on the Continental Shelf, and explicitly recognized in the Submerged Lands Act, 43 U.S.C.A. § 1301 et seq. This Act
further provides (43 U.S.C.A. § 1302) the definition of "natural resources" of the Continental Shelf:

Nothing in this chapter shall be deemed to affect in any wise
the rights of the United States to the natural resources of that portion of the subsoil and seabed of the Continental Shelf lying seaward and outside of the area of lands beneath navigable waters,
as defined in Section 1301 of this title, all of which natural resources appertain to the United States, and the jurisdiction and
control of which by the United States is confirmed.

Section 1301, referred to within the above-quoted section, defines
"natural resources" as including, *"without limiting the generality
thereof,* oil, gas, and all other minerals, and *fish,* shrimp, oysters,
clams, crabs, lobsters, sponges, kelp, *and other marine animal* and
plant *life* * * *." (Emphasis supplied.) 43 U.S.C.A. § 1301(e).

Article 2, paragraph 4, of the Geneva Convention on the Continental Shelf includes in its definition of "natural resources" both
living and non-living resources, for it defines the term as consisting
of " * * * mineral and other non-living resources of the seabed and
subsoil together with living organisms belonging to sedentary species.
* * *"

Having thus concluded that the United States has the exclusive
right for purposes of exploration and exploitation of the reefs, there
remains only the question of whether injunctive relief was improper-

ly denied to the Government on its first count which alleged trespass.

Although the complaint is inaccurately framed in terms of trespass in count one, the Government repeatedly stresses that it is not claiming ownership of the reefs. We do not question the District Court's conclusion that the Government's interest, being something less than fee simple, cannot support a common law action for trespass quare clausum fregit. But we do not understand that claim to seek such a remedy, despite the language in which the petition is couched. Damages, an inseparable element in the common law action for trespass, are not sought here, and the only relief requested is restraint from interference with rights to an area which appertains to the United States and which under national and international law is subject not only to its jurisdiction but its control as well. It is in this light that we consider the allegations of amended count one.

Neither ownership nor possession is, however, a necessary requisite for the granting of injunctive relief. This principle is implicit in the companion decisions of the Supreme Court, United States v. State of Louisiana, 339 U.S. 699, 70 S.Ct. 914, 94 L.Ed. 1216 (1950); United States v. State of Texas, 339 U.S. 707, 70 S.Ct. 918, 94 L.Ed. 1221 (1950), in which injunctive relief was granted to protect "paramount rights" of the United States beyond the territorial limits of Louisiana and Texas, to distances farther out in international waters than that involved here and at a time when those rights had not yet been statutorily established.

* * *

The evidence overwhelmingly shows that the Government has a vital interest, from a practical as well as an aesthetic viewpoint, in preserving the reefs for public use and enjoyment. The protective underwater crannies of the reefs serve as a haven and spawning ground for myriad species of tropical and game fish. The unique and spectacular formations of the submerged coral deposits attract scores of water sports enthusiasts, skin divers, nature students, and marine researchers. Certain organisms living on the reefs contain substances useful in pharmacology. The reefs protect the inland waters from the heavy wave action of the open sea, thus making the area conducive to boating and other water sports. Congress, intent on conserving the value and natural beauty of the area, recently enacted the Biscayne National Monument Bill establishing the area, which includes both Triumph and Long Reefs, as a national monument. The reefs are a part of the series of coral reefs which dot the coastal and international waters extending out from southeastern Florida. Slightly to the south and west of the Triumph and Long Reefs, and straddling the three-mile dividing line between federal and state waters, is the huge federal-approved John Pennekamp Coral Reef State Park, also known as Key Largo Coral Reef Preserve. The fact that the area is worthy of preservation is abundantly demonstrated by the evidence. But more importantly, the evidence shows that protective action by the Government to prevent despoliation of these unique natural resources is of tantamount importance. There was convincing evidence that the activities of defendants in dredging and filling the reefs has and would continue to kill the sensitive corals by smothering them; that the construction would constitute a navigational hazard to pleasure craft, and would destroy a very productive marine area and other natural resources. Obviously the United States has an important interest to protect in preventing the establishment of a new sovereign nation within four and one-half miles of the Florida Coast, whether it be Grand Capri Republic or Atlantis, Isle of Gold.

The rights of the United States in and to the reefs and the vital interest which the Government has in preserving the area require full and permanent injunctive relief against any interference with those rights by defendants and intervenor.

* * *

Affirmed in part, reversed in part.

SUMMARY OF PROVISIONS OF DRAFT PROPOSED BY THE UNITED STATES FOR A "UNITED NATIONS CONVENTION ON THE INTERNATIONAL SEA BED AREA," AUGUST 3, 1970

65 American Journal of International Law 179 (1971).

[The United Nations Committee on the Peaceful Uses of the Seabed and the Ocean Floor Beyond the Limits of National Jurisdiction met in Geneva during the month of August, 1970. On August 3, the United States Delegation tabled, as a working paper, a Draft United Nations Convention on the International Seabed Area. The following summary of the provisions of that draft was prepared by John R. Stevenson, The Legal Adviser of the Department of State.]

On May 23, 1970, President Nixon announced a new oceans policy for the United States and stated that the United States would make specific proposals at the U.N. Seabeds Committee in August with regard to the proposed regime for the seabeds beyond national jurisdiction which he set forth in broad outline in his announcement. The submission of a draft "United Nations Convention on the International Seabed Area" to the Seabeds Committee as a working paper for discussion within that committee as well as with other governments and within the United States, implements the President's announcement. The draft convention and its appendices raise a number of questions with respect to which further detailed study is clearly necessary and do not necessarily represent the definitive views of the United States Government.

The basic structure of the convention reflects the President's proposals that states should by international agreement renounce their sovereign rights in the seabed under the high seas [3] beyond a water depth of 200 meters; establish an international regime for the area beyond with certain basic principles and general rules applicable throughout this area; authorize coastal states as Trustees for the international community to carry out the major administrative role in licensing the exploration and exploitation of natural resources from the limit of coastal state national jurisdiction to the edge of the continental margin, and to share in the international revenues from the Trusteeship Area which they administered; and establish international machinery to perform similar functions in the area beyond the continental margin.

Basic Principles

Among the basic principles which would become applicable to the entire International Seabed Area (including the International Trusteeship Area) under the convention would be the following:

The International Seabed Area would be the common heritage of mankind and no state could exercise sovereignty or sovereign rights over this area or its resources or, except as provided in the convention, acquire any right or interest therein.

The International Seabed Area would be open to use by all states without discrimination, except as otherwise provided in the convention, and would be reserved exclusively for peaceful purposes.

Provision would be made for the collection of revenues from mineral production in the Area to be used for international community purposes including economic advancement of developing countries and for promotion of the safe, efficient and economic exploitation of the mineral resources of the seabed.

Exploration and exploitation of the natural resources of the Area must not result in unjustified interference with other activities in the marine environment, and all activities in the Area must be conducted with adequate safeguards against pollution and for the protection of human life and the marine environment.

A contracting party would be responsible for insuring that those authorized by it (as Trustee in the Trusteeship Area) or sponsored by it (in the area beyond) complied with the convention. Contracting parties would also be responsible for any damage caused by those authorized or sponsored by them.

---

3. The President also referred to the U.S. proposals to fix the boundary between the territorial sea and the high seas at a maximum of 12 nautical miles with free transit through international straits and carefully defined preferential fishing rights for coastal states on the high seas.

The general rules would be as follows:

Mineral Resources

All exploration and exploitation of the mineral deposits in the Area would be licensed by the appropriate Trustee in the Trusteeship Area and by the International Seabed Resource Authority in the area beyond, subject to general provisions relating to the terms of licenses included in appendices forming part of the convention, a number of which allow greater discretion to the Trustee State in the case of the Trusteeship Area. The contracting parties would have primary responsibility for inspecting activities licensed or sponsored by them. The International Seabed Resource Authority would also have authority to inspect and determine if a licensed operation violates the convention. Licenses would be revoked only for cause and in accordance with the convention. Expropriation of investments made, or unjustifiable interference with operations conducted pursuant to a license, would be prohibited.

Living Resources of the Seabed

All contracting parties would have the right to explore and exploit these resources (e. g., king crab) subject to necessary conservation measures and the right of the Trustee in the Trusteeship Area to decide whether and by whom such resources should be exploited.

Protection of the Marine Environment, Life, and Property

The International Seabed Resource Authority would be authorized to prescribe rules to protect against pollution of the marine environment and injury to persons and resources resulting from exploration and exploitation and to prevent unjustifiable interference with other activities in the marine environment.

Scientific Research

Each party would agree to encourage, and to obviate interference with, scientific research and to promote international cooperation in scientific research.

International Trusteeship Area

The provisions of the convention relating to the International Trusteeship Area would define the outer limit of this area as a line beyond the base of the continental slope where the downward inclination of the seabed reaches a specified gradient. Such gradient would be determined by technical experts who would take into account, among other factors, ease of determination, the need to avoid dual administration of single resource deposits, and the avoidance of including excessively large areas in the Trusteeship Area. Other provisions would limit the Trustee's rights to those set forth in the convention. These rights of the Trustee State would include the issuing, suspending and revoking of mineral exploration and exploitation licenses subject to the rules set forth in the convention and its appendices, full discretion to decide whether a license should be issued and to whom a license should be issued, exercise of criminal and civil jurisdiction over its licensees, and retention of a portion (a figure between 33⅓ percent and 50 percent is suggested for consideration) of the fees and payments required under the convention for activities in the Area. The Trustee State would also be able to collect and retain additional license and rental fees to defray its administrative expenses and to collect other additional payments, retaining the same portion as indicated above of such other additional payments.

International Seabed Resource Authority

The principal organs of the proposed International Seabed Resource Authority would be an Assembly of all contracting parties; a Council of 24 members, including the six most industrially advanced contracting states, at least 12 developing countries and at least two landlocked or shelf-locked states; and a Tribunal of from five to nine judges elected by the Council.

The Assembly, which would meet at least once every 3 years, would elect members of the Council, approve budgets proposed by the Council, approve proposals of the Council for changes in allocation of net income within the limits prescribed in an appendix to the convention, and make recommendations.

The Council, which would make decisions only with the approval of a majority of both the six most industrially advanced contracting states and of the 18 other contracting states, would appoint the commissions provided for in the convention, submit to the Assembly budgets and proposals for changes in the allocation of net income within the limits prescribed in an appendix, and could issue emergency orders at the request of a contracting party to prevent serious harm to the marine environment.

The Tribunal would decide all disputes and advise on all questions relating to the interpretation and application of the convention. It would have compulsory jurisdiction in respect of any complaint brought by a contracting party against another contracting party for failure to fulfill its obligations under the convention, or whenever the Operations Commission, on its own initiative or at the request of any licensee, considered that a contracting party or licensee had failed to fulfill its obligations under the convention. If the Tribunal found the contracting party or licensee in default, such party or licensee would be obligated to take the measures required to implement the Tribunal's judgment. The Tribunal would have the power to impose fines of not more than $1,000 for each day of an offense as well as to award damages to the other party concerned. Where the Tribunal determined that a licensee had committed a gross and persistent violation of the provisions of the convention and within a reasonable time had not brought its operations into compliance, the Council could either revoke the license or request the Trustee Party to do so. Where a contracting party failed to perform the obligations incumbent on it under a judgment of the Tribunal, the Council, on application of the other party to the case, could decide upon measures to give effect to the judgment, including, when appropriate, temporary suspension of the rights of the defaulting party under the convention (the extent of such suspension to be related to the extent and seriousness of the violation). In addition, any contracting party, and any person directly affected, could bring before the Tribunal the question of the legality of any measure taken by the Council, or one of its commissions, on the ground of violation of the convention, lack of jurisdiction, infringement of important procedural rules, unreasonableness, or misuse of powers; and the Tribunal could declare such measure null and void.

The convention also provides for the establishment of three commissions, each of from five to nine members. The Rules and Recommended Practices Commission would consider and recommend to the Council adoption of annexes as described below. The Operations Commission would issue licenses for mineral exploration and exploitation in the area beyond the International Trusteeship Area and supervise the operations of licensees in cooperation with the Trustee or sponsoring party, but not itself engage in exploration or exploitation. The International Seabed Boundary Review Commission would review the delineation of boundaries submitted by the contracting parties for approval in accordance with the convention, negotiate differences among the parties and if the differences were not resolved initiate appropriate proceedings before the Tribunal, and render advice to contracting parties on boundary questions.

The members of the Rules and Recommended Practices Commission and the International Seabed Boundary Review Commission would not be full-time employees of the Authority.

The Secretariat of the Authority would consist of a Secretary General appointed by the Council and a staff appointed by the Secretary General under the general guidelines established by the Council.

Any amendment of the convention or the appendices would require the approval of the Council and a two-thirds vote of the Assembly and would come into force only when ratified by two-thirds of the contracting parties, including each of the six most industrially advanced contracting states.

Appendices, which are integral parts of the convention, are included in the draft convention by way of example only, as they require extensive consideration of the questions involved by technically qualified experts.

*   *   *

Prospects for the proposed convention. As pointed out on p. 153, the Committee on Peaceful Uses of the Seabed held meetings in 1971 and 1972 and reached agreement on some draft articles of seabed

principles.   But the principles in these articles are very general.
Even then, not all of the principles involved had been put in the form
of draft articles by the end of the meeting of July 17–August 18,
1972, and no drafting had been done on the more substantive provisions which are to follow the articles containing the principles.   At
the meeting, the representative of the United States continued to urge
the establishment of an international regime for the seabed along the
lines of the draft convention proposed by the United States.   For his
statement on this and other aspects of the law of the sea under consideration by the committee, see U.S. Calls for Prompt International
Action to Settle Problems of Law of the Sea, 67 U.S.Dept.State Bull.
382 (1972).

HENKIN, SEA BED PACT WOULD HELP UNITED STATES

The Washington Post, Aug. 8, 1971, Sec. B, at 2, col. 1.*

A year ago President Nixon presented to the world a proposal
for dealing with the mineral resources of the seabed.   It has been
studied by all governments and will loom large in United Nations discussions beginning this month.   Although the Nixon proposal skill-
fully accommodated various interests of the United States and the domestic political forces that represent them, a Senate Interior subcommittee has struck at the heart of the President's plan.

* * *

The Senate Interior subcommittee, arguing dubious law and wav-
ing a flimsy flag of "sovereignty" in its report, would have the United
States claim exclusive rights to the resources of the entire submerged
continental land mass, and insist on laissez-faire and the right to exploit at will beyond.   Essentially the same position has been taken by
the National Petroleum Council.

* * *

In my view the legal basis for claiming the resources of the
entire submerged land mass is flimsy.   But if there were a respectable
legal case for it, the United States would still be foolish and shortsighted to fall to that temptation.   The paramount interests of the United
States require maximum freedom in maximum sea, subject to commonly agreed regulations to prevent pollution and preserve common
uses and interests.   The only hope for maintaining that freedom is in
restored law and re-established order in the coastal seas.   That can
be achieved only by isolating the few states that desire coastal expansion above all else, and persuading many other states, including many
coastal states, that their interests do not require general expansion,
that they have more to gain from self-restraint and from respecting
and promoting common interests in as much of the seas as possible.

* * *

The Senate subcommittee wishes the United States to tell other coastal states instead that while we can distort the 1958 conventions for our purposes they cannot do so for theirs; that while we can claim sovereignty to a wide seabed for minerals they cannot claim sovereignty over that seabed to remove our military devices; that while we insist on a monopoly in coastal minerals they cannot have a monopoly in coastal fish; that while we claim sovereignty in the seabed they must not claim it in the waters or air above to exclude our submarines or destroyers or oil tankers or aircraft.

* * *

Oil is important to the United States but more oil is not most important. In any event, under the Nixon proposal—and it may go too far—the United States as "trustee" would control the exploitation and disposition of the oil at issue. Some American oil companies, naturally, would prefer to deal with the United States as regards oil off our coasts rather with some unfamiliar international authority. Under the Nixon proposal they would deal with the United States as regards precisely the area of greatest interest to them.

TREATY ON THE PROHIBITION OF THE EMPLACEMENT OF NUCLEAR WEAPONS AND OTHER WEAPONS OF MASS DESTRUCTION ON THE SEA–BED AND THE OCEAN FLOOR AND IN THE SUBSOIL THEREOF, FEBRUARY 11, 1972

T.I.A.S. 7337.

Article I

1. The States Parties to this Treaty undertake not to emplant or emplace on the sea-bed and the ocean floor and in the subsoil thereof beyond the outer limit of a sea-bed zone as defined in Article II any nuclear weapons or any other types of weapons of mass destruction as well as structures, launching installations or any other facilities specifically designed for storing, testing or using such weapons.

2. The undertakings of paragraph 1 of this Article shall also apply to the sea-bed zone referred to in the same paragraph, except that within such sea-bed zone, they shall not apply either to the coastal State or to the sea-bed beneath its territorial waters.

3. The States Parties to this Treaty undertake not to assist, encourage or induce any State to carry out activities referred to in paragraph 1 of this Article and not to participate in any other way in such actions.

Article II

For the purpose of this Treaty the outer limit of the sea-bed zone referred to in Article I shall be coterminous with the twelve-mile outer limit of the zone referred to in Part II of the Convention ✓ on the Territorial Sea and the Contiguous Zone, signed in Geneva on 29 April 1958, and shall be measured in accordance with the provisions of Part I, Section II, of this Convention and in accordance with international law.

SECTION D. CONTROL OF VESSELS

PUBLIC MINISTRY v. MOGENS GLISTRUP

Denmark, Maritime and Commercial Court, 1967.
95 Journal du Droit International 979 (1968).[a]

A vessel belonging to a Danish corporation and registered in Denmark and flying the Danish flag, was bareboat chartered [b] to an American company which used it in Nigerian waters. While the vessel was under charter, it had a crew which did not meet the conditions of the Danish Act on the Manning of Ships of 1965. According to paragraph 1, the act applies to all Danish vessels. The director of the American corporation had interpreted this provision as applying only to vessels under actual Danish control.

The court held however that the act applied to all Danish vessels even when bareboat chartered. The law of the flag controls. Otherwise, said the court, a vessel flying the Danish flag could escape all legislation or public control [of Denmark].

Even though Denmark has not ratified the Geneva Convention on the High Seas, the rule in Article 5 of the convention which makes the nationality of vessels depend upon the existence of a genuine link between the state and vessels flying its flag, must be considered without any question to be a part of public international law. The decision [therefore] seems to be perfectly in accord with the principle expressed in that article: genuine link means that the state effectively exercises its jurisdiction and its control * * *.

---

1. *Article 5 of the 1958 Convention on the High Seas.* The article provides, in paragraph 1:

Each state shall fix the conditions for the grant of its nationality to ships, for the registration of ships in its territory, and for the right to fly its flag. Ships have the nationality of

---

a. Translation by the editors. Reprinted by permission of Editions Techniques, S.A., Paris.

b. Leased without provision of officers or crew by the owner.

the state whose flag they are entitled to fly. There must exist a genuine link between the state and the ship; in particular, the state must effectively exercise its jurisdiction and control in administrative, technical and social matters over ships flying its flag.

2. *Problem.* What is the function of the "genuine link" requirement? If it does not exist between the flag state and the ship, does the ship fail to have the nationality of the flag state? Does the ship have any nationality in such a case? Whose? The state with which there does exist a genuine link, even though the ship does not fly its flag? Or does the "genuine link" have nothing to do with nationality? If it does not, then, again, what is its function?

Consider in connection with these questions the statement made before the United States Senate Committee on Foreign Relations by Mr. Arthur H. Dean, the head of the delegation of the United States at the 1958 Geneva Conference. He said:

The International Law Commission did not decide upon a definition of the term "genuine link." This article as originally drafted by the Commission would have authorized other states to determine whether there was a "genuine link" between a ship and the flag state for purposes of recognition of the nationality of the ship.

It was felt by some states attending the Conference on the Law of the Sea that the term "genuine link" could, depending upon how it were defined, limit the discretion of a state to decide which ships it would permit to fly its flag. Some states, which felt their flag vessels were at a competitive disadvantage with vessels sailing under the flags of other states, such as Panama and Liberia, were anxious to adopt a definition which states like Panama and Liberia could not meet.

By a vote of 30 states, including the United States, against 15 states for, and 17 states abstaining, the provision was eliminated which would have enabled states other than the flag state to withhold recognition of the national character of a ship if they considered that there was no "genuine link" between the state and the ship.

Thus, under the Convention on the High Seas, it is for each state to determine how it shall exercise jurisdiction and control in administrative, technical and social matters over ships flying its flag. The "genuine link" requirement need not have any effect upon the practice of registering American built or owned vessels in such countries as Panama or Liberia. The existence of a "genuine link" between the state and the ship is not a condition of recognition of the nationality of a ship; that is, no state can claim the right to determine unilaterally that no genuine link exists between a ship and the flag state. * * * Excerpt from Executive Report No. 5—Law of the Sea Conventions, 106 Cong.Rec. 11189, 11190 (1960).

THE PEOPLE v. ROBERT J. THOMAS

Eire, Supreme Court, 1954.
22 Int'l L.Rep. 295 (1958).

THE FACTS. The accused was convicted of the manslaughter of one Humphries. The accused and Humphries were travelling together on the Irish ship Munster, from Liverpool to Dublin. They had both been drinking, when, some 15 miles out from the Welsh coast, about midnight, there was a fight in which Humphries went overboard and was lost. Thomas was not an Irish citizen.

There was an appeal on the ground, first, of alleged lack of evidence, and secondly on the ground that the Court had no jurisdiction to try an offence of manslaughter on an Irish ship where the death did not occur on board the ship, or within the jurisdiction.

Held (affirming the Court of Criminal Appeal): that the appeal failed on both grounds. [A portion of the opinion of the court appears below.]

* * * The next ground of appeal is that there was no jurisdiction in the Central Criminal Court to try the appellant for manslaughter as the death did not occur on board the ship and so was not within the jurisdiction of the Court. It is clear that the Central Criminal Court has all the jurisdiction formerly exercised by the Admiral and later exercised by the Commissioners of Oyer and Terminer appointed to exercise the Admiralty jurisdiction in criminal cases (11, 12, 13 Jac. 1, c. 2 (Ir.)). This was not contested. Mr. Bell [Counsel for the accused] contended that the jurisdiction was confined to the trial of persons committing offences on board an Irish ship on the high seas where such offences were committed and completed on the ship. Manslaughter, Mr. Bell says, is a complex crime consisting of two essential ingredients. The first is some unlawful act or culpable neglect, which causes the death, and the second is the fact of death itself. The death admittedly did not take place on the ship. The crime, therefore, according to the argument, not being completed on board the ship was not committed within the jurisdiction. Mr. Bell referred at length to the case of The Queen v. Keyn, 2 Ex.D. 63. Keyn, a foreigner, was in command of a foreign ship which ran into a British ship within three miles of the English shore and sank her. A passenger on board the English ship was drowned. The facts were such as would in English law amount to

manslaughter. On his being indicted for that offence in the Central
Criminal Court the jury found Keyn guilty. Counsel for the prisoner objected that the Court had no jurisdiction. Pollock B., the
trial Judge, stated a case on the point for the opinion of the Court
for Crown Cases Reserved. The majority of the Court held that as
the offence was not committed on a British ship there was no jurisdiction to try the prisoner, even though the ship at the time of the
occurrence was within what has become known as the "three-mile
limit."

* * *

Applying these observations to the present case, the contention
on behalf of the appellant is that since the death took place, if at all,
in the water, the crime was not complete upon the Irish ship and
therefore no crime in fact or in law took place on the ship, and it
follows that the jurisdiction of the Central Criminal Court which is
confined in its admiralty jurisdiction to trying cases of crimes committed in Irish ships is not brought into operation. If the argument
is correct it would appear that there is no jurisdiction in any Court
of this country to try either a citizen or foreigner on an Irish ship
who by culpable negligence or design throws another overboard with
the result that death occurs in the water.

* * *

It will be convenient in discussing the matter of the Admiral's
jurisdiction to consider it from two aspects. First, what jurisdiction
the Admiral had as regards the place where the crime was committed, and, secondly, in respect of what persons that jurisdiction operated.

* * *

The other aspect of the jurisdiction now requires consideration.
It is not necessary for the purposes of this case to enumerate all
persons over whom the jurisdiction may extend. It is sufficient to
say that it is clear law that the jurisdiction extends to a foreigner
on an Irish ship.

It being undoubted that crimes committed by foreigners on
board British or Irish ships are cognizable by British or Irish Courts,
as the case may be, without any statute, is there anything in the
origins or the legal theory giving rise to this rule of law to indicate
that whatever jurisdiction attaches is limited to the punishment of a
crime begun and completed on board the ship, as distinct from a
crime completed by the death taking place in the water surrounding
the ship?

The basis of the jurisdiction is the right of the country to
which the ships belong to control the conduct of those on board from
the point of good order and the prevention of crime by virtue of the
protection afforded to such persons while sailing in such ship. In
The Queen v. Anderson, 1 Cr.Cas.Res. 161, Blackburn, J., at p. 169

says: "There are a vast number of cases which decide that when a ship is sailing on the high seas and bearing the flag of a particular nation, the ship forms a part of that nation's country, and all persons on board of her may be considered as within the jurisdiction of that nation whose flag is flying on the ship, in the same manner as if they were within the territory of that nation."   Coke says: "Protectio trahit subjectionem et subjectio protectionem."   Lord Coleridge in The Queen v. Carr, 10 Q.B.D. 76, says, at p. 85: "The true principle is, that a person who comes on board a British ship where English law is reigning, places himself under the protection of the British flag, and as a correlative, if he thus becomes entitled to our law's protection, he becomes amenable to its jurisdiction, and liable to the punishment it inflicts upon those who there infringe its requirements."   He adds that there is no distinction to be drawn between a member of the crew and a passenger.

* * *

The verdict of manslaughter in this case involved a finding of fact that Humphries is dead.   The evidence points only to a death by drowning on the high seas.   The other ingredient of the crime, the act or omission causing the death, occurred on board the M.V. "Munster", an Irish ship.   Thus the event leading to the death also took place upon the high seas.   The two elements necessary to give jurisdiction were thus both present.   The crime was committed on the high seas and the appellant was at the time of its commission on an Irish ship.   The appellant was, therefore, properly triable in the Central Criminal Court.

The appeal in so far as it was based on want of jurisdiction also fails.

This Court does not see any reason for interfering with the sentence.

Question.   Consider the discussion by the court of The Queen v. Keyn in which it was held that "as the offense was not committed on a British ship there was no jurisdiction to try the prisoner, even though the ship at the time of the occurrence was within what has become known as the three-mile limit."   Was this a statement of a rule of international law in view of the materials considered heretofore in this chapter?

RE BIANCHI

Argentina, Cámara Nacional Especial, 1957.
24 Int'l L.Rep. 173 (1961).

THE FACTS.   The appellant, Gerónimo C. Bianchi, a member of
the crew of the R. T., a ship of Argentine registry, was charged with
the commission of a theft on board the ship while it was anchored
in the harbour of Río de Janeiro, Brazil.   In the absence of any action in the matter by Brazilian authorities, charges were brought
against Bianchi in Argentina.   It was unsuccessfully argued for the
defendant that the Argentine court lacked jurisdiction over an offence which had been committed in foreign territorial waters.   On
appeal,

Held: that the judgment appealed from must be affirmed.   Where
local authorities did not take jurisdiction over an offence committed
on board a ship anchored in foreign territorial waters, jurisdiction
reverted to the courts of the State of registry of the ship.

[A portion of the opinion of the court appears below].

*   *   *   According to the record of proceedings in the trial
Court, an inquiry was made into a theft which was allegedly committed on board the R. T., a ship of Argentine registry, while it was at
anchor in the port of Río de Janeiro.   Article 1, para. 1, of the Penal
Code provides that this Code is applicable (inter alia) to offences committed in places subject to the national jurisdiction.   According to the
rules of public international law, which have not been reproduced
for obvious reasons in the said Article but which are none the less
binding upon Argentine courts, offences committed on board a private
ship fall within the jurisdiction of the courts of the flag State if
the ship is on the high seas, and fall within the jurisdiction of a foreign State only in the event that such offences have been committed
while the ship is in the territorial waters of that other State.

This latter principle is not an absolute rule, however, for if the
foreign State does not choose to exercise its right to institute proceedings because it considers that the act has not affected the community at large or the peace of the port (as maintained in French
and Italian doctrine), the flag State may then assert full authority
over the ship for the purpose of restoring order and discipline on
board or protecting the rights of the passengers (Herrera, La Reforma
Penal, p. 134).   We may reasonably conclude with regard to the case
before us, given the fact that the preliminary hearing was apparently
held "en route", that the Brazilian authorities had relinquished jurisdiction over the alleged offence, so that this offence then became
subject to the jurisdiction of the Argentine courts.   As this reasoning accords with the judgment of the trial Court and with the opinion
of the Fiscal of this Court regarding the case, the judgment under appeal is affirmed.

SPECIAL MARITIME AND TERRITORIAL JURISDICTION OF THE UNITED STATES

18 U.S.C. § 7.

The term "special maritime and territorial jurisdiction of the United States", as used in this title, includes:

(1) The high seas, any other waters within the admiralty and maritime jurisdiction of the United States and out of the jurisdiction of any particular State, and any vessel belonging in whole or in part to the United States or any citizen thereof, or to any corporation created by or under the laws of the United States, or of any State, Territory, District, or possession thereof, when such vessel is within the admiralty and maritime jurisdiction of the United States and out of the jurisdiction of any particular State.

(2) Any vessel registered, licensed, or enrolled under the laws of the United States, and being on a voyage upon the waters of any of the Great Lakes, or any of the waters connecting them, or upon the Saint Lawrence River where the same constitutes the International Boundary Line.

* * *

---

1. *Crimes included in special maritime jurisdiction of the United States.* Title 18 of the United States Code defines as criminal a number of acts that are performed within the special maritime jurisdiction of the United States: Sections 113, assaults; 114, maiming; 661, theft; 662, receiving stolen goods; 1111, murder; 1112, manslaughter; 1113, attempt to commit murder or manslaughter; 2031, rape; 2032, statutory rape; 2111, robbery. (See, also Title 49, Section 1472(k), dealing with these same crimes when committed within the "special aircraft jurisdiction of the United States." This jurisdiction is discussed in Chapter 4.)

2. *Vessels included in special maritime jurisdiction of the United States.*

In civil matters involving vessels on the high seas such as collision and salvage, the United States as well as other states apply the rules of maritime law to foreign flag vessels as well as to vessels sailing under their national flag. The general law maritime is not itself a part of international law. Rather, it is a body of rules reflecting the universal interest of states in achieving a substantial degree of uniformity in the handling of civil claims arising on the high seas. In the application of such rules, each state may use its own understanding or domestic version of the rules without subjecting itself thereby to a claim under international law by another state.

But would it be valid under international law for the United States to apply rules of criminal law under Section 7 of Title 18 to vessels "owned" by United States citizens or corporations if the vessels were registered under a foreign flag?

3. *The law of nations, the law merchant, and the law maritime; an earlier, undifferentiated universalism explained.* In an article entitled, The Law of Nations as Part of the Law of the United States, 101 U.Pa.L.Rev. 26 (1952),* Dickinson wrote:

It is to be emphasized at the outset that the Law of Nations in the eighteenth century embraced a good deal more than the body of practice and agreement which came later to be called public international law. In the De Jure Belli ac Pacis of Hugo Grotius and in the treatises of his successors, it had been expounded as a universal law binding upon all mankind. In countries of the common law, at least, arbitrary distinctions between private and public right or duty were still far in the future. The universal law was law for individuals no less than for states. As such, it was concerned somewhat indiscriminately with matters between individuals, between individuals and states, and between states. As yet unhindered by the dogmas of more restrictive classification, its major divisions were essentially the product of historical evolution. English lawyers were accustomed to identify the major divisions as the law of merchants, the law maritime, and what, for want of a better name, we may call the law of states.

The law of merchants was of ancient lineage and throughout much of its history had been intimately related to the law maritime. Like the latter, it had become a peculiar heritage of traders, whether subject or alien, and like the latter also it had grown up in customary observances and had long been administered by separate courts. In its application to the internal trade of England, it had been largely absorbed into the common law by the end of the sixteenth century; and by the end of the seventeenth century it had been similarly absorbed in its application to foreign trade without losing its distinctive character as a species of jus gentium. In resolving the case for the indorsee against the drawer of a foreign bill of exchange drawn by a merchant of London on a merchant of Rotterdam, Justice Eyres had observed in 1691: "it is no more than the law of merchants, and that is jus gentium, and we are to take notice of it." Other justices agreed, Chief Justice Holt remarking: "the time is well enough by the law of merchants, and that is the same with our law." The adoption of the law of merchants into the common law reached maturity in the eighteenth century, with eloquent emphasis upon its international character, in the great opinions of Lord Mansfield. Blackstone was only summarizing the understandings of his time when he said:

> Whereas no municipal laws can be sufficient to order and
> determine the very extensive and complicated affairs of traffic

and merchandize; neither can they have a proper authority for this purpose. For as these are transactions carried on between the subjects of independent states, the municipal laws of one will not be regarded by the other. For which reason the affairs of commerce are regulated by a law of their own, called the law merchant or lex mercatoria, which all nations agree in and take notice of. And in particular the law of England does in many cases refer itself to it, and leaves the causes of merchants to be tried by their own peculiar customs; and that often even in matters relating to inland trade, as for instance with regard to the drawing, the acceptance, and the transfer, of bills of exchange.

The law maritime boasted an even greater antiquity and a more impressive universality. As developed in customs and formulated in early codes for the regulation of sea-borne commerce, it had been fostered in the mediaeval shipping centers of the Mediterranean, had moved later up the west coast of Europe, and had established its authority over the North Sea and in the Baltic wherever carriage by sea was of commercial consequence. It had been received at a very early date in England, where its administration became the responsibility of a separate branch of the judiciary and where its practice was long the exclusive province of a bar trained in the Civil Law. The High Court of Admiralty, notwithstanding the impairment which its jurisdiction suffered in conflicts with Lord Coke in the seventeenth century, had been able to maintain and develop the law maritime as an important part of English law. This court had found frequent occasion to emphasize the proposition that it was administering a branch of the universal jus gentium. Again, it was pre-eminently Lord Mansfield in the eighteenth century who took up the proposition broadly and made it a postulate of the common law. About midway in the century, there came before Mansfield a shipowner's suit to recover the freight earned on fish shipped from Newfoundland to Lisbon. The vessel had been taken by the French, retaken by an English privateer, and brought into an English port, where it was abandoned to insurers. The shipper having accepted his fish at the English port and forwarded them to another market, the case turned upon his asserted obligation to pay the shipowner freight pro rata. Holding that he was required to pay, Lord Mansfield supported his conclusion by citing the Rhodian laws, the Consolato del Mare, the laws of Oléron, the laws of the Hanse Towns, the laws of Wisbuy and the Ordinance of Louis XIV. The great judge declared: "the maritime law is not the law of a particular country, but the general law of nations." Such, needless to emphasize, became accepted English doctrine in the eighteenth century. The law maritime was a branch of the Law of Nations. It had been received in England and was to be applied by English courts, on the common law side no less than in admiralty, whenever matters appropriate for its application were duly presented.

A third major division of the Law of Nations as understood by English lawyers of the eighteenth century we have called the law of states. The term, it is to be emphasized, is one of convenience. It is without pride of ancestry and presumably without hope of posterity. It may serve nevertheless to denote the amorphous but considerable body of usage and agreement with respect to international matters which had come into being with a rise of a European state system, which had been enriched by borrowings and adaptations from the Roman law and by recourse to a Law of Nature, and which, though by no means inapplicable to individuals inter se or in relation to states, was generally of more immediate concern to states than either the law of merchants or the civil law maritime. Ultimately most of it would be absorbed in one way or another into the so-called public international law of a later age. Meanwhile, on the criminal side, it served to define at least a few individual offences. The familiar examples were piracy and attacks upon ambassadors. On the civil side, it sought to encompass and order an expanding body of international relationships in their impact upon individuals and upon states. Men of learning in the eighteenth century were wont to find apt examples in usage or agreement with respect to captures, diplomatic privilege and treaties.

McCULLOCH, CHAIRMAN, NATIONAL LABOR RELATIONS BOARD v. SOCIEDAD NACIONAL de MARINEROS de HONDURAS

United States Supreme Court, 1963.
372 U.S. 10, 83 S.Ct. 671.

MR. JUSTICE CLARK delivered the opinion of the Court.

These companion cases, involving the same facts, question the coverage of the National Labor Relations Act, as amended, 61 Stat. 136, 73 Stat. 541, 29 U.S.C.A. § 151 et seq. A corporation organized and doing business in the United States beneficially owns seagoing vessels which make regular sailings between United States, Latin American and other ports transporting the corporation's products and other supplies; each of the vessels is legally owned by a foreign subsidiary of the American corporation, flies the flag of a foreign nation, carries a foreign crew and has other contacts with the nation of its flag. The question arising is whether the Act extends to the crews engaged in such a maritime operation. The National Labor Relations Board in a representation proceeding on the application of the National Maritime Union held that it does and ordered an election. 134 N.L.R.B. 287. The vessels' foreign owner sought to enjoin the Board's Regional Director from holding the election, but the District Court for the Southern District of New York denied the requested relief. 200 F.Supp. 484. The Court of Appeals for the Second Circuit reversed, holding that the Act did not apply to the maritime operations here and thus the Board had no power to direct the election. 300 F.2d 222.   The N. M. U. had intervened in the proceeding, and it petitioned for a writ of certiorari (No. 93), as did the Regional Director (No. 91).   Meanwhile, the United States District Court for the District of Columbia, on application of the foreign bargaining agent of the vessels' crewmen, enjoined the Board members in No. 107.   201 F.Supp. 82.   We granted each of the three petitions for certiorari, 370 U.S. 915, 82 S.Ct. 1559, and consolidated the cases for argument.

We have concluded that the jurisdictional provisions of the Act do not extend to maritime operations of foreign-flag ships employing alien seamen.

I.

The National Maritime Union of America, AFL–CIO, filed a petition in 1959 with the National Labor Relations Board seeking certification under § 9(c) of the Act, 29 U.S.C.A. § 159(c), as the representative of the unlicensed seamen employed upon certain Honduran-flag vessels owned by Empresa Hondurena de Vapores, S.A., a Honduran corporation. The petition was filed against United Fruit Company, a New Jersey corporation which was alleged to be the owner of the majority of Empresa's stock. Empresa intervened and on hearing it was shown that United Fruit owns all of its stock and elects its directors, though no officer or director of Empresa is an officer or director of United Fruit and all are residents of Honduras. In turn the proof was that United Fruit is owned by citizens of the United States and maintains its principal office at Boston. Its business was shown to be the cultivation, gathering, transporting and sale of bananas, sugar, cacao and other tropical produce raised in Central and South American countries and sold in the United States.

United Fruit maintains a fleet of cargo vessels which it utilizes in this trade. A portion of the fleet consists of 13 Honduran-registered vessels operated [2] by Empresa and time chartered to United Fruit, which vessels were included in National Maritime Union's representation proceeding. The crews on these vessels are recruited by Empresa in Honduras. They are Honduran citizens (save one Jamaican) and claim that country as their residence and home port. The crew are required to sign Honduran shipping articles, and their wages, terms and condition of employment, discipline, etc., are controlled by a bargaining agreement between Empresa and a Honduran union, Sociedad Nacional de Marineros de Honduras. Under the Honduran Labor Code only a union whose "juridic personality" is recognized by Honduras and which is composed of at least 90% of Honduran citi-

---

2. Ten of the 13 vessels are owned and operated by Empresa. Three are owned by Balboa Shipping Co., Inc., a Panamanian subsidiary of United Fruit. Empresa acts as an agent for Balboa in the management of the latter vessels.

zens can represent the seamen on Honduran-registered ships. The N. M. U. fulfils neither requirement. Further, under Honduran law recognition of Sociedad as the bargaining agent compels Empresa to deal exclusively with it on all matters covered by the contract. The current agreement in addition to recognition of Sociedad provides for a union shop, with a no-strike-or-lockout provision, and sets up wage scales, special allowances, maintenance and cure provisions, hours of work, vacation time, holidays, overtime, accident prevention, and other details of employment as well.

United Fruit, however, determines the ports of call of the vessels, their cargoes and sailings, integrating the same into its fleet organization. While the voyages are for the most part between Central and South American ports and those of the United States, the vessels each call at regular intervals at Honduran ports for the purpose of taking on and discharging cargo and, where necessary, renewing the ship's articles.

II.

The Board concluded from these facts that United Fruit operated a single, integrated maritime operation within which were the Empresa vessels, reasoning that United Fruit was a joint employer with Empresa of the seamen covered by N. M. U.'s petition. Citing its own West India Fruit & Steamship Co. opinion, 130 N.L.R.B. 343 (1961), it concluded that the maritime operations involved substantial United States contacts, outweighing the numerous foreign contacts present. The Board held that Empresa was engaged in "commerce" within the meaning of § 2(6) of the Act [3] and that the maritime operations "affected commerce" within § 2(7),[4] meeting the jurisdictional requirement of § 9(c)(1).[5] It therefore ordered an election to be held among the seamen signed on Empresa's vessels to determine

3.   29 U.S.C.A. § 152(6):
"The term 'commerce' means trade, traffic, commerce, transportation, or communication among the several States, or between the District of Columbia or any Territory of the United States and any State or other Territory, or between any foreign country and any State, Territory, or the District of Columbia, or within the District of Columbia or any Territory, or between points in the same State but through any other State or any Territory or the District of Columbia or any foreign country."

4.   29 U.S.C.A. § 152(7):
"The term 'affecting commerce' means in commerce, or burdening or obstructing commerce or the free flow of com-

merce, or having led or tending to lead to a labor dispute burdening or obstructing commerce or the free flow of commerce."

5.   29 U.S.C.A. § 159(c)(1):
"Whenever a petition shall have been filed * * * the Board shall investigate such petition and if it has reasonable cause to believe that a question of representation affecting commerce exists shall provide for an appropriate hearing * * *."
Section 10(a) of the Act, 29 U.S.C.A. § 160(a), imposes the same requirement, empowering the Board to "prevent any person from engaging in any unfair labor practice * * * affecting commerce."

whether they wished N. M. U., Sindicato Maritimo Nacional de Honduras, or no union to represent them.

* * *

III.

Since the parties all agree that the Congress has constitutional power to apply the National Labor Relations Act to the crews working foreign-flag ships, at least while they are in American waters, The Exchange, 7 Cranch 116, 143 (1812); Wildenhus's Case, 120 U.S. 1, 11, 7 S.Ct. 385 (1887); Benz v. Compania Naviera Hidalgo, 353 U.S. 138, 142, 7 S.Ct. 699 (1957), we go directly to the question whether Congress exercised that power. Our decision on this point being dispositive of the case, we do not reach the other questions raised by the parties and the amici curiae.

The question of application of the laws of the United States to foreign-flag ships and their crews has arisen often and in various contexts. As to the application of the National Labor Relations Act and its amendments, the Board has evolved a test relying on the relative weight of a ship's foreign as compared with its American contacts. That test led the Board to conclude here, as in West India Fruit & Steamship Co., supra, that the foreign-flag ships' activities affected "commerce" and brought them within the coverage of the Act. Where the balancing of the vessel's contacts has resulted in a contrary finding, the Board has concluded that the Act does not apply.

Six years ago this Court considered the question of the application of the Taft-Hartley amendments to the Act in a suit for damages "resulting from the picketing of a foreign ship operated entirely by foreign seamen under foreign articles while the vessel [was] temporarily in an American port." Benz v. Compania Naviera Hidalgo, supra, 353 U.S., at 139, 77 S.Ct., at 700. We held that the Act did not apply, searching the language and the legislative history and concluding that the latter "inescapably describes the boundaries of the Act as including only the workingmen of our own country and its possessions." Id., at 144, 77 S.Ct., at 702, 703. * * *

It is contended that this case is nonetheless distinguishable from Benz in two respects. First, here there is a fleet of vessels not temporarily in United States waters but operating in a regular course of trade between foreign ports and those of the United States; and, second, the foreign owner of the ships is in turn owned by an American corporation. We note that both of these points rely on additional American contacts and therefore necessarily presume the validity of the "balancing of contacts" theory of the Board. But to follow such a suggested procedure to the ultimate might require that the Board inquire into the internal discipline and order of all foreign vessels calling at American ports. Such activity would raise considerable disturbance not only in the field of maritime law but in our international relations as well. In addition, enforcement of Board orders would project the courts into application of the sanctions of the Act to foreign-flag ships on a purely ad hoc weighing of contacts basis.[9] This would inevitably lead to embarrassment in foreign affairs and be entirely infeasible in actual practice. The question, therefore, appears to us more basic; namely, whether the Act as written was intended to have any application to foreign registered vessels employing alien seamen.

Petitioners say that the language of the Act may be read literally as including foreign-flag vessels within its coverage. But, as in Benz, they have been unable to point to any specific language in the Act itself or in its extensive legislative history that reflects such a congressional intent. Indeed, the opposite is true as we found in Benz, where we pointed to the language of Chairman Hartley characterizing the Act as "a bill of rights both for American workingmen and for their employers." 353 U.S., at 144, 77 S.Ct., at 702. We continue to believe that if the sponsors of the original Act or of its amendments conceived of the application now sought by the Board they failed to translate such thoughts into describing the boundaries of the Act as including foreign-flag vessels manned by alien crews. Therefore, we find no basis for a construction which would exert United States jurisdiction over and apply its laws to the internal management and affairs of the vessels here flying the Honduran flag, contrary to the recognition long afforded them not only by our State Department[11] but also by the Congress.[12] In addition, our attention is called to the well-established rule of international law that the law of the flag state ordinarily governs the internal affairs of a ship. See Wildenhus's Case, supra, 120 U.S., at 12, 7 S.Ct., at 387; Colombos, The International Law of the Sea (3d rev. ed. 1954), 222–223. The possibility of international discord cannot therefore be gainsaid. Especially is this true on account of the concurrent application of the Act and the Honduran Labor Code that would result with our approval of juris-

---

9. Our conclusion does not foreclose such a procedure in different contexts, such as the Jones Act, 46 U.S.C.A. § 688, where the pervasive regulation of the internal order of a ship may not be present. As regards application of the Jones Act to maritime torts on foreign ships, however, the Court has stated that "[p]erhaps the most venerable and universal rule of maritime law relevant to our problem is that which gives cardinal importance to the law of the flag." Lauritzen v. Larsen, 345 U.S. 571, 584, 73 S.Ct. 921 (1953); see Romero v. International Terminal Operating Co., 358 U.S. 354, 381–384, 79 S.Ct. 468 (1959); Boczek, op. cit., supra, note 7, at 178–180.

11. State Department regulations provide that a foreign vessel includes "any vessel regardless of ownership, which is documented under the laws of a foreign country." 22 CFR § 81.1 (f).

12. Article X of the Treaty of Friendship, Commerce and Consular Rights between Honduras and the United States, 45 Stat. 2618 (1927), provides that merchant vessels flying the flags and having the papers of either country "shall, both within the territorial waters of the other High Contracting Party and on the high seas, be deemed to be the vessels of the Party whose flag is flown."

diction. Sociedad, currently the exclusive bargaining agent of Empresa under Honduran law, would have a head-on collision with N. M. U. should it become the exclusive bargaining agent under the Act. This would be aggravated by the fact that under Honduran law N. M. U. is prohibited from representing the seamen on Honduran-flag ships even in the absence of a recognized bargaining agent. Thus even though Sociedad withdrew from such an intramural labor fight—a highly unlikely circumstance—questions of such international import would remain as to invite retaliatory action from other nations as well as Honduras.

The presence of such highly charged international circumstances brings to mind the admonition of Mr. Chief Justice Marshall in The Charming Betsy, 2 Cranch 64, 118 (1804), that "an act of congress ought never to be construed to violate the law of nations if any, other possible construction remains . . . ." We therefore conclude, as we did in Benz, that for us to sanction the exercise of local sovereignty under such conditions in this "delicate field of international relations there must be present the affirmative intention of the Congress clearly expressed." 353 U.S., at 147, 77 S.Ct., at 704. Since neither we nor the parties are able to find any such clear expression, we hold that the Board was without jurisdiction to order the election. This is not to imply, however, "any impairment of our own sovereignty, or limitation of the power of Congress" in this field. Lauritzen v. Larsen, 345 U.S. 571, 578, 73 S.Ct. 921 (1953). In fact, just as we directed the parties in Benz to the Congress, which "alone has the facilities necessary to make fairly such an important policy decision," 353 U.S., at 147, we conclude here that the arguments should be directed to the Congress rather than to us. Cf. Lauritzen v. Larsen, supra, 345 U.S., at 593, 73 S.Ct., at 933, 934.

The judgment of the District Court is therefore affirmed in No. 107. The judgment of the Court of Appeals in Nos. 91 and 93 is vacated and the cases are remanded to that court, with instructions that it remand to the District Court for dismissal of the complaint in light of our decision in No. 107. It is so ordered.

Mr. Justice Douglas, Concurring. * * * The practical effect of our decision is to shift from all the taxpayers to seamen alone the main burden of financing an executive policy of assuring the availability of an adequate American-owned merchant fleet for federal use during national emergencies. * * *

Question. Suppose the Congress of the United States had specifically provided that the National Labor Relations Act applied to flag of convenience vessels. Would the application of the act be consistent with international law? See p. 481 dealing with the extraterritorial reach of the anti-trust laws of the United States.

Chapter 4

CONTROL OF AIRSPACE, SPACE AND
CELESTIAL BODIES

———

When the 20th Century began, the techniques of air flight and space exploration were almost all in the future. Little in the way of positive law existed for the regulation of the technology that exploded in the first decade of the century and that has periodically advanced with astonishingly new and unforeseen capacities. It is instructive to observe the ways in which international law has been created by a process that either anticipated unpredictable changes or reacted to events that had not been foreseen.

———

SECTION A. ACTIVITIES IN AIRSPACE

———

1. AERIAL TRANSIT

DRAFT CONVENTION, REGIME OF AEROSTATS AND WIRELESS TELEGRAPHY (1906)

21 Annuaire de l'Institut de Droit International 293, 327 (1907).[a]

Mr. Fauchille, rapporteur, * * * summarizes the main conclusions in his report.

* * *

The fundamental difficulty * * * concerns the nature of airspace and the rights of states in the atmosphere. How can this question be solved? First of all, it must be defined. The atmosphere can be divided in three zones. Above 5000 meters [there is] a zone where breathing is impossible and where balloons cannot penetrate. Close to earth, [there is] a zone [which is] subject to appropriation through building up to, at present, a height of 330 meters since the highest construction today, the Eiffel Tower, is 300 meters high and the highest telegraphic masts reach 30 meters. But even in that situation, one cannot say that airspace is subject to appropriation by the state. What is state property is not airspace but the constructions in the airspace. Thus, it is only in that airspace from the

a. Translation by the editors. The text in the Annuaire is a summary minute of what the rapporteur said   rather than the verbatim transcript of his statement.

244

ground up, where there are no constructions, and up to 5000 meters, that there exists a [third] zone whose [legal] regime must be determined.

Two absolute theories have been advanced.

In the one * * * airspace is completely free in all its zones, be it for aerial navigation or for radio telegraphy. In the other, the subjacent state has a right of property or sovereignty in airspace within a limit, according to one view, * * * [equivalent] to the range of a cannon, or according to another view, * * * within limits to be determined by an international agreement similar to the one proposed by the Netherlands in 1895 for territorial waters.

Mr. Fauchille objects that the first system does not take into account the dangers for states in the matter of espionage, especially, and the operation of radio telegraphy, [which would result] from the passage of aerostats at low altitude. To the second system * * * he objects that [since] the range of a cannon varies widely and may attain, it is said, a range of 4800 meters, it would follow that aerial navigation would in fact become impossible. * * * [To the extent] the second system involves determining the rights of the subjacent state by international agreement, he objects that the determination, not having any rational basis, would be arbitrary. To both aspects of this second system, he replies with a single observation: airspace, *by its very nature*, is not susceptible of appropriation or subjection to sovereignty.

The rapporteur proposes, accordingly, a combination of two uncontested principles: (1) airspace is not susceptible of appropriation or subjection to sovereignty, and therefore is free; (2) a state has a right of self-preservation and of self-defense to guaranty the essential elements of its existence, both in a material sense and as a legal person. Hence this formula: airspace is free, subject to the right of self-preservation and self-defense of the subjacent state.

Two consequences follow from the proposal:

(1) What is the most serious danger from aerostats? Espionage. What form does this danger take? Photography. But useful photography of a country's fortifications can be made only at an altitude of less than 1500 meters. Thus, under 1500 meters, the navigation of aerostats should be forbidden.

(2) What is today the most serious problem for wireless telegraphy? It is the possibility of interference with telephone communications and ordinary telegraphy. (at 293).

* * *

[The following article was adopted by the Institute]

Article 1. Airspace is free. States have in it, in time of peace or in time of war, only the rights necessary for their self-preservation. (at 327).

FROM THEORY TO TREATY LAW

McNair, The Law of the Air 4 (Kerr & Evans, 3d ed. 1964).

* * * Until after the war of 1914–18 the only aspects of aerial navigation which had engaged the serious attention of English lawyers, and, indeed, of the lawyers of almost any country, were the rules of public international law and of the Conflict of Laws which ought to govern it. * * *

Over the high seas it was generally admitted that the airspace was free. * * *

(1) *That the airspace is free, subject only to the rights of states required in the interests of their self-preservation.* This theory, which will always be associated with the name of its champion, Fauchille, was adopted by the Institute of International Law in 1906. * * *

(2) The second theory was that *upon the analogy of the maritime belt or territorial waters there is over the land and waters of each state a lower zone of territorial airspace, and a higher, and unlimited, zone of free airspace.*

(3) The third theory was *that a state has complete sovereignty in its superincumbent airspace to an unlimited height,* thus applying the *cujus est solum* maxim in its crude form.

(4) The fourth theory was the third *with the addition of a servitude of innocent passage for foreign non-military aircraft,* akin to the right of innocent passage of merchant ships through territorial waters.

The war of 1914–18 brought about a realisation of the importance of aerial navigation and of its potential danger to the subjacent state and its inhabitants. It is therefore not surprising to find now the almost universal adoption by international treaty and by national legislation of the theory of complete sovereignty (No. (3) above), subject to a mutual, carefully safeguarded, and easily determinable treaty right of free entry and passage for the non-military aircraft of foreign countries.

Thus, the first Article of the Paris Convention of 1919 [a] was as follows:

> The High Contracting Parties recognise that every Power has complete and exclusive sovereignty over the air space above its territory.

> For the purpose of the present Convention the territory of a State shall be understood as including the national territory, both that of the Mother Country and of the Colonies, and the territorial waters adjacent thereto.

a. 11 L.N.T.S. 174.

GOEDHUIS, CIVIL AVIATION AFTER THE WAR

36 American Journal of International Law 596, 605 (1942).

The unprecedentedly accelerated speed of change in the last thirty years has been such that, politically, air navigation has already passed through many of the phases which it took sea navigation centuries to span.

As to air navigation, it may be observed that in 1910 the states were preoccupied only with guaranteeing the safety of their territory; the necessity of permitting other states to navigate freely to and over their territory was recognized to the fullest extent where this freedom did not affect the security of the state. The period 1910–1919 can thus be compared with that period in the history of shipping in which the adjacent seas were appropriated primarily to secure the land from invasion.

In 1919 the first consideration was still the security of the states, but the study of the minutes of the meetings held by the Aëronautical Commission of the Peace Conference reveals the fact that some small clouds were already appearing on the horizon of the free sky. In the minds of some of the delegates the idea took shape to use the power of the state over the air to protect its own air navigation against foreign competition. As in shipping, the pretensions to the appropriation of the sea and the power to restrict foreign sea commerce grew in proportion to the increase of the direct profits to be expected from them, so in aviation the pretensions to unrestricted sovereignty—not in doctrine but in practice—grew in proportion to the development of aviation during the period from 1919 to 1929.

THE CHICAGO CONVENTION (THE CONVENTION ON INTERNATIONAL CIVIL AVIATION OF DECEMBER 7, 1944): THE HISTORY

[1944] 2 Foreign Relations of the United States 599 (1967).

The Chairman of the American Delegation to the International Civil Aviation Conference (Berle) to President Roosevelt

[Chicago,] December 7, 1944

My Dear Mr. President: I have the honor to report the results of the International Civil Aviation Conference, held at Chicago from November 1 to December 7, 1944.

* * *

(a) International Organization

The first problem discussed was that of the power of an international organization. We stated very bluntly that we simply could not cede dispositive power over United States air traffic to any international body in the present state of affairs. For one thing, there was no method or project of creating an impartial regulatory body: instead, the memberships in that body were to be apportioned among states and would represent political interests. Under these circumstances, any international body had to be in the position of applying exact defined rules agreed to by all hands. The fundamental problem was therefore drafting of the rules.

We said we could agree to an international body primarily to stimulate consultation and to make recommendations; and that if recommendations were not satisfactory, the international body might get together the interested parties and cause them to work out their difficulties. The enforcing power would have to remain in the several countries,—an international body at this stage of the game would have neither the machinery nor the prestige to enforce orders. The British finally acceded to this position, agreeing that obligations taken by treaty or agreement were quite adequate to meet the situation. Accordingly, agreement was reached on an international Council responsible to an international Assembly, the Council to have recommendatory powers; and failure to agree to recommendation would give rise to a prompt process of diplomatic consultation.

(b) Avoidance of Rate Wars

The second problem related to rates. There was general agreement that some method ought to be found of avoiding rate wars and other violences of competition which have disfigured transportation history. Substantial agreement was finally reached on a clause to the general effect that rates should be agreed upon by conferences of air operators analogous to ship operators conferences—a procedure which is specifically authorized by the Civil Aeronautics Act of 1938, and to which the United States can therefore agree. We were fortified in this by an opinion of the Attorney General to the general effect that such agreements were legal provided they were approved by the Civil Aeronautics Board. Since under the recommendatory procedure these agreements would come back to the various countries for acceptance, the procedure would be to have such operators agreements referred to the Civil Aeronautics Board. While the Civil Aeronautics Board does not have general power of enforcement, it could make it plain to any United States operator who violated an agreement that he would thereby forfeit diplomatic protection for his landing and transit rights abroad. It was the opinion of our operating advisers that no airline would violate an agreement thus made. By consequence, we felt that we had an adequate machinery.

* * *

(c) Rights of Commercial Entry

Third, we then got down to the main problem of commercial air rights. The British wanted agreements which would severely limit

international rights in air transport. They were prepared to concede
the so-called "freedoms of the air", namely:

    (1) Freedom of innocent transit;

    (2) Freedom of technical stop;

    (3) Freedom to take traffic from the homeland out to other
countries;

    (4) Freedom to take traffic from other countries back to
the homeland—and possibly, to a limited extent,

    (5) Freedom to pick up and discharge traffic between
points en route—

if, but only if, their operations were severely limited, traffic routes
parceled out, and so forth, by an international body, or conceivably
by rules appearing in a convention.

    *   *   *

    *   *   *   [A]fter ten days of extremely difficult negotiation,
we reported out to the Conference the points on which we had been
able to agree; and also our alternative plans. The British plan was
one of limitation, as above described; ours was a plan by which each
country, having established its transport lines, might increase capacity as rapidly as its planes filled up.

    There followed the tensest debate at the Conference. Lord
Swinton presented the British view, urging the necessity of protecting small nations from competition. I presented the United States
view which was for freedom of the air, with competition, and without cartel or other similar agreements, and without limitation except
for the proposed arrangement against rate wars, and the "full plane"
clause.

    (The debate was in fact a modern version of the old controversy
when Grotius argued for the freedom of the seas, and Selden argued
for the closed seas; a debate which went on in the 17th century until
it was finally settled by the British adopting the freedom of the
seas. Another almost exact historical analogy is the debate which
went on in this country when Livingston in New York tried to argue
for limitation and allocation of steamship transportation as against
Fulton and Daniel Webster who argued for open transportation and
freedom of development of steamships.)

    *   *   *

    The close of the debate was dramatic and somewhat unexpected.
Fifteen small countries in quick succession got up and protested
against the British position. They said it meant strangulation and,
far from protecting them, it virtually excluded them from the air.
This position, which was supported by all the expert opinion of the
Conference, was most ably argued by the Netherlands * * * At
the close of it, the British position was smashed flat, even the Ca-
nadians deserting the British and the New Zealanders declining to
support their position.

The following day, after consultation, the United States Delegation proposed that all matters which had been agreed upon be embodied in a convention; and that a side agreement consisting of the mutual grant of the "five freedoms" be drawn, open to those countries which wished the exchange as between themselves. This was done after consultation with the Chinese, who urged it; with the delegates of the 19 other American republics, who asked that this be done; and with the delegates of the Scandinavian bloc, which was very firm for some such arrangement. The Netherlanders, Turks, and Spaniards likewise urged some such arrangement.

We accordingly drafted and put in a document along this line.

* * *

* * * [T]he British stated that they were prepared to accept agreement covering the "two freedoms"—right of transit and technical stop. This in turn surprised us, because Swinton had steadily and bitterly opposed any such agreement throughout the entire Conference—saying that they could not touch freedom of transit and technical stop except as a part of an agreement including the "controls" on which we had been unable to agree.[a] Thereupon, taking the United States document proposing mutual exchange of the "five freedoms", the British drafted an almost exactly similar document containing mutual exchange of the "two freedoms" among the countries signatory to it. This, as a second side agreement, was proposed and approved by the Conference.

For the United States, this was a real gain.

The countries which agreed to exchange between themselves the "five freedoms" were isolated blocs in various parts of the world—and the blocs could not interconnect. But with freedom of transit and technical stop these countries could interconnect and thereby enable commerce to be carried on.

* * *

a. In a footnote to his report, Mr. Berle stated:

I think that part of the reason for this was that everyone by this time knew exactly the real interests involved. Freedom of transit and technical stop meant on the British part grant of stop at Newfoundland, which makes transit possible across the Atlantic. At the moment, there is no commercial route across the Atlantic which does not involve the transit of Newfoundland and a stop at a Newfoundland point—this being the nearest North American landing both to Iceland and to the Azores. On our side, freedom of transit means permitting a stop at Hawaii or the Aleutians, thereby making it possible to connect Australia and New Zealand with Canada, an old and entirely legitimate ambition. Had the British opposed publicly the "two freedoms", they would have been in a position of keeping Australia and Canada disconnected, and at the same time of endeavoring to prevent American commercial crossings in the Atlantic—a position which would have been hard to justify before the public opinion both of the United States and of the British Commonwealth.

In result, we have:

(1) A permanent convention providing for permanent international organization * * *

(3) A document by which the signatories thereto mutually exchange rights of freedom of transit and freedom of non-traffic stop (document of the "two freedoms") * * *

(4) A document by which the signatories reciprocally grant to each other the "five freedoms" (commonly known as the "five freedoms" or United States document) * * *

(5) A set of completed or partially completed negotiations for bilateral agreements between the United States and a considerable number of countries in various parts of the world.

So far as the strictly American interest is concerned, the combination of bilateral agreements, right of transit and technical stop, and "five freedoms" agreements vastly enlarged possibilities presently available to American aviation. The full benefits for American aviation cannot be completely ascertained until the negotiations for bilateral agreements are concluded; but the commitments obtained are such as to make it plain that these, if properly handled, can be brought to prompt fruition.

On the international side, the great issue of air transport has been faced and met; the positions are fully understood; an international organization capable of administering the agreements made has been established, and the same organization is charged with the duty of carrying forward further study in those respects on which agreement was not reached.

* * *

Finally, a substantial beginning has been made towards opening the air to commerce. It is not too much to say that we entered the Conference in the law and atmosphere of the 17th century; and we came out with a fair prospect of obtaining 20th century conditions.

THE CHICAGO CONVENTION: EXCERPTS

61 Stat. 1180, 15 U.N.T.S. 295.

[The Convention is applicable only to civil (not state) aircraft.]

Article 1

Sovereignty

The contracting States recognize that every State has complete and exclusive sovereignty over the airspace above its territory.

Article 2

Territory

For the purposes of this Convention the territory of a State shall be deemed to be the land areas and territorial waters adjacent thereto under the sovereignty, suzerainty, protection or mandate of such State.

Article 5

Right of non-scheduled flight

Each contracting State agrees that all aircraft of the other contracting States, being aircraft not engaged in scheduled international air services shall have the right, subject to the observance of the terms of this Convention, to make flights into or in transit non-stop across its territory and to make stops for non-traffic purposes without the necessity of obtaining prior permission and subject to the right of the State flown over to require landing. Each contracting State nevertheless reserves the right, for reasons of safety of flight, to require aircraft desiring to proceed over regions which are inaccessible or without adequate air navigation facilities to follow prescribed routes, or to obtain special permission for such flights.

Such aircraft, if engaged in the carriage of passengers, cargo, or mail for remuneration or hire on other than scheduled international air services, shall also, subject to the provisions of Article 7, have the privilege of taking on or discharging passengers, cargo, or mail, subject to the right of any State where such embarkation or discharge takes place to impose such regulations, conditions or limitations as it may consider desirable.

Article 6

Scheduled air services

No scheduled international air service may be operated over or into the territory of a contracting State, except with the special permission or other authorization of that State, and in accordance with the terms of such permission or authorization.

Article 17

Nationality of aircraft

Aircraft have the nationality of the State in which they are registered.

---

1. *I.C.A.O.* The convention creates the International Civil Aviation Organization, an intergovernmental organization the ob-

jectives of which are to "develop the principles and techniques of international air navigation and to foster the planning and development of international air transport."

The convention entered into force for the United States on April 4, 1947. As of January 1, 1972, 122 states were parties to the convention, including the United States and the USSR.

2. *Subsequent treaty developments.* In 1945 the United States became a party to the International Air Services Transit Agreement, 59 Stat. 1693; 84 U.N.T.S. 389. Article 1, Section 1, provides the so-called "two freedoms" for scheduled air services:

> Each contracting State grants to the other contracting States the following freedoms of the air in respect of scheduled international air services:
>
> (1) The privilege to fly across its territory without landing;
>
> (2) The privilege to land for non-traffic purposes.
>
> The privileges of this section shall not be applicable with respect to airports utilized for military purposes to the exclusion of any scheduled international air services. In areas of active hostilities or of military occupation, and in time of war along the supply routes leading to such areas, the exercise of such privileges shall be subject to the approval of the competent military authorities.

As of January 1, 1972, 80 states were parties to the Transit Agreement.

3. The United States also became a party in 1945 to the International Air Transport Agreement, 59 Stat. 1701. So few states became parties to this agreement that the United States withdrew as a party in 1947. Article 1, Section 1, provides the so-called "five freedoms" for scheduled air service:

> Each contracting State grants to the other contracting States the following freedoms of the air in respect of scheduled international air services:
>
> (1) The privilege to fly across its territory without landing;
>
> (2) The privilege to land for non-traffic purposes;
>
> (3) The privilege to put down passengers, mail and cargo taken on in the territory of the State whose nationality the aircraft possesses;
>
> (4) The privilege to take on passengers, mail and cargo destined for the territory of the State whose nationality the aircraft possesses;
>
> (5) The privilege to take on passengers, mail and cargo destined for the territory of any other contracting

State and the privilege to put down passengers, mail and cargo coming from any such territory.

With respect to the privileges specified under paragraphs (3), (4) and (5) of this Section, the undertaking of each contracting State relates only to through services on a route constituting a reasonably direct line out from and back to the homeland of the State whose nationality the aircraft possesses.

* * *

LISSITZYN, BILATERAL AGREEMENTS ON AIR TRANSPORT

30 Journal of Air Law and Commerce 248 (1964).*

There is no widely accepted multilateral treaty which provides for the granting of traffic rights to foreign airlines. * * * Consequently, the operation of international scheduled airlines depends on the consent of the states to or through the territory of which they fly.

The possession of these privileges by a foreign airline depends either on a unilateral grant by a state, or on a bilateral agreement between the state of the airline and the other state. Since World War II, close to a thousand bilateral agreements concerning these privileges have been made between the states of the world.

Before World War II, the United States government generally permitted its airlines to obtain operating rights abroad through their own arrangements with the foreign governments concerned. In that period, few governments outside North America desired reciprocal rights in the United States for their airlines. During the war, however, the policy of the United States was changed in favor of operating rights abroad being obtained by inter-governmental agreements, whenever feasible, and the United States has bilateral air transport agreements with some fifty nations. Such agreements are concluded as "executive agreements" rather than "treaties," and are negotiated by teams composed of officials of the Department of State and Civil Aeronautics Board, with the Department of State having the primary responsibility. * * * A representative of the United States air carriers sits in during the negotiations as an observer. * * *

* * *

A typical bilateral air transport agreement of the United States contains numerous provisions, many of which are standard and non-controversial. The provisions which have given rise to most of the difficulties and criticisms have been of two related categories: (1)

* Reprinted with permission of the Board
of Editors of the Journal of Air Law
and Commerce.

Route descriptions; (2) Standards designed to govern the types of traffic carried and the capacity operated. Provisions concerning rates may also give rise to some problems.

The route descriptions, which are usually set forth in special annexes or schedules, are designed to limit the access of the airlines of one party to the traffic to or from the territory of the other party. They specify, in terms of greater or lesser generality, not only the traffic points in territories of the two contracting parties, but also the points in third states which may be served under the agreement.

* * *

The purpose of restricting the opportunities of a foreign airline to compete for traffic is further served by provisions setting forth certain standards with respect to the type of traffic (especially so-called Fifth Freedom traffic) permitted to be carried and the capacity permitted to be operated by the foreign airline. In the bilateral agreements of the United States made immediately after the Chicago Conference of 1944, no such restrictive standards were set forth. The airlines designated under these agreements were to be permitted to carry international traffic, including so-called Fifth Freedom traffic, on the specific routes, and no restrictions on capacity were mentioned. At that time, the United States was in favor of maximum freedom of operation for international airlines. Since foreign airlines were then too weak to offer effective competition, many foreign governments, including that of the United Kingdom, were unwilling to grant such unrestricted freedom. In a compromise achieved at Bermuda in February 1946, the United States and the United Kingdom agreed to include in the bilateral agreement they signed the so-called Bermuda formula governing traffic and capacity. * * * This formula avoided the "predetermination" of capacity which had been favored by the British but opposed by the United States. Yet it imposed restrictions, though in very general terms. Probably the most significant element in the formula is the "understanding" that "the primary objective" of a service is to provide "capacity adequate to the traffic demands between the country of which such airline is a national and the country of ultimate destination of the traffic," that is, Third and Fourth Freedom traffic, which has consequently come to be called "primary justification" or "primary entitlement" traffic. If either government felt that an airline of the other party was not conforming to these restrictions, there was to be consultation between the aeronautical authorities of the two parties—or what came to be known as ex post facto review. Provision was thus made for a flexible administration of the capacity standards, which are evidently open to more than one interpretation in practice. Subject to these standards, the Fifth Freedom was mutually accorded.

The Bermuda Agreement became a model for all subsequent United States agreements, and the capacity formula was incorporated, in some cases with minor changes, not only in such agreements, but also, with the consent of the other parties, in many of the agreements previously made. * * *

* * *

Regulation of rates. Rates have been established by use of "conference" machinery set up by the International Air Transport Association (IATA), a private association of airlines, sometimes referred to as a "cartel." For analysis of problems in this area, involving relationship of rate-making practices to the United States anti-trust laws and the authority of the United States Civil Aeronautics Board in the rate-making process, see Schwartz, Free Enterprise and Economic Organization 558–584 (4th ed. 1972).

For a revealing picture of the bewildering array of fare options available to international air travelers, see Lowenfeld, Aviation Law III–85 (§ 4.6) (1972).

POWERS CASE

Union of Soviet Socialist Republics, Supreme Court
Military Collegium, 1960.
30 Int'l L.Rep. 69 (1966).

* * * On May 1, 1960, at 5 hours 36 minutes, Moscow time, a military unit of the Soviet anti-aircraft defence in the area of the city of Kirovabad, the Tajik S.S.R., at an altitude of 20,000 metres, unattainable for planes of the civil air fleet, spotted an unknown aircraft violating the State frontier of the U.S.S.R.

The military units of the Soviet anti-aircraft defence vigilantly followed the behaviour of the plane as it flew over major industrial centres and important objectives, and only when the intruder plane had penetrated 2,000 kilometres into Soviet territory and the evil purpose of the flight, fraught with disastrous consequences for world peace in an age of thermonuclear weapons, become absolutely obvious, a battery of ground-to-air missiles brought the aggressor plane down in the area of Sverdlovsk at 8 hours 53 minutes as ordered by the Soviet Government.

The pilot of the plane baled out and was apprehended upon landing. On interrogation, he gave his name as Francis Gary Powers, citizen of the United States of America. Examination of the wreckage of the plane which had been brought down showed that it was of American make, specially designed for high altitude flights and fitted with various equipment for espionage reconnaissance tasks.

In view of this, the pilot Powers was arrested and committed for trial on charges of espionage against the Soviet Union.

During the court hearings, the defendant Powers testified in detail about his espionage activity and the circumstances connected with the violation of Soviet air space on May 1, 1960.

In 1950 Powers volunteered for the American army, completed his training at an Air Force school, and served as pilot at various United States Air Force bases with the rank of Senior Lieutenant.

In April 1956, Powers was recruited by the Central Intelligence Agency of the United States for special intelligence missions in high-altitude aircraft.

After he had concluded a secret contract with the United States Central Intelligence Agency for a term of two years, Powers was allotted a high salary of 2,500 dollars a month for espionage activity. He underwent special training and was assigned to the intelligence air detachment under the code name of "Ten-Ten", stationed at the American-Turkish war base of Incirlik, near the town of Adana, in Turkey.

The Court has established that the detachment "Ten-Ten" is a special combination of the United States military and civilian intelligence designed for espionage against the Soviet Union with the help of reconnaissance planes sent into Soviet air space.

Starting with 1956 Powers systematically flew on espionage missions along the Soviet Union's frontiers with Turkey, Iran and Afghanistan, on orders from the "Ten-Ten" detachment's commander. In May 1958, Powers renewed his secret contract with the Central Intelligence Agency of the United States for a term of two years, and in January 1960 for yet another year.

The Materials of the case and the testimony of defendant Powers have established that the criminal intrusion into the air space of the Soviet Union, committed by him on May 1, 1960, was carefully prepared long before it took place.

On April 27, 1960, Powers, together with the commander of the detachment "Ten-Ten", the American Colonel Shelton and a group of technical personnel intended for preparing the U–2 plane for its flight, were brought in a United States Air Force transport aircraft from the Incirlik base to the Peshawar airport in Pakistan.

Another pilot ferried the U–2 plane in which Powers was to violate the air space of the Soviet Union to this same airfield from Turkey on April 30 of this year.

On the night of April 30, 1960, Colonel Shelton gave Powers the assignment to fly over the territory of the Soviet Union at an altitude of 20,000 metres along the following course: Peshawar, the Aral Sea, Sverdlovsk, Kirov, Archangel, Murmansk, and to land in Norway, at Bodoe airport, with which Powers familiarized himself back in 1958.

Flying over Soviet territory, Powers, on Shelton's orders, was to switch on at definite points his special equipment for aerial photography and the registration of the operation of Soviet anti-aircraft defence radar stations. Powers was to give special attention to two spots—in one of them American intelligence suspected the presence of missile launching ramps and in the other a particularly important defence objective.

The material evidence of the case and his testimony has established that Powers fulfilled the criminal mission given him.

Having taken off from Peshawar airport in Pakistan, Powers flew over the territory of Afghanistan and for more than 2,000 kilometres over the Soviet Union in accordance with the established course. Besides Powers' testimony, this is confirmed by the American flight map discovered in the debris of the U–2 plane and submitted to the Court, bearing the route plotted out by Major Dulak, navigator of the detachment "Ten-Ten", and also notes and signs made by Powers, who marked down on this map several important defence objectives of the Soviet Union he had spotted from the plane.

Throughout the flight, to the very moment the plane was shot down, Powers switched on his special intelligence equipment, photographed important defence objectives and recorded signals of the country's anti-aircraft radar installations. The development of the rescued aerial photography films established that defendant Powers photographed from the U–2 plane industrial and military objectives of the Soviet Union—plants, depots, oil storage facilities, communication routes, railway bridges and stations, electric transmission lines, aerodromes, the location of troops and military equipment.

The numerous photos of the Soviet Union's territory, taken by defendant Powers from an altitude of 20,000 metres, in possession of the Military Collegium of the U.S.S.R. Supreme Court, make it possible to determine the nature of industrial establishments, the design of railway bridges, the number and type of aircraft on the airfields, the nature and purpose of military material.

Powers tape-recorded impulses of certain radar stations of the Soviet Union with a view to detecting the country's anti-aircraft defence system.

According to the conclusion of experts, the information collected by defendant Powers during his flight in Soviet air space on May 1, 1960, constitutes a State and military secret of the Soviet Union, which is specially guarded by law.

Powers testified to the Court that the U–2 plane was provided with demolition devices, intended for the destruction of the plane in case of a forced landing on Soviet territory, and that before the flight on May 1, 1960, Colonel Shelton impressed upon him the necessity of committing suicide in case he were to fall into the hands of Soviet authorities and were tortured. It was precisely for this purpose that Colonel Shelton gave him a special poison needle.

Besides the poison needle, the following objects were confiscated from Powers during his apprehension: a noiseless pistol with cartridges, a dagger, fishing gear, a pneumatic boat, topographical maps of the Soviet Union, means for making camp fires, signal boxes, an electric torchlight, compasses, a saw, food concentrates, drugs, 7,500 roubles in Soviet currency, and valuables (gold coins, rings, wrist watches) which, as Powers testified, were intended for bribing Soviet people in case of a forced landing of the U-2 in Soviet territory.

The Military Collegium of the U.S.S.R. Supreme Court has also examined other evidence confirming that a Soviet rocket unit brought down on May 1, 1960, an aircraft belonging to the United States Air Force.

Despite the fact that the plane which was brought down lacked identification marks, the experts have determined through the examination of the wreckage of the plane and the equipment on board that it was a subsonic U-2 reconnaissance aircraft of the American Lockheed company with one turbo-jet engine.

The equipment and parts of the plane had trade-marks of various American companies, which show, in particular, that the turbo-jet engine was manufactured by the Pratt-Whitney company, and the starting and electrical supply equipment by the Hamilton-Standard and General Electric companies. Furthermore, the equipment had markings indicating that it belonged to the United States military establishment.

The material evidence put before defendant Powers was recognized by him as belonging to the U-2 aircraft in which he violated the air space of the Soviet Union on May 1, of this year.

The identification card AFI 288,068, found on Powers and included in the materials of the case, carried the emblem of the United States Defence Department and the inscription: "Defence Department. United States of America."

Thus, the court hearings have established definitely that the Lockheed U-2 reconnaissance aircraft belonged to the United States Air Force and that defendant Powers was a secret agent of the Central Intelligence Agency of the United States of America.

Powers was an obedient executor of the perfidious designs of the Central Intelligence Agency of the United States of America, carried out with the consent of the American Government.

Powers himself admitted that he realized when intruding into the air space of the Soviet Union that he was violating the national sovereignty of the U.S.S.R. and flying over its territory on an espionage mission, whose main purpose consisted of detecting and marking down missile launching sites.

Examined by the court, witnesses V. P. Surin and A. F. Cheremis-in, L. A. Chuzhakin, and P. E. Asabin testified that they witnessed the falling of the plane in the area of Sverdlosvk and the landing of the parachutist, whom they apprehended and disarmed.

The detained person proved to be Powers.

*   *   *

Article 2 [of the Law on Criminal Responsibility for State Crimes] provides:

Espionage

The giving away, theft or collection with the intention of con-veying to a foreign Power, a foreign organization, or their agents, of information constituting a State or military secret, as well as the giving away or collection on the instructions of foreign in-telligence agencies of other information to be used against the in-terests of the U.S.S.R., if the espionage is committed by a foreign-er or by a stateless person—is punishable by deprivation of lib-erty for a period of from seven to fifteen years with confisca-tion of property, or by death and confiscation of property.

*   *   *   In considering the Powers case, the Military Collegium of the U.S.S.R. Supreme Court takes into account that the intrusion of the American military intelligence plane constitutes a criminal breach of a generally recognized principle of international law, which establishes the exclusive sovereignty of every State over the air space above its territory. This principle, laid down by the Paris Convention of October 13, 1919, for the regulation of aerial navigation, and sev-eral other subsequent international agreements, is proclaimed in the national legislations of different States, including the Soviet Union and the United States of America.

Violation of this sacred and immutable principle of international relations creates in the present conditions a direct menace to uni-versal peace and international security.

At the present level of military technology, when certain States possess atomic and hydrogen weapons, as well as the means of de-livering them quickly to targets, the flight of a military intelligence plane over Soviet territory could have directly preceded a military attack. This danger is the more possible in conditions when the United States of America, as stated by American generals, constantly keeps bomber patrols in the air, always ready to drop bombs on earlier marked-out targets of the Soviet Union.

Under these conditions the aggressive act of the United States of America, carried out on May 1 of this year by defendant Powers, created a threat to universal peace.

Material evidence at the disposal of the Military Collegium of the Supreme Court leaves no doubt that, by his aggressive intrusion into the air space of the Soviet Union, defendant Powers implemented far-reaching plans of reactionary quarters of the United States of America, calculated to aggravate international tension.

After the head of the Soviet Government, N. S. Khrushchov, announced at the session of the Supreme Soviet of the U.S.S.R. on May 5 of the current year that an American plane had been shot down over the territory of the Soviet Union, the State Department of the United States of America, having recognized as "fully possible" the fact of the violation of the Soviet frontier by an American plane, tried to mislead world public opinion.

Such was the purpose of the fabricated statements by the United States National Aeronautics and Space Administration and the State Department about the U–2 plane accidentally straying off course while allegedly conducting scientific research.

In his winding-up speech at the session of the Supreme Soviet of the U.S.S.R. on May 7, Comrade N. S. Khrushchov exposed the falsity of these allegations.

After that the American leaders—President Eisenhower, Vice-President Nixon and State Secretary Herter—admitted that spying flights over Soviet territory by American planes constitute part of the "calculated policy of the United States of America".

Thus, the leaders of the United States of America proclaimed the violation of the sovereignty of other States and espionage against them as the official State policy of America.

The subsequent events confirmed that the aggressive intrusion of the U–2 intelligence plane into the air space of the Soviet Union on May 1 was deliberately prepared by reactionary quarters of the United States of America in order to torpedo the Paris Summit meeting, to prevent the easing of international tension, to breathe new life into the senile cold war policy which is hated by all the peoples.

The Military Collegium of the Supreme Court of the Soviet Union has established that Powers could not have carried out the spy missions assigned to him without the use by the United States of America, for aggressive purposes, of the war bases and aerodromes on the territories of the States neighbouring on the Soviet Union, including the territories of Turkey, Iran, Pakistan and Norway.

Powers' flight has proved that the Government of the United States of America, having bound Turkey, Iran, Pakistan, Norway and other States by bilateral military agreements, has established war bases and aerodromes on their territories for dangerous provocative actions, making these States accomplices in the aggression against the Soviet Union.

Having examined the materials of the case, material and other evidence and expert findings, and having heard the testimony of the defendant and the witnesses, the speeches of the State Prosecutor and of the Defence Counsel, and also the last plea of the defendant, the Military Collegium of the U.S.S.R. Supreme Court holds established that defendant Powers was for a long time an active secret agent of the United States Central Intelligence Agency, directly fulfilling espionage missions of this agency against the Soviet Union; and that on May 1, 1960, with the knowledge of the Government of the United States of America, in a specially equipped U–2 intelligence plane, he intruded into Soviet air space and with the help of special radio-technical and photographic equipment collected information of stra- tegical importance, which constitutes a State and military secret of the Soviet State, thereby committing a grave crime covered by Article 2 of the Soviet Union's Law "On Criminal Responsibility for State Crimes".

At the same time, weighing all the circumstances of the given case in the deep conviction that they are inter-related, taking into account Powers' sincere confession of his guilt and his sincere re- pentance, proceeding from the principles of socialist humaneness, and guided by Articles 319 and 320 of the Code of Criminal Procedure of the Russion Federation, the Military Collegium of the U.S.S.R. Su- preme Court

Sentences

Francis Gary Powers, on the strength of Article 2 of the U.S.S.R. Law "On Criminal Responsibility for State Crimes", to ten years' confinement with the first three years to be served in prison.

The term of punishment, including the preliminary detention, shall be counted as from May 1, 1960.

The material evidence is to be kept with the file of the case. The money and valuables taken from Powers shall be forfeited to the State treasury.

In conformity with Article 44 of the "Fundamental Principles of the Criminal Procedure of the Soviet Union and the Union Re- publics", the sentence is final and not subject to appeal or cassa- tion.

---

1. *Sanctions against aircraft entering airspace.* Does the fact that a state has jurisdiction to prescribe law governing an event mean that it has freedom of choice in the methods used to exercise that jurisdiction? Does a state have a right to shoot down any plane that enters its airspace? In 1955, an El Al Israel Airlines Ltd. commercial airplane, with passengers aboard, entered the airspace of Bulgaria for "some unknown reason." Bulgarian fighter aircraft fired at the plane; it exploded in flight and crashed in Bulgarian territory. All fifty-eight persons aboard were killed, including American and British passengers. Proceedings were instituted against Bulgaria in the In-

ternational Court of Justice by Israel, the United States and the United Kingdom, protesting the inhuman and excessive use of force by the Bulgarians, the lack of adequate warning, the failure of Bulgaria to recognize the right of entry in distress. The cases did not proceed to the merits because of Bulgaria's having failed to consent to the jurisdiction of the Court.   9 Whiteman, Digest of International Law 326–340 (1963).

2. *Excessive use of force: analogies from the law of the sea.* The I'm Alone, 1935, III U.N.Rep.Int'l Arb. Awards 1609 involved a dispute between Canada and the United States arising out of the sinking of a Canadian rum-running vessel. A convention between the United States and Great Britain permitted search and seizure by the United States of British vessels suspected of liquor smuggling if the vessels were found close to, though outside, United States territorial waters. The "hot pursuit" of the I'm Alone ended 200 miles away from the Louisiana coast in the Gulf of Mexico. The commanding officer of the pursuing American coast guard cutter ordered the I'm Alone to stop and informed the commander of the I'm Alone that it would be sunk unless it stopped. After warning shots were fired, the United States vessel put enough shots into the hull of the I'm Alone to sink her. Commissioners appointed to report on this event stated:

> The question is whether, in the circumstances, the Government of the United States was legally justified in sinking the I'm Alone.

> The answer given to this question is as follows:—

UNJUSTIFIED

> On the assumptions stated in the question, the United States might, consistently with the Convention, use necessary and reasonable force for the purpose of effecting the objects of boarding, searching, seizing and bringing into port the suspected vessel; and if sinking should occur incidentally, as a result of the exercise of necessary and reasonable force for such purpose, the pursuing vessel might be entirely blameless. But the Commissioners think that, in the circumstances stated in paragraph eight of the Answer, the admittedly intentional sinking of the suspected vessel was not justified by anything in the Convention.

> *   *   *

> It will be recalled that the I'm Alone was sunk on the 22nd day of March, 1929, on the high seas, in the Gulf of Mexico, by the United States revenue cutter Dexter. By their interim report the Commissioners found that the sinking of the vessel was not justified by anything in the Convention. The Commissioners now add that it could not be justified by any principle of international law. (at 1617)

Are there special risks associated with aircraft that require peremptory use of destructive force?

3. *Beyond trespass: espionage as a state offense.* Issues other than "technical" trespass of Soviet airspace were involved in the U–2 incident. The criminal charge against Powers in the Soviet Union was of espionage as defined in the domestic law of that state. In the tradition of the international spy, fictional and real, the espionage agent is "out in the cold" all by himself. He expects to be disowned if caught. And the conventional practice of states is not overtly to charge another state with espionage but to counter-attack in kind, in what Dean Acheson once called "the underworld of international relations." In the U–2 case, however, although Powers was caught and prosecuted under Soviet law, the USSR openly charged the United States with responsibility, calling for condemnation by the Security Council of the United Nations of the aggressive acts of the United States. President Eisenhower responded with the unprecedented admission that the United States was responsible for Powers' flight, justifying it " 'to obtain information now concealed behind the iron curtain' in order to lessen the danger of surprise attack on the free world   *   *   *." Wright, Legal Aspects of the U–2 Incident, 54 Am. J.Int'l L. 836, 838 (1960).

Are there, therefore, issues of espionage at the international level? That is, is the law of espionage purely domestic, directed at the individual only, or is there state responsibility to the state spied upon? In view of the practices of states over centuries, it is not possible to find a consentio juris that spying per se is an offense under customary law. Has it become so under the United Nations Charter, either as to (a) conventional espionage through the penetration of the state's ground frontier, or (b) aerial espionage through the penetration of airspace? See Article 2(4).

---

2.   OFFENSES ABOARD AIRCRAFT

General Offenses

SILBERWACHT v. ATTORNEY–GENERAL

Israel, District Court of Tel-Aviv, 1953.
20 Int'l L.Rep. 153 (1957).

The Facts. This was an appeal from a decision of the Magistrate's Court convicting the appellant of smuggling and of being in possession of smuggled goods. The appellant was employed at Lydda Airport where there existed a clandestine organization for purchasing tinned food from South African airmen and bringing it on to the market without customs examination and payment of customs duty. By s. 2 of the Customs Ordinance smuggling is defined as:

> Any importation, exportation, carriage coastwise or over the land frontiers, or attempted importation, exportation, carriage coastwise or over the land frontiers, of goods, with intent to defraud the revenue or to evade any prohibition of, restriction on, or regulations as to, the importation, exportation, carriage coastwise or over the land frontiers of any goods; and 'smuggle' and 'smuggled goods' have corresponding meanings.

One of the grounds of appeal was that when the tins were removed from the aircraft by the aircrew they had already been smuggled by the South African crew and were therefore smuggled goods, so that the appellant could not be convicted of smuggling.

Held: that the appeal must be admitted and the conviction dismissed.   [A portion of the opinion of the court appears below]

  * * * This ground of appeal raises several important questions of public international law * * * The question whether the removal of the goods from the aircraft (which, it seems, was a South African aircraft, although it is not clear whether it was privately owned or a State aircraft) constitutes their importation into Israel, or whether the goods entered Israel at the moment when the aircraft entered Israel, is connected with the question whether an aircraft has to be regarded as foreign territory. Although the rule is nowhere explicitly laid down, it seems that the law of Israel presupposes that the law governing territorial sovereignty (from the point of view of jurisdiction) is similar to the concept of ownership of land, and includes authority not only over the surface of the land but also down to its depth and also in the skies above jusque ad coelum. The general opinion in public international law is similar. See Article I of the Chicago Air Agreement of 1944. * * *

  It also seems that this supposition regarding the extent of sovereignty in the air has formed the basis for many international air conventions, whose provisions have been given validity in the municipal law of Israel by virtue of Orders-in-Council issued under powers conferred by the Air Navigation Act, 1920, which is still in force in Israel despite the fact that in 1949, after the date of the establishment of the State of Israel, it was repealed and replaced in England. According to the different Orders-in-Council, the crews of foreign aircraft are permitted to transport in their aircraft goods in transit, and although such goods are exempt from customs, the aircraft themselves are not immune from control by the authorities of the State in which the aerodrome is situated.

  Since for certain limited purposes the law of the air has developed to some extent parallel with the law of the sea and for some purposes aircraft are subject to a legal régime similar to that of seagoing vessels, there has grown up a more general theory concerning this parallelism. The better opinion, however, denies the validity of any such theory. See Shawcross and Beaumont on Air Law, 2nd edition (1951), pp. 17, 86–88. It seems that counsel for the prosecution has based himself on this erroneous theory in trying to apply to this aircraft analogies taken from the sea. However, even if we were to accept this theory, we could not agree that the aircraft is to be regarded as "foreign territory", and this for the following reasons. It has always been an accepted principle of international law that the concept of "the law of the flag" applies in regard to jurisdiction over what occurs in a ship. That is to say, the State whose flag a ship flies and in which the vessel is registered, is entitled to try offenders against that State's laws for acts done on board even when the vessel is within the territorial waters of another State. From this starting point a further question arises, namely: Is the State within whose territorial waters the ship has anchored, entitled to try persons on a foreign vessel for offences which they committed on board that ship? To word it differently, is the vessel considered as foreign territory when she is lying in the territorial waters of another State?

On this point the opinions of the writers on international law are divided. It is not within our province to decide which view is correct. * * *

This problem was considered by the Judicial Committee of the Privy Council in London, on appeal from the Supreme Court of Hong Kong, in Chung Chi Cheung v. The King (see Annual Digest, 1938–1940, Case No. 87). The accused had been suspected of an offence committed on board a ship belonging to the Chinese Government which had come to rest in the territorial waters of Hong Kong, where he had been arrested, tried and convicted. The Government of China was entitled to try the man for an offence committed under its flag but it was not interested in so doing and raised no objection to the action of the British authorities. In the Privy Council the discussion centered on the contradictory theories prevalent in international law. Oppenheim starts from the assumption that, from the point of view of international law, a vessel is to be regarded as foreign territory, a sort of floating island. On the other hand, counsel for the accused relied upon the views of Brierly, who points out that the floating island theory is a pure fiction by which it is implied that the flag State is entitled to try the offender as if the act had been committed within its territory although in fact the act has been committed within the territorial waters of the coastal State—a fact to which international law does not close its eyes. The jurisdictional power of the flag State is parallel and not exclusive. It results therefore that the coastal State is not prevented from trying the accused since a foreign ship within its territory is not foreign territory. Brierly's opinion prevailed, and the Privy Council advised accordingly.

To return to the matter before us, the result will be that even if South Africa has jurisdiction over acts performed in her aircraft in accordance with South African laws regarding the air and regarding jurisdiction (assuming that the existence of exterritorial laws of that character is not contrary to international law and the public policy of Israel)—nevertheless the foreign aircraft is not foreign territory. The result, therefore, is that the act of smuggling came to an end when the pilot imported the tins into Israel with the intention of defrauding the customs. The act of smuggling did not commence at the moment when the tins were removed from the aircraft since they were already within Israel. * * *

Judge Avissar, dissenting, said: "As to the smuggling, it seems to me to make no difference to the appellant whether the pilot who landed at Lydda airport with the tinned goods on board and intending to smuggle them was guilty of an offence or not. * * * When the appellant received the goods from the aircraft and removed them from Lydda Airport without paying customs—as has been proved to have occurred—he committed the offence. The position of a person who receives goods from an aircraft at an airport cannot be any different from the position of a person who receives goods from a ship within the territorial waters of the country and imports them by smuggling. At all events, such a person is to be considered as an importer in the sense of the definition of smuggling contained in section 2 of the Customs Ordinance; and why should any discrimination be made in favour of the man who commits the smuggling by receiving the goods from an aircraft which has landed at an airport? * * *"

Problem. A South African commercial aircraft is making a non-stop transit through the airspace of Israel on a flight to Iran at an altitude of 30,000 feet. No Israeli nationals are on board the plane. A passenger in the plane asaults a stewardess. Both are South African nationals. If the passenger subsequently travels to Tel Aviv, and is arrested and tried there for assault, does South Africa have any basis for complaint under international law?

UNITED STATES v. CORDOVA

United States District Court, E.D. New York, 1950.
89 F.Supp. 298.

KENNEDY, DISTRICT JUDGE. On March 30, 1949, an information was filed against the defendant Cordova, along with one Santano, the charge consisting of four counts: 1) that on August 2, 1948 Cordova assaulted one Machada, pilot of an airplane owned by Flying Tigers,

Inc., an American corporation, while the plane was flying over the high seas from San Juan, Puerto Rico, to New York; 2) that at the same time and place Cordova assaulted one Santiago, stewardess of the air carrier; 3) that at the same time and place Cordova assaulted the codefendant Santano; and 4) that at the same time and place Santano assaulted Cordova.

The statutory bases for jurisdiction alleged in the information are respectively (a) the act forbidding striking, wounding and beating and simple assault within the admiralty and maritime jurisdiction of the United States, 18 U.S.C.A. § 455, now 18 U.S.C.A. § 113(d) and (e), (b) the act defining the admiralty and maritime jurisdiction, 18 U.S.C.A. § 451, now 18 U.S.C.A. § 7, and (c) the venue statute for the prosecution of crimes within the admiralty and maritime jurisdiction, 28 U.S.C.A. § 102, now 18 U.S.C.A. § 3238. The pertinent portions of these statutes, as they existed on August 2, 1948, the date of the alleged offenses, are given in the margin: [1]

As will appear shortly, after the facts have been outlined, the revision of the criminal code has no bearing on the case: the relevant statutes are substantially the same now as they were at the time of the offenses set forth in the information.

When the trial commenced, the government moved to dismiss the fourth count of the information (which charges the codefendant Santano with assault upon the defendant Cordova), a jury was waived, and the cause was tried to the court. Motions appropriate to challenge the jurisdiction of the court over the offenses charged were made at every stage of the case. * * *

The facts are simple and clear. At 6:42 P.M., New York time, the carrier plane DC–4 No. NC–90911 took off from San Juan Air-

---

1. Title 18 U.S.C.A. § 451, reads in part: "Places and waters applicable; on board American vessel on high seas or Great Lakes; on land under exclusive control of United States; guano islands. The crimes and offenses defined in this chapter shall be punished as herein prescribed:
"First. When committed upon the high seas, or on any other waters within the admiralty and maritime jurisdiction of the United States and out of the jurisdiction of any particular State, or when committed within the admiralty and maritime jurisdiction of the United States and out of the jurisdiction of any particular State on board any vessel belonging in whole or in part to the United States or any citizen thereof, or to any corporation created by or under the laws of the United States, or of any State, Territory, or District thereof."

Title 18 U.S.C.A. § 455 (part of the same chapter) is entitled "Felonious assaults; to murder or rape; other felony; with weapons; beating; simple assault," and reads in part: "Whoever shall unlawfully strike, beat, or wound another, shall be fined not more than $500, or imprisoned not more than six months or both. Whoever shall unlawfully assault another, shall be fined not more than $300, or imprisoned not more than three months, or both."
Title 28 U.S.C.A. § 102 is entitled "Offenses on the high seas," and reads:
"The trial of all offenses committed upon the high seas, or elsewhere out of the jurisdiction of any particular State or district, shall be in the district where the offender is found, or into which he is first brought."

field in Puerto Rico, bound for New York. The plane is the property of Flying Tigers, Inc., an American corporation, and at the time of the flight was under charter to Air America, Inc., another American corporation, organized under the laws of California. On board when the flight began were 60 passengers and 6 crew members. Of the passengers 43 were adults, 11 were children under 2 years of age, and 6 were children over that age.

At 8:15 P.M. on August 2, 1948 the plane, travelling at an air speed of 180 m. p. h., was over the Atlantic Ocean on a course 324 degrees true bound for Charleston, S. C., having been on her course for 1½ hours. This means that the plane was to the northward of the Bahama Islands at a point approximately 270 miles northwest of San Juan, Puerto Rico. The plane's altitude was 8,500 feet. At that time (8:15 P.M., August 2, 1948) the plane became tail heavy, and her indicated air speed fell from 180 miles per hour to 150 miles per hour. The nose was rising so fast that the automatic pilot could not make corrections which would keep the ship on an even keel, and it became necessary to adjust the instrument. At this juncture the steward notified the pilot Machada that there was a fight going on in the passenger compartment. Machada turned the controls over to his First Officer and went aft. What he found was a brawl in progress between the passengers Cordova and Santano, which the steward and the stewardess (one Santiago) had been attempting to stop in vain. The passengers had crowded aft to watch the fight; it was because of this fact that the plane had become tail heavy.

Machada intervened, with the result that the defendant Cordova bit him on the shoulder, and during this portion of the fracas Cordova struck not only his adversary Santano, but also the stewardess Santiago.

The story of the origin of the fight is an old one. Apparently when these planes leave from San Juan, the relatives and friends of the passengers participate in a bon voyage celebration, the principal attraction being Puerto Rican rum in large quantities. And to fortify themselves for the flight, on this particular occasion many of the passengers, including Cordova and Santano, had boarded the plane with bottles of rum in paper shopping bags, which they took to their seats. Cordova and Santano had been toasting each other effusively for the first part of the flight, but soon a dispute arose over a missing bottle. Cordova seems literally to have gone beserk: while the main object of his viciousness was Santano, anyone else who crossed his path, including the captain of the plane, was in danger. The efforts of Machada (the captain) to subdue Cordova were reasonable. He began by attempting to hold Cordova's arms. At that time the weather being warm, Machada was wearing no flight jacket, and Cordova, attempting to free himself, bit Machada in the shoulder, drawing blood and necessitating first aid treatment. Eventually Cordova was locked up in a compartment.

The plane landed at La Guardia Field at 4:45 A.M. on August 3, 1948. Cordova and Santano were immediately apprehended in this District and charged with assault. It thus appears that the venue requirements of the statute, 28 U.S.C.A. § 102, heretofore quoted in the margin, are satisfied if a crime within the jurisdiction of the United States Courts was committed. It is also plain that Cordova did, in fact, and without just cause or excuse strike and bite Machada (count 1), Santiago (count 2), and Santano (count 3). The case under the third count is weaker than the others, because Santano was at least in the beginning himself an active participant in the fight. Later, however, he attempted to retreat when the pilot of the plane and the stewardess intervened and the striking or biting which were then committed by Cordova on all three victims clearly violated the terms of the specific substantive statute, 18 U.S.C.A. § 455, heretofore quoted in the margin.

But the statute condemning striking, wounding and beating, and simple assault, within the admiralty and maritime jurisdiction of the United States does not become operative unless the acts complained of meet one of two tests, 18 U.S.C.A. § 451: (1) Were those acts committed on the high seas, or on any other waters within the admiralty and maritime jurisdiction of the United States and out of the jurisdiction of any particular State? or (2) Were those acts committed within the admiralty and maritime jurisdiction of the United States and out of the jurisdiction of any particular State on board any vessel belonging in whole or in part to the United States or any citizen thereof or any corporation created by or under the laws of the United States, or of any State, Territory or District thereof?

The second question gives less difficulty than the other, and perhaps should be dealt with first. The answer that ought to be made turns on the question whether an airplane is a vessel, within the meaning of the statute, and obviously the answer should be in the negative.

* * *

* * * [W]hen, 18 U.S.C.A. § 451, Congress speaks of a "vessel" within the admiralty and maritime jurisdiction of the United States, it evokes in the common mind a picture of a ship, not of a plane.

* * *

It now becomes necessary to return to the first branch of the statute, which denounces certain crimes committed on the high seas or other waters within the admiralty and maritime jurisdiction of the United States and out of the jurisdiction of any particular state, 18 U.S.C.A. § 451. Beyond any doubt, Cordova's misconduct took place over the high seas. Is it proper, then, in a criminal case, to extend federal criminal jurisdiction to a plane in flight over the high seas under a statute which speaks of crimes committed upon the high seas or on any other waters within the admiralty and maritime jurisdiction of the United States? * * *

It is perhaps irrelevant, but I have little doubt that had it wished to do so Congress could, under its police power, have extended federal criminal jurisdiction to acts committed on board an airplane owned by an American national, even though such acts had no effect upon national security.[2] In U. S. v. Flores, 1933, 289 U.S. 137, 53 S.Ct. 580, 77 L.Ed. 1086, the Supreme Court of the United States went the extreme length of holding that the criminal jurisdiction of the United States, under this very statute, 18 U.S.C.A. § 451, was broad enough to include acts committed on an American flag vessel, even though she was within the territorial waters of another sovereign. The Court has even suggested that a State of the union may make a regulation valid and effective to rule conduct on the high seas, so long as the federal government has not occupied the field. Skiriotes v. Florida, 1941, 313 U.S. 69, 61 S.Ct. 924, 85 L.Ed. 1193. And on occasion the Supreme Court has not been over technical to ascertain whether the crime was committed on the ship itself or in adjacent waters. United States v. Holmes, 1820, 5 Wheat. 412, 5 L.Ed. 122. For such a case the expression "high seas" was held to have a general meaning, and a similar result was reached when the Court was dealing with the question whether the term "high seas" was applicable to the Great Lakes. United States v. Rodgers, 1893, 150 U.S. 249, 14 S.Ct. 109, 37 L.Ed. 1071.

But none of these cases, nor the principles on which they rest, would justify the extension of the words "high seas" to the air space over them. It is at this point that the case at bar, I think, becomes one of first impression. * * *

The acts for which Cordova stands charged were vicious in the extreme. He jeopardized the lives of others on the plane, including a considerable number of infants. But it seems to me clear that those acts have not been denounced by a statute which forbids them when committed on board an American "vessel", or when committed on the "high seas".

The situation may call for correction. There has been for some years discussion by experts in the field of aeronautic law of how the problem can be solved. For example, the so-called de Wisscher Draft

2. The reason I mention "national security" is this. It seems clear that Congress can denounce as crimes acts affecting the well-being of the government, and committed by American nationals, even when those acts take place on land within the jurisdiction of a foreign sovereign. U. S. v. Bowman, 1922, 260 U.S. 94, 43 S.Ct. 39, 67 L.Ed. 149; United States v. Chandler, D.C.Mass.1947, 72 F.Supp. 230, affirmed 1 Cir., 1949, 171 F.2d 921, certiorari denied 1949, 336 U.S. 918, 69 S.Ct. 640, rehearing denied 1949, 336 U.S. 947, 69 S.Ct. 809. But Congressional power over vessels on the high seas, or in admiralty waters outside the jurisdiction of any state, is even wider. It can be exercised to punish acts (such as assault) which have no relationship to national security. A different theory of jurisdiction comes into play, namely, that the American flag vessel is itself territory of the United States. There are no international complications, as there might be for land crimes against a person.

Convention of 1937 suggests that crimes of this character ought to be punishable under the laws of the state of which the victim is a national, or of which the accused is a national, or of the state where the airplane arrives, if, in the latter case, what was done affects its security interests. The British Air Navigation Act of 1920 provides that any offense committed on a British aircraft shall be deemed committed in any place where the offender may for the time be. It is my understanding that French criminal law applies to French aircraft in flight any place in the world. Air Nav.Law 1924, Title V, Art. 20. Italian law, I have been told, also applies to Italian planes in flight anywhere, although this may be merely a civil code.

What I gather is that there is little likelihood, if any, of an international agreement involving, as it necessarily would, difficult and delicate questions of sovereignty. However that may be, as the law now stands, acts like those committed by Cordova will go unpunished, unless the law of the domicile of the corporation can be considered to cover them.

I, therefore, find Cordova guilty of the acts charged. But I must arrest judgment of conviction since there is no federal jurisdiction to punish those acts.

I feel very strongly that the government should have the opportunity to review this decision. And I draw the attention of the United States Attorney to the procedure followed in U. S. v. Flores, supra, and also to the criminal appeals statute in its present form, 18 U.S. C.A. § 3731, which seems to give ample protection against appeal to the wrong court. For what it may be worth, I certify that my decision turns on no issue of fact, but merely the determination of a question of law, namely, the construction of 18 U.S.C.A. § 451 and § 455.[4]

---

1. *Special maritime and territorial jurisdiction of the United States.* As discussed on p. 235, the special maritime and territorial jurisdiction of the United States is defined in Title 18, Section 7 of the United States Code. Shortly after the Cordova decision was rendered, the definition was amended to include:

> (5) Any aircraft belonging in whole or in part to the United States, or any citizen thereof, or to any corporation created by or under the laws of the United States, or any State, Territory,

---

4. It is true that I have found the facts against Cordova, including intent, wilfullness, and lack of excuse. But I have construed the statute on the basis of what the information says concerning the place of the offenses, and this is a fact not in dispute nor capable of debate. It may seem odd that fact-finding and a verdict of guilty are combined with an order in arrest of judgment because of want of jurisdiction. But I thought this procedure wise because, in the event my decision is wrong, I can proceed to sentence under the mandate, and save another trial.

district, or possession thereof, while such aircraft is in flight over the high seas, or over any other waters within the admiralty and maritime jurisdiction of the United States and out of the jurisdiction of any particular State.

Title 18 defines as criminal a number of acts that are performed within the special maritime and territorial jurisdiction. For a list of such acts, see Chapter 3, p. 235. Title 49, Section 1472(k) of the United States Code deals with these same crimes when committed within the "special aircraft jurisdiction of the United States." See p. 277.

2. *Problem.* All the facts are the same as in the Cordova case, except that the aircraft is privately owned by an American citizen and is registered in State X. The United States prosecution is based upon Title 18, Section 113, of the United States Code (assaults within the special maritime and territorial jurisdiction) and Title 18, Section 7 (5), of the United States Code, (above). [Cf. Title 49, Section 1301 (32) and 1472(k) of the United States Code.]

a. Are the events in the case covered by the statute?

b. Would they be covered if the defendant were not a national of the United States? Section 113 provides: "Whoever, within the special maritime and territorial jurisdiction of the United States, is guilty of an assault shall be punished as follows: * * * "

c. If the defendant convicted and punished were not a United States national, would State X have a basis for complaint against the United States under international law? See Article 17 of the Chicago Convention, p. 252.

3. *Identification zones.* The United States has established air defense identification zones (ADIZ) and a distant early warning identification zone (DEWIZ) in areas of the airspace over the high seas adjacent to its coasts. Similar zones have been established by some other states. Aircraft operating in or penetrating such zones are subject to requirements with respect to filing flight plans; pilots of aircraft entering the United States through an ADIZ or a DEWIZ are required to report positions. 14 C.F.R., Part 99. Since these zones extend seaward several hundreds of miles, do they entail a violation of international law respecting the jurisdiction of the United States over airspace? Can the United States lawfully prescribe rules regulating activity in these zones on the ground that obedience to the rules is a condition to entry into the territory of the United States? See Restatement of the Foreign Relations Law of the United States, Comment d to Section 17 and Comment e to Section 21 (1965).

GOOD
&
QUESTION

HIJACKING

A passenger in a commercial airplane threatens to explode a bomb which, he asserts, is in a handbag he is carrying. The pilot diverts the flight of the plane to a destination demanded by the passenger. The passenger leaves the plane at that destination and the plane is flown to its original destination.

Even in this simple example there may be a number of problems of domestic and international law. The plane may be registered in the United States or in some other country. The passenger may hijack the plane on the ground in New York, or while it is over the Atlantic on its way to London, or while it is on the ground in London. The hijacker may be a United States national, or the national of another state. He may or may not eventually return to the United States and thus be subject to its enforcement jurisdiction. The United States may ask the government of the foreign state in which the hijacker is located to return him to the United States by extradition proceedings. The government of a state to which the hijacker has fled may decide to try him even though that state has had no connection with the event other than having become a place of refuge.

1. *International Conventions.*

a.   The Tokyo Convention (Convention on Offenses and Certain Other Acts Committed on Board Aircraft, 20 U.S.T. 2941; Documentary Supplement) was drafted under the auspices of the International Civil Aviation Organization and signed in 1963. It entered into force for the United States on December 4, 1969. 49 states were parties to the convention on January 1, 1972.

The convention is concerned broadly with the question of crimes on board aircraft in flight, on the surface of the high seas or any other area outside the jurisdiction of a nation state. A special purpose of the convention is to provide that there be no lapse of jurisdiction with respect to such crimes. To that end Article 3(1) provides that at least one state shall have jurisdiction: "The State of registration of the aircraft is competent to exercise jurisdiction over offenses and acts committed on board." This jurisdiction is not exclusive, however. The convention deals in detail with the powers of the aircraft commander to "off-load" and to restrain offenders or suspected offenders. Article 11 deals specifically with hijacking:

1.   When a person on board has unlawfully committed by force or threat thereof an act of interference, seizure, or other wrongful exercise of control of an aircraft in flight or when such an act is about to be committed, Contracting States shall take all appropriate measures to restore control of the aircraft to its lawful commander or to preserve his control of the aircraft.

2.   In the cases contemplated in the preceding paragraph, the Contracting State in which the aircraft lands shall permit its passengers and crew to continue their journey as soon as practicable, and shall return the aircraft and its cargo to the persons lawfully entitled to possession.

The provision on extradition (Article 16) is relatively weak:

　　1.　Offences committed on aircraft registered in a Contracting State shall be treated, for the purpose of extradition, as if they had been committed not only in the place in which they have occurred but also in the territory of the State of registration of the aircraft.

　　2.　Without prejudice to the provisions of the preceding paragraph, nothing in this Convention shall be deemed to create an obligation to grant extradition.

(b) The Hague Convention (Convention for the Suppression of Unlawful Seizure of Aircraft, TIAS 7192; Documentary Supplement) was also the product of the work of the ICAO. It was approved at a diplomatic conference at The Hague in 1970 and entered into force for the United States on October 14, 1971. 19 states were parties to the Convention on January 1, 1972; a substantial number of states became parties during 1972. In contrast to the Tokyo Convention, the Hague Convention is directed narrowly to the question of hijacking. Its major provisions create universal jurisdiction for the prosecution of hijackers and impose an obligation on the states either to prosecute the hijacker or to extradite him:

Article 1

Any person who on board an aircraft in flight:

　　(a) unlawfully, by force or threat thereof, or by any other form of intimidation, seizes, or exercises control of, that aircraft, or attempts to perform any such act, or

　　(b) is an accomplice of a person who performs or attempts to perform any such act

commits an offence (hereinafter referred to as "the offence").

Article 4

　　1.　Each Contracting State shall take such measures as may be necessary to establish its jurisdiction over the offence and any other act of violence against passengers or crew committed by the alleged offender in connection with the offence, in the following cases:

　　(a) when the offence is committed on board an aircraft registered in that State;

　　(b) when the aircraft on board which the offence is committed lands in its territory with the alleged offender still on board;

　　(c) when the offence is committed on board an aircraft leased without crew to a lessee who has his principal place of business or, if the lessee has no such place of business, his permanent residence, in that State.

2.   Each Contracting State shall likewise take such measures as may be necessary to establish its jurisdiction over the offence in the case where the alleged offender is present in its territory and it does not extradite him pursuant to Article 8 to any of the States mentioned in paragraph 1 of this Article.

3.   This Convention does not exclude any criminal jurisdiction exercised in accordance with national law.

Article 7

Absolute Obligation of Prosecution

The Contracting State in the territory of which the alleged offender is found shall, if it does not extradite him, be obliged, without exception whatsoever and whether or not the offence was committed in its territory, to submit the case to its competent authorities for the purpose of prosecution.

Those authorities shall take their decision in the same manner as in the case of any ordinary offence of a serious nature under the law of that State.

Article 8

1.   The offence shall be deemed to be included as an extraditable offence in any extradition treaty existing between Contracting States.   Contracting States undertake to include the offence as an extraditable offence in every extradition treaty to be concluded between them.

2.   If a Contracting State which makes extradition conditional on the existence of a treaty receives a request for extradition from another Contracting State with which it has no extradition treaty, it may at its option consider this Convention as the legal basis for extradition in respect of the offence.   Extradition shall be subject to the other conditions provided by the law of the requested State.

3.   Contracting States which do not make extradition conditional on the existence of a treaty shall recognize the offence as an extraditable offence between themselves subject to the conditions provided by the law of the requested State.

4.   The offence shall be treated, for the purpose of extradition between Contracting States, as if it had been committed not only in the place in which it occurred but also in the territories of the States required to establish their jurisdiction in accordance with Article 4, paragraph 1.

2.   *United States legislation.*   Do the provisions of the United States Code set forth below satisfy the obligations of the United States under article 4 of the Hague Convention?

Title 49, Section 1301.

As used in this chapter, unless the context otherwise requires—

*   *   *

(32) The term "special aircraft jurisdiction of the United States" include the following aircraft while in flight—

(a) civil aircraft of the United States;

(b) aircraft of the national defense forces of the United States; and

(c) any other aircraft—

(i) within the United States, or

(ii) outside the United States which has its next scheduled destination or last point of departure in the United States provided that in either case it next actually lands in the United States. For the purpose of this definition, an aircraft is considered to be in flight from the moment when power is applied for the purpose of takeoff until the moment when the landing run ends.

Title 49, Section 1472.

(i) (1) Whoever commits or attempts to commit aircraft piracy, as herein defined, shall be punished—

MANDATORY

(A) by death if the verdict of the jury shall so recommend, or, *DEATH* in the case of a plea of guilty, or a plea of not guilty where the *PENALTY* defendant has waived a trial by jury, if the court in its discretion shall so order; or

(B) by imprisonment for not less than twenty years, if the death penalty is not imposed.

(2) As used in this subsection, the term "aircraft piracy" means any seizure or exercise of control, by force or violence or threat of force or violence and with wrongful intent, of an aircraft within the special aircraft jurisdiction of the United States.

(j) Whoever, while aboard an aircraft within the special aircraft jurisdiction of the United States, assaults, intimidates, or threatens any flight crew member or flight attendant (including any steward or stewardess) of such aircraft, so as to interfere with the performance by such member or attendant of his duties or lessen the ability of such member or attendant to perform his duties, shall be fined not more than $10,000 or imprisoned not more than twenty years, or both. Whoever in the commission of any such act uses a deadly or dangerous weapon shall be imprisoned for any term of years or for life.

(k) (1) Whoever, while aboard an aircraft within the special aircraft jurisdiction of the United States, commits an act which, if committed within the special maritime and territorial jurisdiction of the United States, as defined in section 7 of Title 18, would be in violation of section 113, 114, 661, 662, 1111, 1112, 1113, 2031, 2032 or 2111 of such Title 18 shall be punished as provided therein.

(2) Whoever, while aboard an aircraft within the special aircraft jurisdiction of the United States, commits an act, which, if

committed in the District of Columbia would be in violation of section 9 of the Act entitled "An Act for the preservation of the public peace and the protection of property within the District of Columbia", approved July 29, 1892, as amended (D.C.Code, sec. 22–1112), shall be punished as provided therein.

3. *French legislation.* France deposited its ratification to the Hague Convention on September 18, 1972. The following legislation, Law 72–623,[a] was enacted July 5, 1972:

    *   *   *

Art. L.121–7. French courts have jurisdiction over any infraction committed aboard an airplane registered in France. They have jurisdiction as well over any crime or tort committed against such plane outside of the French territory.

Art. L.121–8. French courts have jurisdiction with respect to a crime or a tort committed aboard a plane which is not registered in France when the author or the victim has French nationality, when the plane lands in France after the commission of the crime or tort, or when the infraction was committed aboard a plane which is rented without crew to a person who has his principal place of establishment or, if there be none, his permanent residence in France.

Moreover, in case a plane is forced off its course [i. e. hijacked] which is not registered in France, French courts have jurisdiction over the infraction and over every other act of violence against the passengers or the crew done by the person alleged to have forced the plane off its course in the commission of [literally, in direct relationship to] the offense, when the person is found in France. 92 Gazette du Palais (Legislation) 360 (1972).

    *   *   *

4. *Question.* Does the seizure of aircraft by a passenger or passengers constitute piracy as defined by the law of nations? See p. 194.

Title 18, Section 1651 of the United States Code provides:

> Whoever, on the high seas, commits the crime of piracy as defined by the law of nations, and is afterwards brought into or found in the United States, shall be imprisoned for life.

SABOTAGE

The Sabotage Convention (Convention for the Suppression of Unlawful Acts Against the Safety of Civil Aviation) was adopted by a Conference on International Air Law at Montreal in 1971. T.I.A.S. 7570, Documentary Supplement. It entered into force on January 26,

---

a. Translation by the editors.

1973.   The scope of the convention is described by the head of the United States delegation to the conference as follows:

> Although this convention is similar to the Hijacking Convention in many respects, it is significantly distinct: It does not, basically, require states to define any new offenses—it covers acts which already are common crimes; it does not, for the most part, establish new crimes to fall within the extradition process— most of the acts already are extraditable crimes.   These were important elements of the Hijacking Convention.   It might be said that states could punish offenders or extradite them without this convention.

> What this convention does is to impose an obligation on states *requiring* them to prosecute or extradite offenders.   It serves as a warning to any person who contemplates such acts that the international community has responded with unanimity to condemn such acts.   In this respect it is like the Hijacking Convention.

> And in an important respect this convention does more than the Hijacking Convention.   It covers acts against aircraft in a state's domestic service, even when the acts take place wholly within that same state, if the offender escapes to another state. While this element is not critical for the Hijacking Convention, it is crucial for the effectiveness of the convention we have concluded, because of the possibility that offenders may escape before they are discovered.   This convention declares that no one who sabotages a civil aircraft—whether in domestic or international service—no one who places a bomb on board such an aircraft, no evildoer who commits violence aboard such an aircraft in flight, no criminal of this character shall ever find sanctuary anywhere in the world, no matter how deviously he may seek to evade retribution for his deeds.   The parties to this convention have declared that this despicable criminal shall be pursued without respite. 65 U.S. Dep't State Bull. 464 (1971)

EXTRADITION AND AIRCRAFT OFFENSES

IN RE KAVIC, BJELANOVIC AND ARSENIJEVIC

Switzerland, Federal Tribunal, 1952.
19 Int'l L.Rep. 371 (1957).

THE FACTS.   This was a request by Yugoslavia for the extradition of three Yugoslav nationals, members of the crew of a Yugoslav passenger plane, who had diverted the plane from its lawful destination in Yugoslavia to Switzerland, and had there sought asylum. During the flight the other members of the crew were subjected to constraint, and extradition was requested for that offence as well as for the offences of endangering the safety of public transport and of wrongful appropriation of property. It was contended on behalf of the accused that extradition should be refused on the grounds, inter alia, that the offence was not committed on Yugoslav territory, and that it was a political offence.

Held: that extradition could not be granted. The offences in question had a political character. [A portion of the opinion of the court appears below.]

The question whether the request for extradition must be granted, must be decided in conformity with the Federal Law concerning Extradition of January 22, 1892, and the Extradition Treaty between Switzerland and Serbia of November 28, 1897, since the Kingdom of Yugoslavia and now the Federal Republic of Yugoslavia are the successors of the Kingdom of Serbia, and have taken over international conventions concluded by it. * * *

The accused contend that, according to the principle of territoriality, extradition cannot be granted, since the offences in question were not committed on or over Yugoslav territory, but on or over that of Switzerland, and of Austria and Italy. * * *

(a) This contention is unfounded in so far as it is attempted to deduce from the preamble to Article 1 of the Extradition Treaty that extradition can be granted only for offences committed in Yugoslavia. An earlier decision of this Tribunal (A.T.F., 34, I, p. 781) taking this view in reference to an identical provision in the Swiss-Italian Extradition Treaty, was essentially based on the fact of the lack of competence of Italian courts to deal with offences committed outside Italy. Yugoslav law, on the other hand, provides for the competence of Yugoslav courts also in respect of offences committed by Yugoslav nationals abroad, if the offender is arrested in Yugoslavia, or extradited. * * *

(b) On the other hand, the question arises whether extradition must not be refused on the ground that the offences in question were committed on Swiss territory, to which, both according to international and to municipal law, the airspace above it belongs (Article 1 of the Convention of December 7, 1944, concerning International Civil Aviation; and Article 11, paragraph 1, of the Federal Law concerning Aviation of December 21, 1948). The principle that extradition is not granted for offences committed on Swiss territory is laid down in Article 12 of the Extradition Law; it is valid even in relation to States with whom an extradition treaty is in force which does not contain that principle. It applies not only to offences committed exclusively in Switzerland, but also to offences committed both in Switzerland and in the requesting State, e. g., when the action was carried out in Switzerland and had its effect in the other State, or when acts committed in both countries are considered by criminal law to form one entity. The question whether extradition must be denied on this ground can, however, be left open, since, as will be seen below, it is excluded on another ground.

In accordance with Article 10 of the Extradition Law and Article VI of the Extradition Treaty, extradition is not granted for political offences. This applies not only to offences directed against the State, which are described as purely political offences—and which, in any case, are not amongst the extraditable offences listed—but also to so-called relative political offences, which consist in the commission of a common offence, but which, by virtue of the circumstances and, in particular, the motive, of their commission, acquire a political colouring. Moreover, there are common offences which are committed not for their own sake, but for the purpose of preparing or ensuring the success of purely political offences, and common offences which also constitute a purely political offence. * * *

 * * *

In this connection there can also be applied the principle that the relation between the purpose and the means adopted for its achievement must be such that the ideals connected with the purpose are sufficiently strong to excuse, if not justify, the injury to private property, and to make the offender appear worthy of asylum (A.T.F., 56, I, p. 462). Freedom from the constraint of a totalitarian State must be regarded as an ideal in this sense. In the present case the required relationship undoubtedly exists; for, on the one hand, the offences against the other members of the crew were not very serious, and, on the other, the political freedom and even existence of the accused was at stake, and could only be achieved through the commission of these offences.

----

1. *A summary of extradition law.* If an individual goes from State Z to State A, there is no rule of international law that requires State A to return that individual to State Z. This is true even though State Z claims the individual as its national and, indeed, even though the individual admits that he is State Z's national. This is true also even though the individual has committed a crime in State Z, no matter what the nature of that crime may be.

The practice of extradition has been developed to moderate the absolute inability of a state to procure the return of a person who has committed or been convicted of a crime in its territory and thereafter fled to another state. Under extradition practice, State A will honor State Z's request to return an individual claimed by State Z to have committed (or to have been convicted of) a crime in Z. Under United States law, such a request will not be honored unless the United States has entered into a treaty with the requesting state. *Valentine v. United States ex rel. Neidecker,* 299 U.S. 5, 57 S.Ct. 100 (1936). The United States has over 80 bilateral extradition treaties in force. The extradition treaty between the United States and Argentina which entered into force on Sept. 15, 1972 is set forth in full in the Documentary

Supplement.   An extradition treaty entered into by the United States typically contains a list of offenses; the states agree that they will extradite to each other persons charged with or convicted of those offenses committed in the territory of the requesting state.   See, for example, the schedule of offenses covered by the United States-Argentina treaty.   On the other hand,   " * * * most modern extradition treaties make no attempt to list the offences, and the problem of listing would make it impossible to draft a multilateral treaty on the subject."   2 O'Connell, International Law 722 (2d ed. 1970).

At times, treaties will provide for an exception from obligatory extradition of a person who is a national of the requested state; that exception is provided for in the treaty with Argentina.   The United States will surrender its own national unless the treaty provides otherwise.   Charlton v. Kelly, 229 U.S. 447, 33 S.Ct. 945 (1913).   A major exception in extradition treaties is for crimes of a political character, which creates problems in the event that extradition is sought for an act of killing which formally fits the schedule of extraditable crimes (such as "murder") but was committed with a political motive.   See 2 O'Connell, International Law 726–729 (2d ed. 1970).

2.   *Extradition under the Hague Convention.*   Article 8(1) of the Hague Convention provides, in effect, for the automatic amendment of extradition treaties to add hijacking to the list of extraditable crimes.   What, then, of the individual who seeks to escape from a country which refuses to allow him to emigrate by hijacking a plane in the domestic air service of that country and requiring the pilot to fly the plane to a country of refuge?   If the underlying extradition treaty provides for the usual exception for crimes of a "political character," can the requested state consider that hijacking under those circumstances is such a crime?   If it does so consider it and refuses to extradite, the obligation to prosecute, under Article 7 of the Hague Convention, comes into play.

3. POLLUTION OF AIRSPACE

TRAIL SMELTER CASE (UNITED STATES v. CANADA)

Arbitral Tribunal, 1941.
III U.N.Rep. Int'l Arb. Awards 1905, 1907 (1949).

CONVENTION FOR SETTLEMENT OF DIFFICULTIES ARISING FROM
OPERATION OF SMELTER AT TRAIL, B.C.

* * *

ARTICLE III.

The Tribunal shall finally decide the questions, hereinafter referred to as "the Questions", set forth hereunder, namely:

(1) Whether damage caused by the Trail Smelter in the State of Washington has occurred since the first day of January, 1932, and, if so, what indemnity should be paid therefor?

(2) In the event of the answer to the first part of the preceding Question being in the affirmative, whether the Trail Smelter should be required to refrain from causing damage in the State of Washington in the future and, if so, to what extent?

(3) In the light of the answer to the preceding Question, what measures or régime, if any, should be adopted or maintained by the Trail Smelter?

(4) What indemnity or compensation, if any, should be paid on account of any decision or decisions rendered by the Tribunal pursuant to the next two preceding Questions?

ARTICLE IV.

The Tribunal shall apply the law and practice followed in dealing with cognate questions in the United States of America as well as international law and practice, and shall give consideration to the desire of the high contracting parties to reach a solution just to all parties concerned.

* * *

DECISION

REPORTED ON MARCH 11, 1944, TO THE GOVERNMENT OF THE UNITED STATES OF AMERICA AND TO THE GOVERNMENT OF THE DOMINION OF CANADA, UNDER THE CONVENTION SIGNED APRIL 15, 1935.

*   *   *   *   *   *   *   *   *   *

On April 16, 1938, the Tribunal reported its "final decision" on Question No. 1, as well as its temporary decisions on Questions No. 2 and No. 3, and provided for a temporary régime thereunder. The decision reported on April 16, 1938, will be referred to hereinafter as the "previous decision". * * *

In conclusion (end of Part Two of the previous decision), the Tribunal answered Question No. 1 as follows:

Damage caused by the Trail Smelter in the State of Washington has occurred since the first day of January, 1932, and up to October 1, 1937, and the indemnity to be paid therefor is seventy-eight thousand dollars ($78,000), and is to be complete and final indemnity and compensation for all damage which occurred between such dates. Interest at the rate of six per centum per year will be allowed on the above sum of seventy-eight thousand dollars ($78,000) from the date of the filing of this report and decision until date of payment. This decision is not subject to alteration or modification by the Tribunal hereafter. The fact of existence of damage, if any, occurring after October 1, 1937, and the indemnity to be paid therefor, if any, the Tribunal will determine in its final decision.

*   *   *

In 1896, a smelter was started under American auspices near the locality known as Trail, B.C. In 1906, the Consolidated Mining and Smelting Company of Canada, Limited, obtained a charter of incorporation from the Canadian authorities, and that company acquired the smelter plant at Trail as it then existed. Since that time, the Canadian company, without interruption, has operated the Smelter, and from time to time has greatly added to the plant until it has become one of the best and largest equipped smelting plants on the American continent. In 1925 and 1927, two stacks of the plant were erected to 409 feet in height and the Smelter greatly increased its daily smelting of zinc and lead ores. This increased production resulted in more sulphur dioxide fumes and higher concentrations being emitted into the air. In 1916, about 5,000 tons of sulphur per month were emitted; in 1924, about 4,700 tons; in 1926, about 9,000 tons— an amount which rose near to 10,000 tons per month in 1930. In other words, about 300–350 tons of sulphur were being emitted daily in 1930. (It is to be noted that one ton of sulphur is substantially the equivalent of two tons of sulphur dioxide or SO_2.)

From 1925, at least, to 1937, damage occurred in the State of Washington, resulting from the sulphur dioxide emitted from the Trail Smelter as stated in the previous decision.   *   *   *

The second question under Article III of the Convention is as follows:

In the event of the answer to the first part of the preceding question being in the affirmative, whether the Trail Smelter should be required to refrain from causing damage in the State of Washington in the future and, if so, to what extent?

Damage has occurred since January 1, 1932, as fully set forth in the previous decision. To that extent, the first part of the preceding question has thus been answered in the affirmative.   *   *   *

FOLLOW MUNICIPAL OR I L ?

The first problem which arises is whether the question should be answered on the basis of the law followed in the United States or on the basis of international law. The Tribunal, however, finds that this problem need not be solved here as the law followed in the United States in dealing with the quasi-sovereign rights of the States of the Union, in the matter of air pollution, whilst more definite, is in con- *in conformity* formity with the general rules of international law.

Particularly in reaching its conclusions as regards this question as well as the next, the Tribunal has given consideration to the desire of the high contracting parties "to reach a solution just to all parties concerned".

As Professor Eagleton puts in (Responsibility of States in International Law, 1928, p. 80): "A State owes at all times a duty to protect other States against injurious acts by individuals from within *DUTY* its jurisdiction." A great number of such general pronouncements by leading authorities concerning the duty of a State to respect other States and their territory have been presented to the Tribunal. These and many others have been carefully examined. International decisions, in various matters, from the Alabama case onward, and also earlier ones, are based on the same general principle, and, indeed, this principle, as such, has not been questioned by Canada. But the real difficulty often arises rather when it comes to determine what, pro subjecta materie, is deemed to constitute an injurious act.

A case concerning, as the present one does, territorial relations, decided by the Federal Court of Switzerland between the Cantons of Soleure and Argovia, may serve to illustrate the relativity of the rule. Soleure brought a suit against her sister State to enjoin use of a shooting establishment which endangered her territory. The court, in granting the injunction, said: "This right (sovereignty) excludes * * * not only the usurpation and exercise of sovereign rights (of another State) * * * but also an actual encroachment which might prejudice the natural use of the territory and the free movement of its inhabitants." As a result of the decision, Argovia made plans for the improvement of the existing installations. These, however, were considered as insufficient protection by Soleure. The Canton of Argovia then moved the Federal Court to decree that the shooting be again permitted after completion of the projected improvements. This motion was granted. "The demand of the Government of Soleure", said the court, "that all endangerment be absolutely abolished apparently goes too far." The court found that all *TOO FAR* risk whatever had not been eliminated, as the region was flat and absolutely safe shooting ranges were only found in mountain valleys; that there was a federal duty for the communes to provide facilities for military target practice and that "no more precautions may be demanded for shooting ranges near the boundaries of two Cantons than are required for shooting ranges in the interior of a Canton". (R.O. 26, I, p. 450, 451; R.O. 41, I, p. 137; see D. Schindler, "The Administration of Justice in the Swiss Federal Court in Intercantonal Disputes", American Journal of International Law, Vol. 15 (1921), pp. 172–174.)

No case of air pollution dealt with by an international tribunal has been brought to the attention of the Tribunal nor does the Tribunal know of any such case. The nearest analogy is that of water pollution. But, here also, no decision of an international tribunal has been cited or has been found.

There are, however, as regards both air pollution and water pollution, certain decisions of the Supreme Court of the United States which may legitimately be taken as a guide in this field of international law, for it is reasonable to follow by analogy, in international cases, precedents established by that court in dealing with controversies between States of the Union or with other controversies concerning the quasi-sovereign rights of such States, where no contrary rule prevails in international law and no reason for rejecting such precedents can be adduced from the limitations of sovereignty inherent in the Constitution of the United States.

In the suit of the State of Missouri v. the State of Illinois (200 U.S. 496, 521) concerning the pollution, within the boundaries of Illinois, of the Illinois River, an affluent of the Mississippi flowing into the latter where it forms the boundary between that State and Missouri, an injunction was refused. "Before this court ought to intervene", said the court, "the case should be of serious magnitude, clearly and fully proved, and the principle to be applied should be one which the court is prepared deliberately to maintain against all considerations on the other side. (See Kansas v. Colorado, 185 U.S. 125.)" The court found that the practice complained of was general along the shores of the Mississippi River at that time, that it was followed by Missouri itself and that thus a standard was set up by the defendant which the claimant was entitled to invoke.

As the claims of public health became more exacting and methods for removing impurities from the water were perfected, complaints ceased. It is significant that Missouri sided with Illinois when the other riparians of the Great Lakes' system sought to enjoin it to desist from diverting the waters of that system into that of the Illinois and Mississippi for the very purpose of disposing of the Chicago sewage.

In the more recent suit of the State of New York against the State of New Jersey (256 U.S. 296, 309), concerning the pollution of New York Bay, the injunction was also refused for lack of proof, some experts believing that the plans which were in dispute would result in the presence of "offensive odors and unsightly deposits", other equally reliable experts testifying that they were confidently of the opinion that the waters would be sufficiently purified. The court, referring to Missouri v. Illinois, said: ".   .   . the burden upon the State of New York of sustaining the allegations of its bill is much greater than that imposed upon a complainant in an ordinary suit between private parties. Before this court can be moved to exercise its extraordinary power under the Constitution to control the conduct of one State at the suit of another, the threatened invasion of *STIPULATION* rights must be of serious magnitude and it must be established by clear and convincing evidence."

What the Supreme Court says there of its power under the Constitution equally applies to the extraordinary power granted this Tribunal under the Convention. What is true between States of the Union is, at least, equally true concerning the relations between the United States and the Dominion of Canada.

In another recent case concerning water pollution (283 U.S. 473), the complainant was successful. The City of New York was enjoined, at the request of the State of New Jersey, to desist, within a reasonable time limit, from the practice of disposing of sewage by dumping it into the sea, a practice which was injurious to the coastal waters of New Jersey in the vicinity of her bathing resorts.

In the matter of air pollution itself, the leading decisions are those of the Supreme Court in the State of Georgia v. Tennessee Copper Company and Ducktown Sulphur, Copper and Iron Company, Limited. Although dealing with a suit against private companies, the decisions were on questions cognate to those here at issue. Georgia stated that it had in vain sought relief from the State of Tennessee, on whose territory the smelters were located, and the court defined the nature of the suit by saying: "This is a suit by a State for an injury to it in its capacity of quasi-sovereign. In that capacity, the State has an interest independent of and behind the titles of its citizens, in all the earth and air within its domain."

On the question whether an injunction should be granted or not, the court said (206 U.S. 230):

It (the State) has the last word as to whether its mountains shall be stripped of their forests and its inhabitants shall breathe pure air. * * * It is not lightly to be presumed to give up quasi-sovereign rights for pay and * * * if that be its choice, it may insist that an infraction of them shall be stopped. This court has not quite the same freedom to balance the harm that will be done by an injunction against that of which the plaintiff complains, that it would have in deciding between two subjects of a single political power. Without excluding the considerations that equity always takes into account * * * it is a fair and reasonable demand on the part of a sovereign that the air over its territory should not be polluted on a great scale by sulphurous acid gas, that the forests on its mountains, be they better or worse, and whatever domestic destruction they may have suffered, should not be further destroyed or threatened by the act of persons beyond its control, that the crops and orchards on its hills should not be endangered from the same source. * * * Whether Georgia, by insisting upon this claim, is doing more harm than good to her own citizens, is for her to determine. The possible disaster to those outside the State must be accepted as a consequence of her standing upon her extreme rights.

Later on, however, when the court actually framed an injunction, in the case of the Ducktown Company (237 U.S. 474, 477) (an agreement on the basis of an annual compensation was reached with the most important of the two smelters, the Tennessee Copper Company), they did not go beyond a decree "adequate to diminish materially the present probability of damage to its (Georgia's) citizens".

Great progress in the control of fumes has been made by science in the last few years and this progress should be taken into account.

The Tribunal, therefore, finds that the above decisions, taken as a whole, constitute an adequate basis for its conclusions, namely, that, under the principles of international law, as well as of the law of the United States, no State has the right to use or permit the use of its territory in such a manner as to cause injury by fumes in or to the territory of another or the properties or persons therein, when the case is of serious consequence and the injury is established by clear and convincing evidence.

The decisions of the Supreme Court of the United States which are the basis of these conclusions are decisions in equity and a solution inspired by them, together with the régime hereinafter prescribed, will, in the opinion of the Tribunal, be "just to all parties concerned", as long, at least, as the present conditions in the Columbia River Valley continue to prevail.

Considering the circumstances of the case, the Tribunal holds that the Dominion of Canada is responsible in international law for the conduct of the Trail Smelter. Apart from the undertakings in the Convention, it is, therefore, the duty of the Government of the Dominion of Canada to see to it that this conduct should be in conformity with the obligation of the Dominion under international law as herein determined.

The Tribunal, therefore, answers Question No. 2 as follows: (2) So long as the present conditions in the Columbia River Valley prevail, the Trail Smelter shall be required to refrain from causing any damage through fumes in the State of Washington; the damage herein referred to and its extent being such as would be recoverable under the decisions of the courts of the United States in suits between private individuals. The indemnity for such damage should be fixed in such manner as the Governments, acting under Article XI of the Convention, should agree upon.

The third question under Article III of the Convention is as follows: "In the light of the answer to the preceding question, what measures or régime, if any, should be adopted and maintained by the Trail Smelter?"

Answering this question in the light of the preceding one, since the Tribunal has, in its previous decision, found that damage caused by the Trail Smelter has occurred in the State of Washington since January 1, 1932, and since the Tribunal is of opinion that damage may occur in the future unless the operations of the Smelter shall be subject to some control, in order to avoid damage occurring, the Tribunal now decides that a régime or measure of control shall be applied to the operations of the Smelter and shall remain in full force unless and until modified in accordance with the provisions hereinafter set forth. * * *

---

1. *Jurisdiction to legislate with respect to air pollution.* Does either the State of Washington or the United States have jurisdiction to prescribe laws regulating the pollution of Washington or United States airspace by Canadian polluters?

2. *Applicable Law.* Heretofore in this chapter the law governing events occurring in airspace has been domestic law and the inquiry has been whether or not a state has jurisdiction to prescribe the relevant rule. In what respect does the Trail Smelter case present a different problem? What is the source of the governing rule?

Why is Canada held responsible in this case? By what standard is its conduct measured? Does international law impose an obligation on Canada only after a showing of historical injury, or would a showing of potential injury be sufficient? For a discussion of the implications of the Trail Smelter case for situations in which modern technological developments threaten the environment (e. g., weather modification), see Kirgis, Technological Challenge to the Shared Environment: United States Practice, 66 Am.J.Int'l L. 290 (1972).

McDOUGAL AND SCHLEI, THE HYDROGEN BOMB TESTS IN PERSPECTIVE: LAWFUL MEASURES FOR SECURITY [a]

64 Yale Law Journal 648 (1955).[b]

* * *

The first thermonuclear bomb tests conducted by the United States, in March and April of 1954 in the Pacific Proving Grounds,

a. The article is in part a response to Margolis, The Hydrogen Bomb Experiments and International Law, 64 Yale L.J. 629 (1955).

b. Reprinted by permission of The Yale Law Journal Company and Fred B. Rothman & Company.

demonstrated the enormous destructive power of the new weapon, and caused great concern the world over. Through a series of miscalculations, a number of Marshallese, Japanese, and Americans were injured by the test of March 1st, and the test series as a whole in some measure disrupted the activities of a segment of the Japanese fishing industry. * * *

*   *   *

The basic issue in legal policy * * * in this conflict between the claim of the United States to conduct the hydrogen bomb tests and the demands of others for their discontinuance, is therefore, whether the United States and its associates are authorized by relevant world prescription to continue measures which they deem essential to their defense or whether such measures must be condemned as unlawful, either through derivations from the customary international law of the sea or by application of special commitments undertaken in the United Nations Charter and the Trusteeship Agreement.

THE FACTS

The Trust Territory of the Pacific Islands is composed of 98 island groups (2000 islands) with a total dry land area of 846 square miles, spread over some 3,000,000 square miles of the North Pacific Ocean. The United States governs the Territory as a strategic trusteeship territory under an agreement with the United Nations which entered into force July 18, 1947.

Testing of atomic weapons in the Pacific began with the test series conducted at Bikini Atoll in July 1946, before the Pacific Islands became a Trust Territory. On July 23, 1947, the AEC announced establishment of the Pacific Proving Grounds, and in December chose Eniwetok Atoll, near Bikini in the Marshall Islands, as a site for subsequent testing activities. The U.N. Security Council was advised by the United States that the atoll and its territorial waters had been closed for security reasons, in accordance with Article 13 of the Trusteeship Agreement, in order to enable the AEC to conduct atomic tests.

Because of the anticipated danger to ships approaching too near to Bikini while tests were in progress in 1946, mariners were advised through normal channels, during the months May through August, that the waters in an area of approximately 180,000 square miles surrounding the atoll should be avoided. With the removal of testing operations to Eniwetok, mariners were warned, in January 1947, and thereafter, that a zone of approximately 30,000 square milles would be dangerous to all ships, aircraft, and personnel, and at times of actual danger the area was patrolled to ensure that no ships or aircraft entered inadvertently. In May 1953, the warning area was expanded to include Bikini and its surrounding waters, and from that date until the most recent test series, the warning area included approximately 50,000 square miles. In March 1954, when it had become apparent that the warning area then in effect was inadequate, it was extended to include a total area of approximately 400,000 square miles. On May 21, 1954, 57 days later, all warning zones were canceled. Bikini and Eniwetok, and their territorial waters, remained closed areas.

The magnitude of the test explosion of March 1, 1954, was underestimated by half, and the error in advance calculations was compounded by erroneous wind predictions. This series of miscalculations resulted in minor injuries to twenty-eight Americans and approximately eighty-two Marshallese on islands outside the warning zone. Injuries which eventually became serious were suffered by the twenty-seven man crew of the Japanese fishing craft Fukuryu Maru, which apparently lay some fourteen miles clear of the warning zone at the time of the explosion, and did not arrive in Japan until some weeks later.

The extent to which fish contaminated by radioactive fallout were found outside the immediate vicinity of the tests is not clear. In any event, Japanese authorities inaugurated a system of monitoring for radioactivity the catches of ships reaching port from a wide area in the North Pacific, and condemned a considerable quantity of fish. None of the rumors of injury from contaminated fish have been substantiated, and it seems certain that none ever occurred.

The United States meanwhile took swift action to mitigate the effects of the test mishaps. Injured Marshallese were given immediate medical care at naval facilities on nearby Kwajalein Atoll; expert medical personnel were rushed to their assistance, and to that of the injured Japanese fishermen as soon as their plight became known; and prompt assurances were given that all financial loss would be made good. Two million dollars has been paid to Japan for damages resulting from the tests, including both personal injuries suffered by the crew of the Fukuryu Maru and damage to the Japanese fishing industry. Settlement of all Marshallese claims is in immediate prospect.

      *   *   *

THE ATTACK UPON LEGALITY

Those who attack the legality of the Pacific tests ordinarily begin by implying that any use of atomic and thermonuclear weapons would be unlawful and that this conclusion has some relevance to the legality of the tests. Their principal attack is, however, cast in terms of so-called "traditional and universally accepted rules"   *   *   *

      *   *   *

It is our belief that all of these arguments are unsound in law and in policy   *   *   *.

THE REGIME OF THE HIGH SEAS—A PROCESS OF COMMUNITY PROTECTION OF UNILATERAL CLAIMS

The Process of Asserting and Adjusting Claims

Throughout the centuries of its development, one may observe the regime of the high seas as, not a static body of absolute rules, but rather a living, growing, customary law, grounded in the claims, practices, and sanctioning expectations of nation-states, and changing as the demands and expectations of decision-makers are changed by the exigencies of new social and economic interests, by the imperatives of an ever developing technology and by other continually evolving conditions in the world arena. From the perspective of realistic description, the public order of the high seas is not a mere body of rules, but a whole decision-making process, including both a structure of authorized decision-makers and a body of highly flexible, inherited prescriptions: it is a continuous process of interaction in which the decision-makers of individual nation-states unilaterally put forward claims of the most diverse and conflicting character to the use of the world's seas, and in which other decision-makers, external to the demanding nation-state and including both national and international officials, weigh and appraise these competing claims in terms of the interests of the world community and of the rival claimants and ultimately accept or reject them.

The competing claims asserted by nation-state decision-makers to the use of the high seas, the events to which the "regime of the high seas" is a response, vary enormously in the comprehensiveness and particularity of the interests sought to be secured, in the location and size of area affected, and in the duration of the claim. They range from the comprehensive and continuous claim to all competence in the "territorial sea," through the continuous but limited claims to navigation, fishing, and cable-laying upon the "high seas," to the relatively temporary and limited claims to exercise authority and control beyond territorial boundaries for a vast array of national purposes: security and self-defense, enforcement of health, neutrality, and customs regulations, conservation or monopolization of fisheries, exploitation of the sedentary fisheries and mineral resources of the seabed and continental shelf, the conducting of naval maneuvers, military exercises, and other peacetime defensive activities, and so on.

* * *

* * * The technical prescriptions of the "freedom of the seas," on the one hand, and of "territorial sea," "contiguous zone," "jurisdiction," and so on, on the other, are not arbitrary, inelastic dogmas, but rather are highly flexible policy preferences invoked by decision-makers to record or justify whatever compromise or adjustment of competing claims they may reach in any particular controversy. And for all types of controversies the one test that is invariably applied by decision-makers is that simple and ubiquitous, but indispensable, standard of what, considering all relevant policies and all variables in context, is reasonable as between the parties.   *   *   *

          *   *   *

[The authors analyze the "great range of unilateral claims honored in community practice," such as claims to freedom of the seas for navigation and fishing, comprehensive claims to a territorial sea and limited purpose claims to a contiguous zone.   They argue that special deference has been accorded to claims for security.]

The Hydrogen Bomb Tests As Reasonable Measures for Security

The claim of the United States which is under discussion may be described factually as a claim to use territory (Bikini and Eniwetok Atolls) over which it has jurisdiction, for the purpose of conducting tests of thermonuclear weapons, a use which has the effect of excluding others temporarily from large surrounding areas of the high seas. The United States has established warning zones from time to time which serve to inform mariners of the extent of the area in which danger exists.   No authority to enforce observance of warning zones has been asserted, but as a practical matter observance follows because of the danger from the tests themselves.

The extent to which the bomb tests have actually interfered with commercial navigation in spite if the size of the area affected, is virtually nil.   *   *   *

          *   *   *

Plainly no existing prescriptions in the regime of the high seas are literally applicable to the unique problem presented by the tests. The United States claim bears no similarity whatever to those which, historically, "freedom of the seas" was intended to combat. Others are not excluded from the area affected in order to enable the United States to grant fishing monopolies to its nationals or to pursue the commercial aggrandizement of the United States in any way.   It is apparent, also, that the claim of the United States offers no serious interference with the policies of promoting commercial navigation and fishing which underlie "freedom of the seas." Moreover, the claim does not offend against the subordinate policies against international friction which are involved in claims to exercise police powers on the high seas.   No ships are seized or condemned, nor is civil or criminal jurisdiction of any kind asserted.

What is relevant, and can be applied without irrational extrapolation, to this new problem from prior prescriptions in the regime of the high seas is the test of reasonableness which underlies them all— the test by which the decision-makers of the world community have consistently during modern times decided between claims to navigation and fishing and all that great variety of claims, recounted above, which may interfere with navigation and fishing, and ranging, as we have seen, through all the labels of "territorial sea," "contiguous zones," "piracy," "self-defense," "continental shelf," and so on, even to "freedom of the seas" itself.   *   *   *

The claim of the United States is in substance a claim to prepare for self-defense. It is not, as commonly in self-defense, a claim to respond with force to an attack; it is no claim to invade territory or to sink fleets in anticipation of attack or to take any of the other measures of drastic interference with others commonly subsumed under self-defense. It is, however, a claim to take certain preparatory measures under conditions comparable to those traditionally held to justify measures in self-defense. It is a claim to take certain actions in contiguous zones and upon the high seas, with the minimum possible interference with others, under conditions of high necessity. The conditions of this grave necessity and the absence of reasonable alternatives are familiar knowledge. The contemporary development of instruments of destruction makes it possible for a war-bent nation-state utterly to destroy an opponent and perhaps much of the world. It has not been possible to establish, under the United Nations, commitments and procedures of global scope which offer reasonable assurance against aggression. As expectations of imminent violence in the world arena have become ever more realistic and intense, many of the nations of the free world have organized themselves, under appropriate provisions of the U. N. Charter, into regional groupings for their more effective self-defense. The United States has undertaken its program of atomic and thermonuclear weapons development to ensure that these coalitions of free nations are not lacking in the retaliatory power which may deter aggression, or in the weapons of self-defense if deterrence fails.

*   *   *

THE BALANCING OF SECURITY AND POLLUTION IN DETERMINING REASONABLENESS

The argument against the tests based on "pollution" introduces no principle or policy not already considered in connection with the law of the sea in general: it merely focuses attention upon one modality of possible interference with the competing uses of navigation and fishing. No international tribunal has ever held a nation-state liable in damages for pollution of the sea, or declared the existence of a duty to desist. The international regulation of pollution is at its merest inception, with prescriptions yet to be formulated. In this state of affairs, a decision-maker confronted with competing claims with respect to pollution and freedom of navigation and fishing can only resort to such sources as "general principles of law recognized by civilized nations," and considerations "ex aequo et bono." The decision-maker thus resorting to national prescriptions with respect to "nuisance" generally, and the pollution of waters in particular, finds himself, despite an elaborate facade of technical terms, instructed only to apply the familiar and indispensable test of reasonableness. The innumerable forms which such controversies may indeed take makes it impracticable to adopt any standard more explicit than that of reasonableness, determined by the familiar process of balancing the "utility of the conduct" causing damage, and the "gravity of the harm" to the injured party. In applying municipal law to controversies between nation-states, there is, however, one new and most significant factor which must be taken into account in determining reasonableness, and that is the factor of security. Any balancing of interests which failed to take account of the demands for security which states must make in the contemporary world would, of course, be most unrealistic.

The attack upon the legality of the tests attempted by Dr. Margolis is, thus, not only couched in terms of an inadequate formulation of doctrine, but depends ultimately upon analogies which are fantastically inapt in both fact and policy. By focusing upon "serious magnitude" of damage as the sole legal test, he neglects to consider the most important element in the problem: the overriding utility of the tests to the free world. This one-sided method of calculation is, of course, not to be found in the very cases he cites. The principal case relied upon, the Trail Smelter arbitration, is indeed a passable illustration of the balancing process upon which the law of nuisance depends. But the fact that a copper company in British Columbia was required to take measures available to it to minimize damage to a downwind agricultural community, scarcely reflects policies relevant for appraising the reasonableness of measures taken in mid-ocean by a nation-state faced with imminent threats of atomic attack. Similarly, cases in which the United States Supreme Court settles internal disputes between member-states of the union are relevant only for their emphasis upon the underlying policy of reasonableness. Such internal disputes do not raise the issues of external security, since under our federal system it is the national government which is charged with responsibility for security and most other problems relating to the high seas.

The facts available as to the extent to which water and fish were made radioactive by the tests, and in what areas, leave much to be desired. Newspaper reports originating with segments of the Japanese press unfriendly to the United States, for various reasons, exaggerated the effects of the tests with "evident malice," and no complete, authoritative reports are yet available. It is not clear whether fish found to be dangerously radioactive were caught within or without the largest warning zone, established after the effects of the March 1st test became apparent, so that it is not possible to say whether safety measures in addition to the establishment of an adequate warning zone would be necessary if and when future tests are conducted. It seems clear that no injuries whatever resulted from consumption or handling of fish rendered radioactive by the tests, or from radioactive sea water. The safety measures taken by the Japanese Government were understandably drastic, resulting in the condemnation of some 176 tons of fish, but were 100 per cent effective. Domestic tuna prices in Japan plummeted to 50 per cent of normal in April 1954, after sensationalized accounts of the test effects were published, but exports were unaffected. In view of all the facts now known, any serious attempt to balance the stake of the free world in the tests against the damage resulting from pollution—damage which has taken the exclusive form of financial damage for which compensation has been paid—must reach, we submit, the conclusion that the tests are reasonable and hence lawful.

It might of course be concluded, by analogy from municipal law, that although under all criteria of reasonableness a nation-state is entitled to conduct such tests under contemporary conditions, it should still be held responsible in damages for any inevitable injuries to innocent parties. In every mature legal system the balancing process which determines whether liability exists is repeated in answering the entirely separate question whether the liability-creating conduct may be continued. No international tribunal has yet unequivocally faced the issue whether a state may continue to carry on conduct for which it is liable in damages, but sound policy decrees that international law should parallel municipal law in this respect. Although no legal issues were formally resolved between Japan and the United States, the settlement in fact reached a desirable legal result. Japan explicitly refused to demand that the United States discontinue its tests, and the United States paid two million dollars in damages "without reference" to questions of legal liability. Only third parties, unembarrassed by responsibilities for the defense and security of the free world, seem unable to perceive the need for an appropriate discrimination between remedy for damage and mutual tolerance for vital interests.

*   *   *

1. *Nuclear test ban treaty.* The Treaty Banning Nuclear Weapon Tests in the Atmosphere, in Outer Space and Under Water, 4 U.S.T. 1313, 480 U.N.T.S. 43, Documentary Supplement, entered into force for the United States on October 10, 1963. The preamble to the Treaty recites that the parties desired "to put an end to the contamination of man's environment by radio-active substances." There were 105 parties to the treaty on January 1, 1972.

2. *Question.* France and Communist China are not parties to the Nuclear Test Ban Treaty. They have continued to perform tests in the atmosphere. Are they violating international law in continuing to test during the decade of the 1970's? If you knew more facts could you answer that question? Or is the question one of law only?

SECTION B.   ACTIVITIES IN SPACE

LAY AND TAUBENFELD, THE LAW RELATING TO ACTIVITIES OF MAN IN SPACE, 39 (1970)*

The Upward Extent of Sovereignty

Since it is by now clear that every national state claims and, to the extent it can do so, exercises complete sovereignty in superjacent airspace, and since airspace remains legally undefined for most purposes with no generally accepted limit to its extent, we come directly to a multifaceted dilemma. Of course, the term "airspace" or "atmospheric space" is found in most treaties, but it is only in the last decade that man has been able to send objects and humans beyond what all could readily agree is "airspace."   *   *   *   Where then does "airspace" end? And is this a critical question for pursuit at this time?   *   *   *

Government Views: The United States

It is clear from the outset that, despite the suggestions of many commentators, the states, at least the major powers, have been quite   SECURITY
unready to set specific limits by altitude to their claims to sovereign rights. Unlike the case of lower reaches of airspace, it appears to be the security problem almost exclusively, rather than a mixture of economic and security issues, which has led to this result.

But in the early post-Sputnik period, at least a few states took the position that an airspace boundary should be set and set soon. Sweden, for example, urged a decision as to "the altitude where this [outer] space   *   *   *   begins." At different times, representatives of Spain, Canada, France, Chile, and Italy have all suggested a formal limitation by altitude on the extent of national sovereignty in space.

Formal statements of the United States' position on the outward extent of its sovereignty in space indicate a notable shift in the course of the first space decade. In the earlier years, official policy called for a slow, step-by-step approach to space problems with the "utmost flexibility and freedom of action with regard to future events" retained for the United States. It was acknowledged that the Chicago Convention left it unclear where "airspace" and national sovereignty ended and that, since traces of the atmosphere might be found up to 10,000 miles, "it follows that it would be perfectly rational for us to maintain that under the Chicago Convention the sovereignty of the United States extends 10,000 miles from the surface of the earth."   *   *   *

     *   *   *

In more recent years, although the United States has continued to note its right to defend itself wherever an apprehended source of danger might be located, there has been a shift away from the notion that this might call for an extension of "sovereignty" outward. The boundary line between airspace and outer space is still undetermined, but it is taken as a fact that all satellites orbited to date operate in "outer space" and that, hence, "airspace" must be at least limited below the orbital height of satellites. As we shall see, the United States now persistently relies in many contexts on this concept that orbiting satellites are now in "free" outer space and are not within any state's "territory" nor subject to any state's "territorial" jurisdiction. Thus, while the United States has given little support to the notion of drawing any single "line" and certainly to a very close-in line, there is evidence of tacit support for the principle that outer space begins (and "sovereign" airspace at a maximum must consequently end) at some point equal to or more probably somewhere below that at which an unpowered satellite can be maintained in orbit.

* * *

Government Views: The Soviet View

Soviet writers have suggested a wide variety of approaches to the question of the upward extent of sovereignty. The Soviet claim to complete sovereignty in airspace is the basis for all discussions and received thorough airings both in connection with the alleged appearance of United States weather balloons in Soviet airspace in the mid-1950's and with the U-2 incident. Throughout the mid-1950's a commonly expressed view was that there was no limit to the upward extent of national sovereignty.

If all nations made unlimited claims upward, the flight of Sputniks would of course have violated the sovereign rights of every subjacent state and Soviet writers were quick to shift their approach. In 1958 and thereafter, there were suggestions of a limit based on aerodynamic lift, on "effective control," and on "national security." Although this last is hardly a limiting definition, it does avoid the dangers to national security found by Soviet writers in the other two.

In their quest for security, Soviet authors have rejected a search for traces of the atmosphere or the "density of the gas cloud at one or another distance from the earth" and all other alleged physical criteria. Soviet writers in general, however, have not made claims to the infinite; they seem to agree that at some point in space, out "far enough" from earth, a nation would be sufficiently secure to permit the "free" use of these reaches by all for activities beyond that point. For most activities, the "peaceful" ones, this might be the area where satellite orbits begin, thus again protecting the Sputnik flights as "legal" and according with more recent United States views.

Recently, the emphasis has been, as in the United States, on the nature of the activity, not on the altitude at which it takes place.

Thus, to Soviet spokesmen, "espionage," as they define it, whether
by land, by sea, by U–2, or by reconnaissance satellite, is "illegal" in
international law.   In their words, high-altitude nuclear tests by the
United States, even before the Test Ban Treaty of 1963, are "illegal" as is the scattering of copper needles by the United States
(Project West Ford) ; private "monopoly" enterprise in outer space
is "piratical" and incompatible with the concept of "free" space.

Certainly, however, the Communist writers have been as consistent as those in the West in urging that, at least at some point,
outer space and the celestial bodies are free for the peaceful activities of all men.   As the Polish scholar Machowski put it: "The
* * * question, whether state sovereignty extends into outer
space, has already been tacitly answered negatively by practice and
lack of protests on the part of any states in connection with the
orbiting of space objects over their respective territories."   Thus,
the official view of the United States and that of the Soviet Union,
as far as it can be determined, are similar on most points.   Both agree
that national sovereignty ends at some point "out," but each retains
its right to counter deleterious acts, wherever they occur.   Neither encourages the formal drawing of a line delimiting sovereign claims
based on a territorial concept, but both agree that satellites fly in non-
sovereign outer space, although there is no overall agreement on all
issues concerning legally permissible activities.   The views of other
powers conform, in general, to the position of the major space powers.

The Writers

The literature concerning the desirability of establishing a precise overall boundary to the outward extent of national sovereignty
is vast and its beginnings predate the flight of Sputnik I.   While it
seems clear that the nations are not likely to adopt any single line or
division for all purposes, a brief review of the suggestions proposed
on various bases by writers around the world is still useful since the
argument is a continuing one.   * * *

Granting that nations are sovereign in superjacent airspace, a
vast number of scholars have for these and other reasons proposed
limiting the extent of this iron control by limiting the definition of
airspace itself.   Of course the definition varies depending on the
criteria used for calculation.   Scientists themselves agree generally
that "atmosphere" itself has no single scientific meaning, and indeed
the various sciences disagree since they look to different characteristics.   Recall, too, that the Chicago Convention of 1944 itself nowhere defines airspace.

To proceed logically (if naively from the political point of view),
it is possible to suggest a "scientific" limitation in airspace as the
height at which a human can live without artificial breathing apparatus, conceivably as high as ten miles.   With perhaps more operational
meaning, the maximum height to which aircraft can ascend has been

offered as a definition, at least within the outlook of the civil aviation conventions, for airspace or "atmospheric" space. This would place it, given present technology, at about twelve miles for conventional aircraft or perhaps twenty to twenty-five for the ram jet. Several years ago, for example, Cooper wrote: "After many years of careful research, I am convinced that the term airspace, as used in the Paris Convention in 1919, was there meant to include only those parts of the atmosphere above the surface of the earth where gaseous air is sufficiently dense to support balloons and airplanes, the only types of aircraft then in existence."

Focusing more directly upon the somewhat elliptical terminology of the conventions has not in itself led to uniformity. Thus airspace or atmospheric space might be limited, for purposes of sovereignty and jurisdiction, to what scientists tell us is the "geophysical limit of the atmosphere"; or it is "infinite, at least in theory" or "without limit or height"; or it is all regions "accessible to man"; or it is the outside limit of the earth's atmosphere, perhaps 60,000 miles, etc.

Actually, it is reasonably clear that those who drafted the Chicago Convention, and certainly those who created the Paris Convention, simply never considered the problem of vehicles moving above what would be considered by all to be airspace. * * *

One special problem of the use of the concept of aerodynamic lift and "aircraft," whether considered under the terms of the civil air-law conventions or not, is that, due to technological change, it no longer has an operationally clear justification. Thus, "hybrid" craft, the American X–15, and others noted earlier in chapter 2, possess the characteristics of both aircraft and spacecraft; the X–15 has already flown at heights over 65 miles above the earth. Its performance does not fit neatly within the proposed definitions and limitations, and several of its pilots have won American astronaut wings by piloting it at or above an altitude of 50 miles, the altitude administratively established by military regulation as the basis for qualifying a pilot for such award.

Other "scientific" definitions of "airspace," not necessarily tied to the conventions, have also been offered to support altitudes greater than those at which conventional aircraft can fly. Ambrosini has suggested a height of about 100 kilometers as supported by "physical" considerations. Reintanz, of East Germany, has also supported this height of about 62 miles as "the upper limit of national airspace." Professor Cheng at one time found the limit of airspace at the base of the exosphere, perhaps "300–500 miles above the surface of the earth," and offered this as "the upper limit of national airspace." Others, thinking in terms of "air" or "atmosphere" also reach distances of 10,000 miles or more, since at least oxygen particles can be found a great distance from the earth. At such distances, the "line" then becomes functionally meaningless; most important, close-in space activities will take place within the area bounded by such a line and such regions will be difficult to police, or at least it would be too expensive, given the foreseeable risks.

Other suggestions for fixing a "natural" or "scientific" or "logical" boundary have called for combinations of physical factors including velocity, gravitation, centrifugal force, and the like. One of the more vigorously asserted proposals is that espoused by Haley and others and called generally the Von Karman line. As noted in The Law of Outer Space: [a]

> [I]t accepts the basic concept of aerodynamic lift but argues that such lift need not be the only "support" and that present law could be interpreted as extending sovereignty up to the point where any aerodynamic lift is available. For an object traveling at 25,000 feet per second, that line is said to be about 275,000 feet from the earth's surface. While this line is thought to have more stability than the proposal first put forward, it would also vary with atmospheric conditions and with design changes and other factors affecting the flight of objects.

Others have suggested about the same height for similar or related reasons. Moreover, the International Astronautical Federation now classifies all flight above 62 miles (100 km) as "space flight." It should also be noted that the David Davies Memorial Institute in both its Draft Code of Rules on the Exploration and Uses of Outer Space and in its Draft Rules Concerning Changes in the Environment of the Earth defines airspace as "the volume of space between the surface of the earth at sea level and an altitude of 80,000 meters above it." This would place the upper line at about the distance of the Von Karman line.

One other suggestion deserves special mention. It was perhaps first advanced in recent times by Kelsen in commenting, in 1944, on the Paris Convention and suggests that claims to sovereignty reach as far out as a state can exercise effective control. There would thus be several boundaries, since some states are more technologically advanced than others. The diversity question could be eliminated by placing the line at maximum height which any state could exercise control. This same problem was extensively debated at the time of the U–2 incident. The instability of any such boundary or set of boundaries has been often remarked and the proposal is infrequently heard today.

Limits based on technology, whether it is the technology of flight characteristics or of the ability of a ground state to interdict the flight, have the great defects of instability and uncertainty. New materials, new techniques, new military developments might alter the line significantly, eliminating the alleged certainty which proponents

a. The reference is to Lipson and Katzenbach, The Law of Outer Space, 12–13 (1961).

offer as the basic utility of having a known, "scientifically" sound line. * * *

A few writers have also suggested the use of more than one line, a division into zones. There might be, for example, a fairly low area of complete national control, an intermediate zone free for non-military transit or other internationally agreed uses, and "outer space," free for the peaceful use of all. Haley, for example, also, suggested at one time that states should continue supreme in airspace (up to about 37.3 miles), and in the area of the "astronautic regime," starting about 3,728 miles (except for earth satellites which are in it at any altitude), states should have a limited competence, and that the "escape corridor" between the two altitudes needs further study and consideration. Despite the possible lure of these proposals as analogous to known patterns on the seas, they have thus far attracted little national support.

* * *

---

1. *Problem.* The United States launches a series of a dozen space satellites carrying photographic equipment. The satellites are put into orbits that cross over the earth's poles and sweep over the territory of the Soviet Union, taking continuous photographs as they go. In some cases the satellites emit capsules bearing photographs. As the capsules parachute to earth over the Pacific Ocean, they are snared by United States airplanes. In other cases, photographic information is broadcast back to the United States to listening stations there when the orbiting craft fly over its territory. Although the craft orbit at a distance from the earth's surface of over 100 miles, the photographs reveal objects on the surface in great detail.

In what respects do the legal aspects of this activity differ from those pertaining to the Powers case, p. 256? Compare note 3, "Beyond trespass: espionage as a state offense," p. 264.

How relevant is state practice in determining the answer to the foregoing question? As early as 1964, Premier Khrushchev, in the course of a talk with a United States senator, suggested that space photography had eliminated the need for United States air reconnaissance flights over Cuba. He is quoted as saying "If you wish, I can show you photos of military bases taken from outer space. I will show them to President Johnson if he wishes." N. Y. Times, p. 1, col. 6, May 30, 1964. The Soviet Union, the United States, China and perforce all the rest of the world have ceased to complain about regular surveillance from space.

Would you support positive international law for a right of national freedom from surveillance, or for a national right of privacy?

Why, or why not? If you would not, would you support a positive rule of international law that even penetration of airspace for observation purposes is no longer illegal so long as it is done at sufficiently great heights above the territory?

As to television signals to the populace of a state from space communications satellites (direct broadcasting), an overwhelming majority of states voted in the General Assembly in November, 1972 (the United States the sole dissenter) to request the Outer Space Committee to elaborate principles governing such broadcasting, with the view to concluding an international agreement. IX U.N. Monthly Chronicle, December 1972, p. 39. The Soviet Union has been the proponent of national control over television broadcasting directly into home receivers (an as yet undeveloped technology), seeking to avoid a repetition of the Voice of America radio experience. The United States has countered with arguments based on the freedom of expression guarantees of the Universal Declaration of Human Rights (see Documentary Supplement).

2. *International conventions.* As activities in space and manned and unmanned exploration of the moon and the planets go forward, the need has increased for understanding of the law applicable to those events. There have been several approaches to the problem. At the poles, they are:

a. Presently existing earth law is adequate, since it applies to humans and humans are the actors in space.

b. New law should be enacted at once; problems should be anticipated before conflicts arise and before customary law develops and becomes fixed in undesirable ways.

Several international conventions address the legal problems of space.

a. The Outer Space Treaty (Treaty on Principles Governing the Activities of States in the Exploration and Use of Outer Space, Including the Moon and Other Celestial Bodies), 18 U.S.T. 2410, 610 U.N.T.S. 205, Documentary Supplement, entered into force for the United States on October 10, 1967. 64 states were parties on January 1, 1972. The following articles are suggestive of the generality of its provisions:

Article I

The exploration and use of outer space, including the moon and other celestial bodies, shall be carried out for the benefit and in the interests of all countries, irrespective of their degree of economic or scientific development, and shall be the province of all mankind.

Outer space, including the moon and other celestial bodies, shall be free for exploration and use by all States without discrimination of any kind, on a basis of equality and in accordance with international law, and there shall be free access to all areas of celestial bodies.

There shall be freedom of scientific investigation in outer space, including the moon and other celestial bodies, and States shall facilitate and encourage international co-operation in such investigation.

Article III

States Parties to the Treaty shall carry on activities in the exploration and use of outer space, including the moon and other celestial bodies, in accordance with international law, including the Charter of the United Nations, in the interest of maintaining international peace and security and promoting international co-operation and understanding.

In analyzing this treaty, which purports to set general principles, the following questions should be addressed:

    i.   Has the treaty made any change in the law that would be applicable without the treaty? Another way of putting this question is: is a non-party to the treaty freer than a party to do as it wishes in space and, if so, in what respects?

    ii.   Are enough facts known about space to justify a state's committing itself at this stage of technological development to the principles enunciated in the treaty? How can a state protect its interests if startling new facts are discovered about space in the future?

    b.   The Agreement on the Rescue of Astronauts, the Return of Astronauts, and the Return of Objects Launched Into Outer Space, 19 U.S.T. 7570, entered into force for the United States on December 3, 1968. 54 states were parties on January 1, 1972.

    c.   The Convention on International Liability for Damage Caused by Space Objects, Documentary Supplement, entered into force September 1, 1972. The convention provides that the launching state shall be liable for damage caused by its space object absolutely in some cases, or for its fault in others. A claims procedure involves a Claims Commission, whose decision shall be binding if the parties have so agreed or whose award shall be recommendatory "which the parties shall consider in good faith." (Article XIX). The legal principles to be applied in determining compensation are particularly interesting:

Article XII

The compensation which the launching State shall be liable to pay for damage under this Convention shall be determined in accordance with international law and the principles of justice and equity, in order to provide such reparation in respect of the damage as will restore the person, natural or juridical, State or international organization on whose behalf the claim is presented to the condition which would have existed if the damage had not occurred.

SECTION C.   CELESTIAL BODIES

The Outer Space Treaty provides in Article II:

> Outer space, including the moon and other celestial bodies, is not subject to national appropriation by claim of sovereignty, by means of use or occupation, or by any other means.

Suppose that a state discovers a particularly rare and valuable mineral on the moon, which it is able to "mine" cheaply with manned or unmanned equipment. Does the treaty prohibit that state from exploiting the moon's resources for its own exclusive benefit? Can the state set up a "base" over which it has exclusive control so as to prevent another state from exploiting resources within that "base?" See Article XII.

What law governs the state, not a party to the treaty (or one that has withdrawn pursuant to Article XVI) that wishes to claim a portion of the moon as its territory? Do the principles relating to the acquisition of territory on the surface of the earth apply? If so, what facts would support a claim that a state has lawfully acquired a portion of the moon as its territory?

Of some utility in the analysis of the legal problems of celestial bodies is a study of Antarctica. See the Antarctic Treaty, 12 U.S.T. 794, 402 U.N.T.S. 71, which entered into force for the United States on June 23, 1961; 17 states were parties as of January 1, 1972. The treaty is briefly discussed in Chapter 11. The text of the treaty and bibliographic references are also in Lay and Taubenfeld, The Law Relating to Activities of Man in Space 59–62 (1970).

Leech, O. & S. Cs. Int.Legal System UCB—20

Part II

LIMITATIONS ON THE EXERCISE OF JURISDICTION

Chapter 5

THE IMMUNITY OF STATES

SECTION A. EXTENT OF THE IMMUNITY

ALDONA S. v. UNITED KINGDOM

Poland, Supreme Court, 1948.
90 Journal du Droit International 191 (1963).[a]

The facts. The Plaintiff Aldona S. was engaged as typist in the editorial office of the weekly "Voice of England" published in Cracow by the British Foreign Office. On January 31st 1947 she was suddenly dismissed without being paid the rest of her salary due to her, amounting to 52,500 zl. She filed a claim with the District Court of Cracow against the   *   *   *   United Kingdom for payment of the mentioned amount as compensation for work performed.

This was an appeal against the decision of the Court of Appeal of Cracow which confirmed the judgment of the District Court rejecting the claim of the plaintiff as being inadmissible in view of the defendant being a foreign state   *   *   *   In her appeal the plaintiff alleged that the dispute in question concerned relations with regard to a contract of employment of a private person by a weekly magazine which, as an organized commercial entity, constitutes an enterprise which is juridically private property of the Treasury of the United Kingdom of Great Britain. The Court of Appeal enquired with the Ministry of Justice whether a custom exists in Great Britain by virtue of which it is not admissible to sue a foreign state before an English court. The Ministry of Justice, in its statement of March 4, 1948   *   *   *   expressed the opinion that foreign countries may not be summoned   *   *   *,   whereupon the Court of Appeal, on March 10, 1948, approved the appealed decision, concurring completely with the reasons of that decision. It stated in addition that   *   *   * the weekly magazine "Voice of England" is not an enterprise in the sense of article 5, paragraph 2 of Code of Civil Procedure. In the

a. English text in the Journal. Reprinted by permission of Editions Techniques, S.A., Paris.

appeal against that decision, Aldona S. demanded its rejection on the ground that it infringes substantive law and violates the basic rules of procedure. In particular the plaintiff opposed the view of the Court of Appeal considering it as being in conflict with previous judgments of the Supreme Court and with Polish case law. She suggested that a magazine published by a foreign state on Polish territory, is not part of diplomatic but of economic activity. The refusal of legal protection in such cases would render the obligations of a magazine publisher incomplete, and not binding, and, therefore, meaningless. * * * [The activities involved, she argued, were those] of the treasury of a foreign state, based on a private law labour contract, and does not concern the activity of the foreign state itself.

[A portion of the opinion of the court appears below.]

This question has already twice been the subject of deliberations of the Supreme Court, first, in 1926, in the case against the Treasury of the Czechoslovak State for damages incurred in an accident caused by a Czechoslovak government owned automobile * * * and the second time in 1957, in the case against the Treasury of the German Reich, for payment of damages caused by an illegal imposition of taxes * * *

* * *

Contrary to the suppositions of the plaintiff, the solution of the problem of jurisdiction of Polish courts over foreign states cannot be based upon the provisions of articles 4 and 5 Code of Civil Procedure. A foreign state does not fall under the category of a foreigner within the meaning of article 4 of the Code of Civil Procedure, for it is clear that a legislator, conscious of the principles of international law, could not consider a foreign state as a "foreigner sojourning in another state." * * * Therefore, on examining questions concerning immunity from jurisdiction of foreign states, one has to base oneself directly on general principles universally adopted in international relations. The most essential of these principles is the principle of reciprocity among states which results from the fundamental principle of their equality * * * The principle of reciprocity is based on recognition or non-recognition of the immunity from jurisdiction by one state of another in the same measure as the latter recognizes or refuses to recognize immunity from jurisdiction of other states. Absence of reciprocity may simply stem from clear provisions of the law, but it may also be the result of a continuous and well established practice of the courts of a foreign state. In case of doubt, therefore, in this respect, it is necessary to obtain the opinion of the Ministry of Justice which renders it in agreement with the Ministry of Foreign Affairs.

Passing from the above considerations to the present case directed against the Treasury of the United Kingdom of Great Britain, the Supreme Court states the generally known fact that English

Courts have been consistently and rigorously safeguarding the immunity from jurisdiction of foreign States for a long time (Phillimore, p. 153). Thus in the present case, in view of the well established * * * [case law] of English Courts recognizing immunity from jurisdiction of foreign states, i. e., potentially also the Polish State, Polish Courts were unable, given the principle of reciprocity, to accept for deliberation the claim submitted by Aldona S., even if it concerned a commercial enterprise on behalf of the British authorities. However, such is really not the case, for the Court of Appeal held that the publishing house of "Voice of England" is not a commercial enterprise. The objection of the plaintiff that this does not concern diplomatic but economic activity cannot be admitted as valid, for although the activity may not be diplomatic, it is political by its content, and economic only by its form as a result of the laws and regulations of the country (payment of taxes, purchase of registration cards, etc.).

Finally, the last objection of the plaintiff, that refusal of legal protection would render the obligations of the British Foreign Office as a publisher of a magazine in the territory of our State incomplete and unreal, is also unfounded, for, if the plaintiff does not wish to seek justice before English courts, she may take advantage of general international usage in connection with immunity from jurisdiction, and approach the Ministry of Foreign Affairs, which is obliged to take up the matter with the Ministry of Foreign Affairs of a foreign country with a view to obtain satisfaction for a just claim * * * This approach frequently produces speedier results than court procedure.

In view of the principles explained above, the Supreme Court considering the contentions of the plaintiff against the judgment of the Court of Appeal as unfounded and * * * finding no basis for them in the views of the majority Polish jurisprudence, has dismissed the appeal.

Position of socialist states. "Socialist" states are committed to the "absolute theory" of sovereign immunity and claim international law requires that it be granted even in cases where the litigation arises from commercial activities. In many states in western Europe and elsewhere, however, the courts apply "the restrictive theory" and deny immunity to socialist states—and other states—in litigation arising from such activities. Socialist states look upon the denial of immunity in these cases as unwarranted interference with the conduct of their trade abroad through state monopolies. In requiring proof of reciprocal treatment as a condition for granting immunity to the United Kingdom, the Polish decision reflects the opposition of socialist states to the restrictive theory and their attempt to induce general acceptance of the absolute theory.

KRAJINA v. THE TASS AGENCY

England, Court of Appeal, 1949.
[1949] 2 All E.R. 274.

[This was a suit for alleged libel in a news sheet published by Tass.]

COHEN, L. J. This appeal is against an order of BIRKETT, J., dated Dec. 10, 1948, whereby he affirmed an order of Master Simner dated Nov. 29, 1948, by which it was ordered that the writ herein and service of it on the Tass Agency of Moscow be set aside. The writ was issued by the plaintiff on June 2, 1948, the defendants being described as "The Tass Agency (of Moscow) (trading as a firm or corporation at No. 72/78, Fleet Street in the city of London)" * * *. On June 10, 1948, a conditional appearance was entered on behalf of the * * * defendants, to whom I shall refer hereafter as Tass, and on June 23, 1948, Tass issued a summons asking for the order which they ultimately obtained from Master Simner. * * *

In support of the application Tass filed an affirmation by a Mr. Andrienko, who is described as the legal adviser of the trade delegation of the Union of Soviet Socialist Republics in the United Kingdom. The affirmation contains a summary of some of the provisions of the statute concerning Tass, which was published on Jan. 15, 1935, and there was exhibited to it an extract from the statute, which contained the first of its sixteen clauses. In his affirmation Mr. Andrienko described Tass as "the central information organ of the Union of Soviet Socialist Republics" and as "coming under the Council of Ministers of the Union of Soviet Socialist Republics." He did not make any definite statement as to the legal position of Tass, and the only other evidence before the master at the first hearing was an extract under the heading "Tass Agency" from the register kept under the Registration of Business Names Act, 1916. The master rightly did not consider this evidence sufficient to enable him to reach a decision on the matter, and he adjourned the summons for further evidence. On Nov. 20 an affidavit by Percy Charles Smith was filed, to which was exhibited a certificate from the Soviet Ambassador, the material portion of which was in the following terms:

I, Georgi Nikolaevich Zaroubin, ambassador of the Union of Soviet Socialist Republics in Great Britain, hereby certify that the telegraph agency of the Union of Soviet Socialist Republics, commonly known as Tass, or the Tass Agency, constitutes a department of the Soviet State, i. e., the Union of Soviet Socialist Republics, exercising the rights of a legal entity.

On this evidence the master made the order for which Tass asked and that order was confirmed by BIRKETT, J. * * *

* * *

When the present appeal came before us, counsel for the plaintiff asked leave (which was granted) to put in further evidence which consisted of the full text of the statute establishing the Tass agency, and a translation thereof. Clause 1 is in these terms:

> The telegraphic agency of the Union of Soviet Socialist Republics (TASS) is the central information organ of the U.S.S.R. and is attached to the Soviet of People's Commissars of the U.S.S.R.

It will be observed that this translation does not entirely agree with that in the exhibit to Mr. Andrienko's affirmation, the words, "and comes under the Council" in that exhibit being replaced by "is attached to the Soviet", but I do not think that anything turns on that discrepancy. It seems clear that, in the light of the ambassador's certificate, we are bound to come to the conclusion that the Tass Agency is a department of the Soviet State, but whether that State has given this department a separate juridical existence is another matter which I shall consider later. * * *

       * * *

       * * * Counsel for the plaintiff said that, reading the statute as a whole, the effect is that Tass not only has the right of a legal entity, but is also a legal entity * * *. If that is established, certain consequences, it is argued, follow—in particular, the doctrine of sovereign immunity is not applicable, since Tass has a separate juridical existence from that of the sovereign, the U.S.S.R. Counsel for the plaintiff also argued that, even if the Tass agency was a department of the U.S.S.R. without separate legal existence, the nature of its activities was such as to deprive it of sovereign immunity. He admitted that he could not succeed on that point before us in view of the decision of this court in the United States Shipping Board case and the decision in The Porto Alexandre, but he said that the correctness of these decisions had been doubted by LORD MAUGHAM in Compania Naviera Vascongado v. Cristina S.S. For the plaintiff it was also argued that the evidence before the court as to the status of the Tass agency was ambiguous and self-contradictory, and that, as the onus of establishing their right to immunity was on the defendants, their application must fail.

       It is obvious that the first question we have to decide is whether or not the evidence makes out a prima facie case that Tass was a separate legal entity, for, if it was not, it seems quite plain that the evidence does establish that Tass was a department of the Soviet State, and, unless counsel for the plaintiff can establish it to be a separate legal entity, it is not disputed that this appeal, in this court at any rate, must fail. * * *

       * * *

       * * * It seems to me that the evidence as to the nature of Tass must depend on its constitution and must be a question of Russian law, and that we must look at the Russian statutes and to any relevant evidence that is adduced as to Russian law (and for all prac-

tical purposes in this case, that is nil) to determine whether or not
Tass is a separate legal entity. Mr. Taylor, it seems to me, is wholly
incompetent to give evidence on this subject. Even if what he said be
regarded as prima facie evidence, I am bound to say that, looking at
the rest of the evidence, I am unable to accept the view that Tass is a
separate legal entity. * * * The ambassador, if I may say so,
showed a better appreciation of what was relevant, but he, perhaps
not being a lawyer, perhaps out of caution, quotes practically the wording of the statute without expressing any opinion as to its legal effect.
After saying that the Tass agency is a department of the Soviet State,
he says that it exercises the rights of a legal entity. Does that mean
that it is a legal entity? When the argument first started to say that
it meant the same thing seemed an attractive proposition, but on consideration, and having regard to what has happened in this court as
regards departments of State, I am unable to think that we should be
justified in treating this as establishing that Tass has a separate legal
entity.

* * *

* * * Our attention has been called to nothing which can be
said to amount to a declaration that Tass is a corporation sole. It is
said in the translation of the statute and by the ambassador that it
has the rights of a juridical or legal entity, but it seems to me that the
evidence falls far short of that which would be necessary to establish
that Tass is a legal entity and that the Union of Soviet Socialist Republics, by procuring its incorporation, has deprived that particular
department of the immunity which normally attaches to a department
of a sovereign State in accordance with the principles of comity established by international law and recognized by this country.

That is really sufficient to dispose of the case and to lead to the
dismissal of the appeal, but, as the case may go higher, I think I ought
to say just a few words on what the position would be had I come to
the opposite conclusion and been of opinion that the evidence did establish that Tass was given the status of a separate juridical entity.
It does not seem to me necessary to follow that it would thereby have
been deprived of its immunity. The history of the legislation in this
country as regards the departments of State seems to me to show that
it is quite possible that a State may for certain purposes under its
own legislation give some department of State the status and the rights
of a juridical entity without depriving the department of its general
immunity from suit, and it seems to me that it would be impossible
to say—no doubt, our government would not wish to say—that the
Crown had thereby deprived itself of the right to rely on that immunity if an attempt were made to sue it in a foreign country. One
must look in every case at the facts to reach a conclusion whether the
Crown has intended to give up its immunity generally or only for
limited and defined purposes.

* * *

I desire to say one word more on the last point in the argument of counsel for the plaintiff that the evidence was ambiguous and self-contradictory, and that, as the onus of establishing their right to immunity is on the defendants, their application must fail. I think that turns upon what I have already said, that, in my view, the defendants do establish that Tass was, and in essence is, a department of State to the necessary extent to shift the onus of proving that they were a separate legal entity to the plaintiff. That onus, in my opinion, he has failed to discharge. For these reasons I think that the decision of BIRKETT, J., was right and ought to be affirmed.

[Other opinions omitted.]

The position of English courts on sovereign immunity. The adherence of English courts to the absolute theory of sovereign immunity may result from a rigid application of the rule of precedent rather than from a conviction that international law requires them to continue applying the theory.

In The Porto Alexandre, [1920] P. 30 (C.A.), the immunity of foreign states, previously established with respect to litigation arising from an activity which was not commercial, was granted in litigation involving a ship owned by a foreign state and used for trading. In The Cristina, [1938] A.C. 485, several of the Law Lords indicated they doubted the immunity should have been granted with respect to a commercial activity in The Porto Alexandre, and suggested the extension of immunity in the case was not required by the previous decision in point. But the facts in The Cristina did not afford them the opportunity of passing anew on the issue. Thus the theory of absolute immunity remains the rule of law in English courts.

The position of the English courts in the matter was aptly summarized in a statement by Sir Eric Beckett, of the British Foreign Office, when he was appointed by the Institut de Droit International to report on the state of the law of sovereign immunity in his country. This was in 1951. He said: "My own position with regard to the subject matter * * * is that * * * the amount of State immunity accorded by the English courts at present is somewhat wider than is required by the principles of public international law and is perhaps wider than is desirable." 44(1) Annuaire de l'Institut de Droit International 53, 54 (1952).

The precedents established in the United Kingdom with respect to sovereign immunity have been followed generally by courts in the British Commonwealth, though with occasional indications of doubt about the soundness of the absolute theory.

As indicated on p. 338 of this Chapter, the United Kingdom has signed the European Convention on Sovereign Immunity adopted by the Council of Europe on May 16, 1972. The convention embodies the restrictive theory of sovereign immunity and thus, if ratified by the United Kingdom, will terminate the adherence of its courts to the absolute theory.

FUNDAMENTALS OF CIVIL LEGISLATION OF THE UNION OF SOVIET SOCIALIST REPUBLICS, APPROVED BY THE SUPREME SOVIET, DECEMBER 8, 1961, SOVIET LEGISLATION SERIES (MOSCOW, 1961).

Article 11.   Juridical Persons

Juridical persons are such organisations as possess separate property, and may in their own name acquire property and non-property rights and assume duties, and appear as plaintiffs and defendants in a court of law, or before an arbitration or mediation board.

*   *   *

Article 12.   Legal Capacity of Juridical Persons

Juridical persons shall have civil legal capacity in accordance with the established purposes of their activity.

*   *   *

Article 13.   Liability of Juridical Persons for Their Obligations

Juridical persons shall be liable for their obligations in the property they own (and state organisations, in the property assigned to them) which, in accordance with the legislation of the U.S.S.R. and Union Republics, is subject to attachment.

The state shall not be liable for the obligations of state organisations which are juridical persons, nor shall these organisations be liable for the obligations of the state.

*   *   *

ACADEMY OF SCIENCES OF THE U.S.S.R., INSTITUTE OF STATE AND LAW, INTERNATIONAL LAW 305 (MOSCOW, 1961).

*   *   *

Legal Status of Trade Missions. The main definitive act governing the legal status of trade missions abroad and their rights and duties is the Statute on Trade Missions and Agencies of the U.S.S.R. Abroad adopted by the Central Executive Committee and the

Council of People's Commissars of the U.S.S.R. on September 13, 1933.

Under the terms of this Statute, trade missions are an integral part of the diplomatic missions of the U.S.S.R. abroad and enjoy the same privileges as the latter.   Trade missions fulfil three main functions:

(a) the representation of the interests of the U.S.S.R. in the field of foreign trade and the promotion of the commercial and other economic relations between the U.S.S.R. and the country in which the mission is resident;

(b) the regulation of the trade between the U.S.S.R. and the country in which they are resident;

(c) the implementation of the trade between the U.S.S.R. and the country in which they are resident.

Trade missions function on behalf of the Government of the U.S.S.R. and are organs of the Soviet State abroad.   As a result, they enjoy the rights and privileges of diplomatic missions.   It is generally recognised that the trade representative of the U.S.S.R. and his deputies enjoy complete diplomatic immunity.   They have the right of inviolability of person.   They are safeguarded against threats and coercive measures and are exempt from local jurisdiction.

The premises of the trade mission and the property therein are inviolable.   Searches and the removal of property from these premises can take place only with the permission of the trade representative.   The trade mission has the right to use ciphers.   Its correspondence enjoys complete inviolability.

A trade mission enjoys legal immunity in the country in which it is resident.   Even in cases when the Soviet State voluntarily limits its legal immunity and consents to submission to local jurisdiction, local courts have no right to take measures to enforce a suit, to arrest property, to execute judgments by force, to summon the trade representative or his deputy to court, or to take administrative action against the trade mission, since such action constitutes a violation of the sovereign rights of the U.S.S.R.

*   *   *

Trade missions enjoy all the powers necessary for the fulfilment of these functions.   They can conclude all kinds of agreements and contracts on behalf of the U.S.S.R., enter into commitments, including through the issue of promissory notes, give guarantees, conclude agreements regarding the submission of disputes to arbitration courts and in general undertake all legal actions necessary to carry out the responsibilities with which they are vested, including appearing in foreign courts as a plaintiff.   Trade missions can be defendants only in cases arising out of contracts concluded or guaranteed by them in the country concerned, and only in countries in relation to which the Government of the U.S.S.R. has by means of an international treaty or unilateral declaration clearly and precisely expressed its consent to the trade mission being subject to local courts in disputes of the character concerned.

A trade mission is not a legal person. The treasury of the U.S.S.R. is liable for its commitments, since the Soviet State is the subject of foreign trade transactions which it concludes.

* * *

Attempts to Restrict the Rights of Trade Missions. The foreign trade links of the Soviet State based on the foreign trade monopoly have a long history, telling of the Soviet State's constant struggle for its rights in the world market, for equality between the two systems of property ownership, and for normal commercial relations between all States, both large and small.

This struggle was especially bitter during the early years of the Soviet State, when foreign capital made desperate attempts to wreck the monopoly of foreign trade and to subject the Soviet economy to the economies of the capitalist States.

The capitalist countries as a rule did not conclude commercial transactions on the territory of the U.S.S.R. The overwhelming majority of such transactions were concluded abroad.

The work of Soviet trade missions abroad was constantly subjected to every kind of obstacle, from police raids on premises they occupied to the violation of their elementary rights as state organs of the U.S.S.R.

There were cases of the infringement of the rights and privileges of the trade missions: attacks upon trade representatives, non-recognition of their diplomatic immunity and violation of the immunity of premises occupied by trade delegations. Their legal immunity was ignored and their property made the object of illegal action, etc.

In attempts to justify these illegal measures, bourgeois jurists put forward the theory of the "trading State", in accordance with which a trade mission was considered as a "merchant", as an ordinary legal person, allegedly having none of the rights characteristic of a diplomatic mission.

In accordance with these theories, bourgeois courts permitted suits against Soviet Trade Missions, confiscated their property and did not recognise their rights to legal immunity.

The consistent and resolute policy of the Soviet Government led to the defeat of all the attacks upon the foreign trade monopoly and upon the organs carrying it out. The rights of the Soviet State in exercising its monopoly of foreign trade are now recognised by the absolute majority of States.

* * *

1. *Juridical persons and trade missions of the USSR.* According to Fundamentals of Civil Legislation of the USSR, a "juridical person" is one which possesses separate property, can sue and be sued and is liable, rather than the state, for its own obligations. The law of the USSR has its foundation, in part, in the civil law system. In states where that system prevails, the term "juridical person" is a term of art and usually means, prima facie, that the entity involved is separate and distinct from the government.

In the Tass Agency case the evidence showed only that the agency exercised the rights of a "juridical person." Hence it was open to argument whether it exercised such rights because it was in fact a juridical person, or whether it was given the rights of a juridical person though it was not one in fact. This last possibility would be regarded as anomalous in many civil law states.

According to the Soviet textbook on International Law, a Trade Mission of the USSR is not a legal person, is an integral part of a Soviet diplomatic mission, and the treasury of the USSR is liable for its commitments. Apparently, the foreign trade missions of other socialist states are sometimes given "juridical personality." A Czech author writes: "Under the Acts [of 1948 and 1949] establishing * * * [them], foreign trade undertakings [of Czechoslovakia] are autonomous units endowed with juridical personality. They have a separate budget and their property is liable to answer for the obligations assumed by them. Foreign trade undertakings are not answerable for such claims as one may have against the state [and] its organs * * *." Zourek, Some Comments on the Difficulties Encountered in the Judicial Settlement of Disputes Arising from Trade Between Countries with Different Economic and Social Structures, 86 Journal du Droit International 639, 665 (1959).

The author goes on to note that, as a necessary consequence of being endowed with juridical personality, the foreign trade missions of Czechoslovakia are not entitled to immunity in the courts of other states. [at 665]

In the Soviet textbook on International Law, quoted above, the restrictive theory of sovereign immunity is presented as a device invented by bourgeois states for the specific purpose of wrecking the monopoly over foreign trade of the USSR and subjecting the Soviet economy to the economies of the capitalist states.

The statement should be taken with caution. The restrictive theory appeared in western continental Europe in the latter part of the 19th century and was steadily gaining ground by the time the USSR began to engage in trade with European and other nations. It is true, however, that litigation arising from the commercial transactions of the trade missions of the USSR probably gave impetus to the growth of the restrictive theory.

2. *Evolution of the restrictive theory.* The Supreme Court of Belgium adopted the restrictive theory in 1903. Société Anonyme de Chemins de Fer Liègeois Luxembourgeois v. The Netherlands, [1903] Pasicrisie I, 294. In Egypt, the Court of Appeals of the Mixed Courts—then the highest court with jurisdiction over sovereign immunity cases—sanctioned in 1920 the restrictive theory in a litigation involving the United Kingdom. Captain Hall v. Captain Zacarias Bengoa, 33 Bulletin de Legislation et Jurisprudence Egyptiennes 25 (1920–1921). The court had already made clear in a decision of 1912 it would apply the restrictive theory. Dame Marigo Kildani v. The Ministry of Finance of Greece, 24 Bulletin de Legislation et Jurisprudence Egyptiennes 330 (1911–1912).

By 1918, the Supreme Court of Switzerland was applying the restrictive theory. Ministry of Finance of Austria v. Dreyfus, [1918] Journal des Tribunaux 594. The restrictive theory was formulated as early as 1886 by the lower courts of Italy. The Supreme Court of Italy adopted it in 1925 when a trade mission of the USSR became involved in litigation before the Italian courts which arose from its commercial activities. Trade Delegation of the USSR v. Ditta Tesini e Malvezzi, [1925] Giurisprudencia Italiana I, 204.

By 1928 the lower courts in Greece were declining to grant immunity to the USSR in a suit involving a commercial act. X v. USSR, [1927–1928] Ann.Dig. 172 (No. 109). The Supreme Court of France sanctioned in 1929 the restrictive theory, previously declared and applied in the lower courts, when a trade mission of the USSR was sued in connection with its commercial activities in France. USSR v. Association France-Export, [1929] Dalloz Rec.Heb. 161.

In 1921, the Supreme Court of Germany declined to apply the restrictive theory on the ground that it had not yet acquired sufficient support to justify its application. Selling v. United States Shipping Board (The Ice King), 1921, 26 Am.J.Int'l L.Supp. 620 (1932). Since then the courts of the German Federal Republic have become committed to the restrictive theory. Decision of the Federal Constitutional Court, Second Chamber, 1963, 59 Am.J.Int'l L. 654 (1965).

In the Netherlands, the restrictive theory was applied by the lower courts as early as 1916. Thereafter an ambiguous decision of the Supreme Court in date of 1922 left the issue in a state of confusion and divided the lower courts for a long time. De Booij Case, 48 Journal du Droit International 274 (1921), 26 Am.J.Int'l L.Supp. 538 (1932). A similar situation prevailed in Austria where the restrictive theory became a controversial issue as early as 1918. Its supreme court has since become a leading exponent of the restrictive theory. Dralle v. Republic of Czechoslovakia, 17 Int'l L.Rep. 155 (1956).

As a result, apparently, of the development of the restrictive theory and the repeated denial of immunity to its trade missions by

European courts in the years following World War I, the USSR adopted a policy of entering into international agreements whereby its trade missions submit in advance to local jurisdiction with respect to disputes arising from their commercial transactions.

COLLISION WITH FOREIGN GOVERNMENT OWNED MOTOR CAR

Austria, Supreme Court, 1961.
40 Int'l L.Rep. 73 (1970).

The Facts: The plaintiff, an Austrian citizen, alleged that his motor car had been damaged by the negligent driving of a car owned by the Government of the United States of America. He brought an action for damages for negligence against the United States Government. The latter raised a plea to the jurisdiction of the Austrian courts and contended that since at the time of the alleged collision their motor car was carrying mail intended for the United States Embassy, the Austrian courts were not entitled to exercise jurisdiction. The carriage of mail for and on behalf of the United States Embassy constituted the performance of a "sovereign act" by the United States Government.

The Supreme Court reiterated the view previously expressed in Dralle v. Republic of Czechoslovakia that a distinction must be drawn between the acta jure imperii and the acta jure gestionis of a foreign state, and that in respect of the latter a foreign state is subject to the jurisdiction of the Austrian courts.

On the contention that the carriage of mail on behalf of a foreign Government was an exercise of the sovereign authority of the foreign state,

Held: (i) that this contention must be rejected; and (ii) that in determining whether an act performed by a foreign Government was jure imperii or jure gestionis, the Court must consider only the act itself, and not the purpose for which it is performed. Here the United States Government had operated a vehicle on a public road, and such operation belonged to the private sphere. Accordingly, the United States Government was subject to the jurisdiction, and the fact that the motor car had carried mail for the United States Government was irrelevant.

[A portion of the opinion of the court appears below.]

The Supreme Court, in Rule 28 (new), reported in SZ XXIII, p. 143, has dealt with the question whether, and subject to what conditions, a foreign State may be sued in an Austrian court. In that judgment the Court has reviewed all the relevant Austrian and foreign jurisprudence and doctrine. The judgment has been published and it is therefore sufficient to repeat only the most important of the fundamental reasons which have led the Court to lay down the following Rules:

> (i) By international law foreign States are exempt from the jurisdiction of the Austrian courts so far as concerns acts ✓ undertaken by them in the exercise of their sovereign powers.

> (ii) Similarly, by municipal law, foreign States are subject to the jurisdiction of the Austrian courts in relation to all contentious matters arising out of legal relations pertaining to the ✓ realm of private law.

> *   *   *

The Court, in its earlier judgment, reached the conclusion that in respect of acta jure gestionis a limitation by international law can no longer be recognized. Basing ourselves on this premise, all we have to do in this case is to examine the question whether the plaintiff bases his claim on an act performed by the foreign defendant State in its private or in its sovereign capacity. The lower Courts arrived at different conclusions. Whereas the Court of first instance regarded as decisive the purpose of the journey, viz. the *PURPOSE ?* collection of mail for the embassy of the defendant, the Court of Appeal took the view that the defendant State was being sued as the *ACT ?* operator of the vehicle and as a person circulating as a road user.

In its appeal the defendant contends that the means whereby a State exercises its sovereign rights are irrelevant because all means at its disposal belong to the sphere of private law, and that the decisive factor is the act performed by the State with the aid of those *REJECTED* means. It is contended that in this case the motor car was the means *?* whereby the sovereign act (the collection of mail for the embassy) was carried out, and that the case must be judged in accordance with this act. This Court is unable to accept this contention. The distinction between private and sovereign acts is easily understood if one considers the following: Eminent writers, e. g. Schnitzler (Private International Law, at pp. 833 seq.) point out that an act must be deemed to be a private act where the State acts through its agencies in the same way as a private individual can act.[1] An act must be deemed to be a sovereign act where the State performs an act of legislation or administration (makes a binding decision). Sovereign acts are those in respect of which equality between the parties is lacking, and where the place of equality is taken by subordination of one party to the other. Spruth (Jurisdiction over Foreign States) defined this distinction as follows: "To act as a sovereign State means to act in the performance of sovereign rights. To enter into private transactions means to put oneself on the basis of equality with private individuals."   *   *   *

Thus, we must always look at the act itself which is performed by State organs, and not at its motive or purpose. We must always investigate the act of the State from which the claim is derived. Whether an act is of a private or sovereign nature must always be deduced from the nature of the legal transaction, viz. the nature of the action taken or the legal relationship arising. In a Note of 23 April 1928 to the former League of Nations, Switzerland used the following words: * * *

[The quotation is in French and states the view of the Swiss government that in order to be entitled to immunity the act of the foreign state must be of such a nature that it could not be done by a private person.]

Some examples may serve to illustrate this proposition. The purchase of land by a foreign State from a private individual is, even in the opinion of the defendant, a private act. If, as a result of such a purchase, the acquired rights of a third party were to be infringed, the latter, even in the opinion of the defendant, would be entitled to institute an action for the enforcement of his claim against the foreign State before the courts of the forum. If the purpose of the purchase were to be regarded as decisive, then such an action could not be brought against the foreign State if the land was intended to be used as a military base. If a foreign State instructs a local builder to build a house on land owned by the local State, there can be no doubt, even in the opinion of the defendant, that a building contract of this kind is a private contract in respect of which the foreign State can be sued in the local courts. If the purpose were to be regarded as decisive and the building were intended for use as the embassy of the foreign State, then no action could be brought in the local courts. Many instances could be cited to show that the plea of immunity from the jurisdiction is frequently only a pretext to evade contractual obligations. On the other hand, it may be assumed that States intent on meeting their obligations will make payment without further ado, once the factual and legal position has been established.

These examples show the soundness of the view that, in determining whether an action may be brought, it is the act from which the claim is derived which is decisive, and not the object or purpose of the act.

* * *

If we apply the basic principles here outlined to the case before us, we must conclude that the act from which the plaintiff derives his claim for damages against the defendant is not the collection of mail but the operation of a motor car by the defendant and the latter's action as a road user. By operating a motor car and using the public roads the defendant moves in spheres in which private individuals also move. In these spheres the parties face one another on a basis of equality, and there is no indication here of any supremacy and subordination. It follows that, so far as liability for damage is concerned, the foreign State must be treated like a private individual. The damage which the plaintiff alleges was not caused by the collection of mail from the airport but by the operation and management of the motor car and the use of public roads by the defendant. The plaintiff thus derives his claim from a private legal relationship. The development of traffic on public roads and the dangers threatening every road user from such traffic compel us to accept this view. To deny the liability of a foreign State arising from the operation and management of motor vehicles would lead to intolerable results and hardships for private citizens. This is best illustrated by the present case, assuming always that the plaintiff's allegations are true, which will emerge when the case is heard on the merits. * * * There is no doubt that the foreign State, in the event of a collision involving a motor vehicle owned by it, would be entitled to bring an action for damages against a private individual in the local courts and in accordance with local law. The foreign State is thus given rights to invoke the jurisdiction of the courts of another State, and it could do so as it pleases and for its own benefit. Not so the private individual. The latter would have no rights whatever against the foreign State if the management and operation of motor vehicles and the use of public roads by foreign States were to be regarded as a sovereign act. It could be argued that the claims, however well-founded, of a private individual for damage caused by a collision could not be pursued against the foreign State by a separate action or a counterclaim. The State of the forum would have to deny to its citizens rights which it grants to a foreign State.

Finally, the Court must express its views on some of the arguments put forward against the limitation of the exemption of foreign States from the jurisdiction. It is said that it is one of the fundamental rights of a State not to allow another State to subject it to its authority, and that such subordination creates a risk of political complications and prevents the foreign State from performing the tasks which by international usage it is entitled to perform in the territories of other States. Moreover, the "fear of execution" has caused many writers to deny all jurisdiction over foreign States (Spruth, op. cit., at p. 94). The unlimited recognition of such a "fundamental right" in respect of acta jure gestionis would constitute an interference with the sovereignty of the State of the forum. The risk of political complications is far greater if disputes of a private nature are fought out on the diplomatic level before the facts and the legal position have been clarified. Experience shows that the objective judgment of an independent court is more likely to be accepted than a political decision. The foreign State is not in the least hindered in the performance of its tasks if—like all other road users—it is brought before a court to have its liability for an accident determined in accordance with the provisions of civil law. So far as concerns the lack of means to execute a judgment, we need only point out that such means exist under international law within the framework of municipal law. * * *

For all these reasons the Court is of opinion that the operation of a motor vehicle by a foreign State and the use of public roads by the latter belong to the sphere of the private activities of that State even if, as has been contended, such operation and use have occurred in the performance of official functions, and that accordingly the foreign State can be sued for damages in a local court. A traffic accident creates private legal relations between the foreign State and the private individual, on a basis of equal rights between them. In international jurisprudence, likewise, liability arising out of a private contract is treated on the same basis as liability for a tort which has nothing to do with the political order * * *.

The Court is therefore of opinion that this action has been properly brought in the Austrian courts. * * *

---

1. *Distinction between public acts and private acts.* The restrictive theory, which was developed by the courts of states where the civil law system prevails, is not grounded on a distinction between commercial acts and other acts of a state. Commercial acts are part of the larger category of acts which the civilians denominate "private", or "jure gestionis," and distinguish from those they denominate acts of "sovereignty," or of "public power", or "jure imperii."

From its inception the restrictive theory has been based on the distinction between public acts and private acts. Consider, for example, the language used by the Supreme Court of Italy in 1926. The suit was on a contract with the government of Rumania for the supply of leather to its army. The court said:

> It is hardly necessary to mention * * * that in the contract of purchase entered into with Trutta, * * * [Rumania] was not in the exercise of its *public power* but acted in the sphere of its *civil personality* and performed *acts of essentially private nature* which might have been done just as well by any individual. It may well have been induced to buy because of the necessity of supplying * * * its army.
>
> But such purpose does not alter the nature of the contract of purchase, *inasmuch as means were employed for its realization which were extraneous to the exercise of sovereignty and suited to the ordinary course of action of private individuals.* State of Rumania v. Trutta, 26 Am.J.Int'l L.Supp. 629 (1932). [Emphasis supplied.]

The leading decisions from other civil law states also committed to the restrictive theory of immunity usually contain similar language.

As a result, a substantial number of decisions can be found in the case law of such states where immunity was denied in litigation involving acts which were deemed private, though they were not commercial.

2. *Relevance of French administrative law concepts.*[a] A short excursus in the concepts of administrative law developed in France during the 19th century can be of help in understanding the distinction between public and private acts which characterizes the restrictive theory in civil law states.

After the Revolution of 1789, there were established in France two parallel systems of courts, one judicial and the other administrative. For all practical purposes, they are equal in rank and neither is subordinate to the other. As a roughly valid proposition, we may say the judicial system was given jurisdiction over disputes between private parties, while the administrative system was given jurisdiction over disputes between private parties and the state. Thereupon the administrative courts proceeded to develop—on a case by case basis— a body of administrative law which has no exact counterpart in England or the United States, but has become the basis of administrative law in much of continental Europe and has influenced the administrative law of a number of states elsewhere.

It cannot be entirely an accident that states whose courts led the development of the restrictive theory, or eventually adopted it, are also, in the main, those where French administrative law was followed or acquired influence. For in a French type of administrative law, a fundamental distinction is drawn between situations where the state exercises its public power, and hence litigation concerning such situations belongs to the administrative courts, and situations where the state acts in its private capacity, and hence litigation concerning them is left to the judicial system of courts. The distinction is elementary to civil law lawyers, even though it is subject in its application to exceptions, qualifications and refinements as complex as those surrounding the application of the concept of "due process" in American courts.

In the administrative law of France, for example, the property of the state is divided in two categories: the "public domain" and the "private domain." The first is owned by the state in its public capacity and includes such things as the territorial sea, the sea shore, navigable waters and public roads. This public domain is governed by rules of administrative law which are not found in private law and, generally speaking, litigation concerning it belongs to the administrative courts. The private domain includes land and structures which are managed and exploited by the state for a commercial or industrial purpose. The state owns such domain in its private capacity and legal questions concerning it are governed, as a general proposition, by rules of private law and adjudicated in the judicial courts.

---

a. In the preparation of this portion of the materials, the editors consulted primarily A. de Laubadère, Traité, Elé- mentaire de Droit Administratif (4th ed. 1968) and L. Brown and J. Garner, French Administrative Law (1967).

3. *Reflection in the restrictive theory of civilian concepts of administrative law.* Because of their experience with concepts of administrative law of the French type, the courts of a number of civil law states were intellectually conditioned by the turn of the century to engage in a critical analysis of the doctrine of sovereign immunity and not take it for granted that all acts of a foreign state needed to be treated as acts of sovereignty. The theory they worked out to delimit acts of sovereignty entitled to immunity, and separate them from other acts not entitled to immunity, borrows the differentiation from administrative law of the French type and uses it as the basis for determining immunity vel non.

Suppose, for example, a state purchases land in the territory of another. In France, the French state may acquire land by exercising its power of eminent domain, an act of sovereignty or public power basically governed by administrative law and within the jurisdiction of the administrative courts. But the French state may also acquire land through an ordinary contract of sale, a private act governed by private law and under the jurisdiction of the judicial courts. Should litigation arise concerning the interest acquired by the foreign state through its purchase of land, is it entitled to immunity?

The answer, in France and other states where French concepts of administrative law have influence, is "no," for the act clearly was not one of sovereignty and could not be considered an exercise of public power even if the purpose of the purchase was to build an embassy upon the land. The courts of such states normally classify the purchase as a private act not entitled to immunity in litigation connected with it. It was so classified by the Supreme Court of Chile as early as 1912. Inscripción de Bienes Raíces del Gobierno de Bolivia, [1912] 2 Gaceta de los Tribunales (No. 1170). On this issue more generally, see p. 336.

Consider now the language used by the Supreme Court of Italy in 1926 while deciding Trutta v. State of Rumania. The court said that in concluding the contract, Rumania "was not in the exercise of its public power," performed an act of "essentially a private nature," and used means for its realization which were "suited to the ordinary course of action of private individuals." The language of the court in denying immunity reflects the distinction drawn in civil law states between administrative contracts concluded by the national state in the exercise of its public power and contracts concluded by it in its private capacity.

4. *Difficulties with the application of the distinction between public and private acts.* In civil law states, the application of the distinction between public and other acts of a state has not always produced consistent results. Some of the inconsistencies, though not all, stem from uneven development of the restrictive theory in different states over a period of time. Some others are due to hesitancies or vacillations among the lower courts in a given jurisdiction until

such time as their Supreme Court could resolve the matter. Finally, ⫿
differences in result in some cases are predicated on reasons which
may be considered to be quite artificial. Two cases involving the
United States and decided by the Court of Appeal of Paris, First
Chamber, are illustrative.

In the first, decided in 1960, a French company had agreed to
build apartment buildings to be rented by personnel of the American
military forces, and the United States had agreed to guarantee the
payment of the rents by such personnel. The company sued for breach
of contract. The court noted that France and the United States had
not entered into any international agreement regarding the building
of dwellings for United States military personnel. It found the contract had been concluded in the forms, and according to the methods
and rules of private law. Hence, it ruled, the United States was not ✓
entitled to immunity even if its purpose was to operate a public service. Société Immobilière des Cités Fleuries Lafayette v. United States
of America, 89 Journal du Droit International 132 (1962).

In the second case, decided in 1962, the suit was on a contract to
build apartment buildings intended for residence by American officials responsible for the operation in France of the "Marshall Plan."
The court noted that the contract was exempt from French taxation
and financed on credit extended by the United States to the end of
furthering the international agreement setting up the Marshall Plan.
It found the contract contained clauses—such as those giving jurisdiction for the settlement of disputes to the American Secretary of
State—derogating from ordinary law. Hence, it ruled, the contract
was concluded by the United States in the exercise of its public power ✓
and for the satisfaction of a public interest. The United States was,
accordingly, entitled to immunity. United States of America v.
Perignon, 89 Journal du Droit International 1017 (1962).

Does the Collision case on p. 318 reveal any similar difficulty as
to the application of the distinction?

UNITED STATES: LETTER FROM THE ACTING LEGAL ADVISER OF THE DEPARTMENT OF STATE TO THE DEPARTMENT OF JUSTICE, MAY 19, 1952.

26 United States Department of State Bulletin 984 (1952).

MY DEAR MR. ATTORNEY GENERAL:

The Department of State has for some time had under consideration the question whether the practice of the Government in granting
immunity from suit to foreign governments made parties defendant in
the courts of the United States without their consent should not
be changed. The Department has now reached the conclusion that

such immunity should no longer be granted in certain types of cases. In view of the obvious interest of your Department in this matter I should like to point out briefly some of the facts which influenced the Department's decision.

A study of the law of sovereign immunity reveals the existence of two conflicting concepts of sovereign immunity, each widely held and firmly established. According to the classical or absolute theory of sovereign immunity, a sovereign cannot, without his consent, be made a respondent in the courts of another sovereign. According to the newer or restrictive theory of sovereign immunity, the immunity of the sovereign is recognized with regard to sovereign or public acts (jure imperii) of a state, but not with respect to private acts (jure gestionis). There is agreement by proponents of both theories, supported by practice, that sovereign immunity should not be claimed or granted in actions with respect to real property (diplomatic and perhaps consular property excepted) or with respect to the disposition of the property of a deceased person even though a foreign sovereign is the beneficiary.

The classical or virtually absolute theory of sovereign immunity has generally been followed by the courts of the United States, the British Commonwealth, Czechoslovakia, Estonia, and probably Poland.

The decisions of the courts of Brazil, Chile, China, Hungary, Japan, Luxembourg, Norway, and Portugal may be deemed to support the classical theory of immunity if one or at most two old decisions anterior to the development of the restrictive theory may be considered sufficient on which to base a conclusion.

The position of the Netherlands, Sweden, and Argentina is less clear since although immunity has been granted in recent cases coming before the courts of those countries, the facts were such that immunity would have been granted under either the absolute or restrictive theory. However, constant references by the courts of these three countries to the distinction between public and private acts of the state, even though the distinction was not involved in the result of the case, may indicate an intention to leave the way open for a possible application of the restrictive theory of immunity if and when the occasion presents itself.

A trend to the restrictive theory is already evident in the Netherlands where the lower courts have started to apply that theory following a Supreme Court decision to the effect that immunity would have been applicable in the case under consideration under either theory.

The German courts, after a period of hesitation at the end of the nineteenth century have held to the classical theory, but it should be noted that the refusal of the Supreme Court in 1921 to yield to pressure by the lower courts for the newer theory was based on the view that that theory had not yet developed sufficiently to justify a change.

In view of the growth of the restrictive theory since that time the German courts might take a different view today.

The newer or restrictive theory of sovereign immunity has always been supported by the courts of Belgium and Italy. It was adopted in turn by the courts of Egypt and of Switzerland. In addition, the courts of France, Austria, and Greece, which were traditionally supporters of the classical theory, reversed their position in the 20's to embrace the restrictive theory. Rumania, Peru, and possibly Denmark also appear to follow this theory.

Furthermore, it should be observed that in most of the countries still following the classical theory there is a school of influential writers favoring the restrictive theory and the views of writers, at least in civil law countries, are a major factor in the development of the law. Moreover, the leanings of the lower courts in civil law countries are more significant in shaping the law than they are in common law countries where the rule of precedent prevails and the trend in these lower courts is to the restrictive theory.

Of related interest to this question is the fact that ten of the thirteen countries which have been classified above as supporters of the classical theory have ratified the Brussels Convention of 1926 under which immunity for goverment owned merchant vessels is waived. In addition the United States, which is not a party to the Convention, some years ago announced and has since followed, a policy of not claiming immunity for its public owned or operated merchant vessels. Keeping in mind the importance played by cases involving public vessels in the field of sovereign immunity, it is thus noteworthy that these ten countries (Brazil, Chile, Estonia, Germany, Hungary, Netherlands, Norway, Poland, Portugal, Sweden) and the United States have already relinquished by treaty or in practice an important part of the immunity which they claim under the classical theory.

It is thus evident that with the possible exception of the United Kingdom little support has been found except on the part of the Soviet Union and its satellites for continued full acceptance of the absolute theory of sovereign immunity. There are evidences that British authorities are aware of its deficiencies and ready for a change. The reasons which obviously motivate state trading countries in adhering to the theory with perhaps increasing rigidity are most persuasive that the United States should change its policy. Furthermore, the granting of sovereign immunity to foreign governments in the courts of the United States is most inconsistent with the action of the Government of the United States in subjecting itself to suit in these same courts in both contract and tort and with its long established policy of not claiming immunity in foreign jurisdictions for its merchant vessels. Finally, the Department feels that the widespread and increasing practice on the part of governments of engaging in commercial activities makes necessary a practice which will enable persons doing business with them to have their rights determined in the courts. For these reasons it will hereafter be the Department's policy to follow the restrictive theory of sovereign immunity in the consideration of requests of foreign governments for a grant of sovereign immunity.

It is realized that a shift in policy by the executive cannot control the courts but it is felt that the courts are less likely to allow a plea of sovereign immunity where the executive has declined to do so. There have been indications that at least some Justices of the Supreme Court feel that in this matter courts should follow the branch of the Government charged with responsibility for the conduct of foreign relations.

In order that your Department, which is charged with representing the interests of the Government before the courts, may be adequately informed it will be the Department's practice to advise you of all requests by foreign governments for the grant of immunity from suit and of the Department's action thereon.

Sincerely yours,

For the Secretary of State:

JACK B. TATE
Acting Legal Adviser

VICTORY TRANSPORT, INC. v. COMISARIA GENERAL DE ABASTECIMIENTOS Y TRANSPORTES

United States Court of Appeals, Second Circuit, 1964.
336 F.2d 354.a

J. JOSEPH SMITH, CIRCUIT JUDGE. This is an appeal from an order of the United States District Court for the Southern District of New York, Thomas F. Murphy, District Judge, granting appellee's motion to compel arbitration and denying appellant's cross motions to vacate service and dismiss the petition. We think the district court's disposition of the motions correct and affirm the order.

The appellant, a branch of the Spanish Ministry of Commerce, voyage-chartered the S.S. Hudson from its owner, the appellee, to transport a cargo of surplus wheat, purchased pursuant to the Agricultural Trade Development and Assistance Act, 7 U.S.C.A. § 1691 et seq., from Mobile, Alabama to one or two safe Spanish ports. The charter agreement contained the New York Produce Arbitration Clause, providing for the arbitration of disputes before three commercial men in New York. The ship was delayed and sustained hull damage in discharging its cargo in Spanish ports that were allegedly

a.   Cert. denied 381 U.S. 934, 85 S.Ct. 1763 (1965).

unsafe for a ship of the Hudson's size. When the appellant failed to pay for the damages or submit the dispute to arbitration, the appellee instituted this proceeding under Section 4 of the United States Arbitration Act, 9 U.S.C.A. § 4, to compel arbitration. On March 22, 1963, appellee secured an ex parte order from the district court permitting service of its petition by registered mail at appellant's Madrid office. Service pursuant to this order was effected on April 1, 1963.[4]

On October 15, 1963 the appellant moved to vacate the extraterritorial service as unauthorized by statute. Appearing specially and supported by an affidavit of the Spanish Consul, who stated that the appellant was a branch of the Spanish Government and immune from suit, counsel for the appellant also moved to dismiss the petition to compel arbitration because of a lack of jurisdiction and sovereign immunity. Rejecting these cross-motions, Judge Murphy held that the court had in personam jurisdiction and granted the appellee's motion to compel arbitration.

Sovereign Immunity

Appellant's primary contention is that as an arm of the sovereign Government of Spain, it cannot be sued in the courts of the United States without its consent, which it declines to accord in this case. There is certainly a great deal of impressive precedent to support this contention, for the doctrine of the immunity of foreign sovereigns from the jurisdiction of our courts was early entrenched in our law by Chief Justice Marshall's historic decision in The Schooner Exchange v. McFaddon, 7 Cranch 116, 3 L.Ed. 287 (U.S.1812). The doctrine originated in an era of personal sovereignty, when kings could theoretically do no wrong and when the exercise of authority by one sovereign over another indicated hostility or superiority. With the passing of that era, sovereign immunity has been retained by the courts chiefly to avoid possible embarrassment to those responsible for the conduct of the nation's foreign relations. See Comment, The Jurisdictional Immunity of Foreign Sovereigns, 63 Yale L.J. 1148 (1954). However, because of the dramatic changes in the nature and functioning of sovereigns, particularly in the last half century, the wisdom of retaining the doctrine has been cogently questioned. See, e. g., Lauterpacht, The Problem of Jurisdictional Immunities of Foreign States, 28 Brit.Y.B.Int'l L. 220 (1951). Growing concern for individual rights and public morality, coupled with the increasing entry of governments into what had previously been regarded as private pursuits, has led a substantial number of nations to abandon the absolute theory of sovereign immunity in favor of a restrictive

---

4. To make doubly sure that the appellant had been properly served, the appellee, on October 22, 1963, sought to take advantage of the recent amendment to Rule 4(i) of the Fed.Rules of Civil Procedure by re-serving the appellant by registered mail without a court order. Since we deem the initial service valid, we need not pass on the validity of the second service.

theory. See Dralle v. Rep. of Czechoslovakia, 17 Int.L.Rep. 155 (Sup. Ct. of Austria 1950); Sucharitkul, State Immunities and Trading Activities in International Law (1959); Lauterpacht, supra.

Meeting in Brussels in 1926, representatives of twenty nations, including all the major powers except the United States and Russia, signed a convention limiting sovereign immunity in the area of maritime commerce to ships and cargoes employed exclusively for public and non-commercial purposes.[5] After World War II the United States began to restrict immunity by negotiating treaties obligating each contracting party to waive its sovereign immunity for state-controlled enterprises engaged in business activities within the territory of the other party. Fourteen such treaties were negotiated by our State Department in the decade 1948 to 1958. Setser, The Immunity Waiver for State-Controlled Business Enterprises in United States Commercial Treaties, Proceedings of Am.Soc.Int'l L. 89 (1961). And in 1952 our State Department, in a widely publicized letter from Acting Legal Adviser Jack B. Tate to the Acting Attorney General Philip B. Perlman, announced that the Department would generally adhere to the restrictive theory of sovereign immunity, recognizing immunity for a foreign state's public or sovereign acts (jure imperii) but denying immunity to a foreign state's private or commercial acts (jure gestionis). 26 Dept. State Bull. 984 (1952).

In delineating the scope of a doctrine designed to avert possible embarrassment to the conduct of our foreign relations, the courts have quite naturally deferred to the policy pronouncements of the State Department. National City Bank of New York v. Republic of China, 348 U.S. 356, 360–361, 75 S.Ct. 423, 99 L.Ed. 389 (1955). See generally, Cardozo, Judicial Deference to State Department Suggestions: Recognition of Prerogative or Abdication to Usurper, 48 Corn.L.Q. 461 (1963). The Supreme Court's dictum in Republic of Mexico v.

---

5. International Convention for the Unification of Certain Rules Concerning the Immunities of State Ships. The French text of the Convention is set out in Harvard Research in International Law, 426–429 (1931). An English translation prepared by the Department of State may be found in Allen, The Position of Foreign States Before National Courts, 303–308 (1933).

Article I of the Convention provided:

Seagoing vessels owned or operated by States, cargoes owned by them, and cargoes and passengers carried on Government vessels, and the States owning or operating such vessels, or owning such cargoes, are subject in respect of claims relating to the operation of such vessels or the carriage of such cargoes, to the same rules of liability and to the same obligations as those applicable to private vessels, cargoes, and equipments.

Article II provided that these liabilities and obligations may be enforced by the same rules and procedure applied to private ships and cargoes, while Article III excepted from the application of the first articles "ships of war, Government yachts, patrol vessels, hospital ships, auxiliary vessels, supply ships, and other craft owned or operated by a State and used at the time a cause of action arises exclusively on Governmental and noncommercial service * * *" However, Article III did provide for certain remedies before the courts of the sovereign owning or operating a vessel as a public activity.

Hoffman, 324 U.S. 30, 35, 65 S.Ct. 530, 533, 89 L.Ed. 729 (1945)—
"It is therefore not for the courts to deny an immunity which our government has seen fit to allow, or to allow an immunity on new grounds which the government has not seen fit to recognize"—has been variously construed, but we think it means at least that the courts should deny immunity where the State Department has indicated, either directly or indirectly, that immunity need not be accorded. It makes no sense for the courts to deny a litigant his day in court and to permit the disregard of legal obligations to avoid embarrassing the State Department if that agency indicates it will not be embarrassed. Cf. National City Bank v. Republic of China, supra, 348 U.S. at 360–361, 75 S.Ct. 423 (1955). Moreover, "recognition by the courts of an immunity upon principles which the political department of government has not sanctioned may be equally embarrassing to it in securing the protection of our national interests and their recognition by other nations." Republic of Mexico v. Hoffman, supra, 324 U.S. at 36, 65 S.Ct. at 533.

This is not to say that the courts will never grant immunity unless the State Department specifically requests it. A claim of sovereign immunity may be presented to the court by either of two procedures. The foreign sovereign may request its claim of immunity be recognized by the State Department, which will normally present its suggestion to the court through the Attorney General or some law officer acting under his direction. Alternatively, the accredited and recognized representative of the foreign sovereign may present the claim of sovereign immunity directly to the court. Ex parte Muir, 254 U.S. 522, 41 S.Ct. 185, 65 L.Ed. 383 (1921). In some situations the State Department may find it expedient to make no response to a request for immunity. Where, as here,[7] the court has received no communication from the State Department concerning the immunity of the Comisaría General, the court must decide for itself whether it

---

7. The plea of sovereign immunity for the Comisaría General in the district court was supported only by a conclusionary affidavit of the Spanish Consul in New York. A consul is supposedly clothed with authority to act for his government only in commercial matters. Since nothing in the record indicates that the Spanish Consul was specially authorized to interpose a claim of sovereign immunity, the affidavit was plainly insufficient. The Sao Vicente, 260 U.S. 151, 43 S.Ct. 15, 67 L.Ed. 179 (1922); The Anne, 16 U.S. 435, 3 Wheat. 435, 4 L.Ed. 428 (1818); The Secundus, 13 F.2d 469 (E.D.N.Y.1926); Harris & Co. Adv. Inc. v. Republic of Cuba, 127 So.2d 687 (D.C.App.Fla.1961).
On appeal the Spanish Ambassador to the United States has written a letter directly to this court claiming immunity for the Comisaría General and has moved for permission to appear specially in the proceeding. We find it unnecessary to decide whether this procedure is sufficient to raise the claim of sovereign immunity or whether the defense has been waived through a failure to present it properly. Under the view we take of sovereign immunity, permitting the Spanish Ambassador to intervene at this stage in the proceedings will not materially prejudice the appellee, who does not dispute appellant's sovereign status. We therefore grant the motion of the Spanish Ambassador and treat the claim of sovereign immunity as properly presented to the court.

is the established policy of the State Department to recognize claims
of immunity of this type. Republic of Mexico v. Hoffman, supra, 324
U.S. at 36, 65 S.Ct. 530.

Through the "Tate letter" the State Department has made it clear
that its policy is to decline immunity to friendly foreign sovereigns in
suits arising from private or commercial activity. But the "Tate letter" offers no guide-lines or criteria for differentiating between
a sovereign's private and public acts. Nor have the courts or commentators suggested any satisfactory test. Some have looked to the
nature of the transaction, categorizing as sovereign acts only activity
which could not be performed by individuals. While this criterion is
relatively easy to apply, it ofttimes produces rather astonishing results, such as the holdings of some European courts that purchases of
bullets or shoes for the army, the erection of fortifications for defense, or the rental of a house for an embassy, are private acts. See
Allen, The Position of Foreign States Before National Courts 31
(1933) and cases cited therein. Furthermore, this test merely postpones the difficulty, for particular contracts in some instances may be
made only by states. Others have looked to the purpose of the transaction, categorizing as jure imperii all activities in which the object
of performance is public in character. But this test is even more unsatisfactory, for conceptually the modern sovereign always acts for
a public purpose. Lauterpacht, supra, 28 Brit.Y.B.Int'l L. at 224.
Functionally the criterion is purely arbitrary and necessarily involves
the court in projecting personal notions about the proper realm of
state functioning. See Lalive * * *, 3 Recueil Des Cours at
260 (1953). See also, Friedmann, The Growth of State Control Over
the Individual and Its Effect Upon the Rules of International State
Responsibility, 19 Brit.Y.B.Int'l L. 118, 128 (1938) ; Setser, The Immunities of the State and Government Activities, 24 Law & Cont.
Probs. 291, 309 (1959).

The conceptual difficulties involved in formulating a satisfactory
method of differentiating between acts jure imperii and acts jure gestionis have led many commentators to declare that the distinction is
unworkable. However, the Supreme Court has made it plain that
when the State Department has been silent on the question of immunity in a particular case, it is the court's duty to determine
for itself whether the foreign sovereign is entitled to immunity "in
conformity to the principles accepted by the department of the government charged with the conduct of foreign relations." Republic of
Mexico v. Hoffman, supra, 324 U.S. at 35, 65 S.Ct. at 532. And since
the State Department has publicly pronounced its adherence to the
distinction, we must apply it to the facts of this case.

The purpose of the restrictive theory of sovereign immunity is
to try to accommodate the interest of individuals doing business with
foreign governments in having their legal rights determined by the
courts, with the interest of foreign governments in being free to per-

form certain political acts without undergoing the embarrassment or hindrance of defending the propriety of such acts before foreign courts. Sovereign immunity is a derogation from the normal exercise of jurisdiction by the courts and should be accorded only in clear cases. Since the State Department's failure or refusal to suggest immunity is significant, we are disposed to deny a claim of sovereign immunity that has not been "recognized and allowed" by the State Department unless it is plain that the activity in question falls within one of the categories of strictly political or public acts about which sovereigns have traditionally been quite sensitive. Such acts are generally limited to the following categories:

(1) internal administrative acts, such as expulsion of an alien.

(2) legislative acts, such as nationalization.

(3) acts concerning the armed forces.

(4) acts concerning diplomatic activity.

(5) public loans.

We do not think that the restrictive theory adopted by the State Department requires sacrificing the interests of private litigants to international comity in other than these limited categories. Should diplomacy require enlargement of these categories, the State Department can file a suggestion of immunity with the court. Should diplomacy require contraction of these categories, the State Department can issue a new or clarifying policy pronouncement.

The Comisaría General's chartering of the appellee's ship to transport a purchase of wheat is not a strictly public or political act. Indeed, it partakes far more of the character of a private commercial act than a public or political act.

The charter party has all the earmarks of a typical commercial transaction. It was executed for the Comisaría General by "El Jefe del Servicio Commercial," the head of its commercial division. The wheat was consigned to and shipped by a private commercial concern. And one of the most significant indicators of the private commercial nature of this charter is the inclusion of the arbitration clause. The French Court of Appeal, in dismissing a claim of sovereign immunity where the governmental charterer had agreed to arbitration, pointed out:

> A contract relating to maritime transport is a private contract where the owner merely puts his ship and the ship's crew at the disposal of the State and does not take a direct part in the performance of the public service undertaken by the State in the latter's capacity as a charterer. The charter party does not contain any clause peculiar to public law or unusual in private law. It provides for a time charter of the vessel which is put at the disposal of the State chartering it. The insertion of the arbitra-

tion clause underlines the intention of the parties to make their agreement subject to private law. Myrtoon Steamship Company v. Agent Judicaire Du Tresor, 24 Int.L.Rep. 205, 206 (1957).

Maritime transport has been included among the commercial or business activities specifically mentioned in recent United States treaties restricting sovereign immunity.[15] And the 1926 Brussels Convention, the first major international attempt to restrict sovereign immunity, which Spain signed but never ratified, denied immunity to all maritime governmental activities except vessels operated exclusively on non-commercial service, such as warships, patrol vessels, or hospital ships.

Even if we take a broader view of the transaction to encompass the purchase of wheat pursuant to the Surplus Agricultural Commodities Agreement to help feed the people of Spain, the activity of the Comisaría General remains more in the commercial than political realm. Appellant does not claim that the wheat will be used for the public services of Spain; presumptively the wheat will be resold to Spanish nationals. Whether the Comisaría General loses money or makes a profit on the sale, this purchasing activity has been conducted through private channels of trade. Except for United States financing, permitting payment in pesetas, the Comisaría General acted much like any private purchaser of wheat.

Our conclusion that the Comisaría General's activity is more properly labelled an act jure gestionis than jure imperii is supported by the practice of those countries which have adopted the restrictive theory of sovereign immunity. Thus the Commercial Tribunal of Alexandria declined to grant immunity to this same Spanish instrumentality in a more difficult case—a suit arising from the Comisaría's purchase of rice to help feed the people of neutral Spain during wartime.

> It is not contended in the present case that the rice in question was bought by the Comisaría General for the needs of the Spanish public services. On the contrary, it seems clearly established that the rice was bought for the feeding of the Spanish population during a difficult period. In negotiating this purchase herself, instead of leaving the matter to private enterprise, Spain proceeded in much the same manner as any other Spanish trader would have done who wanted to buy rice in Egypt; that

15. A typical provision is contained in Article XVIII (Par. 3) of the FCN Treaty with Israel, signed August 23, 1951:

No enterprise of either Party, including corporations, associations, and government agencies and instrumentalities, which is publicly owned or controlled shall, if it engages in commercial, manufacturing, processing, shipping or other business activities within the territories of the other Party, claim or enjoy, either for itself or for its property, immunity therein from taxation, suit, execution of judgment or other liability to which privately owned and controlled enterprises are subject therein. Quoted in Setser, 1961 Proceedings of Am. Soc. Int'l L. at 90.

is to say, she got it out of Egypt with the necessary permits and carried it to Spain in a Spanish ship in order to re-sell it on the usual commercial lines. This being so, the Comisaría General cannot claim immunity from jurisdiction, and the judgment entered against it must be confirmed.

Though there are a few inconsistencies, the courts in those countries which have adopted the restrictive theory have generally considered purchasing activity by a state instrumentality, particularly for resale to nationals, as commercial or private activity.

Finally, our conclusion that the Comisaría General's claim of sovereign immunity should be denied finds support in the State Department's communication to the court in New York and Cuba Mail S. S. Co. v. Republic of Korea, 132 F.Supp. 684, 685 (S.D.N.Y.1955). There the Republic of Korea was allegedly responsible for damaging a ship while assisting in the unloading of a cargo of rice for distribution without charge to its civilian and military personnel during the Korean War. Though suggesting that Korea's property was immune from attachment, the State Department refused to suggest immunity "inasmuch as the particular acts out of which the cause of action arose are not shown to be of a purely governmental character." If the wartime transportation of rice to civilian and military personnel is not an act jure imperii, a fortiori the peacetime transportation of wheat for presumptive resale is not an act jure imperii.[20]

* * *

Jurisdiction

Though in most cases jurisdiction over a foreign sovereign is obtained in an in rem proceeding, there is no bar to the assertion of in personam jurisdiction. * * *

We hold that the district court had in personam jurisdiction to enter the order compelling arbitration. By agreeing to arbitrate in New York, where the United States Arbitration Act makes such agreements specifically enforceable, the Comisaría General must be deemed to have consented to the jurisdiction of the court that could compel the arbitration proceeding in New York. To hold otherwise would be to render the arbitration clause a nullity. * * *

* * *

Service of Process

The appellant has also challenged the propriety of the extraterritorial service employed here. But since the appellant has consented beforehand to the jurisdiction of the district court, the sole function

20. Since in our view sovereign immunity does not apply, we find it unnecessary to consider whether the agreement to arbitrate constituted an implied waiver of sovereign immunity.

Compare Duff Development Company, Ltd. v. Government of Kelantan, L.R. [1924] A.C. 797 with Ben Aiad c. Gouvernement tunisien, Dalloz 305 (Cour de Cassation 1897).

of process in this case was, as Judge Murphy correctly noted below, to notify the appellant that proceedings had commenced. This function was certainly performed. * * * No rule of international law requires special treatment for serving branches of foreign sovereigns. See Sucharitkul, supra, at 350, 351.

* * *

The order of the district court is affirmed.

---

1. *Distinction between public acts and commercial acts.* In the Tate letter, the Department of State committed itself to the civil law distinction between the public acts and the private acts of a state. The court so noted in the Victory Transport case and went on to say that since the department had announced its adherence to the distinction, it was its duty to apply it. It then proceeded to classify in five categories those acts of a state which it considered to be "strictly political or public acts" and said the act involved in the case "partakes far more of the character of a private commercial act than a public or political act." Did the court apply the civil law distinction between public acts and private acts or a distinction between public acts and commercial acts?

As pointed out at p. 322, the restrictive theory developed by courts in civilian jurisdictions is not grounded on a distinction between commercial and other acts of a state. Commercial acts are part of the larger category of acts which civilians denominate private. Nevertheless, the Department of State has tended at times to construe the Tate letter as if it set forth a distinction between public and commercial acts. Thus in 1969, a Deputy Legal Adviser to the Department of State said: " * * * [T]he Tate letter tried to draw a distinction between governmental and commercial activities." Belman, New Departures in the Law of Sovereign Immunity, 1969 Proceedings of the American Society of International Law 182, 183–184.

There are, literally, hundreds of decisions dealing with sovereign immunity. Of those, many are decisions by courts in civil law states where immunity was denied because the activity of the foreign state giving rise to the litigation was commercial and hence classified as a private act not entitled to immunity. In a large number of these cases, common law courts would also characterize the activity involved as commercial in nature and it would not make much difference if they did not approach the issue in terms of public versus private acts. They could, if they wanted to, reach the same result, i. e. deny immunity, just as the court did in the Victory Transport case.

Difficulties arise, however, when the test of public versus private acts does not yield the same result as the test of public versus commercial acts. Consider again, for example, the case of Trutta v. State of Rumania, already discussed at p. 324, and the contract involved, i. e. the supply of leather to the army of Rumania. If the purpose of the transaction were looked upon as controlling, the contract could be regarded as involving a public purpose rather than a commercial one and hence as covered by sovereign immunity. The Supreme Court of Italy, however, did not approach the issue in these terms. Instead it ruled the contract was not of the kind which only a state, in the exercise of its public power, could conclude and hence Rumania was not entitled to immunity in litigation on the contract.

The illustration indicates the basic cleavage between the two tests involved. A public purpose and an act of public power are not, in the view of courts from civil law states, the same thing. They would agree a state always acts for a public purpose, but say the relevant question is whether or not it accomplishes its public purpose by an act of public power. When, however, the purpose of the act is made the criterion, the issue becomes whether the act of the foreign state has only a public purpose or, if it has also a commercial purpose, whether the one should be considered as more controlling than the other.

When the issue is framed in terms of the purpose of the act, inconsistent determinations often follow. Thus Belman, the Deputy Legal Adviser of the Department of State whose interpretation of the Tate Letter has just been discussed above, would take the view that a contract for the supply of leather to an army is a commercial act. 1969 Proceedings 183. Yet the court in the Victory Transport case declares it "astonishing" that immunity should be denied in purchases of bullets or shoes for the army. According to Belman again, the purchase by a state of rifles for its Olympic team is probably a public act. 1969 Proceedings 183–184. How do you think the court in the Victory Transport case would classify such a purchase?

2. *Pending United States legislation codifying the restrictive theory.* On January 22, 1973, the Secretary of State and the Attorney General sent to the President of the Senate a joint letter and attached draft bill on sovereign immunity for his consideration and appropriate reference. The bill, S. 566, was introduced on January 26, 1973 and referred to the Committee on the Judiciary. 119 Cong.Rec. 1297 (daily ed. Jan. 26, 1973). The materials appearing in the Congressional Record include the bill, which is in the form of an amendment to 28 U.S.C. and would become Chapter 95 of that title, Sections 1602–1611, the letter of transmittal, and a section by section analysis. Identical materials were also forwarded to the Speaker of the House of Representatives. For the text of the bill, see the Documentary Supplement.

The analysis of "Sec. 1602, Findings and declaration of purpose", states: "There is ＊ ＊ ＊ general acceptance of the restrictive principle of immunity. It is this principle that has been applied by the Department of State and by the courts since the 'Tate letter' ＊ ＊ ＊

and which is incorporated and codified in this Chapter." The analysis of the section further states: "The existing case law, both United States and foreign, could be drawn upon in aid of the interpretation and application of the provisions of this Act." The letter of transmittal says: "The draft bill would give appropriate guidance, grounded in the restrictive theory of immunity, on the standards to be employed. They are consistent with those applied in other developed legal systems."

Section 1605(2) denies immunity to a foreign state in any case "in which the action is based upon a commercial activity carried on in the United States by the foreign state." Section 1603(b) defines a "commercial activity" as follows:

> For the purpose of this chapter, a "commercial activity" means either a regular course of commercial conduct or a particular commercial transaction or act. The commercial character of an activity shall be determined by reference to the nature of the course of conduct or particular transaction or act, *rather than by reference to its purpose.* [Emphasis supplied.]

The analysis of Section 1603(b) states:

> * * * [A] single contract if of the same character as *a contract which might be made by private persons,* can constitute a "particular commercial transaction or act." The fact that the goods or services to be procured through the contract are to be used for a public purpose is irrelevant. Such a contract should be considered to be a commercial contract, *even if its object is to assist in a public function.*

> The courts will have a good deal of latitude in determining what is a "commercial activity." * * * It would include * * * such diverse activities as a contract to manufacture army boots for a foreign government or the sale by a foreign government of a service or product. [Emphasis supplied.]

3. *Questions.* Would Section 1603(b), with its specific exclusion of the purpose of the act as a criterion, effect a substantial rapprochement between the application of the restrictive theory in the United States and its application in civil law states?

How would the Collision case on p. 318, be decided by a court in the United States under the bill if it became law? See Section 1605 (5), Documentary Supplement.

4. *European Convention on Sovereign Immunity: comparison with pending legislation in the United States.* The convention was prepared by the Council of Europe, agreed upon by the member states on May 16, 1972, and signed as of May 24, 1972, by Austria, Belgium, the Federal Republic of Germany, Luxembourg, the Netherlands, Switzerland and the United Kingdom. It embodies the restrictive theory. The text of the convention is in the Documentary Supplement.

It is interesting to note the similarity of techniques employed in the drafting of the legislation proposed for the United States and in the drafting of the European convention. Neither attempts to define the public acts of a foreign state. Rather both provide that a foreign state has immunity except as otherwise stated and list specifically the situations in which it is not entitled to immunity. The European convention is substantially more detailed than the legislation proposed for the United States and appears to be more restrictive of immunity in some respects. For example, it denies immunity to a foreign state, subject to certain conditions, in proceedings relating to a contract of employment between the state and an individual. See Article 5.

While the whole of the convention is not made in terms to turn upon a distinction between public and private acts of a state, it is obvious that it reflects throughout this conceptual distinction. For example Article 4 denies immunity in proceedings relating to contracts which are to be performed in the state of the forum, but exempts from this rule contracts concluded on the territory of the foreign state when they are "governed by its administrative law." It is useful in order to appreciate this exception to have some understanding of the civilian concepts of administrative law and their influence on the development of the restrictive theory of immunity in civil law states, as discussed on p. 323 of this Chapter.

The convention includes provisions requiring a contracting state to give effect to judgments rendered against it by the courts of another contracting state, and provisions for a special European Tribunal to resolve disputes arising under the convention. See Articles 20–23 and the Additional Protocol. On the other hand, the United States proposes to amend its declaration of acceptance of the compulsory jurisdiction of the International Court of Justice, should the pending legislation become law, in order to submit to it disputes concerning the immunity of foreign states which might arise under the bill. The letter of transmittal of the bill so states.

EXCERPTS FROM SWEENEY, THE INTERNATIONAL LAW OF SOVEREIGN IMMUNITY

24–25, 52–55.
(United States Department of State Publication 1963).

[In the excerpts which follow, references to some 80 cases from some 20 states have been eliminated. Consult the original text for the names of these cases and the alphabetical table of cases at pp. 4–17 of the publication for the citations.]

Interests in Immovables and Estates

The immunity from jurisdiction of a foreign state does not extend to actions for the determination of an interest in immovable—or real—property in the territory.

This limitation on the immunity of the state is of long standing. Early cases sometimes stated the limitation as if it applied only to ownership interests in real property. In Ziemer v. Rumanian State (1882), the Court of Conflicts of Berlin said:

> According to a firmly established principle of international law, no state exercises jurisdiction over another state * * *. It is true that limitations on this rule exist in cases of voluntary submission by the foreign state to local jurisdiction, namely with respect to ownership of immovable property. 26 Am.J.Int'l L. Supp. 588 (1932).

Usually, however, the limitation has been stated in broad terms indicating that other interests in real property, including possession, are covered. * * * In Selling v. U. S. S. B. (Germany, 1921) * * * the Supreme Court of Germany said by way of dictum:

> * * * [P]roceedings concerning immovable property situated within the country can be instituted in the local courts also against a foreign state * * * Accordingly, in German law, in claims concerning the ownership, a servitude or freedom from a servitude, the boundary, partition or the possession of immovable property, the court within the district of which such property is situated has exclusive jurisdiction * * *. This factual and legal situation the foreign state must reckon with prior to acquiring land and soil in another state. 26 Am.J.Int'l L.Supp. 587 (1932).
>
> * * *

The litigation must relate to an interest in the property, rather than involving the property in some other way, before jurisdiction will be exercised. * * * In Syquia v. Lopez (Philippines, 1949),[a] the action was for an order to vacate the building and for damages. The [supreme] court would not entertain the suit against the United States on the ground that the remedy sought would require a judgment for damages. In Hungarian Ecclesiastical & Pontifical Institute v. Academy of Hungary in Rome (Italy, 1960),[b] regulation of access to a [Hungarian] library and of its use was considered to be a matter outside of the jurisdiction of the court.

In actions with respect to interests in immovable property, the foreign state does not have immunity from measures of compulsion and its representatives can be ordered to evacuate the premises or threatened with expulsion by force * * * [provided they are not entitled to some other immunity such as diplomatic immunity].

A foreign state does not have any immunity in actions to determine interests in estates locally administered. * * * (at 24–25)

* * *

a. 18 Int'l L.Rep. 228 (1957).   b. 23 Int'l L.Rep. 203 (1960).

By Whom Immunity May Be Claimed

1.   Entities Which Are Not States

Sovereign immunity avails only a sovereign state.   *   *   *.

Sovereign immunity does not extend to the members of a federat- ✓
ed state because they do not qualify as states in the international law
sense.   *   *   *   Similarly, it does not extend to political subdivisions
in a state which is not a federated state.   *   *   *   Sovereign immunity
does not extend to a municipality.   *   *   *

In Hunttiger v. La Société des Chemins de Fer du Congo (France,
1934),[c] the state of the Congo was granted immunity after it had
lost its independence on the ground that the act from which the litigation arose took place while it was still independent.   In Ter K. v.
State of Netherlands, Surinam and Indonesia (Netherlands, 1951),[d]
Indonesia became an independent state after the beginning of the
action.   It was granted immunity and its appearance in the case up to
the moment it became independent was held not to be recognition of
the jurisdiction of the courts.

2.   The Personal Sovereign

The courts of France and Italy distinguish between the public and
private acts of the personal sovereign.   The immunity does not extend
to his private acts.   *   *   *   The immunity extends to his official
acts.   *   *   *   The immunity does not extend after the abdication of
the personal sovereign.   *   *   *   The British courts do not draw a distinction between public and private acts of the personal sovereign.
*   *   *   Immunity extends to both.   *   *   *

In the courts of India the immunity of former rulers of Indian
states is controlled to a large extent by statutory provisions.   *   *   *

3.   Public Officials and Agents

Public officials of a state are entitled to the immunity of the state
for acts done in their official capacity, if the suit is in effect a suit
against the state.   *   *   *

Public officials of the state do not have immunity from personal
liability even for acts carried out in their official capacity.   This would
appear to be the point of S.T.E.F. v. Minister of Finance and Officer
Commanding the United States Defense Force at Keilavik (Iceland,
1956).[e]   The plaintiff claimed damages for non-payment by the Defense Force of royalties in respect of musical works broadcast by the
Defense Force.   It was held that the claim could be maintained against
the commanding officer of the United States Defense Force.   In Saor-
stat & Continental Steamship Company, Ltd. v. Rafael de las Morenas
(Eire, 1944),[f] the defendant was a colonel in the Spanish army who

c.   62 Journal du Droit International 623   e.   23 Int'l L.Rep. 260 (1960).
     (1935).

                                                   f.   [1943–1945] Ann.Dig. 97 (No. 25).
d.   18 Int'l L.Rep. 223 (1957).

had come to Eire as head of a commission of the Spanish government to purchase horses for the use of the Spanish army. He entered into a contract for the shipment of the horses and was sued for breach of contract when he failed to deliver the horses for shipment. The defense of immunity was rejected on the ground that he was being sued in his personal capacity.

A person who is not an official of the state but who is acting as its agent is also entitled to immunity if the suit is in effect a suit against the state. * * *

When a consul of a foreign state is impleaded, he is entitled to the immunity of the state for which he acts, provided that the act from which the suit arises was done in his official capacity. * * * In Spanish State v. Canal (France, 1951),ᵍ the lower court had ordered the consul of Spain to surrender gold, jewels and other valuables which had been turned over to him for return to Spain pursuant to an agreement between France and Spain. The court of appeal reversed on the ground that his act in receiving the valuables was an act of public power.

The immunity to which an official is entitled for acts done in his official capacity is to be distinguished from other specialized immunities such as diplomatic immunities. * * * In Claim Against Foreign Embassy Case (Yugoslavia, 1956),ʰ it was held that an ambassador could not be served in a suit for injuries caused by a car of his embassy and that the suit, if admissible at all, would have to be directed against the state itself.

4. Agencies of the State

In Civil Law states, a distinction is drawn between agencies which are part of the government and those which are separate legal entities. The former are entitled to the immunity of the state. * * * Agencies which are separate legal entities are usually not entitled as such to the immunity of the state. * * * When the courts in Civil Law states deny immunity to an agency on the ground that it is an entity distinct from the government, they frequently base their decision on the alternate ground that the suit arises from a commercial activity of the agency, for which it is not entitled to immunity in any event.

In Common Law states, the test of whether a state agency is entitled to the immunity of the state is more flexible. In each case, it must be determined whether the relationship between the agency and the state creating it is such as to make it in fact a part of the government. In Compania Mercantil Argentina v. United States Shipping Board (England, 1924),ⁱ the United States Shipping Board was held

g.   79 Journal du Droit International 220   i.   40 T.L.R. 601 (1924).
     (1952).

h.   23 Int'l L.Rep. 431 (1960).

to be an agency of the United States government and therefore entitled to the immunity.   *   *   *   In Baccus S.R.L. v. Servicio Nacional del Trigo (England, 1956),[j] the defendant agency was regarded as a department of the government of Spain and as such entitled to immunity notwithstanding that it was created as a separate entity.   *   *

The determination of the status of the agency in relation to the government that created it is made by the forum and great weight is attached to the views of the foreign government involved.   *   *   *

5.   Corporations Owned or Controlled by the State

In Civil Law states, corporations in which the government has an interest are not usually entitled to immunity because they are entities distinct and separate from the state.   A corporation may, however, plead immunity for a particular act accomplished on behalf of the foreign state by application of the ordinary rules of agency.   The act is the act of the state, not that of the corporation, and will result in the immunity of the corporation if it would normally avail the state itself.   *   *   *

In Common Law states, a corporation may be entitled to immunity if it acts on the same basis and in the same manner as agencies of the state.   *   *   *   (at 52–55)

     *   *   *

United States pending legislation and European convention on sovereign immunity.   Compare the statements in the excerpts which appear above, so far as they concern interests in immovables, interests in estates, and political subdivisions, agencies or other instrumentalities, with the relevant provisions of both the pending United States legislation and the European convention.

NATIONAL CITY BANK OF NEW YORK v. REPUBLIC OF CHINA ✦

United States Supreme Court, 1955.
348 U.S. 356, 75 S.Ct. 423.

MR. JUSTICE FRANKFURTER delivered the opinion of the Court.

The Shanghai-Nanking Railway Administration, an official agency of respondent Republic of China, established a $200,000 deposit account in 1948 with the New York head office of petitioner National City Bank of New York.   Subsequently, respondent sought to with-

j.   [1957] 1 Q.B. 438 (C.A.).

draw the funds, but petitioner refused to pay, and respondent brought suit in Federal District Court under 48 Stat. 184, as amended, 12 U.S.C.A. § 632.

In addition to various defenses, petitioner interposed two counterclaims seeking an affirmative judgment for $1,634,432 on defaulted Treasury Notes of respondent owned by petitioner. After a plea of sovereign immunity, the District Court dismissed the counterclaims, 108 F.Supp. 766, and entered judgment on them pursuant to Rule 54 (b), Federal Rules of Civil Procedure. Petitioner appealed, and while the appeal was pending sought leave from the District Court to amend the counterclaims by denominating them setoffs and including additional data. The District Court denied leave. 14 F.R.D. 186. The Court of Appeals for the Second Circuit affirmed the dismissal and the denial on the ground that the counterclaims were not based on the subject matter of respondent's suit (whether they be treated as requests for affirmative relief or as setoffs) and, therefore, it would be an invasion of respondent's sovereign immunity for our courts to permit them to be pursued. 208 F.2d 627. Because of the importance of the question and its first appearance in this Court, we granted certiorari. 347 U.S. 951.

The status of the Republic of China in our courts is a matter for determination by the Executive and is outside the competence of this Court. Accordingly, we start with the fact that the Republic and its governmental agencies enjoy a foreign sovereign's immunities to the same extent as any other country duly recognized by the United States. See Guaranty Trust Co. v. United States, 304 U.S. 126, 137–138.

The freedom of a foreign sovereign from being haled into court as a defendant has impressive title-deeds. Very early in our history this immunity was recognized, De Moitez v. The South Carolina, Bee 422, 17 Fed.Cas. 574, No. 9,697 (Admiralty Court of Pa., 1781, Francis Hopkinson, J.), and it has since become part of the fabric of our law. It has become such solely through adjudications of this Court. Unlike the special position accorded our States as party defendants by the Eleventh Amendment, the privileged position of a foreign state is not an explicit command of the Constitution. It rests on considerations of policy given legal sanction by this Court. * * *

    * * *

And so we come to the immediate situation before us. The short of the matter is that we are not dealing with an attempt to bring a recognized foreign government into one of our courts as a defendant and subject it to the rule of law to which nongovernmental obligors must bow. We have a foreign government invoking our law but resisting a claim against it which fairly would curtail its recovery. It wants our law, like any other litigant, but it wants our law free from the claims of justice. * * * As expounded in The Schooner

Exchange, the doctrine is one of implied consent by the territorial sovereign to exempt the foreign sovereign from its "exclusive and absolute" jurisdiction, the implication deriving from standards of public morality, fair dealing, reciprocal self-interest, and respect for the "power and dignity" of the foreign sovereign.

* * *

(c) Respondent urges that fiscal management falls within the category of immune operations of a foreign government as defined by the State Department's 1952 pronouncement. This is not to be denied, but it is beside the point. A sovereign has freely come as a suitor into our courts; our State Department neither has been asked nor has it given the slightest intimation that in its judgment allowance of counterclaims in such a situation would embarrass friendly relations with the Republic of China.

(d) It is recognized that a counterclaim based on the subject matter of a sovereign's suit is allowed to cut into the doctrine of immunity. This is proof positive that the doctrine is not absolute, and that considerations of fair play must be taken into account in its application. But the limitation of "based on the subject matter" is too indeterminate, indeed too capricious, to mark the bounds of the limitations on the doctrine of sovereign immunity. There is great diversity among courts on what is and what is not a claim "based on the subject matter of the suit" or "growing out of the same transaction." * * * No doubt the present counterclaims cannot fairly be deemed to be related to the Railway Agency's deposit of funds except insofar as the transactions between the Republic of China and the petitioner may be regarded as aspects of a continuous business relationship. The point is that the ultimate thrust of the consideration of fair dealing which allows a setoff or counterclaim based on the same subject matter reaches the present situation. The considerations found controlling in The Schooner Exchange are not here present, and no consent to immunity can properly be implied.

* * *

The judgment of the Court of Appeals must be reversed and the case remanded to the District Court with directions to reinstate the counterclaims and for further proceedings not inconsistent with this opinion.

Reversed.

[Mr. Justice Douglas did not participate in the consideration or decision of the case. Dissenting opinions omitted].

United States pending legislation and European convention on sovereign immunity. On the questions of waiver by institution of proceedings by the foreign state and counterclaims, see the relevant provisions of both the pending United States legislation and the European convention. With respect to waiver in advance, Section 1605(1) of the pending legislation provides that a foreign state shall not be immune in any case "in which the foreign state has waived its immunity either explicitly or by implication, notwithstanding any withdrawal of the waiver which the foreign state may purport to effect after the claim arose." The European convention contains a similar provision in Article 2.

SECTION B. ROLE OF THE UNITED STATES EXECUTIVE BRANCH

EX PARTE REPUBLIC OF PERU

United States Supreme Court, 1943.
318 U.S. 578, 63 S.Ct. 793.

MR. CHIEF JUSTICE STONE delivered the opinion of the Court.

This is a motion for leave to file in this Court the petition of the Republic of Peru for a writ of prohibition or of mandamus. The petition asks this Court to prohibit respondent, a judge of the District Court for the Eastern District of Louisiana, and the other judges and officers of that court, from further exercise of jurisdiction over a proceeding in rem, pending in that court against petitioner's steamship Ucayali, and to direct the district judge to enter an order in the proceeding declaring the vessel immune from suit. The questions for decision here are whether this Court has jurisdiction to issue the writ, whether such jurisdiction should in our discretion be exercised in petitioner's behalf, and whether petitioner's appearance and defense of the suit in the district court was, as that court has ruled, a waiver of its claim that the vessel, being that of a friendly sovereign state, is immune from suit brought by a private party in the court of the United States.

On March 30, 1942, Galban Lobo Co., S. A., a Cuban corporation, filed a libel in the district court against the Ucayali for its failure to carry a cargo of sugar from a Peruvian port to New York, as required by the terms of a charter party entered into by libelant with a Peruvian corporation acting as agent in behalf of the Peruvian Government. On April 9, 1942, the Republic of Peru, acting by the master of the vessel, intervened in the district court by filing a claim to the vessel, averring that the Republic of Peru was sole owner, and stating: "The filing of this claim is not a general appearance and is without prejudice to or waiver of all defenses and objections which may be available to respondent and claimant, particularly, but not exclusively, sovereign immunity."

On the same day, petitioner procured the release of the vessel by filing a surety release bond in the sum of $60,000, on which petitioner was principal. The bond, which contained a reservation identical with that appearing in petitioner's claim to the vessel, was conditioned upon payment of any amount awarded to libelant by the final decree in the cause. On April 11th petitioner proceeded in the cause to take the testimony of the master on the merits, and spread on the record a statement that the testimony was taken with like "full reservation and without waiver of all defenses and objections which may be available to respondent and claimant, particularly, but not exclusively, sovereign immunity." Petitioner also stated that "the appearance of counsel for the Government of Peru and the Steamship Ucayali is for the special purpose only of taking the testimony of the master under the reservation aforesaid."

On April 18th, and again on May 10th and on May 29th, petitioner moved for and obtained an order of the district court extending its time within which to answer or otherwise plead to the libel. Each motion was made "with full reservation and without waiver of any defenses and objections which may be available to mover, particularly, but not exclusively, sovereign immunity."

In the meantime, petitioner, following the accepted course of procedure (see Ex parte Muir, 254 U.S. 522, 41 S.Ct. 185; Compania Espanola v. The Navemar, 303 U.S. 68, 58 S.Ct. 432), by appropriate representations, sought recognition by the State Department of petitioner's claim of immunity, and asked that the Department advise the Attorney General of the claim of immunity and that the Attorney General instruct the United States Attorney for the Eastern District of Louisiana to file in the district court the appropriate suggestion of immunity of the vessel from suit. These negotiations resulted in formal recognition by the State Department of the claim of immunity. This was communicated to the Attorney General by the Under Secretary's letter of May 5, 1942. The letter requested him to instruct the United States Attorney to present to the district court a copy of the Ambassador's formal claim of immunity filed with the State Department, and to say that "this Department accepts as true the statements of the Ambassador concerning the steamship Ucayali, and recognizes and allows the claim of immunity."

Pursuant to these instructions the United States Attorney, on June 29th, filed in the district court a formal statement advising the court of the proceedings and communications mentioned, suggesting to the court and praying "that the claim of immunity made on behalf of the said Peruvian Steamship Ucayali and recognized and allowed by the State Department be given full force and effect by this court"; and "that the said vessel proceeded against herein be declared immune from the jurisdiction and process of this court." On July 1st, petitioner moved for release of the vessel and that the suit be dismissed. The district court denied the motion on the ground that petitioner had waived its immunity by applying for extensions of time within which to answer, and by taking the deposition of the master—steps which the district court thought constituted a general appearance despite petitioner's attempted reservation of its right to assert its immunity as a defense in the suit. 47 F.Supp. 203.

The first question for our consideration is that of our jurisdiction. * * *

* * *

We conclude that we have jurisdiction to issue the writ as prayed. And we think that—unless the sovereign immunity has been waived—the case is one of such public importance and exceptional character as to call for the exercise of our discretion to issue the writ rather than to relegate the Republic of Peru to the circuit court of appeals, from which it might be necessary to bring the case to this Court again by certiorari. The case involves the dignity and rights of a friendly sovereign state, claims against which are normally presented and settled in the course of the conduct of foreign affairs by the President and by the Department of State. When the Secretary elects, as he may and as he appears to have done in this case, to settle claims against the vessel by diplomatic negotiations between the two countries rather than by continued litigation in the courts, it is of public importance that the action of the political arm of the Government taken within its appropriate sphere be promptly recognized, and that the delay and inconvenience of a prolonged litigation be avoided by prompt termination of the proceedings in the district court. If the Republic of Peru has not waived its immunity, we think that there are persuasive grounds for exercising our jurisdiction to issue the writ in this case and at this time without requiring petitioner to apply to the circuit court of appeals * * *.

This case presents no question of the jurisdiction of the district court over the person of a defendant. Such jurisdiction must be acquired either by the service of process or by the defendant's appearance or participation in the litigation. Here the district court acquired jurisdiction in rem by the seizure and control of the vessel, and the libelant's claim against the vessel constituted a case or controversy which the court had authority to decide. Indeed, for the purpose of determining whether petitioner was entitled to the claimed immunity, the district court, in the absence of recognition of the immunity by the Department of State, had authority to decide for itself whether all the requisites for such immunity existed—whether the vessel when seized was petitioner's, and was of a character entitling it to the immunity. See Ex parte Muir, supra; The Pesaro, 255 U.S. 216, 41 S.Ct. 308; Berizzi Bros. Co. v. The Pesaro, 271 U.S. 562, 46 S.Ct. 611; Compania Espanola v. The Navemar, supra.

Therefore the question which we must decide is not whether there was jurisdiction in the district court, acquired by the appearance of petitioner, but whether the jurisdiction which the court had already acquired by seizure of the vessel should have been relinquished in conformity to an overriding principle of substantive law.

That principle is that courts may not so exercise their jurisdiction, by the seizure and detention of the property of a friendly sovereign, as to embarrass the executive arm of the Government in conducting foreign relations. "In such cases the judicial department of this government follows the action of the political branch, and will not embarrass the latter by assuming an antagonistic jurisdiction." United States v. Lee, 106 U.S. 196, 209, 1 S.Ct. 240. More specifically, the judicial seizure of the vessel of a friendly foreign state is so serious a challenge to its dignity, and may so affect our friendly relations with it, that courts are required to accept and follow the executive determination that the vessel is immune. When such a seizure occurs the friendly foreign sovereign may present its claim of immunity by appearance in the suit and by way of defense to the libel. * * * But it may also present its claim to the Department of State, the political arm of the Government charged with the conduct of our foreign affairs. Upon recognition and allowance of the claim by the State Department and certification of its action presented to the court by the Attorney General, it is the court's duty to surrender the vessel and remit the libelant to the relief obtainable through diplomatic negotiations. * * * This practice is founded upon the policy, recognized both by the Department of State and the courts, that our national interest will be better served in such cases if the wrongs to suitors, involving our relations with a friendly foreign power, are righted through diplomatic negotiations rather than by the compulsions of judicial proceedings.

We cannot say that the Republic of Peru has waived its immunity. It has consistently declared its reliance on the immunity, both before the Department and in the district court. Neither method of asserting the immunity is incompatible with the other. Nor, in view of the purpose to be achieved by permitting the immunity to be asserted, are we able to perceive any ground for saying that the district court should disregard the claim of immunity, which a friendly sovereign is authorized to advance by way of defense in the pending suit, merely because the sovereign has seen fit to preserve its right to interpose other defenses. The evil consequences which might follow the seizure of the vessel are not any the less because the friendly state asserts other grounds for the vessel's release.

Here the State Department has not left the Republic of Peru to intervene in the litigation through its Ambassador as in the case of Compania Espanola v. The Navemar. The Department has allowed the claim of immunity and caused its action to be certified to the district court through the appropriate channels. The certification and the request that the vessel be declared immune must be accepted by the courts as a conclusive determination by the political arm of the Government that the continued retention of the vessel interferes with the proper conduct of our foreign relations. Upon the submission of this certification to the district court, it became the court's duty, in conformity to established principles, to release the vessel and to proceed no further in the cause. We have no occasion to decide whether the court should surrender the vessel and dismiss the suit on certification of sovereign immunity by the Secretary, made after the friendly sovereign has once unqualifiedly assented to a judicial determination of the controversy.

The motion for leave to file is granted. We assume that, in view of this opinion, formal issuance of the writ will be unnecessary, and we direct that the writ issue only on further application by the petitioner.

[Concurring and dissenting opinions omitted.]

REPUBLIC OF MEXICO v. HOFFMAN

United States Supreme Court, 1945.
324 U.S. 30, 65 S.Ct. 530.

[The owner of an American ship filed a libel in rem against a Mexican ship, for damages caused by the latter. It was found at trial that the Mexican government owned the libelled ship and had delivered it to a privately owned and operated Mexican corporation under a five-year contract. The corporation operated the ship in a private venture on the high seas. The officers and crews were selected, controlled and paid by the Mexican corporation. The corporation agreed to pay the Mexican government fifty percent of the net profits of the venture but agreed to bear all net losses.

During trial in the district court, the United States attorney filed a State Department communication stating that it accepted as true the contention of the Mexican government that the ship was the property of the Mexican government. The State Department took no position with respect to the immunity of the Mexican ship which had been suggested by the Mexican ambassador. Both the district court and circuit court denied the immunity on the ground that the ship was not in the possession or service of the Mexican government. The Supreme Court affirmed. Portions of the opinion delivered for the Court by MR. CHIEF JUSTICE STONE, and of the concurring opinion of MR. JUSTICE FRANKFURTER, appear below.]

In the absence of recognition of the claimed immunity by the political branch of the government, the courts may decide for themselves whether all the requisites of immunity exist. That is to say, it is for them to decide whether the vessel when seized was that of a foreign government and was of a character and operated under conditions entitling it to the immunity in conformity to the principles accepted by the department of the government charged with the conduct of our foreign relations. See Ex parte Peru, * * *

Every judicial action exercising or relinquishing jurisdiction over the vessel of a foreign government has its effect upon our relations with that government. Hence it is a guiding principle in determining whether a court should exercise or surrender its jurisdiction in such cases, that the courts should not so act as to embarrass the executive arm in its conduct of foreign affairs. * * *

It is therefore not for the courts to deny an immunity which our government has seen fit to allow, or to allow an immunity on new grounds which the government has not seen fit to recognize. * * *

* * *

* * * Here both courts have found that the Republic of Mexico is the owner of the seized vessel. The State Department has certified that it recognizes such ownership, but it has refrained from certifying that it allows the immunity or recognizes ownership of the vessel without possession by the Mexican government as a ground for immunity. It does not appear that the Department has ever allowed a claim of immunity on that ground, and we are cited to no case in which a federal court has done so. * * *

* * *

[W]e think controlling in the present circumstances, is the fact that, despite numerous opportunities like the present to recognize immunity from suit of a vessel owned and not possessed by a foreign government, this government has failed to do so. We can only conclude that it is the national policy not to extend the immunity in the manner now suggested, and that it is the duty of the courts, in a matter so intimately associated with our foreign policy and which may profoundly affect it, not to enlarge an immunity to an extent which the government, although often asked, has not seen fit to recognize. * * *

MR. JUSTICE FRANKFURTER, concurring.

In Berizzi Bros. Co. v. The Pesaro, 271 U.S. 562, 46 S.Ct. 611, this Court held for the first time that "merchant ships owned and operated by a foreign government have the same immunity that warships have." It did so not because the Department of State by appropriate suggestion or through its established policy had indicated that due regard for our international relations counseled such an abnegation of jurisdiction over government-owned merchantmen. On the contrary. In answer to an inquiry by Judge Mack, before whom the Pesaro's claim to immunity was first raised, the Department of State took this position: "It is the view of the Department that government-owned merchant vessels or vessels under requisition of governments whose flag they fly employed in commerce should not be regarded as entitled to the immunities accorded public vessels of war. The Department has not claimed immunity for American vessels of this character." The Pesaro, 277 F. 473, 479–480, note 3; and see 2 Hackworth, Digest of International Law, pp. 429–430, 438–439. Thus, in Berizzi Bros. Co. v. The Pesaro, supra, this Court felt free to reject the State Department's views on international policy and to formulate its own judgment on what wise international relations demanded. The Court now seems to indicate, however, that when, upon the seizure of a vessel of a foreign government, sovereign immunity is claimed, the issue is whether the vessel "was of a character and operated under conditions entitling it to the immunity in conformity with the principles accepted by the department of the government charged with the conduct of our foreign relations."

If this be an implied recession from the decision in Berizzi Bros. Co. v. The Pesaro, I heartily welcome it. * * * I appreciate that the disposition of the present case turns on the want of possession by the Republic of Mexico. My difficulty is that "possession" is too tenuous a distinction on the basis of which to differentiate between foreign government-owned vessels engaged merely in trade that are immune from suit and those that are not. Possession, actual or constructive, is a legal concept full of pitfalls. Even where only private interests are involved the determination of possession, as bankruptcy cases, for instance, abundantly prove, engenders much confusion and conflict. Ascertainment of what constitutes possession or where it is, is too subtle and precarious a task for transfer to a field in which international interests and susceptibilities are involved.

If the Republic of Mexico now saw fit to put one junior naval officer on merchantmen which it owns but are operated by a private agency under arrangements giving that Government a financial interest in the venture, it would, I should suppose, be embarrassing to find that Mexico herself did not intend to be in possession of such ships. And, certainly, the terms of the financial arrangement by which the commercial enterprise before the Court is carried on can readily be varied without much change in substance to manifest a relation to the ship by Mexico which could not easily be deemed to disclose a want of possession by Mexico.

The fact of the matter is that the result in Berizzi Bros. Co. v. The Pesaro, supra, was reached without submission by the Department of State of its relevant policies in the conduct of our foreign relations and largely on the basis of considerations which have steadily lost whatever validity they may then have had. Compare the overruling of The Thomas Jefferson, 10 Wheat. 428 (1825), by The Genesee Chief, 12 How. 443 (1851). The views of our State Department against immunity for commercial ships owned by foreign

governments have been strongly supported by international conferences, some held after the decision in the Pesaro case. See Lord
Maugham in Compania Naviera Vascongado v. The Cristina [1938]
A.C. 485, 521–523. But the real change has been the enormous
growth, particularly in recent years, of "ordinary merchandising"
activity by governments. See The Western Maid, 257 U.S. 419, 432,
42 S.Ct. 159, 160. Lord Maugham in the Cristina thus put the matter:

> Half a century ago foreign Governments very seldom em-
> barked in trade with ordinary ships, though they not infrequent-
> ly owned vessels destined for public uses, and in particular hos-
> pital vessels, supply ships and surveying or exploring vessels.
> These were doubtless very strong reasons for extending the
> privilege long possessed by ships of war to public ships of the
> nature mentioned; but there has been a very large development
> of State-owned commercial ships since the Great War, and the
> question whether the immunity should continue to be given to
> ordinary trading ships has become acute. Is it consistent with
> sovereign dignity to acquire a tramp steamer and to compete
> with ordinary shippers and ship-owners in the markets of the
> world? Doing so, is it consistent to set up the immunity of a
> sovereign if, owing to the want of skill of captain and crew,
> serious damage is caused to the ship of another country? Is it
> also consistent to refuse to permit proceedings to enforce a right
> of salvage in respect of services rendered, perhaps at great risk,
> by the vessel of another country? [1938] A.C. 485, 521–522.

And so, sensible as I am of the weight to which the decision in
the Pesaro is entitled, its implications in the light of the important
developments in the international scene that twenty years have
brought call for its reconsideration. The Department of State, in
acting upon views such as those expressed by Lord Maugham, should
no longer be embarrassed by having the decision in the Pesaro remain
unquestioned, and the lower courts should be relieved from the duty
of drawing distinctions that are too nice to draw.

It is my view, in short, that courts should not disclaim jurisdiction which otherwise belongs to them in relation to vessels owned by
foreign governments however operated except when "the department
of the government charged with the conduct of our foreign relations," or of course Congress, explicitly asserts that the proper conduct of these relations calls for judicial abstention. Thereby responsibility for the conduct of our foreign relations will be placed where
power lies. And unless constrained by the established policy of our
State Department, courts will best discharge their responsibility by
enforcement of the regular judicial processes.

MR. JUSTICE BLACK joins in this opinion.

CHEMICAL NATURAL RESOURCES, INC. v. REPUBLIC OF VENEZUELA

United States, Supreme Court of Pennsylvania, 1966.
420 Pa. 134, 215 A.2d 864 a.

OPINION BY MR. CHIEF JUSTICE BELL, * * *

Facts and Averments

Chemical Natural Resources, Inc., and Venezuelan Sulphur Corporation, C.A. sued Venezuela in an action of assumpsit commenced by a writ of foreign attachment which in this case is an action quasi in rem. Chemical is a Delaware Corporation of which not less than 50 percent of its stock is beneficially owned by United States citizens. Sulphur is a corporation organized under the laws of Venezuela and is a wholly owned subsidiary of Chemical.

On October 21, 1963, the plaintiffs (Chemical and Sulphur) commenced their action of assumpsit against Venezuela by filing a (praecipe for a) writ of foreign attachment (together with a complaint) under which writ the sheriff was directed to attach and seize the S.S. Ciudad de Valencia, allegedly the property of defendant Venezuela, which was then in the Port of Philadelphia and in the custody of Stockyard Shipping and Terminal Corp. The complaint demanded damages in the sum of $116,807,258.28.

On October 22, 1963, the day after the writ was issued, the sheriff attached and seized the steamship and took it into his possession. He also served copies of plaintiffs' complaint on the ship's master and on Stockard as garnishee. However, two days later, on October 24, 1963, the attachment was dissolved without prejudice upon the order of plaintiffs' attorney.

Plaintiffs' pertinent allegations in its amended complaint may be thus summarized:

In April of 1952 the plaintiffs, acting through Sulphur, purchased all mineral rights and interest or denouncements located in the Municipality of El Pilar, State of Sucre, Venezuela. Solely by reason of plaintiffs' exploitation, reservoirs of mineral-laden geothermal steam were discovered in El Pilar. Subsequently, plaintiffs through Sulphur entered into several contracts with a department of the Venezuelan Government under which, inter alia, plaintiffs agreed to erect facilities for converting the steam into electrical power and defendant agreed to purchase the resulting power. Plaintiffs expended large sums of money in order to carry out their part of the contract. Thereafter, Venezuela unilaterally and without any justifiable cause cancelled the contract and confiscated plaintiffs' property and property rights with a resulting loss to plaintiffs of over $116,000,000.

a. Cert. denied 385 U.S. 822, 87 S.Ct. 50 (1966).

Plaintiffs further averred that Venezuela operates its merchant vessels, including the ship which was seized, through a nationalized company wholly owned by Venezuela and thus was engaged in a commercial and private or proprietary capacity as distinguished from a Governmental or public capacity. Plaintiffs further averred that they could not obtain Justice in any Venezuelan Court.

Venezuela has never entered a general appearance in this action, but improperly entered a special appearance for the purpose of challenging the jurisdiction of the Court of Common Pleas. * * *

Venezuela also sought and obtained the intervention of the United States Department of State which, by the United States Attorney for the Eastern District of Pennsylvania acting under orders of the Attorney General of the United States, filed a "Suggestion of Immunity", *which included a prayer to dismiss plaintiffs' action against Venezuela* because of a certification of Sovereign Immunity which was recognized and allowed by the Department of State. The Attorney General acted upon a request received from the Legal Adviser of the State Department dated January 13, 1964—after all parties had been wisely given a hearing by the Legal Adviser both on the facts and the law—reading pertinently:

> The Department recognizes and allows the sovereign immunity of the Republic of Venezuela, defendant in the above suit, from the jurisdiction of the Court of Common Pleas of Philadelphia County, Pennsylvania, and it will be appreciated if appropriate instructions can be issued to the United States Attorney in that jurisdiction to file a suggestion of immunity with the Court.

On December 18, 1964, the Court below entered the following Order: "In re the Suggestion of Immunity

> And Now, this 18th day of December, 1964, in re the Suggestion of Immunity, the motion of the defendant, the Republic of Venezuela, to dismiss the complaint is overruled, with leave to the defendant to file an answer within thirty days from date of this Order.

What the Court apparently intended to do was to deny the State Department's prayer and Venezuela's motion to dismiss (which was contained in its preliminary objections), *basing its denial on its determination that Venezuela was not entitled to Sovereign Immunity.* Venezuela then took a timely appeal to this Court * * *.

* * *

Jurisdiction re Foreign Attachment

The Court below undoubtedly acquired jurisdiction by service of the writ of foreign attachment upon the captain of the vessel, and its jurisdiction was not subsequently divested or lost as a result of plaintiffs' voluntary dissolution of the (foreign) attachment without prejudice. Cf. Ex Parte Peru, 318 U.S. 578 and Pa.R.C.P. 1272. For reasons hereinafter appearing we deem it unnecessary to decide whether on the present complicated and controversial record, with so many conflicting averments, Venezuela's preliminary objections could be sustained. Cf. Pa.R.C.P. 1030 and 1017(b)(1) and 1028(c).

      *   *   *

Sovereign Immunity of Foreign Nations

It is a long and well established general rule that *foreign Sovereigns, which are duly recognized by appropriate action by the State Department,* and their property *are not amenable* without their waiver or consent, *to suit* in the Courts of this Country. This widely accepted National and International diplomatic policy has been established among many civilized non-communist Nations on the principle of comity and for the preservation of International friendships and Peace. In order to preserve this policy of Sovereign Immunity from conflict, confusion and erosion, and to prevent a breach of friendly relations or a severance of diplomatic relations or a possible war with a foreign nation, *the Supreme Court of the United States* has held that in the realm of Foreign Relations or Foreign Affairs, *a determination of Sovereign Immunity by the Executive branch of our Government,* namely, the State Department, when conveyed to a Court through proper channels or officials, is—in the absence of waiver or consent—*binding and conclusive* upon all our Courts. If and when the State Department concludes that a foreign Nation is entitled to Sovereign Immunity that determination, we repeat, is conclusive no matter how unwise or, in a particular case how unfair or unjust the Department's determination appears to be (a) to injured American citizens and (b) to vast numbers of the American people and (c) to our Courts:
*   *   *

      *   *   *

Chemical and Sulphur (plaintiffs below and appellees here) first contend that The Schooner Exchange, Ex Parte Peru and the Stone cases are restricted and limited in their effect and do not apply to the case at bar because (1) procedurally those cases arose out of a seizure (by libel or writ of foreign attachment) of property of a foreign Government or of its instrumentality and that through appellees' voluntary dissolution of the attachment without prejudice, this is no longer a "seizure" case and (2) consequently friendly foreign relations cannot be jeopardized by this suit. Appellees further contend that in spite of the release by them of the property seized, jurisdiction over the person of the defendant was obtained and still remains by way of the writ of foreign attachment, as well as by actual service of the writ and the complaint on the captain of Venezuela's ship. Appellees' attempted distinction of the Supreme Court cases previously cited in this opinion, and their aforesaid contentions are devoid of merit.

The principle or doctrine of absolute Sovereign Immunity has been attacked for many years by legal writers, by text authorities and by numerous Judges. The absolute doctrine is recognized by only a few countries in the world. These authorities assert and appellees contend that even when Sovereign Immunity has been recognized and suggested by the State Department, the acceptance or rejection thereof is nevertheless a matter for the Courts—whether the action be in rem, or quasi in rem or in personam—and the Courts in their sole discretion may accept or reject the plea of Sovereign Immunity. They further assert that this principle of absolute Sovereign Immunity should be restricted and should apply only to situations and activities in which the foreign Country is acting or is involved in its national or governmental or public capacity and not in a proprietary or a commercial or private or nongovernmental activity or capacity. However, where the State Department has (through appropriate channels) recognized the Sovereign Immunity of the foreign Country which is involved, and that Country has not waived its immunity or consented to the suit, the Supreme Court of the United States has never recognized this proposed *restricted* doctrine.

The Tate Letter

More importantly, appellees rely principally upon the so-called Tate Letter, which they contend (1) is the controlling law, (2) adopts the *restrictive* (foreign) Sovereign Immunity doctrine, and (3) allows American Courts *in every case* to accept or reject a Suggestion (or plea) of Sovereign Immunity by a foreign government (a) acting through the State Department and its appropriate channels or (b) itself raising the issue. We shall quote the relevant parts of the Tate Letter, including the sentences which have caused confusion.

* * *

(1) Does the Tate letter *unqualifiedly* express a new and restrictive policy, practice, and position of the State Department, viz., the Department will no longer recognize the absolute Sovereign Immunity of a foreign Nation, but merely *a restrictive* Sovereign Immunity; and (2) can the State Department privately change or abandon its policy in its sole discretion in each particular case; and (3) is the final determination a matter for the Courts or for the Department?

Although the language of the Tate letter appears to be clear, its exact meaning has caused some confusion. The Tate letter, we repeat, states "For these reasons [the widespread practice on the part of governments of engaging in commercial activities] it will *hereafter* be the Department's policy to follow the *restrictive theory* of sovereign immunity in the consideration of requests of foreign governments for a grant of sovereign immunity.

"It is realized that *a shift in policy* by the executive *cannot control* the courts but it is felt that the courts are less likely to allow a plea of sovereign immunity where the executive has declined to do so."

The above quoted excerpts state in clear and unmistakable language that the Department has abandoned its long established principle of *absolute* governmental immunity and has *for the hereafter* adopted a new and restricted (restrictive) theory or principle of Sovereign Immunity, viz., absolute immunity does not apply to Governments when they are engaged in commercial activities. Furthermore, the Tate letter certainly implies—if indeed it does not clearly state—that the Department's conclusion and suggestion of sovereign immunity "cannot control" the Courts which are free to make their own determination. This would undoubtedly very substantially change, if not nullify, the prior well settled law of this Country on the subject of Sovereign Immunity. Irrespective of its clear meaning, it appears that the State Department has silently abandoned the "revised and restricted policy" set forth in the Tate letter and has substituted a case by case foreign Sovereign Immunity policy, i. e., the State Department will recognize and suggest, or fail to recognize or grant or suggest Sovereign Immunity *in each case* presented to it, depending (a) upon the foreign and diplomatic relations which our Country has at that particular time with the other Country, and (2) the best interests of our Country at that particular time.

* * *

It is our conclusion, therefore, (1) that Sovereign Immunity of foreign Governments is a matter for determination in the first instance by the Executive Branch of the Government, namely, the State Department; and (2) if and when that Department's determination has been made and has been appropriately presented to the Courts, the Department's determination is binding and conclusive upon the Courts.

* * *

We believe that the decisions of the Supreme Court of the United States and of this Court which are hereinabove quoted or cited control this case, and require this Court to grant the writ of prohibition prayed for by Venezuela.

Appeal of Venezuela quashed. A writ of prohibition is issued, directed to the Judges of the lower Court dissolving plaintiffs' attachment and dismissing plaintiffs' complaint.

———

Dissenting opinion by MR. JUSTICE MUSMANNO.

The Majority Opinion in this case is built on an erroneous concept of the law, namely, that once the State Department whispers sovereign immunity the Courts must close their doors to everyone who may come within the breeze of the zephyric suggestion. Fortunately, for the majesty of the law, the dignity of the courts, and the fair-minded administration of justice in America, that is not the case. In fact, that is not even the view of the State Department.

The State Department intervened in this litigation on the basis of a question of law, not policy. In a letter to the President of the plaintiff corporation, Chemical Natural Resources, Inc., the State Department said: "The decision of the Department of State in this matter was made in the light of *legal issues*." (Emphasis supplied.)

* * *

[Concurring opinion by Mr. Justice Jones omitted; an extract from the opinion of Mr. Justice Roberts appears at p. 379 of this Chapter.]

RICH v. NAVIERA VACUBA, S. A.

United States Court of Appeals, Fourth Circuit, 1961.
295 F.2d 24.

PER CURIAM. The vessel Bahia de Nipe sailed on August 8, 1961, from Cuba with a cargo of 5,000 bags of sugar destined for a Russian port. When on August 17 the ship was about 300 miles east of Bermuda the master and ten of his crewmen put the rest of the crew under restraint, turned the vessel towards Hampton Roads, Virginia, and notified the Coast Guard of their intention to seek asylum in the United States. As they crossed the three-mile limit and neared the entrance to the Chesapeake Bay the vessel was met by the Coast Guard and taken to anchorage off Lynnhaven, Virginia.

These proceedings were begun on August 18 by the filing of a libel against the vessel on behalf of two longshoremen who had earlier recovered judgments against the Republic of Cuba and Naviera Vacuba, S. A. The latter owned the vessel before she was taken over by the revolutionary government of Cuba. Shortly thereafter another libel was filed against the ship and cargo by Mayan Lines, S. A. which had previously recovered judgment by consent in a state court of Louisiana in the sum of $500,000 against the Republic of Cuba. A third libel was filed against the cargo only by the United Fruit Sugar Company which claimed that the sugar belonged to it, having been unlawfully confiscated in Cuba by the revolutionary government. Libels for wages were also filed by the defecting master and the ten crew members.

Upon the institution of these suits in the United States District Court for the Eastern District of Virginia at Norfolk, the Clerk, pursuant to law and the practice of the court, issued the customary in rem process and delivered the same to the United States Deputy Marshal to be served upon the ship. Service, however, was prevented by the Coast Guard, which purported to act "pursuant to orders" and in reliance upon the authority of 50 U.S.C.A. § 191. On being advised of this interference with the Marshal in the performance of his duties, the District Judge issued an order directed to the Captain of the Port and the Commander of the Coast Guard, requiring them to appear and to show cause why an order should not be entered permitting the Marshal to board the vessel to execute the writs.

A number of communications from and on behalf of the Secretary of State addressed to the Attorney General were presented to the court by the United States Attorney. While infelicitously expressed, we think these sufficiently set forth the requisites of a valid suggestion for the allowance of sovereign immunity.

Arguments extending over several days were heard by the District Court which then held that the Coast Guard and those who had directed it acted in excess of their authority in preventing the service of the court's process. We likewise do not condone the Coast Guard's refusal to permit the Marshal to serve the process and find no authority therefor in section 191.

We turn to a consideration of the other questions raised. The chief defense, indeed the only one argued by the Government, is that the Republic of Cuba is a sovereign power immune from the jurisdiction of the courts of the United States, and that when the Department of State accepted Cuba's claim of ownership, possession and public operation of the ship, and ownership of the cargo, and so certified to the court and suggested that sovereign immunity be accorded, the court was bound to respect the determination and suggestion of the State Department.

The libellants argue that before sovereign immunity may be granted they should be heard by the court on whether the foreign government is in fact the owner and possessor of the property in question and, as to the ship, whether she was operated by that government not commercially but in a public capacity.

Mayan Lines, S. A. showed in addition that in the state court action wherein its $500,000 judgment was obtained against the Republic of Cuba, the defendant specifically waived its sovereign immunity in respect both to the adjudication of liability and the enforcement of the judgment by execution. It argued that it is both illegal and unconscionable for Cuba to attempt in the present proceedings to repudiate its unlimited waiver, solemnly made in the course of the Louisiana litigation.

For the libellant, United Fruit Sugar Company, evidence was adduced to prove that the very bags of sugar constituting the cargo were its property, expropriated from the company's plants in Cuba. Accordingly, this libellant asserted that release of the cargo under the doctrine of sovereign immunity, upon the mere certificate of the State Department without opportunity for further inquiry, would deprive it of its property without due process of law in violation of the Fifth Amendment. Similar contentions under the Fifth Amendment were advanced by the other libellants.

Despite these contentions, we conclude that the certificate and ✓
grant of immunity issued by the Department of State should be accepted by the court without further inquiry. * * *

We think that the doctrine of the separation of powers under our
Constitution requires us to assume that all pertinent considerations
have been taken into account by the Secretary of State in reaching
his conclusion.

The fact that the Mayan Lines' judgment was rendered in the
Louisiana court after a specific waiver of immunity by the Cuban
Government, both with respect to liability and enforcement of the
judgment, does not significantly distinguish its position from that of
the other libellants, in view of the controlling effect that must be
given the State Department's action. We do not mean to suggest that
the contention raised by this libellant as to the effect to be given the
waiver would not be a suitable subject of inquiry in the absence of
State Department action. In that case the question would be a proper
one for the court to consider. The certification and suggestion of
immunity, however, which has been made by the State Department in
this matter affecting our foreign relations, withdraws it from the
sphere of litigation. Especially is this so when the presence of the
ship within the territorial jurisdiction of the court is made possible
only by the barratry of the shipmaster. Refusal of the State Department in these circumstances to enforce Cuba's earlier waiver over its
present assertion of immunity is within the Department's authority,
and constitutes no violation of the libellant's rights under the Fifth
Amendment.

     * * *

The order of the District Court is affirmed.

Executive suggestion of immunity and due process. Assume that
the Department of State suggests that immunity be granted a foreign
state in a case where it is clear such immunity is required by international law. The court grants the immunity. Is it a reasonable
argument that the plaintiff is not thereby denied his constitutional
right of due process, but only compelled to seek his remedy in a different way?

Suppose, however, the Department suggests, and the court grants,
immunity in a case where it is clear international law does not require
it be given the foreign state. Is it a denial of procedural due process
(notice and hearing) or a taking of property without compensation
unnecessarily to deprive the plaintiff of his judicial remedy and compel him to place his claim in the hands of the Department of State for
eventual settlement by diplomatic negotiation?

Consider that the plaintiff may be able to sue in the courts of some other state or to induce the Department of State to espouse his claim internationally.

These issues were raised, but not resolved, in proceedings before the Supreme Court of the United States for a stay of the mandate by the Court of Appeals in the Rich case. I International Legal Materials 276, at 300 and 305 (1962). The issues, however, will become moot should the pending United States legislation on sovereign immunity become law. See on this point the material at p. 367 of this Chapter.

ISBRANDTSEN TANKERS, INC. v. PRESIDENT OF INDIA

United States Court of Appeals, Second Circuit, 1971.
446 F.2d 1198 [a].

J. JOSEPH SMITH, CIRCUIT JUDGE: Appellant shipowner instituted suit in the United States District Court for the Southern District of New York against the defendant-appellee, seeking damages resulting from alleged delays of its vessels during October and November of 1966 near the port of Calcutta. The District Court * * * dismissed one of the three causes of action alleged in appellant's second amended complaint, and the shipowner appeals. We find no error and affirm the dismissal.

The dismissal * * * was premised upon a formal written suggestion of immunity by the United States Department of State, transmitted through the office of the United States Attorney General, after hearings and the filing of briefs with the State Department.

Appellant shipowner and appellee entered into a charter party in July of 1966 for the transportation of grain to India. The shipment was part of a massive effort on the part of the Indian government to end a food shortage, resulting from an extreme drought in 1965 and 1966. The cause of action which is the subject of this appeal sought damages for improper and unreasonable detention of appellant's vessels, preventing discharge of their cargo and causing substantial loss of time and money. Appellant contends that notwithstanding the advisory letter from the State Department recommending immunity, the District Court has jurisdiction in this matter because of the existence of a waiver of immunity by appellee, said to be contained in paragraph 34 of the contract charter between the parties.[3] Addi-

---

a. Cert. denied 404 U.S. 985, 92 S.Ct. 452 (1971).

3. Paragraph 34 of the charter party provides:
Any and all differences and disputes arising under this Charter Party are to be determined by the U.S. Courts for the Southern District of New York, but this does not preclude a party from pursuing any in rem proceedings in another jurisdiction or from submission by mutual agreement of any differences or disputes to arbitration.

tionally, appellant argues that the appearance by appellee by means of serving and filing answering papers constitutes a waiver of any sovereign immunity that may have previously existed.

Whether or not these arguments possess logical force, in cases involving the governments of foreign powers the judiciary has candidly admitted that there exist interests beyond those of purely legal concern. A judicial decision against the government of a foreign nation could conceivably cause severe international repercussions, the full consequences of which the courts are in no position to predict. As this court noted in Victory Transport, Inc. v. Comisaria General, 336 F.2d 354, 358 (2d Cir. 1964), cert. denied, 381 U.S. 934, 85 S.Ct. 1763, 14 L.Ed.2d 698 (1965), "[i]n delineating the scope of a doctrine designed to avert possible embarrassment to the conduct of our foreign relations, the courts have quite naturally deferred to the policy pronouncements of the State Department." * * *

Appellant emphasizes that traditionally, sovereign immunity has been afforded to foreign governments only in regard to actions of a public, as opposed to a private/commercial, nature. Here, it is contended, the actions of the Indian government were wholly concerned with a commercial purchase of grain, and therefore do not concern matters of public policy or governmental discretion. This argument is premised upon the famed letter of Jack B. Tate, Acting Legal Advisor to the State Department, to Philip B. Perlman, Acting Attorney General, dated May 19, 1952 [appearing in 26 State Dept. Bull. 984 (1952)], indicating that it was the policy of our government to adopt the restrictive theory of sovereign immunity, i. e. to grant immunity to acts of a public nature, and to deny it to those of a private nature.

This proposed distinction between acts which are jure imperii (which are to be afforded immunity) and those which are jure gestionis (which are not), has never been adequately defined, and in fact has been viewed as unworkable by many commentators. In Victory Transport, this court adopted the view that acts which are jure imperii would be limited to the following:

    (1) internal administrative acts, such as expulsion of an alien;

    (2) legislative acts, such as nationalization;

    (3) acts concerning the armed forces;

    (4) acts concerning diplomatic activity;

    (5) public loans. 336 F.2d at 360.

Were we required to apply this distinction, as defined, to the facts of the present case, we might well find that the actions of the Indian government were, as appellant contends, purely private commercial decisions.

It is true that the mere fact that a contract with a private commercial interest is involved does not automatically render the acts of the foreign government private and commercial. As this court recently noted:

> The view that all contracts, regardless of their purpose, should be deemed "private" or "commercial" acts would lead to the conclusion that a contract by a foreign government for the purchase of bullets for its army or for the erection of fortifications do not constitute sovereign acts—a result we viewed as "rather astonishing" in Victory Transport, 336 F.2d at 359. * * *

In Victory Transport, the contract was, as here, for the carriage of grain, and in the absence of State Department action, jurisdiction was upheld. * * *

In situations where the State Department has given a formal recommendation, however, the courts need not reach questions of this type. The State Department is to make this determination, in light of the potential consequences to our own international position. Hence once the State Department has ruled in a matter of this nature, the judiciary will not interfere. * * *

Appellant attempts to distinguish the precedents in this area by noting that in none of them had the foreign sovereign contracted to waive its immunity. It is true that in situations where the Executive Branch has made no formal recommendation a foreign sovereign may be held to have waived its immunity. In National City Bank of New York v. Republic of China, supra, 348 U.S. at 364, 75 S.Ct. 423, for example, the Supreme Court held that where a sovereign has itself brought suit, it is not immune from a counterclaim arising out of the same subject matter as the suit itself. In that same opinion, however, the Court noted that "[t]he status of the Republic of China in our courts is a matter for determination by the Executive and is outside the competence of this Court." 348 U.S. at 358, 75 S.Ct. at 425.

The potential harm or embarrassment resulting to our government from a judicial finding of jurisdiction, in the face of an Executive recommendation to the contrary, may be just as severe where the foreign sovereign had initially contracted to waive its claim of sovereign immunity as where it had not done so. Though we sympathize with appellant because of the difficult position in which such a holding places it, we have no alternative but to accept the recommendation of the State Department.

The order of the District Court dismissing appellant's second cause of action is affirmed.

NOTE, INTERNATIONAL LAW—SOVEREIGN IMMUNITY— THE LAST STRAW IN JUDICIAL ABDICATION

46 Tulane Law Review 841 (1972).

* * *

The Department of State's announced espousal of the restrictive theory of sovereign immunity, coupled with the principle that Department suggestions are binding upon the courts, could have moved the United States into the group of progressive states that follow the restrictive theory—a more realistic approach to the problems and disputes arising from the extensive commercial trading activities in which almost all modern governments engage. However, the principle that Department of State suggestions of immunity are conclusive upon the courts and the Department's irregular adherence to the Tate letter doctrine of restrictive immunity have resulted in an absurd state of affairs clearly illustrated by Isbrandtsen. Notwithstanding India's agreement to waive its sovereign immunity as to any disputes arising under the charter party between it and Isbrandtsen Tankers, Inc., the court still felt bound by the Department of State's suggestion of immunity and dismissed the case.

The illogical Isbrandtsen decision demands a re-evaluation by the courts of the relative roles of the judiciary and the Department of State in questions of sovereign immunity. The courts have regarded the Department of State's decisions as unassailable, refusing to inquire into the circumstances under which the suggestions were made. However, the doctrine of immunity does not specifically derive from the Constitution, but instead is based upon policy considerations sanctioned by the Supreme Court. A doctrine judicially created may be judicially modified as present circumstances reveal that the Department of State is not the proper agency to decide questions of sovereign immunity.

The existence or non-existence of an express waiver of immunity is a legal issue requiring judicial resolution. In Isbrandtsen, the court considered the waiver issue subsumed by the Department of State's suggestion of immunity. The court contended that the embarrassment that might result to our government from a judicial denial of immunity when the executive had recommended the contrary might be just as severe when there was a contractual waiver of immunity as when there had been no such waiver. Any subsequent embarrassment that may arise would be caused solely by the executive's unwise recommendation of immunity in a situation where immunity was clearly unwarranted, and not, as the court implies, by judicial impairment of the Department of State's role in the conduct of foreign affairs. The Restatement (Second) of Foreign Relations Law of the United States takes the position that a state may waive immunity by agreement with a private party.

Although no cases have applied this rule, the courts should not hesitate to do so in the future. There is no reason why a foreign state should not be bound by an agreement with a private party to waive immunity as to any disputes that might arise between the contracting parties. The foreign state could not justly complain that its sovereign rights were violated when a United States court assumed jurisdiction over the case, for the court would merely be effectuating the contractual stipulation as to the forum for disputes. By permitting the Department of State to override the express waiver of immunity, the Isbrandtsen court perpetuates an unnecessary legal anachronism.

Recognizing that there existed "interests beyond those of a purely legal concern" in cases involving foreign governments, the court in Isbrandtsen stressed possible international repercussions from a decision against a foreign government. This apprehension by the court is merely a restatement of the courts' traditional rationale for conclusively accepting the Department of State's immunity suggestion, which is that the judiciary must not embarrass the executive in the conduct of foreign relations. One commentator trenchantly declared that this is "one of the most overrated arguments in the annals of American legal history." The courts of other countries have successfully adjudicated disputes involving foreign governments without executive interference, and no catastrophical international repercussions have resulted.

Whether judicial abdication of responsibility to determine whether immunity is warranted will in fact bring about any improvement in international relations is debatable. The Department of State is singularly ill-equipped to render impartial decisions on whether a state should be granted immunity. The executive's legal inquiry is unavoidably tainted by reference to a political evaluation of the litigants. Consequently, the Department of State is markedly subjective in its final determinations and indulges in widespread abuse of discretion by frequently bowing to the whims and caprices of foreign governments. The judiciary, applying principles of municipal and international law, not international politics, can more objectively resolve questions of immunity; the judicial—not the executive—branch of government must interpret the law of the United States, including international law. The independence of the judiciary in questions of sovereign immunity would clearly evidence this country's firm commitment to the principles of international law in the resolution of disputes. The present doctrine of deference to the executive is "antipathetic to the growth of world legal order." The courts must apply rules of law in disputes involving foreign governments rather than executive fiat, which is often little more than a decision based upon changing political expediencies. A judicial determination is much less likely to create embarrassment than an unpredictable edict by the Department of State.

     *   *   *

Elimination of the role of the executive in pending United States legislation. The practice of the courts of the United States to let the Department of State control the grant or denial of immunity is unique in the international legal system. In no other state in the world, so far as can be ascertained, is a suggestion of immunity, or its denial, considered binding by the courts. A major effect of the bill on sovereign immunity now pending in Congress is to leave the determination of immunity entirely to the courts and eliminate the role of the Department of State in the matter.

The operative provision in point in the pending bill is Section 1602. See Documentary Supplement. The letter of transmittal of the proposed bill contains comments on its effect in this respect which read as follows:

> The central principle of the draft bill is to make the question of a foreign state's entitlement to immunity an issue justiciable by the courts, without participation by the Department of State. As the situation now stands, the courts normally defer to the views of the Department of State, which puts the Department in the difficult position of effectively determining whether the plaintiff will have his day in court. If the Department suggests immunity, the court will normally honor the suggestion, and the case will be dismissed for want of jurisdiction. If the Department does not suggest immunity, the court may either take the silence of the Department as an indication that immunity is not appropriate or will determine the question itself, with due regard for the policy of the Department and the views expressed in the past by the courts. While the Department has attempted to provide internal procedures which will give both the plaintiff and the defendant foreign state a hearing, it is not satisfactory that a department, acting through administrative procedures, should in the generality of cases determine whether the plaintiff will or will not be permitted to pursue his cause of action. Questions of such moment appear particularly appropriate for resolution by the courts, rather than by an executive department.

> The transfer of this function to the courts will also free the Department from pressures by foreign states to suggest immunity and from any adverse consequences resulting from the unwillingness of the Department to suggest immunity. The Department would be in a position to assert that the question of immunity is entirely one for the courts.

> Plaintiffs, the Department of State, and foreign states would thus benefit from the removal of the issue of immunity from the realm of discretion and making it a justiciable question.

SECTION C. PROBLEMS OF PROCESS IN COURTS IN THE UNITED STATES

OSTER v. DOMINION OF CANADA

United States District Court, N.D. New York, 1956.
144 F.Supp. 746.[a]

BRENNAN, CHIEF JUDGE. The problem involved in each of the above actions is one of jurisdiction. The question is similar in each case and this decision will apply in each of the above entitled actions.

Practically, Canada is the defendant in each of the claims. It is suggested that the correct denomination of the defendant is "Her Majesty Queen Elizabeth II in Right of Canada, the Sovereign of Canada". No point is made however of any error in the titles as they appear.

As far as important here, the actions seek the recovery of money damages to property claimed to have been caused by the elevation of the water level of Lake Ontario. The damages demanded are large in amount and represent the claims of many United States citizens. Action, Civil 5704, purports to be a class action in that it attempts to recover damages for persons who are similarly situated. The factual background of the claims will be briefly referred to.

The international boundary line between the United States and Canada, near the City of Ogdensburg, N. Y., passes between Adams Island, which is in Canadian territory, and Les Galops Island, which is within the United States. Due to difficulties in navigation on the St. Lawrence River, negotiations were had between the United States and Canada whereby Canada constructed a dam known as the Gut Dam between the two islands with the apparent purpose of facilitating the passage of down-going vessels in the channel to the north of Adams Island. It was proposed that Canada build the dam which would, to some extent, be located upon United States territory. Negotiations were carried on between the two nations on a diplomatic level. Congressional approval to the erection of the dam was given. Plans therefor were approved in accordance with the statute, subject however to the condition quoted below—

> 2.—That if the construction and operation of the said dam shall cause damage or detriment to the property owners of Les Galops Island, or to the property of any other citizens of the United States, the government of Canada shall pay such amount of compensation as may be agreed upon between the said government and the parties damaged, or as may be awarded the said

a. Aff'd sub nom. Clay v. Dominion of   cert. denied 353 U.S. 936, 77 S.Ct. 813
     Canada, 238 F.2d 400 (2d Cir. 1956),   (1957).

parties in the proper court of the United States before which claims for damage may be brought.

Formal assurance of the acceptance of the condition was made by the Canadian authorities to the government of the United States or to the Secretary of War. The dam was thereafter constructed about 1903 and continued performing its functions until 1952 or 1953 when it was removed.

Jurisdiction in each action is based upon Title 28 U.S.C.A. §§ 1331 and 1332(a) (2) which sections refer to actions arising under the laws of the United States and actions based upon diversity of citizenship. In each of the actions a "suggestion" that this Court had no jurisdiction has been filed by the Ambassador of Canada to the United States.

* * *

* * * The burden of the suggestions filed in these cases is to the effect that the <u>defendant is a sovereign and is immune from suit in this Court</u>, such immunity not having been waived. It is also asserted in the suggestions filed that the service of process in these cases is insufficient to obtain jurisdiction over the person of the defendant.

* * * [I]t is concluded that there is a lack of jurisdiction and the actions should be dismissed.

These are in personam actions and the presence of the defendant is an essential element of the jurisdiction of this Court. * * * If there is a failure of jurisdiction, it arises either from insufficient service of process or the defendant's immunity from suit.

Service upon the defendant in each of these actions was made by the delivery of a copy of the summons and complaint to the Consul General of Canada or some one connected with his office at New York City. It is apparent from the whole record that the sufficiency of such service was disputed at the time. * * *

No authority exists for the service of process in a manner other than that set forth in the Federal Rules of Civil Procedure. Clark County, Nev. v. City of Los Angeles, D.C., 92 F.Supp. 28. Concededly there is no precedent which recognizes as valid the type of service of process made here. The argument that these actions came to the attention of the Canadian authorities and thereby performed their notice-giving function as referred to in Hickman v. Taylor, 329 U.S. 495, 67 S.Ct. 385, 91 L.Ed. 451, is unavailing since the above decision refers to the function of pleadings rather than to the function of process.

The limitations upon the authority of a consul is discussed in The Anne, 3 Wheat. 435, at page 446, 4 L.Ed. 428. In fact a photostat copy of the appointment of the consul upon whom service was made in these cases is found among the papers in the Oster action and his power is limited by the terms thereof to the protection of the interests of Canadian citizens within his consular district. He is in no sense a managing agent.

It is beyond argument that jurisdiction of the person in this type of action is a necessary requisite to the overall jurisdiction of the Court to adjudicate the claim submitted. Such jurisdiction must be acquired either by the service of process or by the defendant's appearance. Ex parte Republic of Peru, 318 U.S. 578, at page 587, 63 S.Ct. 793, 87 L.Ed. 1014. Here the defendant has not appeared in any manner in these actions and a consideration of the effect of a holding that service upon a consul is service upon a sovereign is sufficient to conclude that the service of process here is ineffective to obtain jurisdiction over the person of the defendant.

Having arrived at the above conclusion, it would seem unnecessary to discuss and decide whether or not the immunity, ordinarily granted to a friendly sovereign, is available to the defendant in these cases. * * *

The decision here rests upon the lack of jurisdiction over the person of the defendant. Such defect is sufficient authority for the dismissal of these cases. * * * Since there appears to be no chance of the curing of the defect, referred to above, by a proper service of process upon the defendant, each of the above actions will be and is dismissed and it is

So Ordered.

PETROL SHIPPING CORP. v. KINGDOM OF GREECE, MINISTRY OF COMMERCE

United States Court of Appeals, Second Circuit, 1966.
360 F.2d 103.[a]

J. JOSEPH SMITH, CIRCUIT JUDGE. Respondent Kingdom appeals from an order of the United States District Court for the Southern District of New York, Wilfred Feinberg, District Judge, directing it to proceed to arbitration. We find no error and affirm the order.

Petrol Shipping, as owner of the tanker Atlantis, entered into a written charter party with respondent dated February 12, 1960, in New York City, and agreed thereby to transport grain acquired by respondent from the United States government pursuant to an agreement between the two governments. * * *

* * * The ship sustained bottom damage at the discharge berth in Piraeus, allegedly due to an unsafe berth, but the charterer disclaimed responsibility. The shipowner alleged damages were about $287,000.

a.   Cert. denied 385 U.S. 931, 87 S.Ct. 291 (1966).

The charter party contained the following arbitration clause:

Should any dispute arise between Owners and the Charterers, the matter in dispute shall be referred to three persons at New York, one to be appointed by each of the parties hereto, and the third by the two so chosen; their decision or that of any two of them, shall be final, and for the purpose of enforcing any award, this agreement may be made a rule of the Court. The Arbitrators shall be commercial men.

By letter of September 29, 1961 the shipowner named its arbitrator, and demanded that the charterer appoint its; a further demand was made on December 15, 1961. Although respondent said that it had advised its Foreign Trade Administration in Washington to proceed, no arbitrator was named.

On January 14, 1963 Petrol brought this petition in the District Court for the Southern District of New York, under § 4 of the United States Arbitration Act, 9 U.S.C. § 4. Service of process was allegedly effected by ordinary mail to respondent's Ministry of Trade, State Purchase Directorate, Washington; to Becker & Greenwald, described as proctors for the Directorate; and to respondent's Ministry of Commerce, Purchase Directorate, New York City.

The charterer appeared specially, and submitted a suggestion of the Greek Ambassador, that as Greece was a friendly sovereign and therefore immune, the court lacked jurisdiction. No advice from the State Department was transmitted to the court. The District Court, Judge Dawson, denied the petition to compel arbitration on February 21, 1963, on the ground of sovereign immunity.

This judgment was affirmed by a panel of this court, 326 F.2d 117 (2 Cir. 1964), with Judge Clark dissenting, and suggesting the matter should be reversed and remanded to ascertain the position of the State Department. On rehearing en banc, 332 F.2d 370 (2 Cir. 1964), per curiam, the United States Department of Justice having submitted an amicus curiae brief, the matter was remanded for further development of facts. * * *

Before the District Court heard the case on remand, a panel of this court decided Victory Transport, Inc. v. Comisaria General de Abastecimientos y Transportes, 336 F.2d 354 (2 Cir. 1964), cert. den. 381 U.S. 934, 85 S.Ct. 1763, 14 L.Ed.2d 698 (1965), a case substantially similar in its facts to the present case, holding that a branch of the Spanish Ministry of Commerce could be sued without its consent in that suit, and despite its plea of immunity.

On remand to this case, the parties entered into a stipulation in lieu of a hearing, and introduced exhibits, including the Charter Party and certain documents of correspondence with the State Department. These documents were a request by the Greek Ambassador to the State Department for recognition of immunity and a letter from counsel for petitioner to the Legal Advisor of the State Department asking that the Department decline the Ambassador's request, and citing Victory Transport; the reply of the State Department, declining to recognize any sovereign immunity in the case, on the ground that the matter was jure gestionis, and referring the Ambassador to the Tate letter; and a reply of the Legal Advisor to counsel for petitioner, noting that the Department had declined to intervene.

The District Court requested an amicus curiae brief from the United States, but the government declined, in view of the controlling nature of Victory Transport. By opinion of June 4, 1965, the court directed the Kingdom to proceed to arbitration, refusing to recognize any immunity, relying on Victory Transport. 37 F.R.D. 437 (S.D. N.Y.1965). The Kingdom appeals.

The proper theoretical approach to the issues in this case as indicated by the brief of the United States as amicus curiae in the rehearing en banc. There, at page 17, the brief states,

> the immunity of sovereign did not present a "jurisdictional" defect such as improper service might. Under the Supreme Court's analysis [in Ex Parte [Republic of] Peru, 318 U.S. 578 [63 S.Ct. 793, 87 L.Ed. 1014] (1943)], it appears that in an action against a sovereign just as in any other suit, jurisdiction must be acquired either by service of process, or by the defendant's appearance in court, or in rem by seizure and control of property. Only after such jurisdiction is acquired, does the sovereign immunity defense property [sic] come into consideration. Instead of being a "jurisdictional" matter in the same sense as acquiring jurisdiction over a person or property, sovereign immunity presents a ground for relinquishing the jurisdiction previously acquired.

The first issues, then, deal not with immunity, but rather with jurisdiction in personam and the adequacy of service.

I. Jurisdiction

In Farr & Co. v. Cia Intercontinental de Navegacion, 243 F.2d 342 (2 Cir. 1957), this court held that in a suit under the Arbitration Act, where the parties had agreed to arbitrate and that "this submission may be made a rule of court by either party," by agreeing to arbitrate in New York a party "makes himself as amenable to suit as if he were physically present in New York." 243 F.2d at 347. Farr was followed in Orion S. & T. Co. v. Eastern States Petro. Corp. of Panama, 284 F.2d 419 (2 Cir. 1960), where the contract read, "for the purpose of enforcing awards this agreement shall be made a Rule of of [sic] Court." Although the suit was to compel arbitration, not to enforce an award, the court concluded that as in Farr the parties were as if physically present. We conclude that this states a rule of federal law, under the Arbitration Act.

Here the contract reads, "for the purpose of enforcing any award, this agreement may be made a rule of the Court." This is not appreciably different from the Orion contract, and as was said in Victory Transport, "the fine distinction" between a submission to enforce an award and a general submission "did not trouble this court in Orion * * *. Implicit in the agreement to arbitrate is consent to enforcement of that agreement." 336 F.2d at 363, 4.

The fact that one party is a branch of a foreign sovereign does not affect the conclusion that by entering into an arbitration agreement containing a submission such as here, the sovereign becomes amenable to suit. The question of immunity does not bear on the question of amenability, or personal jurisdiction. What Farr and Orion compel is that the Kingdom be treated as if it is physically present.

Moreover, the branch of respondent being sued is actually present. The Purchase Directorate maintains an office in New York, the one served; and it negotiated the charter party in New York, perhaps at that same office. Thus no doctrine of constructive presence by consent is necessary.

II. Service

Regardless, however, of what theory makes the Purchase Directorate present, service must be adequate. Here Farr again arguably controls. Farr may be read as meaning that an arbitration agreement such as construed there gives consent to service by any method designed to give adequate notice, as well as consent to personal jurisdiction, all as a matter of federal law. In fact, however, Farr says that applicable New York law is that consent to jurisdiction includes consent to service by any method consistent with due process.

Farr was a suit against a foreign corporation. Once it was held that service was adequate under New York law, that service sufficed in federal court by virtue of Rule 4(d)(7), Federal Rules of Civil Procedure. But that provision applies only to parties described in Rule 4(d)(1) or (3), and in our view respondent is not one of them.

It is, of course, not an individual, and Rule 4(d)(1) is inapplicable. Rule 4(d)(3) is not a catch-all for categories of parties not otherwise considered in Rule 4. The only entity covered in 4(d)(3) that is remotely like respondent is "other unincorporated association which is subject to suit under a common name." Beyond a doubt, if the Purchase Directorate is subject to suit, it may be sued under a common name, because a right under the Arbitration Act is surely "a substantive right existing under the * * * laws of the United States." Rule 17(b); see United Mine Workers of America v. Coronado Coal Co., 259 U.S. 344, 42 S.Ct. 570, 66 L.Ed. 975 (1922). The only question, then, is whether respondent is an association.

An association ought not to be defined to include an entity which lacks membership; respondent is essentially merely an agency of the Greek government. Neither Rule 4(d)(3), nor any other part of Rule

4, provides for service on such a party. And even if respondent were within Rule 4(d)(3), so that service according to state practice sufficed, since New York does not provide for service on respondent in the manner used here, there would be some difficulty in service.[1]

But the fact that Rule 4 does not provide a method for service on respondent does not mean that no service could be effective. Rule 83 permits "each district court, by action of a majority of the judges thereof" to "make and amend rules governing its practice not inconsistent with these rules." The Rule goes on to say, "in all cases not provided for by rule, the district courts may regulate their practice in any manner not inconsistent with these rules." See also 28 U.S.C.A. § 2071.

* * * And when there is no Federal Rule, and no local rule, the court may fashion one not inconsistent with the Federal Rules. Rule 83, supra; see In re United Corp., 283 F.2d 593 (3 Cir. 1960). * * *

But if neither service under Rule 4, or under a local rule was available here, and, for some reason, that part of Rule 83 authorizing ad hoc rules could not be used, then the court may fashion a rule outside the Federal Rules altogether, although this really amounts to the same thing as the ad hoc provisions of Rule 83. * * *

* * *

In our view there is no inconsistency with the Rules in approving service in this case by ordinary mail on the respondent at its address within the state. Since Rule 4 is silent as to respondent, there is no competing method of service authorized by the Rules which may be said to have been intended to be exclusive. And the fact that service here is in a method which the Rules do not adopt directly for other types of parties is not a compelling distinction; state rules often adopt differing modes of service, and these are used in the federal courts through Rule 4(d)(7).

---

1. There is no general provision for service on an association because under New York law an unincorporated association may not sue or be sued in its own name, Kirkman v. Westchester Newspapers, 261 App.Div. 181, 24 N.Y. S.2d 860 (1st Dept.1941), aff'd 287 N. Y. 373, 39 N.E.2d 919 (1942); Rosen v. Alleghany Corp., 133 F.Supp. 858, 867 (S.D.N.Y.1955), although it may be sued in the name of its president or treasurer, N. Y. General Associations Law, McKinney's Consol.Laws, c. 29, § 13. See Commentary accompanying McKinney's N.Y.C.P.L.R. 311, p. 499. Rule 4(d)(7) permits service "in the manner prescribed by the law of the state * * * for the service of a summons or other like process upon any such defendant [as appears in Rule 4(d) (3)] in an action brought in the courts of general jurisdiction of that state." For arbitration actions in New York service at the time of this suit was governed by N.Y.C.P.A. § 1450, providing for personal service, substituted service, or service as the court directs, none of which occurred here. Contrast N.Y.C.P.L.R. 403(c), which now governs service in all special proceedings. Since in our view respondent is not within Rule 4(d) (3), we do not decide whether the power to direct proper service under § 1450 subsumed the power to approve service later.

Since respondent is not one of the parties dealt with in Rule 4(d) (3), our decision in Arrowsmith v. United Press International, 320 F.2d 219 (2 Cir. 1963) that whether a foreign corporation has done enough to make it present so that service on it under that Rule and under Rule 4(d) (7) will give jurisdiction is to be determined in the first instance by state law, is not directly in point. Moreover, we do not equate "presence," or amenability to suit, with service of process, as our treatment of these two questions here indicates, and we regard Rule 4 as speaking to service alone, and not both service and amenability. * * *

* * * We deal here with a casus omissus both in the Federal Rules and in New York law. The absence of provision in either as to the manner of serving a foreign government cannot reasonably be considered to manifest a policy that no in personam actions against foreign sovereigns could ever be brought. It reflects rather that until the treaties and declarations of the decade beginning in 1948, restricting immunity of foreign governments to public or sovereign acts, see Victory Transport, Inc., supra, 336 F.2d at 357–358, there was no occasion to make provision for service upon them, and that legislators and rulemakers have failed to catch up in their procedural provisions with the more substantive developments in this field of law. Moreover, in sharp contrasts to diversity actions against foreign corporations, the fashioning of provisions with respect to service on foreign governments is a task peculiarly appropriate for federal courts. Compare Banco Nacional de Cuba v. Sabbatino, 376 U.S. 398, 423–427, 84 S.Ct. 923, 11 L.Ed.2d 804 (1964).

In the light of the above, we are not disposed to follow Oster v. Dominion of Canada, 144 F.Supp. 746 (N.D.N.Y.), aff'd 238 F.2d 400 (2 Cir. 1956), cert. den. 353 U.S. 936, 77 S.Ct. 813, 1 L.Ed.2d 759 (1957), or Purdy Co. v. Argentina, 333 F.2d 95 (7 Cir. 1964), cert. den. 379 U.S. 962, 85 S.Ct. 653, 13 L.Ed.2d 557 (1965), to the extent they hold that a sovereign cannot be served in federal court. See also Berlanti Const. Co. v. Republic of Cuba, 190 F.Supp. 126 (S.D.N.Y. 1960), where personal service in Havana, Cuba, on the Minister of the Presidency of the Republic of Cuba, was held invalid under Rule 4(d)(7).

This is not to say that service on the sovereign may be effected on any representative of the sovereign. See Hellenic Lines, Ltd. v. Moore, 345 F.2d 978 (D.C.Cir. 1965). We hold only that service on the branch which is a party to the contract sued on is sufficient.

Finally, it has not been suggested, nor do we believe, that the service here was inconsistent with due process.

III. Immunity

On the question of sovereign immunity this case is identical to Victory Transport, Inc., supra. There this court held that the claim of sovereign immunity would be denied when made by a branch of the Spanish Ministry of Commerce which entered into a voyage charter containing the same arbitration clause as here, for the transport of wheat purchased under the Agricultural Trade Development and Assistance Act, as here. Suit was to compel arbitration.

Moreover, although in Victory Transport, Inc. there had been no advice from the State Department to the court, here there is in evidence the letter from the Department to the Kingdom's representative, rejecting the claim of sovereign immunity, on the ground that "the acts on which the suit is brought are private acts (jure gestionis)," and appending the Tate letter adopting the restrictive theory of sovereignty.

Affirmed.

UNITED STATES, FEDERAL RULES OF CIVIL PROCEDURE, PROCESS

28 U.S.C., App., Rule 4.

(d) Summons: Personal Service. The summons and complaint shall be served together. The plaintiff shall furnish the person making service with such copies as are necessary. Service shall be made as follows:

(1) Upon an individual other than an infant or an incompetent person, * * *

(2) Upon an infant or an incompetent person, * * *

(3) Upon a domestic or foreign corporation or upon a partnership or other unincorporated association which is subject to suit under a common name, * * *

(4) Upon the United States, * * *

(5) Upon an officer or agency of the United States, * * *

(6) Upon a state or municipal corporation or other governmental organization thereof subject to suit, * * *

(7) Upon a defendant of any class referred to in paragraph (1) or (3) of this subdivision of this rule, it is also sufficient if the summons and complaint are served in the manner prescribed by any statute of the United States or in the manner prescribed by the law of the state in which the district court is held for the service of summons or other like process upon any such defendant in an action brought in the courts of general jurisdiction of that state.

(e) Same: Service Upon Party Not Inhabitant of or Found Within State. Whenever a statute of the United States or an order of court thereunder provides for service of a summons, or of a notice, or of an order in lieu of summons upon a party not an inhabitant of or found within the state in which the district court is held, service may be made under the circumstances and in the manner prescribed by the statute or order, or, if there is no provision therein prescribing the manner of service, in a manner stated in this rule. Whenever a statute or rule of court of the state in which the district court is held provides (1) for service of a summons, or of a notice, or of an order in lieu of summons upon a party not an inhabitant of or found within the state, or (2) for service upon or notice to him to appear and respond or defend in an action by reason of the attachment or garnishment or similar seizure of his property located within the state, service may in either case be made under the circumstances and in the manner prescribed in the statute or rule.

      *   *   *

(i) Alternative Provisions for Service in a Foreign Country.

(1) Manner. When the federal or state law referred to in subdivision (e) of this rule authorizes service upon a party not an inhabitant of or found within the state in which the district court is held, and service is to be effected upon the party in a foreign country, it is also sufficient if service of the summons and complaint is made: (A) in the manner prescribed by the law of the foreign country for service in that country in an action in any of its courts of general jurisdiction; or (B) as directed by the foreign authority in response to a letter rogatory, when service in either case is reasonably calculated to give actual notice; or (C) upon an individual, by delivery to him personally, and upon a corporation or partnership or association, by delivery to an officer, a managing or general agent; or (D) by any form of mail, requiring a signed receipt, to be addressed and dispatched by the clerk of the court to the party to be served; or (E) as directed by order of the court. Service under (C) or (E) above may be made by any person who is not a party and is not less than 18 years of age or who is designated by order of the district court or by the foreign court. On request, the clerk shall deliver the summons to the plaintiff for transmission to the person or the foreign court or officer who will make the service.

UNITED STATES, ILLINOIS CIVIL PRACTICE ACT, PROCESS

Ill.Rev.Stat.1968, ch. 110, §§ 16–17.

§ 16.   Personal service outside State

(1) Personal service of summons may be made upon any party outside the State. If upon a citizen or resident of this State or upon a person who has submitted to the jurisdiction of the courts of this State, it shall have the force and effect of personal service of summons with-

in this State; otherwise it shall have the force and effect of service by publication.

* * *

§ 17.   Act submitting to jurisdiction—Process

(1) Any person, whether or not a citizen or resident of this State, who in person or through an agent does any of the acts hereinafter enumerated, thereby submits such person, and, if an individual, his personal representative, to the jurisdiction of the courts of this State as to any cause of action arising from the doing of any such acts:

(a) The transaction of any business within this State;

(b) The commission of a tortious act within this State;

(c) The ownership, use, or possession of any real estate situated in this State;

(d) Contracting to insure any person, property or risk located within this State at the time of contracting;

(e) With respect to actions of divorce and separate maintenance, the maintenance in this State of a matrimonial domicile at the time the cause of action arose or the commission in this State of any act giving rise to the cause of action.

(2) Service of process upon any person who is subject to the jurisdiction of the courts of this State, as provided in this Section, may be made by personally serving the summons upon the defendant outside this State, as provided in this Act, with the same force and effect as though summons had been personally served within this State.

(3) Only causes of action arising from acts enumerated herein may be asserted against a defendant in an action in which jurisdiction over him is based upon this Section.

(4) Nothing herein contained limits or affects the right to serve any process in any other manner now or hereafter provided by law.

* * *

UNITED STATES, JURISDICTION OF FEDERAL DISTRICT COURTS

28 U.S.C. §§ 1331(a), 1332(a), 1333.

§ 1331.   Federal question; amount in controversy; costs

(a) The district courts shall have original jurisdiction of all civil actions wherein the matter in controversy exceeds the sum or value of $10,000, exclusive of interest and costs, and arises under the Constitution, laws, or treaties of the United States.

* * *

§ 1332.   Diversity of citizenship; amount in controversy; costs

(a) The district courts shall have original jurisdiction of all civil actions where the matter in controversy exceeds the sum or value of $10,000, exclusive of interest and costs, and is between—

(1) citizens of different States;

(2) citizens of a State, and foreign states or citizens or subjects thereof; and

(3) citizens of different States and in which foreign states or citizens or subjects thereof are additional parties.

* * *

§ 1333.   Admiralty, maritime and prize cases

The district courts shall have original jurisdiction, exclusive of the courts of the States, of:

(1) Any civil case of admiralty or maritime jurisdiction, saving to suitors in all cases all other remedies to which they are otherwise entitled.

(2) Any prize brought into the United States and all proceedings for the condemnation of property taken as prize.   * * *

CHEMICAL NATURAL RESOURCES, INC. v. REPUBLIC OF VENEZUELA

United States, Supreme Court of Pennsylvania, 1966.
420 Pa. 134, 215 A.2d 864, 877–880.[a]

[The opinion of the Court appears at p. 354 above.]

Concurring and Dissenting Opinion by MR. JUSTICE ROBERTS:
* * *

I dissent, too, from the majority's instruction to the court below to dissolve plaintiff's writ of attachment. In my view, such an order is entirely unnecessary. As the majority recites and the record clearly establishes, on October 24, 1963, the attachment was dissolved by direction of plaintiff. I, therefore, fail to find any legal basis or need for today's order to dissolve an attachment which has been dissolved and nonexistent for more than two years.

* * *

By virtue of the writ of attachment, the Sheriff of Philadelphia County seized the S.S. Ciudad De Valencia, a merchant ship registered in the name of a foreign corporation wholly owned by defendant, and served both the master and the Stockard Shipping and Terminal Corporation as garnishees.

a.   Cert. denied 385 U.S. 822, 87 S.Ct. 50 (1966).

Subsequently, some discussion between the parties having ensued, the attachment of the S.S. Ciudad De Valencia was dissolved "without prejudice" by direction of counsel for plaintiff. * * *

* * *

* * * [A] serious jurisdictional question is raised by plaintiff's ex parte dissolution of the attachment of the S.S. Ciudad De Valencia. Although defendant did not raise the matter of the dissolution of the attachment in its preliminary objections, it may and should be raised by this Court sua sponte. Sovereign immunity involves the exercise of restraint on the part of the court, in deference to the political arm of the government, with respect to jurisdiction which has once attached. If, because of some irregularity in the manner by which plaintiff has proceeded, neither defendant nor its property is properly before the court, then the question of sovereign immunity need not and should not be reached.

I see no justification for proceeding to a consideration of a question which, in my view, is not properly before us. The matter of defendant's claim to immunity should not be considered by this Court until the court below enters an order which is in legal effect adverse to and appealable by one of the parties. The issue which the majority prematurely reaches on the merits might well be obviated by a favorable ruling in the court below on defendant's jurisdictional objections or a finding that the ex parte dissolution of the attachment by plaintiff deprived the court of jurisdiction. I am even more opposed to such premature action when such is done through the medium of prohibition.

Appellant, in order to avoid the thrust of these arguments, urges that extraordinary intervention is required to prevent delay in the disposition of what it characterizes as "a public question of overriding importance." It contends that the delay attendant to the determination of its preliminary objections in the regular course of the proceedings is potentially injurious to the relations between our governments. It also seeks to concede that the dissolution of the attachment in no way affected any jurisdiction which may have been initially acquired thereby.

I am not convinced that defendant's arguments should carry the day. Defendant's view as to the effect of plaintiff's dissolution of the attachment is not dispositive. Foreign attachment is a matter governed by statute and the Rules of Civil Procedure. See Act of June 13, 1836, P.L. 568, § 43, 12 P.S. § 2861 et seq.; Pa.R.C.P. 1251–79. The parties may well not be empowered to depart from these provisions.

Plaintiff, in urging that jurisdiction was not lost by reason of its dissolution of the attachment, asserts that its action was pursuant to an understanding of the parties that the ship would be viewed as though remaining within the control of the attachment process and cites a number of cases in support of the proposition that such an agreement will suffice to support jurisdiction. However, the cases upon which plaintiff relies are not dispositive in that they arise under federal admiralty practice, not under our attachment procedure. Moreover, all appear to involve written stipulations between the parties that any final judgment would be respected by the "claimant." The effect of such stipulations is the creation of a contractual undertaking in lieu of bond. In the instant case, there is nothing of record to disclose any such undertaking between the parties. Therefore, a question is presented as to whether the court below retained a sufficient nexus with defendant or its property to ground jurisdiction. A determination as to the understanding of the parties, if such was the case, and its legal effect would appear required before this Court proceeds to hold that jurisdiction was not affected by the dissolution. I venture no view on the merits but believe the matter to be one requiring a determination by the court below in the first instance.

Any possible contention which might arise by reason of the restraint of defendant's property has been obviated by plaintiff's dissolution, *without bond*, of the S.S. Ciudad De Valencia. Defendant is as free to pursue its engagements, and has been so free for over two years, as it was prior to the commencement of this litigation. No affront should arise merely because defendant is required to seek relief in accordance with the demands of an orderly judicial system. In light of these considerations, the circumstances do not warrant the intrusion the majority makes today.

In my view, the only appropriate disposition is to remand the matter to the court below so that it may pass upon the effect of the dissolution of the attachment * * *

* * *

NEW YORK & CUBA MAIL S. S. CO. v. REPUBLIC OF KOREA

United States District Court, S.D. New York, 1955.
132 F.Supp. 684.

WEINFELD, DISTRICT JUDGE. On filing this suit in admiralty to recover for damages sustained by libellant's steamship, process in personam with writ of foreign attachment issued pursuant to which respondent's funds on deposit in New York banks were attached.

The respondent, Republic of Korea, appearing specially, moves to vacate the attachment and to dismiss the libel on the ground that as a recognized sovereign and independent state it is immune from suit.

The libel alleges that on April 18, 1951 libellant's ship, The Virginia City Victory, which had unloaded a cargo of rice at the port of

Pusan, Korea, was damaged by respondent's lighter which had assisted in the unloading operation. The respondent alleges that the cargo of rice had been acquired by it—not for sale, resale, barter or exchange —but for free distribution to its civilian population and military personnel in Korea.

     * * *

Following the attachment of the bank accounts in the pending suit the Korean Ambassador made formal representation to the Secretary of State of the United States requesting the assistance of the State Department in establishing the immunity of the Republic of Korea from suit, and of its funds from attachment. On this motion the United States Attorney for the Southern District of New York, acting under the direction of the Attorney General, has filed a suggestion with the Court. Attached to the suggestion are copies of the Ambassador's communication to the Secretary of State and the latter's letter to the Attorney General setting forth the Department's position.

     * * * [T]he following quotation therefrom is appropriate for consideration of the issue posed on this application:

> The letter from the Secretary of State of the United States to the Attorney General of the United States recognizes that under international law property of a foreign government is immune from attachment and seizure, and that the principle is not affected by a letter dated May 19, 1952, from the Acting Legal Adviser to the Department of State to the Acting Attorney General of the United States, in which the Department of State indicated its intention to be governed by the restrictive theory of sovereign immunity in disposing of requests from foreign governments that immunity from suit be suggested in individual cases. The Department of State accordingly has requested that a copy of the note of the Ambassador of Korea be presented to the Court and that the Court be informed of the Department of State's agreement with the contention of the Ambassador that property of the Republic of Korea is not subject to attachment in the United States.

> The Department of State, however, has not requested that an appropriate suggestion of immunity be filed, inasmuch as the particular acts out of which the cause of action arose are not shown to be of purely governmental character.

Thus the State Department has taken a direct and unequivocal position with respect to the Republic of Korea's claim that its funds are immune from attachment, but has declined to make the requested suggestion of immunity from suit, asserting that upon the facts as presented it does not appear the claim rests upon acts of a purely governmental character.

     * * *

   *   *   * Lest an untoward incident disturb amicable relations between the two sovereigns, it has long been established that the Court's proper function is to enforce the political decisions of our Department of State on such matters. This course entails no abrogation of judicial power; it is a self-imposed restraint to avoid embarrassment of the executive in the conduct of foreign affairs.

The suggestion before me states explicitly that the principle of the immunity of a foreign government's property from attachment and seizure is not affected by the State Department's favorable attitude towards the restrictive theory of sovereign immunity, and that the Department is in agreement with the respondent's contention that its property "is not subject to attachment in the United States." Thus by its own interpretation of its liberal policy against unrestricted immunity, the Department of State declares in unmistakable language that it adheres to the doctrine that the property of a foreign government is immune from attachment. Indeed the principle is so well established that but for the letter of May 19, 1952 its applicability here could hardly be open to doubt. To borrow a phrase, "Deposits may be the life-blood necessary for national existence."   *   *   *

   *   *   *

Since jurisdiction here rests on the seizure under the writ of attachment, the lifting of the attachment makes it unnecessary for the Court to decide the interesting question of whether the Republic of Korea would otherwise be entitled to immunity from suit even under the restrictive theory.   *   *   *

The motion to vacate the attachment is granted.

   *   *   *

IL precludes levy by attachment or property

WEILAMANN v. CHASE MANHATTAN BANK

United States, New York Supreme Court, 1959.
21 Misc.2d 1086, 192 N.Y.S.2d 469.

[An action in aid of a warrant of attachment was issued against property of the USSR (accounts in defendant bank). The USSR made a claim, through the United States Department of State, that its property in the bank was immune from seizure under the warrant of attachment. A portion of the Court's opinion appears below.]

   *   *   *

   *   *   * The Department of State has recognized this claim of the USSR; and, through the U. S. Attorney for Southern District of New York, has filed in this action a suggestion of interest of the United States to the effect that property of the USSR in the United States is immune "from execution or other action analogous to execution" and that, "this court should proceed forthwith to release any property of the State of the Union of Soviet Socialist Republics hitherto attached in this proceeding and to deny any pending motion for execution or action analogous to execution."

*   *   *

It is true that the suggestion of interest indicating the position of the Department of State would not deprive this court of determining any question left open by such Department for decision by this court.   *   *   *   In this connection, the plaintiffs contend that the Department of State has heretofore recognized a distinction between "immunity from jurisdiction" and "immunity from execution"; that, consequently, it has been its position not to extend the doctrine of immunity so as to bar an attachment of property of a foreign nation for purpose of obtaining jurisdiction, but that its policy was merely directed to opposing the execution of a judgment against the property of a foreign nation.   In this connection, the plaintiffs point out that the suggestion of interest filed herein is stated to be based upon a position of the State Department that the property of the USSR should be "immune from execution or other action analogous to execution."   Thus, the plaintiffs argue that this court should retain jurisdiction to determine whether or not this action is to be regarded as a proceeding looking toward the execution of a judgment in favor of the plaintiff Weilamann.   In this connection, the plaintiffs contend that this action, being one in aid of an attachment, is merely a step in the court toward the perfecting of the attachment for the purpose of vesting the court with jurisdiction, and, therefore, may not be said to constitute action looking toward the execution of a judgment against the USSR.

Now, it does appear that the former action of the plaintiff Weilamann against the USSR, on default of appearance of the latter, has proceeded to judgment in plaintiff's favor for the sum of $77,154.66. Under these circumstances, a recovery by the said plaintiff and the sheriff in the action now brought by them in aid of the attachment would result in the application of the funds from the attached bank accounts to the satisfaction of the judgment. See, Civil Practice Act, § 943 and § 922, subd. 3. Thus, the proceeding with this action here is, in effect, the taking of action for the purpose of the execution of a judgment.

In any event, it is clear that we should not be concerned here with classifying this particular action for the purpose of determining whether or not, technically speaking, under the law of this state, it is in the nature of "action analogous to execution on the property" of the USSR. We are to be concerned solely with the position which is taken by the State Department; and its position with respect to the immunity of the particular bank accounts must be honored by this court. The court may not proceed contrary thereto in this or any similar case and thereby jeopardize international relations. Here, the

State Department's position, as indicated by the suggestion of interest and the letter of March 9, 1959, is clearly to the effect that this court should deny to plaintiffs the relief sought in this action.

The complaint is dismissed without costs.   *   *   *

Pending United States legislation on sovereign immunity. Section 1608 of the proposed legislation requires two methods of notice: (1) mailing of a copy of the summons and of the complaint to the ambassador and (2) transmittal of the same documents, through diplomatic channels, to the ministry of foreign affairs of the defendant state. The initiation of actions through attachment would be no longer appropriate if the pending bill should become law.

SECTION D.   PROBLEMS OF SATISFACTION OF JUDGMENTS

RESTATEMENT OF THE FOREIGN RELATIONS LAW OF THE UNITED STATES

Reporters' Notes to Section 69 (1965).*

2.   *Immunity from execution.*

*   *   *

The view indicated by the State Department in the Weilamann case, that execution by levy upon the attached property is precluded by international law, appears to be inconsistent with the views expressed in a number of cases in foreign states. In these states, a distinction is made between property of the state connected with its public acts (or political acts or acts jure imperii) and its private acts (or acts of a civil nature or acts jure gestionis, which include commercial acts). Property of the state connected with its public acts is entitled to immunity from execution. Property of the state connected with its private acts is not.

Cases supporting execution upon property of a state that is connected with its private acts include: Soviet Distillery in Austria Case, Administrative Court, Austria, Jan. 13, 1954, 9 VwGH (F)5 (1954), 83 Clunet 86 (1956), [1954] Int'l L. Rep. 101; Socobelge v. Greek State, Civil Tribunal of Brussels, Belgium, April 30, 1951, 79 Clunet 244, [1951] Int'l L.Rep. 3 (No. 2), 47 Am.J.Int'l L. 508 (1953); Decision of the Supreme Court, Czechoslovakia, Decision No. R.I. 305/28,

May 8, 1928, 64 Clunet 394 (1937), 26 Am.J.Int'l L.Supp. 585 (1932);
Jacovidis v. Monopoly of Tobacco in Turkey, Court of Appeals (M.C.),
Egypt, Jan. 22, 1930, 42 Bulletin de Legislation et de Jurisprudence
Egyptiennes 212 (1929–1930); Egyptian Delta Rice Mills Co. v. Com-
isaria General de Abastecimientos y Transportes de Madrid, Com-
mercial Tribunal of Alexandria (M.C.), Egypt, March 29, 1943, 55
Bulletin de Legislation et de Jurisprudence Egyptiennes 114 (1942–
1943), [1943–1945] Ann.Dig. 103 (No. 27); Procureur Général près
la Cour de Cassation v. Vestwig, Cour de Cassation, France, Feb. 5,
1946, [1947] Sirey I. 137, 73–76 Clunet 1 (1946–1949), [1946] Ann.
Dig. 78 (No. 32); State of Yugoslavia v. S. A. Sogerfin, Supreme
Court, Switzerland, Oct. 7, 1938, [1939] S.J. 327; U. A. R. v. Dame
X., Supreme Court, Switzerland, Feb. 10, 1960, 55 Am.J.Int'l L. 167
(1961), 88 Clunet 459 (1961); see also Kingdom of Greece v. Banque
Julius Bar, Tribunal Federal, Switzerland, June 6, 1956, 82 R.O. 75
(1956).

It does not appear that states whose property involved with private acts has been executed upon have as a rule protested against the
execution as being a violation of international law. See Lauterpacht,
The Problem of Jurisdictional Immunities of Foreign States, 28 Brit.
Yb.Int'l L. 220, 242–243 (1951). From an examination of the cases
in point, a number of writers have concluded that there is no rule of
international law prohibiting execution upon property of a state connected with its private acts. See Lalive, L'Immunité de Juridiction
des Etats et des Organisations Internationales, 84 Rec. des Cours 205,
274–75 (1953); Garcia Mora, Sovereign Immunity of Foreign States
and its Recent Modifications, 42 Va.L.Rev. 335, 359 (1956); Sorensen,
Principes de Droit International Public, 101 Rec. des Cours 1, 172
(1960).

In certain situations the United States approves the subjecting
to execution of state-owned property that is connected with its commercial activities. Indications to this effect are to be found in international agreements to which it is a party. Between 1948 and 1958,
the United States concluded treaties with fourteen states, each of
which provides that state enterprises engaged in business activities
in the territory of the other cannot claim immunity from execution
upon their property. See, for example, Article XVIII(3) of the
Treaty of Friendship, Commerce and Navigation with Israel of August 23, 1951, [1954] 1 U.S.T. & O.I.A. 550, T.I.A.S. No. 2948, 219
U.N.T.S. 237. The United States has also ratified the Convention on
the Territorial Sea and the Contiguous Zone of April 27, 1958, and
under Article 21 of the Convention, measures of enforcement may
be taken against government vessels operated for commercial purposes
while they are exercising the right of innocent passage, to the same
extent that they may be taken against private vessels. U.N.Doc.
A/Conf.13/L.38, 38 Dep't State Bull. 1111 (1958), 52 Am.J.Int'l L.
834 (1958).

HARRIS AND CO. ADVERTISING, INC. v.
REPUBLIC OF CUBA

United States, District Court of Appeal of Florida, 1961.
127 So.2d 687.

BARNS, PAUL D., ASSOCIATE JUDGE. The appellant-plaintiff, Harris and Company Advertising, Inc., brought an action in assumpsit against the appellee-defendant, Republic of Cuba, and procured the issuance and execution of various writs of attachment against chattels of the defendant and attachments by garnishment of debts owing the defendant by various garnishable defendants. The action was in personam but the remedy sought was in rem; hence a quasi-in-rem action.

Thereafter, a pseudo motion to dismiss was filed on July 15, 1960; and motions to strike said motion to dismiss were filed July 26, 1960. On July 26, 1960, plaintiff's attorneys gave notice of a hearing of all pending motions, said hearing to be on July 27th. At said hearing, the judge sustained the motion to dismiss and overruled the motions to strike the motion to dismiss, and orders were entered accordingly.

After the conclusion of the foregoing hearing, an ex parte motion to dissolve excessive attachments was presented to the judge by one not a party to the action, and an order was made, on July 27, 1960, dissolving all attachments and garnishments other than the attachment by garnishment of some $98,000 in United States currency held by the Florida National Bank & Trust Company.

Thereafter, on August 3, 1960, the plaintiff entered its appeal from (1) the order dismissing the action; (2) the order dissolving writs of attachment and garnishment as excessive; and (3) the order denying plaintiff's motions to strike the motion to dismiss.   *   *   *
    *   *   *

It is well known that the traditional rule of international law denied one sovereign the right to sit in court over another sovereign.
*   *   *

        *   *   *

In this country, the Department of State, in the well-known Tate letter, made clear its position that it will not intervene in favor of sovereign immunity in cases where non-governmental functions are involved.   *   *   *

In this case, it appears that the defendant, through its agency, established to promote the business of tourism (Instituto Nacional de la Industria Turistica), hired the plaintiff's advertising agency to do promotional work in this country. From the uncontroverted allegations in the complaint it appears that the defendant has, through the "Instituto Nacional," hired plaintiff to perform services on its behalf, namely, promote the industry of tourism in this country. This shows clearly that such activity is not governmental in character. First of all, it is evident that the functions of promoting tourism in Cuba have been, at least within this country, simply subcontracted to a local private corporation, which could not have been a governmental function; furthermore, governmental functions as contrasted with commercial activities, could not have exercised within this country without an express consent of the Government of the United States. Just because it was purely commercial in nature, it was possible to have it performed in this country.

Thus it appears that the activity on the part of the defendant government is clearly non-governmental in nature and, consequently, cannot be invoked as a ground for sovereign immunity.

A final problem would remain, namely that of the nature of assets attached under the writ in the court below. In this regard, no special allegation has been made by the defendant that the property attached would be immune and, thus, could not have been used to establish quasi-in-rem jurisdiction and, in case plaintiff should be successful, for the satisfaction of its demand. Since the case of The Schooner Exchange v. M'Faddon, 1812, 7 Cranch 116, 11 U.S. 116, 3 L.Ed. 287, it is well settled that only governmental instrumentalities, like warships, are exempt from the jurisdiction of our courts. * * *

In the present case, deposits in various banks have been attached, which, until it is shown by preponderance of the evidence that they are directly related to activities jure imperii, cannot be deemed immune from the powers of the courts within the territories of which they are kept by the decision of the foreign government itself. It would not be compatible with the principle of judicial powers of a sovereign nation if funds deposited as private funds in a private bank in this country, particularly if derived, used, or intended to be used in business type of activities here, would be clothed in a veil radiating foreign sovereignty.

* * *

Appellee's contention is that Chapter 48, Fla.Stat., F.S.A., providing for constructive service of process, has no application when the defendant is a foreign nation. Section 48.01(1) specifically makes said chapter applicable against the parties "mentioned in § 48.02" (ib) in any action "(7) in which there shall have been issued and executed any writ of replevin, garnishment or attachment"; and § 48.02, supra, authorizes process by publication "upon any party, natural or corporate," including "any corporation or other legal entity." The Republic of Cuba is an entity because it exists and it is a legal entity because it exists in contemplation of law and it is a "party" to the action. To hold otherwise would require us to hold that a nation is not a legal entity. A foreign nation is within the scope of the class of parties who may be served with process by publication, but, of course, any judgment rendered adverse to such nation may not be in personam unless the court acquires personal jurisdiction of the defendant.

*   *   *

Reversed and remanded.

F. W. STONE ENGINEERING CO. v. PETROLEOS MEXICANOS

United States, Supreme Court of Pennsylvania, 1945.
352 Pa. 12, 42 A.2d 57.

OPINION BY MR. JUSTICE JONES, April 13, 1945:

The question in this case is whether the State Department's recognition of the defendant corporation as a governmental instrumentality of the Republic of Mexico, with an attendant right to sovereign immunity, required the court below to release property of the defendant from the grasp of the court's process, viz., a writ of foreign attachment issued by the plaintiff against funds of the defendant on deposit in a local bank. The learned judge of the court below thought that it did and, accordingly, entered an order dissolving the writ, from which the plaintiff appeals.

By an agreement entered into November 16, 1938, the plaintiff, an Ohio corporation, agreed to supply, according to specifications, the equipment and materials necessary for the construction by the defendant, under the plaintiff's supervision, of a manufacturing plant in Mexico for the defendant's use. On December 7, 1938, the parties to the construction agreement, together with the Butler County National Bank & Trust Company, of Butler, Pennsylvania, entered into an escrow agreement. By the terms of that agreement the defendant was required to deposit with the bank, as escrow agent, the sum of $125,000 to secure payment to the plaintiff of the sums due for the purchase of the equipment and materials necessary for the construction of the defendant's plant under the contract. The escrow agreement provided that the last $50,000 of the money so deposited was not to be paid to the plaintiff until certification by the latter to the escrow agent that all of the terms of the construction contract had been complied with and a like certification by the defendant that the completed plant fulfilled the specifications and requirements of the contract. All but $25,000 of the money deposited in escrow had been paid to the plaintiff by August 18, 1944. On that date, the plaintiff, claiming to have complied with all of the terms of the construction contract and having so certified to the escrow agent, caused the balance on deposit to be attached by virtue of a writ of foreign attachment issued out of the court below against the defendant and summoning the depositary bank as garnishee. The issue here involved is unrelated to any controversy as to the plaintiff's performance of the construction contract. The sole question is whether the court below had jurisdiction to entertain the attachment proceeding in view of the following admitted or undenied facts.

On October 2, 1944, the Mexican Charge d'Affairs ad interim addressed a communication to the Honorable Cordell Hull, Secretary of State, informing him of the attachment involved in this case and requesting that the court "be apprised of the immunity of Petroleos Mexicanos and of its funds from suit and attachment". * * *

As a result of the communication from the Mexican Charge d'Affairs, Secretary Hull on October 4, 1944, addressed a letter to the Honorable Francis Biddle, Attorney General of the United States, which, in part here material, reads as follows: "The [State] Department accepts as true the statements made by the Charge d'Affairs ad interim of Mexico that the defendant, Petroleos Mexicanos, is a public agency or instrumentality of the sovereign state of Mexico; and I may add that it has heretofore been recognized as such by this Government. Consequently, this Government recognizes and allows the claim of the Government of Mexico that Petroleos Mexicanos is immune from suit and its property from attachment. * * * "

* * *

When the Department of State makes known its determination with respect to political matters growing out of or incidental to our Government's relations with a friendly foreign state, it is the duty of the courts to abide by the status so indicated or created and to refrain from making independent inquiries into the merit of the State Department's determination or from taking any steps that might prove embarrassing to the Government in the handling of its foreign relations. * * *

* * *

Concluding, as we do, that the goods and property of the defendant in the instant case are immune from seizure or detention under process issuing out of a court of this State, but one question remains and that is whether the defendant's right to immunity was waived. The learned judge of the court below was unable to find any waiver; and, likewise, neither can we, either in the construction contract, the escrow agreement or elsewhere in the record now before us. * * *

* * *

The order appealed from is affirmed.

---

1. *What is the worth of a judgment which cannot be executed?* At the conclusion of a chapter designed to provide a detailed examination of the immunity of a foreign state from the jurisdiction of another and of the handling of the issue in the United States, you find you probably will not be able to execute a judgment against a foreign

state in American courts even if you were fortunate enough to obtain one in the first place.

Was it ever important then to secure a judgment at all? Would it be just as sensible to present the claim to the Department of State and let it be settled through diplomatic channels? Or should the question be reversed and be phrased why should a foreign state ever bother to plead immunity since it knows that even if a judgment should be given against it, it is not possible for the plaintiff to secure execution on the judgment?

There are two answers to these questions. The first is that states, like individuals, have credit ratings, and outstanding judgments are always an embarrassment and affect their ability to conduct commercial transactions. The second is that litigation for a foreign state is in the hands of domestic lawyers and lawyers cannot resist, as a rule, resorting to all defensive pleas available to them, including the plea of sovereign immunity.

2. *United States pending legislation and European convention on sovereign immunity.* In the legislation which has been introduced in the Congress of the United States, Section 1610 provides, subject to certain qualifications, that property held by a foreign state for commercial purposes should be available for the satisfaction of judgments rendered in connection with commercial activities. In the letter of transmittal of the draft bill, the change from the present situation is described as follows:

> Under the present law, a plaintiff who is able to bring his action against a foreign state because it relates to a commercial act (jure gestionis) of that state may be denied the fruits of his judgment against the foreign state. The immunity of a foreign state from execution has remained absolute. The draft bill would permit execution on the assets of a foreign state if the foreign state had waived its immunity from execution or if the assets were held for commercial purposes in the United States. The plaintiff could thus recover against commercial accounts, but not against those maintained for governmental purposes. The successful plaintiff would also be precluded from levying on funds deposited in the United States in connection with central banking activities and on military property.

In the European convention, Article 23 provides that no measures of execution may be taken against the property of a contracting state in the territory of another, except where and to the extent that the contracting state has expressly consented to execution in writing in any particular case. But Article 20, subject to qualifications in Articles 21 and 22, provides that a contracting state "shall give effect to a judgment against it by a court of another contracting state." Hence there is no need for measures of execution in the territory of the state where the judgment was rendered, so far as concerns the parties to the convention.

Chapter 6

THE ACT OF STATE DOCTRINE

Judicial disinclination to pass on the legitimacy of an otherwise determinative rule of foreign law. Courts in one state are sometimes faced with this problem: a private party claims against another private party, and the defendant says that plaintiff has no case under the legal rule of another state that should apply to the issue. Plaintiff rejoins that the foreign rule is invalid and therefore should not be applied. The plaintiff may make this contention in a normal conflict of laws context, i. e., that the foreign rule, although a part of the everyday legal system of the other state, is so deeply shocking to fundamental values as seen at the forum as to require rejection as against the "public policy" of the forum. But, if circumstances warrant, the plaintiff may contend that the foreign rule is unconstitutional in the foreign legal system or that the rule violates international law.

If the plaintiff contends along the first line, the issue is joined in an entirely private law context; and the forum court will not ordinarily be apprehensive that its decision will be taken as intrusive or insulting in the foreign state.

But if the foreign rule stems from some fairly extraordinary exercise of sovereignty by the foreign state and the plaintiff is seeking to attack the fundamental validity of that course of conduct by the foreign state, the forum judge will become more cautious. When that happens, the problems considered in this Chapter arise.

In the Anglo-American legal world a legal consequence deriving from high-level state action—a legal result outside the ordinary field of private law—is given the rather awesome label, "Act of State." In Great Britain the term is usually, but not exclusively, used to refer to the principle that an Officer of the Crown when personally sued for an act committed abroad against a foreigner may defend that he acted at the Crown's command. (He is not allowed this defense as against an assertion of personal responsibility as to acts committed within British territory.) As to the use by courts in Britain of the principle of non-examination of the acts of a foreign state, see the United States Supreme Court's note 21 to its opinion in Banco Nacional de Cuba v. Sabbatino, p. 404.

The United States Supreme Court also makes brief reference in this note to the manner in which tribunals in civil law systems use the principle against examination of the legitimacy of an otherwise applicable foreign legal rule. The term "act of state," however, is rarely used in these systems.

Yet another problem of semantics arises, because the civil law systems will not apply an otherwise applicable foreign rule that is violative of the public order of the forum state, and this notion of "public order" is not the same as that of a common law court when, in a routine conflict of laws case it has to decide whether the foreign law should not be chosen to apply, because against the "public policy" of the forum. The civilian doctrine of "ordre public" concerns itself only with exceptional or highly significant manifestations of the foreign sovereign will and with whether in certain situations it clashes with an equally highly-held principle of proper governance and national interest in the forum state.

An unresolved question exists whether the widely-shared disinclination to declare invalid an act of governance of another state is, internationally, a principle of international relations or a rule of international law. Even if not required by international law, act of state is nonetheless significant in the international legal system.

In the United States the earlier cases on the act of state doctrine were of the classic sort mentioned at the outset, where the plaintiff and the defendant are both private parties and the plaintiff mounts the attack. The major cases in recent years, however, have involved a foreign state as plaintiff; and the defendant has attacked the legitimacy of the foreign law on which the plaintiff relies. In the older cases the immunity of a state was not involved at all. In the later cases, with the foreign state as plaintiff, inter-relationships between immunity as to counterclaims and act of state may be involved. In the most recent development, see Chapter 17, a private party is suing a state engaged in trade for an alleged invalid act of nationalization (nationalization is almost always deemed an act of state), and before the act of state (or ordre public) issue is reached, an issue of immunity from suit has to be resolved.

Note that the new legislation on sovereign immunity proposed to the United States Congress by the Department of State—see Documentary Supplement—contains a provision, § 1605(3), that property nationalized without compensation as required by international law and now in the United States, or a foreign state agency that itself has acted with respect to such property, will not be immune from suit in the United States in actions in which rights in such property are in issue. The Department of State seeks to make it clear that non-immunity under such circumstances would exist regardless of the applicability or non-applicability to the taking of the act of state doctrine.

SECTION A.   THE COURT–MADE DOCTRINE
IN THE UNITED STATES

JIMENEZ v. ARISTEGUIETA

United States Court of Appeals, Fifth Circuit, 1962.
311 F.2d 547.a

ESTES, DISTRICT JUDGE.   This is an appeal from the judgment of
the United States District Court for the Southern District of Florida,
Judge Wm. A. McRae, Jr., dated August 23, 1961, dismissing the original and amended petitions for habeas corpus filed by appellant, Mar-
cos Perez Jimenez, and discharging the original and amended orders
to show cause issued on the petitions for habeas corpus.   The petitions for habeas corpus incorporate by reference the entire file in an
international extradition proceeding under 18 U.S.C. § 3184 et seq.,
filed in the United States District Court for the Southern District
of Florida, Miami Division, on August 24, 1959, by Manuel Ariste-
guieta, Consul General of the Republic of Venezuela, on behalf of
appellee, the Republic of Venezuela (Venezuela), in which the return
to Venezuela of appellant, a former president of Venezuela, now in
Miami, Florida, is sought under the Treaty of Extradition between the
United States and Venezuela (43 Stat. 1698).

*   *   *

The extradition proceeding was concluded by orders entered by
Judge Whitehurst, under 18 U.S.C. § 3184, finding that the proof did
not establish probable cause on the charges of murder and participation in murder.   He further found that probable cause had been shown
as to each of the financial crimes which were separately and independently alleged in plaintiff's Second Amended Complaint and that
the acts charged constituted crimes named in the specified provisions
of the Treaty of Extradition, and he committed the appellant to the
custody of the appellee United States Marshal to await the action of
the Secretary of State under 18 U.S.C. § 3186.   The order of commitment was entered by Judge Whitehurst on June 16, 1961.   His
findings and order of certification to the Secretary of State, entered
June 23, 1961, attach a copy of the Second Amended Complaint in the
extradition proceeding, to which certain sections of the certification
order specifically refer.

Venezuela's Second Amended Complaint, upon which the extradition proceeding and orders under attack were based, charged appellant, chief executive of Venezuela (first as a member of a three-
man junta, then as provisional President, and later as President, having legal responsibility for the administration of the funds and con-

a.   Cert. denied sub nom. Jimenez v.
Hixon, 373 U.S. 914, 83 S.Ct. 1302
(1963).

tracting authority of Venezuela, with two distinct groups of crimes committed in Venezuela during the years 1948–1958, the first group composed of four charges of murder and participation in murder as an accessory before the fact, the second group comprised financial crimes for his own private personal gain. The financial crimes are separately and independently charged in the complaint and are based on certain alleged transactions briefly summarized as follows:

1.   The appellant secured commissions or kickbacks in ten specific instances on Venezuelan Government contracts, some of which the appellant himself had executed.

2.   Through a "front" or alter ego the appellant secured a portion of the compensation paid by the Venezuelan Government for two tracts of land expropriated by decrees promulgated by him.

3.   By his twenty per cent ownership of EVICSA, a construction company, the appellant secured a portion of the compensation paid by the Venezuelan Government on construction contracts with the appellant's Ministry of Development, with the connivance of two of his ministers, one of whom was head of that ministry.

4.   The appellant secured improvements on and maintenance of his private, personal estate at public expense at specified times.

The charges of financial crimes allege that the transactions numbered 1 through 4 above make appellant guilty of embezzlement or criminal malversation by a public officer as provided in paragraph 14 of Article II of the Treaty, guilty of fraud or breach of trust as provided in paragraph 20 of Article II of the Treaty, and that the transactions numbered 1 through 3 above make him guilty of receiving money or valuable securities knowing the same to have been unlawfully obtained as provided in paragraph 18 of Article II of the Treaty.

The same charges are pending in the Supreme Court of Justice (formerly the Federal Court), the highest court of Venezuela, upon petition of the Attorney General of Venezuela with a substantial quantity of supporting evidence. The Supreme Court of Justice determined that if the charges are proved they would constitute violations of the penal code of Venezuela and that such charges are crimes specified in the Treaty of Extradition Article II, paragraphs 14, 18 and 20; found that good cause had been shown for prosecution and issued its warrant of arrest. The proceedings before the Supreme Court of Justice, with a substantial amount of evidence from its record—all documentary—were transmitted to the United States through appropriate diplomatic channels. Venezuela invokes these Treaty provisions in its complaint and requisition for surrender of appellant.

Appellant contends that Judge McRae erred in not discharging appellant from custody on the grounds that: (1) Judge Whitehurst did not have jurisdiction to conduct the extradition proceeding,

(2) appellant was not accorded due process of law in the proceeding before Judge Whitehurst, sitting as extradition magistrate, (3) the acts for which appellant's extradition is sought are acts in the exercise of sovereign authority or acts of state the legality of which the judicial authorities of the United States have no authority to determine, (4) failure of the extradition magistrate to determine whether the claim for extradition was for any crime or offense of a political character or for acts connected with such crimes or offenses, (5) the decision of Judge Whitehurst was not based on legal, competent and adequate evidence, (6) the alleged financial crimes were not within the Treaty of Extradition, and (7) the extradition magistrate was without jurisdiction by virtue of Article XII of the Treaty of Extradition, inasmuch as the Venezuelan government had failed to lay legal evidence of criminality before the extradition magistrate within the two months prescribed by the Treaty.

      *   *   *

Appellant contends that the acts with which he is charged are "acts done in the exercise of or in color of his sovereign authority and by virtue of the law of nations as stated in Underhill v. Hernandez, 168 U.S. 250, 18 S.Ct. 83, 42 L.Ed. 456, was entitled to be discharged from custody inasmuch as the judicial authorities cannot review the acts done by a sovereign in his own territory to determine illegality".[6]

Seizing upon Venezuela's characterization of appellant as a "dictator" he argues that as a "dictator" he himself would be the sovereign —the government of Venezuela—and that all his acts constituting the financial crimes with which he is charged and as to which probable cause of guilt has been found are acts of state or sovereign acts, the legality of which the Act of State Doctrine precludes an extradition judge or magistrate from adjudicating.

Essentially the Act of State Doctrine is "the principle that the conduct of one independent government cannot be successfully ques-

---

6. Appellant relies on Subdivision (c) (4) of 28 U.S.C. § 2241 the habeas corpus statute, which provides that the writ shall extend to citizens and domiciliaries of a foreign state "in custody for an act done or omitted under any alleged right, title, authority, privilege, protection, or exemption claimed under the commission, order or sanction of any foreign state, or under color thereof, the validity and effect of which depend upon the law of nations."

This is only a jurisdictional provision conferring no substantive right on appellant to discharge from custody merely upon allegation of jurisdictional facts. See Horn v. Mitchell, 223 F. 549, affirmed 232 F. 819 (1 Cir. 1916), appeal dismissed 243 U.S. 247, 37 S.Ct. 293, 61 L.Ed. 700.

"The Act of State Doctrine, briefly stated, holds that American courts will not pass on the validity of the acts of foreign governments performed in their capacities as sovereigns within their own territories. * * * This doctrine is one of the conflict of laws rules applied by American courts; it is not itself a rule of International Law." Banco Nacional de Cuba v. Sabbatino, 2 Cir., 307 F.2d 845, p. 855.

"International law is derived indeed from the customs and usages of civilized nations, but its concepts are subject to generally accepted principles of morality whether most men live by these principles or not." Id., p. 860.

tioned in the courts of another * * *." Oetjen v. Central Leather Co., 246 U.S. 297, 303, 38 S.Ct. 309, 311, 62 L.Ed. 726 (1918).

Even though characterized as a dictator, appellant was not himself the sovereign—government—of Venezuela within the Act of State Doctrine. He was chief executive, a public officer, of the sovereign nation of Venezuela. It is only when officials having sovereign authority act in an official capacity that the Act of State Doctrine applies. Bernstein v. Van Heyghen Freres, S. A., 163 F.2d 246, 249 (2d Cir.1947), cert. den. 332 U.S. 772, 68 S.Ct. 88, 92 L.Ed. 357 (1947); Banco de Espana v. Federal Reserve Bank, 114 F.2d 438, 444 (2d Cir. 1940).

Appellant's acts constituting the financial crimes of embezzlement or malversation, fraud or breach of trust, and receiving money or valuable securities knowing them to have been unlawfully obtained as to which probable cause of guilt had been shown were not acts of Venezuela sovereignty. Judge Whitehurst found that each of these acts was "for the private financial benefit" of the appellant. They constituted common crimes committed by the Chief of State done in violation of his position and not in pursuance of it. They are as far from being an act of state as rape which appellant concedes would not be an "Act of State".

A policy underlying the Act of State Doctrine is that to adjudicate the validity of an act of a foreign government under its own law in the courts of the United States would "imperil the amicable relations between governments and vex the peace of nations." Oetjen v. Central Leather Co., supra.

The judiciary abstains from decision in the ordinary Act of State case in deference to the executive, the branch of government charged with international relations. In a comprehensive and discriminating opinion on the Act of State Doctrine by Judge Waterman of the Second Circuit, in Banco Nacional de Cuba v. Sabbatino, it was held that

> * * * when the executive branch of our Government announces that it does not oppose inquiry by American courts into the legality of foreign acts, an exception to the judicial abnegation required by the act of state doctrine has arisen.

In this extradition case the executive branch, through its representation of the appellee United States Marshal, has manifested its desire that the judiciary act and decide this case on its merits.

Underhill v. Hernandez does not support appellant's claim of sovereign immunity. In that case a citizen of the United States brought an action in United States courts for damages for unlawful detention and assault in Venezuela by soldiers in the revolutionary forces in Venezuela under the command of Hernandez. The Supreme Court held that Hernandez, as a military commander representing a de facto government in the prosecution of a war, was not civilly responsible for those acts; pointed out that Hernandez was not "actuated by malice or any personal or private motives;" and made it clear that its decision would have been otherwise had defendant's action been differently motivated, as is the case here. Judge Whitehurst expressly found that the acts of appellant establishing probable cause of guilt of the financial crimes were "for the private financial benefit of the defendant".

The very reason for this extradition case is that the United States has agreed with Venezuela for the extradition of persons charged with crimes enumerated in the Treaty. This Treaty deals expressly in paragraph 14 of Article II with embezzlement or criminal malversation by public officers. Appellant notes that a public officer is one who exercises "in part sovereign power". The two governments intended the tribunals to act when the accused is a public officer charged with crimes enumerated in the Treaty. The acts constituting crimes charged for which the extradition of appellant is sought are not "acts of Venezuela" as in Hernandez, and the Act of State Doctrine is no bar to this extradition proceeding or justification for the discharge from custody of appellant.

* * *

The record contains no reversible error and the judgment of the District Court dismissing the appellant's petition for habeas corpus and discharging the orders to show cause issued thereon is hereby Affirmed. The mandate of the Court will issue forthwith.

BANCO NACIONAL DE CUBA v. SABBATINO, RECEIVER

United States Supreme Court, 1964.
376 U.S. 398, 84 S.Ct. 923.a

MR. JUSTICE HARLAN delivered the opinion of the Court.

The question which brought this case here, and is now found to be the dispositive issue, is whether the so-called act of state doctrine serves to sustain petitioner's claims in this litigation. Such claims are ultimately founded on a decree of the Government of Cuba expropriating certain property, the right to the proceeds of which is here in controversy. The act of state doctrine in its traditional formulation precludes the courts of this country from inquiring into the validity of the public acts a recognized foreign sovereign power committed within its own territory.

a. See Chapter 12, Section A, for that part of the opinion which declares irrelevant the fact that the United States had severed diplomatic relations with Cuba.

I.

In February and July of 1960, respondent Farr, Whitlock & Co., an American commodity broker, contracted to purchase Cuban sugar, free alongside the steamer, from a wholly owned subsidiary of Compania Azucarera Vertientes-Camaguey de Cuba (C. A. V.), a corporation organized under Cuban law whose capital stock was owned principally by United States residents. Farr, Whitlock agreed to pay for the sugar in New York upon presentation of the shipping documents and a sight draft.

On July 6, 1960, the Congress of the United States amended the Sugar Act of 1948 to permit a presidentially directed reduction of the sugar quota for Cuba. On the same day President Eisenhower exercised the granted power. The day of the congressional enactment, the Cuban Council of Ministers adopted "Law No. 851," which characterized this reduction in the Cuban sugar quota as an act of "aggression, for political purposes" on the part of the United States, justifying the taking of countermeasures by Cuba. The law gave the Cuban President and Prime Minister discretionary power to nationalize by forced expropriation property or enterprises in which American nationals had an interest. Although a system of compensation was formally provided, the possibility of payment under it may well be deemed illusory. Our State Department has described the Cuban law as "manifestly in violation of those principles of international law which have long been accepted by the free countries of the West. It is in its essence discriminatory, arbitrary and confiscatory."

Between August 6 and August 9, 1960, the sugar covered by the contract between Farr, Whitlock and C. A. V. was loaded, destined for Morocco, onto the S. S. Hornfels, which was standing offshore at the Cuban port of Jucaro (Santa Maria). On the day loading commenced, the Cuban President and Prime Minister, acting pursuant to Law No. 851, issued Executive Power Resolution No. 1. It provided for the compulsory expropriation of all property and enterprises, and of rights and interests arising therefrom, of certain listed companies, including C. A. V., wholly or principally owned by American nationals. The preamble reiterated the alleged injustice of the American reduction of the Cuban sugar quota and emphasized the importance of Cuba's serving as an example for other countries to follow "in their struggle to free themselves from the brutal claws of Imperialism." In consequence of the resolution, the consent of the Cuban Government was necessary before a ship carrying sugar of a named company could leave Cuban waters. In order to obtain this consent, Farr, Whitlock, on August 11, entered into contracts, identical to those it had made with C. A. V., with the Banco Para el Comercio Exterior de Cuba, an instrumentality of the Cuban Government. The S. S. Hornfels sailed for Morocco on August 12.

Banco Exterior assigned the bills of lading to petitioner, also an instrumentality of the Cuban Government which instructed its agent in New York, Societe Generale, to deliver the bills and a sight draft in the sum of $175,250.69 to Farr, Whitlock in return for payment. Societe Generale's initial tender of the documents was refused by Farr, Whitlock, which on the same day was notified of C. A. V.'s claim that as rightful owner of the sugar it was entitled to the proceeds. In return for a promise not to turn the funds over to petitioner or its agent, C. A. V. agreed to indemnify Farr, Whitlock for any loss. Farr, Whitlock subsequently accepted the shipping documents, negotiated the bills of lading to its customer, and received payment for the sugar. It refused, however, to hand over the proceeds to Societe Generale. Shortly thereafter, Farr, Whitlock was served with an order of the New York Supreme Court, which had appointed Sabbatino as Temporary Receiver of C. A. V.'s New York assets, enjoining it from taking any action in regard to the money claimed by C. A. V. that might result in its removal from the State. Following this, Farr, Whitlock, pursuant to court order, transferred the funds to Sabbatino, to abide the event of a judicial determination as to their ownership.

Petitioner then instituted this action in the Federal District Court for the Southern District of New York. Alleging conversion of the bills of lading, it sought to recover the proceeds thereof from Farr, Whitlock and to enjoin the receiver from exercising any dominion over such proceeds. Upon motions to dismiss and for summary judgment, the District Court, 193 F.Supp. 375, sustained federal in personam jurisdiction despite state control of the funds. It found that the sugar was located within Cuban territory at the time of expropriation and determined that under merchant law common to civilized countries Farr, Whitlock could not have asserted ownership of the sugar against C. A. V. before making payment. It concluded that C. A. V. had a property interest in the sugar subject to the territorial jurisdiction of Cuba. The court then dealt with the question of Cuba's title to the sugar, on which rested petitioner's claim of conversion. While acknowledging the continuing vitality of the act of state doctrine, the court believed it inapplicable when the questioned foreign act is in violation of international law. Proceeding on the basis that a taking invalid under international law does not convey good title, the District Court found the Cuban expropriation decree to violate such law in three separate respects: it was motivated by a retaliatory and not a public purpose; it discriminated against American nationals; and it failed to provide adequate compensation. Summary judgment against petitioner was accordingly granted.

The Court of Appeals, 307 F.2d 845, affirming the decision on similar grounds, relied on two letters (not before the District Court) written by State Department officers which it took as evidence that the Executive Branch had no objection to a judicial testing of the

Cuban decree's validity. The court was unwilling to declare that any one of the infirmities found by the District Court rendered the taking invalid under international law, but was satisfied that in combination they had that effect. We granted certiorari because the issues involved bear importantly on the conduct of the country's foreign relations and more particularly on the proper role of the Judicial Branch in this sensitive area. 372 U.S. 905, 83 S.Ct. 717. For reasons to follow we decide that the judgment below must be reversed.

* * *

IV.

The classic American statement of the act of state doctrine, which appears to have taken root in England as early as 1674, Blad v. Bamfield, 3 Swans. 604, 36 Eng.Rep. 992, and began to emerge in the jurisprudence of this country in the late eighteenth and early nineteenth centuries, see, e. g., Ware v. Hylton, 3 Dall. 199, 230; Hudson v. Guestier, 4 Cranch 293, 294; The Schooner Exchange v. M'Faddon, 7 Cranch 116, 135, 136; L'Invincible, 1 Wheat. 238, 253; The Santissima Trinidad, 7 Wheat. 283, 336, is found in Underhill v. Hernandez, 168 U.S. 250, p. 252, 18 S.Ct. 83, at p. 84, where Chief Justice Fuller said for a unanimous Court:

MUTUAL RESPECT---

> Every sovereign State is bound to respect the independence of every other sovereign State, and the courts of one country will not sit in judgment on the acts of the government of another done within its own territory. Redress of grievances by reason of such acts must be obtained through the means open to be availed of by sovereign powers as between themselves.

Following this precept the Court in that case refused to inquire into acts of Hernandez, a revolutionary Venezuelan military commander whose government had been later recognized by the United States, which were made the basis of a damage action in this country by Underhill, an American citizen, who claimed that he had been unlawfully assaulted, coerced, and detained in Venezuela by Hernandez.

None of this Court's subsequent cases in which the act of state doctrine was directly or peripherally involved manifest any retreat from Underhill. See American Banana Co. v. United Fruit Co., 213 U.S. 347, 29 S.Ct. 511; Oetjen v. Central Leather Co., 246 U.S. 297, 38 S.Ct. 309; Ricaud v. American Metal Co., 246 U.S. 304; Shapleigh v. Mier, 299 U.S. 468, 57 S.Ct. 261; United States v. Belmont, 301 U.S. 324, 57 S.Ct. 758; United States v. Pink, 315 U.S. 203, 62 S.Ct. 552. On the contrary in two of these cases, Oetjen and Ricaud, the doctrine as announced in Underhill was reaffirmed in unequivocal terms.

Oetjen involved a seizure of hides from a Mexican citizen as a military levy by General Villa, acting for the forces of General Carranza, whose government was recognized by this country subsequent to the trial but prior to decision by this Court. The hides were sold to a Texas corporation which shipped them to the United States and assigned them to defendant. As assignee of the original owner, plaintiff replevied the hides, claiming that they had been seized in violation of the Hague Conventions. In affirming a judgment for defendant, the Court suggested that the rules of the Conventions did not apply to civil war and that, even if they did, the relevant seizure was not in violation of them. 246 U.S., at 301–302, 38 S.Ct. at 310. Nevertheless, it chose to rest its decision on other grounds. It described the designation of the sovereign as a political question to be determined by the legislative and executive departments rather than the judicial department, invoked the established rule that such recognition operates retroactively to validate past acts, and found the basic tenet of Underhill to be applicable to the case before it.

> The principle that the conduct of one independent government cannot be successfully questioned in the courts of another is as applicable to a case involving the title to property brought within the custody of a court, such as we have here, as it was held to be to the cases cited, in which claims for damages were based upon acts done in a foreign country, for it rests at last upon the highest considerations of international comity and expediency. To permit the validity of the acts of one sovereign State to be reëxamined and perhaps condemned by the courts of another would very certainly "imperil the amicable relations between governments and vex the peace of nations." Id., 246 U.S. at 303–304, 38 S.Ct. at 311.

In Ricaud the facts were similar—another general of the Carranza forces seized lead bullion as a military levy—except that the property taken belonged to an American citizen. The Court found Underhill, American Banana, and Oetjen controlling. Commenting on the nature of the principle established by those cases, the opinion stated that the rule

> does not deprive the courts of jurisdiction once acquired over a case. It requires only that, when it is made to appear that the foreign government has acted in a given way on the subject-matter of the litigation, the details of such action or the merit of the result cannot be questioned but must be accepted by our courts as a rule for their decision. To accept a ruling authority and to decide accordingly is not a surrender or abandonment of jurisdiction but is an exercise of it. It results that the title to the property in this case must be determined by the result of the action taken by the military authorities of Mexico * * *. 246 U.S., at 309, 38 S.Ct. at 314.

To the same effect is the language of Mr. Justice Cardozo in the Shapleigh case, supra, where, in commenting on the validity of a Mexican land expropriation, he said (299 U.S., at 471, 57 S.Ct. at 262): "The question is not here whether the proceeding was so conducted as to be a wrong to our nationals under the doctrines of international law, though valid under the law of the situs of the land. For wrongs of that order the remedy to be followed is along the channels of diplomacy."

In deciding the present case the Court of Appeals relied in part upon an exception to the unqualified teachings of Underhill, Oetjen, and Ricaud which that court had earlier indicated. In Bernstein v. Van Heyghen Freres Societe Anonyme, 2 Cir., 163 F.2d 246, suit was brought to recover from an assignee property allegedly taken, in effect, by the Nazi Government because plaintiff was Jewish. Recognizing the odious nature of this act of state, the court, through Judge Learned Hand, nonetheless refused to consider it invalid on that ground. Rather, it looked to see if the Executive had acted in any manner that would indicate that United States Courts should refuse to give effect to such a foreign decree. Finding no such evidence, the court sustained dismissal of the complaint. In a later case involving similar facts the same court again assumed examination of the German acts improper, Bernstein v. N. V. Nederlandsche-Amerikaansche Stoomvaart-Maatschappij, 2 Cir., 173 F.2d 71, but, quite evidently following the implications of Judge Hand's opinion in the earlier case, amended its mandate to permit evidence of alleged invalidity, 210 F.2d 375, subsequent to receipt by plaintiff's attorney of a letter from the Acting Legal Adviser to the State Department written for the purpose of relieving the court from any constraint upon the exercise of its jurisdiction to pass on that question.[18]

This Court has never had occasion to pass upon the so-called Bernstein exception, nor need it do so now. For whatever ambiguity may be thought to exist in the two letters from State Department officials on which the Court of Appeals relied,[19] 307 F.2d, at 858, is now

18. The letter stated:
    1. This government has consistently opposed the forcible acts of dispossession of a discriminatory and confiscatory nature practiced by the Germans on the countries or peoples subject to their controls.
       * * *
    3. The policy of the Executive, with respect to claims asserted in the United States for the restitution of identifiable property (or compensation in lieu thereof) lost through force, coercion, or duress as a result of Nazi persecution in Germany, is to relieve American courts from any restraint upon the exercise of their jurisdiction to pass upon the validity of the acts of Nazi officials. State Department Press Release, April 27, 1949, 20 Dept. State Bull. 592.

19. Abram Chayes, the Legal Advisor to the State Department, wrote on October 18, 1961, in answer to an inquiry regarding the position of the Department by Mr. John Laylin, attorney for amici:
    The Department of State has not, in the Bahia de Nipe case or elsewhere, done anything inconsistent with the position taken on the Cuban nationalizations by Secretary Herter. Whether or not these nationalizations will in the future be given effect in the United States is, of course, for the courts to determine. Since the Sabbatino case and other similar cases are at present before the courts, any comments on this question by the Department of State would be out of place at this time. As you yourself point out, statements by the executive

removed by the position which the Executive has taken in this Court on the act of state claim; respondents do not indeed contest the view that these letters were intended to reflect no more than the Department's then wish not to make any statement bearing on this litigation.

The outcome of this case, therefore, turns upon whether any of the contentions urged by respondents against the application of the act of state doctrine in the premises is acceptable: (1) that the doctrine does not apply to acts of state which violate international law, as is claimed to be the case here; (2) that the doctrine is inapplicable unless the Executive specifically interposes it in a particular case; and (3) that, in any event, the doctrine may not be invoked by a foreign government plaintiff in our courts.

V.

Preliminarily, we discuss the foundations on which we deem the act of state doctrine to rest, and more particularly the question of whether state or federal law governs its application in a federal diversity case.[20]

Act of State We do not believe that this doctrine is compelled either by the
Not inherent nature of sovereign authority, as some of the earlier decisions
Compelled seem to imply, see Underhill, supra; American Banana, supra; Oetjen,
By : supra, 246 U.S. at 303, 38 S.Ct. at 311, or by some principle of international law. If a transaction takes place in one jurisdiction and the forum is in another, the forum does not by dismissing an action or by applying its own law purport to divest the first jurisdiction of its territorial sovereignty; it merely declines to adjudicate or makes applicable its own law to parties or property before it. The refusal of one country to enforce the penal laws of another (supra, pp. 932–933) is a typical example of an instance when a court will not entertain a cause of action arising in another jurisdiction. While historic notions of sovereign authority do bear upon the wisdom of employing the act of state doctrine, they do not dictate its existence.

That international law does not require application of the doctrine is evidenced by the practice of nations. Most of the countries rendering decisions on the subject fail to follow the rule rigidly.[21]

branch are highly susceptible of misconstruction.

A letter dated November 14, 1961, from George Ball, Under Secretary for Economic Affairs, responded to a similar inquiry by the same attorney:

I have carefully considered your letter and have discussed it with the Legal Adviser. Our conclusion, in which the Secretary concurs, is that the Department should not comment on matters pending before the courts.

20. Although the complaint in this case alleged both diversity and federal question jurisdiction, the Court of Appeals reached jurisdiction only on the former ground, 307 F.2d at 852. We need not decide, for reasons appearing hereafter, whether federal question jurisdiction also existed.

21. In English jurisprudence, in the classic case of Luther v. James Sagor & Co., [1921] 3 K.B. 532, the act of state doctrine is articulated in terms not unlike those of the United States

No international arbitral or judicial decision discovered suggests that international law prescribes recognition of sovereign acts of foreign governments, see 1 Oppenheim's International Law, § 115aa (Lauterpacht, 8th ed. 1955), and apparently no claim has ever been raised before an international tribunal that failure to apply the act of state doctrine constitutes a breach of international obligation. If international law does not prescribe use of the doctrine, neither does it forbid application of the rule even if it is claimed that the act of state in question violated international law. The traditional view of international law is that it establishes substantive principles for determining whether one country has wronged another. Because of its peculiar nation-to-nation character the usual method for an individual to seek relief is to exhaust local remedies and then repair to the executive authorities of his own state to persuade them to champion his claim in diplomacy or before an international tribunal. See United States v. Diekelman, 92 U.S. 520, 524. Although it is, of course, true that United States courts apply international law as a part of our own in appropriate circumstances, Ware v. Hylton, 3 Dall. 199, 281; The Nereide, 9 Cranch 388, 423; The Paquete Habana, 175 U.S. 677, 700, 20 S.Ct. 290, the public law of nations can hardly dictate to a country which is in theory wronged how to treat that wrong within its domestic borders.

Despite the broad statement in Oetjen that "The conduct of the foreign relations of our Government is committed by the Constitution to the Executive and Legislative * * * Departments," 246 U.S., at 302, 38 S.Ct. at 311, it cannot of course be thought that "every case or controversy which touches foreign relations lies beyond judicial cognizance." Baker v. Carr, 369 U.S. 186, 211, 82 S.Ct. 691. The text of the Constitution does not require the act of state doctrine;

---

cases. See Princess Paley Olga v. Weisz, [1929] 1 K.B. 718. But see Anglo-Iranian Oil Co. v. Jaffrate, [1953] 1 Weekly L.R. 246, [1953] Int'l L.Rep. 316 (Aden Sup.Ct.) (exception to doctrine if foreign act violates international law). Civil law countries, however, which apply the rule make exceptions for acts contrary to their sense of public order. See, e. g., Ropit case, Cour de Cassation (France), [1929] Recueil Général Des Lois et Des Arrêts (Sirey) Part I, 217; 55 Journal Du Droit International (Clunet) 674 (1928), [1927–1928] Ann. Dig., No. 43; Graue, Germany: Recognition of Foreign Expropriations, 3 Am.J.Comp.L. 93 (1954); Domke, Indonesian Nationalization Measures Before Foreign Courts, 54 Am.J.Int'l L. 305 (1960) (discussion of and excerpts from opinions of the District Court in Bremen and the Hanseatic

Court of Appeals in N. V. Verenigde Deli-Maatschapijen v. Deutsch-Indonesische Tabak-Handelsgesellschaft m. b. H., and of the Amsterdam District Court and Appellate Court in Senembah Maatschappij N. V. v. Republiek Indonesie Bank Indonesia); Massouridis, The Effects of Confiscation, Expropriation, and Requisition by a Foreign Authority, 3 Revue Hellénique De Droit International 62, 68 (1950) (recounting a decision of the court of the first instance of Piraeus); Anglo-Iranian Oil Co. v. S. U. P. O. R. Co., [1955] Int'l L.Rep. 19 (Ct. of Venice), 78 Il Foro Italiano Part I, 719; 40 Blätter für Zürcherische Rechtsprechung No. 65, 172–173 (Switzerland). See also Anglo-Iranian Oil Co. v. Idemitsu Kosan Kabushiki Kaisha, [1953] Int'l L.Rep. 312 (High Ct. of Tokyo).

it does not irrevocably remove from the judiciary the capacity to review the validity of foreign acts of state.

The act of state doctrine does, however, have "constitutional" underpinnings. It arises out of the basic relationships between branches of government in a system of separation of powers. It concerns the competency of dissimilar institutions to make and implement particular kinds of decisions in the area of international relations. The doctrine as formulated in past decisions expresses the strong sense of the Judicial Branch that its engagement in the task of passing on the validity of foreign acts of state may hinder rather than further this country's pursuit of goals both for itself and for the community of nations as a whole in the international sphere. Many commentators disagree with this view;[22] they have striven by means of distinguishing and limiting past decisions and by advancing various considerations of policy to stimulate a narrowing of the apparent scope of the rule. Whatever considerations are thought to predominate, it is plain that the problems involved are uniquely federal in nature. If federal authority, in this instance this Court, orders the field of judicial competence in this area for the federal courts, and the state courts are left free to formulate their own rules, the purposes behind the doctrine could be as effectively undermined as if there had been no federal pronouncement on the subject.

We could perhaps in this diversity action avoid the question of deciding whether federal or state law is applicable to this aspect of the litigation. New York has enunciated the act of state doctrine in terms that echo those of federal decisions decided during the reign of Swift v. Tyson, 16 Pet. 1. In Hatch v. Baez, 7 Hun 596, 599 (N.Y. Sup.Ct.), Underhill was foreshadowed by the words, "the courts of one country are bound to abstain from sitting in judgment on the acts of another government done within its own territory." More recently, the Court of Appeals in Salimoff & Co. v. Standard Oil Co., 262 N.Y. 220, 224, 186 N.E. 679, 681, has declared, "The courts of one independent government will not sit in judgment upon the validity of the acts of another done within its own territory, even when such government seizes and sells the property of an American citizen within its boundaries." Cf. Dougherty v. Equitable Life Assurance Society, 266 N.Y. 71, 193 N.E. 897; Holzer v. Deutsche Reichsbahn-Gesellschaft, 277 N.Y. 474, 14 N.E.2d 798. But cf. Frenkel & Co. v. L'Urbaine Fire Ins. Co., 251 N.Y. 243, 167 N.E. 430. Thus our conclusions might

---

22. See, e. g., Association of the Bar of the City of New York, Committee on International Law, A Reconsideration of the Act of State Doctrine in United States Courts (1959); Domke, supra, note 21; Mann, International Delinquencies Before Municipal Courts, 70 L.Q.Rev. 181 (1954); Zander, The Act of State Doctrine, 53 Am.J.Int'l L. 826 (1959). But see, e. g., Falk, Toward a Theory of the Participation of Domestic Courts in the International Legal Order: A Critique of Banco Nacional de Cuba v. Sabbatino, 16 Rutgers L.Rev. 1 (1961); Reeves, Act of State Doctrine and the Rule of Law —A Reply, 54 Am.J.Int'l L. 141 (1960).

well be the same whether we dealt with this problem as one of state law, see Erie R. Co. v. Tompkins, 304 U.S. 64, 58 S.Ct. 817; Klaxon Co. v. Stentor Elec. Mfg. Co., 313 U.S. 487, 61 S.Ct. 1020; Griffin v. McCoach, 313 U.S. 498, 61 S.Ct. 1023, or federal law.

However, we are constrained to make it clear that an issue concerned with a basic choice regarding the competence and function of the Judiciary and the National Executive in ordering our relationships with other members of the international community must be treated exclusively as an aspect of federal law.[23] It seems fair to assume that the Court did not have rules like the act of state doctrine in mind when it decided Erie R. Co. v. Tompkins. Soon thereafter, Professor Philip C. Jessup, now a judge of the International Court of Justice, recognized the potential dangers were Erie extended to legal problems affecting international relations.[24] He cautioned that rules of international law should not be left to divergent and perhaps parochial state interpretations. His basic rationale is equally applicable to the act of state doctrine.

The Court in the pre-Erie act of state cases, although not burdened by the problem of the source of applicable law, used language sufficiently strong and broad-sweeping to suggest that state courts were not left free to develop their own doctrines (as they would have been had this Court merely been interpreting common law under Swift v. Tyson, supra). The Court of Appeals in the first Bernstein case, supra, a diversity suit, plainly considered the decisions of this Court, despite the intervention of Erie, to be controlling in regard to the act of state question, at the same time indicating that New York law governed other aspects of the case. We are not without other precedent for a determination that federal law governs; there are enclaves of federal judge-made law which bind the States. A national body of federal-court-built law has been held to have been contemplated by § 301 of the Labor Management Relations Act, Textile Workers v. Lincoln Mills, 353 U.S. 448, 77 S.Ct. 912. Principles formulated by federal judicial law have been thought by this Court to be necessary to protect uniquely federal interests, D'Oench, Duhme & Co. v. Federal Deposit Ins. Corp., 315 U.S. 447, 62 S.Ct. 676; Clearfield Trust Co. v. United States, 318 U.S. 363, 63 S.Ct. 573. Of course the federal interest guarded in all these cases is one the ultimate statement of which is derived from a federal statute. * * *

* * * We conclude that the scope of the act of state doctrine must be determined according to federal law.[25]

23. At least this is true when the Court limits the scope of judicial inquiry. We need not now consider whether a state court might, in certain circumstances, adhere to a more restrictive view concerning the scope of examination of foreign acts than that required by this Court.

24. The Doctrine of Erie Railroad v. Tompkins Applied to International Law, 33 Am.J.Int'l L. 740 (1939).

25. Various constitutional and statutory provisions indirectly support this determination, see U.S.Const., Art. I, § 8, cls. 3, 10; Art. II, §§ 2, 3; Art. III,

VI.

If the act of state doctrine is a principle of decision binding on federal and state courts alike but compelled by neither international law nor the Constitution, its continuing vitality depends on its capacity to reflect the proper distribution of functions between the judicial and political branches of the Government on matters bearing upon foreign affairs. It should be apparent that the greater the degree of codification or consensus concerning a particular area of international law, the more appropriate it is for the judiciary to render decisions regarding it, since the courts can then focus on the application of an agreed principle to circumstances of fact rather than on the sensitive task of establishing a principle not inconsistent with the national interest or with international justice. It is also evident that some aspects of international law touch much more sharply on national nerves than do others; the less important the implications of an issue are for our foreign relations, the weaker the justification for exclusivity in the political branches. The balance of relevant considerations may also be shifted if the government which perpetrated the challenged act of state is no longer in existence, as in the Bernstein case, for the political interest of this country may, as a result, be measurably altered. Therefore, rather than laying down or reaffirming an inflexible and all-encompassing rule in this case, we decide only that the Judicial Branch will not examine the validity of a taking of property within its own territory by a foreign sovereign government, extant and recognized by this country at the time of suit, in the absence of a treaty or other unambiguous agreement regarding controlling legal principles, even if the complaint alleges that the taking violates customary international law.

There are few if any issues in international law today on which opinion seems to be so divided as the limitations on a state's power to expropriate the property of aliens.[26] There is, of course, authority, in

---

§ 2; 28 U.S.C. §§ 1251(a)(2), (b)(1), (b)(3), 1332(a)(2), 1333, 1350–1351, by reflecting a concern for uniformity in this country's dealings with foreign nations and indicating a desire to give matters of international significance to the jurisdiction of federal institutions. See Comment, The Act of State Doctrine—Its Relation to Private and Public International Law, 62 Col.L. Rev., 1278, 1297, n. 123; cf. United States v. Belmont, supra; United States v. Pink, supra.

26. Compare, e. g., Friedman, Expropriation in International Law 206–211

(1953); Dawson and Weston, "Prompt, Adequate and Effective": A Universal Standard of Compensation? 30 Fordham L.Rev. 727 (1962), with Note from Secretary of State Hull to Mexican Ambassador, August 22, 1938, V Foreign Relations of the United States 685 (1938); Doman, Postwar Nationalization of Foreign Property in Europe, 48 Col.L.Rev. 1125, 1127 (1948). We do not, of course, mean to say that there is no international standard in this area; we conclude only that the matter is not meet for adjudication by domestic tribunals.

international judicial [27] and arbitral [28] decisions, in the expressions of national governments,[29] and among commentators [30] for the view that a taking is improper under international law if it is not for a public purpose, is discriminatory, or is without provision for prompt, adequate, and effective compensation. However, Communist countries, although they have in fact provided a degree of compensation after diplomatic efforts, commonly recognize no obligation on the part of ✓ the taking country.[31] Certain representatives of the newly independent and underdeveloped countries have questioned whether rules of state responsibility toward aliens can bind nations that have not consented to them [32] and it is argued that the traditionally articulated standards governing expropriation of property reflect "imperialist" interests and are inappropriate to the circumstances of emergent states.[33]

The disagreement as to relevant international law standards reflects an even more basic divergence between the national interests of capital importing and capital exporting nations and between the social ideologies of those countries that favor state control of a considerable portion of the means of production and those that adhere to a free enterprise system. It is difficult to imagine the courts of this country embarking on adjudication in an area which touches more sensitively the practical and ideological goals of the various members of the community of nations.[34]

[handwritten margin notes: BASIC SOCIO- ECONOMIC IDEOLOGICAL DIVERGENCE]

27. See Oscar Chinn Case, P.C.I.J., ser. A/B, No. 63, at 87 (1934); Chorzow Factory Case, P.C.I.J., ser. A., No. 17, at 46, 47 (1928).

28. See, e. g., Norwegian Shipowners' Case (Norway/United States) (Perm. Ct.Arb.) (1922), 1 U.N.Rep.Int'l Arb. Awards 307, 334, 339 (1948), Hague Court Reports, 2d Series, 39, 69, 74 (1932); Marguerite de Joly de Sabla, American and Panamanian General Claims Arbitration 379, 447, 6 U.N. Rep.Int'l Arb. Awards 358, 336 (1955).

29. See, e. g., Dispatch from Lord Palmerston to British Envoy at Athens, Aug. 7, 1846, 39 British and Foreign State Papers 1849–1850, 431– 432. Note from Secretary of State Hull to Mexican Ambassador, July 21, 1938, V Foreign Relations of the United States 674 (1938); Note to the Cuban Government, July 16, 1960, 43 Dept. State Bull. 171 (1960).

30. See, e. g., McNair, The Seizure of Property and Enterprises in Indonesia, 6 Netherlands Int'l L.Rev. 218, 243– 253 (1959); Restatement, Foreign Relations Law of the United States

(Proposed Official Draft 1962), §§ 190– 195.

31. See Doman, supra, note 26, at 1143– 1158; Fleming, States, Contracts and Progress, 62–63 (1960); Bystricky, Notes on Certain International Legal Problems Relating to Socialist Nationalisation, in International Assn. of Democratic Lawyers, Proceedings of the Commission on Private International Law, Sixth Congress (1956), 15.

32. See Anand, Role of the "New" Asian-African Countries in the Present International Legal Order, 56 Am.J. Int'l L. 383 (1962); Roy, Is the Law of Responsibility of States for Injuries to Aliens a Part of Universal International Law? 55 Am.J.Int.'l L. 863 (1961).

33. See 1957 Yb.U.N.Int'l L. Comm'n (Vol. 1) 155, 158 (statements of Mr. Padilla Nervo (Mexico) and Mr. Pal (India)).

34. There are, of course, areas of international law in which consensus as to standards is greater and which do not represent a battleground for conflict-

When we consider the prospect of the courts characterizing foreign expropriations, however justifiably, as invalid under international law and ineffective to pass title, the wisdom of the precedents is confirmed. While each of the leading cases in this Court may be argued to be distinguishable on its facts from this one—Underhill because sovereign immunity provided an independent ground and Oetjen Ricaud, and Shapleigh because there was actually no violation of international law—the plain implication of all these opinions, and the import of express statements in Oetjen, 246 U.S., at 304, 38 S.Ct. at 311, and Shapleigh, 299 U.S., at 471, 57 S.Ct. at 262, is that the act of state doctrine is applicable even if international law has been violated. In Ricaud, the one case of the three most plausibly involving an international law violation, the possibility of an exception to the act of state doctrine was not discussed. Some commentators have concluded that it was not brought to the Court's attention,[35] but Justice Clarke delivered both the Oetjen and Ricaud opinions, on the same day, so we can assume that principles stated in the former were applicable to the latter case.

The possible adverse consequences of a conclusion to the contrary of that implicit in these cases is highlighted by contrasting the practices of the political branch with the limitations of the judicial process in matters of this kind. Following an expropriation of any significance, the Executive engages in diplomacy aimed to assure that United States citizens who are harmed are compensated fairly. Representing all claimants of this country, it will often be able, either by bilateral or multilateral talks, by submission to the United Nations, or by the employment of economic and political sanctions, to achieve some degree of general redress. Judicial determinations of invalidity of title can, on the other hand, have only an occasional impact, since they depend on the fortuitous circumstance of the property in question being brought into this country.[36] Such decisions would, if the acts involved were declared invalid, often be likely to give offense to the expropriating country; since the concept of territorial sovereignty is so deep seated, any state may resent the refusal of the courts of another sovereign to accord validity to acts within its territorial borders. Piecemeal dispositions of this sort involving the probability of affront to another state could seriously interfere with negotiations being carried on by the Executive Branch and might prevent or render less favorable the terms of an agreement that could otherwise be

ing ideologies. This decision in no way intimates that the courts of this country are broadly foreclosed from considering questions of international law.

35. See Restatement, Foreign Relations Law of the United States, Reporters' Notes (Proposed Official Draft 1962), § 43, note 3.

36. It is, of course, true that such determinations might influence others not to bring expropriated property into the country, * * * so their indirect impact might extend beyond the actual invalidations of title.

reached.   Relations with third countries which have engaged in similar expropriations would not be immune from effect.

The dangers of such adjudication are present regardless of whether the State Department has, as it did in this case, asserted that the relevant act violated international law.   If the Executive Branch has undertaken negotiations with an expropriating country, but has refrained from claims of violation of the law of nations, a determination to that effect by a court might be regarded as a serious insult, while a finding of compliance with international law, would greatly strengthen the bargaining hand of the other state with consequent detriment to American interests.

Even if the State Department has proclaimed the impropriety of the expropriation, the stamp of approval of its view by a judicial tribunal, however impartial, might increase any affront and the judicial decision might occur at a time, almost always well after the taking, when such an impact would be contrary to our national interest. Considerably more serious and far-reaching consequences would flow from a judicial finding that international law standards had been met if that determination flew in the face of a State Department proclamation to the contrary.   When articulating principles of international law in its relations with other states, the Executive Branch speaks not only as an interpreter of generally accepted and traditional rules, as would the courts, but also as an advocate of standards it believes desirable for the community of nations and protective of national concerns.   In short, whatever way the matter is cut, the possibility of conflict between the Judicial and Executive Branches could hardly be avoided.

Respondents contend that, even if there is not agreement regarding general standards for determining the validity of expropriations, the alleged combination of retaliation, discrimination, and inadequate compensation makes it patently clear that this particular expropriation was in violation of international law.   If this view is accurate, it would still be unwise for the courts so to determine.   Such a decision now would require the drawing of more difficult lines in subsequent cases and these would involve the possibility of conflict with the Executive view.   Even if the courts avoided this course, either by presuming the validity of an act of state whenever the international law standard was thought unclear or by following the State Department declaration in such a situation, the very expression of judicial uncertainty might provide embarrassment to the Executive Branch.

Another serious consequence of the exception pressed by respondents would be to render uncertain titles in foreign commerce, with the possible consequence of altering the flow of international trade.   If the attitude of the United States courts were unclear, one buying expropriated goods would not know if he could safely import them into this country.   Even were takings known to be invalid, one would have difficulty determining after goods had changed hands several times whether the particular articles in question were the product of an ineffective state act.

Against the force of such considerations, we find respondents' countervailing arguments quite unpersuasive. Their basic contention is that United States courts could make a significant contribution to the growth of international law, a contribution whose importance, it is said, would be magnified by the relative paucity of decisional law by international bodies. But given the fluidity of present world conditions, the effectiveness of such a patchwork approach toward the formulation of an acceptable body of law concerning state responsibility for expropriations is, to say the least, highly conjectural. Moreover, it rests upon the sanguine presupposition that the decisions of the courts of the world's major capital exporting country and principal exponent of the free enterprise system would be accepted as disinterested expressions of sound legal principle by those adhering to widely different ideologies.

It is contended that regardless of the fortuitous circumstances necessary for United States jurisdiction over a case involving a foreign act of state and the resultant isolated application to any expropriation program taken as a whole, it is the function of the courts to justly decide individual disputes before them. Perhaps the most typical act of state case involves the original owner or his assignee suing one not in association with the expropriating state who has had "title" transferred to him. But it is difficult to regard the claim of the original owner, who otherwise may be recompensed through diplomatic channels, as more demanding of judicial cognizance than the claim of title by the innocent third party purchaser, who, if the property is taken from him, is without any remedy.

Respondents claim that the economic pressure resulting from the proposed exception to the act of state doctrine will materially add to the protection of United States investors. We are not convinced, even assuming the relevance of this contention. Expropriations take place for a variety of reasons, political and ideological as well as economic. When one considers the variety of means possessed by this country to make secure foreign investment, the persuasive or coercive effect of judicial invalidation of acts of expropriation dwindles in comparison. The newly independent states are in need of continuing foreign investment; the creation of a climate unfavorable to such investment by wholesale confiscations may well work to their long-run economic disadvantage. Foreign aid given to many of these countries provides a powerful lever in the hands of the political branches to ensure fair treatment of United States nationals. Ultimately the sanctions of economic embargo and the freezing of assets in this country may be employed. Any country willing to brave any or all of these consequences is unlikely to be deterred by sporadic judicial decisions directly affecting only property brought to our shores. If the political branches are unwilling to exercise their ample powers to effect compensation, this reflects a judgment of the national interest which the judiciary would be ill-advised to undermine indirectly.

It is suggested that if the act of state doctrine is applicable to violations of international law, it should only be so when the Executive Branch expressly stipulates that it does not wish the courts to pass on the question of validity. See Association of the Bar of the City of New York, Committee on International Law, A Reconsideration of the Act of State Doctrine in United States Courts (1959). We should be slow to reject the representations of the Government that such a reversal of the Bernstein principle would work serious inroads on the maximum effectiveness of United States diplomacy. Often the State Department will wish to refrain from taking an official position, particularly at a moment that would be dictated by the developing of private litigation but might be inopportune diplomatically. Adverse domestic consequences might flow from an official stand which could be assuaged, if at all, only by revealing matters best kept secret. Of course, a relevant consideration for the State Department would be the position contemplated in the court to hear the case. It is highly questionable whether the examination of validity by the judiciary should depend on an educated guess by the Executive as to probable result and, at any rate, should a prediction be wrong, the Executive might be embarrassed in its dealings with other countries. We do not now pass on the Bernstein exception, but even if it were deemed valid, its suggested extension is unwarranted.

However offensive to the public policy of this country and its constituent States an expropriation of this kind may be, we conclude that both the national interest and progress toward the goal of establishing the rule of law among nations are best served by maintaining intact the act of state doctrine in this realm of its application.

* * *

The judgment of the Court of Appeals is reversed and the case is remanded to the District Court for proceedings consistent with this opinion.

It is so ordered.

Mr. JUSTICE WHITE, dissenting.

I am dismayed that the Court has, with one broad stroke, declared the ascertainment and application of international law beyond the competence of the courts of the United States in a large and important category of cases. I am also disappointed in the Court's declaration that the acts of a sovereign state with regard to the property of aliens within its borders are beyond the reach of international law in the courts of this country. However clearly established that law may be, a sovereign may violate it with impunity, except insofar as the political branches of the government may provide a remedy. This backward-looking doctrine, never before declared in this Court, is carried a disconcerting step further: not only are the courts power-less to question acts of state proscribed by international law but they are likewise powerless to refuse to adjudicate the claim founded upon a foreign law; they must render judgment and thereby validate the lawless act. Since the Court expressly extends its ruling to all acts of state expropriating property, however clearly inconsistent with the international community, all discriminatory expropriations of the property of aliens, as for example the taking of properties of persons belonging to certain races, religions or nationalities, are entitled to automatic validation in the courts of the United States. No other civilized country has found such a rigid rule necessary for the sur-vival of the executive branch of its government; the executive of no other government seems to require such insulation from international law adjudications in its courts; and no other judiciary is apparently so incompetent to ascertain and apply international law.[1]

1. The courts of the following coun-tries, among others, and their terri-tories have examined a fully "execut-ed" foreign act of state expropriating property:

England: Anglo-Iranian Oil Co. v. Jaff-rate, [1953] Int'l L.Rep. 316 (Aden Sup. Ct.); N. V. de Bataafsche Petroleum Maatschappij v. The War Damage Comm'n, [1956] Int'l L.Rep. 810 (Sing-apore Ct.App.).

Netherlands: Senembah Maatschappij N. V. v. Republiek Indonesie Bank In-donesia, Nederlandse Jurisprudentie 1959, No. 73, p. 218 (Amsterdam Ct. App.), excerpts reprinted in Domke, In-donesian Nationalization Measures Be-fore Foreign Courts, 54 Am.J.Int'l L. 305, 307–315 (1960).

Germany: N. V. Verenigde Deli-Maats-chapijen v. Deutsch-Indonesische Tabak-Handelsgesellschaft m. b. H. (Bremen Ct.App.), excerpts reprinted in Domke, supra, at 313–314 (1960); Confiscation of Property of Sudeten Germans Case, [1948] Ann.Dig. 24, 25 (No. 12) (Amtsgericht of Dingolfing).

Japan: Anglo-Iranian Oil Co. v. Idem-itsu Kosan Kabushiki Kaisha, [1953] Int'l L.Rep. 305 (Dist.Ct. of Tokyo), aff'd, [1953] Int'l L.Rep. 312 (High Ct. of Tokyo).

Italy: Anglo-Iranian Oil Co. v. S. U. P. O. R. Co., [1955] Int'l L.Rep. 19 (Ct. of Venice); Anglo-Iranian Oil Co. v. S. U. P. O. R. Co., [1955] Int'l L.Rep. 23 (Civ.Ct. of Rome).

France: Volatron v. Moulin, [1938–1940] Ann.Dig. 24 (Ct. of App. of Aix);

Société Potasas Ibericas v. Nathan Bloch, [1938–1940] Ann.Dig. 150 (Ct. of Cassation).

The Court does not refer to any country which has applied the act of state doc-trine in a case where a substantial international law issue is sought to be raised by an alien whose property has been expropriated. This country and this Court stand alone among the civilized nations of the world in ruling that such an issue is not cognizable in a court of law.

The Court notes that the courts of both New York and Great Britain have articulated the act of state doctrine in broad language similar to that used by this Court in Underhill v. Hernan-dez, 168 U.S. 250, 18 S.Ct. 83, and from this it infers that these courts recog-nize no international law exception to the act of state doctrine. The cases relied on by the Court involved no international law issue. For in these cases the party objecting to the valid-ity of the foreign act was a citizen of the foreign state. It is significant that courts of both New York and Great Britain, in apparently the first cases in which an international law issue was squarely posed, ruled that the act of state doctrine was no bar to examination of the validity of the for-eign act. Anglo-Iranian Oil Co. v. Jaffrate, [1953] Int'l L.Rep. 316 (Aden Sup.Ct.): "[T]he Iranian Laws of 1951 were invalid by international law, for, by them, the property of the company was expropriated without any com-pensation." Sulyok v. Penzintezeti Kozpont Budapest, 279 App.Div. 528,

I do not believe that the act of state doctrine as judicially fashioned in this Court, and the reasons underlying it, require American courts to decide cases in disregard of international law and of the rights of litigants to a full determination on the merits.

[The remaining text of MR. JUSTICE WHITE's extensive dissenting opinion is omitted.]

How much of United States foreign affairs law is conclusively determinable only by the United States Supreme Court, despite the doctrine of Erie R. R. Co. v. Tomkins? Students of federal courts law, admiralty, and conflict of laws will recognize the possibilities inherent in the breadth of the court's statement covering its holding that the act of state doctrine falls, even in diversity of citizenship cases, within the penumbra of federal interest, i. e. where the federal courts "find" or "make" law: " * * *   [W]e are constrained to make clear that an issue concerned with a basic choice regarding the competence and function of the judiciary and the National Executive in ordering our relationships with other members of the international community *must* be treated *exclusively* as an aspect of federal law." [Emphasis supplied].   This statement is certainly sufficient to cover all the concerns about the Erie decision that Jessup had in mind in his 1939 article, cited in the court's note 24.   Additionally, it could serve to expand the authority of the federal courts to declare the rules governing private rights and duties in a variety of international transactions situations.   The trend, as is well known, has been for the Supreme Court to enlarge the sectors of "federal interest" in which, even in diversity cases, the federal courts "make" or "find" rules where there is no specific federal statutory norm, as is slowly the continual development of the "general law maritime," which governs even in state court proceedings.

111 N.Y.S.2d 75, aff'd, 304 N.Y. 704, 107 N.E.2d 604 (foreign expropriation of intangible property denied effect as contrary to New York public policy).

SECTION B. LEGISLATIVE AND EXECUTIVE INFLUENCES ON JUDICIAL APPLICATION OR NON-APPLICATION OF THE DOCTRINE IN THE UNITED STATES

UNITED STATES: THE "HICKENLOOPER AMENDMENTS" TO THE FOREIGN ASSISTANCE ACT

22 U.S.C. § 2370.

Prohibitions against furnishing assistance

* * *

(e) (1) The President shall suspend assistance to the government of any country to which assistance is provided under this chapter or any other Act when the government of such country or any government agency or subdivision within such country on or after January 1, 1962—

(A) has nationalized or expropriated or seized ownership or control of property owned by any United States citizen or by any corporation, partnership, or association not less than 50 per centum beneficially owned by United States citizens, or

(B) has taken steps to repudiate or nullify existing contracts or agreements with any United States citizen or any corporation, partnership, or association not less than 50 per centum beneficially owned by United States citizens, or

(C) has imposed or enforced discriminatory taxes or other exactions, or restrictive maintenance or operational conditions, or has taken other actions, which have the effect of nationalizing, expropriating, or otherwise seizing ownership or control of property so owned,

and such country, government agency, or government subdivision fails within a reasonable time (not more than six months after such action, or, in the event of a referral to the Foreign Claims Settlement Commission of the United States within such period as provided herein, not more than twenty days after the report of the Commission is received) to take appropriate steps, which may include arbitration, to discharge its obligations under international law toward such citizen or entity, including speedy compensation for such property in convertible foreign exchange, equivalent to the full value thereof, as required by international law, or fails to take steps designed to provide relief from such taxes, exactions, or conditions, as the case may be; and such suspension shall continue until the President is satisfied that appropriate steps are being taken, and no other provision of this chapter shall be construed to authorize the President to waive the provisions of this subsection.

Upon request of the President (within seventy days after such action referred to in subparagraphs (A), (B), or (C) of this paragraph), the Foreign Claims Settlement Commission of the United States (established pursuant to Reorganization Plan No. 1 of 1954, 68 Stat. 1279) is hereby authorized to evaluate expropriated property, determining the full value of any property nationalized, expropriated, or seized, or subjected to discriminatory or other actions as aforesaid, for purposes of this subsection and to render an advisory report to the President within ninety days after such request. Unless authorized by the President, the Commission shall not publish its advisory report except to the citizen or entity owning such property. There is hereby authorized to be appropriated such amount, to remain available until expended, as may be necessary from time to time to enable the Commission to carry out expeditiously its functions under this subsection.

(2) Notwithstanding any other provision of law, no court in the United States shall decline on the ground of the federal act of state doctrine to make a determination on the merits giving effect to the principles of international law in a case in which a claim of title or other right to property is asserted by any party including a foreign state (or a party claiming through such state) based upon (or traced through) a confiscation or other taking after January 1, 1959, by an act of that state in violation of the principles of international law, *including the principles of compensation and the other standards set out in this subsection: Provided,* That this subparagraph shall not be applicable (1) in any case in which an act of a foreign state is not contrary to international law or with respect to a claim of title or other right to property acquired pursuant to an irrevocable letter of credit of not more than 180 days duration issued in good faith prior to the time of the confiscation or other taking, or (2) in any case with respect to which the President determines that application of the act of state doctrine is required in that particular case by the foreign policy interests of the United States and a suggestion to this effect is filed on his behalf in that case with the court. [Emphasis supplied.]

*   *   *

BANCO NACIONAL DE CUBA v. FARR, WHITLOCK & CO.

United States Court of Appeals, Second Circuit, 1967.
383 F.2d 166.[a]

WATERMAN, CIRCUIT JUDGE. This is an appeal from a judgment of the United States District Court for the Southern District of New York dismissing the appellant's complaint and the defendant's complaint against impleaded third parties. This litigation has been the subject of three much-discussed previous opinions. In the original hearing of the action before the district court summary judgment was

a.   Cert. denied 390 U.S. 956, 88 S.Ct. 1038 (1968).

granted in favor of the defendants, D.C., 193 F.Supp. 375 (1961). This disposition was affirmed by this court (307 F.2d 845 (1962)), but reversed by the Supreme Court, Banco Nacional de Cuba v. Sabbatino, 376 U.S. 398, 84 S.Ct. 923, 11 L.Ed.2d 804 (1964). The facts have been fully stated in these opinions, see e. g., the opinion of Mr. Justice Harlan for the Court, 376 U.S. 398 at 401–408, 84 S.Ct. 923. On remand the district court has again ruled in favor of the defendants in an opinion reported at 243 F.Supp. 957 (July 30, 1965), later supplemented by opinion of November 16, 1965, 272 F.Supp. 836, at the time judgment was entered.

This action, which has served as the test case [1] for litigation concerning Cuban expropriations, involves the disposition of the proceeds of the sale of a cargo of sugar which was expropriated by the Castro government while the cargo was in Cuban territorial waters.

During February and July of 1960 appellee Farr, Whitlock & Co. (a copartnership hereinafter referred to as Farr, Whitlock) an American commodity broker, contracted with a wholly-owned Cuban subsidiary of appellee Compania Azucarera Vertientes-Camaguey de Cuba (C. A. V.) for the purchase of Cuban sugar. The sugar was to be delivered free alongside the steamer in Cuba, and payment was to be made in New York by Farr, Whitlock upon presentation of shipping documents and a sight draft.

Pursuant to the contracts, 22,000 bags of sugar were loaded on board the German vessel S.S. Hornfels which was standing offshore at the Cuban port of Jucaro. The loading took place between August 6 and August 9, 1960. On August 6, 1960 the Cuban government passed a resolution [2] providing for the compulsory expropriation of all prop-

---

1. It is stated in the district court's opinion that thirty-five cases "involving a wide spectrum of questions arising out of Cuban expropriations" remain before the court below awaiting the final determination of this case. 243 F.Supp. 957, 962 (1965).

2. The resolution, which was promulgated by the Cuban President and Prime Minister provides:

Whereas, the attitude assumed by the Government and the Legislative Power of the United States of North America, of continued aggression, for political purposes, against the basic interests of the Cuban economy, as evidenced by the amendment to the Sugar Act adopted by the Congress of said country, whereby exceptional powers were conferred upon the President of said nation to reduce the participation of Cuban sugars in the sugar market of said country, as a weapon of political action against

Cuba, was considered as the fundamental justification of said law.

Whereas, the Chief Executive of the Government of the United States of North America, making use of said exceptional powers, and assuming an obvious attitude of economic and political aggression against our country, has reduced the participation of Cuban sugars in the North American market with the unquestionable design to attack Cuba and its revolutionary process.

Whereas, this action constitutes a reiteration of the continued conduct of the government of the United States of North America, intended to prevent the exercise of its sovereignty and its integral development by our people thereby serving the base interests of the North American trusts, which have hindered the growth of our economy and the consolidation of our political freedom.

* * *

erty located within Cuban territory of appellee C. A. V., a corporation organized under Cuban law but owned to the extent of more than ninety per cent of its capital stock by residents of the United States. As a result of the resolution the consent of the Cuban government was necessary before the S.S. Hornfels was allowed to sail from Cuban waters. This consent was obtained on August 11 when Farr, Whitlock entered into contracts identical to its prior contracts with the subsidiary of C. A. V. with Banco Para el Commercio Exterior de Cuba (Banco Exterior), an instrumentality of the Cuban government. On August 12 the S.S. Hornfels sailed to Morocco with its cargo of sugar.

Banco Exterior assigned the bills of lading to appellant Banco Nacional de Cuba (Banco Nacional), the financial agent of the Cuban government. Banco Nacional sent them to Societe Generale, a French bank which acted as its New York agent, for presentation to Farr, Whitlock in New York. Farr, Whitlock gained possession of the bills of lading on August 29, 1960 without making payment upon presentation. The funds were claimed from Farr, Whitlock on behalf of C. A. V.,[3] and Farr, Whitlock for this reason refused to make payment to Societe Generale or to return the bills of lading.

The present action was commenced by Banco Nacional in the United States District Court for the Southern District of New York on October 10, 1960, alleging that Farr, Whitlock had converted the bills of lading by its refusal to return them or to pay over their proceeds to

Whereas, it is the duty of the peoples of Latin America to strive for the recovery of their native wealth by wrestling it from the hands of the foreign monopolies and interests which prevent their development, promote political interference, and impair the sovereignty of the underdeveloped countries of America.

* * *

Now, Therefore: In pursuance of the powers vested in us, in accordance with the provisions of Law No. 851, of July 6, 1960, we hereby

Resolve:

First. To order the nationalization, through compulsory expropriation, and, therefore, the adjudication in fee simple to the Cuban State, of all the property and enterprises located in the national territory, and the rights and interests resulting from the exploitation of such property and enterprises, owned by the juridical persons who are nationals of the United States of North America, or operators of enterprises in which nationals of said country have a predominating interest, as listed below, to wit:

* * *

22. Compania Azucarera Vertientes Camaguey de Cuba.

* * *

3. Farr, Whitlock received notice on August 23, 1960 that Peter L. F. Sabbatino on August 16 had been appointed Temporary Receiver for the assets of C. A. V. within New York State pursuant to N.Y.Civ.Prac.Act, § 977-b.

On August 26th Farr, Whitlock was notified by officers of C. A. V. that C. A. V., not the Cuban government, was the rightful owner of the sugar covered by the bills of lading which Societe Generale held. Farr, Whitlock and C. A. V. entered into an agreement on that day that Farr, Whitlock would retain the proceeds of the sugar shipments unless compelled to turn them over by court order. In return for this, C. A. V. would indemnify Farr, Whitlock against any claims and defend any suits against Farr, Whitlock for the sugar or the proceeds therefrom. In addition, C. A. V. promised to pay Farr, Whitlock ten per cent of the proceeds if C. A. V. were ultimately successful in obtaining them.

Societe Generale. On October 24, 1960, pursuant to an order of the New York Supreme Court, Kings County, Farr, Whitlock transferred the proceeds of the bills of lading, a total of $173,936.31, to a New York court appointed Temporary Receiver, Sabbatino. The complaint in the present action was amended on October 31, 1960 to include Sabbatino as a defendant.

On March 31, 1961 the district court, acting on various motions of the parties before it, held that it had jurisdiction over the subject matter of the action despite state court control of the funds at issue. It granted summary judgment for the defendants, holding that the taking of the sugar by the Cuban government violated international law in three respects: it was motivated by a retaliatory purpose, not a legitimate public purpose; it discriminated against nationals of the United States; and it failed to provide adequate compensation for the property taken; and inasmuch as the taking violated international law, Cuba did not acquire good title to the sugar upon which to base its claim of conversion.

We affirmed this judgment on July 6, 1962, holding that the failure of the Cuban government to pay adequate compensation to C. A. V. for the taking of its property, combined with the evident retaliatory purpose and the discriminatory effect of the taking upon the rights of American nationals, constituted a violation of international law. We rejected, just as the district court had previously rejected, the appellant's contention that the act of state doctrine applied to this case; and we based in part our conclusion on two letters written by State Department officers evidencing the fact that the Executive Branch had no objection to a judicial determination of the merits of the controversy.

The Supreme Court granted certiorari, 372 U.S. 905, 83 S.Ct. 717, 9 L.Ed.2d 715 (1963), and reversed us on March 23, 1964, 376 U.S. 398, 84 S.Ct. 923, 11 L.Ed.2d 804. The Court held that the act of state doctrine did apply to this case, and therefore the courts of the United States were prevented from examining the validity of the acts of the Cuban government under international law "in the absence of a treaty or other unambiguous agreement regarding controlling legal principles * * *."   376 U.S. at 428, 84 S.Ct. at 941. The Court declared that the act of state doctrine had " 'constitutional' underpinnings" arising out of the "basic relationships between branches of government in a system of separation of powers." 376 U.S. at 423, 84 S.Ct. at 938.[4] The Court did not reach the issue of whether the taking in this case violated international law. See 376 U.S. at 433, 84 S.Ct. 923. It remanded the case to the district court to hear and decide any liti-

---

4. Our view that the two letters written by State Department officers indicated that the Executive Branch had no objection to a judicial determination as to the validity of Cuba's actions under international law proved erroneous when the Executive Branch formally filed an amicus brief in the Supreme Court on the side of Banco Nacional and participated in the oral argument before the Court.

gable issues of fact which might develop and for "proceedings consistent with this opinion." 376 U.S. at 439, 84 S.Ct. at 946.

On March 28, 1963, one year before the decision of the Supreme Court was handed down, Banco Nacional, Farr, Whitlock, C. A. V., and Sabbatino agreed that Lehman Brothers would hold a sum of money in escrow to satisfy the final judgment in this case, and Sabbatino transferred $225,000 to Lehman Brothers for this purpose. The agreement also provided that C. A. V. would indemnify Farr, Whitlock for any excess of any judgment against it over the amount in the escrow fund. Thereafter the New York state Temporary Receivership was terminated by order of the New York Supreme Court and Sabbatino was eliminated as a party to this case by a stipulation of the parties.

After this case was remanded to the district court appellant moved for final judgment in its favor but judgment was not entered due to a miscellany of complications, see 243 F.Supp. 957, at 961–962, and while the proceedings relative to the entry of judgment on remand were pending the Hickenlooper Amendment[5] was enacted into law on October 7, 1964. It provided:

> Notwithstanding any other provision of law, no court in the United States shall decline on the ground of the federal act of state doctrine to make a determination on the merits giving effect to the principles of international law in a case in which a claim of title or other right is asserted by any party including a foreign state (or a party claiming through such state) based upon (or traced through) a confiscation or other taking after January 1, 1959, by an act of that state in violation of the principles of international law, including the principles of compensation and the

---

5. The Hickenlooper Amendment, which has also been referred to elsewhere as the Sabbatino Amendment or the Rule of Law Amendment, was attached to the Foreign Assistance Act of 1964 and became Section 301(d)(4) of that act. (Pub.L. 88–633, 78 Stat. 1009, 1013.)

The Amendment was reenacted in 1965 when the next Congress adopted the Foreign Assistance Act of 1965 (Pub. L. 89–171, 79 Stat. 653) which became law on September 6, 1965. The re-enactment contained a slightly different version of the Hickenlooper Amendment, and is found in Section 301(d)(2) of that Public Law. Incorporated into the U.S.Code it is found at 22 U.S.C. § 2370(e)(2). The only change was the substitution of "other right to property" for "other right" in two instances, and the deletion of Proviso 3, which had formerly made the Amendment inapplicable to any case in which the proceedings had not been commenced before January 1, 1966.

These changes in no way affect the case before us, and when we have discussed the Amendment throughout our opinion we have made no attempt to differentiate the Amendment in effect from October 7, 1964 from the Amendment in effect from September 6, 1965 to date. The Amendment, as first adopted, appears here in the text, the re-enacted version is incorporated into footnote 20. It is interesting to note that these language changes became law during the 60 day period when the court below was awaiting word from the Executive before ordering the entry of judgment. See footnote 1 in Judge Bryan's supplemental opinion. D.C., 272 F.Supp. 837.

other standards set out in this subsection: Provided, That this subparagraph shall not be applicable (1) in any case in which an act of a foreign state is not contrary to international law or with respect to a claim of title or other right acquired pursuant to an irrevocable letter of credit of not more than 180 days duration issued in good faith prior to the time of the confiscation or other taking, or (2) in any case with respect to which the President determines that application of the act of state doctrine is required in that particular case by the foreign policy interests of the United States and a suggestion to this effect is filed on his behalf in that case with the court, or (3) in any case in which the proceedings are commenced after January 1, 1966.

On November 12, 1964 an order was entered impleading C. A. V. and Lehman Brothers as third party defendants pursuant to Fed.R. Civ.P. 14.

Defendant Farr, Whitlock and the third-party defendants moved for summary judgment dismissing the complaint, based on the Hickenlooper Amendment. On July 30, 1965 the district court granted these motions, withholding final judgment for sixty days to allow the President to exercise his rights under the second proviso of the Amendment. Final judgment was entered on November 17, 1965 after the Court was notified that the Executive Branch did not intend to intervene and to suggest application of the act of state doctrine in this case.[7]

The district court in a scholarly and well-reasoned opinion held that the Hickenlooper Amendment applied to the case at bar, that the Amendment was constitutional, and that it was bound by our prior determination, 307 F.2d 845 (1962), that the expropriation by the Cuban government violated international law. The same issues are raised before us, and in disposing of them we reach the same result the lower court reached, adopting as our own much of the discussion and points made by the learned judge below.

I.   The Applicability of the Hickenlooper Amendment

Appellant first claims that the Hickenlooper Amendment was not intended to apply to "transactions" completed before the date of its enactment. If this is so and the expropriation here is a "transaction" the present case would be excluded from the effect of the amendment,

---

7. The court received a letter from the United States Attorney for the Southern District of New York dated September 29, 1965 which reads:

In its decision of July 30, 1965 this Court afforded the Executive Branch the opportunity to file a suggestion indicating whether the application of the act of state doctrine is required by the foreign policy interests of the United States, as provided for in Section 620(e)(2) of the Foreign Assistance Act of 1961, as amended (22 U.S.C. § 2370(e)(2).) I am instructed to inform the Court that no determination has been made that application of the act of state doctrine is required in this case by the foreign policy interests of the United States.

So that there will be no ambiguity, the Court is advised that no such determination is contemplated.

for the expropriation in this case occurred on August 6, 1960, and the Amendment was not enacted until October 7, 1964.

* * *

* * *   The Senate Report stated:

The amendment is intended to reverse in part the recent decision of the Supreme Court in Banco de Nacional de Cuba v. Sabbatino. The act of state doctrine has been applied by U. S. courts to determine that the actions of a foreign sovereign cannot be challenged in private litigation. The Supreme Court extended this doctrine in the Sabbatino decision so as to preclude U. S. courts from inquiring into acts of foreign states, even though these acts had been denounced by the State Department as contrary to international law.

In the Sabbatino case, the Banco Nacional de Cuba sued to recover the proceeds of a sale of Cuban sugar by an American-owned company on the ground that the sugar, which had been expropriated, belonged to the Cuban Government. The lower courts dismissed the suit, but the Supreme Court reversed these decisions and remanded the case for further proceedings on the ground that it would not inquire into the act of the Cuban State.

The effect of the amendment is to achieve a reversal of presumptions. Under the Sabbatino decision, the courts would presume that any adjudication as to the lawfulness under international law of the act of a foreign state would embarrass the conduct of foreign policy unless the President says it would not. Under the amendment, the Court would presume that it may proceed with an adjudication on the merits unless the President states officially that such an adjudication in the particular case would embarrass the conduct of foreign policy.

The bill, including the amendment, was then passed by the Senate and sent to a conference committee. The conference report explains several of the provisions which appear in the final version of the amendment before us:

The managers on the part of the House regretted that there had not been an opportunity for thorough study and full hearings on the subject. The committee of conference amended the Senate language to pinpoint its precise effect, making it clear that it does not apply if no violation of international law principles is found, or if the case involves a short term irrevocable letter of credit issued in good faith prior to the taking of property by a foreign state. The exception in those individual cases in which the President determines that judicial review of the foreign government's action is not in the U. S. foreign policy interest is preserved. An additional change was added to limit the application of the amendment to cases in which the proceedings are commenced before January 1, 1966. This limitation was approved with the understanding that the congressional committees concerned will make a full review and study of the matter during the next Congress and make a determination on the need for permanent legislation.

* * *

In summary, the legislative history provides some support for both parties on the issue of whether the Hickenlooper Amendment was intended to apply to pending cases, but obviously it is stronger in favor of their inclusion. Certainly this legislative history contains nothing which would make us doubt our conclusion based upon the unambiguous words of the statute that the language of the Amendment demonstrates that the statute was intended to apply to cases pending at the time of its enactment as well as to cases which might subsequently be instituted.

* * *

Thus we hold that Congress intended that the Hickenlooper Amendment should apply to cases pending at the time of its enactment, including this case.

[The Court then discussed the constitutionality of the Hickenlooper Amendment, (e)(2).]

* * *

III. Legality of the Cuban Seizure under International Law

Inasmuch as we have found the Hickenlooper Amendment not to be unconstitutional and to be applicable to this case, we must follow its injunction and " * * * make a determination on the merits giving effect to the principles of international law" as to whether the taking in this case was "in violation of the principles of international law, including the principles of compensation and other standards set out in this subsection * * *."

On this question of whether the taking violated the principles of international law, we said on the previous appeal:

> Since the Cuban decree of expropriation not only failed to provide adequate compensation but also involved a retaliatory purpose and a discrimination against United States nationals, we hold that the decree was in violation of international law. 307 F.2d at 868.

This holding of ours, as noted by the court below, was unaffected when the Supreme Court reversed the result we had reached. The Supreme Court based its resolution of the case upon an application of the act of state doctrine and, as appellant concedes, found it unnecessary to decide whether international law had been violated in this case. See 376 U.S. at 433, 84 S.Ct. at 942, cf. 376 U.S. at 428–430, 84 S.Ct. at 940–941.

We do not feel compelled to follow our former holding under the "law of the case" rule, but see Zdanok v. Glidden Co., 327 F.2d 944 (2

Cir.), cert. denied, 377 U.S. 934, 84 S.Ct. 1338, 12 L.Ed.2d 298 (1964), but we are unable to find any convincing reason, based on argument or new authority, for altering our holding in the original appeal. Accordingly, we will not extensively discuss the international law issue but reaffirm the discussion that is contained in our opinion on the first appeal. See 307 F.2d at 859–868. We will only comment briefly on several aspects of international law involved.

It may be noted that the Hickenlooper Amendment requires us to judge the taking here by principles of international law "including the principles of compensation and other standards set out in this subsection." The subsection referred to, 22 U.S.C.A. § 2370(e), contains, besides the Hickenlooper Amendment, a provision requiring the President to suspend assistance to any country which expropriates or discriminates against property owned by United States citizens or owned by business associations which are more than 50 per cent beneficially owned by United States citizens, unless the expropriating country promptly makes arrangement to compensate for such taking at full value. It is clear that if these domestic statutory standards are different from the international law standards which we applied when we decided this case formerly, the statutory standards tend to be more exacting upon the expropriating nations. As we held that the taking before us violated international law under the possibly less exacting standards which we then applied, the application of the new statutory standards would not affect our decision here. This allows us to leave undecided whether the standard set forth in the Hickenlooper Amendment differs from the standard which we applied on the former appeal, and which we now apply again. It also allows us to avoid the question of whether Congress can thus specify how our United States courts must decide questions of international law, though "The Congress shall have Power * * * To *define* and punish Piracies and Felonies committed on the high Seas, and Offences against the Law of Nations," U.S.Const. Art. I, § 8, cl. 10 (emphasis supplied), see Banco Nacional de Cuba v. First Nat. City Bank, 270 F.Supp. 1004 (SDNY July 25, 1967). But see Falk, The Aftermath of Sabbatino 40–41 (1965); Henkin, Comments on Domke, Act of State Doctrine: Sabbatino in the Courts and in Congress, 3 Colum.J.Transnat'l L. 99, 107, 112–13 (1965).

Appellant has urged strongly that we were in error in our prior determination that it is of no particular significance that C. A. V. is a corporation organized under Cuban law. 307 F.2d at 861, see 376 U.S. at 433, n. 37, at 943. This would be significant if the corporation were owned by resident Cuban citizens, see F. Palico y Compania v. Brush, 256 F.Supp. 481 (SDNY 1966), aff'd per curiam, 375 F.2d 1011 (2 Cir. 1967), but such is not the case here. We repeat with emphasis our earlier language:

When a foreign state treats a corporation in a particular way because of the nationality of its shareholders, it would be inconsistent, for us in passing on the validity of that treatment to look only to the "nationality" of the corporate fiction.   307 F.2d 861.

Here it is clear from the resolution of expropriation, see footnote 2, supra, that the property of C. A. V. was expropriated because it was largely owned by "nationals of the United States of North America," and it is interesting to note that the resolution makes no mention whatever of the nationality of the corporation. The situation is clearly distinguishable from cases cited by appellant, such as the Standard Oil Tankers case, 22 Am.J.Int'l L. 404 (1918), in which a sovereign took action against a corporation because of the nationality of the corporation and not because of the nationality of the shareholders.

Also, to the extent that Congress might impose its standards in the decision of these issues, as discussed supra, we would be required to ignore the nationality of the corporation. The congressional standard requires full compensation for any taking of a corporation or other business association more than 50 per cent beneficially owned by United States citizens irrespective of the nominal nationality of the corporation.

Inasmuch as we thus reaffirm our previous holding that the Cuban taking is invalid under international law, we hold that there is no basis for appellant's assertion of title to the bills of lading involved in this case and its assertion that the proceeds of the sale of the sugar were tortiously converted by defendant. Appellant's claim must fail.

Affirmed.

––––––––––

1. *The Hickenlooper Amendments and international law and practice as to nationalization.* The first Hickenlooper amendment to the Foreign Assistance Act, Section 2370(e)(1), lays down a set of standards as to what Congress evidently assumed customary international law requires of a state that nationalizes or otherwise impairs the economic interests of an American citizen or corporation. These standards should be reviewed, as a later note will suggest, after the material in Chapter 17, Section B has been studied. The same standards are, of course, the basis for the directive to the courts in the second Hickenlooper amendment, Section 2370(e)(2).

Section 2370(e)(1) requires appropriate affirmative action, under international law (as interpreted by the standards in the legislation), within not more than 6 months after the act of taking, or, in the event that referral is made to the Foreign Claims Settlement Commission of the United States, within 20 days after that body has passed on the validity of the claim or claims submitted to it. As the alternative of referral to the commission has not been used so far in recent instances of nationalization, the effective deadline is usually six months. Within that period the statute requires the nationalizing state " * * * to take appropriate steps, which may include arbitration, to discharge its obligations * * * " to the satisfaction of the President of the United States. This is a far shorter time span than the usual period required for reaching an assured solution to a nationalization problem by diplomatic means, including an agreement to arbitrate or to refer the case to adjudication. Moreover, a number of developing countries that have nationalized adamantly refuse to accept arbitration or external adjudication.

2. *The short time period for settlement.* The requirement that the President be satisfied within six months of an assured solution to a nationalization problem has created foreign affairs problems under Sub-section (e)(1), which requires the President to cut off foreign assistance to the developing country concerned. Under some other provisions of Section 2370, which lists a number of instances in which foreign assistance shall be suspended, the President has authority to waive suspension when he finds that it is in the foreign policy interests of the United States to do so. But not as to Sub-section (e)(1). (Proposals for an amendment permitting presidential waiver have been advanced.)

In 1968, a military regime in Peru nationalized the properties of the International Petroleum Company, entitled in its own right or through its parent, the Standard Oil Company of New Jersey, to United States diplomatic protection. Peru has set off against any compensation that otherwise might have been payable a much larger claim for "unjust enrichment," based upon a contention that the company and its predecessors never had the legal right to take out oil. All legal remedies in Peru seem to have been exhausted, and the offset is not acceptable to the claimant or to the United States, on grounds that seem, at the least, reasonably arguable. However, Sub-section (e)(1) has not yet formally been applied. Within the first six months after the taking, while efforts at diplomatic settlement were still active, the executive branch consulted with key congressional figures and obtained their tacit agreement to non-application. A major reason for this informal amendment of the law is that Sub-section (e) (1) is a diplomatic blockbuster that if used would have serious adverse effects on United States foreign policy and possibly on private interests of other Americans in Peru and elsewhere. Sub-section (e) (1) has, as a matter of fact been used only once (as to Ceylon), with indifferent results as to its investment-protection objective.

Although the amendment has not been invoked, Peru and Chile have complained that the United States has not in fact entered into new bilateral aid arrangements with them and has opposed international lending agency development assistance to them, and that such conduct is illicit "intervention."

3. *The second Hickenlooper Amendment and the six months period.* In decisions that follow we shall see that the courts have

not been prone to apply Sub-section (e)(2) any more widely than exactly as written. It remains to be seen whether the problems outlined above as to the running of time for Sub-section (e)(1) will be taken into account by courts in Sub-section (e)(2) cases. Suppose, for example, that oil now in the United States is identifiable as having been refined at an IPC refinery in Peru, and a private purchaser is sued for conversion here during the current period of informal suspension of Sub-section (e)(1). What effect will be given by a court to Sub-section (e)(2) if the Department of State chooses not to express a position to the court? What if the Department of State suggests that Sub-section (e)(2) should be applied by the court, even though the executive branch has not applied Sub-section (e)(1)?

FIRST NATIONAL CITY BANK v. BANCO NACIONAL DE CUBA

United States Supreme Court, 1972.
406 U.S. 759, 92 S.Ct. 1808.

MR. JUSTICE REHNQUIST announced the judgment of the Court, and delivered an opinion in which THE CHIEF JUSTICE and MR. JUSTICE WHITE, join.

In July 1958, petitioner loaned the sum of $15 million to a predecessor of respondent. The loan was secured by a pledge of United States Government bonds. The loan was renewed the following year, and in 1960 $5 million was repaid, the $10 million balance was renewed for one year, and collateral equal to the value of the portion repaid was released by petitioner.

Meanwhile, on January 1, 1959, the Castro government came to power in Cuba. On September 16, 1960, the Cuban militia, allegedly pursuant to decrees of the Castro government, seized all of the branches of petitioner located in Cuba. A week later the bank retaliated by selling the collateral securing the loan, and applying the proceeds of the sale to repayment of the principal and unpaid interest. Petitioner concedes than an excess of at least $1.8 million over and above principal and unpaid interest was realized from the sale of the collateral. Respondent sued petitioner in the Federal District Court to recover this excess, and petitioner, by way of set-off and counterclaim asserted the right to recover damages as a result of the expropriation of its property in Cuba.

The District Court recognized that our decision in Banco Nacional de Cuba v. Sabbatino, 376 U.S. 398, 84 S.Ct. 923, 11 L.Ed.2d 804 (1964), holding that generally the courts of one nation will not sit in judgment on the acts of another nation within its own territory would bar the assertion of the counterclaim, but it further held that congres- ✓ sional enactments since the decision in Sabbatino had "for all practical purposes" overruled that case.   Following summary judgment in favor of the petitioner in the District Court on all issues except the amount by which the proceeds of the sale of collateral exceeded the amount which could properly be applied to the loan by petitioner, the parties stipulated that in any event this difference was less than the damages which petitioner could prove in support of its expropriation claim if that claim were allowed.   Petitioner then waived any recovery on its counterclaim over and above the amount recoverable by respondent on its complaint, and the District Court then rendered judgment dismissing respondent's complaint on the merits.

On appeal, the Court of Appeals for the Second Circuit held that the congressional enactments relied upon by the District Court did not govern this case, and that our decision in Sabbatino barred the assertion of petitioner's counterclaim.   We granted certiorari and vacated the judgment of the Court of Appeals for consideration of the views of the Department of State which had been furnished to us following the filing of the petition for certiorari.   400 U.S. 1019, 91 S.Ct. 581, 27 L.Ed.2d 630 (1971).   Upon reconsideration, the Court of Appeals by a divided vote adhered to its earlier decision.   We again granted certiorari, First National City Bank v. Banco Nacional de Cuba, 404 U.S. 820, 92 S.Ct. 79, 30 L.Ed.2d 48.

We must here decide whether, in view of the substantial difference between the position taken in this case by the Executive Branch and that which it took in Sabbatino, the act of state doctrine prevents petitioner from litigating its counterclaim on the merits.   We hold that it does not.

* * *

In Sabbatino, the Executive Branch of this Government, speaking through the Department of State, advised attorneys for amici in a vein which the Court described as being "intended to reflect no more than the Department's then wish not to make any statement bearing on this litigation."   376 U.S., at 420, 84 S.Ct., at 936.   The United States argued before this Court in Sabbatino that the Court should not "hold for the first time that Executive silence regarding the act ✓ of state doctrine is equivalent to executive approval of judicial inquiry into the foreign act."

In the case now before us, the Executive Branch has taken a quite different position.   The Legal Adviser of the Department of State advised this Court on November 17, 1970,[a] that as a matter of principle where the Executive publicly advises the Court that the act of state doctrine need not be applied, the Court should proceed to examine the legal issues raised by the act of a foreign sovereign within

a.   The letter from the Legal Adviser is
discussed and reproduced in part on
p. 434.

its own territory as it would any other legal question before it. His letter refers to the decision of the Court below in Bernstein v. N. V. Nederlandsche Amerikaansche, etc., 210 F.2d 375 (CA 2 1954), as representing a judicial recognition of such a principle, and suggests that the applicability of the principle was not limited to the *Bernstein* case. The Legal Adviser's letter then goes on to state:

> The Department of State believes that the act of state doctrine should not be applied to bar consideration of a defendant's counterclaim or set off against the government of Cuba in this or like cases.

The question which we must now decide is whether the so-called *Bernstein* exception to the act of state doctrine should be recognized in the context of the facts before the Court. In Sabbatino, the Court said:

> This Court has never had occasion to pass upon the so-called *Bernstein* exception, nor need it do so now. 276 U.S., at 420, 84 S.Ct., at 936.

* * *

The line of cases from this Court establishing the act of state doctrine justify its existence primarily on the basis that juridical review of acts of state of a foreign power could embarrass the conduct of foreign relations by the political branches of the government.

* * *

United States v. Belmont, 301 U.S. 324, 57 S.Ct. 758, 81 L.Ed. 1134, is another case that emphasized the exclusive competence of the executive branch in the field of foreign affairs. A year earlier, the Court in United States v. Curtiss-Wright Corp., 299 U.S. 304, 319, 57 S.Ct. 216, 220, 81 L.Ed. 255, had quoted with approval the statement of John Marshall when he was a member of the House of Representatives dealing with this same subject:

> The President is the sole organ of the nation in its external relations, and its sole representative with foreign nations.

* * *

We think that the examination of the foregoing cases indicates that this Court has recognized the primacy of the Executive in the conduct of foreign relations quite as emphatically as it has recognized the act of state doctrine. The Court in Sabbatino throughout its opinion emphasized the lead role of the executive in foreign policy, particularly in seeking redress for American nationals who had been the victims of foreign expropriation, and concluded that any exception to the act of state doctrine based on a mere silence or neutrality on the part of the executive might well lead to a conflict between the executive and judicial branches. Here, however, the Executive Branch has expressly stated that an inflexible application of the act of state doctrine by this Court would not serve the interests of American foreign policy.

The act of state doctrine is grounded on judicial concern that application of customary principles of law to judge the acts of a foreign sovereign might frustrate the conduct of foreign relations by the political branches of the government. We conclude that where the Executive Branch, charged as it is with primary responsibility for the conduct of foreign affairs, expressly represents to the Court that the act of state doctrine would not advance the interests of American foreign policy, that doctrine should not be applied by the courts. In so doing, we of course adopt and approve the so-called *Bernstein* exception to the act of state doctrine. We believe this to be no more than an application of the classical common-law maxim that "the reason of the law ceasing, the law itself also ceases" (Black's Law Dictionary, p. 288).

Our holding is in no sense an abdication of the judicial function to the Executive Branch. The judicial power of the United States extends to this case, and the jurisdictional standards established by Congress for adjudication by the federal courts have been met by the parties. The only reason for not deciding the case by use of otherwise applicable legal principles would be the fear that legal interpretation by the judiciary of the act of a foreign sovereign within its own territory might frustrate the conduct of this country's foreign relations. But the branch of the government responsible for the conduct of those foreign relations has advised us that such a consequence need not be feared in this case. The judiciary is therefore free to decide the case free from the limitations that would otherwise be imposed upon it by the judicially created act of state doctrine.

*   *   *

The act of state doctrine, as reflected in the cases culminating in Sabbatino, is a judicially accepted limitation on the normal adjudicative processes of the courts, springing from the thoroughly sound principle that on occasion individual litigants may have to forego decision on the merits of their claims because the involvement of the courts in such a decision might frustrate the conduct of the Nation's foreign policy. It would be wholly illogical to insist that such a rule, fashioned because of fear that adjudication would interfere with the conduct of foreign relations, be applied in the face of an assurance from that branch of the Federal Government which conducts foreign relations that such a result would not obtain. Our holding confines the courts to adjudication of the case before them, and leaves to the Executive Branch the conduct of foreign relations. In so doing, it is both faithful to the principle of separation of powers and consistent with earlier cases applying the act of state doctrine where we lacked the sort of representation from the Executive Branch which we have in this case.

We therefore reverse the judgment of the Court of Appeals, and remand the case to it for consideration of respondent's alternative bases of attack on the judgment of the District Court.

Reversed.

MR. JUSTICE DOUGLAS, concurring in the result.

Banco Nacional de Cuba v. Sabbatino, 376 U.S. 398, 84 S.Ct. 923, 11 L.Ed.2d 804, does not control the central issue in the present case. Rather, it is governed by National City Bank v. Republic of China, 348 U.S. 356, 75 S.Ct. 423, 99 L.Ed. 389.

WHY?

* * *

It would offend the sensibilities of nations if one country, not at war with us, had our courthouse door closed to it. It would also offend our sensibilities if Cuba could collect the amount owed on liquidation of the collateral for the loan and not be required to account for any setoff. To allow recovery without more would permit Cuba to have her cake and eat it too. Fair dealing requires allowance of the setoff to the amount of the claim on which this suit is brought— a precept that should satisfy any so-called rational decision.

* * *

MR. JUSTICE POWELL, concurring in the judgment.

Although I concur in the judgment of reversal and remand, my reasons differ from those expressed by MR. JUSTICE REHNQUIST and MR. JUSTICE DOUGLAS. While Banco Nacional de Cuba v. Sabbatino, 376 U.S. 398, 419–420, 84 S.Ct. 923, 935–936, 11 L.Ed.2d 804 (1964), technically reserves the question of the validity of the *Bernstein* exception, as MR. JUSTICE BRENNAN notes in his dissenting opinion, the reasoning of Sabbatino implicitly rejects that exception. Moreover, I would be uncomfortable with a doctrine which would require the judiciary to receive the executive's permission before invoking its jurisdiction. Such a notion, in the name of the doctrine of separation of powers, seems to me to conflict with that very doctrine.

* * *

I nevertheless concur in the judgment of the Court because I believe that the broad holding of Sabbatino was not compelled by the principles, as expressed therein, which underly the act of state doctrine. As Mr. Justice Harlan stated in Sabbatino, the act of state doctrine is not dictated either by "international law [or] the Constitution," but is based on a judgment as to "the proper distribution of functions between the judicial and the political branches of the Government on matters bearing upon foreign affairs." 376 U.S., at 427–428, 84 S.Ct., at 940. Moreover, as noted in Sabbatino, there was no intention of "laying down or reaffirming an inflexible and all-encompassing rule. * * *" Id., at 428, 84 S.Ct., at 940.

I do not disagree with these principles, only with the broad way in which Sabbatino applied them. Had I been a member of the Sabbatino Court, I probably would have joined the dissenting opinion of Mr. Justice White. The balancing of interests, recognized as appropriate by Sabbatino, requires a careful examination of the facts in each case and of the position, if any, taken by the political branches of government. I do not agree, however, that balancing the functions of the judiciary and those of the political branches compels the judiciary to eschew acting in all cases in which the underlying issue is the validity of expropriation under customary international law. Such a result would be an abdication of the judiciary's responsibility to persons who seek to resolve their grievances by the judicial process.

Nor do I think the doctrine of separation of powers dictates such an abdication. To so argue is to assume that there is no such thing as international law but only international political disputes that can be resolved only by the exercise of power. Admittedly, international legal disputes are not as separable from politics as are domestic legal disputes, but I am not prepared to say that international law may never be determined and applied by the judiciary where there has been an "act of state." Until international tribunals command a wider constituency, the courts of various countries afford the best means for the development of a respected body of international law. There is less hope for progress in this long neglected area if the resolution of all disputes involving "an act of state" is relegated to political rather than judicial processes.

Unless it appears that an exercise of jurisdiction would interfere with delicate foreign relations conducted by the political branches, I conclude that federal courts have an obligation to hear cases such as this. This view is not inconsistent with the basic notion of the act of state doctrine which requires a balancing of the roles of the judiciary and the political branches. When it is shown that a conflict in those roles exists, I believe that the judiciary should defer because, as the Court suggested in Sabbatino, the resolution of one dispute by the judiciary may be outweighed by the potential resolution of multiple disputes by the political branches.

In this case where no such conflict has been shown, I think the courts have a duty to determine and apply the applicable international law. I therefore join in the Court's decision to remand the case for further proceedings.

MR. JUSTICE BRENNAN, with whom MR. JUSTICE STEWART, MR. JUSTICE MARSHALL, and MR. JUSTICE BLACKMUN join, dissenting.

The Court today reverses the judgment of the Court of Appeals for the Second Circuit that declined to engraft the so-called *"Bernstein"* exception upon the act of state doctrine as expounded in Banco Nacional de Cuba v. Sabbatino, 376 U.S. 398, 84 S.Ct. 923, 11 L.Ed.2d 804 (1964). The Court, nevertheless, affirms the Court of Appeals' rejection of the *"Bernstein"* exception. Four of us in this opinion unequivocally take that step, as do MR. JUSTICE DOUGLAS and MR. JUSTICE POWELL in their separate concurring opinions.

The anomalous remand for further proceedings results because three colleagues, MR. JUSTICE REHNQUIST, joined by THE CHIEF JUSTICE and MR. JUSTICE WHITE, adopt the contrary position, while MR. JUSTICE DOUGLAS finds National City Bank v. Republic of China, 348 U.S. 356, 75 S.Ct. 423, 99 L.Ed. 389 (1955), dispositive in the circumstances of this case and MR. JUSTICE POWELL rejects the specific holding in Sabbatino, believing it was not required by the principles underlying the act of state doctrine. [Remainder of dissenting opinion omitted.]

---

1. *Excerpts from the letter of the Legal Adviser, Department of State.* The full text of the latest executive branch viewpoint on the act of state doctrine (referred to by the Supreme Court in the text of its opinion at footnote a, p. 429) is carried as an appendix to the second consideration of this case by the Court of Appeals for the Second Circuit, 442 F.2d 530, 536 (1971). The Legal Adviser of the Department of State referred to the first decision by the court of appeals in the First National City Bank case [i. e. Section 2370(e) (2) of Title 22 of the United States Code did not apply to the claim and hence the act of state doctrine as laid down by the Supreme Court in the Sabbatino case did apply] ª and stated that the decision involved matters of importance to the foreign policy of the United States, called attention to the Bernstein exception, disagreed with the non-application of it in the first opinion by the court of appeals, and continued as follows:

> While the Department of State in the past has generally supported the applicability of the act of state doctrine, it has never argued or implied that there should be no exceptions to the doctrine. In its Sabbatino brief, for example, it did not argue for or against the Bernstein principle; rather it assumed that judicial consideration of an act of state would be permissible when the Executive so indicated, and argued simply that the exchange of letters relied on by the lower courts in Sabbatino constituted "no such expression in this case." Brief of the United States, page 11.

a. Because the property at issue in the case (the excess of collateral over debt) was not the property (banks in Cuba) actually taken by Castro. The court said:
* * * [W]e can find no basis for holding that the present case is one "in which a claim of title or other right to property is asserted by [First National City] * * * based upon (or traced through) a confiscation or other taking * * *" 22 U.S.C. § 2370(e)(2). To do so would stand the statute on end. * * * 431 F.2d 394, 402 (1970).

Recent events, in our view, make appropriate a determination by the Department of State that the act of state doctrine need not be applied when it is raised to bar adjudication of a counterclaim or setoff when (a) the foreign state's claim arises from a relationship between the parties existing when the act of state occurred; (b) the amount of the relief to be granted is limited to the amount of the foreign state's claim; and (c) the foreign policy interests of the United States do not require application of the doctrine.

The 1960's have seen a great increase in expropriations by foreign governments of property belonging to United States citizens. Many corporations whose properties are expropriated, financial institutions for example, are vulnerable to suits in our courts by foreign governments as plaintiff, for the purpose of recovering deposits or sums owed them in the United States without taking into account the institutions' counterclaims for their assets expropriated in the foreign country.

The basic considerations of fairness and equity suggesting that the act of state doctrine not be applied in this class of cases, unless the foreign policy interests of the United States so require in a particular case, were reflected in National City Bank [of New York] v. Republic of China, 348 U.S. 356 [75 S.Ct. 423, 99 L.Ed. 389] (1956), in which the Supreme Court held that the protection of sovereign immunity is waived when a foreign sovereign enters a U. S. court as plaintiff. While the Court did not deal with the act of state doctrine, the basic premise of that case—that a sovereign entering court as plaintiff opens itself to counterclaims, up to the amount of the original claim, which could be brought against it by that defendant were the sovereign an ordinary plaintiff—is applicable by analogy to the situation presented in the present case.

In this case, the Cuban government's claim arose from a banking relationship with the defendant existing at the time the act of state—expropriation of defendant's Cuban property—occurred, and defendant's counterclaim is limited to the amount of the Cuban government's claim. We find, moreover, that the foreign policy interests of the United States do not require the application of the act of state doctrine to bar adjudication of the validity of a defendant's counterclaim or set-off against the Government of Cuba in these circumstances.

The Department of State believes that the act of state doctrine should not be applied to bar consideration of a defendant's counterclaim or set-off against the Government of Cuba in this or like cases.

2. *Some questions suggested by the First National City Bank case.*

a.   Why did the Department of State change its general attitude as to the weight that should be given to executive branch viewpoints as to the applicability or not of the act of state doctrine in nationalization cases? This was a Cuban nationalization case. What do you guess the Department of State would advise the court as to act of state in the Peruvian hypothetical case at p. 428? What procedure, as to notice, hearing, and the like, if any, do you think the Department of State should provide—or be required to provide—as a prelude to its taking of a position very likely to control the outcome of the case?

b.   This case was remanded " * * * for the consideration of respondent's alternative bases of attack on the judgment of the District Court * * * ". What law, federal or state, will govern as to issues on remand not covered by federal statutes? See p. 415.

c.   What do you think of Justice Douglas' treatment of the case as one of immunity in regard to a counterclaim against a foreign state when it has sued as plaintiff? See p. 343.

d.   What does Justice Powell's opinion suggest as to the future of the act of state doctrine?

e.   Considering the second Hickenlooper amendment and the decision of the Supreme Court in the instant case, do you think that the courts have any assured independence of the Congress or the executive with respect to the application of the act of state doctrine?

f.   If your answer is "No," does the doctrine have any remaining utility in the foreign affairs law of the United States?

g.   If your answer is "Yes," what is the probable future of the doctrine in this country?

h.   What would be your impartial professional attitude as to a federal statute to simplify the present situation by striking the present second Hickenlooper Amendment and substituting the following:

"The so-called Act of State doctrine shall never be available as a bar to consideration of any case on the merits in any court in the United States with jurisdiction over the parties and the subject matter, unless the President, through his authorized representative, shall state to the court that he has no objection to the application of the said doctrine to bar the suit."

The policy and legal issues raised by the present status of the act of state doctrine in the United States are examined in Lowenfeld, Act of State and Department of State: First National City Bank v. Banco Nacional de Cuba, 66 Am.J.Int'l Law 795 (1972).

SECTION C. PROBLEMS AS TO THE SCOPE OF THE DOCTRINE IN THE INTERNATIONAL SYSTEM

1. PROPERTY LOCALIZED OUTSIDE THE NATIONALIZING STATE

REPUBLIC OF IRAQ v. FIRST NATIONAL CITY BANK

United States Court of Appeals, Second Circuit, 1965.
353 F.2d 47.[a]

FRIENDLY, CIRCUIT JUDGE. King Faisal II of Iraq was killed on July 14, 1958, in the midst of a revolution in that country which led to the establishment of a republic, recognized by the United States in August. On July 19, 1958, the new government issued Ordinance No. 23 which decreed that "all property [of the dynasty] * * * whether moveable or immoveable * * * should be confiscated." At the time of his death King Faisal had a balance of $55,925 and 4,008 shares of Canada General Fund, Ltd., a Canadian investment trust, in deposit and custody accounts with Irving Trust Company in New York. In October 1958, the Surrogate's Court for New York County issued to the defendant letters of administration with respect to King Faisal's New York assets. During that month the Consul General of the Republic of Iraq notified Irving Trust that the Republic claimed all assets of King Faisal by virtue of Ordinance No. 23. Notwithstanding the notice, Irving Trust subsequently transferred to the administrator the balance in the account and certificates for the shares, which were later sold.

In March 1962, the Republic brought this action against the administrator in the District Court for the Southern District of New York to recover the bank balance and the proceeds of the shares. From a judgment dismissing the complaint, 241 F.Supp. 567 (1965), the Republic appeals. We affirm.

The District Court properly held that it had jurisdiction of the action. Under 28 U.S.C. § 1332(a) the district courts are vested with original jurisdiction of all civil actions "where the matter in controversy exceeds the sum or value of $10,000, exclusive of interest and costs, and is between * * * (2) citizens of a State, and foreign states or citizens or subjects thereof." Although this general language does not grant jurisdiction to probate a will or administer an estate, it has been established by a long series of decisions "that federal courts of equity have jurisdiction to entertain suits 'in favor of creditors, legatees and heirs' and other claimants against a decedent's estate 'to establish their claims' so long as the federal court does not interfere with the probate proceedings or assume general

a.   Cert. denied 382 U.S. 1027, 86 S.Ct. 648 (1966).

jurisdiction of the probate or control of the property in the custody of the state court." Markham v. Allen, 326 U.S. 490, 494, 66 S.Ct. 296, 298, 90 L.Ed. 256 (1946), citing Waterman v. Canal-Louisiana Bank & Trust Co., 215 U.S. 33, 43, 30 S.Ct. 10, 54 L.Ed. 80 (1909), and other cases.

The principal questions raised in this appeal are the proper definition of the act of state doctrine and its application to foreign confiscation decrees purporting to affect property within the United States. Although difficulty is sometimes encountered in drawing the line between an "act of state" and more conventional foreign decrees or statutes claimed to be entitled to respect by the forum, the Ordinance involved in this case is nowhere near the boundary. A confiscation decree, which is precisely what Ordinance No. 23 purported to be, is the very archetype of an act of state. See ALI, Restatement of Foreign Relations Law of the United States § 41c (Proposed Official Draft, 1962) [hereinafter cited as Restatement].

The Supreme Court has declared that a question concerning the effect of an act of state "must be treated exclusively as an aspect of federal law." Banco Nacional de Cuba v. Sabbatino, 376 U.S. 398, 423–427, 84 S.Ct. 923, 939, 11 L.Ed.2d 804 (1964). We deem that ruling to be applicable here even though, as we conclude below, this is not a case in which the courts of the forum are bound to respect the act of the foreign state. Like the traditional application of the act of state doctrine to preclude judgment with respect to another government's acts concerning property within its own territory at the time, see Underhill v. Hernandez, 168 U.S. 250, 18 S.Ct. 83, 42 L.Ed. 456 (1897); Oetjen v. Central Leather Co., 246 U.S. 297, 38 S.Ct. 309, 62 L.Ed. 726 (1918); Ricaud v. American Metal Co., 246 U.S. 304, 38 S.Ct. 312, 62 L.Ed. 733 ((1918), the exercise of discretion whether or not to respect a foreign act of state affecting property in the United States is closely tied to our foreign affairs, with consequent need for nationwide uniformity. It is fundamental to our constitutional scheme that in dealing with other nations the country must speak with a united voice. See United States v. Belmont, 301 U.S. 324, 331, 57 S.Ct. 758, 81 L.Ed. 1134 (1937); United States v. Pink, 315 U.S. 203, 233–234, 62 S.Ct. 552, 86 L.Ed. 796 (1942). It would be baffling if a foreign act of state intended to affect property in the United States were ignored on one side of the Hudson but respected on the other; any such diversity between states would needlessly complicate the handling of the foreign relations of the United States. The required uniformity can be secured only by recognizing the expansive reach of the principle, announced by Mr. Justice Harlan in Sabbatino, that all questions relating to an act of state are questions of federal law, to be determined ultimately, if need be, by the Supreme Court of the United States.

Under the traditional application of the act of state doctrine, the principle of judicial refusal of examination applies only to a taking by a foreign sovereign of property within its own territory, see Ehrenzweig, Conflict of Laws § 48 at 172 (1962); cf. Banco Nacional de Cuba v. Sabbatino, supra, 376 U.S. at 401, 428, 432, 84 S.Ct. 923; when property confiscated is within the United States at the time of the attempted confiscation, our courts will give effect to acts of state "only if they are consistent with the policy and law of the United States." Restatement § 46.

In this case, neither the bank account nor the shares in the Canadian investment trust can realistically be considered as being within Iraq simply because King Faisal resided and was physically present there at the time of his death; in the absence of any showing that Irving Trust had an office in Iraq or would be in any way answerable to its courts, we need not consider whether the conclusion would differ if it did. Cf. United States v. First Nat'l City Bank, 379 U.S. 378, 85 S.Ct. 528, 13 L.Ed.2d 365 (1965). So far as appears on this record, only a court in the United States could compel the bank to pay the balance in the account or to deliver the certificates it held in custody. The property here at issue thus was within the United States. Although the nationality of King Faisal provided a jurisdictional basis for the Republic of Iraq to prescribe a rule relating to his property outside Iraq, Restatement § 30(1)(b), this simply gives the confiscation decree a claim to consideration by the forum which, in the absence of such jurisdiction, it would not possess —not a basis for insisting on the absolute respect which, subject to the qualifications of Sabbatino, 376 U.S. at 428, 84 S.Ct. 923, the decree would enjoy as to property within Iraq at the time.

Extra-territorial enforcement of the Iraqi ordinance as to property within the United States at the date of its promulgation turns on whether the decree is consistent with our policy and laws. We perceive no basis for thinking it to be. Confiscation of the assets of a corporation has been said to be "contrary to our public policy and shocking to our sense of justice," Vladikavkazsky Ry. Co. v. New York Trust Co., 263 N.Y. 369, 378, 189 N.E. 456, 460, 91 A.L.R. 1426 (1934); see also Zwack v. Kraus Bros. & Co., 237 F.2d 255, 259 (2 Cir. 1956) (partnership); Plesch v. Banque Nationale de la République d'Haiti, 273 App.Div. 224, 77 N.Y.S.2d 43 (1st Dept.), aff'd, 298 N.Y. 573, 81 N.E.2d 106 (1948). Confiscation of the assets of an individual is no less so, even if he wears a crown. Compare Banco de Vizcaya v. Don Alfonso de Borbon y Austria, [1935] 1 K.B. 140. Our Constitution sets itself against confiscations such as that decreed by Ordinance No. 23 not only by the general guarantees of due process in the Fifth and Fourteenth Amendments but by the specific prohibitions of bills of attainder in Article I. See United States v. Brown, 381 U.S. 437, 85 S.Ct. 1707, 14 L.Ed.2d 484 (1965), and cases cited therein. It is true that since these provisions are addressed to action by the United States or a state, they might not prevent a court of the United States from giving effect to a confiscatory act of a foreign state with respect to property in the United States. But at least they show that, from its earliest days under the Constitution, this nation has had scant liking for legislative proscription of members of a defeated faction, although—or perhaps because—many states, in their dealings with property of the loyalists immediately after the Revolution, had practiced exactly that. See United States v. Brown, supra, 381 U.S. at 441–446, 85 S.Ct. 1707. Foreigners entrusting their property to custodians in this country are entitled to expect this historic policy to be followed save when the weightiest reasons call for a departure. In saying this we are not guilty of disrespect to the recitals in the preamble of Ordinance No. 23, see fn. 1; subject to the narrow exception discussed below, the policy of the United States is that there is no such thing as a "good" confiscation by legislative or executive decree.

The only cases cited to us that might seem to suggest a deviation from this view are United States v. Belmont, 301 U.S. 324, 57 S.Ct. 758 (1937), and United States v. Pink, 315 U.S. 203, 62 S.Ct. 552 (1942). Language in the latter opinion did indeed lead "some commentators to protest that the Court had laid down the revolutionary doctrine that recognition requires the recognizing state to give extraterritorial effect to all acts of state of the recognized government." Stevenson, Effect of Recognition on the Application of Private International Law Norms, 51 Colum.L.Rev. 710, 720 & n. 54 (1951); see Borchard, Extraterritorial Confiscations, 36 Am.J.Int'l L. 275 (1942); Jessup, The Litvinov Assignment and the Pink case, id. at 282. The facts of the cases, however, required no such overturn of established principles. By the Litvinov agreement our Government had procured, as an incident to recognition, an assignment of the Soviet Union's claims to American assets of nationalized Russian companies, for the benefit of United States nationals whose property in the Soviet Union had been confiscated. Such action of the Chief Executive, taken under his power to conduct the foreign relations of the United States, was considered to make the Soviet confiscation decrees consistent with the law and policy of the United States from that time forward, and, as we now know from Sabbatino, federal law controls. See Restatement § 46, comment (c) and the discussion of United States v. Pink. In this case, by contrast, nothing remotely resembling the Litvinov agreement is present; on the contrary, the Department of State has disclaimed any interest of the executive department in the outcome of the litigation.[5]

5. The Deputy Legal Adviser to the Department of State said in a letter dated January 15, 1965, to defendant's counsel:

   While the recognition of and maintenance of diplomatic relations with a foreign government are political matters within the province of the executive department of the Federal Government, questions regarding the administration of estates and the determination of rights and interests in property in the United States ordinarily are matters for determination by the courts of competent jurisdiction. Accordingly, the Department considers that the legal effect of Ordinance No. 23 as it may pertain to title

Appellant insists that, however this may be, a New York court would give effect to Ordinance No. 23 because of the New York Decedent Estate Law, McKinney's Consol.Laws, c. 13, § 47, which provides:

> Except where special provision is otherwise made by law, the validity and effect of a testamentary disposition of any other property [i. e., other than real estate] situated within the state, and the ownership and disposition of such property, where it is not disposed of by will, are regulated by the laws of the state or country, of which the decedent was a resident, at the time of his death.

As already indicated, we read Sabbatino to mean that New York could not, by application of its choice of law rules, give a foreign act of state an effect, whether less or greater, differing from that dictated by federal law. But appellant's position would be baseless in any event. Not only does § 47 refer to the law existing at the time of decedent's death, but no state has been stronger in its opposition to foreign confiscation decrees than New York, see, e. g., Vladikavkazsky Ry. Co. v. New York Trust Co., supra; Plesch v. Banque Nationale de la République d'Haiti, supra. Indeed, it was this opposition that required the Supreme Court's intervention in the Pink case. We are thus confident that the courts of New York would not strain to read the general language of the Decedent Estate Law to include what on its face is a confiscation decree.

Since the district judge properly concluded the complaint to be lacking in merit, we do not reach the question whether dismissal would have been required in any event on the ground that a prior decree of the Surrogate's Court distributing the assets of the estate operated as res judicata despite the sovereign character of the Republic of Iraq and the pendency of this suit. See Restatement § 71, comment (e).

Affirmed.

The problem of jurisdiction to nationalize. A number of decisions in other countries also hold that a state's purported act of state in seeking to take into public ownership assets not localized within its territory will not be recognized. These decisions either hold that the act of state doctrine does not apply to such situations, that such takings are clearly against ordre public, or that the state has no jurisdiction to nationalize property that is within the jurisdiction to nationalize of the forum state or some third state. Prob-

to property in the United States of King Faisal II is a question for deter- mination by the competent United States court.

lems of extraterritorial nationalization, then, are clearly distinguishable from the act of state doctrine, and decisions denying recognition of extraterritorial nationalization are not properly to be counted as decisions rejecting the act of state doctrine where the extraterritorial issue is not present. See Reeves, The Sabbatino Case and the Sabbatino Amendment: Comedy—or Tragedy—of Errors, 20 Vand.L. Rev. 429 (1966–1967), especially Appendix II.

As in conflict of laws, there is a problem as to the localization— or ascribed situs—of intangibles, in a range from unliquidated claims against a debtor to negotiable securities. Most nationalization cases, however, involve either land or movables that are capable of having an actual physical location. Illustration: when President Nasser nationalized the assets of the Universal Suez Canal Corporation, he got the canal, but the big investment portfolio of the company kept in Europe remained beyond his grasp.

----

2. INVALIDATION OF TITLE AND RESTITUTION AS REMEDIES FOR NATIONALIZATION

In the Sabbatino case, the lower federal courts demonstrated a somewhat remarkable determination to correct nationalization injustices by judicial dead-reckoning. Both the district court and the court of appeals decided that the Supreme Court's prior creation, the act of state doctrine, did not bar judicial examination of the legitimacy under customary international law of a taking in Cuba. In this they were held in error.

In its first Sabbatino decision, the court of appeals also addressed the remedy issue squarely: if the act of state doctrine is no bar to examination and if examination shows that the taking by Cuba did violate customary international law, what is the remedy? The court's answer, in no uncertain terms, was that the old owner still has title to his property. The act of nationalization was a legal nullity. This is corroborated by the disposition of the case: the Banco Nacional had sued the sugar broker for conversion of the proceeds of the sale of the sugar from the nationalized sugar mill. The district judge granted the defendant's motion for summary judgment, and the court of appeals affirmed—i. e., no conversion; the proceeds were defendant's.

In this decision, 307 F.2d 845 (2d Cir. 1962), the court of appeals said:

> * * * We need not at present go into the question whether the granting of this type of remedy is a feature of international law or of domestic law. But we do suggest that the failure of an international tribunal to give a remedy of this type results from the inability of that kind of court to enforce its awards

and is not a result of the dictates of substantive international law principles *   *   *

To this statement the court added in a note that it did not hope to resolve a "chicken-and-egg" issue on rights and remedies, and continued:

> *   *   * If one believes legal rights exist separate from and prior to the existence of legal remedies, he may interpret our holding to mean that we have recognized an international wrong and have fashioned an appropriate remedy. If, on the other hand, the reader believes legal rights cannot exist in the absence of legal remedies, he is free to interpret our words as meaning that since municipal courts can grant a remedy which divests an international title, the appellant's title is invalid.

This decision led to a great debate in the literature; but, as has been seen, the Supreme Court did not reach the issue, because act of state barred further inquiry. Then, the second Hickenlooper amendment was passed, and its specific retroactive application to the Supreme Court's order in the Sabbatino Case was upheld by the court of appeals in the Farr Case. There also the court of appeals ruled that its prior decision on the international law issue had not been affected by the Supreme Court decision, which had reversed on act of state alone. But in Farr the remedies issue in relationship to international law was not separated for re-examination from the issue of validity of taking under international law. The parties disputed the remedies issue in the certiorari pleadings, and the petitioner (Banco Nacional de Cuba) also advanced the viewpoint that in this case, which involved only the proceeds of the sale of the sugar, "damages" and "restitution" are identical. However, the United States Supreme Court denied certiorari without any indication of viewpoint on the international law issues, including the remedies issue as distinct from the violation-in-the-taking issue.

Thus, there is some authority in the United States that, where the act of state doctrine does not apply and the taking violates international law, the remedy of invalidation of title or of specific restitution is available.

The cases that follow are representative of decisions in other states on the subject matter of this chapter. What do they hold on remedies?

ANGLO–IRANIAN OIL CO., LTD. v. JAFFRATE
(THE ROSE MARY).

Aden, Supreme Court, 1953.
20 Int'l L.Rep. 316 (1957).

THE FACTS: On June 17, 1952, the Rose Mary, flying the flag of Honduras, arrived in Aden harbour with a cargo of crude oil which had been loaded at Bundar Mashur in Southern Iran. The Anglo-Iranian Oil Company Limited brought this action in the Supreme Court of the Colony of Aden in detinue, claiming delivery up to them of this oil or, alternatively, a declaration that it was their property. The action was brought against Captain Guiseppe Jaffrate, the then master, the Compania de Navegacion Teresita S.A. of Panama City, Panama, the owners, and Bubenberg A.G. of Spiez, Switzerland, the charterers, of the Rose Mary.

The plaintiffs claimed the property in, or the immediate right to possession of, the oil by virtue of the Convention between them and the Imperial Government of Persia concluded on April 29, 1933, by which they were granted the exclusive right within the territory of a specified concession to search for and extract petroleum for a period ending on December 31, 1993. The agreement provided, by Article 21, that it should not be altered by legislation and, by Article 22, that in the event of any disputes they were to be referred to arbitration—a procedure which Iran now declined to adopt. The oil in question, the plaintiffs alleged, was produced by plants established by them in the concession in Southern Iran, and this was admitted by all the defendants.

The owners of the Rose Mary refused to give possession of the cargo to the plaintiffs on the ground that the title to it was in dispute, but stated that it was loaded against their instructions. The master pleaded that the Rose Mary entered Aden harbour under duress, and that, accordingly, the Aden Court had no jurisdiction in the matter. He also claimed that the cargo belonged to the charterers. The charterers also alleged duress, and, alternatively, relied on the Iranian Laws of March and May 1951, which purported to nationalize and expropriate as from May 1, 1951, all property vested in the plaintiffs by the concession of 1933.

Held: that the Company were entitled to the oil, which had remained their property and to which the Government of Iran had acquired no title, since (1) "the Iranian Laws of 1951 were invalid by international law, for, by them, the property of the company was expropriated without any compensation;" and (2) "British courts treated international law as incorporated into their domestic law so far as it was not inconsistent with their own rules (per Lord Atkin in Chung Chi Cheung v. Rex (1939) A.C. 160, 168; 55 T.L.R. 184; [1938] All E.R. 786)". It was further held that "the principle in

Aksionairnoye Obschestvo A. M. Luther Co. v. James Sagor and Co. [1921] 3 K.B. 532; 37 T.L.R. 777, and Princess Paley Olga v. Weisz [1929] 1 K.B. 718; 45 T.L.R. 365, that a court would not inquire into the legality of acts done by a foreign government in respect of property situate in that government's territory applied only where the property was that of the government's own subjects; and * * * accordingly, following international law as incorporated in the domestic law of Aden, the court must refuse validity to the Iranian Laws of 1951." Judgment was, therefore, given for the plaintiffs.

[A portion of the opinion of the court appears below.]

[IV. The Question of Compensation before Municipal and International Courts.]—I have been referred to a number of foreign decisions. In Société Potasas Ibericus v. Nathan Bloch (Annual Digest of Public International Law Cases, 1938–1940, p. 150) the French Court of Cassation held that decrees of expropriation by the Government of Catalonia were invalid in France on the ground that, as no just compensation had been provided for, they were against French Public Policy. In U.R.S.S. v. Société La Ropit (Annual Digest of Public International Law Cases, 1927–1928, p. 67) the same Court held that

> although the principle that the courts of a State faced with a juridical situation governed by foreign legislation should apply the foreign law must be admitted, this rule is only obligatory in so far as the application of the foreign law and respect for the rights acquired thereby are not incompatible with those principles and provisions of their national law which are held essential for ordre publique.

The Court then proceeded to disallow the intervention of the Russian Government to get possession of merchant ships which had been nationalised and were berthed at Marseilles.

In relying on French cases, however, it must be borne in mind that the domestic law of France is very explicit regarding the right of private ownership. In Article 545 of Civil Code it is laid down that:

> No one in France can be forced to give up his property except in the public interest and in return for a fair and prepaid compensation.

The decisions in the two cases I have just mentioned actually referred to this section. But although in Aden there is no statutory enactment so far as I know similar to this section, it is nevertheless part of the common law. The cases therefore have some authority.

In Poland the Supreme Court in Siuta v. Guzkowski (Annual Digest of Public International Law Cases, 1919–1922, p. 480) refused validity to a requisition by Ukrainian troops in Poland of horses which they sold to local inhabitants. Its decision was based mainly on Article 52 of the Hague Rules, which forbids requisitions except for the needs of the occupying forces. Nevertheless, it is applicable here inasmuch as the principle was laid down that whether or not the Hague Rules are binding on the parties (and it would seem that they were not binding on the Ukrainians who were not recognised as belligerents) the Polish courts regard confiscation such as this contrary to the "cardinal principle of international custom". And if an act was contrary to international custom they would grant it no validity in Poland.

In Germany the Provincial Court of Kassel and the District Court of Waiblingen, dealing in 1947 and 1948 with cases relating to the sequestration of property of Germans qua Germans, living in Czechoslovakia, held that such sequestration was contrary to international law and refused to recognise it. Where such property came into their jurisdiction they ordered its return to its owners. The cases are to be found in New Juridical Weekly Review, 1947, p. 628, and Monthly Review of German Law, 1949, p. 163, respectively. The Provincial Court of Hildersheim, in a similar case to be found in the South German Lawyers' Review, 1948, p. 143, came to a different conclusion. But they gave no reasons for their decision.

In Italy the Tribunal of Florence, in Lucchesi v. Malfatti (II Foro Italiano, vol. 69 (1944–1946), p. 985 [Annual Digest, 1946, p. 382]) had to decide the subsequent ownership of a motor car which had been requisitioned by the Germans but not for the requirements of the occupying troops. They had seized it from the plaintiff and given it to the defendant on the ground that he was an invalid of the Great War. The Tribunal found that the requisition was unlawful and ordered the return of the car to its former owner. This case, like others previously mentioned, arises out of events which took place in time of war and partly depends on the law of war. But it would seem also applicable to peace time. For if a court is willing to hold that a seizure is illegal in time of war a fortiori it would be unwilling to recognise the same in time of peace.

I now come to the Norwegian Ships case, 1922 [A.J., vol. 17 (1923), p. 362]: The Government of the United States of America had, in 1917, requisitioned certain Norwegian ships. The two Governments submitted the question of compensation to an arbitration tribunal under the auspicies of the Permanent Court of Arbitration at The Hague. Although compensation was the only issue there are several observations in the award which seem relevant to the present case. At page 67 [of the Award] it is said:

> The fifth amendment of the Constitution of the United States provides: "No person shall be deprived of life, liberty or property without due process of law; nor shall private property be taken for public use, without just compensation."

It is common ground that in this respect the public law of the Parties is in complete accord with the international public law of all civilised countries.

At page 69:

Whether the action of the United States was lawful or not, just compensation is due to the claimants under the municipal law of the United States, as well as the international law, based upon the respect for private property.

In deciding what is meant by the word "compensation" in international law the Tribunal said at page 73:

Just compensation implies a complete restitution of the status quo ante, based not upon future gains of the United States or other powers, but upon the loss of profits of the Norwegian owners as compared with other owners of similar property.

Lastly at page 4 it is laid down that:

International law and justice are based upon the principle of equality between States. No state can exercise towards the citizens of another civilized State the "power of eminent domain" without respecting the property of such foreign citizens, or without paying just compensation as determined by an impartial tribunal if necessary.

In the case of the De Sabla Claim (Annual Digest of Public International Law Cases, 1933–1934, p. 241), the specially appointed Claims Commission enquired into the expropriation by the Government of Panama of land belonging to a national of the United States of America. In its judgment the Commission stated:

The Commission concludes that the adjudications and the licences granted by the authorities on Bernadino constituted wrongful acts for which the Government is responsible internationally. It is axiomatic that acts of a government in depriving an alien of his property without compensation impose international responsibility.

In 1938 the Government of Mexico nationalised its oil. A long correspondence then took place between the Government of Mexico and Mr. Cordell Hull the Secretary of State of the United States. In many communications the latter contended that confiscation of the property of aliens is contrary to, and will not be recognised by, international law. He argued that confiscation does not cease to be so because there may be the express desire to pay at some time in the future. The plaintiffs invoke this correspondence in aid. They say that it is not only the opinion of the writer but, as he was then Secretary of State, it is a statement of the opinion, and this is an expression of what would be the practice, of the Government of the United States. This may well be, but it is an opinion set out when arguing a brief and as such I think it cannot have the weight which should be given

to a judicial opinion. It has not got that salutary check upon the
writer of the overhanging shadow of a Court of Appeal. How I think
the plaintiffs are entitled to invoke the dispute in their aid is by
reason of the fact that throughout the argument the Mexican Government does not appear to have denied the main premise of their
adversary's argument. They refer to the blood of Mexico's sons shed
in the revolutionary struggle and assert that their acts were inspired
by legitimate causes and the aspirations of social justice. But they do
not deny the principles of compensation.

The defendants have cited Paley v. Weisz and Luther v. Sagor
as being in their favour. The first of these does no more than lay
down the principle, as enunciated by Russell L.J. at p. 736 of the
report, that:

> This court will not enquire into the legality of acts done
> by a foreign government against its own subjects in respect of
> property situate in its own territory.

It said nothing regarding property of those not its own subjects.

The second case, Luther v. Sagor, also concerned confiscation of
property belonging to subjects of the confiscating Government. It
was also held that the confiscation was valid and would be upheld
by the English court. The dicta in the judgments on which the defendants seek to rely are chiefly those of Scrutton L.J. At p. 556 of
the report he says:

> Should there be any government which appropriates other
> people's property without compensation, the remedy appears to
> be to refuse to recognise it as a sovereign state.

At page 558, he says:

> But it appears a serious breach of international comity, if a
> state is recognised as a sovereign independent state, to postulate
> that its legislation is contrary to essential principles of justice
> and morality.

The court was considering the effect of the conduct of a sovereign
State in regard to its subjects. If Scrutton L.J. had been specifically
considering such conduct in regard to aliens, a far wider question of
international law, I feel no confidence that he would have expressed
the same opinion. His remarks were a good deal wider than necessary
for the decision of the case.

On the whole I think that the relevance to this case of a great
part of the judgment in Luther v. Sagor is more apparent than real
and that the case is in no way decisive here.

The case of Santos v. Illidge, (1860) 8 C.B. (N.S.) 861, might also
appear at first to favour the argument of the defendants. Here the
non-delivery of slaves in Brazil under a contract made there which
was lawful according to Brazilian law was held actionable in England
though the sale would have been criminal in England. The slaves were

acquired by the defendants in Brazil after the passing of the Slave Trade Act, 1824, but before the passing of the Slave Trade Act, 1843. It would seem that the reason why the court did not refuse to entertain the claim was that no statute prohibited the holding of slaves in Brazil even though the purchasing of them might be a felony in a British subject. That well known case, known as Somersett's case, (1772) 20 State Trials, where an escaped slave successfully sued out a writ of habeas corpus on the ground that although slavery may be recognised and lawful in the Colonies it was not allowed and approved of by the law of England was, therefore, not overruled.

British courts are inclined towards resting international law on practice and precedent rather than on the opinions of speculative writers however unanimous or eminent they may be. Nevertheless I have examined the opinions of jurists on international law in such of their writings as are available here. The conclusion I arrive at is that Dicey, Oppenheim, Cheshire, Fachiri and Hackworth endorse the view that expropriation without compensation is contrary to international law. I can find no opinions to the contrary though the defendants have referred me to Martin Wolff.

For the reasons set out above I am satisfied that following international law as incorporated in the domestic law of Aden, this Court must refuse validity to the Persian Oil Nationalisation Law in so far as it relates to nationalised property of the plaintiffs which may come within its territorial jurisdiction. I find the oil in dispute to be still the property of the plaintiffs. * * *

I therefore find that the plaintiffs are entitled to succeed in this action and that the cargo of oil must be returned to them. A decree will issue against all three defendants to this effect as each has or had a measure of control over the cargo.

* * *

ANGLO–IRANIAN OIL COMPANY LTD. v. S.U.P.O.R. CO.

Italy, Court of Venice, 1953.
22 Int'l L.Rep. 19 (1958).

THE FACTS: The respondent Company had purchased in Persia certain oil which was shipped in the *Miriella* from Abadan and lay in store in Venice. The Anglo-Iranian Oil Company (A.I.O.C.) claimed the oil on the ground that the Persian Law of May 1, 1951, nationalizing the petroleum industry had not affected the ownership of A.I.O.C. in this particular cargo of oil and that in any event the Oil Nationalization Law could not properly be enforced by an Italian court as it violated the principles of Italian "public order". The A.I.O.C. applied for "judicial sequestration" [an order for interim custody] of the oil pending the hearing of their claim. S.U.P.O.R. objected on the ground that for the Court to grant such an order would amount to prejudging the substantive claim and so to "annulling" the law of a foreign sovereign State, namely, the Persian Oil Nationalization Law.

Held: that the application must fail. Although the respondents were in error in contending that the Court had no power to examine, and if necessary to refuse to apply, the law of a foreign State, on the merits of the substantive claim the Court found that the Persian Oil Nationalization Law was not contrary to Italian "public order"; the applicant Company therefore had no claim to the ownership of the oil in question. [A portion of the opinion of the court appears below.]

If, however, the question is tested by examining the Nationalization Law in regard to public order, which has been referred to at some length in the contentions put forward on behalf of A.I.O.C., the claim of ownership appears unjustified, which supports the rejection of the request for sequestration.

* * *

It can be seen, therefore, that the Nationalization Law does not exclude the payment of compensation to A.I.O.C.; moreover, it unequivocally recognizes the right to claim such compensation. In fact, whilst Article 2 envisages a deposit to meet the claims of the Company, Article 3 contains the solemn undertaking on the part of the Persian Government to examine, in addition to its own claims, those of the Company; these claims, which are not specified in Article 2 but which are "likely" ("probable" in the English text produced by A.I.O.C.), are in Article 3 defined as being "rightful", and the argument maintained by A.I.O.C. that among these legitimate claims the Law does not include the claim for compensation—which is the most likely and most legitimate, though not the only one—must be regarded as being an entirely arbitrary view.

Little importance, from a legal point of view, can be attached to the argument of A.I.O.C. that the Law does not fix the measure of compensation nor require promptness in payment. Even considering the exceptional nature of the question, which—it must be recognized— as compared with the normal application of a foreign Law almost touches the limits contemplated by Article 31 of the Preliminary Rules, the Persian Law can be examined only with a view to establishing whether it fails to provide for the payment of any compensasion, so as to be contrary to our Constitution, the provisions of which present the principle of public order and which admits expropriation "provided that compensation is paid". And other questions, such as the measure of compensation, its form, and promptness in payment, do not concern the public order; these are accessory elements which should be agreed upon on the basis of present historical, political, social and economic conditions, which should be proportionate to the nature and importance of the property in question, and which do not enter the sphere of public order provided that they do not in practice annul the compensation and make it illusory.

* * *

ANGLO–IRANIAN OIL CO. v. IDEMITSU KOSAN KABUSHIKI KAISHA

Japan, District Court of Tokyo (Civil Ninth Division), 1953.
High Court of Tokyo (First Civil Affairs Section), 1953.
20 Int'l L.Rep. 305 (1957).

THE FACTS. This was an application for an interim order for the placing in the custody of the Court of certain petrol and light oil (hereinafter called "the oil") imported from Iran into Japan by the respondents. The oil had been purchased in April 1953 by the respondents from the National Iranian Oil Co., but the applicants claimed the ownership of the oil on the ground that the National Iranian Oil Co. had had no right to sell it and the respondents had therefore acquired no title to the oil.

The oil was part of certain oil extracted and refined by the applicants under a Concession Agreement (hereinafter called "the Concession Agreement") dated April 29, 1933, and made between the Government of Persia (the former name of Iran) and the Anglo-Persian Oil Co., Ltd. (as the applicants were formerly called). The extraction and refinement took place before the coming into force on May 1, 1951, of the Oil Nationalization Law of Iran (hereinafter called "the Nationalization Law").

The applicants contended that even if the oil in question had not been refined before the Nationalization Law came into force, then in view of the fact that it was loaded in Southern Iran and had a high octane value, it must have been actually produced in the concession district granted to the applicants and refined in one of the applicants' refineries; therefore the oil should be held to be the property of the applicants. Under the Nationalization Law, on May 1, 1951, all the rights and interests in Iran of the applicants under the Concession Agreement were nationalized and acquired by the National Iranian Oil Company. The Nationalization Law deprived the applicants of their rights and interests without compensation contrary to the principle of international law that "No rights or interests of foreigners shall be infringed without payment of reasonable compensation" and for that reason it was invalid, the expropriation was invalid, and the National Iranian Oil Company was not entitled to the rights and interest in the oil of the applicants. * * *

* * *

The Iranian Oil Nationalization Law was a law enacted and enforced by a sovereign State; no court outside Iran therefore (it was contended) had power to judge the validity or invalidity of that Law. The Law did not aim at confiscating the applicants' oil industry in Iran but was a law to expropriate it with compensation. The question of compensation, the question of the effect of the act of expropriation of rights and interests and the question of ownership of the oil were all entirely different questions; compensation was a matter that arose after expropriation had taken effect. * * *

The respondents also contended that the principle that a court cannot judge whether the law of a foreign independent State is valid or not, should be followed.

[Held by the District Court of Tokyo that the application must be dismissed. A portion of the opinion of the District Court appears below.]

* * * The first point raised by the applicants is that the Nationalization Law is a confiscatory law by which an alien's interest has been confiscated without compensation; that it is therefore invalid in the eyes of international law; and that the courts of other countries cannot therefore uphold the validity thereof. It cannot be denied that there exists a rule of international law which makes an act of confiscating without compensation a foreign interest in a country a wrongful act under international law. As a result of that rule, a foreigner who suffers from such an act of confiscation, or his own Government acting in his interests, will naturally demand, and press the confiscating Government for, payment of compensation. However, the question whether or not the courts of a third State have power to declare such an act of another State invalid, or to deny the effect of the act, is quite a different proposition. This Court is not convinced that there exists a universally established principle of international law which answers the question in the affirmative. This Court considers that, if it were called upon to give effect within its own jurisdiction to a nationalization law promulgated by a State for the promotion of its own public welfare, then so long as the law does not violate the public policy of this country and also having regard to the requirements of international comity and of mutual respect for sovereign power between nations, this Court could not refuse to recognize the result of the application of such a law. Subject to the question whether the Nationalization Law is a confiscatory law or not, the applicants do not dispute the fact that the Nationalization Law is a law regularly enacted in accordance with the established legislative procedure of Iran. Consequently, the said Law must be regarded as a valid law in Iran.

[Held by the High Court of Tokyo that the appeal must be dismissed. A portion of the opinion of the High Court appears below.]

* * *

II.   The Right to Adjudicate on the Validity of Foreign Nationalization Laws.   Presumption in favour of Conformity with International Law.   Because Iran enacted, as stated above, the Oil Nationalization Law which caused the oil industry in Iran to be nationalized, and purported to nationalize the appellants' rights under the said Agreement with Iran, there has arisen a dispute between the contracting parties as to whether such rights and interests were or were not actually nationalized by Iran.   According to evidence submitted by the appellants, the Iranian Government have by the Nationalization Law expropriated the appellants' rights under the said Agreement, subject to the payment of compensation; if this Law is valid the appellants have no rights [in the oil which is the object of this application], and if the Law is invalid the appellants have retained their rights therein * * *

(a) There is an established principle of international law that in the event of a violent social reform or revolution in a State, whether or not the property of the nationals of that State is confiscated, property belonging to foreign nationals can only be expropriated with compensation; it cannot be confiscated.   Moreover, such compensation must be "adequate, efficient and immediate compensation". This has been confirmed by the practice of many States, by precedents, and by the writings of acknowledged authorities.

(b) As to whether the courts of a third country must recognize the effect of a law which is, as the Nationalization Law was, properly enacted by another State, or whether it is permissible to examine the validity or invalidity of such a law and then possibly refuse to recognize it, the practice of the various States is still divided, and no universally accepted principle of international law that the effect of a foreign law may be adjudged invalid by the courts of a State has yet been established * * *   This Court considers that the Oil Nationalization Law was enacted in Iran's own interests and in accordance with the Resolution of the General Assembly of the United Nations relating to the exploitation of the natural resources of the various countries.   Furthermore, as stated in the conclusions, in view of the fact that the Nationalization Law is not a completely confiscatory law, contrary to the rights and interests of foreign nationals, but a law of expropriation subject to payment of compensation, the Court feels bound to hold that it cannot try the validity or invalidity of such a law by examining the compensation and seeing whether or not it is "adequate, effective and immediate".   If, however, we take the view that we cannot pass on the validity or invalidity of such a law, we do in effect thereby actually recognize the validity of the law. But if the contents of the law contravene public policy and good morals, then, in view of the provisions of Article 30 of the Hōrei, they ought not to be enforced in this country.   (This point is dealt with later.)   Unless they are contrary to public order, etc., the result mentioned above will be in conformity with the principles of inter-

national comity based on the necessity of mutually respecting the
sovereignty of, and maintaining friendly relations among, independent sovereigns.   It is true that Iran has not yet ratified the Peace
Treaty with Japan of September 8, 1951, so that the two countries
have not entered into normal diplomatic relations.   That fact is well
known to this Court.   In view, however, of the fact that normal
diplomatic relations will be established sooner or later between the
two countries, it is proper for our country to act in conformity with
the principles of international comity.   Accordingly, the appellants'
claim that the Nationalization Law is contrary to international law
and therefore invalid may be regarded as groundless to the extent
that there is no need to deal with further points in dispute.

*   *   *

III.   Nationalization of Expropriated Oil Already Extracted
when the Nationalization Law Came into Force.   It has been proved
in evidence that on September 20, 1951, a large quantity of oil was
stored in the tanks at Abadan and Bandar Mashur (Iran), which had
been extracted by the appellants under the above-mentioned Concession Agreement.   Although there may be some doubt whether or
not it was the intention of the Nationalization Law to nationalize oils
which had been extracted and stored at the date when the Law
came into force, little guidance on that point can be obtained from
the Nationalization Law itself.   The Law provides that "The Government [of Iran]   *   *   *   shall promptly expropriate the property
of [the appellants]", and further, in Article 4, that "All and any oil
revenue and oil products shall be the undeniable property of the
State of Iran as from the 20th day of March 1951   *   *   *."   On the
basis of these provisions, we tend to the opinion that, as the respondents allege, the oil which had already been extracted at that time
was caught by the Nationalization Law and was expropriated by
the Iranian Government.   On the other hand, the appellants apparently admit the fact that the interpretation given to the Law by
the Iranian Government was that the oil which had been extracted at
that time was expropriated, and the oil was dealt with as such.   If
that be the case, admitting that there is left some room for argument
as to the interpretation of the Nationalization Law and unless the
interpretation given to it by the Government of Iran is an impossible
interpretation, it would be advisable for us as the court of a third
country to show a high regard for the Iranian Government's interpretation, and that from the standpoint of and by reason of international comity, which arises from the necessity for the respect of
sovereign power and the maintenance of friendly relations between
independent sovereigns.   Therefore, the oil which was in the tanks
above-mentioned must be regarded as having been expropriated by
the Iranian Government.

IV.   Ownership of the Expropriated Oil.   It is difficult to decide on the evidence whether the oil which is the subject of the present

appeal was part of the oil which had already been extracted at the time when the Nationalization Law came into force, or was part of the oil extracted after the nationalization. However, if the oil in question had already been extracted at the time of the coming into force of the Nationalization Law, then, as already explained, it is part of the property expropriated by Iran under that Law, so that it must be held that in consequence thereof the appellants lost their right to that oil. If, on the other hand, the said oil was extracted after the Law came into force, even if it was produced from the district of which formerly the appellants held a lease, and was refined at one of the refineries which formerly belonged to the appellants, it cannot be regarded as the property of the appellants so long as the Nationalization Law is held to be valid. And in view of the provision of Article 10 of the Japanese Hōrei, which lays down that the acquisition or loss of ownership of movables and immovables shall be determined by the law of the place where the object in question is situated at the time of the occurrence of the fact or facts constituting the cause of such acquisition or loss, it is obvious that the appellants have, as previously explained in detail, lost their right under Iranian municipal law, which is the law of the place governing the oil in question. Accordingly, this Court has no alternative but to hold that the appellants are not entitled to the oil in question.

The appellants claim that to recognize the effect of the Nationalization Law or to hold that the appellants have lost their rights in the oil in question would infringe the terms of Article 30 of the Hōrei; but, as explained above, the Nationalization Law cannot simply be regarded as a law by which the rights of foreign nationals are confiscated. And the present Court, which has failed to find any established rules of international law governing the matter, has confined itself to taking the attitude that it is impossible to pass on the validity or invalidity of the said Law and has not concluded positively that the Law is valid. This has had indirectly the same effect as if we recognized the Nationalization Law as valid; and that has resulted in our denying the appellants' ownership of the oil in question. We do not, however, think that these matters are contrary to the public policy of this country. Therefore the appellants' arguments in regard to this point also must be rejected.

DECISION ON EXPROPRIATION

Federal Republic of Germany, Oberlandesgericht, Bremen, 1959.
90 Journal du Droit International 1127 (1963).[a]

During the period under review, as in previous years, the German courts have had to devote a great part of their attention to the question how far they are bound to respect the expropriation of subjective rights by foreign States where such rights are the subject of an internal dispute.

In a judgment of 21 August 1959 the High Court of Bremen adjudicated on a case of breach of public international law by measures of foreign expropriation (AWD 1959, 207 JIR 984 et seq., reproducing a slightly different extract). Application was made to the Court for measures of conservation against a German-Indonesian trading company which had shipped to Bremen tobacco grown on the plantations of two Netherlands firms expropriated by the Indonesian State. The Court began by finding that the Plaintiffs had not established their ownership of the 1958 crop of tobacco (prior to expropriation) because they had no genuine right of usufruct over the land cultivated by them. Even if they had become the owners of the tobacco, continued the Court, they would have lost the ownership by virtue of the acts of expropriation; in effect, even assuming that these measures were contrary to the jus gentium, there is nothing to establish the existence of an international rule requiring the German courts automatically to treat expropriation effected contrary to the jus gentium as being null and void. The judgment concludes that, since the controversy on this question leaves the Court full discretion to recognize either the confiscation contrary to the jus gentium or the claims of the former owners, it takes the former course, mainly in the light of "the positive effect of the principle of territoriality" which is, moreover, in keeping with the interests of universal peace and world trade. Furthermore, the Court questioned whether the Indonesian expropriation law was contrary to the jus gentium from the angle of discrimination according to nationality, or as a means of political pressure. It considered that, in any event, the law was not contrary to German public policy, even though there was a sufficiently close link with the German courts.

The expropriation of things in action raises a more delicate problem than that of immovable property. Some decisions continue to be based on the idea that a claim is "located" solely in the debtor's country of domicile, even where the debtor owns property in other countries. * * *

---

a. English text in the Journal. The text is a summary of the decision rather than a translation of it. Re- printed by permission of Editions Techniques, S. A., Paris.

The decisions of French courts.   In Chapter 17, p. 1121, the text is given of a decision by a French tribunal of general jurisdiction— i. e., a court equivalent in status to a district court in the federal system of the United States—in a suit brought by the Kennecott Copper Corporation, whose assets in Chile were nationalized, in order to obtain the invalidation of title to a shipment of copper ore brought to France by the Chilean state company which took over the Kennecott mines in Chile.

The parties to the case invoke or contest previous decisions by French courts bearing on the issue of invalidation of title of nationalized property.   Most of these decisions have been discussed in the past by commentators in French law reviews, and some have also been discussed or cited in learned American publications.   A summary of some of these cases follow.

Union des Républiques Socialistes Soviétiques v. Intendant Général Bourgeois ès qual. et Soc. La Ropit, Court of Cassation, 1928, [1927–1928] Ann.Dig. 67 (No. 43).   The ships of the Russian company La Ropit were nationalized by decree while they were in Odessa. Odessa at the time was not yet under the control of the Soviet revolutionary government and a number of the ships escaped to Marseilles.   After being recognized by France, the government of the USSR sued in the French courts claiming title to the ships.   The supreme court rejected the claim because giving effect in France to foreign legislation expropriating property without compensation would conflict with French "established order" [i. e., ordre public].

Société Potasas Ibericas v. Bloch, Court of Cassation, [1939] Dalloz Rec.Heb. 257.   The plaintiff was a corporation whose mines and other facilities in Spain had been nationalized.   Bloch was the consignee of a shipment of chemical products from the Spanish state company which had taken over the facilities.   The plaintiff claimed title to the shipment.   A first decree of nationalization had been issued on August 8, 1936, against industries belonging to absent owners, but without specific mention of the plaintiff and without provision for compensation.   The shipment arrived in France before the issuance of a second decree which specifically took the property of the plaintiff and provided for compensation.   The court held that the second decree could not take effect retroactively in France with respect to a shipment already there and hence the consignee could not justify his possession of it.

Société Hardmuth, Court of Appeal of Paris, 1950, 44 Revue Critique de Droit International 501 (1955).   Hardmuth, a corporation in Czechoslovakia, was nationalized.   Its new directors claimed the property of the corporation in France as against the former owners. The court rejected the claim insofar as concerned the tangible property in France, such as buildings, because measures of nationalization without compensation could not be given effect in France.   But it recognized the claim so far as concerns the trademarks. Their nationalization was effective in Czechoslovakia and their protection in France was required by a convention on industrial property to which France and Czechoslovakia were parties.

Martin v. Bank of Spain, Court of Cassation, 1952, 42 Revue Critique de Droit International Privé 425 (1953). Spanish law required bills of Spanish currency, especially those coming in from France, to be embossed with a special seal in order to be legal tender. The plaintiff acquired in France bills of Spanish currency which were not so embossed and presented them for exchange against valid ones at the Spanish customs. They were given a receipt, but no money. Their invalid bills were turned over to the Bank of Spain. They sued the bank for payment in valid currency of the amount of their receipt. The court said that, even if the principle of immunity were disregarded, the refusal to pay the plaintiffs in valid currency "constituted acts of authority outside the control of the French courts."

De Keller v. Maison de la Pensée Francaise, Tribunal Civil de la Seine (référés) 1954, 44 Revue Critique de Droit International Privé 502 (1955). The plaintiff invoked an emergency and summary procedure by which the court was requested to take temporary custody of 37 out of 49 paintings by Pablo Picasso exhibited by the defendant, a nonprofit organization. The defendant had the 37 Picassos on loan from the Russian state art galleries in Leningrad and Moscow. The plaintiffs alleged that the paintings in issue belonged to their deceased father, whose private art gallery the Russian state had confiscated in 1918, and contended they would establish their title to them in further proceedings. The court denied the request. It would have to determine whether the presence in France of paintings acquired by a foreign state in its own territory, and by a method legally valid there, violated to such a degree the French "juridical order" that it was imperative to end the situation. Such a determination raised difficult questions which could not be resolved in the instant procedure without prejudging the merits as well as the jurisdiction of the French courts in the matter.

The Algerian nationalization cases. The nationalizations in Algeria gave rise in France to a great deal of litigation. On April 23, 1969, the supreme court decided a series of cases involving nationalizations. For a list of them, see Lachaume, Chronique de Jurisprudence Francaise Relative au Droit International Public 1969, Annuaire Francais de Droit International 1970, at 874, 898 (1971). So far as could be ascertained, the cases did not involve issues of invalidation of title.

Chapter 7

RESOLUTION OF JURISDICTIONAL CONFLICTS

As demonstrated above, particularly in Chapter 2, international law recognizes a number of bases of jurisdiction. No one base can serve to exclude another. In The Queen v. Anderson, p. 143, an American citizen committed a murder on board a British vessel within the territorial waters of France. International law recognizes that all three states have jurisdiction to prescribe a rule of law governing that event. Thus if the man were in the custody of any one of the states, that state could properly try him for a violation of its own law of homicide. It could, therefore, make a real difference to the accused to be tried in one state rather than another; a defense of insanity or of intoxication might be treated much more favorably in one of these states than in either of the other two.

In the fields of income and death taxation, multiple bases of jurisdiction to tax create serious problems as to burdens on international transactions and about fiscal fairness. To illustrate: it is universally recognized that states may tax income at its source, and most income tax systems do so. But it is also permissible to tax income to its recipients upon the basis of nationality or even "alien resident" status. Some developing countries, particularly in Latin America, object on policy and interest grounds—but not on legal grounds—to United States income taxation on the nationality basis of business income sourced in their territories. Resolution of jurisdictional conflicts in the taxation fields is usually by international agreement. The modern ones are called treaties for the elimination or reduction of "double" (it could even be triple or quadruple in some cases) taxation. These treaties commonly provide, item by item and situation by situation, which of two states, each with valid jurisdiction to tax, shall actually exercise jurisdiction. Some of the older consular and "FCN" [Friendship, Commerce and Navigation] treaties between the United States and another country still govern as to the death taxation of assets within a particular state owned at death by a national of another. Generally, see Wilson, United States Commercial Treaties and International Law, Ch. VI (1960).

In at least one instance, that of visiting naval vessels, a general practice of states has given the international legal system an accommodation (without treaty) that allocates, to one of the two states having bases for the exercise of jurisdiction, exclusive authority as to its exercise. It would be difficult to deny any jurisdiction to a territorial state whose ports are visited by an aircraft carrier or a cruiser of another state; but "it just isn't done" that the territorial host state, uninvited, should, for example, send a squad on board to make an arrest. Another device, for the resolution of the territory-nationality conflict as to non-naval vessels, is the "peace of the port doctrine," exemplified in Wildenhus's Case, p. 162. Here, for vessels other than public vessels in naval service, the principle of customary international law evolved from a few earlier bilateral treaties.

Jurisdictional conflicts may result from the presence within the territory of a state of a visiting foreign military force, which as an organized unit, naturally, has its own internal system of law and discipline. The problems and the lines of resolution (or reduction) of conflicts in the exercise of jurisdiction over military personnel in a visiting foreign force are suggested by the cases and materials in Section B of this Chapter.

Until comparatively recent times the United States was practically the only country in the world with an antitrust law to enforce or with a strong interest in applying it to transnational economic activities. In those earlier times much debate took place as to whether international law authorized the exercise of prescriptive jurisdiction, as to a defendant fairly and properly before the courts here, on the basis that economic activity outside the United States had effects on the economy of the United States. Today a number of law-making authorities, such as the Federal German Republic and the European Economic Community, join with the United States in affirming that the state where economic consequences are felt may apply its law on that basis alone. But multinational economic activity may have economic effects in many countries, and the problem of resolving conflicts of jurisdiction in this field is just beginning to be faced. A number of writers, and some states, still contend, however, that the sole problem is created by resort to the economic effects doctrine, which is denounced as contrary to territorialistic limitations on prescriptive jurisdiction. In this situation, therefore, the resolution or reduction of conflicts is more involved—as well as frequently highly charged with emotion.

The greater part of this chapter is directed toward an exploration of ways in which the conflicts thus generated are being or may be resolved. One way, obviously, is to reduce or eliminate the differences in the rules that would govern the outcomes of decisions, e. g., by the development in the international legal system of uniform rules for stating the legal consequences of particular types of conduct. Another is to accept, for the time being at least, the reality of divisiveness as to the governing rules and to develop within the international legal system *rules* or *methods*, or both, for the resolution of conflicts. An effort along this line was Section 40 of the Restatement of the Foreign Relations Law of the United States (1965).

SECTION A.   MULTINATIONAL TAXATION

TAX DECISION

Federal German Republic, Supreme Tax Court, 1971.
12 European Taxation II/36.*

I.   THE FACTS

Since the taxpayer, to be known as A, in this case was deceased, his heirs were a party to the proceedings. A was a United States citizen who was domiciled in Italy and who had neither a domicile (Wohnsitz) nor a residence (gewöhnliche Aufenthalt) in Germany.

He had concluded, with a Panamanian company to be known as X, a contract under which X could offer A's services to other companies, in particular movie companies. On May 5, 1958, X concluded a contract with a German company to be known as Y under which A would make a movie for Y. Both companies would be entitled to copies of the film and the right to rent those films to movie theaters. Y paid to X an amount of $200,000 (approximately DM 840,000) as a fee plus granted X a right to a percentage of the movie rentals. The work was performed by A both in Germany and in Italy and it was established that 28/82 and 54/82 of the work was performed in each country respectively.

In 1959 Y paid DM 536,491 to X of which amount the latter kept DM 82,026 and the remainder of DM 454,465 was paid to A.

The German tax administration assumed that the DM 536,491 was income from employment derived by A through X and imposed income tax (wage tax) in the following manner:

15% on $^{28}/_{82}$ of DM 536,491.60 =   DM 27,478.81
25% on $^{54}/_{82}$ of DM 536,491.60 =   DM 88,324.76

                             DM 115,803.57

II.   THE LAW

Section 49(4) of the Individual Income Tax Law (Einkommensteuergesetz) provides that nonresident individuals receiving income from employment which is either carried out in Germany or "utilized" in Germany (this term denotes that the economic effect of the work performed abroad is of direct benefit to the German economy) are subject to German individual income tax with respect to such employment income.

Section 50a(2) of the Individual Income Tax Law provides that in the case of an artist—such as a movie star like A—the rate of the income tax is 15% for that part of the income derived for work

* Reprinted with the permission of the
International Bureau of Fiscal Documentation, Amsterdam.

performed in Germany and 25% for that part which is performed abroad, but utilized in Germany. Article 7 of the German-Italian Tax Treaty of October 21, 1925 (which is still in force), provides that "impersonal" taxes are levied only on income from labor by the State where the personal activity from which the income is derived is carried on. Article 1 defines the term "impersonal" tax as, inter alia, the German individual income tax (Einkommensteuer) insofar as it is levied without regard to the nationality, domicile or residence of the taxpayer, i. e., the individual income tax as it was levied in the present case would be considered an "impersonal" tax.

Article XI of the Friendship, Trade and Shipping Treaty of October 29, 1954, between Germany and the United States provides that citizens of one of the two contracting States who are resident in the other contracting State may not be subjected to any taxation which is more burdensome than the taxation to which citizens of the other State in the same circumstances are or may be subjected.

III. The Issue

The issue was whether A was subject to German individual income tax with respect to the work performed abroad.

It was contended for the taxpayer that only part of this work could be deemed to be "utilized" in Germany, since although all the films were shown in Germany, these domestic showings accounted for only 15% of total usage of the films. Consequently only a minor part of the salary for the work performed abroad could be subject to income tax in Germany.

The tax administration, on the other hand, contended that A had assisted in producing a German movie and consequently the work performed abroad was fully "utilized" in Germany, whether the films were shown in Germany or abroad. The taxpayer therefore was fully taxable with respect to his salary.

IV. The Decision of the Lower Tax Court (Finanzgericht) of Munich of October 23, 1967

The Lower Tax Court of Munich supported the taxpayer's opinion and ruled that only 15% of the work performed abroad could be considered as "utilized" in Germany. It also ruled that A was employed by X so that the salary he received was DM 536,491.60 less DM 82,026 (i. e., the amount which was actually paid by X to A).

*   *   *

V. The Decision of the Supreme Tax Court (Bundesfinanzhof) of September 15, 1971

The Supreme Tax Court held that the Lower Tax Court of Munich had not sufficiently examined the facts and referred the case back to the same Court.

The Supreme Tax Court made the following important statements.

* * *

2.   The Supreme Tax Court agreed that either the amount of DM 454,465 or DM 536,491 (depending on whether A would be considered an employee of X or of Y respectively) was at least $^{28}\!/_{82}$ subject to the 15% rate of individual income tax.   However, the Supreme Tax Court rejected the Lower Tax Court's opinion that $^{54}\!/_{82}$ of the above amounts should only be partially subject to individual income tax in Germany, holding instead that the work performed by A abroad was fully "utilized" in Germany.   The crucial point is where the work is utilized and not—as in the Lower Tax Court's opinion— where the result of the work is utilized.   The fact that the films were also shown abroad is therefore for this case immaterial.   Thus the Supreme Tax Court found that in this case the work performed abroad (i. e., in Italy) was indeed fully utilized in Germany, since (i) the movie as such was produced in Germany, and (ii) the copyrights were initially acquired by a German company (Y) (although they were to a large extent later transferred to X).

3.   The Supreme Tax Court also rejected the view that Germany would be denied the right to impose individual income tax on the work performed in Italy and utilized in Germany, by virtue of the German-Italian Tax Treaty of October 21, 1925.   According to the Court's view, this Treaty exclusively applies to citizens of Germany and Italy and since A was a United States citizen he cannot benefit from any of its provisions.   It is true that the Treaty does not expressly provide that its provisions only apply to income derived by German and Italian citizens, but the Supreme Tax Court formed its opinion from some of the Treaty provisions themselves in connection with the historical development of the Treaty.

4.   The Supreme Tax Court also rejected the view that the article XI of the Friendship, Trade and Shipping Treaty of October 29, 1954, would apply since the provisions of this Treaty apply only to residents of Germany and the United States.   As A was a resident of Italy, neither he nor his heirs can benefit thereof.

ILLUSTRATIVE ARTICLES OF A MODERN TAX TREATY

Cyprus-United Kingdom (Income) Tax Arrangement
Supplementary Service to European Taxation
No. 3, March, 1970, § C.*

ARTICLE 3

(1) The industrial or commercial profits of a United Kingdom enterprise shall not be subject to Cyprus tax unless the enterprise

* Reprinted with the permission of the
International Bureau of Fiscal Documentation, Amsterdam.

is engaged in trade or business in Cyprus through a permanent establishment situated therein. If it is so engaged, tax may be imposed on those profits by Cyprus but only on so much of them as is attributable to that permanent establishment.

(2) [Reciprocally for Cyprus enterprise in the United Kingdom]

(3) Where an enterprise of one of the territories is engaged in trade or business in the other territory through a permanent establishment situated therein, there shall be attributed to that permanent establishment the industrial or commercial profits which it might be expected to derive from its activities in that other territory if it were an independent enterprise engaged in the same or similar activities under the same or similar conditions and dealing at arm's length with the enterprise of which it is a permanent establishment.

(4) No portion of any profits arising from the sale of goods or merchandise by an enterprise of one of the territories shall be attributed to a permanent establishment situated in the other territory by reason of the mere purchase of the goods or merchandise within that other territory.

Article 5

Notwithstanding the provisions of paragraphs 3 and 4, profits which a resident of one of the territories derives from operating ships or aircraft shall be exempt from tax in the other territory.

Article 6

(1) Dividends paid by a company resident in one of the territories to a resident of the other territory who is subject to tax in that other territory in respect thereof and not engaged in trade or business in the first-mentioned territory through a permanent establishment situated therein, shall be exempt from any tax in that first-mentioned territory which is chargeable on dividends in addition to the tax chargeable in respect of the profits or income of the company.

(2) Where a company which is a resident of one of the territories derives profits or income from sources within the other territory, the Government of that other territory shall not impose any form of taxation on dividends paid by the company to persons not resident in that other territory, or any tax in the nature of an undistributed profits tax on undistributed profits of the company, by reason of the fact that those dividends or undistributed profits represent, in whole or in part, profits or income so derived.

(3) If the recipient of a dividend is a company which owns 10 per cent. or more of the class of shares in respect of which the dividend is paid then sub-paragraph (1) shall not apply to the dividend to the extent that it can have been paid only out of profits which the company paying the dividend earned or other income which it received in a period ending twelve months or more before the relevant date. For the purposes of this sub-paragraph the term "relevant date" means the date on which the beneficial owner of the dividend became

the owner of 10 per cent. or more of the class of shares in question. Provided, that this sub-paragraph shall not apply if the beneficial owner of the dividend shows that the shares were acquired for bona fide commercial reasons and not primarily for the purpose of securing the benefit of this paragraph.

Article 9

(1) An individual who is a resident of the United Kingdom shall be exempt from Cyprus tax on profits or remuneration in respect of personal (including professional) services performed within Cyprus in any year of assessment if—

    (a) he is present within Cyprus for a period or periods not exceeding in the aggregate 183 days during that year, and

    (b) the services are performed for or on behalf of a person resident in the United Kingdom, and

    (c) the profits or remuneration are subject to United Kingdom tax.

(2) An individual who is a resident of Cyprus shall be exempt from United Kingdom tax on profits or remuneration in respect of personal (including professional) services performed within the United Kingdom in any year of assessment if—

    (a) he is present within the United Kingdom for a period or periods not exceeding in the aggregate 183 days during that year, and

    (b) the services are performed for or on behalf of a person resident in Cyprus and

    (c) the profits or remuneration are subject to Cyprus tax.

(3) The provisions of this paragraph shall not apply to the profits or remuneration of public entertainers such as stage, motion picture or radio artists, musicians and athletes.

Article 11

The remuneration derived by a professor or teacher who is ordinarily resident in one of the territories, for teaching, during a period of temporary residence not exceeding two years, at a university, college, school or other educational institution in the other territory, shall be exempt from tax in that other territory.

Article 12

A student or business apprentice from one of the territories who is receiving full-time education or training in the other territory shall be exempt from tax in that other territory on payments made to him by persons in the first-mentioned territory for the purposes of his maintenance, education or training.

Article 14

(1) The taxation authorities of the United Kingdom and Cyprus shall exchange such information (being information available under

their respective taxation laws) as is necessary for carrying out the provisions of this Arrangement or for the prevention of fraud or the administration of statutory provisions against legal avoidance in relation to the taxes which are the subject of this Arrangement. Any information so exchanged shall be treated as secret and shall not be disclosed to any persons other than those concerned with the assessment and collection of the taxes which are the subject of this Arrangement. No information shall be exchanged which would disclose any trade secret or trade process.

(2) As used in this paragraph, the term "taxation authorities" means the Commissioners of Inland Revenue or their authorised representative in the case of the United Kingdom and the Commissioner of Income Tax or his authorised representative in the case of Cyprus.

IMPERIAL TOBACCO CO. OF INDIA, LTD. v. COMMISSIONER OF INCOME TAX

Pakistan, Supreme Court, 1958.
27 Int'l L.Rep. 103 (1963).

THE FACTS.—The appellant, the Imperial Tobacco Company of India, Ltd., was assessed to income-tax as a "resident" by an Income-tax Officer in Pakistan. The assessment was for the year 1948–49, for which the previous year was the financial year 1947–48. The registered office of the Company and the control and management of its affairs throughout the previous year was in Calcutta, India, though the Company carried on some business in Pakistan in that year. The Income-tax Officer, the Appellate Assistant Commissioner, the Appellate Tribunal and the High Court of West Pakistan at Karachi all held that the Company was rightly taxed as a "resident" under the Pakistan Income-Tax Law, with the result that the Company's profits which accrued to it in India and not in Pakistan during the previous year were taxed. The Company appealed to the Supreme Court.

Held: that the appeal must be allowed. It was a rule of international law that a State was entitled to tax foreigners only if they earned or received income within the territory of that State, and municipal legislation must not be construed as abrogating international law unless its language clearly had that result. [A portion of the opinion of the court appears below].

* * * To appreciate the question involved, it is necessary to refer to the provisions of our Income-Tax Law which deal with the taxability of income. * * * The principle underlying these provisions is that income may be taxed on two bases: (1) receipt of income and (2) accrual of income. If a person is not resident in Pakistan all that can be taxed is the income that he receives in Pakistan or that accrues to him in Pakistan during the previous year. But if he is resident in Pakistan the income is taxable if it is received by him in Pakistan or if it accrues to him in Pakistan or outside Pakistan during the previous year. On this principle the appellant Company's profits in India during the previous year could be taxed only if the Company were held to be resident in Pakistan during the previous year. The simple issue therefore is whether the Company having its registered office outside Pakistan throughout the previous year could be held to be resident in Pakistan. * * *

     * * * [T]he definition of "resident" * * * is:

A company is resident in British India in any year (a) if the control and management of its affairs is situated wholly in British India in that year. * * *

     * * * Under the Pakistan Income-Tax Law the taxable territory can only be Pakistan, and if this definition were to be applied to-day a company would be resident in any year in Pakistan only if the control and management of its affairs were situated wholly in Pakistan in that year. On this definition, it was conceded by the learned advocate for the Commissioner of Income-Tax that the Department would have no authority to tax the company as a resident company. * * * This interpretation is in accordance with, and gives full effect to, the principle that statutes are not to be construed as abrogating international law unless their language clearly leads to that result, and that extraterritorial operation of a statute over foreigners is not to be presumed as having been intended unless it is expressly so stated. * * *

     Thus, the Pakistan authorities' power to tax the foreign income of a company, the registered office of which has throughout the previous year been in Calcutta, is not to be easily inferred and unless the words of the statute unmistakably lend themselves to a contrary result, full effect must be given to the principle recognized by our own Income-Tax Law, that if a foreigner earns or receives income in Pakistan, that income alone is liable to income-tax and not the income earned by him in the country of his origin or elsewhere * * *.

This construction is consistent with the words and the sense of the definition of "British India" as well as with the principle observed in Section 4 of the Income-Tax Act, and the rule of international law that a legislature has authority to tax its citizens wherever they be, and to tax foreigners only if they earn or receive income in the country for which that legislature has the authority to make laws. The interpretation adopted by the Departmental authorities and by the High Court is opposed to these principles and leads to this absurdity, that the Pakistan income-tax authorities may tax the foreign income of a company even if that company had its registered office for only a day during the previous year in Pakistan.

     For the reasons given above, we allow this appeal and hold that the assessee Company was not resident within the meaning of Section

4–A(c) of the Income-Tax Act so as to be taxed by the Pakistan income-tax authorities under Section 4(1)(b)(ii). The Department must pay the appellant's costs.

——————

1. *Mutual state interests as to taxation.* As has been observed more than once, taxation is an intensely practical matter. If any one of the states having jurisdiction to tax acts unreasonably in making its claim, or in refusing to take into account in some way, through some channel or other, the tax expectations of another state with jurisdiction to tax, the tax source itself is apt to be affected to the common fiscal detriment of the states concerned. Hence through networks of international agreements (although the German-Italian-United States agreements did not help the American actor in the case at p. 461) or the granting of credits against the national tax for foreign taxes of the same sort paid to another state having jurisdiction, multiple taxation of the same increment of economic power is reduced or eliminated.

2. *Parallel problem within the United States.* It is a curious fact, that, as between the states of the Union, the interstate compact approach to the reduction or avoidance of multistate death and income taxation has been so little used in the United States. Some degree of uniformity of treatment of resident and nonresident income exists in the various state income tax laws, and there is a practice of informal consultation between state taxing authorities as to both death and income taxes. The threat of multistate taxation within the United States became greater when the United States Supreme Court abandoned the view that substantive due process of law limited jurisdiction to tax in particular instances to a single state among a number of states having tax "contacts." The problem of multistate tax claims tends to become more serious in the state income field as rates rise above the 1–4% that formerly characterized state income taxation.

——————

SECTION B.   VISITING FOREIGN FORCES

———

Persons in the armed services are still people. They may fail in the performance of their military duties, and they may make mistakes or misbehave when off duty and amidst the civilian community. Or they may deviate from the performance of their official duty while on a mission off-post, with resultant injury to someone who is not a member of the military. In general, the problems of conflicts of jurisdiction that arise when a state receives within its territory an organized military unit of a friendly state, usually an ally, are like those that arise between the military and civilian authorities in the environs of any domestic military installation. For some types of conduct, all agree that the military person should be responsible only to the law of his military unit. At the opposite extreme, all agree that in other instances he should be treated like anyone else within the civilian jurisdiction in which he has acted. As experience with friendly foreign forces present at the invitation of the territorial state has accumulated, principles have been worked out for the allocation of "primary" jurisdiction to one or the other of the states concerned. As the following cases show, applications of the rules of allocation may present problems inherently more difficult than the concoction of the rules themselves. Behind the problem there may be one involving a protected human right against double jeopardy or denial of the defenses of prior acquittal or prior conviction.

WHITLEY v. AITCHISON

France, Court of Cassation, 1958.
26 Int'l L.Rep. 196 (1963).

THE FACTS.—Article VII(3) (b) of the N.A.T.O. Status of Forces Agreement of June 19, 1951, provides that in the case of offences not arising out of acts done in the performance of the official duty of a member of a visiting force, "the authorities of the receiving State shall have the primary right to exercise jurisdiction". Subparagraph (c) of the same paragraph provides that "if the State having the primary right decides not to exercise jurisdiction, it shall notify the authorities of the other State as soon as practicable * * *." Article VII (8) of the Agreement provides:

> Where an accused has been tried by the authorities of one Contracting Party and has been acquitted, or has been convicted and is serving, or has served, his sentence or has been pardoned, he may not be tried again for the same offence within the same territory by the authorities of another Contracting Party.

On November 25, 1953, the appellant, a major of the United States Air Force stationed in France under the provisions of the North Atlantic Treaty, was driving his car at high speed along a road within the judicial district of the French town of Corbeil. He was carrying as a passenger one Aitchison, an officer in the Royal Canadian Air Force. As subsequently found, the applicant drove negligently and as a result of his driving the car crashed and Aitchison was killed. It was also found that when driving the car the appellant was not acting in the performance of his official duty; and in accordance with Article VII(3)(b) of the Agreement of June 19, 1951, the primary right of jurisdiction was vested in the French courts. The United States military authorities requested the French authorities to waive their primary right of jurisdiction, and this request was approved by the French Ministry of Justice and the Prosecutor of the Court of Corbeil. The French authorities duly notified the United States military authorities in accordance with Article VII(3)(c) of the Agreement that they had decided not to exercise jurisdiction.

Notwithstanding the waiver of their primary right of jurisdiction by the French authorities, however, the widow of Aitchison (the respondent herein) instituted proceedings against the appellant for damages as *"partie civile"*, as is customary under French law in connection with criminal proceedings arising out of the same set of facts. At that time the United States military authorities had not yet made any decision as to the manner in which they intended to proceed against the appellant in the exercise of the right of jurisdiction granted to them by the French authorities, but subsequently they decided not to take any action against the appellant.

The appellant objected to the jurisdiction of the French court on the ground that the waiver by the French authorities of their primary right of jurisdiction was irrevocable, and that the right once waived could not be revived by the decision of the United States authorities not to prosecute. The Court of Corbeil overruled the objection and held itself competent to adjudicate upon the respondent's claim for damages, and the Court of Appeal of Paris dismissed the appellant's appeal against that decision.[1]

On further appeal to the Court of Cassation,

Held: (i) that the appeal must be allowed. Once the French authorities had waived their right to primary jurisdiction and notified the United States military authorities of the waiver, their right to exercise jurisdiction was incapable of being revived, notwithstanding that the United States military authorities had decided not to prosecute the appellant.

(ii) Even though under French municipal law a prosecutor cannot definitively waive the right to prosecute, the Agreement, in accordance with Article 26 of the French Constitution of October 27, 1946, must take precedence and as, according to the Agreement, a right of primary jurisdiction once waived cannot be revived, the French courts were no longer competent. [A portion of the opinion of the court appears below.]

* * * The notice of appeal alleges, in addition to the matters raised before the Courts below, a violation of Articles VII(3)(c) and XX(3) of the N.A.T.O. Status of Forces Agreement of June 19, 1951, promulgated by Decree dated October 13, 1952; a violation of Articles 26 et seq. of the Constitution of October 27, 1946; of Articles 3 and 182 of the Code of Criminal Procedure; and of Article 7 of the Law

---

1. The judgment of the Court of Appeal of Paris is reported in International Law Reports, 1956, p. 255.

of April 20, 1810. It is contended that the judgment under appeal, notwithstanding the waiver of the right of primary jurisdiction by the Minister of Justice as well as by the Prosecutor of the Court of Corbeil, in favour of the United States authorities, wrongly considered the Magistrates' Court of Corbeil entitled to deal with the civil action and the criminal prosecution. The Court of Corbeil, it is said, took this view on the ground that a waiver by the authorities of the country entitled to the right of primary jurisdiction is neither irrevocable nor unconditional, and that in order to be final and irrevocable and generally binding, a waiver must be subject to the requirement of the existence of a judgment against the accused. As long as such a judgment has not come into existence the victim, according to the view expressed by the lower courts, cannot be deprived of his right to bring proceedings in the criminal courts with a view to obtaining damages for the injury sustained. Neither the Minister of Justice nor the Public Prosecutor, according to this view, is in full control of the criminal proceedings, and they cannot waive these because such waiver would have no legal effect and could not, in any event, deprive the claimant ("partie civile") of his own rights which the law confers on him.

If the host State which has the right of primary jurisdiction decides to waive this right, there arises a genuine lack of competence for the benefit of the other State which is not entitled to the right of primary jurisdiction. The State which has waived its right can no longer exercise jurisdiction unless the State which benefits from the waiver decides not to exercise jurisdiction and notifies the State which has waived its right. International conventions have the force of law even if they conflict with municipal law, and they must be applied instead of the latter where occasion demands. The provisions of the North Atlantic Treaty necessarily imply that it is the Public Prosecutor's department which is entitled to waive the right of primary jurisdiction, and that when the right has been waived the French courts are no longer competent, notwithstanding that according to French municipal law the Public Prosecutor cannot waive the right to institute criminal proceedings. The victim of the criminal offence, who can always bring his claim before the civil courts, cannot question a renunciation of competence which has been made for reasons of international courtesy.

Article VII(3)(c) of the Agreement of June 19, 1951, between the Parties to the North Atlantic Treaty, as published in the Decree dated October 11, 1952, provides as follows:

> If the State having the primary right decides not to exercise jurisdiction, it shall notify the authorities of the other State as soon as practicable. The authorities of the State having the primary right shall give sympathetic consideration to a request from the authorities of the other State for a waiver of its right in cases

where that other State considers such waiver to be of particular importance.

Where, in accordance with this provision, the authorities of the State which has the right of primary jurisdiction have, at the request of the other State, waived that right, their decision is final, and the criminal courts of the State concerned can no longer exercise jurisdiction over facts in respect of which there has been a waiver. There is no need to enquire whether the State in whose favour the right has been waived has exercised jurisdiction through its own courts. The only exception to this would be the case where the State which has been granted the right to exercise jurisdiction by the State in which the primary right was vested, expressly informs the latter that it does not wish to exercise jurisdiction and leaves the matter to the judicial authorities of the other Contracting Party.

According to Article 26 of the Constitution of October 27, 1946, international treaties duly ratified and published have the force of law even if they conflict with French municipal law. After the death of Aitchison, the latter's widow instituted proceedings against Whitley before the criminal court of Corbeil-Essonnes in whose district the accident had occurred, alleging involuntary homicide committed against her husband while Whitley was not acting in the performance of his official duties. That Court, in arriving at a finding that the subsidiary civil action (action de la partie civile) was subject to the jurisdiction, held that if before the institution of these proceedings the Minister of Justice and the Public Prosecutor of Corbeil-Essonnes agreed, at the request of the United States authorities and in accordance with the [N.A.T.O. Status of Forces] Agreement, to waive the right of primary jurisdiction, this did not imply a waiver of the right subsequently to exercise jurisdiction if, as in this case, the alleged offender has not been tried by the judicial authorities of his home State, because the Agreement itself contemplates the case of an accused who has not been tried in the home State and of an accused who, though convicted, has not served his sentence—unless there has been an amnesty.

The judgment under appeal has misinterpreted the provisions of the Agreement of June 19, 1951, and violated the provisions referred to in the notice of appeal, because it arrived at its finding notwithstanding the absence of any express declaration by the home State that it waived its right to exercise jurisdiction, which jurisdiction had been recognized by France when that country agreed not to exercise its primary right of jurisdiction. The judgment of the Court of Appeal of Paris is therefore reversed, and there is no need for the case to be sent back.

* * *

WILSON, SECRETARY OF DEFENSE v. GIRARD

United States Supreme Court, 1957.
354 U.S. 524, 77 S.Ct. 1409.

PER CURIAM.   Japan and the United States became involved in a controversy whether the respondent Girard should be tried by a Japanese court for causing the death of a Japanese woman. * * *

Girard, a Specialist Third Class in the United States Army, was engaged on January 30, 1957, with members of his cavalry regiment in a small unit exercise at Camp Weir range area, Japan.   Japanese civilians were present in the area, retrieving expended cartridge cases. Girard and another Specialist Third Class were ordered to guard a machine gun and some items of clothing that had been left nearby. Girard had a grenade launcher on his rifle.   He placed an expended 30-caliber cartridge case in the grenade launcher and projected it by firing a blank.   The expended cartridge case penetrated the back of a Japanese woman gathering expended cartridge cases and caused her death.

The United States ultimately notified Japan that Girard would be delivered to the Japanese authorities for trial.   Thereafter, Japan indicted him for causing death by wounding.   Girard sought a writ of habeas corpus in the United States District Court for the District of Columbia.   The writ was denied, but Girard was granted declaratory relief and an injunction against his delivery to the Japanese authorities.   152 F.Supp. 21.   The petitioners appealed to the Court of Appeals for the District of Columbia, and, without awaiting action by that court on the appeal, invoked the jurisdiction of this Court under 28 U.S.C.A. § 1254(1).   Girard filed a cross-petition for certiorari to review the denial of the writ of habeas corpus.   We granted both petitions.   U.S. Supreme Court Rule 20; 354 U.S. 928, 77 S.Ct. 1390.

A Security Treaty between Japan and the United States, signed September 8, 1951, was ratified by the Senate on March 20, 1952, and proclaimed by the President effective April 28, 1952.   Article III of the Treaty authorized the making of Administrative Agreements between the two Governments concerning "[t]he conditions which shall govern the disposition of armed forces of the United States of America in and about Japan * * *."   Expressly acting under this provision, the two Nations, on February 28, 1952, signed an Administrative Agreement covering, among other matters, the jurisdiction of the United States over offenses committed in Japan by members of the United States armed forces, and providing that jurisdiction in any case might be waived by the United States.   This Agreement became effective on the same date as the Security Treaty (April 28, 1952) and was considered by the Senate before consent was given to the Treaty.

Article XVII, paragraph 1, of the Administrative Agreement provided that upon the coming into effect of the "Agreement between the

Parties to the North Atlantic Treaty regarding the Status of their Forces," signed June 19, 1951, the United States would conclude with Japan an agreement on criminal jurisdiction similar to the corresponding provisions of the NATO Agreement. The NATO Agreement became effective August 23, 1953, and the United States and Japan signed on September 29, 1953, effective October 29, 1953, a Protocol Agreement pursuant to the covenant in paragraph 1 of Article XVII.

Paragraph 3 of Article XVII, as amended by the Protocol, dealt with criminal offenses in violation of the laws of both Nations and provided:

3. In cases where the right to exercise jurisdiction is concurrent the following rules shall apply:

(a) The military authorities of the United States shall have the primary right to exercise jurisdiction over members of the United States armed forces or the civilian component in relation to

(i) offenses solely against the property or security of the United States, or offenses solely against the person or property of another member of the United States armed forces or the civilian component or of a dependent;

(ii) offenses arising out of any act or omission done in the performance of official duty.

(b) In the case of any other offense the authorities of Japan shall have the primary right to exercise jurisdiction.

(c) If the State having the primary right decides not to exercise jurisdiction, it shall notify the authorities of the other State as soon as practicable. The authorities of the State having the primary right shall give sympathetic consideration to a request from the authorities of the other State for a waiver of its right in cases where that other State considers such waiver to be of particular importance.

Article XXVI of the Administrative Agreement established a Joint Committee of representatives of the United States and Japan to consult on all matters requiring mutual consultation regarding the implementation of the Agreement; and provided that if the Committee " * * * is unable to resolve any matter, it shall refer that matter to the respective Governments for further consideration through appropriate channels."

In the light of the Senate's ratification of the Security Treaty after consideration of the Administrative Agreement, which had already been signed, and its subsequent ratification of the NATO Agreement, with knowledge of the commitment to Japan under the Administrative Agreement, we are satisfied that the approval of Article III of the Security Treaty authorized the making of the Administrative

Agreement and the subsequent Protocol embodying the NATO Agreement provisions governing jurisdiction to try criminal offenses.

The United States claimed the right to try Girard upon the ground that his act, as certified by his commanding officer, was "done in the performance of official duty" and therefore the United States had primary jurisdiction. Japan insisted that it had proof that Girard's action was without the scope of his official duty and therefore that Japan had the primary right to try him.

The Joint Committee, after prolonged deliberations, was unable to agree. The issue was referred to higher authority, which authorized the United States representatives on the Joint Committee to notify the appropriate Japanese authorities, in accordance with paragraph 3(c) of the Protocol, that the United States had decided not to exercise, but to waive, whatever jurisdiction it might have in the case. The Secretary of State and the Secretary of Defense decided that this determination should be carried out. The President confirmed their joint conclusion.

A sovereign nation has exclusive jurisdiction to punish offenses against its laws committed within its borders, unless it expressly or impliedly consents to surrender its jurisdiction. The Schooner Exchange v. M'Faddon, 7 Cranch 116, 136. Japan's cession to the United States of jurisdiction to try American military personnel for conduct constituting an offense against the laws of both countries was conditioned by the covenant of Article XVII, section 3, paragraph (c) of the Protocol that

> * * * The authorities of the State having the primary right shall give sympathetic consideration to a request from the authorities of the other State for a waiver of its right in cases where that other State considers such waiver to be of particular importance.

The issue for our decision is therefore narrowed to the question whether, upon the record before us, the Constitution or legislation subsequent to the Security Treaty prohibited the carrying out of this provision authorized by the Treaty for waiver of the qualified jurisdiction granted by Japan. We find no constitutional or statutory barrier to the provision as applied here. In the absence of such encroachments, the wisdom of the arrangement is exclusively for the determination of the Executive and Legislative Branches.

The judgment of the District Court in No. 1103 is reversed, and its judgment in No. 1108 is affirmed.

[MR. JUSTICE DOUGLAS took no part in the consideration or decision of this case.]

Background facts for appraisal. In a Joint Statement of the Secretaries of State and Defense appended to the opinion as Appendix B, at 545, the following account is given of the facts of this case:

The incident occurred in a maneuver area provided by the Japanese Government for part-time use of United States forces. The Japanese Defense Force uses the same area about 40% of the time. When the area is not in use by either the United States or Japanese armed forces, Japanese civilians are permitted to farm or otherwise use the area.

Efforts to keep civilians away from the area during such military exercises have not proved effective. In this particular case, red boundary flags were, as customary, erected as a warning to civilians to keep off, and local authorities were notified of the proposed exercises. But, as was frequently the case, a number of Japanese civilians were in the area gathering empty brass cartridge cases at the time of the incident. These civilians had created such a risk of injury to themselves in the morning exercises when live ammunition was used that the American officer in charge withdrew live ammunition from the troops prior to the afternoon exercises. In the interval between two simulated attacks during the afternoon, Girard and another soldier, Specialist 3rd Class Victor M. Nickel, were ordered by their platoon leader, a Lieutenant, to guard a machine gun and several field jackets at the top of a hill. Girard and Nickel were not issued live ammunition for this duty.

It was while these soldiers were performing this duty that the incident occurred. Mrs. Naka Sakai, a Japanese civilian, died a few moments after being hit in the back by an empty brass rifle shell case fired by Girard from his rifle grenade launcher. She was not over 30 yards from Girard and was going away from him when he fired the rifle. Girard had previously fired similarly in the vicinity of a Japanese man, who was not hit.

Girard's action in firing empty shell cases from the rifle grenade launcher was not authorized. He asserted that he fired from the waist, intending only to frighten the Japanese civilians. Others stated, but Girard denied, that empty shell cases were thrown out to entice the Japanese to approach.

JAPAN v. GIRARD

Japan, District Court of Maebashi, 1957.
26 Int'l L.Rep. 203 (1963).

THE FACTS.—The accused, William S. Girard, was charged with the offence of bodily injury resulting in death. The accused was a member of the United States Army stationed in Japan in accordance with the Administrative Agreement under Article 3 of the Security Treaty concluded between Japan and the United States in 1952. At the time of the offence he was a driver with the rank of Specialist Third Class in a cavalry regiment.

On January 30, 1957, the accused took part as a rifleman in an exercise in a manoeuvre area near a Japanese village. Japanese and American authorities had previously set up "no admittance" signs at strategic points surrounding the manoeuvre area and, in addition, whenever exercises were to be held, the residents in the area were notified in advance through the offices concerned. On the actual day of the manoeuvre, red flags were flown at easily visible and specific points around the area. Warnings were issued prohibiting entry into the area because of danger, and local Japanese police authorities undertook various measures to keep out the public. The Japanese and American authorities concerned held frequent discussion meetings and planned counter measures to make these precautions effective. But effective control could not be achieved as originally intended for various reasons, including the fact that the scrap metal from rifle cartridge casings and fragments from artillery shells could be sold at a high price. As a result, many of the local residents entered the manoeuvre area to collect scrap, and eventually they came to ignore the warnings and entered the area even during exercises.

On the day in question, some sixty or seventy brass pickers entered the manoeuvre area and their activities were such that the lives of both soldiers and brass pickers were endangered. The live ammunition exercise was halted and only blank ammunition was used for the afternoon exercise. The accused and another private, Nickel, were ordered to guard a light machine gun and other items on a piece of high ground. Many brass pickers were gathered on the slopes below them. The two men threw some empty cartridge casings down the slopes and the accused called out to one of them, a woman, and pointed to a foxhole indicating that there were cartridge cases there. The woman, Naka Sakai, approached the foxhole, whereupon the accused, having placed an empty cartridge case into the mouth of the grenade launcher attached to his rifle, suddenly turned toward the woman and chased after her, shouting at her. He fired a blank shell from his rifle and the gas pressure from this caused the cartridge casing to be ejected from the launcher. The woman was hit, and died from her injuries.

It was argued for the defence that the accused's act was a crime resulting from an act done in the course of official duty as stipulated in Article 17, paragraph 3(a)(ii), of the Administrative Agreement under Article 3 of the Security Treaty between Japan and the United States. On this basis, the defence contended that the military authorities of the United States had the primary right to exercise jurisdiction. It was further contended that although the United States had notified Japan that they would not exercise jurisdiction in this instance, this notification differed from the case in which the primary right of jurisdiction was waived at the request of the Japanese authorities. Consequently, the notification could not be regarded as meaning that Japan automatically obtained the right of secondary jurisdiction. Alternatively, it was contended that Japan did not have jurisdiction because the provisions of paragraph 6(a) of Article 17 of the Administrative Agreement had not been fulfilled in that the Japanese authorities did not show to the military authorities certain statements made to the Japanese procurators, and that, therefore, the proceedings had been instituted in breach of the stipulations of mutual assistance concerning the collection and production of evidence and the investigation of a crime by the authorities of both countries.

Held: on the submissions regarding jurisdiction, that Japan had jurisdiction in this case. It was a case of concurrent jurisdiction within Article 17, paragraph 1(a) and (b), of the Administrative Agreement. The notification by the United States authorities had the same effect as a waiver so far as the loss of jurisdiction by the United States military authorities, in Japan was concerned. The Court also held that there had been no breach of the provisions of paragraph 6 (a) of Article 17. These provisions did not demand that the authorities of either country submit to the authorities of the other all the evidential material of the case concerned. [A portion of the opinion of the court appears below.]

     *   *   *   The defense, in viewing the offense in this case, have regarded it as a crime resulting from an act done in the course of official duty as stipulated in Article 17, paragraph 3(a)(ii), of the Administrative Agreement, based on Article 3 of the Security Treaty between the United States and Japan, and, on this premise, the defense have advocated that the military authorities of the United States have the primary right to exercise jurisdiction in this case. The defense further have contended that although the United States of America has notified Japan that they will not exercise jurisdiction in this case, this notification differs from the case in which the primary right of jurisdiction is waived at the request of the Japanese authorities.

Thus, the above notification cannot be regarded as meaning that Japan automatically has obtained the right of secondary jurisdiction.

However, in the present case, regardless of whether the crime resulted from an act done in the course of the performance of official duty or not, this is a case based on Article 17, paragraph 1(a) and (b), where both Japan and the military authorities of the United States have concurrent jurisdiction. Thus, in this case of concurrent jurisdiction, the provision of paragraph 3 of the above Article applies. Since the military authorities of the United States notified Japan in a letter dated May 17, 1957, in accordance with (c) of paragraph 3 of the above Article, to the effect that they would not exercise criminal jurisdiction in this case, it stands to reason that this should be interpreted as meaning that the United States military authorities have lost jurisdiction in Japan over this case.

Further, the above notification of non-exercise of jurisdiction differs, as advocated by the defense, from the case of waiving jurisdiction at the request of the authorities of the other State. In other words, it differs from the case stipulated in the latter part of (c) of paragraph 3 of the above Article. However, it must be said that in either of the above cases it is absolutely the same so far as the loss of jurisdiction by the United States military authorities in Japan, is concerned. Consequently, there is no doubt that a Japanese court has jurisdiction in this case, in accordance with the terms of Article 17, paragraph 1(b), of the Administrative Agreement.

So the question of whether Japanese authorities or whether the United States military authorities have the primary right to exercise jurisdiction in this case is already a matter of the past, and there is no advantage in dilating further on this point. Thus, from an absolute point of view, there is no need to determine whether this a case of a crime committed in the course of the performance of official duty or not. However, in another sense, since the Court recognizes that this is an important point of contention, it will dwell further on this point as follows:

Although the Court is able to recognize that this offense took place while the accused was on official duty and that it occurred at the place of duty, the act has no direct connection whatsoever with the execution of the duty of guarding a light machine gun, etc., as ordered by a senior officer. Thus, it is self-evident from the facts found by this Court that the act was not committed in the process of carrying out one's official duty. Moreover, as is clear from the various points of evidence listed above, the Court does not recognize the existence of any concrete anxieties with respect to the light machine guns and field jackets being either damaged or stolen by brass pickers. Rather, the brass pickers were only intent on collecting expended cartridges.

It is for this reason that Specialist Third Class Nickel, who, together with the accused, was ordered to guard duty, was resting at a place toward the eastern part of the saddle a little distance removed from the location of the light machine gun. And, as indicated in the Court findings, Nickel is to be regarded as having thrown a number of empty cartridges a number of times without any specific meaning or, in other words, just to pass the time away. Further, the fact that the accused fired at brass pickers is not limited to the case of Naka Sakai alone, as indicated in the findings of the Court. Just prior to this, there is the case of Eiji Onozeki. Onozeki, one of the brass pickers mentioned in the Court findings, was descending the east slope of the West Peak, when the accused ran towards him. The said brass picker was surprised at this, and began running away. The accused then, aiming towards Onozeki's immediate vicinity from behind, fired an empty cartridge. This has been indicated in the Court findings. Such actions as inviting brass pickers to approach and then of chasing them away, cannot in any sense be regarded as necessary to the performance of official duty. Furthermore, the firing of a blank cartridge by inserting an empty cartridge in a grenade launcher and thereby projecting the casing is a practice that is not permitted by the United States military authorities because it damages the weapons. In addition, the firing of blank cartridges at close distance towards any person without cause is also forbidden. In this case before the Court, the act can only be regarded as excessive mischief, completely irrelevant to the performance of the duty of guarding light machine guns and other items and as having no subjective or objective relationship   *   *   *   an action simply carried out for the sole purpose of satisfying the momentary caprice of the accused himself. Thus, this behaviour cannot be accepted, as contended by the defence, as corresponding to a justifiable action as stipulated in Article 35 of the Criminal Code.

     *   *   *

SECTION C. REGULATION OF ECONOMIC ACTIVITY

Multiple state regulatory interests. On a small planet the economic activities of significant persons and business associations can involve the regulatory, or governmental, interests of several different states and of at least one new association of states, the European Economic Community. If it is accepted that international law permits the exercise of prescriptive jurisdiction on the basis of economic effects within the territory of a state, and hence that several states have jurisdiction to regulate the same economic activity, actual regulation by all states that have jurisdiction would be chaotic, as well as unjust. What state then, under what circumstances, and in what way and by what means, should "yield" the exercise of its jurisdiction to another?

Where economic or social conduct is involved, the question is difficult, because the easy-to-formulate allocation devices considered in the preceding Sections are not relevant. Ideally, what is needed is some way of quantifying state regulatory interests and of leaving the whole regulatory job to the law-making authority with the highly preponderant interest. But how are such interests to be determined and what is the authority of the law-appliers in one state to disregard its own law?

Clearly in the situation of transnational business activity trespassing on the interests of two or more national states, just as in the case of everyday conflicting police power interests of two states of the Union, neither law as rules nor law as method has yet given clear-cut and reliable solutions. Perhaps such methods for the partial resolution of conflicts as we shall consider below might be thought to yield the conclusion that the resolution approach will not work and that the conflict must be reduced by the adoption of new rules. What rules? Rules to narrow the bases of national jurisdiction? Or new universal rules that would replace the welter of national regulatory laws?

_____

1. THE "REACH" OF THE ANTI–TRUST LAWS OF THE UNITED STATES

Hypothetical case to illustrate the differences between antitrust laws. Assume that all the law enforcement authorities involved in the hypothetical case below know and can prove that the producers of 95% of the world supply of a certain basic chemical, some thirty corporations nationals of ten countries, conform to a pattern in which each national market is left to the companies organized there and total production by all the companies is adjusted to total demand in such a way as to keep prices stable and relatively high. However, it is not possible to prove that the thirty companies have made any contractual arrangement to these ends. [This is a simple and classic antitrust problem, that of "concerted action" to allocate markets and control price by restricting production of a single product.]

1. In some of the ten countries even a contractual cartel arrangement would not violate any law; and, indeed, a breach of such a contract would be actionable.

2. In the United States the concerted action would violate the Sherman Act, even if it did not result in market dominance, i. e., a per se violation. Moreover, the sanctions would include invalidation of the contract, criminal prosecution, equitable enforcement by imprisonment or fines for civil contempt, or treble damages to injured competitors outside the cartel arrangement.

3. In the Federal German Republic the supreme court has held that the Cartel Law, p. 130, does not reach concerted actions where there is no contract.

4. In the United States and in the Federal German Republic an antitrust violation under national law, if otherwise actionable, exists if the companies' conduct, wherever it took place, has economic effects within the territories of these states.

5. But in Germany, unlike the United States, criminal and civil contempt sanctions would not lie; the fine is the major sanction.

6.   In Great Britain, prior to its entry into the European Communities,[a] the cartel arrangement would have to be considered by one or the other of two commissions, the Restrictive Practices Commission or the Monopolies Commission, most likely the former, before any sanction whatsoever might be applied.   Also, if certain British scholarly voices should be heeded by the relevant commission and/or the courts on judicial review, customary international law would limit British regulation to conduct within Great Britain having its effects within Great Britain.

7.   In Great Britain, now that it has entered the European Communities, the Economic Community antitrust law, as elaborated by the Court of the Communities will be directly applicable to British (or any other Community) nationals involved in the cartel.   Also the Community Court has decided that, although not explicit in the Treaty of Rome, concerted action without contract as to allocation of markets and the control of production and prices violates Article 85–1 of the Treaty of Rome.   It has also held, p. 131, that the Rome Treaty rule will apply to any such conduct carried on within the Community by an out-of-Community corporation through its controlled subsidiaries within the Community.

8.   But the Economic Community rule does not preempt and render nugatory the various national antitrust laws (if any) of member states.   Thus, subject to a superior, valid demand from the Commission of the Communities (e. g., on the authority of the decision of the Court of the Communities), France may continue to deal with the cartel on the basis that its actions interfere with the French price controls laws.

9.   The Economic Community antitrust law uses fines as the sanction, permits tentative immunity to companies that have registered their anti-competitive agreements and have not been told that they are deemed violations; and, in any event, authorizes the commission to except certain otherwise anti-competitive arrangements if found to "contribute to the improvement of the production or distribution of goods or to the promotion of technological or economic progress while reserving to consumers an equitable share in the profit resulting therefrom," and which:

(a)   neither impose on the enterprises concerned any restrictions not indispensable to the attainment of the above objectives;

(b)   nor enable such enterprises to eliminate competition in respect of a substantial proportion of the goods concerned. [Treaty of Rome, Art. 85–3]

Such variances from liability are unknown in United States antitrust practice, but there is no rule specifying when the Department of

---

a.   The European Communities are described, as to their three constituent elements, created by different treaties, at p. 879.   The Treaty of Rome, 1958, created the element involved in this problem, the European Economic Community (EEC), informally known as the "Common Market."

Justice must prosecute an antitrust case or that the Federal Trade Commission must begin an administrative proceeding.

Now, suppose that by coincidence antitrust proceedings are brought in all legal systems except those in the first category. In the United States proceeding, to the shock of the Europeans, there is a criminal count against the executives of the companies in the cartel, only a few of which can be personally served. Also, in the United States, foreign corporations that cannot otherwise be served with process in the proceedings against the corporations are served through companies organized in the United States as subsidiaries of the foreign companies but which, the United States claims, are really the parent companies and control the foreign companies. The United States also demands of the corporations so served that they produce for an American grand jury the books and records kept abroad by the ostensible foreign parent company.

What results if:

i.   A state in the first category objects under customary international law to every aspect of the United States proceeding, insofar as its citizens and companies organized under its law are concerned. What do you think the counts in this legal protest would be, and the proper legal response of the Department of State?

ii. The Ambassador of the United States to the European Economic Communities, acting on the instruction of his government, asks the commission not to proceed with its case against the cartel, as the matter is being prepared for trial in the United States, the world's largest consumer of the chemical involved. What is a proper response of the commission to the ambassador?

iii. The Commission of the Communities grants an exception under Article 85–3 of the Treaty of Rome, the United States thereafter proceeds to final judgment against all members of the cartel that can be served in the United States, and the commission protests to the American ambassador. What is a proper legal and policy response from him?

iv. Is there any better way to deal with these conflicts of regulatory law? What it is?

[CCH, Common Market Reporter, is a useful source in English of the antitrust laws (or the lack of them) in European states. There is extensive discussion of the divergencies between national legal systems in this regard, and of the problems these create, in the Report of the International Law Association, Fifty-first Conference, Tokyo 1964, at 304–592 (1965), with summaries of national laws beginning at 417.]

THE SHERMAN ACT[a]

15 U.S.C. §§ 1–2.

Sec. 1. Every contract, combination in the form of trust or otherwise, or conspiracy, in restraint of trade or commerce among the several States, or with foreign nations, is [hereby] declared to be illegal * * *

Sec. 2. Every person who shall monopolize, or attempt to monopolize, or combine or conspire with any other person or persons, to monopolize any part of the trade or commerce among the several States, or with foreign nations shall be deemed guilty of a misdemeanor * * *

[To the declarations of invalidity and the criminal penalties provided above, the United States antitrust laws contain as sanctions the use of injunctions, with the corresponding power to punish for civil contempt, and treble damages for injured private parties. European antitrust laws in many instances provide only for fines; such is the case with the provisions against restraints of trade (Article 85) and monopoly power misused (Article 86) of the Treaty of Rome, which establishes the European Economic Community.]

AMERICAN BANANA CO. v. UNITED FRUIT CO.

United States Supreme Court, 1909.
213 U.S. 347, 354, 29 S.Ct. 511.

[This was a private suit for treble damages brought under the Sherman Act. The court summarized the complaint of the plaintiff as follows:]

* * * The plaintiff is an Alabama corporation, organized in 1904. The defendant is a New Jersey corporation, organized in 1899. Long before the plaintiff was formed, the defendant, with intent to prevent competition and to control and monopolize the banana trade, bought the property and business of several of its previous competitors, with provision against their resuming the trade, made contracts with others, including a majority of the most important, regulating the quantity to be purchased and the price to be paid, and acquired a controlling amount of stock in still others. For the same purpose it organized a selling company, of which it held the stock, that by agreement sold at fixed prices all the bananas of the combining parties. By this and other means it did monopolize and restrain the trade and maintained unreasonable prices. The defendant being in this ominous attitude, one McConnell in 1903 started a banana plantation in Panama, then part of the United States of Colombia, and began to build a

---

a. The original and still basic federal antitrust law, now supplemented by legislation such as the Clayton Act and the Federal Trade Commission Act.

railway (which would afford his only means of export), both in accordance with the laws of the United States of Colombia. He was notified by the defendant that he must either combine or stop. Two months later, it is believed at the defendant's instigation, the governor of Panama recommended to his national government that Costa Rica be allowed to administer the territory through which the railroad was to run, and this although that territory had been awarded to Colombia under an arbitration agreed to by treaty. The defendant, and afterwards, in September, the government of Costa Rica, it is believed by the inducement of the defendant, interfered with McConnell. In November, 1903, Panama revolted and became an independent republic, declaring its boundary to be that settled by the award. In June, 1904, the plaintiff bought out McConnell and went on with the work, as it had a right to do under the laws of Panama. But in July, Costa Rican soldiers and officials, instigated by the defendant, seized a part of the plantation and a cargo of supplies and have held them ever since, and stopped the construction and operation of the plantation and railway. In August one Astua, by ex parte proceedings, got a judgment from a Costa Rican court, declaring the plantation to be his, although, it is alleged, the proceedings were not within the jurisdiction of Costa Rica, and were contrary to its laws and void. Agents of the defendant then bought the lands from Astua. The plaintiff has tried to induce the government of Costa Rica to withdraw its soldiers and also has tried to persuade the United States to interfere, but has been thwarted in both by the defendant and has failed. The government of Costa Rica remained in possession down to the bringing of the suit.

As a result of the defendant's acts the plaintiff has been deprived of the use of the plantation, and the railway, the plantation and supplies have been injured. The defendant also, by outbidding, has driven purchasers out of the market and has compelled producers to come to its terms, and it has prevented the plaintiff from buying for export and sale. This is the substantial damage alleged. There is thrown in a further allegation that the defendant has "sought to injure" the plaintiff's business by offering positions to its employés and by discharging and threatening to discharge persons in its own employ who were stockholders of the plaintiff. But no particular point is made of this. It is contended, however, that, even if the main argument fails and the defendant is held not to be answerable for acts depending on the coöperation of the government of Costa Rica for their effect, a wrongful conspiracy resulting in driving the plaintiff out of business is to be gathered from the complaint and that it was entitled to go to trial upon that. (at 354–355)

[The Court affirmed the dismissal of the complaint as not setting forth a cause of action. Justice Holmes stated in the opinion of the Court:]

It is obvious that, however stated, the plaintiff's case depends on several rather startling propositions. In the first place the acts causing the damage were done, so far as appears, outside the jurisdiction of the United States and within that of other states. It is surprising to hear it argued that they were governed by the act of Congress.

* * *

* * * The general and almost universal rule is that the character of an act as lawful or unlawful must be determined wholly by the law of the country where the act is done. * * *

For another jurisdiction, if it should happen to lay hold of the actor, to treat him according to its own notions rather than those of the place where he did the acts, not only would be unjust, but would be an interference with the authority of another sovereign, contrary to the comity of nations, which the other state concerned justly might resent. * * *

* * *

The foregoing considerations would lead in case of doubt to a construction of any statute as intended to be confined in its operation and effect to the territorial limits over which the lawmaker has general and legitimate power. "All legislation is prima facie territorial." Ex parte Blain, In re Sawers, 12 Ch.Div. 522, 528; State v. Carter, 27 N.J. (3 Dutcher) 499; People v. Merrill, 2 Parker, Crim. Rep. 590, 596. Words having universal scope, such as "Every contract in restraint of trade," "Every person who shall monopolize," etc., will be taken as a matter of course to mean only every one subject to such legislation, not all that the legislator subsequently may be able to catch. In the case of the present statute the improbability of the United States attempting to make acts done in Panama or Costa Rica criminal is obvious, yet the law begins by making criminal the acts for which it gives a right to sue. We think it entirely plain that what the defendant did in Panama or Costa Rica is not within the scope of the statute so far as the present suit is concerned. Other objections of a serious nature are urged but need not be discussed.

For again, not only were the acts of the defendant in Panama or Costa Rica not within the Sherman Act, but they were not torts by the law of the place and therefore were not torts at all, however contrary to the ethical and economic postulates of that statute. The substance of the complaint is that, the plantation being within the de facto jurisdiction of Costa Rica, that state took and keeps possession of it by virtue of its sovereign power. But a seizure by a state is not a thing that can be complained of elsewhere in the courts. Underhill v. Hernandez, 168 U.S. 250. The fact, if it be one, that de jure the estate is in Panama does not matter in the least; sovereignty is pure fact. The fact has been recognized by the United States, and by the implications of the bill is assented to by Panama.

* * *

* * * Giving to this complaint every reasonable latitude of interpretation we are of opinion that it alleges no case under the act of Congress and discloses nothing that we can suppose to have been a tort where it was done. A conspiracy in this country to do acts in another jurisdiction does not draw to itself those acts and make them unlawful, if they are permitted by the local law.
* * *

Questions

To what extent does the court's ruling depend upon the Act of State Doctrine? Upon the fact that the "acts of the defendant in Panama or Costa Rica * * * were not torts by the law of the place"? How would the court have ruled if the Costa Rican government had not been involved in the oppression of the Banana Company?

UNITED STATES v. ALUMINUM CO. OF AMERICA

United States Court of Appeals, Second Circuit, 1945.
148 F.2d 416.

[This was a prosecution for violation of the Sherman Act. One of the defendants was Aluminum Limited, a Canadian corporation formed to take over properties of the Aluminum Company of America outside the United States. (Not quite half of each company's shares were owned by the same group of individuals.) The court was concerned about the participation of each company in a foreign "cartel," called the "Alliance." The court concluded that the American company, Alcoa, was not a party to the "Alliance" and "did not join in any violation of § 1 of the Act, so far as concerned foreign commerce." Judge Learned Hand's opinion continued: (at p. 442)]

Whether "Limited" itself violated that section depends upon the character of the "Alliance." It was a Swiss corporation, created in pursuance of an agreement entered into on July 3, 1931, the signatories to which were a French corporation, two German, one Swiss, a British, and "Limited." The original agreement, or "cartel," provided for the formation of a corporation in Switzerland which should issue shares, to be taken up by the signatories. This corporation was from time to time to fix a quota of production for each share, and each shareholder was to be limited to the quantity measured by the number of shares it held, but was free to sell at any price it chose. The corporation fixed a price every year at which it would take off any shareholder's hands any part of its quota which it did not sell. No shareholder was to "buy, borrow, fabricate or sell" aluminum produced by anyone not a shareholder except with the consent of the board of governors, but that must not be "unreasonably withheld." * * *

The agreement of 1936 abandoned the system of unconditional quotas, and substituted a system of royalties. Each shareholder was to have a fixed free quota for every share it held, but as its production exceeded the sum of its quotas, it was to pay a royalty, graduated progressively in proportion to the excess; and these royalties the "Alliance" divided among the shareholders in proportion to their shares. This agreement—unlike the first—did not contain an express promise that the "Alliance" would buy any undisposed of stocks at a fixed price, although perhaps § 3 of Subdivision A, of Part X may have impliedly recognized such an obligation. Probably, during the two years in which the shareholders operated under this agreement, that question did not arise for the demand for aluminum was very active. Nevertheless, we understand from "Limited's" answer to an interrogatory that the last price fixed under the agreement of 1931 was understood to remain in force. Although this agreement, like its predecessor, was silent as to imports into the United States, when that question arose during its preparation, as it did, all the shareholders agreed that such imports should be included in the quotas. The German companies were exempted from royalties—for obvious reasons—and that, it would seem, for practical purposes put them out of the "cartel" for the future, for it was scarcely possible that a German producer would be unable to dispose of all its production, at least within any future period that would be provided for. The shareholders continued this agreement unchanged until the end of March, 1938, by which time it had become plain that, at least for the time being, it was no longer of service to anyone. Nothing was, however, done to end it, although the German shareholders of course became enemies of the French, British and Canadian shareholders in 1939. The "Alliance" itself has apparently never been dissolved; and indeed it appeared on the "Proclaimed List of Blocked Nationals" of September 13, 1944.

Did either the agreement of 1931 or that of 1936 violate § 1 of the Act? The answer does not depend upon whether we shall recognize as a source of liability a liability imposed by another state. On the contrary we are concerned only with whether Congress chose to attach liability to the conduct outside the United States of persons not in allegiance to it. That being so, the only question open is whether Congress intended to impose the liability, and whether our own Constitution permitted it to do so: as a court of the United States, we cannot look beyond our own law. Nevertheless, it is quite true that we are not to read general words, such as those in this Act, without regard to the limitations customarily observed by nations upon the exercise of their powers; limitations which generally correspond to those fixed by the "Conflict of Laws." We should not impute to Congress an intent to punish all whom its courts can catch, for conduct which has no consequences within the United States. American Banana Co. v. United Fruit Co., 213 U.S. 347, 357, 29 S.Ct. 511, 53 L.Ed. 826, 16 Ann.Cas. 1047; United States v. Bowman, 260 U.S. 94, 98, 43 S.Ct. 39, 67 L.Ed. 149; Blackmer v. United States, 284 U.S. 421, 437, 52 S.Ct. 252, 76 L.Ed. 375. On the other hand, *it is settled law*—as "Limited" itself agrees—*that any state may impose liabilities, even upon persons not within its allegiance, for conduct outside its borders that has consequences within its borders which the state reprehends;* [a] and these liabilities other states will ordinarily recognize. Strassheim v. Daily, 221 U.S. 280, 284, 285, 31 S.Ct. 558, 55 L.Ed. 735; Lamar v. United States, 240 U.S. 60, 65, 66, 36 S.Ct. 255, 60 L.Ed. 526; Ford v. United States, 273 U.S. 593, 620, 621, 47 S.Ct. 531, 71 L.Ed. 793; Restatement of Conflict of Laws § 65. It may be argued that this Act extends further. Two situations are possible. There may be agreements made beyond our borders not intended to affect imports, which do affect them, or which affect exports. Almost any limitation of the supply of goods in Europe, for example, or in South America, may have repercussions in the United States if there is trade between the two. Yet when one considers the international complications likely to arise from an effort in this country to treat such agreements as unlawful, it is safe to assume that Congress certainly did not intend the Act to cover them. Such agreements may on the other hand intend to include imports into the United States, and yet it may appear that they have had no effect upon them. That situation might be thought to fall within the doctrine that intent may be a substitute for performance in the case of a contract made within the United States; or it might be thought to fall within the doctrine that a statute should not be interpreted to cover acts abroad which have no consequence here. We shall not choose between these alternatives; but for argument we shall assume that the Act does not cover agreements, even though intended to affect imports or exports, unless its performance is shown actually to have had some effect upon them. Where both conditions are satisfied, the situation certainly falls within such decisions as United States v. Pacific & Artic R. & Navigation Co., 228 U.S. 87, 33 S.Ct. 443, 57 L.Ed. 742; Thomsen v. Cayser, 243 U.S. 66, 37 S.Ct. 353, 61 L.Ed. 597, Ann.Cas.1917D, 322 and United States v. Sisal Sales Corporation, 274 U.S. 268, 47 S.Ct. 592, 71 L.Ed. 1042. (United States v. Nord Deutcher Lloyd, 223 U.S. 512, 32 S.Ct. 244, 56 L.Ed. 531, illustrates the same conception in another field.) * * *

Both agreements would clearly have been unlawful, had they been made within the United States; and it follows from what we have just said that both were unlawful, though made abroad, if they were intended to affect imports and did affect them. Since the shareholders almost at once agreed that the agreement of 1931 should not cover imports, we may ignore it and confine our discussion to that of 1936:

a. Emphasis supplied by the editors.

indeed that we should have to do anyway, since it superseded the earlier agreement. The judge found that it was not the purpose of the
agreement to "suppress or restrain the exportation of aluminum to
the United States for sale in competition with Alcoa." By that we
understand that he meant that the agreement was not specifically directed to "Alcoa," because it only applied generally to the production
of the shareholders. If he meant that it was not expected that the
general restriction upon production would have an effect upon imports, we cannot agree, for the change made in 1936 was deliberate
and was expressly made to accomplish just that. It would have been
an idle gesture, unless the shareholders had supposed that it would,
or at least might, have that effect. The first of the conditions which
we mentioned was therefore satisfied; the intent was to set up a quota
system for imports.

The judge also found that the 1936 agreement did not "materially
affect the * * * foreign trade or commerce of the United States";
apparently because the imported ingot was greater in 1936 and 1937
than in earlier years. We cannot accept this finding, based as it was
upon the fact that, in 1936, 1937 and the first quarter of 1938, the
gross imports of ingot increased. It by no means follows from such an
increase that the agreement did not restrict imports; and incidentally
it so happens that in those years such inference as is possible
at all, leads to the opposite conclusion. It is true that the average imports—including "Alcoa's"—for the years 1932–1935 inclusive were
about 15 million pounds, and that for 1936, 1937 and one-fourth of
1938 they were about 33 million pounds; but the average domestic
ingot manufacture in the first period was about 96 million and in the
second about 262 million; so that the proportion of imports to domestic ingot was about 15.6 per cent for the first period and about 12.6
per cent for the second. We do not mean to infer from this that the
quota system of 1936 did in fact restrain imports, as these figures
might suggest; but we do mean that nothing is to be inferred from
the gross increase of imports. We shall dispose of the matter therefore upon the assumption that, although the shareholders intended to
restrict imports, it does not appear whether in fact they did so. Upon
our hypothesis the plaintiff would therefore fail, if it carried the burden of proof upon this issue as upon others. We think, however, that,
after the intent to affect imports was proved, the burden of proof
shifted to "Limited." In the first place a depressant upon production
which applies generally may be assumed, ceteris paribus, to distribute
its effect evenly upon all markets. Again, when the parties took the
trouble specifically to make the depressant apply to a given market,
there is reason to suppose that they expected that it would have some
effect, which it could have only by lessening what would otherwise
have been imported. If the motive they introduced was over-balanced
in all instances by motives which induced the shareholders to import,
if the United States market became so attractive that the royalties did

not count at all and their expectations were in fact defeated, they to whom the facts were more accessible than to the plaintiff ought to prove it, for a prima facie case had been made. Moreover, there is an especial propriety in demanding this of "Limited," because it was "Limited" which procured the inclusion in the agreement of 1936 of imports in the quotas.

There remains only the question whether this assumed restriction had any influence upon prices   *   *   *   To that Socony-Vacuum Oil Co. v. United States, supra, 310 U.S. 150, 60 S.Ct. 811, 84 L.Ed. 1129, is an entire answer.   *   *   *   The underlying doctrine was that all factors which contribute to determine prices, must be kept free to operate unhampered by agreements. For these reasons we think that the agreement of 1936 violated § 1 of the Act.

------

2.   RECIPROCAL JUDICIAL DEFERENCE

The ICI-DuPont-Nylon Spinners Cases: Basic Facts for Three Cases. DuPont invented nylon; and, as is customary, patented its invention in all—or certainly all industrial—countries, including the United Kingdom. The patent for exploitation of the British market was transferred to Imperial Chemicals Industries (ICI). The United States Department of Justice charged that this transfer was one item in an arrangement whereby the large United States chemical company and the very big British one had pooled their patents and divided the world between them as to markets for products deriving from all the patents in the pool. ICI was properly served in the United States and unsuccessfully contended before the United States court that British law and patent policy favored such territorial divisions in patent cases. The trial judge ordered the dissolution of the pool and directed ICI by an affirmative decree in equity to open the British nylon patent to all wishing to use the patent on payment of standard royalties.

ICI accepted its defeat in the United States with apparent good grace, only to be met, doubtless to its surprise, with a suit for specific performance in a British court. The plaintiff was British Nylon Spinners, Ltd. It had not been served in the United States case and claimed an exclusive assignment by ICI to it of the British nylon patent before the litigation in the United States had begun. The United States was not represented in the British proceeding, and the question of affiliation between the British plaintiffs and defendants was not put in issue in the British suit in equity.

UNITED STATES v. IMPERIAL CHEMICAL INDUSTRIES, LTD.

United States District Court, S.D. of New York, 1951.
100 F.Supp. 504.

* * *

The complaint was filed under * * * the Sherman Anti-Trust Act—to restrain and prevent alleged continuing violations of Section 1 of the Act.

In essence, the complaint charges a conspiracy among the defendants, having as its purpose a division of world markets and the elimination of competition among themselves and between them and third parties in the trade and commerce of chemical products, sporting arms and ammunition. The complaint alleges the achievement of this purpose by the execution of unlawful contracts, agreements, arrangements and understandings and the establishment and maintenance of jointly-owned foreign companies; and the continued existence and accomplishment of this conspiracy and its purposes despite various temporary arrangements necessitated by the war. By reason of this, it is alleged that judicial remedy is necessary to restore competition among the defendants and between them and third parties. The complaint prays that the combination and conspiracy and the practices alleged be decreed unlawful and that defendants be perpetually enjoined from continuing, reviving or renewing any of the said violations.

Generally, the several answers of the defendants consist of a denial that any of them violated the anti-trust laws.

* * *

[The bulk of a very long opinion is omitted.]

We have found that the various patents and processes agreements were made in furtherance of the conspiracy alleged. These agreements, irrespective of their per se legality, were instruments designed and intended to accomplish the world-wide allocation of markets; their object was to achieve an unlawful purpose—an illegal restraint of trade prohibited by Section 1 of the Sherman Act. The agreements are unlawful because they provided a means for the accomplishment of this purpose and objective. We have also found that these agreements did, in operation, result in restraints of United States trade.

We have found that the jointly-owned companies were means designed and used by duPont and ICI to avoid and prevent competition between themselves and with others in the non-exclusive territories. They were a means used for the accomplishment of the basic understanding for the division of world-wide territories. We have found that not only were they intended to affect the export and import trade of the United States but that the limitations placed on duPont and other American companies on the exports to these jointly-owned companies and the restrictions placed on these companies with respect to sales and exports by them to the United States did achieve the purpose and end for which they were organized. Cf. United States v. Aluminum Co. of America, 2 Cir., 1945, 148 F.2d 416, 443–444. The operations of these jointly-owned companies were in violation of the law. United States v. National Lead Co., D.C.S.D.N.Y.1945, 63 F. Supp. 513, 524. * * *

After an exhaustive examination of the voluminous evidence presented in this case, we conclude that the Government has proved its case: the defendants had entered into a conspiracy to divide markets, and the agreements considered in this opinion were instruments of that conspiracy.

In the face of this finding, the law is crystal clear: a conspiracy to divide territories, which affects American commerce, violates the Sherman Act. United States v. Timken Roller Bearing Co., D.C., 83 F.Supp. 284, affirmed 341 U.S. 593, 71 S.Ct. 971; United States v. National Lead Co., D.C., 63 F.Supp. 513, affirmed 332 U.S. 319, 67 S.Ct. 1634, 91 L.Ed. 2077; United States v. General Electric Co., D.C., 80 F.Supp. 989. So settled is the law on this that in the National Lead case, supra, Judge Rifkind wrote: "No citation of authority is any longer necessary to support the proposition that a combination of competitors, which by agreement divides the world into exclusive trade areas, and suppresses all competition among the members of the combination, offends the Sherman Act." 63 F.Supp., at page 523.

* * *

Proposed decrees may be filed within thirty days from the date of the filing of this opinion and thereafter all will be heard on due notice.

UNITED STATES v. IMPERIAL CHEMICAL INDUSTRIES, LTD.

United States, Federal District Court, S.D. New York, 1952.
105 F.Supp. 215.

RYAN, DISTRICT JUDGE. We now approach the task of formulating a final decree designed to prevent and restrain the violations of law which we have found. 15 U.S.C.A. § 4.

Our objective is to fashion, in the terms of a decree, means by which the agreement found to exist is terminated, its revival prevented and its effects destroyed by the reestablishment of competitive conditions insofar as they pertain to United States exports and imports. * * *

Where competition has been eliminated, it must be restored. Only those provisions reasonably necessary to accomplish correction and adjustment of a dislocated competitive situation may be applied.

The essence of the violation found was the unlawful agreement to divide world territories. It was this enduring and basic understanding which was fundamental to all of the dealings of the conspirators. It was to accomplish this purpose and end that the various means were adopted.

The decree will contain injunctions prohibiting agreements and arrangements between the defendants dividing territory and allocating customers and markets so as to unlawfully limit the commerce of the United States. * * *

* * * The decree, however, must contain additional provisions to implement these injunctive directions, so that they are made probable of observance. The jointly-owned companies and the patents, processes and technologies of the defendants must be brought within the scope of the judgment. * * *

The restraints sought to be accomplished were achieved also in part by the patents and processes agreements. * * *

* * *

We decree compulsory licensing because the patent rights which were granted the defendants were misused. The failure to export products manufactured under the patents resulted from the agreement to divide territories. What might have been done lawfully by one, acting as a result of his own decision, became unlawful because it was brought about by common agreement. The failure to export, which might have been legal in itself, also became unlawful because of the purpose and end it was employed to accomplish. One of the means employed was the patents and processes agreements. The needs and requirements of local markets from which the patentee was excluded by the underlying agreement were met by patent grants to fellow conspirators. Thus, the patents themselves and the right to grant licenses under them were used to implement and carry out the allotment of territories. The use of these existing patents must be regulated because of their past abuse.

* * *

The Government does not seek a decree directing ICI to grant compulsory licenses of its British patents. The Government requests that ICI be required to grant immunity under its foreign patents which correspond to the United States patents which we have made subject to compulsory licensing. * * * We have had testimony offered on behalf of ICI by an expert in British law that a provision for granting immunities is contrary to British public policy and that a British court will not enforce such a provision in the judgment of a court of a foreign jurisdiction. As to this, we observe that, acting on the basis of our jurisdiction in personam, we are merely directing ICI to refrain from asserting rights which it may have in Britain, since the enforcement of those rights will serve to continue the effects of wrongful acts it has committed within the United States affecting the foreign trade of the United States.

We are not unmindful that under British law there are restrictions upon exports from the United States by reason of the existence of the British patents owned by ICI. The exclusion of unlicensed imports and the prohibition of unlicensed sales is enforceable because of the legal rights which attach to a British patent.

* * *

While it is true that these rights exist independent of any provision in the patents and processes agreements, they were granted to ICI by the disclosure or assignment of inventions by duPont pursuant to the terms of these agreements. Inventions were also licensed by ICI to duPont for its exclusive use and exploitation in the United States in accordance with the agreements. In the first instance the patents were employed to restrain duPont's exports to Great Britain, in plain violation of American anti-trust laws; in the second instance, the patents were used as a means to prevent ICI exports to the United States and placed a restraint upon the foreign trade of Great Britain, in violation of her declared policy, if not her laws. It does not seem presumptuous for this court to make a direction to a foreign defendant corporation over which it has jurisdiction to take steps to remedy and correct a situation, which is unlawful both here and in the foreign jurisdiction in which it is domiciled. Two evils have resulted from the one understanding of ICI and duPont—restraints upon the foreign trade and commerce of the United States as well as on that of Great Britain. It is not an intrusion on the authority of a foreign sovereign for this court to direct that steps be taken to remove the harmful effects on the trade of the United States.

We recognize that substantial legal questions may be raised with respect to our power to decree as to duPont's foreign patents as well as those issued to ICI. Here, we deal with the regulation of the exercise of rights granted by a foreign sovereign to a domestic corporate defendant and to a foreign corporate defendant. Our power so to regulate is limited and depends upon jurisdiction in personam; the effectiveness of the exercise of that power depends upon the recognition which will be given to our judgment as a matter of comity by the courts of the foreign sovereign which has granted the patents in question.

* * *

The history of the basic British nylon patents reveals a studied and continued purpose on the part of ICI and duPont to remove these patents from within the scope of any decree which might ultimately be made by this court (Op. pp. 115, 116, 197, 198). These British patents were issued to duPont. By the agreement of March 30, 1939, ICI received an exclusive license under them; in January, 1940, ICI granted irrevocable and exclusive rights to make nylon yarn from nylon polymer (which is manufactured by ICI) to British Nylon Spinners, Ltd. (BNS). ICI has a stock interest of 50% in BNS, the remaining 50% is held by Courtaulds, Inc. BNS is in the business of manufacturing and distributing nylon yarn. Not content with this arrangement and with the deliberate purpose to "materially reduce the risk of any loss of rights" as a result of this suit (Ex. 708, p. 2705), duPont pursuant to the nylon agreement of 1946 assigned the basic British nylon patents to ICI. It is now urged that we may not decree with reference to these British patents so as to direct ICI to remove restrictions on imports into Great Britain of nylon polymer or nylon yarn from the United States. It is argued that the sum total of all these agreements is not to create by itself any restrictions against American imports, and that those which exist arise from the right to be free from competition which is inherent in the British patents and cannot possibly be repugnant to the American anti-trust laws.

BNS is not before this court; although they were knowing participants in acts designed to thwart the granting of full relief, we may not direct our decree to them. The lack of majority stock ownership in ICI likewise prevents control of the future acts of BNS by this means; however, we are not without some remedy still available.

Objection is raised by ICI that we are without power to decree that the British nylon patents may not be asserted to prevent the importation of nylon polymer and nylon yarn into Great Britain because BNS has rights which exist independent of those processed by ICI. This overlooks the circumstances under which BNS acquired its rights to these patents by licenses from ICI.

    *   *   *

    *   *   * Throughout all these negotiations it appears that BNS was advised of the dealings between ICI and duPont concerning the British nylon patents. Both ICI and duPont are parties to the instant suit; they were advised in fact and realized that the further use and control of the rights pertaining to the British nylon patents were subject to a decree of this court to be entered in this suit.   *   *   *

We do not hesitate therefore to decree that the British nylon patents may not be asserted by ICI to prevent the importation of nylon polymer and of nylon yarn into Great Britain. What credit may be given to such an injunctive provision by the courts of Great Britain in a suit brought by BNS to restrain such importations we do not venture to predict. We feel that the possibility that the English courts in an equity suit will not give effect to such a provision in our decree should not deter us from including it.

In any event it appears that BNS would have the right under Section 63 of the Patents Act of 1949, as the exclusive licensee to bring suit for infringement against an importer of yarn and staple fiber. There would then be a speedy determination of the effectiveness of the immunity provision of the decree with reference to these products.

If the British courts were not to give credit to this provision, no injury would have been done; if the holding of the British courts were to the contrary, a remedy available would not have been needlessly abandoned.

* * *

BRITISH NYLON SPINNERS LD. v. IMPERIAL CHEMICAL INDUSTRIES LD.

England, Court of Appeal, 1952.
[1953] Ch. 19.

Interlocutory appeal from Upjohn J.

By an agreement made on December 31, 1946, the defendants, Imperial Chemical Industries Ld. and an American corporation, du Pont de Nemours & Co. Inc., the latter agreed to assign to the defendants certain patents and applications for patents scheduled to the agreement, such assigned patents to be registered as British patents in the United Kingdom.

On March 5, 1947, the defendants entered into a contract in England with the plaintiffs, British Nylon Spinners Ld., an English corporation. The plaintiffs claimed that under this contract they had a licence or the right to be granted a licence to exercise and practise within a defined field all the inventions covered by the patents and applications for patents in the schedule to the agreement of December 31, 1946, between the defendants and the American corporation.

In June, 1952, the plaintiffs asked the defendants' solicitors to execute formal licences under the assigned patents to enable the plaintiffs to register them, and were informed that, owing to the existence of legal proceedings in the United States, the defendants could not execute any documents relating to the patents in question.

On July 30, 1952, in the United States District Court of New York, his Honour Sylvester J. Ryan delivered a final judgment in an action brought by the United States of America against the defendants, du Pont de Nemours & Co. Inc., and others under the anti-trust law known as the Sherman Act: United States of America v. Imperial Chemical Industries Ld. and Others. The plaintiffs were not parties to those proceedings.

By a clause in that judgment the United States court ordered that the agreement of December 31, 1946, between the defendants and du Pont de Nemours & Co. Inc. be cancelled, and that the defendants should reconvey within 90 days all the patent rights assigned to them under that agreement.

Other clauses in the judgment forbade any disposition of foreign patents by the defendants unless they obtained from the grantee an undertaking in writing to hold licences subject to the right of American manufacturers to import goods manufactured in accordance with the patents freely into any foreign country.

The plaintiffs thereupon issued a writ claiming declarations as to their rights to licences, and asking for an order that the defendants should execute formal grants of those licences, and for specific performance of the contract of March 5, 1947. They also asked for an injunction to restrain the defendants from assigning or dealing with or parting with any of the patent rights in question in obedience to the order of the United States court.

On August 13, 1952, Upjohn J. granted an interlocutory injunction to restrain the defendants from assigning the patents until judgment or further order.

The defendants appealed.

* * *

EVERSHED M. R. stated the facts and continued:—This is an interlocutory matter, and, therefore, it is inappropriate for the court to say more about the case, or the merits of the case, than is necessary to make clear the grounds of the conclusion which it reaches. It is plain that there is here a question of the comity which subsists between civilized nations. In other words, it involves the extent to which the courts of one country will pay regard and give effect to the decisions and orders of the courts of another country. I certainly should be the last to indicate any lack of respect for any decision of the district courts of the United States. But I think that in this case there is raised a somewhat serious question, whether the order, in the form that it takes, does not assert an extraterritorial jurisdiction which the courts of this country cannot recognize, notwithstanding any such comity. Applied conversely, I conceive that the American courts would likewise be slow (to say the least) to recognize an assertion on the part of the British courts of jurisdiction extending (in effect) to the business affairs of persons and corporations in the United States.

Having said that much, I must make one reference to a passage in the second of the opinions which his Honour delivered, dated May, 1952. It is plain that the judge considered this matter most carefully, and indeed, as Upjohn J. pointed out, expressed his own doubts whether, in giving effect, as he felt it his duty to do, to the implications of the Sherman Act, he might not be going beyond the normally recognized limits of territorial jurisdiction. He said: "It is not an intrusion on the authority of a foreign sovereign for this court to direct that steps be taken to remove the harmful effects on the trade of the United States." If by that passage the judge intended to say (as it seems to me that he did) that it was not an intrusion on the authority of a foreign sovereign to make directions addressed to that foreign sovereign or to its courts or to nationals of that foreign Power effective to remove (as he said) "harmful effects on the trade of the United States," I am bound to say that, as at present advised, I find myself unable to agree with it.

Questions affecting the trade of one country may well be matters proper to be considered by the government of another country. Tariffs are sometimes imposed by one country which obviously affect the trade of another country, and the imposition of such tariffs is a matter for the government of the particular country which imposes them. And if that observation of the judge were conversely applied to directions designed to remove harmful effects on the trade, say, of Great Britain or British nationals in America, I should myself be surprised to find that it was accepted as not being an intrusion on the rights and sovereign authority of the United States.

On the other hand, there is no doubt that it is competent for the court of a particular country, in a suit between persons who are either nationals or subjects of that country or are otherwise subject to its jurisdiction, to make orders in personam against one such party—directing it, for example, to do something or to refrain from doing something in another country affecting the other party to the action. As a general proposition, that would not be open to doubt. But the plaintiffs in this case (unlike Imperial Chemical Industries) are neither subjects nor nationals of the United States, nor were they parties to the proceedings before his Honour, nor are they otherwise subject to his jurisdiction.

What the precise relationship, commercially or otherwise, is between the plaintiffs and the defendants we have not at this stage of the proceedings considered at all, and I proceed on the assumption (and I am not to be taken as hinting that the contrary is the fact) that the plaintiffs are an independent trade corporation and entitled to be treated as independent of Imperial Chemical Industries Ld. Being so independent, they have beyond question, according to the laws of England, certain rights, certain choses in action, by virtue of the contract of 1947, which the courts of this country, in pursuance of the laws which the courts of this country claim to be entitled to administer, will in this country protect and enforce. Broadly, the right which they have may be described as their right under the contract, being an English contract made between English nationals and to be performed in England, to have it performed and, if necessary, to have an order made by the courts of this country for its specific performance. That is a right—it might be said, a species of property, seeing particularly that it is related to patents—which is English in character and is subject to the jurisdiction of the English courts; and it seems to me that the plaintiffs have at least established a prima facie case for saying that it is not competent for the courts of the United States or of any other country to interfere with those rights or to make orders, observance of which by our courts would require that our courts should not exercise the jurisdiction which they have and which it is their duty to exercise in regard to those rights.

But I think that the matter goes somewhat further. The subject-matter of the contract of December, 1946, is a number of English and Commonwealth patents. An English patent is a species of English property of the nature of a chose in action and peculiar in character. By English law it confers certain monopoly rights, exercisable in England, on its proprietor. A person who has an enforceable right to a licence under an English patent appears therefore to have at least some kind of proprietary interest which it is the duty of our courts to protect. And, certainly so far as the English patents are concerned, it seems to me, with all deference to his Honour's judgment, to be an assertion of an extraterritorial jurisdiction which we do not recognize for the American courts to make orders which would destroy or qualify those statutory rights belonging to an English national who is not subject to the jurisdiction of the American courts.

* * *

I think it undesirable that I should say more, except to reaffirm the proposition that the courts of this country will, in the natural course, pay great respect and attention to the superior courts of the United States of America; but I conceive that it is none the less the proper province of these courts, when their jurisdiction is invoked, not to refrain from exercising that jurisdiction if they think that it is their duty so to do for the protection of rights which are peculiarly subject to the protection of the English courts. In so saying, I do not conceive that I am offending in any way against the principles of comity which apply between the two countries; and, like Upjohn J., I take some comfort from the doubts which Judge Sylvester Ryan himself entertained about the extent to which this order might, if carried to its logical conclusion, go.

* * *

DENNING L. J. I agree. It would be a serious matter if there were a conflict between the orders of the courts of the United States and the orders of these courts. The writ of the United States does not run in this country, and, if due regard is had to the comity of nations, it will not seek to run here. But, as I read this judgment of the United States court, there is a saving clause which prevents any conflict, because although Imperial Chemical Industries has been ordered to do certain acts by the United States court, nevertheless there is a provision which says that nothing in the judgment shall operate against the company for action taken in complying with the law of any foreign government or instrumentality thereof to which the company is for the time being subject. With that saving clause, I hope that there will be no conflict between the orders.

ROMER L. J. I also agree, and there is nothing that I wish to add.

Appeal dismissed.

BRITISH NYLON SPINNERS, LTD. v. IMPERIAL CHEMICAL INDUSTRIES, LTD.

England, Court of Chancery, 1954.
[1955] Ch. 37.

July 9. DANCKWERTS, J., read the following judgment: * * *

The view thus asserted by the Master of the Rolls seems to me to be entirely in accordance with the decision of the Court of Appeal in Kleinwort, Sons & Co. v. Ungarische Baumwolle Industrie Akt. & Hungarian General Creditbank (2), in which Du Parcq, L. J., said ([1939] 3 All E.R. 44):

> One starts with the rule that English law is the law which governs the performance of this contract. An elementary principle of English law is that people should keep their contracts and carry them out.

It was argued on behalf of the defendant company that this court would not enforce a contract which involved the deliberate violation of the laws of a friendly country, and I was referred to Dicey's Conflict of Laws, 6th ed., p. 607, and to Foster v. Driscoll (3), which was a case of a contract, the object of which was the illegal importation of whisky into the United States of America. There is no evidence before me that the object of the contract of Mar. 5, 1947, was to do anything contrary to the law of the United States of America and no evidence that the plaintiff company was party to or had knowledge of any conspiracy contrary to the law of the United States when that contract was entered into. It is impossible for me to accept the conclusions of the United States court as findings of fact binding in this action against the plaintiff company which was not a party to the American proceedings. * * *

There are, however, further considerations which also lead to the same result. I had the advantage of the evidence of Mr. Marshall Konopak Skadden, a member of the Bar of the State of New York, practising in the relevant United States courts. His evidence was that the British court would be accepted under the law of the United States as an appropriate court having jurisdiction for the enforcement of the contract under consideration in the present case. Further, his evidence was that, if the defendant company, though prohibited from doing so by a judgment of a court in the United States, complied with an order of a British court and executed a licence, this would not be treated by an American court as a contempt of court. Mr. Skadden referred to a number of decisions of American courts in support of those propositions. This evidence indicates to me that the American courts would not regard a judgment of this court in the present circumstances enforcing against the defendant company the contract of Mar. 5, 1947, as in any way inappropriate, and there does not appear, therefore, to be any difficulty in regard to comity between the courts of the two countries in this case.

Furthermore, it would appear that the judgments of His Honour JUDGE SYLVESTER RYAN recognised this principle and were intended to provide for and limit his own judgment in this very respect. This appears to be the intention of art. IV, para. 3, of the judgment of July 30, 1952:

> No provision of this judgment shall operate against [the defendant company] for action taken in compliance with any law of the United States Government, or of any foreign government or instrumentality thereof, to which [the defendant company] is at the time being subject, and concerning matters over which, under the law of the United States, such foreign government or instrumentality thereof has jurisdiction.

"Instrumentality" of a government is an inaccurate, and, indeed, repellent, description of an English court; but it appears, none the less, that the learned judge was using the word in this manner from his observations on the occasions of further applications which were made to him. On Oct. 27, 1952, His Honour said:

> The court understands that and expects [the defendant company] to obey all orders and regulations that I have enumerated, of all government agencies and of the courts having jurisdiction over the matter on which they seek a ruling   *   *   *. And that is provided for in another section of the decree, I forget which one.

On counsel referring him to art. IV, para. 3, he added: "I think that provision covers this situation". On the same occasion His Honour said:

> Suppose they did, it was a suit in the nature of a declaratory action and I would not see anything contemptuous about such an act. Both [the defendant company] and [the plaintiff company], I think, are well within their rights to have it judicially determined by the courts of Great Britain and as to just what effect will be given to the provisions of the decree of this court which affect the British patents. I do not find anything wrong with that at all.

A further instance is, I think, to be found in the limitation contained in art. IX, para. 4 [of the judgment of July 30, 1952], in which, "until June 30, 1977, to the extent they have the legal right to do so," the American company and the defendant company are directed to make certain grants of immunities. It was argued by counsel for the defendant company that this limitation of the order could not apply to the plaintiff company's rights under the agreement of Mar. 5, 1947, because these rights were only equitable and not legal. I do not, however, read the language of the judgment in that way. I regard the words "to the extent they have the legal right to do so" as equivalent to "so far as they may lawfully do so", that is, not in breach of their obligations, including the equitable as well as the legal rights of other persons, as long as such rights are enforceable in a court of appropriate jurisdiction. Consequently, the prohibition, in art. IX, para. 13(b) [of the judgment of July 30, 1952] of dispositions of foreign patents or rights thereunder, which deprive them of the power or authority to issue the grants of immunity required by the judgment, is similarly limited, as the judgment does not require the issue of grants of immunity which du Pont and the defendant company may not lawfully grant.

These passages indicate to me that His Honour JUDGE SYLVESTER RYAN has been careful so to limit his judgment that neither his judgment, nor any judgment of mine which the law of England requires me to give, will disturb the comity which the courts of the United States and the courts of England are so anxious and careful to observe. I would only add that counsel for the defendant company fully carried out to the best of his ability, in somewhat difficult circumstances, the desire expressed by His Honour that the considerations which led the American court to reach the conclusions and make the order that it did should be before this court.

In the result, my conclusion is that, notwithstanding the judgment of the United States court of July 30, 1952, the defendant company is bound by English law to carry out the agreement of Mar. 5, 1947, and I ought to make the declaration which is asked by the amended statement of claim, and grant specific performance of the contract.

Judgment for the plaintiffs.

Questions. 1. Suppose the United States had thereafter moved before Judge Ryan to adjudge ICI guilty of civil contempt. What judicial response? Do you suppose the Department of Justice would have made any such request? Why or why not?

2. Having considered the United States and the United Kingdom set of opinions, what seems to you to be the utility of "judicial deference" in the resolution of conflicts of jurisdiction?

UNITED STATES v. THE WATCHMAKERS OF SWITZERLAND INFORMATION CENTER, INC.

United States District Court, S. D. New York, 1965.
1965 CCH Trade Cases ¶ 71, 352.*

[In the original proceeding in the United States antitrust case that follows, the contention was strongly made by the defendants, charged as being corporate and trade association members of a non-

* Reproduced by permission from Trade   in 1966 by Commerce Clearing House,
Cases 1965, published and copyrighted   Inc., Chicago, Ill., 60646.

governmental Swiss effort to control and monopolize the watch-making industry through control of the export of watch-making machinery, that it was illicit for the United States to apply its antitrust laws to ventures having their roots and principal places of activity in Switzerland, particularly when these activities were entirely compatible with Swiss law and policy. The trial judge reserved jurisdiction to modify his decree upon any showing that defendants might under it be required to act contrary to Swiss law. The order below illustrates one way in which conflicts can be reconciled, viz. making it clear that a person will not be subject to contempt proceedings in the United States for acting as required by the law of his nationality.]

Memorandum

CASHIN, DISTRICT JUDGE: On January 22, 1964 this court entered a Final Judgment in the captioned action. Under Section XIII (A) of that Judgment I retained jurisdiction for the purpose of enabling the parties to apply for modifications of any of the provisions thereof. Plaintiff, United States of America, now moves to modify the Judgment as follows:—

*   *   *

Revision of Section XI

*   *   *

[The decree will not restrain.]

(E) *   *   *   any defendant, FH member or any other person from:

(1) Performing any act in Switzerland which is required of it under the law of Switzerland;

(2) Refraining from any act in Switzerland which is illegal under the law of Switzerland;

(3) Taking any joint or individual action, consistent with the applicable law of the nation where the party taking such action is domiciled, to comply with conditions for the export of watch parts from Switzerland established by valid ordinances, or rules and regulations promulgated thereunder, of the Swiss Government;

(4) Taking any joint or individual action required by the scheme of regulation of the Swiss watch industry based on Article 31 bis of the Swiss Constitution, with respect to imports of watch parts into Switzerland other than from U. S. companies;

(5) Advocating the enactment of laws, decrees or regulations or urging upon any Swiss governmental body, department, agency or official the taking of any official action;

(6) Furnishing to the Swiss Government or any body, department, agency or official thereof, its independent advice or opinion when requested to do so.

Revision of Section XII

(A)(3) Upon receipt of such a written request for books, ledgers, accounts, correspondence, memoranda, and other records and documents in the possession or under the control of defendants FH, Ebauches, Eterna A. G., Gruen S. A., and Wittnauer-Geneva, particularized or identified in the request to the extent reasonably practicable, and relating to any of the matters as to which such defendants are enjoined or directed to take action pursuant to any of the terms of this Final Judgment, reasonable access during office hours to duly authenticated copies thereof at any office in the City of New York designated by such defendant, provided, however, that no such defendant shall be obligated to bring to the United States any books or other records, or any copies thereof, except upon order of this Court specifically so providing; and provided further that no defendant shall be required to bring to the United States any books or other records, or any copies thereof, when such action is prohibited by the law of Switzerland and such defendant has exercised good faith efforts to obtain the permission of the appropriate authorities but such permission has not been secured.

* * *

Several grounds have been advanced in support of the requested modifications. They are as follows:—

(1) Since the entry of the judgment, the Swiss Confederation has issued official regulations with respect to the issuance of export permits for parts from Switzerland;

(2) The United States Department of State has indicated to the Justice Department that a resolution of this litigation on a basis consistent with United States antitrust laws and the basic objectives of the judgment would be advantageous from the standpoint of American foreign policy;

(3) The termination of the litigation, without any appeal, would give immediate relief in restoring free and open competition in the United States production, import, export and sale of watches, watch parts and watchmaking machinery. In this connection it should be pointed out that more than ten years have elapsed since the complaint herein was filed in October 1954, and if appeals were taken an additional number of years would inevitably be consumed before final relief could be granted. On the other hand, if the proposed modifications are made, the defendants have agreed that they will not appeal the Final Judgment herein, subject to the withdrawal of the appeals by the other defendants.

It is the Court's opinion that the modifications requested do not affect the crucial objectives sought to be achieved in the Final Judgment heretofore filed, and that the above circumstances in their totality justify the granting of the motion. Moreover, these modifications will prevent any situation from arising such as has occurred in other litigation in the past when there was believed to be a possible conflict between a decree of a United States court and the sovereignty of a foreign nation. See United States v. Imperial Chemicals, 105 F. Supp. 215 (S.D.N.Y.1952), and British Nylon Spinners Limited v. Imperial Chemical Industries, Limited, 1 Ch. 19 (1953). In the main the modifications relate to peripheral areas of the judgment which might have been construed to have bearing upon the sovereignty of the Swiss Confederation.

The defendants in this action have filed stipulations with the court consenting to a dismissal of their joint appeal from the Final Judgment if this court sees fit to grant the modifications of that Judgment requested by the plaintiff. (Rule 14(1) of the Revised Rules of the Supreme Court of the United States). They have also stipulated, along with the plaintiff, to waive any right to appeal from said Final Judgment as so modified.

The motion of the plaintiff, United States of America, is granted on the condition that one of the parties enter an order dismissing the joint appeal as provided for in the stipulations. The plaintiff shall submit an order incorporating the modifications granted.

The cross-motion of defendants, Gruen Watch Manufacturing Company, S. A. and Wittnauer et Cie., S. A., that Section XII(D) of the Final Judgment be further modified, is denied as premature.

It is so ordered.

---

3. IS MODERATION OF ENFORCEMENT JURISDICTION REQUIRED BY INTERNATIONAL LAW?

APPLICATION OF THE CHASE MANHATTAN BANK

United States Court of Appeals, Second Circuit, 1962.
297 F.2d 611.

LEONARD P. MOORE, CIRCUIT JUDGE. This is an appeal by the Government from an order of the district court, the effect of which was to modify a grand jury subpoena duces tecum addressed to and directing appellee, The Chase Manhattan Bank (Chase), to produce, inter alia, records in the possession of a branch located in the Republic of Panama. The subpoena was served on Chase, a New York corporation, in New York, its principal place of business, on January 17, 1961. It required Chase to appear before the United States Grand Jury for the Southern District of New York on January 27, 1961, and produce certain banking records "wherever held" relating to the accounts of four individuals and one corporation.

On January 19, 1961, Chase, by its attorneys, advised the United States Attorney that on the return day of the subpoena, Chase would produce all relevant records in Chase's possession in New York, but that any relevant records in the possession of its Panamanian branches would not be produced unless Chase was assured by Panamanian counsel that production of such records would not violate Panamanian law. On the same day, Chase requested the Panamanian branch to obtain a legal opinion with respect to the production of pertinent records as soon as possible.

On January 27, 1961, counsel for Chase produced the New York records, but advised the Grand Jury that the legal opinion with respect to production of Panamanian records had not yet been received. An adjournment was requested, and the Grand Jury instructed Chase to produce the Panamanian records on January 30, 1961. Chase then telephoned the Panamanian branch and learned that it had just received a written legal opinion to the effect that production in New York of records in the possession of the branch, without the consent of local authorities, would violate Panamanian law. On January 30, 1961, Chase by order to show cause why the subpoena should not be modified as to the Panamanian records, commenced the proceeding now before us on appeal. On the same day, the President of Panama signed Law No. 17, enacted by the Legislature on the previous day. A copy of this new law was submitted to the court on February 2, 1961, the return day of the order to show cause, and it is upon this law that the district court's opinion rests.

Article 89 of Law No. 17 provides in part:

The merchant furnishing a copy or reproductions of the contents of his books, correspondence and other documents for use in an action abroad, in compliance with an order of an authority not of the Republic of Panama, shall be penalized with a fine not greater than one hundred balboas (B/100.00).

Article 93 of Law No. 17 provides:

"The account books, correspondence and other documents which the merchant must keep shall be maintained in his establishment in order that they may be examined by the authority competent therefor. It is forbidden to remove them outside of the country. Violation of this prohibition shall be penalized with a fine not greater than one hundred balboas (B/100.00).

In its original order on February 9, 1961, the lower court explicitly accepted the principle that a subpoena duces tecum should be modified if compliance would necessitate a violation of foreign law. However, it denied the motion to modify the subpoena on the grounds that Chase had not adequately established that Law No. 17 would be interpreted to apply, commenting on the lack of any affidavits from Panamanian sources.

On February 15, 1961, Chase moved by an order to show cause for reargument of the application to modify and for a hearing at which to present the testimony of a Panamanian legal expert. The motion was granted and at a hearing on February 24, 1961, Chase produced Senor Carlos Icaza, its Panamanian counsel. He testified that in his opinion, Chase could not respond to the subpoena without subjecting itself to penalties under Panamanian law, and that American authorities could gain access to Panamanian records of American firms only by making application through the Panamanian courts. He also stated that Law No. 17 is the only Panamanian law containing any sanctions with respect to production of records in response to foreign process, and that a violation of the Panamanian law would be equivalent to a misdemeanor under our criminal law. The Government offered no evidence.

Following the rehearing, the district court ruled that Chase had sufficiently shown that production of these records would violate Panamanian law and held that under these circumstances "the next move is up to the Government." The subpoena was left outstanding to insure that Chase complied with its "duty of actively cooperating with the Government" if the Government asked the Panamanian authorities to authorize the Panama branch to produce the documents.

The result reached by the court below is in accord with our previous decision in First National City Bank v. Internal Revenue Service, 2 Cir., 1959, 271 F.2d 616, cert. denied, 361 U.S. 948, 80 S.Ct. 402, 4 L.Ed.2d 381 (1960). There we reinstated a subpoena duces tecum on the ground that there was no showing that the law of Panama would be violated by compliance. We stated (271 F.2d p. 619) that if in fact production of branch records located in Panama "would require action by personnel in Panama in violation of the constitution and laws of Panama * * * production * * * should not be ordered" by the courts of this country.

In the instant case, the Government argues that compliance will not violate Panamanian law, since the subpoena is not directed to personnel in Panama but only to the head office in New York. Upon the assumption that "authority" as used in Article 89 means government official (Senor Icaza so testified), the Government concludes that one not a government official (such as a bank official) could, consistently with Panamanian law, order the production of specified records and that the Panamanian branch could legally respond to a request by the Chase head office in New York. However, this would be nothing more than an attempt to circumvent the Panamanian law. Such a maneuver scarcely reflects the kind of respect which we should accord to the laws of a friendly foreign sovereign state. Just as we would expect and require branches of foreign banks to abide by our laws applicable to the conduct of their business in this country, so should we honor their laws affecting our bank branches which are permitted to do business in foreign countries.

The Government also argues that First National City Bank stands for the proposition that the foreign law prohibiting production must provide criminal sanctions to justify the court in modifying the subpoena. But we need not now decide whether the sanctions must always be criminal. The testimony before the district court was to the effect that violation of the Panama statute would be "equivalent to a misdemeanor" under our criminal law.

Finally, the Government contends that before the district court could modify the subpoena, Chase had to show a good faith effort to comply. However, Chase will still be required to demonstrate its good faith, since the court left the subpoena outstanding. This will insure Chase's cooperation with the Government when and if the Government seeks to obtain the records by application to the Panamanian authorities. On the facts of this case, there is nothing unreasonable about modifying the subpoena so as to leave the next move up to the Government.

The Government, as well as other litigants, has a real interest in civil and criminal cases in obtaining evidence wherever located. However, we also have an obligation to respect the laws of other sovereign states even though they may differ in economic and legal philosophy from our own. As we recently said in modifying subpoenas *duces tecum* in another case, "upon fundamental principles of international comity, our courts dedicated to the enforcement of our laws should not take such action as may cause a violation of the laws of a friendly neighbor or, at the least, an unnecessary circumvention of its procedures." Ings v. Ferguson, 2 Cir., 1960, 282 F.2d 149.

Affirmed.

_____

UNITED STATES OF AMERICA v. FIRST NATIONAL CITY BANK

United States Court of Appeals, Second Circuit, 1968.
396 F.2d 897.

KAUFMAN, CIRCUIT JUDGE. The issue presented on this appeal is of considerable importance to American banks with branches or offices in foreign jurisdictions. We are called upon to decide whether a domestic bank may refuse to comply with a valid Grand Jury subpoena duces tecum requiring the production of documents in the possession of a foreign branch of the bank on the ground that compliance would subject it to civil liability under the law of the foreign state.

*   *   *

On March 7, 1968, First National City Bank of New York [Citibank] was served with a subpoena duces tecum in connection with a federal Grand Jury investigation of certain alleged violations of the antitrust laws by several of its customers. The subpoena required the production of documents located in the bank's offices in New York City and Frankfurt, Germany, relating to any transaction in the name of (or for the benefit of) its customers C. F. Boehringer & Soehme, G.m.b.H., a German corporation, and Boehringer Mannheim Corporation, a New York corporation [referred to jointly hereinafter as "Boehringer"]. Citibank complied with the subpoena insofar as it called for the production of material located in New York but failed to produce or divulge any documents reposited in Frankfurt. Indeed, the bank even refused to inquire or determine whether any relevant papers were overseas. Instead, William T. Loveland, Citibank's vice-president responsible for the decision to defy the subpoena, appeared before the Grand Jury and asserted that the bank's action was justified because compliance would subject Citibank to civil liability and economic loss in Germany.

On May 8, 1968, Judge Pollack conducted an initial hearing at which the sole witness was Dr. Martin Domke, an expert in German law. He testified on behalf of Citibank that under the "bank secrecy law" of Germany, a bank—including a foreign bank (such as Citibank) licensed to do business in Germany—cannot divulge information relating to the affairs of its customers even in response to the process of a court of the United States. To do so, he claimed, would amount to a breach of the bank's "self evident" contractual obligation which flows from the business relationship between bank and customer. Domke made it clear that bank secrecy was not part of the statutory law of Germany; rather, it was in the nature of a privilege that could be waived by the customer but not the bank. He insisted that a violation of bank secrecy could subject the bank to liability in contract or tort but not to criminal sanctions or their equivalent. But, he made it plain, that it was a simple matter for a bank customer to obtain an ex parte restraining order enjoining a bank from disclosing privileged material and that a violation of such an injunction would be punished under a general provision of the criminal law governing violations of court orders. As a result of this testimony, the district judge appropriately decided to adjourn this hearing in order to afford an opportunity to Citibank to ascertain whether its customers would obtain such an injunction and which would have the effect of subjecting the bank to criminal penalties if it complied with the subpoena. This did not prove fruitful however, for the very next day, the court was advised by Citibank's counsel that Boehringer did not intend to take advantage of the readily available injunctive procedures under German law. Instead, the judge was told that Boehringer had informed Citibank that it would have to "suffer the consequences" if it obeyed the subpoena. It was suggested that Boehringer would sue the bank for breach of contract and would also use its influence within German industrial circles to cause Citibank to suffer business losses.

In any event, Citibank remained adamant in its refusal to produce the documents located in Frankfurt and on May 21, 1968, a second hearing was held, this time on the government's order to show cause why the bank and Loveland should not be held in civil contempt. Domke testified once again as did a government expert, Dr. Magdalena Schoch. Both witnesses discussed with great particularity the precise nature of German bank secrecy and Citibank's prospective liability under German law if it were sued for disclosing privileged information. Domke made the point that compulsion by an American court would not be accepted as an excuse for violating bank secrecy and that in a civil suit under German law the court would determine "in its free discretion" the amount of damages, if any. Schoch insisted, however, that Citibank would have a number of valid defenses in the event Boehringer ever sued. Moreover, Schoch's testimony made clear that in a criminal proceeding in Germany bank secrecy does not provide a basis for refusing to obey a court order to provide evidence.

In a reasoned opinion, Judge Pollack concluded that Citibank had failed to present a legally sufficient reason for its failure to comply with the subpoena. He determined that it was manifest that Citibank would not be subject to criminal sanctions or their equivalent under German law, that it had not acted in good faith, and that there was only a "remote and speculative" possibility that it would not have a valid defense if it were sued for civil damages. Accordingly, he adjudged the bank and Loveland to be in civil contempt and fined the bank $2,000 per day for its failure to act; he sentenced Loveland to 60 days' imprisonment. For the reasons stated below, we conclude that Judge Pollack's order was justified and affirm.

The basic legal question confronting us is not a total stranger to this Court. With the growing interdependence of world trade and the increased mobility of persons and companies, the need arises not infrequently, whether related to civil or criminal proceedings, for the production of evidence located in foreign jurisdictions. It is no longer open to doubt that a federal court has the power to require the production of documents located in foreign countries if the court has in personam jurisdiction of the person in possession or control of the material. See, e. g., First National City Bank of New York v. Internal Revenue Service etc., 271 F.2d 616 (2d Cir. 1959), cert. denied, 361 U.S. 948, 80 S.Ct. 402, 4 L.Ed.2d 381 (1960). Thus, the task before us, as Citibank concedes, is not one of defining power but of developing rules governing the proper exercise of power. The difficulty arises, of course, when the country in which the documents are located has its own rules and policies dealing with the production and disclosure of business information—a circumstance not uncommon. This problem is particularly acute where the documents are sought by an arm of a foreign government. The complexities of the world being what they are, it is not surprising to discover nations having diametrically opposed positions with respect to the disclosure of a wide range of information. It is not too difficult, therefore, to empathize with the party or witness subject to the jurisdiction of two sovereigns and confronted with conflicting commands. For an example of a comparable dilemma resulting from the application of the antitrust laws, see British Nylon Spinners Ltd. v. Imperial Chemical Industries, Ltd., [1953] 1 Ch. 19. See also Note, Limitations on the Federal Judicial Power to Compel Acts Violating Foreign Law, 63 Colum.L.Rev. 1441 (1963); Note, Subpoena of Documents Located in Foreign Jurisdictions, 37 N.Y.U.L.Rev. 295 (1962).

In any event, under the principles of international law, "A state having jurisdiction to prescribe or enforce a rule of law is not precluded from exercising its jurisdiction *solely* because such exercise requires a person to engage in conduct subjecting him to liability under the law of another state having jurisdiction with respect to that conduct." Restatement (2d), Foreign Relations Law of the United States, § 39(1) (1965) (emphasis supplied). It is not asking too much however, to expect that each nation should make an effort to minimize the potential conflict flowing from their joint concern with the prescribed behavior. Id. at § 39(2). Compare Report of Oral Argument, 25 U.S.L.W. 3141 (Nov. 13, 1956), Holophane Co. v. United States, 352 U.S. 903, 77 S.Ct. 144, 1 L.Ed.2d 114 (1956). Where, as here, the burden of resolution ultimately falls upon the federal courts, the difficulties are manifold because the courts must take care not to impinge upon the prerogatives and responsibilities of the political branches of the government in the extremely sensitive and delicate area of foreign affairs. See, e. g., Chicago & Southern Air Lines v. Waterman S. S. Corp., 333 U.S. 103, 111, 68 S.Ct. 431, 92 L.Ed. 568 (1948). Mechanical or overbroad rules of thumb are of little value; what is required is a careful balancing of the interests involved and a precise understanding of the facts and circumstances of the particular case.

With these principles in mind, we turn to the specific issues presented by this appeal. Citibank concedes, as it must, that compliance with the subpoena does not require the violation of the criminal law of a foreign power, as in Societe Internationale etc. v. Rogers, 357 U.S. 197, 78 S.Ct. 1087, 2 L.Ed.2d 1255 (1958) (discovery under the Federal Rules of Civil Procedure); Ings v. Ferguson, 282 F.2d 149, 152, 82 A.L.R.2d 1397 (2d Cir.1960), or risk the imposition of sanctions that are the substantial equivalent of criminal penalties, as in Application of Chase Manhattan Bank, 297 F.2d 611, 613 (2d Cir. 1962), or even conflict with the public policy of a foreign state as expressed in legislation, compare Restatement, supra, § 39, Reporters' Notes at p. 113. Instead, all that remains, as we see it, is a possible prospective civil liability flowing from an implied contractual obligation between Citibank and its customers that, we are informed, is considered implicit in the bank's license to do business in Germany.

But, the government urges vigorously, that to be excused from compliance with an order of a federal court, a witness, such as Citibank must show that following compliance it will suffer criminal liability in the foreign country. We would be reluctant to hold, however, that the mere absence of criminal sanctions abroad necessarily mandates obedience to a subpoena. Such a rule would show scant respect for international comity; and, if this principle is valid, a court of one country should make an effort to minimize possible conflict between its orders and the law of a foreign state affected by its decision. Cf. Restatement, supra, § 39(2); Ings v. Ferguson, supra, 282 F.2d at 152. The vital national interests of a foreign nation, especially in matters relating to economic affairs, can be expressed in ways other than through the criminal law. For example, it could not be questioned that, insofar as a court of the United States is concerned, a statement or directive by the Bundesbank (the central bank of Germany) or some other organ of government, expresses the public policy of Germany and should be given appropriate weight. Equally important is the fact that a sharp dichotomy between criminal and civil penalties is an imprecise means of measuring the hardship for requiring compliance with a subpoena. * * * It would be a gross fiction to contend that if the Bundesbank were to revoke the license of Citibank for a violation of bank secrecy the impact would be less catastrophic than having to pay an insignificant fine because the revocation is theoretically not "equivalent to a misdemeanor" or criminal sanction. We are not required to decide whether penalties must be under the "criminal law" to provide a legally sufficient reason for noncompliance with a subpoena; but, it would seem unreal to let all hang on whether the label "criminal" were attached to the sanction and to disregard all other factors. In any event, even were we to assume arguendo that in appropriate circumstances civil penalties or liabilities would suffice, we hold that Citibank has failed to provide an adequate justification for its disobedience of the subpoena.

In evaluating Citibank's contention that compliance should be excused because of the alleged conflict between the order of the court below and German law, we are aided materially by the rationale of the recent Restatement (2d), Foreign Relations Law of the United States, § 40 (1965):

Where two states have jurisdiction to prescribe and enforce rules of law and the rules they may prescribe require inconsistent conduct upon the part of a person, each state is required by international law to consider, in good faith, moderating the exercise of its enforcement jurisdiction, in the light of such factors as

(a) vital national interests of each of the states,

(b) the extent and the nature of the hardship that inconsistent enforcement actions would impose upon the person,

(c) the extent to which the required conduct is to take place in the territory of the other state,

(d) the nationality of the person, and

(e) the extent to which enforcement by action of either state can reasonably be expected to achieve compliance with the rule prescribed by that state.

In the instant case, the obvious, albeit troublesome, requirement for us is to balance the national interests of the United States and Germany and to give appropriate weight to the hardship, if any, Citibank will suffer.

The important interest of the United States in the enforcement of the subpoena warrants little discussion. The federal Grand Jury before which Citibank was summoned is conducting a criminal investigation of alleged violations of the antitrust laws. These laws have long been considered cornerstones of this nation's economic policies, have been vigorously enforced and the subject of frequent interpretation by our Supreme Court. We would have great reluctance, therefore, to countenance any device that would place relevant information beyond the reach of this duly impaneled Grand Jury or impede or delay its proceedings. * * *

We examine the importance of bank secrecy within the framework of German public policy with full recognition that it is often a subtle and difficult undertaking to determine the nature and scope of the law of a foreign jurisdiction. There is little merit, however, in Citibank's suggestion that the mere existence of a bank secrecy doctrine requires us to accept on its face the bank's assertion that compliance with the subpoena would violate an important public policy of Germany. * * * While we certainly do not intend to deprecate the importance of bank secrecy in the German scheme of things, neither can we blind ourselves to the doctrine's severe limitations as disclosed by the expert testimony. We have already made the assumption that the absence of criminal sanctions is not the whole answer to or finally determinative of the problem. But, it is surely of considerable significance that Germany considers bank secrecy simply a privilege that can be waived by the customer and is content to leave the matter of enforcement to the vagaries of private litigation. Indeed, bank secrecy is not even required by statute. See Restatement, supra, § 40, comment (c): "A state will be less likely to refrain from exercising its jurisdiction when the consequence of obedience to its order will be a civil liability abroad." See also Restatement, supra, § 39, Reporters' Notes at p. 113.

Moreover, Section 300 of the Criminal Code of Germany provides that:

Anybody who without authority discloses the secrets of another, shall be punished by imprisonment for a term not to exceed six months or by a fine, if the secret was intrusted or became known to him in his capacity as a

>   (1) Physician, dentist, pharmacist [and similar professions]

>   (2) Attorneys, patent attorney, notary public, defense counsel, auditor, Certified Public Accountant, or tax consultant.

It is not of little significance that a German court has noted, "The fact that bank secrecy has not been included in the penal protection of Section 300 of the Criminal Code must lead to the conclusion that the legislature did not value the public interest in bank secrecy as highly as it did the duty of secrecy of doctors and attorneys." District Court of Frankfurt (1953). Further, Section 53 of the German Code of Criminal Procedure grants the right of refusal to testify to a number of persons, ranging from clergymen and mid-wives to publishers and printers; again, reference to bankers is conspicuously absent. It would be anomalous if Citibank, deprived of any right to assert bank secrecy in a criminal investigation conducted in Germany, could—in the absence of statutes imposing greater limitations upon foreign governments, cf. First National City Bank of New York v. Internal Revenue Service etc., supra, 271 F.2d at 619–620—benefit from German bank secrecy in a criminal investigation in the United States.

In addition, it is noteworthy that neither the Department of State nor the German Government has expressed any view on this case or indicated that, under the circumstances present here, enforcement of the subpoena would violate German public policy or embarrass German-American relations. * * * We are fully aware that when foreign governments, including Germany, have considered their vital national interests threatened, they have not hesitated to make known their objections to the enforcement of a subpoena to the issuing court. See, e. g., In re Grand Jury Investigation of the Shipping Industry, 186 F.Supp. 298, 318 (D.C.1960). So far as appears, both the United States and German governments have voiced no opposition to Citibank's production of the subpoenaed records.

We turn now to the nature and extent of the alleged hardships to which Citibank would be subjected if it complied with the subpoena. It advances two grounds on which it will suffer injury. First, it states that it will be subjected to economic reprisals by Boehringer and will lose foreign business that will harm it and the economic interests of the United States. It paints a dismal picture of foreign companies boycotting American banks for fear that their business records will be subject to the scrutiny of our courts. A partial answer is that the protection of the foreign economic interests of the United States must be left to the appropriate departments of our government, especially since the government is the moving litigant in these proceedings. Cf. United States v. First National City Bank, supra. Moreover, and not without importance, is the fact that the alleged economic reprisals are of doubtful legal relevance in light of the Supreme Court's rejection of a similar argument in First National City Bank (Omar), see 379 U.S. at 402, 85 S.Ct. 528 (dissenting opinion of Justice Harlan), and this Court's decision in First National Bank of New York v. Internal Revenue Service, etc., supra, 271 F.2d at 619, n. 2; and the factual underpinning for this claim is quite feeble considering Citibank's overseas growth following the decision in First National City Bank (Omar), supra.

Second, Citibank complains that it will be subjected to civil liability in a suit by Boehringer. The importance of the possible financial loss Citibank might suffer as a result of such a suit must be viewed in light of Loveland's statement that: "[W]e were not concerned with this isolated case and what one individual might do. The importance [sic], I believe, is the effect that it would have on our operations all over the world * * *." We have already rejected the contention that Citibank's alleged loss of business abroad is a sound justification for disobedience of the subpoena. In any event, Judge Pollack concluded that risk of civil damages was slight and speculative, and we agree. The chance that Boehringer will suffer compensable damages is quite remote and Citibank appears to have a number of valid defenses if it is sued, both under the terms of the contract and principles of German civil law. In addition, as we have noted, German courts are given wide latitude in determining whether to award any damages even in the face of liability. In the unlikely event that Boehringer were to sue Citibank, we cannot believe that Boehringer's adamant refusal to apply for a readily available injunction will pass unnoticed by the Court.

Finally, additional factors support our conclusion that the district judge was correct in citing Citibank and Loveland for civil contempt. As noted above, Citibank has failed to produce or segregate documents or records which reflect the bank's own work product. And, the expert testimony indicated that disclosure of such material would not violate any policy of bank secrecy. Moreover, one of the companies being investigated by the Grand Jury—Boehringer Mannheim Corporation—is incorporated in New York. Whatever one may think of requiring disclosure of records of a German corporation reposited in a bank in Germany, surely an American corporation cannot insulate itself from a federal Grand Jury investigation by entering into a contract with an American bank abroad requiring bank secrecy. Compare Restatement, supra, § 40, Comment (c). If indeed Citibank might suffer civil liability under German law in such circumstances, it must confront the choice mentioned in First National City Bank of New York v. Internal Revenue Service etc., supra, 271 F.2d at 620— the need to "surrender to one sovereign or the other the privileges received therefrom" or, alternatively a willingness to accept the consequences.

Since the life of the Grand Jury is rapidly drawing to a close, we direct that the mandate issue forthwith but that it be stayed for a period of seven days from the date of the filing of this opinion to permit Citibank, if it so chooses, to apply to the Supreme Court or a Justice thereof for a further stay or other relief.

Affirmed.

_____

1. *Section 40 of the Restatement of the Foreign Relations Law of the United States.*   The Restatement position is that international law requires a court, administrative body, or similar institution in any state to consider the interests of the other state concerned before finally fashioning the rule that is to be applied where there is a conflict of prescriptive jurisdiction to regulate economic activity.   This principle is probably as far as any national decision-maker under known national legal systems can go; and in some systems and under some doctrines, perhaps he cannot go this far under national law, whatever international law may require.

2. *Parallel problem in United States conflict of laws.*   Compare the view of the late Brainerd Currie that a court should always apply forum law, if the legislature at that forum has indicated that the state has a governmental interest in the application of its own law. Later, Currie modified his advocacy of this rigorous "homeward trend" in conflict of laws by conceding that in interpreting the governmental interest of its own legal system, the forum should act in a restrained and enlightened manner.   The analysis of state interest ("interest analysis") in the United States conflict of laws has, generally speaking, taken a comparative approach—i. e. looking at the interests of both states concerned.   See generally, Cramton and Currie, Conflict of Laws, 251–54, 286–290 (1968) ; Traynor, Conflict of Laws: Professor Currie's Restrained and Enlightened Forum, 49 Cal. L.Rev. 845 (1961).

_____

4. LINES OF SOLUTION

What lines of solution?   Several possibilities, some of rules, some of method, have been suggested already.   An interesting question arises whether, as the industrialized nations of the world move toward the specific regulation of the same types of activity (restrictive trade practices and monopolization), the differences in their approaches, remedies, and tolerations will exacerbate or relieve conflicts of jurisdiction.   From one point of view, that of achieving the general objective of social control of particular types of economic conduct, it does not seem to make much difference which set of rules actually gets applied.   But administrators and legislators in nation states as well as in the European Economic Community proceed in economic matters from localized senses of mission. Thus the increased number of potentially applicable sets of rules may threaten the effective conduct of transnational business enterprise and create a common need for some system of rationalization or harmonization of regulatory principles. In the period 1948–52, roughly, the first major effort to create a set of international rules for restrictive trade practices and monopoly, the "Havana Charter" of the aborted International Trade Organization (see p. 1044), failed through lack of sufficient agreement among states. Later efforts for the creation of new, positive, universal law in this sector has been slight so far. But perhaps circumstances are changing, due both to the increased array of particularistic regulatory systems and the growth of multinational enterprise.

Part III

THE INDIVIDUAL IN THE INTERNATIONAL
LEGAL SYSTEM

Chapter 8

PROTECTION AND ALLEGIANCE

A basic feature of today's system of nation states is the relative helplessness of the individual. At birth he finds himself a member of some political institution (typically a "state" in the international system) which, more or less, protects him from the violence of other individuals and groups of individuals. In the domestic legal system of that state, its police and courts may offer protection from harm inflicted within the state; its army may protect him from harm caused by aggression from outside the state.

If the individual steps outside "his" state and is injured by someone in another state, he is largely on his own. He must look for redress, if any, in the courts of that other state. Doctrines of sovereign immunity may bar him from redress for injuries caused by that state. As a last resort the individual must appeal to his own state's government to help him. If it chooses, it may come to his aid by espousing a claim against the wrongdoing state through diplomatic channels (or possibly through arbitration or through judicial means such as the International Court of Justice).

For the protection it offers him at home and the protection it may afford him against foreign injuries, the state demands obligations of the individual in return: to obey its laws, to pay its taxes, to help to defend it against aggression.

The physical fact of an individual's presence within a state has been the major basis from which the state exerts its power to protect the individual and to demand his allegiance. But the processes of history have developed legal relationships between the state and the individual that do not depend solely upon his physical presence in the territory of the state. The state has a special relationship to those it designates as its "nationals". In broad and inexact terms, the state's nationals are entitled to greater rights than non-nationals (e. g., in states with voting systems, the national is permitted to vote, the non-national is not); the state is more ready to demand that the national perform obligations (e. g., the national may be subject to laws prescribed by his state even though he is not physically present in its territory).

The practices of states in creating the class of people upon whom they confer nationality vary widely. Some states accord nationality to individuals born within the territory; this right of nationality is referred to as jus soli. Some states accord nationality at birth only to individuals born of parents who are already nationals: this right of nationality is referred to as jus sanguinis. An increasing number of states recognize both bases. In addition to according nationality based upon facts associated with birth, states afford "naturalization" processes by which individuals may apply for and be granted nationality. With such a variety of bases for nationality existing in the international system it is possible for an individual to be designated a national and thus to have "dual nationality" or even "multiple nationality." Indeed, there are circumstances under which he may have no nationality at all and thus be "stateless."

From the perspective of the international legal system, several important questions arise:

    1.   Is a state free to set its own standards for conferring its nationality upon an individual? Or does international law set some minimum standard?

    2.   What is the significance of nationality as a base for the state's requiring the performance of obligations by an individual? For example, can the state draft into its army someone who is not its national?

This chapter explores these two questions. In succeeding chapters the question will be asked whether the developments in the law of human rights and individual responsibility significantly modify the legal situation of the individual as sketched above.

SECTION A. NATIONALITY: LOSS OF ITS BENEFITS

RE IMMIGRATION ACT AND HANNA

Canada, Supreme Court of British Columbia, 1957.
21 Western Weekly Rep. 400.*

SULLIVAN, J. This is a "hard case" of the kind of which it is said that bad law is made.

The applicant George Christian Hanna, whom I shall refer to as "Hanna" in these reasons for judgment, is a young man without a country—one of those unfortunate "stateless" persons of the world

* Reprinted by permission of Burroughs
& Co., Ltd., Calgary, Alberta, Canada.

whose status is a matter of concern to humanitarians and has prompted men and women of good will of all countries to seek relief for such persons through the agency of the Economic and Social Council of the United Nations. A convention was adopted by that council in September, 1954, to which, however, Canada is not a signatory.

The matter comes before me by way of habeas corpus with certiorari in aid. Hanna seeks a judicial declaration that his detention under a deportation order made by F. Wragg, an immigration officer (acting as a special inquiry officer) dated January 18, 1957, and confirmed on appeal to an immigration appeal board duly constituted under the provisions of the Immigration Act, RSC, 1952, ch. 325, is illegal, (1) Because the deportation order is defective, incomplete, impossible of interpretation or enforcement and beyond the statutory authority of Mr. Wragg to make; and (2) Because the immigration appeal board improperly denied Hanna the right to be heard, either in person or by counsel, at the appeal proceedings before such board.

[handwritten margin notes: (1) INHERENT FAULT (2) NO DUE PROCESS]

The issues thus presented for my determination are strictly legal in nature and narrow in their scope. I have no right to reflect upon and must guard against the danger that the strictly legal opinion which I am required to express should be influenced in any degree by considerations of human sympathy for this unfortunate (23-year-old) young applicant in the frustrating dilemma with which fate seems to have confronted him throughout his lifetime prior to his last arrival in Canada as ship-bound prisoner aboard a tramp motor-ship in her ceaseless meanderings from port to port throughout the world.

The deportation order in question is in the words and figures following:

CANADA

DEPARTMENT OF CITIZENSHIP AND IMMIGRATION

DEPORTATION ORDER AGAINST

CHRISTIAN GEORGE HANNA

of Djbuti, French Somaliland

under section 28 of the Immigration Act.

On the basis of the evidence adduced at an inquiry held at the Immigration Building, Vancouver, B.C. on January 18, 1957 I have reached the decision that you may not come into or remain in Canada as of right and that you are a member of the prohibited class described in paragraph (t) of Section 5 of the Immigration Act, in that you do not fulfil or comply with the conditions or requirements of Subsection (1) Subsection (3) and Subsection (8) of Section 18 of the Immigration Regulations.

I hereby order you to be detained and to be deported to the place whence you came to Canada, or to the country of which you are a national or citizen, or to the country of your birth, or to such country as may be approved by the minister.

Date 18 January 1957   [Sgd.] F. WRAGG
                                               Special Inquiry Officer

Service Hereof Acknowledged by
   [Sgd.] C. G. HANNA.

Subsecs. (1), (3) and (8) of sec. 18 of the regulations to which said deportation order refers require that an immigrant possess a passport and visa; and that his passport or other travel document bear a medical certificate in approved form.

It should be stated at the outset that no Canadian court has power to assist Hanna in his plea that he be given right of residence in Canada. That is a decision for immigration officials, and for them alone, to make. Similarly all right of exercise of discretionary power to exempt from strict compliance with the requirements of the Immigration Act or regulations made thereunder is vested in and is the prerogative of only the minister, deputy minister, director, or such other persons as may be authorized to act for the director. * * *

   * * *

It may be helpful to outline Hanna's history and background in brief detail as it is disclosed by the scanty material before me. Most of such material consists of Hanna's sworn testimony, given in the English language, when he was before Mr. Wragg on January 18, 1957, at which time his knowledge and proficiency in the use of our language was not as great as it may be now. He says that he was born at sea and that no known record of his birth is extant. The name of the vessel aboard which he was born, and particulars of her nationality or port of registry are unknown. His father was named George Hanna and supposedly travelled to French Somaliland from Liberia, a small republic situate on the west coast of Africa. His mother's maiden name was Marian Marika and she was a native of Ethiopia (or Abyssinia)—a country whose status either as empire or vassal of Italy at any given time can be determined only by reference to historical data bearing upon Emperor Haille Selassie's struggles in warfare with the late Benito Mussolini. Hanna understands that his parents met and were married at Djibouti, the capital city of French Somaliland. The accuracy of his information in this respect should be easy to check. French Somaliland is a very small country. It has been a French colony for about 80 years, and one imagines that statistical records of births, deaths and marriages are available at the capital city—a comparatively small place of about 22,000 population. Hanna was the only child born of his parents' marriage and both of his parents are dead. Continuing the narrative according to Hanna's understanding of events, his father left his mother to seek employment in Liberia. Subsequently his mother, being pregnant at the time, and seeking to rejoin her husband, took passage on a ship sailing out of Djibouti. She became ill and gave birth to Hanna when the ship was one day at sea, and because of her illness the ship was put about and returned to Djibouti where she and her newborn child were placed in a hospital or home for women. Thereafter Hanna was cared for by his mother who worked at various times at Addis Ababa and Dire Wawa (both in Ethiopia) and at Djibouti in French Somaliland, until Hanna was six years of age. She then died and thereafter Hanna more or less "raised himself" as he puts it, with some assistance from a kindly old Turkish gentleman at Djibouti and others, including a Japanese gentleman at Dire Wawa in Ethiopia.

During his years of infancy and adolescence Hanna seems to have crossed and recrossed the international boundaries of Ethiopia, French Somaliland, British Somaliland and Eritrea (formerly an Italian colony but now a province of Ethiopia by virtue of the recommendation of a United Nations' committee adopted by the General Assembly in 1952) without encountering difficulty with the immigration officials of those countries. I suppose that youth was in his favour at the outset, and I suppose, too, that the international boundaries referred to were not too well defined at that time. That still seems to be the case. I understand that the accurate fixation of the international borders convergent upon the small area of French Somaliland is a problem which presently engages the attention of the United Nations' General Assembly.

In this way Hanna lived and worked from time to time (inter alia) in the ports of Zeila and Berbera in British Somaliland where he picked up a smattering of English. He says that his mother spoke English and, although he never saw his father, it is his understanding that his parents conversed in English. This would be consistent with Hanna's theory that his father was a native of Liberia—a republic which most people look upon as a virtual protectorate of the United States of America, and where English is spoken.

As he grew older Hanna seems to have encountered and had difficulty with the immigration officers of these adjacent countries, in none of which he could claim right of residence. He thereby learned that possession of a birth certificate is an indispensable requirement of modern society. He learned "the hard way" that some of the fundamental human rights with which all men are endowed by their Creator at birth were not his to enjoy without the intervention and benevolent assistance of some temporal power—a power to be exercised in many cases according to the whim or opinion of immigration officers whose numbers are legion in most sovereign states. That is not to say, of course, that he or anyone else possesses an inherent right to enter or remain in Canada unless born here. The late Right Honourable W. L. Mackenzie King, Prime Minister of Canada, said in the House of Commons on May 1, 1947, that

It is not a "fundamental human right" of an alien to enter Canada. It is a privilege. It is a matter of domestic policy.

The same thing might be said with respect to every sovereign state of the world, but one doubts that the Prime Minister intended his statement to be a repudiation of Canadian interest or sympathy in such a case of distress at this one, the like of which, I venture to say, has little chance of recurring. It is probable that the Prime Minister made use of the term "alien" in the popular sense of reference to a person who resides or seeks to reside in a country other than his own; and in that connotation it could be argued that a stateless person like Hanna is not an "alien" since he has no country of his own.

I think I should stop there by reminding myself again that the issue before me is a strictly legal one which I am required to divorce from any considerations of equity or humanitarianism. Those things must be deemed to have been embodied in the statute at the time of its enactment.

Almost three years ago, when he was in the port of Massaua, Eritrea, Hanna stowed away in an Italian tramp steamer in the hope of being carried in her to some country which would grant him asylum and right of residence. His plan met with frustration because upon arrival of such ship at any port he was immediately locked up and denied permission to land. After a year or more of such aimless wandering and imprisonment, Hanna escaped from the Italian vessel when she called at Beirut in the republic of Lebanon, and concealed himself in the hold of the Norwegian motor-ship "Gudveig." As a stowaway in such latter vessel he fared no better than before. He was held prisoner aboard The "Gudveig" for more than 16 months and made three or more trips to Canada in her until his release under writ of habeas corpus in these proceedings. He first came before Clyne, J. upon return of a show cause summons on January 18, 1957, wherein he challenged the legality of his detention by the master of The "Gudveig." My learned brother there held (correctly, in my respectful opinion) that the master's detention of Hanna was not illegal since the master was subject to and bound by the regulations applicable to "stowaways" as passed pursuant to the provisions of the Immigration Act. Thereafter Hanna made application to enter Canada and his status was thereby changed from that of "stowaway" to that of "immigrant." An immigrant is defined by sec. 2(i) of the Immigration Act as follows:

> (i) "immigrant" means a person who seeks admission to Canada for permanent residence.

* * * And so, at a time when it had become a widely publicized matter of general public knowledge or repute that Hanna possessed no proof of birth nor documents of any kind, he was granted the privilege of appearing before three separate departmental tribunals for the purpose of proving—if he could—that he did in fact possess

such documents. Of course, he was unable to discharge that onus, and
the deportation order followed which is now under attack in these proceedings.

I now come to an examination of that deportation order. Was
it an order which the special inquiry officer had legal authority to
make in all of the circumstances existing at the time of its making?
It contains four separate directives which are stated in the alternative and, presumably, in the order of their importance.

The most important directive is, No. 1, that Hanna be deported to
the place whence he came to Canada.

The next directive is, No. 2, that he be deported to the country of
which he is a national or citizen.

The next is, No. 3, that he be deported to the country of his birth.

The final alternative is, No. 4, that he be deported to such country as may be approved by the minister.

The No. 4 directive is meaningless in the absence of anything to
show a possibility of the minister ever finding a country which would
be willing to admit this young man in the face of Canada's refusal to
admit him. It cannot be assumed that travel documents are of less
significance in other countries than here. The thing goes further
than that, however, because sec. 40(2) of our Act makes the minister's
power of designation and approval of "such country" conditional upon
the owners of the M.S. "Gudveig" first making request for such
ministerial approval. Even then, as I interpret the statute, the approval of the minister could have no effect unless after finding "a
country that is willing to receive him," Hanna were to indicate that
such country is "acceptable" to him.

Directives No. 2 and No. 3 referring, respectively, to country of
nationality or citizenship and country of birth, may be discussed together. Neither of these directives could possibly be complied with.
In the absence of satisfactory evidence of nationality of a legitimate
father and lack of any evidence as to the nationality or registry of
the ship aboard which Hanna was born, these directives of the deportation order are meaningless.

The inescapable fact is that Hanna is a "stateless person," and the
efforts of the department to prove otherwise have not been impressive.
I was presented with evidence (consisting of affidavits by lawyers in
Oslo, Norway, and a Canadian immigration officer) in support of the
submission that Hanna is not "stateless" and that the words of the
directive "country of your birth," therefore, are not meaningless. The
trouble is that whilst the affidavit of the immigration officer fixes
Hanna's birthplace as Djibouti in French Somaliland, the Norwegian
lawyers suggest that he is an Egyptian who was born at Alexandria.
None of this conflicting evidence is credible. It is all based on hearsay
and, perhaps, the least said about it, the better.

That brings me to the consideration of directive No. 1—that Hanna be deported to the place whence he came to Canada. What does it mean?

The department's position, as I understand it, is that it could mean a number of things which it leaves to other people to determine for themselves. The place whence Hanna came to Canada might be the port of Beirut in the republic of Lebanon since that is the place where he first stowed away in the M.S. "Gudveig." Perhaps that interpretation is favoured by the department since it has presented certain material tending to show that if Lebanese authorities can be satisfied that Hanna stowed away at Beirut, they might permit him to land in their country—a country, incidentally, which is quite as foreign to Hanna as it is to me. Then again the department seems to suggest that the place whence Hanna came to Canada could be the United Kingdom and an affidavit is presented for the purpose of showing that The "Gudveig" sailed non-stop from the United Kingdom to Vancouver on her last voyage with Hanna aboard. Perhaps the place whence Hanna came to Canada could be the port of Massaua in Eritrea, since that was the starting point of his aimless wanderings as a stowaway in search of a country which would give him right of residence. Other interpretations are possible, but it seems to me that the matter of correct interpretation is of comparative unimportance here. The thing of importance, as I see it, is that the special inquiry officer here delegated to the master or owners of The "Gudveig" the responsibility for saying what his deportation order means; and, apart from the circumstances that he himself does not seem to know what it means, I am of opinion that he has not that power of delegation under the Act.

I have had reference to the authorities cited by counsel wherein it was held that deportation orders made (as this one was) in form approved by the minister were valid and enforceable notwithstanding their multiplicity of alternative directives, but in none of such cases were the facts comparable to the extraordinary facts of this amazing case. In each of such cases the meaning of the deportation order in the form used was clearly apparent to everyone concerned or affected by it. In no case did the deportation order require subsequent inquiry or investigation by anyone for determination of its meaning. In none of such cases was there a necessarily incidental delegation of his authority by the special inquiry officer who made the order for deportation. These are some of the things which, in my opinion, distinguish Hanna's case from all others.

From whatever angle one views it, so far as Hanna is concerned, this deportation order amounted to a sentence of imprisonment aboard The "Gudveig" for an indefinite term, and in my opinion and finding, no immigration officer has the legal right to exercise such drastic power.

* * *

For the reasons previously expressed, there will be judgment for Hanna in these proceedings, with costs. That does not mean that he has established any legal right to enter or remain in Canada. As previously stated, it is for immigration officials and for them alone to grant or withhold that privilege. This judgment does not mean that Hanna may not be deported legally from Canada by further proceedings properly instituted and conducted in accordance with the provisions and intent of the Immigration Act. It means only that the present deportation order is illegal and that Hanna is entitled to be released from detention thereunder; and I so order.

LIMITED

* * *

Consequences of Statelessness

1. What happens to Hanna now? In Staniszewski v. Watkins, 80 F.Supp. 132 (S.D.N.Y.1948), a "stateless" seaman was released after being detained at Ellis Island for about seven months at the expense of his employer. The court observed that the government was "willing that he go back to the ship, but if he were sent back aboard ship and sailed to the port . . . from which he last sailed to the United States, he would probably be denied permission to land." The court said, "There is no other country that would take him without proper documents." (at 134) The court sustained the seaman's writ of habeas corpus and ordered his release: "He will be required to inform the immigration officials at Ellis Island by mail on the 15th of each month, stating where he is employed and where he can be reached by mail. If the government does succeed in arranging for petitioner's deportation to a country that will be ready to receive him as a resident, it may then advise the petitioner to that effect and arrange for his deportation in the manner provided by law." (at 135).

Similarly, in Public Prosecutor v. Zinger, France, Tribunal of the Seine, 1936 [1935–37] Ann.Dig. 307 (No. 138), the court ordered the release of a stateless person who had been imprisoned for failure to obey expulsion orders. The court weighed the alternatives of releasing the man or imprisoning him "at the cost of the French taxpayer" for an offence which he could not help committing, since he was unable to leave French territory. The court concluded that "release is the best solution from the legal point of view."

DON'T BURDEN TAXPAYER

2. If a stateless person is allowed to remain in the United States, is he treated differently from an alien who has the nationality of some other state? Aliens have been held entitled to the benefits of the Fifth Amendment guarantee against expropriation of property without compensation. But suppose that the United States should discriminate between aliens with nationality and those without nationality, to the disadvantage of the latter? Would there be any interna-

tional consequence? A state whose national has been the subject of discrimination could call the United States to account under international law. Who would, or could, espouse the claim of the stateless alien?

3. Suppose a stateless person is allowed to remain in the United States, and does reside there for a number of years. Thereafter he enters a foreign state where he is subject to severe injury at the hands of state officials (e. g., he is imprisoned for a long period without charges or trial and is subjected to torture and other inhumane treatment). Will the United States espouse a claim on his behalf? Section 1732 of Title 22 of the United States Code provides as follows:

> Whenever it is made known to the President that any citizen of the United States has been unjustly deprived of his liberty by or under the authority of any foreign government, it shall be the duty of the President forthwith to demand of that government the reasons of such imprisonment; and if it appears to be wrongful and in violation of the rights of American citizenship, the President shall forthwith demand the release of such citizen, and if the release so demanded is unreasonably delayed or refused, the President shall use such means, not amounting to acts of war, as he may think necessary and proper to obtain or effectuate the release; and all the facts and proceedings relative thereto shall as soon as practicable be communicated by the President to Congress.

The protection of the United States is not confined to native-born citizens. Title 22, Section 1731 of the United States Code provides:

> All naturalized citizens of the United States while in foreign countries are entitled to and shall receive from this Government the same protection of persons and property which is accorded to native-born citizens.

Suppose it is decided by the United States that it will espouse the stateless alien's claim. Is it permitted by international law to do so? See the Nottebohm case, below.

4. Statelessness has resulted from a state's decree that members of a whole class of persons are no longer citizens of the state. During World War II, Germany withdrew German nationality from Jews permanently resident abroad. In France, this loss of nationality relieved an individual from the strictures applied by French law to enemy [German] subjects, even though the denationalization law was repealed by the Allies at the end of the war. Terhoch v. Daudin et Assistance Publique France, Court of Appeal of Paris, 1947, [1947] Ann.Dig. 121 (No. 54).

5. Congress has provided that a person who is a national of the United States by birth or by naturalization shall lose his nationality for a variety of reasons. 8 U.S.C. § 1481. What is the meaning of

the statutory phrase "lose his nationality"?   In Kennedy v. Mendoza-Martinez, 372 U.S. 144, 160, 83 S.Ct. 554, 563 (1963), the court said:

> We recognize at the outset that we are confronted here with an issue of the utmost import.   Deprivation of citizenship—particularly American citizenship, which is "one of the most valuable rights in the world today," Report of the President's Commission on Immigration and Naturalization (1953), 235—has grave practical consequences.   An expatriate who, like Cort, had no other nationality becomes a stateless person—a person who not only has no rights as an American citizen, but no membership in any national entity whatsoever.   "Such individuals as do not possess any nationality enjoy, in general, no protection whatever, and if they are aggrieved by a State they have no means of redress, since there is no State which is competent to take up their case.   As far as the Law of Nations is concerned, there is, apart from restraints of morality or obligations expressly laid down by treaty * * * no restriction whatever to cause a State to abstain from maltreating to any extent such stateless individuals."   I Oppenheim, International Law (8th ed., Lauterpacht, 1955), § 291, at 640.   The calamity is "[n]ot the loss of specific rights, then, but the loss of a community willing and able to guarantee any rights whatsoever * * *"   Arendt, The Origins of Totalitarianism (1951), 294.

In holding that denationalization as a punishment is barred by the Eighth Amendment, the court said in Trop v. Dulles, 356 U.S. 86, 101, 78 S.Ct. 590, 598 (1958):

> There may be involved no physical mistreatment, no primitive torture.   There is instead the total destruction of the individual's status in organized society.   It is a form of punishment more primitive than torture for it destroys for the individual the political existence that was centuries in the development.   The punishment strips the citizen of his status in the national and international political community.   His very existence is at the sufferance of the country in which he happens to find himself.   While any one country may accord him some rights, and presumably as long as he remained in this country he would enjoy the limited rights of an alien, no country need do so because he is stateless.   Furthermore, his enjoyment of even the limited rights of an alien might be subject to termination at any time by reason of deportation.   In short, the expatriate has lost the right to have rights.

It is not only in Trop v. Dulles, supra, that the denationalization provisions have suffered badly at the hands of the United States Supreme Court.   Although in Perez v. Brownell, 356 U.S. 44, 78 S.Ct. 568 (1958), the court had held that it was within Congress' foreign relations power to provide for loss of citizenship by one who votes in a foreign election, this case was overruled in Afroyim v. Rusk, 387 U.S.

253, 87 S.Ct. 1660 (1967). In the Kennedy case, the court held that the provision for loss of nationality by remaining outside the United States to avoid military service was punitive and could not stand constitutionally because it lacked due process safeguards guaranteed by the Constitution of the United States. And in Schneider v. Rusk, 377 U.S. 163, 84 S.Ct. 1187 (1964), the court struck down the provision for loss of nationality by a naturalized citizen who had continuously resided for three years in the country of his origin.

One of the grounds for loss of nationality is "making a formal renunciation of nationality before a diplomatic or consular officer of the United States in a foreign state." 8 U.S.C. § 1481(a)(6). If a citizen of the United States wishes such a renunciation and seeks return to the United States, can he be excluded? If he is later found in the United States, can he be deported? To what state? See Jolley v. Immigration and Naturalization Service, 441 F.2d 1245 (5th Cir. 1971), cert. denied 404 U.S. 946, 92 S.Ct. 302 (1971).

SECTION B.   INTERNATIONAL CRITERIA FOR STATE PROTECTION

NOTTEBOHM CASE (LIECHTENSTEIN v. GUATEMALA)

International Court of Justice, 1955.
[1955] I.C.J.Rep. 4.

By the Application filed on December 17th, 1951, the Government of Liechtenstein instituted proceedings before the Court in which it claimed restitution and compensation on the ground that the Government of Guatemala had "acted towards the person and property of Mr. Friedrich Nottebohm, a citizen of Liechtenstein, in a manner contrary to international law". In its Counter-Memorial, the Government of Guatemala contended that this claim was inadmissible on a number of grounds, and one of its objections to the admissibility of the claim related to the nationality of the person for whose protection Liechtenstein had seised the Court.

It appears to the Court that this plea in bar is of fundamental importance and that it is therefore desirable to consider it at the outset.

Guatemala has referred to a well-established principle of international law, which it expressed in Counter-Memorial, where it is stated that "it is the bond of nationality between the State and the individual which alone confers upon the State the right of diplomatic protection". * * *

Liechtenstein considers itself to be acting in conformity with this principle and contends that Nottebohm is its national by virtue of the naturalization conferred upon him.

Nottebohm was born at Hamburg on September 16th, 1881. He was German by birth, and still possessed German nationality when, in October 1939, he applied for naturalization in Liechtenstein.

In 1905 he went to Guatemala. He took up residence there and made that country the headquarters of his business activities, which increased and prospered; these activities developed in the field of commerce, banking and plantations. Having been an employee in the firm of Nottebohm Hermanos, which had been founded by his brothers Juan and Arturo, he became their partner in 1912 and later, in 1937, he was made head of the firm. After 1905 he sometimes went to Germany on business and to other countries for holidays. He continued to have business connections in Germany. He paid a few visits to a brother who had lived in Liechtenstein since 1931. Some of his other brothers, relatives and friends were in Germany, others in Guatemala. He himself continued to have his fixed abode in Guatemala until 1943, that is to say, until the occurrence of the events which constitute the basis of the present dispute.

In 1939, after having provided for the safeguarding of his interests in Guatemala by a power of attorney given to the firm of Nottebohm Hermanos on March 22nd, he left that country at a date fixed by Counsel for Liechtenstein as at approximately the end of March or the beginning of April, when he seems to have gone to Hamburg, and later to have paid a few brief visits to Vaduz where he was at the beginning of October 1939. It was then, on October 9th, a little more than a month after the opening of the second World War marked by Germany's attack on Poland, that his attorney, Dr. Marxer, submitted an application for naturalization on behalf of Nottebohm.

The Liechtenstein Law of January 4th, 1934, lays down the conditions for the naturalization of foreigners, specifies the supporting documents to be submitted and the undertakings to be given and defines the competent organs for giving a decision and the procedure to be followed. The Law specifies certain mandatory requirements, namely, that the applicant for naturalization should prove: (1) "that the acceptance into the Home Corporation (Heimatverband) of a Liechtenstein commune has been promised to him in case of acquisition of the nationality of the State"; (2) that he will lose his former nationality as a result of naturalization, although this requirement may be waived under stated conditions. It further makes naturalization conditional upon compliance with the requirement of residence for at least three years in the territory of the Principality, although it is provided that "this requirement can be dispensed with in circumstances deserving special consideration and by way of exception". In addition, the applicant for naturalization is required to submit a number of documents, such as evidence of his residence in the territory of the Principality, a certificate of good conduct issued by the competent authority of the place of residence, documents relating to his property and income and, if he is not a resident in the Principality, proof that he has concluded an agreement with the Revenue authorities, "subsequent to the revenue commission of the presumptive home commune having been heard". The Law further provides for the payment by the applicant of a naturalization fee, which is fixed by the Princely Government and amounts to at least one half of the sum payable by the applicant for reception into the Home Corporation of a Liechtenstein commune, the promise of such reception constituting a condition under the Law for the grant of naturalization.

* * *

As to the consideration of the application by the competent organs and the procedure to be followed by them, the Law provides that the Government, after having examined the application and the documents pertaining thereto, and after having obtained satisfactory information concerning the applicant, shall submit the application to the Diet. If the latter approves the application, the Government shall submit the requisite request to the Prince, who alone is entitled to confer nationality of the Principality.

* * *

This was the legal position with regard to applications for naturalization at the time when Nottebohm's application was submitted.

On October 9th, 1939, Nottebohm, "resident in Guatemala since 1905 (at present residing as a visitor with his brother, Hermann Nottebohm, in Vaduz)", applied for admission as a national of Liechtenstein and, at the same time, for the previous conferment of citizenship in the Commune of Mauren. He sought dispensation from the condition of three years' residence as prescribed by law, without indicating the special circumstances warranting such waiver. He submitted a statement of the Crédit Suisse in Zurich concerning his assets, and undertook to pay 25,000 Swiss francs to the Commune of Mauren, 12,500 Swiss francs to the State, to which was to be added the payment of dues in connection with the proceedings. He further stated that he had made "arrangements with the Revenue Authorities of the Government of Liechtenstein for the conclusion of a formal agreement to the effect that he will pay an annual tax of naturalization amounting to Swiss francs 1,000, of which Swiss francs 600 are payable to the Commune of Mauren and Swiss francs 400 are payable to the Principality of Liechtenstein, subject to the proviso that the payments of these taxes will be set off against ordinary taxes which will fall due if the applicant takes up residence in one of the Communes of the Principality". He further undertook to deposit as security a sum of 30,000 Swiss francs. He also gave certain general information as to his financial position and indicated that he would never become a burden to the Commune whose citizenship he was seeking.

* * *

A document dated October 15th, 1939, certifies that on that date the Commune of Mauren conferred the privilege of its citizenship upon Mr. Nottebohm and requested the Government to transmit it to the Diet for approval. A certificate of October 17th, 1939, evidences the payment of the taxes required to be paid by Mr. Nottebohm. On October 20th, 1939, Mr. Nottebohm took the oath of allegiance and a final arrangement concerning liability to taxation was concluded on October 23rd.

This was the procedure followed in the case of the naturalization of Nottebohm.

A certificate of nationality has also been produced, signed on behalf of the Government of the Principality and dated October 20th, 1939, to the effect that Nottebohm was naturalized by Supreme Resolution of the Reigning Prince dated October 13th, 1939.

Having obtained a Liechtenstein passport, Nottebohm had it visa-ed by the Consul General of Guatemala in Zurich on December 1st, 1939, and returned to Guatemala at the beginning of 1940, where he resumed his former business activities and in particular the management of the firm of Nottebohm Hermanos.

* * * Liechtenstein requests the Court to find and declare, first, "that the naturalization of Mr. Frederic Nottebohm in Liechtenstein on October 13th, 1939, was not contrary to international law", and, secondly, "that Liechtenstein's claim on behalf of Mr. Nottebohm as a national of Liechtenstein is admissible before the Court".

The Final Conclusions of Guatemala, on the other hand, request the Court "to declare that the claim of the Principality of Liechtenstein is inadmissible", and set forth a number of grounds relating to the nationality of Liechtenstein granted to Nottebohm by naturalization.

Thus, the real issue before the Court is the admissibility of the claim of Liechtenstein in respect of Nottebohm. Liechtenstein's first submission referred to above is a reason advanced for a decision by the Court in favour of Liechtenstein, while the several grounds given by Guatemala on the question of nationality are intended as reasons for the inadmissibility of Liechtenstein's claim. The present task of the Court is limited to adjudicating upon the admissibility of the claim of Liechtenstein in respect of Nottebohm on the basis of such reasons as it may itself consider relevant and proper.

In order to decide upon the admissibility of the Application, the Court must ascertain whether the nationality conferred on Nottebohm by Liechtenstein by means of a naturalization which took place in the circumstances which have been described, can be validly invoked as against Guatemala, whether it bestows upon Liechtenstein a sufficient title to the exercise of protection in respect of Nottebohm as against Guatemala and therefore entitles it to seise the Court of a claim relating to him. In this connection, Counsel for Liechtenstein said: "the essential question is whether Mr. Nottebohm, having acquired the nationality of Liechtenstein, that acquisition of nationality is one which must be recognized by other States". This formulation is accurate, subject to the twofold reservation that, in the first place, what is involved is not recognition for all purposes but merely for the purposes of the admissibility of the Application, and, secondly, that what is involved is not recognition by all States but only by Guatemala.

The Court does not propose to go beyond the limited scope of the question which it has to decide, namely whether the nationality conferred on Nottebohm can be relied upon as against Guatemala in justification of the proceedings instituted before the Court. It must decide this question on the basis of international law; to do so is consistent with the nature of the question and with the nature of the Court's own function.

    * * *

Since no proof has been adduced that Guatemala has recognized the title to the exercise of protection relied upon by Liechtenstein as being derived from the naturalization which it granted to Nottebohm, the Court must consider whether such an act of granting nationality by Liechtenstein directly entails an obligation on the part of Guatemala to recognize its effect, namely, Liechtenstein's right to exercise its protection. In other words, it must be determined whether that unilateral act by Liechtenstein is one which can be relied upon against Guatemala in regard to the exercise of protection. The Court will deal with this question without considering that of the validity of Nottebohm's naturalization according to the law of Liechtenstein.

It is for Liechtenstein, as it is for every sovereign State, to settle by its own legislation the rules relating to the acquisition of its nationality, and to confer that nationality by naturalization granted by its own organs in accordance with that legislation. It is not necessary to determine whether international law imposes any limitations on its freedom of decision in this domain. Furthermore, nationality has its most immediate, its most far-reaching and, for most people, its only effects within the legal system of the State conferring it. Nationality serves above all to determine that the person upon whom it is conferred enjoys the rights and is bound by the obligations which the law of the State in question grants to or imposes on its nationals. This is implied in the wider concept that nationality is within the domestic jurisdiction of the State.

But the issue which the Court must decide is not one which pertains to the legal system of Liechtenstein. It does not depend on the law or on the decision of Liechtenstein whether that State is entitled to exercise its protection, in the case under consideration. To exercise protection, to apply to the Court, is to place oneself on the plane of international law. It is international law which determines whether a State is entitled to exercise protection and to seise the Court.

The naturalization of Nottebohm was an act performed by Liechtenstein in the exercise of its domestic jurisdiction. The question to be decided is whether that act has the international effect here under consideration.

* * *

* * * International arbitrators, having before them allegations of nationality by the applicant State which were contested by the respondent State, have sought to ascertain whether nationality had been conferred by the applicant State in circumstances such as to give rise to an obligation on the part of the respondent State to recognize the effect of that nationality. In order to decide this question arbitrators have evolved certain principles for determining whether full international effect was to be attributed to the nationality invoked. The same issue is now before the Court: it must be resolved by applying the same principles.

The courts of third States, when confronted by a similar situation, have dealt with it in the same way. They have done so not in connection with the exercise of protection, which did not arise before them, but where two different nationalities have been invoked before them they have had, not indeed to decide such a dispute as between the two States concerned, but to determine whether a given foreign nationality which had been invoked before them was one which they ought to recognize.

International arbitrators have decided in the same way numerous cases of dual nationality, where the question arose with regard to the exercise of protection. They have given their preference to the real and effective nationality, that which accorded with the facts, that based on stronger factual ties between the person concerned and one of the States whose nationality is involved. Different factors are taken into consideration, and their importance will vary from one case to the next: the habitual residence of the individual concerned is an important factor, but there are other factors such as the centre of his interests, his family ties, his participation in public life, attachment shown by him for a given country and inculcated in his children, etc.

Similarly, the courts of third States, when they have before them an individual whom two other States hold to be their national, seek to resolve the conflict by having recourse to international criteria and their prevailing tendency is to prefer the real and effective nationality.

The same tendency prevails in the writings of publicists and in practice. This notion is inherent in the provisions of Article 3, paragraph 2, of the Statute of the Court. National laws reflect this tendency when, inter alia, they make naturalization dependent on conditions indicating the existence of a link, which may vary in their purpose or in their nature but which are essentially concerned with this idea. The Liechtenstein Law of January 4th, 1934, is a good example.

The practice of certain States which refrain from exercising protection in favour of a naturalized person when the latter has in fact, by his prolonged absence, severed his links with what is no longer for him anything but his nominal country, manifests the view of these States that, in order to be capable of being invoked against another State, nationality must correspond with the factual situation.   *   *   *

The character thus recognized on the international level as pertaining to nationality is in no way inconsistent with the fact that international law leaves it to each State to lay down the rules governing the grant of its own nationality. The reason for this is that the diversity of demographic conditions has thus far made it impossible for any general agreement to be reached on the rules relating to nationality, although the latter by its very nature affects international relations. It has been considered that the best way of making such rules accord with the varying demographic conditions in different countries is to leave the fixing of such rules to the competence of each State. On the other hand, a State cannot claim that the rules it has thus laid down are entitled to recognition by another State unless it has acted in conformity with this general aim of making the legal bond of nationality accord with the individual's genuine connection with the State which assumes the defence of its citizens by means of protection as against other States.

The requirement that such a concordance must exist is to be found in the studies carried on in the course of the last thirty years upon the initiative and under the auspices of the League of Nations and the United Nations.   *   *   *

According to the practice of States, to arbitral and judicial decisions and to the opinions of writers, nationality is a legal bond having as its basis a social fact of attachment, a genuine connection of existence, interests and sentiments, together with the existence of reciprocal rights and duties. It may be said to constitute the juridical expression of the fact that the individual upon whom it is conferred, either directly by the law or as the result of an act of the authorities, is in fact more closely connected with the population of the State conferring nationality than with that of any other State. Conferred by a State, it only entitles that State to exercise protection vis-à-vis another State, if it constitutes a translation into juridical terms of the individual's connection with the State which has made him its national.

Diplomatic protection and protection by means of international judicial proceedings constitute measures for the defence of the rights of the State. As the Permanent Court of International Justice has said and has repeated, "by taking up the case of one of its subjects and by resorting to diplomatic action or international judicial proceedings on his behalf, a State is in reality asserting its own rights— its right to ensure, in the person of its subjects, respect for the rules of international law" (P.C.I.J., Series A, No. 2, p. 12, and Series A/B, Nos. 20–21, p. 17).

Since this is the character which nationality must present when it is invoked to furnish the State which has granted it with a title to the exercise of protection and to the institution of international judicial proceedings, the Court must ascertain whether the nationality granted to Nottebohm by means of naturalization is of this character or, in other words, whether the factual connection between Nottebohm and Liechtenstein in the period preceding, contemporaneous with and following his naturalization appears to be sufficiently close, so preponderant in relation to any connection which may have existed between him and any other State, that it is possible to regard the nationality conferred upon him as real and effective, as the exact juridical expression of a social fact of a connection which existed previously or came into existence thereafter.

TEST

Naturalization is not a matter to be taken lightly. To seek and to obtain it is not something that happens frequently in the life of a human being. It involves his breaking of a bond of allegiance and his establishment of a new bond of allegiance. It may have far-reaching consequences and involve profound changes in the destiny of the individual who obtains it. It concerns him personally, and to consider it only from the point of view of its repercussions with regard to his property would be to misunderstand its profound significance. In order to appraise its international effect, it is impossible to disregard the circumstances in which it was conferred, the serious character which attaches to it, the real and effective, and not merely the verbal preference of the individual seeking it for the country which grants it to him.

At the time of his naturalization does Nottebohm appear to have been more closely attached by his tradition, his establishment, his interests, his activities, his family ties, his intentions for the near future to Liechtenstein than to any other State?

* * *

The essential facts are as follows: At the date when he applied for naturalization Nottebohm had been a German national from the time of his birth. He had always retained his connections with members of his family who had remained in Germany and he had always had business connections with that country. His country had been at war for more than a month, and there is nothing to indicate that the application for naturalization then made by Nottebohm was motivated by any desire to dissociate himself from the Government of his country.

MOTIVE

He had been settled in Guatemala for 34 years. He had carried on his activities there. It was the main seat of his interests. He returned there shortly after his naturalization, and it remained the centre of his interests and of his business activities. He stayed there until his removal as a result of war measures in 1943. He subsequently attempted to return there, and he now complains of Guatemala's refusal to admit him. There, too, were several members of his family who sought to safeguard his interests.

In contrast, his actual connections with Liechtenstein were extremely tenuous. No settled abode, no prolonged residence in that country at the time of his application for naturalization: the application indicates that he was paying a visit there and confirms the transient character of this visit by its request that the naturalization proceedings should be initiated and concluded without delay. No intention of settling there was shown at that time or realized in the ensuing weeks, months or years—on the contrary, he returned to Guatemala very shortly after his naturalization and showed every intention of remaining there. If Nottebohm went to Liechtenstein in 1946, this was because of the refusal of Guatemala to admit him. No indication is given of the grounds warranting the waiver of the condition of residence, required by the 1934 Nationality Law, which waiver was implicitly granted to him. There is no allegation of any economic interests or of any activities exercised or to be exercised in Liechtenstein, and no manifestation of any intention whatsoever to transfer all or some of his interests and his business activities to Liechtenstein. It is unnecessary in this connection to attribute much importance to the promise to pay the taxes levied at the time of his naturalization. The only links to be discovered between the Principality and Nottebohm are the short sojourns already referred to and the presence in Vaduz of one of his brothers: but his brother's presence is referred to in his application for naturalization only as a reference to his good conduct. Furthermore, other members of his family have asserted Nottebohm's desire to spend his old age in Guatemala.

These facts clearly establish, on the one hand, the absence of any bond of attachment between Nottebohm and Liechtenstein and, on the other hand, the existence of a long-standing and close connection between him and Guatemala, a link which his naturalization in no way weakened. That naturalization was not based on any real prior connection with Liechtenstein, nor did it in any way alter the manner of life of the person upon whom it was conferred in exceptional circumstances of speed and accommodation. In both respects, it was lacking in the genuineness requisite to an act of such importance, if it is to be entitled to be respected by a State in the position of Guatemala. It was granted without regard to the concept of nationality adopted in international relations.

Naturalization was asked for not so much for the purpose of obtaining a legal recognition of Nottebohm's membership in fact in the population of Liechtenstein, as it was to enable him to substitute for his status as a national of a belligerent State that of a national of a neutral State, with the sole aim of thus coming within the protection of Liechtenstein but not of becoming wedded to its traditions, its interests, its way of life or of assuming the obligations—other than fiscal obligations—and exercising the rights pertaining to the status thus acquired.

Guatemala is under no obligation to recognize a nationality granted in such circumstances. Liechtenstein consequently is not entitled to extend its protection to Nottebohm vis-à-vis Guatemala and its claim must, for this reason, be held to be inadmissible.

The Court is not therefore called upon to deal with the other pleas in bar put forward by Guatemala or the Conclusions of the Parties other than those on which it is adjudicating in accordance with the reasons indicated above.

For these reasons, THE COURT, by eleven votes to three,

Holds that the claim submitted by the Government of the Principality of Liechtenstein is inadmissible.

        *   *   *

Judges KLAESTAD and READ, and M. GUGGENHEIM, Judge ad hoc, have availed themselves of the right conferred on them by Article 57 of the Statute and have appended to the Judgment statements of their dissenting opinion.

[Dissenting opinions omitted.]

---

1. *Earlier adjudication in the Permanent Court of International Justice.* In its Advisory Opinion on Nationality Decrees in Tunis and Morocco (France and Great Britain), 1923, P.C.I.J., Ser. B, No. 4, the court was asked whether a dispute between France and Great Britain as to nationality decrees in Tunis and Morocco was or was not, by international law, solely a matter of domestic jurisdiction under Article 15, paragraph 8, of the Covenant of the League of Nations. Apparently on the ground that the relations between France and Great Britain and their protectorates were determined by international agreements and that "it will be necessary to resort to international law in order to decide what the value of an agreement of this kind may be as regards third States," the court expressed the opinion that the dispute was not, by international law, solely a matter of domestic jurisdiction. But for the existence of the agreements, however, the court presumably would not have taken jurisdiction:

The question whether a certain matter is or is not solely within the jurisdiction of a State is an essentially relative question; it depends upon the development of international relations. Thus, in the present state of international law, questions of nationality are, in the opinion of the Court, in principle within this reserved domain. (at 24)

2. *How far does Nottebohm reach?* Liechtenstein's claim was asserted against a state, Guatemala, with which Nottebohm had, in the language of the court, "a long-standing and close connection", "a link which his naturalization in no way weakened."

a. The opinion reveals that Nottebohm had been sent by Guatemala to the United States for internment during World War II. Suppose that the United States had injured Nottebohm by seizing and retaining, without compensation, property he had removed to a bank in the United States. Liechtenstein now brings an action against the United States in the International Court of Justice; the United States asks the court to declare the claim inadmissible on the grounds that Liechtenstein has no standing. How should the court rule? See Flegenheimer Case, XIV Rep. of Int'l Arb. Awards 327 (Italian-United States Conciliation Commission, 1958), p. 547 of this Chapter.

b. Refer to the Hanna case, p. 520. Suppose that Hanna has resided in Canada for a period of fifteen years, is married there, raises a family and conducts a business. As a result of the international operation of his business, he accumulates large sums of money in a bank in State X. State X expropriates his bank account without compensation. Although he has not been declared a "national" by Canada, Canada espouses his claim against State X and eventually brings an action against State X in the International Court of Justice. State X asks the court to declare the claim inadmissible on the ground that Hanna is not Canada's national. How should the court rule?

If Canada has in fact accorded Hanna its protection domestically over the years, and if in fact he has established a close link or tie with Canada, with its acquiescence, is the formal grant of nationality by Canada necessary? See Leigh, Nationality and Diplomatic Protection, 20 Int'l. & Comp.L. 453 (1971). What interest does State X have in Canada's according Hanna formal nationality?

c. If a stateless person is able to persuade *any* state to espouse his claim against a wrongdoing state with which he has previously had no link, why should that state not be permitted to claim on his behalf in the court?

d. Suppose a national of Czechoslovakia is kidnapped by Soviet agents and subjected to inhumane treatment in a USSR prison. His efforts from prison to enlist the aid of the Czechoslovakian government are in vain. At his request, communicated to the United States government, the United States brings an action against the USSR in the International Court of Justice. The USSR asks the court to declare the claim inadmissible on the ground that he is not a national of the United States. How should the court rule?

3. *Continuity of nationality of individual claimant.*

a. Oppenheim

A State which puts forward a claim before a claims commission or other international tribunal must be in a position to show that it has locus standi for that purpose. The principal, and almost the exclusive, factor creating that locus standi is the nationality of the claimant, and it may be stated as a general principle that from the time of the occurrence of the injury until the making of the award the claim must continuously and without interruption have belonged to a person or to a series of persons (a) having the nationality of the State by whom it is put forward, and (d) not having the nationality of the State against whom it is put forward. International Law 347 (8th ed. 1955) (Vol. I).*

b. Judge Van Eysinga

Those who maintain that this is a hard and fast rule rely mainly on the jurisprudence of the Claims Commissions (Mixed Commissions) * * *

The Mixed Commissions are set up by treaty when, especially after stormy events such as a revolution or civil war, a great number of the nationals of both parties to the treaty have suffered injury. A desire to liquidate all these claims leads the two parties to refer them by treaty to a commission set up especially to deal with them. Accordingly the commission is a special tribunal for certain groups of the nationals of both sides, and it is obvious that such treaties have in view only the nationals of the two parties who have suffered injury but not non-nationals, who may be in the same situation and who, in order to take advantage of the existence of the commission, get themselves naturalized, or nationals who may have bought the claims of non-nationals. In the domain of treaties setting up Mixed Commissions, the rule relied on by the Lithuanian Agent is perfectly comprehensible and perhaps in this sphere it is possible to speak of a rule of international law in the sense that, in the absence of a definite treaty provision, it must be observed by the Mixed Commissions. Panevezys-Saldutiskis Railway Case (Estonia v. Lithuania), 1939, P.C.I.J., Ser. A/B, No. 76, at 33.

c. Schwarzenberger

International judicial practice interprets this test so strictly as to demand the continuity of nationality from the time of the injury (dies a quo) until the date of judgment (dies ad quem). If protection of the individual were the ratio legis behind the rule on the continuity of nationality, the hardships resulting from this rule would lay it open to serious objections. For instance, if, before the award is delivered, the

* Reprinted by permission of David Mc-
Kay & Company, Inc., New York, and
Longmans, Green & Co., Ltd., London.

claimant dies and his heirs have a different nationality, the claim lapses. Yet, in fact, the rule serves a completely different purpose. It is to limit intervention in the domestic affairs of other States even if, in marginal cases, this object can be attained only at the price of considerable hardship to the individual. A Manual of International Law 176 (5th ed. 1967).

MERGÉ CASE

Italian-United States Conciliation Commission, 1955.
XIV U.N.Rep. Int'l Arb. Awards 236.

I. THE FACTS

On October 26, 1948, the Embassy of the United States of America in Rome submitted to the Ministry of the Treasury of the Italian Republic on behalf of Mrs. Florence Strunsky Mergé, a national of the United States of America, a claim based upon Article 78 of the Treaty of Peace with Italy for compensation for the loss as a result of the war of a <u>grand piano</u> and other personal property located at Frascati, Italy, and owned by <u>Mrs. Mergé</u>.

As the Italian Ministry of the Treasury had rejected the claim on the grounds that Mrs. Mergé is to be deemed, under Italian law, an Italian national by marriage, the Agent of the United States of America, on August 28, 1950, submitted to this Commission the dispute which had arisen between the two Governments with respect to the claim of Mrs. Mergé.

* * *

The following facts relating to the two nationalities, Italian and United States, possessed by Mrs. Mergé are revealed by the record:

Florence Strunsky was born in New York City on April 7, 1909, thereby acquiring United States nationality according to the law of the United States.

On December 21, 1933, at the age of 24, Florence Strunsky married Salvatore Mergé in Rome, Italy. As Mr. Mergé is an Italian national, Florence Strunsky acquired Italian nationality by operation of Italian law.

The United States Department of State issued a passport to Mrs. Mergé, then Miss Strunsky, on March 17, 1931. This passport was renewed on July 11, 1933, to be valid until March 16, 1935.

Mrs. Mergé lived with her husband in Italy during the four years following her marriage until 1937. Her husband was an employee of the Italian Government, working as an interpreter and translator of the Japanese language in the Ministry of Communications. In 1937 he was sent to the Italian Embassy at Tokyo as a translator and interpreter.

Mrs. Mergé accompanied her husband to Tokyo, travelling on Italian passport No. 681688, issued on August 27, 1937 by the Ministry of Foreign Affairs in Rome. The passport was of the type issued by the Italian Government to employees and their families bound for foreign posts.

After her arrival in Japan, Mrs. Mergé on February 21, 1940 was registered, at her request, as a national of the United States at the • American Consulate General at Tokyo.

Mrs. Mergé states that, when hostilities ceased between Japan and the United States of America, she refused to be returned to the United States by the United States military authorities, having preferred to remain with her husband.

On December 10, 1948, the American Consulate at Yokohama issued an American passport to Mrs. Mergé, valid only for travel to the United States, with which she travelled to the United States. She remained in the United States for nine months, from December, 1946, until September, 1947. The American passport issued to her at Yokohama and valid originally only for travel to the United States, was validated for travel to Italy, and the Italian Consulate General at New York, on July 31, 1947, granted Mrs. Mergé a visa for Italy as a visitor, valid for three months.

On September 19, 1947, Mrs. Mergé arrived in Italy where she has since resided with her husband.

Immediately after returning to Italy, on October 8, 1947, Mrs. Mergé registered as a United States national at the Consular Section of • the American Embassy in Rome. On October 16, 1947, Mrs. Mergé executed an affidavit before an American consular officer at the American Embassy in Rome for the purpose of explaining her protracted residence outside of the United States. In that affidavit she lists her mother and father as her only ties with the United States, and states that she does not pay income taxes to the Government of the United States.

On September 11, 1950 Mrs. Mergé requested and was granted by the Consular Section of the American Embassy at Rome a new American passport to replace the one which had been issued to her on December 10, 1946, by the American Consulate at Yokohama and which had expired. In her application for the new American passport, Mrs. Mergé states that her "legal residence" is at New York, New York, and that she intends to return to the United States to reside permanently at some indefinite time in the future.

So far as the record indicates, Mrs. Mergé is still residing with her husband in Italy.

II. THE ISSUE

It is not disputed between the Parties that the claimant possesses both nationalities. The issue is not one of choosing one of the two, but rather one of deciding whether in such case the Government of the

United States may exercise before the Conciliation Commission the rights granted by the Treaty of Peace with reference to the property in Italy of United Nations nationals (Articles 78 and 83).

* * *

(1).   Position of the Government of the United States of America:

(a) The Treaty of Peace between the United Nations and Italy provides the rules necessary to a solution of the case.   The first sub-paragraph of paragraph 9(a) of Article 78 states:

> "United Nations nationals" means individuals who are nationals of any of the United Nations, or corporations or associations organized under the laws of any of the United Nations, at the coming into force of the present Treaty, provided that the said individuals, corporations or associations also had this status on September 3, 1943, the date of the Armistice with Italy.

All United Nations nationals are therefore entitled to claim, and it is irrelevant for such purpose that they possess or have possessed Italian nationality as well.

* * *

(c) The principle, according to which one State cannot afford diplomatic protection to one of its nationals against a State whose nationality such person also possesses, cannot be applied to the Treaty of Peace with Italy because such principle is based on the equal sovereignty of States, whereas this Treaty of Peace was not negotiated between equal Powers but between the United Nations and Italy, a State defeated and obliged to accept the clauses imposed by the victors who at that time did not consider Italy a sovereign State.

(2).   Position of the Italian Government:

* * *

(b) A defeated State, even when it is obliged to undergo the imposition of the conqueror, continues to be a sovereign State.   From the juridical point of view, the Treaty of Peace is an international convention, not a unilateral act.   In cases of doubt, its interpretation must be that more favourable to the debtor.

(c) There exists a principle of international law, universally recognized and constantly applied, by virtue of which diplomatic protection cannot be exercised in cases of dual nationality when the claimant possesses also the nationality of the State against which the claim is being made.

* * *

V.   CONSIDERATIONS OF LAW

(1).   The rules of the Hague Convention of 1930 and the customary law manifested in international precedents and in the legal writings of the authors attest the existence and the practice of two principles in the problem of diplomatic protection in dual nationality cases.

The first of these, specifically referring to the scope of diplomatic protection, as a question of public international law, is based on the sovereign equality of the States in the matter of nationality and bars protection in behalf of those who are simultaneously also nationals of the defendant State.

The second of the principles had its origin in private international law, in those cases, that is, in which the courts of a third State had to resolve a conflict of nationality Laws. Thus, the principle of effective nationality was created with relation to the individual. But decisions and legal writings, because of its evident justice, quickly transported it to the sphere of public international law.

(2). It is not a question of adopting one nationality to the exclusion of the other. Even less when it is recognized by both Parties that the claimant possesses the two nationalities. The problem to be explained is, simply, that of determining whether diplomatic protection can be exercised in such cases.

(3). A prior question requires a solution: are the two principles which have just been set forth incompatible with each other, so that the acceptance of one of them necessarily implies the exclusion of the other? If the reply is in the affirmative, the problem presented is that of a choice; if it is in the negative, one must determine the sphere of application of each one of the two principles.

The Commission is of the opinion that no irreconcilable opposition between the two principles exists; in fact, to the contrary, it believes that they complement each other reciprocally. The principle according to which a State cannot protect one of its nationals against a State which also considers him its national and the principle of effective, in the sense of dominant, nationality, have both been accepted by the Hague Convention (Articles 4 and 5) and by the International Court of Justice (Advisory Opinion of April 11, 1949 and the Nottebohm Decision of April 6, 1955). If these two principles were irreconcilable, the acceptance of both by the Hague Convention and by the International Court of Justice would be incomprehensible.

(4). The International Court of Justice, in its recent decision in the Nottebohm Case, after having said that " * * * international law leaves to each State to lay down the rules governing the grant of its own nationality", adds: "On the other hand, a State cannot claim that the rules it has thus laid down are entitled to recognition by another State unless it has acted in conformity with this general aim of making the legal bond of nationality accord with the individual's genuine connexion with the State which assumes the defence of its citizens by means of protection as against other States." * * * "Conferred by a State, it only entitles that State to exercise protection vis-à-vis another State, if it constitutes a translation into juridical terms of the individual's connexion with the State which has made him its national." (Judgment of April 6, 1955, p. 23.)

For even greater reason, this theory must be understood to be applicable to the problem of dual nationality which concerns the two contesting States, in view of the fact that in such case effective nationality does not mean only the existence of a real bond, but means also the prevalence of that nationality over the other, by virtue of facts which exist in the case.

(5).   The principle, based on the sovereign equality of States, which excludes diplomatic protection in the case of dual nationality, must yield before the principle of effective nationality whenever such nationality is that of the claiming State. But it must not yield when such predominance is not proved because the first of these two principles is generally recognized and may constitute a criterion of practical application for the elimination of any possible uncertainty.

(6).   * * *   In view of the principles accepted, it is considered that the Government of the United States of America shall be entitled to protect its nationals before this Commission in cases of dual nationality, United States and Italian, whenever the United States nationality is the effective nationality.

In order to establish the prevalence of the United States nationality in individual cases, habitual residence can be one of the criteria of evaluation, but not the only one. The conduct of the individual in his economic, social, political, civic and family life, as well as the closer and more effective bond with one of the two States must also be considered.

(7).   It is considered that in this connexion the following principles may serve as guides:

(a) The United States nationality shall be prevalent in cases of children born in the United States of an Italian father and who have habitually lived there.

(b) The United States nationality shall also be prevalent in cases involving Italians who, after having acquired United States nationality by naturalization and having thus lost Italian nationality, have reacquired their nationality of origin as a matter of law as a result of having sojourned in Italy for more than two years, without the intention of retransferring their residence permanently to Italy.

(c) With respect to cases of dual nationality involving American women married to Italian nationals, the United States nationality shall be prevalent in cases in which the family has had habitual residence in the United States and the interests and the permanent professional life of the head of the family were established in the United States.

(d) In case of dissolution of marriage, if the family was established in Italy and the widow transfers her residence to the United States of America, whether or not the new residence is of an habitual nature must be evaluated, case by case, bearing in mind also the widow's conduct, especially with regard to the raising of her children, for the purpose of deciding which is the prevalent nationality.

(8). United States nationals who did not possess Italian nationality but the nationality of a third State can be considered "United Nations nationals" under the Treaty, even if their prevalent nationality was the nationality of the third State.

(9). In all other cases of dual nationality, Italian and United States, when, that is, the United States nationality is not prevalent in accordance with the above, the principle of international law, according to which a claim is not admissible against a State, Italy in our case, when this State also considers the claimant as its national and such bestowal of nationality is, as in the case of Italian law, in harmony (Article 1 of the Hague Convention of 1930) with international custom and generally recognized principles of law in the matter of nationality, will reacquire its force.

VI. DECISION

Examining the facts of the case in bar, in the light of the aforementioned criteria, especially paragraph 6, in relation to paragraph 7 (c), the Commission holds that Mrs. Mergé can in no way be considered to be dominantly a United States national within the meaning of Article 78 of the Treaty of Peace, because the family did not have its habitual residence in the United States and the interests and the permanent professional life of the head of the family were not established there. In fact, Mrs. Mergé has not lived in the United States since her marriage, she used an Italian passport in travelling to Japan from Italy in 1937, she stayed in Japan from 1937 until 1946 with her husband, an official of the Italian Embassy in Tokyo, and it does not appear that she was ever interned as a national of a country enemy to Japan.

Inasmuch as Mrs. Mergé, for the foregoing reasons, cannot be considered to be dominantly a United States national within the meaning of Article 78 of the Treaty of Peace, the Commission is of the opinion that the Government of the United States of America is not entitled to present a claim against the Italian Government in her behalf.

* * *

"*Effective nationality.*" Number (8) of the commission's "Considerations of Law" was further amplified in its 1958 decision in the Flegenheimer Case, Italian-United States Conciliation Commission, XIV Rep. of Int'l Arb.Awards 327. Flegenheimer's claim (for cancellation of a sale of stock made under duress) depended upon his being a United States national. The commission found that he had lost his United States nationality upon acquiring German nationality in 1894 (and that this German nationality had been lost in 1940, so that he became stateless). Therefore, the claim was dismissed.

It had been argued by Italy, however, that because of close ties between Flegenheimer and Germay during the long period from 1894 until 1940 when he was a German national, "Italy therefore considers that no effective bond of nationality exists between the United States and Albert Flegenheimer, even if it were to be admitted that he was an American national on purely legal and nominal grounds." Thus, "the United States is not entitled to exercise, in his behalf, the right of diplomatic protection, nor can they resort to the commission to plead his case." (at 375). The commission's opinion further stated:

> The Commission is of the opinion that it is doubtful that the International Court of Justice intended to establish a rule of general international law in requiring, in the Nottebohm Case, that there must exist an effective link between the person and the State in order that the latter may exercise its right of diplomatic protection in behalf of the former. * * *

* * *

> The theory of effective or active nationality was established, in the Law of Nations, and above all in international private law, for the purpose of settling conflicts between two national States, or two national laws, regarding persons simultaneously vested with both nationalities, in order to decide which of them is to be dominant, whether that described as nominal, based on legal provisions of a given legal system, or that described as effective or active, equally based on legal provisions of another legal system, but confirmed by elements of fact (domicile, participation in the political life, the center of family and business interests, etc.). It must allow one to make a distinction, between two bonds of nationality equally founded in law, which is the stronger and hence the effective one.

* * *

> But when a person is vested with only one nationality, which is attributed to him or her either jure sanguinis or jure soli, or by a valid naturalization entailing the positive loss of the former nationality, the theory of effective nationality cannot be applied without the risk of causing confusion. It lacks a sufficiently positive basis to be applied to a nationality which finds support in a state law. There does not in fact exist any criterion of proven effectiveness for disclosing the effectiveness of a bond with a political collectivity, and the persons by the thousands who, because of the facility of travel in the modern world, possess the positive legal nationality of a State, but live in foreign States where they are domiciled and where their family and business center is located, would be exposed to nonrecognition, at the international level, of the nationality with which they are undeniably vested by virtue of the laws of their national State, if this doctrine were to be generalized. (at 376–377).

SECTION C. OBLIGATIONS OF NATIONALITY
OR ALLEGIANCE

It is not uncommon for a state to apply its law to acts performed by its own nationals beyond the territorial limits of the state. As stated by Mr. Chief Justice Hughes in Blackmer v. United States, 284 U.S. 421, 436, 52 S.Ct. 252, 254 (1932):

While it appears that the petitioner removed his residence to France in the year 1924, it is undisputed that he was, and continued to be, a citizen of the United States. He continued to owe allegiance to the United States. By virtue of the obligations of citizenship, the United States retained its authority over him, and he was bound by its laws made applicable to him in a foreign country. Thus although resident abroad, the petitioner remained subject to the taxing power of the United States. For disobedience to its laws through conduct abroad he was subject to punishment in the courts of the United States * * * With respect to such an exercise of authority, there is no question of international law, but solely of the purport of the municipal law which establishes the duties of the citizen in relation to his own government. * * *

The basis for the rule permitting this reach of a state's law was the subject of speculation by the Mexican Supreme Court in a case involving jurisdiction over an offense committed by a Mexican national in Texas:

It is well known that it is the federal judge who has jurisdiction notwithstanding that it is the principle of territoriality which fundamentally regulates the special application of the penal law in accordance with Article 4 of the Federal Criminal Code, even though this precept, in its first hypothesis—a crime committed abroad by a Mexican national—admits the principle of personal law. This is so because of the respect due * * * to the ties of allegiance which should bind the subject to his State, or because it is not possible to conceive that a State should be transformed into a safe refuge for its own nationals who have committed crimes outside its frontiers, or because the rule of prosecution is merely a just corollary to the nonextradition of nationals, which is the practice of the majority of countries. Re Gutierrez, 24 Int'l L.Rep. 265, 266 (1961).

Should this reach of a state's laws based upon the relationship of the individual with the state be confined to those who have the state's nationality? The question is posed below in connection with laws relating to (1) the crime of treason, (2) taxation and (3) compulsory military service.

1. THE CRIME OF TREASON

JOYCE v. DIRECTOR OF PUBLIC PROSECUTIONS

England, House of Lords, 1946.
[1946] A.C. 347.

Appeal from the Court of Criminal Appeal.

The facts, stated by LORD JOWITT L.C. and LORD PORTER, were as follows: The appellant, William Joyce, was charged at the Central Criminal Court on three counts, upon the third of which only he was convicted. That count was as follows

Statement of offence.

High Treason by adhering to the King's enemies elsewhere than in the King's Realm, to wit, in the German Realm, contrary to the Treason Act, 1351.

Particulars of offence.

William Joyce, on September 18, 1939, and on divers other days thereafter and between that day and July 2, 1940, being then—to wit on the several days—a person owing allegiance to our Lord the King, and whilst on the said several days an open and public war was being prosecuted and carried on by the German Realm and its subjects against our Lord the King and his subjects, then and on the said several days traitorously contriving and intending to aid and assist the said enemies of our Lord the King against our Lord the King and his subjects did traitorously adhere to and aid and comfort the said enemies in parts beyond the seas without the Realm of England to wit, in the Realm of Germany by broadcasting to the subjects of our Lord the King propaganda on behalf of the said enemies of our Lord the King.

* * *

The appellant was born in the United States of America, in 1906, the son of a naturalized American citizen who had previously been a British subject by birth. He thereby became himself a natural born American citizen. At about three years of age he was brought to Ireland, where he stayed until about 1921, when he came to England. He stayed in England until 1939. He was then thirty-three years of age. He was brought up and educated within the King's Dominions, and he settled there. On July 4, 1933, he applied for a British passport, describing himself as a British subject by birth, born in Galway. He asked for the passport for the purpose of holiday touring in Belgium, France, Germany, Switzerland, Italy and Austria. He was granted the passport for a period of five years. The document was not produced, but its contents were duly proved. In it he was

described as a British subject. On September 26, 1938, he applied
for a renewal of the passport for a period of one year. He again
declared that he was a British subject and had not lost that national
status. His application was granted. On August 24, 1939, he again
applied for a renewal of his passport for a further period of one year,
repeating the same declaration. His application was granted, the
passport, as appears from the endorsement on the declaration, being
extended to July 1, 1940. On some day after August 24, 1939, the
appellant left the realm, his parents, his brothers and his sister remaining in England. The exact date and manner of his departure
were not proved. On his arrest in the year 1945 there was found on
his person a "work book" issued by the German State on October 4,
1939, from which it appeared that he had been employed by the German radio company of Berlin as an announcer of English news from
September 18, 1939. In this document his nationality was stated to
be "Great Britain" and his special qualification "English." The
passport was not found and nothing further was known of it. It
was proved by uncontradicted evidence that he had, between September 3, 1939, and December 10, 1939, broadcast propaganda on
behalf of the enemy. He did not give evidence but in a statement
made after his arrest in Germany he said (inter alia): "In 1940 I
acquired German nationality * * * As, by reason of my opinions,
I was not conscientiously disposed to fight for Britain against Germany, I decided to leave the country * * * Realizing, however,
that at this critical juncture I had declined to serve Britain I drew
the logical conclusion that I should have no moral right to return to
that country of my own free will and that it would be best to apply
for German citizenship and make my home in Germany." After argument on the law, TUCKER J. said to counsel for the Crown and for
the appellant: "I shall direct the jury on count 3 that on August 24,
1939, when the passport was applied for, the prisoner beyond a shadow of doubt owed allegiance to the Crown of this country and that
on the evidence given, if they accept it, nothing happened at the material time thereafter to put an end to the allegiance that he then
owed. It will remain for the jury, and for the jury alone, as to
whether or not at the relevant dates he adhered to the King's enemies with intent to assist the King's enemies. If both or either of
you desire to address the jury on that issue, of course now is your
opportunity." Both counsel proceeded to address the jury, the defence submitting that the appellant had not adhered to the King's
enemies and the Crown that he had. No other topic was touched on
and no argument was addressed to the question whether the appellant still had the passport in his possession and retained it for use
or whether he still owed allegiance to the British Crown. TUCKER
J. then summed up and the appellant was found guilty on the third
count of the indictment, and sentenced to death on September 19,
1945. An appeal was brought to the Court of Criminal Appeal on

the following grounds: "(1.) The court wrongly assumed jurisdiction to try an alien for an offence against British law committed in a foreign country. (2.) The learned judge was wrong in law in holding, and misdirected the jury in directing them, that the appellant owed allegiance to His Majesty the King during the period from September 18, 1939, to July 2, 1940. (3.) That there was no evidence that the renewal of the appellant's passport afforded him or was capable of affording him any protection or that the appellant ever availed himself or had any intention of availing himself of any such protection. * * * " On November 7, 1945, the Court of Criminal Appeal dismissed the appeal. The Attorney-General certified under s. 1, sub-s. 6, of the Criminal Appeal Act, 1907, that the decision of the Court of Criminal Appeal involved a point of law of exceptional public importance and that in his opinion it was desirable in the public interest that a further appeal should be brought. The appellant accordingly appealed to the House of Lords.

* * *

December 18, 1945. LORD JOWITT L.C. I have come to the conclusion, in common with the majority of your Lordships, that the appeal should be dismissed. I should propose to deliver my reasons at a later date.

* * *

February 1, 1946. Their Lordships delivered their reasons.

LORD JOWITT, L.C.

* * * [I]t is clear that the question for your Lordships' determination is whether an alien who has been resident within the realm can be held guilty and convicted in this country of high treason in respect of acts committed by him outside the realm. This is in truth a question of law of far-reaching importance. * * *

The House is called upon in the year 1945 to consider the scope and effect of a statute of the year 1351, the twenty-fifth year of the reign of Edward III. That statute, as has been commonly said and as appears from its terms, was itself declaratory of the common law: * * * "Whereas divers opinions have been before this time in what case treason shall be said and in what not; the King, at the request of the Lords and of the Commons hath made a declaration in the manner as hereafter followeth, that is to say:" [amongst other things] "if a man do levy war against our Lord the King in his realm, or be adherent to the King's enemies in his realm, giving them aid and comfort in the realm, or elsewhere" then (I depart from the text and use modern terms) he shall be guilty of treason. It is not denied that the appellant has adhered to the King's enemies giving them aid and comfort elsewhere than in the realm. Upon this part of the case the single question is whether, having done so, he can be and in the circumstances of the case is guilty of treason. Your Lordships will observe that the statute is wide enough in its terms to cover any man anywhere, "if a man do levy war," etc. Yet it is clear that some limitation must be placed upon the generality of the language, for the context in the preamble poses the question "in what case treason shall be said and in what not." It is necessary then to prove not only that an act was done but that, being done, it was a treasonable act. This must depend upon one thing only, namely the relation in which the actor stands to the King to whose enemies he adheres. An act that is in one man treasonable, may not be so in another. In the long discussion which your Lordships have heard upon this part of the case attention has necessarily been concentrated on the question of allegiance. The question whether a man can be guilty of treason to the King has been treated as identical with the question whether he owes allegiance to the King. An act, it is said, which is treasonable if the actor owes allegiance, is not treasonable if he does not. As a generalization, this is undoubtedly true and is supported by the language of the indictment but it leaves undecided the question by whom allegiance is owed * * *

* * * Allegiance is owed to their sovereign Lord the King by his natural born subjects; so it is by those who, being aliens, become his subjects by denization or naturalization (I will call them all "naturalized subjects"); so it is by those who, being aliens, reside within the King's realm. Whether you look to the feudal law for the origin of this conception or find it in the elementary necessities of any political society, it is clear that fundamentally it recognizes the need of the man for protection and of the sovereign lord for service. * * * The natural-born subject owes allegiance from his birth, the naturalized subject from his naturalization, the alien from the day when he comes within the realm. By what means and when can they cast off allegiance? The natural-born subject cannot at common law at any time cast it off. * * * Nor can the naturalized subjects at common law. It is in regard to the alien resident within the realm that the controversy in this case arises. Admittedly he owes allegiance while he is so resident, but it is argued that his allegiance extends no further. Numerous authorities were cited by the learned counsel for the appellant in which it is stated without any qualification or extension that an alien owes allegiance so long as he is within the realm and it has been argued with great force that the physical presence of the alien actor within the realm is necessary to make his act treasonable. It is implicit in this argument that during absence from the realm, however brief, an alien ordinarily resident within the realm cannot commit treason; he cannot in any circumstances by giving aid and comfort to the King's enemies outside the realm be guilty of a treasonable act. My Lords in my opinion this which is the necessary and logical statement of the appellant's case is not only at variance with the principle of the law, but is inconsistent with authority which your Lordships cannot disregard. I refer first to authority. It is said in Foster's Crown

Cases (3rd ed.), p. 183—"Local allegiance is founded in the protection a foreigner enjoyeth for his person, his family or effects, during his residence here; and it ceaseth, whenever he withdraweth with his family and effects." And then on p. 185 comes the statement of law upon which the passage I have cited is clearly founded "Section 4. And if such alien, seeking the protection of the Crown, and having a family and effects here, should during a war with his native country, go thither, and there adhere to the King's enemies for purposes of hostility, he might be dealt with as a traitor. For he came and settled here under the protection of the Crown; and, though his person was removed for a time, his effects and family continued still under the same protection. This rule was laid down by all the judges assembled at the Queen's command January 12, 1707." * * * In my view therefore it is the law that in the case supposed in the resolution of 1707 an alien may be guilty of treason for an act committed outside the realm. The reason which appears in the resolution is illuminating. The principle governing the rule is established by the exception: "though his person was removed for a time, his family and effects continued under the same protection," that is, the protection of the Crown. The vicarious protection still afforded to the family, which he had left behind in this country required of him a continuance of his fidelity. It is thus not true to say that an alien can never in law be guilty of treason to the sovereign of this realm in respect of an act committed outside the realm. My Lords, here no question arises of a vicarious protection. There is no evidence that the appellant left a family or effects behind him when he left this realm. I do not for this purpose regard parents or brother or sisters as a family. But though there was no continuing protection for his family or effects, of him too it must be asked, whether there was not such protection still afforded by the sovereign as to require of him the continuance of his allegiance. * * *

* * * The material facts are these, that being for long resident here and owing allegiance he applied for and obtained a passport and, leaving the realm, adhered to the King's enemies. It does not matter that he made false representations as to his status, asserting that he was a British subject by birth, a statement that he was afterwards at pains to disprove. It may be that when he first made the statement, he thought it was true. Of this there is no evidence. The essential fact is that he got the passport and I now examine its effect. The actual passport issued to the appellant has not been produced, but its contents have been duly proved. The terms of a passport are familiar. It is thus described by Lord Alverstone C. J., in R. v. Brailsford: "It is a document issued in the name of the sovereign on the responsibility of a minister of the Crown to a named individual, intended to be presented to the governments of foreign nations and to be used for that individual's protection as a British subject in foreign countries." By its terms it requests and requires

in the name of His Majesty all those whom it may concern to allow the bearer to pass freely without let or hindrance and to afford him every assistance and protection of which he may stand in need. It is, I think, true that the possession of a passport by a British subject does not increase the sovereign's duty of protection, though it will make his path easier. For him it serves as a voucher and means of identification. But the possession of a passport by one who is not a British subject gives him rights and imposes upon the sovereign obligations which would otherwise not be given or imposed. It is immaterial that he has obtained it by misrepresentation and that he is not in law a British subject. By the possession of that document he is enabled to obtain in a foreign country the protection extended to British subjects. By his own act he has maintained the bond which while he was within the realm bound him to his sovereign. The question is not whether he obtained British citizenship by obtaining the passport, but whether by its receipt he extended his duty of allegiance beyond the moment when he left the shores of this country. As one owing allegiance to the King he sought and obtained the protection of the King for himself while abroad.

* * * What is this protection upon which the claim to fidelity is founded? To me, my Lords, it appears that the Crown in issuing a passport is assuming an onerous burden, and the holder of the passport is acquiring substantial privileges. * * * Armed with that document the holder may demand from the State's representatives abroad and from the officials of foreign governments that he be treated as a British subject, and even in the territory of a hostile state may claim the intervention of the protecting power. * * * In these circumstances I am clearly of opinion that so long as he holds the passport he is within the meaning of the statute a man who, if he is adherent to the King's enemies in the realm or elsewhere commits an act of treason. There is one other aspect of this part of the case with which I must deal. It is said that there is nothing to prevent an alien from withdrawing from his allegiance when he leaves the realm. I do not dissent from this as a general proposition. It is possible that he may do so even though he has obtained a passport. But that is a hypothetical case. Here there was no suggestion that the appellant had surrendered his passport or taken any other overt step to withdraw from his allegiance, unless indeed reliance is placed on the act of treason itself as a withdrawal. That in my opinion he cannot do. For such an act is not inconsistent with his still availing himself of the passport in other countries than Germany and possibly even in Germany itself. * * *

The second point of appeal * * * was that in any case no English court has jurisdiction to try an alien for a crime committed abroad and your Lordships heard an exhaustive argument upon the construction of penal statutes. There is, I think, a short answer to this point. The statute in question deals with the crime of treason committed within or * * * without the realm: it is general in its terms and I see no reason for limiting its scope except in the way that I indicated earlier in this opinion, viz.: that, since it is declaratory of the crime of treason, it can apply only to those who are capable of committing that crime. No principle of comity demands that a state should ignore the crime of treason committed against it outside its territory. On the contrary a proper regard for its own security requires that all those who commit that crime, whether they commit it within or without the realm should be amenable to its laws.

    * * *

Finally * * * it was urged on behalf of the appellant that there was no evidence that the renewal of his passport afforded him or was capable of affording him any protection or that he ever availed himself or had any intention of availing himself of any such protection, * * * The document speaks for itself. It was capable of affording the appellant protection. He applied for it and obtained it, and it was available for his use. * * *

    * * *

[Other opinions omitted.]

REX v. NEUMANN

South Africa, Special Criminal Court of Transvaal, 1946.
[1949] 3 So.African L.Rep. 1238, 1263.

[Neumann was indicted for high treason; he was charged with having enlisted and served in the military forces of Germany and with questioning members of the military forces of South Africa and its allies to obtain secret information for Germany. All the alleged acts took place outside the territory of South Africa while that state was at war with Germany. Although it was admitted by the Crown that the defendant was a German by birth and not naturalized in South Africa, the court declined to dismiss the indictment. After the Crown's evidence was heard, the court rejected the defendant's application for discharge (thus requiring the defendant to proceed with his defense). Portions of the court's opinion on the defendant's application appear below:]

    * * * Some years before the outbreak of the present war the accused, a German national by birth, assumed permanent residence in the Cape Peninsula, and became domiciled in the Union. He married a Union national and established a home for her and their children in the vicinity of Cape Town. At one stage he had a business there, which for financial reasons he abandoned shortly before war broke out. He contemplated becoming naturalised and took certain steps in this direction, which were however not carried to completion. In 1940 he enlisted in the armed forces of the Union and in

connection therewith took a certain oath to which reference in greater detail will be made later. He proceeded out of the Union as a member of such armed forces, firstly to Abyssinia and thereafter to Cyrenaica. He allotted portion of his military pay to his wife, to whom it was in due course paid. He was a member of such forces when captured by the German Forces. On various occasions even after capture he expressed his fixed intention to return to the Union. Shortly after his capture he was seen wearing an alleged German uniform. There is evidence that he was then interrogating Union and Allied prisoners of war. Later he served, with distinction, in a German military unit operating in Italy.

* * *

The present is, of course, a case of a conflict between two allegiances: on the one hand there is the accused's allegiance to the state of which he is a born subject. Of this allegiance he has never formally divested himself by the acquisition of citizenship by naturalisation. On the other hand there is the qualified, the less extensive, allegiance which was created by his having come to settle in the Union and having become a Union soldier.

It seems to be beyond question, from the authorities quoted to us, that not only in the law of England but also in the Roman-Dutch law an alien resident in a sovereign state foreign to him owes a qualified allegiance to that state, even when that state and his own are at war with one another. * * *

Without doubt, then, allegiance is required of a resident alien while he himself is physically present in this country. Such allegiance does not, in my view, immediately terminate as soon as he departs from the country. * * * The leaving of his family behind may per se involve a continuation, in respect of the family and for his benefit, of the protection until then enjoyed by him for himself and his family. It seems to me that where it is clear that his departure is of a purely temporary character, accompanied by a definite intention to return for permanent residence, the protection previously acquired does not cease on departure. Any uncertainty on this point, however, appears to disappear when his departure is permitted or facilitated by some positive act on his part, as in Joyce's case * * * whereby he secures the extension, beyond the territorial limits of the country of residence, of the protection which he enjoyed in that country, and in return for which he incurred the *subjectio* referred to. If on principle (which I think is the case) it is the *protectio* which creates the obligation of allegiance, this Court should, in my opinion, follow the principle to be found in Joyce's case and hold that when the accused left the country temporarily in consequence of his enlistment as a soldier in the Union Forces, his existing allegiance continued precisely in the same way as if he had left the country after securing a Union passport.

When the accused enlisted in the Union Forces he stated clearly in his attestation form that he was a German subject and the military authorities accepted him as a soldier of this State with full knowledge of the allegiance he bore to Germany. There is the additional fact that * * * it must have been realised (had the matter ever received specific consideration) that on the general principles of international law even naturalisation as a Union national during the existence of hostilities between the Union and the German Reich would in all probability not have been recognised by the German authorities.

On the other hand, the accused undertook certain obligations. On reference to the form of oath it will be seen that the first matter he swore to was to be faithful and bear true allegiance to His Majesty King George VI, his heirs and successors, according to law (meaning thereby in our view to be faithful and bear allegiance to the State of the Union of South Africa). In the next place he agreed to perform, to the best of his ability, the duties assigned to him as a volunteer member of the Union Defence Forces; he thirdly agreed that in accordance with the resolution of Parliament he would serve in the voluntary full-time Active Citizen Force in Africa, whether within or outside of the limits of South Africa, for the duration of the war; and, finally, agreed to subject himself in so serving to the provisions of the South Africa Defence Act, as amended, and to the regulations in force from time to time and the Military Discipline Code. * * *

The Attorney-General has submitted that the effect of the above oath, read in conjunction with the War Regulations permitting service outside the Union, and the raising of a foreign legion, was entirely to override the accused's natural allegiance to the Reich and to place him in exactly the same position as a Union national. I cannot agree that this is the correct position. * * * The oath taken by the accused was not contended by the Attorney-General to involve the creation of a new allegiance. At most it amounted to a reaffirmation, possibly an extension, of an existing allegiance. I am, therefore, not prepared to go as far as the Crown here contends, and to treat the accused in all matters of allegiance on an equality with a Union citizen by birth or naturalisation. But at the same time I am of opinion that the allegiance in question did not terminate, ipso facto, on the accused's capture * * * Leaving aside the problem presented by a case of voluntary desertion from the Union ranks, followed by enlistment in the German forces, it seems to be an impossible situation that the very moment after his capture the accused could with impunity have seized a rifle and opened fire on his previous comrades in arms, the members of the Union forces. * * *

It seems to me that the only way to reconcile these two allegiances is to hold that even after capture by the German forces the accused was obliged to do nothing *voluntarily* to impair the safety of the Union or participate in any attack on the Union. If, while in German hands, he remained passive, he would not be committing a breach of his allegiance to the state of his birth, nor, obviously, to the Union of South Africa. But if without any compulsion from the German authorities, civil or military, he voluntarily (whether out of a sense of duty or not) embarked upon any course of action which, had he been a Union national, would have constituted an act or acts of high treason, then in my view he has deliberately failed to observe the *subjectio* which he incurred when on leaving South Africa he secured an extension of the *protectio* afforded to him. And if so he has, in my view, committed treason against the Union. If, on the other hand, all he has done is the result of enforcement by the German authorities of their claims against him as a natural-born citizen of the Reich, it seems that no complaint can fairly be made by the State of the Union of South Africa, which had full knowledge of his paramount allegiance when it accepted him as a Union soldier.

In the result, therefore, the question still to be ascertained is whether such otherwise treasonable acts as the accused performed after capture were performed voluntarily or under compulsion from the German authorities. I am not prepared to assume they were performed under compulsion. That question will have to be determined when the defence evidence has been heard. Until then there is a case for the accused to meet, and the application for discharge must be refused. * * *

2. TAXATION

As noted in Chapter 7, p. 459, international law has recognized a number of bases for the imposition of taxes. Here as elsewhere it is essential to distinguish between a state's jurisdiction to prescribe a rule imposing a tax and its jurisdiction to enforce such a rule. The practical difficulties of enforcing taxes upon persons not physically within its territory and not owning property within its territory realistically limit the voraciousness of the tax collecting state. International controversy as to jurisdiction to tax has been relatively infrequent. Consequently the only evidence of the international law on the subject is state practice.

The territorial base supports state taxation measured by property located and income produced within the state. States impose such taxes on the individuals owning such property, or producing or claiming such income, even though the individuals do not have a personal relationship with the taxing state such as that of nationality. At the other extreme, states impose taxes upon their own nationals, even though the nationals are physically located outside the state and their property is located and income produced outside the state.

Will international law permit taxation measured by property located outside the state or income produced outside the state when the individual to be taxed is not its national? The United States, for example, imposes income tax upon aliens who are resident within the United States. "Resident aliens are, in general, taxable the same as citizens of the United States; that is, a resident alien is taxable on income derived from all sources, including sources without the United States." 26 C.F.R. Part 1, § 1.871–1. Residence is defined in the regulations as follows:

> An alien actually present in the United States who is not a mere transient or sojourner is a resident of the United States for purposes of the income tax. Whether he is a transient is determined by his intentions with regard to the length and nature of his stay. A mere floating intention, indefinite as to time, to return to another country is not sufficient to constitute him a transient. If he lives in the United States and has no definite intention as to his stay, he is a resident. One who comes to the United States for a definite purpose which in its nature may be promptly accomplished is a transient; but, if his purpose is of such a nature that an extended stay may be necessary for its accomplishment, and to that end the alien makes his home temporarily in the United States, he becomes a resident, though it may be his intention at all times to return to his domicile abroad when the purpose for which he came has been consummated or abandoned. An alien whose stay in the United States is limited to a definite period by the immigration laws is not a resident of the United States within the meaning of this section, in the absence of exceptional circumstances. 26 C.F.R. Part 1, § 1.871–2(b).

Consider the following more general definition of "residence":

> It appears that most governments consider that an alien who remains in its territory for a certain period of time, six months or more, is resident in such territory for purposes of income taxation. Asst. Sec. of State Macomber to U. S. Senator Carl Hayden, letter quoted in 8 Whiteman, Digest of International Law 536 (1967).

If, then, nationality is not a necessary prerequisite to taxability, is there some minimum personal connection that must exist before a state can lawfully prescribe a tax based on events that occur outside the state? What should that connection be? Could a state lawfully tax a "mere transient or sojourner"? What would be a lawful measure of such a tax? "On the one hand it is agreed that a State cannot tax a transient on the whole of his year's income as if he were a resident, but on the other it is equally agreed that his presence may render him subject to poll tax, and sojourn tax, which, indeed, could be of an equivalent amount." 2 O'Connell, International Law 717 (2d ed. 1970).

3. COMPULSORY MILITARY SERVICE

UNITED STATES v. RUMSA

United States Court of Appeals, Seventh Circuit, 1954.
212 F.2d 927.a

SWAIM, CIRCUIT JUDGE. This opinion disposes of two appeals
by Antanas Juratis Rumsa, the first being an appeal in a criminal
case and the second being an appeal from the order and judgment of
the District Court dismissing Rumsa's amended complaint in an action to enjoin the defendants from inducting and causing him to be
inducted and for a declaratory judgment.

*   *   *

We shall first consider the appeal of Rumsa from the judgment
of the District Court entered on a verdict of guilty on an indictment
which charged him with refusing to submit to induction into the
armed forces of the United States in violation of Section 462, Title 50
Appendix, United States Code Annotated, and the prescribed rules
and regulations thereunder.

The defendant was born in Lithuania on October 9, 1929, and
resided there until sometime in 1944 when the Russians invaded that
country and the defendant was forced to flee to Western Germany.
In Germany he was placed in a labor camp and kept there until he was
finally liberated by the American forces. On February 27, 1950, the
defendant executed a printed form of Application for Immigration
Visa and Alien Registration. This form stated that the defendant's
purpose in going to the United States was "to reside" and that he
intended "to remain permanently." This form also indicated that the
defendant had had five years in elementary school and eight years in
secondary school and that he was able to speak, read and write Lithuanian and a little English and German. The American Vice Consul
approved this application and granted the immigration visa to the
defendant as a displaced person pursuant to Public Law 774, 50 U.S.
C.A.Appendix, § 1951 et seq. Pursuant to the authority granted by
the United States on this application, the defendant was admitted
to, and did, enter the United States on April 6, 1950, coming to Chicago, Illinois, to live. On August 12, 1950, he registered under the
Selective Service Act with Local Board No. 65, located at 63rd Street
and Western Avenue in Chicago. A little more than a month later,
September 15, 1950, the defendant filled out a Selective Service Ques-
tionnaire and on October 9, 1950, he was classified I–A (ready for
service). On January 11, 1951, the defendant was ordered by the
local board to report for physical examination on January 29, 1951.

*   *   *

a. Cert. denied 348 U.S. 838, 75 S.Ct. 36 (1954).

The defendant seems to contend that, since he is an alien, he cannot be required to submit to induction into the armed forces of the United States; that requiring him to be inducted violates international law and also violates the Fifth Amendment to our Constitution; that, further, as a temporary resident alien, he had the right to be deferred from military service by waiving the right ever to become an American citizen; that by his executing and filing Form 130, he did waive his right to ever become an American citizen; and that he thereby acquired the right to be permanently classified as IV–C, a right to exemption which could not thereafter be taken away from him even by a change in the law by Congress.

It is true that the Selective Training and Service Act which was in effect when Rumsa came to this country and when he first registered did provide that any citizen or subject of a neutral country should be relieved from liability for training and service if, prior to his induction, he had made application (Form 130) to be relieved of such liability. But in 1951 the Congress, alarmed by the international situation, determined that the safety of this nation required that more men be inducted for training and service. See legislative history of Universal Military Training Act in U. S. Code Congressional and Administrative Service for 1951, Volume 2, pages 1472–1521. On page 1512 of this history, in the Conference Report, we find the recommendation that the law should be so changed that "All aliens admitted for permanent residence in the United States shall be immediately liable for induction into the Armed Forces or the National Security Training Corps under the same conditions applicable to citizens. * * * "

There can be no question but that the Universal Military Training and Service Act as amended authorized the selection and induction of aliens who had been admitted to the United States for permanent residence. Section 454(a) of 50 U.S.C.Appendix, § 4(a) of the Universal Military Training and Service Act, as amended June 19, 1951, expressly provided: "Except as otherwise provided in this title * * * every male alien *admitted for permanent residence* * * * shall be liable for training and service in the Armed Forces of the United States * * *." And Section 456 of 50 U.S.C.Appendix, which gave to the President broad powers to exempt various classes of aliens, expressly provided: " * * * except that *aliens admitted for permanent residence* in the United States shall not be so exempted." (Our emphasis.) This Act also provided, 50 U.S.C.Appendix, § 467(a): "Except as provided in this title all laws or any parts of laws in conflict with the provisions of this title are repealed." Such clear language leaves no ambiguity for interpretation. We may only apply such a law as it is written.

* * *

It necessarily remained within the province and was the duty of Congress to be constantly alert to impending danger, to appraise such danger, and to raise and support armies of a sufficient number of men to be able to meet the danger successfully. Signs of increasing danger in 1951 were apparent to all. This naturally called for increased numbers in the armed services. The increased numbers could be secured only by enlarging the field from which to draw. This was accomplished by certain amendments which, among other things, reduced the age at which men were eligible, reduced the physical and mental standards required for induction *and made all aliens admitted for permanent residence in the United States immediately available for induction.* No classification of any individual could be considered permanent as against changes in the law, changes in the circumstances of the individual on which the classification was made or changes in valid regulations promulgated under the changed law. To hold that a classification, once made, was binding on the Government regardless of changing conditions and amended laws to meet such changing conditions might, in effect, destroy the power of Congress to raise and support armies.

The defendant had come to the United States from Germany in 1950 with his father and mother. On August 12, 1950, he registered for Selective Service, giving the family address in Chicago as his residence. At that time he had already secured work with the National Video Corporation, and a short time later he enrolled in the Chicago Navy Pier Branch of the University of Illinois. He was a national of Lithuania and, since the Russians had taken over that country and had set up a puppet government, it was uncertain when, if ever, he might be able to return to his native land.

* * *

The conscription law which the defendant violated by refusing to submit to induction does not say that aliens who have come here intending to stay permanently shall be subject to military service; instead it says that those who are qualified for and who are *admitted* for permanent residence are to be inducted. The emphasis is therefore on the intention of the officials who approve the Application for Immigration Visa and those who consent to the alien's admission into the United States, not necessarily on the intention of the alien. With an application for a visa such as we have here before the officials whose duty it was to decide as to his admission, there cannot be much doubt but that Rumsa was *admitted* to the United States for permanent residence regardless of what his secret intention may actually have been.

When we consider this record as a whole, including the conflicting and patently untrue statements in the defendant's letters frantically urging that he be excused from military service, we have no hesitation in saying that there was a factual basis for the action of the local board in finding that he was admitted to the United States for permanent residence, and that he was, therefore, properly classified in January 1952 as I–A. Under the rule of the Cox and Estep decisions of the Supreme Court the District Court properly decided this and then left to the jury only the question of whether the defendant had "wilfully and knowingly failed, neglected or refused to submit to induction as ordered by his local board," a question which the jury decided against the defendant. The burden was on the defendant to establish facts before the local board which showed his right to exemption from military service. * * *

Counsel for the defendant have earnestly argued to us that the conscription of aliens is extremely bad policy on the part of the United States; that prior to the enactment of the Universal Military Training and Service Act the United States and most other nations had consistently refused to draft aliens; that the new policy which Congress adopted in 1951, if followed, will in effect invite other nations to force our nationals who may be residing in those countries to submit to service in their armies; and that, therefore, none of our nationals residing abroad will be safe from conscription by those countries or from the many dangers which service in foreign armies entail.

Even if all this be true there is nothing the courts can do about it. The question of whether or not aliens should be conscripted is a question of policy—a political question which is for the executive and legislative branches of the Government to solve. Such questions are entirely outside the realm of the judicial branch. * * *

The grant of power to Congress to raise and support armies is certainly sufficient to authorize the adoption of the present policy to conscript aliens. It is, of course, also within the power of Congress to change the conscription law to again excuse aliens from service in our armed forces at any time Congress determines that the services of aliens are either unnecessary or should not as a matter of policy be required. And as to this defendant and other aliens who have been convicted of violations of the present draft law, a pardon is always within the power of the President. Neither of these courses is open to the judiciary.

Finding no error, the judgment of the District Court is affirmed.

----

1. *United States legislation on the drafting of aliens.* During World War I, citizens and "male persons not alien enemies who have declared their intention to become citizens" were subject to the draft. Act of May 18, 1917, ch. 15, § 2, 40 Stat. 76.

The Selective Training and Service Act of 1940, ch. 720, § 3(a), 54 Stat. 885, contained similar provisions until amended in 1941, ch. 602, § 2, 55 Stat. 844. This World War II amendment made liable for training and service every male citizen and every other male person "residing in the United States," with the proviso that a citizen or subject of a neutral country could apply for and be granted relief, "but any person who makes such application shall thereafter be debarred from becoming a citizen of the United States." The phrase "residing in the United States" was held in McGrath v. Kristensen, 340 U.S. 162 (1950), not to include a Danish citizen who entered the United States on August 17, 1939 as a temporary visitor for sixty days (to attend the New York World's Fair and visit relatives) and was prevented from returning to Denmark by the outbreak of World War II in September of that year.

The Selective Service Act of 1948, ch. 625, § 4(a), 62 Stat. 604, broadened the category of resident aliens able to apply for relief to include "any citizen of a foreign country," retaining the provision for debarring such an applicant from citizenship.

The dramatic change in policy in the 1951 Universal Military Training and Service Act, ch. 144, § 1(d), 65 Stat. 75, as pointed out in the Rumsa case, was to apply the draft even-handedly to United States citizens and aliens admitted for permanent residence, with no provisions for relief. Non-resident aliens were also subject to the draft, but only if they had remained in the United States for a period exceeding one year; the provisions for application for relief (and debarring from citizenship) were retained as to those non-resident aliens. (In addition, the Act provided for "exemption of certain non-immigrant aliens holding diplomatic positions and of other non-immigrant aliens as determined by the President.) Thus, non-resident aliens might remain in the United States for up to one year without being subject to the draft; selected groups of non-resident aliens might remain for longer periods under exemptions provided by law and regulations. For the text of the relevant statutes referred to above in this note, see 8 Whiteman, Digest of International Law 549 (1967).

By amendments in 1971, which changed the title of the draft statute to "Military Selective Service Act," a wider exclusion of aliens from the draft was provided for. The draft now applies to every male citizen and "every other male person residing in the United States" but not to any alien lawfully admitted as a "nonimmigrant" as defined in a long list of categories in the Immigration and Nationality Act. 8 U.S.C. § 1101(a)(15). In addition, induction of an alien who is draftable is not to take place until "such alien shall have resided in the United States for one year." Thus the statute applies to aliens admitted for permanent residence, who can be drafted only after a year's residence. There is no authorization for drafting any other class of aliens and no provision for application for relief or debarring from citizenship. 85 Stat. 348. Notwithstanding these changes in the draft statute, the Immigration and Nationality Act continues to provide in Title 18 of the United States Code, Section 1426(a): " * * * [A]ny alien who applies or has applied for exemption or discharge from training or service in the Armed Forces * * * on the ground that he is an alien, and is or was relieved or discharged from such training * * * on such ground, shall be permanently ineligible to become a citizen of the United States." Is this provision still viable? In McGrath v. Kristensen, 340 U.S. 162, 71 S.Ct. 224 (1950), in which the court was interpreting the provisions of the Selective Training and Service Act of 1940 debarring aliens from citizenship, the court stated: "As there was no 'liability' for service, his act in applying for relief from a non-existent duty could not create the bar against naturalization. By the terms of the statute, that bar only comes into existence when an alien resident liable for service asks to be relieved." (at 172).

2. *International law on the drafting of aliens.* " * * * On the other hand, an alien does not fall under the personal supremacy of the local State; therefore he cannot, unless his own state consents, be made to serve in its army or navy, and cannot, like a citizen, be treated according to discretion." I Oppenheim, International Law 681 (Lauterpacht, 8th ed. 1955). Is this the law today? If a state should require military service of all persons *present* in its territory, whether resident or not and without regard to the length of time that person was present, would that state be in violation of international law? Does the state lack *jurisdiction* to prescribe a rule of law requiring military service of such a person in fact physically present in the state? If there is no lack of jurisdiction, for what reason is the state precluded from exercising that jurisdiction? Is the alien who is only temporarily within the state entitled to something akin to "immunity" ? Can such an "immunity" be grounded on the customary behavior of states; on the expectations of aliens who are temporarily sojourning in host states?

3. *French point of view on the drafting of aliens.* In Chronique des Faits Internationaux, 71 Revue Générale de Droit International Public 143, 174 (1967), Rousseau comments on the Australian legislation of August 10, 1966. It subjected immigrant aliens to compulsory military service and hence some of them to duty in South Vietnam. Greece and Italy formally protested the legislation and Rousseau comments: "The most surprising aspect of the situation is that only two governments seem to have protested an act which constitutes a clear violation of the traditional status of aliens." (at 179).

He qualifies the French practice of declining even voluntary military service by aliens in time of peace as "perhaps [showing] an excessive respect for foreign sovereignty." He then discusses an exception to the practice, i. e., voluntary service in the French Foreign Legion and the difficulties to which this voluntary service had given rise between France and other states, notably Belgium, Germany and Switzerland. He reviews in particular a serious diplomatic dispute with Switzerland in 1959, concerning the service in the Foreign Legion of Swiss citizens who falsified documents to make it appear they were 21 years of age at the time they enlisted, but were in fact still below that age. Once they enlisted, the Foreign Legion refused to release them.

In time of war, Rousseau points out, the French practice is to permit voluntary military service by aliens and to subject them to compulsory service in the labor force. He then states that "Anglo-Saxon states" have a different point of view in the matter of drafting aliens and reviews critically the dispute between France and the United States with respect to the drafting of French citizens in the American forces under the service Act of 1951, the drafting of aliens by the United Kingdom during World War II, and an Australian decision of 1945 upholding the domestic validity of World War II legislation for the drafting of aliens while recognizing it was in violation of international law.

The Australian decision to which Rousseau refers is Polites v. The Commonwealth, and Kandiliotes v. The Commonwealth, High Court of Australia, 1945, [1943–1945] Ann.Dig. 208 (No. 61).

4. *Military service of Swiss nationals in the United States.* The report of the Federal Council of Switzerland for the year 1965 discusses the dispute between Switzerland and the United States concerning the drafting of Swiss nationals in the United States forces. It points out that a treaty of 1850 exempts the nationals of each from service in the forces of the other. Swiss nationals continue to be called for service in the United States, the report points out, but upon request by the Swiss Ambassador, they are issued a deferment and hence do not actually serve. The report concludes that, even though the practical solution is satisfactory, the issue of principle needs to be resolved as soon as possible. XXIII Annuaire Suisse de Droit International 1966, at 88 (1967).

TELLECH (UNITED STATES) v. AUSTRIA AND HUNGARY

Tripartite Claims Commission, 1928.
VI U.N.Rep. Int'l Arb.Awards 248.

This claim is put forward by the United States on behalf of Alexander Tellech for compensation for time lost and for alleged suffering and privation to which he was subjected, first through internment in Austria, and then through enforced military service in the Austro-Hungarian army. The claimant was born in the United States of Austrian parents on May 14, 1895. Under the Constitution and laws of the United States he was by birth an American national. Under the laws of Austria he also possessed Austrian nationality by parentage. This created a conflict in citizenship, frequently described as "dual nationality". When the claimant was five years of age he accompanied his parents to Austria, where he continued to reside.

In August, 1914, the claimant, while residing in Austria a short distance from the Russian border, was subjected to preventive arrest as an agitator engaged in propaganda in favor of Russia. After investigation he was interned and confined in internment camps for 16 months. He then took the oath of allegiance to the Emperor of Austria and King of Hungary and was impressed into service in the Austro-Hungarian army. A decision of the sharply controverted claim that this oath was taken under duress and that he protested that he was an American citizen is not necessary to a disposition of this case. It appears that in 1915 and later representatives of the Government of the United States in Austria interested themselves in securing his release, but the application was denied.

In July, 1916, the claimant deserted from the Austro-Hungarian army and escaped into Russia, where he was arrested and held by the Russian army authorities as a prisoner of war until the outbreak of the Kerensky revolution, when he was released and thereupon returned to Prague, where he still lives and where he is practicing medicine.

The action taken by the Austrian civil authorities in the exercise of their police powers and by the Austro-Hungarian military authorities, of which complaint is made, was taken in Austria, where claimant was voluntarily residing, against claimant as an Austrian citizen. Citizenship is determined by rules prescribed by municipal law. Under the law of Austria, to which claimant had voluntarily subjected himself, he was an Austrian citizen. The Austrian and the Austro-Hungarian authorities were well within their rights in dealing with him as such. Possessing as he did dual nationality, he voluntarily took the risk incident to residing in Austrian territory and subjecting himself to the duties and obligations of an Austrian citizen arising under the municipal laws of Austria.

Assuming that the claimant suffered the loss and injury alleged and had not lost his American citizenship by taking the Austrian Army oath, the Commissioner finds no provision of the Treaty of Vienna or of Budapest obligating Austria and/or Hungary to make compensation therefor.

Wherefore the Commission decrees that under the Treaty of Vienna and the Treaty of Budapest the Government of Austria and the Government of Hungary are not obligated to pay to the Government of the United States any amount on behalf of the claimant herein.

---

1. *Authoritativeness of the Tellech decision.* The decision was rendered by a commissioner appointed under an agreement between the United States and Austria and Hungary to determine amounts to be paid by the latter two states under Treaties of Vienna and Budapest previously entered into with the United States in 1921. In Adminis-

trative Decision No. 1, VI U.N.Rep.Int'l Arb.Awards 203, 207, the commissioner stated:

> The liability of Austria and/or Hungary must be determined by the application of the terms of the Treaty or Treaties to the facts of each case. The Treaties embody in their terms contracts by which Austria and Hungary accorded to the United States, as one of the conditions of peace, rights in behalf of American nationals which had no prior existence. While these doubtless include some obligations of Austria and/or Hungary arising from violation of rules of international law or otherwise and existing prior to and independent of the Treaties, they also include obligations of Austria and/or Hungary which were created and fixed by their terms. All of these obligations, whatever their nature, are merged in and fixed by the Treaties. The Commission's inquiry in this respect is confined solely to determining whether or not Austria and/or Hungary by the terms of the Treaty or Treaties assumed the pecuniary obligation asserted or accepted responsibility for the act causing the damage claimed, and it is not concerned with the quality of that act or whether it was legal or illegal as measured by rules of international law.

Does the opinion in the Tellech case embody any conclusions of significance to international law?

2. *Military service by the dual national.* If mere presence of the individual in the territory of a state is not sufficient to support the state's requiring him to perform military service, is the fact of nationality sufficient? The issue will not arise unless a state which claims that a person is its national complains to the drafting state and the latter defends its action on the ground that the individual was (also) its national.

In re M. M. and X. M.

Greece, Conseil d'Etat, 1934 (No. 2).
[1933–1934] Ann.Dig. 295 (No. 117).

THE FACTS. The petitioners were born in England of a Greek father, in 1895 and 1898 respectively. By the Greek Law of Nationality (of October 9, 1856, amended by Law 120 of 1914) children of a Greek father, wheresoever they may be born, are Greek. Greek nationality is lost (i) by naturalisation with the consent of the Greek Government, (ii) in certain circumstances, by entering foreign public service, and (iii) by leaving Greek territory with no intention of returning. The petitioners contended (I) that they were British subjects, having opted for British nationality by declarations made at the British Consulate at Patras and by entering themselves as British subjects on the British census of 1915; that they had voted at an election in England; and that they had travelled with British passports.

They contended (II) that they had not registered as Greek nationals with the Greek Consulate in London, had no Greek domicile, and had not done their military service in Greece.

Held: that they were nevertheless Greek subjects. They had in fact two nationalities. The facts recited under (I) above were matters entirely for British law, which was irrelevant in this case. The facts recited under (II) were not sufficient to effect loss of Greek nationality. The provisions of Greek law for the loss of nationality were precise and were to be construed restrictively. Mere acquisition of a foreign nationality without the consent of the Greek Government did not entail loss of Greek nationality (although this was so before the passing of the Law of 1914).

[handwritten marginal note: mere acquisition of one or another nationality does not automatically entail loss]

———

1. *Problem.* Although the foregoing case of M. M. and X. M. did not involve the question of Greece's right to draft those individuals, consider in the light of the Greek law of nationality expressed in the opinion the following problem:

> Client's son was born in the United States. Client is a wealthy Greek alien resident of the U. S. The son went AWOL from the United States Army in Germany and began hitchhiking through Europe. In Greece he was picked up while visiting relatives in a remote village and inducted into the Greek army.

> Client wants you to do all you can, vis-a-vis the Department of State, the Greek Embassy, and if necessary vis-a-vis the authorities in Greece, to get the son released from Greek military service. The son is presently serving a military prison sentence for insubordination, at hard labor along the Corinth Canal. The client says he would rather take chances on the AWOL charge (U. S.) than to leave his boy in the Greek military prison.

Does the state with whom an individual has a more effective link have a claim *on the merits* against the drafting state?

2. *The law in treaties.* The United States is a party to a Protocol Relating to Military Obligations in Certain Cases of Double Nationality which was concluded at the Hague April 12, 1930 and entered into force for the United States May 25, 1937. 50 Stat. 1317. Only 23 states were parties to this international agreement as of January 1, 1972. Article 1 provided: "A person possessing two or more nationalities who habitually resides in one of the countries whose nationality he possesses, and who is in fact most closely connected with that country, shall be exempt from all military obligations in

the other country or countries. This exemption may involve the loss of the nationality of the other country or countries."

For bilateral agreements to which the United States is a party, dealing not only with the drafting of dual nationals but also with the drafting of aliens, see 8 Whiteman, Digest of International Law 561–573 (1967).

The Convention on the Reduction of Cases of Plurality of Nationalities and on Military Obligations in Cases of Plurality of Nationalities of May 6, 1963, was prepared by the Council of Europe. The provisions in Chapter 11 of the convention are designed to insure that a person having two or more nationalities shall discharge his military obligations only once and be dispensed from serving them again in other states parties to the convention. Documents, 95 Journal du Droit International 760, 781 (1968).

Chapter 9

THE GROWTH OF STATE RESPONSIBILITY TO INDIVIDUALS

The catalog of abuses to which men have subjected their fellow-men is one of unrelieved horror. Abuses range from murder through physical torture to the slaughter of religious and racial masses. They include human slavery, forced labor and deprivations of liberty of movement from one place or one state to another. Freedom to speak, to practice one's religion, to select one's own occupation, to marry whom one pleases have been repressed. Arbitrary arrest, imprisonment without trial, unfair trials and degrading punishments have been common ingredients of life. This has been true throughout history. And, what is worse, still is.

All of these abuses to the human personality, to what has been called in recent years "human dignity," are committed by men upon men. Some, such as murder, are often matters of private endeavor. Others are perpetrated by men in some capacity as a part of the organizations of state. Protections against these abuses are frequently afforded by the internal laws of the state. Domestic laws are designed not only to deter private individuals from harming their fellows but also, as in the case of the United States Constitution, to protect the individual from abuses rendered by the state. But suppose the machinery of domestic law fails to operate to protect the individual, either in the United States or elsewhere? Does the international legal system offer any protection to the individual? In particular, does it afford protection against abuses by the individual's own state? As recently as 1955, it was suggested in a somewhat chilling phrase that a state could treat its own citizens "according to discretion." I Oppenheim, International Law 682 (Lauterpacht, 8th ed.1955). Can this be the law today?

In this chapter, questions such as the following will be explored: what substantive legal norms have been developed in the international system for the protection of the individual; what classes of individuals are protected by such norms, aliens alone or citizens of the acting state as well; by what processes are those norms applied and the protections afforded?

SECTION A. RESPONSIBILITY OF STATES FOR INJURIES TO ALIENS

As the nation-state became the organizing unit of the European peoples there was an early, if halting, recognition that, in some circumstances, a state might be circumscribed in the way it treated some of its own nationals. <u>Doctrines of natural law</u> furnished a major impetus. Pressure for such recognition came from states to which those persons had formerly been attached. "The treaties by which States bound themselves to treat their own nationals in a certain way appear only as isolated phenomena inspired first by political interest and later by considerations of humanity. The series of particular agreements inaugurated in 1660 by the Treaty of Oliva after a century and a half of religious commotions bore this aspect. In these, states receiving cessions of territory guaranteed to the ceding states the continuance and protection of the religion existing in the ceded territories. This protection, granted first to individuals, was gradually extended to minority groups, to religious minorities first and afterwards ethnic or national minorities." DeVisscher, Theory and Reality in Public International Law 122 (Corbett trans., 1957).

This process of looking after one's own kind is reflected in the practice of "diplomatic protection" in the 18th and 19th centuries. By this practice the state sought protection for its own nationals when they had left its territory to travel, reside or trade in a foreign state. See Chapter 8, p. 519. If its nationals were injured by the foreign state, diplomatic protests were made, asserting that the foreign state had violated its treaty obligations or, in many cases, obligations imposed by international law generally. In theory, rights of the protecting state had been violated, not the rights of the injured individual. In the absence of an international judiciary in which the rights of the offended state could be litigated, states occasionally resorted to arbitration and authorized ad hoc tribunals to decide claims based upon alleged injuries to individuals. A substantial body of "precedent," establishing a primitive law of human rights, was developed until the practice of arbitrating violations of personal rights began to slacken after World War II. <u>The diplomatic protest</u> remains a major vehicle for the assertion of human rights claims.

---

1.   THE PRINCIPLE OF DIPLOMATIC PROTECTION

The theory that a claim for injury to an alien is the claim of the state of which he is a national has remained the underlying theory of international practice. But the reality of the claim as one on behalf of the individual has been recognized, as shown in the decision which follows.

ADMINISTRATIVE DECISION NO. V

Mixed Claims Commission, (United States—Germany), 1924.
VII U.N.Rep. Int'l Arb. Awards 119, 152.

Ordinarily a nation will not espouse a claim on behalf of its national against another nation unless requested so to do by such na-

REQUEST
BY
VICTIM

tional. When on such request a claim is espoused, the nation's absolute right to control it is necessarily exclusive. In exercising such
control it is governed not only by the interest of the particular claimant but by the larger interests of the whole people of the nation and
must exercise an untrammeled discretion in determining when and
how the claim will be presented and pressed, or withdrawn or compromised, and the private owner will be bound by the action taken.
Even if payment is made to the espousing nation in pursuance of an
award, it has complete control over the fund so paid to and held by it
and may, to prevent fraud, correct a mistake, or protect the national
honor, at its election return the fund to the nation paying it or otherwise dispose of it. But where a demand is made on behalf of a designated national, and an award and payment is made on that specific
demand, the fund so paid is not a national fund in the sense that the
title vests in the nation receiving it entirely free from any obligation
to account to the private claimant, on whose behalf the claim was ar-
serted and paid and who is the real owner thereof. Broad and misleading statements susceptible of this construction are found in cases
where lump-sum awards and payments have been made to the demanding nation covering numerous claims put forward by it and where
the tribunal making the award did not undertake to adjudicate each
claim or to allocate any specified amount to any designated claim. It
is not believed that any case can be cited in which an award has been
made by an international tribunal in favor of the demanding nation
on behalf of its designated national in which the nation receiving payment of such award has, in the absence of fraud or mistake, hesitated
to account to the national designated, or those claiming under him,
for the full amount of the award received. So far as the United States
is concerned it would seem that the Congress has treated funds paid
the nation in satisfaction of specific claims as held "in trust for citizens of the United States or others".

The Umpire agrees with the American Commissioner that the
control of the United States over claims espoused by it before this
Commission is complete. But the generally accepted theory formulated by Vattel, which makes the injury to the national an injury to
the nation and internationally therefore the claim a national claim
which may and should be espoused by the nation injured, must not be
permitted to obscure the realities or blind us to the fact that the ultimate object of asserting the claim is to provide reparation for the private claimant * * *.

  *   *   *

COMMUNIST CHINESE NATIONALS IN INDONESIA

V International Legal Materials 775 (1966).

Chinese Note of April 12, 1966

The Ministry of Foreign Affairs of the People's Republic of China presents its compliments to the Embassy of the Republic of Indonesia in China and has the honor to state the following:

Since October 1965 the Indonesian rightwing reactionary forces have launched massive campaigns against the Chinese nationals in an organized and planned way.

In all parts of Indonesia they have organized large numbers of hooligans for the unbridled persecution of innocent Chinese nationals. The houses and shops of thousands of Chinese nationals have been ransacked or burned up. Many associations and schools of Chinese nationals have been smashed up or seized. Large numbers of Chinese nationals have been beaten up or unwarrantedly arrested. Many have been murdered in cold blood, or even beheaded, disemboweled, dismembered, or burned alive. Not only did the army authorities in some places shield these atrocities, they even issued permits for hooligans to stage "demonstrations" and sent armed men and military vehicles to take a direct part in them. The racist persecution of the Chinese nationals by the Indonesian rightwing reactionary forces, which grossly violates principles of international relations, has reached shocking proportions. The Chinese people are extremely indignant at the above-mentioned atrocities.

The Chinese nationals have resided in Indonesia for generations. They have always lived in amity with the Indonesian people and have made positive contributions to Indonesia's economic life. They have worked for the promotion of friendly relations between China and Indonesia and actively supported the Indonesian people in their struggle against imperialism, colonialism, and neocolonialism. The aim of the Indonesian rightwing reactionary forces in wantonly persecuting Chinese nationals is obviously to meet the needs of imperialism and deliberately to undermine the relations between China and Indonesia and the solidarity of the two peoples in the struggle against imperialism. No matter what pretexts they may fabricate, the Indonesian rightwing reactionary forces are unable to cover up these despicable designs.

Under the treaty and agreements signed by the Chinese and Indonesian governments on the question of the overseas nationals of the two countries, the Indonesian Government has the unshirkable obligation to protect the proper rights and interests of the Chinese nationals. But instead of fulfilling this obligation, it has connived at or even shielded the wild persecution of Chinese nationals by the rightwing reactionary forces and completely ignored the repeated protests and representations of the Chinese Government. Through the military authorities in Djakarta and other places, it has recently gone so far as to issue orders viciously slandering the associations and schools of Chinese nationals as "lairs of saboteurs and counterrevolutionaries" and closed down or disbanded these associations and schools on this pretext. This shows that the Indonesian Government has gone farther in supporting the rightwing reactionary forces' criminal persecution of the Chinese nationals and thereby assumed the inescapable responsibility for further worsening the relations between the two countries.

At present, thousands of persecuted Chinese nationals, having become homeless and bankrupt and lost the means of living, are urgently asking the Indonesian Government to help them return to their motherland. Their request is entirely reasonable and justified. Having failed either to protect them effectively from persecution or give them relief and rehabilitation, the Indonesian Government naturally has the duty of sending back to China those persecuted Chinese nationals who desire to return of their own will. Therefore, the Chinese Government requests the Indonesian Government to do the following:

1. Immediately arrange ships to transport back to China the above-said Chinese nationals who desire to return of their own will.

2. Allow them to bring back their own effects and funds.

3. Insure their safety on the way to the ports; provide them with food and accommodation while they are at the ports; facilitate their departure from Indonesia for China.

4. Protect the Chinese officials to be appointed by the Chinese Embassy and consulates in Indonesia for assisting in the return of those Chinese nationals who desire to come back to China of their own will; provide the said Chinese officials with the necessary facilities.

The Indonesian Government is asked to give a speedy reply to the above request.

The Ministry of Foreign Affairs avails itself of this opportunity to renew to the embassy the assurances of its highest consideration.

Chinese Note of April 25, 1966 (Partial Text)

Since the middle of January this year the Indonesian rightwing reactionary forces have never stopped their racist persecution of the Overseas Chinese in Bima, inflicting serious losses of life and property on them.

A little after 11 p. m. on 11 January, the military authorities of Bima arrested, in the name of giving them "protection," five local Overseas Chinese, Lai Hsiehchien, Huang Hsien-chung, Huang Yin-chang, Huang Che-liu, and Kao Che-ling.

Meanwhile, directed by the army, a large number of reactionary hooligans armed with swords and axes broke into the houses of the Chinese nationals at Raba, Bima County, and forced all of them to leave their homes.   Then the hooligans looted everything in their houses.

Sometime after 3 a. m. the next day, this crowd of hooligans rushed to Bima where they joined another crowd of hooligans swelling the total to more than 2,000.   Then they threw themselves wildly on the more than 140 Overseas Chinese families, with knives, axes, and clubs. They forced their way into Chinese shops and houses, beating up everybody they saw and driving everybody, man or woman, old or young, outdoors.   As a result, 15 Chinese including 3 women were wounded by cutting and beating, and numberless others were hit, kicked, and clubbed.   Huang Cheng-tsai, a Chinese national, died of serious wounds and loss of blood despite emergency medical aid.   First aid proved futile.   The infant of Huang Chia-cheng died of fright. Wu Shan-i was stabbed deep in the abdomen with a dagger and was in a critical state.   Huang Ti-hsin suffered a cut in the head by a sharp weapon and had fingers chopped off, thus becoming disabled.

In the name of "protecting the security" of the Chinese nationals who had been driven outdoors, the army and people forcibly transported them in prearranged vehicles to the Raba prison and the county assembly hall where they were concentrated.   At that time all these Chinese had nothing but what they wore on their backs and were forbidden to take any other clothing or articles with them.

A few hours later, at around 6 a. m. on 12 January, led by the troops and police, hordes of hooligans reentered the Chinese shops and houses where they looted and wrecked things without any restraint. All valuable goods and furniture, as well as clothing, wristwatches and jewelry, were carried away.   This outrage lasted until noon.

Then again in the name of giving "protection," the local government collected whatever articles and furniture remained after the looting and removed them to the football field at Raba and the anteroom of the local assembly.   These things were looted again by hooligans in the evening.

In addition, the Chinese nationals' transport vehicles were requisitioned.   Goods in their warehouses and newly arrived goods from Surabaya were all confiscated and auctioned.

Thus, the Overseas Chinese in Bima lost everything they had and even doors and windows and nails were carried away.

The waves of outrageous crimes then spread to towns and villages in the vicinity of Bima.   More than 100 Chinese nationals at Sape and more than 10 others at Kore were arrested and taken to Bima on 14 and 29 January after they had been robbed of their personal belongings.   At Bima they were detained at a concentration camp together with more than 800 other Chinese nationals.   There they were treated as prisoners, deprived of freedom and movement, and subjected to all kinds of maltreatment.   For instance, the more than 300 Chinese nationals at Raba prison were forced to live in five confinement cells

5 by 5 meters each. They had no clothes to change into, were forbidden to take showers, and remained in semistarvation. Quite a number of old people, women, and children fell ill because of such inhuman treatment.

To cover up their monstrous crimes, the authorities at Bima even attempted a political frameup of these innocent Chinese victims. Through "trials" they tried to force these victims to confess crimes on trumped-up charges, admit as "legitimate" the brigandage committed by the army and police in collaboration with the hooligans, and "waive their claims for compensation" for losses. They unscrupulously tried to set the Overseas Chinese against their motherland.

When all such vicious attempts failed and when they had to release these Chinese nationals after having illegally detained them for more than one month, the authorities at Bima still openly forced the Chinese victims to attend a so-called "ceremony to pledge allegiance" under the "supervision" of the representatives of the local pantatunggal and the rightwing reactionary organizations.

The authorities at Bima tried by every possible means to impose a tight embargo of all news about the outrages. For about two months from 12 January, they forbade the Chinese nationals in Bima to leave the county and those in other places to enter it. They threatened the Chinese victims: "If you report the truth to the Chinese Embassy and Radio Peking broadcasts it, you will pay dearly for it."

Up to now, Huang Hsien-chung, Huang Yin-chang, Huang Che-liu, Kao Che-ling, Kao Che-shui, Fu Sun-chung and other Overseas Chinese are still detained as hostages.

The racist outrages perpetrated by the Indonesian rightwing reactionary forces at Bima were shocking. Facts fully show that these crimes were committed by the local authorities at Bima, the armed forces, and the hooligans of rightwing organizations; they were a carefully planned big conspiracy. The authorities at Bima tried to shut out the heavens with their hands and imposed a tight news blackout. But the just voice cannot be embargoed. The monstrous crimes committed by the rightwing reactionary forces were finally exposed completely; the truth is now out.

DEMANDS: The Chinese Embassy demands that the Indonesian Government immediately release all Overseas Chinese still under detention, severely punish the instigators and organizers of the outrages, pay pensions to families of those Chinese nationals killed and compensation to those who suffered losses, and insure the safety of all Chinese nationals.

The embassy also demands that the Indonesian Government reply promptly to the note of 12 April of the Chinese Foreign Ministry concerning the repatriation of Overseas Chinese to their motherland and, in accordance with the reasonable four-point demand in that note, help, first of all, those Chinese nationals now in deep suffering at Bima to return to their homeland as soon as possible.

Question. Is there a legal basis for the Communist Chinese complaint against Indonesia? Are the Chinese asserting that Indonesian law has been violated? There is a reference to the "treaty and agreements signed by the Chinese and Indonesian governments." Are these the sole basis for the Chinese protest? Would the Communist Chinese government have a basis for complaint if no treaty had existed? By sending these notes and making its demands, is the Communist Chinese government intervening in the internal affairs of Indonesia? In what way is Indonesia as a state implicated in the events detailed in the notes: as the actor; for failing to take measures to protect the Chinese; for failing to prosecute private wrongdoers?

Compare the case of Lynching of Italians at New Orleans, 6 Moore, Digest of International Law 837 (1906).

---

2. THE INTERNATIONAL MINIMUM STANDARD

ROBERTS (UNITED STATES) v. UNITED MEXICAN STATES

General Claims Commission, 1926.
IV U.N.Rep. Int'l Arb. Awards 77.

1. This claim is presented by the United States of America in behalf of Harry Roberts, an American citizen who, it is alleged in the memorial, was arbitrarily and illegally arrested by Mexican authorities, who held him prisoner for a long time in contravention of Mexican law and subjected him to cruel and inhumane treatment throughout the entire period of confinement.

2. From the memorial filed by the Government of the United States and accompanying documents, the allegations upon which the claim is based are briefly stated as follows: Harry Roberts, together with a number of other persons, was arrested by Mexican Federal troops on May 12, 1922, in the vicinity of Ocampo, Tamaulipas, Mexico, charged with having taken part in an assault on the house of E. F. Watts, near Ebano, San Luis Potosí, Mexico, on the night of May 5, 1922. The claimant was taken prisoner and brought to Tampico, whence he was taken to Ciudad Valles, San Luis Potosí, where he was held under detention until he was placed at liberty on December 16, 1923, a period of nearly nineteen months. It is alleged that there were undue delays in the prosecution of the trial of the accused which was not instituted within one year from the time of his arrest, as required by the Constitution of Mexico. These delays were brought to the notice of the Government of Mexico, but no corrective measures were taken. During the entire period of imprisonment, he was subject to rude and cruel treatment from which he suffered great physical pain and mental anguish.

3.   The United States asks that an indemnity be paid by the Government of Mexico in the sum of $10,000.00 for the wrongful treatment of the accused.   It is stated in the memorial that Roberts earned prior to the time of his arrest $350.00 a month; that he would have earned $6,650.00 during the nineteen months that he was under arrest; and that he spent $1,000.00 in fees paid to a lawyer resident in the United States to assist in obtaining his release.   A total indemnity is asked in the sum of $17,650.00 together with a proper allowance of interest.

4.   The evidence presented by the Agency of the United States consists of affidavits made by Roberts and by other persons; correspondence which Roberts and fellow prisoners exchanged with the American Consul at Tampico, and correspondence exchanged by the Consul with Mexican authorities and with the Department of State. The Mexican Government on its part presented records of judicial proceedings, including proceedings instituted against Roberts and others.

5.   It does not appear from this evidence that the Mexican authorities had not serious grounds for apprehending Roberts and his companions.   The record of the proceedings instituted by the Mexican authorities shows that at about twelve o'clock on the night of May 5, 1922, the Chief of the Detachment in the Ebano Station, San Luis Potosí, received a telephone message from Mr. Eduardo F. Watts to the effect that, at that moment, there had appeared in front of his house, which is situated on the limits of a small village, a band of outlaws consisting of several men, mounted and armed; that the officer immediately left with the men under his orders to render assistance; that, upon arriving at the house he discovered several persons in hiding; that, having seen flashes of light and heard discharges from firearms, he ordered his men to return fire, whereupon the persons lying in ambush fled and succeeded in escaping due to their being mounted; that he picked up a dead man named Monte Michaels, who was suspected of being implicated in the blowing-up of a train belonging to a petroleum company; that the officer also picked up a rifle having a burnt cartridge and an unused one in the breech, a saddled mule, and other things; and that Watts furnished the information that the fugitives were three Americans.   It further appears that an examination of Watts' house disclosed the impacts of several shots fired at the premises; that on May 12th, Harry Roberts and two of his companions were apprehended in the neighborhood of Chamal, where they had fled and where forces had been sent to capture them; that upon their being arrested, their preliminary statements were taken, in which they did not deny that they were the persons who were surprised by the detachment from Ebano on the night of May 5th in front of Watts' house, although they asserted that they had not gone there with criminal purposes.   It is further shown by the official Mexican records that on May 15th, the prisoners were placed at the disposition of the

agent of the Federal District Attorney, who immediately ordered a preliminary investigation; that from this time until the date when Roberts was placed at liberty judicial proceedings continued, first before the First District Court of Tampico, Tamaulipas, and afterwards before the Judge of First Instance of the District of Valles, San Luis Potosí; and that in the record of the proceedings instituted before those officials there are found statements of the accused and testimony of other persons indicating that there were grounds for suspecting that Harry Roberts and his companions had committed a crime—grounds sufficient to warrant the authorities to proceed with the arrest and trial of the accused.

6.   The Commission is not called upon to reach a conclusion whether Roberts committed the crime with which he was charged. The determination of that question rested with the Mexican judiciary, and it is distinct from the question whether the Mexican authorities had just cause to arrest Roberts and to bring him to trial. Aliens of course are obliged to submit to proceedings properly instituted against them in conformity with local laws. In the light of the evidence presented in the case the Commission is of the opinion that the Mexican authorities had ample grounds to suspect that Harry Roberts had committed a crime and to proceed against him as they did. The Commission therefore holds that the claim is not substantiated with respect to the charge of illegal arrest.

7.   In order to pass upon the complaint with reference to an excessive period of imprisonment, it is necessary to consider whether the proceedings instituted against Roberts while he was incarcerated exceeded reasonable limits within which an alien charged with crime may be held in custody pending the investigation of the charge against him. Clearly there is no definite standard prescribed by international law by which such limits may be fixed. Doubtless an examination of local laws fixing a minimum length of time within which a person charged with crime may be held without being brought to trial may be useful in determining whether detention has been unreasonable in a given case. The Mexican Constitution of 1917, provides by its Article 20, section 8, that a person accused of crime "must be judged within four months if he is accused of a crime the maximum penalty for which may not exceed two years' imprisonment, and within one year if the maximum penalty is greater." From the judicial records presented by the Mexican Agent it clearly appears that there was a failure of compliance with this constitutional provision, since the proceedings were instituted on May 17, 1922, and that Roberts had not been brought to trial on December 16, 1923, the date when he was released. It was contended by the Mexican Agency that the delay was due to the fact that the accused repeatedly refused to name counsel to defend him, and that as a result of such refusal on his part proceedings were to his advantage suspended in order that he might obtain satisfactory counsel to defend him. We do not consider that this con-

tention is sound. There is evidence in the record that Roberts constantly requested the American Consul at Tampico to take steps to expedite the trial. Several communications were addressed by American diplomatic and consular officers in Mexico to Mexican authorities with a view to hastening the trial. It was the duty of the Mexican judge under Article 20, section 9, of the Mexican Constitution to appoint counsel to act for Roberts from the time of the institution of the proceedings against him. The Commission is of the opinion that preliminary proceedings could have been completed before the lapse of a year after the arrest of Roberts. Even though it may have been necessary to make use of rogatory letters to obtain the testimony of witnesses in different localities, it would seem that that could have been accomplished at least within six or seven months from the time of the arrest. In any event, it is evident in the light of provisions of Mexican law that Roberts was unlawfully held a prisoner without trial for at least seven months. With respect to this point of unreasonably long detention without trial, the Mexican Agency contended that Roberts was undoubtedly guilty of the crime for which he was arrested; that therefore had he been tried he would have been sentenced to serve a term of imprisonment, of more than nineteen months; and that, since, under Mexican law, the period of nineteen months would have been taken into account in fixing his sentence of imprisonment, it cannot properly be considered that he was illegally detained for an unreasonable period of time. The Commission must reject this contention, since the Commission is not called upon to pass upon the guilt or innocence of Roberts but to determine whether the detention of the accused was of such an unreasonable duration as to warrant an award of indemnity under the principles of international law. Having in mind particularly that Roberts was held for several months without trial in contravention of Mexican law, the Commission holds that an indemnity is due on the ground of unreasonably long detention.

8. With respect to the charge of ill-treatment of Roberts, it appears from evidence submitted by the American Agency that the jail in which he was kept was a room thirty-five feet long and twenty feet wide with stone walls, earthen floor, straw roof, a single window, a single door and no sanitary accommodations, all the prisoners depositing their excrement in a barrel kept in a corner of the room; that thirty or forty men were at times thrown together in this single room; that the prisoners were given no facilities to clean themselves; that the room contained no furniture except that which the prisoners were able to obtain by their own means; that they were afforded no opportunity to take physical exercise; and that the food given them was scarce, unclean and of the coarsest kind. The Mexican Agency did not present evidence disproving that such conditions existed in the jail. It was stated by the Agency that Roberts was accorded the same treatment as that given to all other persons, and with respect to the food Roberts received, it was observed in the answer that he was given "the

food that was believed necessary, and within the means of the municipality." All of the details given by Roberts in testimony which accompanies the memorial with respect to the conditions of the jail are corroborated by a statement of the American Consul at Tampico who visited the jail. Facts with respect to equality of treatment of aliens and nationals may be important in determining the merits of a complaint of mistreatment of an alien. But such equality is not the ultimate test of the propriety of the acts of authorities in the light of international law. That test is, broadly speaking, whether aliens are treated in accordance with ordinary standards of civilization. We do not hesitate to say that the treatment of Roberts was such as to warrant an indemnity on the ground of cruel and inhumane imprisonment.

9. The respondent Government has not denied that, under the convention of September 8, 1923, acts of authorities of San Luis Potosí may give rise to claims against the Government of Mexico. The Commission is of the opinion that claims can be predicated on such acts.

10. As has been stated, the Commission holds that damages may be assessed on two of the grounds asserted in the American memorial, namely, (1) excessively long imprisonment—with which the Mexican Government is clearly chargeable for a period of seven months, and (2) cruel and inhumane treatment suffered by Roberts in jail during nineteen months. After careful consideration of the facts of the case and of similar cases decided by international tribunals, the Commission is of the opinion that a total sum of $8,000.00 is a proper indemnity to be paid in satisfaction of this claim.

Decision

11. For the reasons stated above the Commission decides that the Government of the United Mexican States must pay to the Government of the United States of America on behalf of Harry Roberts $8,000.00 (eight thousand dollars) without interest.

Equality versus international minimum standard. The commission rejects as the "ultimate" test "equality of treatment of aliens and nationals" and adopts a test of whether aliens are treated in accordance with "ordinary standards of civilization." When European nationals began to travel for colonization and trade, their governments became concerned for their personal safety. In diplomatic protests on behalf of their nationals, the European states asserted that there existed a "minimum standard of justice" to which all states must adhere in their treatment of aliens. See Dawson and Head, International Law, National Tribunals and the Rights of Aliens, Chapter I (1971). Does such a minimum standard in fact exist as a matter of international law? Or must a state merely assure that aliens are not treated any worse than the state treats its own nationals? What standards are (or are supposed to be) comprehended by the minimum standard?

CANTERO HERRERA v. CANEVARO & CO.

Peru, Supreme Court, 1927.
[1927–28] Ann.Dig. 219 (No. 149).

THE FACTS: Cantero Herrera, a Cuban national residing in Lima, Peru, filed suit, on 22 July, 1913, as agent for certain non-resident Cuban citizens, against a Peruvian national named Cesar Saco y Flores, in the Civil Court of Lima, for the partition and distribution of an inheritance in the estate known as "Huayto." Later, on 29 September, 1913, the Sociedad Canevaro & Cia, also of Lima, was made a co-defendant as the purchaser of the estate from Saco y Flores, and the Court was asked to declare the sale to it void.

The court of first instance, on 10 January, 1919, decided against Cantero Herrera and his co-plaintiffs on three grounds: (a) That they had shown no right to the distribution prayed for; (b) that the sale by Saco y Flores to Canevaro & Cia was a valid one; and (c) that the action was barred by the statute of limitations. This judgment was affirmed by the Superior Court on 23 September, 1920, and by the Supreme Court on 21 August, 1921.

Nothing further was done by the plaintiffs, but on 28 January, 1927, the Cuban Envoy Extraordinary and Minister Plenipotentiary at Lima addressed a Note to the Foreign Minister of Peru, which impugned generally the above-mentioned judgments, laid particular stress on alleged errors of law on the question of the "prescription" of the action, and concluded by alleging that the judgments were tantamount to a denial of justice to the plaintiffs on the ground that they were contrary to Peruvian law; wherefore he called upon the Government of Peru to acknowledge that there had been a denial of justice and to make due reparation. The matter was referred by the Executive to the Supreme Court.

Held: That the claim, in so far as it is based on denial of justice, must fail. [A portion of the opinion of the court follows.]

Between Peru and Cuba there is no treaty regarding foreigners; but the tenor of our laws and the principles generally accepted, especially those proclaimed in American international law, are sufficient to make the question raised by the diplomatic representative of Cuba doctrinally simple.

The condition of foreigners in Peru, from the point of view of private rights, is not left entirely to the provisions of international convenience, nor subordinated to the simple fact of reciprocity, since

Articles 32 and 33 of our Civil Code provide that "civil rights are independent of the status of the citizen," and that "foreigners enjoy in Peru all rights concerning the security of their persons and property and the free administration of the same."

Equality between natives and foreigners before the Civil Law implies their equality as to judicial competency and form of proceeding in the same subject-matter; hence, foreigners enjoy in Peru the same rights, means, recourses and guarantees as nationals to sue for and defend their rights; the cautio judicatum solvi (which, as a dilatory objection against the alien plaintiff, transient or without known assets, was allowed under the Code abrogated in 1912) is no longer in force, notwithstanding that it is still sanctioned by a legislation of some countries, including that of Cuba   *   *   *

The diplomatic representative of Cuba agrees, as must be true, that the ordinary suit commenced by Cantero Herrera against Saco and Canevaro came to a close with the judgment of the Supreme Court, dated 11 August, 1921. As a result, that judgment has placed a final, absolute and definitive seal upon all questions of a legal and juridical character ventilated in the litigation between the said parties, in conformity with the precepts of the Constitution and the laws of Peru, from whose sovereignty the foreigner litigating in the national jurisdiction cannot abstract himself, and which merely give positive expression to the old classic adage res judicata pro veritate habetur.   *   *   *

There is no doubt that nations reciprocally owe one another justice, and are bound to extend it to foreigners having recourse to their tribunals and to give them the opportunity to obtain it in the like measure with nationals; but the good understanding among them, harmonising all interests, has raised to the category of an international law the authority of the thing adjudged, and no self-respecting country will countenance that any other country should impeach the force and legality of an executed judgment, rendered regularly by its authorities, as an emanation of sovereignty.

It is on this account that, in keeping with our political Constitution, it belongs to the President of the Republic, who represents abroad the national sovereignty, "to enforce, obligatorily, the judgments and resolutions of the tribunals and courts" (Article 121, par. 10); and Article 39 of the same Constitution contains this important provision, which it is timely to mention with respect to a claim growing out of litigation over territorial property: "foreigners are, as to their property, in the same condition as Peruvians, and cannot in any case invoke with regard thereto an exceptional situation, nor have recourse to diplomatic claims.   *   *   *."

It is erroneous to suppose that the conclusion of a proceeding in which a foreigner has failed, marks the occasion for the transference of the issue to the diplomatic plane. If it were so, the passions accumulated around matters of an entirely private nature would constantly poison the best cemented international relations.

In the relations of nation to nation, the rule is respect for the sovereignty of friendly powers, typified in the authority of its judges and of its decisions. The exception is the claim based on the motive of denial of justice; but to make such claim conformably with the principles and usages of international law, it is necessary that the case be one of the utmost seriousness, that the denial of justice be manifest or notorious, that is, that the hearing which the foreigner claims, or the recourse which he interposes, has been denied him, and in general that the exercise of his rights and rights of action is interfered with contrary to law, or is subjected to unwarranted delays; because all this involves and constitutes an odious exception, a legal infringement which can be established objectively, without offending the jurisdiction of the country, and which compromises the responsibility of the State.

Cantero Herrera has not been denied a hearing by our tribunals, nor the interposition of any recourse or means of defence permitted by the law, nor has he been subjected to any objectionable treatment. Neither can he aver, as has been alleged in other cases, that he has been cited before a court lacking jurisdiction, or has been judged without being summoned; being the plaintiff, he has selected the court and the proceeding, and with the most absolute freedom has pleaded at every stage, by word of mouth and in writing, everything he has deemed necessary in support of his right. Of what, then, does he complain? Of not having won the action? It is not on that condition, nor on any other, that the portals of justice are thrown open to the public authorities, to foreigners, or to any one else. * * *

---

1. *Standard for determining that there has been a "denial of justice."* By what standard would the Peruvian Supreme Court decide that there has been a "denial of justice?" Must the complaining party show that there has been a failure to meet the standards of Peruvian law? Or may the standards of Peruvian law be so high that a failure to meet those high standards is not, of itself, a "denial of justice?" Would the Peruvian court hold, on the other hand, that even though the standards of Peruvian law have been met there may be a denial of justice because those standards do not meet the higher standards of international law?

2. *The position of Latin American jurists.* These jurists have been in the forefront of those who deny that there is an international standard to which each state's jurisprudence must attain. A frequently stated position is that the alien is entitled only to equality of treatment with nationals. In analyzing this proposition it should be

noted that the broad question of state responsibility for injury to aliens has been discussed somewhat indiscriminately in connection with two types of problems: injury to an alien individual in his personal rights (e.g., rights to physical security and personal freedom, rights to fair trial in cases involving personal liberty) on one hand and, on the other, the alien individual's (or corporation's) rights to property. In recent years, the latter rights have been the subject of considerable controversy, particularly with respect to the expropriation of property by states socializing and collectivizing the means of production. See Chapter 17.

Would you expect a system of international law to be more protective of personal rights than of property rights?

3. *Influence of the creation of new states on the question of the international standard.* The debate that was carried on in the Western World prior to World War II on the question of an international minimum standard versus a standard of national treatment may be viewed as one within an established legal system in which the members of that system sought to delineate the contours of a body of customary law acceptable to them. With the influx of new states in the last two decades, mostly former colonies, the debate has taken on a different tone:

> The international community in its inception was confined to only some Christian states of Europe. It expanded within very narrow limits to embrace, first, the other Christian states of Europe and next their own offshoots in other continents. It thus retained until recently its racial exclusiveness in full and its geographical and other limitations in part. The international law which the worldwide community of states today inherits is the law which owes its genesis and growth, first, to the attempts of these states to regulate their mutual intercourse in their own interests and, secondly, to the use made of it during the period of colonialism.

> The contacts of the members of the restricted international community of the past with other states and peoples of the much larger world outside its own charmed circle were not governed by any law or scruples beyond what expediency dictated. The history of the establishment and consolidation of empires overseas by some of the members of the old international community and of the acquisition therein of vast economic interests by their nationals teems with instances of a total disregard of all ethical considerations. A strange irony of fate now compels those very members of the community of nations on the ebb tide of their imperial power to hold up principles of morality as shields against the liquidation of interests acquired and held by an abuse of international intercourse. Rights and interests acquired and consolidated during periods of such abuse cannot for obvious reasons carry with them in the mind of the victims of that abuse any-

thing like the sanctity the holders of those rights and interests may and do attach to them. To the extent to which the law of responsibility of states for injuries to aliens favors such rights and interests, it protects an unjustified status quo or, to put it more bluntly, makes itself a handmaid of power in the preservation of its spoils.

* * *

The law of responsibility then, is not founded on any universal principles of law or morality. Its sole foundation is custom, which is binding only among states where it either grew up or came to be adopted. It is thus hardly possible to maintain that it is still part of universal international law. Whatever the basis of obligation in international law in the past, when the international community was restricted to only a few states, including those, fewer still, admitted into it from time to time, the birth of a new world community has brought about a radical change which makes the traditional basis of obligation outmoded.

Once it is found that the right of diplomatic protection of their nationals abroad, claimed by states as a customary right, is not universally binding, the structure of this law as part of universal international law crumbles, for this right is assumed to be the sole basis of a state's claim to stretch out its protecting hand to its nationals in the territory of another state independently of its consent. Its elimination from universal international law necessarily means that, even outside the limited zone of the applicability of this law, the responsibility of a state for injuries to aliens remains in every case in which it may be held to be responsible exactly in the same way as in the case of its own nationals, but it remains its responsibility not to the home state of the injured alien but to the injured alien himself. In other words, it ceases to be an international responsibility and becomes a responsibility only under the municipal law of the state concerned. Guha-Roy, Is the Law of Responsibility of States for Injuries to Aliens a Part of Universal International Law? 55 Am.J.Int'l L. 863, 866, 888 (1961).

CHATTIN (UNITED STATES) v. UNITED MEXICAN STATES

General Claims Commission, 1927.
IV U.N.Rep. Int'l Arb. Awards 282.

VAN VOLLENHOVEN, PRESIDING COMMISSIONER:

1. This claim is made by the United States of America against the United Mexican States on behalf of B. E. Chattin, an American national. Chattin, who since 1908 was an employee (at first freight conductor, thereafter passenger conductor) of the Ferrocarril Sud-

Pacifico de Mexico (Southern Pacific Railroad Company of Mexico) and who in the Summer of 1910 performed his duties in the State of Sinaloa, was on July 9, 1910, arrested at Mazatlán, Sinaloa, on a charge of embezzlement; was tried there in January, 1911, convicted on February 6, 1911, and sentenced to two years' imprisonment; but was released from the jail at Mazatlán in May or June, 1911, as a consequence of disturbances caused by the Madero revolution. He then returned to the United States. It is alleged that the arrest, the trial and the sentence were illegal, that the treatment in jail was inhuman, and that Chattin was damaged to the extent of $50,000.00, which amount Mexico should pay.

* * *

3. The circumstances of Chattin's arrest, trial and sentence were as follows. In the year 1910 there had arisen a serious apprehension on the part of several railroad companies operating in Mexico as to whether the full proceeds of passenger fares were accounted for to these companies. The Southern Pacific Railroad Company of Mexico applied on June 15, 1910, to the Governor of the State of Sinaloa, in his capacity as chief of police of the State, co-operating with the federal police, in order to have investigations made of the existence and extent of said defrauding of their lines within the territory of his State. On or about July 8, 1910, one Cenobio Ramírez, a Mexican employee (brakeman) of the said railroad, was arrested at Mazatlán on a charge of fraudulent sale of railroad tickets of the said company, and in his appearance before the District Court in that town he accused the conductor Chattin—who since May 9, 1910, had charge of trains operating between Mazatlán and Acaponeta, Nayarit—as the principal in the crime with which he, Ramírez, was charged; whereupon Chattin also was arrested by the Mazatlán police, on July 9, (not 10), 1910. On August 3 (not 13), 1910, his case was consolidated not only with that of Ramírez, but also with that of three more American railway conductors (Haley, Englehart and Parrish) and of four more Mexicans. After many months of preparation and a trial at Mazatlán, during both of which Chattin, it is alleged, lacked proper information, legal assistance, assistance of an interpreter and confrontation with the witnesses, he was convicted on February 6, 1911, by the said District Court of Mazatlán as stated above. The case was carried on appeal to the Third Circuit Court at Mexico City, which court on July 3, 1911, affirmed the sentence. In the meantime (May or June, 1911) Chattin had been released by the population of Mazatlán which threw open the doors of the jail in the time elapsing between the departure of the representatives of the Diaz regime and the arrival of the Madero forces.

* * *

Irregularity of court proceedings

12.   The next allegation on the American side is that Chattin's trial was held in an illegal manner. The contentions are: (a) that the Governor of the State, for political reasons, used his influence to have this accused and three of his fellow conductors convicted; (b) that the proceedings against the four conductors were consolidated without reason; (c) that the proceedings were unduly delayed; (d) that an exorbitant amount of bail was required; (e) that the accused was not duly informed of the accusations; (f) that the accused lacked the aid of counsel; (g) that the accused lacked the aid of an interpreter; (h) that there were no oaths required of the witnesses; (i) that there was no such a thing as a confrontation between the witnesses and the accused; and (j) that the hearings in open court which led to sentences of from two years' to two years and eight months' imprisonment lasted only some five minutes. It was also contended that the claimant had been forced to march under guard through the streets of Mazatlán; but the Commission in paragraph 3 of its opinion in the Faulkner case (Docket No. 47) rendered November 2, 1926, has already held that such treatment is incidental to the treatment of detention, and suspicion, and cannot in itself furnish a separate basis for a complaint.

13.   As to illegal efforts made by the Governor of Sinaloa to influence the trial and the sentence (allegation a), the only evidence consists in hearsay or suppositions about such things as what the Governor had in mind, or what the Judge has said in private conversation; hearsay and suppositions which often come from persons connected with those colleagues of Chattin's who shared his fate. To uncorroborated talk of this kind the Commission should not pay any attention. *   *   *

*   *   *

15.   For undue delay of the proceedings (allegation c), there is convincing evidence in more than one respect. The formal proceedings began on July 9, 1910. Chattin was not heard in court until more than one hundred days thereafter. The stubs and perhaps other pieces of evidence against Chattin were presented to the Court on August 3, 1910; Chattin, however, was not allowed to testify regarding them until October 28, 1910. Between the end of July, and October 8, 1910, the Judge merely waited. *   *   *   Another remarkable proof of the measure of speed which the Judge deemed due to a man deprived of his liberty, is in that, whereas Chattin appealed from the decree of his formal imprisonment on July 11, 1910—an appeal which would seem to be of rather an urgent character—"the corresponding copy for the appeal" was not remitted to the appellate Court until September 12, 1910; this Court did not render judgment until October 27, 1910; and though its decision was forwarded to Mazatlán on October 31, 1910, its receipt was not established until November 12, 1910.

16.   The allegation (d) that on July 25, 1910, an exorbitant amount of bail, to-wit a cash bond in the sum of 15,000.00 pesos, was required for the accused is true; but it is difficult to see how in the present case this can be held an illegal act on the part of the Judge.

17.   The allegation (e) that the accused has not been duly informed regarding the charge brought against him is proven by the record, and to a painful extent.   The real complainant in this case was the railroad company, acting through its general manager; this manager, an American, not only was allowed to make full statements to the Court on August 2, 3, and 26, 1910, without ever being confronted with the accused and his colleagues, but he was even allowed to submit to the Court a series of anonymous written accusations, the anonymity of which reports could not be removed (for reasons which he explained); these documents created the real atmosphere of the trial.   Were they made known to the conductors?   Were the accused given an opportunity to controvert them?   There is no trace of it in the record, nor was it ever alleged by Mexico.   It is true that, on August 3, 1910, they were ordered added to the court record; but that same day they were delivered to a translator, and they did not reappear on the court record until after January 16, 1911, when the investigations were over and Chattin's lawyer had filed his briefs. The court record only shows that on January 13, and 16, 1911, the conductors and one of their lawyers were aware of the existence, not that they knew the contents, of these documents.   *   *   *

18.   The allegations (f) and (g) that the accused lacked counsel and interpreter are disproven by the record of the court proceedings. *   *   *

19.   The allegation (h) that the witnesses were not sworn is irrelevant, as Mexican law does not require an "oath" (it is satisfied with a solemn promise, protesta, to tell the truth), nor do international standards of civilization.

20.   The allegation (i) that the accused has not been confronted with the witnesses—Delgado and Sarabia—is disproven both by the record of the court proceedings and by the decision of the appellate tribunal.   *   *   *

21.   The allegation (j) that the hearings in open court lasted only some five minutes is proven by the record.   This trial in open court was held on January 27, 1911.   It was a pure formality in which only confirmations were made of written documents, and in which not even the lawyer of the accused conductors took the trouble to say more than a word or two.

22.   The whole of the proceedings discloses a most astonishing lack of seriousness on the part of the Court.   There is no trace of an effort to have the two foremost pieces of evidence explained. *   *   *

There is no trace of an effort to find one Manuel Virgen, who, according to the investigations of July 21, 1910, might have been mixed in Chattin's dealings, nor to examine one Carl or Carrol Collins, a dismissed clerk of the railroad company concerned, who was repeatedly mentioned as forging tickets and passes and as having been discharged for that very reason.   One of the Mexican brakemen, Batriz, stated on August 8, 1910, in court that "it is true that the American conductors have among themselves schemes to defraud in that manner the company, the deponent not knowing it for sure"; but again no steps were taken to have this statement verified or this brakeman confronted with the accused Americans.   No disclosures were made as to one pass, one "half-pass" and eight perforated tickets shown to Chattin on October 28, 1910, as pieces of evidence; * * * No investigation was made as to why Delgado and Sarabia felt quite certain that June 29 was the date of their trip, a date upon the correctness of which the weight of their testimony wholly depended.   No search of the houses of these conductors is mentioned.   Nothing is revealed as to a search of their persons on the days of their arrest; when the lawyer of the other conductors, Haley and Englehart, insisted upon such an inquiry, a letter was sent to the Judge at Culiacán, but was allowed to remain unanswered.   Neither during the investigations nor during the hearings in open court was any such thing as an oral examination or cross-examination of any importance attempted. It seems highly improbable that the accused have been given a real opportunity during the hearings in open court, freely to speak for themselves.   It is not for the Commission to endeavor to reach from the record any conviction as to the innocence or guilt of Chattin and his colleagues; but even in case they were guilty, the Commission would render a bad service to the Government of Mexico if it failed to place the stamp of its disapproval and even indignation on a criminal procedure so far below international standards of civilization as the present one.   If the wholesome rule of international law as to respect for the judiciary of another country * * * shall stand, it would seem of the utmost necessity that appellate tribunals when, in exceptional cases, discovering proceedings of this type should take against them the strongest measures possible under constitution and laws, in order to safeguard their country's reputation.

          * * *

Conviction on insufficient evidence

24.   In Mexican law, as in that of other countries, an accused can not be convicted unless the Judge is convinced of his guilt and has acquired this view from legal evidence.   An international tribunal never can replace the important first element, that of the Judge's being convinced of the accused's guilt; it can only in extreme cases, and then with great reserve, look into the second element, the legality and sufficiency of the evidence.

          * * *

26.   From the record there is not convincing evidence that the proof against Chattin, scanty and weak though it may have been, was not such as to warrant a conviction.   Under the article deemed applicable the medium penalty fixed by law was imposed, and deduction made of the seven months Chattin had passed in detention from July, 1910, till February, 1911.   It is difficult to understand the sentence unless it be assumed that the Court, for some reason or other, wished to punish him severely.   The most acceptable explanation of this supposed desire would seem to be the urgent appeals made by the American chief manager of the railroad company concerned, the views expressed by him and contained in the record, and the dangerous collection of anonymous accusations which were not only inserted in the court record at the very last moment, but which were even quoted in the decision of February 6, 1911, as evidence to prove "illegal acts of the nature which forms the basis of this investigation".   The allegation that the Court in this matter was biased against American citizens would seem to be contradicted by the fact that, together with four Americans, five Mexicans were indicted as well, four of whom had been caught and have subsequently been convicted—that one of these Mexicans was punished as severely as the Americans were— and that the lower penalties imposed on the three others are explained by motives which, even if not shared, would seem reasonable.   The fact that the Prosecuting Attorney who did not share the Judge's views applied merely for "insignificant penalties"—as the first decision establishes—shows, on the one hand, that he disagreed with the Court's wish to punish severely and with its interpretation of the Penal Code, but shows on the other hand that he also considered the evidence against Chattin a sufficient basis for his conviction.   If Chattin's guilt was sufficiently proven, the small amount of the embezzlement (four pesos) need not in itself have prevented the Court from imposing a severe penalty.

27.   It has been suggested as most probable that after Chattin's escape and return to the United States no demand for his extradition has been made by the Mexican Government, and that this might imply a recognition on the side of Mexico that the sentence had been unjust.   Both the disturbed conditions in Mexico since 1911, and the little chance of finding the United States disposed to extradite one of its citizens by way of exception, might easily explain the absence of such a demand, without raising so extravagant a supposition as Mexico's own recognition of the injustice of Chattin's conviction.

Mistreatment in prison

28.   The allegation of the claimant regarding mistreatment in the jail at Mazatlán refers to filthy and unsanitary conditions, bad food, and frequent compulsion to witness the shooting of prisoners. It is well known   *   *   *   how dangerous it would be to place too great a confidence in uncorroborated statements of claimants regard-

ing their previous treatment in jail. * * * The hot climate of Mazatlán would explain in a natural way many of the discomforts experienced by the prisoners; the fact that Chattin's three colleagues were taken to a hospital or allowed to go there when they were ill and that one of them had the services of an American physician in jail might prove that consideration was shown for the prisoner's conditions. Nevertheless, if a small town as Mazatlán could not afford—as Mexico seems to contend—a jail satisfactory to lodge prisoners for some considerable length of time, this could never apply to the food furnished, and it would only mean that it is Mexico's duty to see to it that prisoners who have to stay in such a jail for longer than a few weeks or months be transported to a neighboring jail of better conditions. The statement made in the Mexican reply brief that "a jail is a place of punishment, and not a place of pleasure" can have no bearing on the cases of Chattin and his colleagues, who were not convicts in prison, but persons in detention and presumed to be innocent until the Court held the contrary. On the record as it stands, however, inhuman treatment in jail is not proven.

Conclusion

29. Bringing the proceedings of Mexican authorities against Chattin to the test of international standards (paragraph 11), there can be no doubt of their being highly insufficient. Inquiring whether there is convincing evidence of these unjust proceedings (paragraph 11), the answer must be in the affirmative. Since this is a case of alleged responsibility of Mexico for injustice committed by its judiciary, it is necessary to inquire whether the treatment of Chattin amounts even to an outrage, to bad faith, to wilful neglect of duty, or to an insufficiency of governmental action recognizable by every unbiased man (paragraph 11); and the answer here again can only be in the affirmative.

30. An illegal arrest of Chattin is not proven. Irregularity of court proceedings is proven with reference to absence of proper investigations, insufficiency of confrontations, withholding from the accused the opportunity to know all of the charges brought against him, undue delay of the proceedings, making the hearings in open court a mere formality, and a continued absence of seriousness on the part of the Court. Insufficiency of the evidence against Chattin is not convincingly proven; intentional severity of the punishment is proven, without its being shown that the explanation is to be found in unfairmindedness of the Judge. Mistreatment in prison is not proven. Taking into consideration, on the one hand, that this is a case of direct governmental responsibility, and on the other hand, that Chattin, because of his escape, has stayed in jail for eleven months instead of for two years, it would seem proper to allow in behalf of this claimant damages in the sum of $5,000.00 without interest.

[Opinion of Nielsen, Commissioner, omitted.]

Decision

The Commission decides that the Government of the United Mexican States is obligated to pay to the Government of the United States of America, on behalf of B. E. Chattin, $5,000.00 (five thousand dollars), without interest.

Dissenting Opinion, FERNANDEZ MACGREGOR, COMMISSIONER.

* * *

19. I consider that this is one of the most delicate cases that has come before the Commission and that its nature is such that it puts to a test the application of principles of international law. It is hardly of any use to proclaim in theory respect for the judiciary of a nation, if, in practice, it is attempted to call the judiciary to account for its minor acts. It is true that sometimes it is difficult to determine when a judicial act is internationally improper and when it is so from a domestic standpoint only. In my opinion the test which consists in ascertaining if the act implies damage, wilful neglect, or palpable deviation from the established customs becomes clearer by having in mind the damage which the claimant could have suffered. There are certain defects in procedure that can never cause damage which may be estimated separately, and that are blotted out or disappear, to put it thus, if the final decision is just. There are other defects which make it impossible for such decision to be just. The former, as a rule, do not engender international liability; the latter do so, since such liability arises from the decision which is iniquitous because of such defects. To prevent an accused from defending himself, either by refusing to inform him as to the facts imputed to him or by denying him a hearing and the use of remedies; to sentence him without evidence, or to impose on him disproportionate or unusual penalties, to treat him with cruelty and discrimination; are all acts which per se cause damage due to their rendering a just decision impossible. But to delay the proceedings somewhat, to lay aside some evidence, there existing other clear proofs, to fail to comply with the adjective law in its secondary provisions and other deficiencies of this kind, do not cause damage nor violate international law. Counsel for Mexico justly stated that to submit the decisions of a nation to revision in this respect was tantamount to submitting her to a régime of capitulations. All the criticism which has been made of these proceedings, I regret to say, appears to arise from lack of knowledge of the judicial system and practice of Mexico, and, what is more dangerous, from the application thereto of tests belonging to foreign systems of law. For example, in some of the latter the investigation of a crime is made only by the police magistrates and the trial proper is conducted by the Judge. Hence the reluctance in accepting that one same judge may have the two functions and that, therefore, he may have to receive

in the preliminary investigation (instrucción) of the case all kinds of data, with the obligation, of course, of not taking them into account at the time of judgment, if they have no probative weight. It is certain that the secret report, so much discussed in this case, would have been received by the police of the countries which place the investigation exclusively in the hands of such branch. This same police would have been free to follow all the clues or to abandon them at its discretion; but the Judge is criticized here because he did not follow up completely the clue given by Ramirez with respect to Chattin. The same domestic test—to call it such—is used to understand what is a trial or open trial imagining at the same time that it must have the sacred forms of common-law and without remembering that the same goal is reached by many roads. And the same can be said when speaking of the manner of taking testimony of witnesses, of cross-examination, of holding confrontations, etc.

20. In view of the above considerations, I am of the opinion that this claim should be disallowed.

---

1. *What variations in legal systems are comprehended by the international minimum standard?* National legal systems differ considerably as to how they deal with an accused in a criminal proceeding pending trial on the merits. In some countries, the accusation of a criminal offense results in the accused being put into detention pending investigation by a magistrate on the question of whether there is a probable case against him. In some of these countries, bail is not allowed, either for this period or pending trial. In many developing countries, and perhaps in some developed countries, the physical conditions of detention centers are rather grim. In many civil law countries, moreover, exclusionary rules of evidence are sparse and the defendant is not allowed in all cases to confront the witnesses against him. In view of these differences, it cannot be said that the international minimum standard of criminal procedural justice takes its contents from Anglo-American procedures. Does this mean that there is no international minimum standard? Or does this suggest that the task of determining the content of such a standard does not consist of asking whether the foreign state has conformed to the requirements of the United States Constitution as interpreted by the Supreme Court from time to time? Consider what elements in the Chattin case, in view of the differences in the criminal law systems of the United States and Mexico, violated any international minimum standard.

2. *Theory and practice.* Even states that in claims settlement proceedings assert the international minimum standard find it difficult to insure its application to their nationals as a basis for im-

mediate relief.   Consider for example the following announcement of the United States Department of State warning travelers of penalties for drug violations abroad:

At the end of May 1971, there were 747 Americans under detention in the jails of 50 foreign countries for violating local narcotic and marihuana laws.   This represents an alarming fourfold increase in 2 years.   Detentions in May 1969 totaled 190, and by May 1970 had risen to 556.

With more than 2 million Americans expected to go abroad this summer, the Department of State again warns travelers, particularly young Americans, of the serious consequences that may result from arrests abroad on charges of possessing, trafficking in, or smuggling illegal drugs.

The possibility of arrest is of particular concern because of the severe penalties involved, the primitive penal conditions in some countries, and the very limited ability of U. S. officials to assist those arrested.

Many of the young Americans arrested appear to have been under the impression that foreign governments are more tolerant of drug use and more permissive in their drug laws and law enforcement than is the case in the United States.   In fact, however, prosecution of offenders is being intensified, partly as a result of the international effort to suppress the illicit drug trade, an effort in which the present administration has taken the lead.   In many countries, the consequences of narcotics and marihuana violations are severe, ranging up to the death penalty.

*   *   *

Possession alone can result in a jail term of 6 years and a heavy fine in some countries.   In others, possession or trafficking can result in sentences of 1 to 3 years in a detoxification asylum, usually a mental hospital.   Penalties for trafficking can mean sentences of 10 years, 20 years, or life.   Many countries have no provision for bail on drug charges and pretrial detention may be prolonged, in some cases up to a year.

Prison conditions in some countries are primitive: overcrowding, lack of sanitary facilities and bedding; limited, poor-quality food; little or no heat or light; damp, underground locations; rats and vermin; sometimes solitary confinement.

Case histories like the following illustrate the dangers facing Americans abroad who violate local drug laws:

—Two years ago a young American teacher, arrested in the Middle East for possessing a small quantity of hashish, spent several months in the one-room women's section of a provincial jail.   The only light in the room filtered through the bars of the cell door, which, when covered to keep out winter drafts, left the cell in complete darkness.

—The diet of one young man has been nothing but beans and tortillas since his incarceration almost a year ago in a South American country on a drug charge. He has no money, and there are no local charitable sources to help supplement his diet. He has another year and a half to serve.

* * *

—A Latin American cabdriver urged a young American married couple to buy two marihuana cigarettes for 50 cents. Although they had not been looking for marihuana, they finally accepted the offer. The next night secret police arrested them as they sat by the waterfront smoking the cigarettes. They were placed in separate prisons. He was put with 14 other prisoners in a cell where wall bunks were designed to sleep four. Many slept on the cell floor. There were no sheets, blankets, or pillows. It was 6 months before the couple was brought to trial.

American travelers abroad are not protected by U. S. laws. They are subject solely to the laws of the country they are visiting. The authority of American consular officers to intercede on their behalf is very limited. The U. S. Government can only **EQUAL TREATMENT** seek to insure that the American is not discriminated against; that is, that he receives the same treatment as do nationals of the country in which he is arrested who are charged with the same offense.

When a U. S. citizen is arrested abroad, U. S. consular officials move as quickly as possible to protect his rights, but the laws of the country where the arrest takes place determine what those rights are.

Whenever possible, an American consular officer visits the detainee on learning of his arrest, informs him of his rights, and provides him with a list of local attorneys from which to select defense counsel. If the detainee wishes, the consul helps him contact his family or friends to let them know what has happened and seek their assistance.

The consul reports the arrest and subsequent developments to the Department of State. He is in regular contact with the detainee, his attorney, and local officials to determine how the detainee is being treated and to make sure that processing of the legal charges is not unduly delayed. He also does whatever is possible to solve any difficulties which may result from the conditions of detention. (For example, in some foreign prisons a bare subsistence diet is provided, and families are expected to supply most of the prisoner's food.)

Under U. S. law, official U. S. funds cannot be used to pay ✓ legal fees or other expenses for an indigent American detainee. 65 Dep't State Bull. 56 (1971).

3. *NATO Status of Forces Agreement.* The United States has concluded agreements with states on whose territory American military forces are stationed. Among other matters, these agreements deal with the division of jurisdiction, over criminal offenses committed by members of the forces, between the United States and the state on whose territory the forces are stationed. In general, military or duty-related offenses are triable by the United States, other offenses by the receiving state. In the Agreement between the Parties to the North Atlantic Treaty Regarding the Status of their Forces, June 19, 1951, [1953] 4 U.S.T. 1792, 199 U.N.T.S. 67, express provision is made regarding the principles which must govern a criminal trial conducted by the receiving state when it exercises its jurisdiction. Paragraph 9 of Article VII of the agreement provides:

Whenever a member of a force or civilian component or a dependent is prosecuted under the jurisdiction of a receiving State he shall be entitled

(a) to a prompt and speedy trial; (6th)

(b) to be informed, in advance of trial, of the specific charge or charges made against him; (notice)

(c) to be confronted with the witnesses against him; (6th)

(d) to have compulsory process for obtaining witnesses in his favor, if they are within the jurisdiction of the receiving State;

(e) to have legal representation of his own choice for his defence or to have free or assisted legal representation under the conditions prevailing for the time being in the receiving State; (6th)

(f) if he considers it necessary, to have the services of a competent interpreter; and

(g) to communicate with a representative of the Government of the sending State and, when the rules of the court permit, to have such a representative present at his trial.   — MUCH HIGHER —

Are these guarantees different from those which would be provided under the international minimum standard as defined in the Roberts case, p. 579 ("ordinary standards of civilization")? Would all the members of NATO provide these guarantees without reference to the agreement? Does paragraph 9 incorporate into status of forces jurisprudence the procedural guarantees of the United States Constitution?

* * * [T]he United States Senate, in advising ratification of the Status of Forces Agreement, resolved that the laws of all NATO countries be reviewed and analyzed to determine

whether their legal systems afford the fundamental procedural safeguards of the Constitution of the United States, 99 Cong. Rec. 8780 (1953). If there is an absence or denial of these fundamental safeguards the military officials of the United States "shall request the authorities of the receiving state to waive jurisdiction." *Ibid.* In the operation of the jurisdictional aspects of the Agreement, the several territorial states have been co-operative with the United States authorities. Although the Agreement reserves primary jurisdiction to the territorial state in a substantial number of cases, practice indicates that the territorial state has often waived its right to exercise jurisdiction in response to a request by the military authorities of the United States. See generally, the annual Hearings before a Subcommittee of the Senate Committee on Armed Services to Review Operation of Art. VII of the Status of Forces Agreement. Reporters' Note (a) to Section 62 of the Restatement of the Foreign Relations Law of the United States (1965).*

4. *Law applicable in international arbitrations.* In appraising the utility as precedent for international law, of such arbitral decisions as Roberts, p. 579, and Chattin, it is extremely important to determine the legal context in which the opinion was rendered. As noted in Chapter 1, p. 83, arbitrations are customarily conducted in accordance with an agreement between the contending states (the compromis) which not only sets the terms under which the arbitration will be conducted but also may indicate the governing rules to be applied by the arbitrators. In Roberts and Chattin those rules were set forth in the Convention of September 8, 1923 between the United States and Mexico. 43 Stat. 1730, IV U.N.Rep. Int'l Arb.Awards 11. The first article of the convention provided for the application of "principles of international law, justice and equity."

In Perry (United States) v. Panama, General Claims Commission, 1933, VI U.N.Rep. Int'l Arb.Awards 315, the commission was similarly authorized to decide in accordance with these principles. In awarding the United States the sum of $10,000 because of Panama's arrest and imprisonment of an American citizen "without a proper order," who "remained imprisoned through the failure of the authorities to give to his case proper attention," the majority of the commissioners stated: "There is no reason to scrutinize whether these terms" [i. e. international law, justice, and equity] "embody an indivisible rule or mean that international law, justice and equity have to be considered in the order in which they are mentioned, because either of these constructions leads to the conclusion that the omission shall be guided rather by broad conceptions than by narrow interpretations." The dissenting Panamanian Commissioner stated that the majority opinion suggests "the Tribunal believes it proper to award Perry damages for simple reasons of equity."

NEER AND NEER (UNITED STATES) v. UNITED MEXICAN STATES

General Claims Commission, 1926.
IV U.N.Rep.Int'l Arb.Awards 60.

1. This claim is presented by the United States against the United Mexican States in behalf of L. Fay H. Neer, widow, and Pauline E. Neer, daughter, of Paul Neer, who, at the time of his death, was employed as <u>superintendent of a mine</u> in the vicinity of Guanaceví, State of Durango, Mexico. On November 16, 1924, about eight o'clock in the evening, when he and his wife were proceeding on horseback from the village of Guanaceví to their home in the neighborhood, they were stopped by a number of armed men who engaged Neer in a conversation, which Mrs. Neer did not understand, in the midst of which bullets seem to have been exchanged and <u>Neer was killed</u>. It is alleged that, on account of this killing, his wife and daughter, American citizens, sustained damages in the sum of $100,-000.00; that the Mexican authorities showed an unwarrantable lack of diligence or an unwarrantable lack of intelligent investigation in prosecuting the culprits; and that therefore the Mexican Government ought to pay to the claimants the said amount.

2. As to the nationality of the claim, which is challenged, * * *. On the record as presented the Commission decides that the claimants were by birth, and have since remained, American nationals.

3. As to <u>lack of diligence, or lack of intelligent investigation, on the part of the Mexican authorities</u>, after the killing of Paul Neer had been brought to their notice, it would seem that in the early morning after the tragedy these authorities might have acted in a more vigorous and effective way than they did, and moreover, that both the special agent of the Attorney General of Durango (in his letter of November 24, 1924), and the Governor of that State, who proposed the removal of the Judge of Guanaceví, have shared this opinion. The Commission is mindful that the task of the local Mexican authorities was hampered by the fact that the only eyewitness of the murder was unable to furnish them any helpful information. There might have been reason for the higher authorities of the State to intervene in the matter, as they apparently did. But in the view of the Commission there is a long way between holding that a more active and more efficient course of procedure might have been pursued, on the one hand, and holding that this record presents such lack of diligence and of intelligent investigation as constitutes an international delinquency, on the other hand.

4. The Commission recognizes the difficulty of devising a general formula for determining the boundary between an international delinquency of this type and an unsatisfactory use of power included in national sovereignty. * * * Without attempting to announce a precise formula, it is in the opinion of the Commission possible to go a little further than the authors quoted, and to hold (first) that the propriety of governmental acts should be put to the test of international standards, and (second) that the treatment of an alien, in order to constitute an international delinquency, should amount to an outrage, to bad faith, to wilful neglect of duty, or to an insufficiency of governmental action so far short of international standards that every reasonable and impartial man would readily recognize its insufficiency. Whether the insufficiency proceeds from deficient execution of an intelligent law or from the fact that the laws of the country do not empower the authorities to measure up to international standards is immaterial.

5. It is not for an international tribunal such as this Commission to decide, whether another course of procedure taken by the local authorities at Guanaceví might have been more effective. On the contrary, the grounds of liability limit its inquiry to whether there is convincing evidence either (1) that the authorities administering the Mexican law acted in an outrageous way, in bad faith, in wilful neglect of their duties, or in a pronounced degree of improper action, or (2) that Mexican law rendered it impossible for them properly to fulfil their task. No attempt is made to establish the second point. The first point is negatived by the full record of police and judicial authorities produced by the Mexican Agent, though the Commission feels bound to state once more that in its opinion better methods might have been used. From this record it appears that the local authorities, on the very night of the tragedy, November 16, went to the spot where the killing took place and examined the corpse; that on November 17 the Judge proceeded to the examination of some witnesses, among them Mrs. Neer; that investigations were continued for several days; that arrests were made of persons suspected; and that they were subsequently released for want of evidence. The American Agency in rebuttal offers nothing but affidavits stating individual impressions or suppositions. In the light of the entire record in this case the Commission is not prepared to hold that the Mexican authorities have shown such lack of diligence or such lack of intelligent investigation in apprehending and punishing the culprits as would render Mexico liable before this Commission.

Decision

6. The Commission accordingly decides that the claim of the United States is disallowed.

[Separate opinion omitted.]

3. SUMMARY OF THE PRECEDENTS

INTERNATIONAL LAW COMMISSION REPORT ON STATE RESPONSIBILITY
GARCIA AMADOR, SPECIAL RAPPORTEUR

Yearbook of the International Law Commission
173, 181 (1956, vol. II).

41. An analysis of the traditional doctrine and practice shows that the acts or omissions which give rise to international responsibility fall into the one or other of the following two categories of wrongful acts: (a) acts which affect a State as such, i. e., those which injure the interests or rights of the State as a legal entity; and (b) acts which produce damage to the person or property of its nationals. The first category comprises the most diverse acts or omissions, some being ill-defined or even undefinable. Acts in this category include failure to comply with the terms of a treaty, whatever the nature or purpose of the treaty, failure to respect diplomatic immunities and, in general, the violation of any of the rights which are intrinsic attributes of the personality of the State—political sovereignty, territorial integrity, property rights. The second category includes acts or omissions which give rise to the "responsibility of States for damage done in their territories to the person or property of foreigners". This is the principal subject of the literature, private and official codifications and judicial decisions which treat of the responsibility of States.

42. As will be seen hereunder, the above classification, from the traditional point of view, is more concerned with form than with substance, for it has been said that, whichever category they fall into, the acts or omissions in question have this in common: they damage interests which, in the final analysis, vest in the State exclusively. Apart from this aspect of the question, which will be examined in its proper context in a later chapter (chapter V) the classification may become meaningless in some cases which come within the scope of both categories. An example of such a case would be the nonperformance of a treaty, where the interests of the nationals of one of the contracting States are prejudiced and the claim is based on this prejudice. In any case, for the specific purposes of the present chapter, we shall now consider what acts or omissions are more generally regarded as giving rise to an international responsibility on the part of the State.

43. Acts in the second category have been subdivided into: STATE (i) acts or omissions on the part of the authorities of the State; and ACTION (ii) acts of private persons, which include internal disturbances. PRIVATE Within the first subdivision, a further distinction is drawn according ACTION to whether it is the legislature, the judicature or the executive which has committed the wrongful act. The acts of the legislature may give rise to international responsibility on the part of the State, for example if a measure is enacted which discriminates between nationals

and aliens, or if nationalization and compulsory expropriation legislation is passed which affects the property of aliens in a manner contrary to the rules established by international law. The judicature may involve the State in responsibility if it acts, or fails to act, in such a way that a "denial of justice" to an alien may be said to have occurred (e. g., unwarranted delay in the proceedings, or judgment manifestly unjust or arbitrary from the point of view of international law). In practice, however, wrongful acts or omissions on the part of the executive offer perhaps the commonest and the most varied instances. These include abuses by police officers, which can be very serious (physical ill-treatment; killing without any death sentence having been pronounced; the improper collection of fines or illegal contributions; illegal confiscation of property). Lastly, this group of wrongful acts or omissions includes the non-performance by the State—through the agency of any of its organs—of a contract entered into by the State with an alien, in which case the State is responsible for non-performance.

44. Within the second subdivision, too, the wrongful acts capable of giving rise to responsibility on the part of the State are not all of the same character. Although in these cases the international responsibility does not originate in the act itself but rather in the conduct of the State in relation to the act (failure to exercise due diligence, connivance, manifest complicity, etc.), the nature of the act committed by a private person or of acts committed during internal disturbances is bound to influence the way in which the law regards the State's conduct as a source of international responsibility. Typical examples of wrongful acts which can be committed by private persons are: attacks or insults against a foreign State, in the person of the head of that State, its agencies or diplomatic representatives; acts offensive to its national flag; and illegal acts—whatever their degree of seriousness may be—which cause damage to the person or property of the nationals of a foreign State. When disturbances occur in a State, the acts concerned are usually of a more serious character; in some cases, they are specifically intended to cause damage to the property or person of foreigners.

45. Although not exhaustive, the foregoing enumeration presents a fairly accurate picture of the acts and omissions which according to traditional doctrine and practice, give rise to international responsibility on the part of the State. In any case, it makes it possible to define the character of those acts and so to determine the type of responsibility to which they can give rise.

1. *Exhaustion of local remedies.* "The rule that local remedies must be exhausted before international proceedings may be instituted is a well-established rule of customary international law; the rule has

been generally observed in cases in which a state has adopted the cause of its national where rights are claimed to have been disregarded in another State in violation of international law. Before resort may be had to an international court in such a situation, it has been considered necessary that the State where the violation occurred should have an opportunity to redress it by its own means, within the framework of its own domestic legal system." Interhandel Case (Switzerland v. United States), [1959] I.C.J.Rep. 6, 27. As stated, the rule is applicable to claims based upon violations of personal human rights as well as to claims arising from violations of rights of property. Detailed examination of the rule is deferred to Chapter 17, dealing with economic interests.

It is said that the rule is subject to exceptions; for example, if it is clear that exhaustion of local remedies would not be effective, there is no need to pursue them. Should there be an exception from the requirement of exhaustion of local remedies in such cases as the alleged mistreatment of Chinese by Indonesia, p. 575? Should the rule apply to diplomatic protests, or only to claims in litigation, before the International Court of Justice or an arbitral tribunal?

In view of the exhaustion of local remedies rule, how can a claimant state assert that the acting state has violated its own law? If, for example, an individual has been imprisoned for a long time before trial and complains of this through appropriate court proceedings until a court of final appeal has ruled that the local law does not prohibit such imprisonment, can an international tribunal properly hold that there has been a violation of local law? See the Roberts case, at p. 581 where the commission asserted that Roberts' imprisonment was a violation of the Mexican Constitution. Does the answer to this question lie in the fact that the compromis governing the Roberts arbitration provided in Article V as follows?

> The High Contracting Parties, being desirous of effecting an equitable settlement of the claims of their respective citizens thereby affording them just and adequate compensation for their losses or damages, agree that no claim shall be disallowed or rejected by the Commission by the application of the general principle of international law that the legal remedies must be exhausted as a condition precedent to the validity or allowance of any claim.

2. *A new view of the older precedents.* The flow of third party decisions on questions of violation of personal human rights practically ceased with World War II. It has been observed that the desire of states for freedom to act unilaterally has been strong during the whole life of the United Nations and that states have been reluctant to take disputes to the International Court of Justice. "It may be noted in this context that, whereas the number of arbitral decisions since 1945 was not spectacular, it was not insignificant, although it is probably true that, as the Secretary General of the United Nations

pointed out, 'most of them concerned minor questions, many of them of a commercial nature, which were not in the least likely to disturb peace and security.' "   Gross, The International Court of Justice: Consideration of Requirements for Enhancing its Rôle in the International Legal Order, 65 Am.J.Int'l L. 253, 268 (1971).

This fact has meant that the body of arbitral precedent on personal human rights is static; it has failed to keep up with vast changes in world society and politics.   How reliable then is this body of precedent?   And how useful in today's world?

An even more significant reason for questioning the reliability of the older precedents is the fact that the United Nations has been developing new legal norms in the field of human rights.   This development is described immediately hereafter.   Query whether an arbitral tribunal deciding a case like Roberts or Chattin or Neer today would ignore the Universal Declaration of Human Rights or the relevant draft covenants and conventions that have flowed from the United Nations and regional organizations in recent years.

SECTION B. THE HUMAN RIGHTS PROGRAM OF THE UNITED NATIONS

---

1. HUMAN RIGHTS PROVISIONS OF THE CHARTER OF THE UNITED NATIONS

CHARTER OF THE UNITED NATIONS

Article 1

The Purposes of the United Nations are:

* * *

3.   To achieve international cooperation in solving international problems of an economic, social, cultural, or humanitarian character, and in promoting and encouraging respect for human rights and for fundamental freedoms for all without distinction as to race, sex, language, or religion. * * *

* * *

Article 2

The Organization and its Members, in pursuit of the Purposes stated in Article 1, shall act in accordance with the following Principles.

* * *

2.   All Members, in order to ensure to all of them the rights and benefits resulting from membership, shall fulfil in good faith the obligations assumed by them in accordance with the present Charter.

*   *   *

Article 55

With a view to the creation of conditions of stability and well-being which are necessary for peaceful and friendly relations among nations based on respect for the principle of equal rights and self-determination of peoples, the United Nations shall promote:

a.   higher standards of living, full employment, and conditions of economic and social progress and development;

b.   solutions of international economic, social, health, and related problems; and international cultural and educational cooperation; and

c.   universal respect for, and observance of, human rights and fundamental freedoms for all without distinction as to race, sex, language or religion.

Article 56

All Members pledge themselves to take joint and separate action in cooperation with the Organization for the achievement of the purposes set forth in Article 55.

———————

Highlights of the drafting history of Chapter IX, Article 56 of the Charter.   The question has been raised throughout the life of the United Nations whether Article 56 imposes on states an international legal obligation immediately to take national action to correct internal deficiencies in the area of human rights or serves merely as a statement of political principle, i. e., that states intend to "do something" about human rights.

The history of the drafting of Article 56 at the San Francisco Conference on International Organization discloses that two significant questions were discussed: one, the question of domestic jurisdiction and, two, the question of the nature of the commitment states should undertake.

The United States was particularly concerned that nothing in Chapter IX of the Charter should "be construed as giving authority to the Organization to intervene in the domestic affairs of member states." 10 U.N.Conf.Int'l Org. 83 (1945). The United States was, at one point, of the opinion that the reservation for domestic jurisdiction in Article 2(7) of the Charter would not alone be sufficient to keep human rights from becoming matters of "international concern" if Article 56 were worded to include a "pledge" by members "to take such independent action as they deem appropriate to achieve these purposes within their own territories." 10 U.N.Conf.Int'l Org. 140 (1945). Nevertheless, the United States ultimately supported the language of Article 56 as it appears in the Charter, without insisting upon a special reservation to retain domestic jurisdiction over human rights matters. 10 U.N.Conf.Int'l Org. 161 (1945).

As to the nature of the commitment, the following submission from a drafting sub-committee was rejected:

"All members undertake to cooperate jointly and severally with the Organization for the achievement of these purposes." 10 U.N.Conf.Int'l Org. 394 and 139 (1945).

The proposal noted above, for a pledge to take "independent action", was likewise not accepted. The ultimate language as found in the Charter includes "*separate action* in cooperation with the Organization" [emphasis supplied].

What in fact was agreed to at San Francisco?

The Meaning of Article 56.

THE QUESTION OF RACE CONFLICT IN SOUTH AFRICA RESULTING FROM THE POLICIES OF APARTHEID

United Nations, Resolution 721 (VIII) Adopted by the General Assembly, Dec. 8, 1953

U.N.Gen.Ass., Off.Rec., 8th Sess.1953 Supp. No. 17(A/2630).

The General Assembly,

Having considered the report of the United Nations Commission on the Racial Situation in the Union of South Africa established by resolution 616 A (VII) of 5 December 1952,

Noting with concern that the Commission, in its study of the racial policies of the Government of the Union of South Africa, has concluded that these policies and their consequences are contrary to the Charter and the Universal Declaration of Human Rights,

Noting that the Commission had also concluded that:

(a) "It is highly unlikely, and indeed improbable, that the policy of apartheid will ever be willingly accepted by the masses subjected to discrimination", and

(b) That the continuance of this policy would make peaceful solutions increasingly difficult and endanger friendly relations among nations,

Noting further that the Commission considers it desirable that the United Nations should request the Government of the Union of South Africa to reconsider the components of its policy towards various ethnic groups, * * *

Considering * * * the Commission's view that one of the difficulties encountered by it was the lack of cooperation from the Government of the Union of South Africa and, in particular, its refusal to permit the Commission to enter its territory,

1.   Reaffirms its resolutions 103 (I) of 19 November 1946, 377 A (V), section E, of 3 November 1950 and 616 B (VII) of 5 December 1952, particularly the passages in those resolutions which state respectively that "it is in the higher interests of humanity to put an immediate end to religious and so-called racial persecution and discrimination"; that "enduring peace will not be secured solely by collective security arrangements against breaches of international peace and acts of aggression, but that a genuine and lasting peace depends also upon the observance of all the Principles and Purposes established in the Charter of the United Nations, * * * and especially upon respect for an observance of human rights and fundamental freedoms for all and on the establishment and maintenance of conditions of economic and social well-being in all countries"; and that "in a multi-racial society harmony and respect for human rights and freedoms and the peaceful development of a unified community are best assured when patterns of legislation and practice are directed towards ensuring the equality before the law of all persons regardless of race, creed or colour, and when economic, social, cultural and political participation of all racial groups is on a basis of equality" ;

2.   Expresses appreciation of the work of the United Nations Commission on the Racial Situation in the Union of South Africa;

*   *   *

4.   Requests the Commission:

(a) To continue its study of the development of the racial situation in the Union of South Africa: * * *

(b) To suggest measures which would help to alleviate the situation and promote a peaceful settlement;

5.   Invites the Government of the Union of South Africa to extend its full co-operation to the Commission;

6.   Requests the Commission to report to the General Assembly at its ninth session.

United Nations, Extracts From Debate In Ad Hoc
Political Committee

U.N.Gen.Ass.Off.Rec., 8th Sess., Ad hoc Political Committee
20 Nov. 1953—5 Dec. 1953.

[In the course of the debate, the foregoing resolution was considered in draft form and adopted; a South African resolution denying the competence of the committee to deal with the matters covered by the resolution was defeated.]

* * *

At the invitation of the Chairman, Mr. Santa Cruz, Chairman and Rapporteur of the Commission, took a seat at the Committee table.

5.   Mr. SANTA CRUZ (Chairman and Rapporteur of the Commission appointed to study the racial situation in the Union of South Africa)   * * *

* * *

7.   The Commission had felt it necessary to include a chapter in the report in which it examined the question of its competence to deal with the racial problem in South Africa.   * * *   It had concluded   * * *   that the Assembly was empowered to undertake any investigations and make any recommendations to Member States that it deemed desirable concerning the application and enforcement of the purposes and principles of the Charter, and that, since the Commission was a subsidiary body of the Assembly, it was therefore not restricted in its activities by the provisions of the Charter. Finally, it had concluded that the exercise of the powers and functions devolving on the Assembly in such matters did not constitute an intervention within the meaning of Article 2, paragraph 7.   Those conclusions were in keeping with the jurisprudence of the principal organs of the United Nations; they had been endorsed by the majority of Member States and were based on the views of the most eminent jurists who had dealt with the question.   * * *

* * *

10.   The Commission had assumed a formal obligation on the part of signatories to the Charter, who had undertaken, by adopting Article 56, to take the necessary measures to bring about the purposes of Article 55, including universal respect for human rights and fundamental freedoms, without distinction as to race, sex, language or religion.   That obligation could not, however, mean that States were obliged either to eliminate overnight every internal situation which was contrary to the Charter or to be regarded as having violated it. It would be unreal to ignore the fact that in nearly all countries existing conditions were not always in accordance with the ideal principles proclaimed in the Charter.   Imperfections in the social structure derived from historical circumstances and were associated with social, economic and religious factors which could not be eliminated by legislation.   The obligation, therefore, amounted only to an undertaking by the signatories to do their best in good faith to amend their legislation and customs in accordance with those principles as quickly as practicable.   No situation changing for the better should be regarded as contrary to the obligations laid down in the Charter.   It was for that reason that the Commission had, when comparing the discriminatory legislation of the Union of South Africa with the

provisions of the Charter and of the Universal Declaration of Human Rights, limited itself to analysing only those acts which had been promulgated since the Charter.

11. On the question of competence, the Commission had also come to the conclusion that United Nations agencies had the power to decide whether a matter concerning violation of fundamental human rights was "essentially within the domestic jurisdiction of any State". It was, however, the general conclusion, supported by the opinion of eminent jurists, that United Nations agencies should not use their right in an arbitrary manner, and should avoid converting an institution meant to serve the interests of peace and human progress into an instrument of discord to make barren and unjustified attacks on one of its Members.

* * *

1. Mr. JOOSTE (Union of South Africa) said that his delegation was very conscious of the serious implications of the debate upon which the Committee was about to embark. The South African delegation represented a sovereign and independent Member of the United Nations, with obligations under the Charter with which it was endeavouring to comply to the utmost of its ability and with rights which had been guaranteed to it and which it could expect to be honoured. Those rights were now at stake. The history of the matter before the Committee was well known to its members; as were the events that had culminated in the establishment on 5 December 1952 of a commission whose terms of reference amounted, despite his Government's most solemn protests, to intervention in the internal affairs of his country.

* * *

5. It would probably be pointed out once again that the question had already been considered by the General Assembly and that that in itself rendered the Assembly competent in the matter. If that contention were accepted, the fact that the United Nations had asserted that it was itself competent to examine a question would ipso facto mean that the United Nations legally possessed such competence. In other words, a majority vote could render valid any action of the General Assembly which might be contrary to the provisions of the Charter. The argument that the United Nations had dealt with the matter in the past could therefore not justify the intervention of the General Assembly in the question of racial conflict in South Africa, unless the provisions of the Charter authorized the Assembly to intervene in matters of essentially domestic concern or the item in question did not relate to matters essentially within the domestic jurisdiction of South Africa. He wished to dwell upon those two points.

6. With regard to the first question, the Commission appointed to study the racial situation in the Union of South Africa had found

it necessary to pronounce itself and had endeavoured to prove that the legal position of the Government of the Union of South Africa was not a valid one.   But the Charter of the United Nations was a solemn contract between members of the family of nations, and must be interpreted as such.   The Charter imposed obligations on all Members of the United Nations and guaranteed them certain rights; those obligations and rights were defined in the Charter.   At San Francisco the great Powers had wished to safeguard their positions by reserving the right of veto.   All Member States, and particularly the smaller States, had safeguarded themselves by introducing into Chapter I of the Charter a clause protecting them against any interference by the United Nations in their domestic affairs.   That clause was contained in Article 2, paragraph 7.   It contained both an obligation and a right: an obligation on the United Nations not to intervene in the internal affairs of Members States; and the right of Member States to maintain absolute sovereignty in that field.

7.   His delegation believed that the word "nothing" in Article 2, paragraph 7, precluded any intervention by the United Nations in domestic affairs, with the exception of the application of enforcement measures under Chapter VII of the Charter, which in any case lay outside the competence of the General Assembly.   The word "intervene" in the same paragraph had the meaning assigned to it in dictionaries, and not the artificial, technical meaning given to it by certain jurists.   The word necessarily included the act of interference. It could not be restricted to the meaning of "dictatorial interference", for if it were to be so restricted it would not apply to a measure taken by the General Assembly, which had only the power to recommend.

* * *

9.   The South African delegation, therefore, reaffirmed its faith in the provisions of Article 2, paragraph 7, of the Charter as a protection against any interference in matters within the domestic jurisdiction of States; it did not recognize the United Nations as having any right to take action which would amount to such interference.

10.   Turning to the question as to whether the racial conflict in South Africa could be regarded as essentially within the domestic jurisdiction of the Union of South Africa, he drew attention to the matters to which that conflict related: legislation on land tenure, conditions of employment in public services, regulation of transport, suppression of communism, combat service in the armed forces, nationality, the franchise, movement of population, residence, immigration, the work and practice of the professions, social security, education, public health, criminal law, taxation, housing, regulation of the liquor traffic, regulation of labour and wages, marriage, food subsidies, local government, pensions and workmen's compensation.   Ob-

viously, all those matters were without any doubt essentially within the domestic jurisdiction of the Union of South Africa; they covered the whole field of domestic administration in a modern State. To accept the thesis that the United Nations was entitled to intervene in such matters was tantamount to denying the principle and attributes of national sovereignty and to repudiating the provisions of Article 2, paragraph 1, of the Charter; it would signal the end of the United Nations as an organization of sovereign States.

11.   It had been contended that the matters in question were outside the domestic jurisdiction of South Africa because they involved human rights; the Commission appointed to study the racial situation in the Union of South Africa had supported that contention. It should be pointed out, first, that human rights were not defined in the Charter of the United Nations and that the Charter imposed no obligation on States in respect of them; secondly, that the Universal Declaration of Human Rights was not a legally binding document; and lastly, that there was as yet no international covenant of human rights in which such rights were defined. That was an especially important consideration, for the fact that the United Nations had deemed it necessary to embark on the drafting of an international covenant defining human rights clearly demonstrated that they had not yet been defined and that there was as yet no international instrument imposing specific obligations on Member States with respect to them.

12.   Those who had attempted to justify intervention by the United Nations by alleging that human rights were involved had gone so far as to claim that the racial policy of the Union Government constituted a threat to international peace, and the Commission, in its report, had suggested that that policy was likely to impair friendly relations among nations and therefore called for action under Article 14 of the Charter.

13.   Those preposterous and mischievous allegations reflected a desire to exploit the fundamental purpose of the United Nations, the maintenance of international peace and security, for tendentious purposes. It could not be seriously argued that the racial situation in South Africa constituted a threat to international peace. A threat to international peace could exist only when the territorial integrity or political independence of a State was threatened directly or indirectly. It could hardly be charged that the domestic laws of a State constituted such a threat.

*   *   *

12.   Mr. DAYAL (India)

*   *   *   [I]t was clear that the policy of apartheid was based on the idea that the interests of the white minority in South Africa could only be protected by a policy of racial domination. It was unnecessary to point out that such a solution was contrary to the Charter and was not supported by the experience of history or by the practice

of the United Nations. It was true that racial differences existed, but it was perfectly possible to overcome them by recognizing the rights of each of the races concerned. A solution based on force and domination was no solution at all. It could only generate hatred and eventually make change by violence inevitable.

* * *

25. But social discrimination was the most humiliating type of discrimination. Apartheid did not manifest itself simply in the Group Areas Act or in measures designed to confine the native Bantu populations to reservations. It was practised in shops, hospitals, post offices, theatres, public parks and gardens, libraries, etc. It even existed in telephone booths and elevators. He quoted a series of examples, some of which had been given in the Commission's report.

26. The South African Government was not, of course, the only one to apply measures of racial and social discrimination. Such measures existed in other countries which had signed the United Nations Charter. But there was a vital difference between those countries, which had undertaken to implement the provisions of the Charter without discrimination, and South Africa, which proclaimed that those measures were the only way to preserve white civilization. In all the other countries, discrimination was a diminishing social practice which enlightened opinion everywhere condemned. In South Africa, it was a norm of social behaviour, sanctified by the ideology of the State and enjoying the Government's full support. In the circumstances, a white citizen of South Africa who wished conscientiously to observe the provisions of the United Nations Charter would be guilty of a multitude of offences. Thus, the policy of apartheid not only contravened the Charter, but made the application of the Charter impossible and illegal in the territory of the Union.

27. The memoranda submitted by the Governments of India and Pakistan, and reproduced in the annexes to the Commission's report, cited no less than twenty discriminatory laws promulgated in the Union after 1945, that was to say, after the signing of the Charter. Chapter VIII of the Commission's report alone cited ten of those laws which, according to the Commission, were not in harmony with the Universal Declaration of Human Rights. The non-European population of South Africa had, on 26 June 1952, embarked on a campaign of passive resistance to that policy of discrimination which was growing stronger. That campaign had been suspended soon after the Christmas holidays of 1952, after 8,065 persons had been sentenced to imprisonment. The Union Government had done its utmost to destroy the morale of the resisters by imposing excessively long prison terms, forced labour and corporal punishment. It had repeatedly utilized the Suppression of Communism Act to deal with resisters and had acquired very broad powers by promulgating the Public Safety Act and the Criminal Law Amendment Act which, according

to the Rand Daily Mail, had been tantamount to setting up a dictatorship or reverting to barbaric despotism.

*   *   *

29. The conclusions to be drawn from those facts were clear and the United Nations Commission had formulated them in unambiguous terms. It had stated that the doctrine of racial differentiation and superiority was scientifically false, extremely dangerous to internal peace and international relations, and contrary to the dignity and worth of the human person. The policy arising from it was contrary to the solemn declaration in the Preamble to the Charter, to Articles 55 and 56, to the Universal Declaration of Human Rights, to resolution 377 (V) entitled "Uniting for peace", to resolutions 103 (I) and 616B (VII) of the General Assembly—in short, to the whole doctrine upheld by the United Nations.

*   *   *

1. Sir Walter HANKINSON (United Kingdom) said that in his delegation's opinion the item raised but one question, namely whether the United Nations was competent to discuss the question of apartheid. That did not mean, as he had pointed out at the 435th plenary meeting of the General Assembly, that the United Kingdom's support for the progressive elimination of racial discrimination in the world was any less constant than it had always been.

2. Nevertheless, the United Kingdom Government considered that the item under discussion was outside the competence of the General Assembly for it related to matters essentially within the domestic jurisdiction of the Union of South Africa. That view was borne out by the provisions of Article 2, paragraph 7, of the Charter which should prevail over all other Articles of the Charter.

*   *   *

4. It was often said that by virtue of Articles 55 and 56 of the Charter, questions relating to human rights ceased to be purely domestic problems and acquired an international character. That interpretation was manifestly inaccurate, for if it were to be accepted the United Nations would acquire the right to intervene in all the internal affairs of its Member States, including economic, social and cultural problems. That argument would be valid only if specific international obligations were created with respect to particular rights. Article 56, however, created no such obligations. It merely pledged the Member States to cooperate with the Organization for the achievement of the purposes set forth in Article 55.

5. For all those reasons his delegation thought that the Commission appointed to study the racial situation in the Union of South Africa, whose report the Ad Hoc Political Committee was discussing, had been established illegally and that all its activities were therefore illegal.

*   *   *

8.   The word "intervene", the key word in Article 2, had been interpreted by the Commission with an equal lack of objectivity. The authors of the report considered that the word related only to "dictatorial interference" and cited various authors in support of their view. On the other hand, they avoided mentioning authors holding the contrary view and in particular Professor Preuss himself who had said that the framers of the Charter had probably not even considered so direct and drastic a type of intervention and that nowhere in the Charter, save in Chapter VII, had they vested in any organ of the United Nations the power to interfere dictatorially in the domestic affairs of States. Elsewhere in his monograph Professor Preuss had expressed the view that United Nations practice hardly justified so restrictive an interpretation of the word "intervention" and had concluded that if recommendations and a general discussion were consistent with the pledge of States to undertake joint and separate action in co-operation with the United Nations for achieving the economic and social objectives set forth in the Charter, any specific recommendation relating to a matter within the domestic jurisdiction of a State would undoubtedly constitute interference, which the framers of the Charter had plainly wished to prohibit. * * *

12.   In short, the section of the report dealing with competence was by no means convincing. Consequently, he would support the South African draft resolution * * * relating to competence.

* * *

21.   Mrs. BOLTON (United States of America) said that the question of race conflict in South Africa brought before the General Assembly the entire programme of a Member State's policy and legislation concerning the status and treatment of its nationals on the basis of their racial origins.

22.   At the beginning of the session, the United States delegation had voted for the inclusion of the item in the agenda, stating that its attitude was governed by the fact that at its seventh session the Assembly had established a Commission and had asked it to report to the present session. It had noted on that occasion that an item of that character invited questions about the competence of the General Assembly under Article 2, paragraph 7, of the Charter; that the United States had observed with increasing concern the tendency of the General Assembly to place on its agenda subjects the international character of which was doubtful; and that that problem in the view of the United States, deserved most careful consideration by all Member Governments in preparing for the conference in reviewing the Charter.

23.   Some delegations, in particular that of the Union of South Africa, had contended that the General Assembly could not even discuss the item, in view of the reservation made in Article 2, paragraph 7.   Most delegations, including that of the United States, did not

share such an extreme view of the effect of the paragraph in question. At the same time, the United States was keenly aware of the serious problems in which the Organization might become involved in dealing with matters of that character if it did not constantly keep in mind the provision in the Charter on domestic jurisdiction.

24.   Many Member States considered that the programme of apartheid of the Government of the Union of South Africa imposed an inferior status on large sections of the population, by reason of their race, in disregard of provisions of the Charter, particularly of Articles 55 and 56.   It was difficult to say how the United Nations could best play the part laid down for it in the Charter with respect to the advancement of human rights everywhere.   The provisions on human rights in the Charter represented an important innovation in international political life.   Action must be taken with the greatest circumspection and the highest degree of responsibility, in order not to blight the prospects of steady and wholesome growth for that new element in international relations.   When the United Nations considered human rights problems within a particular country it should keep in mind developments throughout the world in the field of human rights and should state general conclusions relating to the objectives which all Member States should pursue in that field.

*   *   *

26.   The United States delegation had already had occasion to emphasize that progress in the field of race relations was necessarily slow.   The important thing was that there should be progress;   no one could claim to have reached perfection.   The United States, from its own experience recognized the difficulty of the problems confronting the Union of South Africa, and appreciated how acute the problems of racial relations could be rendered by shifts of population, consequent upon economic development and industrialization, and by the state of development of different groups within a population.   In South Africa those problems were further complicated by the numerical proportions of the various racial groups.   But for all that, the problem was not insoluble;   in some parts of the United States and its territories the populations of different racial origins were approximately equal in number, but that did not prevent progress in the improvement of race relations.

*   *   *

MOVCHAN, THE HUMAN RIGHTS PROBLEM IN PRESENT-DAY INTERNATIONAL LAW

Contemporary International Law 233, 239 (Moscow 1969).

The Soviet science of international law is unequivocal in its claim that the "legal position of individuals is determined by national and not international law".   Professor S. B. Krylov, for instance, writes in his work on the U.N. history that the "individual is protected not directly by international law but only with the aid of national law".

International law proceeds from the recognition of the individual as a subject of national law and does not admit the direct protection of his rights by any international organ in circumvention of the state and disregard of the jurisdiction of the state organs in this sphere since this would be tantamount to interference in the domestic affairs of states and to impingement upon their sovereignty.

These principles are challenged by only a few international jurists (Scelle and Politis among them) who support the theory that the individual is a subject of international law, a theory advanced in the West before the Second World War and backed by some British and American scholars (Lauterpacht, Jessup and others.)

This theory alleges that the individual is a subject of international law, enjoys international rights and, consequently, his rights must be defended not only by the state but directly by international organs with the aid of various measures involving interference in the domestic affairs of states. The exponents of such a cosmopolitan interpretation of human rights in essence completely negate the sovereignty of states and in fact, negate international law by replacing it with "human right".

The theory that the individual is a subject of international law is incompatible with the nature of international law as interstate law and has very few supporters among international jurists.

---

1. *Domestic jurisdiction and Article 56.* If the position of the South African and United Kingdom representatives is correct, how is a state's performance under its "pledge" in Article 56 to be judged? Would it be irrational for a state to say that it has indeed accepted an obligation to promote human rights in its own territory but that it alone shall be the judge of both (a) the standard of human rights it is obligated to promote and (b) whether its own performance has reached that standard? Irrespective of the rationality of that position, is that what the Charter of the United Nations has provided?

2. *The contents of the obligations in Article 56.* If Article 56 has imposed an obligation upon members of the United Nations, what is the content of that obligation? Is a member state under an obligation to provide fair hearings in criminal cases, to guarantee freedom of expression, to ensure universal suffrage? Or is a member state merely under an obligation to move affirmatively toward some unstated ideal of rights and freedom? Or not to move negatively away from such an ideal? Or merely not to make distinctions, in the enjoyment of whatever rights may exist, in its domestic law, on the basis of race, sex, language or religion?

3. *Protracted debate in the United Nations.* The foregoing extract from the debates in the United Nations is but one example of a long line of similar discussions in which similar arguments have been made repeatedly. The United Nations' concern with South Africa's racial practices was first voiced in 1946 and continues to be expressed without significant effect. More recent resolutions of the Security Council and the General Assembly have been grounded in part upon the effect of those practices on "international peace and security." This basis for United Nations action with respect to South Africa will be examined in Chapter 20.

ADVISORY OPINION ON THE CONTINUED PRESENCE OF SOUTH AFRICA IN NAMIBIA (SOUTH WEST AFRICA) [a]

International Court of Justice, 1971.
[1971] I.C.J.Rep. 16.

[At the conclusion of World War I, South Africa accepted a Mandate with respect to German South West Africa pursuant to the Covenant of the League of Nations. Upon the demise of the League, South Africa refused to accept the principle urged upon it by the United Nations that the latter had the right to supervise its administration of South West Africa. After fruitless negotiations, and the rendering of advisory opinions on various aspects of the matter by the International Court of Justice, the General Assembly adopted a resolution terminating the Mandate for South West Africa, now called Namibia by the United Nations. South Africa having failed to alter its policies with respect to South West Africa, the Security Council adopted a resolution declaring the continued presence of South Africa in Namibia to be illegal and called on states to act accordingly.

The council thereafter requested the court to render an advisory opinion on the question: "What are the legal consequences for States of the continued presence of South Africa in Namibia, notwithstanding Security Council resolution 276 (1970)?"

In the course of a comprehensive opinion answering this question, the following passages occurred.]

128. In its oral statement and in written communications to the Court, the Government of South Africa expressed the desire to supply the Court with further factual information concerning the purposes and objectives of South Africa's policy of separate development or apartheid, contending that to establish a breach of South

---

a. The full name of the case is: Legal Consequences for States of the Continued Presence of South Africa in Namibia (South West Africa), notwithstanding Security Council Resolution 276 (1970), Advisory Opinion.

Africa's substantive international obligations under the Mandate it would be necessary to prove that a particular exercise of South Africa's legislative or administrative powers was not directed in good faith towards the purpose of promoting to the utmost the well-being and progress of the inhabitants. It is claimed by the Government of South Africa that no act or omission on its part would constitute a violation of its international obligations unless it is shown that such act or omission was actuated by a motive, or directed towards a purpose other than one to promote the interests of the inhabitants of the Territory.

129.   The Government of South Africa having made this request, the Court finds that no factual evidence is needed for the purpose of determining whether the policy of apartheid as applied by South Africa in Namibia is in conformity with the international obligations assumed by South Africa under the Charter of the United Nations. In order to determine whether the laws and decrees applied by South Africa in Namibia, which are a matter of public record, constitute a violation of the purposes and principles of the Charter of the United Nations, the question of intent or governmental discretion is not relevant; nor is it necessary to investigate or determine the effects of those measures upon the welfare of the inhabitants.

130.   It is undisputed, and is amply supported by documents annexed to South Africa's written statement in these proceedings, that the official governmental policy pursued by South Africa in Namibia is to achieve a complete physical separation of races and ethnic groups in separate areas within the Territory. The application of this policy has required, as has been conceded by South Africa, restrictive measures of control officially adopted and enforced in the Territory by the coercive power of the former Mandatory. These measures establish limitations, exclusions or restrictions for the members of the indigenous population groups in respect of their participation in certain types of activities, fields of study or of training, labour or employment and also submit them to restrictions or exclusions of residence and movement in large parts of the Territory.

131.   Under the Charter of the United Nations, the former Mandatory had pledged itself to observe and respect, in a territory having an international status, human rights and fundamental freedoms for all without distinction as to race. To establish instead, and to enforce, distinctions, exclusions, restrictions and limitations exclusively based on grounds of race, colour, descent or national or ethnic origin which constitute a denial of fundamental human rights is a flagrant violation of the purposes and principles of the Charter.[a]

a. For an analysis of this passage, see Schwelb, The International Court of Justice and the Human Rights Clauses of the Charter, 66 Am.J.Int'l L. 337 (1972).

THE QUESTION OF THE SELF-EXECUTING CHARACTER
OF ARTICLE 56

SEI FUJII v. STATE

United States, Supreme Court of California in Banc, 1952.
38 Cal.2d 718, 242 P.2d 617 (1952).

The text of the opinion appears at p. 1026.

The court says that "The provisions in the charter pledging co-operation in promoting observance of fundamental freedoms lack the mandatory quality and definiteness which would indicate an intent to create justiciable rights in private persons immediately upon ratification." Is the court correct in its appraisal of the lack of "mandatory quality" of those provisions such as Article 56? Should the result of the case be different if "mandatory quality" were found? Can the "self-executing" analysis of the court lead to the conclusion, in a particular case, that the state is obligated internationally at *some* time after ratification not to discriminate on the basis of alienage but that the alien is at *no* time after ratification protected by internal law?

Compare Riesenfeld, Editorial Comment, The Doctrine of Self-Executing Treaties and GATT: A Notable German Judgment, 65 Am. J.Int'l L. 548, 550 (1971):

> Does it make sense to search for the intent of the parties, if some of the parties could not have had such an intent with respect to their own sphere? The United Kingdom is believed to be the standard example of such a party. Although the doctrine looking to the intent of the parties is widely supported by practice and theory, it seems much more reasonable to consider the self-executing or executory nature of international conventions a matter depending primarily upon the constitutional law of each nation rather than upon a dubious intent of the parties. Consequently in the United States a treaty ought to be deemed self-executing if it: (a) involves the rights and duties of individuals; (b) does not cover a subject for which legislative action is required by the Constitution; and (c) does not leave discretion to the parties in the application of the particular provision.

2.   THE UNIVERSAL DECLARATION OF HUMAN RIGHTS [a]

The Declaration was adopted by the United Nations General Assembly, Resolution 217A (III), on December 10, 1948, by a vote of 48 to 0, Gen.Ass.Off.Rec., 3rd Sess., Part 1, Resolutions, p. 71.   Although there were no dissenting votes, the following states abstained: Byelorussia S.S.R., Czechoslovakia, Poland, Saudi Arabia, Ukranian S.S.R., U.S.S.R., Union of South Africa and Yugoslavia.

[handwritten margin note: ABSTENTIONS]

CONTENTS OF THE DECLARATION

The text of the Universal Declaration is set forth in full in the Documentary Supplement.   The General Assembly of the United Nations proclaims the listed rights as a "common standard of achievement."   These rights are applicable to "all human beings," to "everyone."   The rights include such personal rights as equal protection of the law, right to a fair hearing, to be presumed innocent, to freedom of movement and asylum, to marry and found a family.   Also included are economic and social rights such as to social security, to work, to form and join trade unions, to a standard of living adequate for health and well-being, to education.   For example:

Article 5

No one shall be subjected to torture or to cruel, inhuman or degrading treatment or punishment.

Article 9

No one shall be subjected to arbitrary arrest, detention or exile.

Article 10

Everyone is entitled in full equality to a fair and public hearing by an independent and impartial tribunal, in the determination of his rights and obligations and of any criminal charge against him.

a.   Other Human Rights Declarations. In addition to the Universal Declaration, a number of other declarations dealing with particular aspects of human rights have been adopted by the General Assembly.   Among them are:

1.   Declaration of the Rights of the Child, November 20, 1959, G.A.Res. 1386(XIV), U.N.Gen.Ass.Off.Rec., 14th Sess., Supp. 16(A/4354), p. 19.

2.   Declaration on the Granting of Independence to Colonial Countries and Peoples, December 14, 1960, G.A.Res. 1514(XV), U.N.Gen.Ass.Off.Rec., 15th Sess., Supp. 16(A/4684), p. 66.

3.   United Nations Declaration on the Elimination of All Forms of Racial Discrimination, November 20, 1963, G.A.Res.   1904(XVIII),   U.N.Gen.Ass. Off.Rec., 18th Sess., Supp. 15(A/5515), p. 35.

4.   Declaration on the Elimination of Discrimination Against Women, November 7, 1967, G.A.Res. 2263(XXII), U.N.Gen.Ass.Off.Rec., 22nd Sess., Supp. 16(A/6716), p. 35.

5.   Declaration on Territorial Asylum, December 14, 1967, G.A.Res. 2312 (XXII),   U.N.Gen.Ass.Off.Rec.,   22nd Sess., Supp. 16(A/6716), p. 81.

THE QUESTION OF THE DECLARATION AS LAW

A DRAFTSMAN'S VIEW

5 Whiteman, Digest of International Law 243 (1965).

As the General Assembly neared its final vote on the Declaration, Mrs. Franklin D. Roosevelt, as the Chairman of the Commission on Human Rights and a representative of the United States in the Assembly, stated:

> In giving our approval to the declaration today, it is of primary importance that we keep clearly in mind the basic character of the document. It is not a treaty; it is not an international agreement. It is not and does not purport to be a statement of law or of legal obligation. It is a declaration of basic principles of human rights and freedoms, to be stamped with the approval of the General Assembly by formal vote of its members, and to serve as a common standard of achievement for all peoples of all nations.

A DIPLOMATIC VIEW

II Kiss, Repertoire de la Pratique Francaise en Matiere de Droit International Public 651 (1966).[a]

Declaration of the French Government of August 1, 1951

The French Government has followed with the greatest attention the measures of deportation taken in Hungary against numerous components of the population [which have been] suddenly declared 'undesirable.' According to the information received [by the French Government] these measures appear to have been extraordinarily far reaching and harsh and to strike pitilessly a great diversity of persons within the population.

Such acts constitute a flagrant violation of the principle of respect for human beings and the rights of man [which is] recognized by the international community and embodied in the Declaration of the United Nations of December 10, 1948.

The French Government notes with the greatest concern that the information has now been confirmed by official statements of the Hungarian authorities. Faithful to its traditions, the French Government regards it as its duty solemnly to denounce practices which openly violate the human rights that the Government of the People's Republic of Hungary has formally committed itself to observe in the Peace Treaty of February 10, 1947.[b]

---

a. Translation by the editors. Reprinted by permission of Editions du Centre National de la Recherche Scientifique, Paris.

b. The treaty of peace with Hungary, the signing of which antedated the Universal Declaration by twenty-two months, provides in Article 2:

1. Hungary shall take all measures necessary to secure to all persons under Hungarian jurisdiction, without distinction as to race, sex, language or religion, the enjoyment of human rights and of the fundamental freedoms, including freedom of expression, of press and publication, of religious worship, of political opinion and of public meeting.

2. Hungary further undertakes that the laws in force in Hungary shall not, either in their content or in their ap-

plication, discriminate or entail any discrimination between persons of Hungarian nationality on the ground of their race, sex, language or religion, whether in reference to their persons, property, business, professional or financial interests, status, political or civil rights or any other matter.

A PUBLICIST'S VIEW

Humphrey, The UN Charter and the Universal Declaration of Human Rights, The International Protection of Human Rights 51 (Luard, ed. 1967).

Even more remarkable than the performance of the United Nations in adopting the Declaration has been its impact and the role which it almost immediately began to play both within and outside the United Nations—an impact and a role which probably exceed the most sanguine hopes of its authors. No other act of the United Nations has had anything like the same impact on the thinking of our time, the best aspirations of which it incorporates and proclaims. It may well be that it will live in history chiefly as a statement of great moral principles. As such its influence is deeper and more lasting than any political document or legal instrument. Men of affairs, however, are more apt to be impressed by the political and legal authority which it has established for itself. Its political authority is now second only to that of the charter itself. Indeed its reception at all levels has been such that, contrary to the expressed intention of its authors, it may have now become part of international law.

A JURIST'S VIEW

Separate Opinion of Vice-President Ammoun in Advisory Opinion on the Continued Presence of South Africa in Namibia (South West Africa) [1971] I.C.J. Reports 16, 76.

The Advisory Opinion takes judicial notice of the Universal Declaration of Human Rights. In the case of certain of the Declaration's provisions, attracted by the conduct of South Africa, it would have been an improvement to have dealt in terms with their comminatory nature, which is implied in paragraphs 130 and 131 of the Opinion by the references to their violation.

In its written statement the French Government, alluding to the obligations which South Africa accepted under the Mandate and assumed on becoming a Member of the United Nations, and to the norms laid down in the Universal Declaration of Human Rights, stated that there was no doubt that the Government of South Africa had, in a very real sense, systematically infringed those rules and those obligations. Nevertheless, referring to the mention by resolution 2145(XXI) of the Universal Declaration of Human Rights, it objected that it was plainly impossible for non-compliance with the norms it enshrined to be sanctioned with the revocation of the Mandate, inasmuch as that Declaration was not in the nature of a treaty binding upon States.

Although the affirmations of the Declaration are not binding qua international convention within the meaning of Article 38, paragraph 1(a), of the Statute of the Court, they can bind States on the basis of custom within the meaning of paragraph 1(b) of the same Article, whether because they constituted a codification of customary law as was said in respect of Article 6 of the Vienna Convention on the Law of Treaties, or because they have acquired the force of custom through a general practice accepted as law, in the words of Article 38, paragraph 1(b), of the Statute. One right which must certainly be considered a preexisting binding customary norm which the Universal Declaration of Human Rights codified is the right to equality, which by common consent has ever since the remotest times been deemed inherent in human nature.

The equality demanded by the Namibians and by other peoples of every colour, the right to which is the outcome of prolonged struggles to make it a reality, is something of vital interest to us here, on the one hand because it is the foundation of other human rights which are no more than its corollaries and, on the other, because it naturally rules out racial discrimination and apartheid, which are the gravest of the facts with which South Africa, as also other States, stands charged. The attention I am devoting to it in these observations can therefore by no means be regarded as exaggerated or out of proportion.

It is not by mere chance that in Article 1 of the Universal Declaration of the Rights of Man there stands, so worded, this primordial principle or axiom: "All human beings are born free and equal in dignity and rights."

From this first principle flow most rights and freedoms. * * * The ground was thus prepared for the legislative and constitutional process which began with the first declarations or bills of rights in America and Europe, continued with the constitutions of the nineteenth century, and culminated in positive international law in the San Francisco, Bogota and Addis Ababa charters, and in the Universal Declaration of Human Rights which has been confirmed by numerous resolutions of the United Nations, in particular the above-mentioned declarations adopted by the General Assembly in resolutions 1514(XV), 2625(XXV) and 2627(XXV). The Court in its turn has now confirmed it.

*   *   *

---

3.   THE HUMAN RIGHTS COVENANTS

Under the aegis of the League of Nations and the United Nations, a number of conventions on particular human rights matters have been prepared by a variety of conferences, committees and commissions. Drafts of these conventions have progressed through a variety of stages. They are typically given final approval by some plenary international body before being submitted to states for ratification or other indication of intention to be bound. In some cases that approval has been given by resolution of the General Assembly of the United Nations. In others, the final text is prepared and approved by an ad hoc United Nations conference. In still other cases, the final text has come from a specialized agency, such as the International Labor Organization.

The variety and range of the matters which have been dealt with concretely by "international legislation" are illustrated in the Documentary Supplement by lists of conventions dealing with human rights. Most of these conventions were in force as of January 1, 1972; some had not yet received a sufficient number of ratifications to bring them into force. The United States is a party to very few of these conventions. (See Supplement.)

Included among the conventions not yet in force are two that are the most general in scope of all of the human rights conventions. These are the International Covenant on Economic, Social and Cultural Rights and the International Covenant on Civil and Political Rights, set forth in full in the Documentary Supplement. These two covenants comprehensively carry into detailed treaty form most of the provisions of the Universal Declaration of Human Rights, although it should be observed that they do not parallel the declaration. A close comparison should be made between the declaration on one hand and the covenants on the other. For example, the declaration provides for the right to asylum; the matter is not treated in the covenants. The right to compensation for unlawful arrest or detention is provided for by the Covenant on Civil and Political Rights, but not by the declaration. Other disparities include the right to own property and the right of self-determination. What other disparities exist? Is the fact of these disparities significant? Does the fact that certain rights were included in the declaration but not in the more detailed "legislation" weaken the general legal significance that has been accorded the declaration? Does the fact that certain rights approved in the covenants but not in the declaration (such as self-determination) suggest that they are less than "universal," that they do not reflect general principles of international law? Or does the worldwide recognition of a particular right as international law depend upon factors more complex than whether the verbal recognition of that right was made in the declaration or one or the other of the covenants? If so, what are the factors?

The covenants were the product of many years' work, first in the Commission on Human Rights (from 1949 until 1954) and thereafter in the Third Committee of the General Assembly of the United Nations (from 1954 until 1966) and finally at the plenary session of the assembly in 1966. Although the original conception in the commission had been to prepare a single draft covenant, the insistence by some states that the covenant include provisions for economic, social and cultural rights resulted in a decision by the General Assembly while the draft covenant was still under consideration by the commission that two covenants be drafted, one dealing with those rights and the other with civil and political rights. Contrast the language of the two covenants as ultimately adopted with respect to the sense of assurance by which the various rights are asserted in each of the documents. Contrast also the wide difference between the two covenants with respect to methods of implementation. See p. 629 on questions of implementation.

The detail with which the Covenant on Civil and Political Rights has amplified and added to the rights that were listed in the Universal Declaration of Human Rights is illustrated by the excerpt which follows.

INTERNATIONAL COVENANT ON CIVIL AND POLITICAL RIGHTS

G.A. Res. 2200A(XXI) Dec. 16, 1966.
U.N. Gen. Ass. Off. Rec., 21st Sess., Supp. No. 16 (A/6316), p. 52.

Article 14

1. All persons shall be equal before the courts and tribunals. In the determination of any criminal charge against him, or of his rights and obligations in a suit at law, everyone shall be entitled to a fair and public hearing by a competent, independent and impartial tribunal established by law. The Press and the public may be excluded from all or part of a trial for reasons of morals, public order (ordre public) or national security in a democratic society, or when the interest of the private lives of the parties so requires, or to the extent strictly necessary in the opinion of the court in special circumstances where publicity would prejudice the interests of justice; but any judgment rendered in a criminal case or in a suit at law shall be made public except where the interest of juvenile persons otherwise requires or the proceedings concern matrimonial disputes or the guardianship of children.

2. Everyone charged with a criminal offence shall have the right to be presumed innocent until proved guilty according to law.

3. In the determination of any criminal charge against him, everyone shall be entitled to the following minimum guarantees, in full equality:

> (a) To be informed promptly and in detail in a language which he understands of the nature and cause of the charge against him;

(b) To have adequate time and facilities for the preparation of his defence and to communicate with counsel of his own choosing;

(c) To be tried without undue delay;

(d) To be tried in his presence, and to defend himself in person or through legal assistance of his own choosing; to be informed, if he does not have legal assistance, of this right; and to have legal assistance assigned to him, in any case where the interests of justice so require, and without payment by him in any such case if he does not have sufficient means to pay for it;

(e) To examine, or have examined, the witnesses against him and to obtain the attendance and examination of witnesses on his behalf under the same conditions as witnesses against him;

(f) To have the free assistance of an interpreter if he cannot understand or speak the language used in court;

(g) Not to be compelled to testify against himself or to confess guilt.

4. In the case of juvenile persons, the procedure shall be such as will take account of their age and the desirability of promoting their rehabilitation.

5. Everyone convicted of a crime shall have the right to his conviction and sentence being reviewed by a higher tribunal according to law.

6. When a person has by a final decision been convicted of a criminal offence and when subsequently his conviction has been reversed or he has been pardoned on the ground that a new or newly discovered fact shows conclusively that there has been a miscarriage of justice, the person who has suffered punishment as a result of such conviction shall be compensated according to law, unless it is proved that the non-disclosure of the unknown fact in time is wholly or partly attributable to him.

7. No one shall be liable to be tried or punished again for an offence for which he has already been finally convicted or acquitted in accordance with the law and penal procedure of each country.

---

1. *Comparison with the precedents on "State Responsibility."* How do the rights provided for in such conventions as the Covenant on Civil and Political Rights compare with those recognized in such cases as Chattin? Who is entitled to these rights? Aliens only? Others? Are the substantive standards different?

2. *Policy problems facing the United States in considering becoming a party.* There are a number of questions which have been

raised under the United States Constitution with respect to the ratification of various human rights conventions. See Chapter 16. Irrespective of the constitutional issues there are policy questions which the public, the President, and the Senate must face when considering whether the United States should become a party to any such convention. What questions of legislative judgment do you see in the human rights conventions set forth in the Documentary Supplement (Convention on Economic, Social and Cultural Rights, Convention on Civil and Political Rights, Convention on Racial Discrimination, Genocide Convention)? Does the United States already provide, by constitution or statute, the protection covered by those conventions? To the extent that it does, what is to be gained by binding the United States *by treaty* to provide for those rights? What is to be lost? To the extent that those rights are not already provided for by constitution or statute in the United States, should they be? Would becoming a party to a treaty be a good way to provide for those rights? Consider, in particular, Article 2(1)(d) of the Racial Discrimination Convention: "Each State Party shall prohibit and bring to an end, by all appropriate means, including legislation as required by circumstances, racial discrimination by any persons, group or organization."

As indicated above, the United States is a party to only a very few of the human rights conventions already in force. *Why is this so?*

SECTION C. INTERNATIONAL IMPLEMENTATION OF THE LAW OF HUMAN RIGHTS [a]

It has been shown above that the violation of the human rights of an alien can be vindicated at the international level through diplomatic protest by the injured individual's state, or through the processes of international arbitration or adjudication put in motion by the individual's state. The recent developments in human rights law under the aegis of the United Nations have emphasized that, either by the growth of international law or by convention, an individual's substantive rights may be claimed by him against even his own state. How can those rights be vindicated at the international level if the individual's state fails or refuses to accord them to him?

The problem in the next sub-section illustrates one factual and legal context (adjudication) in which the question arises. A number of possible procedures are explored thereafter. Test these procedures in the light of the immense variety of circumstances which may in fact arise, e. g., a political opponent to a government is jailed, without

---

a. In preparing this Section, the editors have freely consulted Carey, U.N. Protection of Civil and Political Rights (1970).

charges, hearing or counsel; physical torture is applied to induce confession or the giving of information; a person is arbitrarily deprived of his citizenship, property, or means of livelihood.

---

1. INTERNATIONAL ADJUDICATION

There is no universal court in which an individual can maintain an action to enforce the rights that international law has begun to recognize substantively. The only universal court is the International Court of Justice and only states may be parties in cases before the court. Are there nevertheless means by which an individual's rights can be vindicated in this court?

Problem: N is a national of State D, a party to the International Convention on the Elimination of All Forms of Racial Discrimination. Documentary Supplement. N claims that because of his race he has been denied equal opportunity by State D with respect to housing and employment, in violation of Article 5 of the convention. N persuades the foreign office of State P to become interested in his case by reason of the opportunity it affords State P to publicly embarrass State D over its racial policies. State P is unsuccessful in procuring any change in State D's policies or its treatment of N. All of the procedures provided for in the convention ᵃ are exhausted without effect. Pursuant to Article 22 of the convention, State P refers its dispute with State D, over D's treatment of N, to the International Court of Justice. (Article 22 provides: "Any dispute between two or more States Parties with respect to the interpretation or application of this Convention, which is not settled by negotiation or by the procedures expressly provided for in this Convention, shall, at the request of any of the parties to the dispute, be referred to the International Court of Justice for decision, unless the disputants agree to another mode of settlement.")

Will the court take jurisdiction of such a claim? Will it recognize the "standing" or "interest" of the complainant state?

NOTTEBOHM CASE (LIECHTENSTEIN v. GUATEMALA)

International Court of Justice, 1955.
[1955] I.C.J. Rep. 4.

The opinion of the Court is set forth at p. 530.

In the Problem case the individual, N, whose rights were allegedly violated, is not a national of State P by any definition of nationality. Does the reasoning of Nottebohm suggest that P cannot maintain this proceeding?

a. These procedures are discussed at p. 644.

SOUTH WEST AFRICA CASES (ETHIOPIA v. SOUTH AFRICA; LIBERIA v. SOUTH AFRICA)

International Court of Justice, 1966.
[1966] I.C.J.Rep. 6.

* * *

1. In the present proceedings the two applicant States, the Empire of Ethiopia and the Republic of Liberia (whose cases are identical and will for present purposes be treated as one case), acting in the capacity of States which were members of the former League of Nations, put forward various allegations of contraventions of the League of Nations Mandate for South West Africa, said to have been committed by the respondent State, the Republic of South Africa, as the administering authority.

2. In an earlier phase of the case, which took place before the Court in 1962, four preliminary objections were advanced, based on Article 37 of the Court's Statute and the jurisdictional clause (Article 7, paragraph 2) of the Mandate for South West Africa, which were all of them argued by the Respondent and treated by the Court as objections to its jurisdiction. The Court, by its Judgment of 21 December 1962, rejected each of these objections, and thereupon found that it had "jurisdiction to adjudicate upon the merits of the dispute".

3. In the course of the proceedings on the merits, * * * the Parties put forward various contentions on such matters as whether the Mandate for South West Africa was still in force,—and if so, whether the Mandatory's obligation under Article 6 of the Mandate to furnish annual reports to the Council of the former League of Nations concerning its administration of the mandated territory had become transformed by one means or another into an obligation to furnish such reports to the General Assembly of the United Nations, or had, on the other hand, lapsed entirely;—whether there had been any contravention by the Respondent of the second paragraph of Article 2 of the Mandate which required the Mandatory to "promote to the utmost the material and moral well-being and the social progress of the inhabitants of the territory",—whether there had been any contravention of Article 4 of the Mandate, prohibiting (except for police and local defence purposes) the "military training of the natives", and forbidding the establishment of military or naval bases, or the erection of fortifications in the territory. The Applicants also alleged that the Respondent had contravened paragraph 1 of Article 7 of the Mandate (which provides that the Mandate can only be modified with the consent of the Council of the League of Nations) by attempting to modify the Mandate without the consent of the General Assembly of the United Nations which, so it was contended, had replaced the Council of the League for this and other purposes. There were other allegations also, which it is not necessary to set out here.

4. * * * In this connection, there was one matter that appertained to the merits of the case but which had an antecedent character, namely the question of the Applicants' standing in the present phase of the proceedings,—not, that is to say, of their standing before the Court itself, which was the subject of the Court's decision in 1962, but the question, as a matter of the merits of the case, of their legal right or interest regarding the subject-matter of their claim, as set out in their final submissions.

* * *

10. The mandates system, as is well known, was formally instituted by Article 22 of the Covenant of the League of Nations. As there indicated, there were to be three categories of mandates, designated as "A", "B" and "C" mandates respectively, the Mandate for South West Africa being one of the "C" category. The differences between these categories lay in the nature and geographical situation of the territories concerned, the state of development of their peoples, and the powers accordingly to be vested in the administering authority, or mandatory, for each territory placed under mandate. But although it was by Article 22 of the League Covenant that the system as such was established, the precise terms of each mandate, covering the rights and obligations of the mandatory, of the League and its organs, and of the individual members of the League, in relation to each mandated territory, were set out in separate instruments of mandate which, with one exception to be noted later, took the form of resolutions of the Council of the League.

11. These instruments, whatever the differences between certain of their terms, had various features in common as regards their structure. For present purposes, their substantive provisions may be regarded as falling into two main categories. On the one hand, and of course as the principal element of each instrument, there were the articles defining the mandatory's powers, and its obligations in respect of the inhabitants of the territory and towards the League and its organs. These provisions, relating to the carrying out of the mandates as mandates, will hereinafter be referred to as "conduct of the mandate", or simply "conduct" provisions. On the other hand, there were articles conferring in different degrees, according to the particular mandate or category of mandate, certain rights relative to the mandated territory, directly upon the members of the League as individual States, or in favour of their nationals. Many of these rights were of the same kind as are to be found in certain provisions of ordinary treaties of commerce, establishment and navigation concluded between States. Rights of this kind will hereinafter be referred to as "special interests" rights, embodied in the "special interests" provisions of the mandates. * * * [The "special interest" provisions of "C" mandates] were confined to provisions for freedom for missionaries ("nationals of any State Member of the League of Nations") to "enter into, travel and reside in the territory for the

purpose of prosecuting their calling"—(Mandate for South West Africa, Article 5).   In the present case, the dispute between the Parties relates exclusively to the former of these two categories of provisions, and not to the latter.

* * *

13.   In addition to the classes of provisions so far noticed, every instrument of mandate contained a jurisdictional clause which, with a single exception to be noticed in due course, was in identical terms for each mandate, whether belonging to the "A", "B" or "C" category. The language and effect of this clause will be considered later; but it provided for a reference of disputes to the Permanent Court of International Justice and, so the Court found in the first phase of the case, as already mentioned, this reference was now, by virtue of Article 37 of the Court's Statute, to be construed as a reference to the present Court.

* * *

33.   * * *   [E]ven in the time of the League, even as members of the League when that organization still existed, the Applicants did not, in their individual capacity as States, possess any separate self-contained right which they could assert, independently of, or additionally to, the right of the League, in the pursuit of its collective, institutional activity, to require the due performance of the Mandate in discharge of the "sacred trust".   This right was vested exclusively in the League, and was exercised through its competent organs. * * *   But no right was reserved to them, individually as States, and independently of their participation in the institutional activities of the League, as component parts of it, to claim in their own name,— still less as agents authorized to represent the League,—the right to invigilate the sacred trust,—to set themselves up as separate custodians of the various mandates.   This was the role of the League organs.

34.   To put this conclusion in another way, the position was that under the mandates system, and within the general framework of the League system, the various mandatories were responsible for their conduct of the mandates solely to the League—in particular to its Council—and were not additionally and separately responsible to each and every individual State member of the League.   If the latter had been given a legal right or interest on an individual "State" basis, this would have meant that each member of the League, independently of the Council or other competent League organ, could have addressed itself directly to every mandatory, for the purpose of calling for explanations or justifications of its administration, and generally to exact from the mandatory the due performance of its mandate, according to the view which that State might individually take as to what was required for the purpose.

35.   Clearly no such right existed under the mandates system as contemplated by any of the relevant instruments.   It would have in-

volved a position of accountability by the mandatories to each and every member of the League separately, for otherwise there would have been nothing additional to the normal faculty of participating in the collective work of the League respecting mandates.

*   *   *

HUMANITARIANISM
DOES NOT
CREATE
LEGAL RIGHT

49. * * * Throughout this case it has been suggested, directly or indirectly, that humanitarian considerations are sufficient in themselves to generate legal rights and obligations, and that the Court can and should proceed accordingly. The Court does not think so. It is a court of law, and can take account of moral principles only in so far as these are given a sufficient expression in legal form. Law exists, it is said, to serve a social need; but precisely for that reason it can do so only through and within the limits of its own discipline. Otherwise, it is not a legal service that would be rendered.

50. Humanitarian considerations may constitute the inspirational basis for rules of law, just as, for instance, the preambular parts of the United Nations Charter constitute the moral and political basis for the specific legal provisions thereafter set out. Such considerations do not, however, in themselves amount to rules of law. All States are interested—have an interest—in such matters. But the existence of an "interest" does not of itself entail that this interest is specifically juridical in character.

*   *   *

60. It is however contended that, even if the Judgment of 1962 was, for the above-mentioned reasons, not preclusive of the issue of the Applicants' legal right or interest, it did in essence determine that issue because it decided that the Applicants were entitled to invoke the jurisdictional clause of the Mandate, and that if they had a sufficient interest to do that, they must also have a sufficient interest in the subject-matter of their claim. This view is not well-founded. The faculty of invoking a jurisdictional clause depends upon what tests or conditions of the right to do so are laid down by the clause itself. To hold that the parties in any given case belong to the category of State specified in the clause,—that the dispute has the specified character,—and that the forum is the one specified,—is not the same thing as finding the existence of a legal right or interest relative to the merits of the claim. The jurisdictional clause of the Mandate for South West Africa (Article 7, paragraph 2), which appeared in all the mandates, reads as follows:

> The Mandatory agrees that, if any dispute whatever should arise between the Mandatory and another Member of the League of Nations relating to the interpretation or the application of the provisions of the Mandate, such dispute, if it cannot be settled by negotiation, shall be submitted to the Permanent Court of International Justice provided for by Article 14 of the Covenant of the League of Nations.

*   *   *

62.   It is next contended that this particular jurisdictional clause has an effect which is more extensive than if it is considered as a simple jurisdictional clause: that it is a clause conferring a substantive right,—that the substantive right it confers is precisely the right to claim from the mandatory the carrying out of the "conduct of the Mandate" provisions of the instrument of mandate,—and that in consequence, even if the right is derivable from no other source, it is derivable from and implicit in this clause.

*   *   *

64.   In truth however, there is nothing about this particular jurisdictional clause to differentiate it from many others, or to make it an exception to the rule that, in principle, jurisdictional clauses are adjectival not substantive in their nature and effect.   *   *   *   It is a universal and necessary, but yet almost elementary principle of procedural law that a distinction has to be made between, on the one hand, the right to activate a court and the right of the court to examine the merits of the claim,—and, on the other, the plaintiff party's legal right in respect of the subject-matter of that which it claims,—STANDING— which would have to be established to the satisfaction of the Court.

65.   In the present case, that subject-matter includes the question whether the Applicants possess any legal right to require the performance of the "conduct" provisions of the Mandate.   This is something which cannot be predetermined by the language of a common-form jurisdictional clause such as Article 7, paragraph 2, of the Mandate for South West Africa.   This provision, with slight differences of wording and emphasis, is in the same form as that of many other jurisdictional clauses.   The Court can see nothing in it that would take the clause outside the normal rule that, in a dispute causing the activation of a jurisdictional clause, the substantive rights themselves which the dispute is about, must be sought for elsewhere than in this clause, or in some element apart from it,—and must therefore be established aliunde vel aliter.   Jurisdictional clauses do not determine whether parties have substantive rights, but only whether, if they have them, they can vindicate them by recourse to a tribunal.

66.   Such rights may be derived from participation in an international instrument by a State which has signed and ratified, or has acceded, or has in some other manner become a party to it; and which in consequence, and subject to any exceptions expressly indicated, is entitled to enjoy rights under all the provisions of the instrument concerned.   Since the Applicants cannot bring themselves under this head, they must show that the "conduct" provisions of the mandates conferred rights in terms on members of the League as individual States, in the same way that the "special interests" provisions did. It is however contended that there is a third possibility, and that on the basis of the jurisdictional clause alone, the Applicants, as members of the League, were part of the institutional machinery of control relative to the mandates, and that in this capacity they had a right

of action of the same kind as, for instance, members of the League Council had under the jurisdictional clauses of the minorities treaties of that period, for the protection of minority rights. On this footing the essence of the contention is that the Applicants do not need to show the existence of any substantive rights outside the jurisdictional clause, and that they had—that all members of the League had—what was in effect a policing function under the mandates and by virtue of the jurisdictional clause.

67. The Court has examined this contention, but does not think that the two cases are in any way comparable. When States intend to create a right of action of this kind they adopt a different method. Such a right has, in special circumstances, been conferred on States belonging to a body of compact size such as the Council of the League of Nations, invested with special supervisory functions and even a power of intervention in the matter, as provided by the jurisdictional clause of the minorities treaties—see for instance Article 12 of the minorities treaty with Poland, signed at Versailles on 28 June 1919, which was typical. Even so the right, as exercisable by members of the League Council, in effect as part of the Council's work, with which they would ex hypothesi have been fully familiar, was characterized at the time by an eminent Judge and former President of the Permanent Court as being "in every respect very particular in character" and as going "beyond the province of general international law". The intention to confer it must be quite clear; and the Court holds that for the reasons which have already been given, and for others to be considered later, there was never any intention to confer an invigilatory function of this kind on each and every member of the League.

* * *

69. The Court finds itself unable to reconcile the two types of case except upon the assumption, strongly supported by every other factor involved, that, as regards the mandates, the jurisdictional clause was intended to serve a different purpose, namely to give the individual members of the League the means, which might not otherwise be available to them through League channels, of protecting their "special interests" relative to the mandated territories. In the minorities case, the right of action of the members of the Council under the jurisdictional clause was only intended for the protection of minority populations. No other purpose in conferring a right of action on members of the League Council would have been possible in that case.

* * *

70. In this last connection it is of capital importance that the right as conferred in the minorities case was subjected to certain characterizations which were wholly absent in the case of the jurisdictional clause of the mandates. Any "difference of opinion" was characterized in advance as being justiciable, because it was to be "held to be a dispute of an international character" within the meaning of Article 14 of the Covenant (this was the well-known "deem-

ing" clause), so that no question of any lack of legal right or interest could arise. The decisions of the Court were moreover, to be final and, by means of a reference to Article 13 of the Covenant, were given an effect erga omnes as a general judicial settlement binding on all concerned. The jurisdictional clause of the mandates on the other hand, was essentially an ordinary jurisdictional clause, having none of the special characteristics or effects of those of the minorities treaties.

* * *

99. In the light of these various considerations, the Court finds that the Applicants cannot be considered to have established any legal right or interest appertaining to them in the subject-matter of the present claims, and that, accordingly, the Court must decline to give effect to them.

100. For these reasons,

THE COURT, by the President's casting vote—the votes being equally divided, decides to reject the claims of the Empire of Ethiopia and the Republic of Liberia.

* * *

DISSENTING OPINION OF JUDGE JESSUP.

* * *

The Applicants have not asked for an award of damages or for any other material amend for their own individual benefit. They have in effect, and in part, asked for a declaratory judgment interpreting certain provisions of the Mandate for South West Africa. The Court having decided in 1962 that they had standing (locus standi) to bring the action, they are now entitled to a declaratory judgment without any further showing of interest. (at 328)

* * *

In the minority treaties, one sees a further illustration of the fact that the statesmen of 1919 recognized the right of States to invoke the jurisdiction of the Court in the interest of special groups even when their individual interests were not affected. This is brought out very clearly in the dissenting opinion of Judge Huber in the case of Minority Schools in Upper Silesia (P.C.I.J., Series A, No. 15 (1928), at p. 50):

> Article 72, paragraph 3 [of the Geneva Convention] is the literal reproduction of Article 12 of the Minorities Treaty of June 28th, 1919, and of analogous provisions of other treaties. The jurisdiction conferred by this clause is in every respect very particular in character and goes beyond the province of general international law; for Article 72, paragraph 3, confers on every Power being a Member of the Council, *even if it is not a contracting Party to the Minority Treaties* or to the Geneva Convention, the right of appealing to the Court, and *such judicial action is based upon stipulations which relate not to rights of the applicant State or to those of its nationals on whose behalf it might take*

action, but to the relations between the respondent State and its own nationals. (Italics added.)

The principle that States were entitled to bring to the Court cases which did not involve their own direct interests is not affected by the fact that the right of recourse in the minority treaties was limited to Members of the Council of the League. Although in the Memel case, the Powers who could resort to the Court were all parties to the treaty, in several of the minority cases, the right of recourse belonged not only to the Permanent Members of the Council who may have been parties, but also to the non-permanent Members who were elected from time to time and who, as Judge Huber pointed out, did not need to be, and often were not, parties to the minority treaties which gave them the right to invoke the Court. The States in question derived their "standing" before the Court from the adjudication clause, not from some other conferment of a substantive right. (at 377)

* * *

My separate opinion in 1962 also called attention (at p. 426) to the fact that in more recent times, the same general appreciation of a right to turn to the International Court of Justice for interpretation, application or fulfilment of a treaty having a broad humanitarian interest, is recognized in—

the Genocide Convention, which came into force on 12 January 1951 on the deposit of the twentieth ratification. [It] provides in Article IX:

Disputes between the Contracting Parties relating to the interpretation, application or fulfilment of the present Convention, including those relating to the responsibility of a State for genocide or for any of the other acts enumerated in article III, shall be submitted to the International Court of Justice at the request of any of the parties to the dispute. (Vol. 78, United Nations Treaty Series, pp. 278 at 282).

As this Court said of the Genocide Convention: "In such a convention the contracting States do not have any interests of their own; they merely have, one and all, a common interest, namely the accomplishment of those high purposes which are the raison d'être of the convention. Consequently, in a convention of this type one cannot speak of individual advantages or disadvantages to States, or of the maintenance of a perfect contractual balance between rights and duties. The high ideals which inspired the Convention provide, by virtue of the common will of the parties the foundation and measure of all its provisions." (I.C.J. Reports 1951, at p. 23.) (at 379)

* * *

1. *Comparison of the Mandate for South West Africa with the International Convention on the Elimination of All Forms of Racial Discrimination.* Is the convention comparable to the mandate so as to bring the Article 22 provisions (for reference of a dispute to the court) under the same strictures as to "interest" and "standing" that were articulated in the South West Africa cases? Are there comparable institutional arrangements in the convention which would suggest that state parties cannot bring each other directly into the court? Does the convention contain both "special interest" provisions and "conduct" provisions? Is a state limited, in referring a dispute to the court under Article 22, to disputes relating to its own "special interests" in its own nationals? Do the references in the opinions to the "minorities treaties" suggest that the court would deal differently with the convention than it dealt with the mandate?

2. *The Case concerning the Barcelona Traction, Light and Power Company, Limited (Belgium v. Spain).* It was decided in 1970, [1970] I.C.J.Rep. 3. The text of the decision appears in Chapter 17. The case concerned claimed injury to a corporation's property. In the course of an opinion dealing with the question of the proper state to maintain an action to redress this injury, the court stated:

33.   When a State admits into its territory foreign investments or foreign nationals, whether natural or juristic persons, it is bound to extend to them the protection of the law and assumes obligations concerning the treatment to be afforded them. These obligations, however, are neither absolute nor unqualified. In particular, an essential distinction should be drawn between the obligations of a State towards the international community as a whole, and those arising vis-à-vis another State in the field of diplomatic protection. By their very nature the former are the concern of all States. In view of the importance of the rights involved, all States can be held to have a legal interest in their protection; they are obligations erga omnes.

34.   Such obligations derive, for example, in contemporary international law, from the outlawing of acts of aggression, and of genocide, as also from the principles and rules concerning the basic rights of the human person, including protection from slavery and racial discrimination. Some of the corresponding rights of protection have entered into the body of general international law (Reservations to the Convention on the Prevention and Punishment of the Crime of Genocide, Advisory Opinion, I.C.J. Reports 1951, p. 23); others are conferred by international instruments of a universal or quasi-universal character.

35.   Obligations the performance of which is the subject of diplomatic protection are not of the same category. It cannot be held, when one such obligation in particular is in question, in a specific case, that all States have a legal interest in its observance. In order to bring a claim in respect of the breach of such

an obligation, a State must first establish its right to do so, for the rules on the subject rest on two suppositions:

> The first is that the defendant State has broken an obligation towards the national State in respect of its nationals. The second is that only the party to whom an international obligation is due can bring a claim in respect of its breach. (Reparation for Injuries Suffered in the Service of the United Nations, Advisory Opinion, I.C.J. Reports 1949, pp. 181–182.)

* * *

3. *Remedies.* If a state refers to the court a dispute about a second state's treatment of the second state's own nationals, what relief should be requested or granted? Would monetary relief be administrable? Would a declaratory judgment be more workable? Would it be effective? See Judge Jessup's dissenting opinion in the South West Africa cases, [1966] I.C.J.Rep. at 329.

4. *Advisory Opinions.* How could an individual injured by his own state seek relief by way of an advisory opinion? The individual would need the support of some other state, to enlist the aid of the General Assembly or the Security Council (or some other body authorized under Article 65 of the Statute of the International Court of Justice) to ask for the opinion. The question put to the court would have to be constructed in terms that would permit the court to find it had been asked for an opinion on a "legal question" under Article 65 of the statute. In addition, the court might have to be persuaded it was not in effect deciding a dispute involving a state without that state's consent to its jurisdiction. Cf. Status of Eastern Carelia, P.C.I.J., Ser. B, No. 5 (1923), (Advisory Opinion).

5. *The Statute of the Administrative Tribunal of the United Nations.* The statute is suggestive of a procedure which might be adopted by the General Assembly to encourage the rendering of advisory opinions relative to the violation of an individual's human rights. Under the statute, a committee has been established whose function it is to hear objections to judgments of the tribunal (e.g., errors of law) and to decide whether to ask for an advisory opinion of the court on the matter; the committee is authorized to request the opinion. See the Documentary Supplement.

---

2. AD HOC INVESTIGATION AND PRONOUNCEMENT BY UN POLITICAL BODIES

An individual whose substantive rights have been violated by his own state may try to "enforce" them through the political bodies of the United Nations. An authoritative pronouncement on his case by such a body may serve to induce the wrongdoing state to afford redress to the individual or to change its patterns of behavior. The use of individual petitions (discussed below) has only recently come to be formally recognized as an appropriate method of activating United Nations bodies; the practice of employing ad hoc investigative groups has been fairly common.

The problem of apartheid in South Africa has given rise to several ad hoc groups charged with investigating and publicizing human rights violations. Although their charges are too specialized to serve the purposes of many individuals whose complaints do not deal with the particular problems of apartheid, they serve as a model for other groups which could be created to investigate classes of human rights violations, such as the maintenance of degrading prison conditions or the failure to provide political freedoms.

An example of the kind of inquiry that is referred to here is the work of the Special Committee on the Policies of Apartheid of the Government of the Republic of South Africa. Established by the General Assembly of the United Nations, Resolution 1761 (XVII) of November 6, 1962, its mandate is to "keep the racial policies of the Government of South Africa under review when the Assembly is not in session" and to "report either to the Assembly or to the Security Council or to both, as may be appropriate, from time to time." 1962 Year Book of the United Nations 100.

A minor part of the committee's work has been to comb the public press for cases involving individuals and to publicize the findings in its "Review of Developments in South Africa", as with the case of one Sandra Laing, and the case of the six children of Mr. and Mrs. E. J. Dickson (involving the "reclassification" of their race) (Report of the Special Committee to General Assembly, 23rd Session, 87–88) and the case of one James Lenkoe (was death of a detainee under the Terrorism Act by suicide or by electric shock treatment?) (Report of the Special Committee to General Assembly, 24th Session, 68).

A so-called Ad Hoc Working Group of Experts, established by the Human Rights Commission by Resolution 2 (XXIII) of March 6, 1967, was charged with investigation of the "charges of torture and ill-treatment of prisoners, detainees or persons in police custody in South Africa." Its charge was later expanded by both the Commission and ECOSOC. The legal foundations of the group were the subject of debate and are therefore of interest to anyone attempting to set up a new ad hoc group to investigate a human rights violation. (For discussion of the legal foundations of the group, see Carey, UN Protection of Civil and Political Rights (1970), at 98–99, and fn 15 at 99.)

The Working Group conducted its inquiries by examining live witnesses. At least in one instance, the group's report was the basis for a resolution adopted by the General Assembly by which a particular individual's rights deprivations were publicized. Resolution 2714

(XXV), December 15, 1970, U.N.Gen.Ass.Off.Rec., 25th Sess., Supp. 28 (A/8028), p. 79. In the resolution the General Assembly commended the group for its report and then stated that it *"Reaffirms* that * * * Mr. James Lenkoe, a political prisoner in South Africa, did not commit suicide as reported, but died as a result of electric shocks administered to various parts of his body * * *."

The political pressure behind the creation of such groups as those described above is grounded in the strong anti-apartheid feelings of a large number of UN members. In considering whether an ad hoc committee or group can be created to address itself to other kinds of human rights violations, there is the question whether sufficient political interest can be generated among the relevant UN members. It seems unlikely in the case of one individual or one isolated instance. Can a standing group be created which could be called upon in particular instances to investigate an individual case?

---

3. INDIVIDUAL PETITIONS

The Human Rights Commission and the Economic and Social Council decided in 1947 that the Commission "has no power to take any action in regard to any complaints concerning human rights." ECOSOC Off.Rec., 4th Sess., Supp. 3, Report of the Commission on Human Rights, First Sess., p. 6. Although attempts were made for two decades to reverse this position, the many communications from individuals that come to the United Nations informally each year have not been acted upon, although a state named in a complaint is sent an anonymous copy.

1. *Gross and reliably attested violations.* The situation has now been altered in a way that may be significant by ECOSOC Resolution 1503 (XLVIII) of May 27, 1970, ECOSOC Off.Rec., Resumed 48th Sess., Resolutions, Supp. 1A, p. 8. It provides that the Sub-Commission on Prevention of Discrimination and Protection of Minorities may appoint a working group to consider communications from individuals and to bring to the sub-commission's attention those communications "which appear to reveal a consistent pattern of gross and reliably attested violations of human rights and fundamental freedoms within the terms of reference of the sub-commission." The resolution provides for consideration of the communications by the sub-commission, with reference thereafter to the Human Rights Commission and possibly a study and report by the commission or an investigation by an ad hoc committee appointed by the commission and recommendation to ECOSOC. Limitations of significance are that the ad hoc investigation can be made only with the consent of the state concerned and that the matter must remain confidential until the commission decides to make a recommendation to ECOSOC. The text of the resolution is set forth in the Documentary Supplement.

Under a resolution of the Human Rights Commission in 1949, the terms of reference of the Sub-Commission on the Prevention of Discrimination and Protection of Minorities was "clarified and extended" as follows:

(a) To undertake studies, particularly in the light of the Universal Declaration of Human Rights and to make recommendations to the Commission on Human Rights concerning the prevention of discrimination of any kind relating to human rights and fundamental freedoms and the protection of racial, national, religious and linguistic minorities; and

(b) To perform any other functions which may be entrusted to it by the Economic and Social Council or the Commission on Human Rights.   ECOSOC Off.Rec., 9th Sess., Supp. 10, Report of the Commission on Human Rights, 5th Sess., p. 6.

For a broader reading of these terms in the light of decisions since that date, see Schwelb, The International Court of Justice and the Human Rights Clauses of the Charter, 66 Am.J.Int'l L. 337 (1972). He states that "the new procedure is meant to be applicable not only in regard to dependent territories and to questions of racial discrimination, but is aimed at the stopping of violations of human rights 'wherever they may occur.'"   (at 346)

Provisional procedures to carry out ECOSOC Resolution 1503 were adopted by the sub-commission in August 1971.   The text of the procedures is set forth in the Documentary Supplement.   Paragraph 2 of the procedures discloses that a broad range of persons and groups is empowered to originate communications.   Paragraph 1 indicates that the procedures are useful for a single individual only if he is a victim of a "consistent pattern of gross and reliably attested violations of human rights and fundamental freedoms."   It is significant, however, that the injured person can communicate directly with the United Nations without the necessity of enlisting the aid of a foreign state.

2.   *Racial discrimination.*   A procedure for hearing individual communications is contained in the International Convention on the Elimination of All Forms of Racial Discrimination and a Committee on the Elimination of Racial Discrimination exists under Article 8 of that convention.   Under Article 14 of the convention, no communication from individuals is to be received by the committee if it concerns a state party that has not made a declaration recognizing the competence of the committee.

3.   *Civil and political rights.*   The right to make individual communications is also provided by the Optional Protocol to the International Covenant on Civil and Political Rights.   This right is currently academic, since the covenant is not yet in force.

4. THE "OMBUDSMAN" APPROACH

The frequently discussed "High Commissioner for Human Rights" may become a channel for the individual to vindicate his rights. The matter is presently academic, since the post has not been created.

---

5. THE SECRETARIAT OF THE UNITED NATIONS

Again in the apartheid area, where the UN members' interest is highly intense, the General Assembly authorized the creation by the Secretary-General of a Unit on Apartheid which, Carey reports, has "issued releases such as a 15-page list of persons subjected to South African 'banning orders.' " Carey, U. N. Protection of Civil and Political Rights 156 (1970).

A further example in the same area of apartheid is General Assembly Resolution 2547A (XXIV) of December 11, 1969. 23 Yearbook of the United Nations 1969, at 508. In this resolution the assembly requested the Secretary-General of the United Nations "to establish, maintain and publicize an up-to-date register of persons subjected to imprisonment, detention, banishment and other restrictions, and of persons who have been victims of brutality, for their opposition to apartheid and racial discrimination, as well as of captured freedom fighters held [in named African countries.]"

---

6. CONCILIATION PROCEDURES BY CONVENTION

The International Convention on the Elimination of All Forms of Racial Discrimination, set forth in the Documentary Supplement, provides for a two-step process leading toward conciliation. A party to the convention may bring to the attention of the committee on the Elimination of Racial Discrimination the fact that it considers "that another State Party is not giving effect to the provisions" of the convention. (Article 11) If processes of adjustment at the committee stage fail, the matter is referred to an ad hoc conciliation commission. (Article 12) Ultimately, if the matter is not settled by the disputants, the commission's recommendations for solution of the dispute are communicated to the other parties to the convention. (Article 13) It will be noted, as discussed above, that the convention provides also for a process of individual communications, if a party recognizes the competence of the committee to consider them, and for ultimate reference of a dispute to the International Court of Justice.

---

7. SELF-HELP: ASYLUM AND REFUGE

So long as the level of human rights protections varies among the states of the world, the individual will continue the age-old human practice of leaving a state where he is oppressed to live in another state where, he believes, his rights will be protected. But it is said: "The reception of aliens is a matter of discretion, and every state is by reason of its territorial supremacy competent to exclude aliens from the whole, or any part, of its territory." I Oppenheim, International Law 675 (Lauterpacht, 8th ed. 1955). The writer further asserts that the Universal Declaration of Human Rights does not give an alien a right to demand asylum. The Declaration provides:

Article 13

1. Everyone has the right to freedom of movement and residence within the borders of each State.

* * *

Article 14

1. Everyone has the right to seek and to enjoy in other countries asylum from persecution.

2. This right may not be invoked in the case of prosecutions genuinely arising from non-political crimes or from acts contrary to the purposes and principles of the United Nations.

If an alien cannot lawfully demand that a state grant him asylum, what is the content of the "right to seek asylum?"

The United Nations adopted a Declaration on Territorial Asylum, Resolution 2312 (XXII) of December 14, 1967, U.N.Gen.Ass.Off.Rec., 22nd Sess., Supp. 16 (A/6716), p. 81. It stated:

Article 1

1. Asylum granted by a State, in the exercise of its sovereignty, to persons entitled to invoke article 14 of the Universal Declaration of Human Rights, including persons struggling against colonialism, shall be respected by all other States.

* * *

Article 3

1. No person referred to in article 1, paragraph 1, shall be subjected to measures such as rejection at the frontier or, if he has already entered the territory in which he seeks asylum, expulsion or compulsory return [a] to any State where he may be subjected to persecution.

* * *

It is doubtful that the international community is presently prepared to accept an absolute obligation on the part of each state to grant asylum. In the preparation of a draft convention designed to

---

a. A provision similar to this prohibition against expulsion or return ("refoulement") appears in a treaty in force, the Convention Relating to the Status of Refugees, 1951, 189 U.N. T.S. 137, as amended by the Protocol of 1967, 606 U.N.T.S. 267.

give real effect to the apparent rights proclaimed in Article 14, what interests should be taken into account? Do the events of 1972 in India (the mass influx of refugees from East Pakistan) suggest one of the limits of the problem? Would a convention binding a state to "use its best endeavors to grant asylum in its territory" promote the humanitarian objectives of the Universal Declaration of Human Rights?

Several additional problems concerning asylum and the reception of refugees require notice. (1) Is a state that grants asylum to the national of another state violating the rights of that state? See the language of Article 1 of the Declaration on Territorial Asylum, above. (2) If a state admits individuals seeking asylum or refuge, how must they be treated? On a basis of equality with other aliens; with nationals of the asylum state? See the Convention Relating to the Status of Refugees, 1951, noted in the Documentary Supplement.

At what locations may a state receive persons seeking asylum so as not to violate the rights of the state of which he is a national or from which he is fleeing? Compare the following two cases.

DEFECTION FROM THE "UKRAINA"

8 Whiteman, Digest of International Law 669 (1967).

In connection with the circumstances in which a refugee escaping from a Soviet fishing fleet off Shetland was pursued by Soviets across British soil in June 1958, the Secretary of State for the Home Department and Lord Privy Seal, R. A. Butler, furnished the House of Commons with the following information:

> A man named Erich Teayn, stated to be an Estonian, came ashore in the Shetland Islands early this morning from the Russian fishing vessel "Ukraina", one of three Russian trawlers anchored in a bay at Walls. He made his way to a crofter's house and indicated that he did not want to go back to the Russian vessel. He was followed by a party of Russians, said to number about 30, who landed from two small boats in pursuit of him. He was taken into custody for interrogation under the Aliens Order. Three Russians subsequently called at Lerwick police station and sought access to him. This was refused. * * *

In response to a question whether immediate protest would be made to the Russians if the facts as stated were confirmed, and the person involved were a genuine political refugee, Mr. Butler replied: "First, we have to examine the case. If this man asks for political asylum, it will certainly be considered." * * *

ASYLUM ON A VESSEL

II Hackworth, Digest of International Law 641 (1941).

The American Minister in Guatemala reported to the Department of State, in October 1922, that in reply to an inquiry of the

Mexican Minister as to whether a certain Guatemalan to whom the Mexican Legation had given asylum would be safe from arrest if placed aboard an American vessel in a Guatemalan harbor, he had informed the Minister that the Guatemalan authorities would have the right to effect the arrest of a person in such circumstances so long as the vessel was within Guatemalan waters. In an instruction of November 3, 1922 the Department approved the attitude assumed by the Minister.

Would the result be different if the Guatemalan were placed aboard a United States *naval* vessel in Guatemalan waters? That is, could Guatemala lawfully arrest the man; would Guatemala have a basis for diplomatic protest in such a case? Asylum on diplomatic premises is dealt with at p. 836.

For the United States Department of State statement of general policy for dealing with requests for asylum by foreign nationals, see 66 U.S.Dept. of State Bull. 124 (1972).

SECTION D. THE HUMAN RIGHTS PROGRAMS OF REGIONAL ORGANIZATIONS

---

1. THE COUNCIL OF EUROPE

The Council of Europe was created in 1949 by European states with the aim, in the language of the statute, 87 U.N.T.S. 103, "to achieve a greater unity between its Members for the purpose of safeguarding and realising the ideals and principles which are their common heritage," this aim to be pursued "by discussion of questions of common concern * * * and in the maintenance and further realization of human rights and fundamental freedoms." Pursuant to that aim, and in the light of the Universal Declaration of Human Rights, the European Convention for the Protection of Human Rights and Fundamental Freedoms was brought into force in 1953, 213 U.N.T.S. 221.[a] Compare with counterpart provisions of the International Covenant on Civil and Political Rights the following provisions in the convention which are set forth below.

a. States that had ratified the Convention as of Dec. 1, 1971, were Austria, Belgium, Cyprus, Denmark, Germany (Fed.Rep.), Iceland, Ireland, Italy, Luxembourg, Malta, Netherlands, Norway, Sweden, Turkey and the United Kingdom. Members of the Council that had not ratified were France and Switzerland. (The Council is not to be confused with the European Communities.)

EUROPEAN CONVENTION FOR THE PROTECTION OF HUMAN RIGHTS AND FUNDAMENTAL FREE-DOMS OF NOVEMBER 4, 1950

213 U.N.T.S. 221.

Article 5

(1) Everyone has the right to liberty and security of person.

No one shall be deprived of his liberty save in the following cases and in accordance with a procedure prescribed by law:

(a) the lawful detention of a person after conviction by a competent court;

(b) the lawful arrest or detention of a person for non-compliance with the lawful order of a court or in order to secure fulfilment of any obligation prescribed by law;

(c) the lawful arrest or detention of a person effected for the purpose of bringing him before the competent legal authority on reasonable suspicion of having committed an offence or when it is reasonably considered necessary to prevent his committing an offence or fleeing after having done so;

(d) the detention of a minor by lawful order for the purpose of educational supervision or his lawful detention for the purpose of bringing him before the competent legal authority;

(e) the lawful detention of persons for the prevention of the spreading of infectious diseases, of persons of unsound mind, alcoholics or drug addicts or vagrants;

(f) the lawful arrest or detention of a person to prevent his effecting an unauthorised entry into the country or of a person against whom action is being taken with a view to deportation or extradition.

(2) Everyone who is arrested shall be informed promptly, in a language which he understands, of the reasons for his arrest and of any charge against him.

(3) Everyone arrested or detained in accordance with the provisions of paragraph 1(c) of this Article shall be brought promptly before a judge or other officer authorised by law to exercise judicial power and shall be entitled to trial within a reasonable time or to release pending trial. Release may be conditioned by guarantees to appear for trial.

(4) Everyone who is deprived of his liberty by arrest or detention shall be entitled to take proceedings by which the lawfulness of his detention shall be decided speedily by a court and his release ordered if the detention is not lawful.

(5) Everyone who has been the victim of arrest or detention in contravention of the provisions of this Article shall have an enforceable right to compensation.

Article 6

(1) In the determination of his civil rights and obligations or of any criminal charge against him, everyone is entitled to a fair and public hearing within a reasonable time by an independent and impartial tribunal established by law. Judgment shall be pronounced publicly but the press and public may be excluded from all or part of the trial in the interests of morals, public order or national security in a democratic society, where the interests of juveniles or the protection of the private life of the parties so require, or to the extent strictly necessary in the opinion of the court in special circumstances where publicity would prejudice the interests of justice.

(2) Everyone charged with a criminal offence shall be presumed innocent until proved guilty according to law.

(3) Everyone charged with a criminal offence has the following minimum rights:

(a) to be informed promptly, in a language which he understands and in detail, of the nature and cause of the accusation against him;

(b) to have adequate time and facilities for the preparation of his defence;

(c) to defend himself in person or through legal assistance of his own choosing or, if he has not sufficient means to pay for legal assistance, to be given it free when the interests of justice so require;

(d) to examine or have examined witnesses against him and to obtain the attendance and examination of witnesses on his behalf under the same conditions as witnesses against him;

(e) to have the free assistance of an interpreter if he cannot understand or speak the language used in court.

Article 7

(1) No one shall be held guilty of any criminal offence on account of any act or omission which did not constitute a criminal offence under national or international law at the time when it was committed. Nor shall a heavier penalty be imposed than the one that was applicable at the time the criminal offence was committed.

(2) This Article shall not prejudice the trial and punishment of any person for any act or omission which, at the time when it was committed, was criminal according to the general principles of law recognised by civilised nations.

The convention is notable because it is a working system for the international protection of human rights. The international organs of enforcement are the European Commission on Human Rights and the European Court of Human Rights; these organs have established a substantial body of precedent under the convention. The function of the commission is to ascertain the facts as to alleged breaches of the Convention and to secure a "friendly settlement." There are two ways in which the commission can be activated. One, any state party to the convention may refer an alleged breach by another party. Second, individual victims [a] of a violation by a state party can petition the commission; but this right of petition can be exercised against a state only if it has declared that it recognizes the competence of the commission to receive petitions. The commission has received hundreds of petitions but, under provisions of the convention relating to admissibility (such as the requirement of the exhaustion of domestic remedies), has declared only a small number of them to be admissible. In the event a friendly settlement is not reached through its conciliation processes, the commission renders a report in which it states "its opinion as to whether the facts found disclose a breach by the State concerned of its obligations under the Convention." The convention provides for further decision and the requirement of measures by the Committee of Ministers, an organ of the Council of Europe.

The court on the other hand, has a jurisdiction which is more remote from the individual. Its jurisdiction comprises cases referred to it by the commission or by a state party to the convention; a state may refer the case to the court if its national is alleged to be a victim, or if it referred the case to the commission or was the state against which the complaint had been lodged. As in the case of the International Court of Justice, jurisdiction depends upon the consent of the state concerned. A case cannot be brought to the court until after the commission's efforts for a friendly settlement have failed. From the individual victim's point of view, he is protected only derivatively in a case before the court. Why are states, even in a regional organization of states with a "common heritage," reluctant to permit individuals to have direct access to a court of human rights?

Article 15 of the European Convention on Human Rights contains a provision similar to Article 4 of the International Covenant on Civil and Political Rights, permitting derogation from certain obligations under the convention in emergencies:

Article 15

(1) In time of war or other public emergency threatening the life of the nation any High Contracting Party may take measures derogating from its obligations under this Convention to the extent strictly required by the exigencies of the situation, provided that such measures are not inconsistent with its other obligations under international law.

---

a. Article 25 of the convention: "Any person, non-governmental organization or group of individuals claiming to be the victim of a violation * * *."

(2) No derogation from Article 2 [right to life], except in respect of deaths resulting from lawful acts of war, or from Articles 3 [punishment], 4 (paragraph 1) [slavery] and 7 [ex post facto crime] shall be made under this provision.

(3) Any High Contracting Party availing itself of this right of derogation shall keep the Secretary-General of the Council of Europe fully informed of the measures which it has taken and the reasons therefor. It shall also inform the Secretary-General of the Council of Europe when such measures have ceased to operate and the provisions of the Convention are again being fully executed.

In Lawless v. Government of the Republic of Ireland, 31 Int'l. L.Rep. 276 (1966) (Preliminary Objections) and 31 Int'l.L.Rep. 290 (1966) (Merits), the European Court of Human Rights considered a case referred to the court by the commission. The case involved the complaint of an Irish national against the Republic of Ireland. Lawless complained that he was arrested on suspicion of being a member of an illegal organization (IRA) and was detained without charge or trial from July 13, 1957 until December 11, 1957. He alleged that his detention was a breach of Articles 5 and 6 of the European Convention on Human Rights and claimed damages for wrongful imprisonment. The commission decided that the detention "did not constitute a violation of the provisions of the European Convention of Human Rights, in view of the state of emergency existing in the Republic of Ireland at the time and of the right of the Irish Government, under Article 15 of the Convention, to take measures derogating from its obligations under the Convention, to the extent strictly required by the exigencies of the situation." The court agreed with these conclusions.

----

2.   THE ORGANIZATION OF AMERICAN STATES

In the Charter of the Organization of American States, which entered into force on December 13, 1951, the American states "proclaim the fundamental rights of the individual without distinction as to race, nationality, creed or sex. 2 U.S.T. 2394, 119 U.N.T.S. 3. (Amendments to the Charter entered into force February 27, 1970; 21 U.S.T. 607 (1970).[a]

At the 1948 Conference of the American States which gave birth to the Charter, there was also adopted the American Declaration of the Rights and Duties of Man. In 1959, by resolution of the Ministers of Foreign Affairs meeting as an organ of the Organization, the

a. Members of the organization are the states of the Western Hemisphere except Canada. The present government of Cuba has been declared by two-thirds of the member states to have "voluntarily placed itself outside the inter-American system."

Inter-American Commission on Human Rights was created. In addition to its powers of study and advice, the commission has been given the power to receive and examine individual communications charging the violation of fundamental human rights set forth in the American Declaration and to make recommendations to governments with respect thereto.

A conference in 1969 approved the American Convention on Human Rights, which contains provisions widening the American Declaration and establishing the Inter-American Court of Human Rights. Individuals do not have access to the court, since only states parties and the commission have the right to submit a case to the court; as usual, the court's jurisdiction depends upon the state's consenting thereto. Article 28, a "federal clause," is of special interest to the United States since it imposes immediate responsibility for enacting legislation implementing the convention only on the national government.

The convention was not yet in force as of Oct. 1, 1972.

See, generally, Inter-American Commission on Human Rights, Handbook of Existing Rules Pertaining to Human Rights (O.A.S.), OEA/Ser. L/V/II.23, Doc. 21 (English) Rev., Dec. 17, 1970.

SECTION E. GENOCIDE: BORDERLINE OF STATE AND INDIVIDUAL RESPONSIBILITY UNDER INTERNATIONAL LAW

THE UNITED STATES AND THE GENOCIDE CONVENTION REPORT OF SECRETARY OF STATE ROGERS TO PRESIDENT NIXON

62 U.S.Dept. of State Bull. 351 (1970).[a]

The Convention was adopted unanimously by the General Assembly of the United Nations on December 9, 1948, and signed by the United States two days later. It was submitted to the Senate by President Truman on June 16, 1949 (Executive O, 81st Congress, 1st Session). Hearings were held in 1950 by a Subcommittee of the Foreign Relations Committee which reported it favorably to the full Committee. Neither the Committee nor the Senate as a whole has yet taken action on the Convention.

The Convention entered into force on January 12, 1951. So far seventy-four countries have become parties. It is anomalous that the United States, which firmly opposes the crime of genocide and which played a leading role in bringing about the recognition of

---

a. See Documentary Supplement, for the text of the convention.

genocide as a crime against international law, is not among the parties to the Convention.

Genocide has been perpetrated many times throughout history. Although man has always expressed his horror at this crime, little was done to prevent or punish it before the 1930's. World War II witnessed the most drastic series of genocidal acts ever committed. The revulsion of civilized society manifested itself in a United Nations General Assembly resolution of December 11, 1946, declaring genocide to be a crime under international law and recommending international cooperation in its prevention and punishment. This resolution was the impetus for the drafting of the Convention on the Prevention and Punishment of the Crime of Genocide.

* * *

The contracting parties undertake to enact legislation necessary to give effect to the provisions of the Convention "in accordance with their respective constitutions." It is clear, therefore, that the Convention was not expected to be self-executing. I do not recommend, however, that the Executive Branch propose any specific implementing legislation at this time. The Departments of State and Justice will be prepared to discuss this question should the Congress request our views.

* * *

[President Nixon urged the senate to give its advice and consent to ratification of the convention. 62 U. S. Dept. of State Bull. 350 (1970).]

Questions. Does the convention impose any obligations upon the state aside from the obligation to enact legislation under Article V? If legislation is enacted making genocide a domestic crime, is the state under an obligation to use that legislation? Even if legislation is not enacted, does the state (as distinct from the individuals under its jurisdiction) have any treaty obligation not to commit genocide?

If a state has not become a party to the convention, does it violate international law if it commits genocide as a matter of state policy? If it condones genocide by individuals under its jurisdiction? Or if it fails to take action to prevent or punish genocide by individuals?

MASSACRE IN THE HEART OF AFRICA

The New York Times, June 4, 1972.
Sec. 4, p. 2, col. 1.*

Bujumbura, Burundi—Just before Christmas of 1968, Ntare V, the 19-year-old Mwame, or King, of Burundi, paid a visit to the neighboring country of the Congo, or Zaire, as it now calls itself. * * * He left behind a ceremonial drum, a symbol of his power.

During the King's absence, the commander of the Burundi army, Capt. Michel Micombero, drove up to the royal palace, seized the drum, went to the state radio station and proclaimed himself President.

So began an internecine struggle that in the past two months has grown into bloody civil war. Reports in this Burundi capital indicate that the toll in lives has been as high as 120,000.

King Ntare and President Micombero are both members of the Tutsi tribe, a tall race of warriors that for centuries has dominated the less bellicose Hutus, who account for 85 per cent of the country's 3.5 million people. Within the Tutsi tribe, however, the King and the army commander belonged to rival factions. It is out of this rivalry that the 1968 coup emerged.

As self-proclaimed President, Captain—now Colonel—Micombero ruled Burundi with an iron hand. Earlier this year, he decided that he had consolidated his power sufficiently to let the King return from exile in West Germany. (Burundi had once been a German—and later a Belgian—colony.) The President gave assurances for the monarch's safety.

But shortly after the King's return at the end of March, the authorities announced discovery of a royalist plot. Ntare was placed under arrest. Then, on April 29, an abortive attempt to overthrow the Micombero regime was staged by Tutsi royalists backed by Hutus, who have been supporters of the monarchy. In the melée, Ntare was assassinated.

Thereupon the Hutus, taking advantage of the general confusion, launched an insurrection of their own. The Burundi authorities claim that 50,000 persons, mostly members of the Tutsi tribe, were killed. Independent sources put the number at 20,000. Members of President Micombero's family and the families of many of his army officers were among the slain, though he himself is safe.[a]

The Tutsi minority had lived in dread of just such a Hutu rebellion ever since the bloody events of a decade ago in the sister republic of Rwanda. There too the Tutsi tribe was in control and the Hutus were the overwhelming majority. There too the Hutus rebelled. They overthrew the Tutsi regime of Rwanda, massacred 20,000 Tutsis and forced the rest into exile.

But in Burundi the Hutu rebellion was met head-on. The country's Tutsi-dominated army, police and militant youth organization retaliated savagely. Some 100,000 Hutus are reported to have been killed in the past few weeks.

Word of the massacres has been carried by missionaries and other foreign residents and by refugees who have fled to Zaire. According

a. Tribal rivalries have endured for centuries, are to a degree associated with sorcery, and often exceedingly bloody. Pamphlets have been found on Hutu rebels against the Burundian Tutsi aristocracy, saying: "Kill every man, woman and child. Do not take prisoners. Do not judge. Kill every Tutsi." Sulzberger, "To Be Obscurely Massacred," New York Times, July 2, 1972, Sec. 4, p. 9, col. 1.

to these reports, the Tutsis have waged a deliberate campaign to wipe out the Hutu elite. Those slain are said to have included three Hutu ministers in the Micombero Cabinet, Parliamentary deputies, teachers, church leaders and even school children.

"They have eliminated the Hutu intellectuals for the next generation," said one missionary who fled the country last week. Another churchman who had just crossed the border into Zaire said, "It's worse than Biafra ever was."

Last week, however, the picture apparently began to change. According to foreign sources in this Burundi capital, the Government sought to curb the violence. Army and police chiefs have been counseled to show moderation and punish those of their men who take the law into their own hands.

The Government's efforts came in response to growing international concern over the bloodshed in Burundi. Pope Paul, in a public address last Sunday, denounced the "organized massacre of innocent people." Belgium, which exercised a trusteeship over Burundi for 40 years and still provides aid that constitutes 25 per cent of Burundi's national budget, has threatened to cut off all further assistance. At the same time, the Burundi state radio has begun to talk about "an imperialist plot," alleging that the Belgians were behind the Hutu rising.

An uneasy calm reigns over this bucolic city of 75,000 where life seems to have resumed its quiet routine despite the gruesome tales from the interior. The only evidence of the troubles here is an 8 P.M. curfew and an occasional paratroop patrol.

Yet, the outlook in Burundi remains grim. There is fear that the Hutus in the northern section of the country, who have played a passive role thus far, may mount a violent response to the Tutsi repression. "That," as one foreign observer put it last week, "would be the blood bath to end all blood baths."

Do the actions of the rival tribes in Burundi fall within the definition of genocide in Article II of the convention? Is the answer affected by the fact that the tribes are engaged, in part at least, in a struggle for control of the government of the state, i. e., a "civil war?" ✷ (Note, however, that neither Burundi nor Rwanda is a party to the Genocide Convention.)

What is the legal position of the individuals responsible for the Burundian massacres? The Burundian domestic law of murder is relevant. There is probably no domestic law of genocide such as that described in Article V of the convention. Is there, beyond the domestic law, an international responsibility imposed upon the individual? See the preamble to the convention and consider the significance of the Nuremberg precedent, discussed in the next chapter.

Chapter 10

THE GROWTH OF INDIVIDUAL RESPONSIBILITY

SECTION A. "TRADITIONAL" WAR CRIMES

JUDGMENT IN CASE OF LIEUTENANTS DITHMAR
AND BOLDT
HOSPITAL SHIP "LLANDOVERY CASTLE"

Germany, Supreme Court of Leipzig, 1921.
16 American Journal of International Law 708 (1922).

* * *

Up to the year 1916 the steamer Llandovery Castle, had, according to the statements of the witnesses Chapman and Heather, been used for the transport of troops. In that year she was commissioned by the British Government to carry wounded and sick Canadian soldiers home to Canada from the European theatre of war. The vessel was suitably fitted out for the purpose and was provided with the distinguishing marks, which the Tenth Hague Convention of the 18th October, 1907 (relating to the application to naval warfare of the principles of the Geneva Convention) requires in the case of naval hospital ships. The name of the vessel was communicated to the enemy powers. From that time onwards she was exclusively employed in the transport of sick and wounded. She never again carried troops, and never had taken munitions on board. * * *

* * *

At the end of the month of June, 1918, the Llandovery Castle was on her way back to England from Halifax, after having carried sick and wounded there. She had on board the crew consisting of 164 men, 80 officers and men of the Canadian Medical Corps, and 14 nurses, a total of 258 persons. There were no combatants on board, and, in particular, no American airmen. The vessel had not taken on board any munitions or other war material. * * *

In the evening of 27th June, 1918, at about 9:30 (local time) the Llandovery Castle was sunk in the Atlantic Ocean, about 116 miles south-west of Fastnet (Ireland), by a torpedo from the German U-boat 86. Of those on board only 24 persons were saved, 234 having been drowned. The commander of U-boat 86 was First-Lieutenant Patzig, who was subsequently promoted captain. His present whereabouts are unknown. ‖The accused Dithmar was the first officer of the watch, and the accused Boldt the second‖ Patzig recognized the character of the ship, which he had been pursuing for a long time, at the latest when she exhibited at dusk the lights prescribed for hos-

656

pital ships by the Tenth Hague Convention. In accordance with international law, the German U-boats were forbidden to torpedo hospital ships. According both to the German and the British Governments' interpretation of the said Hague Convention, ships, which were used for the transport of military persons wounded and fallen ill in war on land, belonged to this category. The German Naval Command had given orders that hospital ships were only to be sunk within the limits of a certain barred area. However, this area was a long way from the point we have now under consideration. Patzig knew this and was aware that by torpedoing the Llandovery Castle he was acting against orders. But he was of the opinion, founded on various information (including some from official sources, the accuracy of which cannot be verified, and does not require to be verified in these proceedings), that on the enemy side, hospital ships were being used for transporting troops and combatants, as well as munitions. He, therefore, presumed that, contrary to international law, a similar use was being made of the Llandovery Castle. In particular, he seems to have expected (what grounds he had for this has not been made clear) that she had American airmen on board. Acting on this suspicion, he decided to torpedo the ship, in spite of his having been advised not to do so by the accused Dithmar and the witness Popitz. Both were with him in the conning tower, the accused Boldt being at the depth rudder.

The torpedo struck the Llandovery Castle amidship on the port side and damaged the ship to such an extent that she sank in about 10 minutes. There were 19 lifeboats on board. Each could take a maximum of 52 persons. Only two of them (described as cutters) were smaller, and these could not take more than 23 persons. Some of the boats on the port side were destroyed by the explosion of the torpedo. A good number of undamaged boats were, however, successfully lowered. The favorable weather assisted life-saving operations. There was a light breeze and a slight swell.

The men who were saved from the Llandovery Castle do not agree as regards the number of boats which got away safely. This is sufficiently explained by the circumstances, and particularly by the state of excitement, into which the majority of them were plunged, by the torpedoing and sinking of the ship. *   *   *

It is quite possible that out of these five boats which left the steamer safely, one or two may have been drawn into the vortex made by the sinking ship. But the evidence has shown that at least three of these five boats survived the sinking of the ship. *   *   *

*   *   *

Thus, after the sinking of the Llandovery Castle, there were still left three of her boats with people on board.

Some time after the torpedoing, the U-boat came to the surface and approached the lifeboats, in order to ascertain by examination whether the Llandovery Castle had airmen and munitions on board. The witness Popitz, who was steersman on board the U-boat, took part in the stopping of several lifeboats for that purpose.   *   *   *

*   *   *

**FIRED
AT
LIFEBOAT**

After passing by the second time, the U-boat once more went away.   The lifeboat, which had hoisted a sail in the meantime, endeavored to get away.   But after a brief period, the occupants of the boat noticed firing from the U-boat.   The first two shells passed over the lifeboat.   Then firing took place in another direction; about 12 to 14 shots fell all told.   The flash at the mouth of the gun and the flash of the exploding shells were noticed almost at the same time, so that, as the expert also assumes, the firing was at a very near target.   After firing had ceased, the occupants of the lifeboat saw nothing more of the U-boat.

The captain's boat cruised about for some 36 hours altogether. On the 29th June, in the morning, it was found by the English destroyer Lysander.   The crew were taken on board and the boat left to its fate.   During the 29th June, the commander of the English Fleet caused a search to be made for the other lifeboats of the Llandovery Castle.   The English sloop Snowdrop and four American destroyers systematically searched the area, where the boats from the sunken ship might be drifting about.   The Snowdrop found an undamaged boat of the Llandovery Castle 9 miles from the spot on which the Lysander had found the captain's boat.   The boat was empty, but had been occupied, as was shown by the position of the sail.   *   *   *   Otherwise the search which was continued until the evening of the 1st July, in uniformly good weather, remained fruitless.   No other boat from the Llandovery Castle and no more survivors were found.

The firing from the U-boat was not only noticed by the occupants of the captain's boat.   It was also heard by the witnesses Popitz, Knoche, Ney, Tegtmeier and Käss, who were members of the crew of the U-boat.   According to their statements a portion of the crew of the U-boat were on deck during the evolutions of the U-boat, during the holding up of the lifeboat and during the interrogation of the Englishmen.   *   *   *

After the examination was completed the command "Ready for submerging" was given.   *   *   *   [T]he whole of the crew went below deck, as is the case when the order to be ready for diving is given. There only remained on deck Commander Patzig, the accused, as his officers of the watch and, by special order, the first boatswain's mate, Meissner, who had since died.   *   *   *   Firing commenced some time after the crew had gone below.   The witnesses heard distinctly that only the stern gun, a 8.8 c/m gun was in action.   While firing, the U-boat moved about.   It did not submerge even after the firing had ceased, but continued on the surface.

The prosecution assumes that the firing of the U-boat was directed against the lifeboats of the Llandovery Castle. The court has arrived at the same conclusion as the result of the evidence given at this time.   *   *   *

     *   *   *

In this connection we must refer to the opinion of the actual witnesses, both English and German. [The court analyzes the testimony of the witnesses.]

     *   *   *

If finally the question is asked—what can have induced Patzig to sink the lifeboats, the answer is to be found in the previous torpedoing of the Llandovery Castle. Patzig wished to keep this quiet and to prevent any news of it reaching England. He may not have desired to avoid taking sole responsibility for the deed. This fits in with the descriptions given of his personality. He may have argued to himself that, if the sinking of the ship became known (the legality of which he, in view of the fruitlessness of his endeavors to prove the misuse of the ship, was not able to establish) great difficulties would be caused to the German Government in their relations with other powers. Irregular torpedoings had already brought the German Government several times into complications with other states and there was the possibility that this fresh case might still further prejudice the international position of Germany. This might bring powers, that were still neutral, into the field against her. Patzig may have wished to prevent this, by wiping out all traces of his action. The false entries in the log-book and the chart, which have already been mentioned, were intended, having regard to his position in the service, to achieve this object. This illusion could be, however, of but short duration, if the passengers in the lifeboats, some of whom had been on board the U-boat, and who, therefore could fully describe it, were allowed to get home. It was, therefore, necessary to get rid of them, if Patzig did not wish the sinking of the Llandovery Castle to be known. Herein is to be found the explanation of the unholy decision, which he came to and promptly carried out after his fruitless examination of the boats.

On these various grounds the court has decided that the lifeboats of the Llandovery Castle were fired on in order to sink them. This is the only conclusion possible, in view of what has been stated by the witnesses. It is only on this basis that the behavior of Patzig and of the accused men can be explained.

The court finds that it is beyond all doubt that, even though no witness had direct observation of the effect of the fire, Patzig attained his object so far as two of the boats were concerned.   *   *   *

For the firing on the lifeboats only those persons can be held responsible, who at the time were on the deck of the U-boat; namely Patzig, the two accused and the chief boatswain's mate Meissner.

Patzig gave the decisive order, which was carried out without demur in virtue of his position as commander. It is possible that he asked the opinion of the two accused beforehand, though of this there is no evidence. As Meissner was the gunlayer and remained on deck by special orders, it may be assumed with certainty that he manned the after gun which was fired. In the opinion of the naval expert, he was able to act without assistance. According to this view, owing to the nearness of the objects under fire, there was no need for the fire to be directed by an artillery officer, such as the accused Dithmar. The only technical explanation, which both the accused have given and which fits in with the facts, is that they themselves did not fire. Under the circumstances this is quite credible. They confined themselves to making observations while the firing was going on. The naval expert also assumes that they kept a look-out. Such a look-out must have brought the lifeboats, which were being fired on, within their view. By reporting their position and the varying distances of the lifeboats and such like, the accused assisted in the firing on the lifeboats, and this, quite apart from the fact that their observations saved the U-boat from danger from any other quarter, and that they thereby enabled Patzig to do what he intended as regards the lifeboats. The statement of the accused Boldt that "so far as he took part in what happened, he acted in accordance with his orders" has reference to the question whether the accused took part in the firing on the lifeboats. He does not appear to admit any participation. But the two accused must be held guilty for the destruction of the lifeboats.

With regard to the question of the guilt of the accused, no importance is to be attached to the statements put forward by the defence, that the enemies of Germany were making improper use of hospital ships for military purposes, and that they had repeatedly fired on German lifeboats and shipwrecked people. * * * [T]hroughout the German fleet it was a matter of general belief that improper use of hospital ships was made by the enemy. It must, therefore, be assumed for the benefit of the accused, that they also held this belief. Whether this belief was founded on fact or not, is of less importance as affecting the case before the court, than the established fact that the Llandovery Castle at the time was not carrying any cargo or troops prohibited under clause 10 of the Hague Convention.

The act of Patzig is homicide, according to para. 212 of the Penal Code. By sinking the lifeboats he purposely killed the people who were in them. On the other hand no evidence has been brought forward to show that he carried out this killing with deliberation. Patzig, as to whose character the court has no direct means of knowledge, may very well have done the deed in a moment of excitement, which prevented him from arriving at a clear appreciation of all the circumstances, which should have been taken into consideration. The crew of a submarine, in consequence of the highly dangerous nature of their work, live in a state of constant tension. This is liable to become greater if a torpedoing takes place, particularly in the case of the commander, who is responsible for the act. Several factors were present in this case, which tended specially to deprive Patzig of the power to arrive at a calm decision. He had said that he would torpedo a hospital ship, with all its characteristic markings, in the expectation of being able to prove that it was being used for improper purposes. His hope was in vain. In spite of the most minute investigation, it was not possible for him to obtain any confirmation of his assumption. Then arose the question, how he could avert the evil consequences of his error of judgment. He had to decide quickly: he had to act quickly. Under this pressure of circumstances, he proceeded in a manner which the naval expert rightly described as imprudent. In the darkness of the night there was only a small chance of hitting all the boats. The fact that, as explained above, this did not restrain him from the act, points to the consideration that he did not allow himself time to think the matter over, so little was the idea in his mind of the far-reaching effect of his action.

In view of this state of excitement, which under the circumstances has to be taken into account, the execution of the deed cannot definitely be called deliberate (in the sense implied in para. 211 of the Penal Code).

The firing on the boats was an offence against the law of nations. In war on land the killing of unarmed enemies is not allowed (compare the Hague regulations as to war on land, para. 23(c)), similarly in war at sea, the killing of shipwrecked people, who have taken refuge in lifeboats, is forbidden. It is certainly possible to imagine exceptions to this rule, as, for example, if the inmates of the lifeboats take part in the fight. But there was no such state of affairs in the present case, as Patzig and the accused persons were well aware, when they cruised around and examined the boats.

Any violation of the law of nations in warfare is, as the Senate has already pointed out, a punishable offence, so far as in general, a penalty is attached to the deed. The killing of enemies in war is in accordance with the will of the State that makes war, (whose laws as to the legality or illegality on the question of killing are decisive), only in so far as such killing is in accordance with the conditions and limitations imposed by the law of nations. The fact that his deed is a violation of international law must be well-known to the doer, apart from acts of carelessness, in which careless ignorance is a sufficient excuse. In examining the question of the existence of this knowledge, the ambiguity of many of the rules of international law, as well as the actual circumstances of the case, must be borne in mind, because in war time decisions of great importance have frequently to be made on very insufficient material. This consideration, however, cannot be applied to the case at present before the court. The rule of international law, which is here involved, is simple and is universally known. No possible doubt can exist with regard to the question of its applicability. The court must in this instance affirm Patzig's guilt of killing contrary to international law.

The two accused knowingly assisted Patzig in this killing, by the very fact of their having accorded him their support in the manner, which has already been set out. It is not proved that they were in agreement with his intentions. The decision rested with Patzig as the commander. The others who took part in this deed carried out his orders. It must be accepted that the deed was carried out on his responsibility, the accused only wishing to support him therein. A direct act of killing, following a deliberate intention to kill, is not proved against the accused. They are, therefore, only liable to punishment as accessories. (Para. 49 of the Penal Code.)

Patzig's order does not free the accused from guilt. It is true that according to para. 47 of the Military Penal Code, if the execution of an order in the ordinary course of duty involves such a violation of the law as is punishable, the superior officer issuing such an order is alone responsible. According to No. 2, however, the subordinate obeying such an order is liable to punishment, if it was known to him that the order of the superior involved the infringement of civil or military law. This applies in the case of the accused. It is certainly to be urged in favor of the military subordinates, that they are under no obligation to question the order of their superior officer, and they can count upon its legality. But no such confidence can be held to exist, if such an order is universally known to everybody, including also the accused, to be without any doubt whatever against the law. This happens only in rare and exceptional cases. But this case was precisely one of them, for in the present instance, it was perfectly clear to the accused that killing defenceless people in the lifeboats could be nothing else but a breach of the law. As naval officers by profession they were well aware, as the naval expert Saalwächter has strikingly stated, that one is not legally authorized to kill defenceless people. They well knew that this was the case here. They quickly found out the facts by questioning the occupants in the boats when these were stopped. They could only have gathered, from the order given by Patzig, that he wished to make use of his subordinates to carry out a breach of the law. They should, therefore, have refused to obey. As they did not do so, they must be punished.

The witnesses, Vice-Admiral (retired) von Trotha, and Toepffer, the President of the District Court (the latter acted during the war as an adviser to the Navy on the law relating to war), admitted frankly that in the German fleet, the impression prevailed that a naval officer, who in the course of a fight exceeded the bounds of the law, was not thereby rendered liable to punishment, although he might be answerable for his action to his superiors. The statements of these two witnesses relate, however, to the point of view, which was held by the higher command in the fleet at the time. They did not maintain that the accused shared this opinion. It appears that neither of these witnesses applied himself to the application of these ideas to the incidents now in question. These opinions are based on a misunderstanding of the law and are irrelevant here. They are of no avail for the accused, because the sinking of the lifeboats was not done in the course of a fight, neither in an attack on the enemy nor in defence against him. Although a submarine, while cruising, must continually and in a special degree be ready for fighting, and is always (in the sense of para. 11 of the Military Penal Code) "before the enemy," nevertheless it can do things which are not concerned with fighting.

The defence finally points out that the accused must have considered that Patzig would have enforced his orders, weapon in hand, if they had not obeyed them. This possibility is rejected. If Patzig had been faced by refusal on the part of his subordinates, he would have been obliged to desist from his purpose, as then it would have been impossible for him to attain his object, namely, the concealment of the torpedoing of the Llandovery Castle. This was also quite well-known to the accused, who had witnessed the affair. From the point of view of necessity (para. 52 of the Penal Code), they can thus not claim to be acquitted.

In estimating the punishment, it has, in the first place, to be borne in mind that the principal guilt rests with Commander Patzig, under whose orders the accused acted. They should certainly have refused to obey the order. This would have required a specially high degree of resolution. A refusal to obey the commander on a submarine would have been something so unusual, that it is humanly possible to understand that the accused could not bring themselves to disobey. That certainly does not make them innocent, as has been stated above. They had acquired the habit of obedience to military authority and could not rid themselves of it. This justifies the recognition of mitigating circumstances. In determining the punishment under para. 213, 49, para. 2, 44 of the State Penal Code, a severe sentence must, however, be passed. The killing of defenceless shipwrecked people is an act in the highest degree contrary to ethical principles. It must also not be left out of consideration that the deed throws a dark shadow on the German fleet, and specially on the submarine weapon which did so much in the fight for the Fatherland. For this reason a sentence of four years' imprisonment on both the accused persons has been considered appropriate.

In accordance with Section 34, para. 1, No. 2, Section 40, para. 1, No. 1, and Section 36 of the Military Penal Code, the accused, Dithmar, is dismissed from the service, and the accused, Boldt, is condemned to lose the right to wear officer's uniform.

The behavior of the accused during the proceedings has not been such as to justify reducing the period of imprisonment by the comparatively short period, during which they have already been detained.

* * *

TAYLOR, NUREMBERG AND VIETNAM 20 (1970)*

What, then, are the "laws of war"? They are of ancient origin, and followed two main streams of development. The first flowed from medieval notions of knightly chivalry. Over the course of the centuries the stream has thinned to a trickle; it had a brief spurt during the days of single-handed aerial combat, and survives today in rules (often violated) prohibiting various deceptions such as the use of the enemy's uniforms or battle insignia, or the launching of a war without fair warning by formal declaration.

The second and far more important concept is that the ravages of war should be mitigated as far as possible by prohibiting needless cruelties, and other acts that spread death and destruction and are not reasonably related to the conduct of hostilities. The seeds of such a principle must be nearly as old as human society, and ancient literature abounds with condemnation of pillage and massacre. In more recent times, both religious humanitarianism and the opposition of merchants to unnecessary disruptions of commerce have furnished the motivation for restricting customs and understandings. In the 17th century these ideas began to find expression in learned writings, especially those of the Dutch jurist-philosopher Hugo Grotius.

The formalization of military organization in the 18th-century brought the establishment of military courts, empowered to try violations of the laws of war as well as other offenses by soldiers. During the American Revolution, both Captain Nathan Hale and the British Major John André were convicted as spies and ordered to be hanged, the former by a British military court and the latter by a "Board of General Officers" appointed by George Washington. During the Mexican War, General Winfield Scott created "military commissions," with jurisdiction over violations of the laws of war committed either by American troops against Mexican civilians, or vice versa.

Up to that time the laws of war had remained largely a matter of unwritten tradition, and it was the United States, during the Civil War, that took the lead in reducing them to systematic, written form. In 1863 President Lincoln approved the promulgation by the War Department of "Instructions for the Government of Armies of the United States in the Field," prepared by Francis Lieber, a German veteran of the Napoleonic wars, who emigrated to the United States and became professor of law and political science at Columbia University. These comprised 159 articles, covering such subjects as "military necessity," "punishment of crimes against the inhabitants of hostile countries," "prisoners of war," and "spies." It was by a military commission appointed in accordance with these instructions

---

* Reprinted with permission of Quadrangle Books, Inc., New York.

that Mary Surratt and the others accused of conspiring to assassinate Lincoln were tried.

In the wake of the Crimean War, the Civil War and the Franco-Prussian War of 1870 there arose, in Europe and America, a tide of sentiment for codification of the laws of war and their embodiment in international agreements. The principal fruits of that movement were the series of treaties known today as the Hague and Geneva Conventions. For present purposes, the most important of these are the Fourth Hague Convention of 1907, and the Geneva Prisoner of War, Red Cross, and Protection of Civilians Conventions of 1929 and 1949.

"The right of belligerents to adopt means of injuring the enemy is not unlimited," declared Article 22 of the Fourth Hague Convention, and ensuing articles specify a number of limitations: Enemy soldiers who surrender must not be killed, and are to be taken prisoner; captured cities and towns must not be pillaged, nor "undefended" places bombarded; poisoned weapons and other arms "calculated to cause unnecessary suffering" are forbidden. Other provisions make it clear that war is not a free-for-all between the populations of the countries at war; only members of the armed forces can claim protection of the laws of war, and if a noncombatant civilian takes hostile action against the enemy he is guilty of a war crime. When an army occupies enemy territory, it must endeavor to restore public order, and respect "family honor and rights, the lives of persons, and private property, as well as religious convictions and practices."

Rules requiring humane treatment of prisoners, and for protection of the sick and wounded, are prescribed in the Geneva Conventions. While there is no general treaty on naval warfare, the Ninth Hague Convention prohibited the bombardment of undefended "ports," and the London Naval Treaty of 1930 condemned submarine sinkings of merchant vessels, unless passengers and crews were first placed in "safety."

In all of these treaties, the laws of war are stated as general principles of conduct, and neither the means of enforcement nor the penalties for violations are specified. The substance of their provisions, however, has been taken into the military law of many countries, and is often set forth in general orders, manuals of instruction, or other official documents. In the United States, for example, the Lieber rules of 1863 were replaced in 1914 by an army field manual which, up-dated, is still in force under the title "The Law of Land Warfare." It is set forth therein that the laws of war are part of the law of the United States, and that they may be enforced against both soldiers and civilians, including enemy personnel, by general courts-martial, military commissions, or other military or international tribunals.

Comparable though not identical publications have been issued by the military authorities of Britain, France, Germany and many other countries. These documents, and the treaties on which they are largely based, are regarded as a comprehensive but not necessarily complete exposition of what is really a body of international common law—the laws of war.

Since the mid-19th century, with increasing frequency, the major powers have utilized military courts for the trial of persons accused of war crimes. An early and now famous trial, depicted in a successful Broadway play, was the post-Civil War proceeding against the Confederate Major Henry Wirz on charges of responsibility for the death of thousands of Union prisoners in the Andersonville prison camp, of which he had been commandant. War crimes tribunals were convened by the United States after the Spanish-American War, and by the British after the Boer War.

Following the defeat of Germany in the First World War, the Allies demanded that nearly 900 Germans accused of war crimes, including military and political leaders, be handed over for trial on war crimes charges. The Germans resisted the demand, and in the upshot they were allowed to try their own "war criminals." The trials in 1921 and 1922 were not conducted by military courts, but by the Supreme Court of Germany, sitting in Leipzig. From the Allied standpoint they were a fiasco, as only a handful of accused were tried, and of these nearly all were acquitted or allowed to escape their very short prison sentences. The German court did, however, affirm that violations of the laws of war are punishable offenses, and in the Llandovery Castle case sentenced two German U-boat officers to four-year prison terms (from which both soon escaped) for complicity in the torpedoing of a British hospital ship and the shelling and sinking of her life-boats.

IN RE YAMASHITA

United States Supreme Court, 1946.
327 U.S. 1, 66 S.Ct. 340.

MR. CHIEF JUSTICE STONE delivered the opinion of the Court.

No. 61 Miscellaneous is an application for leave to file a petition for writs of habeas corpus and prohibition in this Court. No. 672 is a petition for certiorari to review an order of the Supreme Court of the Commonwealth of the Philippines (28 U.S.C. § 349), denying petitioner's application to that court for writs of habeas corpus and prohibition. * * *

From the petitions and supporting papers it appears that prior to September 3, 1945, petitioner was the Commanding General of the Fourteenth Army Group of the Imperial Japanese Army in the Philippine Islands. On that date he surrendered to and became a prisoner of war of the United States Army Forces in Baguio, Philippine

Islands. On September 25th, by order of respondent, Lieutenant General Wilhelm D. Styer, Commanding General of the United States Army Forces, Western Pacific, which command embraces the Philippine Islands, petitioner was served with a charge prepared by the Judge Advocate General's Department of the Army, purporting to charge petitioner with a violation of the law of war. On October 8, 1945, petitioner, after pleading not guilty to the charge, was held for trial before a military commission of five Army officers appointed by order of General Styer. The order appointed six Army officers, all lawyers, as defense counsel.

* * *

On the same date a bill of particulars was filed by the prosecution, and the commission heard a motion made in petitioner's behalf to dismiss the charge on the ground that it failed to state a violation of the law of war. On October 29th the commission was reconvened, a supplemental bill of particulars was filed, and the motion to dismiss was denied. The trial then proceeded until its conclusion on December 7, 1945, the commission hearing two hundred and eighty-six witnesses, who gave over three thousand pages of testimony. On that date petitioner was found guilty of the offense as charged and sentenced to death by hanging.

The petitions for habeas corpus set up that the detention of petitioner for the purpose of the trial was unlawful for reasons which are now urged as showing that the military commission was without lawful authority or jurisdiction to place petitioner on trial, as follows:

(a) That the military commission which tried and convicted petitioner was not lawfully created, and that no military commission to try petitioner for violations of the law of war could lawfully be convened after the cessation of hostilities between the armed forces of the United States and Japan;

(b) That the charge preferred against petitioner fails to charge him with a violation of the law of war;

* * *

On the same grounds the petitions for writs of prohibition set up that the commission is without authority to proceed with the trial.

The Supreme Court of the Philippine Islands, after hearing argument, denied the petition for habeas corpus presented to it, on the ground, among others, that its jurisdiction was limited to an inquiry as to the jurisdiction of the commission to place petitioner on trial for the offense charged, and that the commission, being validly constituted by the order of General Styer, had jurisdiction over the person of petitioner and over the trial for the offense charged.

In Ex parte Quirin, 317 U.S. 1, 63 S.Ct. 2, we had occasion to consider at length the sources and nature of the authority to create military commissions for the trial of enemy combatants for offenses against the law of war. We there pointed out that Congress, in the exercise of the power conferred upon it by Article I, § 8, Cl. 10 of the Constitution to "define and punish * * * Offences against the Law of Nations * * *" of which the law of war is a part, had by the Articles of War (10 U.S.C.A. §§ 1471–1593) recognized the "military commission" appointed by military command, as it had previously existed in United States Army practice, as an appropriate tribunal for the trial and punishment of offenses against the law of war. Article 15 declares that the "provisions of these articles conferring jurisdiction upon courts martial shall not be construed as depriving military commissions * * * or other military tribunals of concurrent jurisdiction in respect of offenders or offenses that by statute or by the law of war may be triable by such military commissions * * * or other military tribunals." * * *

We further pointed out that Congress, by sanctioning trial of enemy combatants for violations of the law of war by military commission, had not attempted to codify the law of war or to mark its precise boundaries. Instead, by Article 15 it had incorporated, by reference, as within the preexisting jurisdiction of military commissions created by appropriate military command, all offenses which are defined as such by the law of war, and which may constitutionally be included within that jurisdiction. It thus adopted the system of military common law applied by military tribunals so far as it should be recognized and deemed applicable by the courts, and as further defined and supplemented by the Hague Convention, to which the United States and the Axis powers were parties.

We also emphasized in Ex parte Quirin, as we do here, that on application for habeas corpus we are not concerned with the guilt or innocence of the petitioners. We consider here only the lawful power of the commission to try the petitioner for the offense charged. * * * If the military tribunals have lawful authority to hear, decide and condemn, their action is not subject to judicial review merely because they have made a wrong decision on disputed facts. Correction of their errors of decision is not for the courts but for the military authorities which are alone authorized to review their decisions. * * *

Finally, we held in Ex parte Quirin, supra, 24, 25, as we hold now, that Congress by sanctioning trials of enemy aliens by military commission for offenses against the law of war had recognized the right of the accused to make a defense. * * * It has not foreclosed their right to contend that the Constitution or laws of the United States withhold authority to proceed with the trial. It has not withdrawn, and the Executive branch of the Government could not, unless there was suspension of the writ, withdraw from the courts the duty and power to make such inquiry into the authority of the commission as may be made by habeas corpus.

* * *

* * * [W]e turn to the question whether the authority to create the commission and direct the trial by military order continued after the cessation of hostilities.

An important incident to the conduct of war is the adoption of measures by the military commander, not only to repel and defeat the enemy, but to seize and subject to disciplinary measures those enemies who, in their attempt to thwart or impede our military effort, have violated the law of war. * * * The trial and punishment of enemy combatants who have committed violations of the law of war is thus not only a part of the conduct of war operating as a preventive measure against such violations, but is an exercise of the authority sanctioned by Congress to administer the system of military justice recognized by the law of war. That sanction is without qualification as to the exercise of this authority so long as a state of war exists—from its declaration until peace is proclaimed. * * * The war power, from which the commission derives its existence, is not limited to victories in the field, but carries with it the inherent power to guard against the immediate renewal of the conflict, and to remedy, at least in ways Congress has recognized, the evils which the military operations have produced. * * *

We cannot say that there is no authority to convene a commission after hostilities have ended to try violations of the law of war committed before their cessation, at least until peace has been officially recognized by treaty or proclamation of the political branch of the Government. In fact, in most instances the practical administration of the system of military justice under the law of war would fail if such authority were thought to end with the cessation of hostilities. For only after their cessation could the greater number of offenders and the principal ones be apprehended and subjected to trial.

No writer on international law appears to have regarded the power of military tribunals, otherwise competent to try violations of the law of war, as terminating before the formal state of war has ended. In our own military history there have been numerous instances in which offenders were tried by military commission after the cessation of hostilities and before the proclamation of peace, for offenses against the law of war committed before the cessation of hostilities.

The extent to which the power to prosecute violations of the law of war shall be exercised before peace is declared rests, not with the courts, but with the political branch of the Government, and may itself be governed by the terms of an armistice or the treaty of peace. Here, peace has not been agreed upon or proclaimed. Japan, by her acceptance of the Potsdam Declaration and her surrender, has acquiesced in the trials of those guilty of violations of the law of war. The conduct of the trial by the military commission has been authorized by the political branch of the Government, by military command, by international law and usage, and by the terms of the surrender of the Japanese government.

The charge. Neither congressional action nor the military orders constituting the commission authorized it to place petitioner on trial unless the charge preferred against him is of a violation of the law of war. The charge, so far as now relevant, is that petitioner, between October 9, 1944 and September 2, 1945, in the Philippine Islands, "while commander of armed forces of Japan at war with the United States of America and its allies, unlawfully disregarded and failed to discharge his duty as commander to control the operations of the members of his command, permitting them to commit brutal atrocities and other high crimes against people of the United States and of its allies and dependencies, particularly the Philippines; and he * * * thereby violated the laws of war."

Bills of particulars, filed by the prosecution by order of the commission, allege a series of acts, one hundred and twenty-three in number, committed by members of the forces under petitioner's command during the period mentioned. The first item specifies the execution of "a deliberate plan and purpose to massacre and exterminate a large part of the civilian population of Batangas Province, and to devastate and destroy public, private and religious property therein, as a result of which more than 25,000 men, women and children, all unarmed noncombatant civilians, were brutally mistreated and killed, without cause or trial, and entire settlements were devastated and destroyed wantonly and without military necessity." Other items specify acts of violence, cruelty and homicide inflicted upon the civilian population and prisoners of war, acts of wholesale pillage and the wanton destruction of religious monuments.

It is not denied that such acts directed against the civilian population of an occupied country and against prisoners of war are recognized in international law as violations of the law of war. Articles 4, 28, 46, and 47, Annex to the Fourth Hague Convention, 1907, 36 Stat. 2277, 2296, 2303, 2306–7. But it is urged that the charge does not allege that petitioner has either committed or directed the commission of such acts, and consequently that no violation is charged as against him. But this overlooks the fact that the gist of the charge is an unlawful breach of duty by petitioner as an army commander to control the operations of the members of his command by "permitting them to commit" the extensive and widespread atrocities specified. The question then is whether the law of war imposes on an army commander a duty to take such appropriate measures as are within his power to control the troops under his command for the prevention of the specified acts which are violations of the law of war and which are likely to attend the occupation of hostile territory by an uncontrolled soldiery, and whether he may be charged with personal responsibility for his failure to take such measures when violations result. That this was the precise issue to be tried was made clear by the statement of the prosecution at the opening of the trial.

It is evident that the conduct of military operations by troops whose excesses are unrestrained by the orders or efforts of their commander would almost certainly result in violations which it is the purpose of the law of war to prevent. Its purpose to protect civilian populations and prisoners of war from brutality would largely be defeated if the commander of an invading army could with impunity neglect to take reasonable measures for their protection. Hence the law of war presupposes that its violation is to be avoided through the control of the operations of war by commanders who are to some extent responsible for their subordinates.

This is recognized by the Annex to the Fourth Hague Convention of 1907, respecting the laws and customs of war on land. Article 1 lays down as a condition which an armed force must fulfill in order to be accorded the rights of lawful belligerents, that it must be "commanded by a person responsible for his subordinates." 36 Stat. 2295. Similarly Article 19 of the Tenth Hague Convention, relating to bombardment by naval vessels, provides that commanders in chief of the belligerent vessels "must see that the above Articles are properly carried out." 36 Stat. 2389. And Article 26 of the Geneva Red Cross Convention of 1929, 47 Stat. 2074, 2092, for the amelioration of the condition of the wounded and sick in armies in the field, makes it "the duty of the commanders-in-chief of the belligerent armies to provide for the details of execution of the foregoing articles, [of the convention] as well as for unforeseen cases * * *" And, finally, Article 43 of the Annex of the Fourth Hague Convention, 36 Stat. 2306, requires that the commander of a force occupying enemy territory, as was petitioner, "shall take all the measures in his power to restore, and ensure, as far as possible, public order and safety, while respecting, unless absolutely prevented, the laws in force in the country."

These provisions plainly imposed on petitioner, who at the time specified was military governor of the Philippines, as well as commander of the Japanese forces, an affirmative duty to take such measures as were within his power and appropriate in the circumstances to protect prisoners of war and the civilian population. This duty of a commanding officer has heretofore been recognized, and its breach penalized by our own military tribunals. A like principle has been applied so as to impose liability on the United States in international arbitrations. Case of Jeannaud, 3 Moore, International Arbitrations, 3000; Case of The Zafiro, 5 Hackworth, Digest of International Law, 707.

We do not make the laws of war but we respect them so far as they do not conflict with the commands of Congress or the Constitution. There is no contention that the present charge, thus read, is without the support of evidence, or that the commission held petitioner responsible for failing to take measures which were beyond his control or inappropriate for a commanding officer to take in the circumstances. We do not here appraise the evidence on which petitioner was convicted. We do not consider what measures, if any, petitioner took to prevent the commission, by the troops under his command, of the plain violations of the law of war detailed in the bill of particulars, or whether such measures as he may have taken were appropriate and sufficient to discharge the duty imposed upon him. These are questions within the peculiar competence of the military officers composing the commission and were for it to decide. See Smith v. Whitney, 116 U.S. 167, 178, 6 S.Ct. 570, 576. It is plain that the charge on which petitioner was tried charged him with a breach of his duty to control the operations of the members of his command, by permitting them to commit the specified atrocities. This was enough to require the commission to hear evidence tending to establish the culpable failure of petitioner to perform the duty imposed on him by the law of war and to pass upon its sufficiency to establish guilt.

* * *

Petitioner further urges that by virtue of Article 63 of the Geneva Convention of 1929, 47 Stat. 2052, he is entitled to the benefits afforded by the 25th and 38th Articles of War to members of our own forces. Article 63 provides: "Sentence may be pronounced against a prisoner of war only by the same courts and according to the same procedure as in the case of persons belonging to the armed forces of the detaining Power." Since petitioner is a prisoner of war, and as the 25th and 38th Articles of War apply to the trial of any person in our own armed forces, it is said that Article 63 requires them to be applied in the trial of petitioner. But we think examination of Article 63 in its setting in the Convention plainly shows that it refers to sentence "pronounced against a prisoner of war" for an offense committed while a prisoner of war, and not for a violation of the law of war committed while a combatant.

* * *

It thus appears that the order convening the commission was a lawful order, that the commission was lawfully constituted, that petitioner was charged with violation of the law of war, and that the commission had authority to proceed with the trial, and in doing so did not violate any military, statutory or constitutional command. We have considered, but find it unnecessary to discuss, other contentions which we find to be without merit. We therefore conclude that the detention of petitioner for trial and his detention upon his conviction, subject to the prescribed review by the military authorities, were lawful, and that the petition for certiorari, and leave to file in this Court petitions for writs of habeas corpus and prohibition should be, and they are denied.

MR. JUSTICE JACKSON took no part in the consideration or decision of these cases.

[Dissenting opinions omitted.]

NOTE, THE GENEVA CONVENTION AND THE TREATMENT OF PRISONERS OF WAR IN VIETNAM

80 Harvard Law Review 851 (1967).*

As early as the spring of 1965 the International Committee of the Red Cross took the position that: "The hostilities raging at the present time in Vietnam both North and South of the 17th parallel have assumed such proportions recently that there can be no doubt they constitute an armed conflict to which the regulations of humanitarian law as a whole should be applied." The Committee was referring to the four Geneva Conventions of 1949,[3] which not only set out provisions for the benefit of war victims, both civilian and military, in case of armed conflict between two or more of the signatory States but also establish in Article 3, common to all four Conventions, minimum standards to be respected even in the case of civil war.

The actual participants in the Vietnam conflict have disputed among themselves the applicability of the Conventions, even though all are signatories except the Viet Cong's political arm—the National Liberation Front of South Vietnam (NLF).[4] The United States, the Republic of Vietnam (South Vietnam), and New Zealand support the

---

3. Geneva Convention for the Amelioration of the Condition of the Wounded and Sick in Armed Forces in the Field, Aug. 12, 1949, [1955] 3 U.S.T. 3114, T.I.A.S. No. 3362, 75 U.N.T.S. 31; Geneva Convention for the Amelioration of the Condition of Wounded, Sick and Shipwrecked Members of Armed Forces at Sea, Aug. 12, 1949, [1955] 3 U.S.T. 3217, T.I.A.S. No. 3363, 75 U.N.T.S. 85; Geneva Convention Relative to the Treatment of Prisoners of War, Aug. 12, 1949, [1955] 3 U.S.T. 3316, T.I.A.S. No. 3364, 75 U.N.T.S. 135 [hereinafter cited as Convention]; Geneva Convention Relative to the Protection of Civilian Persons in Time of War, Aug. 12, 1949, [1955] 3 U.S.T. 3516, T.I.A.S. No. 3365, 75 U.N.T.S. 287.

4. Prior to partition, Vietnam acceded to the Prisoners of War Convention, 181 U.N.T.S. 351 (1953), and North Vietnam acceded separately in 1957, 274 U.N.T.S. 339. The Soviet Union—which has military advisers serving in North Vietnam, N.Y. Times, Oct. 3, 1966, at 1, col. 1—ratified in 1954, 191 U.N.T.S. 365, and Communist China acceded in 1956, 260 U.N.T.S. 442. The United States ratified in 1955, 213 U.N.T.S. 383; the Philippines in 1952, 141 U.N.T.S. 384; Australia in 1958, 314 U.N.T.S. 332; and New Zealand in 1959, 330 U.N.T.S. 356. Thailand acceded in 1954, 202 U.N.T.S. 332, and South Korea has recently acceded as well, 6 Int'l Rev. of the Red Cross 547 (1966). The last five countries are allies of the United States with forces fighting in Vietnam. See N.Y. Times, Sept. 28, 1966, at 1, col. 1.

Red Cross opinion, but the Democratic Republic of Vietnam (North Vietnam) and the NLF consider the Conventions inapplicable, though both avow that the prisoners they hold are accorded humane treatment. This Note will evaluate the claims of the NLF and North Vietnam in relation to the Geneva Convention Relative to the Treatment of Prisoners of War.

The 143 articles of this Convention regulate, among other things, the internment, the labor, the medical care, the discipline, and the trial of captives. They provide for the safeguarding of prisoners' rights by the supervision of protecting powers and by the punishment of "grave breaches" of the Convention according to national legislation which each party agrees to enact. * * *

* * *

North Vietnam maintains that it need not treat American captives as prisoners of war under the Convention. One reason given is that neither country has formally declared war. Article 2 states that "the present Convention shall apply to all cases of declared war or of any other armed conflict which may arise between two or more of the High Contracting Parties, even if the state of war is not recognized by one of them"; the argument seems to be that a formal recognition by at least one country is necessary, based on the negative implication of the last phrase and aided by the fact that preliminary drafts of the Article provided for application even when no participant recognizes a state of war. But the language of the article as a whole can also be read plausibly to suggest that the Convention was intended to apply to all armed conflicts between signatories. Moreover in light of the purposes of the Convention, no legitimate interest could be served by the narrower reading. A declaration of war is not an empty formality, and it should have important legal consequences as to some issues, but lack of a declaration in no way makes less necessary the humanitarian safeguards established by the Convention.

North Vietnam also seeks to justify its position by alleging that American pilots who have bombed its territory are war criminals under the Nuremberg Charter.[a] * * *

* * * But North Vietnam has also alleged perpetration of traditional war crimes and crimes against humanity—the second and third categories [of the Nuremberg Charter.] * * *

Even if North Vietnam can assert colorable charges of war crimes within one of the Nuremberg categories, American pilots would still be entitled to substantial protection under the Geneva Convention. Article 85 declares: "Prisoners of war prosecuted under the laws of the Detaining Power for acts committed prior to capture shall retain, even if convicted, the benefits of the present Convention." This provision was adopted in response to a line of decisions following

---

a. The Nuremberg Charter and its application are dealt with at p. 694.

the Second World War which held that prisoners of war charged with the commission of war crimes before capture were not guaranteed certain safeguards of the 1929 Geneva Convention (the immediate predecessor to the current treaty). The leading case was In re Yamashita, in which a Japanese general, sentenced to death for failure to restrain his troops from committing atrocities against Americans and their allies, sought a writ of habeas corpus in the United States Supreme Court on the ground that the procedure at his trial violated Article 63 of the 1929 Convention. That article required the detaining power to try prisoners of war by the same procedure used in trials of its own soldiers, and hearsay and opinion evidence had been admitted at Yamashita's trial, even though the American Articles of War proscribed the use of such evidence in trials of American soldiers. The Court held that "examination of Article 63 in its setting in the Convention plainly shows that it refers to sentence 'pronounced against a prisoner of war' for an offense committed while a prisoner of war, and not for a violation of the law of war committed while a combatant."

One case after Yamashita arrived at the same conclusion by relying not only on the "setting" of Article 63 in the 1929 Convention but also on a rule of customary law that those who have abused the laws of war are not entitled to the protection they offer. But the tendency of these decisions was to prejudge the guilt of the accused by denying him the guarantees of a prisoner of war before he was proved to be a war criminal. Article 85 not only cures this defect but accomplishes a major change in the rule of customary law by continuing the guarantees even after conviction. This does not mean, however, that prisoners of war may no longer be tried, convicted, and executed for war crimes. It does mean that the determination of guilt must be made according to the same procedures used by the detaining power for trial of its own military personnel and in conformity with certain minimal standards established in the Convention. For example:

> The prisoner of war shall be entitled to assistance by one of his prisoner comrades, to defence by a qualified advocate or counsel of his own choice, to the calling of witnesses and, if he deems necessary, to the services of a competent interpreter.

The Soviet-bloc countries, however, have made reservations to Article 85; the Soviet Union's statement is generally representative:

> The Union of Soviet Socialist Republics does not consider itself bound by the obligation, which follows from Article 85, to extend the application of the Convention to prisoners of war who have been convicted under the law of the Detaining Power, in accordance with the principles of the Nuremberg trial, for war crimes and crimes against humanity, it being understood that persons convicted of such crimes must be subject to the conditions obtaining in the country in question for those who undergo their punishment.

The Soviet Union has given its assurance that this reservation does not alter the effect of Article 85 until "the sentence has become legally enforceable." If so, the result of the reservation is to maintain the rule that war criminals do not enjoy the privileges of a prisoner of war, but to reject Yamashita's deprivation of such privileges before conviction.

The North Vietnamese reservation varies only slightly from the Soviet Union's, and the difference may well have been accidental. Potentially, however, this difference may be of considerable significance:

> The Democratic Republic of Viet-Nam declares that prisoners of war *prosecuted for and convicted of* war crimes or crimes against humanity, in accordance with the principles established by the Nuremberg Tribunal, will not enjoy the benefits of the provisions of the present Convention as provided in article 85.

[The note continues with a detailed analysis of the reservations problem. Reservations to multipartite international agreements are considered at p. 949.]

UNITED STATES v. GRIFFEN

United States, Board of Review (Army), 1968.
39 Court Martial Reports 586.

PORCELLA, JUDGE ADVOCATE: In this contested case, the accused was found guilty of acting jointly with others in committing an unpremeditated murder in violation of Article 118 of the Uniform Code of Military Justice. After reducing the period of confinement from ten years, the convening authority approved a sentence of total forfeitures, confinement at hard labor for seven years and reduction to the lowest enlisted grade.

In their assignment of errors, counsel for the appellant contend that the law officer erred prejudicially in failing to instruct the court on the applicable law of the defense of obedience to superior orders. In considering this contention, we will recite those facts which appear pertinent to our disposition of the case.

On 4 April 1967, in Vietnam, a platoon of the 1st Cavalry Division was providing security for an engineer element near Bong Son. About 10 o'clock in the morning, members of the platoon apprehended an indigenous male of military age who, after evacuation and interrogation by a higher echelon, was "confirmed" to be a member of the hostile Viet Cong. Later that day, as the platoon was preparing to cross a large, open rice paddy, a security element on the right flank found an unarmed male native about 40 to 45 years old in a bunker. He was brought to the command post area, and a helicopter was requested for his evacuation. Meanwhile, the accused noticed that activities of his platoon were being observed by a native he suspected might be a member of the Viet Cong. A patrol was dispatched to apprehend him. However, the search was unsuccessful. While the patrol was reconnoitering by fire and discharging grenades in bunkers, one of its members was injured by a secondary explosion. Using radio communications, overheard by several witnesses, Lieutenant Patrick, the platoon leader, conversed with Captain Ogg, the company commander. He arranged for the air evacuation of the wounded man but was told this prisoner would not be evacuated by helicopter. The precise conversation concerning the disposition of the prisoner is not clear. However, the understanding of Captain Ogg's order appears to have been that the prisoner should be killed. There is evidence that Lieutenant Patrick gave the accused a direct order to the same effect. Specialist Garcia, the medical technician attached to the platoon, removed the prisoner from the command post area and escorted him, his hands tied behind his back, to an embankment, where the accused and Private First Class Woods each fired several shots at him with M–16 rifles. The prisoner expired as a result. His body contained numerous fragments from M–16 bullets.

The accused testified, in part, to the following effect: He overheard Captain Ogg state in his radio transmission that the prisoner should be killed. Then Lieutenant Patrick said: "Sergeant Griffen, take him down the hill and shoot him. Come back and let me know." The accused admitted firing his rifle at the prisoner and thereafter reporting back to Lieutenant Patrick. He committed the act because he had been ordered to do so and for the safety of his men. He believed the order to be legal because his platoon leader, a lieutenant, had once been relieved when a prisoner who had been securely tied escaped during the night. Also, he felt that the security of the platoon would have been violated if the prisoner were kept, since their operations had already been observed by another suspect. In addition, several months earlier, all the members of his platoon had either been killed or wounded in that same general area after their positions had been observed.

Prior to argument, the defense submitted a proposed instruction on obedience of orders as a defense to the offense charged. The law officer did not give the requested instruction. Rather, he instructed the court as follows on this subject:

> Now, the general rule is that the acts of a subordinate, done in good faith in compliance with his supposed duty or orders, are justifiable. This justification does not exist, however, when those acts are manifestly beyond the scope of his authority, or the order is such that a man of ordinary sense and understanding would know it to be illegal.
>
> I tell you as a matter of law that if instructions or orders were received over that radio or were given to the accused in this

case to kill the prisoner suspect who was helpless there before them, such an order would have been manifestly an illegal order. You are advised as a matter of law, any such command, if in fact there was such a command, was an illegal order.

A soldier or airman is not an automaton but a reasoning agent who is under a duty to exercise judgment in obeying the orders of a superior officer to the extent, that where such orders are manifestly beyond the scope of the issuing officer's authority and are so palpably illegal on their face that a man of ordinary sense and understanding would know them to be illegal, then the fact of obedience to the order of a superior officer will not protect a soldier for acts committed pursuant to such illegal orders. This is the law in regard to superior orders.

In deciding the issues in this case, we will assume that a superior officer ordered the accused to kill the native male then in the platoon's custody.

The intentional killing of another person without premeditation, provocation, justification, or excuse and not while in the perpetration of a felony is unpremeditated murder (U.C.M.J., Art. 118, 10 U.S.C.A. § 918). However, a homicide committed in the proper performance of a legal duty is justifiable and not a crime. Thus, killing to prevent the escape of a prisoner if no other reasonably apparent means are adequate or killing an enemy in battle are cases of justifiable homicide (M.C.M., U.S.1951, ¶ 197b). Conversely, the killing of a docile prisoner taken during military operations is not justifiable homicide. In this connection, section 85, Department of the Army Field Manual 27–10, Law of Land Warfare, July 1956, promulgates the following doctrine:

85. Killing of Prisoners

A commander may not put his prisoners to death because their presence retards his movements or diminishes his power of resistance by necessitating a large guard, or by reason of their consuming supplies, or because it appears certain that they will regain their liberty through the impending success of their forces. It is likewise unlawful for a commander to kill his prisoners on grounds of self-preservation, even in the case of airborne or commando operations, although the circumstances of the operation may make necessary rigorous supervision of and restraint upon the movement of prisoners of war.

The general rule is that the acts of a subordinate, done in good faith in compliance with his supposed duty or orders are, subject to certain qualifications, justifiable.   (M.C.M., U.S., 1951, ¶ 197b).   In his authoritative work, Winthrop stated:

> That the act charged as an offense was done in obedience to the order—verbal or written—of a military superior, is, in general, a good defense at military law.
>
> *   *   *
>
> *   *   *   Where the order is apparently regular and lawful on its face, he is not to go behind it to satisfy himself that his superior has proceeded with authority, but is to obey it according to its terms, the only exceptions recognized to the rule of obedience being cases of orders so manifestly beyond the legal power of discretion of the commander as to admit of no rational doubt of their unlawfulness.   (Winthrop, Military Law and Precedents, 2d Ed. (1920 Reprint) 296–297.)

The Manual for Courts-Martial, U. S. Army, 1921 (¶ 415, page 355) stated:

> To justify from a military point of view a military inferior in disobeying the order of a superior, the order must be one requiring something to be done which is palpably a breach of law and a crime or an injury to a third person, or is of a serious character (not involving unimportant consequences only) and if done would not be susceptible of being righted.   An order requiring the performance of a military duty or act can not be disobeyed with impunity unless it has one of these characteristics.

The Manual for Courts-Martial, United States, 1951 (¶ 197b, p. 351) contains the following discussion relating to the defense of duty or orders as justification for a homicide:

> *   *   *   the acts of a subordinate, done in good faith in compliance with his supposed duties or orders are justifiable. *This justification does not exist, however, when* those acts are manifestly beyond the scope of his authority, or *the order is such that a man of ordinary sense and understanding would know it to be illegal* *   *   *   (Emphasis supplied.)

(Substantially similar provisions appeared in the M.C.M., U.S.A., 1928, ¶ 148a and M.C.M., U.S.A., 1949, ¶ 179a.)

In C.M. 326604, Gusik, 75 Board of Review 265, 279, the Board of Review said:

> It will be seen, therefore, that, indispensable to the shield of immunity from criminal responsibility afforded one for homicide committed pursuant to lawful orders of his superior, and in the performance of a public duty, are the following:
>
> (a) That the order or authority was lawful or of such character that he had a right under the circumstances to believe and did believe it to be lawful,

(b) That he acted reasonably within the scope of such authority, and

(c) Not with malice, cruelty, or by willful oppression flowing from a wicked heart.

A well known treatise contains the following comments (36 Am.Jur. Homicide § 72, p. 208) :

> * * * But an order which is illegal in itself and not justified by the rules and usages of War, or which is, in its substance, clearly illegal, so that a man of ordinary sense and understanding would know as soon as he heard the order read or given that it was illegal, will afford no protection for a homicide, provided the act with which he may be charged has all the ingredients in it which may be necessary to constitute the same a crime in law.

Also to the same effect, see 1 Wharton's Criminal Law and Procedure by Anderson, Defenses § 118, p. 258 (1957)[1]; United States v. Clark, 31 Fed. 710, 716 (E.D.Mich., 1887); 40 C.J.S. Homicide § 107, p. 967 (1944).

United States doctrine expressed in Department of the Army Field Manual 27–10, The Law of Land Warfare, July 1956, is as follows:

> The fact that the law of war has been violated pursuant to an order of a superior authority, whether military or civil, does not deprive the act in question of its character of a war crime, nor does it constitute a defense in the trial of an accused individual, unless he did not know and could not reasonably have been expected to know that the act ordered was unlawful. In all cases where the order is held not to constitute a defense to an allegation of war crime, the fact that the individual was acting pursuant to orders may be considered in mitigation of punishment.

Having considered the foregoing authorities, we accept the following principle for application in this case (¶ 197b, M.C.M., U.S., 1951, quoted supra) : The act of a subordinate, done in good faith in compliance with the supposed order of a superior, is not justifiable when the order is such that a man of ordinary sense and understanding would know it to be illegal. (See A.C.M. 7321, Kinder, 14 C.M.R. 742, 773 (1954)).

We now turn to the question: Did the law officer err in failing to give an appropriate instruction on justification as a defense to a homicide committed in good faith compliance with the order of a su-

---

1. A general discussion of the assertion of superior orders as a defense appears in the opinion in "The Einsatzgruppen Case" (United States of America vs. Otto Ohlendorf, et al., Case No. 9) IV Trials of War Criminals before the Nuremberg Military Tribunals, p. 1, 470.

perior? As previously noted, the defense counsel made a request for such an instruction, but the law officer instructed contradictorily. He informed the court to the effect that if an order to kill the prisoner had been given, it would have been manifestly illegal.

A law officer is required to give an appropriate instruction when there is some evidence that will allow a reasonable inference that a defense is in issue (United States v. Black, 12 U.S.C.M.A. 571, 31 C.M. R. 157 (1961). Evaluating the record, we find the evidence clear and convincing that an unarmed, unresisting prisoner whose hands were bound behind his back was killed at close range by rifle fire discharged by the accused and another soldier. We note no evidence which could provide an inference suggestive of self-defense, or that the killing was to prevent the escape of the prisoner, or for that matter, any other justification or excuse for the killing. Also, there are strong moral, religious, and legal prohibitions in our society against killing others which should arouse the strongest scruples against killings of this kind. In fact, it is difficult to conceive of a military situation in which the order of a superior would be more patently wrong. Accordingly, we view the order as commanding an act so obviously beyond the scope of authority of the superior officer and so palpably illegal on its face as to admit of no doubt of its unlawfulness to a man of ordinary sense and understanding. As there was no evidence which would have allowed a reasonable inference that the accused justifiably killed the prisoner pursuant to the order of a superior officer, it follows, as a matter of law, that this defense was not in issue, the law officer did not err by refusing to give an instruction on it, and that the law officer properly instructed the court that such an order would have been manifestly illegal.

With respect to the law officer's instructions on sentence, appellate defense counsel contend and government appellate counsel concede that the failure of the law officer to instruct the court-martial that it could adjudge reduction in grade as punishment rendered that portion of the sentence excessive. We find the contention meritorious and will act appropriately (United States v. Crawford, 12 U.S.C.M.A. 203, 30 C.M.R. 203 (1961)).

Further, with respect to the sentence, we observe that the accused was caught up in a rapidly moving sequence of events at the time of the incident. This factor lends mitigating weight to his assertion that he acted without reflection and in honest obedience of a superior's orders. In addition, the accused had approximately eight years of prior service at the time of trial and there were no previous convictions introduced against him. Also, no punitive discharge was adjudged. The staff judge advocate notes in his review, that the accused testified for the prosecution in a subsequent homicide trial of another soldier involving the same incident and that he is "intrinsically remorseful and has a fervent desire to be rehabilitated." He also notes that the two officers involved in this offense were acquitted.

Other records of trial before this board of review show that Specialist-Five Raul Garcia was tried by a general court-martial for the same offense and that his approved sentence provides for bad conduct discharge, total forfeitures, confinement at hard labor for three years and reduction. Private First Class David L. Woods was similarly tried. His approved sentence is confinement at hard labor for twelve months, total forfeitures, and reduction to the lowest enlisted grade.

In view of the foregoing, the board of review finds the findings of guilty and sentence as approved by proper authority correct in law and fact and determines on the basis of the entire record that only so much of the sentence as provides for confinement at hard labor for two years and forfeiture of all pay and allowances should be approved. The sentence is modified accordingly. The findings of guilty and the sentence as thus modified are affirmed.

COMMENT, PUNISHMENT FOR WAR CRIMES: DUTY OR DISCRETION?

69 Michigan Law Review 1312 (1971).*

* * * Immediately prior to the adoption of the 1949 Conventions, it was remarked in reference to one of these earlier conventions that "[i]t is one of the greatest weaknesses of the existing rules on prisoners of war that they do not contain definite and written provisions on sanctions." In view of such criticisms and the ad hoc measures taken to deal with the war crimes of World War II, negotiators in 1949 agreed that specific provisions for punishment of breaches of the new Conventions were essential. Accordingly, each of the Four Conventions adopted in 1949 contained an article requiring each Party to "enact any legislation necessary to provide effective penal sanctions for persons committing * * * grave breaches" of the Conventions.

On March 16, 1968, the most notorious American atrocity yet documented in the Vietnam war took place in the Vietnamese province of Quang Ngai. Soldiers of the United States Army's Americal Division participated in an operation in which scores of unarmed South Vietnamese civilians were slain. If the 1949 Conventions are applicable in the Vietnam War and to the civilian victims at My Lai, the massacre undoubtedly was a grave breach of the standards of wartime conduct imposed on the Parties by the Conventions. Thus, the United States, as a Party to the Conventions, would be obligated to act in compliance with the penal-sanctions provision of the applicable Convention or Conventions. Acting consistently with the possible existence of such an obligation, the United States brought to trial, and convicted of murder, Army First Lieutenant William L. Calley, Jr.,

* Reprinted by permission of the Michigan Law Review.

Paul Meadlo's platoon leader.[22]   Because of his disclosures on national television, Meadlo, by then discharged from the Army, was subpoenaed as a witness for the prosecution.   Meadlo, however, invoked his fifth amendment privilege against self-incrimination and refused to testify.   Although granted a writ of immunity from military prosecution by the Commanding General of Fort Benning, Georgia, where the trial by court-martial of Lieutenant Calley was conducted, Meadlo consistently refused to testify until the Government issued a federal immunity order protecting him from civilian prosecution.   Finally, under threat of arrest for further refusal to testify after having been granted federal immunity, Meadlo took the witness stand on January 11, 1971.   Ten days later, Assistant United States Attorney General William H. Rehnquist struck a disquieting note that has been overlooked in the wake of the Calley conviction: Has the United States violated its treaty obligation under the 1949 Geneva Conventions to prosecute those persons accused of "grave breaches" of the Conventions by granting immunity to a confessed participant in the My Lai slayings?

BISHOP, THE QUESTION OF WAR CRIMES

Commentary [Magazine] 85, 88 (Dec. 1972).*

* * * I know of no instance in which North Vietnam or any other totalitarian government has ever accused a member of its own forces of a violation of the Geneva Conventions or any other war crime.   But the most recent figures I have been able to find show that, as of April 1971, American courts-martial had tried 117 servicemen, and convicted 60, on charges of murdering civilians in Vietnam; an unknown, but probably larger, number had been tried for lesser offenses, such as rape and robbery, against civilians.   Murder and other violence against the persons of noncombatants or captured enemies violate the Geneva Conventions, but they are also, of course, violations of the Uniform Code of Military Justice and have been charged as such.   The main practical difference is that trial by court-martial for a violation of the Code guarantees the accused procedural protections and appellate review to which he might not be entitled if he were tried by a military commission for a war crime.

22. * * * Lieutenant Calley was charged with the premeditated murder of 102 civilians in violation of art. 118, Uniform Code of Military Justice, 10 U.S.C.A. § 918 (1964), as amended (Supp. V, 1965–1969) [hereinafter U.C. M.J.].   N.Y. Times, Jan. 21, 1970, § 1, at 17, col. 1.   Lieutenant Calley was found guilty of premeditated murder and sentenced to life imprisonment. N.Y. Times, March 30, 1971, § 1, at 1, col. 8; id., April 1, 1971, § 1, at 1, col. 8.

* Reprinted from Commentary, by permission; Copyright © 1972 by the American Jewish Committee.

Some of the acquittals were probably unjustified, and in at least one case, that of Captain Ernest Medina, the acquittal may have been based on the military judge's erroneous instruction that Medina had no responsibility for the My Lai massacre unless he had "actual knowledge" of it: the law, as laid down by the Supreme Court in General Yamashita's case, is that a commander is responsible for war crimes committed by his subordinates, if he knew or should have known that they were going on and failed to do what he could to prevent or punish them. It is also safe to assume that many war crimes committed by Americans have never been investigated, tried, or punished. The Pentagon has not shown much enthusiasm for investigating the possible failures of commanders at divisional and higher levels to take adequate measures to prevent and punish war crimes. Moreover, the Department of Justice seems to take the position that an honorably discharged serviceman cannot be tried for a war crime committed prior to his discharge. The Supreme Court did hold some years ago that such a discharged soldier could not be court-martialed for an ordinary offense—i. e., one which was not a war crime—committed prior to his discharge. But it had earlier held, in World War II, that a Nazi saboteur who was an American civilian could constitutionally be tried by a military commission for a war crime, and it did not overrule that decision. I am myself of the opinion (though I seem to be in the minority) that a discharged serviceman can be tried by a military court on a charge of violating the law of war. In any case, Congress could and should give the federal courts jurisdiction to try such cases under the Geneva Conventions; in fact the United States is obligated to "enact any legislation necessary to provide effective penal sanctions" for persons committing "grave breaches."

THE LAW OF LAND WARFARE

United States, Department of the Army Field Manual
[FM 27–10] at 4 (1956).

4. Sources

The law of war is derived from two principal sources:

a. Lawmaking Treaties (or Conventions), such as the Hague and Geneva Conventions.

b. Custom. Although some of the law of war has not been incorporated in any treaty or convention to which the United States is a party, this body of unwritten or customary law is firmly established by the custom of nations and well defined by recognized authorities on international law.

Lawmaking treaties may be compared with legislative enactments in the national law of the United States and the customary law of war with the unwritten Anglo-American common law.

5.　Lawmaking Treaties

　　a.　Treaties to Which the United States Is a Party. The United States is a party to the following conventions pertinent to warfare on land:

　　(1)　Hague Convention No. III of 18 October 1907, Relative to the Opening of Hostilities (36 Stat. 2259, Treaty Series 538), cited herein as H. III.

　　(2)　Hague Convention No. IV of 18 October 1907, Respecting the Laws and Customs of War on Land (36 Stat. 2277; Treaty Series 539), cited herein as H. IV, and the Annex thereto, embodying the Regulations Respecting the Laws and Customs of War on Land (36 Stat. 2295; Treaty Series 539), cited herein as HR.

　　(3)　Hague Convention No. V of 18 October 1907, Respecting the Rights and Duties of Neutral Powers and Persons in Case of War on Land (36 Stat. 2310; Treaty Series 540), cited herein as H. V.

　　(4)　Hague Convention No. IX of 18 October 1907, Concerning Bombardment by Naval Forces in Time of War (36 Stat. 2351; Treaty Series 542), cited herein as H. IX.

　　(5)　Hague Convention No. X of 18 October 1907, for the Adaptation to Maritime Warfare of the Principles of the Geneva Convention (36 Stat. 2371; Treaty Series No. 543), cited herein as H. X.

　　(6)　Geneva Convention Relative to the Treatment of Prisoners of War of 27 July 1929 (47 Stat. 2021; Treaty Series 846), cited herein as GPW 1929.

　　(7)　Geneva Convention for the Amelioration of the Condition of the Wounded and Sick of Armies in the Field of 27 July 1929 (47 Stat. 2074; Treaty Series 847), cited herein as GWS 1929.

　　(8)　Treaty on the Protection of Artistic and Scientific Institutions and Historic Monuments of 15 April 1935 (49 Stat. 3267; Treaty Series 899), cited herein as the Roerich Pact. Only the United States and a number of the American Republics are parties to this treaty.

　　(9)　Geneva Convention for the Amelioration of the Condition of the Wounded and Sick in Armed Forces in the Field of 12 August 1949 (T.I.A.S. 3362), cited herein as GWS.

　　(10)　Geneva Convention for the Amelioration of the Condition of Wounded, Sick and Shipwrecked Members of Armed Forces at Sea of 12 August 1949 (T.I.A.S. 3363), cited herein as GWS Sea.

(11) Geneva Convention Relative to the Treatment of Prisoners of War of 12 August 1949 (T.I.A.S. 3364), cited herein as GPW.

(12) Geneva Convention Relative to the Protection of Civilian Persons in Time of War of 12 August 1949 (T.I.A.S. 3365), cited herein as GC.

* * *

6. Custom

Evidence of the customary law of war, arising from the general consent of States, may be found in judicial decisions, the writings of jurists, diplomatic correspondence, and other documentary material concerning the practice of States. Even though individual States may not be parties to or otherwise strictly bound by H. IV and GPW 1929, the former convention and the general principles of the latter have been held to be declaratory of the customary law of war, to which all States are subject.

The Preamble to the HR specifically provides:

Until a more complete code of the laws of war has been issued, the High Contracting Parties deem it expedient to declare that, in cases not included in the Regulations adopted by them, the inhabitants and the belligerents remain under the protection and the rule of the principles of the law of nations, as they result from the usages established among civilized peoples, from the laws of humanity, and the dictates of the public conscience.

Similarly, a common article of the Geneva Conventions of 1949 (GWS, art. 63; GWS Sea, art. 62; GPW, art. 142; GC, art. 158) provides that the denunciation of (withdrawal from) any of the Geneva Conventions of 1949

* * * shall in no way impair the obligations which the Parties to the conflict shall remain bound to fulfil by virtue of the principles of the law of nations, as they result from the usages established among civilized peoples, from the laws of humanity and the dictates of the public conscience.

* * *

SECTION II. FORBIDDEN CONDUCT WITH RESPECT TO PERSONS

28. Refusal of Quarter

It is especially forbidden * * * to declare that no quarter will be given. (HR, art. 23, par. (d).)

29. Injury Forbidden After Surrender

It is especially forbidden * * * to kill or wound an enemy who having laid down his arms, or having no longer means of defense, has surrendered at discretion. (HR, art. 23, par. (c).)

30.   Persons Descending by Parachute

The law of war does not prohibit firing upon paratroops or other persons who are or appear to be bound upon hostile missions while such persons are descending by parachute. Persons other than those mentioned in the preceding sentence who are descending by parachute from disabled aircraft may not be fired upon.

31.   Assassination and Outlawry

HR provides:

It is especially forbidden * * * to kill or wound treacherously individuals belonging to the hostile nation or army. (HR, art. 23, par. (b).)

This article is construed as prohibiting assassination, proscription, or outlawry of an enemy, or putting a price upon an enemy's head, as well as offering a reward for an enemy "dead or alive". It does not, however, preclude attacks on individual soldiers or officers of the enemy whether in the zone of hostilities, occupied territory, or elsewhere.

32.   Nationals Not To Be Compelled to Take Part in Operations Against Their Own Country

A belligerent is likewise forbidden to compel the nationals of the hostile party to take part in the operations of war directed against their own country, even if they were in the belligerent's service before the commencement of the war. (HR, art. 23, 2d par.)

SECTION III.   FORBIDDEN MEANS OF WAGING WARFARE

33.   Means of Injuring the Enemy Limited

a.   Treaty Provision.

The right of belligerents to adopt means of injuring the enemy is not unlimited. (HR, art. 22.)

b.   The means employed are definitely restricted by international declarations and conventions and by the laws and usages of war.

34.   Employment of Arms Causing Unnecessary Injury

a.   Treaty Provision.

It is especially forbidden * * * to employ arms, projectiles, or material calculated to cause unnecessary suffering. (HR art. 23, par. (e).)

b.   Interpretation.   What weapons cause "unnecessary injury" can only be determined in light of the practice of States in refraining from the use of a given weapon because it is believed to have that effect. The prohibition certainly does not extend to the use of explosives contained in artillery projectiles, mines, rockets, or hand grenades. Usage has, however, established the illegality of the use of lances with barbed heads, irregular-shaped bullets, and projectiles filled with glass, the use of any substance on bullets that would tend unnecessarily to inflame a wound inflicted by them, and the scoring of the surface or the filing off of the ends of the hard cases of bullets.

35. Atomic Weapons

The use of explosive "atomic weapons," whether by air, sea, or land forces, cannot as such be regarded as violative of international law in the absence of any customary rule of international law or international convention restricting their employment.

36. Weapons Employing Fire

The use of weapons which employ fire, such as tracer ammunition, flamethrowers, napalm and other incendiary agents, against targets requiring their use is not violative of international law. They should not, however, be employed in such a way as to cause unnecessary suffering to individuals.

37. Poison

a. Treaty Provision.

It is especially forbidden * * * to employ poison or poisoned weapons. (HR, art. 23, par. (a).)

b. Discussion of Rule. The foregoing rule does not prohibit measures being taken to dry up springs, to divert rivers and aqueducts from their courses, or to destroy, through chemical or bacterial agents harmless to man, crops intended solely for consumption by the armed forces (if that fact can be determined).

38. Gases, Chemicals, and Bacteriological Warfare

The United States is not a party to any treaty, now in force, that prohibits or restricts the use in warfare of toxic or nontoxic gases, of smoke or incendiary materials, or of bacteriological warfare. A treaty signed at Washington, 6 February 1922, on behalf of the United States, the British Empire, France, Italy, and Japan (3 Malloy, Treaties 3116) contains a provision (art. V) prohibiting "The use in war of asphyxiating, poisonous or other gases, and all analogous liquids, materials, or devices," but that treaty was expressly conditioned to become effective only upon ratification by all of the signatory powers, and, not having been ratified by all of the signatories, has never become effective. The Geneva Protocol "for the prohibition of the use in war of asphyxiating, poisonous, or other gases, and of bacteriological methods of warfare," signed on 17 June 1925, on behalf of the United States and many other powers (94 League of Nations Treaty Series 65), has been ratified or adhered to by and is now effective between a considerable number of States. However, the United States Senate has refrained from giving its advice and consent to the ratification of the Protocol by the United States, and it is accordingly not binding on this country.

SECTION IV. BOMBARDMENTS, ASSAULTS, AND SIEGES

39. Bombardment of Undefended Places Forbidden

The attack or bombardment, by whatever means, of towns, villages, dwellings, or buildings which are undefended is prohibited. (HR, art. 25.)

40. Defended Place Defined

Investment, bombardment, assault, and siege have always been recognized as legitimate means of land warfare. Defended places in the sense of Article 25, HR, include:

a. A fort or fortified place.

b. A city or town surrounded by detached defense positions, which is considered jointly with such defense positions as an indivisible whole.

c. A place which is occupied by a combatant military force or through which such a force is passing. The occupation of such a place by medical units alone is not sufficient to make it a defended place.

Factories producing munitions and military supplies, military camps, warehouses storing munitions and military supplies, ports and railroads being used for the transportation of military supplies, and other places devoted to the support of military operations or the accommodation of troops may also be attacked and bombarded even though they are not defended.

41. Unnecessary Killing and Devastation

Particularly in the circumstances referred to in the preceding paragraph, loss of life and damage to property must not be out of proportion to the military advantage to be gained. Once a fort or defended locality has surrendered, only such further damage is permitted as is demanded by the exigencies of war, such as the removal of fortifications, demolition of military buildings, and destruction of stores (GC, art. 147; par. 502 herein).

42. Aerial Bombardment

There is no prohibition of general application against bombardment from the air of combatant troops, defended places, or other legitimate military objectives.

43. Notice of Bombardment

a. Treaty Provision.

The officer in command of an attacking force must, before commencing a bombardment, except in cases of assault, do all in his power to warn the authorities. (HR, art. 26.)

b. Application of Rule. This rule is understood to refer only to bombardments of places where parts of the civil population remain.

c.   When Warning is To Be Given.   Even when belligerents are not subject to the above treaty, the commanders of the United States ground forces will, when the situation permits, inform the enemy of their intention to bombard a place, so that the noncombatants, especially the women and children, may be removed before the bombardment commences.

*   *   *

SECTION III.   GENERAL PROTECTION OF PRISONERS OF WAR

84.   Duration of Protection

a.   Treaty Provision.

The present Convention shall apply to the persons referred to in Article 4 from the time they fall into the power of the enemy and until their final release and repatriation * * *.   (GPW, art. 5; see par. 71 herein.)

b.   Power of the Enemy Defined.   A person is considered to have fallen into the power of the enemy when he has been captured by, or surrendered to members of the military forces, the civilian police, or local civilian defense organizations or enemy civilians who have taken him into custody.

85.   Killing of Prisoners

A commander may not put his prisoners to death because their presence retards his movements or diminishes his power of resistance by necessitating a large guard, or by reason of their consuming supplies, or because it appears certain that they will regain their liberty through the impending success of their forces.   It is likewise unlawful for a commander to kill his prisoners on grounds of self-preservation, even in the case of airborne or commando operations, although the circumstances of the operation may make necessary rigorous supervision of and restraint upon the movement of prisoners of war.

88.   Responsibility for the Treatment of Prisoners

Prisoners of war are in the hands of the enemy Power, but not of the individuals or military units who have captured them. Irrespective of the individual responsibilities that may exist, the Detaining Power is responsible for the treatment given them.

Prisoners of war may only be transferred by the Detaining Power to a Power which is a party to the Convention and after the Detaining Power has satisfied itself of the willingness and ability of such transferee Power to apply the Convention.   When prisoners of war are transferred under such circumstances, responsibility for the application of the Convention rests on the Power accepting them while they are in its custody.

Nevertheless, if that Power fails to carry out the provisions of the Convention in any important respect, the Power by whom the prisoners of war were transferred shall, upon being notified by the Protecting Power, take effective measures to correct the situation or shall request the return of the prisoners of war. Such requests must be complied with.   (GPW, art. 12.)

89.   Humane Treatment of Prisoners

Prisoners of war must at all times be humanely treated. Any unlawful act or omission of the Detaining Power causing death or seriously endangering the health of a prisoner of war in its custody is prohibited, and will be regarded as a serious breach of the present Convention.   In particular, no prisoner of war may be subjected to physical mutilation or to medical or scientific experiments of any kind which are not justified by the medical, dental or hospital treatment of the prisoner concerned and carried out in his interest.

Likewise, prisoners of war must at all times be protected, particularly against acts of violence or intimidation and against insults and public curiosity.

Measures of reprisal against prisoners of war are prohibited. (GPW, art. 13.)

90.   Respect for the Person of Prisoners

Prisoners of war are entitled in all circumstances to respect for their persons and their honour.

Women shall be treated with all the regard due to their sex and shall in all cases benefit by treatment as favourable as that granted to men.

Prisoners of war shall retain the full civil capacity which they enjoyed at the time of their capture.   The Detaining Power may not restrict the exercise, either within or without its own territory, of the rights such capacity confers except in so far as the captivity requires.   GPW, art. 14.)

* * *

497.   Reprisals

a.   Definition.   Reprisals are acts of retaliation in the form of conduct which would otherwise be unlawful, resorted to by one belligerent against enemy personnel or property for acts of warfare committed by the other belligerent in violation of the law of war, for the purpose of enforcing future compliance with the recognized rules of civilized warfare.   For example, the employment by a belligerent of a weapon the use of which is normally precluded by the law of war would constitute a lawful reprisal for intentional mistreatment of prisoners of war held by the enemy.

b.   Priority of Other Remedies.   Other means of securing compliance with the law of war should normally be exhausted before resort is had to reprisals.   This course should be pursued unless the safety of the troops requires immediate drastic action and the persons who actually committed the offenses cannot be secured. Even when appeal to the enemy for redress has failed, it may be a matter of policy to consider, before resorting to reprisals, whether the opposing forces are not more likely to be influenced by a steady adherence to the law of war on the part of their adversary.

c. Against Whom Permitted. Reprisals against the persons or property of prisoners of war, including the wounded and sick, and protected civilians are forbidden (GPW, art. 13; GC, art. 33). Collective penalties and punishment of prisoners of war and protected civilians are likewise prohibited (GPW, art. 87; GC, art. 33). However, reprisals may still be visited on enemy troops who have not yet fallen into the hands of the forces making the reprisals.

d. When and How Employed. Reprisals are never adopted merely for revenge, but only as an unavoidable last resort to induce the enemy to desist from unlawful practices. They should never be employed by individual soldiers except by direct orders of a commander, and the latter should give such orders only after careful inquiry into the alleged offense. The highest accessible military authority should be consulted unless immediate action is demanded, in which event a subordinate commander may order appropriate reprisals upon his own initiative. Ill-considered action may subsequently be found to have been wholly unjustified and will subject the responsible officer himself to punishment for a violation of the law of war. On the other hand, commanding officers must assume responsibility for retaliative measures when an unscrupulous enemy leaves no other recourse against the repetition of unlawful acts.

e. Form of Reprisal. The acts resorted to by way of reprisal need not conform to those complained of by the injured party, but should not be excessive or exceed the degree of violence committed by the enemy.

f. Procedure. The rule requiring careful inquiry into the real occurrence will always be followed unless the safety of the troops requires immediate drastic action and the persons who actually committed the offense cannot be ascertained.

g. Hostages. The taking of hostages is forbidden (GC, art. 34). The taking of prisoners by way of reprisal for acts previously committed (so-called "reprisal prisoners") is likewise forbidden. (See GC, art. 33.)

* * *

502. Grave Breaches of the Geneva Conventions of 1949 as War Crimes

The Geneva Conventions of 1949 define the following acts as "grave breaches," if committed against persons or property protected by the Conventions:

a.   GWS and GWS Sea.

Grave breaches to which the preceding Article relates shall be those involving any of the following acts, if committed against persons or property protected by the Convention: wilful killing, torture or inhuman treatment, including biological experiments, wilfully causing great suffering or serious injury to body or health, and extensive destruction and appropriation of property, not justified by military necessity and carried out unlawfully and wantonly.   (GWS, art. 50; GWS Sea, art. 51.)

b.   GPW.

Grave breaches to which the preceding Article relates shall be those involving any of the following acts, if committed against persons or property protected by the Convention: wilful killing, torture or inhuman treatment, including biological experiments, wilfully causing great suffering or serious injury to body or health, compelling a prisoner of war to serve in the forces of the hostile Power, or wilfully depriving a prisoner of war of the rights of fair and regular trial prescribed in this Convention. (GPW, art. 130.)

c.   GC.

Grave breaches to which the preceding Article relates shall be those involving any of the following acts, if committed against persons or property protected by the present Convention: wilful killing, torture or inhuman treatment, including biological experiments, wilfully causing great suffering or serious injury to body or health, unlawful deportation or transfer or unlawful confinement of a protected person, compelling a protected person to serve in the forces of a hostile Power, or wilfully depriving a protected person of the rights of fair and regular trial prescribed in the present Convention, taking of hostages and extensive destruction and appropriation of property, not justified by military necessity and carried out unlawfully and wantonly.   (GC, art. 147.)

503.   Responsibilities of the Contracting Parties

No High Contracting Party shall be allowed to absolve itself or any other High Contracting Party of any liability incurred by itself or by another High Contracting Party in respect of breaches referred to in the preceding Article. (GWS, art. 51; GWS Sea, art. 52; GPW, art. 131; GC, art. 148.)

504.   Other Types of War Crimes

In addition to the "grave breaches" of the Geneva Conventions of 1949, the following acts are representative of violations of the law of war ("war crimes") :

a.   Making use of poisoned or otherwise forbidden arms or ammunition.

b.   Treacherous request for quarter.

c.   Maltreatment of dead bodies.

d.   Firing on localities which are undefended and without military significance.

e.   Abuse of or firing on the flag of truce.

f.   Misuse of the Red Cross emblem.

g.   Use of civilian clothing by troops to conceal their military character during battle.

h.   Improper use of privileged buildings for military purposes.

i.   Poisoning of wells or streams.

j.   Pillage or purposeless destruction.

k.   Compelling prisoners of war to perform prohibited labor.

l.   Killing without trial spies or other persons who have committed hostile acts.

m.   Compelling civilians to perform prohibited labor.

n.   Violation of surrender terms.

SECTION B.   THE INNOVATIONS OF NUREMBERG: CRIMES AGAINST PEACE AND CRIMES AGAINST HUMANITY

CHARTER OF THE INTERNATIONAL MILITARY TRIBUNAL

59 Stat. 1544, 1546.

Article 1.   In pursuance of the Agreement signed on the 8th day of August 1945 by the Government of the United States of America, the Provisional Government of the French Republic, the Government of the United Kingdom of Great Britain and Northern Ireland and the Government of the Union of Soviet Socialist Republics, there shall be established an International Military Tribunal (hereinafter called "the Tribunal") for the just and prompt trial and punishment of the major war criminals of the European Axis.

Article 2.   The Tribunal shall consist of four members, each with an alternate.   One member and one alternate shall be appointed by each of the Signatories.   *   *   *

Article 6. The Tribunal established by the Agreement referred to in Article 1 hereof for the trial and punishment of the major war criminals of the European Axis countries shall have the power to try and punish persons who, acting in the interests of the European Axis countries, whether as individuals or as members of organizations, committed any of the following crimes.

The following acts, or any of them, are crimes coming within the jurisdiction of the Tribunal for which there shall be individual responsibility:

(a) CRIMES AGAINST PEACE: namely, planning, preparation, initiation or waging of a war of aggression, or a war in violation of international treaties, agreements or assurances, or participation in a common plan or conspiracy for the accomplishment of any of the foregoing;

(b) WAR CRIMES: namely, violations of the laws or customs of war. Such violations shall include, but not be limited to, murder, ill-treatment or deportation to slave labor or for any other purpose of civilian population of or in occupied territory, murder or ill-treatment of prisoners of war or persons on the seas, killing of hostages, plunder of public or private property, wanton destruction of cities, towns or villages, or devastation not justified by military necessity;

(c) CRIMES AGAINST HUMANITY: namely, murder, extermination, enslavement, deportation, and other inhumane acts committed against any civilian population, before or during the war;[1] or persecutions on political, racial or religious grounds in execution of or in connection with any crime within the jurisdiction of the Tribunal, whether or not in violation of the domestic law of the country where perpetrated.

Leaders, organizers, instigators and accomplices participating in the formulation or execution of a common plan or conspiracy to commit any of the foregoing crimes are responsible for all acts performed by any persons in execution of such plan.

Article 7. The official position of defendants, whether as Heads of State or responsible officials in Government Departments, shall not be considered as freeing them from responsibility or mitigating punishment.

Article 8. The fact that the Defendant acted pursuant to order of his Government or of a superior shall not free him from responsibility, but may be considered in mitigation of punishment if the Tribunal determines that justice so requires.

Article 9. At the trial of any individual member of any group or organization the Tribunal may declare (in connection with any act

---

[1] [The contracting governments signed a protocol at Berlin on Oct. 6, 1945 * * * which provides that this semicolon in the English text should be changed to a comma.]

of which the individual may be convicted) that the group or organization of which the individual was a member was a criminal organization.

After rec..pt of the Indictment the Tribunal shall give such notice as it thinks fit that the prosecution intends to ask the Tribunal to make such declaration and any member of the organization will be entitled to apply to the Tribunal for leave to be heard by the Tribunal upon the question of the criminal character of the organization. The Tribunal shall have power to allow or reject the application. If the application is allowed, the Tribunal may direct in what manner the applicants shall be represented and heard.

Article 10. In cases where a group or organization is declared criminal by the Tribunal, the competent national authority of any Signatory shall have the right to bring individuals to trial for membership therein before national, military or occupation courts. In any such case the criminal nature of the group or organization is considered proved and shall not be questioned.

Article 11. Any person convicted by the Tribunal may be charged before a national, military or occupation court, referred to in Article 10 of this Charter, with a crime other than of membership in a criminal group or organization and such court may, after convicting him, impose upon him punishment independent of and additional to the punishment imposed by the Tribunal for participation in the criminal activities of such group or organization.

Article 12. The Tribunal shall have the right to take proceedings against a person charged with crimes set out in Article 6 of this Charter in his absence, if he has not been found or if the Tribunal, for any reason, finds it necessary, in the interests of justice, to conduct the hearing in his absence.

Article 26. The judgment of the Tribunal as to the guilt or the innocence of any Defendant shall give the reasons on which it is based, and shall be final and not subject to review.

Article 27. The Tribunal shall have the right to impose upon a Defendant, on conviction, death or such other punishment as shall be determined by it to be just.

JUDGMENT OF THE INTERNATIONAL MILITARY TRIBUNAL, NUREMBERG, GERMANY, 1946

Nazi Conspiracy and Aggression
(U.S. Gov't Printing Office, 1947).

III. The Common Plan of Conspiracy and Aggressive War

The Tribunal now turns to the consideration of the crimes against peace charged in the indictment. Count one of the indictment charges the defendants with conspiring or having a common plan to commit crimes against peace. Count two of the indictment charges the defendants with committing specific crimes against peace by planning, preparing, initiating, and waging wars of aggression against a number of other States. It will be convenient to consider the question of the existence of a common plan and the question of aggressive war together, and to deal later in this judgment with the question of the individual responsibility of the defendants.

The charges in the indictment that the defendants planned and waged aggressive wars are charges of the utmost gravity. War is essentially an evil thing. Its consequences are not confined to the belligerent states alone, but affect the whole world.

To initiate a war of aggression, therefore, is not only an international crime; it is the supreme international crime differing only from other war crimes in that it contains within itself the accumulated evil of the whole.

The first acts of aggression referred to in the indictment are the seizure of Austria and Czechoslovakia; and the first war of aggression charged in the indictment is the war against Poland begun on the 1st September 1939.

Before examining that charge it is necessary to look more closely at some of the events which preceded these acts of aggression. The war against Poland did not come suddenly out of an otherwise clear sky; the evidence has made it plain that this war of aggression, as well as the seizure of Austria and Czechoslovakia, was premeditated and carefully prepared, and was not undertaken until the moment was thought opportune for it to be carried through as a definite part of the preordained scheme and plan.

For the aggressive designs of the Nazi Government were not accidents arising out of the immediate political situation in Europe and the world; they were a deliberate and essential part of Nazi foreign policy.

From the beginning, the National Socialist movement claimed that its object was to unite the German people in the consciousness of their mission and destiny, based on inherent qualities of race, and under the guidance of the Fuehrer.

For its achievement, two things were deemed to be essential: The disruption of the European order as it had existed since the Treaty of Versailles, and the creation of a Greater Germany beyond the frontiers of 1914. This necessarily involved the seizure of foreign territories.

War was seen to be inevitable, or at the very least, highly probable, if these purposes were to be accomplished. The German people, therefore, with all their resources, were to be organized as a great political-military army, schooled to obey without question any policy decreed by the State.

      *   *   *

IV. VIOLATIONS OF INTERNATIONAL TREATIES

The Charter defines as a crime the planning or waging of war that is a war of aggression or a war in violation of international treaties. The Tribunal has decided that certain of the defendants planned and waged aggressive wars against 10 nations, and were therefore guilty of this series of crimes. This makes it unnecessary to discuss the subject in further detail, or even to consider at any length the extent to which these aggressive wars were also "wars in violation of international treaties, agreements, or assurances." These treaties are set out in appendix C of the indictment. Those of principal importance are the following:

(A) Hague Conventions

In the 1899 Convention the signatory powers agreed: "before an appeal to arms * * * to have recourse, as far as circumstances allow, to the good offices or mediation of one or more friendly powers." A similar clause was inserted in the Convention for Pacific Settlement of International Disputes of 1907. In the accompanying Convention Relative to Opening of Hostilities, article I contains this far more specific language:

> The Contracting Powers recognize that hostilities between them must not commence without a previous and explicit warning, in the form of either a declaration of war, giving reasons, or an ultimatum with a conditional declaration of war.

Germany was a party to these conventions.

(B) Versailles Treaty

Breaches of certain provisions of the Versailles Treaty are also relied on by the prosecution—not to fortify the left bank of the Rhine (art. 42–44); to "respect strictly the independence of Austria" (art. 80); renunciation of any rights in Memel (art. 99) and the Free City of Danzig (art. 100); the recognition of the independence of the Czecho-Slovak State; and the Military, Naval, and Air Clauses against German rearmament found in part V. There is no doubt that action was taken by the German Government contrary to all these provisions, the details of which are set out in appendix C. With regard to the Treaty of Versailles, the matters relied on are:

    1. The violation of articles 42 to 44 in respect of the demilitarized zone of the Rhineland.

    2. The annexation of Austria on the 13th March 1938, in violation of article 80.

3.   The incorporation of the district of Memel on the 22d March 1939, in violation of article 99.

4.   The incorporation of the Free City of Danzig on the 1st September 1939, in violation of article 100.

5.   The incorporation of the provinces of Bohemia and Moravia on the 16th March 1939, in violation of article 81.

6.   The repudiation of the military naval and air clauses of the treaty in or about March of 1935.

On the 21st May 1935, Germany announced that, whilst renouncing the disarmament clauses of the treaty, she would still respect the territorial limitations, and would comply with the Locarno Pact. (With regard to the first five breaches alleged, therefore, the Tribunal finds the allegation proved.)

*   *   *

(E) The Law of the Charter

The jurisdiction of the Tribunal is defined in the Agreement and Charter, and the crimes coming within the jurisdiction of the Tribunal, for which there shall be individual responsibility, are set out in Article 6. The law of the Charter is decisive, and binding upon the Tribunal. *AS ANY CONSTITUTION*

The making of the Charter was the exercise of the sovereign legislative power by the countries to which the German Reich unconditionally surrendered; and the undoubted right of these countries to legislate for the occupied territories has been recognized by the civilized world. The Charter is not an arbitrary exercise of power on the part of the victorious nations, but in the view of the Tribunal, as will be shown, it is the expression of international law existing at the time of its creation; and to that extent is itself a contribution to international law.

*   *   *

*   *   *   [T]he very essence of the Charter is that individuals have international duties which transcend the national obligations of obedience imposed by the individual State. He who violates the laws of war cannot obtain immunity while acting in pursuance of the authority of the State if the State in authorizing action moves outside its competence under international law.

It was also submitted on behalf of most of these defendants that in doing what they did they were acting under the orders of Hitler, *"superior orders"* and therefore cannot be held responsible for the acts committed by them in carrying out these orders. The Charter specifically provides in Article 8:

> The fact that the defendant acted pursuant to order of his Government or of a superior shall not free him from responsibility, but may be considered in mitigation of punishment.

The provisions of this Article are in conformity with the law of all nations. That a soldier was ordered to kill or torture in violation of the international law of war has never been recognized as a defense to such acts of brutality, though, as the Charter here provides, the order may be urged in mitigation of the punishment. The true test, which is found in varying degrees in the criminal law of most nations, is not the existence of the order, but whether moral choice was in fact possible.

V. THE LAW AS TO THE COMMON PLAN OR CONSPIRACY

In the previous recital of the facts relating to aggressive war, it is clear that planning and preparation had been carried out in the most systematic way at every stage of the history.

* * *

In the opinion of the Tribunal, the evidence establishes the common planning to prepare and wage war by certain of the defendants. It is immaterial to consider whether a single conspiracy to the extent and over the time set out in the indictment has been conclusively proved. Continued planning, with aggressive war as the objective, has been established beyond doubt. The truth of the situation was well stated by Paul Schmidt, official interpreter of the German Foreign Office, as follows:

> "The general objectives of the Nazi leadership were apparent from the start, namely the domination of the European Continent, to be achieved first by the incorporation of all German-speaking groups in the Reich, and, secondly, by territorial expansion under the slogan "Lebensraum." The execution of these basic objectives, however, seemed to be characterized by improvisation. Each succeeding step was apparently carried out as each new situation arose, but all consistent with the ultimate objectives mentioned above."

The argument that such common planning cannot exist where there is complete dictatorship is unsound. A plan in the execution of which a number of persons participate is still a plan, even though conceived by only one of them; and those who execute the plan do not avoid responsibility by showing that they acted under the direction of the man who conceived it. Hitler could not make aggressive war by himself. He had to have the cooperation of statesmen, military leaders, diplomats, and businessmen. When they, with knowledge of his aims, gave him their cooperation, they made themselves parties to the plan he had initiated. They are not to be deemed innocent because Hitler made use of them, if they knew what they were doing. That they were assigned to their tasks by a dictator does not absolve them from responsibility for their acts. The relation of leader and follower does not preclude responsibility here any more than it does in the comparable tyranny of organized domestic crime.

*   *   *

VI. War Crimes and Crimes Against Humanity

The evidence relating to war crimes has been overwhelming, in its volume and its detail. It is impossible for this judgment adequately to review it, or to record the mass of documentary and oral evidence that has been presented. The truth remains that war crimes were committed on a vast scale, never before seen in the history of war. They were perpetrated in all the countries occupied by Germany, and on the high seas, and were attended by every conceivable circumstance of cruelty and horror. There can be no doubt that the majority of them arose from the Nazi conception of "total war," with which the aggressive wars were waged. For in this conception of "total war" the moral ideas underlying the conventions which seek to make war more humane are no longer regarded as having force or validity. Everything is made subordinate to the overmastering dictates of war. Rules, regulations, assurances, and treaties, all alike, are of no moment; and so, freed from the restraining influence of international law, the aggressive war is conducted by the Nazi leaders in the most barbaric way. Accordingly, war crimes were committed when and wherever the Fuehrer and his close associates thought them to be advantageous. They were for the most part the result of cold and criminal calculation.

On some occasions war crimes were deliberately planned long in advance. In the case of the Soviet Union, the plunder of the territories to be occupied, and the ill-treatment of the civilian population, were settled in minute detail before the attack was begun. As early as the autumn of 1940, the invasion of the territories of the Soviet Union was being considered. From that date onwards, the methods to be employed in destroying all possible opposition were continuously under discussion.

Similarly, when planning to exploit the inhabitants of the occupied countries for slave labor on the very greatest scale, the German Government conceived it as an integral part of the war economy, and planned and organized this particular war crime down to the last elaborate detail.

Other war crimes, such as the murder of prisoners of war who had escaped and been recaptured, or the murder of commandos or captured airmen, or the destruction of the Soviet commissars, were the result of direct orders circulated through the highest official channels.

The Tribunal proposes, therefore, to deal quite generally with the question of war crimes, and to refer to them later when examining the responsibility of the individual defendants in relation to them.   Prisoners of war were ill-treated and tortured and murdered, not only in defiance of the well-established rules of international law, but in complete disregard of the elementary dictates of humanity.   Civilian populations in occupied territories suffered the same fate.   Whole populations were deported to Germany for the purposes of slave labor upon defense works, armament production and similar tasks connected with the war effort.   Hostages were taken in very large numbers from the civilian populations in all the occupied countries, and were shot as suited the German purposes.   Public and private property was systematically plundered and pillaged in order to enlarge the resources of Germany at the expense of the rest of Europe.   Cities and towns and villages were wantonly destroyed without military justification or necessity.

(A) Murder and Ill-Treatment of Prisoners of War

Article 6(b) of the Charter defines war crimes in these words:

War Crimes: namely, violations of the laws or customs of war.   Such violations shall include, but not be limited to, murder, ill-treatment or deportation to slave labor or for any other purpose of civilian population of or in occupied territory, murder or ill-treatment of prisoners of war or persons on the seas, killing of hostages, plunder of public or private property, wanton destruction of cities, towns, or villages, or devastation not justified by military necessity.

In the course of the war, many Allied soldiers who had surrendered to the Germans were shot immediately, often as a matter of deliberate, calculated policy.   *   *   *

*   *   *

When Allied airmen were forced to land in Germany they were sometimes killed at once by the civilian population.   The police were instructed not to interfere with these killings, and the Ministry of Justice was informed that no one should be prosecuted for taking part in them.

The treatment of Soviet prisoners of war was characterized by particular inhumanity.   The death of so many of them was not due merely to the action of individual guards, or to the exigencies of life in the camps.   It was the result of systematic plans to murder.
*   *   *

*   *   *

(B) Murder and Ill-Treatment of Civilian Population

Article 6(b) of the Charter provides that "ill-treatment   *   *   * of civilian population of or in occupied territory   *   *   *   killing of hostages   *   *   *   wanton destruction of cities, towns, or villages" shall be a war crime.   In the main, these provisions are merely declaratory of the existing laws of war as expressed by the Hague Convention, Article 46, which stated:

> Family honor and rights, the lives of persons and private property, as well as religious convictions and practice, must be respected.

The territories occupied by Germany were administered in violation of the laws of war. The evidence is quite overwhelming of a systematic rule of violence, brutality, and terror. On the 7th December 1941, Hitler issued the directive since known as the "Nacht und Nebel Erlass" (night and fog decree), under which persons who committed offenses against the Reich or the German forces in occupied territories, except where the death sentence was certain, were to be taken secretly to Germany and handed over to the SIPO and SD for trial or punishment in Germany. * * *

Even persons who were only suspected of opposing any of the policies of the German occupation authorities were arrested, and on arrest were interrogated by the Gestapo and the SD in the most shameful manner. * * *

* * *

The practice of keeping hostages to prevent and to punish any form of civil disorder was resorted to by the Germans; an order issued by the defendant Keitel on the 16th September 1941, spoke in terms of fifty or a hundred lives from the occupied areas of the Soviet Union for one German life taken. The order stated that "it should be remembered that a human life in unsettled countries frequently counts for nothing, and a deterrent effect can be obtained only by unusual severity." The exact number of persons killed as a result of this policy is not known, but large numbers were killed in France and the other occupied territories in the west, while in the east the slaughter was on an even more extensive scale. * * *

* * *

(D) Slave Labor Policy

Article 6(b) of the Charter provides that the "ill-treatment or deportation to slave labor or for any other purpose, of civilian population of or in occupied territory" shall be a war crime. The laws relating to forced labor by the inhabitants of occupied territories are found in Article 52 of the Hague Convention, which provides:

> Requisition in kind and services shall not be demanded from municipalities or inhabitants except for the needs of the army of occupation. They shall be in proportion to the resources of the country, and of such a nature as not to involve the inhabitants in the obligation of taking part in military operations against their own country.

The policy of the German occupation authorities was in flagrant violation of the terms of this convention. Some idea of this policy may be gathered from the statement made by Hitler in a speech on November 9, 1941:

> The territory which now works for us contains more than 250,000,000 men, but the territory which works indirectly for us includes now more than 350,000,000. In the measure in which it concerns German territory, the domain which we have taken under our administration, it is not doubtful that we shall succeed in harnessing the very last man to this work.

The actual results achieved were not so complete as this, but the German occupation authorities did succeed in forcing many of the inhabitants of the occupied territories to work for the German war effort, and in deporting at least 5,000,000 persons to Germany to serve German industry and agriculture.

* * *

(E) Persecution of the Jews

The persecution of the Jews at the hands of the Nazi Government has been proved in the greatest detail before the Tribunal. It is a record of consistent and systematic inhumanity on the greatest scale. * * *

* * *

* * * Adolf Eichmann, who had been put in charge of this program by Hitler, has estimated that the policy pursued resulted in the killing of 6,000,000 Jews, of which 4,000,000 were killed in the extermination institutions.

(F) The Law Relating to War Crimes and Crimes Against Humanity

* * *

The Tribunal is of course bound by the Charter, in the definition which it gives both of war crimes and crimes against humanity. With respect to war crimes, however, as has already been pointed out, the crimes defined by Article 6, section (b), of the Charter were already recognized as war crimes under international law. They were covered by Articles 46, 50, 52, and 56 of the Hague Convention of 1907, and Articles 2, 3, 4, 46, and 51 of the Geneva Convention of 1929. That violation of these provisions constituted crimes for which the guilty individuals were punishable is too well settled to admit of argument.

But it is argued that the Hague Convention does not apply in this case, because of the "general participation" clause in Article 2 of the Hague Convention of 1907. That clause provided:

> The provisions contained in the regulations (rules of land warfare) referred to in Article I as well as in the present convention do not apply except between contracting powers, and then only if all the belligerents are parties to the convention.

Several of the belligerents in the recent war were not parties to this convention.

In the opinion of the Tribunal it is not necessary to decide this question. The rules of land warfare expressed in the convention undoubtedly represented an advance over existing international law at the time of their adoption. But the convention expressly stated that it was an attempt "to revise the general laws and customs of war," which it thus recognized to be then existing, but by 1939 these rules laid down in the convention were recognized by all civilized nations, and were regarded as being declaratory of the laws and customs of war which are referred to in Article 6(b) of the Charter.

A further submission was made that Germany was no longer bound by the rules of land warfare in many of the territories occupied during the war, because Germany had completely subjugated those countries and incorporated them into the German Reich, a fact which gave Germany authority to deal with the occupied countries as though they were part of Germany. In the view of the Tribunal it is unnecessary in this case to decide whether this doctrine of subjugation, dependent as it is upon military conquest, has any application where the subjugation is the result of the crime of aggressive war. * * *

With regard to crimes against humanity, there is no doubt whatever that political opponents were murdered in Germany before the war, and that many of them were kept in concentration camps in circumstances of great horror and cruelty. The policy of terror was certainly carried out on a vast scale, and in many cases was organized and systematic. The policy of persecution, repression, and murder of civilians in Germany before the war of 1939, who were likely to be hostile to the Government, was most ruthlessly carried out. The persecution of Jews during the same period is established beyond all doubt. To constitute crimes against humanity, the acts relied on before the outbreak of war must have been in execution of, or in connection with, any crime within the jurisdiction of the Tribunal. The Tribunal is of the opinion that revolting and horrible as many of these crimes were, it has not been satisfactorily proved that they were done in execution of, or in connection with, any such crime. The Tribunal therefore cannot make a general declaration that the acts before 1939 were crimes against humanity within the meaning of the Charter, but from the beginning of the war in 1939 war crimes were committed on a vast scale, which were also crimes against humanity; and insofar as the inhumane acts charged in the indictment, and committed after the beginning of the war, did not constitute war crimes, they were all committed in execution of, or in connection with, the aggressive war, and therefore constituted crimes against humanity.

* * *

VERDICTS AND SENTENCES OF THE INTERNATIONAL MILITARY TRIBUNAL

Calvocaressi, Nuremberg 141 (1947).

	Table of								
	Charges Counts				Verdicts Counts				Sentences
	1	2	3	4	1	2	3	4	
Goering [a]	X	X	X	X	X	X	X	X	
Ribbentrop	X	X	X	X	X	X	X	X	
Keitel	X	X	X	X	X	X	X	X	
Jodl	X	X	X	X	X	X	X	X	
Rosenberg	X	X	X	X	X	X	X	X	
Frick	X	X	X	X		X	X	X	Death.
Seyss-Inquart	X	X	X	X		X	X	X	
Sauckel	X	X	X	X			X	X	
Bormann [b]	X		X	X			X	X	
Kaltenbrunner	X		X	X			X	X	
Frank	X		X	X			X	X	
Streicher	X			X				X	
Raeder	X	X	X	X	X	X	X		
Funk	X	X	X	X		X	X	X	Life.
Hess [c]	X	X	X	X	X	X			
Speer	X	X	X	X			X	X	20 years.
Schirach	X			X				X	
Neurath	X	X	X	X	X	X	X	X	15 years.
Doenitz	X	X	X			X	X		10 years.
Fritzsche	X		X	X					
von Papen	X	X							Acquitted.
Schacht	X	X							

Other trials in Germany. In an article entitled The Eichmann Case and the Nuremberg Trials, 48 A.B.A.J. 738 (1962), Lippert states:

> As a follow-up to the International Military Tribunal (IMT) case, the United States had planned to prosecute high-ranking officials of the security and police services, but after investigation it was realized that few were available for trial. Justice Jack-

a. Committed suicide.

b. Tried in absentia; never found.

c. The only defendant still imprisoned.

son's successor as United States Prosecutor, Brigadier General Telford Taylor, reported that "Many of them were known to be dead and others missing could not be located." It cannot be doubted that the missing Eichmann, the very man named by the IMT, was one of those whose trial had been contemplated, such to be held before one of the United States courts that were established in Nuremberg in 1946 after the IMT finished its work.

These courts which were known as United States Military Tribunals, were staffed by judges who were drawn from the Bench and Bar of the United States. Before one or the other of them, there appeared 177 members of the SS and police, doctors, judges, lawyers, industrialists, government ministers and military leaders. Of this total 142 were found guilty, in greater or less degree, of the war crimes, crimes against peace, and crimes against humanity, of which they were charged, and twelve were executed pursuant to the death penalty imposed. The trial of the jurists has become well known by reason of the fictional version of it portrayed in the film "Judgment at Nuremberg".

Moreover, there were still other United States courts in Germany which could have taken jurisdiction of Eichmann's case at the time. Concurrently with the trials in Nuremberg an equally monumental judicial undertaking was in progress in Dachau, a suburb of Munich, and previously the site of one of the infamous extermination camps, complete with gas chamber and ovens. Here the United States Army in a staggering total of 489 trials prosecuted those charged with crimes committed against United States soldiers and those having complicity in the operation of the concentration camps liberated by United States troops. Of the 1,672 persons accused, 1,347 were found guilty and 258 suffered the death penalty. * * *

UNITED STATES v. VON LEEB (THE HIGH COMMAND CASE)

American Military Tribunal (Tribunal V), 1948. XI Trials of War Criminals 462 (1950).

PRESIDING JUDGE YOUNG: The Tribunal will now proceed to read the judgment.

This Tribunal is composed of Presiding Judge John C. Young (formerly Chief Justice of the Supreme Court of Colorado), and Associate Judges Justin W. Harding (formerly U. S. District Judge First Division, District of Alaska) and Winfield B. Hale (Justice Tennessee Court of Appeals, on leave of absence).

It was created under and by virtue of Military Government Ordinance No. 7, effective 18 October 1946 adopted pursuant to Control Council Law No. 10, enacted 20 December 1945, in order to give effect to the London Agreement of 8 August 1945, and the Charter issued pursuant thereto for the prosecution of war criminals.

In Nuernberg, on 28 November 1947, in accordance with Ordinance No. 7 (Article III (a)) supra, an indictment was lodged against the defendants by Telford Taylor, Brigadier General, U.S.A., Chief of Counsel for War Crimes, acting in behalf of the United States of America. A copy of the indictment in the German language was served upon each defendant at least thirty days prior to arraignment on 30 December 1947, at which time each, in the presence of counsel of his own selection, entered a plea of "not guilty."

The indictment named as defendants:

Generalfeldmarschall (General of the Army) Wilhelm von Leeb, Generalfeldmarschall (General of the Army) Hugo Sperrle, Generalfeldmarschall (General of the Army) Georg Karl Friedrich-Wilhelm von Kuechler, Generaloberst (General) Johannes Blaskowitz, Generaloberst (General) Hermann Hoth, Generaloberst (General) Hans Reinhardt, Generaloberst (General) Hans von Salmuth, Generaloberst (General) Karl Hollidt, Generaladmiral (Admiral) Otto Schniewind, General der Infanterie (Lieutenant General Infantry) Karl von Roques, General der Infanterie (Lieutenant General, Infantry) Hermann Reinecke, General der Artillerie (Lieutenant General, Artillery) Walter Warlimont, General der Infanterie (Lieutenant General, Infantry) Otto Woehler, and Generaloberstabsrichter (Lieutenant General, Judge Advocate) Rudolf Lehmann.

* * *

The indictment is in four counts charging (1) crimes against peace; (2) war crimes; (3) crimes against humanity; and (4) a common plan or conspiracy to commit the crimes charged in counts one, two, and three.

* * *

Count one of the indictment, heretofore set out, charges the defendants with crimes against peace.

Before seeking to determine the law applicable it is necessary to determine with certainty the action which the defendants are alleged to have taken that constitutes the crime. As a preliminary to that we deem it necessary to give a brief consideration to the nature and characteristics of war. We need not attempt a definition that is all-inclusive and all-exclusive. It is sufficient to say that war is the exerting of violence by one state or politically organized body against another. In other words, it is the implementation of a political policy by means of violence. Wars are contests by force between political units but the policy that brings about their initiation is made and the actual waging of them is done by individuals. What we have said thus far is equally as applicable to a just as to an unjust war, to the initiation of an aggressive and, therefore, criminal war as to the waging of a defensive and, therefore, legitimate war against criminal aggression. The point we stress is that war activity is the implementation of a predetermined national policy.

Likewise, an invasion of one state by another is the implementation of the national policy of the invading state by force even though the invaded state, due to fear or a sense of the futility of resistance in the face of superior force, adopts a policy of nonresistance and thus prevents the occurrence of any actual combat.

In the light of this general characterization and definition of war and invasions we now consider the charge contained in the indictment. The essence of the charge is *participation in the initiation of* ✓ *aggressive invasions and in the planning, preparation, and waging of aggressive wars.* * * *

The prosecution does not seek, or contend that the law authorizes, a conviction of the defendants simply by reason of their positions as shown by the evidence, but it contends only that such positions may be considered by the Tribunal with all other evidence in the case for such light as they may shed on the personal guilt or innocence of the individual defendants. The prosecution does contend, and we think the contention sound, that the defendants are not relieved of responsibility for action which would be criminal in one who held no military position, simply by reason of their military positions. This is the clear holding of the judgment of the IMT, and is so provided in Control Council Law No. 10, Article II, paragraph 4(a).

The initiation of war or an invasion is a unilateral operation. When war is formally declared or the first shot is fired the initiation of the war has ended and from then on there is a waging of war between the two adversaries. Whether a war be lawful, or aggressive and therefore unlawful under international law, is and can be determined only from a consideration of the factors that entered into its initiation. In the intent and purpose for which it is planned, prepared, initiated and waged is to be found its lawfulness or unlawfulness.

As we have pointed out, war whether it be lawful or unlawful is the implementation of a national policy. If the policy under which it is initiated is criminal in its intent and purpose it is so because the individuals at the policy-making level had a criminal intent and purpose in determining the policy. If war is the means by which the criminal objective is to be attained then the waging of the war is but an implementation of the policy, and the criminality which attaches to ✓ the waging of an aggressive war should be confined to those who participate in it at the policy level.

This does not mean that the Tribunal subscribes to the contention made in this trial that since Hitler was the Dictator of the Third Reich and that he was supreme in both the civil and military fields, he alone must bear criminal responsibility for political and military policies. No matter how absolute his authority, Hitler alone could not formulate a policy of aggressive war and alone implement that policy by preparing, planning, and waging such a war. Somewhere between the Dictator and Supreme Commander of the Military Forces of the nation and the common soldier is the boundary between the criminal and the excusable participation in the waging of an aggressive war by an individual engaged in it. Control Council Law No. 10 does not definitely draw such a line.

It points out in paragraph 2 of Article II certain fact situations and established relations that are or may be sufficient to constitute guilt and sets forth certain categories of activity that do not establish immunity from criminality. Since there has been no other prosecution under Control Council Law No. 10 with defendants in the same category as those in this case, no such definite line has been judicially drawn. This Tribunal is not required to fix a general rule but only to determine the guilt or innocence of the present defendants.

The judgment of the IMT held that:

> The Charter is not an arbitrary exercise of power on the part of the victorious nations, but in view of the Tribunal, as will be shown, it is the expression of international law existing at the time of its creation; and to that extent is itself a contribution to international law.

We hold that Control Council Law No. 10 likewise is but an expression of international law existing at the time of its creation. We cannot therefore construe it as extending the international common law as it existed at the time of the Charter to add thereto any new element of criminality, for so to do would give it an ex post facto effect which we do not construe it to have intended. Moreover, that this was not intended is indicated by the fact that the London Charter of 8 August 1945, is made an integral part of the Control Council Law.

Since international common law grows out of the common reactions and the composite thinking with respect to recurring situations by the various states composing the family of nations, it is pertinent to consider the general attitude of the citizens of states with respect to their military commanders and their obligations when their nations plan, prepare for and initiate or engage in war.

While it is undoubtedly true that international common law in case of conflict with state law takes precedence over it and while it is equally true that absolute unanimity among all the states in the family of nations is not required to bring an international common law into being, it is scarcely a tenable proposition that international common law will run counter to the consensus within any considerable number of nations.

Furthermore, we must not confuse idealistic objectives with realities. The world has not arrived at a state of civilization such that it can dispense with fleets, armies, and air forces, nor has it arrived at a point where it can safely outlaw war under any and all circumstances and situations. In as much as all war cannot be considered outlawed then armed forces are lawful instrumentalities of state, which have internationally legitimate functions. An unlawful war of aggression connotes of necessity a lawful war of defense against aggression. There is no general criterion under international common law for determining the extent to which a nation may arm and prepare for war. As long as there is no aggressive intent, there is no evil inherent in a nation making itself militarily strong. An example in Switzerland which for her geographical extent, her population and resources is proportionally stronger militarily than many nations of the world. She uses her military strength to implement a national policy that seeks peace and to maintain her borders against aggression.

There have been nations that have initiated and waged aggressive wars through long periods of history, doubtless there are nations still disposed to do so; and if not, judging in the light of history, there may be nations which tomorrow will be disposed so to do. Furthermore, situations may arise in which the question whether the war is or is not aggressive is doubtful and uncertain. We may safely assume that the general and considered opinions of the people within states—the source from which international common law springs are not such as to hamper or render them impotent to do the things they deem necessary for their national protection.

ELEMENTS

We are of the opinion that as in ordinary criminal cases, so in the crime denominated aggressive war, the same elements must all be present to constitute criminality. There first must be actual knowledge that an aggressive war is intended and that if launched it will be an aggressive war. But mere knowledge is not sufficient to make participation even by high ranking military officers in the war criminal. It requires in addition that the possessor of such knowledge, after he acquires it shall be in a position to shape or influence the policy that brings about its initiation or its continuance after initiation, either by furthering, or by hindering or preventing it. If he then does the former, he becomes criminally responsible; if he does the latter to the extent of his ability, then his action shows the lack of criminal intent with respect to such policy.

If a defendant did not know that the planning and preparation for invasions and wars in which he was involved were concrete plans and preparations for aggressive wars and for wars otherwise in violation of international laws and treaties, then he cannot be guilty of an offense. If, however, after the policy to initiate and wage aggressive wars was formulated, a defendant came into possession of knowledge that the invasions and wars to be waged, were aggressive and unlawful, then he will be criminally responsible if he, being on the policy level, could have influenced such policy and failed to do so.

If and as long as a member of the armed forces does not participate in the preparation, planning, initiating, or waging of aggressive war on a policy level, his war activities do not fall under the definition of crimes against peace. It is not a person's rank or status, but his power to shape or influence the policy of his state, which is the relevant issue for determining his criminality under the charge of crimes against peace.

International law condemns those who, due to their actual power to shape and influence the policy of their nation, prepare for, or lead their country into or in an aggressive war. But we do not find that, at the present stage of development, international law declares as criminals those below that level who, in the execution of this war policy, act as the instruments of the policy makers. Anybody who is on the policy level and participates in the war policy is liable to punishment. But those under them cannot be punished for the crimes of others. The misdeed of the policy makers is all the greater in as much as they use the great mass of the soldiers and officers to carry out an international crime; however, the individual soldier or officer below the policy level is but the policy makers' instrument, finding himself, as he does, under the rigid discipline which is necessary for and peculiar to military organization.

We do not hesitate to state that it would have been eminently desirable had the commanders of the German armed forces refused to implement the policy of the Third Reich by means of aggressive war. It would have been creditable to them not to contribute to the cataclysmic catastrophe. This would have been the honorable and righteous thing to do; it would have been in the interest of their State. Had they done so they would have served their fatherland and humanity also.

But however much their failure is morally reprimandable, we are of the opinion and hold that international common law, at the time they so acted, had not developed to the point of making the participation of military officers below the policy making or policy influencing level into a criminal offense in and of itself.

International law operates as a restriction and limitation on the sovereignty of nations. It may also limit the obligations which individuals owe to their states, and create for them international obligations which are binding upon them to an extent that they must be carried out even if to do so violates a positive law or directive of state. But the limitation which international common law imposes on national sovereignty, or on individual obligations, is a limitation self-imposed or imposed by the composite thinking in the international community, for it is by such democratic processes that common law comes into being. If there is no generality of opinion among the nations of the world as to a particular restriction on national sovereignty or on the obligations of individuals toward their own state, then there is no international common law on such matter.

By the Kellogg-Briand Pact 63 nations, including Germany, renounced war as an instrument of national policy. If this, as we believe it is, is evidence of a sufficient crystallization of world opinion to authorize a judicial finding that there exist crimes against peace under international common law, we cannot find that law to extend further than such evidence indicates. The nations that entered into the Kellogg-Briand Pact considered it imperative that existing international relationships should not be changed by force. In the preamble they state that they are:

> Persuaded that the time has come when * * * all changes in their relationships with one another should be sought only by pacific means * * *

This is a declaration that from that time forward each of the signatory nations should be deemed to possess and to have the right to exercise all the privileges and powers of a sovereign nation within the limitations of international law, free from all interference by force on the part of any other nation. As a corollary to this, the changing or attempting to change the international relationships by force of arms is an act of aggression and if the aggression results in war, the war is an aggressive war. It is, therefore, aggressive war that is renounced by the pact. It is aggressive war that is criminal under international law.

The crime denounced by the law is the use of war as an instrument of national policy. Those who commit the crime are those who participate at the policy making level in planning, preparing, or in initiating war. After war is initiated, and is being waged, the policy question then involved becomes one of extending, continuing or discontinuing the war. The crime at this stage likewise must be committed at the policy making level.

The making of a national policy is essentially political, though it may require, and of necessity does require, if war is to be one element of that policy, a consideration of matters military as well as matters political.

It is self-evident that national policies are made by man. When men make a policy that is criminal under international law, they are criminally responsible for so doing. This is the logical and inescapable conclusion.

The acts of commanders and staff officers below the policy level, in planning campaigns, preparing means for carrying them out, moving against a country on orders and fighting a war after it has been instituted, do not constitute the planning, preparation, initiation, and waging of war or the initiation of invasion that international law denounces as criminal.

Under the record we find the defendants were not on the policy level, and are not guilty under count one of the indictment. With

crimes charged to have been committed by them in the *manner* in
which they behaved in the waging of war, we deal in other parts of
this judgment.

     *   *   *

---

1. *Trial of Japanese leaders.* An International Military Tribunal for the Far East conducted a trial of Japanese leaders in Tokyo
and rendered a judgment in November, 1948. Examples from the
judgment and other opinions are reported in Sohn, Cases on United
Nations Law 898 (1956).

2. *The Nuremberg principles in the United Nations.* In December, 1946, the General Assembly of the United Nations adopted a
resolution affirming "the principles of international law recognized by
the Charter of the Nuremberg Tribunal and the judgment of the Tribunal." Resolution 95(1). The International Law Commission, an
organ of the United Nations established by the General Assembly to
carry out Article 13 of the Charter, was requested by the General Assembly to "formulate" the Nuremberg principles. In 1950, the Commission submitted a draft of seven principles which were discussed by
the General Assembly but never formally affirmed by the assembly.
Extensive efforts in the United Nations to prepare and agree upon a
Draft Code of Offenses against the Peace and Security of Mankind
and to establish an international criminal court have come to nought.
A detailed report of this work of the United Nations is set forth in
Sohn, Cases on United Nations Law 969–1019 (1956).

SECTION C. UNIVERSAL JURISDICTION AND THE NUREMBERG PRINCIPLES

ATTORNEY GENERAL OF ISRAEL v. EICHMANN

Israel, Supreme Court 1962.
36 Int'l L.Rep. 277 (1968).

1. The appellant, Adolf Eichmann, was found guilty by the
District Court of Jerusalem of offences of the most extreme gravity
against the Nazi and Nazi Collaborators (Punishment) Law, 1950
(hereinafter referred to as "the Law") and was sentenced to death.
These offences may be divided into four groups:

    (a) Crimes against the Jewish people, contrary to Section 1(a)

       (1) of the Law;

(b) Crimes against humanity, contrary to Section 1(a)(2);

(c) War crimes, contrary to Section 1(a)(3);

(d) Membership of hostile organizations, contrary to Section 3.

2.   The acts constituting these offences, which the Court attributed to the appellant, have been specified in paragraph 244 of the judgment of the District Court * * *.

The acts comprised in Group (a) are:

(1) that during the period from August 1941 to May 1945, in Germany, in the Axis States and in the areas which were subject to the authority of Germany and the Axis States, he, together with others, caused the killing of millions of Jews for the purpose of carrying out the plan known as "the Final Solution of the Jewish Problem" with the intent to exterminate the Jewish people;

(2) that during that period and in the same places he, together with others, placed millions of Jews in living conditions which were calculated to bring about their physical destruction, for the purpose of carrying out the plan above mentioned with the intent to exterminate the Jewish people;

(3) that during that period and in the same places he, together with others, caused serious physical and mental harm to millions of Jews with the intent to exterminate the Jewish people;

(4) that during the years 1943 and 1944 he, together with others, "devised measures the purpose of which was to prevent births among Jews by his instructions forbidding child bearing and ordering the interruption of pregnancies of Jewish women in the Theresin Ghetto with the intent to exterminate the Jewish people".

The acts constituting the crimes in Group (b) are as follows:

(5) that during the period from August 1941 to May 1945 he, together with others, caused in the territories and areas mentioned in clause (1) the murder, extermination, enslavement, starvation and deportation of the civilian Jewish population;

(6) that during the period from December 1939 to March 1941 he, together with others, caused the deportation of Jews to Nisco, and the deportation of Jews from the areas in the East annexed to the Reich, and from the Reich area proper, to the German Occupied Territories in the East, and to France;

(7) that in carrying out the above-mentioned activities he persecuted Jews on national, racial, religious and political grounds;

(8) that during the period from March 1938 to May 1945 in the places mentioned above he, together with others, caused the spoliation of the property of millions of Jews by means of mass

terror linked with the murder, extermination, starvation and deportation of these Jews;

(9) that during the years 1940–1942 he, together with others, caused the expulsion of hundreds of thousands of Poles from their places of residence;

(10) that during 1941 he, together with others, caused the expulsion of more than 14,000 Slovenes from their places of residence;

(11) that during the Second World War he, together with others, caused the expulsion of scores of thousands of gipsies from Germany and German-occupied areas and their transportation to the German-occupied areas in the East;

(12) that in 1942 he, together with others, caused the expulsion of 93 children of the Czech village of Lidice.

The acts comprised in Group (c) are:

that he committed the acts of persecution, expulsion and murder mentioned in Counts 1 to 7, in so far as these were done during the Second World War against Jews from among the populations of the States occupied by the Germans and by the other Axis States.

The acts comprised in Group (d) are:

that as from May 1940 he was a member of three Nazi Police organizations which were declared criminal organizations by the International Military Tribunal which tried the Major War Criminals, and as a member of such organizations he took part in acts which were declared criminal in Article 6 of the London Charter of August 8, 1945.

3. The appellant has appealed to this Court against both conviction and sentence.

4. The oral and written submissions of learned counsel who supported the appeal, Dr. Servatius, may, in so far as they are directed against conviction, be classified under two heads:

(1) Purely legal contentions, the principal object of which was to undermine the jurisdiction of a court in Israel to try the appellant for the crimes in question;

(2) Factual contentions the object of which was in essence to upset the finding of the District Court that there was no foundation for the defence of the appellant that he played the part of a "small cog" in the machine of Nazi destruction, that in all the above-mentioned chapters of events he functioned as a minor official without any independent initiative, and that nothing but the compulsion of orders and blind obedience to commands from above guided him in carrying out his work at all stages.

* * *

5.   The District Court has in its judgment dealt with both categories of contentions in an exhaustive, profound and most convincing
manner.   We should say at once that we fully concur, without hesitation or reserve, in all its conclusions and reasons.   *   *   *
[The Jurisdiction of the Court]

6.   Most of the legal contentions of counsel for the appellant
revolve around the argument that in assuming jurisdiction to try
the appellant the District Court acted contrary to the principles of
international law.   These contentions are as follows:

(1) The Law of 1950, which is the only source of the jurisdiction of the Court in this case, constitutes ex post facto penal legislation which prescribes as offences acts that were committed
before the State of Israel came into existence;   therefore the
validity of this Law is confined to its citizens alone.

(2) The offences for which the appellant was tried are "extra-territorial offences", that is to say, offences that were committed outside the territory of Israel by a citizen of a foreign
State, and even though the Law confers jurisdiction in respect
of such offences, it conflicts in so doing with the principle of territorial sovereignty, which postulates that only the country within
whose territory the offence was committed or to which the offender belongs—in this case, Germany—has the right to punish
therefor.

(3) The acts constituting the offence of which the appellant
was convicted were at the time of their commission Acts of State.

(4) The appellant was brought to Israel territory, to be tried
for the offences in question, unwillingly and without the consent
of the country in which he resided, and this was done through
agents of the State of Israel, who acted on the orders of their
Government.

(5) The judges of the District Court, being Jews and feeling
affinity with the victims of the plan of extermination and Nazi
persecution, were psychologically incapable of giving the appellant an objective trial.

*   *   *

7.   We reject all these contentions.

*   *   *

[Portions of the court's opinion dealing with the second contention—
the "extraterritoriality" of the offences—are set forth as follows.]
[Universal Jurisdiction]

12.   *   *   *   [I]t is the universal character of the crimes in question which vests in every State the authority to try and punish those
who participated in their commission.   This proposition is closely

linked with the one advanced in the preceding paragraph, from which indeed it follows as a logical outcome. The grounds upon which it rests are as follows:

(a) One of the principles whereby States assume in one degree or another the power to try and punish a person for an offence is the principle of universality. Its meaning is substantially that such power is vested in every State regardless of the fact that the offence was committed outside its territory by a person who did not belong to it, provided he is in its custody when brought to trial. This principle has wide currency and is universally acknowledged with respect to the offence of piracy jure gentium. But while general agreement exists as to this offence, the question of the scope of its application is in dispute * * *

* * *

(b) The brief survey of views set out above shows that, notwithstanding the differences between them, there is full justification for applying here the principle of universal jurisdiction since the international character of "crimes against humanity" (in the wide meaning of the term) dealt with in this case is no longer in doubt, while the unprecedented extent of their injurious and murderous effects is not to be disputed at the present time. In other words, the basic reason for which international law recognizes the right of each State to exercise such jurisdiction in piracy offences—notwithstanding the fact that its own sovereignty does not extend to the scene of the commission of the offence (the high seas) and the offender is a national of another State or is stateless—applies with even greater force to the above-mentioned crimes. That reason is, it will be recalled, that the interest to prevent bodily and material harm to those who sail the seas and to persons engaged in trade between nations, is a vital interest common to all civilized States and of universal scope * * *.

It follows that the State which prosecutes and punishes a person for piracy acts merely as the organ and agent of the international community and metes out punishment to the offender for his breach of the prohibition imposed by the law of nations * * *

The above explanation of the substantive basis upon which the exercise of the principle of universal jurisdiction in respect of the crime of piracy rests, justifies its exercise in regard also to the crimes which are the subject of the present case.

(c) The truth is—and this further supports our conclusion—that the application of this principle has for some time been moving beyond the international crime of piracy. We have in mind its application to conventional war crimes as well. As we observed in paragraph 11 (c) of this judgment, whenever a "belligerent" country tries and punishes a member of the armed forces of the enemy for an act contrary to "the laws and customs of war", it does so because the matter involves an international crime in the prevention of which the countries of the whole world have an interest. * * *

* * *

(f) We sum up our views on this subject as follows. Not only do all the crimes attributed to the appellant bear an international character, but their harmful and murderous effects were so embracing and widespread as to shake the international community to its very foundations. The State of Israel therefore was entitled, pursuant to the principle of universal jurisdiction and in the capacity of a guardian of international law and an agent for its enforcement, to try the appellant. That being the case, no importance attaches to the fact that the State of Israel did not exist when the offences were committed. Here therefore is an additional reason—and one based on a positive approach—for rejecting the second, "jurisdictional", submission of counsel for the appellant.

* * *

SECTION D. CONTEMPORARY PROBLEMS RELATED TO THE WAR IN VIETNAM

UNITED STATES v. MITCHELL

United States Court of Appeals, Second Circuit, 1966.
369 F.2d 323.

MEDINA, CIRCUIT JUDGE. David Henry Mitchell, III appeals from a conviction, after a trial to Judge Clarie and a jury, of wilful failure to report for induction into the Armed Forces in violation of 50 U.S.C., Appx., Section 462.

After initially registering with Selective Service Local Board 17, appellant "disaffiliated" himself from the Selective Service and thereafter refused to cooperate with his Board in any respect. In August, 1964, appellant was classified 1A and did not appeal. Subsequently, he was ordered to report for induction on January 11, 1965. Appellant acknowledged receipt of this notice by letter but did not report as ordered.

Appellant was indicted for violation of 50 U.S.C., Appx., Section 462, tried and found guilty. This Court reversed the first conviction because the trial judge had failed to allow sufficient time for appellant to obtain counsel. United States v. Mitchell, 354 F.2d 767 (2 Cir. 1966). He was retried before Judge Clarie and a jury. The wilfulness of his failure to report for induction was all too apparent, and he was again convicted and sentenced to five years imprisonment. At trial appellant made no claim to be a conscientious objector but sought to produce evidence to show that the war in Vietnam was being conducted in violation of various treaties to which the United States is a signatory and that the Selective Service system was being operated as an adjunct of this military effort. Judge Clarie ruled out all such evidence as immaterial and this ruling is assigned as error.

The government, citing a line of cases beginning with Falbo v. United States, 320 U.S. 549, 64 S.Ct. 346, 88 L.Ed. 305 (1944), would preclude consideration of appellant's claims because of his failure to exhaust his administrative remedies. But, as appellant does not seek any relief which the Selective Service is empowered to grant, we will assume these cases are not in point. Rather, he seeks a declaration, in effect, that the Service must cease to function. It would be pointless in this case to require appellant to press his claims before a Board which he claims is illegal.

Similarly, as appellant asserts that the Selective Service, and not merely the conduct of the war in Vietnam, is illegal, his defenses would seem not to be premature.

Nevertheless, appellant's allegations are not a defense to a prosecution for failure to report for induction into the Armed Forces and his evidence was properly excluded. Regardless of the proof that appellant might present to demonstrate the correlation between the Selective Service and our nation's efforts in Vietnam, as a matter of law the congressional power "to raise and support armies" and "to provide and maintain a navy" is a matter quite distinct from the use which the Executive makes of those who have been found qualified and who have been inducted into the Armed Forces. Whatever action the President may order, or the Congress sanction, cannot impair this constitutional power of the Congress.

Thus we need not consider whether the substantive issues raised by appellant can ever be appropriate for judicial determination. See United States v. Hogans, 2 Cir., 369 F.2d 359, decided by this Court on November 28, 1966.

Affirmed.

MITCHELL v. UNITED STATES

United States Supreme Court, 1967.
386 U.S. 972, 87 S.Ct. 1162.

Certiorari denied.

MR. JUSTICE DOUGLAS, dissenting.

Petitioner did not report for induction as ordered, was indicted, convicted, and sentenced to five years' imprisonment and his conviction was affirmed. 369 F.2d 323. His defense was that the "war" in Vietnam was being conducted in violation of various treaties to which we were a signatory, especially the Treaty of London of August 8, 1945, 59 Stat. 1544, which in Article 6(a) declares that "waging of a war of aggression" is a "crime against peace" imposing ✓ "individual responsibility." Article 8 provides:

> "The fact that the Defendant acted pursuant to order of his Government or of a superior shall not free him from responsibility, but may be considered in mitigation of punishment if the Tribunal determines that justice so requires."

Petitioner claimed that the "war" in Vietnam was a "war of aggression" within the meaning of the Treaty of London and that Article 8 makes him responsible for participating in it even though he is ordered to do so.[1]

Mr. Justice Jackson, the United States prosecutor at Nuremberg, stated: "If certain acts in violation of treaties are crimes, they are crimes whether the United States does them or whether Germany does them, and we are not prepared to lay down a rule of criminal conduct against others which we would not be willing to have invoked against us." (International Conference on Military Trials, Dept. of State Pub. No. 3080, p. 330.)

Article VI, cl. 2, of the Constitution states that "Treaties" are a part of the "supreme Law of the Land; and the Judges in every State shall be bound thereby."

There is a considerable body of opinion that our actions in Vietnam constitute the waging of an aggressive "war."

This case presents the questions:

(1) whether the Treaty of London is a treaty within the meaning of Art. VI, cl. 2;

(2) whether the question as to the waging of an aggressive "war" is in the context of this criminal prosecution a justiciable question;

(3) whether the Vietnam episode is a "war" in the sense of the Treaty;

(4) whether petitioner has standing to raise the question;

(5) whether, if he has, the Treaty may be tendered as a defense in this criminal case or in amelioration of the punishment.

These are extremely sensitive and delicate questions. But they ✓ should, I think, be answered. Even those who think that the Nuremberg judgments were unconstitutional by our guarantee relating to ex post facto laws would have to take a different view of the Treaty of London that purports to lay down a standard of future conduct for all the signatories.

---

1. The trial court charged the jury that the Treaty of London did not interfere "in any manner in respect to this de- fendant fulfilling his duty under this order."

I intimate no opinion on the merits. But I think the petition for certiorari should be granted. We have here a recurring question in present-day Selective Service cases.[a]

Problem. Analyze the following news article in the light of the Nuremberg principles, from the substantive and procedural points of view. (The question of the legality of the military action, as such, by the United States in Vietnam is dealt with at p. 1233.) The article appeared in The N. Y. Times, Dec. 31, 1972, Sec. 4, at 1.[b]

Saigon—Air raid sirens scream day and night. The earth trembles with the violence of an earthquake, and whole sections of the city crumble in a roar of flames and flying jagged steel. For the first time in the war the people seem afraid.

This is Hanoi under attack by American B–52's, as described by Westerners who have been there. The big bombers, flying in wedges of three, lay down more than 65 tons of bombs at a time in a carpet pattern a mile and a half long and a half mile wide.

For nearly two weeks now the city has been the focal point of a siege by American bombers that has extended across the densely populated heart of North Vietnam. Hundreds, if not thousands, of civilians are believed to have been killed. Even during a 36-hour bombing halt at Christmas, reconnaissance planes swooped over Hanoi keeping the people's nerves on edge.

The destruction, said one Westerner who left Hanoi last week, is "unbelievable."

The B–52's reportedly have destroyed about 80 per cent of the Gia Lam International Airport buildings in the capital. The main railroad station and yards in downtown Hanoi have been smashed, and much of the Bach Mai Hospital also is said to have been reduced to rubble.

Although North Vietnamese officials have been advising city dwellers for some time to move into the countryside as a precaution against just this kind of intensive raids, intelligence sources here say that many persons disregarded the advice and only now are evacuating the prime target areas.

For the first 10 days of the raids that started Dec. 18 the United States military command here maintained official silence on the

---

a. Problems posed by this case are more fully analyzed in Forman, The Nuremberg Trials and Conscientious Objection to War: Justiciability under United States Municipal Law, 1969 Proceedings of the American Society of International Law 157 and comments therein by Telford Taylor and others, 165 ff.

b. © 1972, by the New York Times Company. Reprinted by permission of the publisher.

scope of the operations and the damage, saying that "military security" was at stake.

Last Wednesday it released a report of some 50 targets that had been bombed at least once in the first seven days of the raids. The command further disclosed that there had been more than 1,000 strikes by fighter-bombers during the week and 147 B–52 missions, each presumed to consist of at least three planes.

Nineteen of the targets were within 10 miles of the center of Hanoi. Among them were the city's thermal power plant and its port facilities. Another seven of them were within six miles of the center of Haiphong, including a shipyard, a naval base and an airfield. There were several other targets in and around the cities of Thai Nguyen to the north and Thanh Hoa on the southern coast.

The American command maintained that all of these were "military targets," and spokesmen would not respond to questions about the international airport or the hospital in Hanoi, or even acknowledge that some of the small brick homes with red tiled roofs packed closely together in the cities were being flattened. It also would not acknowledge that there were any civilian casualties.

"We have targeted and continue to target only military targets," Maj. Gilbert L. Whiteman, a spokesman for the command, said.

The command likewise would not comment on reports from Radio Hanoi that B–52's had cut swaths through several of the compact, circular farming villages that dot the fertile delta. Several of the "military targets" were being bombed for the first time, the command admitted, without adding that they had previously been proscribed because to attack them increased the chances of killing civilians.

One of the major reasons that B–52's had not previously been used in North Vietnam in great numbers, a senior Air Force officer said in a recent interview, was the increased threat they posed to the civilian population. "Even with the accuracy we get," the officer said, "we're still not sure we would not get a little more than military targets."

The North Vietnamese Foreign Ministry charged at midweek that the bombing had "caused thousands of deaths [and] destroyed thousands of homes."

Losses on the American side have been grave, too. By Friday evening the American command had acknowledged the loss of 25 aircraft—including 15 B–52's which are valued at about $8-million each—and indicated that at least 82 American airmen were missing or captured. One American official said the losses were a measure of Mr. Nixon's intention to "go all out."

"In May the policy was 'If you lose a B–52 you're in trouble,'" the official said. "When we start losing as many B–52's as we've lost in the last few days, you know that a lot of scruples and constraints have been done away with. We've always tried to avoid civilian casualties, but now it looks like someone has said, 'Well, it may not be nice, but we've just got to do it.' "

It is widely believed here that the massive new bombing is being closely supervised by President Nixon. He has shrouded the operation in extremely tight military security, withholding the sketchiest of information from some of the higest ranking civilian and military officials in Saigon. Informed officers say that the daily staff briefings at the command headquarters here have been restricted to intelligence and operations officers only and their commanders.

Some officials have suggested that part of the reason for this is that the South Vietnamese Government is believed to have been "penetrated" by enemy agents. Other officials and some newsmen, however, said they failed to understand the secrecy and believed strongly that it was a conscious attempt to allow only the barest details of the bombing to reach the American public.

Military spokesmen here and in Washington initially said that the bombing had been ordered to head off preparations for a new offensive by the North. That line of reasoning could have been called into play at almost any time in the history of the conflict because the North Vietnamese have always either been engaged in an offensive or planning one. But officials here said they saw no activity by the North Vietnamese prior to the latest air raids that in itself would have warranted such a massive response.

The only genuine reason universally accepted here for the new bombing was that Mr. Nixon was determined to bring the North Vietnamese to their knees, bludgeoning them with bombs into accepting terms for peace that the President believed were favorable to the United States and South Vietnam.

South Vietnamese Government officials thoroughly endorse the bombing. It might bring about a settlement, some of them say. If not, at least it will weaken the North for future battles.

Part IV

THE STRUCTURE OF THE INTERNATIONAL SYSTEM

Chapter 11

STATEHOOD: ANALYSIS OF THE CONCEPT

In spite of increasing concern for the individual in the international legal system, the fact remains that the fulcrum of that system is still the nation state. It is the major institution governing the affairs of men today. No other institution offers serious competition as the center for law making and for the protection (well or poorly executed) of the interests of individuals. International organizations such as the United Nations have not pushed the state off the power center; religious organizations, the corporation, the tribe and the family are largely subordinate to the state. Political entities such as cities, "states" members of a federal system, commonwealths, trusteeships, mandates and colonies are likewise subordinated to the state.

In a functional sense, the states are the major actors in the international system, the political entities that "operate" the system. Most of them are members of the United Nations; they may be parties in cases before the International Court of Justice, can expect to be accorded immunity in the courts of sister states, can and do prescribe and enforce laws applicable to individuals and institutional aggregates of individuals, send diplomatic representatives to each other, demand from each other protection of their citizens, make protests to sister states over invasions of their territory, territorial seas and airspace, wage war in their-self defense and so forth. These entities in the international community exist for years, even centuries, despite wars, revolutions and changes of government by peaceful or other means.

Up to this point in this book, several major problems of the powers of states have been examined without an exploration of the concept of statehood. For the most part, there has been no need to question whether the institution or entity involved in those cases was a state as that term is understood in international law. Thus, in the Cutting case, p. 116, the United States did not ground its objection to Mexico's extension of its jurisdiction to Mr. Cutting on any notion that Mexico was not a state with general power to legislate. And in Victory-Transport, p. 328, Comisaria General's failure to be accorded

725

immunity did not rest upon Spain's not being a state. But legal controversies do arise in which the concept of statehood becomes significant: a treaty or domestic statute may apply in terms only to states; a rule of positive law may have been articulated in terms of statehood; one or more of the parties may verbalize the controversy in terms of states or statehood. In this chapter, the concept of statehood is examined from the point of view of the international lawyer who must decide specific cases or advise on their resolution.

Analytically, the concept of statehood embraces two very different components: first, the minimum set of facts which must exist before one can say that a state exists; second, the normal legal consequences that follow from the existence of that set of facts.

1. *The question of minimum facts.* The definition of "state" in Section 4 of the Restatement of the Foreign Relations Law of the United States (1965) may be useful: " * * * an entity that has a defined territory and population under the control of a government and that engages in foreign relations." It is instructive to note that this definition does not make reference to any central legal process by which those facts are to be determined. The lack of a central legal process for this purpose stands in contrast to domestic legal systems in which new entities such as "corporations" are created by legal processes: frequently by the issuance of a charter or certificate of incorporation by an official after the applicants have satisfied minimum factual criteria set forth in the relevant statute. In such a domestic system a "corporation" can be defined as an entity that has been created by compliance with that statutorily prescribed process. No such legal process exists in the case of the formation of entities called states.

The nearest analogues are (a) the process by which new members are admitted to the United Nations and (b) the phenomenon known as "recognition" in the international system. These analogues are imperfect. Admission to the United Nations is not automatically accorded to every entity that meets the factual criteria for "statehood", since Article 4 of the Charter lays down additional criteria. As for the process of "recognition," it should be noted that (i) there is no central recognizing authority, for each state in the international community makes its own unilateral determination to recognize a new state (or a new government of an existing state) and (ii) there is disagreement among legal theorists on the question whether the fact of recognition by other states is one of the minimum facts necessary for a new state to come into existence or is merely a neutral acknowledgment of an historical fact, i. e., that a new state has come into existence. (The question of recognition will be explored in Chapter 12.)

2. *The question of the normal legal consequences of statehood.* Once a state exists in the factual sense referred to above (i. e. there exist the elements of territory, population, government and engagement in foreign relations), what normal legal consequences follow

from this? Some of these consequences can be gleaned from an examination of the charters of international organizations. Extracts from the United Nations Charter, the Statute of the International Court of Justice and the Charter of the Organization of American States are set out below.

There are two additional documents of interest in this connection. They appear in the Documentary Supplement: a Draft Declaration on Rights and Duties of States, proposed by the International Law Commission to the General Assembly in 1949, and The Declaration on Principles of International Law Concerning Friendly Relations and Cooperation among States, adopted by the General Assembly.

CHARTER OF THE UNITED NATIONS

Article 2

The Organization and its Members, in pursuit of the Purposes stated in Article 1, shall act in accordance with the following Principles.

1. The Organization is based on the principle of the sovereign equality of all its Members.

* * *

4. All Members shall refrain in their international relations from the threat or use of force against the territorial integrity or political independence of any state, or in any other manner inconsistent with the Purposes of the United Nations.

* * *

6. The Organization shall ensure that states which are not Members of the United Nations act in accordance with these Principles so far as may be necessary for the maintenance of international peace and security.

7. Nothing contained in the present Charter shall authorize the United Nations to intervene in matters which are essentially within the domestic jurisdiction of any state or shall require the Members to submit such matters to settlement under the present Charter; but this principle shall not prejudice the application of enforcement measures under Chapter VII.

Article 3

The original Members of the United Nations shall be the states which, having participated in the United Nations Conference on International Organization at San Francisco, or having previously signed the Declaration by United Nations of 1 January 1942, sign the present Charter and ratify it in accordance with Article 110.

Article 4

1.   Membership in the United Nations is open to all other peace-loving states which accept the obligations contained in the present Charter and, in the judgment of the Organization, are able and willing to carry out these obligations.

Article 31

Any Member of the United Nations which is not a member of the Security Council may participate, without vote, in the discussion of any question brought before the Security Council whenever the latter considers that the interests of that Member are specially affected.

Article 32

Any Member of the United Nations which is not a member of the Security Council or any state which is not a Member of the United Nations, if it is a party to a dispute under consideration by the Security Council, shall be invited to participate, without vote, in the discussion relating to the dispute. The Security Council shall lay down such conditions as it deems just for the participation of a state which is not a Member of the United Nations.

Article 35

1.   Any Member of the United Nations may bring any dispute, or any situation of the nature referred to in Article 34, to the attention of the Security Council or of the General Assembly.

2.   A state which is not a Member of the United Nations may bring to the attention of the Security Council or of the General Assembly any dispute to which it is a party if it accepts in advance, for the purposes of the dispute, the obligations of pacific settlement provided in the present Charter.

* * *

STATUTE OF THE INTERNATIONAL COURT OF JUSTICE

ARTICLE 34—1.   Only states may be parties in cases before the Court.

CHARTER OF THE ORGANIZATION OF AMERICAN STATES

2 U.S.T. 2394, 119 U.N.T.S. 3, as amended February 27, 1967, 21 U.S.T. 607.

Article 1

The American States establish by this Charter the international organization that they have developed to achieve an order of peace and justice, to promote their solidarity, to strengthen their collaboration, and to defend their sovereignty, their territorial integrity and their independence. Within the United Nations, the Organization of American States is a regional agency.

Article 4

All American States that ratify the present Charter are Members of the Organization.

Article 9

States are juridically equal, enjoy equal rights and equal capacity to exercise these rights, and have equal duties. The rights of each State depend not upon its power to ensure the exercise thereof, but upon the mere fact of its existence as a person under international law.

Article 10

Every American State has the duty to respect the rights enjoyed by every other State in accordance with international law.

Article 11

The fundamental rights of States may not be impaired in any manner whatsoever.

Article 12

The political existence of the State is independent of recognition by other States. Even before being recognized, the State has the right to defend its integrity and independence, to provide for its preservation and prosperity, and consequently to organize itself as it sees fit, to legislate concerning its interests, to administer its services, and to determine the jurisdiction and competence of its courts. The exercise of these rights is limited only by the exercise of the rights of other States in accordance with international law.

Article 13

Recognition implies that the State granting it accepts the personality of the new State, with all the rights and duties that international law prescribes for the two States.

Article 14

The right of each State to protect itself and to live its own life does not authorize it to commit unjust acts against another State.

Article 15

The jurisdiction of States within the limits of their national territory is exercised equally over all the inhabitants, whether nationals or aliens.

Article 16

Each State has the right to develop its cultural, political and economic life freely and naturally. In this free development, the State shall respect the rights of the individual and the principles of universal morality.

Article 17

Respect for and the faithful observance of treaties constitute standards for the development of peaceful relations among States. International treaties and agreements should be public.

Article 18

No State or group of States has the right to intervene, directly or indirectly, for any reason whatever, in the internal or external affairs of any other State. The foregoing principle prohibits not only armed force but also any other form of interference or attempted threat against the personality of the State or against its political, economic and cultural elements.

Article 19

No State may use or encourage the use of coercive measures of an economic or political character in order to force the sovereign will of another State and obtain from it advantages of any kind.

Article 20

The territory of a State is inviolable; it may not be the object, even temporarily, of military occupation or of other measures of force taken by another State, directly or indirectly, on any grounds whatever. No territorial acquisitions or special advantages obtained either by force or by other means of coercion shall be recognized.

Article 21

The American States bind themselves in their international relations not to have recourse to the use of force, except in the case of self-defense in accordance with existing treaties or in fulfillment thereof.

Article 22

Measures adopted for the maintenance of peace and security in accordance with existing treaties do not constitute a violation of the principles set forth in Articles 18 and 20.

Minimum facts for statehood not clearly present. It is easy enough to identify entities of long standing as states, and to concede that whatever one normally believes to be the rights and duties of states inheres in those entities. France is a state, without doubt, and has the normal rights and duties of a state. And the same can be said for most of the more than 130 members of the United Nations.

But cases may arise when the factual criteria to support a finding of statehood are either not clearly discernible, or when parties to a controversy take differing views on the existence or non-existence of the facts, or when essential facts clearly do not exist. What, then, are the rights and duties of such an entity? For example, as a result of political compromise it was agreed at the founding of the United Nations that two of the federal states of the Union of Soviet Socialist Republics would be admitted to the United Nations as members: Byelorussian Soviet Socialist Republic and Ukranian Soviet Socialist Republic. This compromise was agreed to by the founders of the United Nations even though these units of the USSR did not freely engage in international relations with the rest of the world.

Thus political entities which did not satisfy the minimum factual criteria for statehood were treated, at least for purposes of membership in the United Nations, as though they were states. Did they thereby become "states"? The international lawyer is not presented with such a question in the abstract. Rather, the question is whether such entities, not fully meeting the factual criteria for statehood, will or will not have one of the legal attributes normally accorded to states, this attribute to be identified as problems arise. Under international law, are the Byelorussian Soviet Socialist Republic and the Ukranian Socialist Soviet Republic proper parties to treaties? See the following list of parties to the Nuclear Test Ban Treaty. Other issues may illustrate the problem. Are these two entities entitled to sovereign immunity in the courts of foreign states, such as the United States? Are such questions to be answered by first determining whether these entities are "states"? Or by an analysis of the purposes which would be served by according these entities in the particular case the particular attribute of statehood in question? If the latter question is the one to be answered, the subsidiary processes of inquiry may be enormously complex.

PARTIES TO THE NUCLEAR TEST BAN TREATY
OF AUGUST 5, 1963

Treaties in Force on Jan. 1, 1972 (United States Department of State)

Ratification, accession or notification of succession deposited by:

Afghanistan
Australia
Austria
Belgium
Bolivia
Botswana

Brazil
Bulgaria
Burma
[Byelorussian   Soviet   Socialist
    Republic] [4]
Canada

4. With reference to the reported signature and deposit of ratification at Moscow by the Byelorussian Soviet Socialist Republic and the Ukrainian Soviet Socialist Republic, the Government of the United States considers those two constituent republics as already covered by the signature and deposit of ratification of the treaty by the Union of Soviet Socialist Republics.

Central African Republic	Korea
Ceylon	Kuwait
Chad	Laos
Chile	Lebanon
China	Liberia
Congo (Kinshasa)	Libya
Costa Rica	Luxembourg
Cyprus	Madagascar
Czechoslovakia	Malawi
Dahomey	Malaysia
Denmark	Malta
Dominican Republic	Mauritania
Ecuador	Mauritius
El Salvador	Mexico
Finland	Mongolia
Gabon	Morocco
Gambia, The	Nepal
[Germany, Dem.Rep.] [8]	Netherlands
Germany, Fed.Rep.	New Zealand
Ghana	Nicaragua
Greece	Niger
Guatemala	Nigeria
Honduras	Norway
Hungary	Panama
Iceland	Peru
India	Philippines
Indonesia	Poland
Iran	Romania
Iraq	Rwanda
Ireland	San Marino
Israel	Senegal
Italy	Sierra Leone
Ivory Coast	Singapore
Japan	South Africa
Jordan	Spain
Kenya	Sudan

8. With reference to the reported signature and deposit of ratification at Moscow by the "German Democratic Republic", attention is called to the following statement in a note of August 16, 1963 from the Government of the United States to the Government of the Union of Soviet Socialist Republics: "In as much as the Government of the United States of America does not recognize the 'German Democratic Republic' as a State or as an entity possessing national sovereignty, it does not accept notice of signature, in behalf thereof. Bearing in mind, however, the purpose of the treaty, the Government of the United States of America notes that the East German regime has signified its intention with respect to the matters dealt with in the treaty". That view was reaffirmed by the Government of the United States in a note of January 24, 1964 to the Government of the Union of Soviet Socialist Republics in connection with reported deposit of ratification.

Swaziland

Sweden

Switzerland

Syrian Arab Rep.

Tanganyika

Thailand

Togo

Trinidad and Tobago

Tunisia

Turkey

Uganda

[Ukrainian   Soviet   Socialist
 Rep.] [4]

Union of Soviet Socialist Republics

United Arab Rep.

United Kingdom

United States

Uruguay

Venezuela

Western Samoa

Yugoslavia

Zambia

Treaty relations with entities not otherwise treated as states.
A number of footnotes to this table have been omitted; these notes
identify the place or places when the parties deposited their accessions or ratifications.   Ratifications and accessions were deposited
in Washington, London and Moscow: sometimes in all those cities,
sometimes in two of them, sometimes in but one.   This means of
recording adherence to the treaty was deliberately chosen instead
of depositing ratifications and accessions at a single place, such as
the Secretariat of the United Nations.   See Chapter 12, p. ——.

The "Holy See" is a party to the Geneva Conventions of 1949
(dealing with prisoners of war, 6 U.S.T. 3316, 75 U.N.T.S. 135;
wounded and sick in armed forces in the field, 6 U.S.T. 3114, 75 U.N.
T.S 31; wounded, sick and shipwrecked members of armed forces at
sea, 6 U.S.T. 3217, 75 U.N.T.S. 85).   "The problem of personality
divorced from territorial base is difficult to isolate because of the
interaction of the Vatican City, the Holy See, and the Roman Catholic
Church."   Brownlie, Principles of Public International Law 59, n. 3
(1966).

Also parties to the Geneva Conventions of 1949 are Korea, the
Democratic Republic of Korea, Germany, the Democratic Republic
of Germany, Vietnam, and the Democratic Republic of Vietnam.

ADMISSION OF RUANDA AND BURUNDI TO
UNITED NATIONS MEMBERSHIP

Higgins, The Development of International Law through the
Political Organs of the United Nations 22 (1963).*

The United Nations role in the coming to nationhood of Ruanda
and Burundi, and their admission to membership at the seventeenth

----

4.   See p. 731.

* From THE DEVELOPMENT OF IN-
TERNATIONAL LAW THROUGH
THE POLITICAL ORGANS OF THE

UNITED NATIONS by Rosalyn Hig-
gins. Published by Oxford University
Press under the auspices of the Royal
Institute of International Affairs.

session of the Assembly, is also of interest in this context. Ruanda-Urundi—originally two separate kingdoms, each headed by a Mwami (King)—came under Belgian administration in 1923, and was a mandate under the League and a trust territory under the United Nations. In 1959 tribal fighting broke out, and in September 1961 a United Nations Commission supervised legislative elections and a referendum on the institution of the Mwami. The result of the vote was a declared preference for two separate states—a republic in Ruanda and a kingdom in Burundi. On 23 February 1962 the General Assembly sent a new commission, which was given certain specific tasks, to Ruanda-Urundi. The Assembly declared at this time its view that the best course for the territory would be to become independent as a single sovereign state. At the end of June 1962 the Assembly discussed the report of the most recent commission. The Commission noted the refusal of the Governments of the two parts to become independent as a single state, and expressed its disappointment with this attitude. The Commission supported the Belgian view that the national forces were in an embryonic state, and that there might well be difficulties in keeping law and order. In Burundi the Government in power had 'indisputable popular support', the Commission reported. It was therefore felt that in spite of the inadequate training of officials and army, the government should prove capable of ensuring law and order in its territory. In Ruanda, where different ethnic groups (primarily the Tutsi aristocracy of warriors and the formerly subservient Hutu majority) had yet to be reconciled, and the question of the future of the Mwami still remained unsettled, the Commission was less hopeful about the ability of the government to maintain order.

Nevertheless, to prevent further tension and violence, it was felt that the scheduled date of 1 July 1962 for independence should be adhered to. But so inadequate were the governmental resources at Burundi's disposal, and so uncertain was the nature and degree of governmental control, that the Commission stated that:

> *   *   *   [T]he granting of independence on July 1 and the simultaneous adoption of a body of measures designed to make up for the country's lack of preparation in the Economic, Social, Educational and other spheres, will be an essential contribution to Burundi's free and independent development.   *   *   *

> The situation in [Ruanda] is not calculated to dispel the many misgivings which the General Assembly has always felt with regard to the conditions in which the people of Ruanda are approaching statehood.

It is quite clear, then, that these two territories, when emerging from trusteeship, lacked at least one of the traditional requirements of statehood. This view is confirmed by an examination of Assembly resolution 1746 (XVI), passed after considering the report of the Commission. This resolution, implicitly acknowledging the difficulties the new Governments will face in keeping law and order, calls for Belgium to withdraw its forces by 1 August 1962—that is to say, a full month after independence. A Soviet amendment to this resolution, which would have called on Belgium to withdraw its troops before independence, was rejected by 24 votes to 46, with 33 abstentions. The Ruanda and Burundi applications for United Nations membership were received soon after their independence, and upon Security Council recommendation they were admitted to the Organization.

The problem is this: that the traditional requirement of a stable and effective government in a territory claiming statehood runs counter to the developments in international law regarding a legal right of self-determination. It is also often at variance with political reality: the anti-colonial pressures upon Western European states, and uneconomic costs for them to remain by force in their colonial possessions, have caused these states in several cases to withdraw from territories which they previously governed before any adequate indigenous system of government has been formed. Are these territories, no longer under colonial rule, to be denied the dignity of statehood, and the rights and duties that follow therefrom? Bearing in mind that such marginal legal problems are invariably graded by policy preference rather than by juridical preference, it can hardly be in the interests of the international community to refuse to acknowledge such territories as states. To do so would be to set up a class of 'territories-in-Limbo', and with it a host of unnecessary problems. It would also seem to involve a visitation on the children of the sins of the fathers. In purely political terms, to adhere rigidly to the requirement of a stable and effective government is in neither the Communist nor the Afro-Asian interest, as these groups perceive it. It becomes more and more doubtful whether it is in the interests of the West either.

Statehood in "United Nations practice". Denial of United Nations membership to a political entity is at best ambiguous on the question of statehood, since Article 4 of the Charter opens membership to "states" that meet other criteria besides statehood. In addition, since admission is not automatic but requires affirmative action by two political bodies, the Security Council and the General Assembly, reasons for non-admission can be both numerous and unspecified. Major political entities that are not members of the United Nations are Switzerland, the two Vietnams, the two Koreas and the two Germanies.

When an entity is admitted to membership in the United Nations before meeting the "standard" minimum criteria for statehood as defined by international law, is one to assume that the members have acted illegally or, at least, "outside" the law? Or are the members saying that the purposes of the Charter may be fulfilled when an entity is well on the way to meeting 'those criteria and that it is thus a "state" as that term is used in Article 4 of the Charter?

What is meant by the "legal right of self-determination" referred to in the extract from Higgins?

THE ARANTZAZU MENDI

England, House of Lords, 1939.
[1939] A.C. 256.

* * *

[The Arantzazu Mendi] was a Spanish ship registered at Bilbao. After that port was captured by General Franco's forces she was requisitioned by the Republican Government. She was then on the high seas, and on August 11, 1937, on her arrival in London, her owners issued a writ in rem for possession, and in pursuance thereof the ship was arrested by the Admiralty Marshal in the Surrey Commercial Docks. To that writ the Republican Government entered a conditional appearance. On March 28, 1938, General Franco issued a decree requisitioning the ship in question and other vessels for public services. On April 11, 1938, the owners' possession action was discontinued, but the vessel still remained under arrest. On April 13 the managing director of the owners made a notarial declaration that he consented to the order of requisition and held the vessel at the disposal of the Nationalist Government. The master made a similar declaration. On the same day the Republican Government issued the present writ, which the Nationalist Government sought to set aside on the ground that it impleaded a foreign sovereign State which was unwilling to submit to the jurisdiction of the Court.

* * *

LORD ATKIN. My Lords, * * * The question is whether the Nationalist Government of Spain represents a foreign sovereign State in the sense that entitles them to immunity from being impleaded in these Courts, and, if so, whether they are impleaded in the action by reason of being in possession of the ship in question. I state the question in that form as being sufficient to dispose of the present case. * * * On the question whether the Nationalist Government of Spain was a foreign sovereign State, Bucknill J. took the correct course of directing a letter, dated May 25, 1938, to be written by the Admiralty Registrar to the Secretary of State for Foreign Affairs, asking whether the Nationalist Government of Spain is recognized by His Majesty's Government as a foreign sovereign State. I pause here to say that not only is this the correct procedure, but that it is the only procedure by which the Court can inform itself of the material fact whether the party sought to be impleaded, or whose property is sought to be affected, is a foreign sovereign State.

* * * The reason is, I think, obvious.   Our State cannot speak with two voices on such a matter, the judiciary saying one thing, the executive another.   Our Sovereign has to decide whom he will recognize as a fellow sovereign in the family of States; and the relations of the foreign State with ours in the matter of State immunities must flow from that decision alone.

The answer of the Foreign Secretary was given in a letter dated May 28, 1938.   After stating that His Majesty's Government recognizes Spain as a foreign sovereign State, and recognizes the Government of the Spanish Republic as the only de jure Government of Spain or any part of it, the letter proceeds:

> 5.   His Majesty's Government recognizes the Nationalist Government as a Government which at present exercises de facto administrative control over the larger portion of Spain.

> 6.   His Majesty's Government recognizes that the Nationalist Government now exercises effective administrative control over all the Basque Provinces of Spain.

> 8.   The Nationalist Government is not a Government subordinate to any other Government in Spain.

My Lords, this letter appears to me to dispose of the controversy. By "exercising de facto administrative control" or "exercising effective administrative control," I understand exercising all the functions of a sovereign government, in maintaining law and order, instituting and maintaining courts of justice, adopting or imposing laws regulating the relations of the inhabitants of the territory to one another and to the Government.   It necessarily implies the ownership and control of property whether for military or civil purposes, including vessels whether warships or merchant ships.   In those circumstances it seems to me that the recognition of a Government as possessing all those attributes in a territory while not subordinate to any other Government in that territory is to recognize it as sovereign, and for the purposes of international law as a foreign sovereign State.   It does not appear to be material whether the territory over which it exercises sovereign powers is from time to time increased or diminished.   In the present case we appear to be dealing with a claim based upon a legislative decree affecting merchant shipping registered at Bilbao in the Basque Provinces, the territory specially designated in the sixth paragraph of the Foreign Office letter.   That the decree therefore emanated from the sovereign in that territory there can be no doubt. There is ample authority for the proposition that there is no difference for the present purposes between a recognition of a State de facto as opposed to de jure.   All the reasons for immunity which are the basis of the doctrine in international law as incorporated into our law exist.   There is the same necessity for reciprocal rights of immunity, the same feeling of injured pride if jurisdiction is sought to be exercised, the same risk of belligerent action if Government property is seized or injured. The non-belligerent State which recognizes two Governments, one de jure and one de facto, will not allow them to transfer their quarrels to the area of the jurisdiction of its municipal Courts.

For these reasons I think that it was established by the Foreign Office letter that the Nationalist Government of Spain at the date of the writ was a foreign sovereign State and could not be impleaded.

*   *   *

*   *   * For these reasons, my Lords, the appeal was, in my opinion, rightly dismissed.

*   *   *

[Other opinions omitted.]

---

1. *Questions.* Lord Atkin says that "the Nationalist Government of Spain at the date of the writ was a foreign sovereign State." Were there, then, two governments of the single territory formerly known as Spain? Or was that territory now divided into two territories, each with its own government? Was it necessary for the court to find that the Nationalist Government was a state in order to reach the result in the case?

2. *Belligerent and insurgent entities.* During the 19th century, processes were developed by which revolutionary groups were treated as something different from merely bands of private persons defying legal governments. As will be discussed in Chapter 19, older ideas about the lawfulness of war have been altered by the Pact of Paris of 1928 and the United Nations Charter; the law of war, civil war, neutrality and intervention has undergone substantial change. Thus the processes of "recognition of belligerency" and "recognition of insurgency" are today more interesting than useful in international practice. They are described in the Reporters' note to Section 94 of the Restatement of the Foreign Relations Law of the United States (1965),* as follows:

> Recognition of belligerency. Recognition of belligerency by a state is an act by which the state, in issuing a declaration of neutrality, asserts that it (a) is neutral in an armed conflict, (b) assumes certain neutral duties toward the parties to the conflict, and (c) has certain rights with respect to trade between its nationals and persons within the territory of the belligerency subject to the rules of international law regarding visitation, search, contraband, blockade, and prize. Recognition of belligerency for an otherwise unrecognized entity or re-

gime may arise from a declaration of neutrality by another state as between a constitutional government and rebels in a civil war. This occurred in the American Civil War when Great Britain recognized the belligerency of the Confederacy, declared its neutrality, and claimed neutral trading rights. It is well-established, as in that instance, that recognition of a rebel's belligerency does not have the effect, standing alone, of committing the second state to treat the rebel regime as the government, or the rebel entity (if one is claimed to have come into existence) as a state.

Recognition of insurgency. In customary practice, recognition of insurgency has considerably less legal significance than recognition of belligerency. Historically, the object of recognition of insurgency by non-contending states was to obtain for rebels carrying on organized military operations the protections given by international law. Recognition of insurgency has often been the first official notice that other states have taken of the eventual possible success of a revolutionary regime.

The more recent tendency has been to rely on ad hoc assurances in revolutionary situations that the basic principles underlying the rules of warfare will be respected. * * *

THE CASE OF KOREA IN THE UNITED NATIONS

United Nations Security Council, Off.Rec., V, No. 24, Aug. 3, 1950; No. 27, Aug. 10, 1950; No. 28, Aug. 11, 1950; No. 31, Aug. 22, 1950; No. 36, Sept. 1, 1950.

[Korea had existed independently for centuries prior to falling under Japanese rule in 1905; it was still under Japanese rule during the Second World War. Allied leaders had first planned to place Korea under a trusteeship after the war, but these plans fell through. As a military matter, Korea was divided at the 38th parallel in 1945, when Japanese troops surrendered to the USSR north of that parallel and to the United States in the south.

The United Nations addressed itself to Korean independence but no way could be found to provide a single government for all Korea. In 1948, elections were held in the south under United Nations supervision and the United Nations General Assembly adopted a resolution declaring that "there has been established a lawful government (the Government of the Republic of Korea) having effective control and jurisdiction over the part of Korea where the Temporary Commission was able to observe and consult and in which the great majority of the people of all Korea reside; that this Government is based on elections which were a valid expression of the free will of the electorate of that part of Korea and which were observed by the Temporary Commission; and that this is the only such Government in Korea." Also in that year, a Democratic People's Republic of Korea was proclaimed by a Supreme People's Assembly. The Republic claimed jurisdiction over all Korea. Elections to the assembly were not observed by the United Nations.

The USSR and the United States announced withdrawal of forces from Korea in 1948 and 1949. The United Nations was informed that the North Koreans had invaded South Korea on June 25, 1950. The Security Council met; the Russians were not present, since they had left the council some months earlier over the refusal of the council to oust the Nationalist Chinese in favor of the Communist Chinese. In a series of resolutions the council recommended "that the members of the United Nations furnish such assistance to the Republic of Korea as may be necessary to repel the armed attack and to restore international peace and security in the area," recommended that the members provide forces to a unified command under the United States, requested the United States to designate the commander of such forces and authorized the "use of the United Nations flag in the course of operations against North Korean forces concurrently with the flags of the various nations participating." [a]

The USSR entered into the debate on the Korean question for the first time when it returned to the council on August 1, 1950, with Mr. Malik then taking his turn in the chair.]

1. *Debate on the Adoption of the Agenda* (No. 24, Aug. 3, 1950).

[The representatives of the following countries were present: China, Cuba, Ecuador, Egypt, France, India, Norway, Union of Soviet Socialist Republics, United Kingdom of Great Britain and Northern Ireland, United States of America and Yugoslavia.

The president of the Security Council, Mr. Malik, had proposed a provisional agenda which included an item entitled "Peaceful Settlement of the Korean Question." The council rejected this item in favor of one proposed by the United States, entitled: "Complaint of Aggression upon the Republic of Korea." In the course of the debate on the adoption of the agenda, the president made a speech, a portion of which appears below.]

THE PRESIDENT (translated from Russian):

* * *

It is clear to anyone with a grain of impartiality that a civil war is in progress in Korea between the North and South Koreans. The military operations between the North and South Koreans are of an internal character; they bear the character of a civil war. There is therefore no justification for regarding these military operations as aggression.

a. These events are more fully described in Higgins, United Nations Peacekeeping, 1946–67, II Asia 153 (1970); Sohn, Cases and Materials on United Nations Law (2d ed. 1967).

Aggression takes place where one State attacks another. The U.S.S.R. Government has taken this line in defining aggression since 1933, when the delegation of the Soviet Union put forward a definition of aggression in the Committee on Security Questions of the Conference for the reduction and limitation of armaments in Geneva. This definition contains instructions for the guidance of international organs which may be called upon to determine the side guilty of attack, the attacking side, in other words, the aggressor.

As is known, this definition of aggression includes such acts as a declaration of war by a State against another State; invasion of a territory by the armed forces of another State even without a declaration of war; the invasion of the territory of one State by the armed forces of another State and so forth.

According to this definition no political, strategic or economic considerations can justify aggression. Nor can the denial that a territory which is attacked has the specific attributes of statehood serve as a justification for an attack. Nor can a revolutionary or counter-revolutionary movement, or a civil war, serve as a justification, or the establishment or the maintenance of a particular political, economic or social order.

* * *

United States armed forces have invaded Korean territory, although without a formal declaration of war. The above-mentioned definition qualifies such action as aggression. United States land, sea and air forces are bombing Korean territory and attacking Korean vessels and aircraft. According to the above-mentioned definition, such acts are acts of aggression, and the United States is the attacking State—the aggressor. United States land, sea and air forces have landed on Korean territory and are carrying on military action there against the Korean people which is at present in a state of domestic civil war. Such acts constitute aggression on the part of the United States. The United States has established a naval blockade of the Korean coast and ports. Such acts constitute aggression in accordance with the definition referred to.

* * *

Thus if the action taken by the United States in Korea is considered in the light of the above definition of aggression, it is clear beyond question that the United States Government has interfered in an internal conflict in Korea between two groups in a single State and has thereby undertaken an act of aggression upon the Korean people.

As regards the war between the North and South Koreans, it is a civil war and therefore does not come under the definition of aggression, since it is a war, not between two States, but between two parts of the Korean people temporarily split into two camps under two separate authorities.

The conflict in Korea is thus an internal conflict. Consequently rules relating to aggression are just as inapplicable to the North and South Koreans as the concept of aggression was inapplicable to the northern and southern states of America, when they were fighting a civil war for the unification of their country. We know that the role of aggressor at that time was played by Great Britain, which attempted to intervene in that civil war and to prevent the unification of the North and South in the United States. Similarly, the United Kingdom is now, together with the United States, intervening in the civil war in Korea in the attempt to impede the unification of that country.

A similar situation arises in China also where, as we know, the struggle between the Chiang Kai-shek group and the national liberation movement of the north has not been regarded as aggression, and foreign Powers have accordingly abstained from intervention in this domestic conflict, in this civil war.

All this goes to show that the only aggressors in Korea are those Powers which are maintaining their forces on Korean territory and are intervening in the struggle between the North and South Koreans, thereby extending the sphere of military operations.

Hence we have in Korea on the one hand an internal conflict between the North and South Koreans—a civil war—and on the other hand the armed intervention of the Government of the United States in this internal Korean civil war in the form of armed aggression, which falls completely within the definition of aggression contained in the declaration on aggression, which was adopted in May 1933 by the League of Nations Committee on Security Questions, on which seventeen States were represented, including the United States of America.

As is known, the United Nations Charter also directly prohibits intervention by the United Nations in the domestic affairs of any State when the conflict is an internal one between two groups within a single State and a single nation. Accordingly, the United Nations Charter provides for intervention by the Security Council only in events of an international rather than of an internal nature.

That is the essence of the Korean question and of the United States armed aggression against the Korean people.

Thus the peoples of the whole world and the United Nations are at present confronted with open armed aggression in Korea on the part of the United States Government and with attempts by the United States to involve the United Nations in that aggression.

* * *

2. *Complaint of Aggression upon the Republic of Korea.* (No. 27, Aug. 10, 1950).

[The agenda having been adopted, Mr. Malik proposed that the council invite representatives of both North and South Korea to the council. The Chinese representative raised a point of order, namely that the council had previously invited a representative of South Korea and should not vote on that matter again. In the course of the debate on the question of invitation of representatives, the following statements were made.]

Mr. Austin (United States of America):

* * * During the recent world war, the leading allies, including the U.S.S.R., pledged the freedom and independence of Korea. By agreement between the United States and the Soviet Union at the time of Japan's surrender, the 38th parallel was selected as an administrative boundary line for convenience in accepting the surrender of Japanese troops. That was a temporary, military, division; it was not a permanent, political, division. It was interpreted differently, however, by the U.S.S.R. Government, which proceeded to turn the 38th parallel into a hard and fast frontier. In an effort to correct that obvious violation of war-time pledges made to the Korean people, my Government has consistently urged the abolition of the military frontier and the creation of a democratic and independent government of unified Korea.

In 1947, in 1948 and in 1949, the General Assembly by an overwhelming majority urged the same things. It has maintained in Korea for nearly three years a Commission charged with the completion of those tasks. The Commission has been denied access to North Korea—that is, that part of Korea north of the 38th parallel—by the Soviet Union as the occupying Power. South of that parallel, the United Nations Commission on Korea has supervised two elections, certified the establishment of a democratic government and verified the withdrawal of United States occupation forces. The General Assembly itself, by its resolution 195 (III), accepted the Government of the Republic of Korea as the only valid and lawful government in Korea. Many Members of the United Nations have recognized the Republic of Korea, whose admission to the United Nations was blocked by the U.S.S.R. veto.

This summary of political history should make it clear what Government has blocked the unity and independence of Korea, what Government has established a puppet government in its zone of military control, and what Government has defied the recommendations of the United Nations.

* * *

If the efforts of the United Nations had not been blocked by the Soviet Union and the authorities in North Korea, then Korea today would be free and independent. Below the line of the 38th parallel, the light of day has shone. The United Nations observers could watch and report. They could tell us what was happening—the faults of a new nation, as well as its virtues. They could certify to us that democracy was having its struggles, but that it was succeeding.

Above that line, all was darkness. The arbitrary action of one great Power—and one great Power alone—kept the United Nations observers from fulfilling, above that line, the task assigned to them by the General Assembly. That great Power was free to pick and choose its instruments as it wished, to carry out its imperialist purposes in North Korea.

* * *

On 25 June, the mists that for five years had covered North Korea parted. Out of the fog came a mighty military machine to launch an unexpected and unprovoked attack on the Republic of Korea.

Although the representative of the Soviet Union did not feel able to attend the meetings of the Security Council called when Korea was invaded, he must have read the reports submitted to us by the United Nations Commission on Korea.

On 24 June, the day before the attack, the observers for the Commission reported that their "principal impression" was that the Republican army "is organized entirely for defence and is in no condition to carry out attack on large scale against forces of north" [S/1518]. The Commission itself, composed of representatives of Australia, China, El Salvador, France, India, the Philippines and Turkey, found on 26 June [S/1507] that "judging from actual progress of operations, Northern régime is carrying out well-planned, concerted, and full-scale invasion of South Korea".

* * *

Subsequent military developments have proved to anyone with a knowledge of warfare that the invasion by the North Koreans was carefully planned and had been prepared over a long period of time. I am sure the representative of the U.S.S.R. will agree that it must have taken many months to train the drivers and gunners who are now massacring their fellow countrymen and defying the United Nations.

In the face of the unprovoked aggression launched by the North Koreans, the Security Council met within twenty-four hours of the attack and adopted [473rd meeting] a resolution calling for the immediate cessation of hostilities, for the withdrawal of the North Korean forces to the 38th parallel, and for the rendering of "every assistance" by all Members to the United Nations "in the execution of this resolution". That was addressed to all Members.

As the attack continued, the President of the United States, at noon on 27 June, announced support for this resolution by ordering the United States air and sea forces to assist the troops of the Korean Government. On the same day, 27 June, the Security Council recommended [474th meeting] that all Members of the United Nations should furnish such aid to the Republic of Korea as might be necessary to repel the attack and restore international peace and security in the area. Since that time, fifty-three Members have supported the Security Council's action to restore peace in Korea. Many of them have offered, and some have already sent, military support or other types of assistance. All are working and fighting together under the United Nations flag and under a Unified Command in a great common effort to put down lawless aggression. To call such a United Nations function "aggréssion" is like calling aid to a peaceful citizen, attacked by a thief in the night, aggression.

Yet the representative of the Soviet Union obstructs all efforts of the Security Council to perform its peacemaking functions by speeches charging the United States as the aggressor.

Those are the facts of recent Korean history.

*   *   *

3. *Complaint of Aggression upon the Republic of Korea, Continued* (No. 28, Aug. 11, 1950).

*   *   *

Sir Gladwyn Jebb (United Kingdom): It is, I fear, only too true that the refusal of our President to admit the representative of the Republic of Korea and his insistence on inviting a representative of the North Korean authorities raise most important and, indeed, basic matters of principle, some of which, but not all, have already been alluded to in the long debate which we have now had on this subject.

. . .

The Soviet Union representative's basic intention, as I understand it, is based on the premise that what we are dealing with in Korea is a civil war. He proceeds to argue that, as is indeed natural, there are two sides to most civil wars and, therefore, two sides to this one. Consequently, if we invite the representative of one side to be present, we are bound in logic and in equity—and, indeed, I think he said in accordance with the dictates of common sense—to invite the representative of the other side also.

This would all be very obvious were it not for the fact that the Soviet Union representative, in his desire to impress public opinion with the rightness of his cause, has omitted to draw attention to the fact that the Government of the Republic of Korea has already been declared the lawful government by the United Nations; that United Nations observers were stationed on its de facto northern frontier; and that, therefore, the whole State was, as it were, existing under the mantle of this great international Organization.

The Government of the Korean Republic was, however, attacked—and I shall not here proceed to demonstrate that it was attacked or to counter Soviet propaganda to the effect that it was Mr. Dulles and Mr. Muccio who attacked the Northern Koreans first—incidently I must apologize for omitting to refer to Mr. Muccio previously, since clearly Mr. Muccio's presence doubled the total number of the interventionist force—since that is so obviously absurd that it is hard to think that it can be swallowed even by the automata who listen to the Moscow radio. It was attacked, I say, by soldiers coming under the authority of a rival Korean government, not acceptable to the United Nations, and established at Pyongyang. It is quite true that the soldiers I refer to were Koreans, and therefore were, so to speak, blood brothers of the people whom they attacked; but to argue that this fact in itself constitutes a civil war, or that it necessarily in itself puts both sides on an equal footing, is patent nonsense. The President made what he thought were some very telling observations regarding the American Civil War, but they would only have been relevant if he had gone on to show that in 1861 either the northern states or the southern had been recognized by an international organization, which he could not do for the simple reason that no international organization existed at that time.

* * *

Quite apart from this, there is absolutely no reason to suppose that wars between people of the same race, even if they do not involve a government which has been set up under the aegis of the United Nations, are necessarily exempt from the decisions of the Security Council. A civil war in certain circumstances might well, under Article 39 of the Charter, constitute a "threat to the peace", or even a "breach of the peace", and if the Security Council so decided, there would be nothing whatever to prevent its taking any action it liked in order to put an end to the incident, even if it should involve two or more portions of the same international entity. Indeed, paragraph 7 of Article 2 of the Charter so provides. This reads:

"Nothing contained in the present Charter shall authorize the United Nations to intervene in matters which are essentially within the domestic jurisdiction of any State or shall require the Members to submit such matters to settlement under the present Charter; but this principle shall not prejudice the application of enforcement measures under Chapter VII."

It will be seen that the last few words make it quite clear that the United Nations has full authority to intervene actively in the internal affairs of any country if this is necessary for the purpose of enforcing its decisions as regards the maintenance of international peace and security. I do honestly hope that, for the reasons given, we shall hear no more of this "civil war" argument from the mouth of the Soviet Union spokesman.

It is equally true that, under the Charter, the Security Council might be unlikely to make a recommendation or a decision under Article 39 in regard to another such incident as the present, since such action could and no doubt would be vetoed by the Soviet Union. But when the Security Council very properly decided that the Government of the Republic of Korea should be defended against a brutal attack, and decided on the appropriate measures to that effect, it did so unanimously, and no permanent member present at this table objected in the slightest degree, or even made any reservations. On the contrary, they were all horrified at the outrage which had occurred, and the

Council machinery therefore worked smoothly and easily and in entire accord with the purposes and principles of the Charter. * * *

* * *

4. *Complaint of Aggression upon the Republic of Korea, Continued* (No. 31, Aug. 22, 1950).

Sir Gladwyn Jebb (United Kingdom):

* * *

Quite apart from this, however, the "civil war" argument simply does not make sense on general grounds. First of all, you divide a State into two, then you organize a special Government in one part of it, not allowing anybody else to see how this Government is formed or what it is doing. You give it full governmental powers and you recognize it, even though most States have recognized the other Government. Then the Government organized in this way, possessing de facto authority over half the territory, attacks the lawful Government of the other half which has been set up under the international protection of the United Nations. Nobody, however, is allowed to interfere with this process on the grounds that it is a "civil war". The result, of course, is that, in defiance of international authority, you get control of the whole country and you get what you want. It is quite easy to think of other cases in which this interesting, if rather sinister, theory might be applied.

* * *

5. *Complaint of Aggression upon the Republic of Korea, Continued* (No. 36, Sept. 1, 1950).

[The president of the council, Mr. Malik, neither invited a representative of South Korea to the council nor put to a vote his proposal to invite a representative of North Korea. At the beginning of the next month, the presidency of the council rotated to Sir Gladwyn Jebb, who immediately invited the South Korean representative to sit at the council table. This action was upheld by the council (the USSR opposed). A draft resolution by the USSR to invite representatives of North and South Korea was interpreted by the president (the council agreeing) to relate only to the question of the representation of North Korea. The USSR draft resolution was rejected. Prior to the vote, the following statements were made.]

Sir Benegal N. Rau (India): * * *

* * *

It has been urged that Article 32 of the Charter requires us to invite the North Korean representative. If this contention were correct, not only must the North Korean representative be invited to our future discussions, but any past proceedings to which he was not invited would stand vitiated as a violation of the Charter. This, to my mind, is a serious matter. Some of these past proceedings have been endorsed by India, and it is therefore necessary for me to examine the contention carefully. I shall proceed to do so even at the risk of being tedious.

The relevant portion of Article 32 provides that any State which is not a Member of the United Nations, "if it is a party to a dispute under consideration by the Security Council", must be invited to participate without vote in the discussion relating to the dispute. So three conditions must be satisfied if the Article is to apply to the present case: North Korea must be a State; so must South Korea; and the Security Council must be considering a dispute between the two. But if North Korea and South Korea are separate States, the contention that the conflict between them is a civil war is untenable. That is by the way. There is, however, a more fundamental flaw in the argument: what we are discussing at present with respect to Korea is not a dispute. If I may use a hackneyed analogy of which some of the members of the Council may be rather tired, when the police are quelling a riot or the fire brigade is putting out a fire, they are not considering a dispute; they are taking action to remove a serious danger.

So, here, at this moment, we are not investigating or considering a dispute; we are in the midst of enforcement action to suppress a dangerous breach of the peace. The two things are quite distinct. The Security Council has, in fact, a dual function under the Charter: it investigates disputes under Chapter VI of the Charter, and it takes action with respect to breaches of the peace under Chapter VII. It is only when it is considering disputes that Article 32 of the Charter applies. The wording, if I may repeat it, makes this clear: "if it is a party to a dispute under consideration by the Security Council".

Of course, when the enforcement action that is now in progress has been concluded, there may supervene a dispute, and at that stage Article 32 may come into operation, if we regard North Korea and South as separate States.

In his recent book on The Law of the United Nations, Professor Kelsen states: "A 'dispute' exists in the relation between two States only if the one has addressed a claim to the other State and if the latter has refused to comply with this claim. When a State attacks another State without previously having demanded anything from the attacked State and without this State's having refused to comply with a demand of the other, there exists a conflict between the two States, but no 'dispute'."

Therefore it seems to me that Article 32 of the Charter has no application to the present situation at this stage. The Council will remember that when we invited the representative of the Republic of Korea on 25 June and subsequent dates, we did so not under Article 32 of the Charter, but under rule 39 of our provisional rules of procedure.[a] This, I hope, is not a small legal point. I think there is more in it than that.

a. Rule 39 provides: "The Security Council may invite members of the secretariat or other persons, whom it considers competent for the purpose, to supply it with information or to give other assistance in examining matters within its competence."

From time to time, we receive reports from the Unified Command describing the progress of the campaign in Korea. I am not a military expert myself but it is conceivable that the contents of these reports, and any disclosures in the course of our discussions upon those reports, might be of value to the enemy. So far as I am aware, no representative of the United Nations is allowed to participate in the discussions conducted by the North Korean authorities on the Korean campaign.

Briefly, what we are engaged in at the present moment is not the discussion of the Korean dispute, but, rather of the Korean campaign. In the view of my Government, the question of hearing the representative of the North Korean authorities cannot arise until the campaign is over; that is to say, until at least hostilities have ceased and withdrawal of the North Korean forces has been agreed upon. I shall therefore have to vote against the proposal that their representative should be invited to the Council table at this stage— and I emphasize the words "at this stage".

Mr. Malik (Union of Soviet Socialist Republics) (translated from Russian): * * *

It is impossible to agree that Article 32 of the Charter is applicable only in the consideration of questions relating to Chapter VI. Article 40, in Chapter VII, provides that in case of international conflict, the Security Council should not rush headlong into that conflict, that it should not make the situation more complicated or allow aggression or military action to spread. It specifically states: "In order to prevent an aggravation of the situation, the Security Council may, before making the recommendations or deciding upon the measures provided for in Article 39, call upon the parties concerned to comply with such provisional measures as it deems necessary or desirable."

Article 41 states: "The Security Council may decide what measures not involving the use of armed force are to be employed to give effect to its decisions".

If the Council considers and decides on such measures, then where in Chapter VII or elsewhere is it said that the representative of the party which, rightly or wrongly, legitimately or illegitimately, is accused of aggression, has no right to be present at the meetings of the Council? Would the jurists show me a sentence, a word, a provision or an Article in the Charter to that effect? There are no such provisions in the Charter and when questions falling within Chapters VI and VII are discussed, the representative of the party against which charges of aggression have been brought must attend in order that the Council may better clarify the facts of the dispute and take all the necessary measures to halt aggression and to prevent the war from spreading.

Was anything done here to that end? No. On 25 June, when the conflict which had arisen in Korea was discussed, no decision was taken as to what Article of the Charter should be applied and on what legal basis action should be taken. The representative of North Korea was not admitted to the meeting. No jurist could have explained, or can explain, on what grounds he was voting against inviting the representative of North Korea; yet when the question of not admitting the representative of North Korea was discussed on 25 June, no decision was taken regarding the application of sanctions, even of illegal ones. I am not even speaking about the illegal character of that resolution. Any truly objective jurist will be obliged to state that the decisions on the Korean question were taken in violation of the Charter, without the participation of two permanent members of the Security Council who were unable to attend the meeting for reasons which are well known, and at a time when one of the permanent members of the Security Council, relying on the support of a group of members of the Council, was blocking the admission to the Council of the legitimate representative of China. This is common knowledge.

What happened on 25 June? On that day the Security Council adopted by a majority the illegal decision to refuse to admit a representative of North Korea to the Security Council meeting. On what grounds was this done, on what legal basis? No objective jurist would find a justification for such a decision. * * *

Lastly, let us take a document such as the definition of aggression proposed by the USSR delegation as early as May 1933 in the Committee on Security Questions of the League of Nations and taken by that Committee as a basis. It contains a specific provision that the fact that a territory has not been recognized as a State cannot be used as a justification for aggression against that State. I can cite the exact words of that document. It states that a people's political, economic or cultural backwardness, or the alleged shortcomings of its administration, may not be used to justify any act of aggression. Nor may the fact that a territory has no distinct attributes of statehood or that its possession of such attributes is denied.

In the present case, the jurist invokes the argument that since there is no State of North Korea, North Korea does not exist at all. This, however, is absurd. There is a North Korea which has nine million or more inhabitants, its own authorities, an army—and a very good one at that, as events have shown; for that army has been able to deal not only with the mercenary troops of the Syngman Rhee regime of South Korea, but also with the troops of the United States aggressor who has invaded foreign territory. How then can it be denied that we are dealing with a people and their authorities? What jurist will take it upon himself to prove the contrary—that there is nothing and no one there?

In any case, the document on the definition of aggression, on the basis of which the organs called upon to consider international conflicts must determine who is the aggressor, and who the victim of aggression, states plainly that the fact that a specific territory is not a State, or lacks the distinguishing signs of a State, cannot be used to justify aggression.

Thus no legal tricks will help in this case. There is a North Korea with a population of from nine to ten million, if not more, a government, an army, local and central authorities and legislative organs. What right has the Security Council to examine the Korean question without inviting and hearing the representatives of those authorities? Only because the United States Government wishes it? That is no reason, and cannot be used as a legal justification, as a ground for not inviting the representative of North Korea. * * *

Commentary and questions. The foregoing extracts, lengthy as they are, are but a small trickle in the torrent of words emanating from the Security Council during the debate on the agenda and the question of representation. The formal issues before the council were the matters of agenda and invitation of representatives. The more pervasive issue was the question of the military operation of the United Nations, although this issue was not precisely focussed by draft resolutions before the council.

What was the relevance of the arguments on Korean statehood on the formal issues of agenda and representation? On the issues of the legality of the United Nations military operations? Analytically Korea could be characterized as one state or two states. Or as no state. Is "characterization" the beginning or the end of the inquiry?

If the legal problem before the council is not to be phrased as "Is Korea a single state?", then what is the problem? By what legal criteria should it be solved?

IN RE HARSHAW CHEMICAL CO.'S PATENT

England, Comptroller of Patents, 1964.
41 Int'l L.Rep. 15 (1970).

THE FACTS. This was an application for an extension of their patent by the Harshaw Chemical Company, the registered proprietors of letters patent relating to a method of bright nickel plating. The application was made under section 24(1) of the Patents Act, 1949, which provides:

"If upon application made by a patentee in accordance with this section the court or the comptroller is satisfied that the patentee as such has suffered loss or damage * * * by reason of hostilities between His Majesty and any foreign state, the court or comptroller may by order extend the term of the patent subject to such restrictions, conditions * * * as may be specified in the order * * *"

Section 24(8) of the Act provides:

"No order shall be made under this section on the application of—

(a) a person who is a subject of such a foreign state as is mentioned in subsection (1) of this section;"

The application was opposed by three other companies.

The applicants asked for an extension of six years based entirely on the shortage of nickel between 1950 and 1957 which they alleged was caused by the Korean war. The opponents contended that the shortage of nickel was not occasioned "by reason of hostilities between His Majesty and any foreign state", and asked that the Comptroller of Patents or one of the opponents should inquire from the Foreign Office as to whether there were any hostilities with a foreign State. The Foreign Office's reply to an inquiry by the Comptroller was in these terms:—

"The United Kingdom was one of the States which as Members of the United Nations participated in the hostilities against the so-called Democratic People's Republic of Korea. These hostilities lasted from June 25, 1950, to July 27, 1953. The decision to send United Kingdom troops to Korea was taken on July 26, 1950; these troops arrived in Korea on August 29, 1950.

The Democratic People's Republic of Korea was not recognized by either His late Majesty's Government or Her Majesty's Government as an independent sovereign State at any time during the above-mentioned period of hostilities, and it has not subsequently been so recognized by Her Majesty's Government."

The remaining facts and the arguments presented by counsel appear from the decision of the Comptroller.

Held: that the application must fail. The patentee had not shown a loss within section 24 because the Democratic People's Republic of Korea was not a "State" recognized by Her Majesty's Government at any relevant time.

The Comptroller stated the facts substantially as set out above * * * [A portion of the decision by the Comptroller appears below.]

Mr. Price argued [for the applicants] that the absence of recognition did not alter the fact that the Democratic People's Republic is a "state". A "state" is merely a country with certain sovereignty, as, for example, a member state of the U.S.A. The Foreign Office statement admits the existence of the Democratic People's Republic as an entity, and it is clear from the reference thereto in Whittaker's Almanac that it is just as much a "state" as the Republic of Korea.

Mr. Ford, on the other hand, submitted [for two of the opponents] that the reference in section 24(8) of the Act to "a person who is a subject of such a foreign state as is mentioned in subsection (1) of this section" necessarily infers that a "state" within the meaning of section 24 must have subjects. This in turn introduces the concept of sovereignty, which the Democratic People's Republic does not possess because it has not been recognised as an "independent sovereign state". Mr. Ford referred to International Law by L. Oppenheim, Volume I, seventh edition, page 145, in support of his contention that recognition is a declaration, on the part of the recognising States, that a foreign community or authority is in possession of the necessary qualifications of statehood, these qualifications being the existence of a people, a country, a government and a sovereign government. It followed that in the absence of recognition there was no evidence that the facts are such that the Democratic People's Republic of Korea comprised a state. Its name implied a claim for authority over the whole state of Korea whereas there existed also a government in South Korea representing the "Republic of Korea". The necessary qualification of sovereignty was therefore not satisfied.

Later, Mr. Ford referred to Halsbury's Laws of England, third edition, volume 15, paragraph 612, on page 336, as the authority that the courts take notice of the existence and titles of foreign states which are recognised by the British Government as independent, and, as appears from the footnote (r), that the existence and status of foreign states not so recognised are not noticed by the judges.

Dr. White [for the third opponent company] supported Mr. Ford's arguments and stressed that the applicants had failed to supply any evidence to prove that the hostilities in Korea were between the Crown and a foreign state. He submitted that section 24 must be construed strictly and that it would be wrong for the Comptroller to hold that the Democratic People's Republic was a state under section 24 in the face of the Foreign Office statement. The history of events shows that Korea was a single unitary state divided in itself, and the United Nations intervened in Korea to restore order and unify the country. Crown intervention in a civil war does not qualify for loss under section 24.

In reply, Mr. Price argued that the Democratic People's Republic clearly possessed all the qualifications of statehood, and it was not necessary for sovereignty to be complete for a "state" to exist. On recognition, the concern in the present case is with facts and not the niceties of international diplomacy. The acceptance of North Korea is evidenced by the references in the Post Office Guide on the sending of letters to North or South Korea, and the Comptroller can act accordingly under section 24 without prejudicing the position of the Crown.

In deciding on this question I am impressed with the force of Dr. White's argument that section 24(1) must be construed strictly. * * Whilst none of the cases mentioned have any direct bearing on the present issue, nevertheless I agree that they point to a strict interpretation of the wording of the relevant sections of the Act. As I see it, therefore, I should regard the word "state" in section 24(1) as meaning a state which exists manifestly with all the qualifications required for statehood in international law, and not just any entity, whatever its status. Indeed, if it was the intention of section 24 to provide relief for loss sustained by reason of any hostilities involving the Crown, then presumably the section would have been worded accordingly. It does not appear to me that such was the intention and I take the view that the reference to "state" in the wording of section 24 is intended to limit the scope of the section. To be effective, therefore, the word "state" must be construed rigidly, and to be consistent it must be defined in accordance with established law as implying independence and sovereignty. This appears to me to follow also from the reference in section 24(8) to a person who is "a subject of such a foreign state", because unless such significance is attached to the word "state" then considerable difficulty may arise in deciding on questions under section 24(8), * * *

Having reached the conclusion that the word "state" must be construed rigidly, then as I see it, on the authority to which Mr. Ford referred, I cannot ignore the dictum that the courts cannot take judicial notice of the existence and status of "states" which are not recognised by the British Government as independent. The footnote (r) to paragraph 612 of Halsbury's Laws of England, which I have already mentioned, refers to a number of cases in which this dictum has been followed and in which it is established that the proper course on any question of the status of a foreign country is to ascertain the facts from H.M. Government, and that the court is bound to act on the information given to it through the proper department. As Lord Atkin stated in the case of The Arantzazu Mendi [1939] A.C. 256, H.L.; at page 264,

> Our state cannot speak with two voices on such a matter, the judiciary saying one thing, the executive another.

This being so, then, in the light of the Foreign Office statement, I am bound to decide that the Democratic People's Republic of Korea, or, as it is more commonly referred to, North Korea, cannot be regarded at any relevant time as comprising a "state" within the meaning of section 24 of the Act. * * *

However, in view of the submissions made at the hearing on the necessary qualifications of statehood and particularly the submission of Mr. Price that the absence of recognition by the Crown does not alter the fact that the Democratic People's Republic of Korea is a "state", it is perhaps desirable that I should also state my views on the matter in the light of these submissions.

The applicants have not adduced any evidence to show that the Democratic People's Republic of Korea constitutes a "state" despite the fact that they have been aware of the Foreign Office statement since the end of May, 1963. Of course, the facts on Korea as set out in Whittaker's Almanac are within recent memory, and it may be that the applicants feel that these known facts are sufficient to prove the existence of the Democratic People's Republic as a "state", but in my view the contrary is the case. As I see it, since the end of Japanese rule in 1945, the country of Korea has been a focal point of East-West conflict, with the country divided into North and South areas. Prior to the outbreak of hostilities in June, 1950, each area had set up its own government and constitution, with South Korea calling itself the "Republic of Korea", and North Korea "The Democratic People's Republic of Korea". It may fairly be said that the Republic of Korea, which was formally inaugurated in August, 1948 and has been recognised by Her Majesty's Government and by most other countries except the U.S.S.R. and her satellites, came into existence in accordance with a resolution passed by the General Assembly of the United Nations in November, 1947. On the other hand, the Democratic People's Republic was set up in September, 1948 under the auspices of the U.S.S.R. and has been recognised by the U.S.S.R. and her satellites.

The names adopted by the two areas each suggest a claim to represent the whole territory of Korea, and certainly the aim of the United Nations at all times has been to bring about the unification of the country. There is but one Korean people and, for reasons which are of no concern in these proceedings, this people is divided among itself. It is significant in this respect that the government of the Republic of Korea did not accept the armistice agreement, signed by the U. N. Commander-in-Chief and the commanders of the North Korean forces in July, 1953, wherein the line of division between North and South Korea remained in the neighbourhood of the 38th parallel.

It seems to me, therefore, that the hostilities in Korea were more in the nature of a civil war rather than a war between two "states". The United Nations intervened on the side of the government of the Republic of Korea, which had come into being under United Nations sponsorship and which was recognised by the majority of the member states of the United Nations including the United Kingdom. The armistice of 1953 brought about the cessation of hostilities, and in 1954 the Geneva Conference discussed Korea with a view to agreeing measures for reunifying the country. No agreement was reached, but the fact that such discussion took place suggests to me that, up to then at least, the Democratic People's Republic was considered to be no more than a "belligerent power". On the facts available to me nothing has happened since to so consolidate the division of Korea as would confer the status of statehood on the so-called Democratic People's Republic. In my view, therefore, the Democratic People's Republic has not at any time been a "state" for the purposes of section 24.

Having reached this conclusion, it is unnecessary for me to decide the second question, namely, whether the hostilities in North Korea were "between His Majesty and any foreign state". I think I should say, however, that if, contrary to this conclusion, I had formed the opinion that the Democratic People's Republic could be regarded as a state for the purposes of section 24. I would have had no hesitation in concluding that the Korean hostilities were hostilities within the meaning of section 24. *   *   *

Questions. The comptroller feels bound by the fact that North Korea had not been recognized by the Foreign Office. Is the "constitutional" question of the relationship between the comptroller and the Foreign Office relevant to the question presented in the application? He also apparently decided on his own analysis of Korean history that the hostilities in Korea were more like a civil war than a war between two "states." By what criteria did he make that determination?

In the opinion that follows, the same issue was before a court five years later, on application of a different patentee. Although the court doubted its own jurisdiction in the peculiar procedural posture of the case, it nevertheless offered its opinion on the merits. By what criteria did the court arrive at a different conclusion from the comptroller? Is "statehood" to be determined by international legal principles? Why did the English Parliament exclude all but hostilities between "states" from the operation of the provisions of Section 24(1) of the Patents Act? Does either opinion consider that question? Should it have?

IN RE AL–FIN CORPORATION'S PATENT

Chancery Division, 1969.
[1969] 2 W.L.R. 1405.

ORIGINATING SUMMONS.

Patentees, Al-Fin Corporation, took out this originating summons in connection with an application for extension of their patent No. 689,129 for the determination of whether on a true construction of section 24 of the Patents Act, 1949, the democratic Peoples Republic of Korea in the events which happened was a foreign state within the meaning of subsection 1 of section 24 at the time of the Korean war.   *   *   *

*   *   *   An affidavit of Mr. Victor Frank dated April 24, 1968, set out a factual account of the history of Korea over the relevant period. By paragraphs 22 to 25:

22.   Elections for local People's Committees were held in November, 1946; only one list of candidates, all members of the National Democratic Front, was presented, and, it was announced, gained 97 per cent. of the votes cast. These local People's Committees appointed a Convention of People's Committees which met in 1947 in Pyongyang. This convention set up a further body, a "Supreme People's Assembly," which drafted and, in April 1948, approved a constitution based on that of the U.S.S.R. Elections for the new Assembly were held in August 1948—360 of the 572 seats being nominally for South Korea, where clandestine "elections" were held by Communist canvassers. In September 1948, the formation of a "people's Democratic Republic of Korea" was announced, and, in October, the Soviet union accorded it diplomatic recognition, the other communist countries following suit. No other members of the United Nations accorded the Government diplomatic recognition. The Soviet Government announced that it had withdrawn all its forces from North Korea by January 1, 1949. Thus, two Governments had been established, one in the South, the other in the North. Both Governments claimed to be Governments of the whole of Korea, and each of them denied its rival any legal or constitutional validity.

23.   When the Russian forces withdrew in 1949 they left behind them in North Korea a government which, though not wholly subject to the direction of the Kremlin, was nonetheless bound both economically and politically to the will of the Soviet Government. The North Korean military forces were built up with Russian arms (and arms captured from the Japanese), by Russian instructors, the members of the forces being conscripted from 1949 onwards by the effective Government of the country. It should be emphasised that between 1949 and 1950 the Government of North Korea exercised effective rule over the area of Korea defined already, that its rule was accepted by the population as being the sole source of civil and military authority in the said area, and that the government entered into diplomatic relations with other sovereign states which recognised its existence.

24.   On June 25, 1950, North Korean forces launched a large scale offensive against the territory of the Republic of Korea. On the same day, the Security Council held a meeting which, in the absence of the Soviet representative, passed a resolution describing the North Korean invasion as a breach of the peace and calling upon

all U.N. member-states "to render every assistance to the United Nations and to refrain from giving assistance to the North Korean authorities." Two days later, in view of an imminent collapse of South Korean resistance, the Security Council adopted a resolution which recommended "that the members of the United Nations furnish such assistance to the Republic of Korea as may be necessary to repel the armed attack and to restore international peace and security in the area." On June 29, 1950, the North Korean authorities rejected the decisions of the U.N. Security Council as "unlawful." In this attitude North Korea was supported by the U.S.S.R. and all other Soviet-orbit states. An overwhelming majority of U.N. member-states, however, endorsed the council's actions. Immediate and substantial naval and air support was furnished by the British Commonwealth. On June 28, the United Kingdom Prime Minister, Mr. Attlee, announced that ships of the Royal Navy then in Japanese waters would be sent to aid the Republic of Korea. In the succeeding months the majority of UN member-states including members of the British Commonwealth, gave further substantial military or economic support to the United Nations action.

25. The attack on the Republic of Korea was an act of war by the effective government of North Korea and was not in any sense comparable to a civil disturbance arising out of an insurrection against a lawful government, or an act of civil war within a single country. The Government of North Korea launched its offensive with the approval and consent of the Soviet Union. Indeed, so close were the political, military and economic ties then existing between North Korea and the Soviet Union, that it could not have made the attack other than with Soviet approval and consent.

Further facts appear from the judgment.

GRAHAM, J. By notice of motion dated July 31, 1967, the applicants the Al-Fin Corporation of 1 Paul Street, Bethel, Connecticut, in the United States of America, ask for the determination of the court of the question whether, on the true construction of section 24 of the Patents Act, 1949, the Democratic People's Republic of Korea in the events which happened was a foreign state within the meaning of section 24(1) at the time of the Korean war. The Comptroller General of Patents Designs and Trade Marks is the respondent to the motion.

The applicants are the owners of British letters patent No. 689,-129, which was applied for on November 9, 1950, and claims priority from an American application dated November 10, 1949. The British letters patent were granted in 1953 and on May 6, 1966, the applicants applied to the comptroller under section 24 for an extension of five years on the ground of war loss due to hostilities between His late Majesty and the government of the Democratic People's Republic of Korea during the period June 25, 1950, until July 27, 1953.

It is sufficient for present purposes to note that the letters patent relate to the use of ferrous metal incorporated in pistons of either a high nickel cast iron or gray cast iron and which require the use of quantities of nickel in their manufacture. It is alleged that by reason of the war in question nickel was in short supply in this country and that the applicants suffered loss because they were not able to manufacture and sell as many pistons as they would have been able to do had there been no such shortage.

*   *   *

The position of North Korea. I will now deal with the question whether North Korea is a "state" within the meaning of section 24 as a preliminary point in the hearing of the application for extension by the court, which I will treat as before the court in accordance with the undertaking to refer previously mentioned.

The question depends primarily on the proper construction of section 24, and the difference between the parties may be succinctly stated as follows: Must the section be read as if the words "recognised as such by Her Majesty" were included after the words "any foreign state" in subsection (1), or is it correct to read the section in a broader sense without the necessity for the qualification of recognition?

Mr. MacCrindle argued that the court is not here construing a contract between parties but ascertaining the intention of the legislature which is an arm of state. The words hostilities "between His Majesty and any foreign state" demonstrate that it is not sufficient to point to any hostilities—they must be hostilities against a "state," and he took the example of the Eoka disturbances in Cyprus which he submitted would clearly not qualify under these words. Section 8, he says, makes it clear that the foreign state is one which has "subjects." Subjects have their counterpart in their sovereign and the former owe allegiance to the latter and it is not enough that those called subjects merely carry out the orders of some government exercising practical authority over them. In English law a person cannot be a national or subject of a foreign state unless by the laws of that state such person is recognised as a subject of that state. So, if a person is alleged to be a subject of North Korea, the approach of the English court would involve the inquiry whether under the system of law which the English courts would regard as valid in North Korea that individual is a subject of North Korea. In establishing the law prevailing in North Korea, the English courts must look and see if the government which has made the law in question is entitled so to do. The court must therefore first inquire which government is recognised as being in authority in the territory of that foreign state and it can consider only laws passed by that government, and on the question of recognition the Foreign Office certificate is conclusive. The corollary follows that, if there is no formal recognition, there is no government and no state whose laws can be inquired into for the purpose of establishing whether a person is the subject of such a state. To apply section 8 you must be able to examine the relevant law as to status and you are not entitled to regard as a competent law giver a foreign body not recognised by Her Majesty as Sovereign. There are insoluble problems, says Mr. MacCrindle, unless you can establish that the person in question is a subject or national of the state in question, since, once the strict legal meaning of "subject" in that sense is abandoned, how far can one go in considering the question of status.

* * *

Mr. Dillon, on the other hand, for the applicants argued that the obvious intention of the section was to give a right to an extension for loss where the applicant could show that hostilities between this country and another country had occasioned such loss, and that the definition of "state" should certainly not be limited in such a way that it depended on the technical fact of recognition. He said the matter must be looked at from a practical point of view and that, if the facts were sufficient to show that there was a government in effective control over a defined area of territory, then this should qualify as a state within the section whether in fact recognition by the Foreign Office had been made or not. In recent times it has frequently been the case that governments for political or other reasons are not prepared to give de facto or de jure recognition of other governments sometimes for short and sometimes for long periods of time after the stability of such other governments has in fact been clearly established. To this the Foreign Office is no exception and the present certificate is interesting in this respect, since, though recognition has not been made, it is clear on the face of the certificate, paragraph 4, that there was a government exercising control over North Korea during the relevant period, and, secondly, from the point of view of the Foreign Office the question in issue here is regarded as one for the court.

As regards the meaning of "subject" in subsection (8), Mr. Dillon argued that the word should be construed in a general sense as meaning a person who was in fact under the control of an established foreign government whether recognised or not, and should be tested by such matters as the fact of such control, the place of his birth, the place of his father's birth, his residence and generally having regard to all the facts relating to his status and freedom of action.

* * *

* * * In my judgment, the correct principle is that the word must be construed in its context and given the meaning which it is considered was intended by the legislature.

Applying these principles to section 24, I have no hesitation in holding that the phrase "any foreign state," although of course it includes a foreign state which has been given Foreign Office recognition, is not limited thereto. It must at any rate include a sufficiently defined area of territory over which a foreign government has effective control. Whether or not the state in question satisfies these conditions is a matter primarily of fact in each case and no doubt there will be difficult cases for decision from time to time, but difficult cases of fact do not prevent the court from coming to a conclusion when the relevant facts are proved before it.

In the present case, * * * there is the evidence of Mr. Frank in his affidavit of April 24, 1968, which satisfies me, see paragraphs 22 to 25 in particular, that at the relevant time North Korea had a defined territory over which a government had effective control and that His late Majesty was engaged in hostilities with this state albeit his troops were under the command and formed part of the United Nations' forces fighting in the area.

I hold therefore that North Korea was a foreign state within the meaning of section 24 and that the applicants are entitled to proceed with the application for extension on that basis.

In so saying it is clear that I consider that the Harshaw case [1965] R.P.C. 97 was on this point wrongly decided for the reasons which I have given above. It is not necessary to analyse the decision in detail, since in my judgment the question is one of construction and the conclusion of the superintending examiner was wrong. * * *

Order accordingly.

———————

Vietnam "statehood."   The "one-state, two-state" issue has arisen in connection with the Vietnam war. At one point, the United States Department of State characterized South Vietnam not as a "state" as such but as "an independent national entity" having the "right to be free from external interference." 53 Department of State Bulletin, 444, 445 (1965). The question of Vietnam's statehood is dealt with in the full context of the war at pp. 1237 and 1244.

———————

THE TERRITORIAL ELEMENT IN STATEHOOD

1. *Acquisition of land territory.* The existence of a state is conditioned upon its occupation of a defined area of the earth, its land territory. Only if it does have such a territory can it also meet the other organic requirements for membership in the international community, i. e. the requirement of a defined population and the requirement of a government in control of it.

Historically, competition for the acquisition of land territory has been a main feature of the rise of the nation-state and the source of bitter and violent conflicts as well. Conquest was a common and legally recognized form of acquisition of title to territory, and this mode of establishing a right to permanent occupation of a defined area of the earth is not extinct, though it occurs much less frequently than it used to. Peaceful means of acquisition of title also developed, such as cession, prescription and occupation. But the last two at least presuppose the availability of earth areas not already occupied or firmly occupied, else conquest would be the only recourse. Yet there are not many land areas left on earth which are not already occupied by a state.

The outstanding exception is the Antartic and it is symptomatic of modern attitudes, and the result as well no doubt of the harsh climate, that states with potential claims of sovereignty in the area, such as Great Britain, Norway, Chile and Argentina, and others which disclaimed any intention of territorial acquisition there, such as the United States, agreed to establish an international regime for Antarctica. Antarctic Treaty of December 1, 1959, 12 U.S.T. 794, 402 U.N.T.S. 71. It entered into force on June 23, 1961, upon the deposit of ratifications by all the signatory states: Argentina, Australia, Belgium, Chile, France, Japan, New Zealand, Norway, Union of South Africa, Union of Soviet Socialist Republics, United Kingdom and the United States.

The intent of the treaty is to ensure that Antarctica shall be used exclusively for peaceful purposes and not become the object of international discord, and to promote freedom of scientific investigation in the area and international cooperation to that end. Article 4 provides that nothing in the treaty shall be interpreted as a renunciation of asserted rights of sovereignty or bases for claims of sovereignty by the parties, or prejudice their recognition or non-recognition of claims by other states. It further states that the acts or activities of the parties taking place in Antarctica shall not constitute a basis for asserting, supporting or denying claims of sovereignty in the area or creating rights of sovereignty therein.

As to the maritime territory of states, see Chapter 3, and as to their airspace above their land and maritime territory, see Chapter 4.

2. *Territorial boundaries.* Over the centuries, many contests between states concerning territorial questions have been over the location of land boundaries delimiting their respective areas of sovereignty. For even when allocations of territory have been agreed upon by two or more states, there still remain the problem of agreeing on the description of the boundaries and the problem of actually laying down the boundaries by demarcation.

In parts of the earth where allocations of territory have been stable for a long time, and descriptions and demarcations of boundaries made long ago, there are still portions of boundaries, often involving small areas, in controversy. The issue may be resolved by litigation before the International Court of Justice, as in the Case Concerning Sovereignty over Certain Frontier Land, (Belgium v.

Netherlands), [1959] I.C.J. 209.   Or it may be resolved on the occasion of some other settlement, as in the Italian Peace Treaty of February 10, 1948, where provisions were made for changes in the Franco-Italian boundary.   61 Stat. 1245, 49 and 50 U.N.T.S.   A border issue was also involved in the case before the International Court of Justice concerning the Temple of Preah Vihear (Cambodia v. Thailand), [1962] I.C.J.Rep. 6.   Hostilities over a border question broke out between India and Pakistan in 1965 and the issue was submitted to arbitration, as briefly discussed on p. 83.   Rann of Kutch Arbitration, 1968, VII International Legal Materials 633 (1968).   Communist China and India have been embroiled over the years in border disputes which flare up occasionally into limited hostilities.

It would be quite pointless to try elucidating from boundary cases specific principles of international law, since the issues nearly always come down to a matter of interpretation of agreements between the parties.   There is an exception to this proposition, however, when the boundary between two states is a navigable river.   In such a case, the location of the boundary is the "thalweg," i. e. the middle of the channel of navigation.   Restatement of the Foreign Relations Law of the United States, § 12 (1965).   The same section also states that when the boundary between two states is a non-navigable river or lake, its location is in the middle of the river or lake.   For the settlement of the Chamizal Boundary Dispute between the United States and Mexico, which involved the Rio Grande, see Chapter 1.

3.   *Newly independent states.*   Since World War II, the breaking-up of colonial empires has proceeded at an accelerated pace.   As a result, a substantial number of independent states have come into being which previously were dependent territories of a colonial power or were subjected in various degrees to administrative control by another state, as in the case of mandate or trusteeships.   The emergency of new states has created difficult problems of "succession," including those concerning succession to treaties concerning the boundaries of their territory or certain uses of their territory.

At its 1972 session, the International Law Commission received from its special rapporteur the final articles of his draft on the Succession of States in respect of Treaties.   See the Report on the Work of Its Twenty-Fourth Session, May 2–July 7, 1972, U.N.Gen.Ass.Off. Rec., Supp. No. 10 (A/8710/Rev. 1).   It considered these and other articles and the complete draft it adopted was transmitted to the governments of states for their consideration (at 8).   Part V of the draft is entitled: "Boundary Regimes or Other Territorial Regimes Established by a Treaty."   It consists of two articles.   Article 29 provides:

Boundary regimes

A succession of States shall not as such affect:

(a)   a boundary established by a treaty; or

(b)   obligations and rights established by a treaty and relating to the regime of a boundary.

The commentary on this article states in part:

There was general agreement in the Commission upon the basic principle that a succession of States does not, as such, affect a boundary or a boundary regime established by treaty. Having regard to the various considerations mentioned * * * and to the trend of modern opinion on the matter, the Commission concluded that it should formulate the rule not in terms of the treaty itself but of a boundary established by a treaty and of a boundary regime so established. Accordingly, article 29 provides that a succession of States shall not as such affect: (a) a boundary established by a treaty; or (b) obligations and rights established by a treaty and relating to the regime of a boundary. In accepting this formulation the Commission underlined the purely negative character of the rule, which goes no further than to deny that any succession of States simply by reason of its occurrence affects a boundary established by a treaty or a boundary regime so established. As already pointed out in paragraph (16), it leaves untouched any legal ground that may exist for challenging the boundary, such as self-determination or the invalidity of the treaty, just as it also leaves untouched any legal ground of defence to such a challenge. The Commission was also agreed that this negative rule must apply equally to any boundary regime established by a treaty, whether the same treaty as established the boundary or a separate treaty.

Article 30 provides:

Other territorial regimes

1.   A succession of States shall not as such affect:

(a) obligations relating to the use of a particular territory, or to restrictions upon its use, established by a treaty specifically for the benefit of a particular territory of a foreign State and considered as attaching to the territories in question;

(b) rights established by a treaty specifically for the benefit of a particular territory and relating to the use, or to restrictions upon the use of a particular territory of a foreign State and considered as attaching to the territories in question.

2.   A succession of States shall not as such affect:

(a) obligations relating to the use of a particular territory, or to restrictions upon its use, established by a treaty specifically for the benefit of a group of States or of all States and considered as attaching to that territory.

(b) rights established by a treaty specifically for the benefit of a group of States or of all States and relating to the use of a particular territory, or to restrictions upon its use, and considered as attaching to that territory.

This article is intended to deal with situations in which the predecessor state granted to another state by treaty certain rights in the territory such as lease of a port in perpetuity, operation of commercial aircraft for certain bases, rights of navigation on rivers or canals, and rights to use water resources.

The commentary states in part:

> Some further precedents of one kind or another might be examined, but it is doubtful whether they would throw any clearer light on the difficult question of territorial treaties. Running through the precedents and the opinions of writers are strong indications of a belief that certain treaties attach a regime to territory which continues to bind it in the hands of any successor State. Not infrequently other elements enter into the picture, such as an allegation of fundamental change of circumstances or the allegedly limited competence of the predecessor State, and the successor State in fact claims to be free of the obligation to respect the regime. Nevertheless, the indications of the general acceptance of such a principle remain. At the same time, neither the precedents nor the opinions of writers give clear guidance as to the criteria for determining when this principle operates. The evidence does not, however, suggest that this category of treaties should embrace a very wide range of so-called territorial treaties. On the contrary, this category seems to be limited to cases where a State by a treaty grants a right to use territory, or to restrict its own use of territory, which is intended to attach to territory of a foreign State or, alternatively, to be for the benefit of a group of States or of all States generally. There must in short be something in the nature of a territorial regime.

It should be noted that draft article 30 restricts the devolution by succession of the types of rights involved to those situations where the right either benefits the particular territory of another state and attaches to it, or benefits a group of states or all states. Can you see why? What would happen to the lease of a port in perpetuity, or to a right to operate commercial aircraft from bases in the territory, under draft article 30?

The draft of the International Law Commission is intended to formulate general principles. Frequently, however, the types of situations to which it refers have been resolved by ad hoc agreements between all interested parties.

4. *Rights over territory short of title.* A state may cede to another a portion of its territory, just as a person may pass title to his property in private law. But just as rights in property may be created in private law which fall short of title, so it is in international law with respect to the territory of a state.

Thus a state may lease to another a portion of its territory for a term of years. The United Kingdom holds Hong Kong in lease from China for 99 years. The convention between the United States and Panama of November 18, 1903, 33 Stat. 2234, grants to the United States "in perpetuity" the use, occupation and control of a 10-mile strip of Panamanian territory for the purpose of constructing and operating a ship canal, and in this zone the United States may exercise all the rights it "would possess and exercise if it were the sovereign of the territory" to the entire exclusion of the exercise by Panama of any such sovereign rights.

The trusteeship system set up under articles 75–91 of the Charter of the United Nations presents obvious analogies to the institution of the trust in the common law system. See the Documentary Supplement for these articles. It does not follow, however, that a state holding a territory in trusteeship is vested with title to it because a trustee is usually vested with title to the trust at common law. The common core of the concept which underlies the system of trusteeship under the Charter of the United Nations and the preceding systems of mandates under the League of Nations is the vesting of power of control in the mandatory and the trustee for the benefit of the people in the territory under mandate or trusteeship. The most absolute power of control available, i. e. title to or sovereignty over the territory, is not given however to the mandatory or the trustee state, though of course the scope of the power is very broad.

The arrangements just described and involving rights over territory falling short of title must be distinguished from arrangements where a state gives to another the right to exercise a certain amount of jurisdiction in its territory with respect to certain persons. Under the system of extraterritorial jurisdiction once in effect in many states of Africa and Asia, the United States like many European states had jurisdiction over its nationals when they were defendants in certain civil and criminal cases. This jurisdiction, based on nationality, was "personal" and did not rest on any right over the territory.

Chapter 12

RECOGNITION OF STATES AND GOVERNMENTS

Recognition is a political act, taken by a government of a state in reference to foreign affairs operations. In this chapter we consider the extent to which the international legal system has rules about the performance of this political act and attempt to project some of the legal-political consequences of the act of recognition, once it has occurred.

THE THEORY OF RECOGNITION

1 O'Connell, International Law 127–128 (2d ed. 1970).*

There is no topic of international law more theoretically confusing than that of recognition. The term "recognition" itself is used with distressing imprecision by both lawyers and political scientists, while only an arbitrary selection and rejection of evidence has made the mass of contradictory State practice on the subject intelligible. Even the most dedicated positivist has been forced into a priori reasoning, and in the result there are several intellectual constructions claiming exclusive authority as to the legal value of an act of recognition and as to its legal consequence. It would seem, however, that too much has been made of the theoretical issue between the rival schools of thoughts. Many of the puzzles of recognition as a legal concept are only linguistic, and careful definition will cause them to vanish. This is not to suggest that the topic is thereby simplified. Far from it. But at least confusion is not worse confounded by mistaking what we are talking about and what we are trying to do.

Recognition as a term covers a variety of factual situations calling for acknowledgment by foreign States. They are: the appearance of new States, changes of government outside the constitutional forms, territorial changes, especially those achieved by force and involving the extinction of States, and the parties to civil war. The common factor in all these cases is that certain governmental authorities claim competence over territory and people, and foreign States are faced with the choice of recognising or not recognising that the claim is valid. Recognition is a political action whereby the recognising State indicates a willingness to acknowledge the factual situation and to bring about certain legal consequences of that acknowledgment. Acknowledgment is not recognition if it is limited to noting the factual situation. The United States knows perfectly well that the Central

---

* Reprinted with the permission of O'Connell and Stevens & Sons, Ltd., London.

People's Government rules China; it does not doubt that fact, nor does it pretend to the contrary. It merely refuses to allow the legal consequences of its knowledge, and this international law would seem to permit it to do.

In order to distinguish an acknowledgment of facts which has consequences in international law from one which has not it is useful to distinguish three processes, cognition, cognisance and recognition. The taking notice of the facts may be described as cognition. Until the facts are noted, and until indeed they are facts, there is no proper cognition, without which there can be no proper recognition. Cognisance is the act of some body other than the executive taking note of the facts and allowing consequences to follow therefrom. This is what a judge does when he draws legal conclusions from the existence of an unrecognised as well as from a recognised State or government. Recognition is the act of the Executive taking note of the facts and indicating a willingness to allow all the legal consequences of that noting to operate. These are consequences in international law. Whether consequences also follow in municipal law is a matter for municipal law itself to determine. In fact most of the material on recognition is not international law at all, but municipal law dealing with the respective roles of the executive and non-executive branches of government inter se in this matter of fact-finding and of drawing legal conclusions. The first point to be settled, therefore, is that there is no necessary logic in the process of recognition, whereby uniform conclusions must be drawn in every legal system, so that the case law of any one system would form part of the corpus of international law.

* * *

Recognition involves only extraordinary political changes. The need for recognition arises only when the appearance on the world scene of a new state or the rise to power of a new government of an existing state is an extraordinary political event. In the case of the recognition of entities as new states, the element of the extraordinary usually occurs only when there has been a revolutionary separation from another state. It is true that every new state holds itself out for recognition, but recognition is routine if the new entity is a peaceful—or at least not militarily contested—separation from an old state.

By far the majority of recognition problems that arise involve recognition of regimes as the governments of already recognized states. If the succession from one government to another is in keeping with the ordinary processes (usually as specified in constitutions) for changes of government, there is no occasion for an act of recognition. It is only when the change of government is discontinuous such as by a coup d'etat or some other departure from legitimacy in the succession, that a question arises as to whether the new regime should be considered for recognition.

Thus there is a close relationship between the need for recognition and the unorthodoxy of how the new political authority in the state came to power. One school of thought and action—so far not the prevailing view—holds that even revolutionary changes of government should not require a new act of recognition. This viewpoint originated in Mexico and is known as the Estrada doctrine, being so named for the foreign minister of Mexico who first asserted it. Mexican motivation for the assertion of such a doctrine—that change by bullets is as valid as change by ballots so far as the external world is concerned—is grounded in that country's feeling that its big neighbor to the north manipulates the withholding of recognition of successful revolutionary regimes to interventionist ends.

The Mexican reaction was brought about by the no doubt well-intentioned efforts of President Woodrow Wilson during the Mexican Revolution (1911–1921) to create a pressure for democratic and orderly changes of government, p. 812. Why should the Mexicans reject so well-intentioned a viewpoint?

SECTION A.   THE EFFECT OF NONRECOGNITION IN JUDICIAL PROCEEDINGS

By far the majority of legal problems concerning recognition and nonrecognition have arisen in domestic courts. The classic problem has been this: in the absence of diplomatic recognition of an entity as a state or of a regime as the government of a state by the department or branch of the forum state government having control of foreign affairs, may such entity or regime be treated by domestic courts as having juridical existence? It might be possible in such cases for the courts of a country to find themselves incapable of acting at all. Or, the courts might feel that the characterizations of parties as state entities or as governments of states should be made for all national purposes by the diplomatic arm. Or, the courts might make such decisions for themselves upon the basis of law. If so, what law? International? Principles of law common to the world's major legal systems? Judicial notice? Analogies to the private law of entities, such as that of corporations? Judicial responses of various types are discernible in the materials that follow in this Section.

1. ON ACTIONS IN DOMESTIC COURTS: STANDING TO SUE AND RIGHT TO CONTROL STATE ASSETS

RUSSIAN SOCIALIST FEDERATED SOVIET REPUBLIC v. CIBRARIO

United States, New York Court of Appeals, 1923.
235 N.Y. 255, 139 N.E. 259.

ANDREWS, J. In Wulfsohn v. Russian Federated Soviet Republic, 234 N.Y. 372, 138 N.E. 24, we held that our courts would not entertain jurisdiction of an action brought without its consent against an existing foreign government, in control of the political and military power within its own territory, whether or not such government had been recognized by the United States. We have now to determine whether such a government may itself become a plaintiff here.

If recognized, undoubtedly it may. * * * Conceivably this right may depend on treaty. But if no treaty to that effect exists the privilege rests upon the theory of international comity. This is so with regard to all foreign corporations. * * * Their power to sue may be regulated as is done by section 15 of our General Corporation Law (Cons.Laws, ch. 23). (Paul v. Virginia, 75 U.S. [8 Wall.] 168.) And except as limited by constitutional provisions the same thing is true of those not citizens of our state. Much more true is it that the right of a foreign government to sue is likewise based upon the same consideration. Neither a natural person nor a corporation, ordinarily we would not recognize it as a proper party plaintiff. * * * It represents, however, the general interests of the nation over which it has authority. We permit it to appear and protect those interests as a body analogous to one possessing corporate rights, but solely because of comity. * * *

Comity may be defined as that reciprocal courtesy which one member of the family of nations owes to the others. It presupposes friendship. It assumes the prevalence of equity and justice. Experience points to the expediency of recognizing the legislative, executive and judicial acts of other powers. We do justice that justice may be done in return. * * *

* * *

Does any rule of comity then require us to permit a suit by an unrecognized power? In view of the attitude of our government should we permit an action to be brought by the Soviet government? To both queries we must give a negative answer.

* * *

We reach the conclusion, therefore, that a foreign power brings an action in our courts not as a matter of right. Its power to do so is the creature of comity. Until such government is recognized by the United States, no such comity exists. The plaintiff concededly has not been so recognized. There is, therefore, no proper party before us. We may add that recognition and consequently the existence of comity is purely a matter for the determination of the legislative or executive departments of the government. Who is the sovereign of a territory is a political question. In any case where that question is in dispute the courts are bound by the decision reached by those departments. * * *

* * *

With regard to the present Russian government the case is still stronger, even did comity not depend on recognition. We not only refuse to recognize it. Our state department gives the reasons. Secretary Colby has stated them in an official note, dated August 10, 1920. He begins by saying that our government will not participate in any plan for the expansion of the armistice negotiations between Russia and Poland into a general European conference, "which would in all probability involve two results, from both of which this country strongly recoils, viz.: The recognition of the Bolshevist regime and a settlement of the Russian problem almost inevitably upon the basis of a dismemberment of Russia." He continues, "We are unwilling that while it is helpless in the grip of a non-representative government whose only sanction is brutal force, Russia shall be weakened still further by a policy of dismemberment, conceived in other than Russian interests. * * * The Bolsheviki, although in number an inconsiderable minority of the people, by force and cunning seized the powers and machinery of government, and have continued to use them with savage oppression to maintain themselves in power. * * * It is not possible for the government of the United States to recognize the present rulers of Russia as a government with which the relations common to friendly governments can be maintained. * * * The existing regime in Russia is based upon the negation of every principle of honor and good faith, and every usage and convention, underlying the whole structure of international law, the negation, in short, of every principle upon which it is possible to base harmonious and trustful relations, whether of nations or of individuals. The responsible leaders of the regime have frequently and openly boasted that they are willing to sign agreements and undertakings with foreign powers while not having the slightest intention of observing such undertakings or carrying out such agreements. * * * They have made it quite plain that they intend to use every means * * * to promote revolutionary movements in other countries. * * * In the view of this government, there cannot be any common ground upon which it can stand with a power whose conceptions of international relations are so entirely alien to its own, so utterly repugnant to its moral sense. There can be no mutual confidence or trust, no respect even, if pledges are to be given and agreements made with a cynical repudiation of their obligations already in the

mind of one of the parties. We cannot recognize, hold official relations with, or give friendly reception to the agents of a government
which is determined and bound to conspire against our institutions,
whose diplomats will be the agitators of dangerous revolt, whose
spokesmen say that they sign agreements with no intention of keeping them."

Our government has not receded from this position. Secretary
Hughes in rejecting trade proposals of the Soviet, said on March 25,
1921, "It is only in the productivity of Russia that there is any hope
for the Russian people, and it is idle to expect resumption of trade
until the economic bases of production are securely established. Production is conditioned upon the safety of life, the recognition by firm
guarantees of private property, the sanctity of contract and the rights
of free labor," and he postpones any consideration of trade relations
until such time as our government has convincing evidence of fundamental changes that will fulfill these conditions.

In the face of these declarations it is impossible to hold that
to-day any such relations exist between the United States and Russia
as call upon our courts to enforce rules in favor of the latter depending on the comity of nations.

The judgment appealed from should be affirmed, with costs.

WULFSOHN v. RUSSIAN SOCIALIST FEDERATED SOVIET REPUBLIC

United States, New York Court of Appeals, 1923.
234 N.Y. 372, 138 N.E. 24.

ANDREWS, J. The Russian Federated Soviet Republic is the existing de facto government of Russia. This is admitted by the plaintiff. Otherwise there is no proper party defendant before the court.
It is claimed by the defendant. The Appellate Division states that it
is a matter of common knowledge. It has not been recognized by the
government of the United States. The plaintiffs owned a quantity of
furs. They were stored in Russia and they were confiscated by the
Russian government. Treating this act as a conversion the present
action is brought. The litigation is not, therefore, with regard to title
to property situated within the jurisdiction of our courts where the
result depends upon the effect to be given to the action of some
foreign government. Under such circumstances it might be that the
theory of the comity of nations would have a place. * * * A different case is presented to us. The government itself is sued for an
exercise of sovereignty within its own territories on the theory that
such an act if committed by an individual here would be a tort under
our system of municipal law. It is said that because of non-recognition
by the United States such an action may be maintained. There is no
relation between the premise and the conclusion.

The result we reach depends upon more basic considerations than recognition or non-recognition by the United States. Whether or not a government exists clothed with the power to enforce its authority within its own territory, obeyed by the people over whom it rules, capable of performing the duties and fulfilling the obligations of an independent power, able to enforce its claims by military force, is a fact not a theory. For it recognition does not create the state although it may be desirable. So only are diplomatic relations permitted. Treaties made with the government which it succeeds may again come into effect. It is a testimony of friendly intentions. * * * We have an existing government sovereign within its own territories. There necessarily its jurisdiction is exclusive and absolute. It is susceptible of no limitation not imposed by itself. This is the result of its independence. It may be conceded that its actions should accord with natural justice and equity. If they do not, however, our courts are not competent to review them. They may not bring a foreign sovereign before our bar, not because of comity, but because he has not submitted himself to our laws. Without his consent he is not subject to them. Concededly that is so as to a foreign government that has received recognition. * * * But whether recognized or not the evil of such an attempt would be the same. "To cite a foreign potentate into a municipal court for any complaint against him in his public capacity is contrary to the law of nations and an insult which he is entitled to resent." (De Haber v. Queen of Portugal, 17 Q.B. 171.) In either case to do so would "vex the peace of nations." In either case the hands of the state department would be tied. Unwillingly it would find itself involved in disputes it might think unwise. Such is not the proper method of redress if a citizen of the United States is wronged. The question is a political one, not confided to the courts but to another department of government. WAIT ON Whenever an act done by a sovereign in his sovereign character is EXE CUTIVE questioned it becomes a matter of negotiation, or of reprisals or of war.

If the complaint and the affidavits upon which the warrant of attachment was based in the case before us clearly indicate that the plaintiffs must ultimately fail the warrant should be vacated. It does so appear in this case.

The orders, therefore, appealed from should be reversed, with costs in all courts, and motions to vacate attachment granted, with costs, and the question certified to us should be answered in the ✓ negative.

HISCOCK, CH. J., HOGAN, CARDOZO, POUND and MCLAUGHLIN, JJ., concur; CRANE, J., dissents.

Ordered accordingly.

UPRIGHT v. MERCURY BUSINESS MACHINES CO.

United States, New York Supreme Court, Appellate Division, 1961.
13 A.D.2d 36, 213 N.Y.S.2d 417.

BREITEL, JUSTICE PRESIDING.

Plaintiff, an individual, sues as the assignee of a trade acceptance drawn on and accepted by defendant in payment for business typewriters sold and delivered to it by a foreign corporation. The trade acceptance is in the amount of $27,307.45 and was assigned to plaintiff after dishonor by defendant.

Involved on this appeal is only the legal sufficiency of the first affirmative defense. It alleges that the foreign corporation is the creature of the East German Government, a government not recognized by the United States. It alleges, moreover, that such corporation is an enterprise controlled by and that it is an arm and instrument of such government.

On motion addressed to its sufficiency Special Term sustained the defense. For the reasons that follow the defense should have been stricken as legally insufficient * * *.

A foreign government, although not recognized by the political arm of the United States Government, may nevertheless have de facto existence which is juridically cognizable. The acts of such a de facto government may affect private rights and obligations arising either as a result of activity in, or with persons or corporations within, the territory controlled by such de facto government. This is traditional law. * * *

In the Russian Reinsurance Co. case, Lehman, J., later Chief Judge, summarized the principles:

"The fall of one governmental establishment and the substitution of another governmental establishment which actually governs, which is able to enforce its claims by military force and is obeyed by the people over whom it rules, must profoundly affect all the acts and duties, all the relations of those who live within the territory over which the new establishment exercises rule. Its rule may be without lawful foundation; but lawful or unlawful, its existence is a fact, and that fact cannot be destroyed by juridical concepts. The State Department determines whether it will recognize its existence as lawful, and, until the State Department has recognized the new establishment, the court may not pass upon its legitimacy or ascribe to its decrees all the effect which inheres in the laws or orders of a sovereign. The State Department determines only that question. It cannot determine how far the private rights and obligations of individuals are affected by acts of a body not sovereign, or with which our government will have no dealings. That question does not concern our foreign relations. It is not a political question, but a judicial question. The courts in considering that question assume as a premise that until recognition these acts are not in full sense law.   Their conclusion must depend upon whether these have nevertheless had such an actual effect that they may not be disregarded.   In such case we deal with result rather than cause.   We do not pass upon what such an unrecognized governmental authority may do, or upon the right or wrong of what it has done; we consider the effect upon others of that which has been done, primarily from the point of view of fact rather than of theory."   *   *   *

So, too, only limited effect is given to the fact that the political arm has not recognized a foreign government.   Realistically, the courts apprehend that political nonrecognition may serve only narrow purposes.   While the judicial arm obligates itself to follow the suggestions of the political arm in effecting such narrow purposes, nevertheless, it will not exaggerate or compound the consequences required by such narrow purposes in construing rights and obligations affected by the acts of unrecognized governments.   *   *   *

*   *   *

Applying these principles, it is insufficient for defendant merely to allege the nonrecognition of the East German Government and that plaintiff's assignor was organized by and is an arm and instrumentality of such unrecognized East German Government.   The lack of jural status for such government or its creature corporation is not determinative of whether transactions with it will be denied enforcement in American courts, so long as the government is not the suitor. (Actually, on the present pleadings no issue is raised that plaintiff assignee is that government, or is an arm of that government, or that the assignment to him of the trade acceptance is invalid or does not represent a genuine transfer.)

*   *   *

This case does not involve the issues, tendered by defendant in its argument, of jural status of the East German corporation, or of its incapacity to transfer title, or even of its capacity to sue in our courts.   These have been long recognized as issues to be resolved by reference to the actual facts—the realities of life—occurring in the territory controlled by a de facto government, unless, of course, the contemplated juridical consequences of such "facts" can be properly related as inimical to the aims and purposes of our public or national policy.   *   *   *   Even the power of a rebel government in one of the Confederate States to create a corporation with capacity to sue the United States Government was admitted where such creation was not directly in furtherance of the rebellion (United States v. Insurance Companies, 22 Wall. 99, 89 U.S. 99, 22 L.Ed. 816).

It is a false notion, if it prevail anywhere, that an unrecognized government is always an evil thing and all that occurs within its governmental purview are always evil works.   There are many things which may occur within the purview of an unrecognized government which are not evil and which will be given customary legal significance in the courts of nations which do not recognize the prevailing de facto government. In a time in which governments with established control over territories may be denied recognition for many reasons, it does not mean that the denizens of such territories or the corporate creatures of such powers do not have the juridical capacity to trade, transfer title, or collect the price for the merchandise they sell to outsiders, even in the courts of nonrecognizing nations (cf. Sokoloff v. National City Bank, 239 N.Y. 158, 165–166, 145 N.E. 917, 918–919, supra).

Of course, nonrecognition is a material fact but only a preliminary one. The proper conclusion will depend upon factors in addition to that of nonrecognition. Such is still the case even though an entity involved in the transaction be an arm or instrumentality of the unrecognized government. Thus, in order to exculpate defendant from payment for the merchandise it has received, it would have to allege and prove that the sale upon which the trade acceptance was based, or that the negotiation of the trade acceptance itself, was in violation of public or national policy. Such a defense would constitute one in the nature of illegality and if established would, or at least might, render all that ensued from the infected transaction void and unenforceable. Defendant buyer cannot escape liability merely by alleging and proving that it dealt with a corporation created by and functioning as the arm of and instrumentality of an unrecognized government.

Put more concretely: The public policy which denies juridical recognition to the East German Government is determined by the refusal of the political arm to recognize it. That means the East German Government cannot sue in our courts. The question whether its corporate instrumentality can sue is not so clear. Perhaps it could sue. But another, not otherwise lacking in capacity to sue, may, by way of transfer or other mesne assignment, sue on the underlying transaction, unless such transaction itself or the assignment is shown to violate the national or public policy. In order for such transaction or the assignment to violate national or public policy, it must be shown either to violate our laws or some definite policy. If the national government does not administratively forbid, or if it facilitates, the purchase and delivery into this country of East German typewriters, and no law forbids it, then defendant buyer will be hard put to show the "illegality" of the underlying transaction, or the assignment, and thereby avoid payment of the price for such merchandise.

Moreover, the status of the East German territory is that of territory, once belligerent, but now occupied by a wartime ally, the Soviet Union, with the consent of the other allies. Nonrecognition, in the past, of the East German Government simply meant that, pending a reunification plan and free secret elections, the State Department refused to recognize the displacement of the Soviet Union as the power responsible for the territory and for the conduct of affairs there.

* * *

Accordingly, the order of Special Term should be reversed, on the law, and the motion to strike the first affirmative defense granted * * *

[Concurring opinion omitted.]

IN RE ALEXANDRAVICUS

United States, New Jersey Superior Court, Appellate Division, 1964.
83 N.J.Super. 303, 199 A.2d 662.

The opinion of the court was delivered by LEWIS, J. A. D.

This is one of several appellate reviews incident to the estate of Joseph Alexandravicus, deceased. Death occurred February 15, 1953, and the litigated issue as to the right to administer decedent's estate is still a matter of controversy.

* * * Jonas Budrys, Consul General of the Republic of Lithuania, instituted proceedings in the Hudson County Court, Probate Division, demanding that he be granted letters of administration. The crucial allegations set forth in his verified complaint may be summarized:

Joseph Alexandravicus of the County of Hudson died intestate leaving him surviving two brothers, Vincas and Antanas, residents of the Republic of Lithuania.

Said Republic was unlawfully subjugated on June 15, 1940, and, shortly thereafter, it was illegally annexed into the Union of Soviet Socialist Republics. The occupied government is not recognized by the United States of America.

Plaintiff's consular status with the Republic of Lithuania is evidenced by an exequatur issued to him by the Government of the United States. Pursuant to the "laws and treaties" of our country and the Republic of Lithuania, he, as consul general has the power and authority to act as attorney-in-fact for his nationals who inherit American property in the State of New Jersey.

The application of Jesse Moskowitz, Esq., for such an appointment was predicated upon a power of attorney (dated February 19, 1959), executed by decedent's two brothers empowering the New York law firm of Messrs. Wolf, Popper, Ross, Wolf & Jones, or its nominee, to apply for letters of administration. Said power was not executed before officials of the Republic of Lithuania * * *.

* * * After a full hearing before the County Court, the trial judge entered an order on August 3, 1962 vacating the order to show cause and dismissing the complaint.

On appeal to this court plaintiff advances two major arguments to support a reversal: (1) the power of attorney and designation under which the authority of Moskowitz emanates is invalid; and (2) the consul general has the exclusive right to be appointed administrator.

* * *

The documentary facts are not in dispute. The identity of the surviving brothers, the authenticity of their signatures and their legal capacity, were certified February 19, 1959 by a notary of the Ministry of Justice of the Lithuanian Soviet Socialist Republic. The notary's qualification and signature were certified by the Chief of the Revisionary Department of the Ministry of Justice of the Lithuanian Soviet Socialist Republic whose signature was visaed by the Consular Administration of the Ministry of Foreign Affairs of U. S. S. R. There was an accompanying certificate by an American consul certifying the authenticity of the Russian minister's signature and the official Russian seal; a caveat thereto stated, "This authentication is not to be interpreted as implying recognition of Soviet sovereignty over Lithuania."

The trial judge received a letter dated January 31, 1962, addressed to him from the United States Department of State which included the following information: the Government of the United States does not recognize the forced incorporation of Lithuania into the Union of Soviet Socialist Republics; it continues to recognize the diplomatic and consular officers of the Republic of Lithuania, and the position of the Department is the same as declared in a communique of October 1, 1959 declaring that the effect to be given a power of attorney executed in the Soviet Union by nationals of Lithuania is for the courts to decide.

It is well settled that the laws, acts, judgments and decrees of foreign governments have extraterritorial effect only as a matter of comity, sometimes called "comity of nations," which in a legal sense is "neither a matter of absolute obligation, on the one hand, nor of mere courtesy and good will, upon the other." Hilton v. Guyot, 159 U.S. 113, 163–164, 16 S.Ct. 139, 143, 40 L.Ed. 95, 108 (1895), approvingly cited in Banco Nacional de Cuba v. Sabbatino, 84 S.Ct. 923 (decided March 23, 1964). Political recognition, however, is exclusively a function of the Executive. Ibid. When our Federal Government has determined upon a policy of recognition of a foreign country, it is binding upon the courts. United States v. Pink, 315 U.S. 203, 229–230, 62 S.Ct. 552, 565, 86 L.Ed. 796, 817 (1942). Similarly, a policy of non-recognition when demonstrated by the Executive must be deemed to be "as affirmative and positive in effect as the policy of recognition." The Maret, 145 F.2d 431, 442 (3 Cir. 1944). Accord, Latvian State Cargo & Passenger S. S. Line v. McGrath, 88 U.S.App. D.C. 226, 188 F.2d 1000, 1003 (D.C.Cir.), cert. denied 342 U.S. 816, 72 S.Ct. 30, 96 L.Ed. 617 (1951).

Appellant contends that because the power of attorney here at
issue was executed in subjugated Lithuania and the notarial acts appended to the power were sealed and consummated by officers of an
unrecognized sovereignty, the document should be declared a total nullity.   He relies upon the authority of cases typified by In re Adler's
Estate, 197 Misc. 104, 93 N.Y.S.2d 416 (Surr.Ct.1949), appeal dismissed 279 App.Div. 745, 109 N.Y.S.2d 175 (App.Div.1951), wherein
it was said that a court may not give effect to an act of an unrecognized government, since to do so would invade the domain of the political authority.   It was then declared, "If, therefore, the court may
not give effect to an act of an unrecognized government, it may not
give effect to an act of an official acting in behalf of that regime."
*   *   *

The argument continues that it would be an anomalous situation
if we were to give recognition to the notarial acts of those appointed
under the laws of the "puppet regime" now in control of Lithuania,
because it would be tantamount to an acknowledgment that the Russian laws were applicable to the Baltic country of Lithuania.   But
that does not necessarily follow.   In the first place, the American consul's certification was specifically qualified to negate such a conclusion, and, secondly, it is not every act of an official of an unrecognized
government that is regarded as a nullity.   While judicially a government that is unrecognized may be viewed as no government at all, it
was pointed out many years ago by Justice (then Judge) Cardozo
that in practice "juridical conceptions are seldom, if ever, carried to
the limit of their logic, the equivalence is not absolute, but is subject
to self-imposed limitations of common sense and fairness   *   *   *."
Sokoloff v. National City Bank, 239 N.Y. 158, 165, 145 N.E. 917, 918,
37 A.L.R. 712 (Ct.App.1924).

It is only where the acts are political in nature that the courts
are precluded from considering their validity and effectiveness.   Russian Reinsurance Co. v. Stoddard, 240 N.Y. 149, 147 N.E. 703 (Ct.App.
1925).   Thus, where the controversy is concerned exclusively with
private rights and obligations of the subjects of an unrecognized state,
the law of that state may prevail.   *   *   *

A significant approach was taken to this issue in the recent case
of In re Luberg's Estate, 19 A.D.2d 370, 243 N.Y.S.2d 747 (App.Div.
1963), wherein two powers of attorney were involved—one executed
and notarized in Estonia and the other at Leningrad, Russia.   In considering the former, it was declared, by way of obiter dictum, that the
judiciary is not required to disregard a power of attorney merely because it was authenticated by an official of a de facto rather than a
de jure government.   If this were not so, rationalized the court,

> many situations would become intolerable.   It would be impossi-
> ble to establish the elementary facts of birth, marriage, death or
> the like where the certification of the same was made by, or the

official before whom proof was to be taken was an appointee of, the unrecognized regime. Moreover, we would perforce have to refuse nationals of the regime that we do recognize access to our shores because the only persons who could in fact authenticate their passports would be officials of the regime that is not recognized. In that way we would be acting in a manner that was in practical effect more oppressive to those nationals whose independence we are seeking to further than is the government which usurped authority over them. * * * (243 N.Y.S.2d, at p. 750.)

* * *

Against the force of the evidence before us, we find appellant's countervailing arguments, attacking the validity of the power of attorney in question, to be unpersuasive.

* * *

We conclude that plaintiff did not have an exclusive right to be appointed administrator and that any standing he might have had prior to February 19, 1959, terminated at that time when decedent's brothers designated attorneys in this country to represent them.

The judgment of the trial court is affirmed.

IN RE ESTATE OF LUKS

United States, New York Surrogate Court, N.Y. County, 1965.
45 Misc.2d 72, 256 N.Y.S.2d 194.

JOSEPH A. COX, SURROGATE. The Consuls General of the governments in exile of Latvia and Estonia have moved for orders dismissing the objections to the Public Administrator's accounts and striking the notices of appearance filed by purported attorneys-in-fact for alleged distributees in the accounting proceedings. The motions are founded upon the alleged invalidity of the powers of attorney. The attorneys-in-fact on their part have moved to strike the appearances of the Consuls General, alleging that they are not proper parties to these proceedings by reason of the designation of specified persons as attorneys-in-fact authorized to appear on behalf of the claimants in these proceedings * * * The Attorney General of the State of New York has joined in the motions to have the powers of attorney declared invalid. Except for the fact that in the Luks case the powers of attorney were executed in Latvia and in the Kask and Tiit cases the powers were executed in Estonia, the fact situations surrounding the execution of the powers and their authentication present like issues.

In each case the powers were executed in the country where the claimants reside and were purportedly acknowledged before a notary in that country whose signature was authenticated by an official of the Notarial Department of the Soviet Latvian or Soviet Estonian Supreme Court as the case might be. The authority of the authenticating official was in turn certified by an official of the Consular Administration of the Ministry of Foreign Affairs of the Union of Soviet Socialist Republics whose signature was attested to by the Consul of the United States in Moscow.   Each certification of the United States Consul contained a provision that the certification was not to be interpreted as implying a recognition of Soviet sovereignty in the occupied country.   In addition to the foregoing documents, Certificates of Conformity have been filed which certify that the powers of attorney conformed to and were executed, acknowledged and authenticated in accordance with the laws of the Union of Soviet Socialist Republics and which attest to the correctness of the translations of the texts of the powers from the Russion into the English language. These Certificates of Conformity are signed by the Third Secretary of the Embassy of the Union of Soviet Socialist Republics at Washington, D. C. who is also the Deputy Chief of the Consular Division of the Embassy of the Union of Soviet Socialist Republics.

The Government of the United States has never recognized the forceful occupation of Estonia and Latvia by the Union of Soviet Socialist Republics nor does it recognize the absorption and incorporation of Latvia and Estonia into the Union of Soviet Socialist Republics. The legality of the acts, laws and decrees of the puppet regimes set up in these countries by the Union of Soviet Socialist Republics is not recognized by the United States, diplomatic or consular officers are not maintained in either Estonia or Latvia and full recognition is given to the Legations of Estonia and Latvia established and maintained here by the governments in exile of those countries.

* * *

The problems here presented arise from the facts that a powerful aggressor nation overwhelmed its small neighboring nations, ousted their chosen governments and installed instead puppet governments not responsive to the needs or wants of the citizens of those nations. The policy of our government has been to refuse recognition to such acts of aggression.   Questions of recognition of governments lie exclusively within the realm of the executive branch of our government and our courts can give no effect to an act of an unrecognized government which either by implication or otherwise would indicate recognition of that government   * * *.

* * *

* * *   In the cases at bar the Certificates of Conformity were issued by a consular official of the Union of Soviet Socialist Republics who certified that the said powers were executed in accordance with the laws of the Union of Soviet Socialist Republics.   This country does not recognize the law of the Union of Soviet Socialist Republics in Latvia and Estonia and, for such reason, the Certificates of Conformity are defective.   As the powers were executed in Latvia and Estonia the Certificates of Conformity must show that they were executed in accordance with the laws of Latvia and Estonia as independent governments.

The acknowledgement of the alleged claimants' signatures by the notaries and the authentications of the notaries' signatures by the Notarial Department of the Soviet Estonian and Soviet Latvian Supreme Courts were acts performed by officials whose presence in and dominion over those countries is not recognized by the United States Government. As such they are invalid from their inception and such invalid acts cannot be validated by the acts of the Soviet officials in Moscow who certified as to the authority of their officials in Estonia and Latvia.

* * * The powers of attorney filed in these matters are not entitled to recognition and the motions to dismiss the objections and the notices of appearance filed by the attorneys-in-fact designated in such powers are granted. The cross-motions to strike the appearances of the Consuls General are denied. The claimants in the above entitled matters are citizens of Latvia and Estonia and the Consuls General of those countries are by treaty vested with power to represent their nationals.

BANK OF CHINA v. WELLS FARGO BANK & UNION TRUST CO.

United States District Court, N.D. California, 1952.
104 F.Supp. 59.[a]

GOODMAN, DISTRICT JUDGE. Plaintiff, a Chinese corporation, filed these actions to recover the total sum of $798,584.64 on deposit in the defendant Bank. Defendant Bank filed answers asserting its willingness to pay the sum, but alleging that it was unable to do so because of conflicting claims of corporate authority to receive payment. Thereafter the attorneys for the plaintiff moved for summary judgment in plaintiff's favor. Later a second group of attorneys, claiming that they were the only attorneys empowered to represent the plaintiff Bank of China, filed a motion to dismiss these actions or in the alternative to substitute themselves as the attorneys for the plaintiff. * * *

* * *

The question now presented is essentially one of law. The attorneys who initiated this action contend that the controlling corporate authority of the Bank of China is vested by its Articles of Association in the Nationalist Government of China. They note that the Bank of China was directed by representatives of that Government when the deposit in suit was made. The Nationalist Government, they point out, not only still exists, but is the only government

a. Reversed as to other issues 209 F.2d 467 (9th Cir. 1953).

of China recognized by the United States. The Bank of China, they assert, still functions under the control of the Nationalist Government at its present seat on the Island of Formosa and at branch offices in various parts of the world. The Bank of China, so functioning, is the plaintiff in this action, they say, and the rightful claimant to the deposit in suit.

The intervening attorneys contend that the Peoples Government of China, as the successor in fact to the Nationalist Government in continental China, has succeeded to the corporate rights of the Chinese State in the Bank of China. They allege that the operations of the Bank of China throughout the Chinese Mainland and in certain branch offices abroad are now conducted by new Government directors appointed by the Peoples Government in conjunction with the directors representing private stockholders. It is only through these banking operations, they argue, that the corporate purposes of the Bank of China are now being realized. Only through operations so conducted, they say, can the rights of the Chinese State as majority stockholder and those of the private investors be given any substance. Such corporate operations, the intervening attorneys urge, are the true indicia of rightful ownership of the deposit.

The issue before the Court has therefore been reduced to a comparatively narrow one. It appears from the record, that there are two Banks of China now functioning. The question is: Which Bank $ 800,000 of China is legally entitled to the deposit in suit? For convenience, the plaintiff will hereafter be referred to as the "Nationalist" Bank of China, and the Bank of China represented by the intervening attorneys as the "Peoples" Bank of China.

At the outset, the Court must determine whether these causes may finally be disposed of by summary judgment. Rule 56(c), F.R. C.P., 28 U.S.C. If there is "a genuine issue as to a material fact," summary disposition of the causes cannot be made. This does not mean that any factual dispute bars summary judgment. The dispute must be as to material facts; and the issue thus resulting must be "genuine."

* * *

The affidavits, certificates, and other documents proffered by the plaintiff and the intervening attorneys are in conflict only in the sense that they allege facts in support of adverse claims to the funds deposited with the defendant Bank. The events and transactions set forth by both sides are not reciprocally denied. Only the legal effect of the factual occurrences and the conclusions to be drawn from them are in dispute. Thus the Court may assume the truth of the facts set forth by both sides and be required to decide only the legal effect. Consequently there is no genuine issue of material fact requiring a further hearing or trial.

* * *

Consequently, we now reach the question: Which Bank of China is legally entitled to the funds deposited with the defendant Bank?

The controlling corporate authority of the Bank of China is effectively vested in the Government of China by virtue of its majority stock ownership, its dominant voice in the managing directorate, and the supervisory powers accorded by the Articles of Association to the Minister of Finance. A determination of what government, if any, should be recognized by this court as now entitled to exercise this corporate authority over the deposit in suit, will govern the disposition of these causes.

The issue thus posed focuses attention at the outset on the fact that of the two governments asserting corporate authority, one is recognized by the United States while the other is not. If this fact, per se, is determinative, the issue is resolved. If whenever this court is called upon to determine whether there is a government justly entitled to act on behalf of a foreign state in respect to a particular matter, the court is bound to say, without regard to the facts before it, that the government recognized by our executive is that government, then nothing more need be said here. To permit this expression of executive policy to usurp entirely the judicial judgment would relieve the court of a burdensome duty, but it is doubtful that the ends of justice would thus be met. It has been argued that such is the accepted practice. But the authorities do not support this view.

* * *

Some more recent decisions of the federal courts, involving Soviet nationalization of corporations of the Baltic states, give great weight to the executive policy of non-recognition. But it cannot be said that these decisions establish an all-embracing rule that no extra-territorial effect may ever be given the acts of an unrecognized government.

* * *

The decisions just set forth, as well as others in this field, reveal no rule of law obliging the courts to give conclusive effect to the acts of a recognized government to the exclusion of all consideration of the acts of an opposing unrecognized government. Nor does it appear that such a sweeping rule would be a sound one.

Even were the court solely concerned with the implementation of our executive foreign policy, it would be presumptuous to blindly effectuate every act of a recognized government or to treat every act of an unrecognized government as entirely fictional. Early in our national history, our recognition policy was generally based on the executive's view of the stability and effectiveness of the government in question. More recently recognition has been granted and withheld at the diplomatic bargaining table. Our policy has thus become equivocal. Conflicting considerations are balanced in the executive decision. Moreover, an act of recognition does not necessarily mark a sudden reversal in executive policy. It may come as a culmination of a gradual change in attitude. Thus the import of recognition or non-recognition may vary with time and circumstance.

Recognition is not intended to sanctify every act, past and future, of a foreign government. The withholding of recognition may cast a mantle of disfavor over a government. But, it does not necessarily stamp all of its acts with disapproval or brand them unworthy of judicial notice. Our executive, on occasion, has even entered into a treaty with an unrecognized government.

This is not to suggest that the courts should regard executive policy in respect to recognition and non-recognition of foreign governments as meaningless or of little consequence. In any particular situation, executive policy may be crucial, as indeed it appears to be in the present case. But, it is a fact which properly should be considered and weighed along with the other facts before the court.

Turning to the record in this case, it appears that two governments are governments in fact of portions of the territory of the State of China. The "Peoples" Government has supplanted the "Nationalist" Government in dominion over the entire Chinese Mainland with an area of more than 3,700,000 square miles, and a population of more than 460,000,000. The "Nationalist" Government controls one of the 35 provinces of China, the Island of Formosa, which has an area of 13,885 square miles and a population in excess of 6,000,000. It is obvious that the "Peoples" Government is now the government in fact of by far the greater part of the territory of the Chinese State. Nevertheless the "Nationalist" Government controls substantial territory, exceeding in area that of either Belgium or the Netherlands, and in population that of Denmark or Switzerland.

Each government, in its respective sphere, functions effectively. Each is recognized by a significant number of the nations of the world. Each maintains normal diplomatic intercourse with those nations which extend recognition. This has been the status quo for more than two years.

Each government is in a position to exercise corporate authority in behalf of the Bank of China. That is, each government is capable of utilizing the corporate structure and certain corporate assets to promote the corporate purposes. The Bank of China was chartered primarily to facilitate Chinese international commercial activities. It was organized as an international exchange bank to deal in domestic and foreign exchange and gold and silver bullion, to discount, purchase, and collect commercial bills and drafts, to issue, service, and redeem government bonds in foreign markets, and to handle public funds deposited abroad. It was also authorized to engage in a general domestic banking business including the acceptance of deposits and valuables for safe keeping, the granting of loans, and the issuance and service of domestic government loans. Each government is in a position to act through the corporate structure of the Bank of China to carry on these international functions in the areas abroad where such Government is recognized and these domestic functions within the territory such Government controls. Each government is in fact doing so. The Bank of China, as controlled by the Nationalist Government, continues to function on the Island of Formosa and through its foreign branches in the United States, Cuba, Australia, Japan, Indo China, and elsewhere where the Nationalist Government is recognized.

The Peoples Government as successor in fact to the Nationalist Government on the Chinese Mainland is exercising the prerogatives of the Government in respect to the Bank of China there. The Peoples Government has not nationalized the Bank of China, nor confiscated its assets, nor denied the rights of private stockholders. It exercises the authority vested in the Government of China as majority stockholder. The Bank of China continues to function in accordance with its Articles of Association under the guidance of the appointees of the Peoples Government and the majority of the directors previously elected by private stockholders on the Chinese Mainland and through branches in London, Hong Kong, Singapore, Penang, Kuala Lumpur, Batavia, Calcutta, Bombay, Karachi, Chittagong, and Rangoon.

* * *

* * * Both the Nationalist and Peoples Governments have maintained and strengthened their positions. Our national policy toward these governments is now definite. We have taken a stand adverse to the aims and ambitions of the Peoples Government. The armed forces of that Government are now engaged in conflict with our forces in Korea. We recognize only the Nationalist Government as the representative of the State of China, and are actively assisting in developing its military forces in Formosa. The Bank of China now operates as two corporate entities, each performing within the area of its operations the functions bestowed upon the Bank of China by its Articles of Association. Each Bank of China is in a position to employ the deposit in suit for corporate purposes.

From a practical standpoint, neither of the rival Banks of China is a true embodiment of the corporate entity which made the deposit in the Wells Fargo Bank. The present Nationalist Bank of China is more nearly equivalent in the sense of continuity of management. The Peoples Bank is more representative in ability to deal with the greater number of private stockholders and established depositors and creditors. Were the Court to adopt a strictly pragmatic approach, it might attempt a division of the deposit between these two banks in the degree that each now exercises the functions of the Bank of China. Or the Court might award the entire deposit to the bank it deems to be the closest counterpart of the corporation contemplated by the Articles of Association.

But this, the Court could not do merely by balancing interests of a private nature. Such a course would ultimately entail determining which bank best serves the corporate interests of the State of China. That determination could not be made, while the State, itself, remains divided, except by an excursion into the realm of political philosophy. Were there only one government, in fact, of the Chinese State, or only one government in a position to act effectively for the State in respect to the matter before the Court, the Court might be justified in accepting such a government as the proper representative of the State, even though our executive declined to deal with it. Here, there coexist two governments, in fact, each attempting to further, in its own way, the interests of the State of China, in the Bank of China. It is not a proper function of a domestic court of the United States to attempt to judge which government best represents the interests of the Chinese State in the Bank of China. In this situation, the Court should justly accept, as the representative of the Chinese State, that government which our executive deems best able to further the mutual interests of China and the United States.

Since the Court is of the opinion that it should recognize the Nationalist Government of China as legally entitled to exercise the controlling corporate authority of the Bank of China in respect to the deposit in suit, the motion for summary judgment in favor of the Bank of China, as controlled by the Nationalist Government, is granted. The motion of the intervening attorneys to dismiss, or, in the alternative, for their substitution as attorneys for the plaintiff, is denied.

* * *

HAILE SELASSIE v. CABLE AND WIRELESS, LTD. (NO. 2)

England, Court of Appeal, 1938.
[1939] Ch. 182.

* * *

SIR WILFRID GREENE M. R. This is an appeal from a judgment of Bennett J. in an action by the late Emperor of Abyssinia against Cable and Wireless Limited. The claim in the action was for an account of all dealings between the plaintiff and the defendant company under a certain agreement, and payment of the amount found due. The agreement in question was an agreement between the competent Minister of the then Government of Ethiopia and the defendant company in relation to the establishment of a wireless station at Addis Ababa, the capital city of Abyssinia. Under that agreement certain sums admittedly became due from the defendant company. The dispute between the parties turned on the fact that the defendants asserted that the plaintiff had no title to sue for those moneys. Bennett J. decided in favour of the plaintiff. At the date of the trial the evidence available which was before the learned Judge, so far as it relates to the essential question raised in this appeal, showed that the annexation of Ethiopia by His Majesty the King of Italy had not yet been recognized by His Majesty's Government, but that His Majesty's Government recognized the plaintiff as the de jure Emperor of Ethiopia, and that His Majesty's Government recognized the Italian Government as the Government de facto of virtually the whole of Ethiopia, and such recognition had existed since the second half of December, 1936, that is to say, since a date earlier than the date of the issue of the writ, which was issued on January 4, 1937. Bennett J. held that the events which had taken place in Ethiopia and the other matters which were established before him were not sufficient to divest the plaintiff as still de jure Emperor of Ethiopia, of the right to recover the debt in suit in this country. From that judgment this appeal is brought. The appeal stood in the list for hearing on November 3 last, and it was called to our attention by Mr. Wynn Parry that, on the day before, an announcement had been made by the Prime Minister in the House of Commons from which it appeared that in the course of a few days, or at any rate a very short time, it was the intention of His Majesty's Government to recognize His Majesty the King of Italy as Emperor of Abyssinia, that is to say, that his position would be recognized de jure and no longer merely de facto. It was obvious from that announcement that, if it were carried into effect, the situation of this action would be profoundly affected, because circumstances would then be brought to the knowledge of the Court which would have a very important bearing upon the position of the plaintiff and his rights in respect of the debt in question in the action. Accordingly we thought right to adjourn the hearing of the appeal until a date after the probable date of recognition. * * * Events have proved that that decision was a right and just one.

What has happened is this. As appears from a certificate signed by the direction of His Majesty's Principal Secretary of State for Foreign Affairs, dated November 30, 1938, His Majesty's Government no longer recognizes His Majesty Haile Selassie as de jure Emperor of Ethiopia; His Majesty's Government now recognizes His Majesty the King of Italy as de jure Emperor of Ethiopia. From that certificate two things emerge as the result of the recognition thereby evidenced. It is not disputed that in the Courts of this country His Majesty the King of Italy as Emperor of Abyssinia is entitled by succession to the public property of the State of Abyssinia, and the late Emperor of Abyssinia's title thereto is no longer recognized as existent. Further, it is not disputed that that right of succession is to be dated back at any rate to the date when the de facto recognition, recognition of the King of Italy as the de facto Sovereign of Abyssinia, took place. That was in December, 1936. Accordingly the appeal comes before us upon a footing quite different to that upon which the action stood when it was before Bennett J. We now have the position that in the eye of

the law of this country the right to sue in respect of what was held
by Bennett J. to be (and no dispute is raised with regard to it) part
of the public State property, must be treated in the Courts of this
country as having become vested in His Majesty the King of Italy as
from a date, at the latest, in December, 1936, that is to say, before the
date of the issue of the writ in this action. Now that being so, the
title of the plaintiff to sue is necessarily displaced. When the matter
was before Bennett J., the de jure recognition not having taken place,
the question that he had to deal with was whether the effect of the de
facto conquest of Abyssinia and the recognition de facto of the Italian
Government's position in Abyssinia, operated to divest the plaintiff
of his title to sue. Whether that decision was right or whether it was
wrong is a question we are not called upon to answer, but what is admittedly the case is that if Bennett J. had had before him the state of
affairs which we have before us, his decision would have been the other way.

  *   *   *

That being so, the order of the Court will be that the appeal be
allowed, that the action be dismissed, but that the order as to costs
made by Bennett J. shall not be disturbed, and there will be no costs
of the appeal.

  *   *   *

———————

 1. *Retroactive effect of recognition.* Suppose that in the Haile
Selassie case, the decision below in favor of the King of Ethiopia had
become final and the next day the King of Italy had been recognized
by the British Government as the de jure sovereign of Ethiopia. If
the Court of Appeal meant literally what it said in stating that, for
the purpose of succession to property, recognition was retroactive to
the time of recognition of the King of Italy as de facto sovereign of
Ethiopia, what would the situation be? Does the statement really
mean that the King of Italy would be entitled to funds that a person
had previously paid to the King of Ethiopia?

 One can argue that in any event the King of Italy would not sue
the King of Ethiopia in the British courts because they would uphold
a defense of sovereign immunity and hence the issue is really moot.
But the same issue can be posed in terms which get around this point.
Consider the case of Gdynia Ameryka Linie v. Boguslawski, [1953]
A.C. 11. The case involved the Polish Government in exile in London
and the Lublin regime in Poland. A department of the Polish Government in exile agreed on behalf of the Polish shipping companies it controlled in England to give severance pay to the seamen of Polish vessels it controlled. The British Government then recognized the Lublin
government. Next some of the crewmen sued one of the Polish ship-

ping companies for the severance pay. It defended that the recognition of the Lublin government retroactively invalidated all the acts of the former government in exile.

The contention was rejected and the result can be explained by pointing out that the British Government had specified it recognized the London government until midnight July 5–6, 1945, and from that moment it recognized the Lublin government. Hence, the explanation runs, the British Government had specified that its recognition had no retroactive effect. Suppose the British Government had not been so careful, and assume further the Polish Government in London had paid the severance pay before recognition. Does it follow that the Lublin government could claim the payment was invalid?

A great deal of confusion has arisen over the meaning of so-called retroactivity in both the British courts and the courts of the United States. Whatever the rationale advanced, the result of the decisions in the United States and the United Kingdom is that rights acquired or obligations incurred by the previously recognized government are not denied effect as a result of the recognition of the successor government. The question then is whether it is proper to speak at all of retroactivity, as the courts do, or whether it would be better to accept the fact that, in the kind of situations presented in the cases appearing in this Subsection, there is neither need nor justification for doing so.

In the kind of situations involved in these cases, the government of a state continues to recognize a government of another state which has lost control of all or a major part of its territory. Even so, the dispossessed government still has some matters under its effective control so long as other governments continue to recognize it. Thus in the Wells Fargo case, the Nationalist Government of China, because it was recognized still as the government of China even though it had lost control of the Chinese territory or most of it, remained in effective control of funds of the state of China. What this really means is that the United States had the choice of continuing the Nationalist Government in effective control of the funds or else shift the effective control of the funds to the communist regime by the simple process of recognizing it.

To speak of retroactivity in this kind of situation is to suggest that the United States, by recognizing the Nationalist Government all along and then recognizing the successor regime, is the real party in error and thus at fault in failing to acknowledge that the successor regime was entitled from the start to control of the assets of China in the United States. Yet the rule of international law in point is precisely the reverse and the issue created by talk of retroactivity is false. The United States, and the United Kingdom, are not under a legal duty to recognize a successor regime even though it occupies the territory at stake, and have a right to maintain the government they recognize in effective control of matters still within its grasp.

NO LEGAL DUTY

In this kind of situation, the effect of recognition is clean cut. One day the King of Ethiopia is entitled to the funds due the state of Ethiopia, and the next day the government of Italy is. One day he can sue in the name of his state and the next day cannot. There is no question of invalidating his act and much less of invalidating the continuing recognition given him by the state in which he has taken refuge. In short there is no issue of retroactivity.

The issue is somewhat different however when the time comes for the newly recognized government to present itself in the courts of the state which has recognized it and discarded, so to speak, the previous government. Though yesterday the King of Italy was told he could not claim the funds of Ethiopia because he was not recognized as its government, today, because of the act of recognition, he cannot be turned down. But what if he should rely for his claim on some act he previously took in the territory of Ethiopia, when he was in effective control of it, and its population, and long before he was recognized? May he be told he was not then the recognized government and cannot therefore be treated now for what he was in fact at the time?

The answer, of course, is No, and the newly recognized government cannot be told there is a vacuum—sometimes of many years duration—between the time it acquired effective control of territory and population and the time the fact was formally acknowledged by way of the act of recognition. What that government did then cannot now be denied and to this extent and in this sense, the act of recognition may be labeled as having a retroactive effect. It operates to suppress the defense of non-recognition with respect to past as well as future occurrences.

This is not to say, nevertheless, that all acts previously done, or which may be done in the future, by the newly recognized government will be given effect by the recognizing state. It simply means that whatever legal rules would be operative aside from non-recognition now come into effect. See the next subsection.

2. *Decisions in other legal systems.* Access to courts has been denied to a non-recognized regime in a number of states outside the common law system. Thus the Soviet Government was refused the right to sue in Soviet Government v. Ericsson, Sweden, Supreme Court, 1921, [1919–1922] Ann.Dig. 54 (No. 30). The outcome was the same in Société Despa v. USSR, Belgium, Court of Appeal of Liège, 1931, Pasicrisie II, 108, 1931. In USSR v. Luxembourg and Saar Company, Luxembourg, Tribunal of Commerce of Luxembourg, 1935, Sirey, IV, 26, 1936, the USSR was allowed to sue but on the ground it had been impliedly recognized by Luxembourg and hence the bar against bringing the suit had been removed. In some cases, however, the unrecognized regime has been allowed to sue even though it may not claim under international law a right to do so. Commercial Representation of the USSR v. Levant Red Sea Coal Co., Egypt, Tribunal

of Alexandria, 1933, 62 Journal du Droit International 199 (1935); Republic of the South Moluccas v. Netherlands New Guinea, Netherlands, District Court of the Hague, 1954, 21 Int'l L.Rep. 48 (1957).

It has been held in France that an unrecognized regime is entitled to sovereign immunity to the extent demanded by international law. Clerget v. Commercial Representation of the Democratic Republic of Vietnam [i. e. North Vietnam], Court of Appeal of Paris (7 Ch.), 1969, 96 Journal du Droit International 895 (1969). The court said that a state becomes part of the international legal order as soon as it exists and this is so the moment it effectively exercises powers of government over a defined territory and its government is obeyed by a majority of the population. Immunity results from the independence and sovereignty of a state and not from its recognition by other states. In this case, the defendant state was not entitled to immunity from jurisdiction, but was entitled to immunity from attachment or execution for its bank assets.

In the case of The Spanish Government v. Felipe Campuzano, Norway, Supreme Court, 1938, 33 Am.J.Int'l 609 (1939), the Spanish minister in Oslo resigned at the start of the Civil War and informed the Norwegian authorities he was joining the party of General Franco. His second in command removed the furniture of the legation, including the archives, and refused to turn them over to the new appointee of the Republican Government, claiming he was holding the articles for the government of General Franco. The court upheld the right to the articles of the representative of the Republican Government so long as it was recognized by the Norwegian Government.

---

2. ON THE LAW–MAKING AUTHORITY OF UNRECOGNIZED GOVERNMENTS

SALIMOFF & CO. v. STANDARD OIL CO. OF NEW YORK

United States, New York Court of Appeals, 1933.
262 N.Y. 220, 186 N.E. 679.

POUND, CH. J. The Soviet government, by a nationalization decree, confiscated all oil lands in Russia and sold oil extracted therefrom to defendants. The former owners of the property, Russian nationals, join in an equitable action for an accounting on the ground that the confiscatory decrees of the unrecognized Soviet government and the seizure of oil lands thereunder have no other effect in law on the rights of the parties than seizure by bandits. (Luther v. Sagor & Co., [1921] 1 K.B. 456; s. c., 3 K.B. 532; cited in Sokoloff v. National City Bank, 239 N.Y. 158, 164, 145 N.E. 917.) The complaints have been dismissed.

The question is as to the effect on the title of a purchaser from the unrecognized confiscating Soviet Russian government. Does title pass or is the Soviet government no better than a thief, stealing the property of its nationals and giving only a robber's title to stolen property? Plaintiffs contend that the Soviet decrees of confiscation did not divest them of title.

When a government which originates in revolution is recognized by the political department of our government as the de jure government of the country in which it is established, such recognition is retroactive in effect and validates all the actions of the government so recognized from the commencement of its existence. (Oetjen v. Central Leather Co., 246 U.S. 297, 38 S.Ct. 309; Terrazas v. Holmes, 115 Tex. 32, 275 S.W. 392.) The courts of one independent government will not sit in judgment upon the validity of the acts of another done within its own territory, even when such government seizes and sells the property of an American citizen within its boundaries. If the Soviet government were a de jure government, it would follow that title to the property in this case must be determined by the result of the confiscatory Soviet decrees.

The status of the Soviet government is defined by the Secretary of State's office as follows:

"1. The Government of the United States accorded recognition to the Provisional Government of Russia as the successor of the Russian Imperial Government, and has not accorded recognition to any government in Russia since the overthrow of the Provisional Government of Russia.

"2. The Department of State is cognizant of the fact that the Soviet regime is exercising control and power in territory of the former Russian Empire and the Department of State has no disposition to ignore that fact.

"3. The refusal of the Government of the United States to accord recognition to the Soviet regime is not based on the ground that that regime does not exercise control and authority in territory of the former Russian Empire, but on other facts."

It follows that the question as to the validity of acts and decrees of a regime, not the subject of diplomatic recognition, becomes a matter to be decided by the courts in an appropriate case. Thus it was held that out of respect for the political departments of the United States government only a recognized government may be a plaintiff in the courts of this State. (Russian Socialist Federated Soviet Republic v. Cibrario, 235 N.Y. 255, 139 N.E. 259.)

It has been held by the Appellate Division: "Whatever may be said of the propriety or justice of the nationalizing decrees promulgated by the Soviet government of Russia, those decrees were made by the de facto government of that country and are there in full force and effect and binding upon all Russian nationals. * * *

"Under well-established principles of international law and in accordance with the decisions of our courts, the Soviet law and decrees must be given internal effect in that country." (237 App.Div. 686, 689, 690, 262 N.Y.S. 693, 697.)

*   *   *

*   *   *   The oil property confiscated was taken in Russia from Russian nationals. A recovery in conversion is dependent upon the laws of Russia. (Riley v. Pierce Oil Corp., 245 N.Y. 152, 154, 156 N.E. 647.) When no right of action is created at the place of wrong, no recovery in tort can be had in any other State on account of the wrong. The United States government recognizes that the Soviet government has functioned as a de facto or quasi government since 1917, ruling within its borders. It has recognized its existence as a fact although it has refused diplomatic recognition as one might refuse to recognize an objectionable relative although his actual existence could not be denied. It tells us that it has no disposition to ignore the fact that such government is exercising control and power in territory of the former Russian empire. As was said by this court in Sokoloff v. National City Bank (supra, p. 165): "Juridically, a government that is unrecognized may be viewed as no government at all, if the power withholding recognition chooses thus to view it. In practice, however, since juridical conceptions are seldom, if ever, carried to the limit of their logic, the equivalence is not absolute, but is subject to self-imposed limitations of common sense and fairness, as we learned in litigations following our Civil War."

As a juristic conception, what is Soviet Russia? A band of robbers or a government? We all know that it is a government. The State Department knows it, the courts, the nations and the man on the street. If it is a government in fact, its decrees have force within its borders and over its nationals. "Recognition does not create the state." (Wulfsohn v. Russian S. F. S. Republic, 234 N.Y. 372, 375, 138 N.E. 24, 25.) It simply gives to a de facto state international status. Must the courts say that Soviet Russia is an outlaw and that the Provisional government of Russia as the successor of the Russian Imperial government is still the lawful government of Russia although it is long since dead? *   *   *   The courts may not recognize the Soviet government as the de jure government until the State Department gives the word. They may, however, say that it is a government, maintaining internal peace and order, providing for national defense and the general welfare, carrying on relations with our own government and others. To refuse to recognize that Soviet Russia is a government regulating the internal affairs of the country, is to give to fictions an air of reality which they do not deserve.

The courts cannot create a foreign wrong contrary to the law of the place of the act. *   *   *   The cause of action herein arose where the act of confiscation occurred and it must be governed by the law of Soviet Russia. According to the law of nations it did no legal wrong when it confiscated the oil of its own nationals and sold it in Russia to the defendants. Such conduct may lead to governmental refusal to recognize Russia as a country with which the United States may have diplomatic dealings. The confiscation is none the less effective. The government may be objectionable in a political sense. It is not unrecognizable as a real governmental power which can give title to property within its limits.

*   *   *

Orders affirmed, etc.

<hr>

PETROGRADSKY M. K. BANK v. NATIONAL CITY BANK OF NEW YORK

United States, New York Court of Appeals, 1930.
253 N.Y. 23, 170 N.E. 479.a

CARDOZO, CH. J. The plaintiff, a Russian bank, chartered in 1869 by the Imperial Russian Government, has deposit accounts with the defendant, opened in 1911 and 1915, with a balance of $66,749.45 to its credit at the trial.

Following the Soviet revolution of November, 1917, the assets of the bank in Russia were seized by the revolutionary government, and the directors driven into exile. By decrees of the Russian Soviet Republic in 1917, the bank was declared to be merged in the People's or State Bank, its assets were confiscated, its liabilities canceled, and its shares extinguished, and by a later decree, in January, 1920, the People's or State Bank was itself abolished, a banking system having been found to be unnecessary to the new economic life.

The terms of the plaintiff's charter or "statutes" are printed in the record. The governing body was to be a directorate consisting of seven members, of whom three were to form a quorum. One of the directors lost his life in the revolution. The other six made their way to Paris, where they held meetings from time to time, and did such business as they could. All six were alive in October, 1925, when this action was begun. Three have since died, but a quorum, three, survive.

At the time of the revolution the bank had assets of large value outside the territorial limits of the Soviet Republic. The refugee directors have sought and are still seeking to bring these assets together at their present domicile in Paris. Branch banks were in existence in London, Paris, Brussels and Geneva. The assets in these branches, with the exception of those in Geneva, have been paid to the directors, and are held in the name of the bank to be distributed hereafter as justice may require. At times the payments have been

a. Cert. denied 282 U.S. 878, 51 S.Ct. 82.

voluntary, and at times in obedience to judgments of the courts. In fulfilment of the same policy, the directors have attempted to collect the balance on deposit with the defendant in New York. They requested payment, but the defendant declined to recognize their authority. They presented a check, signed by directors who had been accredited in former years as competent to draw, but the check was dishonored. In this action, which followed, the defendant insists: (1) That the plaintiff corporation has been dissolved and is no longer a juristic person; (2) that if it be a juristic person, its former directors are without authority to speak for it; and (3) that the court, in any event, should decline jurisdiction since a judgment for the plaintiff will leave the defendant unprotected against the danger of conflicting claims. The Trial Term gave judgment in favor of the defendant, and the Appellate Division unanimously affirmed.

CAN SUE

(1) We think the plaintiff is not dissolved, but is still a juristic person with capacity to sue.

The decrees of the Soviet Republic nationalizing the Russian banks are not law in the United States, nor recognized as law * * *. They are exhibitions of power. They are not pronouncements of authority. "Acts or decrees, to be ranked as governmental, must proceed from some authority recognized as a government de facto" * * *. Exhibitions of power may be followed or attended by physical changes, legal or illegal. These we do not ignore, however lawless their origin, in any survey of the legal scene. They are a source at times of new rights and liabilities. Ex facto jus oritur. Exhibitions of power may couple the physical change with declarations of the jural consequences. These last we ignore, if the consequences, apart from the declaration, do not follow from the change itself * * *. There may be exceptions to this as there are to most principles of equal generality. If so, it is only when "violence to fundamental principles of justice or to our own public policy might otherwise be done" * * *. The every-day transactions of business or domestic life are not subject to impeachment, though the form may have been regulated by the command of the usurping government * * *. To undo them would bring hardship or confusion to the helpless and the innocent without compensating benefit. On the other hand, there is no shelter in such exceptions for rapine or oppression. We do not recognize the decrees of Soviet Russia as competent to divest the plaintiff of the title to any assets that would otherwise have the protection of our law. At least this must be so where the title thus divested is transferred to the very government not recognized as existent. * * *

* * *

Putting aside, then, as irrelevant the fiat of the Soviet Government that the jural consequence shall be death, we are brought to the question whether the law of the Imperial Government of Russia

or of the later Provisional Government would have ascribed the consequence of death to the supervening changes irrespective of the fiat.
These changes in briefest summary are the loss of the Russian assets,
the dispersion of the stockholders, and the exclusion of the directors
as well as all subordinate agents from the soil of the old empire.

* * *

The corporation once existing, the burden was on the defendant
to overthrow the presumption of continuance and to show that life
had ceased * * *. We cannot say upon this record that the burden
has been borne. * * *

* * *

We find no statute or precedent that points with reasonable
clarity to the conclusion that by the law of pre-Soviet Russia there
has been an extinguishment of life as well as a suspension of activity.
We find nothing in the Russian concept of juristic personality that
leads to that conclusion, for there is nothing to show that the concept differs from our own. This being so, the presumption of continuance must tilt the balanced scales. The corporation survives in
such a sense and to such a degree that it may still be dealt with as a
persona in lands where the decrees of the Soviet Republic are not
recognized as law. We think there is no substantial basis in the evidence for an opinion to the contrary * * *.

(2) The corporation surviving, the question must still be answered whether the former directors have authority to speak for it.

* * *

* * * We think their authority is sufficient in default of ✓
other representatives to permit them to sue in our courts in the name
and for the benefit of the corporation they represent * * *.

* * *

(3) The possibility of adverse claims does not relieve the defendant from liability when sued in an action at law by a depositor
who is successful in proving a title to the fund.

* * *

The case comes down to this: A fund is in this State with title
vested in the plaintiff at the time of the deposit. Nothing to divest
that title has ever happened here or elsewhere. The directors who
made the deposit in the name of the corporation or continued it in
that name now ask to get it back. Either it must be paid to the depositor, acting by them, or it must be kept here indefinitely. Either
they must control the custody, or for the present and the indefinite
future it is not controllable by any one. The defendant expresses the
fear that the money may be misapplied if the custody is changed.
The fear has its basis in nothing more than mere suspicion. The
directors, men of honor presumably, will be charged with the duties
of trustees, and will be subject to prosecution, civil or criminal, if

those duties are ignored. The defendant is not required to follow the money into their hands and see how they apply it. Its duty is to pay.

The judgment of the Appellate Division and that of the Trial Term should be reversed and judgment directed in favor of the plaintiff for $66,749.45 with interest from December 21, 1920, and costs in all the courts.

CRANE, LEHMAN, KELLOGG and HUBBS, JJ., concur; POUND and O'BRIEN, JJ., dissent.

Judgment accordingly.

A. M. LUTHER v. JAMES SAGOR & CO.

England, Court of Appeal, 1921.
[1921] 3 K.B. 532.

* * *

BANKES L. J. The action was brought to establish the plaintiff company's right to a quantity of veneer or plywood which had been imported by the defendants from Russia. The plaintiffs' case was that they are a Russian company having a factory or mill at Staraja Russia in Russia for the manufacture of veneer or plywood, and that in the year 1919 the so-called Republican Government of Russia without any right or title to do so seized all the stock at their mill and subsequently purported to sell the quantity in dispute in this action to the defendants. The plaintiffs contended that the so-called Republican Government had no existence as a government, that it had never been recognized by His Majesty's Government, and that the seizure of their goods was pure robbery. As an alternative they contended that the decree of the so-called government nationalizing all factories, as a result of which their goods were seized, is not a decree which the Courts of this country would recognize.

The answer of the defendants was two-fold. In the first place they contended that the Republican Government which had passed the decree nationalizing all factories was the de facto Government of Russia at the time, and had been recognized by His Majesty's Government as such, and that the decree was one to which the Courts of this country could not refuse recognition. Secondly they contended that the plaintiff company was an Esthonian and not a Russian company * * *. Roche J. decided the two main points in the plaintiffs' favour. Upon the evidence which was before the learned judge I think that his decision was quite right. As the case was presented in the Court below the appellants relied on certain letters from the Foreign Office as establishing that His Majesty's Government had recognized the Soviet Government as the de facto Government of

Russia.   The principal letters are referred to by the learned judge in his judgment.   He took the view that the letters relied on did not establish the appellants' contention.   In this view I entirely agree.

In this Court the appellants asked leave to adduce further evidence, and as the respondents raised no objection, the evidence was given.   It consisted of two letters from the Foreign Office dated respectively April 20 and 22, 1921.   The first is in reply to a letter dated April 12, which the appellants' solicitors wrote to the Under Secretary of State for Foreign Affairs, asking for a "Certificate for production to the Court of Appeal that the Government of the Russian Socialist Federal Soviet Republic is recognized by His Majesty's Government as the de facto Government of Russia."   To this request a reply was received dated April 20, 1921, in these terms: "I am directed by Earl Curzon of Kedleston to refer to your letter of April 12, asking for information as to the relations between His Majesty's Government and the Soviet Government of Russia.   (2.)   I am to inform you that His Majesty's Government recognize the Soviet Government as the de facto Government of Russia."   The letter of April 22 is in reply to a request for information whether His Majesty's Government recognized the Provisional Government of Russia, and as to the period of its duration, and the extent of its jurisdiction.   The answer contains (inter alia) the statement that the Provisional Government came into power on March 14, 1917, that it was recognized by His Majesty's Government as the then existing Government of Russia, and that the Constituent Assembly remained in session until December 13, 1917, when it was dispersed by the Soviet authorities.   The statement contained in the letter of April 20 is accepted by the respondents' counsel as the proper and sufficient proof of the recognition of the Soviet Government as the de facto Government of Russia.

*   *   *

*   *   *   [U]pon the construction which I place upon the communication of the Foreign Office to which I have referred, this Court must treat the Soviet Government, which the Government of this country has now recognized as the de facto Government of Russia, as having commenced its existence at a date anterior to any date material to the dispute between the parties to this appeal.

An attempt was made by the respondents' counsel to draw a distinction between the effect of a recognition of a government as a de facto government and the effect of a recognition of a government as a government de jure, and to say that the latter form of recognition might relate back to acts of state of a date earlier than the date of recognition, whereas the former could not.   Wheaton quoting from Mountague Bernard states the distinction between a de jure and a de facto government thus (1): "A de jure government is one which, in the opinion of the person using the phrase, ought to possess the powers of sovereignty, though at the time it may be deprived of them. A de facto government is one which is really in possession of them, although the possession may be wrongful or precarious." For some purposes no doubt a distinction can be drawn between the effect of the recognition by a sovereign state of the one form of government or of the other, but for the present purpose in my opinion no distinction can be drawn. The Government of this country having, to use the language just quoted, recognized the Soviet Government as the Government really in possession of the powers of sovereignty in Russia, the acts of that Government must be treated by the Courts of this country with all the respect due to the acts of a duly recognized foreign sovereign state.

*   *   *

*   *   * Although I consider that upon the materials before him the learned judge's judgment was quite correct, I think that upon the fresh materials before this Court the appeal succeeds and the judgment must be set aside and entered for the appellants. As the respondents succeeded, as I consider, rightly upon the evidence upon which the appellants relied in the Court below, I think that the respondents should have the costs of the action, and the appellants should have the costs of this appeal.

Since writing this judgment a further communication from the Foreign Office dated May 4, 1921, has been supplied by the respondents' solicitors to the members of the Court, and to the appellants' solicitors. The communication was made to a firm of solicitors interested in some other litigation. In the communication the writer states that he is instructed to state that His Majesty's Government recognize the Soviet Government of Russia as the de facto Government of that country as from March 16, 1921. I have ascertained that the words "as from" should be read "as on." So read the communication adds nothing to the information already before the Court and I need not refer to it further.

[Other opinions omitted.]

Decisions in other legal systems. Effect has been denied to acts of an unrecognized regime done in its own territory by a number of courts outside the common law system in cases where they would otherwise have determined the issue by applying their rules of private international law, i. e. conflict of laws. The exclusive reliance on non-recognition as a ground for refusing effect to the act involved has led on occasion to peculiar results.

Lhoest-Siniawskaia v. Officier de l'Etat Civil, Belgium, Tribunal Civil of Liège, 1929, 56 Journal du Droit International 1158 (1929), involved an action to compel the registrar to record an act of marriage established in Russia in 1919. In view of the non-recognition of the USSR by Belgium, there was no Russian official whose act could be recognized as valid in Belgium and in any case the signatures on the document were not certified. In Krimtchansky v. Officier de l'Etat Civil of Belgium, Tribunal Civil of Liège, 1929, 56 Journal du Droit International 1159 (1929), the action was to compel the registrar to accept a document as evidence of a divorce in Russia in 1928 so that the plaintiff could get a marriage license. The document had been recorded in Odessa. But since Belgium did not recognize the government of the USSR, the document, quite apart from other defects, could not be recognized as a valid act by a Russian official.

An heir claimed the money deposited in a bank account by the deceased in Hamarvy v. Credit Lyonnais, Egypt, Tribunal of Alexandria, 1925, 52 Journal du Droit International 475 (1925). Proof of his identity as heir depended on a certification by the appropriate Russian authorities. Since Egypt did not recognize the USSR, however, the proof would have to be furnished by consuls from the former Russian Government who were still in Egypt. In Decision No. 5641, Greece, Tribunal of Athens, 1924, 52 Journal du Droit International 1111 (1925), a will was given effect though contrary to Soviet law which would normally govern, on the ground that since Greece did not recognize the government of the Soviet Union, it would be contrary to the public order to give effect to Soviet law.

There were cases of Russian companies whose directors in France could not, as a practical matter, comply with the Russian law in force prior to the taking of power by the Soviet Government. Still that law controlled, rather than that of the unrecognized regime, and the directors were to follow it as much as feasible and otherwise do the best they could under the circumstances. Vlasto v. Banque Russo Asiatique, France, Tribunal of Commerce of the Seine, 1922, 50 Journal du Droit International 933 (1923); Shramchenko v. Tcheloff, France, Tribunal of Commerce of Marseille, 1920, 51 Journal du Droit International 141 (1924). A similar type of issue and ruling was also involved in Katsikis v. Societá Fati Svoroni di Pallone, Italy, Tribunal of Genoa, 1923, 50 Journal du Droit International 1021 (1923).

In Attorney General v. Salomon Toledano, Morocco, Court of Appeal of Rabat, 1963, 40 Int'l L.Rep. 40 (1970), Toledano was granted by the court below an exequatur [i. e. an order giving full force and effect] for a notarial act executed in Tel Aviv. On appeal by the Attorney General, the order was reversed. Morocco did not recognize Israel as a state; hence it is deemed not to exist, all the rules regulating its functioning are deemed to be non-existent, and the notarial act is non-existent.

Stroganoff-Scherbatoff v. Bensimon, Tribunal of General Jurisdiction of the Seine, 1966, 56 Revue Critique du Droit International Privé 120 (1967) involved the following facts. By laws of succession of 1817 and 1847, Lieutenant Stroganoff became owner of certain properties. In 1918, the Soviet Government abolished the legislation under which he had title to them, took in particular some of the art objects and sold them in Berlin to the defendant company. A nephew of Stroganoff claimed as heir the objects involved. Part of the issue turned on whether the art objects continued to be immovables under the Russian laws of 1817 and 1847 or became movables by the Soviet law of 1918. The court said that the non-recognition of the Soviet Government did not entitle French courts to disregard Soviet legislation on succession enacted before recognition of the Soviet Government by France. It went on to apply the appropriate choice of law rules and found that Lieutenant Stroganoff lost possession of the objects in 1918 and hence the thirty year prescription (i. e. statute of limitations) had run long before the plaintiff brought his action.

3. NONRECOGNITION DISTINGUISHED FROM BREAKING DIPLOMATIC RELATIONS

BANCO NACIONAL DE CUBA v. SABBATINO

United States, Supreme Court, 1964.
376 U.S. 398, 84 S.Ct. 923.

[This case is reported at p. 398, above. Banco Nacional, an instrumentality of the Cuban government, brought an action in the Federal District Court for the Southern District of New York alleging conversion of bills of lading representing sugar previously expropriated by the Cuban government; the action seeks recovery of proceeds from the sale of the sugar. At the outset several procedural questions were presented to the Court, one of which was dealt with when MR. JUSTICE HARLAN delivered the opinion of the Court, as follows.]

It is first contended that this petitioner, an instrumentality of the Cuban Government, should be denied access to American courts because Cuba is an unfriendly power and does not permit nationals of this country to obtain relief in its courts. * * * If the courts of this country should be closed to the government of a foreign state, the underlying reason is one of national policy transcending the interests of the parties to the action, and this Court should give effect to that policy sua sponte even at this stage of the litigation.

Under principles of comity governing this country's relations with other nations, sovereign states are allowed to sue in the courts of the United States, * * * [P]rior to some recent lower court cases which have questioned the right of instrumentalities of the Cuban Government to sue in our courts, the privilege of suit has been denied only to governments at war with the United States * * *.

Respondents, pointing to the severance of diplomatic relations, commercial embargo, and freezing of Cuban assets in this country, contend that relations between the United States and Cuba manifest such animosity that unfriendliness is clear, and that the courts should be closed to the Cuban Government. We do not agree. This Court would hardly be competent to undertake assessments of varying degrees of friendliness or its absence, and, lacking some definite touchstone for determination, we are constrained to consider any relationship, short of war, with a recognized sovereign power as embracing the privilege of resorting to United States courts. Although the severance of diplomatic relations is an overt act with objective significance in the dealings of sovereign states, we are unwilling to say that it should inevitably result in the withdrawal of the privilege of bringing suit. Severance may take place for any number of political reasons, its duration is unpredictable, and whatever expression of animosity it may imply does not approach that implicit in a declaration of war.

It is perhaps true that nonrecognition of a government in certain circumstances may reflect no greater unfriendliness than the severance of diplomatic relations with a recognized government, but the refusal to recognize has a unique legal aspect. It signifies this country's unwillingness to acknowledge that the government in question speaks as the sovereign authority for the territory it purports to control * * *. Political recognition is exclusively a function of the Executive. The possible incongruity of judicial "recognition," by permitting suit, of a government not recognized by the Executive is completely absent when merely diplomatic relations are broken.

The view that the existing situation between the United States and Cuba should not lead to a denial of status to sue is buttressed by the circumstance that none of the acts of our Government have been aimed at closing the courts of this country to Cuba, and more particularly by the fact that the Government has come to the support of Cuba's "act of state" claim in this very litigation.

There are good reasons for declining to extend the principle to the question of standing of sovereign states to sue. Whether a foreign sovereign will be permitted to sue involves a problem more sensitive politically than whether the judgments of its courts may be reexamined, and the possibility of embarrassment to the Executive Branch in handling foreign relations is substantially more acute. Reexamination of judgments, in principle, reduces rather than enhances the possibility of injustice being done in a particular case; refusal to allow suit makes it impossible for a court to see that a particular dispute is fairly resolved. The freezing of Cuban assets exemplifies the capacity of the political branches to assure, through a variety of techniques * * * that the national interest is protected against a country which is thought to be improperly denying the rights of United States citizens.

Furthermore, the question whether a country gives res judicata effect to United States judgments presents a relatively simple inquiry. The precise status of the United States Government and its nationals before foreign courts is much more difficult to determine. To make such an investigation significant, a court would have to discover not only what is provided by the formal structure of the foreign judicial system, but also what the practical possibilities of fair treatment are. The courts, whose powers to further the national interest in foreign affairs are necessarily circumscribed as compared with those of the political branches, can best serve the rule of law by not excluding otherwise proper suitors because of deficiencies in their legal systems.

We hold that this petitioner is not barred from access to the federal courts.

---

4. IN INTERNATIONAL TRIBUNALS

ARBITRATION BETWEEN GREAT BRITAIN AND COSTA RICA (THE TINOCO CLAIMS)

William H. Taft, Sole Arbitrator, 1923.
1 U.N. Rep. Int'l Arb. Awards 375 (1948).

[There has been very little consideration by international tribunals of the subject of recognition, either as to its legal effects in the sense of this Section, or as to international rights and duties in regard to recognition. One of the few legal decisions at the international level is this arbitration by a former President of the United States and (at the time) Chief Justice of the United States. Chief Justice Taft as sole arbitrator had to decide, basically, whether rights against the Costa Rican state could vest in favor of persons entitled to British diplomatic protection as a result of governmental monetary activities and contractual undertakings by a coupist president of Costa Rica whose regime had not been recognized by the United Kingdom, the United States, and a number of other leading countries. After Tinoco had established a new constitution and called elections, his regime fell before elections were held. Thereafter a provisional government was in authority temporarily, elections were held, and a new government took office under the restored old constitution. The new government enacted a Law of Nullities, purporting to invalidate currency issued by Tinoco's regime and held by British subjects and an oil concession granted by Tinoco to a British company. Although the arbitrator found no injury to the plaintiff as to either claim for reasons not relevant at this point, he determined that the Tinoco regime could bind the state internationally. A portion of his award follows.]

Dr. John Bassett Moore, now a member of the Permanent Court of International Justice, in his Digest of International Law, Volume 1, p. 249, announces the general principle which has had such universal acquiescence as to become well settled international law:

Changes in the government or the internal policy of a state do not as a rule affect its position in international law. A monarchy may be transformed into a republic or a republic into a monarchy; absolute principles may be substituted for constitutional, or the reverse; but, though the government changes, the nation remains, with rights and obligations unimpaired.   *   *   *

First, what are the facts to be gathered from the documents and evidence submitted by the two parties as to the de facto character of the Tinoco government?

In January, 1917, Frederico A. Tinoco was Secretary of War under Alfredo Gonzalez, the then President of Costa Rica. On the ground that Gonzalez was seeking reelection as President in violation of a constitutional limitation, Tinoco used the army and navy to seize the government, assume the provisional headship of the Republic and become Commander-in-Chief of the army. Gonzalez took refuge in the American Legation, thence escaping to the United States. Tinoco constituted a provisional government at once and summoned the people to an election for deputies to a constituent assembly on the first of May, 1917. At the same time he directed an election to take place for the Presidency and himself became a candidate. An election was held. Some 61,000 votes were cast for Tinoco and 259 for another candidate. Tinoco then was inaugurated as the President to administer his powers under the former constitution until the creation of a new one. A new constitution was adopted June 8, 1917, supplanting the constitution of 1871. For a full two years Tinoco and the legislative assembly under him peaceably administered the affairs of the Government of Costa Rica, and there was no disorder of a revolutionary character during that interval. No other government of any kind asserted power in the country. The courts sat, Congress legislated, and the government was duly administered. Its power was fully established and peaceably exercised. The people seemed to have accepted Tinoco's government with great good will when it came in, and to have welcomed the change.   *   *   *

But it is urged that many leading Powers refused to recognize the Tinoco government, and that recognition by other nations is the chief and best evidence of the birth, existence and continuity of succession of a government. Undoubtedly recognition by other Powers is an important evidential factor in establishing proof of the existence of a government in the society of nations. What are the facts as to this? The Tinoco government was recognized by Bolivia on May 17, 1917; by Argentina on May 22, 1917; by Chile on May 22, 1917; by Haiti on May 22, 1917; by Guatemala on May 28, 1917; by Switzerland on June 1, 1917; by Germany on June 10, 1917; by Denmark on June 18, 1917; by Spain on June 18, 1917; by Mexico on July 1, 1917; by Holland on July 11, 1917; by the Vatican on June 9, 1917; by Colombia on August 9, 1917; by Austria on August 10, 1917; by Portugal on August 14, 1917; by El Salvador on September 12, 1917; by Roumania on November 15, 1917; by Brazil on November 28,

1917; by Peru on December 15, 1917; and by Ecuador on April 23, 1917.

What were the circumstances as to the other nations?

The United States, on February 9, 1917, two weeks after Tinoco had assumed power, took this action:

> The Government of the United States has viewed the recent overthrow of the established government in Costa Rica with the gravest concern and considers that illegal acts of this character tend to disturb the peace of Central America and to disrupt the unity of the American continent. In view of its policy in regard to the assumption of power through illegal methods, clearly enunciated by it on several occasions during the past four years, the Government of the United States desires to set forth in an emphatic and distinct manner its present position in regard to the actual situation in Costa Rica which is that it will not give recognition or support to any government which may be established unless it is clearly proven that it is elected by legal and constitutional means.

And again on February 24, 1917:

> In order that citizens of the United States may have definite information as to the position of this Government in regard to any financial aid which they may give to, or any business transaction which they may have with those persons who overthrew the constitutional Government of Costa Rica by an act of armed rebellion, the Government of the United States desires to advise them that it will not consider any claims which may in the future arise from such dealings, worthy of its diplomatic support.

The Department of State issued the following in April, 1918:

> The Department of State has received reports to the effect that those citizens of Costa Rica now exercising the functions of government in the Republic of Costa Rica have been led to believe by those persons who are acting as their agents, that the Government of the United States was considering granting recognition to them as constituting the Government of Costa Rica.

> In order to correct any such impression which is absolutely erroneous, the Government of the United States desires to state clearly and emphatically that it has not altered the attitude which it has assumed in regard to the granting of recognition to the above mentioned citizens of Costa Rica and which was conveyed to them in February, 1917, and further that this attitude will not be altered in the future.

Probably because of the leadership of the United States in respect to a matter of this kind, her then Allies in the war, Great Britain, and France and Italy, declined to recognize the Tinoco government. Costa Rica was, therefore, not permitted to sign the Treaty of Peace at

Versailles, although the Tinoco government had declared war against Germany.

The merits of the policy of the United States in this non-recognition it is not for the arbitrator to discuss, for the reason that in his consideration of this case, he is necessarily controlled by principles of international law, and however justified as a national policy non-recognition on such a ground may be, it certainly has not been acquiesced in by all the nations of the world, which is a condition precedent to considering it as a postulate of international law.

The non-recognition by other nations of a government claiming to be a national personality, is usually appropriate evidence that it has not attained the independence and control entitling it by international law to be classed as such. But when recognition vel non of a government is by such nations determined by inquiry, not into its de facto sovereignty and complete governmental control, but into its illegitimacy or irregularity of origin, their non-recognition loses something of evidential weight on the issue with which those applying the rules of international law are alone concerned. What is true of the non-recognition of the United States in its bearing upon the existence of a de facto government under Tinoco for thirty months is probably in a measure true of the non-recognition by her Allies in the European War. Such non-recognition for any reason, however, cannot outweigh the evidence disclosed by this record before me as to the de facto character of Tinoco's government, according to the standard set by international law.

Second.   It is ably and earnestly argued on behalf of Costa Rica that the Tinoco government cannot be considered a de facto government, because it was not established and maintained in accord with the constitution of Costa Rica of 1871. To hold that a government which establishes itself and maintains a peaceful administration, with the acquiescence of the people for a substantial period of time, does not become a de facto government unless it conforms to a previous constitution would be to hold that within the rules of international law a revolution contrary to the fundamental law of the existing government cannot establish a new government. This cannot be, and is not, true. The change by revolution upsets the rule of the authorities in power under the then existing fundamental law, and sets aside the fundamental law in so far as the change of rule makes it necessary. To speak of a revolution creating a de facto government, which conforms to the limitations of the old constitution is to use a contradiction in terms. The same government continues internationally, but not the internal law of its being. The issue is not whether the new government assumes power or conducts its administration under constitutional limitations established by the people during the incumbency of the government it has overthrown. The question is, has it really established itself in such a way that all within its influence recognize its control, and that there is no opposing force assuming to be a government in its place? Is it discharging its functions as a government usually does, respected within its own jurisdiction?

* * *

Liability of the state for acts of ordinary governmental administration by an unrecognized regime. There is international arbitral, as well as national decisional, support for the proposition that even a revolutionary regime that is not successful in establishing itself, albeit temporarily, as the only effective government in a state is capable in territory under its control of creating legal obligations against the state and in favor of aliens as a result of the conduct of ordinary governmental administration, such as collecting and giving quittances for taxes, issuing postal money orders, etc. See generally, Restatement of the Foreign Relations Law of the United States, Reporters' Notes to Section 110 (1965).

It is frequently assumed a fortiori, cf. the Tinoco Arbitration, that a revolutionary regime that does establish itself as the effective government in control of a state can create concession and other investment rights in favor of aliens that will bind a future de jure government. While this may be so in law, the political problems for a foreign investor who has "dealt with a dictator," especially if the transaction is unusually favorable to the investor, can and have been many. Thus, in foreign investment practice there is a very difficult problem for international transactions lawyers whose clients want to know: "Do you advise me to take up or reject this really good opportunity that old General Dictadura is offering me?" Try your hand at responding to hypotheticals that you can easily think of about direct foreign investments involving special acts of grant by, inter alia, the regimes presently in control of Spain, Greece, Turkey, Egypt, Argentina, Bolivia, Brazil, Ecuador, Paraguay, and Peru.

SECTION B. INTERNATIONAL LEGAL EFFECTS OF NATIONAL RECOGNITION POLICIES

---

1. SKETCHES OF NATIONAL POLICIES

1. *Recognition of entities as states.* It is not often that the recognition of a state is in doubt. Most such recognitions are as routine as the acts that bring new states into existence, such as by the voluntary granting of independence to a former colony. The latest extraordinary act of recognition of a new state was in the case

of Bangladesh.   Under these circumstances a classic doctrinal dispute has fallen into desuetude: is recognition of a state *constitutive*, in the sense that the state cannot exist legally as a state without recognition?   Much ink has been spilled on this question, with inconclusive results, because almost all entities (including micro-mini states) that mount drives for statehood get "recognized" as such.   About the only failure is the Island of Anguilla, but it is by no means clear that the Anguillans wanted independence so much as freedom from association in semi-statehood with the neighboring islands of Nevis and St. Kitts.   The Anguillans seemed happy to settle for renewed British colonial status.   The British seemed less happy to have to keep the colony.

2.   *De facto recognition of regimes as governments.*   As an act of cognition, see p. 768, recognition obviously must be based on what is perceived about an entity as a state or a regime as a government. While there is no rule or doctrine of international law that a regime perceived as a government must be recognized as such by the diplomatic arm of another state, the general practice of states is to "recognize" or "extend recognition to" a new regime that has come to power in abnormal ways and is perceived in fact as having established itself as a government.   Therefore, in this sense recognition practice, at least, as to regimes as governments is "de facto"; i. e., based on the facts perceived.   Notwithstanding the simplicity of the basic situation just described, the terms "de facto" and "de jure" have an unfortunate ballast of imprecision in international relations and law. The Restatement of the Foreign Relations Law of the United States (1965)* attempts clarification as follows in Reporters' Note 2 to Section 96:

2.   *Uses of term "de facto" in connection with recognition.* The term de facto is used by writers and in judicial decisions dealing with recognition in a variety of ways.

a.   The term de facto is used to indicate that the recognition extended to a regime is tentative and hence, under the rule stated in Subsection (2) of this Section, may be withdrawn.   In this sense, a regime may be recognized as a de facto government or, to make it even more tentative, as a de facto authority.   For an example of British practice regarding tentative recognition see § 102, Reporters' Note.

b.   The term de facto is used to describe the policy followed by some states in determining whether to extend recognition. Even in this context two separate uses of the term de facto must be distinguished:

(i) The term de facto has been used, in contrast to the term de jure, to describe a recognition policy that does not interpose as an objection to recognition of a government the fact that the government came into power in violation of the constitution of the state.   This sense of the term is now obsolete since no state now requires constitutional legitimacy as a necessary condition for recognition of a new government.

(ii) The term de facto has been used to describe a policy under which a state will recognize any new regime satisfying the requirements stated in § 101 with respect to actual control of the state.   This is in contrast to a policy under which legal considerations, such as the ability and intention of the regime to carry out the obligations of the state under international law and agreements, are applied as additional requirements for recognition.

c.   The term de facto has been used by national courts and international tribunals in dealing with the effect to be given the acts of non-recognized regimes that are in actual control of the state.   Arbitrator Taft referred to the Tinoco regime as the de facto government of Costa Rica in Tinoco Arbitration (Great Britain v. Costa Rica), [1923–1924] Ann.Dig. 34, 176, 177, 379, 380 (Nos. 15, 95, 96, 211, 212), 18 Am.J. Int'l L. 147 (Oct. 18, 1923).   The New York Court of Appeals described the Soviet Union in the same terms in Salimoff & Co. v. Standard Oil Co., 262 N.Y. 220, 186 N.E. 679 (1933)).   In neither case did the court's characterization of the non-recognized regime as a de facto government involve recognition of the regime, although the facts that led to this characterization resulted in a decision, in each case, giving legal effect to the acts of the regime under the rules stated in §§ 109 and 113.

British recognition policy is commonly described as being "de facto" in the sense of both a and b (ii) above.   In the United States, which has oscillated as between a de facto and a de jure policy as to recognition of governments—and which may now have virtually abandoned the act of recognition altogether—de facto recognition was classically stated by Thomas Jefferson, as Secretary of State, and elaborated by his successors in that office, as requiring satisfaction *in fact* that three pre-conditions had been met by the regime being considered for recognition: that (i) it is in substantial control of the territory of the state, (ii) with the acquiescence [not necessarily the electoral approval] of the people, and (iii) is willing to carry out the international obligations of the state.   A scholarly British Ambassador explained British and American recognition policies as follows:

Sir Roger Makins, British Ambassador to the United States, speaking in 1954, discussed American and British viewpoints with reference to diplomatic recognition and explained particularly with reference to the viewpoint of Great Britain:

* * * As you all know, the British Government recognized the Communist Government of China in 1950, in

company with a number of other Governments. We continue to recognize it and have no present intention of changing our position. The United States has not recognized the Peking regime, and the administration has recently reaffirmed its refusal to do so.

Now, there are no differences between us in our objectives in the Far East, even if we sometimes differ on the timing, and the method of our approach to them. We are both equally concerned to oppose and to prevent the spread of Communist imperialism. How is it, therefore, that we should be found at variance on this question of recognition? And what is the significance of this divergent position?

The practice of governments in giving diplomatic recognition to each other has fluctuated through the years, and the attitudes of the British and United States governments have sometimes approximated and sometimes diverged. Broadly speaking, there are two main lines of approach to be found in the writings of the authorities, and in the policies of governments. The one treats recognition as an act based solely on the facts, an act which follows upon the fulfillment of certain objective criteria; the other regards it as an act of policy which signifies something more than the recognition of a situation of fact and law. I shall call the former the de facto principle, the latter the principle of legitimacy. . . .

The practice of Great Britain has always conformed fairly closely to the de facto principle. If a government is in effective control of the country in question; if it seems to have a reasonable expectancy of permanence; if it can act for a majority of the country's inhabitants; if it is able (though possibly not willing) to carry out its international obligations; if, in short, it can give a convincing answer to the question, "Who's in charge here?," then we recognize that government. We are not conferring a favor, we are recognizing a situation of fact. The conduct of foreign affairs (as distinct from the formation of foreign policy) is, after all, not essentially different from the conduct of any other business. You do not have to like a man's face, or manners, or even morals, in doing business with him. And even if you do not want to do business with an ugly customer, shutting your eyes won't make him go away.

* * *

There have been other periods in American history when this realistic, Jeffersonian, de facto-type view of recognition has yielded to the belief that what Chief Justice Taft called "legitimacy" was a further requirement. The Union took that view, naturally enough, under Secretary

Seward at the time of the Civil War, and later, during President Wilson's first term, there were emphatic reversions to the principle of legitimacy. Britain also applied this principle to some extent during the 19th century. For example, in 1870 Britain refused to recognize the government of the Third Republic in France until it had been elected by a constituent assembly, and again in Portugal in 1910 Britain refused to recognize the revolutionary government until a constitution had been voted and a President elected.

But since 1924 Britain has followed the de facto principle closely in a series of cases, the Soviet Union, Chile, Peru, Ecuador, Argentina, and the Nationalist government of Gen. Franco in Spain. So we arrive at the situation today in which Britain and the United States find themselves at opposite points in applying the doctrine of diplomatic recognition in the case of China: we have applied the de facto principle, you are applying a contemporary version of the legitimacy principle.

Before commenting on this there is a question of timing and circumstances to be mentioned. Britain recognized Communist China before the Korean war began, before Chinese intervention in the struggle, before the natural indignation to which these events gave rise. * * *

2 Whiteman, Digest of International Law 110 (1963)

3. *Recognition and revolution.* When a mother country in an orderly manner spins off a former colony as a new state—"mini" or normal—or when a sharp change in political preference within a country comes at the ballot box, recognition is either routine, as in the case of new states, or does not recur at all, as when the Chileans elected Dr. Allende as the world's first freely elected Communist chief of state. Hence both the policy and the consequent legal problems related to recognition are closely linked to abnormal political change within particular geographic areas. Established governments of existing states respond in various ways, over time, to revolutionary changes elsewhere. Not even the United Kingdom has always been rigorously faithful to a "de facto" view of diplomatic recognition. As to the recognition of revolutionary regimes, the United States, although over the longer span being more or less faithful to the "Jeffersonian Prescription" where "old-line" countries and fairly remote new ones have had *coups d'etat,* has followed a zig-zag course as to Latin America and as to revolutionary socialism (the USSR and the Peoples Republic of China).

The most dramatic and possibly still the most far-reaching departure of the United States from a detached and clinical viewpoint as to coups was that of President Woodrow Wilson, who under the influence of his Secretary of State, William Jennings Bryan, withheld recognition of Francisco Madero, and later others, who in Mexico rose up against the dictatorship of Porfirio Diaz.

What had begun with an excess of virtue, p. 769, ended with an excess of national espousal of questionable property rights given to American concerns by Diaz. That is, the Harding Administration withheld recognition of the Obregon Government of Mexico, after conditions had stabilized in the country, until the Government of Mexico agreed, as a condition to recognition by the United States, to validate the Diaz grants of property rights.

These pages of history have had great influences. Out of Latin America's observation of the Wilson-Harding episode came the Estrada doctrine and an attitudinal conditioning in Latin America that the withholding of recognition is an act of inadmissible intervention in the internal affairs of the state that has had the coup. With ethnocentric insensitivity, however, United States diplomatic practice and strong mass media opinion continued to support a United States recognition policy for Latin America different from the one applied to coups elsewhere, excluding the major socialist ones.

In 1962, President Kennedy for nearly a month withheld recognition of a coup in Peru, on the grounds that the change of government had not occurred democratically. But in the 1960's, coup after coup in sub-Sahara Africa and southeast Asia were met with routine applications of the Jeffersonian criteria.

Latin America has become extremely sensitive as to the discrimination. But even before the announcement by President Nixon, pursuant to his "Low Posture" doctrine, that we would deal with governments as we find them—even in Latin America—United States recognition policy had begun to shift toward what might be called a modified Estrada Doctrine. In the Panamanian and Peruvian coups of 1968, the Department of State took the position that the occurrence of a coup did not necessarily mean that a new act of recognition would have to take place. Instead, the practice of the Government came to be to adjust relations in accordance with the stage of the coup and the stability of the regime within the country and to continue relations in such cases and situations as the national interests of the United States might indicate as provident for contact between the United States and the coupists. The ambassadors were not withdrawn, and the resumptions of "full" relations were not marked by formal acts, such as presentations of credentials. The United States did continue a practice of consulting with other members of the Organization of American States and of issuing press statements at the time of return to "full" relationships. These recent practices and utterances have tended to reduce sharply the former difference in treatment of coups in the other American republics from those elsewhere.

Mexico, the home of the Estrada Doctrine, p. 769, which declares that there is no more reason for new recognition following a coup than for one following an election, has not been continually faithful to its basic doctrine. To this day Mexico has not recognized the Franco Regime in Spain, and it was only after President Nixon's visit to Peking that Mexico arranged for an exchange of ambassadors with the Peoples Republic of China.

UNITED STATES POLICY ON NONRECOGNITION OF COMMUNIST CHINA

39 United States Department of State Bulletin 385 (1958).

[Text of a memorandum sent by the Department of State to its missions abroad on United States policy regarding nonrecognition of Communist China.]

Policy toward Communist China has been an important issue since the Communists came to power there, and it is of critical significance to the United States and the free world today. In the United States the issue is a very real one to the vast majority of the people. As a result of Korean and Chinese Communist aggression in Korea, the United States suffered 142,000 casualties, bringing tragedy to communities all over the country. * * *

The basic considerations on which United States policy toward China rests are twofold. First, the Soviet bloc, of which Communist China is an important part, is engaged in a long-range struggle to destroy the way of life of the free countries of the world and bring about the global dominion of communism. The Chinese Communist regime has made no secret of its fundamental hostility to the United States and the free world as a whole nor of its avowed intention to effect their downfall. Today its defiance of and attacks on the non-Communist world have reached a level of intensity that has not been witnessed since the Korean war. The second basic factor is that East Asia is peculiarly vulnerable to the Communist offensive because of the proximity of the free countries of that area to Communist China, the inexperience in self-government of those which have recently won their independence, their suspicions of the West inherited from their colonial past, and the social, political, and economic changes which inevitably accompany their drive toward modernization.

The Chinese Communists see the victory of communism in Asia inevitable; and now that they control the vast population and territory of mainland China they are utilizing the advantages these give to encompass their ends. Chinese Communist leaders have shown by their words and their acts that they are not primarily interested in promoting the welfare of their people while living at peace with their neighbors. Their primary purpose is to extend the Communist revolution beyond their borders to the rest of Asia and thence to the rest of the world.

     *   *   *

In the case of China there are special considerations which influence United States policy with regard to recognition. For one thing, although the Chinese Communists have seized the preponderant bulk of China, they have not completed their conquest of the country. The generally recognized legitimate Government of China continues to exist and in Taiwan is steadily developing its political, economic, and military strength. The Government of the Republic of China controls the strategic island of Taiwan and through its possession of a sizable military force—one of the largest on the side of the free world in Asia—presents a significant deterrent to renewed Chinese Communist aggression. Recognition of Communist China by the United States would seriously cripple, if not destroy altogether, that Government. On the other hand, continued United States recognition and support of the Republic of China enables it to challenge the claim of the Chinese Communists to represent the Chinese people and keeps alive the hopes of those Chinese who are determined eventually to free their country of Communist rule.

     *   *   *

An argument often heard is that the Chinese Communists are here "to stay"; that they will have to be recognized sooner or later; and that it would be the course of wisdom to bow to the inevitable now rather than be forced to do so ungracefully at a later date. It is true that there is no reason to believe that the Chinese Communist regime is on the verge of collapse; but there is equally no reason to accept its present rule in mainland China as permanent. In fact, unmistakable signs of dissatisfaction and unrest in Communist China have appeared in the "ideological remodeling" and the mass campaign against "rightists" which have been in progress during the past year. Dictatorships often create an illusion of permanence from the very fact that they suppress and still all opposition, and that of the Chinese Communists is no exception to this rule. The United States holds the view that communism's rule in China is not permanent and that it one day will pass. By withholding diplomatic recognition from Peiping it seeks to hasten that passing.

In public discussions of China policy one of the proposals that has attracted widest attention is that known as the "two Chinas solution." Briefly, advocates of this arrangement propose that the Chinese Communist regime be recognized as the government of mainland China while the Government at Taipei remains as the legal government of Taiwan. They argue that this approach to the Chinese problem has the merit of granting the Communists only what they already control while retaining for the free world the military strategic bastion of Taiwan. However, it overlooks or ignores certain facts of basic importance. The Republic of China would not accept any diminution of its sovereignty over China and could be expected to resist such an arrangement with all the means at its disposal. If a "two Chinas solution" were to be forcefully imposed against its will, that Government's effectiveness as a loyal ally to the free-world-cause would be destroyed. Peiping, too, would reject such an arrangement. In fact, over the past year Chinese Communist propaganda has repeatedly and stridently denounced the "two Chinas" concept and, ironically, has been accusing the United States Government of attempting to put it into effect. Peiping attaches great importance to the eventual acquisition of Taiwan and has consistently reserved what it calls its "right" to seize Taiwan by force if other means fail. There is no prospect that it would ever acquiesce in any arrangement which would lead to the permanent detachment of Taiwan from China.

The "two Chinas" concept is bitterly opposed by both Peiping and Taipei. Hence, even if such a solution could be imposed by outside authority, it would not be a stable one. Constant policing would be required to avert its violent overthrow by one side or the other. * * *

------

1. *Is implied or inadvertent recognition a danger?* It is recalled from time to time in the press that once at Geneva in the 1950s, United States Secretary of State John Foster Dulles found himself in the same room with Chou En-lai of the People's Republic of China. Fearing a handshake or some other greeting from Chou, Dulles rushed from the room, exclaiming, "I cannot, I cannot!" Aside from personal and ideological factors, the Secretary seems to have been motivated by the fear that an act of social intercourse would amount to recognition of the "Chicoms" as the government of mainland China. In his instructions to American diplomatic missions, Mr. Dulles also expressed great concern lest American foreign service officers, by appearing at the same social functions with representatives of unrecognized regimes representing "international communism," effectuate inadvertent recognition of them.

Need the Secretary have worried? Section 104 of the Restatement of the Foreign Relations Law of the United States (1965), makes the sensible and widely accepted point that, although recognition by implication can occur, a disclaimer is sufficient to negate it. Hence an implication of intention to recognize from propinquity or other associative conduct is largely an illusory fear.

The best recent support of the effect of a disclaimer—mutual in this case—is that in 1971 the President of the United States made an official visit to the government of the People's Republic of China, without previously having extended it recognition. Why has the United States not yet recognized the People's Republic, which now sits in the Chinese state's seats in the United Nations, the Nationalist Chinese (entity or regime?) having been turned out? What has become of the defense commitments of the United States to the Chinese government on Taiwan? Would United States recognition of the People's Republic as the government of the state of China, whose territory the President confirmed at Peiping includes the island of Taiwan, automatically withdraw United States recognition of the Nationalist Republic of China, and if so or not, as the government of what?

2. *What, if anything, should be done to regulate internationally long term or intensive relations without recognition?* The disclaimer principle makes it possible for governments to carry on over many years fairly intensive sets of relationships without recognition. For instance, the United States did not recognize the Bolshevists as the government of the state of Russia until 16 years after the 1917 Russian Revolution. However, in that period trade delegates were exchanged and the largest volume of private sector United States trade and technology transfers to date took place. Franco took Madrid and the Spanish Civil War ended in April 1939. Mexico has and for years has had quite intensive commercial, cultural (including exchanges of bullfighters) and other relations with the Franco regime. There is a Mexican official in Madrid to give visas for travel to Mexico. But Mexico has no diplomatic mission to the Franco regime. Are these peculiarities significant or not in the conduct of international relations? Should diplomatic recognition be regulated by positive international law in this respect? Why or why not? In the case of Spain, is Mexico refusing to recognize or is it implying that recognition is irrelevant and that it simply does not choose to send an ambassador to Franco's palace? See p. 769.

SCHWEBEL, "COGNITION" AND THE PEKING VISIT
IS THE RECOGNITION OF GOVERNMENTS OBSOLETE?

The Washington Post, Feb. 23, 1972.
Sec. A, p. 16, col. 3, 4, 5.*

One of the many extraordinary aspects of President Nixon's visit to Peking is that it is an official visit by the chief of state of a government that does not recognize the government by whose chief of state he has been officially received.

Not only, in fact, does the United States not recognize what it calls the Government of the People's Republic of China as the Government of China; it recognizes another government, the Government of the Republic of China, as the Government of China.

Great importance is attached by the three governments concerned—in Washington, Peking and Taipei—to which government is

* © The Washington Post.

acknowledged as the recognized government. Yet at the same time, as President Nixon's journey so dramatically demonstrates, the content of recognition is, internationally speaking, unimpressive.

For two governments may in fact know, appreciate and act on the conclusion of their respective existence, even though they do not "recognize" one another. They may conclude treaties (such as that for a Korean armistice), conduct negotiations between ambassadors (as with the Warsaw talks), trade (as U. S. citizens may now lawfully do with mainland China), promote cultural exchanges (as of ping-pong teams), collaborate or contest in international organs (such as the United Nations Security Council), attend each other's diplomatic receptions (as in New York), and coordinate their foreign policies (as China and the United States appear to have done, in effect if not by design, on Bengal). Viewed against that background of not inconsiderable relations, President Nixon's official visit to the unrecognized government in Peking seems less anomalous.

Not only does the absence of recognition admit extensive relations; recognition itself does not require substantial, still less cordial relations. For example, the United States recognized the State of Cuba with the Spanish-American War. It recognized the Castro government soon after it seized power. But diplomatic relations between the two governments have been severed for years. Trade is interdicted, travel is limited, the most minimal diplomatic intercourse seems to be carried on through the good offices of third states, indeed sanctions are in force.

If then the reality of recognition is so arid, why the fuss about it? Whether or not one government accords recognition to a foreign state or government remains a matter of much political significance. Sheikh Mujibur Rahman is triumphant when more than a score of states recognize the statehood of Bangladesh. The senators of the opposition scent a political point in the administration's delaying the recognition of Bangladesh, a matter which, ironically enough, President Nixon suggests he will deal with on his return from talks with the unrecognized government in Peking.

Presumably there is something to all this controversy about recognition or there would be less controversy. Something, but not much.

Under international law, an entity is generally acknowledged to be a state if it has a reasonably defined territory, a population, a government substantially independent of other governments, and a measure of stability.

Under international law, a political authority qualifies as a government if it is in effective control of the state.

When these conditions are fulfilled, other governments act as if they know that the entities that fulfill these conditions are there. This they can do short of recognition—as American relations with the government in Peking demonstrate.

And short of recognition, other governments must nevertheless accord unrecognized states and governments certain rights—most notably respect for their territorial integrity. The Arab States are not legally permitted to attack the State of Israel because they do not recognize it; nor is the United States entitled to attack forces of the Government of the People's Republic of China because it does not recognize it.

In other words, short of recognition, there is what the legal adviser of the Swedish Ministry for Foreign Affairs, Hans Blix, terms "cognition." States know when in fact foreign states and governments exist, even though they have not extended recognition to them; and they must act on that knowledge up to a limited point.

What then is left to the function of recognition?

Recognition is a declaration (or occasionally, an action) by which the recognizing government in effect affirms that the new state or regime fulfils the criteria of statehood or government and that it is ready to accept it as such. It implies (but does not require) that the recognizing government is prepared to regularize relations by the establishment of diplomatic relations. It suggests that the recognizing government is ready to extend to the newly recognized at least a measure of cooperation and courtesy.

But recognition does not necessarily manifest readiness for close and cordial relations. Thus, on Sept. 25, 1969, the United States Senate resolved: "*   *   * that it is the sense of the Senate that when the United States recognizes a foreign government and exchanges diplomatic relations with it, this does not of itself imply that the United States approves of the form, ideology or policy of that foreign government."

In other words, recognition, on the international plane, does little more than manifest the willingness of the recognizing government to maintain relations on a more regularized and possibly more intimate basis than heretofore. It may not even imply that. India recognized Israel years ago; it has yet to exchange ambassadors with it.

On the domestic plane, the effects of recognition are larger. In most national courts, questions like the capacity of a foreign state or government to sue, and to claim sovereign immunity from suit, turn on whether it is recognized by the national government in question.

The substantive aridity of recognition on the international level —coupled with the considerable emotional confusion which issues of recognition nevertheless continue to generate—have led to suggestions that the term and concept of recognition be dropped. States would act on the basis of cognition alone. They would establish diplomatic relations, and pragmatically develop other relations, as they please.

Possibly national courts might be left themselves to make decisions about the existence of foreign states and governments as cases arise, without the benefit of executive guidance.

Abandonment of recognition as an international practice would seem to present few problems. One would be that of the choice as to which of two rival governments represents a single state—a problem which the China case poses. As it is, international organizations such as the United Nations make that choice for themselves for their purposes.

Certainly a good deal of international misunderstanding and domestic hyperbole would disappear with the disappearance of the doctrine of recognition. At the very least, President Nixon's trip to Peking furnishes fine occasion to think about it.

ACADEMY OF SCIENCES OF THE U.S.S.R. INSTITUTE OF STATE AND LAW, INTERNATIONAL LAW 117 (MOSCOW, 1961)

* * *

Political factors play a certain part in deciding upon recognition of a State.

Recognition is an act undertaken by a State which expresses the desire of the ruling class of that State. The emergence of a socialist State as a rule gives rise to strong opposition on the part of the imperialist States. This is expressed by their attitude to the problem of recognition (the United States did not recognise the Soviet Union until 1933, and it has still not recognised the Chinese People's Republic).

Something similar may also be observed in the case of the recognition of States emerging as a result of the national-liberation struggle. The governments of some imperialist States not only do not recognise these States, but attempt to keep them in a state of dependence by force of arms, and in this way to maintain unchanged the shameful system of colonialism.

All these measures are illegal, in that they contradict a most important principle of International Law—the principle of the self-determination of nations.

* * *

Governments and diplomatic missions in exile. Charles II, by inheritance from his beheaded father, King of England-Scotland, bided his time (with a modest retinue) on the continent during the Cromwellian era. So also many another ruler or pretender has waited, but it was not until World War II that the phenomenon of governments operating as such in exile occurred. Because of the Nazi occupations, the de jure governments of Belgium, the Netherlands, Norway, Yugoslavia, and Poland had to flee to the territory of allied states, mainly to the United Kingdom, where they arranged to carry on acts of governance. A contemporary legal analysis presented the ensuing legal problems as follows:

The appointment of the American Ambassador to Poland, Mr. Biddle, as diplomatic representative to Belgium, The Netherlands, Norway, and Yugoslavia, raises a nice point of international law and procedure. Is this unique embassy to governments-in-exile in England a fiction or a fact?

When Poland was occupied by Germany, Ambassador Biddle accompanied the Polish Government in its flight and re-established the Embassy near the remnant of Polish sovereignty represented in London. This government exercises no authority whatever within the boundaries of Poland. Can it therefore be truly said that Poland still exists as a member of the family of nations?

The status of Norway and Yugoslavia is similar to that of Poland, but the situation of Belgium and The Netherlands is much different. The King of Belgium, it is true, is a German prisoner, while the Queen of The Netherlands is free to serve as the standardbearer of Dutch sovereignty. The significant fact in the case of both these countries, however, is that they possess vast colonial territories still under the direct administration of their respective governments in London. They continue to exist as international entities and are able to maintain diplomatic relations with other nations.

Poland, Norway, and Yugoslavia, on the other hand, have no territory left on which to find pied à terre. Their governments are in large measure simulacra, symbols rather than active administrative entities. And yet both Poland and Norway possess and control navies and merchant marines. Their airplanes and submarines are inflicting serious damage on Germany.

While the status of these governments-in-exile is unique and not identical in every case, it would seem clear that they are facts and not fictions. Until their countries shall have been definitely integrated with the German Reich they must be considered as international entities. Their sovereignty has not been extinguished. Its freedom of exercise has merely been restricted or suspended.

Military occupation by itself does not confer title or extinguish a nation. Nor does a proclamation of annexation so long as the claims of the occupying Power are effectively challenged and remain unrecognized. The Emperor of Abyssinia in exile never accepted the occupation of his country by Italy and now once again is its sovereign head. Such may be the good fortune of all those nations which have been over-run by the German

armies.   Brown, Sovereignty in Exile, 35 Am.J.Int'l Law 666
(1941).

The analyst was right.   The overrun European states had the
same good fortune as the Emperor of Abyssinia (despite his earlier
setback in the British courts, p. 787).   But the problem continues on
another front, that of the Soviet occupations of the formerly independent states of Estonia, Latvia and Lithuania.   A number of states,
following a practice pioneered by the United States in 1932 at the
time of the Japanese occupation of Manchuria and the creation there
of a puppet state of Manchukuo, have refused to "recognize" (in
what sense?) that these Baltic states and their governments disappeared when the USSR by force reconstituted the old Czarist territorial hegemony in the Baltic area.   However, in the cases of the
three invaded and incorporated Baltic states, the governments did not
escape to set up elsewhere.   Only their diplomatic representatives are
still free of Soviet sway.   What, from the standpoint of the international legal system, especially as to diplomatic immunity, do you think
about the situation described in the extract that follows?

PHANTOM DIPLOMATS CARRY ON IN BRITAIN—
MEN WITH NO COUNTRY

The Wall Street Journal, Dec. 9, 1970, p. 1, col. 4.*

LONDON—By all rights, His Excellency August Torma should
easily qualify as dean of the diplomatic corps here.

Mr. Torma is Estonia's Envoy Extraordinary and Minister
Plenipotentiary—a post he has occupied since 1934, when he presented his credentials to King George V.   "It was on December 12th or
13th," he recalls.

Of 112 foreign envoys here, Mr. Torma alone has had official
business with either King George V or his successor, King Edward
VIII, who became the Duke of Windsor after his abdication.

And yet the 76-year-old Mr. Torma wasn't even invited last
month to the Queen's annual reception for the diplomatic corps at
Buckingham Palace.   In fact, Mr. Torma and Queen Elizabeth II
haven't met since her coronation in 1952, although he knew her as a
young princess during the reign of her father, King George VI.

A Buckingham Palace official, after confirming that last month's
guest list had excluded Mr. Torma, confesses "I didn't know Estonia
had a legation here."

The Royal Family, however, hasn't committed an unpardonable
gaffe by snubbing Mr. Torma.   For the past 30 years, Mr. Torma

* Reprinted with the permission of The
Wall Street Journal.

hasn't existed. At least officially. Mr. Torma is, in effect, an envoy without a country. He and four other such "phantom diplomats" have been granted diplomatic privileges by the British government—but they aren't quite recognized by it.

This unusual state of diplomatic affairs dates to 1940, when Russia invaded Estonia and its Baltic Sea neighbors, Latvia and Lithuania. The three Baltic states were unwillingly "absorbed" by the Soviet Union, which now numbers them among its 15 republics. Britain acknowledges the political realities of the situation. It concedes that Russia occupies and governs the Baltic states—but it doesn't recognize the legality of the Soviet absorption.

"Nothing Changes"

For that reason, the Baltic states continue to enjoy diplomatic privileges and to maintain legations here. But since none of the Baltic governments actually exists, a Foreign Office spokesman notes, none can perform the routine function of appointing new legation officers to replace deceased officials. Over the years, attrition has reduced the three Baltic legations to five accredited officials among them.

Mr. Torma is the last surviving envoy. Lithuania and Estonia are headed by junior officials who assumed the role of charge d'affaires upon the death of their envoys. The Lithuanian delegation consists only of Vincas Balickas, the charge d'affaires. The Foreign Office declines to speculate whether Britain will quietly alter its views of the Lithuanian situation when the legation no longer has an accredited representative.

For his part, Mr. Balickas tries to avoid interviews, which are obviously painful. "We give interviews and nothing changes," he says. "Our countries are still occupied, and the stories give us pain, as if to reproach us for existing. Is something wrong in that?"

Mr. Balickas keeps in touch with the dwindling Lithuanian community, attending social and cultural affairs. "This week, I'll be going to four functions," he says. Although his Lithuanian passport is still valid, he hasn't traveled abroad since 1959. "I hate leaving the office to go away now," he says. "I prefer staying here at my post."

The Baltic legations continue to function—issuing passports, displaying their flags on national holidays, keeping alive memories of their brief period of independence between the two world wars. But they function in diminished elegance, existing mostly on private contributions and carefully watching expenses: Furniture hasn't been replaced in 30 years, rugs are threadbare, old maps curl against faded wallpaper. Only the outside brass plates that identify the stately buildings as legations are kept as shiny as those of the busiest embassy.

Dignity and Irony

Last year, after three decades of controversy, the British government appropriated about $16 million in gold reserves that the Baltic states had on deposit with the Bank of England since before World War II. The money became part of a fund to repay British claims for property lost as a result of Russia's occupation.

"We thought this was very unfair," says Ernst Sarepera of the Estonian legation. "It wasn't our governments that appropriated the property. The money should have been preserved for the legitimate governments as a matter of principle."

Mr. Sarepera, who is Estonia's consul general, accepts the political situation with dignity and irony. Several times a year his duties require his attendance at consular affairs at which Russian and other Iron Curtain officials are also invited. There never are any incidents though face-to-face meetings are minimized. "We're all civilized people," says Mr. Sarepera with a thin smile.

As a consulate, the Estonian legation still issues passports to those Estonian natives who haven't taken out British citizenship. "We aren't as busy as we used to be," says Mr. Sarepera, who observes that the Baltic legations issued documents to tens of thousands of refugees who fled the three states immediately after the war.

Old friends in the diplomatic corps still invite the Baltic legations to social functions. Once a year they go to Buckingham Palace —to an afternoon garden party, not a diplomatic gathering. Among their diplomatic courtesies and privileges, the legations aren't required to pay income taxes. Income has, to be sure, diminished greatly.

The legations firmly hold the view that their states will someday be independent again. "History hasn't stopped today," says Eric Zilinskis, the Latvian legation's secretary. "Who can predict the future?" He keeps books and documents with pictures of Latvians killed or tortured under the Russian occupation. "But we don't demonstrate like hooligans," he says. "Our relations with the world are peaceful—and delicate."

The United States goes beyond Britain and recognizes neither the Soviet Union's legal nor de facto occupation of the Baltic states, a position that gratifies the three legations. "The world owes us some justice," says Mr. Torma, "but we have only right on our side, not might." Nevertheless, he's confident that there will be a change. "Not tomorrow nor the next day and I probably won't see it," he says, "but things won't be like this forever."

Meantime, the phantom diplomats try to remind the world that their nations once existed and governed about six million people without Russian assistance. And, occasionally, European border authorities are reminded of the Baltic states when someone like Mr. Zilinskis presents them with a Latvian passport.

"Of course, only on holiday," he says.   "There are no business trips for me anymore."

----

2.   POSSIBLE INTERNATIONAL LEGAL PROBLEMS

1.   *Withdrawal of recognition of regimes as governments.*   As the basic notion of recognition is cognition or perception, p. 768, there is an inherent illogic in later attempts to say, when no change has intervened, "What we said we saw we now say we no longer see." Withdrawal of the recognition of states, moreover, would involve doctrinal problems about the declaratory versus the constitutive theory of the recognition of states, p. 809.   Some states, including the United States, have viewpoints on record that do not exclude the possibility that the recognition of a regime as a government can be withdrawn; see Restatement of the Foreign Relations Law of the United States (1965), Section 96, and especially Reporters' Note 1. The notion of withdrawal of recognition seems to have no international legal content.   And it is a concept not known to have been used in modern times, except by the unlearned, such as the mass media, which never seem able to distinguish, in the case of the United States and the Government of Cuba, between recognition, derecognition, and the breaking of diplomatic relations; see p. 802.

2.   *Recognition conditioned upon performance.*   Again, here, the situation seems to be one in which state practice in past times has in some instances involved the granting of recognition of a regime as a government upon the basis of its acceptance of some stipulations or pre-conditions by the recognizing state.   In such instances the promise of certain performance by the regime seeking recognition may be sought and obtained in a negotiation relating to recognition; but there is no practice of using a divesting condition subsequent that would authorize the withdrawal of recognition if the promise should not be carried out.

The most famous negotiation leading to recognition was the Litvinov-Roosevelt Agreement of 1933 under which the Soviet Union made several promises (some that it has not yet entirely performed) and was recognized.   The Mexicans and other Latin Americans base a good deal of their objection to the withholding of recognition (seen as an instrument of intervention) upon the fact that well after the Mexican Revolution had settled down into a new government, the United States continued to withhold recognition until Mexico made certain promises about American private property claims in Mexico.

The great recognition case still ahead is that of the Chinese People's Republic by the United States.   Will there be agreements that in any sense could be called "conditions precedent" to recognition? If so, will all these run in favor of the United States? Or, does the regime in control of mainland China see itself as having the capacity to "recognize" the Nixon Administration as the Government of the United States? In such cases as the one just supposed, is it really "recognition" that is involved in negotiations or foreign relations in general, including the exchange of diplomatic missions? To put the question in this way is to suggest, here again, that possible state practice of little or no legal content is involved—except for those in Latin America who contend that withholding, conditioning, or withdrawing recognition is illicit intervention. In a 1966 study of the differences between intervention and collective action, the Latin America members of the Inter-American Juridical Committee of the Organization of American States listed as an illegal act of intervention:

> 1. The abusive use of recognition of governments in contravention of the norms established by international law as a means of obtaining unjustified advantages.

The recommendation of which this entry is one item has not yet been acted upon by the member states through the competent organs of the OAS.

REPORTERS' NOTES TO SECTION 94 OF THE RESTATEMENT OF THE FOREIGN RELATIONS LAW OF THE UNITED STATES (1965) *

1. *Recognition of belligerency.* Recognition of belligerency by a state is an act by which the state, in issuing a declaration of neutrality, asserts that it (a) is neutral in an armed conflict, (b) assumes certain neutral duties toward the parties to the conflict, and (c) has certain rights with respect to trade between its nationals and persons within the territory of the belligerency subject to the rules of international law regarding visitation, search, contraband, blockade, and prize. Recognition of belligerency for an otherwise unrecognized entity or regime may arise from a declaration of neutrality by another state as between a constitutional government and rebels in a civil war. This occurred in the American Civil War when Great Britain recognized the belligerency of the Confederacy, declared its neutrality, and claimed neutral trading rights. It is well-established, as in that instance, that recognition of a rebel's belligerency does not have the effect, standing alone, of committing the second state to treat the rebel regime as the government, or the rebel entity (if one is claimed to have come into existence) as a state.

2. *Recognition of insurgency.* In customary practice, recognition of insurgency has considerably less legal significance than recognition of belligerency. Historically, the object of recognition of insurgency by non-contending states was to obtain for rebels carrying on organized military operations the protections given by international law. Recognition of insurgency has often been the first official notice that other states have taken of the eventual possible success of a revolutionary regime.

The more recent tendency has been to rely on ad hoc assurances in revolutionary situations that the basic principles underlying the rules of warfare will be respected. * * *

---

1. *Legal responsibility for premature recognition.* Recognition problems are almost always closely linked to revolutionary situations, p. 768. Revolutions usually begin as insurgencies, that is, are conducted by organized military or para-military units. In the past century and earlier, the insurgents might later be recognized as belligerents if successful enough to become of economic significance to traders in neutral states. Recognition of belligerency in this sense, one that invoked an elaborate set of rights and duties as between neutrals and belligerents as to trade, is passé. The rules of the Declaration of Paris, 1856, as to free ships make free goods; a blockade to be legal must be effective, etc., were not followed in either of the twentieth century world wars; and today a formal recognition of belligerency, statement of neutrality, and assertion of the right to trade in non-contraband with the rebels—or with the established government in some cases—would surely be treated as a quaint anachronism—and in the United Nations, possibly, as a violation of basic obligations of United Nations membership.

But the fact remains that there have been modern problems about long, drawn out revolutions—or civil wars. If the rebels quickly win or are quickly put down, problems of premature recognition do not often arise. But if the rebels have their successes, acquire control of important state territory and installations, such as ports and airfields, are recognized, and then eventually lose, are the states that have recognized them liable to the established state? A number of only slightly analyzed questions are: (i) Under what circumstances is recognition actionably premature? (ii) Are actual damages caused by premature recognition essential to the cause of action, or does something like punitive damages in domestic law obtain? (iii) Does the cause of action die if later the plaintiff loses the revolution and is ousted (to other territory if a state, to government-in-exile status if a defeated de jure regime)?

Consider, briefly, these examples (some hypothetically varied from history) of lengthy rebellions:

(i) The American Revolution, if the United States had been recognized by Prussia, Russia, and Turkey as a state and the Continental Congress as its government, and then the British had won.

(ii) The American Civil War, if the Confederacy had been recognized by Spain as a new, separate state, and thereafter it was defeated.

(iii) The Spanish Civil War, if after the United Kingdom and other states had recognized the Franco regime as the government of that portion of Spain that it then controlled, the Spanish Republic had won.

(iv) The Nigerian Civil War, if Biafra had been recognized by the United States as an independent state and government, and thereafter it was defeated.

(v) The Chinese Civil War, if after the Nationalists had been forced off the mainland to Taiwan, the Chinese People's Republic had been recognized by France as the government of mainland China and then Chiang had unleashed himself and regained the mainland.

These instances reveal a basic political reality, that foreign recognition of rebels is in every sense a disservice or threat to the established state and its de jure government; and if that state or government is able to overcome the threat to its existence that the rebellion is, it will remember to resent recognition extended to the rebels during the crisis.

At what point does premature recognition become a resentment that the injured state may pursue as a legal claim under international law? There is very little authority in international decisional law. In treatises it is usually assumed that a cause of action exists, although its point of maturation—on the scale of events during the rebellion—is not clearly specified by the writers. See Restatement of the Foreign Relations Law of the United States (1955), Sections 100 and 101.

In the celebrated arbitral award in the *Alabama Claims* (1872), Great Britain was found liable for actual damages inflicted upon Union shipping by Confederate raiders allowed to be fitted out in British ports. This is about as close as one can come so far to an international decision on state responsibility for premature recognition. In this case the status of the Confederacy as a belligerent had been recognized by the United Kingdom. However, it is to be noted that: (i) the award was made under an agreement to arbitrate that excluded decision on principles of international law; (ii) the award was for the damage caused to plaintiff's shipping by the failure of the respondent to use due diligence to prevent the fitting out and arming of Confederate sea raiders within its jurisdiction; and (iii) recognition of belligerency per se was not the burden of the United States claim. Although as a general proposition premature recognition of a rebel group as a state and government would be an a fortiori case for liability if there is liability for a premature recognition of belligerency, the Alabama Claims award does not go to recognition so much as to the improper discharge of neutral duties by Great Britain after the belligerent status of the Confederate States of America had been recognized.

2.   *Problems.*

a.   An insurgency begins in the remote mountain areas of State A, a developing country. The insurgent chieftain is colorful and immensely popular with the foreign mass media. The insurgency is presented by the press to the world as very apt to succeed. As a result 75 states recognize the insurgents as the de jure government of State A, and this causes a severe flight of capital from State A that slows its rate of development from 6% to 1% per year, resulting in an estimated national accounts loss of 1 billion dollars. State A easily puts down the insurgency and then sues the 75 states that recognized the insurgents as the de jure government of State A for the above amount in damages. On the merits, what would be your opinion as a judge of the International Court of Justice?

b.   What if the insurgents had been recognized as the government de facto of State A, all other facts being the same?

3.   *A logical problem about the continued recognition of a government in limbo.* Is a state responsible to another for losses suffered by the latter due to extreme slowness of the respondent state in recognizing the clear authority of a revolutionary government of the plaintiff state to manage and control state assets localized in the territory of the respondent state? Consider the cases in Section A, particularly one such as this variation on the suit of the Bank of China v. Wells Fargo, p. 782.

Chinese state assets in the United States were left to the administration of the Chinese Nationalist Government (Taiwan) after the Federal judge found in the 1950s that in effect the "dust had settled." They are still under the control of the Chinese Nationalist Government, but the Chinese Peoples Republic institutes a new suit in 1973, claiming that it now is entitled to manage these assets, or, in the alternative, that the Chinese Nationalist Government is no longer entitled to use them. The court, in 1973, noting that the United States has not recognized the Chinese Peoples Republic, dismisses the complaint in its entirety. This is upheld on final appeal. The Chinese Peoples Republic then sues the United States in the International Court of Justice for provable post-demand losses to the funds on deposit, claiming that these losses would not have happened but for

(i) the undue delay of the United States in recognizing the plaintiff as the de jure government of China, thus giving it standing under national law to sue and to recover; or (ii) failure to develop and apply a domestic rule of law that the only true government of a foreign country must be permitted to manage state assets in a foreign state, even if that state has not recognized the said true government.

Does the rule that there is no duty to recognize a government, Restatement, Section 99, conclusively govern the outcome of this so far hypothetical case?

Suppose the Department of State should announce that the United States now follows the Estrada Doctrine, p. 769. What, if anything, should the department thereafter suggest to a national court in the above situation?

4. *Reprise on recognition.* On the whole the international relations (political) problems of recognition seem to outweigh the legal effects of recognition. Is it possible that, if the political problems of recognition should decline in importance, either as a result of doctrinal change about recognition, detente between the socialist and the non-socialist states, or a drastic drop in the number of revolutions, the legal problems of recognition would also drop to a very low level of significance, or disappear entirely? There are some straws in the wind that indicate that recognition is not as much of a problem on any front as it used to be.

From one viewpoint, it is seen as unlikely that many more new states will come into existence by revolutionary secession. But, on the other hand, what may happen in the new Africa as tribal boundaries press against the frontiers that new states defend as a result of how the white colonialists in times past drew lines?

One of the greatest pressures on recognition doctrine in recent years has been its complete inability to deal with—or to be permitted to deal with—the all too well-known divided somethings (states or governments?): the two Germanies, the two Koreas, the two Vietnams, the two Chinas. Some of these inelegant stalemates in the cold war now seem to be moving toward political and legal resolution. The existence of two de jure German states seems to be the early result of the Ostpolitik of Chancellor Willy Brandt. It is too early to assess the structural effects of recent thaw between the two Koreas. The issue of one or two Vietnamese states is still in the womb of history. It seems only a question of time before all Chinese territory is held within a single state of China.

Questions remain as to whether puppet statecraft is also vanishing and will be abandoned, and as to whether wars of national liberation or other types of civil wars might be brewing in as yet unidentified quarters.

The material in Chapter 11 is highly relevant to these speculations.

Chapter 13

DIPLOMATIC AND CONSULAR PROTECTION
AND IMMUNITY

SECTION A. PROTECTION OF FOREIGN
REPRESENTATIVES

---

1. *Risks of diplomatic life: in former times.* Diplomatic representation is essential to the operation of the international legal system. As a concomitant of this proposition it has been recognized for a long time that, in order for diplomatic representation to function effectively, diplomatic representatives must be protected from interference with the discharge of their duties by the authorities in the receiving state. Some sense of the early and ready acceptance of this verity is reflected in the entertaining account by Lord Mansfield in Triquet v. Bath of the incident which led to the enactment in England of the Diplomatic Privileges Act of 1708:

> This privilege of foreign ministers and their domestic servants depends upon the law of nations. The Act of Parliament of 7 Ann. c. 12, is declaratory of it. All that is new in this Act, is the clause which gives a summary jurisdiction for the punishment of the infractors of this law.

> The Act of Parliament was made upon occasion of the Czar's Ambassador being arrested. If proper application had been immediately made for his discharge from the arrest, the matter might and doubtless would have been set right. Instead of that, bail was put in, before any complaint was made. An information was filed by the then Attorney General against the persons who were thus concerned, as infractors of the law of nations: and they were found guilty; but never brought up to judgment.

> The Czar took the matter up, highly. No punishment would have been thought, by him, an adequate reparation. Such a sentence as the Court could have given, he might have thought a fresh insult.

> Another expedient was fallen upon and agreed to: this Act of Parliament passed, as an apology and humiliation from the whole nation. It was sent to the Czar, finely illuminated by an ambassador extraordinary, who made excuses in a solemn oration. 3 Burr. 1478, 1480 (K.B.1764).

Protection from the authorities in the receiving state has not always been sufficient, however, to insure the inviolability of diplomatic representatives. Over the many years that diplomatic representation and immunity have existed, private individuals have at times felt compelled physically to vent frustrations of one kind or another upon the persons of foreign ambassadors. A celebrated instance in the history of the United States involved an assault upon a French diplomat, for which the culprit was convicted of a crime against the law of nations. Respublica v. de Longchamps, 1 Dall. 111 (1784).

On the whole, though, interference with the function of diplomatic representation, either by the authorities of the receiving states or by individuals resorting to violence, seems to have been rather minimal in the past. In the last few years, unfortunately, the situation has changed.

2. *Risks of diplomatic life: in modern times.* The Revue Générale de Droit International Public publishes in each of its four yearly issues a "Chronique des Faits Internationaux." This chronicle of diplomatic happenings is kept by Rousseau and is based on official and unofficial sources, including newspapers' reports. Of late it has become a catalogue of violence and other illegal acts against diplomatic (and consular) representation.

For example, the chronicle shows that during the period running from about the fall of 1964 to the fall of 1965, diplomatic premises of the United States were attacked in some sixteen different states. The attacks, by groups large and small, included the breaking down of doors and windows, the ransacking of the interior, the throwing of "Molotov cocktails" or better constructed bombs, and attempted or successful destruction by fire. The embassies or legations involved were those in: Sofia, Nairobi, Khartoum, Ankara, Moscow, Budapest, Djakarta, Kuala Lumpur, Kampala, Manila, Warsaw, Rio de Janeiro, Accra, Tokyo, Tenerife and Quito (Vol. 65 at 120, 154, 155, 461, 479, 482, 483, 485, 803, 804, 806 and 1110).

During the same period, consular premises of the United States and premises of its Information Agency were also attacked. In its library in Cairo, the agency lost some 23,000 volumes to fire (Vol. 65, at 130). The diplomatic premises of other states were not spared. Included in the attacks were those of: Algeria in Brussels; Belgium in Buenos Aires and Prague; the U.S.S.R. in Leopoldville; Egypt in Khartoum; Greece in Ankara; Israel in Caracas; the U.S.S.R. in Rome and Vienna; France in Quito; the Federal Republic of Germany in Baghdad and Taiz (Yemen); Egypt in Tunis; Tunisia in Cairo; The Netherlands in Praetoria; and Brazil in Guatemala City. (Vol. 65 at 108, 111, 118, 123, 131, 171, 176, 177, 443, 474, 762, 770, 794, 1096 and 1106).

There were other disturbing happenings during the period covered. Hidden microphones were discovered in the main rooms of the embassy of the United States in Warsaw, just as similar devices had been found a short time before in its embassy in Moscow.   (Vol. 65 at 483).   Algeria and Zambia joined the group of socialist states which restrict the travel of diplomatic representatives in their territories (Vol. 65 at 107 and 843.)   And the consul of the Federal Republic of Germany was wounded by a grenade while the consul of Yugoslavia in Munich and the consul of the United States in Cordoba were wounded by gunshots; in all cases, the motives of the assailants appeared to have been political.   (Vol. 65 at 761, 1102 and 1104).

The chronicle for the period running from about the spring of 1970 to about the fall of 1971 shows no improvement.   A rough count of attacks on diplomatic premises which involved violence would come to at least thirty-nine, not to mention attacks on consular premises. In addition some diplomatic and consular representatives were personally assaulted or shot at.   What is worse, diplomatic or consular representatives were either kidnapped, or the object of an attempted kidnapping, in at least eleven instances which occurred in Guatemala, Paraguay, Brazil, Uruguay, Venezuela, Spain and Canada.   The ambassador of the Federal Republic of Germany to Guatemala was killed by his abductors when their political demands were not met.   (Vol. 71, at 143, 152, 153, 157, 474, 483, 805, 856, 1087, 1098 and 1107).

3.   *United States legislation to protect foreign representatives.* Threats of violence and violent acts against foreign representatives have also been on the rise in the United States.   The situation in New York, with repeated political demonstrations and attacks on diplomatic representatives to the United Nations, led the General Assembly to pass a resolution urging the United States to take measures for ensuring the protection and security of the United Nations Headquarters and the missions accredited to it and their personnel.   See the statements of the Deputy Under Secretary of State for Management and of the United States Representative to the United Nations, 67 U. S. Dep't State Bull. 609 (1972).   At the request of the United States Department of State, legislation was enacted on October 24, 1972, 86 Stat. 1070.   It makes it a federal offense to commit certain crimes, e. g. murder, kidnapping, assault, harassment, property damage, against foreign embassy personnel and their families and representatives to international organizations and their families.

4.   *Draft international agreement for the protection of diplomats.*   The International Law Commission drafted a convention for consideration by the General Assembly of the United Nations which is designed to deny safe haven to those who attack, kidnap, or inflict grievous bodily harm upon diplomats or officials of foreign governments or international organizations.   The convention would require the state where the offender is found to prosecute him if it did not extradite him.   It was being considered by the General Assembly in its 27th meeting.

SECTION B. DIPLOMATIC IMMUNITY

1. INVIOLABILITY OF DIPLOMATIC PREMISES

FATEMI v. UNITED STATES

United States Court of Appeals, District of Columbia, 1963.
192 A.2d 525.

MYERS, ASSOCIATE JUDGE. These are consolidated appeals of fourteen Iranian nationals from convictions for "unlawful entry" under Title 22 D.C.Code § 3102, 1961 Ed.

Appellants, Iranian students studying in this country, entered the Iranian Embassy to deliver a petition protesting an Iranian land reform referendum. After they had staged an overnight "sleep-in," embassy officials requested the Metropolitan police to come to the embassy. Several police officers, headed by a captain, entered the embassy and talked with the Minister who gave the captain a formal, written request addressed to the Metropolitan Police Department asking the police to enter the embassy, eject the students from the premises and arrest them because, after a lawful entry on the previous day, they had refused to leave upon demand of the person lawfully in charge. The Minister then, in the presence of the police, again asked the students to leave within five minutes, addressing them in both Iranian and English. When they refused to depart they were placed under arrest and bodily carried from the embassy.

Following trial on January 22, 1963, the defendants, having refused a continuance and having chosen not to testify, but at all times fully represented by counsel, were found guilty.

Appellants complain numerous errors were committed below. We are of the opinion that only two alleged errors are worthy of consideration: (1) that the District of Columbia police had no authority to enter the Iranian Embassy and arrest Iranian nationals for a crime committed within the confines of the Embassy; and (2) even if the inviolability of the Embassy could be waived, the Minister had no authority to waive it. Appellants contend that a foreign embassy, protected by the doctrine of inviolability, which extends to diplomatic dwellings, is not subject to the jurisdiction of the local police and courts of the receiving state or to its body of criminal law. We find scant authority to support this contention; indeed the weight of authority is to the contrary.

Since our decision must rest in part upon principles of international law, which is part of the law of the land, we have examined custom, case decisions and the works of the treatise writers to aid in ascertaining the nature of the particular questions here involved. Although case law is not controlling in determining issues of international law, recorded decisions help in analyzing the custom or trend of the law in a given area. We believe that the weight of international case law as reinforced by the treatise writers [5] establishes as a modern rule of international law that (1) a foreign embassy is not to be considered the territory of the sending state; and (2) local police have the authority and responsibility to enter a foreign embassy if the privilege of diplomatic inviolability is not invoked when an offense is committed thereon in violation of local law.

Representatives of a foreign sovereign are given immunity from the operation of the laws of the receiving nation, and the premises and buildings occupied by the diplomatic mission usually are regarded as inviolable by the authorities of the receiving state. This is grounded upon the international law concept that all sovereigns are equal and that the representatives of a particular sovereign serve in the place of the one sending them. "No act of jurisdiction or administration of the receiving Government can take place within [the confines of an embassy] *except by special permission of the envoys.*" (Emphasis added.)

That the diplomatic premises are a part of the territory of the sending state and therefore *always* exempt from local laws does not follow as a matter of course, however. "The modern tendency among writers is toward rejecting the fiction of extraterritoriality * * *." Numerous case decisions bear out this trend. As early as 1867, the doctrine of extraterritoriality was abandoned by European nations. Recently, in the case of R. v. Kent, the British courts held that "A crime committed in a foreign embassy is a crime committed in the United Kingdom and the offender, *if not protected by diplomatic immunity*, is liable to prosecution in British courts." (Emphasis added.)

Appellants have failed to distinguish cases in which the privilege of diplomatic immunity is invoked from those in which it is not. If a member of the diplomatic community asserts his claim to immunity, then the local police are powerless to act. Only if the criminal act being committed by the diplomat is such as to endanger the public may the police disregard the inviolability of an embassy and enter to seize the offender. Even in this situation the police may only hold the accused to prevent injury to the public, and only until the Department of State can request his recall, but the law enforcement officers are powerless to prosecute the offender. Such is not the instant case, in-

---

5. A few selections from the treatises disclose:

(a) * * * If a crime is committed inside the house of an envoy by an individual who does not enjoy personally the privilege of extraterritoriality, the criminal must be surrendered to the local Government. 1 Oppenheim, International Law (8th Ed. Lauterpacht Editor 1955) § 390.

(b) The inviolability of diplomatic premises does not mean that they are to be considered as altogether outside the application of the law of the receiving state—a foreign enclave within its territory. Brierly, The Law of Nations (6th Ed. 1963).

volving an embassy to which the police had been invited in order to arrest and remove Iranian students who have no claim to the privilege of immunity and were violating local law.

Appellants' next contention—that even if the inviolability of the diplomatic dwellings can be waived, the Minister of the embassy had no authority to do so—that the waiver must come only from the Ambassador—is equally without merit.

* * * We do not think it unreasonable to hold that a police captain can enter the Iranian embassy and make an arrest for a misdemeanor committed in his presence when he has been called by one who purports to be the Minister of the embassy and is given a letter on official Iranian stationery asking the local police to disregard, for this one instance, the diplomatic rule of inviolability of the embassy and to lend aid in the ejection of violators. * * *

* * *

Accordingly, we rule that the arrest of the appellants was neither arbitrary nor illegal but orderly and proper under the circumstances, and there being no error concerning the trial, the convictions are

Affirmed.

ASYLUM CASE (COLOMBIA v. PERU)

International Court of Justice, 1950.
[1950] I.C.J. Rep. 266.

* * *

On January 3rd, 1949, * * * [during a coup in Peru, Victor Raul Haya de la Torre, leader of the Aprista party] sought asylum in the Colombian Embassy in Lima. On the next day, the Colombian Ambassador sent the following note to the Peruvian Minister for Foreign Affairs and Public Worship:

> I have the honour to inform Your Excellency, in accordance with what is provided in Article 2, paragraph 2, of the Convention on Asylum signed by our two countries in the city of Havana in the year 1928, that Señor Victor Raúl Haya de la Torre has been given asylum at the seat of this mission as from 9 p. m. yesterday.

> In view of the foregoing, and in view of the desire of this Embassy that Señor Haya de la Torre should leave Peru as early as possible, I request Your Excellency to be good enough to give orders for the requisite safe-conduct to be issued, so that Señor Haya de la Torre may leave the country with the usual facilities attaching to the right of diplomatic asylum.

On January 14th, the Ambassador sent to the Minister a further note as follows:

> Pursuant to instructions received from the Chancellery of my country, I have the honour to inform Your Excellency that the Government of Colombia, in accordance with the right conferred upon it by Article 2 of the Convention on Political Asylum signed by our two countries in the city of Montevideo on December 26th, 1933, has qualified Señor Víctor Raúl Haya de la Torre as a political refugee.

A diplomatic correspondence followed, leading up to the Act of Lima of August 31st, 1949, whereby the dispute which had arisen between the two Governments was referred to the Court.

* * *

The Colombian Government has presented two submissions, of which the first asks the Court to adjudge and declare

> That the Republic of Colombia, as the country granting asylum, is competent to qualify the offence for the purpose of the said asylum, within the limits of the obligations resulting in particular from the Bolivarian Agreement on Extradition of July 18th, 1911, and the Convention on Asylum of February 20th, 1928, and of American international law in general.

If the Colombian Government by this submission intended to allege that Colombia, as the State granting asylum, is competent to qualify the offence only provisionally and without binding effect for Peru, the solution would not remain a matter of doubt. * * *

This is not, however, the meaning which the Colombian Government has put on its submission. It has not claimed the right of qualification for the sole purpose of determining its own conduct. The written and oral arguments submitted on behalf of that Government show that its claim must be understood in the sense that Colombia, as the State granting asylum, is competent to qualify the nature of the offence by a unilateral and definitive decision binding on Peru. Colombia has based this submission partly on rules resulting from agreement, partly on an alleged custom.

The Colombian Government has referred to the Bolivarian Agreement of 1911, Article 18, which is framed in the following terms:

> Aside from the stipulations of the present Agreement, the signatory States recognize the institution of asylum in conformity with the principles of international law.

In recognizing "the institution of asylum", this article merely refers to the principles of international law. But the principles of international law do not recognize any rule of unilateral and definitive qualification by the State granting diplomatic asylum.

* * *

In the case of diplomatic asylum, the refugee is within the territory of the State where the offence was committed. A decision to grant diplomatic asylum involves a derogation from the sovereignty of that State. It withdraws the offender from the jurisdiction of the territorial State and constitutes an intervention in matters which are exclusively within the competence of that State. Such a derogation from territorial sovereignty cannot be recognized unless its legal basis is established in each particular case.

* * *

The Colombian Government further relies on the Havana Convention on Asylum of 1928. This Convention lays down certain rules relating to diplomatic asylum, but does not contain any provision conferring on the State granting asylum a unilateral competence to qualify the offence with definitive and binding force for the territorial State. The Colombian Government contends, however, that such a competence is implied in that Convention and is inherent in the institution of asylum.

A competence of this kind is of an exceptional character. It involves a derogation from the equal rights of qualification which, in the absence of any contrary rule, must be attributed to each of the States concerned; it thus aggravates the derogation from territorial sovereignty constituted by the exercise of asylum. Such a competence is not inherent in the institution of diplomatic asylum. This institution would perhaps be more effective if a rule of unilateral and definitive qualification were applied. But such a rule is not essential to the exercise of asylum.

These considerations show that the alleged right of unilateral and definitive qualification cannot be regarded as recognized by implication in the Havana Convention. Moreover, this Convention, in pursuance of the desire expressed in its preamble of "fixing the rules" which the Governments of the States of America must observe for the granting of asylum, was concluded with the manifest intention of preventing the abuses which had arisen in the previous practice, by limiting the grant of asylum. It did so in a number of ways and in terms which are unusually restrictive and emphatic ("It is not permissible for States. . . ."; "Asylum may not be granted except in urgent cases and for the period of time strictly indispensable. * * *", etc.).

* * *

The Colombian Government has * * * invoked "American international law in general". In addition to the rules arising from agreements which have already been considered, it has relied on an alleged regional or local custom peculiar to Latin-American States.

The Party which relies on a custom of this kind must prove that this custom is established in such a manner that it has become binding on the other Party. The Colombian Government must prove that

the rule invoked by it is in accordance with a constant and uniform *DUTY OF COLOMBIA*
usage practised by the States in question, and that this usage is the
expression of a right appertaining to the State granting asylum and
a duty incumbent on the territorial State. This follows from Article
38 of the Statute of the Court, which refers to international custom
"as evidence of a general practice accepted as law".

In support of its contention concerning the existence of such a *COLOMBIA RAISES THESE TO SUPPORT "CUSTOM"*
custom, the Colombian Government has referred to a large number
of extradition treaties which, as already explained, can have no bearing on the question now under consideration. It has cited conventions
and agreements which do not contain any provision concerning the
alleged rule of unilateral and definitive qualification such as the Montevideo Convention of 1889 on international penal law, the Bolivarian
Agreement of 1911 and the Havana Convention of 1928. It has invoked conventions which have not been ratified by Peru, such as the
Montevideo Conventions of 1933 and 1939. The Convention of 1933
has, in fact, been ratified by not more than eleven States and the Convention of 1939 by two States only.

It is particularly the Montevideo Convention of 1933 which Counsel for the Colombian Government has also relied on in this connexion.
It is contended that this Convention has merely codified principles
which were already recognized by Latin-American custom, and that *ICJ REJECTS*
it is valid against Peru as a proof of customary law. The limited number of States which have ratified this Convention reveals the weakness
of this argument, and furthermore, it is invalidated by the preamble
which states that this Convention modifies the Havana Convention.

Finally, the Colombian Government has referred to a large number of particular cases in which diplomatic asylum was in fact granted
and respected. But it has not shown that the alleged rule of unilateral
and definitive qualification was invoked or—if in some cases it was
in fact invoked—that it was, apart from conventional stipulations, exercised by the States granting asylum as a right appertaining to them
and respected by the territorial States as a duty incumbent on them
and not merely for reasons of political expediency. The facts brought
to the knowledge of the Court disclose so much uncertainty and contradiction, so much fluctuation and discrepancy in the exercise of
diplomatic asylum and in the official views expressed on various occasions, there has been so much inconsistency in the rapid succession
of conventions on asylum, ratified by some States and rejected by
others, and the practice has been so much influenced by considerations of political expediency in the various cases, that it is not possible to discern in all this any constant and uniform usage, accepted as
law, with regard to the alleged rule of unilateral and definitive qualification of the offence.

The Court cannot therefore find that the Colombian Government
has proved the existence of such a custom. But even if it could be
supposed that such a custom existed between certain Latin-Ameri-

can States only, it could not be invoked against Peru which, far from having by its attitude adhered to it, has, on the contrary, repudiated it by refraining from ratifying the Montevideo Conventions of 1933 and 1939, which were the first to include a rule concerning the qualification of the offence in matters of diplomatic asylum.

* * *

For these reasons, the Court has arrived at the conclusion that Colombia, as the State granting asylum, is not competent to qualify the offence by a unilateral and definitive decision, binding on Peru.

For these reasons, THE COURT, on the submissions of the Government of Colombia; by fourteen votes to two,

Rejects the first submission in so far as it involes a right for Colombia, as the country granting asylum, to qualify the nature of the offence by a unilateral and definitive decision, binding on Peru; * * *.

---

2. THE THEORY OF DIPLOMATIC IMMUNITY

The Vienna Convention on Diplomatic Relations was signed on April 18, 1961, at a conference of eighty-one states. It entered into force on April 24, 1964; as of January 1, 1972, 103 states were parties to the convention. For its text, see the Documentary Supplement. The convention entered into force for the United States on December 13, 1972. The long delay between the signature of the convention and its ratification by the United States was caused by efforts of the Department of State to obtain before ratification the enactment of new legislation to resolve inconsistencies between the present legislation and the convention. As of December 31, 1972, the proposed legislation had not been enacted.

Prior to the drafting of the convention, the practice of states in the matter of diplomatic immunity was not uniform. There was a great degree of uniformity in some areas and in respect to those the convention sets up a uniform standard for states to follow. In some instances the convention introduces new rules.

The materials in this Section are designed to explore issues which arose in the operation of the system of diplomatic immunities prior to the convention and provide the necessary background for assessment of the effect of the convention upon pre-existing practice. Many of the issues exposed have been resolved by the convention. Some have not.

HELLENIC LINES, LTD. v. MOORE, UNITED STATES MARSHAL

United States Court of Appeals, D.C. Circuit, 1965.
345 F.2d 978.

BAZELON, CHIEF JUDGE.   Appellant filed a libel in personam against the Republic of Tunisia. D.D.C.Admiralty No. 27–62. A summons was issued addressed to the Republic to be served upon the Tunisian Ambassador to the United States. Appellee, the United States Marshal, made the following return upon the unexecuted summons: "The within named principal agent having Diplomatic Immunity and being listed in the Diplomatic List of the State Department cannot be served at Washington, D. C. * * *." Appellant then filed this mandamus action to compel appellee to serve the summons "in conformity with the dignity and respect to be accorded representatives of a foreign government." The court granted appellee's motion to dismiss.

The only issue is whether the Marshal's return provided an adequate reason for his refusal to serve the summons. The return indicated that the Ambassador was entitled to diplomatic immunity. If the Ambassador's diplomatic immunity would in fact have been violated by service of process, the Marshal's return was sufficient. For although courts will not allow a Marshal to avoid his duty to serve process merely because he notices the availability of a defense to the suit [1] they must protect him if service would violate international law and might subject him to the criminal law of the United States.[2] Since we think that the Ambassador's diplomatic immunity would have been violated by any compulsory service of process on him by

1. The Marshal would not be permitted to refuse service because, for example, he notices that venue is improper, since the defendant might not wish to raise the defense. The defendant might decide that, although venue were improper, defense of the suit in the proper venue would be less convenient or would under Erie R. R. v. Tompkins, 304 U.S. 64, 58 S.Ct. 817, 82 L.Ed. 1188, 114 A.L.R. 1487 (1938), require the application of less desirable law. Similarly, a sovereign sued in the United States might waive its immunity defense because it could more easily present its witnesses and evidence here or because the law would be more favorable here than in courts of alternative forums where it would have no immunity defense. The sovereign might also decide that an airing of the dispute in an independent judicial tribunal would further its domestic policies or its foreign relations.

2. Statutes passed in 1790 make it criminal for any officer to execute any process "whereby the person of any ambassador * * * of any foreign * * * State * * * is arrested or imprisoned, or his goods or chattels are distrained, seized, or attached * * *." 22 U.S.C. §§ 252, 253 (1952). These statutes are liberally construed as being declarative of international law of diplomatic immunity. In re Baiz, 135 U.S. 403, 420, 10 S.Ct. 854, 34 L.Ed. 222 (1890); see Carrera v. Carrera, 84 U.S.App.D.C. 333, 174 F. 2d 496 (1949); Bergman v. De Sieyes, 71 F.Supp. 334 (S.D.N.Y.1946).

the Marshal,[3] we conclude that the return was sufficient, and the district court's dismissal was proper.

Although we have held that diplomatic immunity is violated by joining a diplomatic officer as a defendant to a suit, Carrera v. Carrera, 84 U.S.App.D.C. 333, 174 F.2d 496 (1949), we have never decided whether it is violated by service of process on a diplomatic officer in an attempt to join, not him, but his sending state. There is little authority in international law concerning whether service of process on a diplomatic officer as an agent of his sending country is an "attack on his person, freedom or dignity" prohibited by diplomatic immunity.[4] Because application of the doctrine of diplomatic immunity exempts a person from the legal procedures necessary to ordered society and often deprives others of remedies for harm they have suffered, courts hesitate to invoke the doctrine in a novel situation unless its purposes will certainly be served. These purposes are to "contribute to the development of friendly relations among nations" and "to ensure the efficient performance of the functions of diplomatic missions." Vienna Convention on Diplomatic Relations Signed at Vienna, April 18, 1961, preamble, 55 Am.J.Int'l L. 1064 (1961). We requested the views of the Department of State concerning the effect of service in this type of case on international relations and on the performance of diplomatic duties. The Department replied that service would prejudice the United States foreign relations and would probably impair the performance of diplomatic functions.[5] We con-

FOLLOW
ST. DEPT.
CUE

---

3. We do not decide whether service of process by diplomatic note would violate diplomatic immunity. In reply to our request for information, the Department of State through its Acting Legal Adviser stated, "The Department would not, in the absence of express statutory or treaty provision, attempt to transmit the summons by an official diplomatic note to the embassy of a sending state, unless the embassy indicated a willingness to accept the summons." Letter from Leonard C. Meeker to John W. Douglas, Assistant Attorney General, August 10, 1964.

Although an ambassador may be served if he consents to service, the failure of the Marshal to state on the return that he attempted to ascertain whether the Ambassador would accept service voluntarily did not render the return inadequate. We do not think that the Marshal should be burdened with a duty to investigate whether diplomatic immunity will be waived. Rather that burden should rest on the party seeking service.

4. Article 29 of the Vienna Convention requires that "The person of a diplomatic agent shall be inviolable. He shall not be liable to any form of arrest or detention. The receiving state shall treat him with due respect and shall take all appropriate steps to prevent any attack on his person, freedom or dignity." 55 Am.J.Int'l L. 1064, 1070–1071 (1961).

The Vienna Convention has been signed by 63 states, including the United States. It came into force on April 24, 1964, having been finally accepted by 28 states. The treaty is now before the United States Senate for its advice and consent to ratification. See Maktos, Diplomatic Immunity, 31 D.C. Bar J. 227, 231 (1964).

5. On possible impairment of a diplomatic officer's performance of official duty, the State Department said, "It is quite probable that such impairment would be caused; the degree of it would depend on the circumstances. An ambassador and his government would in all likelihood consider that

clude that the purposes of diplomatic immunity forbid service in this case.[6] Therefore, the Ambassador is not subject to service of process, and the return was adequate.

The judgment is Affirmed.

[Concurring opinion omitted.]

Rationale of immunity of diplomatic agents. In footnote no. 5 of its opinion, the court quotes a letter from the Department of State setting forth the rationale of diplomatic immunity. The letter gives two basic reasons for the prohibition against service of process upon Ⓘ a diplomatic agent. First, it would probably impair the performance of his duties. Second, it might be protested by the foreign state Ⓞ concerned as a failure to protect the person and "dignity" of its ambassador and as such a departure from a "universally accepted rule of international law and practice."

In practice, however, a number of states took the position that "functional" necessity was the sole basis of diplomatic immunity, and rejected "representational" considerations, i.e. those pertaining to the

he had been hampered in the performance of his duties if, for example, (a) the ambassador felt obliged to restrict his movements to avoid finding himself in the presence of a process server; or (b) he were diverted from the performance of his foreign relations functions by the need to devote time and attention to ascertaining the legal consequences, if any, of service of process having been made, and to taking such action as might be required in the circumstances; or (c) the manner of service had been publicly embarrassing to him and called attention to the infringement of his personal inviolability." Moreover, "The maintenance of friendly foreign relations between the United States and the sending state concerned would certainly by prejudiced by service of process on an ambassador against his will. The sending state might well protest to the Department that the United States had failed to protest the person and dignity of its official representative, and might complain particularly that service was by an officer of the United States Government, namely, a United States Marshal. Other governments might interpret the incident as meaning that the Government of the United States had

decided, as a matter of policy, to depart from what they had considered a universally accepted rule of international law and practice." Letter from Leonard C. Meeker, Acting Legal Adviser of the Department of State, to Nathan J. Paulson, Clerk of the United States Court of Appeals for the District of Columbia Circuit, January 13, 1965.

6. "[S]erious and far-reaching consequences would flow from a judicial finding that international law standards had been met if that determination flew in the face of a State Department proclamation to the contrary. When articulating principles of international law in its relations with other states, the Executive Branch speaks not only as an interpreter of generally accepted and traditional rules, as would the courts, but also as an advocate of standards it believes desirable for the community of nations and protective of national concerns." Banco Nacional de Cuba v. Sabbatino, 376 U.S. 398, 432, 84 S.Ct. 923, 942, 11 L. Ed.2d 804 (1964). Our courts have deferred to the views of the State Department as to whether sovereign immunity should be granted. * * *

protection of the personal dignity of diplomatic agents.   The case
which follows is intended to illustrate the point.

RE ARECO LEÓN (MINORS)

Chile, Second Juvenile Court of Santiago, 1955.
23 Int'l L.Rep. 425 (1960).

THE FACTS.   A warrant for arrest was issued against Don Alberto Areco Pittaluga for failure to make alimony payments for a
period of four months.   The defendant pleaded to the jurisdiction on
the ground that as First Secretary of the Uruguayan Embassy in
France he was vested with diplomatic immunity.   He submitted that
according to Articles 578 and 580 of the Chilean Civil Code the present charge must be classified as a "personal" suit or action and that
according to Articles 333 and 337 of the Code of Private International
Law (Bustamante Code) the Courts of the contracting parties could
not take cognizance of "personal" actions in which the defendant was
a foreign diplomatic agent.

Held: that the plea must be rejected.   A diplomat may not invoke
immunity from the jurisdiction of local courts in regard to his personal acts as distinguished from his official acts.

[The court first discussed Article 23 of a Convention Concerning
Diplomatic Officers of February 20, 1928, to which Chile and Uruguay
were parties.   Article 23 provided that diplomatic officers were entitled to immunity while temporarily in a state other than the one to
which they were accredited, if there "during the exercise of their functions" and prior notice of their "position" was given.

The remainder of the opinion of the court appears below.]

According to the record, His Excellency the Ambassador of the
Oriental Republic of Uruguay notified the Ministry of Foreign Relations of Chile that on Friday, March 11, "the First Secretary of Embassy in the Diplomatic Service of Uruguay, Don Alberto Areco
Pittaluga" had arrived in Santiago.   Although it has been shown that
the defendant is "the First Secretary of Embassy in the Diplomatic
Service of Uruguay", that "he is temporarily in Chile", and that both
matters have been brought officially to the attention of the Government of this Republic, these facts do not suffice to establish that
Señor Areco is in Chile "in the exercise of his diplomatic function",
which is the indispensable requisite for the enjoyment of immunity.
Whatever else may have been submitted in the pleadings, there is no
specific statement as to whether Señor Areco came to the capital of
Chile in his official diplomatic capacity or simply as a private citizen;
indeed, the context of the official notification would lead to the latter
conclusion.

In the event that the defendant's plea of diplomatic immunity
were to be sustained, it is appropriate to note that, in the opinion of
the Court, this immunity would suffice to protect him from any judi-

cial consequences arising from contracts or agreements which he might have entered into in pursuance of his official duties in the State in which he was temporarily or permanently stationed. It should be borne in mind, however, that the action giving rise to the present litigation did not arise out of a contract or agreement. It is, instead, the consequence of the application of a substantive legal norm of public order, i. e., that a father is obliged to assume responsibility for the expenses of support and education of his legitimate children (Title IX, Book I, Civil Code) and to provide alimony therefor (Title XVIII, Book I, Civil Code); this legal norm is not comprehended within the scope of diplomatic immunity from local jurisdiction.

This conclusion has been confirmed in the doctrine that diplomats enjoy privileges in and owe obligations to the country in which they are accredited. Among these privileges the most fundamental are personal inviolability and immunity from local jurisdiction; the obligations include respect for the laws of the State in whose territory they reside and the maintenance of irreproachable conduct therein. The eminent publicist Miguel Cruchaga Tocornal, referring to Fiore among other authorities, has stated in his treatise on International Law (vol. I, Editorial Reus, S.A., Madrid) that an act of a diplomat which does not arise out of his official functions must be regarded as a private act for which he may not invoke the privilege of inviolability (p. 473). It cannot be accepted that a diplomatic officer may contract a civil obligation and yet be exempted from the jurisdiction of the courts by reason of his enjoyment of the extraordinary and special privilege of immunity (p. 481). This comment is particularly pertinent to the case sub lite. Fernando Albónico, Professor of Private International Law, commenting in his dissertation upon the privilege of diplomatic immunity, has stated that acts carried out by a diplomat in his private capacity "fall within the competence of the courts" (p. 200). The same view has been advanced by Germán Vallejos Freire in his dissertation in which he has quoted the publicist, Sánchez de Bustamante, whose authority in the field of international law has been demonstrated by the fact that his name was given to the Code of Private International Law: "On the other hand, when diplomats carry out any act or conclude any contract in their private capacity, as distinguished from their official capacity, they are subject to ordinary jurisdiction" (p. 53).

Given the above considerations, it must be concluded that this Court properly has jurisdiction over the present action. * * * Therefore the defendant's plea must be rejected.[a]

a. In a note at the end of the case, the editor of the publication indicates that an appeal from the decision was denied by the Court of Appeals at Santiago.

1. *The distinction between official acts and private acts in practice before the Vienna Convention.* The case did not involve a diplomatic agent accredited to Chile, but the court specifically stated that,
even if it were to treat him as a diplomat temporarily or permanently
stationed in Chile, he would not be entitled to immunity because the
act involved in the litigation was a private act. The statement was in
line with a previous decision by the Supreme Court of Chile indicating
the court would not grant immunity for private acts. In re Scarponi,
1952, 19 Int'l L.Rep. 382 (1957). In 1956, however, a decision of the
Supreme Court of Chile dealing with waiver of diplomatic immunity
included language suggesting it might grant immunity for the private
acts of a diplomatic representative as well as for its official acts.
Acũna de Arce v. Solórzana y Menocal, 23 Int'l L.Rep. 422 (1960).

The possibility of distinguishing between the official acts and the
private acts of a diplomatic representative has an obvious parallel
in the distinction made by many courts in civil law states between the
public acts of a foreign state—for which immunity is granted—and
its private acts—for which no immunity is given. See Chapter 5.
A number of states have applied the distinction to acts involving diplomatic immunity. The courts of France have done so, for example.
Freeborn v. Fou Pei Kouo, Civil Tribunal of the Seine, 1949, [1949]
Ann.Dig. 286 (No. 97). In Italy, the issue was resolved in divergent
ways over a period of time and finally compelled a decision by all the
sections of the Supreme Court [i. e. en banc] which upheld immunity
for the private acts of a diplomatic representative. De Meeus v. For-
zano, Court of Cassation, 1940, [1938–1940] Ann.Dig. 423 (No. 164).

2. *The distinction between official and private acts in the Vienna
Convention.* The Soviet Government was much opposed to making
functional necessity, i. e. granting immunity for official acts and
denying it for private acts, the sole basis of diplomatic immunity in
the Vienna Convention. In an article entitled The Vienna Convention
on Diplomatic Intercourse and Fundamental Questions of the Codification of International Law Regarding Diplomatic Privileges and Immunities, Soviet Year Book of International Law 1961, at 89 (1962),
Romanov stated:

> The delegations of several countries, especially small coun-
> tries, sought to ensure that the principle of functional necessity
> should be set down in the Convention as the sole basis of diplo-
> matic immunities and privileges. The Soviet delegation like
> those of many other countries, pointed out that it was impossible
> to restrict the question to this principle alone, because it is in-
> sufficient to constitute a basis for diplomatic privileges and
> immunities. * * *

> The adherents of the principle of functional requirements
> did not succeed in getting its recognition as the sole basis for
> diplomatic privileges and immunities in the Vienna Convention.
> At the suggestion of the Soviet delegation, a reference to the

representational character of Embassies and Missions as one of the foundations for diplomatic privileges and immunities was included in the Preamble to the Convention.

* * *

The draft convention granted the possibility of civil actions against diplomats unrelated to their official functions. At the conference the representatives of many countries called for the extension of the range of exceptions to immunity from civil jurisdiction envisaged in the draft. It was, for example, proposed that in the event of an action seeking compensation for damages caused by a diplomat as a result of a motor accident, he should enjoy immunity from civil jurisdiction only if an insurance company in the host-state had previously assumed liability for such damage.

The majority of representatives, including that of the U.S. S.R., pointed out that such proposals undermine the very principle of the immunity of the diplomat. If it is possible to take an action for damages caused by a diplomat against an insurance company of the host-country, there is no necessity to include this in the Convention. In so far as such insurance does not exist in all countries, a clause in the Convention to this effect would create inequality in the legal position of diplomats.

A special resolution regarding compensation for damages caused by a diplomat was adopted at the conference. The resolution recommends that in appropriate cases the accrediting state should waive the immunity of officials of its diplomatic mission as regards civil suits by persons in the host-state when this is possible without violation of the function of representation, and that when there is no waiver of immunity, the accrediting state should do everything possible for the legitimate satisfaction of such demands.

See, however, Article 31 of the Convention, Documentary Supplement, which makes exceptions to the immunity of a diplomatic agent from the civil jurisdiction of the receiving state in three types of situations involving his private acts. See also the denial of immunity to members of the administrative and technical staff of a diplomatic mission for all acts performed outside the course of their duties, as discussed on p. 860 of this Section.

3. *Diplomatic agent in transit.* In the Chilean case appearing above, the diplomatic agent was not in transit through Chile on his way to taking up or returning from his post. Suppose he had been in transit for that purpose, however. Would he be entitled to immunity from prosecution for failure to make alimony payments, under the Vienna Convention? See Article 40 of the Convention, Documentary Supplement. Compare Section 78(1) of the Restatement of the Foreign Relations Law of the United States.

3. APPLICABILITY OF DOMESTIC LAW

Applicability of domestic law before obtaining diplomatic status.
The appointment by a foreign state of a diplomatic agent does
not automatically bring him diplomatic immunity. The receiving state must give its consent and, until it does, the diplomatic agent
may be sued or prosecuted if he is already on the territory of the
receiving state. In re Vitianu, Switzerland, Federal Tribunal [1949]
Ann.Dig. 281 (No. 94).

In the case of the head of a diplomatic mission, the sending state
must inquire before nomination whether the proposed envoy is "persona grata," and the receiving state must also express its "agrément,"
before the nomination. As to other members of the diplomatic staff,
"agrément" is not required and the consent to their appointment may
be either express or implied. They are entitled to immunity from the
time they enter the territory of the receiving state if such consent has
been given beforehand.

DICKINSON v. DEL SOLAR

England, Court of Appeal, 1929.
[1930] 1 K.B. 376.

[The plaintiff sought damages from the First Secretary of the
Peruvian Legation for injuries alleged to have been caused by his
negligent driving. The Minister of the Peruvian Legation waived the
immunity of the defendant on the ground that at the time of the
accident the car was being used not for official but for private purposes. The insurance company asserted that the defendant was entitled to immunity and as such had no legal liability to the plaintiff.
Thus it contended it was not bound to indemnify the defendant.]

LORD HEWART C. J. [after making the above statement of facts,
continued:] Diplomatic agents are not, in virtue of their privileges
as such, immune from legal liability for any wrongful acts. The
accurate statement is that they are not liable to be sued in the English
Courts unless they submit to the jurisdiction. Diplomatic privilege
does not import immunity from legal liability, but only exemption
from local jurisdiction. The privilege is the privilege of the Sovereign
by whom the diplomatic agent is accredited, and it may be waived with
the sanction of the Sovereign or of the official superior of the agent
* * * In the present case the privilege was waived and jurisdiction
was submitted to by the entry of appearance * * * and as Mr.
Del Solar had so submitted to the jurisdiction it was no longer open
to him to set up privilege. If privilege had been pleaded as a defence,
the defence could, in the circumstances, have been struck out. Mr.
Del Solar was bound to obey the direction of his Minister in the mat-

ter. In these circumstances it does not appear to me that there has been, on the part of Mr. Del Solar, any breach of the conditions of the policy, and the judgment clearly creates a legal liability against which the insurance company have agreed to indemnify him. It has been argued that by reason of the privilege execution cannot issue against Mr. Del Solar on the judgment. That is perhaps an open question * * *. But in my opinion it is not necessary to decide it. Even if execution could not issue in this country while Mr. Del Solar remains a diplomatic agent, presumably it might issue if he ceased to be a privileged person, and the judgment might also be the foundation of proceedings against him in Peru at any time. I hold therefore that the third parties here are liable.

---

1. *Applicability of domestic law to private acts of diplomatic agent.* As seen on p. 847, domestic law may be enforced against a diplomatic agent with respect to such of his acts as are private and not covered by immunity. Under Article 31 of the Vienna Convention, Documentary Supplement, it may also be enforced, as in the case set forth above, when his act is private and entitled to immunity, but the immunity is waived. See with respect to waiver Article 32 of the Vienna Convention, Documentary Supplement. And it may be enforced as well when the act is private and entitled to immunity, but the function of the diplomatic agent has come to an end. In this later case, the immunity ceases from the moment he leaves the territory of the receiving state, or on expiry of a reasonable period of time to do so. See Article 39 of the Vienna Convention, Documentary Supplement.

2. *Non-applicability of domestic law to official acts of diplomatic agent.* Suppose a diplomatic agent performs an official act such as the preparation of a report on a highly sensitive political matter in the receiving state, at the request of his chief of mission. The report is made public in the sending state and is eventually reprinted in a newspaper in the receiving state. The diplomatic agent retires from the diplomatic service of the sending state and remains in the state where he formerly exercised his function. Thereupon he is sued for libel in the report he prepared as an official act. He is entitled to immunity. See Section 73 of the Restatement of the Foreign Relations Law of the United States (1965). Suppose he is sued while still in the exercise of his diplomatic function, but the immunity is waived. Is he entitled to immunity?

3. *Who may waive the immunity of a diplomatic agent?* Article 32 of the Vienna Convention provides that the immunity may be waived by the sending state. If the diplomatic agent is the head of the mission, this means that the waiver must come from the ministry

of foreign affairs of the sending state. If he is below in rank in the diplomatic mission, presumably the head of the mission, who is in the receiving state the person authorized to speak for the sending state, may waive the immunity. In either case, the waiver must be express. But see the case which follows.

ALI KOUNI v. NAHIBA KHIARI (WIFE OF KOUNI)

Tunisia, Court of Appeal of Tunis, 1963.
95 Journal du Droit International 131 (1968).a

The Court of Appeal of Tunis had to decide in this case an issue concerning the immunity of diplomatic representatives. Mr. Kouni, counsellor of the embassy of the Islamic Republic of Mauritania, brought an action for divorce against his wife, who was of Tunisian nationality, under article 31 of the Tunisian code on personal status. This article provides for discretionary divorce [divorce abusif], a divorce which either spouse may seek without showing fault on the part of the other or obtaining the other spouse's consent. [When thus sought], the divorce is granted by the courts but she has the right to claim, as provided by the article, damages for the injury caused her by a divorce without grounds. The district court in Tunis where the diplomatic agent brought his action therefore had to grant him the divorce. But, in the same judgment, it gave effect to the rights of his wife by accepting her counterclaim and holding Mr. Kouni must pay her 1000 dinars in damages and alimony as well.

Mr. Kouni appealed and made several arguments before the court of appeal.

* * * He relied on his diplomatic immunity, contending that it was a bar to the counterclaim by his wife.

The court of appeal upheld the judgment below * * *. It held, in particular, that in bringing an action for divorce in the Tunisian courts, he impliedly but necessarily waived his diplomatic immunity:

> Whereas * * * it is established * * * by customary international law and the relevant case law that the beneficiary of diplomatic immunity is considered as having impliedly waived his immunity by resorting to the courts of the country where he discharges his diplomatic functions * * * and hence these courts have jurisdiction over the diplomatic agent; accordingly it follows that counterclaims brought against him are valid.

The decision is in conformity with the French law in point. Indeed, the Court of Appeal of Tunis gave in its decision numerous citations to French writers and French decisions. * * *

---

a.   Translation by the editors. Reprinted by permission of Editions Techniques, S.A., Paris.

Waiver of immunity by initiation of proceedings. It is provided for in Article 32 of the Vienna Convention. See Documentary Supplement. There is no requirement in the article that a diplomatic agent obtain authorization from his state prior to initiating the proceeding. It had been previously held there was no need for prior authorization in such a case. Cholam Samsani v. Societa Urbe, Italy Court of Rome, 1940, [1941–1942] Ann.Dig. 369 (No. 111).

Is it consistent to require the express authorization of the state when the diplomatic agent is sued and not require any authorization when he brings the proceeding himself? Can the apparent inconsistency be resolved by saying that, when the diplomatic agent brings a proceeding, it is likely to be a private matter in which the sending state would have little interest?

In the Italian case just cited above, the court barred the counterclaim on the ground that it constituted substantially an independent action rather than a defense to the claim.

----

4. REACH OF DIPLOMATIC IMMUNITY

a. *Organization of a diplomatic mission.* The Vienna Convention divides the personnel of a diplomatic mission into four categories and assigns different privileges and immunities to each. In assessing the difference in treatment of each of these categories, it is useful to know who are the persons in each and what they do. The information below is a simplified table of organization of a diplomatic mission.

The first category is the diplomatic staff. Its members have diplomatic rank. They are the ones who are engaged in the performance of the diplomatic function in the strict sense of the term. These diplomatic agents, as they are called in the Vienna Convention, include the chief of mission (ambassador, or minister or chargé d'affaires), counsellor or deputy chief of mission, the first, second and third secretaries (of embassy), the military attachés (air, army, navy) and such other attachés (for commerce, labor, treasury and other matters) as the receiving state may agree to recognize as diplomatic agents.

The next two categories—which may be looked upon as part of the "official" family of the diplomatic agent—are the administrative and technical staff on the one hand and the service staff on the other. The administrative staff includes administrative officers, persons in charge of communications (code and mail), secretary-typists and file clerks. The service staff includes drivers of the mission cars, butlers, cooks, maids and gardeners. The last category—which may be looked upon as part of the "personal" family of the diplomatic agent—consists of private servants.

b. *Variant state interests as to the reach of immunity.* These variants are caused by such factors as relative costs, felt need for extreme secrecy within the mission and public opinion.

Many diplomatic missions, including those of the United States, make heavy use of "local" employees, i.e. nationals of the host state. A few, such as those of some socialist states, use their own nationals even for driving automobiles, cooking and serving meals, and other "non-sensitive" positions. And the non-socialist states, including, again, the United States, have had reason to be concerned about the position of the local employees before national authorities of the host state. It is in the general interest of states in this latter group to have a fairly wide reach of immunity for all members of the embassy community, including the local employees.

In some of the socialist states, however, this concern is not as great, because formal diplomatic status is sought—and often obtained —for persons who in reality are not carrying on work that is clearly diplomatic in nature (either representationally or functionally). On the other hand, states such as the United States have to take into account the objections of those of their citizens (and their elected representatives) who would develop a sense of outrage if diplomatic immunity were widely accorded to fellow nationals and resident aliens on the basis of being the local employees of a foreign mission.

c. *Effect of nationality upon diplomatic immunity.* Before the Vienna Convention, there was no settled practice on whether immunity must be accorded to diplomatic agents who were nationals of the receiving state. It was the practice of the United States neither to send nor to recognize as diplomatic agents persons who were nationals or residents of the receiving state. As to other personnel, such as employees or domestic servants, international practice also varied if they were nationals of the receiving state. The practice of the United States was to grant immunity to its nationals who were employed by foreign diplomatic missions or were domestic servants, only for acts performed by them in the course of their official duties. See generally 7 Whiteman, Digest of International Law 253–260 (1970).

Under Article 38 of the Vienna Convention, a diplomatic agent who is a national of or a permanent resident in the receiving state is entitled to immunity only in respect of acts performed in the exercise of his functions. Moreover, Article 7 provides that members of the diplomatic staff of a mission should "in principle" be of the nationality of the sending state and their appointment is subject to the consent of the receiving state. As to all other personnel, they are not entitled to any immunity under Article 37 if they are nationals of the receiving state, unless and except to the extent such state cares to accord some. See Documentary Supplement.

PERSONAL FAMILY

CARRERA v. CARRERA

United States Court of Appeals, D.C. Circuit, 1949.
84 U.S.App.D.C. 333, 174 F.2d 496.

WILBUR K. MILLER, CIRCUIT JUDGE. Rosa H. Carrera sued her husband, Amable H. Carrera, in the United States District Court for the District of Columbia for separate maintenance for herself, and for the custody of and support for their fifteen-year old son. The Carreras are nationals of Ecuador, permanently resident in the United States. When the action was instituted, both were domestic servants in the Czechoslovakian Embassy.

Amable moved to quash the return showing service of process upon him and also moved to dismiss the complaint, claiming diplomatic immunity from the action. Such immunity was requested for him by the Czechoslovakian Ambassador in a communication to the Secretary of State. A copy of the Ambassador's note was transmitted to the district judge by the legal adviser to the Secretary of State with the following letter:

> There is enclosed for the information of the District Court of the United States for the District of Columbia a copy of a note received by the Department of State from the Czechoslovak Ambassador in which diplomatic immunity is requested on behalf of Amable Hidalgo Carrera, an Ecuadoran national, employed by the Czechoslovak Ambassador as a butler and chauffeur.

> The name of Mr. Carrera has been previously registered in the Department of State in accordance with Section 254 of Title 22 of the United States Code and has been included in the "List of Employees in the Embassies and Legations in Washington not Printed in the Diplomatic List", commonly known as the "White List", which has been transmitted by the Secretary of State to the Marshal of the District of Columbia.

> It would be appreciated if the Court would take into consideration the request of the Czechoslovak Ambassador and take such action as the Court deems to be appropriate in the circumstances.[1]

---

1. Sections 252, 253 and 254 of Title 22 of the United States Code, Annotated, which have to do with the diplomatic immunity of ambassadors and public ministers, are as follows:

§ 252. Suits against ministers and their domestics prohibited. Whenever any writ or process is sued out or prosecuted by any person in any court of the United States, or of a State, or by any judge or justice, whereby the person of any ambassador or public minister of any foreign prince or State, authorized and received as such by the President, or any domestic or domestic servant of any such minister, is arrested or imprisoned, or his goods or chattels are distrained, seized, or attached, such writ or process shall be deemed void.

✓ The District Court dismissed the complaint on the ground that Amable was diplomatically immune from the action. Rosa appeals.

Her first ground for reversal is that the right of the appellee to diplomatic immunity was not properly presented to the District Court. We find, however, that the process by which the claim of immunity made by the Czechoslovakian Ambassador to the State Department was communicated to the court is that which was approved by the Supreme Court in In re Baiz, 1890, 135 U.S. 403, 421, 10 S.Ct. 854, 34 L.Ed. 222. It is enough that an ambassador has requested immunity, that the State Department has recognized that the person for whom it was requested is entitled to it, and that the Department's recognition has been communicated to the court. "The courts are disposed to accept as conclusive of the fact of the diplomatic status of an individual claiming an exemption, the views thereon of the political department of their government." [2]

The next contention of the appellant is that the inclusion of Amable's name on the so-called "White List" was not sufficient to bring him within the second clause of § 254 which would extend to him the protection of §§ 252 and 253. In support of this proposition the appellant cites Trost v. Tompkins, D.C.Mun.App.1945, 44 A.2d 226. But in the Trost case the court held no more than that, certification of the Secretary of State being absent, a court otherwise having jurisdiction should determine whether the person claiming immunity was properly placed on the "White List." But here, the Secretary having certified Carrera's name as included in the list, judicial inquiry into the propriety of its listing was not appropriate.

It is further suggested by the appellant that this action is not within the purview of § 252 since it is not one in which the defendant's goods or chattels were distrained, seized or attached. The rule of immunity is not confined to those actions which have as a direct objective the distraint, seizure or attachment of goods or chattels. "It

§ 253. Penalty for wrongful suit. Whenever any writ or process is sued out in violation of section 252 of this title, every person by whom the same is obtained or prosecuted, whether as party or as attorney or solicitor, and every officer concerned in executing it, shall be deemed a violator of the laws of nations and a disturber of the public repose, and shall be imprisoned for not more than three years, and fined at the discretion of the court.

§ 254. Exceptions as to suits against servants, etc., of minister; listing servants. Sections 252 and 253 of this title shall not apply to any case where the person against whom the process is issued is a citizen or inhabitant of the United States, in the service of an ambassador or a public minister, and the process is founded upon a debt contracted before he entered upon such service; nor shall section 253 of this title apply to any case where the person against whom the process is issued is a domestic servant of an ambassador or a public minister, unless the name of the servant has, before the issuing thereof, been registered in the Department of State, and transmitted by the Secretary of State to the marshal of the District of Columbia, who shall upon receipt thereof post the same in some public place in his office. All persons shall have resort to the list of names so posted in the marshal's office, and may take copies without fee.

2. II Hyde, International Law, 1268.

has long been a settled rule of law that foreign diplomatic representatives are exempt from all local processes in the country to which they are accredited. 1 Kent's Commentaries 15, 38. The same immunity is not only given to an ambassador himself, but to his subordinates, family and servants as well." 27 Harv.L.Rev. 489 (1914). See also 27 Yale L.J. 392 (1917).

The appellant also invokes the first portion of § 254, which is

> Sections 252 and 253 of this title shall not apply to any case where the person against whom the process is issued is a citizen or inhabitant of the United States, in the service of an ambassador or a public minister, and the process is founded upon a debt contracted before he entered upon such service * * *.

The suggestion is that Amable is an inhabitant of the United States in the service of an ambassador and that the process against him in this case was founded upon a debt contracted before he entered upon such service, in that the child for whom support was sought was born before he began to serve the Ambassador. A parent's moral or legal obligation to support his infant child is not usually considered as a debt within the ordinary significance of the word. We are here concerned with the word "debt" as it is used in § 254; and we do not regard Amable's moral or legal obligation to support his child, which this action sought to enforce, as a "debt contracted before he entered upon" the Ambassador's service.

The final contention of the appellant is that the rule of diplomatic immunity does not apply in the field of domestic relations, in support of which she cites State of Ohio ex rel. Popovici v. Agler, 1930, 280 U.S. 379, 50 S.Ct. 154, 74 L.Ed. 489. But the question of diplomatic immunity was not raised in that case, as Popovici was a vice consul of Rumania, and it is universally recognized as a principle of international law that, in the absence of express agreement therefor, immunity does not extend to consuls, who are merely commercial representatives of foreign states. 16 Am.Jur. 964. Cf. The Sao Vicente, 1922, 260 U.S. 151, 155, 43 S.Ct. 15, 67 L.Ed. 179.

We have no doubt that the case was properly decided by the District Court.

Affirmed.

---

1. *No immunity required for private servants under the Vienna Convention.* Before the convention, the United Kingdom, like the United States, granted complete immunity to the private servants of diplomatic agents. Many other states did not. Argentina, for example. Bregante v. Souviron, Supreme Court, 1943 [1943–1945] Ann.Dig. 242 (No. 76); Re Rodriguez, Criminal Court of the Capital, 1958, 26 Int'l L.Rep. 546 (1963). Under Article 37(4) of the con-

vention, private servants of members of the mission are entitled to immunity only to the extent the receiving state wishes to grant any.

2.   *Effect of Vienna Convention on the practice of the United States with respect to private servants.*   The statutes by which the United States gives complete immunity to private servants are derived from the Act of April 30, 1790, ch. 9, §§ 25–27, 1 Stat. 117. Section 252 of Title 22 of the United States Code expressly bars suits against any "domestic" or "domestic servant" of diplomatic agents. What should a court in the United States do in a situation like the one involved in the Carrera case, now that the Vienna Convention is in force for the United States? Is Article 37(4) of the convention in conflict with the legislation or can the two be harmonized? Is it possible to say that the convention does not affect the legislation since it does not require the United States to deny immunity to private servants, but rather leaves it free to decide how much, if any, immunity it wants to give private servants?

AYALA v. SOCIETE GENERALE DE CONSTRUCTION

France, Court of Cassation, 1958.
85 Journal du Droit International 789 (1958).[a]

* * *

Having regard to the decree of 13 Ventose An II:

Whereas the immunity laid down by this decree in favour of the envoys of foreign governments is an absolute bar to any legal proceedings in France against the wife of the diplomat even in respect of acts performed before the diplomat assumed his functions;

Whereas the Société Générale de Construction on the 27th May 1947 commenced proceedings against Mme de Guiroye or Ayala and her husband Hector de Ayala, Envoy Extraordinary and Minister Plenipotentiary of the Republic of Cuba in Paris, claiming the payment of two million francs acknowledged to be due from the said Mme de Guiroye or Ayala under deed dated 16th November 1932, and whereas the invalidating order now under appeal rejected the plea of demurrer put forward by the said Mme de Guiroye or Ayala, who was the only party to appear, and based on the aforesaid decree, on the grounds that "while the basic principle of immunity from jurisdiction, which is to give the representatives of foreign States the complete independence which is necessary for the discharge of their diplomatic duties, enables this privilege to be extended to the wife of such a representative, it would nevertheless be an abuse of justice if the status of being a diplomat's wife had the effect of enabling her to reject all claims relating to her personal debts contracted before the

a.   English text in the Journal. Reprinted by permission of Editions Techniques, S.A., Paris.

marriage and having no connection with her husband's diplomatic functions";

Whereas by this decision the Court of Appeal has failed to apply the aforesaid decree;

For these reasons,

Quashes * * *.

----

1. *Immunity of family members and dependents of diplomatic agent under the Vienna Convention.* Under Article 37(1) of the Vienna Convention, the members of the family of a diplomatic agent forming part of his household are entitled to the immunity he personally has. See Documentary Supplement. Who the "members of the family" are, however, is left unclear and so is the notion of "household." There was a great diversity of views on the meaning of these terms at the Vienna Conference on Diplomatic Relations. In a letter quoted in 7 Whiteman, Digest of International Law 260 (1970), an Assistant Legal Adviser in the Department of State of the United States stated:

> * * * The Governments represented at the Vienna Conference were unable to agree on a definition of family, for purposes of privileges and immunities. All governments are in general agreement that the wife of a diplomatic agent, his minor children, and perhaps his children who are full-time college students or who are totally dependent on him, are entitled to diplomatic immunity. All governments tend to agree that other relatives forming part of his household who are gainfully employed are not entitled to diplomatic immunity. Other cases, e.g. unmarried adult daughters, dependent parents, and sisters acting as official hostesses, are decided on the basis of the facts in the particular situation and the practice in the receiving state. Under the Vienna Convention, members of the family of a diplomatic agent who are nationals of the receiving state are not entitled to diplomatic immunity.

OFFICIAL FAMILY

RE JURSITIS

Brazil, Supreme Court, 1956.
23 Int'l L.Rep. 429 (1960).

THE FACTS. Jursitis, a Lithuanian national, was employed as a driver by the Austrian Embassy in Rio de Janeiro. On May 22, 1953, while driving a car belonging to the Embassy, he was involved in a collision. He was prosecuted and convicted by a Magistrate's Court under Article 129 of the Penal Code. An application for habeas corpus was made on his behalf on the ground that the Magistrate had no jurisdiction because (a) Jursitis was a member of the Embassy staff and (b) he was an alien.

The Court below held that the application must be dismissed. Jursitis as a driver was not a diplomatic officer and was therefore not entitled to immunity from the jurisdiction of the courts in criminal matters. In any event, he was not an Austrian national.

The applicant appealed from this decision.

Held (Guimarães and da Andrada dissenting) : that the appeal must be dismissed. Diplomatic immunity did not extend to drivers in the service of an embassy.

The Court said: "The immunity must be limited to diplomatic agents, the official staff of the mission and members of their respective families residing with them." Jursitis was of Lithuanian and not Austrian nationality, and even if diplomatic immunity extended to servants employed by an embassy, it covered only those who were of the same nationality as the Head of Mission.

* * *

1. *United States practice with respect to the immunity of service staff.* The practice has been to grant them the same immunity as diplomatic agents. In one incident, the driver of the Minister of Iran was arrested in Maryland for speeding and both he and the minister taken to the police station. A justice of the peace dismissed the driver's fine. Upon protest from Iran, the police officers were prosecuted, fined and removed from duty. See Reeves, the Elkton Incident, 30 Am.J.Int'l L. 95 (1936).

While neither diplomatic representatives nor their drivers were subject to arrest or detention for parking violations, they were expected nevertheless to pay the charges involved or else the Department of State would not authorize the issuance to them of DPL plates. Announcement of April 1, 1964, 58 Am.J.Int'l L. 1001 (1964). The move was the result of increasing violations of parking regulations in the District of Columbia by diplomatic representatives and their drivers.

2. *Effect of Vienna Convention upon the practice of the United States with respect to service staff.* Under Article 37(3) of the Vienna Convention, the members of the service staff have no immunity from criminal jurisdiction and have immunity from civil jurisdiction only for acts performed in the course of their duties. See Documentary Supplement. But the article does not bar the United

States from granting them the broader immunity given them under its present law and practice.

3. *Swiss practice with respect to the application of parking and traffic regulations to diplomatic agents.* In Switzerland, the Political Department of the Federal Government issued in 1962 and 1963 opinions concerning the application of parking and driving regulations to diplomatic agents. A summary of these opinions appears below. Determine whether they are consistent with the relevant provisions of the Vienna Convention.

When the cars of diplomatic representatives are parked in violation of regulations, a distinction must be made between two possible situations. If the car of the diplomat is wrongly parked against "all common sense" and impedes traffic, it can be towed away and the diplomat is expected to pay the cost of towing, for the towing is in the nature of a service to the public interest and its cost is not a penalty. If, on the other hand, it is towed merely because it is parked at the wrong place, the diplomat is not expected to pay for cost. La Pratique Suisse, XXIII Annuaire Suisse de Droit International 1966, at 98, 102–103 (1967).

The Political Department is also of the opinion that the driver's license of a diplomatic representative can be withdrawn if it should become known he is addicted to drinking alcohol, for in such a case he was not entitled to have a driver's license to begin with. Thus, in the view of the Political Department, withdrawal of the license is not a breach of diplomatic immunity, though withdrawal of the license as a sanction for a violation of traffic regulations would be. La Pratique Suisse, XXIII Annuaire Suisse de Droit International 1966, at 98, 103–104 (1967).

The Political Department is not prepared, however, to compel a diplomatic representative to undergo a blood test for determining, in the case of accidents, whether he was driving under the influence of alcohol. It is prepared, apparently, to compel the blood test for persons, such as members of the service staff, who are entitled to immunity only for acts performed in the course of their duties and rejects the argument that the test could be viewed as an interference with the performance of their duties. La Pratique Suisse, XXIII Annuaire Suisse de Droit International 1966, at 98, 104–107 (1967).

ROMANOV, THE VIENNA CONVENTION ON DIPLOMATIC INTERCOURSE AND FUNDAMENTAL QUESTIONS OF THE CODIFICATION OF INTERNATIONAL LAW REGARDING DIPLOMATIC PRIVILEGES AND IMMUNITIES

Soviet Year-Book of International Law 1961, at 92 (1962).

The most prolonged and acute discussion at the Vienna Conference developed around the question of the privileges and immunities of the administrative and technical personnel of Embassies and Missions.

The draft convention drawn up by the International Law Commission envisaged the establishment of general rules which would oblige all signatories to extend all diplomatic privileges and immunities to administrative and technical personnel of Embassies without exception. Such a rule has not hitherto existed in international law, and the practice of states has been extremely varied.

Some delegations proposed that the administrative and technical personnel of Embassies and Missions should enjoy immunity only in regard to actions committed by them in the execution of their duties, which would equate this category of official to the auxiliary personnel of diplomatic missions. A proposal that no general rule envisaging concrete privileges and immunities for administrative and technical personnel should be incorporated in the Convention, as a result of which the question would be left to the discretion of the parties concerned, was also submitted.

The majority of delegations, while not objecting to the granting of diplomatic privileges and immunities to this category of official, considered, however, that the draft convention went too far in fully equating administrative and technical personnel with diplomatic personnel.

* * *

During plenary session the proposal adopted by the Committee was amended somewhat. A reservation was incorporated to the effect that immunity from civil and administrative jurisdiction is granted to administrative and technical personnel only in relation to actions committed in the course of the fulfilment of their official duties. In all other respects the Vienna Convention accords the administrative and technical personnel of Embassies and Missions the same privileges and immunities as diplomats.

Hence, whereas in other respects regarding diplomatic privileges and immunities the Vienna Convention in the main reinforced already-existing rules of international law, it established a new rule as regards the privileges and immunities of the administrative and technical personnel of Embassies and Missions. The Convention substantially alters the legal status of this category of official or diplomatic missions * * *.

1. *Effect of Vienna Convention on the practice of the United States with respect to administrative and technical staff.* The practice of the United States has been to give members of this staff the same immunity as is given diplomatic agents. Under Article 37(2) of the Vienna Convention, the United States is not required to give them immunity from civil jurisdiction for acts performed outside the course of their official duties. See Documentary Supplement. But neither is it barred from granting them the broader immunity given them under present law and practice.

Article 37 of the Vienna Convention, however, grants to families of the members of the administrative and technical staff the same immunity as is granted the members of that staff themselves. Until the Vienna Convention became in force for the United States, it had been its practice not to grant any immunity to their families.

2. *Proving diplomatic status.* Comment i to Section 73 of the Restatement of the Foreign Relations Law of the United States (1965) states with respect to the practice of the United States as to proof of diplomatic status:

> Diplomatic status is established by its recognition as such by the Department of State, on request of the foreign government, and communication of this recognition to the court. Mere inclusion in the Diplomatic List maintained by the Department of State (the "Blue List") is not alone sufficient to foreclose judicial inquiry. Preparation of this list is only a ministerial act and not a determination by the executive branch of a right to diplomatic immunity. Where the Secretary or his designee certifies an individual's name as a person accepted as a diplomatic agent, the certification is conclusive on the court.

Comment b to Section 74 of the Restatement states as to proof of status in United States practice for persons other than diplomatic agents:

> The Department of State maintains a List of Employees of Diplomatic Missions (the "White List") which is comparable to the "Blue List" * * *. The same procedural and legal questions arise with respect to proof of immunity of persons on the "White List" as apply in the case of persons on the "Blue List."

Decisions in matters of diplomatic immunity by the national courts of other states often mention that the ministry of foreign affairs has certified the diplomatic status of the person involved in the case, and thus suggest that decision-making by the executive with respect to diplomatic status is widespread.

A diplomatic passport is not proof of diplomatic status and indeed may be issued on occasion to important officials who are not diplomatic agents. On the other hand, the special identity cards issued by the Department of State to foreign diplomatic agents in the

United States are of great practical value in readily establishing their diplomatic identity.

3. *More favorable treatment than required by Vienna Convention.* The convention sets up a minimum standard of immunity and the Department of State of the United States has taken the position that the immunity provided by the convention may not be sufficient to meet the needs of its diplomatic missions. Hence the legislation it has been seeking would authorize the President of the United States to grant more favorable treatment to foreign diplomatic missions than required by the convention and obtain in return the same more favorable treatment for American diplomatic missions abroad. Harris, Diplomatic Privileges and Immunities: A New Regime Is Soon to be Adopted by the United States, 62 Am.J.Int'l L. 98, at 101–102 (1968).

Should the United States and other states follow the practice of granting and obtaining more immunity than required by the convention, the state of the law in this area will again be characterized by lack of uniformity in certain areas just as it was before the convention.

POTENTIAL
HARM
✓

---

5. PERSONS ASSIMILATED TO DIPLOMATIC STATUS AND SPECIAL MISSIONS

HARRIS, DIPLOMATIC PRIVILEGES AND IMMUNITIES: A NEW REGIME IS SOON TO BE ADOPTED BY THE UNITED STATES

62 American Journal International Law 98 (1968).

[The author discusses the provisions of proposed legislation on diplomatic immunity which the Department of State, as pointed out on p. 840 of this Chapter, has been seeking since 1967.]

* * *

As its third major innovation, the Diplomatic Relations Act will codify into the statutory law of the United States the privileges and immunities which are to be accorded to visiting heads of state, heads of government, foreign ministers, and members of their official parties. In view of the increasing number of such visits, it would appear that this codification is long overdue. Under Section 3 of the Act, the definitional term "foreign diplomatic missions and the personnel thereof" includes "the head of a foreign state or the head of the government of a foreign state, and, when they are on an official visit to or in transit through the United States the foreign minister of a foreign government, and those members of the official party accompanying such officials." The Secretary of State will presumably obtain the authorization of the President under Section 4(a)(1) of the Act "to apply the treatment prescribed by the Vienna Convention, or any part or parts thereof, to those foreign diplomatic missions and the personnel thereof not otherwise entitled to such treatment." The State Department explained this section by indicating "(t)he privileges and immunities which are everywhere accorded to visiting heads of state and heads of government should have some basis in the statutory law of the United States." The transmittal letter of the Secretary of State to the Congress also noted:

> * * *   [T]he Vienna Convention on Diplomatic Relations deals only with permanent diplomatic missions and the personnel thereof, and has no application to foreign heads of state and heads of government and foreign ministers. Such privileges and immunities as have been accorded these three classes of high officials on an ad hoc basis rest generally on the law of nations and custom and comity, and, when applicable, on the doctrine of sovereign immunity.

It goes without saying that a visiting head of state or government should receive no less favorable treatment than the ambassador who is the personal representative of such person, and likewise the ambassador should receive no more than the foreign minister from whom he receives his instructions.

> * * *

---

1. *Denial of immunity to heads of states and other officials for their private acts.* In the case of Ali Ali Reza v. Grimpel, France, Court of Appeals of Paris (1st Ch.), 1961, Gazette du Palais, 1961, 2, 267, a minister of state from Saudi Arabia was denied immunity in a suit for eviction from the apartment he occupied. The case was summarized and commented upon by Siabelli in Survey of French Judicial Decisions, 89 Journal du Droit International 161, 173 (1962). In his comment, he pointed out that the members of the Belgian Government in exile in France during World War I were given the same immunity as Belgian diplomatic representatives. On the other hand, he noted, the same Court of Appeal in Paris had denied diplomatic immunity in 1936 to a minister for foreign affairs. He further stated: "It is not certain that the court would strictly maintain this attitude towards the head of the foreign diplomatic corps * * *." (at 175)

2. *Sovereign immunity for official acts of heads of states and other officials.* In the main case, and in the comment referred to above, the immunity under consideration was immunity for acts of foreign ministers of states which do not involve the performance of official duties. As to official acts, they would be covered by the immunity of their national states—i. e. sovereign immunity, as discussed in Chapter 5—and so would the heads of foreign states and heads of foreign governments. Such is the view expressed in Section 66 of the Restatement of the Foreign Relations Law of the United States (1965).

THE STATE v. MATTEI

United Arab Republic, State Security Tribunal, 1962.
34 Int'l L. Rep. 175 (1967).

THE FACTS. France and the United Arab Republic entered into an Agreement at Zurich on August 22, 1958 (hereinafter called the Zurich Agreement). This Agreement provided for the way in which French property in the Egyptian territory of the United Arab Republic, which had been sequestrated in 1956, should be dealt with: in particular, it provided that, there being no diplomatic relations between France and the United Arab Republic, there should be established in Egypt a French governmental commission to assist with the implementation of the Agreement. It was provided in Article 6 that this commission would enjoy during its mission the facilities necessary for its task, but these facilities were not specified.

In October 1958, the members of the French Property Commission, most of whom were members of the French diplomatic service, established their office in Cairo. Before their arrival in the United Arab Republic no action appears to have been taken to specify the facilities which they were to enjoy. They were, however, issued with non-diplomatic identity cards by the authorities of the United Arab Republic. They were not given diplomatic customs franchise, and their cars were given ordinary private number plates, not the special number plates given to diplomatic agents.

[The United Kingdom and the United Arab Republic then entered into an agreement on financial and commercial relations and the Swiss embassy in Cairo sent a note to the Egyptian government concerning the appointment of a British Property Commission. The Egyptian government in reply stated that certain exceptions and facilities would be given the British commission, including "immunities from legal proceedings." The note went on to state that the same exceptions and facilities would be granted the members of the French Property Commission.]

In September 1959, the United Arab Republic passed Law No. 216 which gave legislative form to the privileges and immunities accorded to the French and British Property Commissions. By Article 1,

> The premises occupied by the [two Commissions] as well as their archives and all the documents they own or possess shall be free and immune from all legal processes on a basis of reciprocity.

Article 2, so far as is relevant here, provided that the Head and members of the Commissions "shall be granted for the duration of their service, the following immunities and privileges on a basis of reciprocity: (i) legal immunity for all their actions in their official capacity." Although this Law did not entirely coincide with the terms of the Note of April 23 to the Swiss Embassy, no action seems to have been taken on behalf of the French Government to bring any discrepancy to the notice of the United Arab Republic Government.

On the night of November 23–24, 1961, three members of the French Property Commission were arrested in Cairo on, in effect, charges of espionage; the former Head of the Commission was also arrested *in absentia.* In ensuing weeks several private citizens (including an employee of the Canadian Embassy in Cairo, who was a local national) were arrested as being involved in the illegal activities which were alleged to have taken place.

At the trial the jurisdiction of the Court was contested on behalf of the French officials. It was argued, first, that the Government of the United Arab Republic was under an international obligation in consequence of their Note to the Swiss Embassy of April 23, 1959, to grant jurisdictional immunity to the members of the French Property Commission; and secondly, that the Government of the United Arab Republic was obliged as a matter of customary international law to grant them jurisdictional immunity.

As to the first contention, the defence argued that the Note set out the terms of an international agreement binding upon the United Arab Republic, * * * The prosecution claimed that the Note did not involve any binding international agreement but was merely a unilateral indication of the intentions of the United Arab Republic Government and that the Court was competent to look only at the terms of Law No. 216, which accorded only a limited jurisdictional immunity, namely, immunity for acts committed in an official capacity. * * *

As to the second contention the defence argued that as a matter of customary international law the members of the French Property Commission, being in the United Arab Republic on an official mission on behalf of the French Government, were entitled to immunity from the jurisdiction of the local courts. The defence relied largely on the contention that the functions of the French Property Commission were essentially those of a diplomatic mission (namely, to act for the protection of the nationals of the sending State, and their property, in their dealings with the authorities of another State) and that any mission performing diplomatic functions, even if only temporarily, was entitled to diplomatic immunities.

The prosecution denied that the French Property Commission in any way possessed diplomatic status since the Note of April 23 made it clear that the proper channel for diplomatic communications between the French and the United Arab Republic Governments was to remain the Swiss Embassy. Being without diplomatic, or even consular, status, the entitlement under customary international law of the French Property Commission to immunities turned on whether the Commission's functions extended to political issues, and the prosecution concluded that the Commission's functions were restricted to economic, property and cultural matters. In the absence of any political complexion, the Commission and its members were not entitled as a matter of international law to any immunities. Notwithstanding this lack of entitlement in international law to immunity, the United Arab Republic had nevertheless granted the mission and its members certain privileges and immunities by Law No. 216, but the jurisdictional immunity was limited to what was done in the course of the official activities which, under the Zurich Agreement, they were sent to the United Arab Republic to perform: for what they did outside this field, such as the conspiracies and espionage alleged in the present case, they were accountable before the courts of the United Arab Republic.

Held: that the members of the French Property Commission were not entitled to immunity from the Court's jurisdiction in respect of the proceedings before the Court. The Court did not at the time give, and has not so far made public, any reasons for its decision.

The Court heard the substantive charges against the accused. Part of the evidence against the accused members of the French Property Commission, to show that they had engaged in activities outside their functions as laid down in the Zurich Agreement, consisted of copies of documents from the archives of the Commission. These documents were obtained when, at the time the members of the Commission were arrested, the United Arab Republic authorities raided the Commission's premises. As already stated, Article 1 of Law No. 216 (although not the terms of the Note of April 23) provided that

> The premises occupied by the [French] Property Commission * * *. as well as their archives and all the documents they own or possess shall be free and immune from all legal processes.

The defence objected to the introduction of evidence obtained in violation of this provision. The Court held that the documents were admissible.

* * *

---

1. *I.L.C. Draft Articles on Special Missions.* The International Law Commission has prepared a set of Draft Articles on Special Missions. See the Report of the commission in 62 Am.J.Int'l L. 244 (1968). The commission had observed that the convention on diplomatic relations dealt only with permanent diplomatic missions and that "diplomatic relations between states also assumed other forms that might be placed under the heading of 'ad hoc diplomacy,' covering itinerant envoys, diplomatic conferences and special missions sent to a state for limited purposes." Id. at 246. Article 29 of the Draft Articles provides for personal inviolability of the persons of the representatives of the sending state in the special mission and of the mem-

bers of its diplomatic staff (as in Article 29 of the Vienna Convention on Diplomatic Relations).   Article 31 of the Draft Articles reproduces Article 31 of the Vienna Convention on Diplomatic Relations except that immunity is not granted to members of special missions with respect to "an action for damages arising out of an accident caused by a vehicle used outside the official functions of the person in question."

2. *Immunities associated with international organizations.* These immunities are considered in Chapter 14.

SECTION C.   CONSULAR IMMUNITY

THE CONSULAR FUNCTION

2 O'Connell, International Law 914 (2d ed. 1970).*

Consular Functions as Compared with Diplomatic Functions

The institution of the consul derives from the practice in medieval Italy of electing a representative from among the foreign merchants resident in a city, and until very recently consular functions were principally commercial and not diplomatic, though judicial jurisdiction over nationals of the consul's State was sometimes vested in consuls, especially in undeveloped countries.   Today, however, the distinction between commercial and diplomatic activity is difficult to maintain. Much formal diplomatic negotiation is in fact trade promotion, and much trade promotion leads to diplomatic overtures.   This fusion of functions has led inevitably to a fusion of the diplomatic and consular services, so that a career officer may be posted on one tour to an embassy secretariat, on the next to a trade mission, and on the next to a consulate proper.   Some embassies make no pretence even of keeping the consular service distinct, and house it in the same building, and to some extent with the same personnel.

Traditionally, consuls were concerned only with commercial and like matters, but in recent times they have come to represent all manner of governmental activity, such as supervising treaty implementation and performing duties with respect to government-owned merchant ships.   These functions are not very distinguishable from those of diplomats.

In 1963 a Convention on Consular Relations was signed at Vienna, and Article 5 lists consular functions at length.

(a) Promotion of commerce.   Consuls prepare trade reports, make trade inquiries, supply commercial information, arrange trade fairs, investigate infractions of commercial treaties, and visa invoices and certificates of origin.

* Reprinted   with   the   permission   of O'Connell   and   Stevens & Sons, Ltd., London.

(b) Supervision of shipping. They also supervise the papers of their national ships, and assist in matters of customs clearance, quarantine, immigration and seamen's regulations. They inspect their national ships to enable them to procure whatever information is necessary to prepare necessary documents. They take protective measures with respect to wrecked national ships. They also settle disputes according to national law among seamen or between seamen and the ship, supervise the signing on of seamen, and their discharge, and arrange their repatriation, or disposal of their property on decease.

(c) Protection of nationals. The United Kingdom Consular Instructions refer to the duty of a consul to watch over and take all proper steps to safeguard the interests of British subjects. These steps include advice and assistance to nationals in their dealings with the local authorities, and intervention where necessary to secure for them the benefit of treaty rights or rights under international law. Consuls report to the diplomatic authorities any failure to secure redress, and intervene in judicial proceedings if a denial of justice occurs. They see that their nationals have proper legal advice, are detained under satisfactory conditions and have necessary access to the outside world. Certain consular conventions require that consuls be informed immediately of the arrest of their nationals.

Sometimes consuls are instructed to assist their nationals who became ill or indigent.

(d) Representational functions. Many countries authorise their consuls to represent their nationals in civil litigation and in the administration of deceased estates. Obviously their competence so to do will depend greatly upon the law of the receiving country. Accordingly, United States consuls are instructed to discharge these functions only if treaty, usage or the local law permits, but in any event are prohibited from acting as agents or trustees of deceased estates. Some legal systems acknowledge the right of foreign consuls to represent their nationals, even in the absence of treaties. The laws of several of the United States tend in this direction, especially those of New York, although in the absence of treaties consuls will not be allowed to exercise rights "personal" to the national. Also, the right of consuls to take bona vacantia as against the right of the host State is dependent upon treaty. The United States has, however, been reluctant to accord foreign consuls broad representative and administrative functions, and the 1949 consular convention with the United Kingdom which contained provisions to this effect, was not ratified, and was replaced in 1951 with a convention conferring on British consuls only the right to receive for transmission abroad the proceeds of a court administration of deceased estates. United States consuls abroad are authorised to take possession of personal estates of deceased nationals, list the assets, dispose of them, collect and pay debts, and account to the successors. United Kingdom consuls may fully or partially administer estates of British subjects if the local law permits and this is reasonably necessary for the protection of British interests. Foreign consuls of countries specified by Order in Council may exercise certain powers relating to the administration of deceased estates in England.

ANDERSON v. VILLELA

United States District Court, D. Massachusetts, 1962.
210 F.Supp. 791.

FORD, DISTRICT JUDGE. This is an action for damages for personal injuries in which one of the two defendants moves for judgment dismissing the action as to him on the ground that the court is without jurisdiction as to him.

The sole basis for jurisdiction set forth in the complaint is 28 U.S.C.A. § 1351, which provides: "The district courts shall have original jurisdiction, exclusive of the courts of the States, of all actions and proceedings against consuls or vice consuls of foreign states." The defendants here are Vasco A. Villela, the owner of the motor vehicle alleged to have caused plaintiff's injuries, and his son Ruy Villela, who is alleged to have been the driver of the vehicle. The complaint alleges that Vasco is a consul and he does not appear to challenge the court's jurisdiction as to the action against him. The sole issue raised by Ruy Villela's motion to dismiss is whether § 1351 gives this court jurisdiction over the action as against him, since no other basis of jurisdiction is alleged in the complaint.

Ruy Villela is not himself a consul or vice consul. However, plaintiff contends that § 1351 should be interpreted as applying to members of the family of a consul as well as to the consul personally. He argues that just as the diplomatic immunity from suit of ambassadors and other envoys extends to members of their families, so the immunity of a consul from suit in a state court should be extended to members of the consul's family. The analogy is not persuasive. The diplomatic immunity of ambassadors and other envoys and the members of their suites rests on a principle of international law which has been recognized and applied by our courts. Under international law a consul does not enjoy any such immunity, at least as to suits not based on his official acts within the scope of his duties as consul. Coppell v. Hall, 7 Wall (74 U.S.) 542, 553, 19 L.Ed. 244; The Anne, 3 Wheat. (16 U.S.) 435, 445, 446, 4 L.Ed. 428; Arcaya v. Paez, D.C., 145 F. Supp. 464, affirmed 2 Cir., 244 F.2d 958. Such immunity as a consul enjoys from suit in a state court is not one based on international law but is conferred solely by statute, and in fact Congress has not always expressly provided for exclusive federal jurisdiction over actions against consuls. Bors v. Preston, 111 U.S. 252, 261, 4 S.Ct. 407, 411, 28 L.Ed. 419. Hence there is no basis for concluding that the scope of any immunity conferred by § 1351 should be co-extensive with the scope of diplomatic immunity under international law.

* * *

The motion of defendant Ruy Villela is allowed and the action will be dismissed as against him.

Vienna Convention on Consular Relations. The Vienna Convention on Consular Relations was signed on April 24, 1963. The convention entered into force on March 19, 1967; as of January 1, 1972, 47 states were parties to the convention. It entered into force for the United States on December 24, 1969. 21 U.S.T. 325, 596 U.N.T.S. 261. The convention provides in part:

Article 31
Inviolability of the Consular Premises

1. Consular premises shall be inviolable to the extent provided in this Article.

2. The authorities of the receiving State shall not enter that part of the consular premises which is used exclusively for the purpose of the work of the consular post except with the consent of the head of the consular post or of his designee or of the head of the diplomatic mission of the sending State. The consent of the head of the consular post may, however, be assumed in case of fire or other disaster requiring prompt protective action.

3. Subject to the provisions of paragraph 2 of this Article, the receiving State is under a special duty to take all appropriate steps to protect the consular premises against any intrusion or damage and to prevent any disturbance of the peace of the consular post or impairment of its dignity.

4. The consular premises, their furnishings, the property of the consular post and its means of transport shall be immune from any form of requisition for purposes of national defence or public utility. If expropriation is necessary for such purposes, all possible steps shall be taken to avoid impeding the performance of consular functions, and prompt, adequate and effective compensation shall be paid to the sending State.

Article 41
Personal Inviolability of Consular Officers

1. Consular officers shall not be liable to arrest or detention pending trial, except in the case of a grave crime and pursuant to a decision by the competent judicial authority.

2. Except in the case specified in paragraph 1 of this Article, consular officers shall not be committed to prison or liable to any other form of restriction on their personal freedom save in execution of a judicial decision of final effect.

3. If criminal proceedings are instituted against a consular officer, he must appear before the competent authorities. Nevertheless, the proceedings shall be conducted with the respect due to him by reason of his official position and, except in the case specified in paragraph 1 of this Article, in a manner which will hamper the exercise of consular functions as little as possible. When, in the circumstances mentioned in paragraph 1 of this Article, it has become necessary to detain a consular officer, the proceedings against him shall be instituted with the minimum of delay.

Article 43

Immunity from Jurisdiction

1. Consular officers and consular employees shall not be amenable to the jurisdiction of the judicial or administrative authorities of the receiving State in respect of acts performed in the exercise of consular functions.

2. The provisions of paragraph 1 of this Article shall not, however, apply in respect of a civil action either:

(a) arising out of a contract concluded by a consular officer or a consular employee in which he did not contract expressly or impliedly as an agent of the sending State; or

(b) by a third party for damage arising from an accident in the receiving State caused by a vehicle, vessel or aircraft.

Chapter 14

INTERNATIONAL ORGANIZATIONS

SECTION A. FUNCTIONS IN THE INTERNATIONAL SYSTEM

JACOB AND ATHERTON, THE DYNAMICS OF INTERNATIONAL ORGANIZATION
18, 681 (1965).*

EVOLUTION OF INTERNATIONAL AGENCIES (at 18)

Three main types of international organization have developed over the last hundred years. First, administrative agencies have been set up for specialized technical tasks, such as regulation of international means of communication. Second, machinery for adjudication or conciliation of international disputes was established. Third, general international organizations were created on either a regional or global basis to provide collective security and promote cooperative action on a broad range of other international problems.

International Administration

International administration started with private associations that attempted to advance their particular interests across national frontiers. The problems of international rail traffic led to organization of the International Railway Union, a body representing the individual railroad managements in Europe. The International Red Cross was created as a private effort to assist the wounded and ease the suffering of other war victims. Gradually, governments agreed to support or even participate in some private bodies; and, ultimately, a number of "public international unions," usually representing only governments, were formed to carry out administrative tasks that required public authority. In 1856, for instance, the Treaty of Paris created two international commissions to regulate and improve navigation on the Danube River. The Universal Postal Union, as mentioned above, was established in 1874, the first International Telegraphic Union in 1865, the International Commission for Air Navigation and the International Labor Organization at the Paris Peace Conference in 1919. The structure and powers of such bodies have changed from time to time. Some have merged into new and different organizations. But the machinery for international administration has expanded and become permanent.

* * *

* Reprinted with permission from Jacob and Atherton, The Dynamics of International Organization (Homeward, Ill. The Dorsey Press, 1965 c.).

League of Nations

The League of Nations was the first attempt to develop a comprehensive global international organization to preserve peace. It was born a compromise between the vision of a world parliament championed by Woodrow Wilson and a pact among the victorious Allies to maintain the peace treaties as demanded by French leaders. It was designed, in part, to provide the machinery for mutual aid among its members if they were victims of attack. At the same time, it had a much broader group of functions aimed at preventing war. It had specific responsibilities for encouraging peaceful settlement of disputes, developing plans for limitation of armaments, and supervising administration of the former German and Turkish colonies. The League was furthermore entrusted with supervision over international agreements relating to traffic in drugs and women and children, collection of information in all matters of international interest, and direction of international bureaus. The organization, though far from a government, nevertheless had broad competence to care for the world's welfare, and it quickly came to occupy a position in international affairs far beyond the status of the more specialized agencies that had previously existed. It served at once as a world forum, an instrument for continuous diplomatic negotiation, an international civil service, and an organ of economic and social collaboration. The League could not fulfill its political role as custodian of international security in the face of the resurgent nationalism of the 1930's and, in particular, the aggressive policies of Nazi Germany, Fascist Italy, and Japan. The organization was also seriously weakened because the United States had failed to become a member; the U. S. Senate insisted on reservations to the Covenant that were unacceptable to President Wilson. But the League's economic, financial, statistical, and social services grew so significant that they were continued even during the second world war.

The United Nations System

The framework of international society was so badly shattered by the war that Britain, Russia, the United States, and China decided not to revive the League but, instead, to build a new general international organization through which they could continue their wartime collaboration and attempt to assure a durable peace. Concrete proposals for the organization were worked out while the war was still in full progress, in joint discussions of the four powers at Dumbarton Oaks (an estate in Washington, D. C.) from August 21 to October 7, 1944. They placed primary emphasis on the security functions of the agency and provided for the big powers to assume major responsibility for the maintenance of peace. On the other hand, formation of the organization was divorced from the process of making the peace with the Axis so that it might be less hampered than the League by identification with the specific settlements imposed by the victors. The Dumbarton Oaks proposals were made public and were discussed intensively for over six months, particularly in the United States and Great Britain. Criticisms and suggestions were invited from other governments, from private organizations, and individuals. In April, 1945, 50 nations assembled at San Francisco for the United Nations Conference on International Organization, which reconsidered the proposals, modified and amended them in important respects, and finally, on June 26, signed the Charter of the United Nations.

The new organization, as tailored by the smaller states, has broader functions and a more democratic division of responsibility than originally envisaged by the four sponsoring powers. It has fused the predominant power interests of the postwar world with the heritage of functional cooperation left by the League of Nations. As a matter of fact, its powers extend well beyond those of the League. In addition to providing for peaceful settlement of international disputes and for collective action to prevent or stop aggression, the Charter endowed the United Nations with very wide responsibility for promoting economic and social welfare, exercising trusteeship over the former mandates, and encouraging respect for human rights and fundamental freedoms. While five powers—Britain, the United States, U.S.S.R., France, and China—received special, prerogatives, particularly in regard to peace and security, all members of the organization, large and small, were given equal voice in most of the other United Nations' activities. The United Nations has been from the beginning, therefore, more than a mere league of victors; it is, in fact, a comprehensive system for the conduct and oversight of the entire range of international affairs.

The basic organization established by the Charter includes six major organs: the General Assembly, the Security Council, the Economic and Social Council, the Trusteeship Council, the Secretariat, and the International Court of Justice. In addition, there is a vast network of subsidiary commissions, committees, and other bodies, some established by the Charter and others by the U.N. organs themselves in the course of their operations. Completing the United Nations "system" are a group of affiliated but autonomous "specialized agencies."

* * *

General Assembly (at 681)

The General Assembly, in which each member is represented equally, is the keystone of the United Nations. It has the sweeping power to discuss and make recommendations on any questions within the scope of the Charter, except that it may not consider a dispute or situation currently before the Security Council. The General Assembly is also responsible for studies and recommendations to promote international cooperation in all fields—political, legal, economic, social, cultural, educational, health, and human rights. It is the highest administrative authority of the United Nations, receiving and considering reports from all other organs, approving the budget, and supervising the work of the Secretariat. It may itself discuss and recommend action to maintain peace and security, or may call dangerous situations to the attention of the Security Council. It elects the other (major) organs of the United Nations. On recommendation of the Security Council, it likewise admits new members and appoints the Secretary-General.

Security Council

The Security Council of eleven members,[a] including the five permanent members (United States, U.S.S.R., Britain, France, and China), has the "primary responsibility for the maintenance of international peace and security." In executing this task, it acts for all members of the United Nations and is accountable to no other body. It is organized to function continuously. The Council may consider any dispute or situation that threatens the peace, recommend measures to settle issues peacefully, or order use of various forceful measures to halt violence and prevent aggression. It may also propose plans for the regulation of armaments. A Military Staff Committee, consisting of the chiefs of staff of the five permanent members, is responsible to the Security Council. The Council was thus conceived as a small body, capable of swift, independent, and effective action in dealing with international crises.

Economic and Social Council

The Economic and Social Council, composed of 18 members[b] elected by the General Assembly, initiates studies and recommends action with respect to international economic, social, cultural, and similar nonpolitical matters, and is also responsible for implementing the Charter's provisions in regard to human rights. Creation of the Council as a major organ in contrast to the perfunctory role originally assigned to it at Dumbarton Oaks was in direct response to widespread demand that economic and social cooperation be considered vital functions of the United Nations. In this regard, the organization of the United Nations represents a great advance over the League of Nations, which had no separate major body responsible for such matters.

Responsible to the Economic and Social Council are a group of regional economic commissions (for Europe, Asia and the Far East, Latin America, and Africa) and several functional commissions (social, human rights, population, statistical, status of women, narcotic drugs, and international commodity trade). Also reporting to

a. By amendment of the Charter of the United Nations which came into force Aug. 31, 1965, the number of members of the Security Council was increased from eleven to fifteen.

b. By amendment of the Charter of the United Nations which came into force Aug. 31, 1965, the number of members of the council was increased from eighteen to twenty-seven.

ECOSCO are a number of operating agencies, created to carry out united programs of social and economic assistance: the United Nations Children's Fund, the Special Fund, the High Commissioner for Refugees, and a peculiar interagency coordinating instrument—the Technical Assistance Board. The activities of these bodies are discussed in later chapters. The Economic and Social Council is itself accountable to the General Assembly.

Trusteeship Council

The Trusteeship Council consists of an equal number of those states that administer trust territories and those that do not. Under the authority of the General Assembly, it supervises the execution of special agreements safeguarding the welfare, human rights, and development toward self-government of the inhabitants of territories placed under trusteeship of the United Nations. Only territories voluntarily brought under the system by the controlling state are subject to the Council's authority; but once this is accomplished, the Council calls for and reviews reports from the administering authority, accepts and examines petitions from the inhabitants or others concerned with conditions in the territory, and sends visiting missions to inspect the territories at firsthand. The Council's powers are considerably more extensive than those of its forerunner, the Permanent Mandates Commission of the League of Nations.

* * *

Secretariat

The Secretariat of the United Nations, headed by the Secretary-General, serves as the staff for all the other organs, putting their decisions into effect, arranging for their meetings, and collecting information needed for their consideration. It is an international civil service, responsible only to the United Nations, with special privileges and immunities to safeguard its international character and independence from external authorities.

Specialized Agencies

In addition to the United Nations organization proper, 12 intergovernmental specialized agencies, functioning under their own constitutions, carry out separate programs of international action in their respective fields. They are, however, related to the United Nations by formal agreements providing that they submit reports and, in some cases, budgets to the Economic and Social Council for its consideration and approval. They agree to consider recommendations made to them by the United Nations and, in particular, to assist the regular organs of the U.N. in carrying out decisions related to the maintenance of peace and security. Most of the specialized agencies are also organizationally involved with the U.N. as participants in the United Nations Expanded Program of Technical Assistance.

Three of these agencies are public international unions that existed prior to creation of the United Nations, but their constitutions are slightly changed in order to bring about their integration with the United Nations system. These are: Universal Postal Union (UPU), established 1875; International Telecommunications Union (ITU), originally established 1865; International Labor Organization (ILO), established 1919.

The other specialized agencies, newly organized during or after the second World War, are:

Food and Agricultural Organization (FAO), 1944.
International Monetary Fund, 1944.
International Bank for Reconstruction and Development, 1944.
United Nations Educational, Scientific, and Cultural Organization (UNESCO), 1945.
World Health Organization (WHO), 1946.
International Civil Aviation Organization (ICAO), 1947.
World Meteorological Organization (WMO), 1950.
International Finance Corporation (IFC), 1956.
Intergovernmental Maritime Consultative Organization (IMCO), 1958.

Another specialized agency, the International Refugee Organization ceased operations at the end of 1951.

The International Atomic Energy Agency (IAEA), established in 1957, has a working relationship with the United Nations, although it is not formally designated a specialized agency.

* * *

1. *Regional organizations and the Charter of the United Nations.* Article 51 (Chapter VII) and Chapter VIII (Articles 52–54) of the Charter make it clear that states members of the universal organization and of the universal specialized international agencies may also belong to regional groupings of states. Chapter VIII does not use the term "regional organizations" but the looser "regional arrangements," a usage criticized by Professor Hans Kelsen in his Law of the United Nations but understandable to negotiators, especially in the light of the problems about regional arrangements that arose at the San Francisco Conference, at which the Charter was prepared in final form.

Behind the San Francisco debates lay a basic question: Should the United Nations be a worldwide association of states or an association of regional associations of states? Within the United States Government the issue was an open one for some time, in part because one of the proposed reservations of the Senate minority that blocked United States ratification of the Covenant of the League of Nations in 1919 had sought to ensure that regional arrangements in the Western Hemisphere would not be affected by the Covenant. Cordell Hull recalls in his Memoirs that President Franklin D. Roosevelt himself made the decision that the United States would support a universalistic concept of a United Nations. The Dumbarton Oaks Draft (U. S.) reflected this viewpoint, but at San Francisco the Latin American countries and smaller states elsewhere (such as Australia) were dissatisfied with the role provided for regional aggregations of states. The Charter reflects what is known as the "Vandenberg Compromise" (proposed by the late Senator Arthur Vandenberg), authorizing collective defense "if an armed attack occurs." The result is that pre-attack treaty arrangements have been made for purposes of collective security within regions (but not limited to states actually within such regions). These "regional arrangements" are always based on Article 51 and sometimes on Chapter VIII as well. Such arrangements and the activities of the institutions created by them must under the Charter be consistent with the Principles and Purposes (Chapter I) of the United Nations. Moreover, Article 53 makes it clear that regional arrangements cannot take enforcement action (as distinguished from collective self-defense) except as authorized or required by the Security Council.

It will be noted that the Charter says nothing for or against regional organizations that are not related to self-defense, collective-security, and peace-keeping. States members of the United Nations are not limited by the Charter as to a preference for regional over universal mechanisms for such things as economic and social development, scientific and cultural improvement, and even common, peaceful political objectives. There are few regional organizations that seem to fit entirely into the category of those not covered at all by the charter. Perhaps the Organization of African Unity does. The Organization of American States (OAS), which did not come into existence until after the Charter of the United Nations was in effect, has many goals and functions that lie outside the force-security-defense field, but the OAS also has subtle and somewhat complicated relationships with its companion arrangement, the Inter-American (Rio) Pact of Reciprocal Assistance. The latter, like the North Atlantic Treaty Organization (NATO) and the eastern socialist bloc's Warsaw Pact, is basically an Article 51 organization for collective self-defense. For its part, though, NATO is seen by some as having evolved a few functions that are not directly related to the primary defense purpose of the organization.

Regional arrangements in some instances have sub-institutions or organs that in name and function overlap similar sub-institutions of the United Nations. Thus, there are an Inter-American Economic and Social Council (IA–ECOSOC) under the OAS and the Economic and Social Council of the United Nations. There are Inter-American and European human rights commissions and also one in the United Nations.

The jurisdictional lines between the UN, the universal international organization, its organs and its linked specialized agencies, and regional organizations and their organs and linked specialized agencies are by no means clear on paper or in practice. The only rule that seems clearly laid down is that a regional organization cannot engage in enforcement action. See Chapter 19. One of the important activities of national decision-makers with a legal bent and a political sense is to decide "which channel to use" to achieve particular objectives, the universal or a regional one. Of course, even with both universal and regional international organizations available, the state-to-state channel may not be foreclosed either. This is particularly so as to agreements related to coordinated or unified positions within such organizations, such as how to vote on particular proposals.

2. *What is the European Community (EC)?* [a] An arrangement between states in a particular area to create free trade between themselves could be a regional international organization. But if free trade were no more than a treaty undertaking, with no transnational structure for administration, the treaty might not create an international organization (entity) at all. Military alliances without structure of earlier centuries are not regarded today—and certainly not then—as entities.

Probably, however, most of the free trade associations and common markets that exist today are regional international organizations, e. g., entities. (As yet there is no worldwide or even transregional free trade area or common arrangement.) The European Free Trade Association (EFTA), the Latin American Free Trade Association (LAFTA), the Central American Common Market (CACM) and the Andean Community (ANCOM) all have some organs of a transnational nature. The Caribbean, African and Southeast Asian trade arrangements are somewhat harder to analyze at this time.

But the European Economic Community, the world's most outstanding economic association of states, has reached such a high level

a. On the basis of the authorities granted to them in the international agreements that create them, there are three European communities with identical state membership. They are the European Coal and Steel Community (ECSC), the European Economic Community (EEC, created by the Treaty of Rome), and the European Atomic Community (EURATOM). The first became operational in 1953, the other two in 1958. In 1965 the member countries entered into a Merger Treaty that provided a single council and a single commission for the three communities. This treaty also provided for a single staff. The assembly and the court were dealt with in the same way in all three of the earlier treaties, so the Merger Treaty did not have to make new provisions as to them. In a technically correct way there are today still three communities, but in ordinary usage the term European Community is correct enough.

of development as to have moved beyond the field of international organizations as they are presently understood. The EEC is more than a common market (with zero tariffs between its members and a common external tariff as to the rest of the world)—thus differing from a free trade association (in which each member state keeps its own tariff structures as against non-members). It is a limited federated structure for some economic and some social purposes.

But, granted its advanced stage of institutional development (council of ministers, commission, court, assembly, large technical staff), *why* is the European Community more akin to a federated state than to an international organization? Its members are still states in every sense. It is because the community has the power, once its relevant organs have reached decisions in accordance with the voting and other allocations of decision-making authority, to act directly within the territory of the member states. The Court of the Communities has even declared national legislation and the national constitutional authority therefor unavailing as against the commands of the Treaty of Rome. The commission, subject to judicial review by the court, can assess nationals of member states for violations of the community antitrust and other regulatory laws.

The "Grand Design" of the first conceptualizers of European unification was that Western Europe would evolve into a new, federated state by movement from a customs union, to economic unification, to a common defense force, to political fusion. Resurgences of nationalism in France have twice slowed or stopped this movement. At the present time the community has expanded from 6 to 9 members; and a new one, the United Kingdom, has just recently called for the strengthening of the assembly, to make it into a law-making, rather than a law-advising body, through direct election of its members by the people of the member states. Such expectations and the growing realization of the member states that they must develop a common monetary policy (which cannot be done without a common budgetary and tax policy) are seen in some quarters as justifying a revival of expectations for the complete federation of Western Europe.

The EC has already developed so much "law-stuff" of its own that its treatment in a general course on intentional law is impossible. Some with long sight and high idealism see in what has and may come to pass in Western Europe the possibility that evolution beyond the present state system will proceed through the development of regional governments to coalescence into world government.

3. *Voting formulas.* A fundamental principle of conventional international relations practice is that all states are juridically and politically equal and sovereign (not subject to external command). Equality requires that each state in a decision-making relationship with another state or states have the same vote as any other state.

Sovereignty means that no state may be compelled without its consent to accept a decision or action. Thus there have developed the twin principles of "one-state, one-vote" and of "unanimity."

As to undertakings looking to future developments, in old-fashioned politico-military alliances, these twin principles did not cause much difficulty. Indeed, sometimes they were seen as having a desirable stabilizing influence or as a protection for one or the other of the parties. Obviously they do not cause problems as to bilateral agreements.

But most types of modern international organizations, universal and regional, are set up primarily to deal with a continuum of events. The international agreements that create the organizations are only frameworks of principles and procedures for decisions that can be made only as events unfold, situations develop, and foreseen general needs become specific. Here the twin principles cannot but get in the way of, complicate, or abort, decision-making. The architects of international organizations have tried in various ways to reduce the dimensions of the problems thus created.

One approach is to reduce the principle of one-state, one-vote. The weighted voting formulas of the World Bank Group and of the International Monetary Fund are examples of this approach. In these organizations decisions are made by a majority of the votes cast, but the votes themselves are mathematical functions of the invested capital of the member states. Needless to say, weighted voting is not popular with states with slight voting rights; but sometimes such states organize themselves into blocs that by aggregation can increase their combined voting strength. Or states with low voting strength may align themselves with one or more of the states with high voting strength.

Weighted voting of a different sort is seen in the rule requiring the concurrence of the permanent members of the Security Council (Article 27 of the Charter).

The other approach to the problem of freeing-up decision-making in international organizations is to reduce the required vote for a decision from "all" to various fractions of "all." The approach leaves all members with equal votes, but the outcome is determined by some type of majority ($\frac{3}{4}$, $\frac{2}{3}$, plurality) of the votes cast. The nearer the required voting strength approaches unanimity, of course, the easier it is for groups of states to band together in blocs to block action.

In your study of the United Nations, you will note various approaches to the definition of effective majorities. See, especially, Article 18, dealing with voting in the General Assembly. In the Organization of American States many types of questions, such as the exclusion or re-inclusion of the Castro Government of Cuba, must be taken by a two-thirds vote, and the votes of Brazil and El Salvador, of the United States and Bolivia, are equal.

The use of voting formulas during the transition period (1958–70) of the EEC, from partial to full economic union as to trade, eased the shift from a strictly national control of events. Even today the allocation among the community members of portions of the total voting strength established for decisions that still require national assent is carefully, almost cunningly, arranged. What is sought is to ensure that possible blocs of two "big" states cannot dominate all the other states of the community (big and small) and that the small ones not be able to form blocs capable of stopping action.

In 1965, France under President de Gaulle almost stopped the evolution—and even threatened the continued existence—of the community. One motivation was fear that majority voting in the final phases of the transition period would permit unacceptable decisions to be forced on France as to the common agricultural policy of the community. France simply quit participating in the Council of Ministers, and the other five decided to do nothing of importance without France's participation. The impasse was finally resolved by a tacit political understanding that the voting strength of the community would never—or almost never—be used against a strongly dissident, important member. Whether this understanding or the careful efforts to anticipate and avoid possible voting blocs will survive in the expanded community is a very interesting and important matter. Perhaps one day a member state whose nationalism has not yet been transferred to the community will have to face the question of what to do if soundly outvoted on an issue of importance to it. The three merged treaties that establish the community do not carry provisions for terms of years, termination, or secession.

4. *The conduct of investigations by the United Nations.* The broad range of functions of the United Nations—from seeking to preserve international peace and security to promoting human rights and freedom—requires that the organization be supplied with information to substantiate its actions. There is no doubt that it would be aided greatly in acquiring such information if it could freely send its agents, commissions, committees and other organs into the territory of states to conduct investigations and enquiries. In practice, the United Nations does not place its fact-finding bodies on the territory of a state without that state's consent.

Aside from the fact that, as a matter of physical power, the United Nations could not force an unwilling state to accept a fact-finding body and to allow it freedom of movement (or could do so only with extreme difficulty), there are legal considerations stemming from the Charter and its interpretation by member states. Although Article 29 provides that the Security Council may establish the subsidiary organs "it deems necessary for the performance of its functions" and although Article 34 gives the council power to investigate disputes and situations in certain circumstances, it has been argued that no state may be required to submit to such investigations unless, possibly, the council is acting under Chapter VII and thus has determined that there is a "threat to the peace, breach of the peace, or act of aggression" (Article 39).

Beyond the argument that the council is simply not given the power to conduct investigations in a non-consenting state (unless there is an Article 39 situation), there are the inhibiting terms of Article 2(7), in which it is stated that the Charter does not authorize the United Nations to intervene in matters essentially within the domestic jurisdiction of a state. There is an extensive jurisprudence on the issue of the meaning of "domestic" and "to intervene" which can be gleaned from the Repertory of Practice of United Nations Organs (1955) and its two Supplements (dated 1958 and 1964 as they relate to Article 2 of the Charter). It is not altogether clear, however, that this provision of the Charter legally bars the council from conducting investigations on the territory of non-consenting states. Aside from the problem whether a fact-finding body could be "intervening" in a "domestic" matter, there is the saving clause of Article 2(7): "but this principle [of non-intervention] shall not prejudice the application of enforcement measures under Chapter VII." Thus the problem is thrown back again to the question whether the council can provide support for a fact-finding mission because of the existence of a "threat to the peace, breach of the peace, or act of aggression."

The matter was ventilated and resolved only inconclusively early in the life of the organization. Beginning with its 147th meeting in June of 1947, the council considered the appointment of a commission to investigate frontier violations on Greece's border with Albania, Bulgaria and Yugoslavia; the commission would have the right to perform its functions on both sides of the border. The resolution to appoint the commission was vetoed by the Soviet Union, as were resolutions determining that there was a threat to the peace (under Article 39). Excerpts from the Security Council debate are to be found in Sohn, Cases on United Nations Law 321 (1967).

For analysis of the United Nations' practice in placing peace-keeping forces on the territory of a state, see Chapter 20.

SECTION B. THE INTERNATIONAL CIVIL SERVANT

Law governing the relationships between the United Nations and its employees. The basic law is, of course, the Charter. Articles of special significance to the question of the status of the employees of the organization ("international civil servants") are Articles 97 through 101, defining the powers and duties of the Secretary-General of the United Nations and his staff, and Articles 104 and 105, dealing with questions of capacity, privileges and immunities.

In addition to the Charter, there are basic international agreements detailing in more specific form the broad provisions of the Charter. A major document is the Convention on the Privileges and Immunities of the United Nations, 21 U.S.T. 1418, 1 U.N.T.S. 15, which came with force early in the life of the organization, but was not ratified by the United States until April, 1970. The organization has also entered into conventions with states in which it has located its principal offices; the agreement governing the United Nations premises in New York City is the Headquarters Agreement with the United Nations, 61 Stat. 756, 11 U.N.T.S. 11.

Beyond agreements of general applicability are those the organization has entered into with states on whose territory it is carrying on a specific, temporary project. For example, the Secretary-General of the United Nations concluded an agreement with the Government of Egypt in 1957 on the status of the United Nations Emergency Forces in that country, dealing with such matters as civil and criminal jurisdiction over members of the force, privileges and immunities and the like. U.N. Doc. A/3526, Gen.Ass.Off.Rec. XI, Annexes, Agenda Item 66, pp. 52–57; Sohn, Recent Cases on United Nations Law 225 (1963).

In determining what law governs a particular situation arising in the United States, it is of course necessary to analyze the several possibly applicable treaties and legislation not only in terms of their substantive provisions but also, in case of conflict, in terms of the chronology of their enactment or coming into force. See p. 27 for a discussion of the relationship between treaties and legislation under the law of the United States.

The Convention on the Privileges and Immunities of the United Nations and excerpts from the Headquarters Agreement and the International Organizations Immunities Act are set forth in the Documentary Supplement.

CONVENTION ON THE PRIVILEGES AND IMMUNITIES OF THE UNITED NATIONS OF FEBRUARY 13, 1946

21 U.S.T. 1418, 1 U.N.T.S. 15.

Article VII

United Nations Laissez-Passer

Section 24. The United Nations may issue United Nations laissez-passer to its officials. These laissez-passer shall be recognized and accepted as valid travel documents by the authorities of Members, taking into account the provisions of Section 25.

Section 25.   Applications for visas (where required) from the holders of United Nations laissez-passer, when accompanied by a certificate that they are travelling on the business of the United Nations, shall be dealt with as speedily as possible.   In addition, such persons shall be granted facilities for speedy travel.

Section 26.   Similar facilities to those specified in Section 25 shall be accorded to experts and other persons who, though not the holders of United Nations laissez-passer, have a certificate that they are travelling on the business of the United Nations.

Section 27.   The Secretary-General, Assistant Secretaries-General and Directors travelling on United Nations laissez-passer on the business of the United Nations shall be granted the same facilities as are accorded to diplomatic envoys.

Section 28.   The provisions of this article may be applied to the comparable officials of specialized agencies if the agreements for relationship made under Article 63 of the Charter so provide.

---

8 WHITEMAN, DIGEST OF INTERNATIONAL LAW
334 (1967)

On July 9, 1959, the United Nations Secretariat addressed the following note to the United States Mission to the United Nations at New York:

* * * the United States Mission has invited the views of the Secretariat as to the implications of a possible accession [to the Convention on the Privileges and Immunities of the United Nations, February 13, 1946, 1 UNTS 15] by the United States subject to a reservation as to the United Nations laissez-passer established by Article VII of the Convention.

In reply the Secretariat wishes to take this opportunity to emphasize the great importance to the United Nations of the fullest recognition of the laissez-passer. Of the States Members of the Organization sixty-one have to date acceded to the Convention and none has yet proposed a reservation with respect to the laissez-passer. Moreover, it has from the beginning been a constant preoccupation of the Organization to obtain from other States, pending their accession, a recognition in practice of the laissez-passer as a valid travel document.

* * * Both its issuance and its use are subject to strict control, with the result that it may be carried only by officials and then only during actual travel in the interests of the Organization; on official duty, on home leave at the expense of the Organization, or in similar circumstances specially authorized

by the Secretary-General. In this manner it serves to establish the identity of United Nations officials; to bring to the attention of various government authorities throughout the world the specific texts, in each of the official languages, of the articles of the Convention determining the legal status of officials; to enable governments to enter visas in a travel document which they can know will be used by the bearer only in his capacity as a member of the staff of the international organization; to serve as a travel document for officials who are stateless or otherwise unable to avail themselves of a national passport for travel on behalf of the Organization; and, finally, to permit members of an international Secretariat to travel strictly as such, without impediments in any particular country which might otherwise be imposed upon bearers of given national passports.

Because of this very real practical importance of the laissez-passer to a world-wide organization, it will be understood that the United Nations must necessarily view with genuine concern any measure which might undermine the effectiveness of this essential travel document. It seems inevitable that a reservation to Article VII of the Convention on the part of the very Government which is host to the Headquarters of the United Nations—the Government to and from whose territory more international personnel must travel than in any other country—must gravely impair the status of the laissez-passer as an effective travel document. In this connection it will also be recalled that a major purpose in the decision to adopt a Convention pursuant to Article 105 of the Charter was to secure "the greatest uniformity in application" of the privileges necessary for the fulfillment of the purposes of the Organization. (First Report of the Sub-Committee on Privileges and Immunities, Official Records of the General Assembly, First Part of the First Session, Sixth Committee, Annex 3 to Summary Records, para. 3.)

In view of the value of the laissez-passer as a practical device to facilitate the travel of United Nations personnel, it is permissible to inquire whether practical advantage would be retained by the United States if it were to enter a reservation to Article VII. To do so could not effect the entry and exit, the transit to the Headquarters, of officials of the United Nations, since Section 18(d) of the Convention would still assure them right of entry and freedom from immigration restrictions for themselves and their immediate families * * * [The United States] has already conferred unimpeded right of transit on such persons by the terms of Section 11(1) of the Headquarters Agreement between the United Nations and the United States.

Inasmuch as it is only officials who are entitled to the United Nations laissez-passer, and inasmuch as this class of persons is already assured transit to and from the Headquarters by Section 11 of the Headquarters Agreement, it would appear that a reservation to Article VII could constitute no more than a reservation to the existence of an official travel document as such, without affecting the substantive right of staff to travel * * *[a]

UNITED STATES CHANGES PROCEDURES GOVERNING TRAVEL OF HUNGARIAN OFFICIALS

45 United States Department of State Bulletin 67 (1961).

The U.S. Government was informed by the Government of the Hungarian People's Republic on June 21, 1961, that, effective July 1, 1961, the existing authorization requirement for travel of U.S. Government personnel in Hungary would be replaced by a procedure under which U.S. personnel may travel within Hungary upon advance notification to the Hungarian Government of the planned travel. The U.S. Government has, therefore, informed the Government of the Hungarian People's Republic that, effective July 1, 1961, personnel of the Hungarian Legation in Washington and the Hungarian Mission to the United Nations in New York may travel within the United States upon advance notification to the U.S. Government of the planned travel.

These procedures apply, as heretofore, only to travel which exceeds a radius of 25 miles from Washington or New York City or 40 kilometers from Budapest, as appropriate.

UNITED STATES AIDE MEMOIRE TO SOVIET MISSION

43 United States Department of State Bulletin 521 (1960).

1. The United States Government has been informed by the Soviet Government that the Chairman of the Council of Ministers of the USSR, N. S. Khrushchev, will head the Soviet Delegation to the Fifteenth General Assembly meeting of the United Nations.

2. The United States Government's concern in this connection is with the provision of adequate security to Mr. Khrushchev and members of the Soviet Delegation in their transit of United States territory for the purpose of attending meetings of the United Nations.

a. When the United States acceded to the Convention it did not enter a reservation to the provisions on laissez-passer. It did, however, enter a reservation to the provisions on privileges and immunities: "Nothing * * * shall be construed to grant any person who has abused his privileges of residence by activities in the United States outside his official capacity exemption from the laws and regulations of the United States regarding the continued residence of aliens * * *". 21 U.S.T. 1418, 1442.

3.   The question of assuring the necessary security for Mr. Khrushchev and the Soviet Delegation has, of course, been complicated by the hostile public statements of the head of the Soviet Government and by the destruction of an American plane over international waters by Soviet action and the continued illegal detention of two American flyers.

4.   The United States Government therefore requests that arrangements be made for Mr. Krushchev to reside in the closest convenient proximity to the headquarters of the United Nations and that his movements other than those connected with arrival and departure be limited to those required by his official mission, not beyond Manhattan Island.

5.   Since security arrangements must be made some time in advance, the United States Government requests the earliest possible notification as to the exact time of arrival, place of residence, length of stay, and time and method of departure.

Question.   May the United States take action, similar to the action in the Soviet and Hungarian cases, with respect to the Secretary-General or other officials or employees of the United Nations?

REPARATION FOR INJURIES SUFFERED IN THE SERVICE OF THE UNITED NATIONS (ADVISORY OPINION)

International Court of Justice, 1949.
[1949] I.C.J. Rep. 174.

The Court,   * * *   gives the following advisory opinion:

On December 3rd, 1948, the General Assembly of the United Nations adopted the following Resolution:

> Whereas the series of tragic events which have lately befallen agents of the United Nations engaged in the performance of their duties raises, with greater urgency than ever, the question of the arrangements to be made by the United Nations with a view to ensuring to its agents the fullest measure of protection in the future and ensuring that reparation be made for the injuries suffered; and

> Whereas it is highly desirable that the Secretary-General should be able to act without question as efficaciously as possible with a view to obtaining any reparation due; therefore

The General Assembly

Decides to submit the following legal questions to the International Court of Justice for an advisory opinion:

> I. In the event of an agent of the United Nations in the performance of his duties suffering injury in circumstances involving the responsibility of a State, has the United Nations, as an Organization, the capacity to bring an international claim against the responsible de jure or de facto government with a view to obtaining the reparation due in respect of the damage caused (a) to the United Nations, (b) to the victim or to persons entitled through him?

> II. In the event of an affirmative reply on point I(b), how is action by the United Nations to be reconciled with such rights as may be possessed by the State of which the victim is a national?

Instructs the Secretary-General, after the Court has given its opinion, to prepare proposals in the light of that opinion, and to submit them to the General Assembly at its next regular session.

    *   *   *

The questions asked of the Court relate to the "capacity to bring an international claim"; accordingly, we must begin by defining what is meant by that capacity, and consider the characteristics of the Organization, so as to determine whether, in general, these characteristics do, or do not, include for the Organization a right to present an international claim.

Competence to bring an international claim is, for those possessing it, the capacity to resort to the customary methods recognized by international law for the establishment, the presentation and the settlement of claims. Among these methods may be mentioned protest, request for an enquiry, negotiation, and request for submission to an arbitral tribunal or to the Court in so far as this may be authorized by the Statute.

This capacity certainly belongs to the State; a State can bring an international claim against another State. Such a claim takes the form of a claim between two political entities, equal in law, similar in form, and both the direct subjects of international law. It is dealt with by means of negotiation, and cannot, in the present state of the law as to international jurisdiction, be submitted to a tribunal, except with the consent of the States concerned.

When the Organization brings a claim against one of its Members, this claim will be presented in the same manner, and regulated by the same procedure. It may, when necessary, be supported by the political means at the disposal of the Organization. In these ways the Organization would find a method for securing the observance of its rights by the Member against which it has a claim.

But, in the international sphere, has the Organization such a nature as involves the capacity to bring an international claim? In order to answer this question, the Court must first enquire whether the Charter has given the Organization such a position that it possesses, in regard to its Members, rights which it is entitled to ask them to respect. In other words, does the Organization possess international personality? This is no doubt a doctrinal expression, which has sometimes given rise to controversy. But it will be used here to mean that if the Organization is recognized as having that personality, it is an entity capable of availing itself of obligations incumbent upon its Members.

* * *

The subjects of law in any legal system are not necessarily identical in their nature or in the extent of their rights, and their nature depends upon the needs of the community. Throughout its history, the development of international law has been influenced by the requirements of international life, and the progressive increase in the collective activities of States has already given rise to instances of action upon the international plane by certain entities which are not States. This development culminated in the establishment in June 1945 of an international organization whose purposes and principles are specified in the Charter of the United Nations. But to achieve these ends the attribution of international personality is indispensable.

The Charter has not been content to make the Organization created by it merely a centre "for harmonizing the actions of nations in the attainment of these common ends" (Article I, para. 4). It has equipped that centre with organs, and has given it special tasks. It has defined the position of the Members in relation to the Organization by requiring them to give it every assistance in any action undertaken by it (Article 2, para. 5), and to accept and carry out the decisions of the Security Council; by authorizing the General Assembly to make recommendations to the Members; by giving the Organization legal capacity and privileges and immunities in the territory of each of its Members; and by providing for the conclusion of agreements between the Organization and its Members. Practice—in particular the conclusion of conventions to which the Organization is a party—has confirmed this character of the Organization, which occupies a position in certain respects in detachment from its Members, and which is under a duty to remind them, if need be, of certain obligations. It must be added that the Organization is a political body, charged with political tasks of an important character, and covering a wide field namely, the maintenance of international peace and security, the development of friendly relations among nations, and the achievement of international co-operation in the solution of problems of an economic, social, cultural or humanitarian character (Article I); and in dealing with its Members it employs political means. The "Convention on the Privileges and Immunities of the United Nations" of 1946 creates rights and duties between each of the signatories and the Organization (see, in particular, Section 35): It is difficult to see how such a convention could operate except upon the international plane and as between parties possessing international personality.

In the opinion of the Court, the Organization was intended to exercise and enjoy, and is in fact exercising and enjoying, functions and rights which can only be explained on the basis of the possession of a large measure of international personality and the capacity to operate upon an international plane. It is at present the supreme type of international organization, and it could not carry out the intentions of its founders if it was devoid of international personality. It must be acknowledged that its Members, by entrusting certain functions to it, with the attendant duties and responsibilities, have clothed it with the competence required to enable those functions to be effectively discharged.

Accordingly, the Court has come to the conclusion that the Organization is an international person. That is not the same thing as saying that it is a State, which it certainly is not, or that its legal personality and rights and duties are the same as those of a State. Still less is it the same thing as saying that it is "a super-State", whatever that expression may mean. It does not even imply that all its rights and duties must be upon the international plane, any more than all the rights and duties of a State must be upon that plane. What it does mean is that it is a subject of international law and capable of possessing international rights and duties, and that it has capacity to maintain its rights by bringing international claims.

The next question is whether the sum of the international rights of the Organization comprises the right to bring the kind of international claim described in the Request for this Opinion. That is a claim against a State to obtain reparation in respect of the damage caused by the injury of an agent of the Organization in the course of the performance of his duties. Whereas a State possesses the totality of international rights and duties recognized by international law, the rights and duties of an entity such as the Organization must depend upon its purposes and functions as specified or implied in its constituent documents and developed in practice. The functions of the Organization are of such a character that they could not be effectively discharged if they involved the concurrent action, on the international plane, of fifty-eight or more Foreign Offices, and the Court concludes that the Members have endowed the Organization with capacity to bring international claims when necessitated by the discharge of its functions.

What is the position as regards the claims mentioned in the request for an opinion? Question I is divided into two points, which must be considered in turn.

Question I(a) is as follows:

In the event of an agent of the United Nations in the performance of his duties suffering injury in circumstances involving the responsibility of a State has the United Nations, as an Organization, the capacity to bring an international claim against the responsible de jure or de facto government with a view to obtaining the reparation due in respect of the damage caused (a) to the United Nations. * * * ?

The question is concerned solely with the reparation of damage caused to the Organization when one of its agents suffers injury at the same time. It cannot be doubted that the Organization has the capacity to bring an international claim against one of its Members which has caused injury to it by a breach of its international obligations towards it. The damage specified in Question I(a) means exclusively damage caused to the interests of the Organization itself, to its administrative machine, to its property and assets, and to the interests of which it is the guardian. It is clear that the Organization has the capacity to bring a claim for this damage. As the claim is based on the breach of an international obligation on the part of the Member held responsible by the Organization, the Member cannot contend that this obligation is governed by municipal law, and the Organization is justified in giving its claim the character of an international claim.

When the Organization has sustained damage resulting from a breach by a Member of its international obligations, it is impossible to see how it can obtain reparation unless it possesses capacity to bring an international claim. It cannot be supposed that in such an event all the Members of the Organization, save the defendant State, must combine to bring a claim against the defendant for the damage suffered by the Organization.

The Court is not called upon to determine the precise extent of the reparation which the Organization would be entitled to recover. It may, however, be said that the measure of the reparation should depend upon the amount of the damage which the Organization has suffered as the result of the wrongful act or omission of the defendant State and should be calculated in accordance with the rules of international law. Amongst other things, this damage would include the reimbursement of any reasonable compensation which the Organization had to pay to its agent or to persons entitled through him. Again, the death or disablement of one of its agents engaged upon a distant mission might involve very considerable expenditure in replacing him. These are mere illustrations, and the Court cannot pretend to forecast all the kinds of damage which the Organization itself might sustain.

Question I(b) is as follows:

* * * has the United Nations, as an Organization, the capacity to bring an international claim * * * in respect of the damage caused

* * * (b) to the victim or to persons entitled through him?

In dealing with the question of law which arises out of Question I(b), it is unnecessary to repeat the considerations which led to an affirmative answer being given to Question I(a). It can now be assumed that the Organization has the capacity to bring a claim on the international plane, to negotiate, to conclude a special agreement and to prosecute a claim before an international tribunal. The only legal question which remains to be considered is whether, in the course of bringing an international claim of this kind, the Organization can recover "the reparation due in respect of the damage caused * * * to the victim. * * *"

The traditional rule that diplomatic protection is exercised by the national State does not involve the giving of a negative answer to Question I(b).

In the first place, this rule applies to claims brought by a State. But here we have the different and new case of a claim that would be brought by the Organization.

In the second place, even in inter-State relations, there are important exceptions to the rule, for there are cases in which protection may be exercised by a State on behalf of persons not having its nationality.

In the third place, the rule rests on two bases. The first is that the defendant State has broken an obligation towards the national State in respect of its nationals. The second is that only the party to whom an international obligation is due can bring a claim in respect of its breach. This is precisely what happens when the Organization, in bringing a claim for damage suffered by its agent, does so by invoking the breach of an obligation towards itself. Thus, the rule of the nationality of claims affords no reason against recognizing that the Organization has the right to bring a claim for the damage referred to in Question I(b). On the contrary, the principle underlying this rule leads to the recognition of this capacity as belonging to the Organization, when the Organization invokes, as the ground of its claim, a breach of an obligation towards itself.

Nor does the analogy of the traditional rule of diplomatic protection of nationals abroad justify in itself an affirmative reply. It is not possible, by a strained use of the concept of allegiance, to assimilate the legal bond which exists, under Article 100 of the Charter, between the Organization on the one hand, and the Secretary-General and the staff on the other, to the bond of nationality existing between a State and its nationals.

The Court is here faced with a new situation. The questions to which it gives rise can only be solved by realizing that the situation is dominated by the provisions of the Charter considered in the light of the principles of international law.

The question lies within the limits already established; that is to say it presupposes that the injury for which the reparation is demanded arises from a breach of an obligation designed to help an agent of the Organization in the performance of his duties. It is not a case in which the wrongful act or omission would merely constitute a breach of the general obligations of a State concerning the position of aliens; claims made under this head would be within the competence of the national State and not, as a general rule, within that of the Organization.

The Charter does not expressly confer upon the Organization the capacity to include, in its claim for reparation, damage caused to the victim or to persons entitled through him. The Court must therefore begin by enquiring whether the provisions of the Charter concerning the functions of the Organization, and the part played by its agents in the performance of those functions, imply for the Organization power to afford its agents the limited protection that would consist in the bringing of a claim on their behalf for reparation for damage suffered in such circumstances. Under international law, the Organization must be deemed to have those powers which, though not expressly provided in the Charter, are conferred upon it by necessary implication as being essential to the performance of its duties. This principle of law was applied by the Permanent Court of International Justice to the International Labour Organization in its Advisory Opinion No. 13 of July 23rd, 1926 (Series B., No. 13, p. 18), and must be applied to the United Nations.

Having regard to its purposes and functions already referred to, the Organization may find it necessary, and has in fact found it necessary, to entrust its agents with important missions to be performed in disturbed parts of the world. Many missions, from their very nature, involve the agents in unusual dangers to which ordinary persons are not exposed. For the same reason, the injuries suffered by its agents in these circumstances will sometimes have occurred in such a manner that their national State would not be justified in bringing a claim for reparation on the ground of diplomatic protection, or, at any rate, would not feel disposed to do so. Both to ensure the efficient and independent performance of these missions and to afford effective support to its agents, the Organization must provide them with adequate protection.

This need of protection for the agents of the Organization, as a condition of the performance of its functions, has already been realized, and the Preamble to the Resolution of December 3rd, 1948 * * *, shows that this was the unanimous view of the General Assembly.

For this purpose, the Members of the Organization have entered into certain undertakings, some of which are in the Charter and others in complementary agreements. The content of these undertakings need not be described here; but the Court must stress the importance of the duty to render to the Organization "every assistance" which is accepted by the Members in Article 2, paragraph 5, of the Charter. It must be noted that the effective working of the Organization—the accomplishment of its task, and the independence and effectiveness of the work of its agents—require that these undertakings should be strictly observed. For that purpose, it is necessary that, when an infringement occurs, the Organization should be able to call upon the responsible State to remedy its default, and, in particular, to obtain from the State reparation for the damage that the default may have caused to its agent.

In order that the agent may perform his duties satisfactorily, he must feel that this protection is assured to him by the Organization, and that he may count on it. To ensure the independence of the agent, and, consequently, the independent action of the Organization itself, it is essential that in performing his duties he need not have to rely on any other protection than that of the Organization (save of course for the more direct and immediate protection due from the State in whose territory he may be). In particular, he should not have to rely on the protection of his own State. If he had to rely on that State, his independence might well be compromised, contrary to the principle applied by Article 100 of the Charter. And lastly, it is essential that—whether the agent belongs to a powerful or to a weak State; to one more affected or less affected by the complications of international life; to one in sympathy or not in sympathy with the mission of the agent—he should know that in the performance of his duties he is under the protection of the Organization. This assurance is even more necessary when the agent is stateless.

Upon examination of the character of the functions entrusted to the Organization and of the nature of the missions of its agents, it becomes clear that the capacity of the Organization to exercise a measure of functional protection of its agents arises by necessary intendment out of the Charter.

The obligations entered into by States to enable the agents of to Organization to perform their duties are undertaken not in the interest of the agents, but in that of the Organization. When it claims redress for a breach of these obligations, the Organization is invoking its own right, the right that the obligations due to it should be respected. On this ground, it asks for reparation of the injury suffered, for "it is a principle of international law that the breach of an engagement involves an obligation to make reparation in an adequate form"; as was stated by the Permanent Court in its Judgment No. 8 of July 26th, 1927 (Series A., No. 9, p. 21). In claiming reparation based on the injury suffered by its agent, the Organization does not represent the agent, but is asserting its own right, the right to secure respect for undertakings entered into towards the Organization.

Having regard to the foregoing considerations, and to the undeniable right of the Organization to demand that its Members shall fulfil the obligations entered into by them in the interest of the good working of the Organization, the Court is of the opinion that, in the case of a breach of these obligations, the Organization has the capacity to claim adequate reparation, and that in assessing this reparation it is authorized to include the damage suffered by the victim or by persons entitled through him.

The question remains whether the Organization has "the capacity to bring an international claim against the responsible de jure or de facto government with a view to obtaining the reparation due in respect of the damage caused (a) to the United Nations, (b) to the victim or to persons entitled through him" when the defendant State is not a member of the Organization.

In considering this aspect of Question I(a) and (b) it is necessary to keep in mind the reasons which have led the Court to give an affirmative answer to it when the defendant State is a Member of the Organization. It has now been established that the Organization has capacity to bring claims on the international plane, and that it possesses a right of functional protection in respect of its agents. Here again the Court is authorized to assume that the damage suffered involves the responsibility of a State, and it is not called upon to express an opinion upon the various ways in which that responsibility might be engaged. Accordingly the question is whether the Organization has capacity to bring a claim against the defendant State to recover reparation in respect of that damage or whether, on the contrary, the defendant State, not being a member, is justified in raising the objection that the Organization lacks the capacity to bring an international claim. On this point, the Court's opinion is that fifty States, representing the vast majority of the members of the international community, had the power, in conformity with international law, to bring into being an entity possessing objective international personality, and not merely personality recognized by them alone, together with capacity to bring international claims.

Accordingly, the Court arrives at the conclusion that an affirmative answer should be given to Question I(a) and (b) whether or not the defendant State is a Member of the United Nations.

* * *

Question II is as follows:

In the event of an affirmative reply on point I(b), how is action by the United Nations to be reconciled with such rights as may be possessed by the State of which the victim is a national?

The affirmative reply given by the Court on point I(b) obliges it now to examine Question II. When the victim has a nationality, cases can clearly occur in which the injury suffered by him may engage the interest both of his national State and of the Organization. In such an event, competition between the State's right of diplomatic protection and the Organization's right of functional protection might arise, and this is the only case with which the Court is invited to deal.

In such a case, there is no rule of law which assigns priority to the one or to the other, or which compels either the State or the Organization to refrain from bringing an international claim. The Court sees no reason why the parties concerned should not find solutions inspired by goodwill and common sense, and as between the Organization and its Members it draws attention to their duty to render "every assistance" provided by Article 2, paragraph 5, of the Charter.

Although the bases of the two claims are different, that does not mean that the defendant State can be compelled to pay the reparation due in respect of the damage twice over. International tribunals are already familiar with the problem of a claim in which two or more national States are interested, and they know how to protect the defendant State in such a case.

The risk of competition between the Organization and the national State can be reduced or eliminated either by a general convention or by agreements entered into in each particular case. There is no doubt that in due course a practice will be developed, and it is worthy of note that already certain States whose nationals have been injured in the performance of missions undertaken for the Organization have shown a reasonable and co-operative disposition to find a practical solution.

* * *

The question of reconciling action by the Organization with the rights of a national State may arise in another way; that is to say, when the agent bears the nationality of the defendant State.

The ordinary practice whereby a State does not exercise protection on behalf of one of its nationals against a State which regards him as its own national, does not constitute a precedent which is relevant here. The action of the Organization is in fact based not upon the nationality of the victim but upon his status as agent of the Organization. Therefore it does not matter whether or not the State to which the claim is addressed regards him as its own national, because the question of nationality is not pertinent to the admissibility of the claim.

In law, therefore, it does not seem that the fact of the possession of the nationality of the defendant State by the agent constitutes any obstacle to a claim brought by the Organization for a breach of obligations towards it occurring in relation to the performance of his mission by that agent.

FOR THESE REASONS, the Court is of opinion

On Question I(a) :

(i) unanimously,

That, in the event of an agent of the United Nations in the performance of his duties suffering injury in circumstances involving the responsibility of a Member State, the United Nations as an Organization has the capacity to bring an international claim against the responsible de jure or de facto government with a view to obtaining the reparation due in respect of the damage caused to the United Nations.

(ii) unanimously,

That, in the event of an agent of the United Nations in the performance of his duties suffering injury in circumstances involving the responsibility of a State which is not a member, the United Nations as an Organization has the capacity to bring an international claim against the responsible de jure or de facto government with a view to obtaining the reparation due in respect of the damage caused to the United Nations.

On Question I(b) :

(i) by eleven votes against four,

That, in the event of an agent of the United Nations in the performance of his duties suffering injury in circumstances involving the responsibility of a Member State, the United Nations as an Organization has the capacity to bring an international claim against the responsible de jure or de facto government with a view to obtaining the reparation due in respect of the damage caused to the victim or to persons entitled through him.

(ii) by eleven votes against four,

That, in the event of an agent of the United Nations in the performance of his duties suffering injury in circumstances involving the responsibility of a State which is not a member, the United Nations as an Organization has the capacity to bring an international claim against the responsible de jure or de facto government with a view to obtaining the reparation due in respect of the damage caused to the victim or to persons entitled through him.

On Question II:

By ten votes against five,

When the United Nations as an Organization is bringing a claim for reparation of damage caused to its agent, it can only do so by basing its claim upon a breach of obligations due to itself; respect for this rule will usually prevent a conflict between the action of the United Nations and such rights as the agent's national State may possess, and thus bring about a reconciliation between their claims; moreover, this reconciliation must depend upon considerations applicable to each particular case, and upon agreements to be made between the Organization and individual States, either generally or in each case.

* * *

[Concurring and dissenting opinions omitted.]

Freedom of the staff of the United Nations Secretariat from national control. Article 100 of the Charter provides that the Secretary-General of the United Nations and his staff "shall not seek or receive instructions from any government or from any other authority external to the organization;" members of the United Nations are committed not to seek to influence the Secretary-General and his staff in the discharge of their responsibilities. In realistic terms the staff can retain freedom from national control only if the staff members are not dependent on their home state. But complete lack of dependency is not attainable, since the United Nations cannot confer a permanent "citizenship" upon its employees. (Indeed, the judges of the International Court of Justice do not have life-time tenure, as do federal judges in the United States).

The opinion of the court in the Reparation case, however, suggests that at least in one area the dependency of the staff member on his state is reduced. The Legal Department of the United Nations Secretariat has interpreted this opinion as conferring on the United Nations a "right of diplomatic protection" which goes beyond the bare right to present a claim to an alleged wrong-doing state: "* * * [W]hen a United Nations staff member is arrested or detained by the authorities of a State, the Organization always has a right to send representatives to visit and converse with him with a view to ascertaining whether or not an injury has occurred to the United Nations or to him through non-observance by the State concerned of its international obligations, and whether or not such injury is connected with the performance of his duties. Furthermore, at least when the staff member is not a national of the detaining State, there are reasons for recognizing a broader interest of the United Nations in the matter, so that the staff member will not have to rely exclusively on the protection of his own State." United Nations Juridical Yearbook 1963, at 191–192; 13 Whiteman, Digest of International Law 187–188 (1968).

KEENEY v. UNITED STATES

United States Court of Appeals, D.C. Circuit, 1954.
218 F.2d 843.

* * *

EDGERTON, CIRCUIT JUDGE. Appellant, a former employee of the United Nations, was a witness before a Subcommittee of the Committee on the Judiciary of the United States Senate. She was asked whether anyone in the State Department had aided her in obtaining employment with the United Nations. She did not answer, and asserted a privilege not to answer by reason of the Charter and the Staff Rules of the United Nations. On the theory that she had "refused" to answer, she was prosecuted for contempt of Congress. Rev. Stat. § 102, as amended, 52 Stat. 942, 2 U.S.C.A. § 192. The District Court overruled her claim of privilege and she was convicted. United States v. Keeney, D.C., 111 F.Supp. 233.

Appellant was not asked whether anyone in the State Department *told her he would try* to aid her. Perhaps it was a mistake not to ask her that question, but if so, the mistake was not hers. We need not speculate whether she would have answered that question if it had been asked, or whether she would have been punishable if she had not answered it. She was asked whether anyone in the State Department *did* aid her: "Did anyone in the State Department aid you in obtaining employment with the United Nations?" Whether she realized it or not, this was equivalent to asking her whether the United Nations officials who decided to appoint her had received and been influenced by communications from anyone in the State Department recommending that she be appointed.

Staff Rule 7 of the United Nations provides that "Staff members shall exercise the utmost discretion in regard to all matters of official business. They shall not communicate to any other person any unpublished information known to them by reason of their official position except in the course of their duties or by authorization of the Secretary-General." In my opinion both the first sentence and the second sentence of this Rule support appellant's failure to answer. (1) Since the appointment of official personnel is official business, appellant could not answer without violating her obligation to "exercise the utmost discretion in regard to all matters of official business." She could not, consistently with "the utmost discretion", even answer that she did not know, for that would have meant that her superiors had not told her. Whether officials do or do not tell an employee who aided her in obtaining employment is a matter of official policy and official business. (2) The question related to "unpublished information". The United Nations does not tell the world what recommendations underlie appointments of staff members. The United Nations Administrative Manual even defines "unpublished information" to include "the appointment * * * [of] or any other confidential information concerning" a staff member. I think it plain that staff members would not have such unpublished and confidential information unless it had been made "known to them by reason of their official position".

The Charter of the United Nations supports Staff Rule 7. The Charter provides:

Article 100

1. In the performance of their duties the Secretary-General and the staff shall not seek or receive instructions from any government or from any other authority external to the Organization. They shall refrain from any action which might reflect on their position as international officials responsible only to the Organization.

2. Each Member of the United Nations undertakes to respect the exclusively international character of the responsibilities of the Secretary-General and the staff and not to seek to influence them in the discharge of their responsibilities. * * *

Article 105

1. The Organization shall enjoy in the territory of each of its Members such privileges and immunities as are necessary for the fulfillment of its purposes.

2. Representatives of the Members of the United Nations and officials of the Organization shall similarly enjoy such privileges and immunities as are necessary for the independent exercise of their functions in connection with the Organization. 59 Stat. 1052, 1053.

Compulsory disclosure of the persons who influence appointments to the staff of the United Nations would not be consistent with the independence of the Organization or "the exclusively international character of the responsibilities of the Secretary-General and the staff * * *." (Art. 100, Par. 2.) And the prospect of such disclosure might influence staff members, in one degree or another, to regulate their official conduct with a view to avoiding embarrassment of sponsors. The privilege of nondisclosure is therefore "necessary for the independent exercise of their functions in connection with the Organization." (Art. 105, Par. 2.)

Thus the Charter and the Staff Rules of the United Nations establish, in my opinion, the privilege on which appellant relied. And her failure to answer is within the spirit if not the letter of the International Organizations Immunities Act, which provides in § 7(b), 59 Stat. 672, 22 U.S.C.A. § 288d(b): "Representatives of foreign governments in or to international organizations and officers and employees of such organizations shall be immune from suit and legal process relating to acts performed by them in their official capacity and falling within their functions as such representatives, officers, or employees except insofar as such immunity may be waived by the foreign government or international organization concerned."

So far in this opinion I speak only for myself. But we all agree that appellant's conviction must be reversed because of errors in the admission of evidence.

* * *

The result of our several opinions is this. The conviction is reversed with instructions to grant a new trial. In so far as the answer depends upon data in the files of the United Nations or upon information derived from those files, it was privileged by the Charter and the Staff Rules and could not legally be revealed. Evidence as to pertinency will be taken in the absence of the jury. The question whether the appellant's action was under all the circumstances a deliberate and intentional refusal to answer will be put to the jury with the other jury issues.

Reversed.

DANAHER, CIRCUIT JUDGE (concurring).

I agree that the conviction should be reversed and a new trial be ordered. The error requiring this result stems from the failure to exclude the jury while highly prejudicial evidence was received to establish the element of pertinency.

From the very outset the jury heard the appellant linked to a nefarious, world-wide Communist movement, with her associates numbered among those performing acts of espionage and sabotage even as they purloined secrets of the United States in favor of the Russian government.

* * *

The witness testified that the Committee was attempting to learn a number of facts about the Institute of Pacific Relations, how it operated, what it sought to accomplish, and the degree to which it had accomplished it. "The Institute of Pacific Relations was an institution which had been taken over by Communists and was being operated for their purposes." The Institute had sought to place and had in fact placed "its persons" in high places in government and elsewhere in positions of influence. The Committee came across the name of Mary Jane Keeney in a document which had been seized from the files of the Institute; the document indicated that appellant was active in the Washington Advisory Committee of the Institute; and "the Committee found that Mrs. Keeney had a long record of what appeared to be Communist affiliation—"

Mr. Donner. I object to this, Your Honor.

The Court. Objection overruled. This testimony is not given as proof of any fact, but merely as proof of the pertinency of the inquiry * * *.

Defense counsel again insisted that the question of pertinency was a matter of law for the court, and upon a ruling that the trial judge saw no reason for excluding the jury, defense counsel moved for a mistrial.

The witness continued that appellant in San Francisco prior to 1940 had attended a number of Communist meetings and after coming to Washington had entered a circle of acquaintanceship which included Communists and suspected Communists, numbering among her friends Nathan Gregory Silvermaster and Leonard Ullman. The Committee had "unevaluated" information that Mrs. Keeney had been placed in the United Nations with the help of persons in the IPR and the assistance of persons in the State Department.

Defense counsel renewed his motion for a mistrial and moved to strike the testimony and both motions were denied. That the admission of such evidence over appellant's objections was highly prejudicial can not be doubted, and the rulings with reference thereto and denial of appellant's motion for mistrial constitute reversible error. A new trial must be granted.

On the record presented we do not, in my view, reach the question of privilege. Appellant in her brief and in oral argument has urged us to adopt the sophistry which both before the Senate committee and the District Court she applied to the question: "Did anyone in the State Department aid you in obtaining employment with the United Nations?"

Cited to us are the United Nations charter, its rules and interpretations, and section 7(b) of the International Organizations Immunities Act, 59 Stat. 669, 22 U.S.C.A. § 288 et seq. The question asked does not lead us within the fold of privilege so predicated. There is not the slightest suggestion at any stage that by virtue of her official position the appellant gleaned knowledge from the official files as to how her employment came about. On the contrary, after her conviction, the appellant took the witness stand and was sworn and testified " . . . I do not know to whom the United Nations wrote for references, *because that information is never disclosed to the applicant*, to the Secretariat * * *" (Emphasis supplied.)

When a witness before the Senate committee, if appellant did not know the answer to the question, all she had to say was "I don't know"—if she did not know. If, either before obtaining employment with the United Nations or after such employment had been terminated, she learned—other than from official sources—that someone in the State Department had aided her in obtaining employment she was bound to answer "Yes." If she had personal knowledge —other than from official sources—that no one in the State Department had been of "aid" in her procuring employment, she was bound to answer "No."

In short, even if we were to reach the question of the claimed privilege, unless she acquired information by virtue of her official position during the period of her employment by the United Nations that someone in the State Department did aid her in obtaining such employment, she was bound to answer according to the fact. Whatever privilege may be said to stem from the charter and the staff rules and regulations of the United Nations would apply only with respect to information known to the witness by reason of official position, past or present.

The International Organizations Immunities Act, § 7(b), 59 Stat. 671, 22 U.S.C.A. § 288d(b), provides: "Representatives of foreign governments in or to international organizations and officers and employees of such organizations shall be immune from suit and legal process *relating to acts performed by them in their official capacity and falling within their functions as such representatives, officers, or employees * * *.*" (Emphasis supplied.) This witness was not subjected to suit or legal process relating to acts performed by her in her official capacity. There is no need to give strained and extended interpretation to the very useful Immunities Act which by its terms has no application here.

After trial when the very question was put to her, with her own particular qualification she answered "I don't know." She specified "that information is never disclosed to the applicant * * *" When she applied for employment in the United Nations she "did not know anyone in the State Department." "Q. Did anyone intercede for you? A. Not to my knowledge."

The answer to the question was clearly within the power of the witness to provide, and a reading of her testimony in the Joint Appendix discloses that the jury might properly be asked to pass upon the issue as to her contumacy as alleged.

* * *

PRETTYMAN, CIRCUIT JUDGE (concurring).

I concur in the result, and I agree with both of my brethren in the parts of their opinions dealing with the reception before the jury of the evidence relating to pertinency.

* * *

On the other point, concerning the accused's privilege not to answer the question put to her, I find myself midway between my two brethren. I think that, in so far as the answer to the question, "Did anyone in the State Department aid you in obtaining employment with the United Nations?", depended upon data in the files of the United Nations or upon information derived from those files, it was privileged by the Charter and the Staff Rules and could not legally be revealed. To that extent the witness could and should have refused to answer. But it is conceivable that wholly apart from any files or information gleaned from them the witness had knowledge that someone at the State Department did aid her in getting employment. Some such matters are frequently known personally and altogether outside official channels. Information thus obtained was not privileged, and if this witness knew of any of that sort in her case she should have said so. If she did not know of any, she should have answered to that effect. As the event turned out, that was the view of the United Nations Secretariat and also the view later adopted by the witness. It seems to me that her initial position in response to the question was not fully protected.

At the same time it seems to me that this witness's course might not be deemed by a jury to be a refusal to answer.

* * *

DUBERG v. UNITED NATIONS EDUCATIONAL, SCIENTIFIC AND CULTURAL ORGANIZATION

International Labor Organization Administrative Tribunal, 1955.
38 I.L.O. Off. Bull. 251.

[Duberg, an American citizen who was employed by the defendant organization, was denied a renewal of his employment contract by the Director-General because he had not complied with an invitation to appear before the International Organizations Employees Loyalty Board of the United States Civil Service Commission in 1953. The Director-General had informed Duberg that his conduct could not be accepted as consistent with "the high standards of integrity which are required of those employed by the Organization."]

(10) By a letter of 10 September 1954 the Director-General received communication of the report of the Loyalty Board (advisory determination) in which it was stated: "It has been determined on all the evidence that there is a reasonable doubt as to the loyalty of Norwood Peter Duberg to the Government of the United States" and that "this determination, together with the reasons therefor, in as much detail as security considerations permit, are submitted for your use in exercising your rights and duties with respect to the integrity of the personnel employed by the United Nations Educational, Scientific and Cultural Organisation";

(11) The complainant was himself informed of the conclusions of the Loyalty Board by letter of the Chairman of the Loyalty Board dated 10 September 1954, and was also informed of the fact that the report of the Loyalty Board had been transmitted to the Director-General of the defendant Organisation;

(12) On 23 September 1954 the complainant submitted an appeal to the U.N.E.S.C.O. Appeals Board asking that the above-mentioned decision should be rescinded;

(13) On 2 November 1954 the Appeals Board, by a majority opinion, expressed the opinion that the decision should be rescinded;

(14) By a letter dated 25 November 1954 the Director-General informed the Chairman of the Appeals Board that he could not act in accordance with this opinion;

(15) Before the Appeals Board had taken its decision the Director-General, on 28 September 1954, set up a Special Advisory Board consisting of members of the staff, whose task was to "examine the cases of certain staff members on the basis of certain information which has been brought to the knowledge of the Director-General, and in the light of the standards of employment and conduct prescribed by the Constitution and Staff Regulations";

(16) The complainant appeared and explained his position before this Special Advisory Board. However, in a letter to the Director-General dated 4 October 1954, he expressed certain reservations to the procedure followed and asked for any measures affecting him which might result from this procedure to be cancelled;

(17) By a letter dated 11 October 1954 the Chief of the Bureau of Personnel and Management informed the complainant of the rejection of this request;

* * *

ON THE SUBSTANCE:

A.　Considering that the defendant Organisation holds that the renewal or the non-renewal of a fixed-term appointment depends entirely on the personal and sovereign discretion of the Director-General, who is not even required to give his reason therefor;

Considering that, if this were to be so, any unmotivated decision would not be subject to the general legal review which is vested in the Tribunal, and would be liable to become arbitrary;

Considering that, in fact, it may be conceived that this might exceptionally be the case when, for example, it is a matter of assessing the technical suitability of the person concerned for carrying out his duties;

Considering, however, that in this matter the question does not affect the issue inasmuch as the Director-General has not only given the reason for the decision taken by him but has also made it public in a communiqué issued to the press;

That this reason is based solely on the refusal of the complainant to co-operate in the measures of investigation provided in respect of certain of its nationals by the Government of the State of which he is a citizen, and in particular on his refusal to appear before a commission invested by that Government with the power to investigate his loyalty to that State;

That the Director-General declares that he concludes from this that he can no longer retain his confidence in the complainant and offer him a new appointment, his attitude being incompatible with the high standards of integrity required of those who are employed by the Organisation and being, furthermore, capable of harming the interests of the Organisation;

Considering in relation hereto that it is necessary expressly to reject all uncertainty and confusion as to the meaning of the expression "loyalty towards a State" which is entirely different from the idea of "integrity" as embodied in the Staff Regulations and Rules; and that this is evident and requires no further proof;

B.   Considering that if the Director-General is granted authority not to renew a fixed-term appointment and so to do without notice or indemnity, this is clearly subject to the implied condition that this authority must be exercised only for the good of the service and in the interest of the Organisation;

Considering that it is in the light of this principle that the facts in this case should be examined;

Considering that Article 1.4 of the Staff Regulations of the defendant Organisation, as it stood at the moment when the decision complained of was taken, was as follows:

> Members of the Secretariat shall conduct themselves at all times in a manner consonant with the good repute and high purposes of the Organisation and their status as international civil servants.   They shall not engage in any activity that is incompatible with the proper discharge of their duties.   They shall avoid any action, and in particular any kind of public pronouncement, which would adversely reflect upon their status.   While they are not expected to give up religious or political convictions or national sentiments, they shall at all times exercise the reserve and tact incumbent upon them by reason of their international responsibilities;

Considering that, in thus clearly establishing the entire freedom of conscience recognised to international officials in respect of both their philosophical convictions and their political opinions, the Regulations impose on them the duty to abstain from all acts capable of being interpreted as associating them with propaganda or militant proselytism in any sense whatever:

That this abstention is rigorously imposed on them by the overriding interest of the international organisation to which they owe their loyalty and devotion;

C.   Considering that, when consulted by the Staff Association of the defendant organisation on the obligation incumbent on members of the staff to reply to questionnaires issued by authorities of their respective countries, the Director-General declared that the answer must depend only on the conscience of the individual, except that he should not lie and should have regard to the consequences which the refusal to reply might have for him;

* * *

Considering that it is desirable to determine whether the attitude adopted by the complainant in this respect may be considered as justifying the loss of confidence pledged by the Director-General;

* * *

E.   Considering that it is quite different when the ground for complaint of the Director-General is based solely on the refusal of the official to participate in measures of verbal or written inquiry to which his national Government considers it necessary to subject him;

That the Director-General of an international organisation cannot associate himself with the execution of the policy of the government authorities of any State Member without disregarding the obligations imposed on all international officials without distinction and, in consequence, without misusing the authority which has been conferred on him solely for the purpose of directing that organisation towards the achievement of its own, exclusively international, objectives;

That this duty of the Director-General is governed by Article VI, paragraph 5 of the Constitution of the defendant Organisation, in the following terms:

> The responsibilities of the Director-General and of the staff shall be exclusively international in character. In the discharge of their duties they shall not seek or receive instructions from any government or from any authority external to the Organisation. They shall refrain from any action which might prejudice their position as international officials. Each State Member of the Organisation undertakes to respect the international character of the responsibilities of the Director-General and the staff, and not to seek to influence them in the discharge of their duties;

Considering that the fact that in this case the matter involved is an accusation of disloyalty brought by a Government which enjoys in all respects the highest prestige must be without any influence upon the consideration of the facts in the case and the determination of the principles whose respect the Tribunal must ensure;

That it will suffice to realise that if any one of the 72 States and Governments involved in the defendant Organisation brought against an official, one of its citizens, an accusation of disloyalty and claimed to subject him to an inquiry in similar or analogous conditions, the attitude adopted by the Director-General would constitute a precedent obliging him to lend his assistance to such inquiry and, moreover, to invoke the same disciplinary or statutory consequences, the same withdrawal of confidence, on the basis of any opposal by the person concerned to the action of his national Government;

That if this were to be the case there would result for all international officials, in matters touching on conscience, a state of uncertainty and insecurity prejudicial to the performance of their duties and liable to provoke disturbances in the international administration such as cannot be imagined to have been in the intention of those who drew up the Constitution of the defendant Organisation;

Considering, therefore, that the only ground for complaint adduced by the Director-General to justify the application to the complainant of an exception to the general rule of renewal of appointments, that is to say his opposal to the investigations of his own Government, is entirely unjustified;

Considering that it results therefrom that the decision taken must be rescinded; but that nevertheless the Tribunal does not have the power to order the renewal of a fixed-term appointment, which requires a positive act of the Director-General over whom the Tribunal has no hierarchical authority;

That in the absence of such a power, and unless the Director-General should consider himself in a position to reconsider his decision in this manner, the Tribunal is none the less competent to order equitable reparation of the damage suffered by the complainant by reason of the discriminatory treatment of which he was the object;

That redress will be ensured ex aequo et bono by the granting to the complainant of the sum set forth below;

Considering that, on the one hand, there should be granted to the complainant the amount of the salary which he would have received had he not been subject to the measure of exception of which he complains, that is to say one year's basic salary;

That, on the other hand, there should be granted to him a second year's basic salary in order to compensate for the moral prejudice and in particular the difficulties which he will encounter in seeking new means of subsistence;

That, in this calculation, there should be added to the salary the statutory amount of children's allowance;

ON THE GROUNDS AS AFORESAID:

The Tribunal,

* * *

Orders the decision taken to be rescinded and declares in law that it constitutes an abuse of rights causing prejudice to the complainant;

In consequence, should the defendant not reconsider the decision taken and renew the complainant's appointment, orders the said defendant to pay to the complainant the sum of 15,500 dollars, plus children's allowance for two years, the whole together with interest at 4 per centum from 1 January 1955;

Orders the defendant Organisation to pay to the complainant the sum of 300 dollars by way of participation in the costs of his defence * * *.

---

1. *"Affirmance" by the International Court of Justice.* The court subsequently rendered an advisory opinion that the administrative tribunal had acted within its jurisdiction in the Duberg and companion cases. Judgments of the Administrative Tribunal of the International Labour Organization upon Complaints Made against the United Nations Educational, Scientific and Cultural Organization, [1956] I.C.J.Rep. 77.

2. *Questions.*

(a) Has the independence of the international civil service been vindicated in this case?

(b) Why did the tribunal not order Mr. Duberg's reinstatement to his job?

(c) Note that the Duberg case arose during the "McCarthy era" in the United States. Suppose that it had recently arisen in respect of a Soviet national. Of a South African national.

(d) How can international organizations deal with the problem of national influence on selection of international civil servants?

SECTION C. CAPACITIES AND IMMUNITIES

BALFOUR, GUTHRIE & CO., LTD. v. UNITED STATES

United States District Court, N.D. California, 1950.
90 F.Supp. 831.

* * *

GOODMAN, DISTRICT JUDGE. The competency of the United Nations to sue the United States in Federal Court under the Suits in

Admiralty Act, 46 U.S.C.A. § 741 et seq., is the principal and unique question tendered by the exceptions to the libel of the United Nations and other joint libelants. As well do the exceptions question the right of the United Nations to maintain the libel against American Pacific Steamship Co., a co-respondent.

The libel alleges that in the autumn of 1947, the United Nations' International Children's Emergency Fund shipped from the ports of Tacoma and Oakland aboard the SS Abraham Rosenberg a large quantity of powdered milk destined for Italy and Greece. A portion of the shipment, it is alleged, was never delivered to the consignee and another portion arrived in a damaged condition. The Abraham Rosenberg was owned by the United States and was operated under a bareboat charter by respondent American Pacific Steamship Company. The United Nations and six other shippers, whose merchandise allegedly suffered a similar fate, have joined in the libel against the United States and the American Pacific Steamship Company.

Whether the United Nations may maintain these proceedings against respondent American Pacific Steamship Company can be first and more easily answered.

The International Court of Justice has held that the United Nations is a legal entity separate and distinct from the member States. While it is not a state nor a super-State, it is an international person, clothed by its Members with the competence necessary to discharge its functions.

Article 104 of the Charter of the United Nations, 59 Stat. 1053, provides that "the Organization shall enjoy in the territory of each of its Members such legal capacity as may be necessary for the exercise of its functions and the fulfillment of its purposes." As a treaty ratified by the United States, the Charter is part of the supreme law of the land. No implemental legislation would appear to be necessary to endow the United Nations with legal capacity in the United States. But the President has removed any possible doubt by designating the United Nations as one of the organizations entitled to enjoy the privileges conferred by the International Organizations Immunities Act, 59 Stat. 669, 22 U.S.C.A. §§ 288–288f. Section 2(a) of that Act, 22 U.S.C.A. § 288a(a), states that "international organizations shall, to the extent consistent with the instrument creating them, possess the capacity—(i) to contract; (ii) to acquire and dispose of real and personal property; (iii) to institute legal proceedings."

The capacity of the United Nations to maintain the libel against the American Pacific Steamship Company is completely consistent with its charter. The libel asserts rights flowing from a contract made by a specialized agency of the United Nations in the performance of its duties. The agency, the International Children's Emergency Fund, was created by resolution of the General Assembly of the United Nations on December 11, 1946. (Resolution 57(1), United

Nations Yearbook 1946–47, 162). Its function is to promote child health generally and in particular to assist the governments of countries, that were the victims of aggression, to rehabilitate their children. The solution of international health problems is one of the responsibilities assumed by the United Nations in Article 55 of its Charter, 59 Stat. 1045.

Whether the United Nations may sue the United States is a more difficult question. It is apparent that Article 104 of the Charter of the United Nations was never intended to provide a method for settling differences between the United Nations and its members. It is equally clear that the International Organizations Immunities Act does not amount to a waiver of the United States' sovereign immunity from suit. The precise question posed is whether the capacity to institute legal proceedings conferred on the United Nations by that Act includes the competence to sue the United States in cases in which the United States has consented to suits by other litigants.

The broad purpose of the International Organizations Immunities Act was to vitalize the status of international organizations of which the United States is a member and to facilitate their activities. A liberal interpretation of the Act is in harmony with this purpose.

The considerations which might prompt a restrictive interpretation are not persuasive. It is true that history has recorded few, if any, instances in which international entities have submitted their disputes to the courts of one of the disputing parties. But international organizations on a grand scale are a modern phenomena. The wide variety of activities in which they engage is likely to give rise to claims against their members that can most readily be disposed of in national courts. The present claim is such a claim. No political overtones surround it. No possible embarrassment to the United States in the conduct of its international affairs could result from such a decree as this court might enter. A claim for cargo loss and damage is clearly susceptible of judicial settlement. Particularly is this so in this litigation inasmuch as the United Nations' claim is one of several of the same nature arising out of the same transaction or occurrence.

International organizations, such as the United Nations and its agencies, of which the United States is a member, are not alien bodies. The interests of the United States are served when the United Nations' interests are protected. A prompt and equitable settlement of any claim it may have against the United States will be the settlement most advantageous to both parties. The courts of the United States afford a most appropriate forum for accomplishing such a settlement.

It may be contended that since international organizations are granted immunity from suit by the International Organizations Immunities Act, an equitable and complete judicial settlement of claims asserted against the United States may not be had. But this possible objection is more fancied than real. For the United Nations submits to our courts when it urges its claim and cannot consequently shut off any proper defenses of the United States.

Finally, it cannot be denied that when the Congress conferred the privileges specified in the International Organizations Immunities Act, it neither explicitly nor implicitly limited the kind or type of legal proceedings that might be instituted by the United Nations. There appears to be no good reason for the judicial imposition of such limitations.

The exceptions of the respondents are severally overruled.

---

1. *Convention on the Privileges and Immunities of the United Nations.* The United States has become a party to the convention since the date of the foregoing opinion. Compare the language of the immunities provision of the convention (Section 2) with the language of the International Organization Immunities Act (22 U.S.C. § 288a; Documentary Supplement) referred to in the opinion. Both provide for express waiver. The act provides for the same immunity "as is enjoyed by foreign governments"; the convention provides for immunity from every form of legal process without mentioning foreign governments. Under the convention, if the United Nations is a plaintiff in a law suit, does it submit to counterclaims by the defendant?

2. *The doctrine of restrictive immunities as applied to international organizations.* If an international organization should engage in activities that, if engaged in by a state, would invoke the doctrine of restrictive immunities, would it be suable, despite the provisions of a convention such as the one above? For example, there have been proposals to aid in United Nations financing through economic activity and that the United Nations engage in various exploitative activities as to the resources of the deep sea bed. Would the considerations underlying the restrictive theory of state immunity necessarily be controlling in the case of a universal international organization such as the United Nations?

INTERNATIONAL REFUGEE ORGANIZATION v. REPUBLIC S. S. CORP.

United States Court of Appeals, Fourth Circuit, 1951.
189 F.2d 858.

PARKER, CHIEF JUDGE. These cases arise out of a controversy between the International Refugee Organization, an agency of the United Nations, and the Republic of Panama, and one Jose Jacintho de Medeiros, a citizen of Portugal. * * * No. 6202 involves a charge of fraud and deceit made by the I.R.O. against the corporation and Medeiros in a suit instituted against them to recover damages and establish a constructive trust.

* * *

The allegations of fraud in both cases are that the corporation and Medeiros obtained $840,000 from I.R.O. by means of false and fraudulent representations with respect to the ownership, title and speed of the S. S. San Francisco, a vessel chartered to the I.R.O. by the Republic Steamship Company represented by Medeiros as president.

In No. 6202, the action against Medeiros and the Republic Steamship Company was dismissed by the lower court for lack of jurisdiction.

* * *

The dismissal for lack of jurisdiction in No. 6202 is based upon the holding that a suit by the I.R.O. is not one of which the federal courts have been given jurisdiction. We think that this is error. The United Nations is an international organization of which the United States is a member, and article 104 of its charter provides that it shall enjoy in the territory of each of its members "such legal capacity as may be necessary for the exercise of its functions and the fulfillment of its purposes". 59 Stat. 1053. Article 13 of the Constitution of the I.R.O., which is an agency of the United Nations, contains a provision to like effect. In the International Organization Immunities Act, 59 Stat. 669, 22 U.S.C.A. § 288a, Congress has undertaken to discharge the obligations assumed under these provisions by providing that international organizations such as I.R.O. shall "to the extent consistent with the instrument creating them, possess the capacity—

"(i) to contract;

"(ii) to acquire and dispose of real and personal property;

"(iii) *to institute legal proceedings*". (Italics supplied.) This means, by necessary implication, that Congress has opened the doors of the federal courts to suits by such international organizations; for the right to institute legal proceedings means the right to go into court, and the federal courts are the only courts whose doors Congress can open.

As pointed out by the Secretary of State (hearings on U. N. Charter, 77th Congress, 1st Session, pp. 33, 134–135) and the Senate Committee on Foreign Affairs (S.Report, exec. No. 8, 77th Congress, 1st Session, p. 6), "It is apparent that an organization like the United Nations which will have offices and employees, will purchase supplies, and presumably rent or purchase office space, must have the legal capacity to enter into contracts, to take title to real and personal property and to appear in court (although its position as a defendant is protected by Article 105). The purpose of Article 104 is to make clear that the Organization has that legal capacity." Certainly an organization like the I.R.O., which is purchasing and chartering vessels and entering into all sorts of contracts in connection with the transportation of refugees, must have the right to go into court for the protection of its rights and interests; and in this country the logical courts for it to go into are the courts of the nation which has adhered to the international organization, not the local courts of the several states which have had no part therein. In determining its rights in this regard, we should give a liberal interpretation to the International Organization Immunities Act.

* * *

We think also that there is jurisdiction to entertain the suit by reason of 28 U.S.C.A. § 1331, which provides that the District Courts shall have jurisdiction of civil actions arising under the "Constitution, laws or treaties of the United States". Under the principles laid down in Osborn v. United States Bank, 9 Wheat. 738, 6 L.Ed. 204, this was certainly a civil action arising not only under the treaties creating the United Nations and the International Refugee Organization into both of which the United States had entered, but also under the act of Congress which gives the right to sue to public international organizations in which the United States participates. The right of federal corporations to invoke the jurisdiction of the federal courts has been curtailed by act of Congress but this involves no limitation of the doctrine of Osborne v. United States Bank, supra. On the contrary, it is an express recognition of that doctrine. It will be noted that the statute, 28 U.S.C.A. § 1349, denying jurisdiction to a corporation created by act of Congress unless the United States is the owner of more than one-half its capital stock can have no application because the I.R.O. is not a corporation created by act of Congress but an international organization to which the United States itself is a party. If, as said by the Supreme Court in the case of Gully v. First National Bank, 299 U.S. 109, 114, 57 S.Ct. 96, 81 L.Ed. 70, there is no thought of disturbing the doctrine of the charter cases, that doctrine must be held to support the jurisdiction here. If a corporation may invoke the federal jurisdiction because created by a law of the United States, an international organization created by treaties to which the United States is a party may invoke the jurisdiction because created by a treaty of the United States. Especially is this true where the international organization is clothed by a law of the United States with the essential corporate functions of contracting, acquiring and disposing of property and suing in court.

It has been suggested that the jurisdiction of the court can be sustained under 28 U.S.C.A. § 1345 on the theory that a suit by an international organization is a suit by the United States as well as by the other nations which are parties to the organization and that jurisdiction of a suit by the United States is not defeated because other parties are joined as plaintiffs in the suit. See Erickson v. United States, 264 U.S. 246, 249, 44 S.Ct. 310, 68 L.Ed. 661. We need not pass upon this, however, as we think there can be no question as to the jurisdiction for the reasons already given.

* * *

WESTCHESTER COUNTY v. RANOLLO

United States, City Court of New Rochelle, 1946.
187 Misc. 777, 67 N.Y.S.2d 31.

RUBIN, ACTING CITY JUDGE.   The defendant, as the operator of a motor vehicle, is charged with having violated the provisions of the ordinances of the Westchester County Park Commission, in that he did on the 17th day of October, 1946, on the Hutchinson River Parkway, a Public Highway in this city, operate said vehicle, for a distance greater than a quarter of a mile, at a rate of speed of fifty miles per hour, the legal limit being forty miles.   Appearing through counsel, the defendant answers that he was operating said motor vehicle at the time and place complained of as an employee of the United Nations, and, in fact, he was accompanied in the vehicle at the time by the Hon. Trygve Lie, Secretary General of the United Nations, and by virtue of these facts he urges that he is immune from prosecution in this Court or, for that matter in any Court.

The claim for immunity rests upon Executive Order 9698, 22 U.S.C.A. § 288 note, U.S.Code, Congressional Service, 1946, p. 1771, promulgated by the President of the United States, February 19, 1946, by virtue of the authority vested in the President by Sec. 1 of the International Organizations Immunities Act approved December 29, 1945, otherwise known as Public Law 291, 79th Congress, 22 U.S.C.A. § 288 et seq.   That statute was enacted and designed to implement the Immunities provisions as embodied in the Charter of the United Nations.

By the provisions of Article 105 of Chapter XVI of the United Nations Charter the signatories, including the United States, covenanted and agreed:

   1.   The Organization shall enjoy in the territory of each of its Members *such privileges and immunities as are necessary for the fulfillment of its purposes.*

   2.   Representatives of the Members of the United Nations and officials of the Organization shall similarly enjoy *such privileges and immunities as are necessary for the independent exercise of their functions in connection with the Organization.* (Italics supplied.)

It is to be noted significantly at this point that the phrase, "such privileges and immunities" is nowhere defined in the Charter.

The Congressional Act (Public Law 291) provides, among other things, that "the privileges, exemptions, and immunities provided for" herein may be accorded, withheld, withdrawn, conditioned or limited by Executive Order of the President (Sec. 1).

By Sec. 7 of the Act, 22 U.S.C.A. § 288d, subd. (b), the national policy on the subject of immunity is laid down in the following words:

> (b) Representatives of foreign governments in or to international organizations and officers and employees of such organizations shall be immune from suit and legal process relating to acts performed by them in their official capacity and falling within their functions as such representatives, officers, or employees except insofar as such immunity may be waived by the foreign government or international organization concerned.

One examines the statute in vain for any definition of the term "legal process" or of the term "in their official capacity and falling within their functions as such representatives, officers, or employees."

Again when we turn to Executive Order 9698, there is a declaration by the President that the United Nations are "entitled to enjoy the privileges, exemptions, and immunities conferred by the said International Organizations Immunities Act," without any attempt to further define or limit or prescribe the extent of the immunities so conferred.

It is urged in behalf of the defendant that the application of these cited provisions requires the exemption from prosecution or suit, criminal or civil, and without regard to the degree of the offense committed, of all personnel accredited to the United Nations as an international organization, without regard to the question as to whether the one so involved is the Secretary General himself or an accredited delegate to the Organization's deliberations, or the humblest servant attached to the personnel of the Organization, and without regard to the importance or unimportance of the functions of the particular individual defendant in the deliberations and workings of the Organization so long as the defendant, at the time of the commission of the offense or the incurring of the liability, be acting in his official capacity. This Court is not prepared to accede to that view.

In the absence of statutory definitions, the question presented must be treated under the general rules of construction applicable to criminal proceedings in this State. Section 21 of the Penal Law very aptly furnishes the rule of construction in the following language:

> The rule that a penal statute is to be strictly construed does not apply to this chapter or any of the provisions thereof, but all such provisions must be construed according to the fair import of their terms, *to promote justice and effect the objects of the law*. (Italics supplied.)

To recognize the existence of a general and unrestricted immunity from suit or prosecution on the part of the personnel of the United Nations, so long as the individual be performing in his official capacity, even though the individual's function has no relation to the importance or the success of the Organization's deliberations, is carrying the principle of immunity completely out of bounds. To establish such a principle would in effect create a large preferred class within our borders who would be immune to punishment on identical facts for which the average American would be subject to punishment. Any such theory does violence to and is repugnant to the American sense of fairness and justice and flouts the very basic principle of the United Nations itself, which in its preamble to its Charter affirms that it is created to give substance to the principle that the rights of all men and women are equal.

Furthermore, the establishment of such a rule of immunity would far exceed any effort heretofore undertaken in the intercourse between nations to recognize the principle of diplomatic immunity, for ambassadors and foreign ministers and members of their households, accredited to a specific nation and enjoying immunity from prosecution here under the provisions of Sec. 25 of the Penal Law, at least, theoretically, were subject to return to their own country for trial and punishment. The United Nations has no tribunal for the trial and punishment of offenders among its personnel, and if blanket immunity were to be recognized as prevailing in this case, then one would have to come to the conclusion that such an offender could escape trial and punishment completely. Certainly no court of justice, and no people who believe in justice, would be prepared to endorse such a position.

It is interesting to note that research discloses a similar attempt to escape punishment by one Avenol in the Courts of the Republic of France in 1934, when he was being held to account for alleged failure to support his family, he then being the Secretary General of the ill fated predecessor to the present International Organization, namely, the League of Nations. The judgment in that instance refused to accord the claimed immunity, with the comment, "No one may claim to be immune from suit in 50 states. That is practically in all the world. Such a privilege would be abhorrent to the fundamental idea of justice."

There can be no disputing of the proposition that if these international legislative bodies are to function properly within the borders of the particular nation that may be housing their activities, a certain amount of immunity, exemption and privilege is necessary to insure their necessary personnel against harassment by way of court proceedings, civil or criminal, and every right thinking American citizen is sincerely anxious that the deliberations of this international body shall proceed uninterruptedly and with a maximum measure of success in every one's interest.

This assurance can be given by interpreting the language of the Charter and the Act of Congress and the Presidential Executive Order as being limited in the application of the principle of immunity to those personnel whose activities are such as to be necessary to the actual execution of the purposes and deliberations of the United Nations as distinguished from those household servants and personnel who merely serve the personal comfort, convenience or luxury of the delegates and Secretariat who actually perform the true functions of the Organization. It is only by the application of such a rule that one can be said to be interpreting the law "According to the fair import of its terms to promote justice and effect the objects of the law."

Our State and national legislators enjoy a measure of immunity so as to insure the proper functioning of the Congress and of the State Legislatures, which falls short of that measure of immunity contended for on behalf of the personnel of the United Nations, and no valid reason exists why the immunity to be accorded to the United Nations should be greater in scope than that found necessary to insure the proper functioning of our own Congress.

It is only by a proper definition of the immunity to be accorded to the personnel of the United Nations and by a proper circumscription of the effect to be given the Congressional language that the American people can be assured that the hospitality accorded the United Nations on American soil will not be abused by conduct on the part of even the humblest member of its personnel in a manner that is hostile to the American concept of the equal administration of justice among our people. This Court feels strongly that the question of immunity under these circumstances should be entrusted, not to the whim or caprice of any individual or committee that might speak for the United Nations Organization, but rather that such immunity should be available only when it is truly necessary to assure the proper deliberations of the Organization—a circumstance that could be readily brought about if the granting of immunity were restricted to those cases where our own State Department certified that the exemption from prosecution or suit was in the public interest.

In the light of the foregoing citations and principles, this Court holds that upon the facts in this case, the defendant is not entitled to immunity as a matter of law without a trial of the issue of fact, and is accordingly required to plead to the information before the Court.

UNITED STATES EX REL. CASANOVA v. FITZPATRICK

United States District Court, S.D. New York, 1963.
214 F.Supp. 425.

* * *

WEINFELD, DISTRICT JUDGE.   The petitioner, Roberto Santi-esteban Casanova, seeks his release from custody on a writ of habeas corpus on the ground of lack of the Court's jurisdiction over his person.   He is under arrest and detention by virtue of a two-count indictment wherein he, two codefendants and two others not named as defendants are charged with conspiracy to commit sabotage and to violate the Foreign Agents Registration Act.   He was originally arrested on a warrant issued by the United States Commissioner, based upon a complaint, and held in $250,000 bail fixed by the Commissioner.   Thereafter, following his indictment by a grand jury, this Court set bail in the sum of $75,000, which it later reduced to $50,-000.   Petitioner has been confined since his arrest in default of bail.

Petitioner contends he is entitled to diplomatic immunity and is not subject to Federal arrest, detention or prosecution.   The basic facts upon which his claim to immunity rests are not in dispute.   He is a Cuban national, appointed by his government as an attache and Resident Member of the Staff of the Permanent Mission of Cuba to the United Nations, hereafter referred to as the "Cuban Mission."   He entered the United States on October 3, 1962 with a diplomatic passport issued by his own government, a nonimmigrant visa issued by our Department of State, and a landing card issued by the Immigration and Naturalization Service.   From the time of his admission to the United States to the date of his arrest on November 16th he was employed as a Resident Member of the staff of the Cuban Mission.

Petitioner contends that he enjoys diplomatic immunity from arrest and prosecution under (1) Article 105 of the United Nations Charter, (2) Section 15(2) of the Headquarters Agreement of the United Nations, and (3) the Law of Nations.   He further contends that even if his claim to immunity is overruled, nonetheless the writ must be sustained, since the Supreme Court of the United States has exclusive and original jurisdiction to try him under Article III of the Constitution of the United States and section 1251 of Title 28, United States Code.

Before considering his contentions, it is desirable to localize the issue with which we deal.   The petitioner is not a member of a diplomatic staff accredited to, and recognized by, the United States Government.   He is not a representative to, or an employee of, the United Nations.   His claim to diplomatic immunity derives solely from his status as a Resident Member of the Cuban Permanent Mission to the United Nations.   Whatever right to immunity exists must be considered within the context of that status.

A. The Claim of Diplomatic Immunity Under the United Nations Charter.

* * *

The thrust of the relator's contention is that the declaration in section 2 is self-executing and requires absolute diplomatic immunity be accorded to representatives of members and their staffs. The argument rests upon the postulate, universally recognized in international law, that diplomatic agents are accorded immunity from judicial process so that their governments may not be hampered in their foreign relations by the arrest or harassment of, or interference with, their diplomatic representatives. Petitioner urges that this rationale applies with equal force to the members of a mission to the United Nations and its staff; that unless they enjoy diplomatic immunity they can be prevented from fulfilling their diplomatic functions vis-a-vis the United Nations, if the host country, in this instance the United States, were able to arrest and detain them—in short, that diplomatic immunity is required to assure the independence of the Organization and its members in the discharge of their duties and functions. Accordingly, he contends that Article 105 intended, and in fact confers, full diplomatic immunity. The language of Article 105, its history, as well as subsequent acts by the United States and the United Nations, require rejection of petitioner's claim that by its own force full diplomatic immunity was either intended or granted by the Article.

* * *

The Court concludes that Article 105 of the Charter does not purport to nor does it confer diplomatic immunity. The broadest claim that can be made is that it is self-operative with respect to functional activities. And even if it were so construed, it avails not the petitioner, since by its very language the immunity is confined to acts necessary for the independent exercise of functions in connection with the United Nations. Conspiracy to commit sabotage against the Government of the United States is not a function of any mission or member of a mission to the United Nations. Accordingly, the Court holds that the petitioner does not enjoy diplomatic immunity against prosecution on the indictment by virtue of Article 105 of the United Nations Charter.

B. The Claim of Diplomatic Immunity Under the Headquarters Agreement.

(1) Is the Court concluded by the certificate of the State Department?

The development and growth of international organizations over the past two decades, particularly the United Nations as a world force, have brought into being new problems and concepts relating to the immunities and privileges to be accorded the organization, its officials and representatives of member states and their staffs. From the start it was evident that unless adequate immunity was provided to protect them in the exercise of their respective functions, the independence of the organization would be undermined and its effectiveness greatly hampered, if not destroyed. The location of the headquarters presents special problems to the host country and the organization. Access to the headquarters to all persons having legitimate business with the organization is required and, on the other hand, the host country is entitled to protection against the admission of persons likely to engage in activities subversive of its national interests and internal security. These matters are usually provided for by the basic charter or constitution, special agreements or national legislation. With the United States as the site of the United Nations headquarters, our Government was particularly sensitive to the problem of assuring the independence and proper functioning of the United Nations, and also to the protection of its own security. The Headquarters Agreement was one of the means adopted to protect the respective interests.

* * *

Under the above provisions, those who come within its embrace are entitled to the broad diplomatic privileges and immunities enjoyed by diplomatic envoys accredited to the United States. And there would appear to be no question that if the petitioner is entitled to the benefits of Article 15, he is immune from prosecution upon the charges contained in the indictment. Petitioner relies upon section 15(2) as conferring diplomatic immunity upon him by reason of his position as an attache and a Resident Member of the Cuban Mission. The Government challenges his claim, pointing out that the subsection expressly provides that immunity thereunder is accorded only to "such resident members * * * as may be agreed upon between the Secretary-General, the Government of the United States and the Government of the Member concerned." It denies that any such agreement was ever manifested, although it admits that an application therefor was made by the Secretary-General of the United Nations pursuant to the request of the Cuban Mission.

The prosecution has filed an authenticated affidavit of the Chief Protocol Officer of the Department of State certifying that the Government of the United States has not agreed to grant diplomatic immunity to petitioner under section 15(2) of the Headquarters Agreement, "and that he does not enjoy any diplomatic privileges and immunities under the aforesaid Article 15 of the Agreement." Accordingly, it presses that the Court is concluded by this certification.

Thus, a threshold question is presented. The precise issue before the Court is whether, in the light of section 15(2) of the Headquarters Agreement, certification by the Department of State that an individual acknowledged to be a resident attache of the Permanent

Cuban Mission to the United Nations has not been "agreed upon" by the Government as entitled to diplomatic privileges and immunities thereunder, concludes the question.

A number of leading authorities do hold that the State Department certification is conclusive where the issue pertains to a diplomatic envoy accredited to the United States. This Court is of the view that such authorities do not control the question here presented. There is a sharp distinction between a diplomatic envoy accredited to the Government of the United States and a representative of a member state to the United Nations, an international organization. The status of each is different and immunity rests upon and is derived from entirely different desiderata.

Acceptance of a diplomatic envoy from a foreign government to the United States rests upon the exercise by our Executive of its power to conduct foreign affairs. It either accepts or rejects the diplomat in its sole and absolute discretion and, if he is received, he thereby is entitled, without more, under the Law of Nations, to full diplomatic immunity. These are political judgments by the Executive Branch of the Government and the Court is concluded thereby. In contrast, a representative of a member state to an international organization, such as the United Nations, is designated by his Government entirely independent of the views of other member states and indeed of the Organization. The United States has no say or veto power with respect to such representative of any member state. These representatives acquire immunity only to the extent that it is granted by legislation, or by agreement, whether under the basic charter, a general convention, or a separate agreement, as in the instant case by the Headquarters Agreement. Accordingly, whether or not a particular individual is entitled to immunity is to be decided within the framework of the applicable document. The Headquarters Agreement simply provides that the three designated parties are to agree upon those entitled to immunity.

* * *

Whether, upon the facts presented by both the Government and the individual involved or his government, immunity exists by reason of the agreement, is not a political question, but a justiciable controversy involving the interpretation of the agreement and its application to the particular facts. In this instance the decision is for the Court and it is not concluded by the unilateral statement of the Government, a party to that agreement and to this controversy, that the individual is not entitled to immunity thereunder.

* * *

The scope of the inquiry is narrowly confined. Did the United States of America, as one of the parties to the Headquarters Agreement, make its decision under section 15(2) either that it agreed or did not agree that petitioner was entitled to diplomatic immunity?

The Government's statement that it did not so agree is evidential but not conclusive. Petitioner asserts that by various acts the necessary agreement was manifested; the Government denies it.

    * * *

Thus we proceed to consider the petitioner's contention upon the merits.

(2) The claim that section 15(2) of the Headquarters Agreement contemplates agreement only as to categories and not as to individuals.

The petitioner's contention is that the clause "such resident members as may be agreed upon" contemplates an agreement with respect to categories of persons and does not require agreement upon persons within the category. The petitioner's main props in support of his contention are comments and reports of committees of the United Nations with respect to immunity proposals. While the unilateral views of any United Nations committee or member cannot serve to defeat the express language of the final agreement (the Headquarters Agreement), nonetheless, analysis of such comments and reports negates rather than supports the plaintiff's position.

    * * *

The argument that unless petitioner's construction of class agreement is adopted the United States would obtain "a discriminatory, unilateral and effective control of and sanctions against nations of equal sovereignty in the United Nations" is unpersuasive. As already demonstrated, full diplomatic immunity is accorded under subdivision 1 of section 15 to top echelon representatives of member nations identical to that accorded to accredited diplomats to the United States. As to their staff members, pending agreement by the United States under section 15(2), which would entitle them to diplomatic immunity, there is available under the International Organizations Immunities Act the immunity necessary for the independent exercise of their functions, apart from Article 105 of the Charter, if in fact it is self-executing. No member state is prevented from appointing whomever it will to serve on the resident staff of its mission to the United Nations, but the United States, under section 15(2), is not required, simply by reason of one's employment in a particular category, to grant diplomatic immunity. It retains the rights thereunder to agree or not to agree that diplomatic immunity shall extend to individuals who qualify under the broad category "Resident Members of their Staffs." While it has exercised this right sparingly, it has refused, in the instance of at least five individuals, to agree to the request for immunity, without objection by either the Secretary-General or the member state who submitted the request.

The construction advanced would mean that a member state of the United Nations which may be hostile to our interests is free to send to the United States individuals designated as resident members of their staffs, to engage in conduct destructive of our national interest and security and yet have them protected from criminal prosecution on the theory that their designated status cloaked them with diplomatic immunity. It would open the flood gates for the entry of saboteurs, agents provocateur and others under a built-in guarantee that no matter what the criminal conduct, the Government could not prosecute them.

The language of the section controls. There is nothing in its history or in the practice under it to support petitioner's claim. To accept his contention would in effect amend section 15(2) by inserting therein the words "classes of" to read "such classes of resident members * * *."

The Court holds that the status of petitioner as an attache and resident member of the Cuban Mission does not by itself entitle him to diplomatic immunity under section 15(2) and that unless there was the agreement of the United States, as provided therein, the prosecution is not barred. The petitioner claims there was such agreement.

(3) The claim that the United States did agree that petitioner was entitled to diplomatic immunity.

The essence of petitioner's claim is that the issuance of the visa and the landing permit constituted, under the facts and law, the agreement of the Government of the United States that he was entitled to diplomatic privileges and immunities under section 15(2) of the Headquarters Agreement. * * *

* * *

I am of the view that petitioner's contention cannot be upheld. To do so is to transmute the G–1 visa issued by the State Department into the agreement of the United States required under section 15(2) before diplomatic immunity extends to staff members of missions to the United Nations. The fact that the G–1 visa recognized that petitioner had the status encompassed within section 15(2) does not mean that by reason thereof the United States gave the required agreement thereunder. The visa was issued at the request of the Cuban Mission upon presentation of a diplomatic passport issued by the Cuban government and its representation of petitioner's appointment as "diplomatic attache." Since the designation rested with the Cuban government, the United States was obligated under sections 11 and 13 of the Headquarters Agreement not to impose any impediment in his transit to and from the Headquarters District and to provide him with the necessary visa. The visa was the basic document of entry into the United States enroute to his post with his mission.

Petitioner argues that the State Department did not have to issue a G–1 visa in order to fulfill its obligations under the Headquarters Agreement; that so long as petitioner was accorded free access to the Headquarters District, the obligations of the United States Government were met. But as the prosecution contends, once the State Department determined that petitioner, upon the documents and representations contained therein, qualified for a G–1 visa, its issuance to the petitioner was pursuant to rules promulgated under the Immigration and Naturalization Act. The question of the agreement of the United States Government to diplomatic immunity was entirely separate from facilitating petitioner's entry to assume his duties with his mission.

I conclude that the Government of the United States did not, by the issuance of the visa and the landing permit, give its agreement that petitioner, on his entry into the United States to assume his duties as a member of the Cuban Mission, was thereby entitled to diplomatic immunity under section 15(2) of the Headquarters Agreement.

C. THE CLAIM OF DIPLOMATIC IMMUNITY UNDER THE LAW OF NATIONS.

Here the petitioner's position is that under the Law of Nations he had diplomatic immunity from the time of his entry until the Government of the United States took definitive action upon the request of the Cuban Mission that he be "agreed upon" for diplomatic immunity under the Headquarters Agreement. Again, the claim centers in part about the G–1 visa and landing permit. He urges in substance that by their issuance the United States acknowledged his status for the purpose of entry into the United States to assume his duties with his mission, aware that he was eligible for diplomatic immunity. Accordingly, he contends that he was entitled to diplomatic immunity from the time of his entry on the same principle as that applicable under the Law of Nations to diplomats awaiting acknowledgment by governments to which they are accredited and which attaches even before they have been received by it—in fine, that until he was either agreed upon or rejected in response to his government's request, he was protected. * * *

> * * *

Petitioner's path is blocked by the same reasoning upon which the Court rejected the Government's position that its unilateral determination that he was not entitled to diplomatic immunity under the Headquarters Agreement was conclusive. As the Government's suggestion of an analogy to diplomats accredited to the United States was refused above, so is petitioner's in this instance. It is the Headquarters Agreement, the Charter and the applicable statutes of the United States that govern the determination of his rights, not the Law of Nations. The Law of Nations comes into play and has applicability in defining the nature and scope of diplomatic immunity only once it is found a person is entitled thereto under an applicable agreement or statute.

The Court concludes that petitioner is not entitled to diplomatic immunity by virtue of the Law of Nations.

D.   The Claim that Petitioner May Only be Prosecuted Before the Supreme Court of the United States.

Finally, petitioner contends that by virtue of the Constitution and the Judicial Code he may be prosecuted and tried only before the Supreme Court of the United States.

Article III, section 2, clause 2, of the Constitution provides:

> In all Cases affecting Ambassadors, other public Ministers and Consuls,   *   *   *   the supreme Court shall have original Jurisdiction.

Section 1251(a) of Title 28 United States Code, provides that the Supreme Court shall have original and exclusive jurisdiction of:

> (2) all actions or proceedings against ambassadors or other public ministers of foreign states or their domestics or domestic servants, not inconsistent with the law of nations.

He argues that the expression "[A]mbassadors or other public [M]inisters," used in the foregoing, embraces all officials performing diplomatic functions, including attaches. Thus he contends under the constitutional provision and the statute that the Supreme Court has not only original, but exclusive jurisdiction and that this Court lacked jurisdiction to receive the indictment from the grand jury, to detain him, or to proceed with the prosecution.

It has already been emphasized that petitioner's entry into the United States was to serve as an attache and Resident Member on the staff of the Cuban Mission to the United Nations. The presence here of the principal representative of his government to the United Nations is solely because of its membership in the United Nations. He, as well as the petitioner herein, serves no function in relation to the Government of the United States. Neither is accredited to the United States. Indeed, in view of the lack of diplomatic relations between the United States and Cuba, petitioner, from the day of his entry to the present, could not have functioned in a diplomatic capacity vis-a-vis the United States; and, of course, this is equally true of the principal representative of the Cuban Mission and its members.

The constitutional provision and the statute are designed to apply to diplomatic representatives of foreign governments accredited to the United States. International organizations which have come into full bloom only in the last several decades were not envisaged by the Founding Fathers; clearly it was not within their contemplation that staff members of missions to such international organizations were included within the term "Ambassadors and other public Ministers." In the light of the foregoing discussion, the petitioner is not a "public minister" within the meaning of the constitutional or statutory provisions. Such an all-embracing definition is not justified.

This Court has jurisdiction of the petitioner under the indictment returned by the grand jury.

The petition for a writ of habeas corpus is dismissed upon the merits.

When the state of nationality of a United Nations employee confers diplomatic rank upon him. United States v. Melekh, 190 F. Supp. 67 (S.D.N.Y.1960) involved an indictment of a Russian citizen for a conspiracy to obtain United States defense information. Melekh was employed in the Secretariat of the United Nations as chief of the Russian language section in the office of Conference Services. Melekh's defense of immunity was based upon the assertion that the Soviet Union had conferred on him the diplomatic rank of Second Secretary of the Ministry of Foreign Affairs of the USSR. The court rejected Melekh's claim of immunity. The defendant had not been designated as a representative of the USSR to the United Nations, was not a member of the staff of the Soviet delegation, was not assigned by the USSR to diplomatic duties with the United States or any other government and had not been received by the United States as a diplomat. Diplomatic immunity was therefore unavailable under 22 U.S.C. § 252 and the Headquarters Agreement. Functional immunity was unavailable under the International Organizations Immunities Act: "* * * the defendant does not argue that the alleged criminal acts * * * grew out of or were incidental to his official activities as a United Nations officer or employee". (at p. 79). The court also found no basis for immunity in Article 105 of the charter or international law. In response to the argument that diplomatic status arose out of the relationship between the defendant's government and the United Nations, the court stated: "It is neither the defendant's position with his own government, as such, nor the relationship of the defendant's government, as such, with the United Nations that is decisive. What counts is the actual position occupied by the defendant in the United Nations and his actual duties and functions in the United Nations." (at p. 85)

Part V

METHODS OF OPERATION IN THE INTERNATIONAL SYSTEM

Chapter 15

INTERNATIONAL AGREEMENTS: THE INTERNATIONAL LAW

---

1. *The wide range of utilization of international agreements.* Undertakings between states are major tools of operations in the international legal system. Customary law derived from the usual modes of conduct of international relations, custom, right reason, judicial decisions, general principles of law common to the world's major legal systems, and the like, usually lag behind developing needs within the international community; and for technologically complicated and politically sophisticated situations they lack specificity. International agreements, on the other hand, are made because the parties thereto have realized a need to reach agreement upon some issue, matter, or common concern. Like contracts or trusts in private law, international agreements are cut to the cloth of the interests of the parties.

Functionally, international agreements cover a wide range of interests, extending from certain types of agreements that are in effect conveyances of real estate (treaties of lease, cession, and admeasurement of boundaries) through mutual promises to pursue common lines of action (military alliances, mutual defense, safety at sea) to organic arrangements that function much as constitutions (the Charter of the United Nations). Some international agreements are regarded as executed internationally as between the parties when made (boundary treaties). Others are executory such as the mutual promises of the members of the North Atlantic Treaty Organization to consider an attack on one an attack on all and to respond effectively in such context.

International agreements carry many labels: treaty, convention, modus vivendi, concordat, charter, articles of agreement, etc. Basically, the labels are not legally significant, except that some are used mainly to denominate agreements of two or at most, several, states, while others refer to multipartite agreements, which, as such, may have special rules governing their applicability (e. g., reservations).

In Chapter 17 we shall see that international agreements have given the international legal system almost all the rules that exist as to trade and investment. In the more traditional "political" areas, international agreements alter or expand customary international law. Also, they may restate or codify it. Finally, given the lack so far of an effective international parallel to national legislatures, international agreements of the multipartite sort are used to make new law such as with respect to pollution of the high seas, uses of the moon, aerial hi-jacking, human rights. Sometimes these latter are referred to as "law-making treaties", and it is with respect to them that the analytical issue whether the rules therein stated are themselves international law comes sharpest. Here it suffices to note that the modern international practitioner must of necessity have a lot to do with international agreements and that the International Court of Justice has subject-matter jurisdiction as to issues concerning international agreements.

One of the most significant new types of international agreements is the Treaty of Rome, which creates the European Economic Community (EEC). It establishes new structures, binds the member states to stated courses of action in the field of the integration of their economies, and has an in-built capacity to generate new rules of law through the operations of the authorized agencies of the Community. Is the legal system of the EEC "international law" among the member states, or is it only a new species of semi-federal domestic law? There is probably no clear answer to this question at this stage of the EEC's life; but, again the law in and deriving from the Treaty of Rome is of great professional interest or concern to lawyers everywhere.

2. *New convention on the law of international agreements.* The Vienna Convention on the Law of Treaties was opened for signature on May 23, 1969. It was not in force as of Jan. 1, 1972. This convention is the product of the International Law Commission (ILC) and of the United Nations Conference on the Law of Treaties, which met in Vienna in 1968 and again in 1969. The ILC's Draft Articles were published, with commentary, in 61 Am.J. Int'l L. 263 (1967). The draft articles adopted at the first session of the Conference (committee of the whole) were published in 7 International Legal Materials 770 (1968). The text of the convention and the final act of the conference were published in VIII International Legal Materials 679 (1969).

In a highly useful report on the conclusion of this convention, it was stated:

The Convention on the Law of Treaties sets forth the code of rules that will govern the indispensable element in the conduct of foreign affairs, the mechanism without which international intercourse could not exist, much less function. It is possible to

[handwritten margin notes: SPECIAL AGENCY REGULATIONS ∨ DISPLACE TREATIES—]

imagine a future in which the treaty will no longer be the stand-ard device for dealing with any and all international problems —a future in which for example, the use of regulations promul-gated by international organizations in special fields of activity, such as the World Health Organization's sanitary regulations, will become the accepted substitute for the lawmaking activity now effected through international agreement. But, in the present state of international development, this is crystal-gaz-ing. For the foreseeable future, the treaty will remain the cement that holds the world community together. Kearney and Dalton, The Treaty on Treaties, 64 Am.J. Int'l Law 495 (1970).

This chapter highlights the major problems in this field of the law, and the convention relates to all of them. It should be consulted in the Documentary Supplement in the course of preparation for appraisal of these problems.

SECTION A. AGREEMENTS AS OBLIGATIONS

THE RULE PACTA SUNT SERVANDA

Kelsen & Tucker, Principles of International Law 456 (2d ed. 1966).*

[handwritten margin note: 2 LEVELS]

The Rule Pacta Sunt Servanda. By concluding a treaty the con-tracting states apply a norm of customary international law—the rule pacta sunt servanda (treaties must be, or ought to be, observed, that is, have binding force)—and at the same time create a norm of inter-national law, the norm which presents itself as the treaty obligation of one or of all of the contracting parties, and as the treaty right of the other or the others. Legal obligations and legal rights are always the function of a legal norm determining the behavior of an in-dividual. The term "norm" designates the objective phenomenon whose subjective reflections are obligation and right. The statement that the treaty has "binding force" means nothing but that the treaty is or creates a norm establishing obligations and rights of the con-tracting parties. Thus the treaty has a law-applying and at the same time a law-creating character. It has a law-applying character be-cause every conclusion of a treaty is the application of the rule of general international law pacta sunt servanda; it has a law-creating function because every treaty constitutes obligations and rights that, prior to the conclusion of the treaty, had not yet existed, obligations and rights which come into existence by the treaty.

Good faith. Before the Vienna Convention, the authorities were not always clearly in agreement as between the notions that the Latin

* Reprinted with the permission of Holt, Rinehart & Winston, Inc.

phrase pacta sunt servanda meant that international agreements should be performed "in good faith" or "with utmost fidelity" (uberrima fides). Article 26 of the convention states the former as the standard; and the negotiating history shows that it would have been difficult to go beyond it, because other differences arose as to the formulation of the article. The ILC draft was adopted in principle to avoid putting the other differences to a vote, and it had used "good faith". Notice that Article 26 states that every treaty in force is binding on the parties and must be performed in good faith, whereas some delegates at Vienna wanted it stated that only valid treaties in force should be so entitled, and some others wished to confine the performance standard to treaties in force in conformity with the convention, which, of course, would have raised a serious retroactivity problem. See the Kearney and Dalton article at p. 516. What is the difference between the two standards?

YALTA CONFERENCE, AGREEMENT REGARDING ENTRY OF THE SOVIET UNION INTO THE WAR AGAINST JAPAN, FEB. 11, 1945

59 Stat. 1823.

The leaders of the three Great Powers—the Soviet Union, the United States of America and Great Britain—have agreed that in two or three months after Germany has surrendered and the war in Europe has terminated the Soviet Union shall enter into the war against Japan on the side of the Allies on condition that:

1. The status quo in Outer-Mongolia (The Mongolian People's Republic) shall be preserved;

2. The former rights of Russia violated by the treacherous attack of Japan in 1904 shall be restored, viz:

    (a) the southern part of Sakhalin as well as all the islands adjacent to it shall be returned to the Soviet Union,

    (b) the commercial port of Dairen shall be internationalized, the preeminent interests of the Soviet Union in this port being safeguarded and the lease of Port Arthur as a naval base of the USSR restored,

    (c) the Chinese-Eastern Railroad and the South-Manchurian Railroad which provides an outlet to Dairen shall be jointly operated by the establishment of a joint Soviet-Chinese Company it being understood that the preeminent interests of the Soviet Union shall be safeguarded and that China shall retain full sovereignty in Manchuria;

3. The Kuril islands shall be handed over to the Soviet Union.

It is understood, that the agreement concerning Outer-Mongolia and the ports and railroads referred to above will require concurrence of Generalissimo Chiang Kai-Shek. The President will take measures in order to obtain this concurrence on advice from Marshal Stalin.

The Heads of the three Great Powers have agreed that these claims of the Soviet Union shall be unquestionably fulfilled after Japan has been defeated.

For its part the Soviet Union expresses its readiness to conclude ✓ with the National Government of China a pact of friendship and alliance between the USSR and China in order to render assistance to China with its armed forces for the purpose of liberating China from the Japanese yoke.

> И. Сталин [a]
> Franklin D. Roosevelt
> Winston S. Churchill

UNITED STATES POSITION ON SOVIET–JAPANESE PEACE TREATY NEGOTIATIONS

35 United States Department of State Bulletin 484 (1956).

Following is the text of an aide memoire which was given to the Japanese Ambassador at Washington on September 7 and to the Japanese Foreign Minister at Tokyo on September 8.

Pursuant to the request made by the Japanese Foreign Minister, Mr. Shigemitsu, in the course of recent conversations in London with the Secretary of State, Mr. Dulles, the Department of State has reviewed the problems presented in the course of the current negotiations for a treaty of peace between the Union of Soviet Socialist Republics and Japan, with particular reference to the interest of the United States as a signatory of the San Francisco Peace Treaty, and on the basis of such review makes the following observations.

The Government of the United States believes that the state of war between Japan and the Soviet Union should be formally ter- ✓ minated. Such action has been overdue since 1951, when the Soviet Union declined to sign the San Francisco Peace Treaty. Japan should also long since have been admitted to the United Nations, for which it is fully qualified; and Japanese prisoners of war in Soviet hands should long since have been returned in accordance with the surrender terms.

a. J. Stalin.

With respect to the territorial question, as the Japanese Government has been previously informed, the United States regards the so-called Yalta agreement as simply a statement of common purposes by the then heads of the participating powers, and not as a final determination by those powers or of any legal effect in transferring territories. The San Francisco Peace Treaty (which conferred no rights upon the Soviet Union because it refused to sign) did not determine the sovereignty of the territories renounced by Japan, leaving that question, as was stated by the Delegate of the United States at San Francisco, to "international solvents other than this treaty".

     *   *   *

DEPARTMENT OF STATE,

     Washington, September 7, 1956.

LEGAL STATUS OF EASTERN GREENLAND
(DENMARK v. NORWAY)

Permanent Court of International Justice, 1933.
P.C.I.J., ser. A/B, No. 53.

     *   *   *

By an Application instituting proceedings, filed with the Registry of the Court on July 12th, 1931, in accordance with Article 40 of the Statute and Article 35 of the Rules of Court, the Royal Danish Government, relying on the optional clause of Article 36, paragraph 2, of the Statute, brought before the Permanent Court of International Justice a suit against the Royal Norwegian Government on the ground that the latter Government had, on July 10th, 1931, published a proclamation declaring that it had proceeded to occupy certain territories in Eastern Greenland, which, in the contention of the Danish Government, were subject to the sovereignty of the Crown of Denmark. The Application, after thus indicating the subject of the dispute, proceeds, subject to the subsequent presentation of any cases, counter-cases and any other documents or evidence, to formulate the claim by asking the Court for judgment to the effect that "the promulgation of the above-mentioned declaration of occupation and any steps taken in this respect by the Norwegian Government constitute a violation of the existing legal situation and are accordingly unlawful and invalid."

     *   *   *

The Danish submission in the written pleading, that the Norwegian occupation of July 10th, 1931, is invalid, is founded upon the contention that the area occupied was at the time of the occupation subject to Danish sovereignty; that the area is part of Greenland, and at the time of the occupation Danish sovereignty existed over all Greenland; consequently it could not be occupied by another Power.

In support of this contention, the Danish Government advances two propositions. The first is that the sovereignty which Denmark now enjoys over Greenland has existed for a long time, has been continuously and peacefully exercised and, until the present dispute, has not been contested by any Power. This proposition Denmark sets out to establish as a fact. The second proposition is that Norway has by treaty or otherwise herself recognized Danish sovereignty over Greenland as a whole and therefore cannot now dispute it.

marginalia: 1. ACTUALLY CONTROLLED E. GREENLAND 2. NORWAY RECOGNIZED D.'S TITLE TO EG

* * *

The Court will now consider the second Danish proposition that Norway had given certain undertakings which recognized Danish sovereignty over all Greenland. These undertakings have been fully discussed by the two Parties, and in three cases the Court considers that undertakings were given.

* * *

3. In addition to the engagements dealt with above, the Ihlen declaration, viz. the reply given by M. Ihlen, the Norwegian Minister for Foreign Affairs, to the Danish Minister on July 22nd, 1919, must also be considered. * * *

* * * [T]he point which must now be considered is whether the Ihlen declaration—even if not constituting a definitive recognition of Danish sovereignty—did not constitute an engagement obliging Norway to refrain from occupying any part of Greenland.

The Danish request and M. Ihlen's reply were recorded by him in a minute, worded as follows:

I. The Danish Minister informed me to-day that his Government has heard from Paris that the question of Spitzbergen will be examined by a Commission of four members (American, British, French, Italian). If the Danish Government is questioned by this Commission, it is prepared to reply that Denmark has no interests in Spitzbergen, and that it has no reason to oppose the wishes of Norway in regard to the settlement of this question.

Furthermore, the Danish Minister made the following statement:

The Danish Government has for some years past been anxious to obtain the recognition of all the interested Powers of Denmark's sovereignty over the whole of Greenland, and it proposes to place this question before the above-mentioned Committee at the same time. During the negotiations with the U.S.A. over the cession of the Danish West Indies, the Danish Government raised this question in so far as concerns recognition by the Government of the U.S.A., and it succeeded in inducing the latter to agree that, concurrently with the conclusion of a convention regarding the cession of the said islands, it would make a declaration to the effect that the Government of the U.S.A. would not object to the Danish Government extending their political and economic interests to the whole of Greenland.

The Danish Government is confident (he added) that the Norwegian Government will not make any difficulties in the settlement of this question.

I replied that the question would be examined.

14/7—19 Ih.

II.   To-day I informed the Danish Minister that the Norwegian Government would not make any difficulties in the settlement of this question.   22/7—19 Ih.

The incident has, therefore, reference, first to the attitude to be observed by Denmark before the Committee of the Peace Conference at Paris in regard to Spitzbergen, this attitude being that Denmark would not "oppose the wishes of Norway in regard to the settlement of this question"; as is known, these wishes related to the sovereignty over Spitzbergen.   Secondly, the request showed that "the Danish Government was confident that the Norwegian Government would not make any difficulty" in the settlement of the Greenland question; the aims that Denmark had in view in regard to the last-named island were to secure the "recognition by all the Powers concerned of Danish sovereignty over the whole of Greenland", and that there should be no opposition "to the Danish Government extending their political and economic interests to the whole of Greenland".   It is clear from the relevant Danish documents which preceded the Danish Minister's démarche at Christiania on July 14th, 1919, that the Danish attitude in the Spitzbergen question and the Norwegian attitude in the Greenland question were regarded in Denmark as interdependent, and this interdependence appears to be reflected also in M. Ihlen's minute of the interview.   Even if this interdependence—which, in view of the affirmative reply of the Norwegian Government, in whose name the Minister for Foreign Affairs was speaking, would have created a bilateral engagement—is not held to have been established, it can hardly be denied that what Denmark was asking of Norway ("not to make any difficulties in the settlement of the [Greenland] question") was equivalent to what she was indicating her readiness to concede in the Spitzbergen question (to refrain from opposing "the wishes of Norway in regard to the settlement of this question").   What Denmark desired to obtain from Norway was that the latter should do nothing to obstruct the Danish plans in regard to Greenland.   The declaration which the Minister for Foreign Affairs gave on July 22nd, 1919, on behalf of the Norwegian Government, was definitely affirmative: "I told the Danish Minister to-day that the Norwegian Government would not make any difficulty in the settlement of this question."

HOLDING:

The Court considers it beyond all dispute that a reply of this nature given by the Minister for Foreign Affairs on behalf of his Government in response to a request by the diplomatic representative of a foreign Power, in regard to a question falling within his province, is binding upon the country to which the Minister belongs.

* * *

It follows that, as a result of the undertaking involved in the Ihlen declaration of July 22nd, 1919, Norway is under an obligation to refrain from contesting Danish sovereignty over Greenland as a whole, and a fortiori to refrain from occupying a part of Greenland.

* * *

FOR THESE REASONS, the court, by twelve votes to two,

(1) decides that the declaration of occupation promulgated by the Norwegian Government on July 10th, 1931, and any steps taken in this respect by that Government, constitute a violation of the existing legal situation and are accordingly unlawful and invalid;

* * *

Dissenting Opinion of MR. ANZILOTTI:

* * *

The question whether the so-called Ihlen declaration was merely a provisional indication (Norwegian contention) or a definitive undertaking (Danish contention) has been debated at length. * * *

The outcome of all this is therefore an agreement, concluded between the Danish Minister at Christiania, on behalf of the Danish Government, and the Norwegian Minister for Foreign Affairs, on behalf of the Norwegian Government, by means of purely verbal declarations.

The validity of this agreement has been questioned, having regard, in the first place, to its verbal form, and to the competence of the Minister for Foreign Affairs.

As regards the form, it should be noted, to begin with, that as both Parties are agreed as to the existence and tenor of these declarations, the question of proof does not arise. Moreover, there does not seem to be any rule of international law requiring that agreements of this kind must necessarily be in writing, in order to be valid.

The question of the competence of the Minister for Foreign Affairs is closely connected with the contents of the agreement in question; and these have already been determined.

No arbitral or judicial decision relating to the international competence of a Minister for Foreign Affairs has been brought to the knowledge of the Court; nor has this question been exhaustively treated by legal authorities. In my opinion, it must be recognized that the constant and general practice of States has been to invest the Minister of Foreign Affairs—the direct agent of the chief of the

State—with authority to make statements on current affairs to foreign diplomatic representatives, and in particular to inform them as to the attitude which the government, in whose name he speaks, will adopt in a given question. Declarations of this kind are binding upon the State.

As regards the question whether Norwegian constitutional law authorized the Minister for Foreign Affairs to make the declaration, that is a point which, in my opinion, does not concern the Danish Government: it was M. Ihlen's duty to refrain from giving his reply until he had obtained any assent that might be requisite under the Norwegian laws.

[Observations and a dissenting opinion omitted.]

RIGHTS AND OBLIGATIONS OF STATES NOT PARTIES TO AN INTERNATIONAL AGREEMENT

Read Articles 34 through 37 of the Vienna Convention, Documentary Supplement.

FREE ZONES OF UPPER SAVOY AND THE DISTRICT OF GEX (FRANCE v. SWITZERLAND)

Permanent Court of International Justice, 1932.
P.C.I.J., ser. A/B, No. 46.

[France contended that the Treaty of Versailles (1919) abrogated certain tariff-free areas within France, on the border with Switzerland in the region of Geneva. Switzerland claimed that her rights in these areas had been provided in the post-Napoleonic settlement of Europe, by various treaties stemming from the Congress of Vienna, in the years 1814–15. The court found that Switzerland had sufficiently participated in the earlier arrangements as to have acquired rights as to the free zones. It also decided that the Treaty of Versailles was not intended to abrogate these rights. Nevertheless, the court expressed a viewpoint on the question whether rights that Switzerland might have acquired as a non-party to the 1814–15 treaties could have been taken away by France and other parties to the Versailles treaty, to which Switzerland was not a party. On third party rights the court made a statement which a common law lawyer would call obiter dictum. It appears below.]

It cannot be lightly presumed that stipulations favourable to a third State have been adopted with the object of creating an actual

[handwritten marginal note: Could rights have been taken away?]

right in its favour. There is however nothing to prevent the will of sovereign States from having this object and this effect. The question of the existence of a right acquired under an instrument drawn between other States is therefore one to be decided in each particular case: it must be ascertained whether the States which have stipulated in favour of a third State meant to create for that State an actual right *which the latter has accepted as such.* [Emphasis supplied.]

[handwritten: MOTIVATION / INTENTION / ACCEPTANCE]

Question. Before the Vienna Convention the statement above was the main authority on the point. Does the convention follow the dictum squarely? See Article 36 of the convention. *(REPRINT)*

Jus Cogens. Are there overriding restrictions on what states may do by international agreements? The Latin term jus cogens (compelling law) may supply an answer.

INTERNATIONAL LAW COMMISSION, DRAFT ARTICLES ON THE LAW OF TREATIES

61 American Journal of International Law 263, 409 (1967).

Article 50 [a]

Treaties conflicting with a peremptory norm of general international law (jus cogens)

A treaty is void if it conflicts with a peremptory norm of general international law from which no derogation is permitted and which can be modified only by a subsequent norm of general international law having the same character.

Commentary

(1) The view that in the last analysis there is no rule of international law from which states cannot at their own free will contract out has become increasingly difficult to sustain, although some jurists deny the existence of any rules of jus cogens in international law, since in their view even the most general rules still fall short of being universal. The Commission pointed out that the law of the Charter concerning the prohibition of the use of force in itself constitutes a conspicuous example of a rule in international law having the charac-

---

a. Draft Article 50, with changes, corresponds to Article 53 in the convention.

ter of jus cogens. Moreover, if some governments in their comments have expressed doubts as to the advisability of this article unless it is accompanied by provision for independent adjudication, only one questioned the existence of rules of jus cogens in the international law of today. Accordingly, the Commission concluded that in codifying the law of treaties it must start from the basis that today there are certain rules from which states are not competent to derogate at all by a treaty arrangement, and which may be changed only by another rule of the same character.

(2) The formulation of the article is not free from difficulty, since there is no simple criterion by which to identify a general rule of international law as having the character of jus cogens. Moreover, the majority of the general rules of international law do not have that character, and states may contract out of them by treaty. It would therefore be going much too far to state that a treaty is void if its provisions conflict with a rule of general international law. Nor would it be correct to say that a provision in a treaty possesses the character of jus cogens merely because the parties have stipulated that no derogation from that provision is to be permitted, so that another treaty which conflicted with that provision would be void. Such a stipulation may be inserted in any treaty with respect to any subject matter for any reasons which may seem good to the parties. The conclusion by a party of a later treaty derogating from such a stipulation may, of course, engage its responsibility for a breach of the earlier treaty. But the breach of the stipulation does not, simply as such, render the treaty void (see Article 26). It is not the form of a general rule of international law but the particular nature of the subject matter with which it deals that may, in the opinion of the Commission, give it the character of jus cogens.

(3) The emergence of rules having the character of jus cogens is comparatively recent, while international law is in process of rapid development. The Commission considered the right course to be to provide in general terms that a treaty is void if it conflicts with a rule of jus cogens and to leave the full content of this rule to be worked out in state practice and in the jurisprudence of international tribunals. Some members of the Commission felt that there might be advantage in specifying, by way of illustration, some of the most obvious and best settled rules of jus cogens in order to indicate by these examples the general nature and scope of the rule contained in the article. Examples suggested included (a) a treaty contemplating an unlawful use of force contrary to the principles of the Charter, (b) a treaty contemplating the performance of any other act criminal under international law, and (c) a treaty contemplating or conniving at the commission of acts, such as trade in slaves, piracy or genocide, in the suppression of which every state is called upon to co-operate. Other members expressed the view that, if examples were given, it would be undesirable to appear to limit the scope of the article to

cases involving acts which constitute crimes under international law; treaties violating human rights, the equality of states or the principle of self-determination were mentioned as other possible examples. The Commission decided against including any examples of rules of jus cogens in the article for two reasons. First, the mention of some cases of treaties void for conflict with a rule of jus cogens might, even with the most careful drafting, lead to misunderstanding as to the position concerning other cases not mentioned in the article. Secondly, if the Commission were to attempt to draw up, even on a selective basis, a list of the rules of international law which are to be regarded as having the character of jus cogens, it might find itself engaged in a prolonged study of matters which fall outside the scope of the present articles.

(4) Accordingly, the article simply provides that a treaty is void "if it conflicts with a peremptory norm of general international law from which no derogation is permitted and which can be modified only by a subsequent norm of general international law having the same character." This provision makes it plain that nullity attaches to a treaty under the article only if the rule with which it conflicts is a peremptory norm of general international law from which no derogation is permitted, even by agreement between particular states. On the other hand, it would clearly be wrong to regard even rules of jus cogens as immutable and incapable of modification in the light of future developments. As a modification of a rule of jus cogens would today most probably be effected through a general multilateral treaty, the Commission thought it desirable to indicate that such a treaty would fall outside the scope of the article. The article, therefore defines rules of jus cogens as peremptory norms of general international law from which no derogation is permitted "and which can be modified only by a subsequent norm of general international law having the same character."

(5) The Commission thinks it desirable to state its point of view with regard to two matters raised in the comments of governments. The first, already mentioned above, concerns the difficulty of applying the article in a satisfactory manner unless it is accompanied by a system of independent adjudication or by some provision for an authoritative determination of the rules which are rules of jus cogens. The Commission considered that the question of the means of resolving a dispute regarding the invalidity of a treaty, if it may have particular importance in connexion with the present article, is a general one affecting the application of all the articles on the invalidity, termination and suspension of the operation of treaties. It has sought, so far as is practicable in the present state of international opinion regarding acceptance of compulsory means of pacific settlement, to cover the question by the procedural safeguards laid down in Article 62. This article is designed to exclude the arbitrary determination of the invalidity, termination or suspension of a treaty by an individu-

al state such as has happened not infrequently in the past and to ensure that recourse shall be had to the means of peaceful settlement indicated in Article 33 of the Charter. In the Commission's view, the position is essentially the same in the cases of an alleged conflict with a rule of jus cogens as in the case of other grounds of invalidity alleged by a state.

(6) The second matter is the non-retroactive character of the rule in the present article. The article has to be read in conjunction with Article 61 (Emergence of a new rule of jus cogens), and in the view of the Commission, there is no question of the present article having retroactive effects. It concerns cases where a treaty is void at the time of its conclusion by reason of the fact that its provisions are in conflict with an already existing rule of jus cogens. The treaty is wholly void because its actual conclusion conflicts with a peremptory norm of general international law from which no states may derogate even by mutual consent. Article 61, on the other hand, concerns cases where a treaty, valid when concluded, becomes void and terminates by reason of the subsequent establishment of a new rule of jus cogens with which its provisions are in conflict. The words *"becomes* void and *terminates"* make it quite clear, the Commission considered, that the emergence of a new rule of jus cogens is not to have retroactive effects on the validity of a treaty. The invalidity is to attach only as from the time of the establishment of the new rule of jus cogens. The non-retroactive character of the rules in Articles 50 and 61 is further underlined in Article 67, paragraph 2 of which provides in the most express manner that the *termination* of a treaty as a result of the emergence of a new rule of jus cogens is not to have retroactive effects.

In his dissenting opinion in the Oscar Chinn case (Belgium v. Great Britain) Judge Schücking expressed the view that it was possible to create jus cogens with the effect that any act adopted in contravention to such a rule would be automatically void. The Court would never apply a convention the terms of which were contrary to public morality. The attitude of the tribunal should, in his opinion, be governed by considerations of international public policy.

In United States against Alfried Krupp and others, a case tried in 1947/1948 by a United States Military Tribunal sitting in Nuremberg, the defendants were charged, with, inter alia, "employment of prisoners of war in . . . work having a direct relation to war operations, including the manufacture and transport of armament and munitions . . .," which was prohibited by Article 31, paragraph 1, of the Geneva Prisoners of War Convention of 1929. In justification of the use of French prisoners of war in armament industry the defense claimed that this had been authorized by an agreement of Germany with the Vichy Government made through the French Ambassador to Berlin. The Tribunal found that there was no credible evidence of any such agreement. It went on to say, however, that, if there was any such agreement *it was void under the law of nations.* If Laval or the Vichy Ambassador to Berlin made any agreement with respect to the use of French prisoners of War in German armament production, it was manifestly contra bonos mores and hence void.

A statute of the Federal Republic of Germany enacted in 1952 imposes taxes for the purpose of raising revenue to be used for the payment of compensation for losses suffered by expellees and certain categories of war victims. A convention between the Federal Republic and Switzerland of the same year permits the application of the statute to Swiss nationals to the extent that it applies to the nationals of the most favored nations. A Swiss company claimed before the German Federal Constitutional Court that the German-Swiss convention violated an alleged general rule of international law to the effect that foreigners could not be compelled to contribute to the raising of revenues for the purpose of paying for expenditures resulting from war. The appellant did not refer to this alleged rule of customary international law as a rule of jus cogens, but the Court interpreted the appellant's contention to this effect, as otherwise it would have made no sense because most rules of customary international law are jus dispositivum and can therefore be validly replaced by a treaty. The Court went on to say that a few elementary legal commands have to be considered as rules of customary international law from which no derogation by treaty is permitted. The quality of such norms of jus cogens may be attributed only to those legal provisions which are firmly rooted in the legal conviction of the community of states, which are indispensable for the existence of international law as an international legal order and the observance of which can be demanded by all members of the community of states. The provision that aliens must not be required to cover consequences of a war would certainly not be one of those peremptory rules of international law (jus cogens).

SCHWELB, SOME ASPECTS OF INTERNATIONAL JUS COGENS AS FORMULATED BY THE INTERNATIONAL LAW COMMISSION

61 American Journal of International Law 946, 949 (1967).

Jurisprudence on International Jus Cogens

The only instances involving the authoritative invocation of something akin to international jus cogens which can be traced are the four judicial pronouncements mentioned below, two of which were dissenting opinions, while the other two were those of national courts. Certain United Nations proceedings on the Cyprus question have also a bearing on the problem. There appears to be no case on record in which an international court or arbitral tribunal decided that an international treaty was void because of repugnancy to a peremptory rule, in which an international political organ made a decision or recommendation to this effect, or where, in settling a dispute, governments have agreed on such a proposition.

In the case of the S. S. Wimbledon the question at issue was whether Germany, as a neutral in the Polish-Russian war, was in 1921 under the obligation to permit contraband destined for Poland to pass through the Kiel Canal. The Court decided that Article 380 of the Peace Treaty of Versailles applied, under which the Canal was to be maintained open to the vessels of all nations at peace with Germany. Mr. Schücking, the German national judge, dissented. One of his arguments was the consideration that, by permitting the passage of the ship carrying contraband, Germany would have violated the duties of a neutral. It cannot have been the intention of the victorious states, he said, to bind Germany to commit offenses against third states. It would have been impossible to give effect to such an intention because it is impossible to undertake by treaty a valid obligation to perform acts which would violate the rights of third parties. Judges Anzilotti and Huber, who also dissented from the decision of the Court, did not adduce an argument based on the partial invalidity of the Peace Treaty article.

State Practice on Jus Cogens

In the Treaty of Guarantee between Cyprus on the one hand and Greece, Turkey and the United Kingdom on the other, signed at Nicosia on August 16, 1960, it is provided that, in the event of a breach of certain provisions of the treaty, the three guarantor Powers undertake to consult together with respect to the representations or measures necessary to insure observance of those provisions. Insofar as common or concerted action may not prove possible, each of the three guaranteeing Powers reserves the right to take action with the sole aim of re-establishing the state of affairs created by the treaty. When, after the outbreak of inter-communal violence on Cyprus in December, 1963, the Security Council was seised of the situation, the treaty provisions just summarized became one of the contested points, particularly the right of unilateral and possibly armed intervention of any of the guaranteeing Powers. One of the reasons adduced in support of the claim that the provision was invalid was the contention that it conflicted with a peremptory rule of international law (jus cogens) within the meaning of what is now Article 50 of the draft articles on the law of treaties, particularly with the rule prohibiting the threat or use of force as formulated in Article 2(4) of the Charter. The claim was also made that the contested provision was an unequal or "leonine" treaty, a concept to which further reference will be made later in the present article. The immediate outcome was the Security Council resolution of March 4, 1964, which recommended the creation of a United Nations peace-keeping force in Cyprus and the designation of a mediator for the purpose of promoting a peaceful solution and an agreed settlement. The Security Council abstained from expressing an opinion on the validity or otherwise of the treaty. It said in the Preamble to the resolution, however, that it considered "the positions taken by the parties in relation to the Treaties signed at Nicosia" and that it "had in mind" the relevant provisions of the Charter and its Article 2, paragraph 4, thus leaving the question open whether or not the treaties were repugnant to the peremptory rule codified in that paragraph.

In 1965 the General Assembly was seised of the Cyprus question and adopted a resolution in which it took "cognizance of the fact that the Republic of Cyprus, as *an equal Member* of the United Nations is, in accordance with the Charter of the United Nations, entitled to enjoy, *and should enjoy*, full sovereignty and complete independence *without any foreign intervention or interference*." The General Assembly further called upon all states, "in conformity with their obligations under the Charter, and in particular Article 2, paragraphs 1 and 4, to respect the sovereignty, unity, independence and territorial integrity of the Republic of Cyprus *and to refrain from any intervention directed against it*." The vote on this resolution indicates, however, that the authority which can be attributed to it is not very great, as only 47 Members voted for it, five against, and 54 Members abstained. For the purposes of the present article it should also be noted that the jus cogens rules which were invoked (sovereign equality and the prohibition of the threat of force) are expressly set forth in the Charter.

THE NEGOTIATING HISTORY OF JUS COGENS AT VIENNA

Kearney and Dalton, Treaty on Treaties, 64 American Journal
of International Law 495, 535 (1970).

From this heated discussion the committee of the whole moved immediately to one of the most controversial articles produced by the Commission—Article 53 on treaties conflicting with a peremptory norm of international law or, as it is customarily described, the Jus Cogens Doctrine. The Commission's proposal was:

A treaty is void if it conflicts with a peremptory norm of general international law from which no derogation is permitted and which can be modified only by a subsequent norm of general international law having the same character.

Although the principle that there are fundamental requirements of international behavior that cannot be set aside by treaty is considered a fairly recent development, it has been incorporated into Section 116 of the Restatement of the Foreign Relations Law of the United States in the following terms:

> An international agreement may be made with respect to any matter except to the extent that the agreement conflicts with
>
> a) the rules of international law incorporating basic standards of international conduct. * * *

Both the Commission's article and the Restatement, however, present the same difficulty: they leave open the question what is a peremptory norm of international law or what is a basic standard of international conduct.

The Commission did not attempt to define a peremptory norm or to provide even an illustrative list of the norms that it considered peremptory. In the commentary to this article, the Commission noted: "The formulation of the article is not free from difficulty, since there is no simple criterion by which to identify a general rule of international law as having the character of jus cogens." The Commission explained the formulation of the article as follows:

> The emergence of rules having the character of jus cogens is comparatively recent, while international law is in process of rapid development. The Commission considered the right course to be to provide in general terms that a treaty is void if it conflicts with a rule of jus cogens and to leave the full content of this rule to be worked out in State practice and in the jurisprudence of international tribunals. * * *

In his second report Waldock had proposed three categories of jus cogens: (a) the use or threat of force in contravention of the principles of the United Nations Charter; (b) international crimes so characterized by international law; (c) acts or omissions whose suppression is required by international law. The discussion in the Commission indicated such varying viewpoints on what constituted jus cogens that the categories were dropped. A comment regarding the resulting draft is pertinent: "Mr. Bartoš explained that the drafting committee had been compelled to refrain from giving any definition of jus cogens whatever, because two-thirds of the Commission had been opposed to each formula proposed."

The position in the conference reflected the position in the Commission. There was no substantial attack made upon the concept of jus cogens. Indeed, it would be very difficult to make a sustainable case that two states are free to make a treaty in which they agree to attack and carve up a third state or to sell some of their residents to each other as slaves. But as Minagawa points out, "examples such as the treaty permitting piracy or re-establishing slavery appear to concern merely 'une pure hypothèse d'école'." The real problem was ✓ how to define the test for recognizing a rule of jus cogens.

The United States proposed a two-part amendment. The first part—that the article applied only to a treaty which "at the time of its conclusion" violated a peremptory norm—was intended to make clear that a rule of jus cogens did not void a treaty retroactively. The second part was designed to incorporate in the article a test by which to determine whether a rule of general international law was jus cogens—recognition "in common by the national and regional legal systems of the world" as a peremptory norm "from which no derogation is permitted." A less stringent requirement that the peremptory character of the norm "be recognized by the international community" was proposed by Finland, Greece and Spain.

The debates, which extended through six meetings, revealed considerable opposition to the United States amendment on the ground it was too restrictive and would block the "evolution of jus cogens." *   *   * The Ukrainian representative waved the red shirt of colonial treaties in connection with the proposals to clarify the article, but this did not touch off any similar denunciations by ex-colonies. The bulk of the criticism was directed to importing the concept of internal law into the jus cogens principle.

The Austrian jurist, Hanspeter Neuhold, gives in his analysis of the 1968 session a lively account of the conclusion of debate:

> After five meetings had been devoted to discussing the various problems of jus cogens, the scene was set for the final showdown at a night meeting on 7 May which lasted almost till midnight. It was fought with all the weapons which the arsenal of the rules of procedure offered the delegates. Thus, the representative of the USA introduced a motion to defer the vote on article [53] and to refer all amendments to the Drafting Committee with a view to working out a more acceptable text. This proposal was endorsed by the United Kingdom and France. Conversely, the Ghanaian delegate, who was supported by the representatives of India and the USSR, moved to take a vote immediately, since the various delegations had made their positions sufficiently clear. Motions to adjourn the debate and to close the discussion were defeated. Other motions requesting a division of the original United States proposal caused considerable confusion. At last, a roll call was taken on the motion submitted by the USA to defer voting on article [53] and the amendments thereto, which failed to obtain the necessary majority by the narrowest margin possible: 42 votes were cast in favour, the same number against, with 7 abstentions! Ironically enough, if a request by Ghana for priority of her motion to vote at once had been adopted and the votes cast in the same way, the United States motion would have prevailed indirectly   *   *   * The

first part of the substantive amendment introduced by the USA which specified the non-retroactive character of article [53]— which had been stressed by the ILC in its commentary—was adopted, whereas reference to recognition of jus cogens by the national and regional legal systems of the world was rejected. The somewhat similar amendment co-sponsored by Finland, Greece and Spain requesting [sic] recognition by the international community of a peremptory norm was, on the contrary, referred to the Drafting Committee * * *

A dispute then arose as to the meaning of that vote and whether the principle of jus cogens had been adopted. The chairman settled the matter by ruling that the jus cogens principle had been adopted and that the drafting committee was to see if the text could be made clearer. In the drafting committee, Dean Sweeney performed superbly in helping frame, against substantial opposition, an addition to Article 53 that achieved the objective of the United States. A peremptory norm was defined as "a norm accepted and recognized by the international community of States as a whole. * * *" At the eightieth meeting, the chairman of the drafting committee, in introducing the revised text, stated that the phrase "as a whole" had been included to avoid any implication that an individual state had a right of veto. The Ghanaian delegate, on the basis that the phrase might be interpreted otherwise, asked for a separate vote on those three words. The phrase was approved 57 votes to 3 with 27 abstentions. No change was made in 1969.

Article 64 is a corollary of Article 53 which provides that if a new peremptory norm of general international law emerges, any existing treaty which is in conflict with that norm becomes void and terminates. There was little discussion of this article at the conference because it is so clearly implicit in the principle of jus cogens. The necessity for it as a separate article springs from the fact that different legal consequences attend a treaty that is entered into in violation of an existing rule of jus cogens (which is considered as void ab initio) and the annulment of an existing treaty by the emergence of a new rule. The differing effects are spelled out in Article 71. In a case falling under Article 53 the parties must:

(a) eliminate as far as possible the consequences of any act performed in reliance on any provision which conflicts with the peremptory norm of general international law; and

(b) bring their mutual relations into conformity with the peremptory norm of general international law.

In an Article 64 case, however, "the termination of the treaty:

(a) releases the parties from any obligation further to perform the treaty;

(b) does not affect any right, obligation or legal situation of the parties created through the execution of the treaty prior to its termination; provided that those rights, obligations or situations may thereafter be maintained only to the extent that their maintenance is not in itself in conflict with the new peremptory norm of general international law."

SECTION B. RESERVATIONS TO INTERNATIONAL AGREEMENTS

---

1. *Why are reservations even made?* A state that is interested in entering into a treaty relationship will attempt during the negotiations to shape the agreement to its wishes. If it succeeds, there is no further problem. But if it cannot convince its negotiating partner or partners and if its wish then is to protect itself against becoming obligated in a manner or to a degree that in the negotiations it unsuccessfully sought to provide against, it may want to attempt to enter into the treaty relationship under the safeguard of a reservation.

Where the negotiations are between two, or at most several, states, reservations have little utility. Either the parties agree or they do not agree during the negotiations; if they do not, there is not going to be any agreement at all. In the context of bilateral negotiations it is sometimes said that a reservation is a counter-offer, which if not accepted by the offeree, means "no contract." If it is accepted, there is a contract on the terms of the counter-offer.

In the case of some multipartite international agreements, such as the Vienna Convention on the Law of Treaties, we have already seen the intensity with which particular issues are disputed and voted on in the negotiating conference. If a state tries hard to make its point and is voted down but still is interested in the general idea of being a party to such a convention, it may consider trying to enter the treaty community thus created with a reservation.

A reservation will be put forward by a state that has made the decision just alluded to simultaneously with its manifestation of intent to become bound. In times past, when most chiefs of state were autocrats, this was at the time their representatives purported to sign for them. But today it is rare indeed that a multipartite convention should come into effect at signing. Today, the signature of the final act of the negotiating conference is almost always ad referendum to an internal authorization process, leading to ratification. Even so, reservations are sometimes made at signature, so as to give a clear showing of viewpoint to the other states involved or to protect the negotiators from criticism at home. An international agreement may provide that it is open for acceptance or accession by states that did not participate in the negotiation. In such cases, obviously, an acceding state wishing to make a reservation would do so at the time of attempted accession.

In many states the internal authorization to become bound involves the consent of the legislative branch. In the case of the United States, as the following chapter discloses, the Senate, by a two-thirds majority of the senators present and voting, gives the legislative authorization. The legislative authorization may itself be conditioned upon the making of a reservation. Under most constitutional systems when this happens the executive has no alternative, if it wishes to go forward with the treaty association, but to put the reservation forward internationally. Such a second stage reservation often reflects imperfect foresight on the part of the executive at the time of the negotiations as to the views of the legislature on the particular point. The classic and tragic case is that of President Woodrow Wilson and a minority (more than one-third) of the Senate as to the Covenant of the League of Nations. In negotiating the Covenant at Paris in 1919, the President did not take into account that "a little group of wilful men", as he called the group of dissident senators, would block the approval of the Covenant unless their reservations were accepted. When he discovered that they did have such power, it was too late. The Covenant was an annex to the Versailles peace treaty with Germany, and a re-convention of the peace conference was politically impossible, as Germany had already recovered sufficiently to have begun the resistance to Versailles that Adolph Hitler concluded.

The relationships between the President and the Senate of the United States with respect to the conclusion of treaties makes for both domestic and international complications. The Restatement of the Foreign Relations Law of the United States (1965) sketches them at pp. 413–425.

2. *Effect of reservation on other states.* When a reservation is put forward, it presents the other states with this problem: shall State X come in on its altered version of the treaty or shall we try to exclude State X from the agreement? This issue has a substantive and a procedural aspect. The old rule was clear: State X could not come in, unless its reservation was unanimously accepted. In modern times as reflected in the Vienna Convention, there has been a shift in this viewpoint with the result that the rules provide greater flexibility. The materials that follow deal with this shift.

RESERVATIONS TO THE CONVENTION ON GENOCIDE (ADVISORY OPINION)

International Court of Justice, 1951
[1951] I.C.J. Rep. 15.

* * *

On November 16th, 1950, the General Assembly of the United Nations adopted the following resolution:

The General Assembly,

Having examined the report of the Secretary-General regarding reservations to multilateral conventions,

Considering that certain reservations to the Convention on the Prevention and Punishment of the Crime of Genocide have been objected to by some States,

Considering that the International Law Commission is studying the whole subject of the law of treaties, including the question of reservations,

Considering that different views regarding reservations have been expressed during the fifth session of the General Assembly, and particularly the Sixth Committee,

1. Requests the International Court of Justice to give an Advisory Opinion on the following questions:

In so far as concerns the Convention on the Prevention and Punishment of the Crime of Genocide in the event of a State ratifying or acceding to the Convention subject to a reservation made either on ratification or on accession, or on signature followed by ratification:

I. Can the reserving State be regarded as being a party to the Convention while still maintaining its reservation if the reservation is objected to by one or more of the parties to the Convention but not by others? *[handwritten: IS RESERVING STATE A PARTY?]*

II. If the answer to Question I is in the affirmative, what is the effect of the reservation as between the reserving State and:

(a) The parties which object to the reservation?

(b) Those which accept it?

III. What would be the legal effect as regards the answer to Question I if an objection to a reservation is made:

(a) By a signatory which has not yet ratified?

(b) By a State entitled to sign or accede but which has not yet done so?

2. Invites the International Law Commission:

(a) In the course of its work on the codification of the law of treaties, to study the question of reservations to multilateral conventions both from the point of view of codification and from that of the progressive development of international law; to give priority to this study and to report thereon, especially as regards multilateral conventions of which the Secretary-General is the depositary, this report to be considered by the General Assembly at its sixth session;

(b) In connection with this study, to take account of all the views expressed during the fifth session of the General Assembly, and particularly in the Sixth Committee;

3. Instructs the Secretary-General, pending the rendering of the Advisory Opinion by the International Court of Justice, the receipt of a report from the International Law Commission and further action by the General Assembly, to follow his prior practice with respect to the receipt of reservations to conventions and with respect to the notification and solicitation of approvals thereof, all without prejudice to the legal effect of objections to reservations to conventions as it may be recommended by the General Assembly at its sixth session.

* * *

The Court observes that the three questions which have been referred to it for an Opinion have certain common characteristics.

All three questions are expressly limited by the terms of the Resolution of the General Assembly to the Convention on the Prevention and Punishment of the Crime of Genocide, and the same Resolution invites the International Law Commission to study the general question of reservations to multilateral conventions both from the point of view of codification and from that of the progressive development of international law. The questions thus having a clearly defined object, the replies which the Court is called upon to give to them are necessarily and strictly limited to that Convention. The Court will seek these replies in the rules of law relating to the effect to be given to the intention of the parties to multilateral conventions.

The three questions are purely abstract in character. They refer neither to the reservations which have, in fact, been made to the Convention by certain States, nor to the objections which have been made to such reservations by other States. They do not even refer to the reservations which may in future be made in respect of any particular article; nor do they refer to the objections to which these reservations might give rise.

Question I is framed in the following terms:

Can the reserving State be regarded as being a party to the Convention while still maintaining its reservation if the reservation is objected to by one or more of the parties to the Convention but not by others?

The Court observes that this question refers, not to the possibility of making reservations to the Genocide Convention, but solely to the question whether a contracting State which has made a reservation can, while still maintaining it, be regarded as being a party to the Convention, when there is a divergence of views between the contracting parties concerning this reservation, some accepting the reservation, others refusing to accept it.

It is well established that in its treaty relations a State cannot be bound without its consent, and that consequently no reservation can be effective against any State without its agreement thereto. It is also a generally recognized principle that a multilateral convention is the result of an agreement freely concluded upon its clauses and that consequently none of the contracting parties is entitled to frustrate or impair, by means of unilateral decisions or particular agreements, the purpose and raison d'être of the convention. To this principle was linked the notion of the integrity of the convention as adopted, a notion which in its traditional concept involved the proposition that no reservation was valid unless it was accepted by all the contracting parties without exception, as would have been the case if it had been stated during the negotiations.

This concept, which is directly inspired by the notion of contract, is of undisputed value as a principle. However, as regards the Genocide Convention, it is proper to refer to a variety of circumstances which would lead to a more flexible application of this principle. Among these circumstances may be noted the clearly universal character of the United Nations under whose auspices the Convention was concluded, and the very wide degree of participation envisaged by Article XI of the Convention. Extensive participation in conventions of this type has already given rise to greater flexibility in the international practice concerning multilateral conventions. More general resort to reservations, very great allowance made for tacit assent to reservations, the existence of practices which go so far as to admit that the author of reservations which have been rejected by certain contracting parties is nevertheless to be regarded as a party to the convention in relation to those contracting parties that have accepted the reservations—all these factors are manifestations of a new need for flexibility in the operation of multilateral conventions.

It must also be pointed out that although the Genocide Convention was finally approved unanimously, it is nevertheless the result of a series of majority votes. The majority principle, while facilitating the conclusion of multilateral conventions, may also make it necessary for certain States to make reservations. This observation is confirmed by the great number of reservations which have been made of recent years to multilateral conventions.

In this state of international practice, it could certainly not be inferred from the absence of an article providing for reservations in a multilateral convention that the contracting States are prohibited from making certain reservations. Account should also be taken of the fact that the absence of such an article or even the decision not to insert such an article can be explained by the desire not to invite a multiplicity of reservations. The character of a multilateral convention, its purpose, provisions, mode of preparation and adoption, are factors which must be considered in determining, in the absence of any express provision on the subject, the possibility of making reservations, as well as their validity and effect.

Although it was decided during the preparatory work not to insert a special article on reservations, it is none the less true that the faculty for States to make reservations was contemplated at successive stages of the drafting of the Convention. In this connection, the following passage may be quoted from the comments on the draft Convention prepared by the Secretary-General: " * * * (1) It would seem that reservations of a general scope have no place in a convention of this kind which does not deal with the private interests of a State, but with the preservation of an element of international order * * *; (2) perhaps in the course of discussion in the General Assembly it will be possible to allow certain limited reservations."

Even more decisive in this connection is the debate on reservations in the Sixth Committee at the meetings (December 1st and 2nd, 1948) which immediately preceded the adoption of the Genocide Convention by the General Assembly. Certain delegates clearly announced that their governments could only sign or ratify the Convention subject to certain reservations.

Furthermore, the faculty to make reservations to the Convention appears to be implicitly admitted by the very terms of Question I.

The Court recognizes that an understanding was reached within the General Assembly on the faculty to make reservations to the Genocide Convention and that it is permitted to conclude therefrom that States becoming parties to the Convention gave their assent thereto. It must now determine what kind of reservations may be made and what kind of objections may be taken to them.

The solution of these problems must be found in the special characteristics of the Genocide Convention. The origins and character of that Convention, the objects pursued by the General Assembly and the contracting parties, the relations which exist between the provisions of the Convention, inter se, and between those provisions and these objects, furnish elements of interpretation of the will of the General Assembly and the parties. The origins of the Convention show that it was the intention of the United Nations to condemn and punish genocide as "a crime under international law" involving a denial of the right of existence of entire human groups, a denial which shocks the conscience of mankind and results in great losses to humanity, and which is contrary to moral law and to the spirit and aims of the United Nations (Resolution 96(I) of the General Assembly,

December 11th 1946). The first consequence arising from this con- /
ception is that the principles underlying the Convention are <u>principles</u> *GEN. PRINCIPES*
which are recognized by civilized nations as binding on States, even
without any conventional obligation. A second consequence is the
universal character both of the condemnation of genocide and of the *UNIV. CARACTÈRE*
co-operation required "in order to liberate mankind from such an
odious scourge" (Preamble to the Convention). The Genocide Convention was therefore intended by the General Assembly and by the
contracting parties to be definitely universal in scope. It was in fact
approved on December 9th, 1948, by a resolution which was unanimously adopted by fifty-six States.

     The objects of such a convention must also be considered. The *HUMANITARIAN MOTIVES*
Convention was manifestly adopted for a purely humanitarian and
civilizing purpose. It is indeed difficult to imagine a convention that
might have this dual character to a greater degree, since its object
on the one hand is to safeguard the very existence of certain human
groups and on the other to confirm and endorse the most elementary
principles of morality. In such a convention the contracting States
do not have any interests of their own; they merely have, one and all,
a common interest, namely, the accomplishment of those high purposes which are the raison d'être of the convention. Consequently,
<u>in a convention of this type one cannot speak of individual advantages
or disadvantages to States</u>, or of the maintenance of a perfect contractual balance between rights and duties. The high ideals which
inspired the Convention provide, by virtue of the common will of
the parties, the foundation and measure of all its provisions.

     The foregoing considerations, when applied to the question of res-
ervations, and more particularly to the effects of objections to reservations, lead to the following conclusions. *GOAL: MAXIMUM*

     The object and purpose of the Genocide Convention imply that *PARTICIPATION*
it was the intention of the General Assembly and of the States which
adopted it that as many States as possible should participate. The
complete exclusion from the Convention of one or more States would
not only restrict the scope of its application, but would detract from
the authority of the moral and humanitarian principles which are its
basis. It is inconceivable that the contracting parties readily contemplated that an objection to a minor reservation should produce
such a result. But even less could the contracting parties have intended to sacrifice the very object of the Convention in favour of a
vain desire to secure as many participants as possible. The object
and purpose of the Convention thus limit both the freedom of making
reservations and that of objecting to them. It follows that it is the
compatibility of a reservation with the object and purpose of the Convention that must furnish the criterion for the attitude of a State in
making the reservation on accession as well as for the appraisal by
a State in objecting to the reservation. Such is the rule of conduct
which must guide every State in the appraisal which it must make,

✓ individually and from its own standpoint, of the admissibility of any reservation.

Any other view would lead either to the acceptance of reservations which frustrate the purposes which the General Assembly and the contracting parties had in mind, or to recognition that the parties to the Convention have the power of excluding from it the author of a reservation, even a minor one, which may be quite compatible with those purposes.

COURT DISAGREES THAT ANY & ALL RESERVATIONS ARE VALID It has nevertheless been argued that any State entitled to become a party to the Genocide Convention may do so while making any reservation it chooses by virtue of its sovereignty. The Court cannot share this view. It is obvious that so extreme an application of the idea of State sovereignty could lead to a complete disregard of the object and purpose of the Convention.

On the other hand, it has been argued that there exists a rule of international law subjecting the effect of a reservation to the express or tacit assent of all the contracting parties. This theory rests essentially on a contractual conception of the absolute integrity of the convention as adopted. This view, however, cannot prevail if, having regard to the character of the convention, its purpose and its mode of adoption, it can be established that the parties intended to derogate from that rule by admitting the faculty to make reservations thereto.

NEITHER ABSOLUTE CONTRACT:
① BUILT-IN FACULTY
② NO RULE OF IL

It does not appear, moreover, that the conception of the absolute integrity of a convention has been transformed into a rule of international law. The considerable part which tacit assent has always played in estimating the effect which is to be given to reservations scarcely permits one to state that such a rule exists, determining with sufficient precision the effect of objections made to reservations. In ✓ fact, the examples of objections made to reservations appear to be too rare in international practice to have given rise to such a rule. It cannot be recognized that the report which was adopted on the subject by the Council of the League of Nations on June 17th, 1927, has had this effect. At best, the recommendation made on that date by the council constitutes the point of departure of an administrative practice which, after being observed by the Secretariat of the League of Nations, imposed itself, so to speak, in the ordinary course of things on the Secretary-General of the United Nations in his capacity of depositary of conventions concluded under the auspices of the League. But it cannot be concluded that the legal problem of the effect of objections to reservations has in this way been solved. The opinion of the Secretary-General of the United Nations himself is embodied in the following passage of his report of September 21st, 1950: "While it is universally recognized that the consent of the other governments concerned must be sought before they can be bound by the terms of a reservation, there has not been unanimity either as to the procedure to be followed by a depositary in obtaining the necessary consent or as to the legal effect of a State's objecting to a reservation."

It may, however, be asked whether the General Assembly of the United Nations, in approving the Genocide Convention, had in mind the practice according to which the Secretary-General, in exercising his functions as a depositary, did not regard a reservation as definitively accepted until it had been established that none of the other contracting States objected to it. If this were the case, it might be argued that the implied intention of the contracting parties was to make the effectiveness of any reservation to the Genocide Convention conditional on the assent of all the parties.

The Court does not consider that this view corresponds to reality. It must be pointed out, first of all, that the existence of an administrative practice does not in itself constitute a decisive factor in ascertaining what views the contracting States to the Genocide Convention may have had concerning the rights and duties resulting therefrom. It must also be pointed out that there existed among the American States members both of the United Nations and of the Organization of American States, a different practice which goes so far as to permit a reserving State to become a party irrespective of the nature of the reservations or of the objections raised by other contracting States. The preparatory work of the Convention contains nothing to justify ✓ the statement that the contracting States implicitly had any definite practice in mind. Nor is there any such indication in the subsequent attitude of the contracting States: neither the reservations made by certain States nor the position adopted by other States towards those reservations permit the conclusion that assent to one or the other of these practices had been given. Finally, it is not without interest to note, in view of the preference generally said to attach to an established practice, that the debate on reservations to multilateral treaties which took place in the Sixth Committee at the fifth session of the General Assembly reveals a profound divergence of views, some delegations being attached to the idea of the absolute integrity of the Convention, others favouring a more flexible practice which would bring about the participation of as many States as possible.

It results from the foregoing considerations that Question I, on account of its abstract character, cannot be given an absolute answer. The appraisal of a reservation and the effect of objections that might be made to it depend upon the particular circumstances of each individual case. *[margin note: DEPENDS UPON EACH CASE.]*

Having replied to Question I, the Court will now examine Question II, which is framed as follows:

If the answer to Question I is in the affirmative, what is the effect of the reservation as between the reserving State and:

(a) the parties which object to the reservation?

(b) those which accept it?

The considerations which form the basis of the Court's reply to Question I are to a large extent equally applicable here. As has been

pointed out above, each State which is a party to the Convention is
✓ entitled to appraise the validity of the reservation, and it exercises
this right individually and from its own standpoint. As no State can
be bound by a reservation to which it has not consented, it necessarily
follows that each State objecting to it will or will not, on the basis
of its individual appraisal within the limits of the criterion of the
object and purpose stated above, consider the reserving State to be a
party to the Convention. In the ordinary course of events, such a
decision will only affect the relationship between the State making
the reservation and the objecting State; on the other hand, as will
be pointed out later, such a decision might aim at the complete exclusion from the Convention in a case where it was expressed by the adoption of a position on the jurisdictional plane.

The disadvantages which result from this possible divergence of
views—which an article concerning the making of reservations could
have obviated—are real; they are mitigated by the common duty of
the contracting States to be guided in their judgment by the compatibility or incompatibility of the reservation with the object and
purpose of the Convention. It must clearly be assumed that the contracting States are desirous of preserving intact at least what is essential to the object of the Convention; should this desire be absent,
it is quite clear that the Convention itself would be impaired both in
its principle and in its application.

It may be that the divergence of views between parties as to the
admissibility of a reservation will not in fact have any consequences.
On the other hand, it may be that certain parties who consider that
the assent given by other parties to a reservation is incompatible with
the purpose of the Convention, will decide to adopt a position on the
jurisdictional plane in respect of this divergence and to settle the dispute which thus arises either by special agreement or by the procedure
laid down in Article IX of the Convention.

Finally, it may be that a State, whilst not claiming that a reservation is incompatible with the object and purpose of the Convention,
will nevertheless object to it, but that an understanding between that
State and the reserving State will have the effect that the Convention
will enter into force between them, except for the clauses affected by
the reservation.

Such being the situation, the task of the Secretary-General would
be simplified and would be confined to receiving reservations and objections and notifying them.

Question III is framed in the following terms:

What would be the legal effect as regards the answer to
Question I if an objection to a reservation is made:

(a) By a signatory which has not yet ratified?

(b) By a State entitled to sign or accede but which has not
yet done so?

The Court notes that the terms of this question link it to Question I. This link is regarded by certain States as presupposing a negative reply to Question I.

The Court considers, however, that Question III could arise in any case. Even should the reply to Question I not tend to exclude, from being a party to the Convention, a State which has made a reservation to which another State has objected, the fact remains that the Convention does not enter into force as between the reserving ◦ State and the objecting State. Even if the objection has this reduced legal effect, the question would still arise whether the States mentioned under (a) and (b) of Question III are entitled to bring about such a result by their objection.

An extreme view of the right of such States would appear to be that these two categories of States have a *right to become* parties to the Convention, and that by virtue of this right they may object to reservations in the same way as any State which is a party to the Convention with full legal effect, i. e. the exclusion from the Convention of the reserving State. By denying them this right, it is said, they would be obliged either to renounce entirely their right of participating in the Convention, or to become a party to what is, in fact, a different convention. The dilemma does not correspond to reality, as the States concerned have always a right to be parties to the Convention in their relations with other contracting States.

From the date when the Genocide Convention was opened for signature, any Member of the United Nations and any non-member State to which an invitation to sign had been addressed by the General Assembly, had the *right to be a party* to the Convention. Two courses of action were possible to this end: either signature, from December 9th, 1948, until December 31st, 1949, followed by ratification, or accession as from January 1st, 1950 (Article XI of the Convention). The Court would point out that the right to become a party to the Convention does not express any very clear notion. It is inconceivable that a State, even if it has participated in the preparation of the Convention, could, before taking one or the other of the two courses of action provided for becoming a party to the Convention, exclude another State. Possessing no rights which derive from the Convention, that State cannot claim such a right from its status as a Member of the United Nations or from the invitation to sign which has been addressed to it by the General Assembly.

The case of a signatory State is different. Without going into the question of the legal effect of signing an international convention, which necessarily varies in individual cases, the Court considers that signature constitutes a first step to participation in the Convention.

It is evident that without ratification, signature does not make the signatory State a party to the Convention; nevertheless, it establishes a provisional status in favour of that State. This status may decrease in value and importance after the Convention enters into force. But, both before and after the entry into force, this status would justify more favourable treatment being meted out to signatory States in respect of objections than to States which have neither signed nor acceded.

As distinct from the latter States, signatory States have taken certain of the steps necessary for the exercise of the right of being a party. Pending ratification, the provisional status created by signature confers upon the signatory a right to formulate as a precautionary measure objections which have themselves a provisional character. These would disappear if the signature were not followed by ratification, or they would become effective on ratification.

Until this ratification is made, the objection of a signatory State can therefore not have an immediate legal effect in regard to the reserving State. It would merely express and proclaim the eventual attitude of the signatory State when it becomes a party to the Convention.

The legal interest of a signatory State in objecting to a reservation would thus be amply safeguarded. The reserving State would be given notice that as soon as the constitutional or other processes, which cause the lapse of time before ratification, have been completed, it would be confronted with a valid objection which carries full legal effect and consequently, it would have to decide, when the objection is stated, whether it wishes to maintain or withdraw its reservation. In the circumstances, it is of little importance whether the ratification occurs within a more or less long time-limit. The resulting situation will always be that of a ratification accompanied by an objection to the reservation. In the event of no ratification occurring, the notice would merely have been in vain.

For these reasons,

THE COURT IS OF OPINION,

In so far as concerns the Convention on the Prevention and Punishment of the Crime of Genocide, in the event of a State ratifying or acceding to the Convention subject to a reservation made either on ratification or on accession, or on signature followed by ratification,

On Question I:

by seven votes to five,

that a State which has made and maintained a reservation which has been objected to by one or more of the parties to the Convention but not by others, can be regarded as being a party to the Convention if the reservation is compatible with the object and purpose of the Convention; otherwise, that State cannot be regarded as being a party to the Convention.

On Question II:

by seven votes to five,

(a) that if a party to the Convention objects to a reservation which it considers to be incompatible with the object and purpose of the Convention, it can in fact consider that the reserving State is not a party to the Convention;

(b) that if, on the other hand, a party accepts the reservation as being compatible with the object and purpose of the Convention, it can in fact consider that the reserving State is a party to the Convention;

On Question III:

by seven votes to five,

(a) that an objection to a reservation made by a signatory State which has not yet ratified the Convention can have the legal effect indicated in the reply to Question I only upon ratification. Until that moment it merely serves as a notice to the other State of the eventual attitude of the signatory State;

(b) that an objection to a reservation made by a State which is entitled to sign or accede but which has not yet done so, is without legal effect.

* * *

[Dissenting opinions omitted.]

----

1. *Vienna Convention provisions on reservations.* See Articles 19–23, Documentary Supplement. These articles are the end product of the General Assembly's invitation to the International Law Commission, referred to in the Genocide Case, to deal with the matter of reservations. How do the convention's provisions compare with the decision of the International Court of Justice? Do other states have to consent to reservations and if so how is consent to be determined? Are the needs of the United Nations Secretariat as a treaty depositary well met in the convention?

2. *Problems:*

a. State X, with nuclear capability, has not yet acceded to the Nuclear Test Ban Treaty, Documentary Supplement. What would be the legal consequences (a) under the Genocide Case and (b) under the Vienna Convention if State X were to deposit the following instrument with the three depositary governments? "State X accedes to the Treaty Banning Nuclear Weapons in the Atmosphere, in Outer Space and under Water done at Moscow, August 5, 1963, subject to the reservation that the treaty shall not be deemed to inhibit the use of nuclear weapons in armed conflict".

b.   State Y, a new state that has just come into existence, proposes to accede to a number of multipartite international agreements open for accession including the Geneva Convention Relative to the Treatment of Prisoners of War, 6 U.S.T. 3316, 75–76 U.N.T.S. 135. It offers for deposit this reservation: "Provided, however, that persons guilty of war crimes shall not be entitled in State Y to treatment as prisoners of war under this Convention". At the time this proposal is made, military personnel of State A, which is engaged in armed conflict with State Y, have been captured in large numbers by State Y.   State A is a party to the Geneva Convention.   Assume the Vienna Convention is in force.   What position would you as the relevant official of State A take as to this reservation under the Vienna Convention?

c.   The United States and Canada negotiated a Treaty Concerning the Uses of the Waters of the Niagara River, 1 U.S.T. 694 (1950). The major purpose of the treaty was to allocate as between the two countries the amount of hydro-static potential each could use for the generation of electrical power.   The Senate resolution of advice and consent included a reservation that the United States for its part reserves the right to provide by legislation for the use of the United States' share of the waters of the Niagara and that no project for the use of the United States' share should be undertaken until specifically authorized by Congress.   This reservation was officially called to the attention of the Government of Canada.   What, if any, response do you think Canada should make?   See Reporters' Note 7 to section 133 of the Restatement of the Foreign Relations Law of the United States. Internal legal aspects of this situation, in relationship to the Federal Power Act of 1920 and the jurisdiction of the Federal Power Commission in the absence of any new legislation, were involved in Power Authority of New York v. Federal Power Commission, 101 U.S.App. D.C. 132, 247 F.2d 538 (1957), cert. vacated as moot 355 U.S. 64, 78 S.Ct. 141 (1957).

SECTION C.   INTERPRETATION OF INTERNATIONAL AGREEMENTS

A contemporary hypothetical problem and the interpretation provisions of the Vienna Convention (Articles 31–33, Documentary Supplement).   Article 5 of the Convention on the High Seas (Documentary Supplement) provides:

Each state shall fix the conditions for the grant of its nationality to ships, for the registration of ships in its territory, and for the right to fly its flag.   Ships have the nationality of the state whose flag they are entitled to fly.   There must exist a genuine link between the state and the ship; in particular, the state must effectively exercise its jurisdiction and control in administrative, technical and social matters over ships flying its flag.

A national of State X wholly owns a vessel registered in and flying the flag of State Y. The law of State Y purports only to impose a small property tax on such vessels. While in a port of State Z, the vessel is nationalized without compensation by State Z, because the military dictator of State Z believes that State X has given military assistance to State A in hostilities between Z and A. State Y asserts a claim against State Z for the taking of the vessel. State Z defends that the vessel does not have for diplomatic protection purposes the nationality of State Y (under a rule of general international law, accepted here arguendo, that such claims can only be espoused by the state of nationality). State Z cites Article 5 of the Convention on the High Seas and the Vienna Convention on the Law of Treaties, both of which, it is assumed, are in force as to all parties concerned. How do you interpret Article 5 of the High Seas Convention in the light of the materials below?

INTERNATIONAL LAW COMMISSION, DRAFT ARTICLES ON THE LAW OF TREATIES

61 American Journal of International Law 255, 349 (1967).

Commentary on Rules of Interpretation

(1) The utility and even the existence of rules of international law governing the interpretation of treaties are sometimes questioned. The first two of the Commission's Special Rapporteurs on the law of treaties in their private writings also expressed doubts as to the existence in international law of any general rules for the interpretation of treaties. Other jurists, although they express reservations as to the obligatory character of certain of the so-called canons of interpretation, show less hesitation in recognizing the existence of some general rules for the interpretation of treaties. * * *

(2) Jurists also differ to some extent in their basic approach to the interpretation of treaties according to the relative weight which they give to:

(a) The text of the treaty as the authentic expression of the intentions of the parties;

(b) The intentions of the parties as a subjective element distinct from the text; and

(c) The declared or apparent objects and purposes of the treaty. * * *

* * *

(3) Most cases submitted to international adjudication involve the interpretation of treaties, and the jurisprudence of international tribunals is rich in reference to principles and maxims of interpretation. In fact, statements can be found in the decisions of international tribunals to support the use of almost every principle or maxim of which use is made in national systems of law in the interpretation of statutes and contracts. Treaty interpretation is, of course, equally part of the everyday work of Foreign Ministries. * * *

　　　　* * *

(11) The article as already indicated is based on the view that the text must be presumed to be the authentic expression of the intentions of the parties; and that, in consequence, the starting point of interpretation is the elucidation of the meaning of the text, not an investigation ab initio into the intentions of the parties. The Institute of International Law adopted this—the textual—approach to treaty interpretation. The objections to giving too large a place to the intentions of the parties as an independent basis of interpretation find expression in the proceedings of the Institute. The textual approach on the other hand, commends itself by the fact that, as one authority has put it, "le texte signé est, sauf de rares exceptions, la seule et la plus récente expression de la volonté commune des parties." Moreover, the jurisprudence of the International Court contains many pronouncements from which it is permissible to conclude that the textual approach to treaty interpretation is regarded by it as established law. In particular, the Court has more than once stressed that it is not the function of interpretation to revise treaties or to read into them what they do not, expressly or by implication, contain.

THE INTERNATIONAL LAW COMMISSION'S DRAFT ARTICLES UPON INTERPRETATION: TEXTUALITY REDIVIVUS

McDougal, 61 American Journal of International Law 992 (1967).

The great defect, and tragedy, in the International Law Commission's final recommendations about the interpretation of treaties is in their insistent emphasis upon an impossible, conformity-imposing textuality. * * *

In explicit rejection of a quest for the "intentions of the parties as a subjective element distinct from the text," the Commission adopts a "basic approach" which demands merely the ascription of a meaning to a text. The only justification offered, and several times repeated as if in an effort to carry conviction, is that "the text [of a treaty] must be presumed to be the authentic expression of the intentions of the parties" and hence that "the starting point of interpretation is the elucidation of the meaning of the text, not an investigation ab initio into the intentions of the parties." This arbitrary presumption is described as "established law" because of approval by the Institute of International Law and pronouncements by the International Court of Justice   *   *   *

      *   *   *

It can scarcely be doubted, further, that the "basic approach" of the Commission in generally arrogating to one particular set of signs— the text of a document—the rôle of serving as the exclusive index of the shared expectations of the parties to an agreement is an exercise in primitive and potentially destructive formalism. The parties to any particular agreement may have sought to communicate their shared expectations of commitment by many other signs and acts of collaboration; and it is hubris of the highest order to assume that the presence or absence of shared subjectivities at the outcome phase of any sequence of communications, much less that of an international agreement, can be read off in simple fashion from a manifest content or "ordinary meaning" of words imprinted or embossed in a document. *   *   *   To foreclose or impede inquiry about features of the process of making and performing agreements which in fact affect the parties' expectations about commitment, and to establish in advance of inquiry fixed hierarchies in significance among features of the process whose significance in fact is a function of the configuration of all other features in any particular context, may be to impose upon one or both of the parties an agreement they never made and completely to disrupt that stability in expectation which is indispensable to effective co-operation. The truth is that in the absence of a comprehensive, contextual examination of all the potentially significant features of the process of agreement, undertaken without the blinders of advance restrictive hierarchies or weightings, no interpreter can be sure that his determinations bear any relation to the genuine shared expectations of the parties. If it be suggested that the Commission's formulations are so vague and imprecise and so impossible of effective application that a sophisticated decision-maker can easily escape their putative limits, surely it must be answered that not all decision-makers are so sophisticated and that it is not the expected function of the International Law Commission to create myth for cloaking arbitrary decision.

The insight had appeared widespread, prior to the appearance of the Commission's formulations, that the most appropriate function of all principles of interpretation, including both "general rules" and "so-called canons," is that of guiding interpreters to potentially relevant features of the process of agreement and its context and, hence, of assisting in the making of that comprehensive and systematic examination regarded as indispensable to rational decision. The great bulk of the principles historically employed by international and national tribunals, as well as by other interpreters, has in fact, with the exception of some formulations of the travaux préparatoires and the "ordinary meaning" principles, been primarily permissive, openir

[handwritten margin notes: "- OPEN UP RATHER THAN RESTRICT" and "- POLITICALLY PRAGMATIC"]

up features for inquiry, rather than restrictive in character; and expositions of relevant principles, whether by authoritative decision-makers or private scholars, have largely differed only in the comprehensiveness and systematization of their presentation. In such a context, it has made little difference whether principles of interpretation were regarded as "obligatory" prescriptions or mere optional aids; only occasional impediments to inquiry have been imposed by even the "obligatory" view. The International Law Commission, in contrast, not only projects the highly restrictive principles which we have noted above, but also recommends that these principles be made obligatory prescription—which of course they will become if the states of the world accept in present form the proposed convention on the law of treaties. * * *

Fortunately, an excellent model both in statement of appropriate goal and in perception of relevant features of the process of agreement and its context is readily available for any critic who may choose to seek alternatives to the Commission's formulations. The Harvard Research in International Law, more than thirty years ago, put the essential understanding for such a model into black-letter nutshell:

> A treaty is to be interpreted in the light of the general purpose which it is intended to serve. The historical background of the treaty, travaux préparatoires, the circumstances of the parties at the time the treaty was entered into, the change in these circumstances sought to be effected, the subsequent conduct of the parties in applying the provisions of the treaty, and the conditions prevailing at the time interpretation is being made, are to be considered in connection with the general purpose which the treaty is intended to serve.[35]

What the Harvard Research does not offer, in implementation of its insight about appropriate goal and necessary context, is a comprehensive and systematic set of principles of content and procedure designed effectively to assist interpreters in the economic examination of particular contexts in pursuit of their appropriate goal. Even the task of fashioning such a set of principles should not, however, be beyond the reach of contemporary scholars who enjoy the advantages both of a rich inheritance in tested principles and of access to modern studies in semantics, syntactics, and other aspects of communication.

35. Harvard Research in International
Law, Law of Treaties, 29 A.J.I.L.Supp.
653 at 937 (1935), Art. 19.

KEARNEY AND DALTON, THE TREATY ON TREATIES

64 American Journal of International Law 495, 518 (1970).

* * *

The articles on interpretation demonstrate that a quite conservative (even old-fashioned) series of rules would be accepted by the conference if endorsed by the Commission. Articles 31 and 32 deal, respectively, with the general rule and supplementary means of interpretation. The Commission's formulation established a hierarchy of sources in which primacy was accorded to the text.

Paragraph 1 of Article 31 requires that a treaty be "interpreted in good faith in accordance with the ordinary meaning to be given to the terms of the treaty in their <u>context</u> and the light of its <u>object and purpose</u>." Context is narrowly defined as comprising, "in addition to the text, including its preamble and annexes," related agreements made by all the parties and instruments made by less than all the parties but accepted by all as related to the treaty. Paragraph 3 of Article 31, listing elements "extrinsic to the text" which shall be "taken into account" in interpretation, is limited to subsequent agreements between the parties, subsequent practice establishing agreement and relevant rules of international law.

Article 32 allows "supplementary means of interpretation" to be resorted to, "including preparatory work on the treaty and the circumstances of its conclusion, in order to confirm the meaning resulting from the application of article 31, or to determine the meaning when the interpretation according to article 31: (a) leaves the meaning ambiguous or obscure; or (b) leads to a result which is manifestly absurd or unreasonable."

A member of the Commission has observed that the method of presentation in both Articles 31 and 32 "is designed to stress the dominant position of the text itself in the interpretative process."

In the Commission Messrs. Briggs, El Erian, Rosenne and Tsuruoka supported a proposal to combine the substance of Articles 31 and 32 into a single article. In addition, Mr. Bartoš stated that he was inclined to favor the proposal, and Mr. Amado that he had no strong feelings either way. Among the governments which in their comments on the Commission's articles criticized treating the travaux préparatoires as a secondary means of interpretation were Hungary and the United States.

In light of the division in the Commission on the subject, the expressions of concern in governmental comments, and the traditional United States position in favor of according equal weight to travaux, the United States formally proposed an amendment, the principal objective of which was to eliminate the hierarchy between the sources of evidence for interpretation of treaties by combining the articles containing the general rule and the supplementary means of interpretation:

> A treaty shall be interpreted in good faith in order to determine the meaning to be given to its terms in the light of all relevant factors, including in particular:
>
> (a) the context of the treaty;
>
> (b) its objects and purposes;
>
> (c) any agreement between the parties regarding the interpretation of the treaty;
>
> (d) any instrument made by one or more parties in connexion with the conclusion of the treaty and accepted by the other parties as an instrument related to the treaty;
>
> (e) any subsequent practice in the application of the treaty which establishes the common understanding of the meaning of the terms as between the parties generally;
>
> (f) the preparatory work of the treaty;
>
> (g) the circumstances of its conclusion;
>
> (h) any relevant rules of international law applicable in the relations between the parties;
>
> (i) the special meaning to be given to a term if the parties intended such term to have a special meaning.

In introducing the amendment Professor McDougal adverted to the practice of Ministries of Foreign Affairs in looking at the travaux when considering a problem of treaty interpretation and to the practice of international tribunals, as illustrated by the Lotus case, of looking at the preparatory work before reaching a decision on the interpretation of a treaty described as "sufficiently clear in itself."

In the ensuing debate in the committee of the whole, the U.S. amendment received scant support. A principal source of arguments against it was the 1950 debates in the Institute of International Law which had adopted the textual approach. Fear was expressed that "too ready admission of the preparatory work" would afford an opportunity to a state which had "found a clear provision of a treaty inconvenient" to allege a different interpretation "because there was generally something in the preparatory work that could be found to support almost any intention." Other arguments advanced included the assertion that recourse to travaux would favor wealthy states with large and well-indexed archives, fear that non-negotiating states would hesitate to accede to multilateral conventions, since they could hardly be aware of or wish to have their rights based on recourse to the travaux, and the characterization of the International Law Commission text as a "neutral and fair formulation of the generally recognized canons of treaty interpretation." Given the tenor of the debate, the rejection of the amendment was a foregone conclusion.

The adoption by the conference of two articles which the United States viewed as somewhat archaic and unduly rigid does not seriously weaken the value of the convention. It seems unlikely that Foreign Offices will cease to take into consideration the preparatory work and the circumstances of the conclusion of treaties when faced with problems of treaty interpretation, or that international tribunals will be less disposed to consult Article 32 sources in determining questions of treaty interpretation.

The reaction of the conference to a United States amendment to Article 33, which deals with interpretation of plurilingual treaties, was more favorable. The amendment was referred to the drafting committee, which incorporated it in paragraph 4. The new rule provides that when a treaty has been authenticated in two or more languages, neither of which has been accorded priority, and a difference in meaning persists after recourse to the other articles on interpretation, "the meaning which best reconciles the texts, having regard to the object and purpose of the treaty, shall be adopted."

FITZMAURICE, VAE VICTIS OR WOE TO THE NEGOTIATORS! YOUR TREATY OR OUR "INTERPRETATION" OF IT?

65 American Journal of International Law 358, 370 (1971).

The length of time which has unfortunately (owing entirely to the procrastinations and backslidings of this reviewer) elapsed since the date when this (by any standards) most original and arresting work was first published in April, 1967,[1] makes it scarcely necessary to supply that systematic description of its contents which, up to a point, any well-ordered review ought to seek to do,—for by this time all those who are interested in its subject matter will have read or at least looked through it. We shall therefore concentrate on those salient aspects of it which, even after the familiarity of three years has softened their outlines, still seem to stand out with special prominence.

Arresting and original—yes. But this is and remains a very difficult work to assimilate and, partly for that reason, to be fair to. We doubt whether we shall in fact succeed in being fair to it, and think it best to declare ourselves in that sense at the outset. Not only do the authors make the task exceptionally difficult, for reasons that will appear and which indeed constitute a major part

1. The Interpretation of Agreements and World Public Order. Principles of Content and Procedure. By Myres S. McDougal, Harold D. Lasswell and James C. Miller. New Haven & London, Yale University Press, 1967, pp. xxii, 410. Index. $9.75; £ 3.60.

of our complaint, but, in addition, the book is peculiarly well cal-culated to run foul of some of our most dearly cherished predilec-tions! Having said this, however, we hope we can claim to have complied, or tried to comply, with at least one of the recommenda-tions the authors make to "decision-makers," namely * * *, to carry out the operation of *"examining the self * * * for bias"* (italics in the original), as a first step towards modifying one's out-look. * * *

* * *

The most striking feature of the authors' system is, however, that it subordinates the interpretation of a treaty—or rather (for the matter has little to do with interpretation stricto sensu) its applica-tion—to the attainment of certain objectives,—a process which is sum-med up * * * under the head of the "policing . . . goal." This is defined in general terms * * * as "requiring the rejec-tion of the parties' explicit expectations which [sc. if and insofar as they] contradict community policies." In other words the intentions of the parties, even if clear and ascertained and—what is even more important—common to them both, or all (in short the intentions of the *treaty*—* * *), are not to be given effect to if, in the opinion of the "decision-maker," such intentions are inconsistent with * * * "the goals of public order." Since it is thus left to the adjudicator to decide not only whether there is such inconsistency but also what *are* the goals of public order (and of which public order) to be taken in-to account, it is evident that on this wideranging, indeed almost il-limitable basis, the parties could never be sure how their treaty would be applied or whether it would be applied at all. The process would, in fact, confer on the "decision-maker" a discretion of a kind alto-gether exceeding the normal limits of the judicial function, amount-ing rather to the exercise of an administrative rôle.

This is well illustrated by the character of the only "community goal" which, so far as this reviewer can see, the authors themselves actually specify, namely, that of the preservation of "human dignity" which is coupled with what is called * * * "the operation of *examining the self* (italics in the original) for predispositions incom-patible with the goal of human dignity"—an admirable desideratum, one aspect of which (the duty of impartiality) has already received some comment earlier herein. No one of course can quarrel with the ideal of the preservation of human dignity, and the avoidance of ac-tion incompatible with it, as an essential objective. But without further and much more precise definition, this criterion and others like it which the authors specify, such as "overriding community goals" or "basic constitutive policies," etc. are too subjective to be of practical value to the adjudicator, or in the alternative would in-vest him with an almost arbitrary power. As Professor Leo Gross has well said, such concepts "are pregnant with ambiguity far great-er than ever confronted an international tribunal in interpreting

TOO MUCH DISCRETION

* * * a treaty." He adds, pointing to a further difficulty: "Reference is apparently made to communities of various orders ranging from a relatively compact community comprising the parties and the tribunal * * * to a world-wide community." Everyone knows, for instance, that in private life some people will regard as an affront to their dignity things which others will not even notice; and in the international field also there is a wide range of possible variables.

At bottom, the theory is one which proposes indirectly to import into treaty law an extensively conceived element of ius cogens without, however, any adequate definition of the ius which is to be "cogendum." The Vienna Convention on the Law of Treaties which, even so, is considered by some to go too far in this respect, does at least, in providing for the voidance of treaties if they conflict with "a peremptory norm of general international law (ius cogens)," define such a norm as being one that is "accepted and recognized by the international community of States as a whole as a norm from which no derogation is permitted and which can be modified only by a subsequent norm of general international law having the same character." This definition may not itself be entirely satisfactory, but it does give the adjudicator something to go by, at all events as to the nature of the notion involved.

Similarly, in the domestic field, the notion of "overriding community goals" is already to a limited extent reflected in the concept of "public policy," but in a highly modified, indeed quite different form. The latter policy is the policy of the law, and only indirectly of the community, considered apart from the law,—and it operates only within the confines of the law. The law will not, for instance, enforce certain types of contracts, as being usurious, as involving gambling transactions, as being directed to immoral purposes, etc. But, except in very special circumstances, these disqualifications are known to the parties in advance, not imposed ex post facto at the discretion of the adjudicator.

Nor is the policing of agreements in the sense of, in effect, voiding them for "conflict with community policies," by any means the only doom with which this work confronts the negotiators. An equal hazard, tending in certain circumstances to bring about, over the parties' heads, an even greater sea-change in a given treaty situation, is to be anticipated from what the authors call their second goal,— the first being * * * to make "a disciplined, responsible effort to ascertain the genuine shared expectations of the * * * parties * * *," because * * * "to defend the dignity of man is to respect *his* (authors' italics) choices and, not, *save for overriding common interest* (our italics here), to impose the choices of others upon him,"—admirable sentiments of course, but we have seen where, in the pursuit of the third (policing) goal, that saving clause about the "overriding common interest" can lead.

The *second* goal contemplates the case where the search for * * * the "genuine shared expectations" of the parties "must falter or fail because of gaps, contradictions or ambiguities" in their "communication"—(an unclear term which might mean in the course of the negotiations leading up to the agreement, or in the agreement itself). In such event (ibid.) "a decision-maker should supplement or *augment* (our italics) the relatively more explicit expressions of the parties [sc. what they actually wrote into the agreement] by making reference to the basic constitutive policies of the larger community * * *." Here again, therefore, community policies come in as a criterion, and also, once more, human dignity,—for (ibid.) "no conceivable alternative goal" could be "in accord with the aspiration to defend and expand a social system compatible with the overriding objectives of human dignity."

This, of course, however excellent, is not law but sociology; and although the aim is said to be "in support of search for the genuine shared expectations of the parties," it would in many cases have—and is perhaps subconsciously designed to have—quite a different effect, namely, in the guise of interpretation, to substitute the will of the adjudicator for that of the parties, since the intentions of the latter are, by definition (in the given circumstances) unascertainable because not sufficiently clearly or fully expressed,—and therefore presumed intentions, based on what the adjudicator thinks would be good for the community, or in accordance with "overriding objectives of human dignity" etc., must be attributed to them.

Now the process of, so to speak, curing the deficiencies of a text is, within certain limits, a perfectly legitimate one, constantly employed by courts and tribunals. For instance, where the intention or object of the agreement is plain, no court would allow a party to get out of what was a clear undertaking, merely on account of some drafting lapse, wrong reference, incorrect description or manifest omission, and such like deficiencies of a technical not substantive character—(this indeed, when the "explicit rationality" is cut away, can be seen to be the real basis of the decision of the International Court in the first (preliminary objection) phase of the Temple case). Another example is afforded by the principle ut res magis valeat quam pereat, the effect of which is that where a text is ambiguous or defective, but a possible, though uncertain, interpretation of it would give the agreement some effect, whereas otherwise it would have none, a court is entitled to adopt that interpretation, on the legitimate assumption that the parties must have intended their agreement to have some effect, not none.

Significantly, however, the maxim ut magis is all too frequently misunderstood as denoting that agreements should always be given their maximum possible effect, whereas its real object is merely ("quam pereat") to prevent them failing altogether. This affords a very good pointer to the limits of a doctrine which, if allowed free play, would result in parties finding themselves saddled with obligations they never intended to enter into, in relation to situations they never contemplated, and which often they could not even have anticipated. Is it unfair to ascribe to the authors of this work the championship of such a doctrine? Let them * * * be heard for themselves:

> Modern logical tools may disclose implications that were undreamed of when the parties were hammering out their understanding.

Of what use then is it to "hammer out" an understanding (not surely any casual process) if implications then "undreamed of" are later to be imported, and given obligatory force?

COMPETENCE OF ASSEMBLY REGARDING ADMISSION TO THE UNITED NATIONS (ADVISORY OPINION)

International Court of Justice, Advisory Opinion, 1950.
[1950] I.C.J.Rep. 4.

* * *

On November 22nd, 1949, the General Assembly of the United Nations adopted the following Resolution:

> The General Assembly,
>
> Keeping in mind the discussion concerning the admission of new Members in the Ad Hoc Political Committee at its fourth regular session,
>
> Requests the International Court of Justice to give an advisory opinion on the following question:
>
>> Can the admission of a State to membership in the United Nations, pursuant to Article 4, paragraph 2, of the Charter, be effected by a decision of the General Assembly when the Security Council has made no recommendation for admission by reason of the candidate failing to obtain the requisite majority or of the negative vote of a permanent Member upon a resolution so to recommend?

* * *

The Request for an Opinion envisages solely the case in which the Security Council, having voted upon a recommendation, has concluded from its vote that the recommendation was not adopted because it failed to obtain the requisite majority or because of the negative vote of a permanent Member. Thus the Request refers to the case in which the General Assembly is confronted with the absence of a recommendation from the Security Council.

It is not the object of the Request to determine how the Security Council should apply the rules governing its voting procedure in regard to admissions or, in particular, that the Court should examine whether the negative vote of a permanent Member is effective to defeat a recommendation which has obtained seven or more votes. The question, as it is formulated, assumes in such a case the non-existence of a recommendation.

The Court is, therefore, called upon to determine solely whether the General Assembly can make a decision to admit a State when the Security Council has transmitted no recommendation to it.

Article 4, paragraph 2, is as follows:

> The admission of any such State to membership in the United Nations will be effected by a decision of the General Assembly upon the recommendation of the Security Council.

The Court has no doubt as to the meaning of this text. It requires two things to effect admission: a "recommendation" of the Security Council and a "decision" of the General Assembly. It is in the nature of things that the recommendation should come before the decision. The word "recommendation", and the word "upon" preceding it, imply the idea that the recommendation is the foundation of the decision to admit, and that the latter rests upon the recommendation. Both these acts are indispensable to form the judgment of the Organization to which the previous paragraph of Article 4 refers. The text under consideration means that the General Assembly can only decide to admit upon the recommendation of the Security Council; it determines the respective roles of the two organs whose combined action is required before admission can be effected: in other words, the recommendation of the Security Council is the condition precedent to the decision of the Assembly by which the admission is effected.

In one of the written statements placed before the Court, an attempt was made to attribute to paragraph 2 of Article 4 a different meaning. The Court considers it necessary to say that the first duty of a tribunal which is called upon to interpret and apply the provisions of a treaty, is to endeavour to give effect to them in their natural and ordinary meaning in the context in which they occur. If the relevant words in their natural and ordinary meaning make sense in their context, that is an end of the matter. If, on the other hand, the words in their natural and ordinary meaning are ambiguous or lead to an unreasonable result, then, and then only, must the Court, by resort to other methods of interpretation, seek to ascertain what the parties really did mean when they used these words. As the Permanent Court said in the case concerning the Polish Postal Service in Danzig (P.C.I.J., Series B, No. II, p. 39):

> It is a cardinal principle of interpretation that words must be interpreted in the sense which they would normally have in their context, unless such interpretation would lead to something unreasonable or absurd.

When the Court can give effect to a provision of a treaty by giving to the words used in it their natural and ordinary meaning, it may not interpret the words by seeking to give them some other meaning. In the present case the Court finds no difficulty in ascertaining the natural and ordinary meaning of the words in question and no difficulty in giving effect to them. Some of the written statements submitted to the Court have invited it to investigate the travaux préparatoires of the Charter. Having regard, however, to the considerations above stated, the Court is of the opinion that it is not permissible, in this case, to resort to travaux préparatoires.

The conclusions to which the Court is led by the text of Article 4, paragraph 2, are fully confirmed by the structure of the Charter, and particularly by the relations established by it between the General Assembly and the Security Council.

The General Assembly and the Security Council are both principal organs of the United Nations. The Charter does not place the Security Council in a subordinate position. Article 24 confers upon it "primary responsibility for the maintenance of international peace and security", and the Charter grants it for this purpose certain powers of decision. Under Articles 4, 5, and 6, the Security Council co-operates with the General Assembly in matters of admission to membership, of suspension from the exercise of the rights and privileges of membership, and of expulsion from the Organization. It has power, without the concurrence of the General Assembly, to reinstate the Member which was the object of the suspension, in its rights and privileges.

The organs to which Article 4 entrusts the judgment of the Organization in matters of admission have consistently interpreted the text in the sense that the General Assembly can decide to admit only on the basis of a recommendation of the Security Council. In particular, the Rules of Procedure of the General Assembly provide for consideration of the merits of an application and of the decision to be made upon it only "if the Security Council recommends the applicant State for membership" (Article 125). The Rules merely state that if the Security Council has not recommended the admission, the General Assembly may send back the application to the Security Council for further consideration (Article 126). This last step has been taken several times; it was taken in Resolution 296 (IV), the very one that embodies this Request for an Opinion.

To hold that the General Assembly has power to admit a State to membership in the absence of a recommendation of the Security Council would be to deprive the Security Council of an important power which has been entrusted to it by the Charter. It would almost nullify the role of the Security Council in the exercise of one of the essential functions of the Organization. It would mean that the Security Council would have merely to study the case, present a report, give advice, and express an opinion. This is not what Article 4, paragraph 2, says.

The Court cannot accept the suggestion made in one of the written statements submitted to the Court, that the General Assembly, in order to try to meet the requirement of Article 4, paragraph 2, could treat the absence of a recommendation as equivalent to what is described in that statement as an "unfavourable recommendation", upon which the General Assembly could base a decision to admit a State to membership.

Reference has also been made to a document of the San Francisco Conference, in order to put the possible case of an unfavourable recommendation being voted by the Security Council: such a recommendation has never been made in practice. In the opinion of the Court, Article 4, paragraph 2, envisages a favourable recommendation of the Security Council and that only. An unfavourable recommendation would not correspond to the provisions of Article 4, paragraph 2.

While keeping within the limits of a Request which deals with the scope of the powers of the General Assembly, it is enough for the Court to say that nowhere has the General Assembly received the power to change, to the point of reversing, the meaning of a vote of the Security Council.

In consequence, it is impossible to admit that the General Assembly has the power to attribute to a vote of the Security Council the character of a recommendation when the Council itself considers that no such recommendation has been made.

For these reasons, THE COURT, by twelve votes to two, is of opinion that the admission of a State to membership in the United Nations, pursuant to paragraph 2 of Article 4 of the Charter, cannot be effected by a decision of the General Assembly when the Security Council has made no recommendation for admission, by reason of the candidate failing to obtain the requisite majority or of the negative vote of a permanent Member upon a resolution so to recommend.

[Concurring and dissenting opinions omitted.]

Three questions:

1. Would the outcome of the case have been different if the standard for interpretation had been that of the United States proposal that was so poorly received at Vienna?

2. What kinds of information, data, and other factual material would the International Court of Justice have had to have before it in order to apply the United States proposal at Vienna?

3.   What kinds of information, data, and other factual material would have been relevant and persuasive under the provision on interpretation in the Vienna Convention? ✱

CASE ON INTERPRETATION OF THE AUSTRIAN STATE TREATY

Seidl-Hohenveldern, Notes on Austrian Judicial Decisions
86 Journal du Droit International 835, 837 (1959).a

The German text of Article 16, Austrian State Treaty (BGBl., Nr. 152/1955; J. O. 2nd Sept. 1955; 49 AJIL, 1955, Off. Doc., p. 162), is worded as follows: "Prohibition relating to Civil Aircraft of German and Japanese Design". "Austria shall not acquire or manufacture civil aircraft which are of German or Japanese design or which embody major assemblies of German or Japanese manufacture or design". Pursuant to this regulation, the Federal Ministry of communications and electric power — Air Navigation Division — denied the request filed by an Austrian glider club for licensing a glider of German construction type; and the glider club, in protest, brought an action before the Vervaltungsgerichtshof. It pointed out, to start with, that in the German language version of the Treaty there was an inherent contradiction, since the Title of Article 16 read "Zivil- flugzeuge" (airplanes), whereas in the Article proper one referred to "Luftfahrtzeugen" (aircraft). In Austrian terminology, the plaintiff asserted, "Zivilflugzeuge" indicates in principle that the plane is engine-driven, while "Luftfahrtzeuge" covers gliders as well. Pursuant to Article 38, State Treaty, the Russian, English, French and German texts are authentic. The French version makes use, for both title and text of Article 16, of the word "Avion", which corresponds to the "Zivilflugzeug" concept, instead of using "aéronef", which would render "Luftfahrtzeug"; and so does the Russian text. The English version, on the contrary, reads — for both title and text of Article 16 — "aircraft", which corresponds to "Luftfahrtzeug", whereas "Zivilflugzeug", in English, would be "airplane".

[margin note: CONFLICT IN LANGUAGE]

The glider club considered that, account being taken of the aforementioned discrepancies between texts, one was faced here, essentially, with an error in the translation into German. Article 16 certainly brings about a limitation of Austrian sovereignty, but even according to the basic principles of international law the existence of diverging authentic texts of a State Treaty results in considering that version which infringes least on sovereignty, as the only one which may be regarded as consonant with the will of the contracting parties and the principles of International Law. Moreover, it claimed, the French

---

a.   English text in the Journal. Reprinted by permission of Editions Techniques, S.A., Paris.

text of the State Treaty is most authoritative, because in the Convention on International Civil Aviation French terminology is clearly defined — French being the official language of ICAO. If taken into account, the French wording does not provide any reason for further limiting Austria's sovereignty.

The Verwaltungsgerichtshof decided that, for the purpose of implementing the State Treaty — which in the domestic sphere is to be regarded as directly applicable law — one must infer from its Article 39, paragraph 1, that the State Treaty in its German version became domestic law. Pursuant to Austrian practice, headings are to be called upon for construing a legal text only in the event that the text proper is not clear or does not make sense — which is not the case here. In the light of the purpose which, among others, underlies Part II of the State Treaty — namely, to prevent coordination of the Austrian Air Force and civilian aviation with those of Germany and Japan —, the importance of civil aviation as a whole in war time, together with the widespread use of all types of aircraft, including gliders and balloons, for war aims, make a prohibition against any aircraft (even one which is not engine-propelled) appear perfectly logical, however harsh such a rule may seem to glider pilots.

Nor is anything to be gained in favour of thus construing this legal text by underlining the existing contradictions between the German version and those in other languages, since the latter turn out to be just as diverging. Therefore, as long as the differences are not settled by an authentic interpretation of Article 16, made in accordance with the procedure provided for in Article 35 of the Treaty — a procedure which can only be initiated at the international public law level —, the Austrian authorities must continue to abide by the German text, application of which as positive law is mandatory for them and in which the wording does not admit — as already pointed out — of the kind of interpretation proposed by the plaintiff. A legal text may be interpreted in the manner most favourable to the sovereignty of the country concerned only when there exists a doubt as to how that regulation ought to be interpreted; since the provisions of Article 16, in its German version, are unambiguous, this does not apply here.

* * *

SECTION D. SUCCESSION TO AND TERMINATION AND SUSPENSION OF INTERNATIONAL AGREEMENTS

1. *Termination and suspension.* Where an international agreement is not made for a term of years, it continues to be in force as a basis of an international obligation until it is terminated. Normal

types of termination are renegotiation (comparable to novation in private law), substitution, and cancellation (sometimes called denunciation) by a party having that capacity under the terms of the treaty or by the practice of states as to treaties of the particular type. Extraordinary types of termination include desuetude for very old and now-inapt international agreements, although ordinarily the problem of over-age treaties is dealt with through a process that begins with national analysis to identify them and continues with a proposal for novation or cancellation by mutual consent. Additionally, extraordinary termination may result, dependent upon the function of the agreement, from external developments, such as the complete disappearance of one or more of the states that entered into a bilateral or several-party treaty, through its absorption into another state and the break-up into a number of states of a former state, no one of which is juridically the same state (now reduced) as the treaty state. The effect of jus cogens, under Article 64 of the Vienna Convention on the Law of Treaties is to give a new extraordinary ground for termination, even of multipartite conventions, inasmuch as the article says that the emergence in future of a new peremptory norm of international law makes void and terminates a pre-existing treaty in conflict therewith.

In some situations, extrinsic happenings are held to suspend rather than end international agreements. Such suspension may be as to mutual promissory and continuing undertakings, or it may arise from the fact that the extrinsic situation gives one of the parties, by stipulation in the agreement or by interpretation, the privilege of not performing a promise until a condition precedent or concurrent has been met.

2. *The durability of an international agreement in relationship to its type and function.* The question whether an international agreement is still a source of national rights and duties does not often arise in international legal disputes or litigation between states. The reason is that in normal relationships between states parties to international agreements, the attitude of one or the other of them as to the continuing validity or not of a treaty arises as a diplomatic issue, thus quite naturally tending toward resolution of the issue by renegotiation. Questions of suspension and termination arise more often in national courts, in terms of the question whether the international agreement still exists at the relevant time and can be the basis of rights of private persons against one another.

As between states themselves, however, some general underlying principles of international politics and law exist: (i) multipartite treaties are much less susceptible to termination or suspension than bilateral ones are; (ii) so long as a state continues to exist, so do its treaty relationships; (iii) treaties that have been fully carried out (executed), especially those that created "vested rights" in territory, are virtually termination-proof. (Suspension is not an issue, as it relates to agreements involving continuing or future performance.)

Bilateral political treaties, especially those as to cooperation and harmonization of the conduct of foreign relations, are the most vulnerable of all types of treaties to termination. But even here, a great deal depends on what the states parties to the agreements have said after the event. In the peace treaties that followed World War II (the one with Germany or the Germanies is still to be negotiated), the parties stipulated which of their pre-war bilateral treaties were to remain in force, and the negotiating history of the peace conferences shows that it was assumed that multipartite conventions were not affected as to continued existence by war.

3. *State continuation and succession and the durability and ambit of applicability of international agreements.* In international practice a state can survive a great deal and continue to exist. The Western Allies of World War II debated, at the time (1950) that they began the process which led to the coming into existence of what is now the Federal German Republic, whether the German state (Reich) had survived defeat, unconditional surrender, and the complete exercise of governmental authority in the territory of the Reich for some years by Allied military governments. The United Kingdom and the United States said that the German state had survived all this. The French thought that the German state had died. The practical issue—there were political ones as well—was about treaty relationships. If the German state had died and the entity in the western zones of occupation of the former Germany was to be a new something, then all treaty relationships would have to be negotiated again by it. Finally, the French gave in, and "Germany's" treaty relationships continued, except for such effects as war might have had on suspension or termination.

Complete split-up of states (the Austro-Hungarian Empire after World War I) and the growth of states by aggregation (the expansion of the Kingdom of Savoy into the Kingdom of Italy) have become historic phenomena. Theoretically, in a complete split-up the pre-existing state would disappear and its treaty relationships with it. The expansion of the territory of a state merely makes its treaty law more widely applicable, unless, of course, the treaty itself contains some indication that the other party should not be held to have impliedly agreed to such a possibility.

The separation of a territory and its people from a metropole through the creation of a new state (a spin-off, to continue the corporate analogy) creates many important problems about state succession. If the spin-off is orderly and itself based upon an international agreement or agreements, there is no problem, usually, as to state succession to the rights and duties of the former mother state, insofar as the territory, installations, and inhabitants of the new state are concerned. New states, of which we have seen there are so many today, are free to decide for themselves what relationships they shall opt for as to those multipartite conventions that are always open for accession, such as the United Nations Charter, the Articles of Association of the International Bank for Reconstruction and Development, the Charter of the Food and Agriculture Organization, and the Convention on Safety of Life at Sea, to list just a sample of the large number of agreements that the foreign affairs decision-makers of such a country have to consider in the light of the interests of the new state as seen by them. It is a politically popular attitude in some of the very new states to exhibit great sensitivity about being bound to pre-existing law. The targets of doubt include customary international law and rules in treaties. In point of fact, except for fully-executed international agreements about such things as boundaries, the new states have had very little law in treaties "imposed" upon them. Nonetheless, from a politico-anthropological viewpoint, the new states in sub-Sahara Africa do have serious problems, where boundaries fixed between colonies by European imperial powers have determined the boundaries of the new states with each other, even though they cut across the territorial dispersion of various tribal groups in Africa. It well may be that the principle that a "deed of grant" type treaty is almost invulnerable as to subsequent changes of circumstances will meet a challenge of survival in Africa. There is nothing in the Vienna Convention on state succession and existing treaties.

The creation of new states (as distinguished from new governments) by violent revolution is not, so far, a common experience of the modern world. It is inferable that states beginning life in this manner will be less subject to pre-existing metropole treaties than states that spun-off peacefully would be, but even in such cases the freezing effect of a boundary or territorial arrangement would probably be felt, because of the interests of a third state or states.

The treaties creating the European Economic Community contain no provisions limiting the life of the association or for withdrawal. Although only an economic union so far, the parallel between these treaties and the Constitution of the United States of America in this particular is striking. Undoubtedly, in both cases omissions were deliberate.

In connection with treaty draftsmanship attention should be paid to whether the matters of duration, effect of hostilities, change of condition and circumstances, hardship, and the like should be dealt with in the negotiations with a view to the inclusion of provisions in the agreement.

4. *Treaty provisions on termination and related matters.* Treaties contained in the Documentary Supplement display a variety of approaches to the question of termination.

a   No express provision appears in the following:

    (i) International Covenant on Economic, Social and Cultural Rights.

    (ii) International Covenant on Civil and Political Rights.

    (iii) Vienna Convention on the Law of Treaties.

    (iv) Vienna Convention on Diplomatic Relations.

    (v) Conventions on the Law of the Sea.

b   Denunciation at anytime by notice to Secretary-General of United Nations (to take effect one year after receipt of notice): International Convention on the Elimination of all forms of Racial Discrimination, Article 21.

c   After ten years, convention in force for successive periods of five years, for parties that have not denounced (by notice to Secretary-General) six months before end of current period: Convention on the Prevention and Punishment of the Crime of Genocide, Article XIV.

d   Notice of withdrawal may be given to Depository Governments after one year after treaty in force (to take effect one year after receipt of notice): Space Treaty, Article XVI.

Some conventions provide an amendment process (e. g. Nuclear Test Ban, Space Treaty, United Nations Charter).

Some conventions provide that parties may request revision by notifying the Secretary-General of the United Nations, in which event the General Assembly shall decide what steps to take (e. g., conventions on Racial Discrimination, the Territorial Sea, the High Seas, the Continental Shelf). The Law of the Sea conventions provide that such requests can be made only after five years from the date the relevant convention has come into force.

Article 56 of the Vienna Convention on the Law of Treaties provides that if there is no provision for termination, denunciation or withdrawal, a treaty is not subject to denunciation unless "it is established that the parties intended to admit the possibility of denunciation or withdrawal" or "a right of denunciation or withdrawal may be implied by the *nature* of the treaty." [Emphasis supplied.]

ACADEMY OF SCIENCES OF THE U.S.S.R., INSTITUTE OF STATE AND LAW, INTERNATIONAL LAW 208 (MOSCOW, 1961)

Annulment of Treaties. The annulment of an international treaty can be defined as a unilateral declaration by a State that it repudiates the treaty concerned.

Annulment may take the form of a recognition of the treaty as having been ineffective from the outset, or regarding its termination in the future.

Not every annulment is impermissible under International Law. The annulment of a treaty by one signatory in the event of the non-fulfilment by the other of key terms is held to be legal.

It will be recalled that the British and French governments, by their remilitarisation of Western Germany, the creation of a West European army and the inclusion of a remilitarised Western Germany in the military groupings of the Western European Union and the North Atlantic bloc—actions directed against the Soviet Union—in effect annulled the Anglo-Soviet Treaty of May 26, 1942 and the Franco-Soviet Treaty of December 10, 1944.

Therefore on May 7, 1955 the Presidium of the Supreme Soviet of the U.S.S.R. annulled these treaties as ineffective.

It has already been noted that unequal treaties and treaties of a similar character are not binding. Their annulment does not contradict generally recognised democratic principles of present-day International Law. From this point of view, the Egyptian Parliament's decision of October 15, 1951 to repudiate the Anglo-Egyptian Treaty of 1936 and the 1899 Convention regarding the condominium over the Sudan was legal in that it corresponded to the principles of democracy supported by all progressive mankind, since these treaties violated the elementary sovereign rights of the Egyptian people.

A treaty may be annulled by the fact that a signatory ceases to exist.

The annulment of an international treaty is justified, in the opinion of some international jurists, by a vital change of circumstances when the signatories based themselves upon the fact that such circumstances could not change (that is, when a treaty is subject to the reservation rebus sic stantibus).

We may cite as examples the Franco-Moroccan Declaration of March 2, 1956, regarding the Treaty of March 30, 1912 and the Franco-Tunisian Protocol of March 22, 1956 regarding the Treaty of May 12, 1881.

It must, however, be borne in mind that this clause is frequently interpreted extremely broadly by capitalist States, in the sense that any change in the international situation gives the right to annul a treaty. Such an interpretation has been used by aggressor countries to justify expansionist foreign policies.[1]

Only a fundamental, radical change in the international situation can constitute grounds for the application of the clause rebus sic stantibus.

---

1. It should at the same time be noted that in bourgeois literature a negative attitude to this reservation is also to be found (See Hans Kelsen, "Théorie du droit international public". Recueil des Cours, t. 84, 1955, pp. 162–64).

The unilateral, arbitrary dissolution of international treaties contradicts International Law.   Nevertheless, it is a frequent phenomenon in the practice of capitalist States, particularly in the period of imperialism.   Imperialist States not only grossly violate the United Nations Charter and the international undertakings which they have assumed during and since the Second World War, but in effect unilaterally annul them.

The U.S.S.R. unswervingly champions the stability of international treaties concluded on the basis of the sovereign equality of the parties.

NEDERLANDSCHE RIJNVAARTVEREENIGING v. DAMCO SCHEEPVAART MAATSCHAPPIJ

Netherlands, District Court of Rotterdam, 1954.
21 Int'l L. Rep. 276 (1957).

THE FACTS.   In Swiss Corporation Tanutra v. N.V. Nederlandsche Rijnvaartvereeniging (see International Law Reports, 1953, p. 164), the same Court, on April 17, 1953, had ex officio declared itself not competent to adjudicate on a claim for damages arising out of a collision which had taken place on the Rhine near Cologne after the British High Commissioner for the Western Zone of Germany had reinstated the Rhine Navigation Courts.   In the present case the collision had taken place at a point between the bridges across the Rhine at Mainz near the thalweg of the river which was the boundary line between the United States and the French Zones of Occupation.   The date of the collision was April 1, 1946.   The claim for damages was presented on November 6, 1948.   During 1946 and 1947 the United States and the French authorities had reinstated the Rhine Navigation Courts in their respective Zones.   It does not appear that either party raised the issue of jurisdiction.   However, the Court raised the matter ex officio.

Held: that the Court's decision in the Tanutra case be adhered to and that, therefore, the Court was not competent to adjudicate in this action.   [A portion of the opinion of the court appears below].

*   *   *   In November 1936 the German Government denounced the Revised Convention of Mannheim of 1868 concerning Navigation on the Rhine [hereinafter called the Rhine Convention] and dissolved the German Rhine Navigation Courts.   Since the Rhine Convention is a treaty which cannot be denounced unilaterally no legal consequences could, therefore, according to international law, follow from such denunciation.   In the Netherlands the Convention remained in full force.   With regard to Germany it could, as a consequence of the dissolution of the German Rhine Navigation Courts, no longer be observed by the other States.   Germany was henceforth not in a position

to demand that the other States should apply the provisions on jurisdiction laid down in Articles 33, 34 and 35 of the Rhine Convention in connection with collisions occurring on the Rhine in Germany. These provisions with regard to Germany remained in force de jure, but they could no longer be observed de facto.   After 1936, the Netherlands courts applied to such collisions the provision concerning competence ratione materiae laid down in Article 543 of the Netherlands Commercial Code.   This was a provisional solution fully justified by Germany's illegal acts.   The multilateral Rhine Convention, which had always remained in full operation between the Netherlands and Belgium, France and Switzerland had, as far as the legal relations between the Netherlands and Germany were concerned, been suspended, according to generally recognized principles of international law, by the outbreak of war between the Netherlands and Germany on May 10, 1940.   That suspension must be deemed to have ended in the autumn of 1945.   At that time all the Governments concerned promoted by their words and acts the restoration of the use of the Rhine for commerce within the scope of the Rhine Convention.   Since the autumn of 1945 the Rhine Convention again completely regulated navigation on the Rhine between the Netherlands and the Occupying Powers which then exercised the sovereignty of the German State. In the course of the years 1946 and 1947, these Occupying Powers established courts which could fulfil the task which the Rhine Convention imposed on the navigation courts envisaged by it.   The present collision took place at a time when navigation on the Rhine was once more controlled by the Rhine Convention save for the fact that the functions allotted to the courts constituted by the Convention could not yet be exercised.   This was, however, possible by the time the writ of summons was served in the present proceedings.   In these circumstances there is no reason why the interim solution based on Article 543 of the Commercial Code should take priority over the time-honoured regulation of the jurisdiction of the Rhine Navigation Courts.

* * *

Outbreak of Hostilities

1.   In Clark v. Allen, 331 U.S. 503, 508, 67 S.Ct. 1431 (1947), the Court said:

We start from the premise that the outbreak of war does not necessarily suspend or abrogate treaty provisions.   Society for the Propagation of the Gospel v. New Haven, 8 Wheat. 464, 494–495.   There may of course be such an incompatibility between a particular treaty provision and the maintenance of a state of war as to make clear that it should not be enforced.

Karnuth v. United States, 279 U.S. 231, 49 S.Ct. 274. Or the Chief Executive or the Congress may have formulated a national policy quite inconsistent with the enforcement of a treaty in whole or in part. This was the view stated in Techt v. Hughes * * * [229 N.Y. 222, 128 N.E. 185 (1920), cert. denied 254 U.S. 643, 41 S.Ct. 14 (1920)] and we believe it to be the correct one. That case concerned the right of a resident alien enemy to inherit real property in New York. Under New York law, as it then stood, an alien enemy had no such right. The question was whether the right was granted by a reciprocal inheritance provision in a treaty with Austria which was couched in terms practically identical with those we have here. The court found nothing incompatible with national policy in permitting the resident alien enemy to have the right of inheritance granted by the treaty.

2. Article 73, Vienna Convention on the Law of Treaties provides: "The provisions of the present Convention shall not prejudge any question that may arise in regard to a treaty * * * from the outbreak of hostilities between States."

BREMEN (FREE HANSA CITY OF) v. PRUSSIA

Germany, Staatsgerichtshof, 1925.
[1925–1926] Ann. Dig. 352 (No. 266).

THE FACTS. A treaty entered into on 21 May, 1904, between Bremen and Prussia provided for an exchange of portions of territory belonging to each of the two States mainly with the view of enabling Bremen to extend the facilities for transport by sea. Article 13 of the Treaty laid down that a specified portion of the territory received by Bremen in exchange should be used by Bremen only for the purpose of constructing ports and other works connected with navigation, and Article 22 provided that no works connected with the fishing industry should be constructed or allowed by Bremen. The area of the territories exchanged was 595 and 597 hectares, but it appears from the judgment that the territory received by Prussia was only useful for agricultural purposes and, therefore, less valuable. Prussia, therefore, asked for a further consideration, and received it in the form of the above restrictive clauses calculated to safeguard the interests of her adjoining provinces menaced by the competition of the neighbouring Bremen fishing industry. Before the Staatsgerichtshof Bremen asked for a rescission of the restrictive clauses, subject, if necessary, to adequate compensation to be paid by her. She claimed that, as a result of the outcome of the War of 1914–1918, there had taken place a total change in the circumstances which underlay the conclusion of the Treaty. It was expected in 1904 that not only would the commercial

INADEQUATE EFFORT TO INVENT DOCTRINE TO SERVE REAL NEED CONDITIONS ALWAYS A SOMEWHAT — DIFFICULT TO ARTICULATE OBJECTIVE TEST TO MEASURE WHEN THEY HAVE A SUFFICIENTLY TO INVOKE THIS ESCAPE —

fleet of Bremen, especially the North German Lloyd, continue to exist, but also that a rapid development of that fleet would take place. It was in view of this expectation that Bremen agreed to the restrictions contemplated in Articles 13 and 22. Bremen pointed out before the court that the Treaty of Versailles effected a complete change in the situation in that the German commercial fleet was handed over to the Allied Powers; that the position of Bremen as a centre of shipping and navigation was irretrievably lost; and that the operation of the restrictive clauses had become most oppressive as the prohibited activities had now become the only sphere open to Bremen as a maritime State.

Held: That the application of Bremen must be refused.

1. International Law recognises to a large extent the possibility of termination of treaties on account of changed circumstances in accordance with the principle rebus sic stantibus.

2. This principle applies also to treaties concluded between State members of the German Reich. Although rules of International Law do not eo ipso form part of German constitutional law, they may be resorted to in order to supplement the latter. The regard for the interests of the other contracting party which International Law expects from a State, cannot be regarded as inequitable and devoid of a legal foundation within the German Federation.

3. However, as the two restrictive clauses formed an integral part of the treaties in question and as Prussia would not, in the opinion of the Court, have agreed to the treaties but for the restrictive clauses they could not be abrogated without her consent.

4. Neither could the clauses in question be abrogated subject to compensation to be paid to Prussia by Bremen. No such alteration of individual provisions of the treaty is admissible as would compel one contracting party to remain subject to the obligation while surrendering what it intended to achieve as the principal object of the treaty, at the time of the conclusion of the treaty.

5. The above decision does not amount in fact to a rejection of the doctrine rebus sic stantibus. The doctrine could still be applied in regard to certain payments or time limits contemplated in several provisions of the treaty.

The clause rebus sic stantibus. The Vienna Convention on the Law of Treaties provides in Article 62 (in somewhat negative language) for terminating, withdrawing from or suspending a treaty because of a "fundamental change of circumstances." This provision should be read in conjunction with the procedures established in Articles 65–68, with respect to invalidity, termination, withdrawal from or suspension of a treaty.

Suppose a state simply ceases to comply with a treaty and is subsequently called to account by the other party. Is rebus sic stantibus a defense? Under the Vienna Convention, is a "fundamental change of circumstances" a defense, i. e., can either doctrine be invoked unilaterally by a state?

In order to "avoid the doctrinal implication" of the term rebus sic stantibus, the International Law Commission decided not to use it either in the text or the title of the article on fundamental change. See the Commentary of the International Law Commission in its draft article 59 (now Treaty Article 62), 61 Am.J.Int'l L. 428 (1967). It is clear, however, that the commission was carefully and narrowly stating its preferred version of the rule of rebus sic stantibus. In its commentary, the commission noted that the International Court of Justice had avoided taking a position on the existence of the rule by finding, in the one case which posed the question, that the facts of that case did not warrant application of the rule. Free Zones of Savoy and Gex, P.C.I.J., 1932, Series A/B, No. 46. The commission further noted that, although municipal courts "have not infrequently recognized the relevance of the principle in international law," they have "always ended by rejecting the application of it in the particular circumstances of the case before them." (One such case was Bremen v. Prussia.) However, the commission found in state practice "a wide acceptance of the view that a fundamental change of circumstances may justify a demand for termination or revision of a treaty."

The doctrine of rebus sic stantibus, either in those terms or in other words, is to be found in the domestic law of states in cases not involving treaties but, rather, commercial contracts between private persons. Article 610 of the German Civil Code provides that one who promises to make a loan can revoke the promise in case of misgivings if a material deterioration develops in the pecuniary circumstances of the other party, through which the claim for repayment is jeopardized. See also Article 321 of the German Civil Code, on bilateral contracts. Article 2–609 of the United States Uniform Commercial Code provides in terms very similar to Article 321 of the German Civil Code: "A contract for sale imposes an obligation on each party that the other's expectation of receiving due performance will not be impaired. When reasonable grounds for insecurity arise with respect to the performance of either party, the other may in writing demand adequate assurance of performance and until he receives such assurance may if commercially reasonable suspend any performance for which he has not already received the agreed return."

If notions of rebus sic stantibus are common to municipal systems of law, why should there be such hesitancy to recognize that the rule is a rule of international law? Are there any peculiar risks to its application in international law that do not exist, or exist to a lesser extent, in municipal law? Is the weakness of international adjudication one such risk?

CHARLTON v. KELLY, SHERIFF

United States Supreme Court, 1913.
229 U. S. 447, 33 S.Ct. 945.

* * *

This is an appeal from a judgment dismissing a petition for a writ of habeas corpus and remanding the petitioner to custody under a warrant for his extradition as a fugitive from the justice of the Kingdom of Italy. * * *

* * *

MR. JUSTICE LURTON * * * delivered the opinion of the court.

* * *

The objections which are relied upon for the purpose of defeating extradition may be conveniently summarized and considered under four heads:

* * *

3. That appellant is a citizen of the United States, and that the treaty in providing for the extradition of "persons" accused of crime does not include persons who are citizens or subjects of the nation upon whom the demand is made.   *[margin note: does not cover U.S. citizens]*

4. That if the word "person" as used in the treaty includes citizens of the asylum country, the treaty, in so far as it covers that subject, has been abrogated by the conduct of Italy in refusing to deliver up its own citizens upon the demand of the United States, and by the enactment of a municipal law, since the treaty, forbidding the extradition of citizens.

We will consider these objections in their order:

* * *

3. By Article I of the extradition treaty with Italy the two governments mutually agree to deliver up all persons, who, having been convicted of or charged with any of the crimes specified in the following article, committed within the jurisdiction of one of the contracting parties, shall seek an asylum in the other, etc. It is claimed by counsel for the appellant that the word "persons" as used in this article does not include persons who are citizens of the asylum country.

That the word "persons" etymologically includes citizens as well as those who are not, can hardly be debatable. The treaty contains no reservation of citizens of the country of asylum. The contention is that an express exclusion of citizens or subjects is not necessary, as by implication, from accepted principles of public law, persons who are citizens of the asylum country are excluded from extradition conventions unless expressly included. * * *

* * * This interpretation has been consistently upheld by the United States, and enforced under the several treaties which do not exempt citizens. That Italy has not conformed to this view, and the effect of this attitude will be considered later. But that the United States has always construed its obligation as embracing its citizens is illustrated by the action of the executive branch of the Government in this very instance. A construction of a treaty by the political department of the Government, while not conclusive upon a court called upon to construe such a treaty in a matter involving personal rights, is nevertheless of much weight. * * *

4. We come now to the contention that by the refusal of Italy to deliver up fugitives of Italian nationality, the treaty has thereby ceased to be of obligation on the United States. The attitude of Italy is indicated by its Penal Code of 1900 which forbids the extradition of citizens, and by the denial in two or more instances to recognize this obligation of the treaty as extending to its citizens.

* * *

This adherence to a view of the obligation of the treaty as not requiring one country to surrender its nationals while it did the other, presented a situation in which the United States might do either of two things, namely: abandon its own interpretation of the word "persons" as including citizens, or adhere to its own interpretation and surrender the appellant, although the obligation had, as to nationals, ceased to be reciprocal. The United States could not yield its own interpretation of the treaty, since that would have had the most serious consequence on five other treaties in which the word "persons" had been used in its ordinary meaning, as including, all persons, and, therefore, not exempting citizens. If the attitude of Italy was, as contended, a violation of the obligation of the treaty, which, in international law, would have justified the United States in denouncing the treaty as no longer obligatory, it did not automatically have that effect. If the United States elected not to declare its abrogation, or come to a rupture, the treaty would remain in force. It was only voidable, not void; and if the United States should prefer, it might waive any breach which in its judgment had occurred and conform to its own obligation as if there had been no such breach.

* * *

That the political branch of the Government recognizes the treaty obligation as still existing is evidenced by its action in this case. In the memorandum giving the reasons of the Department of State for determining to surrender the appellant, after stating the difference between the two governments as to the interpretation of this clause of the treaty, Mr. Secretary Knox said:

> The question is now for the first time presented as to whether or not the United States is under obligation under treaty to surrender to Italy for trial and punishment citizens of

the United States fugitive from the justice of Italy, notwithstanding the interpretation placed upon the treaty by Italy with reference to Italian subjects. In this connection it should be observed that the United States, although, as stated above, consistently contending that the Italian interpretation was not the proper one, has not treated the Italian practice as a breach of the treaty obligation necessarily requiring abrogation, has not abrogated the treaty or taken any step looking thereto, and has, on the contrary, constantly regarded the treaty as in full force and effect and has answered the obligations imposed thereby and has invoked the rights therein granted. It should, moreover, be observed that even though the action of the Italian Government be regarded as a breach of the treaty, the treaty is binding until abrogated, its provisions are operative against us.

The question would, therefore, appear to reduce itself to one of interpretation of the meaning of the treaty, the Government of the United States being now for the first time called upon to declare whether it regards the treaty as obliging it to surrender its citizens to Italy, notwithstanding Italy has not and insists it can not surrender its citizens to us. It should be observed, in the first place, that we have always insisted not only with reference to the Italian extradition treaty, but with reference to the other extradition treaties similarly phrased that the word "persons" includes citizens. We are, therefore, committed to that interpretation. The fact that we have for reasons already given ceased generally to make requisition upon the Government of Italy for the surrender of Italian subjects under the treaty, would not require of necessity that we should, as a matter of logic or law, regard ourselves as free from the obligation of surrendering our citizens, we laboring under no such legal inhibition regarding surrender as operates against the government of Italy. Therefore, since extradition treaties need not be reciprocal, even in the matter of the surrendering of citizens, it would seem entirely sound to consider ourselves as bound to surrender our citizens to Italy even though Italy should not, by reason of the provisions of her municipal law be able to surrender its citizens to us.

The executive department having thus elected to waive any right to free itself from the obligation to deliver up its own citizens, it is the plain duty of this court to recognize the obligation to surrender the appellant as one imposed by the treaty as the supreme law of the land and as affording authority for the warrant of extradition.

Judgment affirmed.

INTERNATIONAL LAW COMMISSION DRAFT ARTICLES ON THE LAW OF TREATIES

61 American Journal of International Law 263, 422 (1967).

Commentary [a]

(1) The great majority of jurists recognize that a violation of a treaty by one party may give rise to a right in the other party to abrogate the treaty or to suspend the performance of its own obligations under a treaty. A violation of a treaty obligation, as of any other obligation, may give rise to a right in the other party to take non-forcible reprisals, and these reprisals may properly relate to the defaulting party's rights under the treaty. Opinion differs, however, as to the extent of the right to abrogate the treaty and the conditions under which it may be exercised. Some jurists, in the absence of effective international machinery for securing the observance of treaties, are more impressed with the innocent party's need to have this right as a sanction for the violation of the treaty. They tend to formulate the right in unqualified terms, giving the innocent party a general right to abrogate the treaty in the event of a breach. Other jurists are more impressed with the risk that a State may allege a trivial or even fictitious breach simply to furnish a pretext for denouncing a treaty which it now finds embarrassing. These jurists tend to restrict the right of denunciation to "material" or "fundamental" breaches and also to subject the exercise of the right to procedural conditions.

(2) State practice does not give great assistance in determining the true extent of this right or the proper conditions for its exercise. In many cases, the denouncing state has decided for quite other reasons to put an end to the treaty and, having alleged the violation primarily to provide a pretext for its action, has not been prepared to enter into a serious discussion of the legal principles involved. The other party has usually contested the denunciation primarily on the basis of the facts; and, if it has sometimes used language appearing to deny that unilateral denunciation is ever justified, this has usually appeared rather to be a protest against the one-sided and arbitrary pronouncements of the denouncing state than a rejection of the right to denounce when serious violations are established.

(3) Municipal courts have not infrequently made pronouncements recognizing the principle that the violation of a treaty may entitle the innocent party to denounce it. But they have nearly always done so in cases where their government had not in point of fact elected to denounce the treaty, and they have not found it necessary to examine the conditions for the application of the principle at all closely.

a. On Draft Article 57 (now Treaty Article 60).

(4) In the case of the Diversion of Water from the Meuse, Belgium contended that, by constructing certain works contrary to the terms of the Treaty of 1863, Holland had forfeited the right to invoke the treaty against it. Belgium did not claim to denounce the treaty, but it did assert a right, as a defence to Holland's claim, to suspend the operation of one of the provisions of the treaty on the basis of Holland's alleged breach of that provision, although it pleaded its claim rather as an application of the principle inadimplenti non est adimplendum. The Court, having found that Holland had not violated the treaty, did not pronounce upon the Belgian contention. In a dissenting opinion, however, Judge Anzilotti expressed the view that the principle underlying the Belgian contention is "so just, so equitable, so universally recognized that it must be applied in international relations also." The only other case that seems to be of much significance is the Tacna-Arica Arbitration. There Peru contended that by preventing the performance of Article 3 of the Treaty of Ancon, which provided for the holding of a plebiscite under certain conditions in the disputed area, Chile had discharged Peru from her obligations under that article. The Arbitrator, after examining the evidence, rejected the Peruvian contention, saying:

> It is manifest that if abuses of administration could have the effect of terminating such an agreement, it would be necessary to establish such serious conditions as the consequence of administrative wrongs as would operate to frustrate the purpose of the agreement, and, in the opinion of the Arbitrator, a situation of such gravity has not been shown.

This pronouncement seems to assume that only a "fundamental" breach of Article 3 by Chile could have justified Peru in claiming to be released from its provisions.

(5) The Commission was agreed that a breach of a treaty, however serious, does not ipso facto put an end to the treaty, and also that it is not open to a state simply to allege a violation of the treaty and pronounce the treaty at an end. On the other hand, it considered that within certain limits and subject to certain safeguards the right of a party to invoke the breach of a treaty as a ground for terminating it or suspending its operation must be recognized. Some members considered that it would be dangerous for the Commission to endorse such a right, unless its exercise were to be made subject to control by compulsory reference to the International Court of Justice. The Commission, while recognizing the importance of providing proper safeguards against arbitrary denunciation of a treaty on the ground of an alleged breach, concluded that the question of providing safeguards against arbitrary action was a general one which affected several articles. It, therefore, decided to formulate in the present article the substantive conditions under which a treaty may be terminated or its operation suspended in consequence of a breach, and to deal with the question of the procedural safeguards in Article 62.

The Geneva Accords of 1954 and treaty breach.   Much of the legal argument about the military action of the United States and North Vietnam in South Vietnam revolves around claims of breaches of the Geneva Accords that accompanied French departure from that area in 1954.   For analyses of the United States position on the law of treaty breach as applied to Vietnam, see Chapter 19.

Chapter 16

INTERNATIONAL AGREEMENTS: THE LAW OF THE UNITED STATES

SECTION A. THE TREATY POWER

CONSTITUTION OF THE UNITED STATES

Article I, Section 10

Clause 3. No State shall, without the Consent of Congress, * * *, enter into any Agreement or Compact with another State or with a foreign Power, * * *

Article II, Section 2

Clause 2. He [the President] shall have Power, by and with the Advice and Consent of the Senate, to make Treaties, provided two-thirds of the Senators present concur; and he shall nominate, and by and with the Advice and Consent of the Senate, shall appoint Ambassadors, other public Ministers and Consuls, * * *

Article II, Section 3

Clause 1. * * * [H]e shall receive Ambassadors and other public Ministers; * * *

Article VI

Clause 2. This Constitution, and the laws of the United States which shall be made in Pursuance thereof; and all Treaties made, or which shall be made, under the Authority of the United States, shall be the supreme Law of the Land; and the Judges in every State shall be bound thereby, any Thing in the Constitution or Laws of any State to the Contrary notwithstanding.

Amendment 10

The powers not delegated to the United States by the Constitution, nor prohibited by it to the States, are reserved to the States respectively, or to the people.

MISSOURI v. HOLLAND

United States, Supreme Court, 1920.
252 U.S. 416, 40 S.Ct. 382.

MR. JUSTICE HOLMES delivered the opinion of the court.

This is a bill in equity brought by the State of Missouri to prevent a game warden of the United States from attempting to enforce the Migratory Bird Treaty Act of July 3, 1918, c. 128, 40 Stat. 755, and the regulations made by the Secretary of Agriculture in pursuance of the same. The ground of the bill is that the statute is an unconstitutional interference with the rights reserved to the States by the Tenth Amendment, and that the acts of the defendant done and threatened under that authority invade the sovereign right of the State and contravene its will manifested in statutes. The State also alleges a pecuniary interest, as owner of the wild birds within its borders and otherwise, admitted by the Government to be sufficient, but it is enough that the bill is a reasonable and proper means to assert the alleged quasi sovereign rights of a State. Kansas v. Colorado, 185 U.S. 125, 142, 22 S.Ct. 552; Georgia v. Tennessee Copper Co., 206 U.S. 230, 237, 27 S.Ct. 618; Marshall Dental Manufacturing Co. v. Iowa, 26 U.S. 460, 462, 33 S.Ct. 168. A motion to dismiss was sustained by the District Court on the ground that the act of Congress is constitutional. 258 Fed. 479. Acc. United States v. Thompson, 258 Fed. 257; United States v. Rockefeller, 260 Fed. 346. The State appeals.

On December 8, 1916, a treaty between the United States and Great Britain was proclaimed by the President. It recited that many species of birds in their annual migrations traversed certain parts of the United States and of Canada, that they were of great value as a source of food and in destroying insects injurious to vegetation, but were in danger of extermination through lack of adequate protection. It therefore provided for specified close[d] seasons and protection in other forms, and agreed that the two powers would take or propose to their law-making bodies the necessary measures for carrying the treaty out. 39 Stat. 1702. The above mentioned Act of July 3, 1918, entitled an act to give effect to the convention, prohibited the killing, capturing or selling any of the migratory birds included in the terms of the treaty except as permitted by regulations compatible with those terms, to be made by the Secretary of Agriculture. Regulations were proclaimed on July 31, and October 25, 1918. 40 Stat. 1812; 1863. It is unnecessary to go into any details, because, as we have said, the question raised is the general one whether the treaty and statute are void as an interference with the rights reserved to the States.

To answer this question it is not enough to refer to the Tenth Amendment, reserving the powers not delegated to the United States,

because by Article II, § 2, the power to make treaties is delegated *supremacy*
expressly, and by Article VI treaties made under the authority of
the United States, along with the Constitution and laws of the United
States made in pursuance thereof, are declared the supreme law
of the land. If the treaty is valid there can be no dispute about the *necessary*
validity of the statute under Article I, § 8, as a necessary and proper *proper*
means to execute the powers of the Government. The language of
the Constitution as to the supremacy of treaties being general, the
question before us is narrowed to an inquiry into the ground upon
which the present supposed exception is placed.

It is said that a treaty cannot be valid if it infringes the Constitution, that there are limits, therefore, to the treatymaking power,
and that one such limit is that what an act of Congress could not do
unaided, in derogation of the powers reserved to the States, a treaty
cannot do. An earlier act of Congress that attempted by itself and
not in pursuance of a treaty to regulate the killing of migratory birds
within the States had been held bad in the District Court. United
States v. Shauver, 214 Fed. 154; United States v. McCullagh, 221
Fed. 288. Those decisions were supported by arguments that migratory birds were owned by the States in their sovereign capacity
for the benefit of their people, and that under cases like Geer v.
Connecticut, 161 U.S. 519, 16 S.Ct. 600, this control was one that
Congress had no power to displace. The same argument is supposed
to apply now with equal force.

Whether the two cases cited were decided rightly or not they
cannot be accepted as a test of the treaty power. Acts of Congress
are the supreme law of the land only when made in pursuance of the
Constitution, while treaties are declared to be so when made under
the authority of the United States. It is open to question whether
the authority of the United States means more than the formal acts
prescribed to make the convention. We do not mean to imply that
there are no qualifications to the treaty-making power; but they
must be ascertained in a different way. It is obvious that there may *qualification*
be matters of the sharpest exigency for the national well being that
an act of Congress could not deal with but that a treaty followed by
such an act could, and it is not lightly to be assumed that, in matters
requiring national action, "a power which must belong to and somewhere reside in every civilized government" is not to be found. Andrews v. Andrews, 188 U.S. 14, 33, 23 S.Ct. 237. What was said
in that case with regard to the powers of the States applies with
equal force to the powers of the nation in cases where the States
individually are incompetent to act. We are not yet discussing the
particular case before us but only are considering the validity of the
test proposed. With regard to that we may add that when we are
dealing with words that also are a constituent act, like the Constitution of the United States, we must realize that they have called into
life a being the development of which could not have been foreseen

FRAMERS

completely by the most gifted of its begetters. It was enough for them to realize or to hope that they had created an organism; it has taken a century and has cost their successors much sweat and blood to prove that they created a nation. The case before us must be considered in the light of our whole experience and not merely in that of what was said a hundred years ago. The treaty in question does not contravene any prohibitory words to be found in the Constitution. The only question is whether it is forbidden by some invisible radiation from the general terms of the Tenth Amendment. We must consider what this country has become in deciding what that Amendment has reserved.

ADAPTIVE

STATES HAVE NO TITLE TO MIGRATORY BIRDS

The State as we have intimated founds its claim of exclusive authority upon an assertion of title to migratory birds, an assertion that is embodied in statute. No doubt it is true that as between a State and its inhabitants the State may regulate the killing and sale of such birds, but it does not follow that its authority is exclusive of paramount powers. To put the claim of the State upon title is to lean upon a slender reed. Wild birds are not in the possession of anyone; and possession is the beginning of ownership. The whole foundation of the State's rights is the presence within their jurisdiction of birds that yesterday had not arrived, tomorrow may be in another State and in a week a thousand miles away. If we are to be accurate we cannot put the case of the State upon higher ground than that the treaty deals with creatures that for the moment are within the state borders, that it must be carried out by officers of the United States within the same territory, and that but for the treaty the State would be free to regulate this subject itself.

As most of the laws of the United States are carried out within the States and as many of them deal with matters which in the silence of such laws the State might regulate, such general grounds are not enough to support Missouri's claim. Valid treaties of course "are as binding within the territorial limits of the States as they are elsewhere throughout the dominion of the United States." Baldwin v. Franks, 120 U.S. 678, 683, 7 S.Ct. 656, 657. No doubt the great body of private relations usually fall within the control of the State, but a treaty may override its power. We do not have to invoke the later developments of constitutional law for this proposition; it was recognized as early as Hopkirk v. Bell, 3 Cranch, 454, with regard to statutes of limitation, and even earlier, as to confiscation, in Ware v. Hylton, 3 Dall. 199. It was assumed by Chief Justice Marshall with regard to the escheat of land to the State in Chirac v. Chirac, 2 Wheat. 259, 275; Hauenstein v. Wynham, 100 U.S. 483; Geofroy v. Riggs, 133 U.S. 258, 10 S.Ct. 295; Blythe v. Hinckley, 180 U.S. 333, 340, 21 S.Ct. 390. So as to a limited jurisdiction of foreign consuls within a State. Wildenhus's Case, 120 U.S. 1, 7 S.Ct. 385. See Ross v. McIntyre, 140 U.S. 453, 11 S.Ct. 897. Further illustration seems unnecessary, and it only remains to consider the application of established rules to the present case.

Here a national interest of very nearly the first magnitude is involved. It can be protected only by national action in concert with that of another power. The subject-matter is only transitorily within the State and has no permanent habitat therein. But for the treaty and the statute there soon might be no birds for any powers to deal with. We see nothing in the Constitution that compels the Government to sit by while a food supply is cut off and the protectors of our forests and our crops are destroyed. It is not sufficient to rely upon the States. The reliance is vain, and were it otherwise, the question is whether the United States is forbidden to act. We are of opinion that the treaty and statute must be upheld. Carey v. South Dakota, 250 U.S. 118, 39 S.Ct. 403.

[handwritten margin note: NATIONAL INTEREST]

Decree affirmed.

MR. JUSTICE VAN DEVANTER and MR. JUSTICE PITNEY dissent.

REID v. COVERT

United States Supreme Court, 1957.
354 U.S. 1, 77 S.Ct. 1222.

MR. JUSTICE BLACK announced the judgment of the Court and delivered an opinion, in which THE CHIEF JUSTICE, MR. JUSTICE DOUGLAS, and MR. JUSTICE BRENNAN join.

These cases raise basic constitutional issues of the utmost concern. They call into question the role of the military under our system of government. They involve the power of Congress to expose civilians to trial by military tribunals, under military regulations and procedures, for offenses against the United States thereby depriving them of trial in civilian courts, under civilian laws and procedures and with all the safeguards of the Bill of Rights. These cases are particularly significant because for the first time since the adoption of the Constitution wives of soldiers have been denied trial by jury in a court of law and forced to trial before courts-martial.

In No. 701 Mrs. Clarice Covert killed her husband, a sergeant in the United States Air Force, at an airbase in England. Mrs. Covert, who was not a member of the armed services, was residing on the base with her husband at the time. She was tried by a court-martial for murder under Article 118 of the Uniform Code of Military Justice (UCMJ). The trial was on charges preferred by Air Force personnel and the court-martial was composed of Air Force officers. The court-martial asserted jurisdiction over Mrs. Covert under Article 2(11) of the UCMJ, which provides:

The following persons are subject to this code:

* * *

(11) Subject to the provisions of any treaty or agreement to ✓ which the United States is or may be a party or to any accepted rule of international law, all persons serving with, employed by, or accompanying the armed forces without the continental limits of the United States * * *

Counsel for Mrs. Covert contended that she was insane at the time she killed her husband, but the military tribunal found her guilty of murder and sentenced her to life imprisonment. The judgment was affirmed by the Air Force Board of Review, 16 CMR 465, but was reversed by the Court of Military Appeals, 6 USCMA 48, because of prejudicial errors concerning the defense of insanity. While Mrs. Covert was being held in this country pending a proposed retrial by court-martial in the District of Columbia, her counsel petitioned the District Court for a writ of habeas corpus to set her free on the ground that the Constitution forbade her trial by military authorities. Construing this Court's decision in United States ex rel. Toth v. Quarles, 350 U.S. 11, 76 S.Ct. 1, as holding that "a civilian is entitled to a civilian trial" the District Court held that Mrs. Covert could not be tried by court-martial and ordered her released from ✓ custody. The Government appealed directly to this Court under 28 U.S.C.A. § 1252. See 350 U.S. 985, 76 S.Ct. 476.

In No. 713 Mrs. Dorothy Smith killed her husband, an Army officer, at a post in Japan where she was living with him. She was tried for murder by a court-martial and despite considerable evidence that she was insane was found guilty and sentenced to life imprisonment. The judgment was approved by the Army Board of Review, 10 CMR 350, 13 CMR 307, and the Court of Military Appeals, 5 USCMA 314. Mrs. Smith was then confined in a federal penitentiary in West Virginia. Her father, respondent here, filed a petition for habeas corpus in a District Court for West Virginia. The petition charged that the court-martial was without jurisdiction because Article 2(11) of the UCMJ was unconstitutional insofar as it authorized the trial of civilian dependents accompanying servicemen overseas. The District Court refused to issue the writ, 137 F.Supp. 806, and while an appeal was pending in the Court of Appeals for the Fourth Circuit we granted certiorari at the request of the Government, 350 U.S. 986, 76 S.Ct. 476.

✓The two cases were consolidated and argued last Term and a majority of the Court, with three Justices dissenting and one reserving opinion, held that military trial of Mrs. Smith and Mrs. Covert for their alleged offenses was constitutional. 351 U.S. 470, 76 S.Ct. 886; 351 U.S. 487, 76 S.Ct. 880. The majority held that the provisions of Article III and the Fifth and Sixth Amendments which require that crimes be tried by a jury after indictment by a grand jury did not protect an American citizen when he was tried by the American Government in foreign lands for offenses committed there and that Congress could provide for the trial of such offenses in any manner it saw fit so long as the procedures established were reasonable and consonant with due process. The opinion then went on to express the view that military trials, as now practiced, were not unreasonable or arbitrary when applied to dependents accompanying members of the armed forces overseas. In reaching their conclusion the majority found it unnecessary to consider the power of Congress "To make Rules for the Government and Regulation of the land and naval Forces" under Article I of the Constitution.

Subsequently, the Court granted a petition for rehearing, 352 U.S. 901, 77 S.Ct. 124. Now, after further argument and consideration, we conclude that the previous decisions cannot be permitted to stand. We hold that Mrs. Smith and Mrs. Covert could not constitutionally be tried by military authorities.

* * *

At the time of Mrs. Covert's alleged offense, an executive agreement was in effect between the United States and Great Britain which permitted United States' military courts to exercise exclusive jurisdiction over offenses committed in Great Britain by American servicemen or their dependents.[29] For its part, the United States agreed that these military courts would be willing and able to try and to punish all offenses against the laws of Great Britain by such persons. In all material respects, the same situation existed in Japan when Mrs. Smith killed her husband.[30] Even though a court-martial does not give an accused trial by jury and other Bill of Rights protections,

29. Executive Agreement of July 27, 1942, 57 Stat. 1193. The arrangement now in effect in Great Britain and the other North Atlantic Treaty Organization nations, as well as in Japan, is the NATO Status of Forces Agreement, 4 U. S. Treaties and Other International Agreements 1792, T.I.A.S. 2846, which by its terms gives the foreign nation primary jurisdiction to try dependents accompanying American servicemen for offenses which are violations of the law of both the foreign nation and the United States. Art. VII, §§ 1(b), 3(a). The foreign nation has exclusive criminal jurisdiction over dependents for offenses which only violate its laws. Art. VII, § 2(b). However, the Agreement contains provisions which require that the foreign nations provide procedural safeguards for our nations tried under the terms of the Agreement in their courts. Art. VII, § 9. Generally, see Note, 70 Harv.L.Rev. 1043.

Apart from those persons subject to the Status of Forces and comparable agreements and certain other restricted classes of Americans, a foreign nation has plenary criminal jurisdiction, of course, over all Americans—tourists, residents, businessmen, government employees and so forth—who commit offenses against its law within its territory.

30. See Administrative Agreement, 3 U. S. Treaties and Other International Agreements 3341, T.I.A.S. 2492.

the Government contends that Art. 2(11) of the UCMJ, insofar as it provides for the military trial of dependents accompanying the armed forces in Great Britain and Japan, can be sustained as legislation which is necessary and proper to carry out the United States' obligations under the international agreements made with those countries. The obvious and decisive answer to this, of course, is that no agreement with a foreign nation can confer power on the Congress, or on any other branch of Government, which is free from the restraints of the Constitution.

Article VI, the Supremacy Clause of the Constitution, declares:

> This Constitution, and the Laws of the United States which shall be made in Pursuance thereof; and all Treaties made, or which shall be made, under the Authority of the United States, shall be the supreme Law of the Land; * * *

There is nothing in this language which intimates the treaties and laws enacted pursuant to them do not have to comply with the provisions of the Constitution. Nor is there anything in the debates which accompanied the drafting and ratification of the Constitution which even suggests such a result. These debates as well as the history that surrounds the adoption of the treaty provision in Article VI make it clear that the reason treaties were not limited to those made in "pursuance" of the Constitution was so that agreements made by the United States under the Articles of Confederation, including the important peace treaties which concluded the Revolutionary War, would remain in effect. It would be manifestly contrary to the objectives of those who created the Constitution, as well as those who were responsible for the Bill of Rights—let alone alien to our entire constitutional history and tradition—to construe Article VI as permitting the United States to exercise power under an international agreement without observing constitutional prohibitions. In effect, such construction would permit amendment of that document in a manner not sanctioned by Article V. The prohibitions of the Constitution were designed to apply to all branches of the National Government and they cannot be nullified by the Executive or by the Executive and the Senate combined.

There is nothing new or unique about what we say here. This Court has regularly and uniformly recognized the supremacy of the Constitution over a treaty.[33] For example, in Geofroy v. Riggs, 133 U.S. 258, 267, 10 S.Ct. 295, 297, it declared:

> The treaty power, as expressed in the Constitution, is in terms unlimited except by those restraints which are found in

---

33. E. g., United States v. Minnesota, 270 U.S. 181, 207–208, 46 S.Ct. 298, 305–306; Holden v. Joy, 17 Wall. 211, 242–243; The Cherokee Tobacco, 11 Wall. 616, 620–621; Doe v. Braden, 16 How. 635, 657. Cf. Marbury v. Madison, 1 Cranch 137, 176–180. We recognize that executive agreements are involved here but it cannot be contended that such an agreement rises to greater stature than a treaty.

that instrument against the action of the government or of its departments, and those arising from the nature of the government itself and of that of the States. It would not be contended that it extends so far as to authorize what the Constitution forbids, or a change in the character of the government or in that of one of the States, or a cession of any portion of the territory of the latter, without its consent.

This Court has also repeatedly taken the position that an Act of Congress, which must comply with the Constitution, is on a full parity with a treaty, and that when a statute which is subsequent in time is inconsistent with a treaty, the statute to the extent of conflict renders the treaty null.[34] It would be completely anomalous to say that a treaty need not comply with the Constitution when such an agreement can be overridden by a statute that must conform to that instrument.

There is nothing in Missouri v. Holland, 252 U.S. 416, 40 S.Ct. 382, which is contrary to the position taken here. There the Court carefully noted that the treaty involved was not inconsistent with any specific provision of the Constitution. The Court was concerned with the Tenth Amendment which reserves to the States or the people all power not delegated to the National Government. To the extent that the United States can validly make treaties, the people and the States have delegated their power to the National Government and the Tenth Amendment is no barrier.

In summary, we conclude that the Constitution in its entirety applied to the trials of Mrs. Smith and Mrs. Covert. Since their court-martial did not meet the requirements of Art. III, § 2 or the Fifth and Sixth Amendments we are compelled to determine if there is anything *within* the Constitution which authorizes the military trial of dependents accompanying the armed forces overseas.

* * *

In No. 701, Reid v. Covert, the judgment of the District Court directing that Mrs. Covert be released from custody is affirmed.

In No. 713, Kinsella v. Krueger, the judgment of the District Court is reversed and the case is remanded with instructions to order Mrs. Smith released from custody.

Reversed and remanded.

34. In Whitney v. Robertson, 124 U.S. 190, 8 S.Ct. 456 at page 458, the Court stated, at p. 194: "By the Constitution a treaty is placed on the same footing, and made of like obligation, with an act of legislation. Both are declared by that instrument to be the supreme law of the land, and no superior efficacy is given to either over the other * * * [I]f the two are inconsistent, the one last in date will control the other * * * " Head Money Cases, 112 U.S. 580, 5 S.Ct. 247; Botiller v. Dominguez, 130 U.S. 238, 9 S.Ct. 525; Chae Chan Ping v. United States, 130 U.S. 581, 9 S.Ct. 623. See Clark v. Allen, 331 U.S. 503, 509–510, 67 S.Ct. 1431, 1435–1436; Moser v. United States, 341 U.S. 41, 45, 71 S.Ct. 553, 555.

MR. JUSTICE WHITTAKER took no part in the consideration or decision of these cases.

MR. JUSTICE FRANKFURTER, concurring in the result.

* * *

A further argument is made that a decision adverse to the Government would mean that only a foreign trial could be had. Even assuming that the NATO Status of Forces Agreement, 4 U. S. Treaties and Other International Agreements 1792, T.I.A.S. 2846, covering countries where a large part of our armed forces are stationed, gives jurisdiction to the United States only through its military authorities, this Court cannot speculate that any given nation would be unwilling to grant or continue such extraterritorial jurisdiction over civilian dependents in capital cases if they were to be tried by some other manner than court-martial. And, even if such were the case, these civilian dependents would then merely be in the same position as are so many federal employees and their dependents and other United States citizens who are subject to the laws of foreign nations when residing there. * * *

[Opinion of Mr. Justice Harlan, concurring in the result, omitted.]

MR. JUSTICE CLARK, with whom MR. JUSTICE BURTON joins, dissenting.

* * *

Before discussing the power of the Congress under Art. I, § 8, cl. 14, of the Constitution it is well to take our bearings. These cases do not involve the jurisdiction of a military court-martial sitting within the territorial limits of the United States. Nor are they concerned with the power of the Government to make treaties or the legal relationship between treaties and the Constitution. Nor are they concerned with the power of Congress to provide for the trial of Americans sojourning, touring, or temporarily residing in foreign nations. Essentially, we are to determine only whether the civilian dependents of American servicemen may constitutionally be tried by an American military court-martial in a foreign country for an offense committed in that country.

* * *

The only alternative remaining—probably the alternative that the Congress will now be forced to choose—is that Americans committing offenses on foreign soil be tried by the courts of the country in which the offense is committed. Foreign courts have exclusive jurisdiction under the principles of international law and many nations enjoy concurrent jurisdiction with the American military authorities pursuant to Article VII of the Agreement Regarding Status of Forces of Parties to the North Atlantic Treaty. Where the American military authorities do have jurisdiction, it is only by mutual agreement with the foreign sovereign concerned and pursuant to carefully drawn agreements conditioned on trial by the American military authorities. Typical of these agreements was the one concluded between the United States and Japan on February 28, 1952, and in force at the time one of these cases arose. Under this and like agreements, the jurisdiction so ceded to the United States military courts will surely be withdrawn if the services are impotent to exercise it. It is clear that trial before an American court-martial in which the fundamentals of due process are observed is preferable to leaving American servicemen and their dependents to the widely varying standards of justice in foreign courts throughout the world. Under these circumstances it is untenable to say that Congress could have exercised a lesser power adequate to the end proposed.

ALTERNATIE

* * *

Questions on the constitutionality of the human rights conventions.

a.   Are there constitutional impediments to the United States becoming a party to the human rights conventions sponsored by the United Nations? Refer in particular to the conventions in the Documentary Supplement: Economic, Social and Cultural Rights; Civil and Political Rights; Elimination of All Forms of Racial Discrimination; Genocide. Consider Article 4 of the Convention on Racial Discrimination and Article 19 of the Convention on Civil and Political Rights. Is Article 5 of the Convention on Civil and Political Rights relevant to the question of the constitutionality of that convention as a whole?

b.   Do the human rights treaties embody a "bargain" with foreign states? Must they, to be within the treaty power? If a "treaty" does not involve a bargaining of concessions between the negotiating states, some have argued that it does not involve a matter of "international concern." If a putative treaty does not involve a matter of international concern, the argument continues, the arrangement is not really a "treaty" within the meaning of the Constitution, and hence the overriding power given to the federal government in Article VI, Clause 2 is not activated. This argument assumes that a decisionmaker, presumably a court, would pass on the question whether the supposedly necessary "international concern" exists in the particular case. Is this evaluation a proper function for courts in the United States? How would the Supreme Court go about making a determination as to whether a treaty was or was not a matter of "international concern?" Could it ever find a treaty not of "international concern" without impugning the good faith of the executive branch, including the President? Of course, even if the courts were not to review a treaty at the constitutional level on the basis of "international concern", senators in giving their advice and consent to the treaty are also obligated, by their oath of office, to consider the question. And even if the senators should find that the treaty is constitutional in this respect, it lies within their responsibilities and prerogatives to determine that the treaty is, nonetheless, undesirable from a policy point of view. The term "international concern" is also used in this latter sense. Nonetheless, as to the human rights treaties, the fundamental question still remains: is it a legitimate use of a treaty power for the President and the Senate to make a human rights treaty supreme law of the land simply if it is desirable to have as many nations as possible promise to adhere to the human rights standards stated in them?

c. What would you have thought of the use of the treaty power under the "supremacy clause" as the legal means of securing equal rights as between the sexes, as an alternative to the proposed amendment the Constitution that is now before the states for ratification? To review your knowledge of the various human rights conventions previously considered, Chapter 9, would any one of them, if acceded to by the United States, have made the new proposed amendment redundant?

SECTION B. PRESIDENTIAL POWERS

The President, the Senate, and the House of Representatives. What institutions of the federal government should participate in the formulation of foreign policy and in the making of internal law by international agreement? Despite the experience of President Washington, detailed below, Senate leaders in recent years have contended that the power as to "advice and consent" to treaties gives the Senate a special role of collaboration with the executive in the formulation of United States foreign policy, even where no specific international agreement is involved.

Leaders of the House of Representatives have not shown much enthusiasm for this concept of senatorial special responsibility. Also, there have been voices in the House that question whether certain types of international agreements in treaty form are valid without House participation, such as a treaty that would scale down or give up the rights of the United States, "as if sovereign", in the Panama Canal Zone. This viewpoint is based on the rule of practice that government property can only be given up by an act of Congress. Sometimes, as in the case of tax treaties, the special responsibility of the House as to revenue measures is respected by the practice of making such treaties subject to the enactment of tax legislation by Congress as a whole.

Further, in a revenue measure, Congress may delegate to the ✓ executive, before the fact, the power to make certain types of international agreements, such as those for the reduction of tariffs. The tariff-cutting delegations fix time limits, state maximum cuts, and require periodic reports to Congress. More recently, they specify procedural steps. See Chapter 17, Section B.

As to the possibility that executive agreements not authorized by Congress might force it to go along with the executive, either as to foreign policy lines of action or as to internal legal effect, concern has from time to time been expressed in both chambers, although the Senate has usually taken the lead in expressing it, as in the celebrated Bricker Amendment crisis in the early 1950s. A review of executive-congressional responsibilities was recently conducted by the Senate Committee on Foreign Relations and resulted in the legislation which appears at p. 1016. The hearings are significant because they cover many current aspects of the basic problem. Selected portions of the hearings appear in the Supplement.

If the people of the United States should ever consider a fullscale review of the Constitution what would you think of making those international agreements that now require the approval of two-thirds of the senators subject only to approval by simple majorities in both Houses? If you are generally favorable, would you wish to see all international agreements subject to such approval? If generally favorable to both suggestions, would you be willing to include in the revision a provision that an international agreement of the United States, as so approved, could not be contradicted by subsequent inconsistent legislation? See Chapter 1, p. 26.

II SCHWARTZ, A COMMENTARY ON THE CONSTITUTION OF THE UNITED STATES: THE POWERS OF GOVERNMENT 101, 150 (1963).*

The conception of the Senate as a Presidential council in the diplomatic field broke down as soon as it was tried in practice. In August, 1789, Washington came personally to the Senate to seek its advice on a proposed treaty. As might have been expected, an independent legislative chamber (even one composed of only twenty-six members) was scarcely suited to perform the role of Council of State. Instead of giving the President the speedy advice he sought, the Senators made lengthy speeches on the procedure to be followed. "This defeats every purpose of my coming here!" Washington ex-

* © Bernard Schwartz 1962; reprinted by permission of the publisher, The Macmillan Company, New York.

claimed. As he left the Senate Chamber, he is reported to have declared "That he would be damned if he ever went there again." The account is probably apocryphal, but the fact remains that, after Washington's experience in this respect, neither he nor any other President ever again sought the formal advice of the Senate on a proposed negotiation. The concept of the Senate as an executive council in the field of foreign affairs was thus all but still-born at the outset of the Republic.

With the passing of the notion of association between the President and Senate in the formation of foreign policy, the conception of the President as the sole organ of external affairs has had the field to itself. * * * (at 101)

* * *

That an executive agreement can, in fact, be employed to accomplish the identical purpose as a treaty covering the same subject-matter is dramatically demonstrated by Theodore Roosevelt's action in connection with a proposed treaty with the Dominican Republic. Plenipotentiaries of the two countries had signed an agreement in 1905 in treaty form providing for the collection and disbursement of Dominican customs revenues. The treaty was submitted to the Senate, but that body failed to give its constitutional consent. President Roosevelt then proceeded to put the proposed treaty provisions into effect as an executive agreement. As T. R. put it in his Autobiography: "Somebody had to do that duty, and accordingly I did it. I went ahead and administered the proposed treaty anyhow, considering it as a simple agreement on the part of the Executive."

Having regard only to the legal questions involved, there is no doubt that any President can do what Theodore Roosevelt did in the case of the Dominican treaty. The executive agreement may thus be used as a means of circumventing the treaty-making procedure prescribed in Article II and avoiding the Senatorial control provided for therein. This can be done by the negotiation, in any particular case, of an executive agreement, which the President alone can make, rather than a treaty, which must be confirmed by the Senate.

This is true because, as this section has shown, there is no hard and fast legal line between executive agreements and treaties and they have come to be employed interchangably in most areas of our foreign relations. That even experts in the field cannot really draw other than a purely formal line between treaties and executive agreements is shown by a request addressed to the State Department by a Senator asking them how to distinguish a treaty, which must be approved by the Senate, from an executive agreement, which need not. The State Department unhelpfully defined a treaty as "something they had to send to the Senate in order to get approval by a two-thirds vote. An executive agreement was something they did not have to send to the Senate." This reply, said the Senator who

had sent the request, "reminded me of the time when I was a boy on the farm, and asked the hired man how to tell the difference between a male and a female pigeon. He said, 'You put corn in front of the pigeon. If he picks it up, it is a he; if she picks it up, it is a she.'"
(at 150)

IN CONTEMPT OF THE CONSTITUTION

The New York Times, Dec. 26, 1971, Editorial,
Sec. E, at 8, col. 2.*

Since World War II, the United States has had the privilege of refueling its military planes at an air base in the Portuguese Azores. This arrangement included port facilities for the U. S. Navy. A so-called "executive agreement" was entered into between this Government and Portugal and regularly renewed until 1962, when the Portuguese allowed it to lapse because of their resentment against the Kennedy Administration's anti-colonial policy in Africa. Use of the facilities continued, however, without a formal agreement. About 1,500 American servicemen have been stationed in the Azores for many years.

Earlier this month, President Nixon revived the agreement and not only renewed it for five years but also granted $435 million in economic aid to Portugal without consulting Congress.

Air and Naval bases, the stationing of troops overseas, the granting of money—these are the very substance of foreign policy. If the Senate is to exercise its constitutional authority to advise and consent in the making of foreign policy, it has an obligation to pass judgment on these issues.

Under the North Atlantic Treaty, of which Portugal is a signer, and under various laws enacted in the past the Nixon Administration can find a color of legality for the latest Azores deal. But the truth is that the President did not submit this agreement to the Senate as a treaty because he knew that he could not get two-thirds approval. It is doubtful if he could get the support of a simple majority. Rather than put the question to a test, he has put himself in contempt of the plain intent of the Constitution. It is an odd posture for a President who claims to be a "strict constructionist."

It is worth recalling that in 1947 when President Truman wanted to extend a smaller amount of aid—$400 million—to Greece and Turkey, he addressed a joint session of Congress and committees of Congress held lengthy hearings before approval was granted.

The amount of assistance granted to Portugal is enormous in terms of that small country's limited budget. It is also politically significant because it eases Portugal's budgetary difficulties when her finances are strained by the cost of combating the guerrilla warfare of the black rebels in the African colonies. Do the American people with their anti-colonial traditions wish to provide a subsidy to this last ramshackle little empire?

Senator Case, Republican of New Jersey, and four other members of the Senate Foreign Relations Committee from both parties have challenged Mr. Nixon's highhanded behavior by introducing a resolution calling upon him to submit the Azores agreement to the Senate for ratification as a treaty. If the Senate wishes to restore its constitutional credibility as a partner in the making of foreign policy, it will adopt this resolution.

UNITED STATES DEPARTMENT OF STATE CIRCULAR NUMBER 175

50 American Journal of International Law 784 (1956).

1. Purpose of Circular

1.1 The purpose of this circular is to insure (a) that the function of making treaties and other international agreements is carried out within traditional and constitutional limits; (b) that the objectives to be sought in the negotiation of particular treaties and other international agreements are approved by the Secretary or Under Secretary; (c) that firm positions resulting from negotiations are not undertaken without the approval of the interested Assistant Secretaries or their Deputies; (d) that the final texts developed are approved by the interested Assistant Secretaries or their Deputies and brought to the attention of the Secretary or Under Secretary a reasonable time before signature; and (e) that authorization to sign the final text is secured and appropriate arrangements for signature are made.

1.2 It is a further purpose of this circular to insure that full implementation shall be given to the policy stated in the Secretary's testimony before the Senate Committee on the Judiciary on April 6, 1953, in which he said:

> The Constitution provides that the President shall have power to make treaties by and with the advice and consent of the Senate. This administration recognizes the significance of the word "advice". It will be our effort to see that the Senate gets its opportunity to "advise and consent" in time so that it does not have to choose between adopting treaties it does not like, or embarrassing our international position by rejecting what has already been negotiated out with foreign governments.

* * * I am authorized by the President to advise this Committee, the Senate Foreign Relations Committee, and the House Foreign Affairs Committee as follows:

It has long been recognized that difficulties exist in the determination as to which international agreements should be submitted to the Senate as treaties, which ones should be submitted to both Houses of the Congress, and which ones do not require any Congressional approval.

* * * the Congress is entitled to know the considerations that enter into the determinations as to which procedures are sought to be followed. To that end, when there is any serious question of this nature and the circumstances permit, the Executive Branch will consult with appropriate Congressional leaders and Committees in determining the most suitable way of handling international agreements as they arise.

2. Scope of the Treaty-Making Power

Treaties should be designed to promote United States interests by securing action by foreign governments in a way deemed advantageous to the United States. Treaties are not to be used as a device for the purpose of effecting internal social changes or to try to circumvent the constitutional procedures established in relation to what are essentially matters of domestic concern.

3. Scope of the Executive Agreement-Making Power

Executive agreements shall not be used when the subject matter should be covered by a treaty. The executive agreement form shall be used only for agreements which fall into one or more of the following categories:

a. Agreements which are made pursuant to or in accordance with existing legislation or a treaty;

b. Agreements which are made subject to Congressional approval or implementation; or

c. Agreements which are made under and in accordance with the President's Constitutional power.

* * *

5. Action Required

* * *

5.2 Questions as to Treaty or Executive Agreement Form

Where there is any serious question as to whether an international agreement should be made in the form of a treaty or in the form of an executive agreement made by the President alone or with the consent of both Houses of Congress, the matter shall be brought to the attention of the Secretary by a memorandum prepared by the officer responsible for the contemplated negotiations. This memorandum shall first be routed to the Legal Adviser and the Assistant Secretary for Congressional Relations for their clearance and comment. Thereafter, whenever circumstances permit, consultation shall be had with appropriate Congressional leaders and committees in determining the most suitable way of handling such international agreements, such consultation to be had by the office responsible for the negotiations with the assistance of the Assistant Secretary for Congressional Relations.

* * *

---

1 O'CONNELL, INTERNATIONAL LAW 206 (2d ed. 1970) *

The Constitution of the United States requires the approval of treaties by a two-third majority of the Senate. If, in constitutional law, a mere agreement is not a treaty, and thereby does not require Senate endorsement, the President may, by resort to informal methods of contracting, oblige the nation without the democratic control that the legislative process aims at. Actually the President is rarely so isolated in the matter of executive agreements from Congressional action of some sort as to be independent of legislative control or approval. The term "executive agreement" is a wide one, designed to mark off the boundary between treaties which require the advice and consent of the Senate and those documents, widely but loosely described in international practices as "treaties," which do not. Three main categories of instruments are comprehended: (a) agreements or understandings entered into pursuant to or in accordance with specific directives or authorisation of Congress given antecedently; (b) those not given effect to without such direction or authorisation given subsequently; and (c) those made by the Executive solely in virtue of its constitutional power. Actually, those in the third category are relatively few. The critics of the executive agreements, therefore, must be taken to be attacking, not principally the dangers of Presidential commitment without legislative check, so much as the constitutional rule concerning the effect internally on the States of informal international agreements; implied in the argument is that State sovereignty is insufficiently protected by Joint Resolution of both Houses, and that the more obstructive process of a two-third Senate majority is necessary.

The principal example of an executive agreement in the third category was the Litvinov Agreement between President Roosevelt and the Soviet Ambassador which affected suits between private claimants and the Soviet. * * *

* * *

* Reprinted with the permission of O'Connell and Stevens & Sons, Ltd., London.

The question is whether an international commitment of the United States is required by the Constitution to be in treaty as distinct from agreement form. The question is usually resolved on an ad hoc basis by consultation between the Executive and Congress, taking into account the extent to which the agreement can be carried out by the former without encroaching on the domain of the latter. Whenever there is a serious doubt as to whether an international agreement should be in the form of a treaty or in the form of an executive agreement the matter must be brought to the attention of the Secretary of State by memorandum with comments of the Legal Adviser. It is then referred to Congress through the office of the Assistant Secretary for Congressional Relations. If it is decided that the matter may be dealt with by executive agreement the next question that arises is whether such agreement should be supported, antecedently or subsequently, by a Joint Resolution or an Act so as to acquire legislative character, or whether it may be left within the President's constitutional authority. It is accepted that this authority is to be deduced from those provisions of the Constitution which confer exclusive power on the President, such as command of the armed forces, and it is quite certain that it is limited by the stated guarantees of the Constitution. Since the field of executive action proper is necessarily limited, the bulk of executive agreements are made with Congressional co-operation, and this, in fact, is the case with some 90 per cent. of those actually contracted.

[handwritten margin note: PROCEDURE TO DISTINGUISH APPROPRIATE SUBJECT MATTER FOR EXEC. AGREEMENTS]

Annex

Select List of Executive Agreements

Category 1 (prior Congressional approval)

Agriculture:	Migration of Mexican agricultural workers. 57 Stat. 70, 73; 58 Stat. 15; 59 Stat. 645; 61 Stat. 55; 50 U.S.C. App. 1355(g). Co-operative agricultural programmes. 61 Stat. 780.
Aid, Foreign:	Assistance agreements with Greece and Turkey. 61 Stat. 103, 610; 62 Stat. 157.
Anthropology:	Co-operation in research. 53 Stat. 1290; 22 U.S.C. 501–502.
Civil Air Routes:	International Civil Aviation Convention. T.I.A.S. 1591; 61 Stat., pt. 2, 1180.

Civil Defence:	Defence Agreement with Canada. Public Law 920, 81st Cong.; 64 Stat. 1245.
Claims:	War Damage Act. 55 Stat. 880; 57 Stat. 66; 59 Stat. 511; 31 U.S.C. 224 d—224 i–1; 63 Stat. 279, 878.
Copyright:	Extension of time agreements. 55 Stat. 732. Rights affected by war. 60 Stat. 568, 940; 61 Stat. 413. Lend-Lease Act. 55 Stat. 732; 22 U.S.C. 411–419.
Economic Co-operation:	Foreign Assistance Act 1948. 62 Stat. 137, 150, 153. Foreign Aid Appropriation Act 1949. 62 Stat. 1054.
Educational Programmes:	Fulbright Act. 61 Stat. 780; 60 Stat. 754; Public Law 584. 79th Cong.
Lend-Lease:	Lend-Lease Act 1941. 55 Stat. 31; 57 Stat. 222; 58 Stat. 223; 59 Stat. 52; 22 U.S.C. 411–419.
Military Service:	Reciprocal agreements for service of aliens. 50 U.S.C. App. 301–318.
Passport Visas:	Abolition of. 43 Stat. 976; 8 U.S.C. 202(i).
Postal Conventions:	Rev.Stat., sec. 398; 48 Stat. 943. This confers on the Postmaster-General power to conclude postal agreements.
Shipping:	International Convention for the Safety of Life at Sea. 50 Stat. 1121.
Taxation, Double:	Internal Revenue Code. 26 U.S.C. 212(b), 231(d).
Trade:	Trade Agreement with Iceland. 57 Stat. 1075, 1094; E.A.S. No. 342; U.N.T.S., Vol. 29, p. 317. GATT (Tariff Act 1950). 19 U.S.C. 1351(a).

Category 2 (subsequent Congressional approval)

ILO	Joint Resolution, 1934, 48 Stat. 1182.
	" "	1938, 62 Stat. 1151.
UNNRA	" "	1944, 58 Stat. 122; 59 Stat. U.S.C. 1571–1578.
PAO	" "	1945, 59 Stat. 539.
IMF	Act	1945, 59 Stat. 512; 22 U.S. C. 286–286K; 59 Stat. 669.
IBRD	ibid.	ibid.
UNESCO	Joint Resolution, 1946, 60 Stat. 712; Act, 59 Stat. 669.
WHO	" "	1948, 62 Stat. 441; Act, 59 Stat. 669.
IRO	" "	1947, 61 Stat. 214; Act, 59 Stat. 669.
U.N.H.Q. Agmt.	" "	1946, 61 Stat. 756; Act, 59 Stat. 669.
Trusteeship Agmt.	" "	1947, 61 Stat. 397.
Fur Seal Agmt. with Canada Act	" "	1944, 58 Stat. 100; 61 Stat. 450; 16 U.S.C. 631a–631r.

Category 3 (inherent executive powers)

Armistice Agreements (five).

Understandings with certain countries after the Second World War that U. S. armed forces were present on their territory with permission.

Understandings with Syria and Lebanon regarding most-favoured-nation treatment to American nationals.

Agreements regarding aid by certain countries to U. S. armed forces stationed in their territory.

Arrangements recognising jurisdiction of the U. S. over criminal offences by U. S. armed forces in foreign countries.

Arrangements dealing with various phases of the movement and treatment of U. S. armed forces.

Arrangements for Red Cross facilities to U. S. armed forces.

Claims settlement not involving rights of U. S. citizens.

Arrangement with the LON for registration of treaties.

Modi vivendi, e. g. Preparatory Commissions for UN, UNESCO, IRO.

Arrangements with Panama for emergency use of highways.

Arrangements for military occupation of territory.

UNITED STATES: LAW ON TRANSMITTAL OF U. S. INTERNATIONAL AGREEMENTS TO CONGRESS

1 U.S.C.A. 112b.

§ 112b. United States international agreements; transmission to Congress

The Secretary of State shall transmit to the Congress the text of any international agreement, other than a treaty, to which the United States is a party as soon as practicable after such agreement has entered into force with respect to the United States but in no event later than sixty days thereafter. However, any such agreement the immediate public disclosure of which would, in the opinion of the President, be prejudicial to the national security of the United States shall not be so transmitted to the Congress but shall be transmitted to the Committee on Foreign Relations of the Senate and the Committee on Foreign Affairs of the House of Representatives under an appropriate injunction of secrecy to be removed only upon due notice from the President.

UNITED STATES v. PINK

United States Supreme Court, 1942.
315 U.S. 203, 62 S.Ct. 552.

[The Litvinov Agreement referred to in the quotation from O'Connell on p. 1012, was the subject of litigation in United States v. Belmont, 301 U.S. 324, 57 S.Ct. 758 (1937) and United States v. Pink. In the Pink case, the relevant document is referred to as the Litvinov Assignment. As an incident to the United States recognition of the USSR on November 16, 1933, the Soviet foreign minister, Litvinov, delivered a letter to the President of the United States by which the Soviet Union assigned to the United States amounts due to the Soviet Union from United States nationals. This assignment was stated to be preparatory to a final settlement mainly of United States claims for nationalization of property of citizens of the United States situated in the USSR. In Pink the United States, assignee of the Soviet Union, sued the New York Superintendent of Insurance, who had succeeded by a court order to the assets of the New York branch of a Russian insurance company (previously nationalized by Soviet law). One defense was that the Russian nationalization decrees were extraterritorial, confiscatory and contrary to the public policy of New York. The New York courts had dismissed the United States complaint, but the Supreme Court reversed.   In the court's opinion, MR. JUSTICE DOUGLAS stated, in part:]

* * *   The powers of the President in the conduct of foreign relations included the power, without consent of the Senate, to determine the public policy of the United States with respect to the Russian nationalization decrees.   "What government is to be regarded here as representative of a foreign sovereign state is a political rather than a judicial question, and is to be determined by the political department of the government."   Guaranty Trust Co. v. United States, supra, 304 U.S. page 137, 58 S.Ct. page 791.   That authority is not limited to a determination of the government to be recognized. It includes the power to determine the policy which is to govern the question of recognition.   Objections to the underlying policy as well as objections to recognition are to be addressed to the political department and not to the courts.   See Guaranty Trust Co. v. United States, supra, 304 U.S. page 138, 58 S.Ct. page 791; Kennett v. Chambers, 14 How. 38, 50–51.   As we have noted, this Court in the Belmont case recognized that the Litvinov Assignment was an international compact which did not require the participation of the Senate.   It stated (301 U.S. pages 330–331, 57 S.Ct. pages 760, 761) : "There are many such compacts, of which a protocol, a modus vivendi, a postal convention, and agreements like that now under consideration are illustrations."   And see Monaco v. Mississippi, 292 U.S. 313, 331, 54 S.Ct. 745, 751; United States v. Curtiss-Wright Corp., 299 U.S. 304, 318, 57 S.Ct. 216, 220.   Recognition is not always absolute; it is sometimes conditional.   1 Moore, International Law Digest (1906), pp. 73–74; 1 Hackworth, Digest of International Law (1940), pp. 192–195.   Power to remove such obstacles to full recognition as settlement of claims of our nationals (Levitan, Executive Agreements, 35 Ill.L.Rev. 365, 382–385) certainly is a modest implied power of the President who is the "sole organ of the federal government in the field of international relations."   United States v. Curtiss-Wright Corp., supra, 299 U.S. page 320, 57 S.Ct. page 221.   Effectiveness in handling the delicate problems of foreign relations requires no less.   Unless such a power exists, the power of recognition might be thwarted or seriously diluted.   No such obstacle can be placed in the way of rehabilitation of relations between this country and another nation, unless the historic conception of the powers and responsibilities of the President in the conduct of foreign affairs (see Moore, Treaties and Executive Agreements, 20 Pol.Sc.Q. 385, 403–417) is to be drastically revised.   It was the judgment of the political department that full recognition of the Soviet Government required the settlement of all outstanding problems including the claims of our nationals.   Recognition and the Litvinov Assignment were interdependent.   We would usurp the executive function if we held that that decision was not final and conclusive in the courts.

"All constitutional acts of power, whether in the executive or in the judicial department, have as much legal validity and obligation as if they proceeded from the legislature, . . . " The Federalist, No. 64. A treaty is a "Law of the Land" under the supremacy clause (Art. VI, Cl. 2) of the Constitution. Such international compacts and agreements as the Litvinov Assignment have a similar dignity. United States v. Belmont, supra, 301 U.S. page 331, 57 S.Ct. page 761. See Corwin, The President, Office & Powers (1940), pp. 228–240.

It is, of course, true that even treaties with foreign nations will be carefully construed so as not to derogate from the authority and jurisdiction of the States of this nation unless clearly necessary to effectuate the national policy. Guaranty Trust Co. v. United States, supra, 304 U.S. page 143, 58 S.Ct. page 793, and cases cited. For example, in Todok v. Union State Bank, 281 U.S. 449, 50 S.Ct. 363, this Court took pains in its construction of a treaty, relating to the power of an alien to dispose of property in this country, not to invalidate the provisions of state law governing such dispositions. Frequently the obligation of a treaty will be dependent on state law. Prevost v. Greneaux, 19 How. 1. But state law must yield when it is inconsistent with, or impairs the policy or provisions of, a treaty or of an international compact or agreement. See Nielsen v. Johnson, 279 U.S. 47, 49 S.Ct. 223. Then, the power of a State to refuse enforcement of rights based on foreign law which runs counter to the public policy of the forum (Griffin v. McCoach, 313 U.S. 498, 506, 61 S.Ct. 1023, 1027) must give way before the superior Federal policy evidenced by a treaty or international compact or agreement. Santovincenzo v. Egan, supra, 284 U.S. 30, 52 S.Ct. 81; United States v. Belmont, supra [301 U.S. 324, 57 S.Ct. 758].

Enforcement of New York's policy as formulated by the Moscow case would collide with and subtract from the Federal policy, whether it was premised on the absence of extraterritorial effect of the Russian decrees, the conception of the New York branch as a distinct juristic personality, or disapproval by New York of the Russian program of nationalization. * * *

UNITED STATES v. GUY W. CAPPS, INC.

United States Court of Appeals, Fourth Circuit, 1953.
204 F.2d 655.[a]

PARKER, CHIEF JUDGE. This is an appeal by the United States from a judgment entered on a verdict directed for the defendant, Guy W. Capps, in an action instituted to recover damages alleged to have been sustained by the United States as the result of alleged

a. Aff'd 348 U.S. 296, 75 S.Ct. 326 (1955.)

breach by defendant of a contract with respect to the importation of seed potatoes from Canada. The District Court denied a motion to dismiss the action. United States v. Guy W. Capps, Inc., 100 F. Supp. 30. Upon the subsequent trial, however, the court directed a verdict and entered judgment for defendant on the ground that there was no sufficient showing of breach of contract or damage to the United States.

The contract sued on has relation to the potato price support program of 1948 and the executive agreement entered into between Canada and the United States through the Canadian Ambassador and the Acting Secretary of State of the United States. Pursuant to the Agricultural Act of 1948, Public Law 897, 80th Cong. 2d Sess., 62 Stat. 1247, the United States committed itself to purchase from eligible potato growers, directly or through dealers, all table stock and seed potatoes that could not be sold commercially at a parity price. The purchase and disposal of potatoes under this program was carried out by the Commodity Credit Corporation. In a manifest attempt to protect the American Potato Market in which this price support program was operating from an influx of Canadian grown potatoes, the Acting Secretary of State of the United States, on November 23, 1948, entered into an executive agreement with the Canadian Ambassador, who was acting for the Canadian Government, to the effect that the Canadian Government would place potatoes in the list of commodities for which export permits were required and that export permits would be granted therefor only to Canadian exporters who could give evidence that they had firm orders from legitimate United States users of Canadian seed potatoes and that "Canadian exporters would also be required to have included in any contract into which they might enter with a United States seed potato importer a clause in which the importer would give an assurance that the potatoes would not be diverted or reconsigned for table stock purposes". In consideration of this agreement on the part of the Canadian Government, the United States Government undertook that it would not impose "any quantitative limitations or fees on Canadian potatoes of the 1948 crop exported to the United States" under the system of regulating the movement of potatoes to the United States outlined in the Canadian proposal and would not consider the Canadian Government's guarantee of a floor price with respect to certain potatoes to be the payment of a bounty or grant and would not levy any countervailing duty on such potatoes under the provisions of section 303 of the Tariff Act of 1930. On November 26, 1948, the Canadian Privy Council added potatoes to the list of products under export permit control and exporters of seed potatoes to the United States could not secure an export permit without complying with the conditions required by the executive agreement.

Defendant, a corporation engaged in business in Norfolk, Virginia, entered into a contract in December 1948 with H. B. Willis, Inc., a Canadian exporter, to purchase 48,544 sacks of Canadian seed potatoes, containing 100 lbs. each, to be shipped on the S. S. Empire Gangway docking in Jacksonville, Florida, in January 1949. Defendant's officers admittedly knew of the agreement with Canada and stated in a telegram to an official of the United States Department of Agriculture that the potatoes were being brought in for seed purposes. Defendant sent a telegram to the exporter in Canada on the same day that the potatoes were billed stating that they were for planting in Florida and Georgia. Defendant sold the potatoes while in shipment to the Atlantic Commission Company, a wholly owned agency of Great Atlantic & Pacific Tea Company, a retail grocery organization. No attempt was made to restrict their sale so that they would be used for seed and not for food, and there is evidence from which the jury could properly have drawn the conclusion that they were sold on the market as food displacing potatoes grown in this country and causing damage to the United States by requiring greater purchases of American grown potatoes in aid of the price support program than would have been necessary in the absence of their importation.

On these facts we think that judgment was properly entered for the defendant, but for reasons other than those given by the District Court. We have little difficulty in seeing in the evidence breach of contract on the part of defendant and damage resulting to the United States from the breach. We think, however, that the executive agreement was void because it was not authorized by Congress and contravened provisions of a statute dealing with the very matter to which it related and that the contract relied on, which was based on the executive agreement, was unenforceable in the courts of the United States for like reason. We think, also, that no action can be maintained by the government to recover damages on account of what is essentially a breach of a trade regulation, in the absence of express authorization by Congress. The power to regulate foreign commerce is vested in Congress, not in the executive or the courts; and the executive may not exercise the power by entering into executive agreements and suing in the courts for damages resulting from breaches of contracts made on the basis of such agreements.

In the Agricultural Act of 1948, Congress had legislated specifically with respect to the limitations which might be imposed on imports if it was thought that they would render ineffective or materially interfere with any program or operation undertaken pursuant to that act. Section 3 of the act, which amended prior statutes, provided in the portion here pertinent, 62 Stat. 1248–1250, 7 U.S.C.A. § 624:

> (a) Whenever the President has reason to believe that any article or articles are being or are practically certain to be im-

ported into the United States under such conditions and in such quantities as to render or tend to render ineffective, or materially interfere with, any program or operation undertaken under this title　*　*　*　he shall cause an immediate investigation to be made by the United States Tariff Commission, which shall give precedence to investigations under this section to determine such facts.　Such investigation shall be made after due notice and opportunity for hearing to interested parties, and shall be conducted subject to such regulations as the President shall specify.

"(b) If, on the basis of such investigation and report to him of findings and recommendations made in connection therewith, the President finds the existence of such facts, he shall by proclamation impose such　*　*　*　quantitative limitations on any article or articles which may be entered　*　*　*　for consumption as he finds and declares shown by such investigation to be necessary in order that the entry of such article or articles will not render or tend to render ineffective, or materially interfere with, any program or operation referred to in subsection (a), of this section　*　*　*　Provided, That no proclamation under this section shall impose any limitation on the total quantity of any article or articles which may be entered　*　*　* for consumption which reduces such permissible total quantity to proportionately less than 50 per centum of the total quantity of such article or articles which was entered　*　*　*　for consumption during a representative period as determined by the President: * * *.

There was no pretense of complying with the requirements of this statute.　The President did not cause an investigation to be made by the Tariff Commission, the Commission did not conduct an investigation or make findings or recommendations, and the President made no findings of fact and issued no proclamation imposing quantitative limitations and determined no representative period for the application of the 50% limitation contained in the proviso.　All that occurred in the making of this executive agreement, the effect of which was to exclude entirely a food product of a foreign country from importation into the United States, was an exchange of correspondence between the Acting Secretary of State and the Canadian Ambassador.　Since the purpose of the agreement as well as its effect was to bar imports which would interfere with the Agricultural Adjustment program, it was necessary that the provisions of this statute be complied with and an executive agreement excluding such imports which failed to comply with it was void.　Morgan v. United States, 304 U.S. 1, 58 S.Ct. 773, 999, 82 L.Ed. 1129; Panama Refining Co. v. Ryan, 293 U.S. 388, 55 S.Ct. 241, 253, 79 L.Ed. 446. As was said by Chief Justice Hughes in the case last cited: "We are not dealing with action which, appropriately belonging to the executive province, is not the subject of judicial review or with the presumptions attaching to executive action. * * * we are concerned with the question of the delegation of legislative power. * * *"

It is argued, however, that the validity of the executive agreement was not dependent upon the Act of Congress but was made pursuant to the inherent powers of the President under the Constitution. The answer is that while the President has certain inherent powers under the Constitution such as the power pertaining to his position as Commander in Chief of Army and Navy and the power necessary to see that the laws are faithfully executed, the power to regulate interstate and foreign commerce is not among the powers incident to the Presidential office, but is expressly vested by the Constitution in the Congress. It cannot be upheld as an exercise of the power to see that the laws are faithfully executed, for, as said by Mr. Justice Holmes in his dissenting opinion in Myers v. United States, 272 U.S. 52, 177, 47 S.Ct. 21, 85, 71 L.Ed. 160, "The duty of the President to see that the laws be executed is a duty that does not go beyond the laws or require him to achieve more than Congress sees fit to leave within his power". * * *

We think that whatever the power of the executive with respect to making executive trade agreements regulating foreign commerce in the absence of action by Congress, it is clear that the executive may not through entering into such an agreement avoid complying with a regulation prescribed by Congress. Imports from a foreign country are foreign commerce subject to regulation, so far as this country is concerned, by Congress alone. The executive may not by-pass congressional limitations regulating such commerce by entering into an agreement with the foreign country that the regulation be exercised by that country through its control over exports. Even though the regulation prescribed by the executive agreement be more desirable than that prescribed by Congressional action, it is the latter which must be accepted as the expression of national policy. * * *

For the reasons stated, we do not think that the United States can maintain the action for damages. The judgment for defendant will accordingly be affirmed.

Affirmed.

Problem. The Nuclear Test Ban Treaty entered into force on October 10, 1963, following its ratification by the United States, the United Kingdom and the Soviet Union. 105 states were parties to the treaty by January 1, 1972. In its operative Article I "Each of the Parties to this Treaty undertakes to prohibit, to prevent, and not to carry out any nuclear weapon test explosion, or any other nuclear explosion, at any place under its jurisdiction or control: **(a)** in the atmosphere; beyond its limits, including outer space; or underwater, including territorial waters or high seas; or **(b)** in any other environment if such explosion causes radioactive debris to be present outside the territorial limits of the State under whose jurisdiction or control such explosion is conducted. * * * " Article II of the treaty provides for amendment as follows:

1. Any Party may propose amendments to this Treaty. The text of any proposed amendment shall be submitted to the Depositary Governments which shall circulate it to all Parties to this Treaty. Thereafter, if requested to do so by one-third or more of the Parties, the Depositary Governments shall convene a conference, to which they shall invite all the Parties, to consider such amendment.

2. Any amendment to this Treaty must be approved by a majority of the votes of all the Parties to this Treaty, including the votes of all of the Original Parties. The amendment shall enter into force for all Parties upon the deposit of instruments of ratification by a majority of all the Parties, including the instruments of ratification of all of the Original Parties.

The resolution of the United States Senate giving its advice and consent to the ratification of the treaty provides as follows:

Whereas the President has submitted a limited nuclear test ban treaty, providing a method of amendment, to the Senate for its advice and consent in accordance with article II, section 2 of the Constitution; and

Whereas the Constitution in article II, section 2, provides "He shall have Power, by and with the Advice and Consent of the Senate, to make Treaties, provided two-thirds of the Senators present concur"; and

Whereas amendments to treaties are subject to this constitutional provision: Now, therefore, be it

Resolved (two-thirds of the Senators present concurring therein), That the Senate advise and consent to the ratification of the treaty banning nuclear weapon tests in the atmosphere, in outer space, and underwater, signed at Moscow on August 5, 1963, on behalf of the United States of America, the United Kingdom of Great Britain and Northern Ireland, and the Union of Soviet Socialist Republics.

If the USSR should wish to agree with the United States to ban testing underground, could the President of the United States lawfully make an executive agreement with the Soviet Union to that effect?

SECTION C. SELF EXECUTION OF INTERNATIONAL AGREEMENTS

ASAKURA v. CITY OF SEATTLE

United States Supreme Court, 1924.
265 U.S. 332, 44 S.Ct. 515.

MR. JUSTICE BUTLER delivered the opinion of the Court.

Plaintiff in error is a subject of the Emperor of Japan, and, since 1904, has resided in Seattle, Washington. Since July, 1915, he has been engaged in business there as a pawnbroker. The city passed an ordinance, which took effect July 2, 1921, regulating the business of pawnbroker and repealing former ordinances on the same subject. It makes it unlawful for any person to engage in the business unless he shall have a license, and the ordinance provides "that no such license shall be granted unless the applicant be a citizen of the United States." Violations of the ordinance are punishable by fine or imprisonment or both. Plaintiff in error brought this suit in the Superior Court of King County, Washington, against the city, its Comptroller and its Chief of Police to restrain them from enforcing the ordinance against him. He attacked the ordinance on the ground that it violates the treaty between the United States and the Empire of Japan, proclaimed April 5, 1911, 37 Stat. 1504; * * * It was shown that he had about $5,000 invested in his business, which would be broken up and destroyed by the enforcement of the ordinance. The Superior Court granted the relief prayed. On appeal, the Supreme Court of the State held the ordinance valid and reversed the decree. * * *

Does the ordinance violate the treaty? Plaintiff in error invokes and relies upon the following provisions: "The citizens or subjects of each of the High Contracting Parties shall have liberty to enter, travel and reside in the territories of the other to carry on trade, wholesale and retail, to own or lease and occupy houses, manufactories, warehouses and shops, to employ agents of their choice, to lease land for residential and commercial purposes, and generally to do anything incident to or necessary for trade upon the same terms as native citizens or subjects, submitting themselves to the laws and regulations there established. * * * The citizens or subjects of each * * * shall receive, in the territories of the other, the most constant protection, and security for their persons and property, * * *."

A treaty made under the authority of the United States "shall be the supreme law of the land; and the judges in every State shall be bound thereby, any thing in the constitution or laws of any State to the contrary notwithstanding." Constitution, Art. VI, § 2.

The treaty-making power of the United States is not limited by any express provision of the Constitution, and, though it does not extend "so far as to authorize what the Constitution forbids," it does extend to all proper subjects of negotiation between our government and other nations.

* * * The treaty was made to strengthen friendly relations between the two nations. As to the things covered by it, the provision quoted establishes the rule of equality between Japanese subjects while in this country and native citizens. Treaties for the protection of citizens of one country residing in the territory of another are numerous, and make for good understanding between nations. The treaty is binding within the State of Washington. * * * The rule of equality established by it cannot be rendered nugatory in any part of the United States by municipal ordinances or state laws. It stands on the same footing of supremacy as do the provisions of the Constitution and laws of the United States. It operates of itself without the aid of any legislation, state or national; and it will be applied and given authoritative effect by the courts. * * *

The purpose of the ordinance complained of is to regulate, not to prohibit, the business of pawnbroker. But it makes it impossible for aliens to carry on the business. It need not be considered whether the State, if it sees fit, may forbid and destroy the business generally. Such a law would apply equally to aliens and citizens, and no question of conflict with the treaty would arise. The grievance here alleged is that plaintiff in error, in violation of the treaty, is denied equal opportunity.

It remains to be considered whether the business of pawnbroker is "trade" within the meaning of the treaty.

* * * The language of the treaty is comprehensive. The phrase "to carry on trade" is broad. That it is not to be given a restricted meaning is plain. * * *

* * * There is nothing in the character of the business of pawnbroker which requires it to be excluded from the field covered by the above quoted provision, and it must be held that such business is "trade" within the meaning of the treaty. The ordinance violates the treaty. * * *

Decree reversed.

Self-executing and non self-executing international agreements. When does an international agreement have domestic effect as law without the need for any further law-making act than the final national action required to bind the promising state internationally? The question does not arise in legal systems that require that the law-making authority of the state, usually its legislature, approve the international agreement in order for it to bind the state internationally. It does arise in constitutional arrangements such as that of the United States, where "laws" are ordinarily passed by both of two legislative chambers but "treaties" (Article 2, Sec. VI, Constitution of the United States) need be approved by only one of them in order to become effective internationally as to that state. And even in the latter type arrangement, the question would not arise if the constitution made it clear that such unicameral approval was not equivalent to a legislative act.

In the case of the United States Constitution, however, the language of the supremacy clause is open to the interpretation, and has been interpreted, to leave open the possibility that the President, two-thirds of the Senate concurring, can put into effect international agreements that also have internal effect ex proprio vigore. Early in the history of United States foreign relations law (at the constitutional level) it was established by executive and judicial practice that a treaty intended to be self-executing could take effect as the law of the land when promulgated by the President, following approval by the Senate. Thomas Jefferson as a commentator on the Constitution considered such self-executing effect as a species of legislation authorized by the Constitution. Thus the possibility of there being self-executing international agreements exists, subject to certain not as yet fully explored limits, such as whether the President and two-thirds of the Senate can define a crime against the United States or the law of nations, appropriate funds, or dispose of property of the United States. In normal operations of the United States Government the executive branch and the Senate avoid trespassing on the institutional expectations of the House of Representatives as to participation in law-making in these fields by making it clear that the treaty was not intended to be self-executing. Intent in this regard can be controlled by stipulations in the international agreement that it shall not be self-executing, or in the President's message to the Senate transmitting the treaty for approval, or by a Senate reservation, see p. 950. This issue aside, whether a treaty is or is not self-executing is determined by the courts through normal interpretative processes.

SEI FUJII v. STATE

United States, Supreme Court of California, in Banc, 1952.
242 P.2d 617, 38 Cal.2d 718.

GIBSON, CHIEF JUSTICE. Plaintiff, an alien Japanese who is ineligible to citizenship under our naturalization laws, appeals from a judgment declaring that certain land purchased by him in 1948 had escheated to the state. There is no treaty between this country and Japan which confers upon plaintiff the right to own land, and the sole question presented on this appeal is the validity of the California alien land law.[1]

---

1. The pertinent portions of the alien land law, 1 Deering's Gen.Laws, Act 261, as amended in 1945, are as follows:

§ 1. All aliens eligible to citizenship under the laws of the United States may acquire, possess, enjoy, use, cultivate, occupy, transfer, transmit and

United Nations Charter

It is first contended that the land law has been invalidated and superseded by the provisions of the United Nations Charter pledging the member nations to promote the observance of human rights and fundamental freedoms without distinction as to race. Plaintiff relies on statements in the preamble and in Articles 1, 55 and 56 of the Charter, 59 Stat. 1035.[2]

It is not disputed that the charter is a treaty, and our federal Constitution provides that treaties made under the authority of the United States are part of the supreme law of the land and that the judges in every state are bound thereby. U.S.Const., art. VI. A treaty, however, does not automatically supersede local laws which are inconsistent with it unless the treaty provisions are self-executing. In the words of Chief Justice Marshall: A treaty is "to be regarded in courts of justice as equivalent to an act of the Legislature, whenever

---

inherit real property, or any interest therein, in this state, and have in whole or in part the beneficial use thereof, in the same manner and to the same extent as citizens of the United States, except as otherwise provided by the laws of this state.

§ 2. All aliens other than those mentioned in section one of this act may acquire, possess, enjoy, use, cultivate, occupy and transfer real property, or any interest therein, in this state, and have in whole or in part the beneficial use thereof, in the manner and to the extent, and for the purposes prescribed by any treaty now existing between the government of the United States and the nation or country of which such alien is a citizen or subject, and not otherwise.

§ 7. Any real property hereafter acquired in fee in violation of the provisions of this act by any alien mentioned in section 2 of this act, * * * shall escheat as of the date of such acquiring, to, and become and remain the property of the state of California. * * *

2. The preamble recites that "We the peoples of the United Nations determined * * * to reaffirm faith in fundamental human rights * * * and for these ends * * * to employ international machinery for the promotion of the economic and social advancement of all peoples, have resolved to combine our efforts to accomplish these aims."

Article 1 states that The Purposes of the United Nations are: * * * 3. To achieve international co-operation in solving international problems of an economic, social, cultural, or humanitarian character, and in promoting and encouraging respect for human rights and for fundamental freedoms for all without distinction as to race, sex, language, or religion; * * *.

Articles 55 and 56 appear in Chapter IX, entitled "International Economic and Social Cooperation." Article 55 provides: "With a view to the creation of conditions of stability and well-being which are necessary for peaceful and friendly relations among nations based on respect for the principle of equal rights and self-determination of peoples, the United Nations shall promote:

a. higher standards of living, full employment, and conditions of economic and social progress and development;

b. solutions of international economic, social, health, and related problems; and international cultural and educational cooperation; and

c. universal respect for, and observance of, human rights and fundamental freedoms for all without distinction as to race, sex, language, or religion.

Article 56 provides: All Members pledge themselves to take joint and separate action in cooperation with the Organization for the achievement of the purposes set forth in Article 55.

it operates of itself, without the aid of any legislative provision. But when the terms of the stipulation import a contract—when either of the parties engages to perform a particular act, the treaty addresses itself to the political, not the judicial department; and the Legislature must execute the contract, before it can become a rule for the court." Foster v. Neilson, 1829, 2 Pet. 253, 314, 7 L.Ed. 415.[3]

In determining whether a treaty is self-executing courts look to the intent of the signatory parties as manifested by the language of the instrument, and, if the instrument is uncertain, recourse may be had to the circumstances surrounding its execution. * * *

In order for a treaty provision to be operative without the aid of implementing legislation and to have the force and effect of a statute, it must appear that the framers of the treaty intended to prescribe a rule that, standing alone, would be enforceable in the courts. * * *

It is clear that the provisions of the preamble and of Article 1 of the charter which are claimed to be in conflict with the alien land law are not self-executing. They state general purposes and objectives of the United Nations Organization and do not purport to impose legal obligations on the individual member nations or to create rights in private persons. It is equally clear that none of the other provisions relied on by plaintiff is self-executing. Article 55 declares that the United Nations "shall promote: * * * universal respect for, and observance of, human rights and fundamental freedoms for all without distinction as to race, sex, language, or religion," and in Article 56, the member nations "pledge themselves to take joint and separate action in cooperation with the Organization for the achievement of the purposes set forth in Article 55." Although the member nations have obligated themselves to cooperate with the international organization in promoting respect for, and observance of, human rights, it is plain that it was contemplated that future legislative action by the several nations would be required to accomplish the declared objectives, and there is nothing to indicate that these provisions were intended to become rules of law for the courts of this country upon the ratification of the charter.

The language used in Articles 55 and 56 is not the type customarily employed in treaties which have been held to be self-executing and to create rights and duties in individuals. For example, the treaty involved in Clark v. Allen, 331 U.S. 503, 507–508, 67 S.Ct. 1431, 1434,

---

3. In Foster v. Neilson, certain treaty provisions were held not to be self-executing on the basis of construction of the English version of the document. Subsequently, upon consideration of the Spanish version, the provisions in question were held to be self-executing. United States v. Percheman, 7 Pet. 51, 8 L.Ed. 604.

Chief Justice Marshall's language in the Foster case, however, has been quoted with approval in later cases. United States v. Rauscher, 119 U.S. 407, 417–418, 7 S.Ct. 234, 239–240, 30 L.Ed. 425; Valentine v. United States, 299 U.S. 5, 10, 57 S.Ct. 100, 103, 81 L.Ed. 5.

91 L.Ed. 1633, relating to the rights of a national of one country to inherit real property located in another country, specifically provided that "such national shall be allowed a term of three years in which to sell the [property] * * * and withdraw the proceeds * * *" free from any discriminatory taxation. See, also, Hauenstein v. Lynham, 100 U.S. 483, 488–490, 25 L.Ed. 628. In Nielsen v. Johnson, 279 U.S. 47, 50, 49 S.Ct. 223, 73 L.Ed. 607, the provision treated as being self-executing was equally definite. There each of the signatory parties agreed that "no higher or other duties, charges, or taxes of any kind, shall be levied" by one country on removal of property therefrom by citizens of the other country "than are or shall be payable in each state, upon the same, when removed by a citizen or subject of such state respectively." In other instances treaty provisions were enforced without implementing legislation where they prescribed in detail the rules governing rights and obligations of individuals or specifically provided that citizens of one nation shall have the same rights while in the other country as are enjoyed by that country's own citizens. * * *

It is significant to note that when the framers of the charter intended to make certain provisions effective without the aid of implementing legislation they employed language which is clear and definite and manifests that intention. For example, Article 104 provides: "The Organization shall enjoy in the territory of each of its Members such legal capacity as may be necessary for the exercise of its functions and the fulfillment of its purposes." Article 105 provides: "1. The Organization shall enjoy in the territory of each of its Members such privileges and immunities as are necessary for the fulfillment of its purposes. 2. Representatives of the Members of the United Nations and officials of the Organization shall similarly enjoy such privileges and immunities as are necessary for the independent exercise of their functions in connection with the Organization." In Curran v. City of New York, 191 Misc. 229, 77 N.Y.S.2d 206, 212, these articles were treated as being self-executory. See, also, Balfour, Guthrie & Co. v. United States, D.C., 90 F.Supp. 831, 832.

The provisions in the charter pledging cooperation in promoting observance of fundamental freedoms lack the mandatory quality and definiteness which would indicate an intent to create justiciable rights in private persons immediately upon ratification. Instead, they are framed as a promise of future action by the member nations. Secretary of State Stettinius, Chairman of the United States delegation at the San Francisco Conference where the charter was drafted, stated in his report to President Truman that Article 56 "pledges the various countries to cooperate with the organization by joint and separate action in the achievement of the economic and social objectives of the organization without infringing upon their right to order their national affairs according to their own best ability, in their own way, and in accordance with their own political and economic institutions and processes." Report to the President on the Results of the San Francisco Conference by the Chairman of the United States Delegation, the Secretary of State, Department of State Publication 2349, Conference Series 71, p. 115; Hearings before the Committee on Foreign Relations, United States Senate [Revised] July 9–13, 1945, p. 106. The same view was repeatedly expressed by delegates of other nations in the debates attending the drafting of article 56. * * *

The humane and enlightened objectives of the United Nations Charter are, of course, entitled to respectful consideration by the courts and Legislatures of every member nation, since that document expresses the universal desire of thinking men for peace and for equality of rights and opportunities. The charter represents a moral commitment of foremost importance, and we must not permit the spirit of our pledge to be compromised or disparaged in either our domestic or foreign affairs. We are satisfied, however, that the charter provisions relied on by plaintiff were not intended to supersede existing domestic legislation, and we cannot hold that they operate to invalidate the alien land law.

Fourteenth Amendment of the Federal Constitution

The next question is whether the alien land law violates the due process and equal protection clauses of the Fourteenth Amendment. * * *

* * *

* * * The California alien land law is obviously designed and administered as an instrument for effectuating racial discrimination, and the most searching examination discloses no circumstances justifying classification on that basis. There is nothing to indicate that those alien residents who are racially ineligible for citizenship possess characteristics which are dangerous to the legitimate interests of the state, or that they, as a class, might use the land for purposes injurious to public morals, safety or welfare. Accordingly, we hold that the alien land law is invalid as in violation of the Fourteenth Amendment.

The judgment is reversed.

* * *

SCHAUER, JUSTICE (dissenting and concurring). * * *

* * *

I agree that the United Nations Charter, as presently constituted and accepted was not intended to, and does not, supersede existing domestic legislation of the United States or of the several states and territories.

I would hold that provisions of the Alien Land Law here invoked by the State of California do not contravene either the federal or state constitutions; and would affirm the judgment of the trial court.

* * *

[Concurring and dissenting opinions omitted.]

Self-execution when the intention of states parties on that issue not specified. Aside from the instances in which the treaty makes it reasonably clear that the only immediate obligation the parties wanted from each was the enactment of legislation (so that the treaty can easily be described as non self-executing), there are instances in which the treaty is fairly opaque on the question of how the parties will put into effect, domestically, what they have promised internationally. Riesenfeld has suggested, as we have seen, p. 621, that it may not be useful to search for the intention of the states parties on this domestic question. At least in multilateral treaties a state may have multiple expectations about what the other parties will do as a matter of domestic law, since some (such as the United Kingdom) must always procure parliamentary action; while others (such as the United States) go to their legislature in some cases and not in others.

The significant first question in the analysis is: did each state expect the other states immediately to be bound to perform the substance that was promised (e.g., to recognize a new boundary, to refrain from going to war, to cease racial discrimination, to pay certain sums of money, to impose criminal sanctions on certain behavior)? If so, according to the Riesenfeld suggestion, the only functional question for the United States is whether by its Constitution it is required to enact legislation as a matter purely of internal law (as presumably it would in cases involving the appropriation of money or the designation of certain behavior as criminal); in such a case the treaty could be described as non self-executing. On the other hand, if a court could constitutionally apply a rule of law without the aid of Congress, as it did in the Asakura case in its invalidation of the local ordinance, then it need not await legislation action; the treaty can then be described as self-executing. The resolution of this problem is especially significant in the field of human rights, since such rights are so frequently of the kind that courts have in the past been able to recognize under our own constitutional Bill of Rights without the aid of legislation.

It bears reiteration, however, that the first question is whether the states expected of each other immediate international responsibility with respect to the substance of the treaty.

LOOK AT STATES' INTENTIONS

RESTATEMENT OF THE FOREIGN RELATIONS LAW OF THE UNITED STATES, REPORTERS' NOTES TO SECTION 154 (1965).*

Relation to constitutional procedures of other states. Under the constitutional law of a number of states self-executing international agreements are not permitted. In the United Kingdom and a number of other countries of the British Commonwealth, for example, only an act of Parliament can have effect as domestic law, and international agreements cannot be applied (with rare exceptions) as determinative of domestic legal relationships unless anticipated under, or subsequently implemented by, an act of Parliament. See McNair, the Law of Treaties 81–100 (1961). Under Article 59(2) of the Basic Law of the Federal Republic of Germany, an international agreement cannot be ratified so as to have international effect until the agreement has been approved, and where necessary implemented, as to its domestic effect by legislative action. For the constitutional situations in these and other states, see generally, Oliver, Contemporary Problems of Treaty Law, 88 Recueil des Cours 421, 439–51 (1955). As to the effect of such constitutional limitations on the scope of authority to enter into an internationally binding commitment as to self-execution, see § 123.

It has been argued against further provisions for self-executing international agreements of the United States that the United States is at a disadvantage in relation to states that do not provide for self-execution. In fact, however, in many (if not most) of such states there exists a cabinet form of government in which executive and legislative powers are merged. In such situations, the government in power is in practice able to get the necessary parliamentary implementation almost as surely and as efficiently as if the agreement were self-executing. In states where the ratification process requires general legislative approval, implementing legislation is introduced as a part of the ratification process.

* * *

---

1. *Executive agreements are inherently self-executing.* The point to be made is not that in this or that constitutional system an executive agreement, which binds the state internationally, is willy-nilly the internal law of the land. In some states, such as the United States, see p. 1006, even a self-executing "treaty" may not always have such an effect. And even where treaties might be law of their own force, executive agreements made by the President alone would not have the same effect as internal law. The emphasis here is on the function sought to be achieved by an executive agreement; and that function is to bind the state at signing, without waiting for any subsequent act of validation, as by Senate consent in the case of the United States.

Once the state is bound by it internationally, there is a pressure, to say the least, on the legislative branch to conform domestic law to the executive agreement, if the undertaking in the executive agreement is based upon the expectation of such conformity. In constitutional systems such as that of the United States the legislature, obviously, does not feel that it is being forced to go along if the executive agreement falls within a prior legislative delegation of power to the executive, p. 1013. Again, in the same constitutional situation, an executive agreement falling within the inherent foreign relations power of the executive, see p. 1015, will not usually deal with a matter that requires legislative action to conform internal law; or, such an executive agreement will be negotiated ad referendum, that is, as a promise contingent upon the willingness of the legislature to implement it, as by an appropriation. Executive agreements in support of existing treaties, p. 1011, usually do not, but could, raise issues as to whether the Senate's prior consent in the treaty could reasonably be taken to authorize the executive agreement.

From an historical viewpoint, executive agreements, as we call them today, were the ways that absolute monarchs in past centuries bound themselves, before chiefs of state came to share national decision-making with legislative bodies. For this reason, also, in an earlier period international agreements were usually taken as effective on signature by the chiefs of state or their authorized agents.

2. *Questions relating to the hearings on the law on transmittal of U. S. international agreements to Congress.*

a. Excerpts from the hearings are in the Documentary Supplement.

b. What do you infer was the immediate cause of the law?

c. What, in your opinion, was the most effective argument against the law advanced by the Legal Adviser of the Department of State?

d. What would you, if you were the Legal Adviser, consider doing about Circular 175, p. 1010, in the light of the enactment of the law (i) internally, that is, within the Executive Branch; (ii) vis-a-vis Congress?

Chapter 17

THE REGULATION OF ECONOMIC ACTIVITY WITHIN THE INTERNATIONAL SYSTEM.

1. *Introductory problems*

Case A. *Trade*

For some years private enterprise in State X has been exporting large quantities of electric razors to consumers in State Y, paying a Y import duty of 10% ad valorem. Suddenly the authorities in State Y rule that to protect the domestic industry no foreign-made razors may be imported anymore. The razor industry in State X is struck a mighty blow, and bankruptcies and serious unemployment result.

Case B. *Economic Interests of Aliens Within a State*

Razor-makers in State X decide to transfer capital to State Y and build razor factories there, using Y labor, for the Y razor market. State Y refuses to permit the entry of the X foreign capital for this use.

Case C. *Same*

A corporation organized in State Z owns 100% a corporation chartered in State Y that under State Y law owns subsurface rights to mine certain minerals. These rights are now worth $50,000,000. State Y expropriates these rights and pays no compensation, charging that the alien group from State Z only paid $500,000 for the rights to begin with and has since profited $100,000,000 from their exploitation.

Case D. *Welfare and Development*

State M has a population growth rate of 3% a year and a Gross National Product per capita of $62 a year—in short a very poor state indeed. It has been receiving from State N and from International Organization O foreign assistance grants to help with its population problem and development loans on concessional terms (below the market cost of the money to the lenders) to support a National Development Plan designed to boost GNP per capita to $200 over ten years. In the fifth year of the assistance program both State N and International Organization O decline to provide additional grant and loan assistance to State M. The development plan is threatened with immediate failure.

2. *Lack of customary international law.* Persons in states and states themselves have long engaged in the movement of goods and capital across national frontiers. The velocity, frequency, and quanti-

ty of such movements has increased tremendously in modern industrial times.

Whether for moral, political or trade investment reasons, a foreign aid dimension has been added to transnational economic activity in response to the troublesome gap, still widening, between rich and poor nations.

Economic power is a prime factor in the assessment of the capacity of a state, a group of states or an international organization to be effective in the achievement of its objectives and values. Where military force is illegal or inadvisable, economic strength is now the principal source of a state's authority in the international system.

Notwithstanding these major activities and needs, there is no customary international law imposing duties and creating correlative rights in the above cases, except possibly Case C, where capital-exporting states (or some of them) would argue that there is a rule of customary law requiring fair compensation and some capital-receiving (usually also poor and "developing") nations would assert the contrary.

Except for the increasingly disputed nationalization area of Case C and some rules about the trading rights of "neutrals" in pre-UN wars—rules that in World War I and II were not followed because the enemy continued to breach closely related rules—the rules of the international legal systems as to economic activity are in international agreements. These rules are incomplete. Despite the modification of rules, customary and by international agreement, the lawyer's role in the transnational economic field is presently active and highly important, although his "international lawyering" takes him more often than not into national centers of law and policy and to the law in treaties, rather than to decisions of international tribunals or the doctrines of international law publicists.

This chapter affords a sketch only of a subject matter that largely falls in the curricula of law schools in the United States to courses in International Transactions or The Regulation of International Trade and Investment.

SECTION A.   THE TRADE LAW OF THE INTERNATIONAL SYSTEM

1.   UNCONDITIONAL MOST-FAVORED NATION TREATMENT OF TRADE

Problem. At a time when its own tariffs were highly protectionist, State A analyzed world trade conditions and came to the conclusion that tariff barriers were undesirably high worldwide including the tariffs of States B, C and D. Up to that time, State A had given another state only such tariff cuts for its exports to State A as were "paid for" by some corresponding cut in that state's duty on State A's exports to it. This requirement of "compensation" applied even where the other state had been promised "most favored nation" treatment in a treaty with State A, and State A had given a cut to a third state, which, in turn, had conceded a trade benefit to State A.

When State A decided to launch a worldwide effort to lower tariff barriers, it announced that it was changing its concept of "most favored nation" provisions to an unconditional form. Thereafter, States A, B, C, and D each entered into unconditional most favored nation agreements [MFNs] with all three other states. States A, B, and C are highly-developed, producing wide ranges of manufactured goods. State D is a less well-developed country, largely an agricultural producer and non-competitive as to costs with A, B, and C insofar as manufactured goods are concerned. If D did not have its very high tariffs on goods (say automobiles) manufactured in A, B, and C, its high cost domestic market would yield to the foreign imports and D would lose scarce foreign exchange to pay for the imports.

States A and B enter into wide-ranging and hard-bargained negotiations that result in average tariff cuts of 50% from schedules on both sides. C and D, under their MFN treaties with A and B, claim the benefits of these cuts but offer none in return, with the result that their tariff walls loom higher than ever as clogs on international trade.

Considering the materials on pp. 1036–1041, answer these questions:

1. Why did A ever move to unconditional MFN?

2. Why did A and B make their arrangement, assuming they knew that C and D would not offer cuts?

3. Could A and B legally withdraw their promises to C and D?

METZGER, INTERNATIONAL LAW, TRADE AND FINANCE: REALITIES AND PROSPECTS 18 (1962)

Under the nation-state system a country can buy what it wants from anyone, or discriminate among foreigners in what it buys and in how it treats the goods at the border; it can exclude foreigners from entering the country for any purpose, including investment purposes; it can sell its goods abroad at any time in any manner, and at any price; it can manipulate its currency any way it pleases; it can maintain exchange controls, quotas, and any other device it chooses under any circumstances; it can broadcast over the entire spectrum at any strength regardless of interference with other countries' radio stations and listeners. These and many other things which in the modern world can result in serious injury to others can be done without trenching upon the customary rules which international law has evolved from days when the problems were different from those which now beset us. The fast pace which the industrial revolution has set in creating more complicated economic arrangements, to speak of only one segment, has created more problems of a complex character than could possibly be coped with by the old tort technique of international law.

What to do? The statutory technique, which was the principal domestic addition to the common law in order to respond to the industrial revolution, was not available because there was no legislature to enact statutes. And there was not ever a court of general compulsory jurisdiction to perform the ancillary functions of interpretation and application. The nations did the best they could with the only available techniques. For centuries they had made many contracts with each other on extremely general and sometimes specific matters. These contracts or treaties established rules of behavior of a limited or general type as between signatories. They were flexible instruments, able to be filled with high-sounding protestations of friendship, or detailed rules regarding customs formalities, or both. They came into increasing use for both purposes. During the past one hundred years, and especially during the past fifty years, it is fair to say that contract rules—or treaty law as it is sometimes called— have far overshadowed customary international law rules, from the viewpoint of coping with the main problems of modern international relations.

PATTERSON, DISCRIMINATION IN INTERNATIONAL TRADE, THE POLICY ISSUES 1945–1965, at 6 (1966).*

Discriminatory policies were sometimes defended on the much wider grounds that they fostered freer trade. In a world in which there are problems of unemployment and in which tariff barriers exist and are reduced by a process of negotiation and exchange of "concessions," in such a world a policy of nondiscrimination (unconditional-most-favored-nation treatment) by A and B reduces their future bargaining power in the quest for larger markets in C and D. The consequence, many held, could easily be a slowing down in tariff reductions all around the world. This case for discrimination was more difficult to deal with by those who favored more liberal trade policies and it was commonly accepted as a potent case for discrimination. Ways were found to partially meet the problem—notably, the development of the "principal supplier" rule and specialized tariff classification [6]—but at the cost of impairing the most-favored-nation principle.[7]

Trade liberalization and the rise of most-favored national treatment in the unconditional form. Broadly, both the conditional and unconditional forms of most favored nation treatment reduce the discrimination that exists in international trade when two states restrict exclusively to themselves the trade advantages they give to each other. Bilateral and strictly exclusive trade bargains were the norm over much of the historical period of the modern state, often being linked to treaties of military and political alliance. To a considerable extent for some countries such arrangements existed until somewhat after World War II in the western world, usually those with foreign exchange difficulties. Bilateral trade arrangements of the exclusive sort still characterize the trading practices of the eastern European socialist bloc.

However, there is evidence that in past centuries states sometimes found it in their respective national interests to make trade liberalization arrangements in the knowledge that there were outstanding most favored nation promises to third states, and in some instances these promises were of the unconditional type.

Between the two World Wars and after the Second down to date, subject to questions that arise in relationship to material to follow in this section, the United States has been the prime mover toward trade liberalization (lower tariffs and the reduction of quotas on imports, i. e. quantitative restrictions). Exclusive trade agreements were not favored by the United States even when political parties favoring highly protective tariffs were in power. Until shortly before the exchange of notes with Brazil that follows, the United States adhered to the practice of entering into conditional most favored nation treaty

---

6. The principal supplier—or chief source—rule requires that a nation negotiate reductions in import barriers on a given product only with the country which had been supplying the greatest portion of the former's import of that product. It is thus intended that each concession will be negotiated with the country having the greatest interest in it. This practice preserves bargaining power when the unconditional - most - favored - nation practice is followed, because there is a tendency under it for some products of prime interest to other countries (those goods for which each is a major supplier) not to be the subject of negotiation between other pairs of countries. Specialized tariff classification facilitates the application of the principal supplier rule by so defining products for trade barrier cutting purposes that fewer, rather than more, of the exports important to those not participating in a given bilateral negotiation qualify for the bilaterally agreed cuts.

7. The argument lost some more of its potency when, immediately after World War II, arrangements were made for simultaneous bilateral negotiations, a procedure which Germany had followed before World War I, and which became the hallmark of the General Agreement on Tariffs and Trade.

relationships.   See Whitney v. Robertson, 124 U.S. 190, 8 S.Ct. 456 (1888), where an importer of goods from "San Domingo" failed to get the lower than tariff schedule rate the United States had given the King of Hawaii on the same product, because the United States treaty with the country of the import's origin was of the conditional most favored nation variety and that country did not give American imports concessions comparable to those that the King of Hawaii had given.   It was so held even though the treaty with Santo Domingo (today the Dominican Republic) had not specifically stated that the United States treaty promise to that country was conditioned upon the giving of such "compensation."

In 1923 the United States through Secretary of State Charles Evans Hughes announced a new policy of negotiating trade treaties in unconditional form as to most favored nation treatment.   The exchange of notes with Brazil preceded by some months the secretary's public statement of general policy in this regard.

Nonetheless, the general level of United States and other tariffs remained high.   What is said to be the highest general level of tariffs in United States history was reached in the Tariff Act of 1930, coinciding with the Great Depression and European defaults on their war debts to the United States, because of the debtor's inability to sell enough for dollars and gold to pay without seriously impairing the credibility of their own monies and their capacity to pay for necessary imports.   Franklin D. Roosevelt came to power in 1933 committed to trade liberalization through the negotiation of bilateral tariff reductions that by unconditional most favored nation treatment would spread throughout the world trading system.   It was assumed that the maximum use of the "principal supplier" technique (see the excerpt from Patterson above) would ensure the requisite network of tariff-cutting agreements.

Congress responded with the Reciprocal Trade Agreements Act of 1933, which as codified and from time to time extended and amplified as to the scope of the President's delegated power to cut tariffs, is still the basis of United States trade liberalization treaties and for United States participation in the General Agreement on Tariffs and Trade (GATT).[a]

a.   80 states were parties as of January 1, 1972.

EXCHANGE OF NOTES BETWEEN THE UNITED STATES AND BRAZIL ACCORDING MUTUAL UNCONDITIONAL MOST-FAVORED NATION TARIFF TREATMENT

[1923] 1 Foreign Relations of the United States 453, 459 (1938).

The Ambassador in Brazil (Morgan) to the Secretary of State

Rio de Janeiro, April 26, 1923–1 p. m.

* * * Brazil is disinclined to state formally that the United States will receive unconditional most-favored-nation clause because she will be forced to change her international tariff policy in which she has been educated by the United States through our annual insistence upon the reissue of our preferential list. This preferential policy the Brazilian Government finds convenient and desires to extend to other nations.

* * *

The Department of State to the Brazilian Embassy, Memorandum

Washington, June 2, 1923.

The Government of the United States has carefully noted the two declarations made by the Brazilian Government in the Memorandum of the Ambassador. It notes with gratification the declaration that the Government of Brazil accepts the customs policy of unconditional most-favored-nation treatment for the purpose of demonstrating its good-will toward the United States and with a view to affirming in a practical way the disposition of the Brazilian Government to bring about more intimate commercial bonds, in mutual accord. The second declaration of the Brazilian Government relates to the subject of the preferences which prior to the present year have been accorded to American commerce. The Government of the United States, in refraining from requesting the renewal of the preference in question for the present year, has not been indifferent to the fact that changes of this character may possibly in some measure interfere with commercial intercourse as conducted on the previously existing basis. However, as stated in the Memorandum recently presented to the Brazilian Government by the American Ambassador at Rio de Janeiro, it is the policy of the United States to offer to all countries and to seek from them unconditional most-favored-nation treatment, making exception only in the case of Cuba, the dependencies of the United States, and the Panama Canal Zone. This policy is expressed by specific provisions in recent tariff legislation of the Congress of the United States, and, in the judgment of the United States, it is the policy best calculated to be of the maximum of advantage in furthering relations of amity and commerce.

The Brazilian Government will readily perceive how inconsistent it would be for the Government of the United States to enter into any arrangement involving a request on its part for special customs treatment or which offered special concessions on the part of the United States, whether in connection with the customs tariff or otherwise, in consideration of the granting to the United States of special customs treatment. It is the opinion of the Government of the United States that the stabilization of commercial relations between Brazil and the United States on the basis proposed could not but promote in the long run the strengthening of the bonds of friendship and commerce which now happily exist between them.

FOREIGN TRADE AGREEMENTS OF THE UNITED STATES: AUTHORITY OF THE PRESIDENT

19 U.S.C. § 1351 (1965).

(1) For the purpose of expanding foreign markets for the products of the United States (as a means of assisting in establishing and maintaining a better relationship among various branches of American agriculture, industry, mining, and commerce) by regulating the admission of foreign goods into the United States in accordance with the characteristics and needs of various branches of American production so that foreign markets will be made available to those branches of American production which require and are capable of developing such outlets by affording corresponding market opportunities for foreign products in the United States, the President, whenever he finds as a fact that any existing duties or other import restrictions of the United States or any foreign country are unduly burdening and restricting the foreign trade of the United States and that the purpose above declared will be promoted by the means hereinafter specified, is authorized from time to time—

(A) To enter into foreign trade agreements with foreign governments or instrumentalities thereof: Provided, That the enactment of the Trade Agreements Extension Act of 1955 shall not be construed to determine or indicate the approval or disapproval by the Congress of the executive agreement known as the General Agreement on Tariffs and Trade.

(B) To proclaim such modifications of existing duties and other import restrictions, or such additional import restrictions, or such continuance, and for such minimum periods, of existing customs or excise treatment of any article covered by foreign trade agreements, as are required or appropriate to carry out any foreign trade agreement that the President has entered into hereunder.

TREATY OF FRIENDSHIP, COMMERCE AND NAVIGATION BETWEEN THE UNITED STATES AND JAPAN OF APRIL 2, 1953

4 U.S.T. 2063, 206 U.N.T.S. 143.

Article XIV

1.   Each Party shall accord most-favored-nation treatment to products of the other Party, from whatever place and by whatever type of carrier arriving, and to products destined for exportation to the territories of such other Party, by whatever route and by whatever type of carrier, with respect to customs duties and charges of any kind imposed on or in connection with importation or exportation or imposed on the international transfer of payments for imports or exports, and with respect to the method of levying such duties and charges, and with respect to all rules and formalities in connection with importation and exportation.

2.   Neither Party shall impose restrictions or prohibitions on the importation of any product of the other Party, or on the exportation of any product to the territories of the other Party, unless the importation of the like product of, or the exportation of the like product to, all third countries is similarly restricted or prohibited.

3.   If either Party imposes quantitative restrictions on the importation or exportation of any product in which the other Party has an important interest:

(a)   It shall as a general rule give prior public notice of the total amount of the product, by quantity or value, that may be imported or exported during a specified period, and of any change in such amount or period; and

(b)   If it makes allotments to any third country, it shall afford such other Party a share proportionate to the amount of the product, by quantity or value, supplied by or to it during a previous representative period, due consideration being given to any special factors affecting the trade in such product.

4.   Either Party may impose prohibitions or restrictions on sanitary or other customary grounds of a noncommercial nature, or in the interest of preventing deceptive or unfair practices, provided such prohibitions or restrictions do not arbitrarily discriminate against the commerce of the other Party.

5.   Nationals and companies of either Party shall be accorded national treatment and most-favored-nation treatment by the other Party with respect to all matters relating to importation and exportation.

6.   The provisions of the present Article shall not apply to advantages accorded by either Party:

(a)   to products of its national fisheries;

(b) to adjacent countries in order to facilitate frontier traffic; or

(c) by virtue of a customs union or free-trade area of which it may become a member, so long as it informs the other Party of its plans and affords such other Party adequate opportunity for consultation.

7.   Notwithstanding the provisions of paragraphs 2 and 3(b) of the present Article, a Party may apply restrictions or controls on importation and exportation of goods that have effect equivalent to, or which are necessary to make effective, exchange restrictions.

*   *   *   However, such restrictions or controls shall depart no more than necessary from the aforesaid paragraphs and shall be conformable with a policy designed to promote the maximum development of nondiscriminatory foreign trade and to expedite the attainment both of a balance-of-payments position and of monetary reserves which will obviate the necessity of such restrictions.

Article XVI

1.   Products of either Party shall be accorded, within the territories of the other Party, national treatment and most-favored-nation treatment in all matters affecting internal taxation, sale, distribution, storage and use.

2.   Articles produced by nationals and companies of either Party within the territories of the other Party, or by companies of the latter Party controlled by such nationals and companies, shall be accorded therein treatment no less favorable than that accorded to like articles of national origin by whatever person or company produced, in all matters affecting exportation, taxation, sale, distribution, storage and use.

Article XXII

1.   The term "national treatment" means treatment accorded within the territories of a Party upon terms no less favorable than the treatment accorded therein, in like situations, to nationals, companies, products, vessels or other objects, as the case may be, of such Party.

2.   The term "most-favored-nation treatment" means treatment accorded within the territories of a Party upon terms no less favorable than the treatment accorded therein, in like situations, to nationals, companies, products, vessels or other objects, as the case may be, of any third country.

GENERAL AGREEMENT ON TARIFFS AND TRADE
OF OCTOBER 30, 1947

61 Stat. Part 5, A12, 55 U.N.T.S. 187.

Article I

1. With respect to customs duties and charges of any kind imposed on or in connection with importation or exportation or imposed on the international transfer of payments for imports or exports, and with respect to the method of levying such duties and charges, and with respect to all rules and formalities in connection with importation and exportation, and with respect to all matters referred to in paragraphs 1 and 2 of Article III, any advantage, favour, privilege or immunity granted by any contracting party to any product originating in or destined for any other country shall be accorded immediately and unconditionally to the like product originating in or destined for the territories of all other contracting parties.

2. The provisions of paragraph 1 of this Article shall not require the elimination of any preferences in respect of import duties or charges which do not exceed the levels provided for in paragraph 3 of this Article and which fall within the following descriptions:

[There follow specified excepted trade preferences, i. e., tariff advantages that are to remain exclusive. Generally, these were those between the United Kingdom and other Commonwealth entities; France and Territories of the French Union; the Customs Union of Belgium, Luxembourg and The Netherlands and the overseas territories of Belgium and The Netherlands; the United States and the Republics of Cuba and The Philippines and dependent territories of the United States; preferences between a few neighboring countries, the United States and Canada-Mexico not being included.]

The institutional history of GATT. The GATT, as a set of multipartite treaty rules about international trade and as a slenderly developed international organization, is all that survives of an ambitious post-World War II, early UN, effort to establish an International Trade Organization (ITO). The Charter of the International Trade Organization died aborning, chiefly because it attempted to regulate internationally restrictive trade practices and cartels and monopolies, as well as tariffs and quotas. GATT was put into effect pending sufficient state approvals to permit the ITO to come into being, which it never did. As the prospects for the ITO dimmed, GATT institutionalized itself, although it still is not, strictly speaking, a full-fledged international organization.

As to the expectations for the ITO, see Rubin, The Judicial Review Problem in the International Trade Organization, 63 Harv.L. Rev. 78 (1949). As to the early period of GATT, consult Gorter, GATT after Six Years, VIII Int'l Orgs. 1 (1954). The failure of the ITO also cost the less-developed countries (LDCs) their effort to write into most favored nation treatment an explicit exception for their development-related exports; the developed countries having agreed to such a principle (Art. XV of the ITO) for the ITO, successfully resisting its inclusion in the GATT part of that arrangement. As things turned out GATT was the only part of the total effort to regulate all major aspects of international trade that went into effect.

---

2. DEPARTURES FROM UNCONDITIONAL MOST FAVORED NATION TREATMENT

Types of departures. The most favored nation principle, along with provisions for national treatment in some instances, has a wider use in modern commercial treaties than terms of trade (tariffs and quotas) alone. Custom has dictated certain exclusions from most favored nation provisions as to the right of an alien to do business within a state: civil aviation, for example. Certain other activities are also excluded, sometimes explicitly or by the general understanding of the mutually promising states: defense industries, administration of aliens' estates, for example. As to trade in the strict sense, there is a customary exclusion of preferences given to "frontier traffic;" see GATT, Art. XXIV(3), which codifies this exception.

The more important departures are those that arise where customs unions and free trade areas provide trade advantages for the participating states in their trade with each other that if extended to non-participating states having most favored nation treaties with the member states individually would destroy a major incentive toward the elimination of tariffs and quotas between the member states. The very important Art. XXIV of GATT lays down the contours of the exception under reference, but in practice few of the arrangements that have been made have fitted GATT like a glove, with the result that waivers have been sought and usually granted, as was the case (with strong United States approval) in the formative period of the European Economic Community (EEC).

The EEC has now completed its transitional phases (except for new entrants), and the general rule is zero tariff between the members. Non-members are subject to a common external tariff, except where the EEC has made special arrangements; and the EEC is bound to unconditional most favored nation treatment with third states only as to its external tariff. The EEC is subject to GATT, because its members are all GATT states. The same general principle applies to the European Free Trade Association (EFTA) as to the tariff and quota preferences the member states give each other. But as there is no common external tariff in EFTA each EFTA state, through GATT, is responsible for dealing properly with third states in the administration of its national tariff. The Central American Common Market (CACM) is in the situation of the EEC; and the Latin American Free Trade Association (LAFTA), allowing for a few uncertainties, is like EFTA, vis-a-vis unconditional most favored nation treatment. Other groupings in developing Africa, Southeast Asia, and Latin America (the Andean Group within LAFTA) are similarly classifiable as either common markets or customs unions.

The greatest problems raised as to departures from unconditional most favored nation treatment are those created by emergency foreign exchange stringencies suffered by a state (whether developed or developing) and by the insistent demands of the developing countries that the rich countries grant them non-reciprocal, non-discriminatory, generalized trade preferences for the products of their industrialization. As to trade preference, the battle lost at ITO/GATT has brought into being the "Group of 77" (actually many more) of the poorer, developing countries, which through the United Nations Conference on Trade and Development (UNCTAD) fight on for preferences and other special trade advantages.

Why do they? What have preferences to do with development? In a nutshell the LDC's argument is: development requires a net inflow of resources in excess of our subsistence needs. We are too poor and too far behind to grow, as urgently we must, from what our societies can save from our internal trade and our disadvantaged exports of agricultural commodities and other raw materials. No matter what comes to us from external assistance and from foreign investment, greater export earnings are absolutely essential as a source of the development capital we need. But our exports are at a comparative disadvantage in world markets, because (i) we are just getting started and our market base is too narrow for economies of scale, (ii) we have to use large components of manpower in our production due to underemployment, (iii) we lack technology. If we have to pay the same tariffs as our developed competitors do in any significant foreign market, we will lose the export opportunity, because our costs are higher. To this they usually add: while developing, we need many kinds of manufactured imports ourselves. They always cost too much and the costs of what we have to buy are always rising faster than the prices of our traditional (raw materials) exports.

This viewpoint is sometimes theorized by poor country groups into seeing in unconditional most favored nation treatment a modern version of Mercantilism. This is hard for grizzled trade liberationists in developed countries to take, if they look back to the battles they have won or tried to win, instead of facing the new reality of Rich Nations-Poor Nations.

The materials that follow point toward a new problem: the legal and policy aspects of a new wave of protectionism. Does the United States 10% surcharge violate GATT, the Reciprocal Trade Agreements Act, general international law, or what?

———

TREATY ESTABLISHING THE EUROPEAN ECONOMIC COMMUNITY OF MARCH 25, 1957

298 U.N.T.S. 3.

Article 9

1. The Community shall be based upon a customs union covering the exchange of all goods and comprising both the prohibition, as between Member States, of customs duties on importation and exportation and all charges with equivalent effect and the adoption of a common customs tariff in their relations with third countries.

* * *

Article 10

1. Products having been entered for consumption in a Member State shall be deemed to be products coming from a third country in cases where, in respect of such products, the necessary import formalities have been complied with and the appropriate customs duties or charges with equivalent effect have been levied in such Member State and where such products have not benefited by any total or partial drawback on such duties or charges. * * *

* * *

Article 18

Member States hereby declare their willingness to contribute to the development of international commerce and the reduction of barriers to trade by entering into reciprocal and mutually advantageous arrangements directed to the reduction of customs duties below the general level which they could claim as a result of the establishment of a customs union between themselves.

Article 19

1. Under the conditions and within the limits laid down below, the duties under the common customs tariff shall be at the level of the arithmetical average of the duties applied in the four customs territories covered by the Community.

* * *

Article 30

Quantitative restrictions on importation and all measures with equivalent effect shall, without prejudice to the following provisions, hereby be prohibited between Member States.

AGREEMENT CONCERNING AUTOMOTIVE PRODUCTS BETWEEN THE UNITED STATES AND CANADA OF JANUARY 16, 1965

17 U.S.T. 1372.

Article II

(a) The Government of Canada, not later than the entry into force of the legislation contemplated in paragraph (b) of this Article, shall accord duty free treatment to imports of the products of the United States described in Annex A [automotive vehicles and parts].

(b) The Government of the United States * * * shall seek enactment of legislation authorizing duty-free treatments of imports of the products of Canada described in [the same products, with the exception of stated percentages of components manufactured outside Canada].

Problems

(1) Mexico complains of the preference given a Canadian-made truck over one made entirely in Mexico, say at the huge, integrated Volkswagen factory at Puebla. Does the United States have a defense as against its unconditional most favored nation promises (if any) to Mexico?

(2) Under the third country component provision in (b) what is legally permissible to Canada as to the claim that a United States "made" small car with a German-made engine and a British transmission is entitled to duty-free entry into Canada?

JOINT DECLARATION OF THE DEVELOPING COUNTRIES OF NOVEMBER 11, 1963

UNCTAD, Basic Documents 8, 10 (1963).

2. International trade could become a more powerful instrument and vehicle of economic development not only through the expansion of the traditional exports of the developing countries, but also through the development of markets for their new products and a general increase in their share of world exports under improved

terms of trade. For this purpose, a new international division of labour, with new patterns of production and trade, is necessary. Only in this way will the economic independence of the developing countries be strengthened and a truly interdependent and integrated world economy emerge. The development of production and the increase in productivity and purchasing power of the developing countries will contribute to the economic growth of the industrialized countries as well, and thus become a means to world-wide prosperity.

3. The existing principles and patterns of world trade still mainly favour the advanced parts of the world. Instead of helping the developing countries to promote the development and diversification of their economies, the present tendencies in world trade frustrate their efforts to attain more rapid growth. These trends must be reversed. The volume of trade of the developing countries should be increased and its composition diversified; the prices of their exports should be stabilized at fair and remunerative levels, and international transfers of capital should be made more favourable to those countries so as to enable them to obtain through trade more of the means needed for their economic development.

4. To achieve these objectives, a dynamic international trade policy is required. This policy should be based on the need for providing special assistance and protection for the less developed parts of the world economy. The removal of obstacles to the trade of the developing countries is important, but the accelerated development of the parts of the world which are lagging behind requires more than the unconditional application of the most-favoured-nation principle and the mere reduction of tariffs. More positive measures aimed at achieving a new international division of labour are essential to bring about the necessary increase in productivity and diversification of economic activity in the developing countries. The measures taken by developed countries to promote the development of the relatively backward areas within their national boundaries provide a guide for the purposeful and dynamic action which needs to be taken in the field of international economic co-operation.

5. The fundamental trade problems of developing countries are well identified. What the world lacks today is, therefore, not the awareness of the problem, but the readiness to act. Many constructive proposals were advanced during the second session of the Preparatory Committee of the United Nations Conference on Trade and Development. The representatives of developing countries making the present Declaration recommend to all Members of the United Nations that they give earnest consideration to these proposals and that they explore, before the beginning of the Conference, all practical means for their implementation, so as to make it possible to reach at the Conference basic agreement on a new international trade and development policy. This policy, in accordance with General Assembly resolution 1785 (XVII) of 8 December 1962, should lead

to the adoption by the Conference of concrete measures to achieve, inter alia, the following:

(a) Creation of conditions for the expansion of trade between countries at a similar level of development, at different stages of development or having different systems of social and economic organization;

(b) Progressive reduction and early elimination of all barriers and restrictions impeding the exports of the developing countries, without reciprocal concessions on their part;

(c) Increase in the volume of exports of the developing countries in primary products, both raw and processed, to the industrialized countries, and stabilization of prices at fair and remunerative levels;

(d) Expansion of the markets for exports of manufactured and semi-manufactured goods from the developing countries;

(e) Provision of more adequate financial resources at favourable terms so as to enable the developing countries to increase their imports of capital goods and industrial raw materials essential for their economic development, and better coordination of trade and aid policies;

(f) Improvement of the invisible trade of the developing countries, particularly by reducing their payments for freight and insurance and the burden of their debt charges;

(g) Improvement of institutional arrangements, including, if necessary, the establishment of new machinery and methods for implementing the decisions of the Conference.

TRADE AND DEVELOPMENT BOARD

UNCTAD, Basic Documents 59.[a]

The resolution of the General Assembly establishing UNCTAD provided, within that framework, for the setting up of a Trade and Development Board as a permanent organ to carry out, when the Conference itself is not in session, the functions that fall within the latter's competence. In laying down the terms of reference of the Board the resolution states that it "shall establish such subsidiary organs as may be necessary to the effective discharge of its functions". At its first session, the Board decided by its resolutions 7 (I), 9(I), 12(I) and 10(I) of 29 April 1965, to set up four main Committees in the fields of Commodities, Manufactures, Shipping, and Invisibles and Financing related to Trade. The Board also decided by its resolution 8(I) of 29 April 1965 to set up an Advisory Committee to the Board and to the Committee on Commodities.

The terms of reference of these bodies are reproduced below:
* * *

a. U.N. Publication; Sales No.: 66.I.14.

Terms of Reference for the Committee on Manufactures

* * *

4.   To assist the Board in its task of keeping under review and taking appropriate action within its competence for the implementation of the recommendations, declarations, resolutions and other decisions of the Conference, as they bear on the exports of manufactured and semi-manufactured articles from developing countries.

Such action by the Board may include, in particular, bringing to the attention of Member Governments recommendations of the Conference in respect of the following subjects, with due regard to the desirability of avoiding duplication with other international bodies dealing with these subjects:

(a) Avoidance of measures leading to a worsening of trading opportunities for developing countries;

(b) Reduction and, wherever possible, elimination of tariff and non-tariff barriers affecting exports of manufactured and semi-manufactured articles from developing countries;

(c) Consideration of the question of establishment by developed countries of a non-reciprocal system of preferences in favour of developing countries; and

(d) Programme of measures and actions for expansion of market opportunities for exports of manufactured and semi-manufactured articles produced in developing countries.

UNITED STATES: FOREIGN ASSISTANCE FOR THE SEVENTIES, THE PRESIDENT'S MESSAGE TO THE CONGRESS, SEPTEMBER 15, 1970

116 Congressional Record 31682 (970).[a]

Reform # 6: I propose that we redirect our other policies which bear on development to assure that they reinforce the new approach outlined in this message. Our goal will be to expand and enhance the contribution to development of trade and private investment, and to increase the effectiveness of government programs in promoting the development process. A number of changes are necessary:

I propose that we move promptly toward initiation of a system of tariff preferences for the exports of manufactured products of the lower income countries in the markets of all of the industrialized countries * * *

* * *

3.   Promoting Effective Development Through Improved Economic Policies.

In addition to a new emphasis on the role of international institutions and a new shape to our bilateral programs, I propose in-

a.   The message also appears in 6 Weekly Compilation of Presidential Documents 1214, Sept. 21, 1970.

itiatives that will enhance the public and private sector contribution to the development process.

To open further the benefits of trade to the lower income countries, I have proposed that the international community initiate a system of tariff preferences for the exports of manufactured and selected primary products of the lower income countries in the markets of all of the industrialized countries.

The lower income countries must expand their exports to be able to afford the imports needed to promote their development efforts, and to lessen their need for concessional foreign assistance.

Market growth for most of the primary commodities which have traditionally been their major sources of export earnings is insufficient to enable them to meet these needs. I will submit legislation to the Congress recommending that we eliminate duties on a wide range of manufactured products purchased from the lower income countries. We will move ahead with this approach as soon as we achieve agreement with the other industrialized countries to join us with comparable efforts * * *

EEC EXPANDS GENERALIZED PREFERENCES TO DEVELOPING COUNTRIES

Press Release from the European Community Information Service, Washington, D. C. June 23, 1971.

CCH, Common Market Reporter, ¶ 9441.*

The European Common Market's Council of Ministers formally agreed to give "generalized preferences" to developing countries starting July 1, 1971.

The decision provides for a system of preferences that cover manufactured and semi-manufactured products, as well as some processed farm products. The one-way preferences are extended initially to 91 developing countries which are members of the "Group of 77" of the UN Conference on Trade and Development (UNCTAD).

Franco Maria Malfatti, President of the European Communities Commission, said that the Council's decision, culminating eight years of work, was the most important international step that the Community had taken since the conclusion of the Kennedy Round. He pointed out that the Community would be the first industrialized power to carry out its offers of generalized preferences. He said that the action was but the beginning of a more active policy for dealing with the problems of development in the world.

The list of generalized preferences conforms to the conclusions adopted by the Council of Ministers on March 30, 1971, on the basis of proposals recommended by the Commission and approved by the European Parliament.

The Community's Offer

The Common Market's offer has been designed to give the maximum advantage possible to the benefiting countries while still safeguarding the interests of industry in the Community and its associated states.

The Community makes a distinction between agricultural products and semi-manufactured and manufactured goods.

(a) Processed agricultural goods (Chapters 1 to 24 of the Brussels Nomenclature). Tariff benefits are granted on about 150 processed agricultural products imported from developing countries, valued at about $30 million. The preferences consist of partial reduction in customs duties or levies, and imports will be admitted without volume limits.

A safeguard clause, based on Article XIX of the General Agreement on Tariffs and Trade, is included, allowing partial or complete reimposition of the duty or levy when the quantity or price of the imports risks causing grave harm to Community production of similar or directly competitive goods. The safeguard clause will apply only to the country or countries causing the harm, thus protecting non-offending recipient countries.

(b) Industrial products (Chapters 25 to 99 of the Brussels Nomenclature). Basic industrial products are not covered by the Community's offer, but almost all imported industrial raw materials already come into the Community duty-free; only 0.6 percent of such goods imported from developing countries ($44 million of a total $700 million) are still dutiable. Of this 0.6 percent, the Community opens tariff quotas with nil or reduced duties on certain non-ferrous metals.

Ceilings, Exemptions, and No Exclusion

The Community's offer, as it applies to semi-manufactured and manufactured goods, has three features: a ceiling system, duty-exemption, and no excluded products.

The ceiling system limiting the volume of preferential imports is counter-balanced by duty-exemption and by the fact that no products are shut out and that there is no safeguard clause.

A ceiling is fixed each calendar year for each product. In general, the ceiling is calculated according to the following formula: the basic amount (level of imports, c. i. f. European Community, from recipient countries in 1968) plus an additional amount (5 percent of the value of imports, c. i. f. European Community, from non-recipient countries, i. e. industrialized countries, in the last year for which statistics are available). This method results in a raising of the ceiling every year, as the "additional amount" will grow as Community trade with industrialized countries increases.

Preferential exemption from duty is to be granted by the Community on all manufactured and semi-manufactured products.

No products are to be shut out. The Community's offer, as distinct from others, makes no exceptions.

The Recipient Countries

The Community has decided to apply its offer, in the first stage, to developing countries which are members of the "Group of 77" of the UN Conference on Trade and Development (which are now actually 91 countries) and to dependent territories of non-member states (including Hong Kong). The Community, in consultation with other industrialized countries, is studying the possibility of including among recipient countries those that are not members of the "77" Group but who desire to benefit.

Long-Range View

The Community's offer is not particularly bold as far as processed agricultural products are concerned, mainly because the idea of generalized preferences is accepted by all for industrial products but has not yet received universal support for processed agricultural products.

The Community is also limited because its organization of agricultural markets seriously narrows the possibilities of reducing duties or levies.

The Community's offer for industrial products is of undoubted advantage to the recipient countries. Of all the donor countries, the Community is practically the only one to grant tariff preferences to textiles, which are regarded as a particularly sensitive area by all industrialized countries. The link set up between the period of validity of the International Long-Term Cotton Textile Agreement and the calculation of ceilings has been worked out in such a way as to give the recipient countries additional export receipts while avoiding undue market expansion which might hurt Community industries. Thus, for sensitive textile products, ceilings opened for the first year are only about $115 million on imports of approximately $110 million.

In the case of other less sensitive products, the situation is much the same. Developing countries are already the main suppliers of the Community for these goods and are very competitive. The first annual ceilings opened for sensitive products (numbering about 40) amount to about $195 million on approximately $150 million of imports from recipient countries. Ceilings for the slightly less sensitive products (also numbering about 40) are in the region of $35 million on $20 million of imports.

For the majority of other products, classed as non-sensitive, the first annual ceilings are about $660 million on imports of approximately $170 million.

As a whole, the first annual ceilings opened by the Community are more than double the value of imports from the Third World in

1968, i. e., more than a billion dollars (total ceilings) as against $450 million (basic amounts) for dutiable products covered by preferences. This jump of $550 million over imports shows the size of the "additional amounts" (5 percent of the value of imports from non-benefiting countries). The Community is using the "additional amount" to establish a link between the growth of its trade with industrialized countries and the increase in the level of its trade with the Third World. The more imports into the Community from developed countries increase, the greater will be the value of the additional amount in the following year, pushing up the ceilings for preferential imports.

The sensitive and slightly less sensitive products mentioned are in practice items which industrialized non-member countries supply in very small quantity to the Community. Thus the ceilings opened will not be much above the level of imports from developing countries and the additional amount will be very small. For the remaining, non-sensitive products already being exported ($170 million) and products which developing countries are not yet exporting to the Community, the working of the additional amount will be an encouragement to production and export and a spur to industrialization.

All manufactured and semi-manufactured industrial goods covered by the Community's offer are subject to a ceiling, that is, the de jure situation. In actual practice, ceilings will not be strictly applied except to sensitive and slightly less sensitive products.

In the case of sensitive products, the Community tariff quota will be the ceiling, and the management of it includes a previous sharing-out between the Member States of the Community. There is no previous sharing-out of a ceiling between the Member States in the case of the slightly less sensitive products: a simple system will arrange for a shut-down, if necessary, for preferential imports when the ceiling is reached. In cases where the ceiling system is strictly applied, imports from the benefiting countries can still continue to enter the Community, but they will pay customs duties, and the preferential arrangements will be started again at the beginning of the following calendar year.

For all other products classed as non-sensitive—the vast majority —there will be neither tariff quotas nor special safeguard machinery, and in practice, preferential imports will be allowed to exceed the ceilings.

The Community decided that it would rather have a ceiling system than safeguarding clauses for industrial products wherever possible.

Industrial producers in the Community, with the ceilings system, will be in a better position to gauge in advance the effects of preferential competition. For the benefiting developing countries, the system gives a measure of assurance of regular outlets in the markets offering preferences.

The ceilings system also offers a fairer sharing among the recipient countries, putting a limit on the most competitive of them in preferential markets for sensitive products. The Community's offer, in fact, states that no recipient country may, as a general rule, get more than 50 percent of the ceiling for each product (30 percent or 20 percent in certain cases). This is the so-called "buffer-clause," framed to give a chance to the less advanced benefiting countries and keep down the pressure from the more competitive suppliers.

Generalized preferences will not provide all the benefiting countries with tangible advantages and the same measure of benefits, nor will they work the miracle of providing a solution to all development problems in the Third World. In the immediate future, only a limited number of the more advanced developing countries, such as Yugoslavia, Iran, India, Pakistan, Brazil, Venezuela, Mexico, Argentina, and the United Arab Republic, will be able to derive substantial advantages from the privileged opening of Community markets.

Even so, generalized preferences will open up additional export opportunities for all developing countries, which they should utilize for the advancement of their interests.

IMPOSITION OF SUPPLEMENTAL DUTY FOR BALANCE OF PAYMENTS PURPOSES BY THE PRESIDENT OF THE UNITED STATES OF AMERICA

36 Fed. Reg. 15724 (1971).

A Proclamation

Whereas, there has been a prolonged decline in the international monetary reserves of the United States, and our trade and international competitive position is seriously threatened and, as a result, our continued ability to assure our security could be impaired;

Whereas, the balance of payments position of the United States requires the imposition of a surcharge on dutiable imports;

Whereas, pursuant to the authority vested in him by the Constitution and the statutes, including, but not limited to, the Tariff Act of 1930, as amended (hereinafter referred to as "the Tariff Act"), and the Trade Expansion Act of 1962 (hereinafter referred to as "the TEA"), the President entered into, and proclaimed tariff rates under, trade agreements with foreign countries;

Whereas, under the Tariff Act, the TEA, and other provisions of law, the President may, at any time, modify or terminate, in whole or in part, any proclamation made under his authority;

Now, Therefore, I, Richard Nixon, President of the United States of America, acting under the authority vested in me by the Constitution and the statutes, including, but not limited to, the Tariff Act, and the TEA, respectively, do proclaim as follows:

A.   I hereby declare a national emergency during which I call upon the public and private sector to make the efforts necessary to strengthen the international economic position of the United States.

B.   (1) I hereby terminate in part for such period as may be necessary and modify prior Presidential Proclamations which carry out trade agreements insofar as such proclamations are inconsistent with, or proclaim duties different from, those made effective pursuant to the terms of this Proclamation.

(2) Such proclamations are suspended only insofar as is required to assess a surcharge in the form of a supplemental duty amounting to 10 percent ad valorem. Such supplemental duty shall be imposed on all dutiable articles imported into the customs territory of the United States from outside thereof, which are entered, or withdrawn from warehouse, for consumption after 12:01 a. m., August 16, 1971, provided, however, that if the imposition of an additional duty of 10 percent ad valorem would cause the total duty or charge payable to exceed the total duty or charge payable at the rate prescribed in column 2 of the Tariff Schedules of the United States, then the column 2 rate shall apply.

C.   To implement section B of this Proclamation, the following new subpart shall be inserted after subpart B of part 2 of the Appendix to the Tariff Schedules of the United States:

Subpart C—Temporary Modifications for
Balance of Payments Purposes

Subpart C headnotes:

1.   This subpart contains modifications of the provisions of the tariff schedules proclaimed by the President in Proclamation 4074.

2.   Additional duties imposed—The duties provided for in this subpart are cumulative duties which apply in addition to the duties otherwise imposed on the articles involved. The provisions for these duties are effective with respect to articles entered on and after 12:01 a. m., August 16, 1971, and shall continue in effect until modified or terminated by the President or by the Secretary of the Treasury (hereinafter referred to as the Secretary) in accordance with headnote 4 of this subpart.

3.   Limitation on additional duties—The additional 10 percent rate of duty specified in rate of duty column numbered 1 of item 948.00 shall in no event exceed that rate which, when added to the column numbered 1 rate imposed on the imported article under the appropriate item in schedules 1 through 7 of these schedules, would result in an aggregated rate in excess of the rate provided for such article in rate of duty column numbered 2.

4.   For the purposes of this subpart—

(a) Delegation of authority to Secretary—The Secretary may from time to time take action to reduce, eliminate or reimpose the rate of additional duty herein or to establish exemption therefrom, either generally or with respect to an article which he may specify either generally or as the product of a particular country, if he determines that such action is consistent with safeguarding the balance of payments position of the United States.

(b) Publication of Secretary's actions—All actions taken by the Secretary hereunder shall be in the form of modifications of this subpart published in the Federal Register.   Any action reimposing the additional duties on an article exempted therefrom by the Secretary shall be effective only with respect to articles entered on and after the date of publication of the action in the Federal Register.

(c) Authority to prescribe rules and regulations—The Secretary is authorized to prescribe such rules and regulations as he determines to be necessary or appropriate to carry out the provisions of this subpart.

5.   Articles exempt from the additional duties—In accordance with determinations made by the Secretary in accordance with headnote 4(a), the following described articles are exempt from the provisions of this subpart:

*   *   *   *   *   *   *   *   *

Item	Article	Rates of duty	
		1	2
948.00	Articles, except as exempted under headnote 5 of this subpart, which are not free of duty under these schedules and which are the subject of tariff concessions granted by the United States in trade agreements.	10% ad val. . . (See headnote 3 of this subpart.)	No change.

D.   This Proclamation shall be effective 12:01 a. m., August 16, 1971.

In Witness Whereof, I have hereunto set my hand this fifteenth day of August in the year of our Lord nineteen hundred and seventy-one, and of the Independence of the United States of America the one hundred and ninety-sixth.

Richard Nixon

Problem. Suppose you had been asked as a member of the Legal Adviser's staff of the Department of State, to analyze the above action while it was still in the planning stage. What would you have concluded as to its legality under international law? Why?

GENERAL AGREEMENT ON TARIFFS AND TRADE OF OCTOBER 30, 1947

61 Stat. Part 5, A12, 55 U.N.T.S. 187.

Article XII

1. Notwithstanding the provisions of paragraph 1 of Article XI [eliminating quotas], any contracting party, in order to safeguard its external financial position and its balance of payments, may restrict the quantity or value of merchandise permitted to be imported, subject to the provisions of the following paragraphs of this Article.

2. (a) Import restrictions instituted, maintained or intensified by a contracting party under this Article shall not exceed those necessary:

  (i) to forestall the imminent threat of, or to stop, a serious decline in its monetary reserves, or

  (ii) in the case of a contracting party with very low monetary reserves, to achieve a reasonable rate of increase in its reserves * * *

  (b) Contracting parties applying restrictions under subparagraph (a) of this paragraph shall progressively relax them as such conditions improve * * *

Article XXXVII

1. The developed contracting parties shall to the fullest extent possible—that is, except when compelling reasons, which may include legal reasons, make it impossible—give effect to the following provisions:

  *   *   *

  (b) refrain from introducing, or increasing the incidence of, customs duties * * * on products currently and potentially of particular export interest to less-developed contracting parties * * *

"COMPELLING REASONS" UNDER GATT

Statement by the United States Assistant Secretary of State for
Inter-American Affairs, Meeting of the Inter-American Economic
and Social Council, OAS, September 15, 1971

65 United States Department of State Bulletin 379, 383 (1971).

* * *

I would like to say at this point that my Government does not
consider that this temporary surcharge is a violation of the standstill
commitment. The standstill to which we have agreed is the one stated
in part IV of the GATT, which was extended to all OAS members at
the Caracas Conference, which permits taking measures in case of
compelling reasons. The situation which my country faced prior to
August 15 clearly constituted compelling reasons, as so many of you
reflected in your statements. We have stated repeatedly on this same
subject that the U. S. Government has no legislative authority to grant
compensation and that the only case in which the United States recognizes the right to compensation is when it is specifically required by
the GATT in return for impairing or withdrawing a tariff concession
previously negotiated, and I believe without being totally expert that
the temporary nature of the surcharge once again sets the surcharge
apart.

I would like, if I might, to refer to a possible misunderstanding
in the trade issue section of the manifesto, in which the reference to
freezing of domestic prices is unclear—at least to me. I think all, or
some of you, do know that the 10-percent surcharge may be passed
directly to the customer as an additional element of cost, and I am
frank to admit that the passage of that 10 percent of cost is a marketing problem, or may be a marketing problem.

———

U. S. RAPPED SOUTH OF THE BORDER
IMPORT SLAP PROVES TOUCHY IN "THIRD WORLD"

The Christian Science Monitor Oct. 27, 1971,
p. 10, col. 2, 3, 4 and 5.*

Lima, Peru

Washington's new economic policies and particularly the 10 percent import surcharge were clearly the major topics of discussion as
foreign ministers from 95 developing nations met here this week.

In preliminary sessions, the Latin-American members of the
group took sharp exception to the import surcharge and accused Washington of having little real interest in the development of Latin America.

The Latin Americans are hoping to get the full membership of the grouping to approve resolutions calling on the developed nations and particularly the United States to take more finished manufactured products from the developing nations—and therefore help with their development.

The U. S. surcharge will come in for searching criticism in the days to come. The Latin Americans point out that they had a net trade deficit with the United States last year of $700 million and that therefore they were not contributing to Washington's economic problems, but that their developing industries are being seriously hurt by the import surcharge.

The talks here, however, range much further afield than Latin America. Foreign ministers from Africa, Asia, the Middle East are also present.

The organization that brings them together is the so-called Group of 77 which now, with the admission of Cuba, has 95 members.

The loose grouping of nations seeks to work out joint strategies on development.

To many of those gathered here, such strategies are made all the more difficult by U. S. economic policies and to a lesser extent by those of other developed nations, including the Western European countries and the Soviet Union and its bloc nations.

Over the weekend numerous delegates from Africa and the Middle East complained privately about European tariff barriers on their goods, and some African delegates spoke of "Soviet imperialism in economic affairs."

Surcharge criticized

But the brunt of comment fell heavily upon the United States, not only from the Latin nations but also from countries in Africa and the Far East. Much of the criticism centered on the import surcharge, an item conference sources say will be a major issue for discussion.

"If Washington really wants to know what the world feels about its economic policies, it should tune in on the talks here," a Latin American delegate said.

The presence of Cuba stirred considerable interest with the arrival of an advance party Saturday and the scheduled arrival of Foreign Minister Rául Roa early Monday. But the Cubans here kept to themselves. What role they will play is not clear.

Cuba was admitted as a member last week in a Latin-American caucus at the United Nations. It marked one more weakening of the political, economic, and diplomatic isolation of Cuba, which dates from the early 1960's and suggests the growing Latin-American desire to end the isolation and resume ties with Cuba.

A range of economies

The nations gathered here represent a wide variety of economies, and the term "developing" is a loose one. Among the grouping's members are Yugoslavia, the only European member; Brazil, with its annual growth rate of 9 percent or more; Haiti, with its tremendous poverty; South Vietnam and South Korea, but not the northern halves of those two lands; Liberia; and Tanzania.

What unifies them is "a common sense of urgency about changing our economic backwardness," as a delegate from a Central African nation said.

Whether the group can form some sort of economic strategy to help protect their interests and to assist in the development is not certain. Though the grouping is influential when it comes to totting up the number of members, its diversities are large.

Marxist-capitalist dialogue

A Peruvian organizer of the conference said over the weekend that when Marxist-oriented Chile and capitalist-oriented Argentina meet, they do not talk the same economic language at first. "But as they get down to the basics, there is more agreement than one might suspect."

The same may well be true of the organization as a whole. Moreover, President Nixon's new economic policies, spelled out last August serve as a common ground. If preconference comment is any indication, Washington is going to get rough verbal treatment here.

Whether the Group of 77 can put any muscle into its unhappiness is yet another question. A document is before it that calls on the developed nations to change their commercial practices to permit the entry of more manufactured and semimanufactured goods from countries that are in the process of development.

Demand is familiar

The proposal has a familiar ring. The Latin Americans have been demanding the same of Washington for years and spelled it out in the declaration of Viña del Mar 2½ years ago.

Washington for a number of years has been committed to a policy of encouraging diversification in Latin America—to move Latin nations away from single-crop economies and single-product exports. In the process, Washington has agreed to take more Latin-American finished goods.

But the Latin Americans say that little has come from that agreement and that now, moreover, the import surcharge defeats whatever progress has been made. The Latin nations feel a sense of urgency about the whole business and are encouraged to get the proposed document approved by the full membership of the grouping in order to put pressure on Washington.

Late in 1971, a group of developing countries,[a] all but two members of the GATT, carried out, for the first time, GATT trade negotiations between themselves alone. The countries included several not normally regarded as clearly and unequivocally "developing," such as Spain and Israel. The negotiation presupposed no most favored nation extension of the preferences to the GATT community generally; other GATT members ["Contracting Parties"], except for the United States, voted for a waiver. The United States objected and said it would consider claiming "compensation" as for breaches of the GATT. Why? Would it be that this arrangement marks the beginning of the end of the unconditional most favored treatment?

GATT DECISION ON WAIVER

Nov. 26, 1971 (L/3636).
Gatt, Basic Instruments and Selected Documents, 18th Supp., 1972, p. 26.

Text of the Decision

The Contracting Parties to the General Agreement have adopted the following Decision:

The Contracting Parties to the General Agreement on Tariffs and Trade,

Recognizing that individual and joint action is essential to further the development of the economies of developing countries and to bring about a rapid advance in the standards of living in these countries;

Noting that the Contracting Parties may enable developing contracting parties to use special measures to promote their trade and development;

Considering that trade negotiations among developing countries have as their objective expanding access on more favourable terms for developing countries in one another's markets through an exchange of tariff and trade concessions directed towards the expansion of their mutual trade;

Recalling that, at the twenty-third session, the Contracting Parties recognized that the establishment of preferences among developing countries, appropriately administered and subject to the necessary safeguards, could make an important contribution to the expansion of trade among developing countries and to the attainment of the objectives of the General Agreement;

Noting that the countries which have participated in these negotiations have drawn up the "Protocol relating to Trade Negotiations among Developing Countries" (hereinafter referred to as the Pro-

------

a. Brazil, Chile, Egypt, Greece, India, Israel, Korea, Mexico, Pakistan, Peru, Philippines, Spain, Tunisia, Turkey, Uruguay and Yugoslavia. (Mexico and the Philippines are not contracting parties to GATT.)

tocol) with rules to govern the arrangements as well as a first list of concessions, and that these countries intend to keep under review the possibility of promoting negotiations for additions or enlargements to the schedules of concessions;

Noting also that while concessions exchanged in the Negotiations will apply among parties to the arrangements set out in the Protocol, the countries participating in these negotiations have undertaken to facilitate the accession of all developing countries on terms consistent with the latters' individual development, financial and trade needs;

Noting further that the Contracting Parties express the hope that all developing countries which have not participated in the arrangements will consider acceding to the Protocol; and

Recognizing that these arrangements should not impede the reduction of tariffs on a most-favoured-nation basis;

Decide:

(a) that without prejudice to any other Article of the General Agreement and subject to the provisions of paragraphs (b)–(e) of this Decision, the provisions of paragraph 1 of Article I of the General Agreement shall be waived to the extent necessary to permit each contracting party participating in the arrangements set out in the Protocol (hereinafter referred to as a participating contracting party) to accord preferential treatment as provided in the Protocol with respect to products originating in other parties to the Protocol, without being required to extend the same treatment to like goods when imported from other contracting parties;

> Provided that any such preferential treatment shall be designed to facilitate trade between participants and not to raise barriers to the trade of other contracting parties;

(b) that any participating contracting party which, pursuant to the arrangements set out in the Protocol, introduces or modifies any preferential concessions shall so notify the Contracting Parties and shall furnish them with all useful information relating to the actions taken;

(c) that each participating contracting party shall afford adequate opportunity for consultations at the request of any other contracting party which considers that any benefit accruing to it under the General Agreement may be or is being impaired unduly as a result of the arrangements set out in the Protocol;

(d) that any contracting party which considers that the arrangements under the Protocol are being applied inconsistently with this Decision or that any benefit accruing to it under the General Agreement may be or is being impaired unduly as a result of the arrangements and that consultations have proved unsatisfactory, may bring the matter before the Contracting Parties, which will examine it promptly and will formulate any recommendation that they judge appropriate; and

(e) that the Contracting Parties will review annually, on the basis of a report to be furnished by the participating countries, the operation of this Decision in the light of the aforementioned objectives and considerations and after five years of its operation carry out a major review in order to evaluate its effects. Before the end of the tenth year the Contracting Parties will undertake another major review of its operation with a view to deciding whether this Decision should be continued or modified. In connexion with such annual reviews and major reviews, the participating contracting parties shall make available to the Contracting Parties relevant information regarding action taken under this Decision.

SECTION B. ECONOMIC INTERESTS OF ALIENS WITHIN A STATE

Dimensions of the problem. This section deals mainly with the "nationalization problem" where aliens' property or economic interests are affected. The existing international legal system is under stress in this area. The problem is an old one; but it has become more acute than ever before, as states, particularly new and developing ones, embark upon various types of social experimentation.

First of all, there is a sharp cleavage between the rich states and some of the developing countries on the question whether there is an "international minimum standard," that is a legal restraint upon the taking state as to the (i) purpose of nationalization and the (ii) payment of compensation.

Second, there is a question as to whether only certain types of traditional property rights are included, or whether impairment of aliens' economic interests more broadly viewed are within the ambit of the rules and principles governing nationalization and its counterpart in diplomacy, the extension of "diplomatic protection" (espousal) by the state of nationality.

A third modern issue, dealt with in Chapter 6 on aspects of the act of state doctrine, concerns the scope of the remedies for nationalizations, especially as to whether invalidation of the title given by the taking state to a purchaser from it is a remedy that customary international law recognizes.

The modern nationalization problem in international law must be viewed against the backdrop of strong psycho-political pressures in certain taking states. These tend to induce irrationality, not only in the decision to nationalize, but also in the stance of the nationalizing state in relationship to its international interests and obligations. Also, the dispossessed alien owners, even when from rich and highly developed states, tend to become emotional about the issues involved. Thus where, as is usually the case, such owners are influential persons in the essentially democratically responsive "rich" nation, both the sending and the host states become involved in escalations of tension that make it necessary for things to cool before either diplomacy or law can act effectively.

However, despite the foregoing, it is reasonably accurate to generalize that in time most nationalization issues get settled, by negotiation, by arbitration, or by adjudication. International claims law is a specialty in international practice; and sometimes, as where there is a lump sum settlement calling for a division among claimants by one of its indigenous institutions, a parallel specialty in domestic law also develops. Also the lawyer who is called upon to counsel foreign investors needs to know about the nationalization problem and its law, both substantive and procedural.

Almost no one is satisfied with the international law of nationalization as it is. It is not only disputed. It is slow. An old quip of its practitioners is that the claims of the grandparents are settled by the parents for the benefit of the children. In the field of foreign capital movements, the accelerated pace of planet-wide activity chafes against the slow, Dickensian tempo of nationalization settlements.

The final and most important question is: what *should* the law be, reliance, rationality, equity, economic development, reasonable universality and effectiveness all considered? Some day, before too long, lawyers and statesmen are going to have to answer the question multinationally, not by legislative fiat in a single state. To answer it effectively they have to know what exists now as to legal regulation of nationalization of aliens' economic interests and go on from there.

---

1. THE NATURE OF STATE RESPONSIBILITY FOR TAKINGS

LAUTERPACHT, THE DEVELOPMENT OF INTERNATIONAL LAW BY THE INTERNATIONAL COURT 314 (1958) *

The Plea of Non-Discrimination

In the sphere of State responsibility the jurisprudence of the Court has assisted—indirectly, but emphatically—in discouraging a view closely connected with an extreme assertion of sovereignty, namely, that a State incurs no international responsibility if, with regard to measures adopted by it, it treats aliens and nationals alike. The Court has repeatedly laid down that the so-called plea of non-

* Reprinted by permission of Frederick A. Praeger, Inc., New York, and Stevens & Sons, Ltd., London.

discrimination is not a valid defence against a charge of violation of international law. This the Court has done in the numerous cases, referred to elsewhere in this book, in which it affirmed the principle that equality of treatment must be an equality of both fact and law, and that a State cannot avoid its obligations by the device of framing its law in general terms equally applicable to all. However, the jurisprudence of the Court goes further than that. A measure, even if genuinely applicable both to nationals and to aliens, does not, for that reason, become lawful if it is otherwise prohibited by treaty. After finding, in the case of Certain German Interests in Polish Upper Silesia, that expropriation without indemnity was contrary to the Convention between Poland and Germany, the Court held expressly that "a measure prohibited by the Convention cannot become lawful under this instrument by reason of the fact that the State applies it to its own nationals." It invoked that principle once more in its Judgment in the Peter Pázmány University case. Previously, in the Advisory Opinion on German Settlers in Poland, the Court considered as irrelevant the fact that in a few instances the Polish law in question applied also to non-German Polish nationals who took as purchasers from original holders of German race.

It is legitimate to assume that these principles apply not only to international obligations established by treaty but also to customary international law. The plea of non-discrimination as a defence against a charge of violation of international law amounts, upon analysis, to a claim of the sovereign State to disregard international law and to erect its own law as the sole standard of the legitimacy of its action so long as such action is of general application. That claim the Court has declined to countenance. The attitude of the Court on the subject is fully in accordance with its repeated affirmation, as a matter of course, of the priority of the obligations of international law over municipal law. It did so in particular by refusing to permit the parties to plead their municipal law as a justification for non-compliance with an international obligation; that, in the words of the Court, "would amount to relying upon the non-fulfilment of an obligation imposed * * * by an international agreement."

Measure of Damages

In connection with State responsibility it is of interest to note the attitude of the Court to the question of the measure of damages due as compensation for a breach of an international obligation. In the international sphere the principle established in general jurisprudence to the effect that damages must, as a rule, include full restitution in integrum did not at first secure ready acceptance by writers. It was asserted that the responsibility of States must be limited to damages arising directly out of the injurious event, to the exclusion of all indirect and consequential damages. This was, to some extent, in accordance with certain tendencies in national law

—now in process of disappearing in countries under the rule of law—to limit both the amenability of the State to suit and the consequences of its liability. While discouraging the award of purely speculative and remotely consequential damages, international jurisprudence has not, in general, accepted these assertions.

The suggestion of a general limitation of the responsibility of States in this matter was rejected by the Court of the Judgment in the case concerning the Chorzów Factory. The Court declined to agree that the compensation due to the German Government was limited to the value of the undertaking at the moment of dispossession, plus interest to the day of payment. The Court distinguished between expropriation which was lawful but for the fact of the State having failed to pay the just price of the property taken—in which case the compensation might properly be limited to the value of the undertaking at the time of the dispossession—and expropriation which had been resorted to in violation of an international undertaking. In the latter case, the Court said, the reparation "must, so far as possible, wipe out all the consequences of the illegal act and re-establish the situation which would, in all probability, have existed if that act had not been committed." The Court laid down in detail the principles governing compensation in these cases: "Restitution in kind, or, if this is not possible, payment of a sum corresponding to the value which a restitution in kind would bear; the award, if need be, of damages for loss sustained which cannot be covered by restitution in kind or payment in place of it." The Court then proceeded to assess compensation for losses in a manner which might have caused a less authoritative tribunal some apprehension lest it be charged with awarding damages for speculative profits.

GERMAN INTERESTS IN POLISH UPPER SILESIA—THE SO-CALLED CASE OF THE FACTORY AT CHORZOW (GERMANY v. POLAND)

Permanent Court of International Justice, 1926.
P.C.I.J., Ser. E, No. 2, 99, 114–115.

[Acting under a national law and claiming authorization therefore under the Treaty of Versailles and a Germano-Polish Convention Concerning Upper Silesia, a Polish tribunal nullified in the land records a conveyance from the German state to a German national made after the Armistice but before the effective date of the Treaty of Versailles. To Germany's claim under general international law, as incorporated into the Convention as a general standard by Heading III thereof the Polish defense was that it did not lie because of what the Court in the excerpt below refers to as treaty "exceptions."]

* * * This right constitutes an exception to the principle of respect for vested rights recognized by international law and con-

firmed as regards Upper Silesia generally under Heading II of the Convention; the derogation is therefore strictly in the nature of an exception and, for this reason, exclusive. Any measure affecting the property, rights and interests of German subjects covered by Head III of the Convention, which would overstep the limits set by the generally accepted principles of international law and were not justified on special grounds taking precedence over the Convention, would be incompatible with the régime established under the Convention.

Again, one of the formal conditions for the exercise of the right of expropriation is that previous notice of an intention to expropriate should be given; this notice must only cover property liable to expropriation and therefore presupposes a preliminary enquiry as to the existence of the necessary conditions. The Court infers from this that there may be no dispossession of property except in the form intended by the Convention, unless it be first established that the Convention is not applicable.

Considering next the law of July 14th, 1920, in the light of these principles, the Court observes that Article 2 of the law treats as null and non-existing rights which private persons may have acquired by deeds of alienation executed by the Crown, the German Reich, etc., if such deeds were drawn after November 11th, 1918. And, by authorizing the Polish Treasury to demand the eviction of any persons who, after the coming into force of the law, remain, in virtue of a contract of the kind contemplated in Article 5, in occupation of one of the landed properties in question, this article, in the Court's view, recognizes a right to disregard even private rights derived from contracts previous to November 11th, 1918. These articles, therefore, may affect private property and withdraw it from the protective régime instituted by Heading III, subjecting it to measures prohibited by the Convention; and they are applied automatically, without any investigation as to the title of ownership or validity of each transfer or contract. No means of redress is given to interested Parties and no indemnification is provided for. The Court arrives at the conclusion that both in form and in substance the application of Articles 2 and 5 of the Polish law is not compatible with the system established by Heading III of the * * * Convention.

THE PANEVEZYS–SALDUTISKIS RAILWAY CASE
(ESTONIA v. LITHUANIA)

Permanent Court of International Justice, 1939
P.C.I.J., Ser. A/B, No. 76, 4, 16.

[This nationalization case turned on issues related to the nationality of the private party and exhaustion of remedies considered at p. 1113. The excerpt that follows tends to show that the parties and the court assumed, in going on to these issues, the existence of an underlying general principle of customary international law as to the taking state's responsibility. To what extent is it valid to argue from such assumptions that the weight of opinion among states supports the underlying principle when it is not specifically challenged in the particular case?]

* * *

In the opinion of the Court, the rule of international law on which the first Lithuanian objection is based is that in taking up the case of one of its nationals, by resorting to diplomatic action or international judicial proceedings on his behalf, a State is in reality asserting its own right, the right to ensure in the person of its nationals respect for the rules of international law. This right is necessarily limited to intervention on behalf of its own nationals because, in the absence of a special agreement, it is the bond of nationality between the State and the individual which alone confers upon the State the right of diplomatic protection, and it is as a part of the function of diplomatic protection that the right to take up a claim and to ensure respect for the rules of international law must be envisaged. Where the injury was done to the national of some other State, no claim to which such injury may give rise falls within the scope of the diplomatic protection which a State is entitled to afford nor can it give rise to a claim which that State is entitled to espouse.

* * *

STATEMENT OF POLICY BY THE PRESIDENT OF THE UNITED STATES CONCERNING THE INTERNATIONAL MINIMUM STANDARD

8 Weekly Compilation of Presidential Documents, 64 (1972).

We live in an age that rightly attaches very high importance to economic development. The people of the developing societies in particular see in their own economic development the path to fulfillment of a whole range of national and human aspirations. The United States continues to support wholeheartedly, as we have done for decades, the efforts of those societies to grow economically—out of our deep conviction that, as I said in my Inaugural Address, "To go forward at all is to go forward together"; that the well-being of mankind is in the final analysis indivisible; and that a better-fed, better-clothed, healthier, and more literate world will be a more peaceful world as well.

* * *

I also wish to make clear the approach of this administration to the role of private investment in developing countries, and in particular to one of the major problems affecting such private investment: upholding accepted principles of international law in the face of expropriations without adequate compensation.

A principal objective of foreign economic assistance programs is to assist developing countries in attracting private investment.   A nation's ability to compete for this scarce and vital development ingredient is improved by programs which develop economic infrastructure, increase literacy, and raise health standards.   Private investment, as a carrier of technology, of trade opportunities, and of capital itself, in turn becomes a major factor in promoting industrial and agricultural development.   Further, a significant flow of private foreign capital stimulates the mobilization and formation of domestic capital within the recipient country.

A sort of symbiosis exists—with government aid efforts not only speeding the flow of, but actually depending for their success upon, private capital both domestic and foreign.   And, of course, from the investor's point of view, foreign private investment must either yield financial benefits to him over time, or cease to be available.   Mutual benefit is thus the sine qua non of successful foreign private investment.

Unfortunately, for all concerned, these virtually axiomatic views on the beneficial role of and necessary conditions for private capital have been challenged in recent and important instances.   U. S. enterprises, and those of many other nations, operating abroad under valid contracts negotiated in good faith, and within the established legal codes of certain foreign countries, have found their contracts revoked and their assets seized with inadequate compensation, or with no compensation.

Such actions by other governments are wasteful from a resource standpoint, shortsighted considering their adverse effects on the flow of private investment funds from all sources, and unfair to the legitimate interests of foreign private investors.

The wisdom of any expropriation is questionable, even when adequate compensation is paid.   The resources diverted to compensate investments that are already producing employment and taxes often could be used more productively to finance new investment in the domestic economy, particularly in areas of high social priority to which foreign capital does not always flow.   Consequently, countries that expropriate often postpone the attainment of their own development goals.   Still more unfairly, expropriations in one developing country can and do impair the investment climate in other developing countries.

In light of all this, it seems to me imperative to state—to our citizens and to other nations—the policy of this Government in future situations involving expropriatory acts.

1.   Under international law, the United States has a right to expect:

—That any taking of American private property will be nondiscriminatory;

—that it will be for a public purpose; and

—that its citizens will receive prompt, adequate, and effective compensation from the expropriating country.

Thus, when a country expropriates a significant U. S. interest without making reasonable provision for such compensation to U. S. citizens, we will presume that the U. S. will not extend new bilateral economic benefits to the expropriating country unless and until it is determined that the country is taking reasonable steps to provide adequate compensation or that there are major factors affecting U. S. interests which require continuance of all or part of these benefits.

2.   In the face of the expropriatory circumstances just described, we will presume that the United States Government will withhold its support from loans under consideration in multilateral development banks.

3.   Humanitarian assistance will, of course, continue to receive special consideration under such circumstances.

4.   In order to carry out this policy effectively, I have directed that each potential expropriation case be followed closely. A special inter-agency group will be established under the Council on International Economic Policy to review such cases and to recommend courses of action for the U. S. Government.

*   *   *

---

1.   *Significance of Presidential statement.* According to the New York Times of January 20, 1972, at 1, col. 1, the foregoing is the first known explicit Presidential statement of the international minimum standard. In the practice of the Department of State, its assertion in diplomatic notes and in claims presentations is well established. Congress, in the two Hickenlooper Amendments, pp. 416–17, 22 U.S.C. § 2370(e)(1) and (2), assumes (and thus asserts) its existence. However, the Supreme Court of the United States has been more reserved. In Banco Nacional de Cuba v. Sabbatino, 376 U.S. 398, 84 S.Ct. 923 (1964), the celebrated act of state decision considered in Chapter 6 above, Mr. Justice Harlan, speaking for the majority, observed:

*   *   *

There are few if any issues in international law today on which opinion seems to be so divided as the limitations on a state's power to expropriate the property of aliens. There is, of course, authority, in international judicial and arbitral decisions, in the expressions of national governments, and among commentators for the view that a taking is improper under international law if it is not for a public purpose, is discriminatory, or is without provision for prompt, adequate, and effective compensation. However, Communist countries, although they have in fact provided a degree of compensation after diplomatic efforts, commonly recognize no obligation on the part of the taking country. Certain representatives of the newly independent and underdeveloped countries have questioned whether rules of state responsibility toward aliens can bind nations that have not consented to them and it is argued that the traditionally articulated standards governing expropriation of property reflect "imperialist" interests and are inappropriate to the circumstances of emergent states.

The disagreement as to relevant international law standards reflects an even more basic divergence between the national interests of capital importing and capital exporting nations and between the social ideologies of those countries that favor state control of a considerable portion of the means of production and those that adhere to a free enterprise system. It is difficult to imagine the courts of this country embarking on adjudication in an area which touches more sensitively the practical and ideological goals of the various members of the community of nations. (at 428–430)

* * *

However, Mr. Justice White, dissenting, stated:

* * *

The Court accepts the application of rules of international law to other aspects of this litigation, accepts the relevance of international law in other cases and announces that when there is an appropriate degree of "consensus concerning a particular area of international law, the more appropriate it is for the judiciary to render decisions regarding it, since the courts can then focus on the application of an agreed principle to circumstances of fact rather than on the sensitive task of establishing a principle not inconsistent with the national interest or with international justice." Ante, p. 428. The Court then, rather lightly in my view, dispenses with its obligation to resolve controversies in accordance with "international justice" and the "national interest" by assuming and declaring that there are no areas of agreement between nations in respect to expropriations. There may not be. But without critical examination, which the Court fails to provide, I would not conclude that a confiscatory taking which discriminates against nationals of another country to retaliate against the government of that country falls within that area of issues in international law "on which opinion seems to be so divided." Nor would I assume, as the ironclad rule of the Court necessarily implies, that there is not likely to be a consensus among nations in this area, as for example upon the illegality of discriminatory takings of alien property based upon race, religion or nationality. But most of all I would not declare that even if there were a clear consensus in the international community, the courts must close their eyes to a lawless act and validate the transgression by rendering judgment for the foreign state at its own request. This is an unfortunate declaration for this Court to make. It is, of course, wholly inconsistent with the premise from which the Court starts, and, under it, banishment of international law from the courts is complete and final in cases like this. I cannot so cavalierly ignore the obligations of a court to dispense justice to the litigants before it. (at 455–56)

* * *

2. *The Calvo doctrine.* The doctrinal source of opposition to the concept of an international minimum standard is to be found in the 1868 treatise on international law of Carlõs Calvo, Argentine diplomat and publicist. As explained in 5 Hackworth, Digest of International Law 635 (1943), the Calvo doctrine is based upon two fundamental propositions: (i) the sovereign equality of states requires that a state be free from foreign state interference "of any sort"; (ii) diplomatic protection of an alien's interests is proscribed interference and hence an alien " * * * may seek redress for grievances only before the local [national] authorities." The result of this doctrine is that the alien is entitled to national treatment and no more, thus negating the concept that, whatever a state does to its nationals, it must treat aliens permitted to enter in accordance with the rules of international law setting a minimum standard for such treatment.

Reporter's Note to § 202, Restatement of the Foreign Relations Law of the United States (1965) gives useful information as to the development of "Calvo Clauses" in constitutions, legislation, and state contracts with aliens. These clauses require the alien, as a condition of entry, to accept the principles of equality of treatment with nationals and to undertake not to seek diplomatic protection from the state of his nationality. See p. 1123.

3. *The Drago doctrine.* Also of Argentinian origin (1902), it rejects specifically the threat of external force to collect past due public debts; see p. 1087. However, it is postulated on the same derivation from concepts of sovereignty, independence, and absolute

equality of states as is the Calvo doctrine. The twin doctrines have received wide doctrinal and governmental application in the other American republics.

NOTE FROM THE MEXICAN MINISTER FOR FOREIGN AFFAIRS (HAY) TO THE AMERICAN AMBASSADOR IN MEXICO (DANIELS)

[1940] 5 Foreign Relations of the United States 1019 (1961).

MEXICO, May 1, 1940.

MR. AMBASSADOR: I have the honor to refer to the note sent on the third of last April by the Government of Your Excellency to the Ambassador of Mexico in Washington. In it Your Excellency was pleased to state that during recent years different matters have arisen between the Government of Mexico and the Government of the United States, some of them of notable interest, the equitable and friendly solution of which would benefit the peoples of the two countries, and that, with a view to arriving at the solution of such matters and to simplifying their prompt settlement, Your Government had suggested a comprehensive and immediate study of the same.

It is added that at that moment the expropriation of petroleum properties belonging to American citizens took place, for which no payment whatever has been made, nor is there any prospect of payment even though the Mexican Government has manifested on various occasions its disposition to pay, as well as its capacity to do so. Once more the Government of the United States admits the right of expropriation which for reasons of public utility pertains to every sovereign State, adding that such right is united to and conditioned by the obligation to make an effective, prompt and adequate compensation. For this purpose, it is recalled that in a previous note the government of Your Excellency stated that the structure of international relations in its different phases rests in the respect of governments and peoples for reciprocal rights, according to International Law, and that a prompt and just compensation was part of that structure; a principle professed by all the governments of the world and to which the Government of Mexico has lent its support.

Based on the indisputable facts, it cannot be denied that my Government has shown its utmost respect, by its legal dispositions, to the principle of compensation, as well as its resolution to put it into effect. In a conciliatory spirit, it has avoided introducing into this matter the point of view supported and confirmed by numerous cases that there is not, in International Law, any accepted universal policy in theory or in practice that makes obligatory the payment of immediate compensation, and therefore that immediate indemnization does not constitute an inherent element or a condition to the right of expropriation. Nevertheless, though on different bases, it is pleasing to my Government to recognize that there does not exist any disagreement with the Government of your country regarding the obligation of making payment of due indemnization as imposed on the Mexican Nation by its own laws.

* * *

The Government of Your Excellency has insisted upon other occasions in sustaining the opinion that expropriation without a just and prompt compensation is confiscation and that it does not cease to be because there may exist the express desire to pay some time in the future. Mexico does not consider itself to be in such a situation, since it has not only expressed its desire to pay but has unequivocably expressed its willingness to do so, having done everything on its part in accordance with its own laws, to the end of establishing the sum to be paid.

It is mentioned, in the note signed by His Excellency, the Secretary of State, that during the last 25 years American interests in Mexico have suffered at the hands of my country's Government, mentioning to this effect, besides the cases mentioned previously, that my Government is not up to date in the service of its foreign debt and the railroad debt. I consider that the suspension of said services does not constitute an exceptional case in the world, since the phenomenon results from causes of a general character, but further still, I should state that the possible renewal of said services was, before expropriation, in a state of very advanced negotiations and if they were suspended it was due to the campaign against Mexico in which the petroleum companies, with the help of some Governments, employed, among other measures, the boycott to totally prohibit the sale of our petroleum in other countries or else to considerably restrict it by means of imposing tariff barriers, especially those called quotas, placing an appreciable limitation on the possibilities of payment by Mexico.

The Government of Your Excellency concludes proposing that both Governments agree to submit to arbitration the petroleum question, investing a court of justice with the necessary authority, not only to determine the amount to be paid to American nationals deprived of their properties, "but also the means so that its decision may be executed and to assure that an effective and adequate compensation be soon paid".

With this in mind, the Government of Your Excellency makes an appeal to continental solidarity for the principle of arbitration, its use being more commendable because it comes at a time when an increasing contempt for order appears to be in the ascendent and there is a tendency to substitute force for peaceful measures in the friendly solution of these matters.

It pleases me to recognize that Mexico concurs with the ideas of the Government of Your Excellency in a manifestation of its persevering and firmly renewed faith that the moment will come when force will be eliminated as a means of resolving conflicts between States, using only the pacific means adopted by our Continent. If a country of America has constantly maintained its faith in arbitration, it has been Mexico, which has always scrupulously fulfilled the arbitral decisions, even in those cases where the award had been adverse, as in the recent case of Clipperton Island; neither has it failed to recognize the utility of using this means of settling international differences, even though as in the case of Chamizal, an award which was favorable to it has been pending fulfillment on the part of the Government of Your Excellency since 1911.

Nevertheless, my Government does not believe that arbitration should be accepted unless the Nation has fully exercised its rights of sovereignty through the action of its tribunals and it can be proved that denial of justice exists.

* * *

My Government indicates to the Government of Your Excellency the desirability of renewing the conversations that were suspended upon the presentation of the petroleum case, in order to discuss and decide other matters pending between both Governments, because the Government of Mexico considers that the prompt solution of all of them will contribute favorably to strengthen the good relations between both countries.

Please receive [etc.]   EDUARDO HAY

PERMANENT SOVEREIGNTY OVER NATURAL RESOURCES
GENERAL ASSEMBLY RESOLUTION 1803 (XVII), DEC. 14, 1962

U.N.Gen.Ass.Off.Rec. 17th Sess., Supp. No. 17 (A/5217), p. 15.

The General Assembly,

Recalling its resolutions 523(VI) of 12 January 1952 and 626 (VII) of 21 December 1952,

Bearing in mind its resolution 1314(XIII) of 12 December 1958, by which it established the Commission on Permanent Sovereignty over Natural Resources and instructed it to conduct a full survey of the status of permanent sovereignty over natural wealth and resources as a basic constituent of the right to self-determination, with recommendations, where necessary, for its strengthening and decided further that, in the conduct of the full survey of the status of the permanent sovereignty of peoples and nations over their natural wealth and resources, due regard should be paid to the rights and duties of

States under international law and to the importance of encouraging international co-operation in the economic development of developing countries,

Bearing in mind its resolution 1515(XV) of 15 December 1960, in which it recommended that the sovereign right of every State to dispose of its wealth and its natural resources should be respected,

Considering that any measure in this respect must be based on the recognition of the inalienable right of all States freely to dispose of their natural wealth and resources in accordance with their national interests, and on respect for the economic independence of States,

Considering that nothing in paragraph 4 below in any way prejudices the position of any Member State on any aspect of the question of the rights and obligations of successor States and Governments in respect of property acquired before the accession to complete sovereignty of countries formerly under colonial rule,

Noting that the subject of succession of States and Governments is being examined as a matter of priority by the International Law Commission,

Considering that it is desirable to promote international co-operation for the economic development of developing countries, and that economic and financial agreements between the developed and the developing countries must be based on the principles of equality and of the right of peoples and nations to self-determination,

Considering that the provision of economic and technical assistance, loans and increased foreign investment must not be subject to conditions which conflict with the interests of the recipient State,

Considering the benefits to be derived from exchanges of technical and scientific information likely to promote the development and use of such resources and wealth, and the important part which the United Nations and other international organizations are called upon to play in that connexion,

Attaching particular importance to the question of promoting the economic development of developing countries and securing their economic independence,

Noting that the creation and strengthening of the inalienable sovereignty of States over their natural wealth and resources reinforces their economic independence,

Desiring that there should be further consideration by the United Nations of the subject of permanent sovereignty over natural resources in the spirit of international co-operation in the field of economic development, particularly that of the developing countries,

I

Declares that:

1. The right of peoples and nations to permanent sovereignty over their natural wealth and resources must be exercised in the interest of their national development and of the well-being of the people of the State concerned.

2. The exploration, development and disposition of such resources, as well as the import of the foreign capital required for these purposes, should be in conformity with the rules and conditions which the peoples and nations freely consider to be necessary or desirable with regard to the authorization, restriction or prohibition of such activities.

3. In cases where authorization is granted, the capital imported and the earnings on that capital shall be governed by the terms thereof, by the national legislation in force, and by international law. The profits derived must be shared in the proportions freely agreed upon, in each case, between the investors and the recipient State, due care being taken to ensure that there is no impairment, for any reason, of that State's sovereignty over its natural wealth and resources.

4. Nationalization, expropriation or requisitioning shall be based on grounds or reasons of public utility, security or the national interest which are recognized as overriding purely individual or private interests, both domestic and foreign. In such cases the owner shall be paid appropriate compensation, in accordance with the rules in force in the State taking such measures in the exercise of its sovereignty and in accordance with international law. In any case where the question of compensation gives rise to a controversy, the national jurisdiction of the State taking such measures shall be exhausted. However, upon agreement by sovereign States and other parties concerned, settlement of the dispute should be made through arbitration or international adjudication.

5. The free and beneficial exercise of the sovereignty of peoples and nations over their natural resources must be furthered by the mutual respect of States based on their sovereign equality.

6. International co-operation for the economic development of developing countries, whether in the form of public or private capital investments, exchange of goods and services, technical assistance, or exchange of scientific information, shall be such as to further their independent national development and shall be based upon respect for their sovereignty over their natural wealth and resources.

7. Violation of the rights of peoples and nations to sovereignty over their natural wealth and resources is contrary to the spirit and principles of the Charter of the United Nations and hinders the development of international co-operation and the maintenance of peace.

8. Foreign investment agreements freely entered into by or between sovereign States shall be observed in good faith; States and international organizations shall strictly and conscientiously respect the sovereignty of peoples and nations over their natural wealth and resources in accordance with the Charter and the principles set forth in the present resolution.

* * *

BARCELONA TRACTION, LIGHT AND POWER CO., LTD. (BELGIUM v. SPAIN)

International Court of Justice, 1970
[1970] I.C.J.Rep. 3.

[The decision was on a narrow issue, the question whether Belgium had standing to espouse claims of its nationals who owned the majority of the shares of a corporation organized in Canada. In the course of 303 pages of "separate opinions" by members of a court that, except for one judge ad hoc, was unanimous in its disposition of the case, almost every aspect of the nationalization problem as it concerns investments in the corporate form is discussed by one or more of the judges. The selections that follow deal with the international minimum standard. It is perhaps revealing that the dispositive opinion and some of the separate opinions assume it exists. Other views, pro and con, are more explicitly stated.]

Separate Opinion of Judge Tanaka at p. 115, 116

* * *

Here, it is not necessary to emphasize the spirit of a universally recognized rule of customary international law concerning every State's right of diplomatic protection over its nationals abroad, that is, a right to require that another State observe a certain standard of decent treatment to aliens in its territory. The spirit of the institution of diplomatic protection is clearly declared by a Judgment of the Permanent Court of International Justice:

> * * * in taking up the case of one of its nationals, by resorting to diplomatic action or international judicial proceedings on his behalf, a State is in reality asserting its own right, the right to ensure in the person of its nationals respect for the rules of international law. This right is necessarily limited to intervention on behalf of its own nationals because * * * it is the bond of nationality between the State and the individual which alone confers upon the State the right of diplomatic protection, and it is as a part of the function of diplomatic protection that the right to take up a claim and to ensure respect for the rules of international law must be envisaged. (Panevezys-Saldutiskis Railway case, P.C.I.J., Series A/B, No 76, p. 16.)

Briefly, the idea of diplomatic protection does not seem to be a blind extension of the sovereign power of a State to the territory of other countries; the spirit of this institution signifies the collaboration of the protecting State for the cause of the rule of law and justice.

* * *

Separate Opinion of Judge Jessup at p. 162, 164–167

* * *

10.   In adjudicating upon the Barcelona Traction case the Court must apply rules from one of the most controversial branches of international law. The subject of the responsibility of States for injuries to aliens (otherwise referred to as the diplomatic protection of nationals), evokes in many current writings recollections of political abuses in past eras. The Court is not involved here in any conflict between great capital-exporting States and States in course of development. Belgium and Spain are States which, in those terms, belong in the same grouping. I do not agree with the Spanish contention on 20 May 1969 that Belgium was merely trying to get the Court to internationalize a private litigation, but it is true that basically the conflict was between a powerful Spanish financial group and a comparable non-Spanish group. This case cannot be said to evoke problems of "neo-colonialism".

Moreover, the Court is not here in the least concerned with such provocative problems as State sovereignty over natural resources or the rules applicable to compensation in case of nationalizations or expropriations. Professor F. V. García Amador, in his sixth report as Special Rapporteur of the International Law Commission on State responsibility (Yearbook of the International Law Commission, 1961, Vol. II, p. 2 at p. 46), set forth an admirable attitude:

> * * *   his purpose was to take into account the profound changes which are occurring in international law, in so far as they are capable of affecting the traditional ideas and principles relating to responsibility. The only reason why, in this endeavour, he rejected notions or opinions for which acceptance is being sought in our time, is that he firmly believes that any notion or opinion which postulates extreme positions—whatever may be the underlying purpose or motive—is incompatible and irreconcilable with the idea of securing the recognition and adequate legal protection of all the legitimate interests involved. That has been the policy followed by the Commission hitherto and no doubt will continue to be its policy in the future.

11.   The institution "of the right to give diplomatic protection to nationals abroad was recognized in * * * the Vienna Convention on Diplomatic Relations, 1961", as Mr. Gros (as he then was) reminded the sub-committee of the International Law Commission (Yearbook of the International Law Commission, 1963, Vol. II, p.

230). The institution of the right to give diplomatic protection is surely not obsolete although new procedures are emerging.

With reference to diplomatic protection of corporate interests, the customary international law began to change in the latter half of the nineteenth century. As Jennings writes, in somewhat picturesque and Kiplingesque language:

> It is small wonder that difficulties arise when 19th century precedents about outrageous behaviour towards aliens residing in outlandish parts are sought to be pressed into service to yield principles apposite to sophisticated programmes of international investment. (121 Hague Recueil 1967, II, p. 473.)

Since the critical date in this case is 1948, developments in the law and procedures during the ensuing last two decades are not controlling.

12. Any court's application of a rule of law to a particular case, involves an interpretation of the rule. Historical and logical and teleological tools may be used by the judge, consciously or unconsciously. If the Court in the instant case had decided to include more factors in its Judgment, it could have clarified the traditional system in the light of clearer understandings of business practices and forms of corporate organization, as these were already well developed two decades ago when the events called into question in this case transpired. Legal norms applicable to those events should not be swept aside on the assumption that they have already become mere cobwebs in the attics of legal history. Corporations today and tomorrow may well utilize other methods of financing and controlling foreign enterprises, and governments will have adapted or will adapt their own laws and practices to meet the realities of the economic factors which affect the general interests of the State. The "law of international economic development" will mature. Thus joint business ventures, State guarantees of foreign investment, the use of international organizations such as the IBRD and UNDP, may in the course of time relegate the case of Barcelona Traction to the status now occupied by Delagoa Bay—a precedent to be cited by advocates if helpful to the pleading of a cause, but not a guiding element in the life of the international business community.

Nevertheless, the Court has the duty to settle a specific dispute between Belgium and Spain which arose out of Spain's exercising jurisdiction over a complex of foreign corporate enterprises.

13. There is a trend in the direction of extending the jurisdictional power of the State to deal with foreign enterprises which have contact with the State's territorial domain; " * * * all that can be required of a State is that it should not overstep the limits which international law places upon its jurisdiction; within these limits, its title to exercise jurisdiction rests in its sovereignty. But what are the limits placed by international law? Do the courts of the United

States, for example, go too far in applying its anti-trust laws to foreign enterprises, following the statement of principle by Judge Hand in Alcoa? But that principle is accepted in at least six other countries. Are the jurisdictional limits on national jurisdiction exceeded in the cases dealing with product liability of a "giant octopus corporation" with multiple subsidiaries abroad? Rules valid enough for interstate conflicts within the constitutional system of the United States, may be improper when placing a burden on international commerce. The Committee on International Law of the Association of the Bar of the City of New York concluded that "*   *   *   the extension of the regulatory and penal provisions of the Securities Exchange Act of 1934   *   *   *   to foreign corporations which have neither listed securities in the United States nor publicly offered securities within the United States is a violation of international law".

14. In States having different types of economic and financial problems, international law has become increasingly permissive of actions involving nationalizations. In place of what used to be denounced as illegal expropriation, the issues now turn largely on the measure of compensation, since even the famous General Assembly Resolution on Permanent Sovereignty Over Natural Resources, provides that compensation is due.

Separate Opinion of Judge Padilla Nervo at p. 244, 246–250

*   *   *

The history of the responsibility of States in respect to the treatment of foreign nationals is the history of abuses, illegal interference in the domestic jurisdiction of weaker States, unjust claims, threats and even military aggression under the flag of exercising rights of protection, and the imposing of sanctions in order to oblige a government to make the reparations demanded.

Special agreements to establish arbitral tribunals were on many occasions concluded under pressure, by political, economic or military threats.

The protecting States, in many instances, are more concerned with obtaining financial settlements than with preserving principles. Against the pressure of diplomatic protection, weaker States could do no more than to preserve and defend a principle of international law, while giving way under the guise of accepting friendly settlements, either giving the compensation demanded or by establishing claims commissions which had as a point of departure the acceptance of responsibility for acts or omissions, where the government was, neither in fact nor in law, really responsible.

In the written and in the oral pleadings the Applicant has made reference, in support of his thesis, to arbitral decisions of claims commissions—among others those between Mexico and the United States, 1923.

These decisions do not necessarily give expression to rules of customary international law, as * * * the Commissions were authorized to decide these claims 'in accordance with principles of international law, justice and equity' and, therefore, may have been influenced by other than strictly legal considerations. (Schwarzenberger, International Law, Vol. I, p. 201.)

In the Special Claims Commission: Mexico-United States, established by the convention of 10 September 1923, Article II states:

* * * each member of the Commission * * * shall make and subscribe a solemn declaration stating that he will * * * examine and decide, according to the best of his judgment and in accordance with the principles of *justice and equity* all claims presented for decision * * * (Italics are mine.)

The second paragraph of the same Article II reads as follows:

The Mexican Government desires that the claims shall be so decided because Mexico wishes that her responsibility shall not be fixed according to the generally accepted rules and principles of international law, but ex gratia feels morally bound to make full indemnification and agrees, therefore * * * (U.N.R.I. A.A., Vol. IV, p. 780.)

Article VI of the same convention makes another exception to the accepted general rules, when it states:

* * * the Mexican Government agrees that the Commission shall not disallow or reject any claim by the application of the general principle of international law that the legal remedies must be exhausted as a condition precedent to the validity or allowance of any claim. (Ibid., p. 781.)

Some of the decisions of claims commissions invoked during the pleadings are not, in my view, relevant precedents in respect to this case.

Now the evolution of international law has other horizons and its progressive development is more promising, as Rosenne wrote:

There is prevalent in the world today a widespread questioning of the contemporary international law. This feeling is based on the view that for the greater part international law is the product of European imperialism and colonialism and does not take sufficient account of the completely changed pattern of international relations which now exists. * * *

Careful scrutiny of the record of the Court may lead to the conclusion that it has been remarkably perceptive of the changing currents of internationalist thought. In this respect it has performed a major service to the international community as a whole, because the need to bring international law into line with present-day requirements and conditions is real and urgent.

(Rosenne, The Law and Practice of the International Court, 1965, Vol. I, pp. 17–18.)

The law, in all its aspects, the jurisprudence and the practice of States change, as the world and the everyday requirements of international life change, but those responsible for its progressive evolution should take care that their decisions do, in the long run, contribute to the maintenance of peace and security and to the betterment of the majority of mankind.

In considering the needs and the good of the international community in our changing world, one must realize that there are more important aspects than those concerned with economic interests and profit making; other legitimate interests of a political and moral nature are at stake and should be considered in judging the behaviour and operation of the complex international scope of modern commercial enterprises.

It is not the shareholders in those huge corporations who are in need of diplomatic protection; it is rather the poorer or weaker States, where the investments take place, who need to be protected against encroachment by powerful financial groups, or against unwarranted diplomatic pressure from governments who appear to be always ready to back at any rate their national shareholders, even when they are legally obliged to share the risk of their corporation and follow its fate, or even in case of shareholders who are not or have never been under the limited jurisdiction of the State of residence accused of having violated in respect of them certain fundamental rights concerning the treatment of foreigners. It can be said that, by the mere fact of the existence of certain rules concerning the treatment of foreigners, these have certain fundamental rights that the State of residence cannot violate without incurring international responsibility; but this is not the case of foreign shareholders as such, who may be scattered all over the world and have never been or need not be residents of the respondent State or under its jurisdiction.

In the case of the Rosa Gelbtrunk claim between Salvador and the United States, the President of the arbitration commission expressed a view which may summarize the position of foreigners in a country where they are resident. This view was expressed as follows:

> A citizen or subject of one nation who, in the pursuit of commercial enterprise, carries on trade within the territory and under the protection of the sovereignty of a nation other than his own, is to be considered *as having cast in his lot* with the subjects or citizens of the State in which he *resides* and carried on business. (Italics added.)

"In this case", Schwarzenberger remarks, "the rule was applied to the loss of foreign property in the course of a civil war. The decision touches, however, one aspect of a much wider problem: the existence of international minimum standards, by which, regarding foreigners, territorial jurisdiction is limited."

As the Permanent Court of International Justice said in the Lotus case in 1927 (P.C.I.J., Series A, No. 10, p. 19)—

> all that can be required of a State is that it should not overstep the limits which international law places upon its jurisdiction; within these limits, its title to exercise jurisdiction rests in its sovereignty.

The rules concerning the treatment of foreigners are a limitation of a State's jurisdiction ratione personae. Schwarzenberger says in this respect:

> States generally exercise exclusive jurisdiction over their nationals within their territory, concurrent jurisdiction over their nationals abroad, and limited jurisdiction over, for example, individuals and groups within their territory who are protected by international customary or treaty law.
>
> While, in principle, territorial sovereignty applies to nationals and foreigners alike, the home State retains a concurrent jurisdiction over its nationals abroad. * * * Furthermore, the unrestricted exercise of territorial jurisdiction over foreigners on the part of the State of residence may be limited by rules of international customary law or treaties. If such exercise of territorial jurisdiction happens to come into conflict with international law, the question turns into an issue between the subjects of international law concerned. The home State is entitled to demand respect for international limitations of territorial jurisdiction, and the State of residence may have to answer for its interference "with the rights which each State may claim for its national in foreign territory." As the World Court laid down in the case of the Mavrommatis Palestine Concessions (1924), "it is an elementary principle of international law that a State is entitled to protect its subjects, when injured by acts contrary to international law committed by another State, from whom they have been unable to obtain satisfaction through the ordinary channels." (Schwarzenberger, International Law, Vol. I, pp. 189–190.)

Much has been said about the justification for not leaving the shareholders in those enterprises without protection.

Perhaps modern international business practice has a tendency to be soft and partial towards the powerful and the rich, but no rule of law could be built on such flimsy bases.

Investors who go abroad in search of profits take a risk and go there for better or for worse, not only for better. They should respect the institutions and abide by the national laws of the country where they chose to go.

* * *

Separate Opinion of Judge Ammoun at p. 287, 290–295

* * *

5.   In this connection, it is essential to stress the trends of Latin-American law and that of Asia and Africa, and their undeniable influence on the development of traditional international law.

It seems indeed that among the principles and norms which have sprung from the regional law peculiar to Latin America are the norms and principles whose aim is to protect countries in that part of the world against the more powerful industrialized States of North America and Europe.

An Afro-Asian law also seems to be developing as a result of the same preoccupations, springing from the same causes. In the field of the responsibility of States and of diplomatic protection, the same points of view have been adopted in the countries of the three continents, thus initiating a form of co-operation which will not be of slight effect on the renewal of law.

The first reaction to the rules of traditional law came however from the countries of Latin America; witness the vehement speech made by Mr. Seijas, a former Venezuelan minister, at the 1891 Session of the Institut de droit international at Hamburg, which was no mere display of bad temper. Evidence of this too is the appearance of the Calvo Clause, excluding recourse to international adjudication in favour of internal remedies, on which the jurists of Latin America have never compromised, because of their lack of confidence in diplomatic protection as conceived by traditional law and the practices of western nations. This reaction on the part of the Latin American States would, moreover, explain their opposition from 1948 onwards to the draft insurance guarantee agreement proposed by the United States, providing for the exercise of diplomatic protection by that power without local remedies having been exhausted.

This attitude on the part of the Hispanic States, which is shared by the Afro-Asian States, is the more readily understandable if the extra-legal forms and means to which diplomatic protection formerly had recourse are borne in mind. It will be recalled that the claims of great States and their nationals abroad often led, during the period preceding the renewal of the law consequent upon two world wars and the creation of a means of international adjudication, to acute conflicts and to acts of deliberate violence going so far as armed intervention and permanent occupation, or to demonstrations of force, against which the Drago doctrine, which was endorsed by the Pan-American Conference of 1906 and has since become one of the basic principles of Latin American international law, has, since 1926, reacted not without success. Recourse to force, subject to an offer of arbitration, was nevertheless tolerated by The Hague Peace Conference of 1907, which admitted intervention sub modo by virtue of the Porter Convention, against which Convention Drago and his Latin

American colleagues vainly protested at the Conference. This was not the least of the contradictions which attended it, contradictions which bespeak the still predominant influence of the colonialist era. Accordingly, one is entitled to suspect certain arbitral decisions of having been agreed to or accepted under duress, those decisions having been preceded by ultimata or menaces or by a deployment of force more or less in the spirit of the said Conference, which was struggling to free itself from a tyrannical tradition.

If the Drago doctrine has finally triumphed, and if the Porter Convention, on the insistence of Mexico, expressing Latin American opinion at the Chapultepec Conference in 1945, is now recognized as incompatible with the terms of Article 103 of the United Nations Charter, it is nevertheless the case that many decisions have not avoided all confusion between reparation sticto sensu, as in private municipal law, and the "satisfaction" demanded by powerful States, which gives reparation lato sensu the character of a measure aimed at deterrence or punishment. This right to punish, which is arrogated to themselves by certain States, and to which such eminent writers as Bluntschli, Liszt and Fauchille, as well as a 1927 resolution of the Institut de droit international have lent their authority, seems to have been rejected by Anzilotti, who noted that in all forms of reaction against the unlawful act there were present "*   *   * an element of satisfaction and an element of reparation, the notion of punishment of the unlawful act and that of reparation for the wrong suffered". Thus, the opposition of Latin American or Afro-Asian jurists to the western conception of responsibility and diplomatic protection is founded not only on memories of a painful past, but also on serious apprehensions.

The development of Latin American thought concerning diplomatic protection and its limits must be particularly stressed in the present discussion, on account of the influence which it can have on the development of that institution. This thought is at present centred on the following aspects of the problem:

A. The 20 States of South and Central America all reject the rule laid down by Vatel and endorsed by the Permanent Court of International Justice, according to which the right of diplomatic protection is "to ensure, in the person of its subjects, respect for the rules of international law". They hold it to be a fiction, which one of their most eminent jurists, Garcia Robles, has described as "a product of Hegelian influence, resulting from the expansionism of the nineteenth century". And all these States, at inter-American conferences, in the writings of publicists, in the positions adopted by governments, are united in their efforts for its elimination, on the understanding that the individual's status as a subject of the law is to be recognized thus enabling him to seek legal redress himself, and not under the cloak of his national State. But before what tribunal? Before an American regional tribunal. The resolution submitted to the Inter-American

Conference at Buenos Aires and adopted almost unanimously reads: "American legal controversies should be decided by American judges * * * and a correct understanding of acts pertaining to the Americas is more readily to be obtained by Americans themselves".

Since the same causes produce the same effects, the States of the Organization of African Unity wrote into the Addis Ababa Charter the same objective of the creation of a regional tribunal.

The countries of Latin America have gone further still. In 1948 they unanimously adopted a resolution at Bogotá whereby they undertook not to bring a claim before a court of international jurisdiction, not excluding the International Court of Justice.

B.   The States of Latin America remain firmly attached to the Calvo Clause, which they habitually insert in contracts entered into with foreign undertakings. Their constitutions and laws generally make it compulsory. Their doctrine with regard thereto, founded upon the two principles of equality between States and non-intervention, was forcefully expressed by Judge Guerrero, a former President of the Court, in the report which he submitted on behalf of the Subcommittee set up by the Committee of Experts of the League of Nations to study the responsibility of States. Several non-American countries were not hostile to this point of view. China, Holland and Finland were frankly favourable to it. Finally, the United States, which had found in Borchard a vigorous defender of the thesis that the individual cannot dispose of a right which, according to Vatelian doctrine, is that of the State and not his own, allowed itself to be won over, with the inauguration of the "good neighbour" policy of F. D. Roosevelt, to the doctrine of its southern neighbours.

C.   The Calvo clause, which on the other side of the Atlantic is regarded merely as a compromise, was destined to prepare the way for the adoption of the Calvo doctrine, which is aimed at nothing less than the abolition of unilateral diplomatic protection in order to substitute for it a protection exercised by the collectivity on the basis of human rights.

The path towards this unconcealed objective is certainly a long and arduous one; its success seems bound up with the progress of mankind towards an inter-American or international organization less removed than the United Nations from the concept of the Super-State.

* * *

It was the more necessary to recall these features of American law in that other States are treading the same path towards the limitation of diplomatic protection. The States of Africa and of Asia, since they too have come to participate in international life, share the same concerns,—as witness the proceedings of the International

Law Commission. At its Ninth Session in 1957, Mr. Padilla Nervo stated that:

> * * * the history of the institution of State responsibility was the history of the obstacles placed in the way of the new Latin American countries—obstacles to the defence of their * * * independence, to the ownership and development of their resources, and to their social integration.

And he added:

> With State responsibility * * * international rules were established, not merely without reference to small States but against them.

And Mr. El-Erian, of the United Arab Republic, stressed the twofold consequence of the privileged condition accorded to nationals of Western countries in their relations with the countries of Africa or Asia, which on the one hand had led to the system of capitulations and on the other afforded a pretext for intervention in the domestic affairs of States.

> The similarity of the essential views and objectives of the States of the three continents of America, Africa and Asia, and the action they are able to take to develop a positive international law of world-wide ambit, will tend to direct them toward a universalist concept of law and bring them back to a system of international adjudication which will no longer be of an exclusive nature but will, through its effective composition, meet the wishes expressed in the United Nations Charter, which would have it represent the main legal systems and principal forms of civilization of the world.

> It is in the light of these preliminary considerations that the connected problem of diplomatic protection and the jus standi of the applicant State should have been approached.

>   * * *

---

2. TYPES OF ECONOMIC INTERESTS TREATED AS ENTITLED TO DIPLOMATIC PROTECTION

Perspective. Here the focus is on what types of economic interests the state of nationality or other state entitled to make the claim will recognize and the host state will accept as constituting a taking of property. In many situations there is no problem in this regard. There is common agreement that land, physical things (artifacts), patents, copyrights, bank balances and other book assets are property for nationalization claims purposes. At the other extreme, the mere prospect of having made a gain is not property. When a business enterprise is taken from an alien the manner in which he holds his ownership interests therein may become important in the context of the present inquiry. In the field of direct foreign investment in minerals extraction and disposal for profit, the civil and the common law tend to have different viewpoints as to whether authorizations to explore, mine or drill, and remove create interests in property. In the common law world they do. The recipient of the authorization either has an estate in determinable fee simple in the subsurface, an incorporeal hereditament (a profit a prendre), or a lessee's rights under a mining lease. But in most of Latin America, all subsurface minerals property pertains to the state, and the state is not authorized to alienate such property. A concession contract in such a country is not a grant of a real property interest; it is a contract with the state under which the private party is licensed to explore, extract and market.

In several notable instances in Latin America, some governments sought to convey to foreign investors property in sub-surface minerals in disregard of this fundamental notion. After these governments were displaced, extraordinarily strong political rejection-reaction developed. Nonetheless, it is usually not argued in extractive industries nationalization cases that a minerals concession is not property. There is less general agreement about losses by aliens due to the cancellation or non-performance by the state of other types of contracts with aliens.

In nationalization cases valuation is often a serious problem. However, in several recent nationalizations in Latin America the regime in control of the state has not contested its general responsibility to pay compensation, or even the amount, but has sought to offset the claim with charges for alleged back taxes, improper exploitation, or illegality ab initio of removals, despite the good faith nature of the alien's operation. Whether such situations will fall into the category of denial of justice or be dealt with as defenses to taking cannot now be foretold.

CREDITORS' CLAIMS: EARLY POLICY OF UNITED STATES DEPARTMENT OF STATE

VI Moore, Digest of International Law 707 (1906).

* * *

How far it may be justifiable or expedient formally to press all the claims upon the French Government for immediate payment is a consideration to be distinguished from the clear opinion which is entertained of their intrinsic justice. Wherever they originated in compulsory measures practiced upon the claimants, they are entitled to a full and immediate interposition of their Government; but where the bills have been received by virtue of voluntary contracts, whether with the agents of the French Government or individuals, the receivers, having regard, as they must have had, to the degree of credit and punctuality ascribed to that Government, at the period of their speculation, any calculation and consequent disappointment ought not to be permitted to embarrass their own Government by binding it to pursue very pointed measures for their relief. (at 707)

You appear not fully to have understood your powers and duties under the law of nations in regard to claims of American citizens on foreign governments. I can not explain these more clearly than by extracting a few sentences from a letter dated on the 11th November, 1847, and addressed by this Department to Vice-President Dallas, in answer to an application made by him in behalf of an American citizen. The extract follows: "It has been the practice of this Department to confine its official action in the recovery of indemnity from foreign governments to tortious acts committed under their authority against the persons and property of our citizens. In the case of violation of contract, the rule has been not to interfere, unless under very peculiar circumstances, and then only to instruct our diplomatic agents abroad to use their good offices in behalf of American citizens with the Governments to which they are accredited. The distinction between claims arising from torts and from contracts is, I believe, recognized by all nations, and the reasons for this distinction will readily occur to your own mind." This letter was carefully considered and adopted by the President and the entire Cabinet. I might add, that if this were not the rule, governments, and especially our Government, would be involved in endless difficulties. Our citizens go abroad over the whole world and enter into contracts with all foreign governments. In doing this they must estimate the character of those with whom they contract and assume the risk of their ability and will to execute their contracts. Upon a different principle, it would become the duty of the Government of our country to enforce the payment of loans made by its citizens and subjects to the government of another country. This might prove exceedingly inconvenient to some of the States of this Union as well as to other sovereign States. (at 708, 709)

     *   *   *

CREDITORS' CLAIMS: PRESENT POLICY OF UNITED STATES DEPARTMENT OF STATE

8 Whiteman, Digest of International Law 933 (1967).

In response to a letter requesting information on steps which the United States Government could take to protect the interests of United States bondholders affected by the default of the Government of Cuba on payments of principal and interest on bonds, the policy of the Department of State with regard thereto was explained as follows:

> A default in the payment of principal or interest on bonds of foreign governments is considered by the Department primarily a matter for direct negotiation and settlement by the American bondholders or their representatives and the foreign government concerned. The Department is, however, always ready to facilitate such negotiations and settlements when possible, but it has been its consistent policy, repeatedly stated by various Secretaries of State, generally to decline to intervene in the enforcement of such obligations, except under very unusual circumstances, as, for example, where American nationals are discriminated against in connection with payments made by a foreign government on its obligations.

> It was because of this policy that the Government in the fall of 1933 encouraged the creation of the Foreign Bondholders Protective Council, a private nonprofit organization, with the view that it would assist the numerous and scattered American holders of defaulted foreign government securities in the protection of their interests. The Council has offices at 90 Broad Street, New York, New York. As it functions entirely independently of the Government, this reference to it is, of course, made without responsibility on the part of the Department.

> The Department will consider the bonds to which you have referred in the event that a general settlement of claims against Cuba becomes feasible or in the event that unusual circumstances arise with respect to the bonds, such as those mentioned above.

> * * *

* * * [The Foreign Bondholders Protective Council, Inc.] was formed in 1933 by its original directors upon request of Mr. Cordell Hull, Secretary of State, Mr. W. H. Woodin, Secretary of the Treasury, and Mr. Charles H. March, Chairman of the Federal Trade Commission, who expressed the need for "an adequate and disinterested organization for the protection of American holders of foreign securities," this problem being of such "great and urgent importance to American investors, and of such public significance as to make its proper handling a public service."

The White House announcement to the press on October 20, 1933 stated that the making of satisfactory arrangements and protecting American interests was "a task primarily for private initiative and interests. The traditional policy of the American Government has been that such loan and investment transactions were primarily private actions, to be handled by the parties directly concerned. The Government realizes a duty, within the proper limits of international law and international amity, to defend American interests abroad. However, it would not be wise for the Government to undertake directly the settlement of private debt situations."

As a consequence, the Council was incorporated December 13, 1933 under the laws of the State of Maryland as a non-stock, non-profit organization. Among the purposes for which the corporation was formed is that of protecting the rights and interests of American holders of publicly offered dollar bonds issued or guaranteed by foreign governments and their political subdivisions.

BOND CLAIMS AGAINST BLOCKED ASSETS

8 Whiteman, Digest of International Law 952 (1967).

Public Law 285, 84th Congress, approved August 9, 1955, further amending the International Claims Settlement Act of 1949, contained provision (section 202) that in accordance with article 29 of the Treaty of Peace with Hungary, which entered into force September 15, 1947, any property blocked by the United States in accordance with Executive Order No. 8389 of April 10, 1940, as amended, and remaining blocked on the date of the Act, and which, as of September 15, 1947, was owned by Hungary or a national thereof, should vest in such officer or agency as the President of the United States might designate, such property to be sold or otherwise liquidated as expeditiously as possible after vesting and the net proceeds thereof to be covered into the U. S. Treasury. (Provision was also contained in the same section for the divesting and restoration to blocked status (subject to release) of property "directly owned at the date of vesting by a natural person".) The 1949 Act as amended, provided (section 302 of title III) that there was thereby created in the U. S. Treasury, the Hungarian Claims Fund comprised of net proceeds of vested Hungarian assets covered into the Treasury (as provided in the Act). By section 303 the Foreign Claims Settlement Commission was authorized to receive and determine "in accordance with applicable substantive law, including international law, the validity and amounts of claims of nationals of the United States" against the Government of Hungary, Bulgaria, and Rumania, for failure to comply with obligations in three categories of cases, the first of which had to do with restoration of or payment for property under the Peace Treaties, the second, with payment of "effective compensation for the nationalization, compulsory liquidation, or other taking, prior to the effective date of this title" of property of U. S. nationals, and the third, with failure to meet obligations expressed in currency of the United States arising out of contractual or other rights acquired by U. S. nationals prior to September 1, 1939 (in the case of Hungary), and which became payable prior to September 15, 1947. The Foreign Claims Settlement Commission made awards in favor of

U. S. nationals in certain bond claims against Hungary.   [The opinion of the commission stated:]

The essential part of this section [303(3)] as it relates to the question provides, for the determination of claims against the Governments of Bulgaria, Hungary, and Rumania, arising out of the failure to meet obligations expressed in dollars arising out of contractual or other rights acquired prior to certain dates and which became payable prior to September 15, 1947.

It has been concluded * * * that under section 303(3) of the Act only those dollar bond claims and interest coupon claims which became payable prior to September 15, 1947, are deemed compensable.

The legislative history of the Act suggests that the term "against the Governments of Bulgaria, Hungary, and Rumania or any of them, arising out of the failure to * * * meet obligations * * *" are claims against the three governments. The Senate Committee on Foreign Relations in reporting on the amendments to the Act in its discussion of H.R. 6382, stated, with respect to section 303(3), the following:

The purpose of the present bill is to establish a claims program for the benefit of American nationals * * * for * * * prewar governmental debt (bond) claims, against the Governments of Bulgaria, Hungary, and Rumania, * * *. (S. Report No. 1050, 84th Congress, 1st Sess., p. 1.)

Prewar government debt claims contemplate those claims based upon the failure of any of these governments to meet their bond obligations or other debts. * * * Claims dealt with in section 303(3) of the bill relate to contractual obligations, principally rights in bonds, issued by the Governments of Bulgaria, Hungary, and Rumania.

Other congressional reports and debates pertaining to section 303(3) further substantiates [sic] the interpretation of this section as claims dealing in bonds issued by the three governments or other contractual obligations of such governments. The legislative history is void of any reference to the contractual obligations of the political subdivisions of the three governments.

* * * [T]his bond issue has never been considered a government bond. These bonds were issued on the credit of the Municipality of the City of Budapest and the purchasers of such bonds did so with the knowledge of this fact. It is a well-established fact that a political subdivision cannot pledge the credit of its national government since they are distinct and separate entities.

Claims based upon bonds of private banking institutions in Hungary were likewise found to be not compensable under Section 303(3) of the Act inasmuch as they involved no obligations for which the Government of Hungary was responsible.

* * *

SAUDI ARABIA v. ARABIAN AMERICAN OIL CO. (ARAMCO)

Arbitration Tribunal, 1958.
27 Int'l L.Rep. 117 (1963).

[This was an arbitration by an ad hoc panel pursuant to an agreement between the Arabian American Oil Co. (ARAMCO), a Delaware corportion, and the State of Saudi Arabia. A 1933 concession arrangement grants the company's predecessor in title (a company with a slightly different name and organized in California) " * * * the exclusive right * * * to explore, prospect, drill for, extract, treat, manufacture, transport, deal with, carry away and export petroleum * * * " within an "Exclusive Area" which included islands, territorial waters, and all offshore areas as to which the Saudi State has or may claim dominion. In 1954 Aristotle Socrates Onassis made an agreement with Saudi Arabia under which Onassis' Saudi Arabian Tankers Company (SATCO) was granted " * * * the right of priority to ship and transport oil and its products exported from Saudi Arabia to foreign countries by way of the sea * * * ". This priority was conditioned upon a "first priority" for shipment by concessionaires up to the extent they actually engaged in the regular transportation of Saudi Arabian oil before December 31, 1953. ARAMCO asked the tribunal to declare the contracts in conflict and the second a nullity as to ARAMCO, i. e., that ARAMCO have an unlimited right to ship oil from Saudi Arabia. A majority of the panel did so declare. The appointee of Saudi Arabia dissented.

A portion of the opinion by the arbitral tribunal appears below.]

* * *

Inasmuch as the law in force in Saudi Arabia did not contain any definite rule relating to the exploitation of oil deposits, because no such exploitation existed in that State before 1933, this lacuna was filled by the 1933 Concession Agreement, whose validity and legality under Saudi Arabian law are not disputed by either side. The present dispute only concerns the effects of the provisions contained in the Agreement.

The Concession Agreement is thus the fundamental law of the Parties, and the Arbitration Tribunal is bound to recognize its particular importance owing to the fact that it fills a gap in the legal system of Saudi Arabia with regard to the oil industry. The Tribunal holds that the Concession has the nature of a constitution which has the effect of conferring acquired rights on the contracting Parties. By reason of its very sovereignty within its territorial domain, the State possesses the legal power to grant rights which it forbids itself to withdraw before the end of the Concession, with the reservation of the Clauses of the Concession Agreement relating to its revocation. Nothing can prevent a State, in the exercise of its sovereignty, from binding itself irrevocably by the provisions of a concession and from granting to the concessionaire irretractable rights. Such rights have the character of acquired rights. Should a new concession contract incompatible with the first, or a subsequent statute, abolish totally or partially that which has been granted by a previous law or concession, this could constitute a clear infringement, by the second contract, of acquired rights or a violation, by the subsequent statute, of the principle of non-retroactivity of laws, with the only exception of rules of public policy. This is because a legal situation acquired by virtue of a previous special statute cannot be abrogated by a subsequent statute—generalia specialibus non derogant—unless the legislator has expressly given retroactive effect to such statute, which the State cannot do in respect of concessions, without engaging its responsibility.

In so far as doubts may remain on the content or on the meaning of the agreements of the Parties, it is necessary to resort to the general principles of law and to apply them in order to interpret, and even to supplement, the respective rights and obligations of the Parties.

The Arbitration Tribunal relies, by analogy, on the precedent of the Lena Goldfields Arbitration between the U.S.S.R. and a British corporation, with respect to mining concessions, and on the award given in that case on 3 September 1930. According to Article 75 of the concession contract, the concessionary company was subject to the whole present and future legislation of the U.S.S.R., but with the following important reservation: "in so far as special provisions are not contained in the present agreement". Further, under Article 76, the Government had undertaken not to modify the contract in any way, by order, by decree or by any other unilateral act, without the approval of the Lena Goldfields Ltd. The arbitrators (in the absence of the Government's arbitrator who refused to take part in the proceedings adopted the following standpoint, in conformity with the submissions of the plaintiff:

> *　*　* On all domestic matters in the U.S.S.R., the laws of Soviet Russia applied except in so far as they were excluded by the contract, and accordingly that in regard to performance of the contract by both parties inside the U.S.S.R. Russian law was the "proper law of the contract."

But * * * for other purposes the general principles of law such as those recognised by Article 38 of the Statute of the Permanent Court of International Justice at The Hague should be regarded as the "proper law of the contract."

The latter solution seemed justified to the arbitrators because several provisions in the Concession called for the application of international law rather than that of municipal law (Cornell Law Quarterly, vol. 36, 1930, p. 50).

A similar decision is found in the Arbitral Award given by Lord Asquith of Bishopstone, in August 1951, in the case of Abu Dhabi. Looking for the law to be applied, the Arbitrator noted that the law of Abu Dhabi was applicable prima facie, as an oil concession was involved, but that this law did not contain any rules on the subject. Having, on the other hand, excluded the application of English law, as unwarranted, the Arbitrator held, therefore, that he had to resort to the general principles of law, as a kind of "modern law of nature" (Petroleum Development [Trucial Coast] Ltd. v. The Shaikh of Abu Dhabi: International and Comparative Law Quarterly, vol. I [4th series] 1952, p. 247).

This award has been relied upon by both Parties in the present arbitration (Government's Memorial, No. 36–37, pp. 26–27; Aramco's Second Memorial, No. 238, p. 125).

This same character of public rights inevitably mixed with the grant of private rights to the concessionaire is to be found in the Aramco Concession Agreement.

Matters pertaining to private law are, in principle, governed by the law of Saudi Arabia but with one important reservation. That law must, in case of need, be interpreted or supplemented by the general principles of law, by the custom and practice in the oil business and by notions of pure jurisprudence, in particular whenever certain private rights—which must inevitably be recognized to the concessionaire if the Concession is not to be deprived of its substance —would not be secured in an unquestionable manner by the law in force in Saudi Arabia.

This solution results directly from the interpretation of Article 35 of the Concession Agreement; although this Article only provides that the English text shall prevail in all cases relating to the obligations of the Company, it supports this solution as follows:

Inasmuch as most of the obligations hereunder are imposed upon the Company and inasmuch as the interpretation of the English text, especially as regards technical obligations and requirements relating to the oil industry, has been fairly well established through long practice and experience in contracts such as the present one, it is agreed that while both texts shall have equal validity, nevertheless in case of any divergence of interpretation as to the Company's obligations hereunder, the English text shall prevail.

In the Tribunal's opinion, this provision is an unequivocal recognition by the Parties of the established custom and practice of the oil industry; such custom and practice can therefore supplement an incomplete legal system.

Aramco's right of ownership in the oil it extracts and the oil derivatives it produces is not expressly mentioned in the 1933 Concession Agreement and it has been questioned by the Government, although the latter admits that the Company does possess private rights of a sacred character. (Answering Memorial No. 46, p. 56.)

In the course of the oral hearings, the Government claimed that this omission was intentional and that neither one nor the other Party had any absolute right of ownership in the oil. Aramco has no such right, it was argued, because it is not entitled to enjoy and dispose freely of the object of the Concession. Under Moslem law, it cannot base its alleged right of ownership on the fact of prior discovery and extraction of the oil because the right of the first discoverer in Hanbali law is not an exclusive right and is only attributed to Moslems and to non-Moslems who are among the residents of the Moslem State (Ahl al Dar); Aramco, it was further argued, cannot claim to be the first discoverer of the oil by virtue of its exclusive right to explore the vast area reserved to it in the Concession for the following reason: as no one else had the right to explore and prospect, Aramco's privilege would destroy the rules of Hanbali law according to which the first discoverer cannot prevent others from taking their needs of the mineral resources he has discovered.

But these rules, evolved some centuries ago in respect of mineral deposits other than oil, have precisely been supplemented by the 1933 Concession Agreement, ratified by Royal Decree No. 1135 in the proper exercise of the powers vested, under Hanbali law, in the Ruler of the State. The right to sell the products of the conceded oil deposits is not disputed by the Government, for it is explicitly mentioned in Article I of the 1933 Concession, as follows:

It is understood, however that such right does not include the exclusive right to sell crude or refined products within the area described below or within Saudi Arabia.

It follows, by an inescapable argument a contrario, that the concessionaire has the exclusive right to sell outside Saudi Arabia. This right of sale, which entails a transfer of title, implies a recognition of Aramco's right of ownership in the oil and oil products.

The arguments proffered in order to dispute the concessionaire's ownership are all the more devoid of foundation since this very right of ownership has been recognized several times in the Government's correspondence and, during the proceedings, in the Government's

Memorials (Answering Memorial of the Government, No. 53–54, pp. 63–65). The proof of this statement can be found in the letter, dated 10 July 1954, corresponding to 9 Zul Quada 1373, from the Minister of Finance to Mr. Davies, Chairman of Aramco's Board of Directors, where Aramco's property right is recognized in the following words:

> If it is admissible that the oil produced within the area which the second article of the Agreement delimits is by principle the property of Aramco, and that to the Government (there belong only) the royalty and taxes, nevertheless this statement requires clarification * * *.

The idea is then expressed that this property right is subject to the laws and decisions of the Government and is inferior in rank to the supreme right of the State in respect of properties and persons within its territorial borders. The same view is expressed in the Government's Answering Memorial (No. 53–57, pp. 63 to 67). The reservations accompanying this recognition in principle of Aramco's property right are not such as to weaken its force. The Company claims nothing more than the respect of its acquired rights, which cannot be unilaterally altered by the State, both Parties being on an equal footing from a contractual standpoint.

In conclusion, this analysis shows that, in Saudi Arabian law as in the laws of Western Countries, the oil concession is an institution which implies an authorization by the State, on the basis of a statute or of a contract, and necessarily entails the grant to the concessionaire of property rights in the oil. As a result of this, the Concession, even in the absence of an express clause to that effect, confers upon Aramco the right to dispose of the oil. Because of this fundamental similarity, the Tribunal will be led, in the case of gaps in the law of Saudi Arabia, of which the Concession Agreement is a part, to ascertain the applicable principles by resorting to the world-wide custom and practice in the oil business and industry; failing such custom and practice, the Tribunal will be influenced by the solutions recognized by world case-law and doctrine and by pure jurisprudence.

As regards the international effects of the Concession, such as the effects of the sale and transport of the oil and oil products to foreign countries, and in particular the f. o. b. sales, the Tribunal holds that these effects are governed by the custom and practice prevailing in maritime law and in the international oil business. Because of the American nationality of the concessionaire, a particular importance must be ascribed, in this connection, to the custom and practice followed by producers in the United States and their buyers all over the world. This does not mean that American law, as the law of the nationality and of the domicile of one of the Parties, should be given any priority in relation to the law of Saudi Arabia, as the national law of the grantor and the law of the place of exploration.

What the Tribunal intends to take into account is only the world-wide practice adopted in the oil industry and business.

Lastly, the Tribunal holds that public international law should be applied to the effects of the Concession, when objective reasons lead it to conclude that certain matters cannot be governed by any rule of the municipal law of any State, as is the case in all matters relating to transport by sea, to the sovereignty of the State on its territorial waters and to the responsibility of States for the violation of its international obligations.

* * *

[Dissenting opinion omitted.]

---

1. *Management-service contracts with the state.* As an alternative to foreign direct investment in enterprises within the territory, some developing countries are paying for foreign skills, technology, and to some extent, capital, by making contracts with foreign enterprise for the conduct of a particular type of economic operation on a fee basis. For example, Mexico, despite its state-owned oil industry and the full rigor of a constitutional prohibition on any kind of foreign-owned capital interest in oil and gas in place, has made several contracts with foreign oil companies for exploration and production of oil and gas. Another example: when in the 1940's the Franco regime in Spain bought out ITT's interest in the Spanish telephone company, an ITT subsidiary was given a contract to operate, maintain, and supply the nationalized public utility. The foreign companies are usually paid an agreed percentage of the net returns from the operation, but they have only contract rights with the host state.

As to espousal of claims based on management-service contracts, so far there has been too little experience with unilateral cancellation, outside of contract stipulations, for any clear trend to have developed as to whether such cancellations would fall into the category of interests of aliens for which espousal is accepted or into that for which espousal is not generally recognized. It is likely that the foreign investment history of such arrangements (that of having developed as alternatives to foreign private sector entrepreneurial activity based on ownership of the means of production) will incline both capital-exporting and capital-importing states to regard management-service contracts as eligible for espousal—if, of course, the receiving country does not under Calvo Clause doctrines or otherwise deny the validity of diplomatic protection in any case.

2. *Question*: Your client has been offered a management-service contract in a state where the constitution requires a Calvo Clause undertaking from a foreign investor. Would you advise your client to reject the offer out of hand? Why or why not?

BREACH OF CONTRACT

Restatement of the Foreign Relations Law of the United States § 193 (1965).

§ 193. When Breach of Contract is Wrongful under International Law

(1) The breach by a state of a contract with an alien, except as indicated in Subsections (2) and (3), is wrongful under international law if either

(a) the breach is effected in an arbitrary manner without bona fide claim of excuse,

(b) the law and practice of the state in effect at the time of the breach do not make reasonable provision for reparation for the breach,

(c) the state entered into the contract with the alien (or an alien assignor of the contract) in his capacity as an alien, or

(d) the circumstances indicate that, when the alien became a party to the contract, the parties contemplated that performance of the contract would involve to a substantial degree foreign commerce, use of foreign resources, or activity outside the territory of the state.

(2) Subsections (1)(a) and (1)(b) are not applicable to a contract for the repayment of money borrowed on the domestic market of the state.

*   *   *

———————

Cancellation of the right to engage in business where no contract, franchise or concession right is involved. Suppose you represent a Brazilian manufacturer of "Saturday night specials" and that Congress enacts legislation prohibiting the sale of such handguns in the United States. The Brazilian manufacturer has a sales agency in the United States and has imported, under proper munitions control procedures, 350,000 Saturday night specials before the effective date of the act of Congress. The Brazilian national stands to lose his normal profit of $22 each on these arms and claims that existing arms control laws in most other countries prevent him from mitigating his damages by removing the arms from the United States for sale elsewhere. Suppose (i) that in an FCN treaty between Brazil and the United States the nationals of either are entitled to engage in general manufactures and commerce in the other; (ii) that there is no such treaty undertaking. Under each assumption: if Brazil espouses the claim, what should the Legal Adviser of the Department of State recommend to the Secretary?

Do the following provisions of the Restatement give you adequate guidance?

PROHIBITION OF GAINFUL ACTIVITY

Restatement of the Foreign Relations Law
of the United States §§ 196, 197 (1965).*

§ 196.   General Rule

(1) Conduct attributable to a state that forbids an alien to engage in previously lawful gainful activity is wrongful under international law unless either

(a) the alien receives reasonable notice and opportunity to engage in other gainful activities or to depart from the territory of the state,

(b) the prohibition is promulgated for bona fide reasons of public policy of the state and is equally applicable to nationals and to aliens similarly situated, or

(c) under the law and practice of the state in effect when the prohibition becomes effective there is reasonable provision for the determination and payment of just compensation.

(2) Failure of a state to pay just compensation under the circumstances, indicated in Subsection (1)(c) is wrongful under international law.

§ 197.   Police Power and Law Enforcement

(1) Conduct attributable to a state and causing damage to an alien does not depart from the international standard of justice indicated in § 165 if it is reasonably necessary for

(a) the maintenance of public order, safety, or health, or

(b) the enforcement of any law of the state (including any revenue law) that does not itself depart from the international standard.

*   *   *

*   *   *

Comment:

a.   General.   The essential criterion in determining whether exercise of police power, or enforcement of a law of a state, that causes damage to an alien is consistent with the international standard, is whether the conduct, in each case, is reasonably necessary to achieve the indicated objective, and whether that objective is consistent with the international standard.

Illustrations:

1.   State A enacts a law requiring periodical inspection of livestock and destruction of animals that are found to have certain

communicable diseases. The law provides for compensation only in cases where more than five percent of a herd is destroyed. Pursuant to such inspection, the state destroys two percent of a herd belonging to X, an alien. The destruction does not violate the rule stated in § 185 regarding the taking of an alien's property without just compensation.

* * *

Questions.

1. Suppose the legislation prohibiting the sale of "Saturday night specials" also provided for their confiscation and destruction? Would Brazil clearly have a claim?

2. Suppose the change of national policy involves, as in land reform, the taking of property from one group (large landowners) and its transfer to another (small holders). What then as to the rights of foreign large landowners?

EL AGUILA NATIONALIZATION

8 Whiteman, Digest of International Law 1272 (1967).

Pursuant to a Decree of the Mexican Government of March 18, 1938, that Government expropriated property, including oilfields in Mexico, of a Mexican joint stock company, Compañía Mexicana de Petróleo El Aguila, S.A. (Mexican Eagle Oil Company), the shareholders of which were mainly British. Article 1 of the decree stated that the company's assets were being expropriated "on grounds of public interest (utilidad publica)". The British Government by a note to the Mexican Government of April 8, 1938, protested and requested restoration of the property to the company. In the note it was stated that "His Majesty's Government in the United Kingdom do not question the general right of a Government to expropriate in the public interest and on payment of adequate compensation; but this principle does not serve to justify expropriations essentially arbitrary in character." In its reply of April 12, 1938, the Government of Mexico took the position that the company was "a Mexican enterprise, and therefore the defence of its interests does not appertain to a foreign State, either in the realm of the internal affairs of the Mexican State or in the sphere of international life." The Mexican Government stated further in this note that it desired to place on record that—

> * * * there is a universally accepted principle of international law which attributes to all sovereign and independent countries the right to expropriate in the public interest with the payment of adequate compensation; moreover, this principle has been considered and held to mean that the grounds of public

interest may be determined by every State at its own discretion, with such latitude as conditions, social and of every other kind, may require in each case.

In a further note of April 20, 1938, the British Government insisted on its right to protect the interest of British shareholders in the company, stating:

> His Majesty's Government are not intervening on behalf of the Mexican Eagle Company but on behalf of the very large majority of shareholders who are of British nationality.

> They are perfectly well aware of the Mexican nationality of the Mexican Eagle Company itself in the sense that it is incorporated under Mexican law, and in no way seek to deny this.

> But the fact remains that the majority of shareholders who are the ultimate sufferers from the action of the Mexican Government are British, and the undertaking in question is essentially a British interest.

> For this reason alone His Majesty's Government have the right, which cannot be affected by anything in the Mexican Constitution, to protest against an action which they regard as unjustified * * *.

The British note pointed out in this connection that—

> If the doctrine were admitted that a Government can first make the operation of foreign interests in its territories depend upon their incorporation under local law, and then plead such incorporation as the justification for rejecting foreign diplomatic intervention, it is clear that the means would never be wanting whereby foreign Governments could be prevented from exercising their undoubted right under international law to protect the commercial interests of their nationals abroad.[a]

By notes exchanged between the two Governments, February 7, 1946, procedure was agreed upon for determining the amount to be paid to British subjects affected by the acts of expropriation or otherwise (subsequent to March 17, 1938) in respect of certain petroleum industrial properties in Mexico. Experts, appointed by the two Governments, were to determine an adequate valuation of the properties, rights, and interests, at the time they were affected by the acts of the Government of Mexico, on the basis of justice and equity. The experts, however, failed to reach agreement within the time allotted (3 months).

* * *

Thereafter, in August 1947, the Government of Mexico and the several companies whose properties were affected as a consequence of

---

a. For a discussion of this type of situation, see paragraph 92 of the opinion of the International court of Justice in the Barcelona Traction case, which appears at p. 1135.

the Mexican Decree of March 18, 1938, reached a settlement whereby the Government of Mexico undertook to pay $81,250,000, with interest, in U. S. currency, to the companies. The Agreement was incorporated in notes exchanged on August 29, 1947, between the British Embassy at Mexico City and the Mexican Foreign Office.   *   *   *

PEACE TREATY BETWEEN THE ALLIED POWERS AND ITALY OF FEBRUARY 10, 1947

61 Stat. 1245, 49 U.N.T.S. 3.

SECTION 1—UNITED NATIONS PROPERTY IN ITALY

Article 78

(1) In so far as Italy has not already done so, Italy shall restore all legal rights and interests in Italy of the United Nations and their nationals as they existed on June 10, 1940, and shall return all property in Italy of the United Nations and their nationals as it now exists.

    *   *   *

(4)(a) The Italian Government shall be responsible for the restoration to complete good order of the property returned to United Nations nationals under paragraph 1 of this Article. In cases where property cannot be returned or where, as a result of the war, a United Nations national has suffered a loss by reason of injury or damage to property in Italy, he shall receive from the Italian Government compensation in lire to the extent of two-thirds of the sum necessary, at the date of payment, to purchase similar property or to make good the loss suffered. In no event shall United Nations nationals receive less favourable treatment with respect to compensation than that accorded to Italian nationals.

(b) United Nations nationals who hold, directly or indirectly, ownership interests in corporations or associations which are not United Nations nationals within the meaning of paragraph 9(a) of this Article, but which have suffered a loss by reason of injury or damage to property in Italy, shall receive compensation in accordance with sub-paragraph (a) above. This compensation shall be calculated on the basis of the total loss or damage suffered by the corporation or association and shall bear the same proportion to such loss or damage as the beneficial interests of such nationals in the corporation or association bear to the total capital thereof.

(c) Compensation shall be paid free of any levies, taxes or other charges. It shall be freely usable in Italy but shall be subject to the foreign exchange control regulations which may be in force in Italy from time to time.

    *   *   *

(9) As used in this Article:

(a) "United Nations nationals" means individuals who are nationals of any of the United Nations, or corporations or associations organised under the laws of any of the United Nations, at the coming into force of the present Treaty, provided that the said individuals, corporations or associations also had this status on September 3, 1943, the date of the Armistice with Italy.

The term "United Nations nationals" also includes all individuals, corporations or associations which, under the laws in force in Italy during the war, have been treated as enemy;

(b) "Owner" means the United Nations national, as defined in sub-paragraph (a) above, who is entitled to the property in question, and includes a successor of the owner, provided that the successor is also a United Nations national as defined in sub-paragraph (a). If the successor has purchased the property in its damaged state, the transferor shall retain his rights to compensation under this Article, without prejudice to obligations between the transferor and the purchaser under domestic law;

(c) "Property" means all movable or immovable property, whether tangible or intangible, including industrial, literary and artistic property, as well as all rights or interests of any kind in property. Without prejudice to the generality of the foregoing provisions, the property of the United Nations and their nationals includes all seagoing and river vessels, together with their gear and equipment, which were either owned by United Nations or their nationals, or registered in the territory of one of the United Nations, or sailed under the flag of one of the United Nations and which, after June 10, 1940, while in Italian waters, or after they had been forcibly brought into Italian waters, either were placed under the control of the Italian authorities as enemy property or ceased to be at the free disposal in Italy of the United Nations or their nationals, as a result of measures of control taken by the Italian authorities in relation to the existence of a state of war between members of the United Nations and Germany.

*   *   *

BARCELONA TRACTION, LIGHT AND POWER CO., LTD.
(BELGIUM v. SPAIN)
International Court of Justice, 1970

[1970] I.C.J. Rep. 3.

Separate Opinion of Judge Jessup at p. 168.

*   *   *

16. In connection with the instant case, the question arises from the argument that there can be no international right to damages for shareholders indirectly injured by damage to the company in which

they hold shares, since no such right is generally established in municipal law. Much reliance is placed upon the proposition that under most systems of municipal law, shareholders have no rights in or to the assets of the corporation until after it is dissolved or wound up. Shareholders' suits are indeed provided by law in the United States and somewhat less extensively in Great Britain. In the United States "The derivative stockholder-plaintiff is not only a nominal plaintiff, but at the same time a real party in interest. He sues not solely upon a corporate cause of action but also upon his own cause of action". See Koessler, "The Stockholder's Suit: A Comparative View", 46 Columbia Law Review 1946, pages 238 and 242. The provisions for shareholder suits in the European countries seem to be somewhat less favourable to the shareholder. But the trend in France is toward more protection of shareholders, as Judge Gros points out in paragraph 11 of his separate opinion.

17. Although the concept of corporate personality is a creature of municipal law, none of the theories evolved in that frame of reference can be relied on universally to explain the legal relations surrounding that "technical legal device".

Gierke's theory was based upon Germanic village communities, medieval guilds and similar truly corporate entities. But such a theory hardly fits the modern holding company * * * The result is that those who administer the law, whether as judges, revenue authorities, or as administrators, in civilian and common law systems alike [and I would add in the international law system] have had to discard all known theories of corporate personality, and to relativise the conception of juristic personality, respecting it for some purposes, disregarding it for others, in accordance with the nature of the problem before them. (Friedmann, Legal Theory, 5th ed. 1967, pp. 522–523. See also p. 571.)

I would paraphrase and adapt a dictum from a recent decision of the Supreme Court of the United States in an anti-trust case: the International Court of Justice in the instant case is "not bound by formal conceptions of" corporation law. "We must look at the economic reality of the relevant transactions" and identify "the overwhelmingly dominant feature". The overwhelmingly dominant feature in the affairs of Barcelona Traction was not the fact of incorporation in Canada, but the controlling influence of far-flung international financial interests manifested in the Sofina grouping.

It may well be that the new structures of international enterprise will be increasingly important, but any glance at the world-wide picture today shows that non-governmental corporations still have a major role to play. That is why so many new States, and the United Nations itself, encourage the investment of private capital.

The Right to Extend Diplomatic Protection to Corporate Enterprises

18.   The decision of the Court, in this case, is based on the legal conclusion that only Canada had a right to present a diplomatic claim on behalf of Barcelona Traction which was a company of Canadian nationality.   My own conclusion is that, for reasons which I shall explain, Canada did not have, in this case, a right to claim on behalf of Barcelona Traction.   As a matter of general international law, it is also my conclusion that a State, under certain circumstances, has a right to present a diplomatic claim on behalf of shareholders who are its nationals.   As a matter of proof of fact, I find that Belgium did not succeed in proving the Belgian nationality, between the critical dates, of those natural and juristic persons on whose behalf it sought to claim.   The Belgian claim must therefore be rejected.

*   *   *

---

1.   *Creeping nationalization.*   It is sometimes difficult to find a formal, positive act of nationalization.   Major political changes in the host country may alter the whole investment climate in reliance on which the investment was made.   Or the tax laws of the host country may become much more severe.   The zeal with which the police power is used may increase.   At some point, in some situations, a design of harassment and discrimination against all, or a particular, foreign investment may become sufficiently clear as to be the basis of a formal or informal diplomatic remonstrance by a state entitled to espouse the interests of the investor affected.   But it is extremely difficult for such diplomatic actions to go to the point of claiming a constructive taking of the alien's economic interests thus making the objection one under international law.

In a few instances, such as in that of a deliberate course of police intimidation of foreign enterprise, some states of nationality have declared that the conduct of the host state was a constructive taking. Other states have been disinclined to make such claims based on "constructive nationalization."

2.   *Question.*   From the standpoint of a host state, if a foreign investment has become internally unpopular or undesirable, why should the state nationalize instead of squeezing the foreign interest out?   Would the host state not have an easier time internationally if it followed the latter course?   Would the Hickenlooper Amendments (see 22 U.S.C. § 2370(e)(1) and (2)) be activated by a program of tightening the noose to the point of practical strangulation of the foreign enterprise, but without taking title?   Mexico has developed some

refined ways of inducing foreign enterprises, such as the American sulphur industry in Mexico, to scale down the foreign stock ownership through sale at fair prices. The inducement in the sulphur case was to cut down almost to zero on export licenses for sulphur, most of which was sold in the world market, not in Mexico. After the American interests sold down to a minority position, export licensing on a large scale was resumed. Eventually the American interest sold out entirely.

IN THE MATTER OF THE CLAIM OF JENO HARTMANN

8 Whiteman, Digest of International Law 1011 (1967).

[Foreign Claims Settlement Commission of the United States, 1958 [a]]

This is a claim under Section 303(2) of the International Claims Settlement Act of 1949, as amended, for $27,901.26 by JENO HARTMANN, a national of the United States since his naturalization in the United States on July 23, 1946, for the nationalization, compulsory liquidation, or other taking of property in Hungary.

The Commission finds that the claimant was the owner of a plot of land at 6 Epreskert Street, Ryiregyhazs, improved with a building containing living quarters and a bakery consisting of installed equipment, and furnishings, all of which belonged to claimant, although the business was conducted by another, to whom any profits belonged. The Government of Hungary nationalized the bakery on January 6, 1950, under the provisions of Law-Decree 1949: 20 tvr. (Magyar Kozlony, December 28, 1949).

The operation of the bakery by the Government of Hungary is made possible only through the use of the claimant's real property, for which he has received no compensation. Although the Government of Hungary has stated that title to the real estate in question has not been taken into state ownership, it is hard to conceive of a more effective method of taking of property than appears in the instant case with respect to claimant's realty. Claimant has been prohibited from entering upon his property, from using and enjoying it, and from alienating it. Accordingly, while the method of taking of claimant's realty utilized in the present situation, leaves the claimant endowed with the indicia of ownership, the Commission nevertheless finds that

a. The decisional law of the commission is important, although it sometimes results from the application of particular statutory principles in the United States authorizing legislation, 64 Stat. 12 (1949), as amended, rather than from general international law. Unfortunately these decisions are not officially published but are included only in semi-annual reports to the Congress. The use by Whiteman of some of them makes the digest the semi-official reporter for Claims Commission decisions—to the extent that the digest reproduces them.

such realty has been effectively taken from claimant within the meaning of Section 303(2) of the International Claims Settlement Act of 1949, as amended.

---

3. THE FUNDAMENTALS OF INTERNATIONAL CLAIMS

1. *Tour d'horizon.* The existing international legal system does not provide very effective rules for assuring direct foreign private sector investors against nationalization. The possibilities for improvement are sketched later on in this chapter. But when a nationalization occurs and the host state does not behave in a normal way, that is, provide that such takings be only for public purposes (including social policy purposes, as in land reform), be executed with procedural fairness, and on the payment of compensation, the injured foreign investor has a natural grievance. When a series of abnormal takings occurs (either in a single country or in a group of countries) or in sensational cases, a degree of neurosis is added to the sense of grievance. The investor under these latter circumstances—or its lawyers (it is usually a corporation that has been nationalized)—wants lessons taught as well as compensation. Probably the subconscious wish in many cases is to be freed of the nationalization threat and to resume business as usual. But usually this wish is not within the range of achievement and this adds to the frustrations.

Thus it is that abnormal nationalizations tend to involve the emotions, as well as the law. Naturally, in such cases, emotions, political or genuinely deeply held, also rise in the nationalizing country if it begins to sense foreign opprobrium or pressure. One result of this syndrome is that time must pass before passions cool and a settlement of the claim can be worked out, whether by private arrangements, diplomatic protection activities, arbitration, adjudication, or other means of conflicts resolution. The truth of this observation can be verified by studying the time-lag in the claims settlements between the United States and Mexico following the highly charged atmosphere engendered by the Mexican Revolution and its aftermath. Also, when will it be that the United States and Cuba will find themselves calmly and clinically able to work out mutual solutions to the wholesale nationalizations carried out by Fidel Castro?

In the main the materials that follow relate to the process of claims settlement in a calm environment. Some of the applications of the principles sketched, it is true, were made during periods of tension. Such uses are often tactical gambits, designed to put off as long as possible—or until tempers have cooled—the real work of settlement. The analyst should always be aware of the psycho-political atmosphere in which a claims settlement rule is being invoked or rejected.

Another consequence of the emotions aroused in certain instances of nationalization is that the aggrieved former owners of expropriated property turn to varieties of self-help, either on their own or through the enlistment of national legislation such as the Hickenlooper Amendments (see p. 416) and, in the case of the United States also, to the registration of claims with the Department of State and, more recently, to pre-international settlement declarations of right to compensation by the Foreign Claims Settlement Commission of the United States. Self-help is also induced, no doubt, by the reality that except through it, save in the rare case of an arbitration contract with the host state, the private party has no standing on his own to pursue his rights by a suit against the nationalizing state.

2. *The fundamentals in a nutshell.* The basic rules for international claims settlements are set out in a number of useful sources, including the Restatement of the Foreign Relations Law of the United States § 184–214 (1965), 8 Whiteman, Digest of International Law 1216–1291 (1967) and 2 O'Connell, International Law, Ch. 33 (1970). Whatever the instrumentality or means of settlement the major rules, usually followed are:

a. Local (nationalizing state) remedies must have been exhausted, if any exist in law and are not clearly unavailable in fact.

b. The private claimant must have had the nationality, through a genuine link, of the espousing state at the time of the taking. This rule creates obvious problems where dual or corporate nationality is involved; distinguish as to the latter the question considered at p. 1104 as to the rights of foreign shareholders in relationship to their equities in corporations of the nationality of the taking state. In the settlements of the nationalizations that occurred in socialist states in Eastern Europe after World War II, sensitive issues arose as to persecuted persons who had had the nationality of the taking state at the time of the taking but had been naturalized in other states before the claims settlement.

c. The claimant must have continued to be a national of the espousing state down to the time of espousal, and possibly to the time of settlement. This rule has also created certain stresses of a politico-moral nature.

d. The most widely recognized remedy is compensation. Restitution or invalidation of title to the nationalized property has not been granted by international adjudication as a clear alternative to compensation possibly because international cases are not presented in the form of suits against private parties purchasing from the nationalizing states. However, some national courts have given these remedies in cases involving such parties, but others have not. See Chapter 6.

e. The doctrine of sovereign immunity bars suits against the taking state in the courts of another state.

f. Internationally the state authorized to espouse the claim has the power to bar it in whole or in part by arrangement with the taking state, even though no—or no adequate—compensation has been obtained.

g. Use of force by the espousing state to redress the injury suffered by the owner whose economic interests are taken in violation of international law is illicit under the United Nations Charter and the Charter of the Organization of American States. Also, for political reasons, it is extremely unlikely today that intervention in pursuit of such redress would be undertaken. The aborted British-French action at Suez, 1956, in redress of the nationalization of the Suez Canal by the United Arab Republic, is likely not to be often imitated. The Bay of Pigs and Dominican Republic actions involved no property protection elements whatsoever. As to the denial by the epousing state of economic advantages or development assistance to the taking state, see p. 1072.

EXHAUSTION OF REMEDIES AND OTHER PRECONDITIONS

LETTER OF ACTING SECRETARY OF STATE WELLES TO SENATOR BUNKER (1942)

8 Whiteman, Digest of International Law 769 (1967).

I have received your letter of April 1 in which you urge that this Government request the British Government to effect a dismissal of the Prize Court proceedings instituted against the oil cargoes of the vessels Chas. Racine and Petter and to transmit the proceeds of the sale of the cargoes to the United States for delivery to Davis and Company, Incorporated, the alleged owner.

It appears from the Department's records that in relation to a similar request which you addressed to Mr. Berle [Assistant Secretary of State] and Mr. Hackworth [The Legal Adviser], respectively, the Secretary [Mr. Hull], on January 28, 1942, informed you of the long standing practice of this Government to decline to intervene in cases of this character pending in the courts of a foreign country.

In view of the fact that statements contained in the first paragraph of your letter of February 4 and in the last paragraph of your letter under acknowledgment tend to indicate that you are under the impression that the position of the Department in this matter is predicated upon rules or regulations promulgated by the British Government, I hasten to assure you that this is not the case. I should like to invite your attention to a few of the many authorities in support of the general rule of international law and practice in this respect.

In an opinion of February 22, 1792, Attorney General Randolph stated that states do not interfere with the regular course of the administration of justice in cases in which an alien is a party until he shall have taken his case to the court of last resort. (1 Op.Atty.Gen.

25, 26). In an opinion of Attorney General Lee it was held that American citizens were bound to apply to the tribunals of the Province of Florida 'for the recovery of their property in that Province, as well as for redress of injury done them there'. (Ibid. 68, 69.)

In a communication of June 1, 1885, to the British Minister, Secretary Bayard cited with approval the following statement of Sir R. Phillimore (International Law, II, 4):

> The State must be satisfied that its citizen has exhausted the means of legal redress offered by the tribunals of the country in which he has been injured.

He also cited the following statement of Chief Justice Waite in the case of New Hampshire vs. Louisiana (108 U.S., 90):

> There is no principle of international law which makes it the duty of one nation to assume the collection of the claims of its citizens against another nation, if the citizens themselves have ample means of redress without the intervention of their Government. (Foreign Relations 1885, Page 458.)

In a report of February 5, 1896 to the President, Secretary Olney stated:

> This position of the French Government—that claims of aliens cognizable by the courts of a foreign country can not be made the subject of diplomatic intervention unless there has been a palpable failure of justice after all local judicial remedies have been exhausted—is one upon which this Government has often insisted and of which it has often availed itself. (Foreign Relations 1895, Part I, Page 259.)

On more than one occasion the Court of Claims has dismissed claims because of the failure of the claimants to exhaust the legal remedies available to them in the courts of a foreign state. (See 29 Ct.Cls. 68, and 45 Ct.Cls. 555.) Similar action has been taken by international arbitral tribunals in a large number of cases.

In the [sic] declining to intervene in the case of the steamship Dacia pending in the French Prize Court, the Department in a communication of August 31, 1915 stated:

> * * * the Department desires to call your attention to the generally accepted rule of international law, that, in cases of the character of the present one, the interested party must exhaust his local legal remedies before diplomatic intervention is appropriate. (Foreign Relations, 1915, Supplement, Page 530.)

The position of the British Government in this regard was set forth in the excerpt from a memorandum, accompanying the British Embassy's note of April 24, 1916, which was quoted in the Secretary's letter to you of January 28, 1942. In that relation I may say that the Department has recently received a despatch from the American Embassy at London reporting the receipt by it of a communication from the Procurator General enclosing a copy of a letter addressed to you by the latter on February 5, 1942 in which it was stated that since the present case is pending in the Prize Court any intervention, whether through the diplomatic channel or otherwise, is in principle inappropriate and inadmissible.

In the light of the foregoing consideration I feel sure that you will appreciate that the Department is not in a position to intervene in the present case. I should also point out the possibility that any rights which Davis and Company, Incorporated, may have in the matter may be seriously prejudiced should the Company fail to present to the Prize Court the evidence and arguments upon which it rests its claim for compensation.

THE AMBATIELOS CLAIM

Commission of Arbitration, 1956.
XII U.N.Rep.Int'l.Arb.Awards 82, 91 (1963).

[This claim arose out of a 1919 contract between Ambatielos, a Greek national, and the United Kingdom Government for the purchase by the former of several vessels being built for the Government at Hong Kong. Ambatielos was unable to complete payment for the vessels, allegedly because an undue delay in their delivery deprived him of favorable freight rates; and he gave mortgages to the British Government for the balance owed on them. On foreclosure proceedings in an English court, the defense of undue delay was rejected and the vessels ordered sold. Ambatielos lost the vessels and what he had paid on them. In the trial court and on appeal Ambatielos tried to get support for his defense from British official files and from the British officials who had negotiated with him. He was unsuccessful, and thereupon Ambatielos abandoned his appeal in the British case and got the Greek Government to espouse the claim. The International Court of Justice held that the United Kingdom was under an international agreement obligation to submit the claim to arbitration, and in the arbitration that followed one of the British defenses was that Ambatielos had not exhausted his remedies in the English courts. Great Britain won the arbitration on "Claim A" on the ground that in fact Ambatielos had not exhausted his domestic judicial remedies, as to calling witnesses. Other claims were rejected because it was found that they had not been presented in the British courts at all.]

In countering the claim of the Greek Government the Government of the United Kingdom relies on the non-exhaustion by Mr. Ambatielos of the legal remedies which English law put at his disposal.

One of the questions which the Commission is requested to determine is "The question raised by the United Kingdom Government of the non-exhaustion of legal remedies in the English Courts in respect of the acts alleged to constitute breaches of the Treaty." The Commission notes that the question raised by the United Kingdom Government covers all the acts alleged to constitute breaches of the Treaty.

The Commission will therefore examine the validity of the United Kingdom objection independently of the conclusions it has reached concerning the validity of the Ambatielos claim under the Treaty of 1886.

The rule thus invoked by the United Kingdom Government is well-established in international law. Nor is its existence contested by the Greek Government. It means that the State against which an international action is brought for injuries suffered by private individuals has the right to resist such an action if the persons alleged to have been injured have not first exhausted all the remedies available to them under the municipal law of that State. The defendant State has the right to demand that full advantage shall have been taken of all local remedies before the matters in dispute are taken up on the international level by the State of which the persons alleged to have been injured are nationals.

In order to contend successfully that international proceedings are inadmissible, the defendant State must prove the existence, in its system of internal law, of remedies which have not been used. The views expressed by writers and in judicial precedents, however, coincide in that the existence of remedies which are obviously ineffective is held not to be sufficient to justify the application of the rule. Remedies which could not rectify the situation cannot be relied upon by the defendant State as precluding an international action.

The Greek Government contends that in the present case the remedies which English law offered to Mr. Ambatielos were ineffective and that, accordingly, the rule is not applicable.

The ineffectiveness of local remedies may result clearly from the municipal law itself. That is the case, for example, when a Court of Appeal is not competent to reconsider the judgment given by a Court of first instance on matters of fact, and when, failing such reconsideration, no redress can be obtained. In such a case there is no doubt that local remedies are ineffective.

Furthermore, however, it is generally considered that the ineffectiveness of available remedies, without being legally certain, may also result from circumstances which do not permit any hope of redress to be placed in the use of those remedies. But in a case of that kind it is essential that such remedies, if they had been resorted to, would have proved to be obviously futile.

Here a question of considerable practical importance arises.

If the rule of exhaustion of local remedies is relied upon against the action of the claimant State, what is the test to be applied by an international tribunal for the purpose of determining the applicability of the rule?

As the arbitrator ruled in the Finnish Vessels Case of 9th May, 1934, the only possible test is to assume the truth of the facts on which the claimant State bases its claim. As will be shown below, any departure from this assumption would lead to inadmissible results.

In the Finnish Vessels Case the issue was whether a means of appeal which had not been used by the claimants ought to be regarded as ineffective.

In the Ambatielos Case, failure to use certain means of appeal is likewise relied upon by the United Kingdom Government, but reliance is also placed on the failure of Mr. Ambatielos to adduce before Mr. Justice Hill evidence which it is now said would have been essential to establish his claims. There is no doubt that the exhaustion of local remedies requires the use of the means of procedure which are essential to redress the situation complained of by the person who is alleged to have been injured.

In paragraph 109 of its Counter-Case, the United Kingdom Government says the following concerning this point:

> The "local remedies" rule . . . finds its principal field of application in the two requirements (a) that the complainant should have availed himself of any right given him by the local law to take legal proceedings in the local courts; and (b) that having done so, he should have exhausted the possibilities of appealing to a higher court against any adverse decision of a lower one. The application of the rule is not, however, confined to these two cases. It also requires that during the progress, and for the purposes of any particular proceedings in one of the local courts, the complainant should have availed himself of all such procedural facilities in the way of calling witnesses, procuring documentation, etc., as the local system provides.

The Commission shares this view in principle. At the same time it feels that it must add some clarifications and reservations to it. Although this question has hardly been studied by writers and although it does not seem, hitherto, to have been the subject of judicial decisions, it is hardly possible to limit the scope of the rule of prior exhaustion of local remedies to recourse to local courts.

The rule requires that "local remedies" shall have been exhausted before an international action can be brought. These "local remedies" include not only reference to the courts and tribunals, but also the use of the procedural facilities which municipal law makes available to litigants before such courts and tribunals. It is the whole system of legal protection, as provided by municipal law, which must have been put to the test before a State, as the protector of its nationals, can prosecute the claim on the international plane. In this sense the statement in paragraph 109 of the Counter-Case seems to be sound.

It is clear, however, that it cannot be strained too far. Taken literally, it would imply that the fact of having neglected to make use of some means of procedure—even one which is not important to the defence of the action—would suffice to allow a defendant State to claim that local remedies have not been exhausted, and that, therefore, an international action cannot be brought. This would confer on the rule of the prior exhaustion of local remedies a scope which is unacceptable.

In the view of the Commission the non-utilisation of certain means of procedure can be accepted as constituting a gap in the exhaustion of local remedies only if the use of these means of procedure were essential to establish the claimant's case before the municipal courts.

It is on the assumption that the statements of the claimant Government are correct that the international tribunal will be able to say whether the non-utilisation of this or that method of procedure makes it possible to raise against a claim a plea of inadmissibility on the ground of non-exhaustion of local remedies.

Have the local remedies been exhausted with regard to Claim A?

Claim A is a claim for compensation for breach of the contract of sale by the United Kingdom Government. The breach alleged is that the vessels which Mr. Ambatielos bought at an agreed price and on condition that they were to be delivered to him on certain fixed dates, which had been agreed upon between the Parties, were not in fact delivered on those dates. Compensation is claimed for the damage caused to Mr. Ambatielos as a result of this breach of contract.

The United Kingdom Government has raised the question of the non-exhaustion of local remedies in the English Courts in so far as concerns the acts which are alleged to constitute breaches of the Treaty of 1886.

The principal act which is alleged by the Greek Government to constitute a breach of that Treaty is the alleged breach of contract aforesaid.

As regards Claim A, the questions of the non-exhaustion of local remedies thus raised are:

(1) In the 1922 proceedings Mr. Ambatielos failed to call (as he could have done) the witnesses who, as he now says, were essential to establish his case.

With regard to Major Laing, the Greek Government has primarily contended that Mr. Ambatielos was prevented from calling Major Laing as a witness before Mr. Justice Hill because Major Laing—though not heard—had been subpoenaed to appear as a witness for the Crown. In the course of the proceedings before the Commission, however, the Parties agreed that the fact that Major Laing had been subpoenaed by the Crown would not, under English law, have precluded

Mr. Ambatielos from calling Major Laing as a witness before Mr. Justice Hill.

The Greek Government further contends that if Mr. Ambatielos had called Major Laing as a witness, the decision of Mr. Justice Hill would have been favourable to him; this is a contention which is disputed by the United Kingdom Government.

It is not possible for the Commission to decide on the evidence before it the question whether the case would have been decided in favour of Mr. Ambatielos if Major Laing had been heard as a witness. The Commission has not heard the witnesses called before Mr. Justice Hill and cannot solely on the documentary evidence put before the Commission form an opinion whether the testimony of Major Laing would have been successful in establishing the claim of Mr. Ambatielos before Mr. Justice Hill. The Commission cannot put itself in the position of Mr. Justice Hill in this respect.

The test as regards the question whether the testimony of Major Laing was essential must therefore be what the claimant Government in this respect has contended, viz. that the testimony of Major Laing would have had the effect of establishing the claim put forward by Mr. Ambatielos before Mr. Justice Hill.

Under English law Mr. Ambatielos was not precluded from calling Major Laing as a witness.

In so far as concerns Claim A, the failure of Mr. Ambatielos to call Major Laing as a witness at the hearing before Mr. Justice Hill must therefore be held to amount to non-exhaustion of the local remedy available to him in the proceedings before Mr. Justice Hill.

It may be that the decision of Mr. Ambatielos not to call Major Laing as a witness, with the result that he did not exhaust local remedies, was dictated by reasons of expediency—quite understandable in themselves—in putting his case before Mr. Justice Hill. This, however, is not the question to be determined. The Commission is not concerned with the question as to whether he was right or wrong in acting as he did. He took his decision at his own risk.

---

1. *Recognition of the exhaustion requirement by international adjudication.* The Interhandel case, abstracted at p. 78, was a 1959 holding by the International Court of Justice that Switzerland could not sue the United States there for a claimed illicit taking of the property of alleged Swiss nationals until it had exhausted its remedies in United States courts. This Swiss resort to the International Court came after a United States federal district court had dismissed with prejudice a Swiss suit in the United States, because the plaintiff refused to permit discovery of records kept in Switzerland and claimed

by the Department of Justice to have a possible bearing on the basic issue being litigated. The issue: was General Aniline and Film Corporation, organized in the United States, beneficially owned by enemy-national Germans or by Swiss? Noting that the Supreme Court of the United States had, shortly after the international suit was instituted, granted certiorari to review a court of appeals affirmance of the above holding of the district court and, further, had, before the instant hearing of preliminary objections in the ICJ, reversed the lower courts as to dismissal with prejudice, the International Court of Justice upheld the United States' objection that domestic remedies had not been exhausted. In doing so the court recognized the rule requiring exhaustion of local remedies before resort to international proceedings as " * * * a well-established rule of customary international law * * * " that clearly " * * * must be observed when domestic proceedings are pending * * * [that] are designed to obtain the same result: the restitution of the assets of Interhandel vested in the United States * * * ".

2. *Questions about "exhaustion."* The Swiss have stringent laws against the unauthorized revelation of business records and usually react negatively to foreign official efforts to command the use as evidence of records kept in Switzerland. Suppose the Swiss, after having suffered dismissal with prejudice on discovery rules grounds in the federal district court, had not appealed to the court of appeals but had dropped the American suit and had sued in the International Court of Justice. Might Switzerland have fared better on the exhaustion of remedies issue? Suppose the district court had dismissed the plaintiff's suit on motion for summary judgment as having failed to make a prima facie case within the divestiture provisions of the United States Trading with the Enemy Act. Would the Swiss, nonetheless, have had to fight their way to a final decision by the United States Supreme Court before having satisfied a condition precedent to suit in the International Court of Justice? Suppose, in either of the above situations, that the Swiss had lost in the United States Supreme Court. Would they have to file a motion for rehearing in the United States Supreme Court as a condition precedent to suing effectively in the International Court of Justice? Or to appeal, after the denial of rehearing, to the Congress and the President to redress an alleged breach of international law compounded by the final action of the Supreme Court?

These questions raise the outer limits of "exhaustion." There is little but opinion authority on this point. The general view that has been expressed is that the claimant must have made reasonable efforts to obtain satisfaction within the domestic legal system. Cf. Restatement of the Foreign Relations Law of the United States, § 207, which seems to assume that legal or quasi-legal trial and appellate systems in the respondent state must normally be exhausted.

3. *Where exhaustion is not required.* Exhaustion as a condition precedent to an international claims action is usually pleaded in bar by a state against a state. It is very rare indeed that a private party plaintiff would be in a litigation situation in which he would attempt to assert that the internal legal system of the respondent state is so under-developed, so corrupt, so unfair, or so predetermined as to make it clear that it would be useless to try to use it. However, in the Kennecott Copper litigation, see p. 1141, the plaintiff in the suits for the copper ore or its proceeds, a private party, does contend that its prior legal efforts in Chile have demonstrated that no relevant institution of the Chilean state will accept jurisdiction to apply international law as against the Chilean president's retrospective assessment of excess profits liabilities.

In state-to-state proceedings the plaintiff state's response to the defense of non-exhaustion must be made with due regard to the sensibilities of the respondent state. The safest contention, of course, is that all relevant local remedies have been tried and have proved to be unavailing.

4. *Waiver of the requirement of exhaustion by agreement.* Naturally, as between states wishing to settle issues between themselves through a general claims or a lump sum arrangement, exhaustion of remedies as to each of a large number of individual claims is waived, either expressly or tacitly. An agreement to waive the requirement of exhaustion also avoids, in sensitive situations (as both parties realize), any possibility of diplomatic indelicacy as to the "honor" of the respondent state's internal system of justice. As to the disputed effect of the existence of an agreement to arbitrate that does not expressly provide for waiver of exhaustion of domestic remedies, see the Reporters' Note to § 208, Restatement, Foreign Relations Law of the United States (1965).

OWNERS OF THE TATTLER (UNITED STATES) v. GREAT BRITAIN

Arbitral Tribunal, Great Britain-United States, 1920
VI U. N. Rep. Int'l Arb. Awards 48 (1955).

[The Canadian authorities in Nova Scotia arrested and detained a fishing vessel of United States nationality on charges of having engaged in fishing in violation of an 1818 treaty between the United States and Great Britain, which in 1886 became internal law in Canada, then and at the time of this suit still a British dominion. The Tattler was released upon the payment of a fine and the signing by the private party of a waiver of further claim.]

The record shows that by an agreement made at Liverpool, Nova Scotia, April 15, 1905 (United States memorial, exhibit 19, enclosure 1), the owners entered into the following undertaking:

"In consideration of the release of the American schooner Tattler of Gloucester, Mass., now under detention at the port of Liverpool, Nova Scotia (on payment of the fine of five hundred dollars, demanded by the Honourable, Minister of Marine and Fisheries of Canada, or by the Collector of Customs at said port), we hereby guarantee His Majesty King Edward the Seventh, his successors and assigns, represented in this behalf by the said Minister, and all whom it doth or may concern, against any and all claims made or to be made on account of or in respect to such detention or for deterioration or otherwise in respect to said vessel or her tackle or apparel, outfits, supplies or voyage, hereby waiving all such claims and right of libel or otherwise before any courts or Tribunal in respect to said detention or to such or any of such claims or for loss or damage in the premises."

It has been observed by the United States Government that on the same day the owners notified the Canadian authorities that the payment of the said sum of $500 was made under protest.

But neither this protest nor the receipt given by the Canadian authorities for the $500 contains any reservation to, or protest against, the guarantee given against "any and all claims made or to be made on account of or in respect to such detention". It does not appear, therefore, that the waiver in the undertaking of any claim or right "before any court or tribunal" was subject to any condition available before this tribunal.

It is proved by the documents that the consent of the British Government to the release of the vessel was given on two conditions, first, on payment of $500, and, second, on the owners undertaking to waive any right or claim before any court, and the protest against the payment does not extend and can not in any way be held by implication to extend to this waiver.

This protest appears to have been a precautionary measure in case the Canadian authorities should have been disposed to reduce the sum. Any protest or reserve as to the waiver of the right to damages would have been plainly inconsistent with the undertaking itself and would have rendered it nugatory if it had been accepted by the other party.

On the other hand, it has been objected that the renunciation of and guarantee against any claims are not binding upon the Government of the United States, which presents the claim.

But in this case the only right the United States Government is supporting is that of its national, and consequently in presenting this claim before this Tribunal, it can rely on no legal ground other than those which would have been open to its national.

For these reasons

This Tribunal decides that the claim relating to the seizure and detention of the American schooner Tattler on and between April 10 and April 16, 1905, must be dismissed.

------

1. *Settlement acceptable to the private claimant.* States usually espouse the claims of their nationals only because the claims have not otherwise been settled. If after causing or threatening to cause diplomatic problems, a claim is settled by the respondent state and the private claimant, the settlement is instinctively supported as final. The potential plaintiff state's officials breathe a sigh of relief and go on to other business. This is clearly so if there is no related but independent plaintiff-state claim and if the settlement is reached before formal espousal has been made. Technically this might not be so for a settlement thereafter, but the resistance to a second settlement that the respondent state would surely interpose makes the technicality rather illusory. The state of nationality, however, will tend to be sensitive to the interests of its national as against undue pressure or duress in the settlement itself.

2. *Waiver as a condition precedent to entry as a foreign contractor or investor; the Calvo clause problem.* Some Latin American states in their constitutions, by statute, or by executive action make it a condition precedent to the entry of a foreign contractor or direct investor that the alien undertake at the time of entry and in consideration therefor not to invoke the diplomatic protection of the state of his nationality and to accept non-discriminatory national treatment as his sole basis of right. Contractually, this is an anticipatory waiver of claims. The foreign minister of Argentina who gave his name in the latter part of the last century to the Calvo doctrine, which the clauses seek to implement, grounded the doctrine firmly on a negation of any right of diplomatic protection inhering in states of nationality and on a denial of the existence of an international minimum standard. See p. 1074.

Inevitably Calvo clauses raise these questions: (i) may the private party bind or bar the state of his nationality? (ii) if the promisor, again the private party, breaches his promise and goes tattling to the state of his nationality, what happens as to: (a) the investor vis-a-vis the state to which he gave his promise, (b) any independent right of action that the state of nationality otherwise might have had?

The questions posed do not have clear and satisfactory answers in either doctrinal writings or in international arbitrations. There have been no International Court decisions on these matters. Analytically, these questions raise the issue whether the notion that a nation-

alization claim is an injury to the state of espousal is an expression
of a fundamental of customary international law, or whether it is
really merely a doctrine of logical convenience, to get around the un-
der-development of individuals' rights in the international legal system.

Capital exporting states other than the United States seem to
have been only rarely troubled by Calvo clauses. So far this device
for subjecting the foreign investor to greater host state control has
not spread throughout the developing half of the world.

In diplomatic correspondence and in the position of at least one
of its appointees to arbitral tribunals, the United States has rejected
the notion that the international cause of action of the United States
could be compromised by an agreement between a foreign state and a
United States citizen. United States Commissioner F. K. Neilsen dissented vigorously in the International Fisheries Case, U. S.–Mexican
General Claims Commission 1926, Op. of Comms. 207 (1927). A majority of the arbitral body in this case followed the general line of a
previous case in the same arbitral series (U. S.–Mexico General
Claims) to the effect that a Calvo clause undertaking must be given
a reasonable and circumspect interpretation. Such an interpretation
includes these elements: (i) the undertaking covers only the economic
and technical aspects of the contract or investment venture, not the
general rights of alien private persons; (ii) a Calvo clause does not
mean that the private party must abstain from pursuing international
legal remedies for denial of procedural justice or outrageous conduct
by the host state; (iii) a state's rights under international law cannot
be taken away by a contract to which it is not a party; (iv) where, in
an arbitration involving a Calvo clause-affected claim, the plaintiff
state acts strictly on behalf of its national and the national does not
resort to (or exhaust) his local remedies but instead complains to his
government and seeks espousal, provisions in the arbitration agreement that exhaustion of remedies will be waived do not apply. That
is, a waiver of exhaustion between the states parties to the agreement
to arbitrate does not cover non-exhaustion in Calvo clause cases.

This is where the legal trail ends at the present time. Consult
Restatement of the Foreign Relations Law of the United States
(1965), Section 202, and particularly the authorities cited in the Reporters' Note. Both the arbitral decisions referred to above and state
practice seem to negate the view that Calvo clauses are nullities in
international claims law and practice. And there is some evidence
that in United States diplomatic practice the presence of a Calvo
clause is a factor in determining either espousal itself, or the degree
and intensity with which the normal diplomatic protection function
of the Department of State is discharged.

3. *Problem.* An American investor makes a Calvo clause investment in State X. Later the investment is nationalized without

compensation satisfactory to the investor. The investor complains to the Department of State but does not pursue his remedies in X, which is under a military dictatorship that has made a big national issue out of this particular nationalization. Strictly on the bases of the two Hickenlooper Amendments, see p. 416, one requiring the President to cut off foreign assistance to a country that does not give reasonable assurance of settling a nationalization claim in accordance with international law within six months of the taking and the other ordering the elimination of the act of state doctrine in Sabbatino-type nationalization cases, insofar as alleged violations of international law are concerned, what should be the effects, if any, of the disregard by the investor of his Calvo clause promises?

4. *Question.* Would it be reasonably accurate to say that the Hickenlooper Amendments are hard-nosed developed state responses to a too-clever developing state doctrinal device for making international law irrelevant in nationalization cases?

Espousal of Claims

General requirement of effective nationality. Judge Jessup discusses this requirement in the Barcelona Traction Case, [1970] I.C.J.Rep. 3, at 182. [A portion of his opinion follows.]

38. There is no question that, under international law, a State has in general a right to extend its diplomatic protection to a corporation which has its nationality, or national character as it is more properly called. The proposition raises two questions:

(1) What are the tests to determine the national character of a corporation?

(2) Assuming the appropriate tests are met, must that national character be "real and effective" as shown by the "link" between the corporation and the State, just as, in the Nottebohm case, this Court decided that a certain claim to nationality is not enough in all situations to justify a State in extending its diplomatic protection to a natural person?

39. There are two standard tests of the "nationality" of a corporation. The place of incorporation is the test generally favoured in the legal systems of the common law, while the siège social is more generally accepted in the civil law systems. (See Kronstein, "The Nationality of International Enterprises", 52 Columbia Law Review (1952), p. 983.) There is respectable authority for requiring that both tests be met.

It is not possible to speak of a single rule for all purposes. The tests used in private international law have their own character, as well brought out by Caflisch, "La nationalité des sociétés commerciales en droit international privé", Annuaire suisse de droit international, Vol. XXIV, 1967, page 119.

Commercial treaties and claims conventions often contain their own definitions of which companies shall be considered to have the nationality of a State for purposes of the treaty. (Cf. Walker, "Provisions on Companies in United States Commercial Treaties", 50 American Journal of International Law, 1956, p. 373; Wilson, United States Commercial Treaties and International Law, 1960; and, for a more comprehensive survey, Ginther, "Nationality of Corporations", Österreichische Zeitschrift für Öffentliches Recht, Vol. XVI, 1966, p. 28 at pp. 31–59.) The tests used for such purposes may be quite different—even in the practice of the same State—from the tests used for other purposes. For example, the "control" test was widely used to determine the enemy character of property during war, but it is not established in international law as a general test of the nationality of a corporation. On the other hand, control may constitute the essential link which, when joined to nationality, gives the State the right to extend diplomatic protection to the corporation. It is a familiar fact that the laws of certain States provide favourable conditions for companies incorporating therein, especially in relation to taxation. Canada is one such State, Liechtenstein is another. In the United States, many companies find it advantageous, for various reasons, to incorporate in Delaware or New Jersey. Charters secured for such reasons may be called "charters of convenience".

40. The Judgment of the Court in Nottebohm, Second Phase, in 1955 (I.C.J. Reports 1955, p. 4), has been widely discussed in the subsequent literature of international law particularly with reference to the so-called "link theory" by which the effectiveness of nationality may be tested.

It has been argued that the doctrine is equally applicable in the case of ships flying "flags of convenience" and in relation to the diplomatic protection of corporations. I have maintained the view that it should apply in both those situations.

41. In the instant case the Parties did not debate the applicability of the link principle to the Barcelona Traction Company, but they were certainly aware of the question. The Spanish side stated:

> * * * the Spanish Government never disputed the effective character of Barcelona Traction's Canadian nationality, because a number of factors were present which were sufficient proof of the existence of a real link between the company and the economic life of Canada. (P.O., 1963, p. 190.)

Counsel for Belgium argued on 4 July 1969 that "if the Canadian Government had been able to espouse in international judicial proceedings the cause of Barcelona Traction, its action could have been challenged on the ground of the lack of sufficient true Canadian interest". Counsel for Spain responded directly to this remark on 21 July.

42.   I am in full agreement with the proposition that the decisions of the International Court of Justice should not be based upon a legal rule or principle which has not been considered by the parties —indeed, I believe that the failure to heed that proposition is the only criticism which can properly be directed at the Court's decision in Nottebohm.   When, however, both Parties have revealed a full awareness of the fact that the "link" principle might be applied to test the national quality of Barcelona Traction, the fact that they did not choose to develop their arguments on the ground of legal principle, rather than of fact, cannot operate to prevent the Court from dealing with the principle.   Of course the question whether the link principle does apply to juristic persons is a question of international law and jura novit curia.   The implication in the pleading of Belgian counsel just cited, intimated a conclusion that the link principle does apply to juristic persons.

It is indeed true that since Spain admitted that Canada had a right to extend diplomatic protection to Barcelona Traction, it may be argued that Spain is estopped to deny such a right although the elements of true estoppel may be lacking and such estoppel could be claimed (if at all) by Canada and not by Belgium.   Aside from the fact that I believe the jurisprudence of the Court has tended to rely too heavily on estoppel or preclusion, the question posed here is in the first place a question of the Court's finding a rule of law.   The Court in its Judgment does not accept the application of the link theory to juristic persons.   Since I have reached the conclusion that the existence of a link between a corporation holding a "charter of convenience" and the State granting the charter, is the key to the diplomatic protection of multinational corporate interests, I cannot avoid the problems of law and fact on any such basis as the application of the doctrine of estoppel in this particular case.

43.   It has also been argued that the Court should not pass judgment on the question whether there existed the necessary link between Canada and Barcelona Traction without hearing argument on behalf of Canada.   Canada might have sought to intervene in the instant case under Article 62 of the Statute, but it did not do so. It is said that after judgment is pronounced in this case of Belgium v. Spain, Canada might find some jurisdictional ground to found an application to institute a case of Canada v. Spain.   It is known that no such jurisdictional ground now exists.   It seems quite unreal to suppose that Spain would now agree with Canada upon a compromise submitting to the Court a Canadian claim on behalf of Barcelona Traction, thus exposing Spain to the new hazard of being required to pay some two hundred millions of dollars of damages.   But if the Court were properly seised of an application by Canada, it would have to take cognizance of the fact that following Article 59 of the Statute, "The decision of the Court has no binding force except between the parties and in respect of that particular case".   Had the

Court endorsed the application of the link principle to juristic persons, in its present decision in Belgium v. Spain, Canada could have argued against that conclusion in the hypothetical case of Canada v. Spain, or might have relied on Spanish admissions that Canada was entitled to protect the company.

44. It seems to be widely thought that the "link" concept in connection with the nationality of claims, originated in the International Court of Justice's Judgment in Nottebohm. I do not agree that in that instance the Court created a new rule of law. Indeed the underlying principle was already well established in connection with diplomatic claims on behalf of corporations. To look for the link between a corporation and a State is merely another example of what is now the familiar practice of "lifting the veil". See, for example Cohn and Simitis " 'Lifting the Veil' in the Company Laws of the European Continent", 12 International and Comparative Law Quarterly (1963), page 189; Drachsler in Report of the Section of International and Comparative Law of the American Bar Association, July 1964, page 29. The practice of such States as the United States and Switzerland had already given weight to the proposition that a corporation would not be protected solely because it was incorporated in the State, i. e., had the State's nationality; some other link was required and that link usually was related to the ownership of shares. Such abstention, being as it were "against interest", has special probative value.

Three years after the decision in Nottebohm, the Italian-United States Conciliation Commission, under the presidence of the late Professor Sauser Hall, in the Flegenheimer case stated:

> The right of challenge of the international court, authorizing it to determine whether, behind the nationality certificate or the acts of naturalisation produced, the right to citizenship was regularly acquired, is in *conformity with the very broad rule* of *effectivity* which dominates the law of nationals entirely and allows the court to fulfill its legal function and remove the inconveniences specified. (Emphasis supplied.) (53 American Journal of International Law, 1959, p. 944.)

* * *

BARCELONA TRACTION, LIGHT AND POWER CO., LTD.
(BELGIUM v. SPAIN)

International Court of Justice, 1970
[1970] I.C.J.Rep. 3.

[In this case, the parent company in the corporate complex involved was incorporated in 1911 in Canada; but after the First World War approximately 85% of its shares came to be held by Belgian nationals, largely through complicated arrangements involving some very large Belgian holding companies. Belgium wished to be allowed to show that its nationals as shareholders had been seriously harmed by actions of the Spanish state after the Spanish Civil War. These included, according to the Belgian memorials in an earlier ICJ case dropped in 1961 in expectation of a diplomatic settlement: denial from 1940 on of foreign exchange licenses to the Traction Company and some of its Spanish subsidiaries to permit service on bonds payable in pounds sterling; a 1948 bankruptcy proceeding in Spain brought by Spanish purchasers of "defaulted" sterling bonds of which the Traction Company itself had not received fair notice; an unfair time limit on appeal in the bankruptcy case; and the eventual passage of very substantial influence over the corporate structures in Spain to one Juan March.

Although the memorials do not mention the matter in just this way, March, known widely as the "Match King" of Spain, was often reported to have been a significant financial supporter of Franco's insurgency against the Spanish Republic and known as a highly skilled and secretive financial operator. The essence of the Belgian claim on the merits in the case that follows would have been that Belgians had been the victims of foreign exchange, bankruptcy, and related official actions that squeezed out the Belgian equity investment in the Barcelona Traction corporate complex. In the jargon of international claims practice the case as seen by Belgium involved "creeping expropriation" and "denial of justice."

A portion of the opinion of the court appears below.]

28. For the sake of clarity, the Court will briefly recapitulate the claim and identify the entities concerned in it. The claim is presented on behalf of natural and juristic persons, alleged to be Belgian nationals and shareholders in the Barcelona Traction, Light and Power Company, Limited. The submissions of the Belgian Government make it clear that the object of its Application is reparation for damage allegedly caused to these persons by the conduct, said to be contrary to international law, of various organs of the Spanish State towards that company and various other companies in the same group.

29. In the first of its submissions, more specifically in the Counter-Memorial, the Spanish Government contends that the Belgian Application of 1962 seeks, though disguisedly, the same object as the Application of 1958, i. e., the protection of the Barcelona Traction company as such, as a separate corporate entity, and that the claim should in consequence be dismissed. However, in making its new Application, as it has chosen to frame it, the Belgian Government was only exercising the freedom of action of any State to formulate its claim in its own way. The Court is therefore bound to examine the claim in accordance with the explicit content imparted to it by the Belgian Government.

30. The States which the present case principally concerns are Belgium, the national State of the alleged shareholders, Spain, the State whose organs are alleged to have committed the unlawful acts complained of, and Canada, the State under whose laws Barcelona Traction was incorporated and in whose territory it has its registered office ("head office" in the terms of the by-laws of Barcelona Traction).

31. Thus the Court has to deal with a series of problems arising out of a triangular relationship involving the State whose nationals are shareholders in a company incorporated under the laws of another State, in whose territory it has its registered office; the State whose organs are alleged to have committed against the company unlawful acts prejudicial to both it and its shareholders; and the State under whose laws the company is incorporated, and in whose territory it has its registered office.

32. In these circumstances it is logical that the Court should first address itself to what was originally presented as the subject-matter of the third preliminary objection: namely the question of the right of Belgium to exercise diplomatic protection of Belgian shareholders in a company which is a juristic entity incorporated in Canada, the measures complained of having been taken in relation not to any Belgian national but to the company itself.

* * *

35. * * * In order to bring a claim in respect of the breach of such an obligation, a State must first establish its right to do so, for the rules on the subject rest on two suppositions:

> The first is that the defendant State has broken an obligation towards the national State in respect of its nationals. The second is that only the party to whom an international obligation is due can bring a claim in respect of its breach. (Reparation for Injuries Suffered in the Service of the United Nations, Advisory Opinion, I.C.J. Reports 1949, pp. 181–182.)

In the present case it is therefore essential to establish whether the losses allegedly suffered by Belgian shareholders in Barcelona Traction were the consequence of the violation of obligations of which

they were the beneficiaries. In other words: has a right of Belgium
been violated on account of its nationals' having suffered infringement of their rights as shareholders in a company not of Belgian nationality?

36. Thus it is the existence or absence of a right, belonging to
Belgium and recognized as such by international law, which is decisive for the problem of Belgium's capacity.

> This right is necessarily limited to intervention [by a State]
> on behalf of its own nationals because, in the absence of a special
> agreement, it is the bond of nationality between the State and the
> individual which alone confers upon the State the right of diplo-
> matic protection, and it is as a part of the function of diplomatic
> protection that the right to take up a claim and to ensure respect
> for the rules of international law must be envisaged. (Pane-
> vezys-Saldutiskis Railway, Judgment, 1939, P.C.I.J., Series A/B,
> No. 76, p. 16.)

It follows that the same question is determinant in respect of Spain's
responsibility towards Belgium. Responsibility is the necessary corollary of a right. In the absence of any treaty on the subject between
the Parties, this essential issue has to be decided in the light of the
general rules of diplomatic protection.

* * *

39. Seen in historical perspective, the corporate personality
represents a development brought about by new and expanding requirements in the economic field, an entity which in particular allows
of operation in circumstances which exceed the normal capacity of
individuals. As such it has become a powerful factor in the economic
life of nations. Of this, municipal law has had to take due account,
whence the increasing volume of rules governing the creation and
operation of corporate entities, endowed with a specific status. These
entities have rights and obligations peculiar to themselves.

* * *

46. It has also been contended that the measures complained of,
although taken with respect to Barcelona Traction and causing it
direct damage, constituted an unlawful act vis-à-vis Belgium, because
they also, though indirectly, caused damage to the Belgian shareholders in Barcelona Traction. This again is merely a different way
of presenting the distinction between injury in respect of a right
and injury to a simple interest. But, as the Court has indicated, evidence that damage was suffered does not ipso facto justify a diplomatic claim. Persons suffer damage or harm in most varied circumstances. This in itself does not involve the obligation to make reparation. Not a mere interest affected, but solely a right infringed involves responsibility, so that an act directed against and infringing

only the company's rights does not involve responsibility towards the shareholders, even if their interests are affected.

* * *

50. In turning now to the international legal aspects of the case, the Court must, as already indicated, start from the fact that the present case essentially involves factors derived from municipal law— the distinction and the community between the company and the shareholder—which the Parties, however widely their interpretations may differ, each take as the point of departure of their reasoning. If the Court were to decide the case in disregard of the relevant institutions of municipal law it would, without justification, invite serious legal difficulties. It would lose touch with reality, for there are no corresponding institutions of international law to which the Court could resort. Thus the Court has, as indicated, not only to take cognizance of municipal law but also to refer to it. It is to rules generally accepted by municipal legal systems which recognize the limited company whose capital is represented by shares, and not to the municipal law of a particular State, that international law refers. In referring to such rules, the Court cannot modify, still less deform them.

51. On the international plane, the Belgian Government has advanced the proposition that it is inadmissible to deny the shareholders' national State a right of diplomatic protection merely on the ground that another State possesses a corresponding right in respect of the company itself. In strict logic and law this formulation of the Belgian claim to jus standi assumes the existence of the very right that requires demonstration. In fact the Belgian Government has repeatedly stressed that there exists no rule of international law which would deny the national State of the shareholders the right of diplomatic protection for the purpose of seeking redress pursuant to unlawful acts committed by another State against the company in which they hold shares. This, by emphasizing the absence of any express denial of the right, conversely implies the admission that there is no rule of international law which expressly confers such a right on the shareholders' national State.

* * *

* * * [T]he process of lifting the veil, being an exceptional one admitted by municipal law in respect of an institution of its own making, is equally admissible to play a similar role in international law. It follows that on the international plane also there may in principle be special circumstances which justify the lifting of the veil in the interest of shareholders.

59. Before proceeding, however, to consider whether such circumstances exist in the present case, it will be advisable to refer to two specific cases involving encroachment upon the legal entity, instances of which have been cited by the Parties. These are: first, the treatment of enemy and allied property, during and after the First and

Second World Wars, in peace treaties and other international instruments; secondly, the treatment of foreign property consequent upon the nationalizations carried out in recent years by many States.

60.   With regard to the first, enemy-property legislation was an instrument of economic warfare, aimed at denying the enemy the advantages to be derived from the anonymity and separate personality of corporations. Hence the lifting of the veil was regarded as justified ex necessitate and was extended to all entities which were tainted with enemy character, even the nationals of the State enacting the legislation. The provisions of the peace treaties had a very specific function: to protect allied property, and to seize and pool enemy property with a view to covering reparation claims. Such provisions are basically different in their rationale from those normally applicable.

61.   Also distinct are the various arrangements made in respect of compensation for the nationalization of foreign property. Their rationale too, derived as it is from structural changes in a State's economy, differs from that of any normally applicable provisions. Specific agreements have been reached to meet specific situations, and the terms have varied from case to case. Far from evidencing any norm as to the classes of beneficiaries of compensation, such arrangements are sui generis and provide no guide in the present case.

62.   Nevertheless, during the course of the proceedings both Parties relied on international instruments and judgments of international tribunals concerning these two specific areas. It should be clear that the developments in question have to be viewed as distinctive processes, arising out of circumstances peculiar to the respective situations. To seek to draw from them analogies or conclusions held to be valid in other fields is to ignore their specific character as lex specialis and hence to court error.

63.   The Parties have also relied on the general arbitral jurisprudence which has accumulated in the last half-century. However, in most cases the decisions cited rested upon the terms of instruments establishing the jurisdiction of the tribunal or claims commission and determining what rights might enjoy protection; they cannot therefore give rise to generalization going beyond the special circumstances of each case. Other decisions, allowing or disallowing claims by way of exception, are not, in view of the particular facts concerned, directly relevant to the present case.

* * *

85.   The Court will now examine the Belgian claim from a different point of view, disregarding municipal law and relying on the rule that in inter-State relations, whether claims are made on behalf of a State's national or on behalf of the State itself, they are always the claims of the State. As the Permanent Court said,

> "The question, therefore, whether the . . . dispute originates in an injury to a private interest, which in point of fact is

the case in many international disputes, is irrelevant from this standpoint." (Mavrommatis Palestine Concessions, Judgment No. 2, 1924, P.C.I.J., Series A, No. 2, p. 12. See also Nottebohm, Second Phase, Judgment, I.C.J. Reports 1955, p. 24.)

86.   Hence the Belgian Government would be entitled to bring a claim if it could show that one of its rights had been infringed and that the acts complained of involved the breach of an international obligation arising out of a treaty or a general rule of law. The opinion has been expressed that a claim can accordingly be made when investments by a State's nationals abroad are thus prejudicially affected, and that since such investments are part of a State's national economic resources, any prejudice to them directly involves the economic interest of the State.

> *   *   *

89.   Considering the important developments of the last half-century, the growth of foreign investments and the expansion of the international activities of corporations, in particular of holding companies, which are often multinational, and considering the way in which the economic interests of States have proliferated, it may at first sight appear surprising that the evolution of law has not gone further and that no generally accepted rules in the matter have crystallized on the international plane. Nevertheless, a more thorough examination of the facts shows that the law on the subject has been formed in a period characterized by an intense conflict of systems and interests. It is essentially bilateral relations which have been concerned, relations in which the rights of both the State exercising diplomatic protection and the State in respect of which protection is sought have had to be safeguarded. Here as elsewhere, a body of rules could only have developed with the consent of those concerned. The difficulties encountered have been reflected in the evolution of the law on the subject.

90.   Thus, in the present state of the law, the protection of shareholders requires that recourse be had to treaty stipulations or special agreements directly concluded between the private investor and the State in which the investment is placed. States ever more frequently provide for such protection, in both bilateral and multilateral relations, either by means of special instruments or within the framework of wider economic arrangements. Indeed, whether in the form of multilateral or bilateral treaties between States, or in that of agreements between States and companies, there has since the Second World War been considerable development in the protection of foreign investments. The instruments in question contain provisions as to jurisdiction and procedure in case of disputes concerning the treatment of investing companies by the States in which they invest capital. Sometimes companies are themselves vested with a direct right to de-

fend their interests against States through prescribed procedures. No such instrument is in force between the Parties to the present case.

* * *

92.   Since the general rule on the subject does not entitle the Belgian Government to put forward a claim in this case, the question remains to be considered whether nonetheless, as the Belgian Government has contended during the proceedings, considerations of equity do not require that it be held to possess a right of protection. It is quite true that it has been maintained that, for reasons of equity, a State should be able, in certain cases, to take up the protection of its nationals, shareholders in a company which has been the victim of a violation of international law. Thus a theory has been developed to the effect that the State of the shareholders has a right of diplomatic protection when the State whose responsibility is invoked is the national State of the company. Whatever the validity of this theory may be, it is certainly not applicable to the present case, since Spain is not the national State of Barcelona Traction.

93.   On the other hand, the Court considers that, in the field of diplomatic protection as in all other fields of international law, it is necessary that the law be applied reasonably. It has been suggested that if in a given case it is not possible to apply the general rule that the right of diplomatic protection of a company belongs to its national State, considerations of equity might call for the possibility of protection of the shareholders in question by their own national State. This hypothesis does not correspond to the circumstances of the present case.

94.   In view, however, of the discretionary nature of diplomatic protection, considerations of equity cannot require more than the possibility for some protector State to intervene, whether it be the national State of the company, by virtue of the general rule mentioned above, or, in a secondary capacity, the national State of the shareholders who claim protection. In this connection, account should also be taken of the practical effects of deducing from considerations of equity any broader right of protection for the national State of the shareholders. It must first of all be observed that it would be difficult on an equitable basis to make distinctions according to any quantitative test: it would seem that the owner of 1 per cent. and the owner of 90 per cent. of the share-capital should have the same possibility of enjoying the benefit of diplomatic protection. The protector State may, of course, be disinclined to take up the case of the single small shareholder, but it could scarcely be denied the right to do so in the name of equitable considerations. In that field, protection by the national State of the shareholders can hardly be graduated according to the absolute or relative size of the shareholding involved.

95.   The Belgian Government, it is true, has also contended that as high a proportion as 88 per cent. of the shares in Barcelona Trac-

tion belonged to natural or juristic persons of Belgian nationality, and it has used this is an argument for the purpose not only of determining the amount of the damages which it claims, but also of establishing its right of action on behalf of the Belgian shareholders. Nevertheless, this does not alter the Belgian Government's position, as expounded in the course of the proceedings, which implies, in the last analysis, that it might be sufficient for one single share to belong to a national of a given State for the latter to be entitled to exercise its diplomatic protection.

96. The Court considers that the adoption of the theory of diplomatic protection of shareholders as such, by opening the door to competing diplomatic claims, could create an atmosphere of confusion and insecurity in international economic relations. The danger would be all the greater inasmuch as the shares of companies whose activity is international are widely scattered and frequently change hands. It might perhaps be claimed that, if the right of protection belonging to the national States of the shareholders were considered as only secondary to that of the national State of the company, there would be less danger of difficulties of the kind contemplated. However, the Court must state that the essence of a secondary right is that it only comes into existence at the time when the original right ceases to exist. As the right of protection vested in the national State of the company cannot be regarded as extinguished because it is not exercised, it is not possible to accept the proposition that in case of its non-exercise the national States of the shareholders have a right of protection secondary to that of the national State of the company. Furthermore, study of factual situations in which this theory might possibly be applied gives rise to the following observations.

* * *

100. In the present case, it is clear from what has been said above that Barcelona Traction was never reduced to a position of impotence such that it could not have approached its national State, Canada, to ask for its diplomatic protection, and that, as far as appeared to the Court, there was nothing to prevent Canada from continuing to grant its diplomatic protection to Barcelona Traction if it had considered that it should do so.

101. For the above reasons, the Court is not of the opinion that, in the particular circumstances of the present case, jus standi is conferred on the Belgian Government by considerations of equity.

103. Accordingly, THE COURT rejects the Belgian Government's claim by fifteen votes to one, twelve votes of the majority being based on the reasons set out in the present Judgment.

* * *

[Declarations, separate opinions and dissenting opinion omitted.]

REMEDIES FOR NATIONALIZATION

RESTATEMENT OF THE FOREIGN RELATIONS LAW OF THE UNITED STATES (1965) *

§ 185. Comment c: *Taking and failure to pay compensation distinguished.* It is often stated that the taking of an alien's property is a violation of international law unless the state pays just compensation. Since payment is frequently delayed until some time after the taking, this would suggest that the legality of the taking may be determined ab initio by subsequent events. Such a theory has practical disadvantages from the point of view of international commerce as to the property taken. For example, if a state were to take property under a program providing for just compensation and otherwise consistent with the rule stated in this Section, the taking would appear to be lawful under international law at the time but might later turn out to be in violation of international law if the compensation were not forthcoming or did not constitute just compensation * * * The subsequent determination could present serious problems to third parties dealing in the property in the territory of states that do not apply the act of state doctrine * * * and treat a taking in violation of international law as ineffective in passing title. On the other hand, some writers have contended that a taking is never per se unlawful (assuming a public purpose and no violation of an international agreement) and that it is only the failure to pay compensation that constitutes a violation of international law. The rule stated in this Section treats a taking as unlawful on the ground of failure to pay just compensation only if it does not appear at the time of taking that just compensation will be provided. * * *

* * *

§ 185. Reporters' Note 6: *Distinction between taking and failure to pay compensation.* The theory, rejected in Comment c, that a taking lawful when made becomes unlawful ab initio upon failure to pay just compensation is illustrated by the reasoning of the arbitrator in Goldenberg (Germany v. Rumania), 2 U.N.Rep.Int'l Arb.Awards 901, 909 (1928). For an exposition of the view that a taking is never per se unlawful (assuming a public purpose and no prohibition by international agreement), see Delson, Whether a Taking of an Alien's Property, Without Compensation, or in Derogation of the Terms of a Contract, is in Violation of Public International Law, Am.Branch, Int'l L.Ass'n, 1959–60 Proceedings 33.

* * *

§ 186. Failure to Pay Just Compensation for Taking

Failure of a state to pay just compensation for taking the property of an alien is wrongful under international law, regardless of whether the taking itself was wrongful under international law.

Comment:

   a. *General.* * * * [C]ertain types of state conduct causing injury to the economic interests of aliens impose a duty to pay just compensation, even though the conduct is not itself wrongful under international law. The taking of an alien's property imposes such a duty. If the taking was wrongful under international law, the failure to pay constitutes a second violation of international law. If the taking was not wrongful under international law, international responsibility does not arise until the state fails to make the payment.

---

   1. *Characterization of the theory of action against the taking state.* Some writers characterize a state that has violated international law (either in the taking itself or by failing to pay compensation) as having been guilty of tortious conduct. Others say that the theory of action is analogous to unjust enrichment, inasmuch as the taking state acquired property without paying for it. The first theory covers both injuries to aliens in their persons and their economic interests while the second does not. Historically, both types of injuries have given rise to international responsibilities, in some instances in the same case. The tort theory, therefore, has the utility of providing a conceptual basis for both situations. If the unjust enrichment theory is followed as to takings of economic interests, it requires further refinement as to situations covered by § 186 of the Restatement, above. That is, as to a taking that ab initio violates international law, is an unjust enrichment theory analytically convincing?

   It should be borne in mind that both these characterizations draw heavily upon analogies to municipal legal systems, and that the analogies cannot be pushed very far beyond the fundamental concepts involved. As is well known, what is "tort", with a whole array of sub-rules as to duty, proximate cause, damages, and the like, to a common law lawyer is not quite the same thing as "civil responsibility" to a civil law lawyer. And while legal systems agree that unjust enrichment should be redressed in some ways in some situations, the doctrines of quasi-contract and quantum meruit at common law are not of universal acceptance. Thus, it would seem inadmissable to derive conclusions about the remedies that international law provides for the taking of an alien's economic interest in violation of international law by logical deduction of explicit rules from these characterizations. If there is an international tort or an international cause of action for unjust enrichment it should be regarded as sui generis, rather than as a detailed transformation of national law into international law.

2. *The remedy of compensation.* There is common agreement that compensation ought to be sufficient in value to make the forcibly disinvested alien whole. The basic problem is what value of what. Valuation is an extremely difficult problem in domestic legal systems, and in such systems, too, there are questions as to what types of interests, expectations, and prospects should be included. A fairly common problem in the international claims arena is as to the valuation of the interests of an oil company lost by the cancellation of its concession. Its physical installations raise only the problems of technique and criteria for fixing the value in money of what has been taken, not that these are simple. [Replacement value? Original cost depreciated? What kind of depreciation? etc.] But what of known but not extracted reserves of oil and gas in place? What of speculative value as to reserves not yet known? There is a natural tendency for claimants to put high valuations on what they have lost by nationalization and an equally natural tendency of the respondent state in any type of claims settlement proceeding to minimize the damage suffered.

Eventually some money value is going to have to be arrived at. On an individual case basis this may be done by diplomatic bargaining, a finding of the damages by an arbitral tribunal or a court (perhaps assisted by a fact-finding aide), or agreement of the parties to engage a professional and disinterested valuation expert to determine "true" value. In instances where a state has engaged in wholesale nationalization, as when Yugoslavia became socialist, a very great many claimants with many different types of losses exist. In such situations the settlement may take the form of the acceptance by the espousing state of a global or lump sum in complete satisfaction and waiver of all the claims included within the scope of the negotiation. The espousing state would, of course, find it necessary to analyze all the claims it had received as to amounts claimed, types of property involved, etc. and come to an overall negotiating figure that it would then use in bargaining with the other state concerned. (In a sense such an approach is not unlike the settlement out of court of a class action in the United States.)

In the Yugoslavian claims settlement negotiations of 1948–49, the United States Department of State received (as a result of published notice) the claims of United States citizens against Yugoslavia for the nationalization program carried on in that country. These submissions were then examined to determine espousibility by the United States and to estimate the degree of inflation or over-statement that might exist in particular claims. During the course of this operation, also, there were consultations with claimants and groups of claimants to explain the process and to seek general concurrence that a lump sum figure of such and such amount (to be divided rateably among the claimants in the proportion of total lump sum recovery to total eligible claims) would be acceptable. Eventually the United

States decided that it could accept $17 million in gold in complete settlement and waiver of a total of espousible claims that, before analysis for overstatement of value, totaled $42 million. After the negotiation of an executive agreement with Yugoslavia for settlement along these lines, the Congress authorized the use of the value of the gold received for the benefit of the private claimants and set up an administrative body, now the Foreign Claims Settlement Commission, to pass upon the individual claims as to eligibility under the terms of the agreement and to award money recoveries.

As to "lump sum settlements" generally, see Lillich, International Claims (1962).

The remedy of compensation is adjectivally stated as having to be "just", "fair", "appropriate", or in the classic United States formulation, "prompt, adequate, and effective." The latter three adjectives are the subject of somewhat wishful further descriptions in standard sources for expression of United States viewpoints on what international law requires, such as Restatement Second: Foreign Relations Law of the United States (1965) §§ 187–190 and the various Department of State digests of international law. As interpretated one of the American trilogy of adjectives, "effective", expresses a clear preference for compensation in cash in freely convertible foreign exchange instead of compensation in inconvertible local currency. The effect of this requirement, if strictly adhered to, would be to prevent a state short of foreign exchange from nationalizing aliens' interests even under programs of social reform. But, of course, it is not adhered to in such cases, beyond a kind of discounted foreign exchange receipt in quittance under lump sum agreements to pay in convertible monetary assets. Payment over time, as by the issuance of government or government-guaranteed bonds, is in state practice "prompt enough" to be acceptable.

Finally, it should be noted that the nationalization of a going enterprise is a business disaster, and compensation under any criteria that the taking state would consider accepting is below the real value of the economic loss. This reality properly justifies the classification of claims settlement as a species of salvage. It is important for lawyers to get salvage for their clients, but the law of salvage is hardly the best body of law to provide a secure and lasting basis for foreign investment that wants to stay in business.

3. *Restitution, invalidation of title, and other specific recovery of property as remedies; cross-reference to Chapter 6.* The question whether customary international law has developed remedies for violations of an international minimum standard in addition to the remedy of fair compensation in state to state proceedings becomes pertinent at this point in consideration of what the injured private party's attorney can do. The cases bearing on the remedies of specific restitution, invalidation of the title derived from the national-

izing state, and other possible types of specific recovery of property have been dealt with in Chapter 6 as a necessary aspect of the act of state doctrine.

It will be recalled that in a few of the cases there arrayed, courts specifically held that a nationalizing state that did not abide by the international minimum standard would not be recognized in the courts of other states as having effectively acquired and transferred title to the property in question, or its proceeds. In other instances the national courts upheld the defendant's title derived from the nationalizing state, either on the ground that the court could not make enquiry as to validity (act of state, United States version) or that the transactions complained of by the plaintiff did not raise issues of the fundamental public policy of the forum state (act of state, continental version). In the two decisions by the Second Circuit Court of Appeals in the Sabbatino Case (one before and one after the second Hickenlooper Amendment), it was seen that the court assumed that if the act of state doctrine did not apply, it followed without more under customary international law that the former owner did not lose title by the illicit nationalization. But commentators on Sabbatino and its progeny have brought out that the court may have leapt too far, from a problem comparable to forum non conveniens, political question, or other devices that prevent a court's having to decide on the merits, to a dubious conclusion about the consentio juris on remedies for legal wrongs by states. A tenable hunch for the practical lawyer at this stage is that the law of remedies for nationalization is in somewhat of a state of flux and that it might well make a big difference where suit is brought, both as between the International Court of Justice and municipal courts, and between the latter in various countries.

4. *The Kennecott Copper Corporation litigation, early stages.* As illustrative of the range of arguments and activities that lawyers for plaintiff and defendant must be prepared for in this period of uncertainty about remedies, a case presently still in the French courts is here sketched. The Kennecott Copper Company owns 100% the Braden Copper Company. Both are incorporated in the United States. Braden owned property rights (not a mere right to exploit under a concession) in copper ore in place at El Teniente, a mine in Chile.

In 1967 Braden transferred its property rights in the copper in place to a Chilean corporation, Sociedad Minera El Teniente, S. A., for 49% of the shares thereof, the 51% shareholder being the Chilean Government through its organ, Copper Corporation.

In 1971, Sociedad Minera El Teniente was nationalized, and Kennecott has failed in all its efforts in Chile to get compensation under Chilean law for the injury to its equity in Braden caused by the taking, because no agency of the Chilean Government will accept competence to examine into the legitimacy of the Chilean Government's claim that an offset of liability for excess profits (Braden's from 1955–1967 under a 1971 Presidential ruling) washes out the amount otherwise due to Braden for the loss of its interest in Sociedad Minera, or in El Teniente mine and the copper ore in place in it.

After the nationalization, Copper Company shipped ore clearly identifiable as coming from the El Teniente mine by sea to Europe. After having been threatened by Kennecott as it approached the original port of destination, the carrying vessel, not of Chilean flag or registry, put unto a French port, where Braden promptly brought a third party attachment proceeding under French law against the French consignee.

The plaintiff's pleading in the French court makes it clear that a property interest in the copper ore shipped is claimed. The possible title thereto of Sociedad Minera El Teniente is claimed by plaintiff to be non-existent under French law, because (plaintiff asserts) under French law the assets of a dissolved corporation revert to the shareholders. Continuing, Braden argues that under French decisions * * * "Copper Corporation cannot argue that the nationalization effected by the Chilean State gave * * *" Copper Corporation title to the ore. Reason: France does not "recognize" nationalizations abroad in such cases, citing cases of Soviet nationalizations, Spanish expropriations, nationalizations in eastern countries, and Algerian nationalizations.[a]

In the present early stage of the contest in the French legal system, argument in the courts has focused on the question whether Copper Corporation is entitled to sovereign immunity (as an organ of the Chilean State) with regard to the French attachment procedure used. Chile argues that such attachment is not merely for the purpose of judicial jurisdiction over the cause of action but also for the levy of execution upon state property if the plaintiff wins on other issues. Once this issue is finally settled, it can be expected that other issues will be considered, including act of state, violation or not of international law in the taking, and the remedy for such violation, if found to have occurred.

The French Tribunal of General Jurisdiction in Paris—i. e. a court equivalent in status to a district court in the federal system of the United States, allowed the attachment, but by agreement of the parties a bond was substituted for the copper ore, which thereupon was free for processing.

a. See Chapter 6, p. 457 for a summary of some previous decisions which are being invoked or relied upon by the parties to the case.

Thereafter, the French court gave the following decision, taken from a translation supplied by the Kennecott Copper Corporation but not controverted as to accuracy by the Embassy of Chile:

November 29, 1972

The Tribunal deciding in public hearing and in summary proceedings on the report of Monsieur Drai, Vice President, after the arguments in public hearing on October 19, 1972 before Monsieur Vassogne, President, Messieurs Olivier, First Vice President, and Drai, Vice President, has delivered in the first instance the following judgment:

Whereas an order of September 30, 1972 has authorized Braden Copper Company to garnish the sums which could be due by the French company Trefimetaux to the Chilean Copper Corporation within the limits of 2,721,720 French Francs, an order dated the same day has authorized Braden Copper Company to garnish the sums which could be due by the French company Groupement d'Importation des Metaux to the Chilean Copper Corporation within the limits of 6,804,-300 French Francs;

Whereas, that in order to obtain these orders, Braden Copper Company presented itself as creditor of said sums which represent the appraisal by Braden of the value of a cargo of copper which belongs to it and which was sold in France in contempt of its rights by the Chilean Copper Corporation; that Braden argued that the nationalization of the copper mines from which the disputed copper was extracted, namely the installations of El Teniente, decided by the Chilean State to the detriment of Braden on July 16, 1971 be deprived of all legal effectiveness on French territory since it was not accompanied by an equitable indemnization;

Whereas, the Chilean Copper Corporation, a national public establishment organized under Chilean law, with its seat in Santiago, Chile, requested that the two orders of September 30, 1972 be repealed and that the garnishments made for their execution on October 2, 1972 be cancelled;

Whereas, the Chilean Copper Corporation argues that it is the central agency by which the Chilean State carries out its policy relating to copper and that being endowed for that purpose with prerogatives of public power, its immunity from jurisdiction and immunity from execution according to principles of international law must be recognized; that it denies the allegations of the Braden Copper Company as to any alleged spoilation of its assets and denies to Braden any real right on the cargo of copper sold to Trefimetaux and to the Groupement d'Importation des Metaux and any right to the sale price of the copper extracted and processed after the law of nationalization;

Whereas, the litigation thus submitted to the Tribunal concerns only a peculiar aspect of a dispute for which the parties should seek the proper ways to ensure a global settlement.

Whereas, the Chilean Copper Corporation appears according to the Chilean legal texts which treated it and which regulated its status as being a national institution having its own legal personality, formally distinct from the central power of the State; that its unique specialized vocation is to promote the production and commercialization of copper and of its by-products, to ensure the regulation and the control of the interior and exterior copper market and that finally its assets are constituted by a legal endowment of properties which come from the carrying out of its purpose;

Whereas, that for the carrying out of its purpose the Chilean Copper Corporation proceeds specially in international transactions according to the ways and forms of the private law of business; that thus the contracts of sale signed with Trefimetaux and the Groupement d'Importation des Metaux exclude any recourse to the methods which are usually connected with the public power; but on the contrary include the pledge of the parties to submit themselves in case of dispute to a private arbitration according to the rules of the International Chamber of Commerce of Paris;

Whereas, that if in these circumstances the Chilean Copper Corporation must be considered as acting in the name and on behalf of the Chilean State for the management and development of the nationalized domain, it cannot, however, on the occasion of the present litigation oppose itself to the examination by the Tribunal, in a conservatory and provisional manner, of a plea which relates to an act of its own management and which is necessarily linked to its commercial mission which could be different in view of the result of the measure of investigation when the question will be the compulsory execution on the funds proceeding from this management.

Whereas, the Chilean State is entitled to sovereignly adopt measures proper to develop the natural resources of its national territory; but

Whereas, no legal effect is recognized in France to a dispossession made by a foreign state without an equitable indemnity so that the dispute between the parties over the reality in this case of such an indemnity makes the recourse to a measure of investigation necessary;

Whereas, that, as the Chilean Copper Corporation recognized that no payment has been made in favor of Braden Copper Company because of the set-off between the amount of indemnity and the excess profits which are charged to Braden, it is necessary to admit the principle of a claim in favor of Braden, taking into account the public order rule hereinabove mentioned and while waiting for the results of the measure of investigation; and

Whereas, the claim of Braden Copper Company, which is not due for immediate payment, shall, without hurting the rights of third parties, be sufficiently guaranteed by the following conditions accompanying the withdrawal of the garnishments.

For These Reasons:

Deciding in summary proceedings;

A.   Rejects the plea of sovereign immunity;

B.   Before deciding the case Appoints Monsieur Thouvenot, 74 Rue Raymond, Paris, with the mission, after having received from the parties all useful documents, to proceed to all investigations:

1.   Determine the appropriate destination and utilization of the funds received by the Chilean Copper Corporation as a consequence of its commercial management.

2.   To appraise the conflicting affirmations of the parties as to the existence of an equitable indemnity for the benefit of Braden Copper Company.

3.   To gather all elements that could permit the global settlement of the dispute by the opposing parties.

C.   States that the agent of the Tribunal can receive help from any specialist of its choice.

D.   Orders the cancellation of the garnishments authorized by the orders of September 30, 1972, on the condition that the Chilean Copper Corporation keeps for itself the sums garnished and produces them in the event that it should be judged as being the debtor.

Made and Decided in Paris on Wednesday, the 29th of November 1972.

5.   *Restitution of looted property distinguished from restitution as a remedy for nationalization of economic interests within the territory.*   The Axis powers in World War II, particularly the German Reich, took by force or duress huge amounts of property of all kinds in territory occupied by them.   These takings went far beyond the recognized requisitioning power of a military occupier.   During the course of the war, on January 5, 1943, the Allied powers issued a declaration that they would do their utmost to defeat these Axis acts of dispossession, and after the surrender of the Axis powers various international agreements and governmental orders in occupied territories provided for the return to former owners of identifiable property looted from owners by force or duress.   This Allied policy is the basis of the Department of States' letter to the court in the second Bernstein Case, p. 403.   It is generally accepted that the above restitution policy has no bearing on the question whether invalidation of the title taken or transferred by a state that nationalizes property within its territory in violation of international law is a commonly recognized remedy in international law, especially in peacetime.   See 8 Whiteman,

Digest of International Law (1967) 1202–03 for some of the looted property declarations.

6. *Investment insurance.* The Marshall Plan (1948) was not only the world's first major foreign assistance program; it also broke new ground in providing that qualified private sector investors (mainly United States companies) could, for fees of approximately ¾ to 1% of the principal per type of risk, receive the promise of the United States to reimburse them for certain types of non-business losses, such as from nationalization without adequate compensation, non-convertibility of earnings in soft currencies into dollars, and damages resulting from hostilities. The investment guaranty, as it was then called, was designed to encourage the outflow of capital from the United States' private sector to help rehabilitate the private sectors of the countries in Europe that were to benefit from the Marshall Plan. [The Soviet Union was included in the Marshall Plan's general invitation to participate, but it declined for itself and its dominated satellites.]

When, approximately a decade later, the United States began to engage for the first time in significant bilateral assistance to the world's poorer and developing countries, the investment guaranty program was extended to them, first for the above three risks, slightly expanded in the third instance (that of physical damage from hostilities, to include losses due to civil insurrection). By that time the writing of investment guaranties for developed countries had stopped. There had been no losses in Europe, but the amounts for which guaranties nonetheless were being sought were becoming too large to be prudently managed on the resource base Congress was willing to provide.

Certain types of "all-risk" guarantees were later developed, especially for Latin America, in the field of low cost housing; see 22 U.S.C. §§ 2181, 2182. Additionally, a government guarantee against loss was authorized for certain types of export credits financed by the Export-Import Bank of the United States, a wholly Government-owned corporation; 12 U.S.C. § 635j. Some other capital-exporting states also have developed forms of insurance or guaranties as to exports, and there is even a slight use elsewhere of the insurance system for direct investments.

From the beginning it was accepted—and it still is—that the United States' contingent liabilities on investment guaranties are not funded with reserves to the same extent that true insurance underwriters generally are required to be. Thus, very heavy losses might require Congress to have to appropriate new money to cover them; but, in general, the investing community assumes that Congress would do this, as it has promised in 22 U.S.C. § 2197(c).

In 1969, as recommended by President Nixon, Congress took the investment guaranty program out of the United States Foreign Assistance Administration (USAID) and turned it over to a wholly-owned government corporation, the Overseas Private Investment Corporation (OPIC); see 22 U.S.C.A. §§ 2191–2200a.

The investment insurance program simplifies the problem of the foreign investor as to getting compensation for new investment, provided the coverage is available. However, there is considerable hostility in Latin America to United States (and probably other foreign country) investment insurance. In part this resistance arose from the insistence of Congress in earlier years on a precondition that an investment-receiving country have entered into a bilateral agreement with the United States accepting the scheme and recognizing the right of the United States Government to be subrogated to any covered claims it might discharge. Legislatures balked in a number of Latin countries as to contract subrogation and its implicit assertion of the international minimum standard. The Andean Investment Code binds the states members of the Andean Common Market (ANCOM) not to give foreign investors better than national treatment (Art. 50), and its Article 51 provides:

> In no instrument relating to investments or the transfer of technology shall there be clauses that remove possible conflicts from the national jurisdiction and competence of the recipient country or allow the subrogation by States to the rights and actions of their national investors.

These Latin strictures do not apply literally to investment guaranties or insurance by multipartite assistance agencies, such as the International Finance Corporation of the World Bank Group. For some time the staff of the latter has worked on a multipartite investment insurance plan. The Latin American states, on the whole, had been reserved even as to this approach.

The recent nationalizations without any actual compensation of foreign copper equity investments in Chile have threatened OPIC with very large claims, in excess, possibly, of the funds available for payment plus the continuation of meaningful programs elsewhere. The claimant copper companies and OPIC are now performing very much as insurance companies and insureds do in tight situations. They are bargaining hard and are prepared to litigate, if necessary.

Recently OPIC's authority was extended to cover certain eastern bloc countries (but not the Soviet Union), and it has announced that it has made a true insurance arrangement with Lloyd's of London to "re-insure" its risks on conventional actuarial terms.

An early doubt about investment insurance (at the time of its first use in the Marshall Plan) was that it might change the nature of overseas investors from venture capitalists to timid dabblers in sure things. This does not seem to have happened. (Would it have been so bad if it had?) The main users of investment insurance, by far, have been well-established overseas investing corporations, many of whom have the alternative of income tax writeoffs where not covered by investment insurance.

----

4. APPROACHES TO THE REDUCTION OR PREVENTION OF TRANSNATIONAL INVESTMENT CONFLICT

The possibility of new foreign investment arrangements. The preceding material in Chapter 17, Section B, deals with the jural pathology of direct foreign investment in the present international legal system. Better treatment of investment diseases, as by better opportunity for authoritative and neutral settlement of investment disputes under existing international law, would help. Also, clarifications and substantive modifications in the rules themselves might reduce fears, suspicions and tensions in both capital-exporting and capital-importing states.

It is rather striking in this regard to note how little trouble creditor investments seem to give. Why? Is it because they are not very much protected by the international legal system, or is there some other reason? Would it help if for international purposes foreign equity investment should come to be regarded as limited rather than perpetual ownership, that is, to arrange the rules so that the foreign ownership investor is entitled to x times his total investment and then must get out?

There is an interesting parallel in the case of Venezuelan oil concessions now coming to the end of their 50 year terms. Under the concession contracts the concessionaires' title to the installations they built with their capital ends with the term of the right to explore, produce and sell oil. True, some problems have arisen. The Venezuelan legislature has recently enacted a Law of Reversions that takes the position that the installations must be turned over in complete good order, rather than run down, and requires the oil companies to set aside special reserve funds to ensure this. Press accounts imply that the oil companies did not expect the termination modalities to be so rigorously policed. Apparently, also, this problem was not forseen in the original contracts.

Foreign investment developments in Venezuela point up another factor that is coming more and more to planning attention in regard to direct foreign ownership investment, that of the effect of development itself upon the stability of investment relationships. In general, investment disputes between the world's industrialized, rich countries (a gross national product per capita of $1000 or over) are very few, except for the administration of prior restraints on entry in France and Japan and for some antitrust problems, especially with the European Economic Community. It is between the private sector ownership investors of rich countries and the governments, politicians and publics of the less well-developed countries that most of the problems arise. To a considerable extent they seem to be related to differences in the levels of managerial skills of the foreign companies and the host country administrators. But technological advances as host countries develop may tend toward the eventual tranquilization of the present general investment situation between the rich and poor halves of the planet and the evolution of more effective legal rules for the governance of relationships between capital exporting and capital receiving countries.

Codification efforts toward new rules for foreign investment have been made. Several proposed codes for foreign investment, to come into effect as law-making international agreements, have been made by groups within developed countries. In general these proposals have found little favor so far in developing countries. Why? Some developing countries individually have provided rules through legislation and administrative practice. These range from prior restraints and foreign ownership maxima to provisions designed actually to attract foreign investment, either generally or into lagging sectors of the national economies. More recently, the six countries in the Andean Group within the Latin American Free Trade Association (LAFTA) have formulated a complete system of regulation designed to be put into effect nationally in each of them a uniform basic law on foreign investment. All of these efforts are parts of a quest for normative order for foreign investment of greater precision and sophistication than that provided by the vague principles of customary international law, which as we have seen sound more in salvage than in prevention.

TREATY OF FRIENDSHIP, ESTABLISHMENT AND NAVIGATION BETWEEN THE UNITED STATES AND BELGIUM OF FEBRUARY 21, 1961

14 U.S.T. 1284, 480 U.N.T.S. 149.

Article 4

(1) Property that nationals and companies of either Contracting Party own within the territories of the other Party shall enjoy constant security therein through full legal and judicial protection.

(2) Neither Party shall take unreasonable or discriminatory measures that would impair the acquired rights and interests within its territories of nationals and companies of the other Party in the enterprises which they have established, in their capital, or in the skills, arts or technology which they have supplied.

(3) Nationals and companies of either Party shall not be expropriated of their property within the territories of the other Party except for public benefit and with the prompt payment of just compensa-

tion. Such compensation shall be in an effectively realizable form and shall represent the full equivalent of the property taken. Furthermore, adequate provision shall have been made not later than the time of taking for the determination and payment thereof.

(4) Nationals and companies of either Party shall in no case be accorded, within the terrritories of the other Party, less than national treatment with respect to the matters set forth in paragraph 3 of the present Article and in paragraph 5 of Article 3. Moreover, enterprises in which nationals and companies of either Party have a substantial interest shall be accorded, within the territories of the other Party, not less than national treatment in all matters relating to the taking of privately owned enterprises into public ownership and to the placing of such enterprises under public control.

DRAFT CONVENTION ON THE PROTECTION OF FOREIGN PROPERTY

Council of the Office of Economic Cooperation and Development, 1967
OECD Document, 1967.*

Article 3

Taking of Property

No Party shall take any measures depriving, directly or indirectly, of his property a national of another Party unless the following conditions are complied with:

(i) The measures are taken in the public interest and under due process of law;

(ii) The measures are not discriminatory; and

(iii) The measures are accompanied by provision for the payment of just compensation. Such compensation shall represent the genuine value of the property affected, shall be paid without undue delay, and shall be transferable to the extent necessary to make it effective for the national entitled thereto.

Article 7

Disputes

(a) Any dispute between Parties as to the interpretation or application of this Convention may be submitted by agreement between them either to an Arbitral Tribunal established in accordance with the provisions of the Annex to this Convention, which shall form an integral part thereof, or to any other international tribunal. If no agreement is reached for this purpose between the Parties within a

* Draft convention prepared by the OECD. Reprinted with the permission of the OECD.

period of sixty days from the date on which written notice of intention to institute proceedings is given, it is hereby agreed that an Arbitral Tribunal established in accordance with that Annex shall have jurisdiction.

(b) A national of a Party claiming that he has been injured by measures in breach of this Convention may, without prejudice to any right or obligation he may have to resort to another tribunal, national or international, institute proceedings against any other Party responsible for such measures before the Arbitral Tribunal referred to in paragraph (a), provided that:

(i) the Party against which the claim is made has accepted the jurisdiction of that Arbitral Tribunal by a declaration which covers that claim; and

(ii) the Party of which he is a national has indicated that it will not institute proceedings under paragraph (a) or, within six months of receiving a written request from its national for the institution of such proceedings, has not instituted them.

(c) The declaration referred to in paragraph (b)(i), whether general or particular, may be made or revoked at any time. In respect of claims arising out of or in connection with rights acquired during the period of the validity of such declaration, it shall continue to apply for a period of five years after its revocation.

(d) At any time after the expiry of the period of six months referred to in paragraph (b)(ii), the Party concerned may institute proceedings in accordance with paragraph (a). In this case proceedings instituted in accordance with paragraph (b) shall be suspended until the proceedings instituted in accordance with paragraph (a) are terminated.

CONVENTION ON SETTLEMENT OF INVESTMENT DISPUTES

International Bank for Reconstruction and Development, 1965
8 Whiteman, Digest of International Law 805 (1967).

In 1965 the International Bank for Reconstruction and Development—after broad consultations with legal experts in some 86 countries and assistance in the actual drafting from specially designated representatives of 61 of its members—opened for signature a Convention on the Settlement of Investment Disputes between States and Nationals of Other States. In submitting the Convention for signature the Executive Directors made it clear that its purpose was the promotion of "an atmosphere of mutual confidence" and thus to stimulate "a larger flow of private international capital into those countries which wish to attract it." To that end, "It would provide facilities for conciliation and arbitration by specially qualified persons of independent judgment carried out according to rules known and accepted in advance by the parties concerned." The Convention (now in effect) ª contemplates consent by parties to the dispute to conciliation or arbitration under the auspices of an International Centre for Settlement of Investment Disputes (which has its seat at the principal office of the Bank unless otherwise decided). Article 25 reads:

(1) The jurisdiction of the Centre shall extend to any legal dispute arising directly out of an investment, between a Contracting State (or any constituent subdivision or agency of a Contracting State designated to the Centre by that State) and a national of another Contracting State, which the parties to the dispute consent in writing to submit to the Centre. When the parties have given their consent, no party may withdraw its consent unilaterally.

(2) "National of another Contracting State" means: * * *

(3) Consent by a constituent subdivision or agency of a Contracting State shall require the approval of that State unless that State notifies the Centre that no such approval is required.

(4) Any Contracting State may, at the time of ratification, acceptance or approval of this Convention or at any time thereafter, notify the Centre of the class or classes of disputes which it would or would not consider submitting to the jurisdiction of the Centre. The Secretary-General shall forthwith transmit such notification to all Contracting States. Such notification shall not constitute the consent required by paragraph (1).

On the subject of exhaustion of local remedies, the Executive Directors of the Bank explain in their Report on the Convention:

32. It may be presumed that when a State and an investor agree to have recourse to arbitration, and do not reserve the right to have recourse to other remedies or require the prior exhaustion of other remedies, the intention of the parties is to have recourse to arbitration to the exclusion of any other remedy. This rule of interpretation is embodied in the first sentence of Article 26. In order to make clear that it was not intended thereby to modify the rules of international law regarding the exhaustion of local remedies, the second sentence explicitly recognizes the right of a State to require the prior exhaustion of local remedies.

Article 26 reads:

Consent of the parties to arbitration under this Convention shall, unless otherwise stated, be deemed consent to such arbitration to the exclusion of any other remedy. A Contracting State may require the exhaustion of local administrative or judicial

a. 62 states were parties as of January 1, 1972.

remedies as a condition of its consent to arbitration under this Convention.

As to "diplomatic protection", article 27 expressly prohibits a Contracting State from giving diplomatic protection, or bringing an international claim, in respect of a dispute which one of its nationals and another Contracting State have consented to submit or shall have submitted to arbitration under the Convention, unless such other Contracting State shall have failed to abide by and comply with the award rendered in that dispute.

FRIEDMANN AND BEGUIN, JOINT INTERNATIONAL BUSINESS VENTURES IN DEVELOPING COUNTRIES 23 (1971) *

* * * [The joint venture] cannot be regarded as a panacea. It is a device to be adopted, rejected, or modified after a sober consideration of the many legal, psychological, and technical factors prevailing in a given situation. Confidence between the partners will overcome the most difficult obstacles; lack of confidence will destroy the most perfect devices. As a major negative factor, we mentioned disparity of outlook between the foreign and local partners:

> * * * In joint ventures between industrially developed countries, such as the United States, Britain, West Germany, the Netherlands, Italy, or Sweden, there is a certain community not only of tradition and of scientific, technical, and legal standards, but there has also been more experience with responsible investment practices and legal supervision, although such standards have often evolved only after disastrous experiences with unscrupulous speculators. In many of the less developed countries, this stage has not yet been reached in the business environment. Power and wealth are often concentrated in relatively few hands, and they are not matched by a corresponding sense of responsibility. The partner from the industrialized country, usually a large corporation with worldwide interests and long experience, generally takes a long-term view of profits, placing the development of the enterprise before quick dividends. Tax considerations may provide an additional incentive to reinvest in a developing foreign enterprise.

> Inflationary conditions may produce the reverse situation: The local partner will want to leave his investment in the enterprise where it is relatively inflation-proof, while the foreign investor will be anxious to take out his earnings before devaluation decimates them.

* Reprinted with the permission of the Columbia University Press.

A similar note is struck by Dr. Pieter Kuin, a member of the Board of Unilever and Chairman of the ICC Commission on International Investments and Economic Development, in his introduction to a report of that Commission on International Joint Business Ventures in Developing Countries:

> * * * The rising tide of national independence and self-reliance in developing countries has created a desire for even more active participation by local people in this process. Shares in the capital and profits of foreign business have sometimes been claimed too readily, without much consideration for mutual performance. But gradually a more mature idea of partnership is taking shape, in which the partners share risks as well as benefits.

> Joint ventures in production are one way of meeting this need for partnership. Like other forms of co-operation they are in themselves neither good nor bad. Their value depends entirely on the degree to which they meet each partner's requirements. Only successful and mutually satisfactory joint ventures serve the cause of world economic development. Contrary to what some enthusiasts seem to believe, joint ventures are not a panacea for progress in the promotion of this cause. Certain conditions must be fulfilled. For private ventures, there must be a local business community from which partners can be recruited. Their industrial and trading traditions must not be caused by incomprehensible behaviour. For any joint venture—with private partners or government agencies—to be successful, the host country should also have at least the beginnings of a managerial class. Without this, a disproportionate number of expatriate managers will prevent the new company from looking like a real joint enterprise. The government and the administration in the host country should in principle be sympathetic, understand the requirements of modern enterprises and be reasonably equipped to meet these. If a government agency is the local partner, it should be fairly free from day-to-day politics.

This is a sober and realistic appraisal of the place of the joint international business venture in contemporary conditions of economic development. It contrasts with the following expression, by Kenneth Weg, Senior Associate Editor of Business International, of a more negative point of view, as it was typical until a few years ago of many American business enterprises:

> * * * Even though joint ventures may currently be in vogue, many firms with extensive international commitments are becoming increasingly dissatisfied with this approach to international business. The case against joint ventures in the less-developed countries rests on two major points: the presence of a local partner contributes to (1) day-to-day operational problems

and policy conflicts, and (2) lack of managerial flexibility in adjusting to new market and investment requirements and opportunities.

Companies with a policy of establishing wholly owned subsidiaries whenever possible have been more fortunate in planning for rationalized operations in both industrialized and less-developed regions. For example, IBM World Trade Corp. has had a conscious policy of 100% ownership ever since it began moving into foreign markets. Today, IBM is an outstanding example of an international corporation in which full-line assembly plants tend to disappear in favor of a very few world production centers for a given product or component.

In rebutting certain statements made by the U. S. State Department and AID in favor of joint ventures, Mr. Weg observed:

The rebuttal is obvious: a wholly owned subsidiary offers all these possibilities, and may even be a better training vehicle since it does not encounter internal opposition to advanced management techniques, as is often the case in joint ventures. In addition, if the growth of the new managerial class follows traditional patterns, many local nationals trained in the wholly owned subsidiary will undoubtedly set out on their own and establish competitive enterprises or ancillary product companies with the know-how they have assimilated.

As far as economic theory is concerned, two factors should be considered. First, a wholly owned venture may make a greater contribution to economic development because of greater efficiency and less internal conflict; second, it may be a fallacy to think that the joint venture will offer more direct material benefits to the public, since in the majority of cases it is the already wealthy and established investor who becomes the joint-venture partner or shareholder.

Mr. Weg, however, declared himself in favor of regional development corporations—which have played an important role in some recent multilateral joint ventures, such as Prolacsa.

* * * What is required is acceptance both by the people and governments of the new nations and by foreign investors of the need for regional development corporations in which all parties would participate. These regional companies would offer their shareholders profits resulting from total regional operations, thereby helping to break down the nationalistic barriers to development, and coordinating production planning on a multinational basis for the most efficient and competitive operations.

On the latter point, there will be general agreement. But the competition argument is highly questionable. In many developing countries there is, at present, no room for more than one enterprise, e. g. in the manufacture of trucks, nylon, or radio equipment, and competition would simply be a waste of precious new materials and foreign exchange. Nor is Mr. Weg's reasoning entirely consistent. For the reason why some giant multinational corporations, such as General Motors or IBM, are not favorable to joint ventures, is their wish to maintain complete technological and managerial control * * *.

Multinational enterprises (MNEs). In recent years there has been great growth in the size and number of corporate families (parents and foreign subsidiaries) that carry on economic activity on multi-country, regional, or even global, bases. Even more growth, both as to the sizes and the numbers of families, is predicted, by all friends and by some foes of MNEs. Growth to date, however, has hardly matched the expansion of the wordage, in scientific, business, and popular media, about MNEs. To long-time observers of direct foreign investments the MNE seems today to be getting the degree of expectant attention that joint ventures enjoyed about a decade ago. Aside from the influence of fashions in thought about business structure, why have the joint venture, earlier, and the MNE now, raised so many expectations as to preferred forms of direct foreign investment? It seems to us that in both instances new ideas for business structure have been or are seen as having utility in removing or reducing the brand of feeling of "foreignness" in host countries.

As is well known to experienced observers, the classic American parent wholly owned foreign subsidiary structure is very definitely tagged as "very foreign" in most host countries; and in socially volatile ones, such as the developing and highly nationalistic states of Latin America, the label can lead to very uncomfortable results. Thus, from the perspective of reducing or preventing transnational investment conflicts, the issue as to the MNE is one of credibility. Is the MNE really something new that does not deserve to be feared, controlled, or discriminated against as "foreign?" Or is the MNE just a new name for an old and basically unchanged and increasingly controversial foreign investment structure?

With regard to this issue, the following viewpoints, culled from current discourses about MNEs, are of some conjectural relevance:

(i) Whether the MNE can establish itself as something new depends upon the way the parent deals with the owned or controlled subsidiaries in various countries. If the parent runs each national subsidiary separately from all the others, instead of directing or permitting fairly free movement of capital, orders, personnel, and technology between the various subsidiaries in different countries, the pattern does not vary enough from the old-fashioned transnational corporate family to be able to establish itself as something new and different. That is to say, if the old pattern was one of a very big developed-country corporation owning 95–100% of the shares in five, six, or more rigorously controlled corporations in as many foreign states, with absolute water-tight compartments between the subsidiaries themselves, and the same pattern is now called an MNE, nothing has really changed. The issue arises, the debate continues, because a widely-*used* definition of an MNE stresses only the transnational parent-subsidiary system, the centralization of decision-making with the parent, and a rather vague "common business policy." It will be noted that the "counter-definition" implicit above limits true MNEs to situations where economic movements across national frontiers are free. Today there is only one such area, the European Economic Community. Hence, some argue, at the present time it is simply not possible to assert seriously that true MNEs can exist in, say South America, where free movement is not yet established.

(ii) The host state acceptability of MNEs vel non, need not turn on national preferences as to consigning particular economic activity to the private or to the public sector, because MNEs need not be limited to the private sector. Some observers aver that substantial interest, and some growth, exist in MNEs that combine private and state capital, even the state capital of socialist countries. Additionally, there is nothing to prevent wholly state-owned MNEs. On the other hand, it is asked: would a foreign state-dominated enterprise really be less objectionable in host countries?

(iii) In the private sector, is the MNE apt to be more or less vulnerable than ordinary foreign enterprises to uncoordinated national controls in host states? Are MNEs seriously threatened by conflicting, overlapping, and in the aggregate, crushing, multinational regulation? Some enthusiasts who actually profess to see the MNE as the next great step beyond the national state in human societal evolution suggest, in taking this view, an undefined, statelike, invulnerability of MNEs to being nibbled or bitten to death. Others reject the notion that the corporate form would ever be acceptable for the governance of people and with it the implicit linking of the MNE to the state's relatively greater armor against external control. In another quarter the debate is over the question whether host countries might not come to see MNEs as so economically and socially effective, and so much a part of the conditions of good life in the host states themselves, that MNEs would be treated with scrupulous fairness in the national interest. A few cynics say that the only way an MNE can be sure that it will not be singled out for harsh control and taxation is for the MNE to be able to subvert the processes of governmental action in the host state, and they point to the re-doubled vulnerability of an MNE when the fact of such subversion surfaces.

(iv) Another approach to the establishment of an effective and credible new economic structure—a "truly true" MNE—is to say that the sole or preponderant nationality factor must be eliminated at all stages: in the ownerships and management of the parent, in the complexion of the executive and labor forces of the corporate family, in the degree of participation by host state nationals, not only in the national subsidiary, but in the whole arrangement. This type of MNE is, at this time only faintly perceptible in the world's structures for business enterprise.

(v) One difficulty the MNE image is apt to have, in developing countries at least, but possibly in others as well, is that some self-styled MNEs—and they fit the definition quoted above also—have been take-over conglomerates. Foreign take-over of the best indigenous enterprise is always politically unpopular. When to this there is added the controversies that swirl around the basic assumption in justification that undefined and largely still personalized asserted management skills make conglomerates economically and socially desirable, the damage that the asserted linkage can do to the general idea of MNEs could be substantial. Another relationship that comes into play at this point is whether the worlds of today and tomorrow (short range) have put aside as no longer relevant the "Curse of Bigness" of late nineteenth century populism and the late Louis D. Brandeis. MNEs are big, and a "little business" MNE is almost unimaginable. Has business learned how to be big, yet agile, adaptive, and efficient at the same time? Here new doctrines of management technology and earlier "folk-doubts" may face a moment of truth before long. Or, if not an intellectual confrontation, then antitrust ones.

(vi) In the United States at the present time, MNE parent corporations are not without their own "at home" problems. Organized labor complains that MNEs are largely responsible for "runaway plants" that take jobs away from American workers and bring in foreign-made goods under freer trade auspices. Others complain that certain self-styled MNEs conspire against, and seek to involve the United States Government in conspiring against, certain foreign governments. Thus, Congress has to face what it will do about proposed legislation against imports here of goods made abroad by American-owned foreign companies, and in the Senate a sub-committee of the Foreign Relations Committee is investigating the influence of MNEs on United States foreign policy. Some observers have seen in recent patterns of European Economic Community antitrust enforcement action a bias against certain large American companies with numerous subsidiaries (some of them by take-over) within the EEC. On the other hand, others say that the industrialized Europeans and the Japanese have enthusiastic ideas of their own about the further use of MNEs. It is sometimes added that more true MNEs are based in Europe—and have been for some time—than in the United States at the present time, because the Europeans, more than the Americans, have found it expedient in past to share participations in capital at the top—and sometimes at lower—levels within the structure of a corporate family.

Student users of these materials—and some of their teachers—will in their professional lifetimes probably be able to see how the foregoing issues and problems work themselves out. Will one straight line projection or its opposite occur? Or will evolution take a now unforeseen twist? Meanwhile, the profession of international lawyering is already considerably involved with the MNE as a new concept, a new rhetoric, or a new reality.

OLIVER, THE ANDEAN FOREIGN INVESTMENT CODE: A NEW PHASE IN THE QUEST FOR NORMATIVE ORDER AS TO DIRECT FOREIGN INVESTMENT

66 American Journal of International Law 763 (1972).

In the broad the Andean Investment Code does these things: (i) classifies equity (or ownership) investment in accordance with its degree of foreignness; (ii) imposes prior restraints upon the entry of new direct foreign investment; (iii) requires disinvestment by existing foreign elements down to minority levels, on pain of denial of the benefits of free movement of goods and services within a common market; (iv) closes certain sectors to foreign investment; (v) regulates repatriation of invested capital and the remittance of profits; (vi) limits the present opportunities of technology owner-transferrors, through patents, trademarks and know-how, to benefit collaterally from their industrial rights; (vii) makes or anticipates some important changes in corporation and tax law.

As promulgated the Code takes no position on the debated question, whether the *consentio juris* recognizes an international minimum standard as to the treatment of the economic interests of aliens. It was probably decided there was no need to re-affirm the traditional Latin American viewpoint on this issue, inasmuch as the Code does not at any point clash, *as law in books*, with whatever general international law is asserted to require by proponents of the international minimum standard. As is well known, prior restraints on entry are not illegal, except as they depart unilaterally from possible commercial treaty obligations. Detailed reporting by investors is merely an exercise of the police power. Disinvestment in most cases is not forced, only induced; and in any event, orderly sale of ownership "overage" to a governmental or private market is envisaged. Article 50, in a sense, approaches the "equality of treatment" viewpoint by the back door, providing that:

> Member countries shall not grant to foreign investors any treatment more favorable than that granted to national investors.

Foreign investors are not guaranteed national treatment. Under Article 50 they cannot have *more than* national treatment, which seems inferentially to negate the notion of a substantive international minimum standard.

The Code definitely links the treatment of foreign investment to development goals, and it assumes that participation in a wider free market will be an incentive that outweighs the disincentives of regulation. In this respect the Code reflects optimism and expectation about the development process that is certainly commendable and reassuring, * * *

In its studies the Board, which formulated the Code that the Commission approved with relatively few alterations, acted upon the bases of technocratic conclusions that, as scientifically stated, mask the intensity of certain conditioning psycho-political attitudes about foreigners, foreignness, and foreign ownership investment in Latin America. * * * In a nutshell, the technocrats of the Code believed that (i) development and integration require continued and significant transfers of developed-country capital and technology; (ii) the Andean Group nations' interest in foreign private investment and know-how is to get it to help fill the gap caused by an insufficient supply of local capital and technology plus public sector development assistance; (iii) certain negative effects historically associated with the presence of foreign ownership investment should be regulated consistently with the recognized needs, stated above. These negative effects of (iii) cluster about too high costs, interference with the growth of a national private sector, and loss of effective national capacity to make and enforce national policies.

Behind these formulations of goals there is a considerable body of Latin American professional know-how about foreign investment. It is a mistake to assume that the Code was written by a group of scholastic ideologues who knew little, if anything, about what they were trying to regulate. Some of the Code's designers are experienced attorneys who for many years represented direct foreign investment in the member countries. Others are skilled economists and administrators, often trained in the United States. Many of them share a continuing dissatisfaction with what they regard as a wry historical change in the way the world finances a nation's development. When he was President of Colombia, Dr. Carlos Lleras Restrepo several times commented that what is most needed from the private sector or developed countries is a supply of long-term, *loan capital*. The developing countries everywhere are faced with the fact that the private sector foreign investor today is almost an *equity* (or ownership) investor. It has been observed in Latin America that when the United States developed, with European capital flows, the foreign investors were mainly creditors and that in time a creditor, inevitably, is got rid of. (He is paid off, defaulted out, or inflated away.) The foreign owner, on the other hand, has a perpetual claim on the productivity, the foreign exchange resources, and the economic utilizations (priorities) in the host country.   Times change and circumstances vary. The Great Depression left North Americans rather favoring equity over creditor investment, as "better" or "more liberal."   It is not seen that way in Latin America today.

"But," the Code's true architects might be imagined as saying, "the Code assumes, the foreign capital and technology that we need is probably not going to change as to the form in which it comes here. Therefore, we must conform its impact to our ends, but without unduly curbing the flow.   Why will ownership capital yet flow, despite these Regulations?   Mainly because the foreign equity owners will be interested in the substantial promise of our Andean Common Market."   And there lies the big issue: Is it true?   Note that we have put the question in terms of "new flow."   It is "new flow" or continued flow, that the Andean countries are primarily interested in.   *   *   *

Profile-lowering devices.   In the United States and in a number of other countries the legal profession, through practitioners specializing in international business transactions, is influential in the structuring of foreign investments.   The reality that clients prefer to be told how they can come somewhere near achieving their objectives, rather than to be told what they cannot do, exists here as in other sectors of practice involving prospective operations.   Knowledge of the existing rules of the international legal system and of the lines along which these rules may evolve is highly important.   It is also important that the lawyer be innovative, sensitive to the psycho-political setting in the potential host country, and free of ideological prejudice.   In particular, it is useful for him to consider ways in which the business venture itself can be organized and operated so as to avoid to the extent possible shifts for the worse in the investment climate after the client has become irrevocably committed to the venture, as by making a foreign investment in fixed assets.   The fundamental principle of economics that such an investment is assuredly retrievable only for its scrap or salvage value should not be overlooked.   Among the possibilities that modern foreign investors ought to be induced to consider, in particular circumstances, are

1.   Management-service contracts as an alternative to ownership interests.   Some countries have already limited the foreign investor to the former in the extractive industries and public utilities.

2.   Joint ventures.

3.   Wider offerings of stock in the host-country operating company to investors of that country, i. e., a departure from the pattern so often found in past of complete foreign stock ownership, except for qualifying shares, usually 3% or less of the total stock in that company.

4.   Due regard to national and regional preferences that foreign investors not dominate particular sectors of the economy, such as defense-related industries, telecommunications, etc.

5.   For the extractive industries, the possibiliy of negotiating the country-company sharing of the proceeds of the business at different ratios during the life of the concession, particularly if the term is a fairly long one.   In many instances minerals concessions now giving the preponderant return to the country were originally contracted for on the basis of a far lower participation by the host, and as time went on pressures built up for changing the sharing that sometimes caused crises in the relationship, and even nationalizations · under emotionally heated circumstances.   It has been suggested that with the utilization of improved techniques of economic forecasting new concessions might be originally negotiated to provide for increasing the host share of the proceeds at successive stages in the life of the concession.

6.   Acceptance of partial disinvestment down to substantial minority stock ownership.   See Hirschman, How to Divest in Latin America, and Why, Princeton Essays in International Finance (No. 76, 1969).

7.   The multinationalization of the foreign ownership, thus reducing the association of the venture with any single foreign nationality.   See Perlmutter, The Tortuous Evolution of the Multinational Corporation, 4 Columbia J. of World Business 9 (1969); Oliver, Speculations on Developing Country Reception of Multinational Enterprise, 11 Va.J. of Int'l Law 192 (1971).

Other possibilities involving legal structuring exist and still others will doubtless develop in the future.   Outside the lawyer's sphere of specialization, but related, are managerial practices as to the use of nationals of the host country in executive suites as well as in the labor force, corporate good citizenship in the host country, maximum use of products of that country in the conduct of a manufacturing or sales business, and the like.

Part VI

THEORIES ABOUT THE INTERNATIONAL
LEGAL SYSTEM

1. *Is theory influential on outcomes under international law and on its development?* If you have taken these materials in the order in which we have arranged them, your study of this Chapter comes after you have had experience with many of the major aspects of law in the international system. You will have begun to form your own ideas about the similarities and differences between the law you have studied here and the public law you study in other courses. For example: putting to one side the difference between the United States Supreme Court and the International Court of Justice as to authorization to decide, do you find these courts acting similarly or in sharply different ways in types of cases that are similar, i. e., where the Supreme Court is sitting in judgment upon the conflicting interests of two or more states of the Union either in a suit in the original jurisdiction of the Supreme Court or in some other type of case?

We have put the theory material this far along for three reasons: (a) we wanted you to begin to grope toward theory on your own as you went along; (b) we wanted you to see from case study that so far as professional methodology and involvement go, international law calls upon the same range of skills as other systems of law do; (c) we wanted to avoid raising too many doubts and prospects before you had matured in the subject matter.

Although underdeveloped, the international legal system has been extensively theorized about. Why so much doctrine for so few rules and effective institutions to apply them? Is it because the scholars who have committed themselves to this field are creating theories and schools casting their expectations and preferences as law simply because they have so little in the way of real law stuff to deal with? Do the materials which follow suggest that scholars are theorizing about reality or their dreams?

2. *Critical independence is indispensable.* International public law, more so than any other bodies of law, tends to be presented in discrete doctrinal packages. "Schools" abound. Learned men encourage disciples. Deviation becomes intellectual heresy. Those who do not agree are dolts. Also, international law is often appealed to by advocates in court or in print highly interested in particular outcomes. This is done either because international law is highly amorphous and hence susceptible to a wide range of assertion or because it becomes an argument of last resort. Sometimes these groups of distorters, the didactic scholars and the argumentative activists, combine forces. As a result there is claimed for the international legal system a competence, a completeness, and a virtue that it may not in

fact possess. See, Oliver, On Saving International Law from its Friends (editorial), 52 Am.J.Int'l L. 498 (1958). In this field the rule of caveat emptor is quite important for would-be shoppers of doctrine.

In methodology, international public law is somewhat old-fashioned by the most modern techniques of some domestic systems. It is highly exegetic, rigorously logical (even when there are errors in the logic), antiseptic, and remote. Quantification technique as to events, things, and attitudes of social groups barely exists. Even the schools that claim for themselves the utmost in realistic modernity are hardly scientific in any sense of association with modern scientific and engineering technology. Major propositions are largely supported by secondary authorities. In large part, perhaps, the generally backward methodological standard reflects the reality that, after all, the international legal system exists by consensus, and world does not yet have a consensus as to what law is and how it should be used.

3. *Basic jurisprudential problems.* International law shares with domestic law certain basic problems. These are the relationship of law and justice, the essential nature of law, and the judicial process in relationship to other types of decision-making.

Beyond these, international law throws into issue other fundamental questions:

(1) Is international law "law" in terms of a general concept of law, whatever that concept is?

(2) If international law is "law" in some sense or other, what is its relationship to other congeries of law, such as natural law, national law, international organizations law, regional systems law?

Chapter 18

THE INFLUENCE OF LEGAL PHILOSOPHY

The excerpts that follow are intended to assist you in the development of your own philosophic outlook about law in the international system, both in terms of what is and what ought to be. You will have been doing this, subliminally at least, as you have gone through the preceding chapters. This is a focusing chapter. There is little here on the history and sources of international law.

We have not here arranged the writers of centuries past into groups upon the basis of their views on the sources and authority of international law; e. g., Naturalists (either via the law of God or the law of nature and right reason); Positivists (state consent to be bound, manifested by express or implied intention); or Eclectics. It is easy to find a great deal on these matters elsewhere. The late twentieth century has inherited a synthesis of history that, on the whole, makes specific philosophic inquiry into the past somewhat irrelevant, except for cultural reasons. It is true that most of the law of the international legal system grew up with the modern state system, that is, within the past 350–500 years; but the question for now and the future is the relationship of the state system itself to legal and social expectations and needs that are larger than any state.

The readings to follow are mainly from twentieth century writers, and they are representative of most of the major current trends in theory about law in the international system. The more important identifications today, which subsume under new rubrics many of the older philosophical classifications, are: (1) idealism versus realism; (2) relative versus absolute values; (3) monism versus pluralism; (4) rules versus modi operandi; (5) lawmen versus other types of experts (social psychologists, economists, etc.) as the preferred decision-makers; (6) law as an instrumentality or tool; (7) the law in international agreements as international law; (8) law generated by the political actions of states and of international organizations; (9) law and political evolution beyond the present international system.

JAMES, THE VARIETIES OF RELIGIOUS EXPERIENCE
516 (1902)

[On the question: If God exists how do we know it?]

God is the natural appellation * * * for the supreme reality * * * I only translate into schematic language what I may call the instinctive belief of mankind: God is real since he produces real effects.

Does similar reasoning lead to the conclusion that international law is real?

---

1 AUSTIN, JURISPRUDENCE 177, 189 (1861)

* * * Speaking with greater precision, international law, or the law obtaining between nations, regards the conduct of sovereigns considered as related to one another.

And hence it inevitably follows, that the law obtaining between nations is not positive law: for every positive law is set by a given sovereign to a person or persons in a state of subjection to its author. As I have already intimated, the law obtaining between nations is law (improperly so called) set by general opinion. The duties which it imposes are enforced by moral sanctions: by fear on the part of nations, or by fear on the part of sovereigns, of provoking general hostility, and incurring its probable evils, in case they shall violate maxims generally received and respected.

A society political but subordinate is merely a limb or member of a society political and independent. All the persons who compose it, including the person or body which is its immediate chief, live in a state of subjection to one and the same sovereign.

Besides societies political and independent, societies independent but natural, society formed by the intercourse of independent political societies, and societies political but subordinate, there are societies which will not quadrate with any of those descriptions. Though, like a society political but subordinate, it forms a limb or member of a society political and independent, a society of the class in question is not a political society. Although it consists of members living in a state of subjection, it consists of subjects considered as private persons.—A society consisting of parents and children, living in a state of subjection, and considered in those characters, may serve as an example.

* * * But if perfect or complete independence be of the essence of sovereign power, there is not in fact the human power to which the epithet sovereign will apply with propriety. Every government, let it be never so powerful, renders occasional obedience to commands of other governments. Every government defers frequently to those opinions and sentiments which are styled international law. And every government defers habitually to the opinions and sentiments of its own subjects. If it be not in a habit of obedience to the commands of a determinate party, a government has all the independence which a government can possibly enjoy.

2 WOLFF, CLASSICS OF INTERNATIONAL LAW
CARNEGIE ENDOWMENT 11, 19 (1934)

§ 7.—Of the society established by nature among nations. Nature herself has established society among all nations and binds them to preserve society. For nature herself has established society among men and binds them to preserve it. Therefore, since this obligation, as coming from the law of nature, is necessary and immutable, it cannot be changed for the reason that nations have united into a state. Therefore society, which nature has established among individuals, still exists among nations and consequently, after states have been established in accordance with the law of nature and nations have arisen thereby, nature herself also must be said to have established society among all nations and bound them to preserve society.

* * *

§ 8.—Of the purpose of that state. Since nature herself has established society among all nations, in so far as she has established it among all men, as is evident from the demonstration of the preceding proposition, since, moreover, the purpose of natural society, and consequently of that society which nature herself has established among men, is to give mutual assistance in perfecting itself and its condition; the purpose of the society therefore, which nature has established among all nations, is to give mutual assistance in perfecting itself and its condition, consequently the promotion of the common good by its combined powers.

* * *

§ 25.—Of the positive law of nations. That is called the positive law of nations which takes its origin from the will of nations. Therefore since it is plainly evident that the voluntary, the stipulative, and the customary law of nations take their origin from the will of nations, all that law is the positive law of nations. And since furthermore it is plain that the voluntary law of nations rests on the presumed consent of nations, the stipulative upon the express consent, the customary upon the tacit consent, since moreover in no other way is it conceived that a certain law can spring from the will of nations, the positive law of nations is either voluntary or stipulative or customary.

* * *

§ 26.—General observation. We shall carefully distinguish the voluntary, the stipulative, and the customary law of nations from the natural or necessary law of nations, nevertheless we shall not teach the former separately from the latter, but when we have shown what things belong to the necessary law of nations, we shall straightway add, where, why, and in what manner that must be changed to the voluntary, and here and there, when we have carefully considered it, we shall add the stipulative and the customary, which are by no means to be confused with the voluntary, especially since they have not been distinguished from it with sufficient care by Grotius. And the method which we have thus far used, both in the law of nature and in the other parts of philosophy already taught by us, and which we shall likewise use in the other parts, to be taught by us in their own time and order, this too we use in the law of nations, although the particular laws peculiar to some nations, which either come from stipulations or are due to customs, we do not consider, inasmuch as they are at variance with our plan, with which only those things which belong to science are in harmony. And why one must use such a method is plain from our proofs and our notes in the Prolegomena to "The Law of Nature."

PHILLIPSON, INTRODUCTION TO GENTILI, DE JURE BELLI LIBRI TRES (II TRANS., CARNEGIE ENDOWMENT, 1933) 22a *

5. Conception of the Law of Nations—Society of States—Civil Basis—Membership of the Society

The law of nations, designated by Gentili ius gentium (the customary expression adapted from Roman Law) is that law which all nations or the greater part of them—"maior parsorbis"—agree upon. It is the law of the society or community of states, of the "Societas gentium". This is a concise and simple description, whereby the ambiguous Roman term is made to refer explicitly to international relations. It is not, of course, an exact definition, as it involves, though unavoidably, a tautologism. Indeed, no satisfactory definition had hitherto been formulated. Grotius adopts substantially the conception of Gentili, when he says that the law of nations (ius gentium) is that law which has received obligatory force from the will of all nations or of many; whilst Vattel, like Gentili, verges on tautology in his statement that the law of nations (droit des gens) is the science of the rights and obligations which exist between nations. Some writers emphasize in their definitions the origin of the law of nations, others the nature of the subject-matter, and others again lay stress on those concerned in and bound by it. * * *

However this may be, the fundamental notion in the use and application of the term is aptly stated by Gentili, although he has not adopted the much better and more precise phraseology "ius inter gentes", which was afterwards consistently used by the English jurist, Richard Zouche, and which was even before foreshadowed by Franciscus de Victoria. Such law regulating the relationships between independent sovereigns or peoples is the result either of express conventions, or of tacit compacts inferred from long-established customs

* Reprinted with the permission of the Carnegie Endowment for International Peace.

generally acquiesced in. Here the conventional character of international law is emphasized. The members of the "societas gentium" are interdependent as well as independent. As human beings are concerned who have interests and needs in common, mutual relationships are inevitable, association and understanding are the conditions precedent to the orderly continuance of these relationships, and so governing laws are necessary to regulate their reciprocal rights and obligations. That is to say (though Gentili does not put it this way) the basic axiom of human solidarity, "ubi societas ibi ius" is as applicable to a group of peoples as it is to a group of individuals. Here Gentili, by his implicit recognition of the principle of solidarity and interdependence of States as an essential limitation of their sovereignty, has anticipated a vital conception of our own times, a conception which, when it comes to be duly realized by the peoples of the world (and more particularly by their ministers and representatives), will facilitate the working of the League of Nations organization, and so will pave the way for the consummation of a rational world polity.

These governing laws, on the one hand, have a positive basis— the "usus gentium"; and, on the other, are due to the exigence of natural reason—those underlying dictates of justice and right which are everywhere and at all times forced on the minds of men. The authority of the ius naturae or ius naturale or ratio naturalis (a legacy of Greek and Roman philosophy and jurisprudence) was invoked by all writers, earlier and later, including Grotius, and even such determined positivists as Bynkershoek and De Martens. But unlike the sixteenth-century writers, especially those among the Jesuit order, with their revived scholasticism and their a priori procedure, Gentili was not addicted to the indiscriminate adoration of this naturalistic principle, and to the elaboration of a multiplicity of theses largely irrelevant and extraneous to the main subject. In the sixteenth century, indeed, investigations into the ius naturae began to be made by writers such as Oldendorp, Hemming, and others, who treated the subject from a wider point of view than the Jesuit or Franciscan theologians had done or were doing. Alberico introduced the principle of natural reason, however, partly to explain the ultimate origin of international law, and partly to fortify the positive sanction; and in so doing he adopted the Protestant conception of ecclesiastical supremacy and secular sovereignty, as against the Roman Catholic notion, enshrined in the canon law, of a universal heirarchy under the papal headship, and, in matters temporal, the idea of an empire under the Emperor as a continuation of the "imperium Romanum" in accordance with the views of the civilians. Very frequently we find that Gentili appeals to the ius naturae in order to test the validity of a particular doctrine or the legitimacy of a certain practice; but usually he disregards the current vague metaphysico-legal significance of that term, and interprets it in the sense of humanity, justice, and the best common sense of mankind. And throughout his exposition he insists on the positive juridical sanction quite as much as on the considerations of ethics or on the behests of divine law, and he is careful to discriminate between the work and objects of theologians and the sphere and functions of jurists.

The pioneer work of Gentili was in harmony with the larger movement of the sixteenth century which witnessed a transformation of society, the establishment of a new spirit and wider outlook, the decline of theocracy, and the rise of the modern State. The political conceptions of the Middle Ages, which identified civil and ecclesiastical authority, were derived on the one hand from Greek and Roman doctrines, and on the other from Hebrew and Christian teaching. Towards the end of the thirteenth century the temporal supremacy of the papacy began to be seriously opposed, especially in France, and its decline was further hastened on by the great schism. The conciliar movement of the fifteenth century spread the theory that sovereign power was of the nature of a trust. The Renaissance and the Reformation, two sides of the same great intellectual and moral awakening, revived humanism, scientific curiosity, established a spirit of independence, political as well as spiritual, and a desire to find a more rational basis than the arbitrary theocratic for human society, and substituted civil for clerical authority, a society of territorial States resting on law and juridical sanction for a theocratic confederation subject to canon law. And at the head of such States are monarchs who, in the view of Gentili, are in the position of guardians or administrators of their respective countries, and not absolute rulers independent of law. Grotius approves St. Thomas's interpretation of the fifty-first Psalm, and cites other authorities from both "sacred and profane history", as to the irresponsibility of princes and their superiority to law—a view that afterwards found expression in Louis XIV's sinister dictum: "L'état c'est moi." Gentili, though writing earlier than Grotius, shows himself to be more in harmony with modern ideas when he asserts that it is a hallucination of theologians, mere adulation on the part of lawyers to represent to kings that they are permitted to do everything and that their sovereignty is absolute.

Finally, having conceived of a "societas gentium" on a civil basis, and a system of rules freed from the bonds of theological casuistry and from other irrelevant intermixture and interpolation, Gentili took a further step—a remarkable one, even though it is a corollary following from his general thesis—and included in this society of States infidel and even barbarian communities, so long as they were independent and politically organized nations. The common opinion of writers was that only Roman Catholic or, at most, Christian princes, could be vested with dominium; but Gentili held that heretics and infidels could legitimately enjoy the right of sovereignty in their own domains. Contrary to the view of the great majority of preceding writers, he maintained that heresy or infidelity or even idolatry was not intrinsically a just cause of war. Treaty relationships may be established with peoples of this character; and they possess also the right of legation. On the other hand, those who have no religion at all are in the position of pirates, as the natural enemies of mankind, and are therefore outside the pale of the society of States; they are on the level of the lowest brutes and are in a sense opposed to God and to nature, and consequently ought to be warred upon and compelled to follow, in this respect, the ways of the rest of mankind. As to brigands and other marauders, it was also a universally accepted rule that they, like pirates, could not enjoy the benefits of the law of nations; and Gentili expresses astonishment at the contrary assertion of Hotman.

6.   International Relations: Freedom of Intercourse, Freedom of the Sea

From the conception of the world as a community of States, autonomous and independent, whose relationships are regularized, whose transactions depend on the indefeasible principle of *societas*, which is itself of the essence of natural law, it follows that, subject to the exercise of territorial sovereignty, both the earth and the seas belong to all. Hence innocent passage over another's territory cannot legitimately be refused, and all have the right to undisturbed maritime navigation, to carry on commercial intercourse in general, to secure shelter in foreign ports, and to enjoy the right of market. To deny such natural rights without good and sufficient cause is a violation of the fundamental principle of *societas*, and consequently is not only an unlawful injury to the party directly involved, but is also an offence against human society at large. And for the purpose of vindicating such rights war may be justly declared. That is why, adds Gentili, war was made on the Turks. Their attempt to refuse passage to the Christians, who were proceeding against the Saracens, was unjustifiable.

The question of the right of passage was long one of the great controversies in which opinions were sharply divided and recorded practices opposed to one another. Gentili, following the view of St. Augustine, decides in the affirmative, on the ground first that it is a right conferred by nature, and secondly that the normal condition of mankind is peace and amity, not war and enmity. * * *

STONE, LEGAL CONTROLS OF INTERNATIONAL CONFLICT liii (1954) *

* * * Is there an international law? In what sense, if any, are its rules binding? To whom are such rules (insofar they exist and bind) directed? Can international law be said to be the law of a

* © Julius Stone 1954. Reprinted with   Wm. W. Gaunt & Sons, Inc., Holmes
the permission of Julius Stone and   Beach, Fla.

society or a community? Nor have the new approaches yielded even substantially new answers to the old questions.

John Austin's denial of the *legal* force of international law lacked, no doubt, the temperateness of Professor Corbett or the passionate cynicism of a Lundstedt; but there is little now said that he did not foreshadow a century ago. Today, as centuries ago, those who champion the cause of international law as "law", find its source of validity either in natural law, as did Vitoria and Suàrez, or in positive enactment, as did Gentili and Zouche, or in a mixture of the two as in Grotius. Even Kelsen's reduction of the relations between international law and international society to the identity of *legal order* and *legal community,* while apparently resolving a traditional perplexity into a mere verbal illusion, has proved to be a new evasion rather than a new solution. Its identification of the international legal order with the international legal community is achieved only by excluding from the notion of "society" the very reference to the world of existence which was the essential source of the exorcised perplexity. Nor will the yearning, shared both by modern believers and modern sceptics, for a "real" world community, stir new emotions in students of the classical civitas maxima, since Dante's fourteenth century vision.

No doubt modern thought has exposed, within the classical field, novel shades and directions of interest, and modes of analysis. Yet for the international lawyer, the novelties of feelings, insights, or analysis of empiricist, phenomenologist, existentialist, or neo-Kantian formalist, have only that point which they can contribute to easing his perplexities.

It may be, for instance, of literary interest to assert with Dr. Schwarzenberger the basic role of force in the relations of States. Yet it adds little in itself to Hobbes' proposition that in politics clubs are trumps; or to that implicit in Austin's denial that international law is law. To produce fruitful novelty the notion of power involved must be carried to finer definition and deeper analysis.

So, too, it may be striking that modern theories as opposed in temper as those of Professors Lauterpacht, Lundstedt and Messner converge by different paths on the importance of recognising the role of the individual in international law. But these questions of the "Aye" or "No" of the international status of individuals are in themselves as old as the natural law of a Suàrez or a Grotius: and mere theory is unlikely to advance them further. What theory rather requires is a fuller understanding of the mediating, distorting or obstructing operation of State entities on human relations.

Such fuller new inquiries do not lend themselves to quick answers, nor at all to armchair answers. The need for long and arduous field research within the most inaccessible and dangerously controversial area of human relations is (it is believed) a basic reason for the modern stalemate in juristic thought concerning international law. If such needed inquiries are shunned, then theory is thrown back on such barren questions as whether the actual self-subordination of States to wider international association, functionally limited, warrants the use of the term "community" to describe such an international association. And since the degrees of such self-subordination are potentially infinite in number, ranging from the most transient association on the battlefield by way of a truce for burying the dead, through the intimate organic association (on paper) of a United Nations Organisation, to the intimacy in fact of a successful federation such as that of the United States or the Commonwealth of Australia, such inquiries are as interminable as they are barren.

Insofar, therefore, as we are concerned with a "living" or "operative" international law, with "law in action" as distinct from "the books", the continuance of armchair debate whether international law is "law", will not advance understanding. Nor does it really advance matters to interpret "law in action", as do Dr. Schwarzenberger and others, to mean the law enounced or applied by tribunals or competent State organs, as distinct from the writings of publicists. So far as concerns the effects of international law *on men,* and *of men on law,* the law of tribunals and State organs may still be "law in the books" rather than "law in action". Nor has Professor Corbett's search for international "law in action", despite its courage and vigour, really faced the preliminary question, what "international law in action" may mean. It is, in the present view, impossible to study "law in action" without relating the law not merely to the supposed interests and conduct of States, but also (and above all) to those of the men and women of particular times and places. And if this be so, then it becomes apparent that the task of assessing the effect on human interests and human conduct of the interposition of State entities between the great aggregations of mankind, is an inescapable preliminary.

Judge Alvarez's and Professor Northrop's calls for an international law based respectively on the "psychology of peoples" or on reconciled national cultures, which have committed the "international" aspect of their lives to international law, do, indeed, show a commendable tendency to transcend the traditional framework of inter-State relations. But despite their earnest efforts, the "psychological" or "inter-cultural" frameworks which they would respectively substitute are still but remotely related to the actual inter-play of State and human claims and conduct. Only because of that remoteness could such theories fail to take account of the grave crisis in human communications (already examined) between populations variously conditioned in the insulated chambers of the several States. That failure is, indeed, understandable in another sense, for the difficulties of taking account of it become almost beyond contemplation when we remember that the relation between each State and its citizens has unique features, forbidding easy generalisation. Yet, the fact remains that it is probably from here that the explanation is to be sought for the stubborn political frustration of the technological drive towards an integrated world community.

It is at least probable, that the magic circle of the unsolved classical problems will not be broken until we cease to assume that the categories, conceptions, and methods of municipal law are sufficient, or even necessarily relevant, either for testing the validity of international law or for understanding its actual operation. Certainly our plight seems to cry out for insights which the classical problems, even when clothed in twentieth century philosophical garb, fail to yield. Such an escape from the classical magic circle might also release intellectual energy for tasks more fruitful than those which now engage them.

KELSEN, THE PURE THEORY OF LAW

51 Law Quarterly Review 517 (1935).*

28. The law, or the legal order, is a system of legal norms. The first question we have to answer, therefore, is this: What constitutes the unity in diversity of legal norms? Why does a particular legal norm belong to a particular legal order? A multiplicity of norms constitutes a unity, a system, an order, when validity can be traced back to its final source in a single norm. This basic norm constitutes the unity in diversity of all the norms which make up the system. That a norm belongs to a particular order is only to be determined by tracing back its validity to the basic norm constituting the order. According to the nature of the basic norm, i. e. the sovereign principle of validity, we may distinguish two different kinds of orders, or normative systems. In the first such system the norms are valid by virtue of their content, which has a directly evident quality compelling recognition. *   *   *

29. With legal norms the case is different. These are not valid by virtue of their content. Any content whatsoever can be legal; there is no human behaviour which could not function as the content of a legal norm. A norm becomes a legal norm only because it has been constituted in a particular fashion, born of a definite procedure and a definite rule. Law is valid only as positive law, that is, statute (constituted) law. Therefore the basic norm of law can only be the fundamental rule, according to which the legal norms are to be produced; it is the fundamental condition of law-making. The individual norms of the legal system are not to be derived from the basic norm by a process of logical deduction. They must be constituted by an act of will, not deduced by an act of thought. If we trace back a single legal norm to its source in the basic norm, we do so by showing that the procedure by which it was set up conformed to the requirements of the basic norm. Thus, if we ask why a particular act

* Reprinted with the permission of Stevens & Sons, Ltd., London.

of compulsion—the fact, for instance, that one man has deprived another of his freedom by imprisoning him—is an act of law and belongs to a particular legal order, the answer is, that this act was prescribed by a certain individual norm, a judicial decision. If we ask, further, why this individual norm is valid, the answer is, that it was constituted according to the penal statute book. If we inquire as to the validity of the penal statute book, we are confronted by the State's constitution, which has prescribed rules and procedure for the creation of the penal statute book by a competent authority. If, further, we ask as to the validity of the constitution, on which repose all the laws and the acts which they have sanctioned, we come probably to a still older constitution and finally to an historically original one, set up by some single usurper or by some kind of corporate body. It is the fundamental presupposition of our recognition of the legal order founded on this constitution that that which the original authors declared to be their will should be regarded as valid norm. Compulsion is to be exercised according to the method and conditions prescribed by the first constitutional authority, or its delegated power. This is the schematic formulation of the basic norm of a legal order.

30.   The Pure Theory of Law operates with this basic norm as with an hypothesis. Presupposed that it is valid, then the legal order which rests on it is valid also. Only under this presupposition can we systematize as law (i. e. arrange as a system of norms) the empirical material which presents itself for legal recognition. On the composition of this material (acts) will depend also the particular content of the basic norm. This norm is only an expression for the necessary presupposition of all positivistic constructions of legal material. In formulating the basic norm, the Pure Theory of Law in no way considers itself as inaugurating a new scientific method of jurisprudence. It is only trying to make conscious in the minds of jurists what they are doing when, in seeking to understand their subject, they reject a validity founded on natural law, yet affirm the positive law, not as a mere factual assembly of motives, but as a valid order, as Norm. With the theory of the basic norm, the Pure Theory of Law is only trying to elucidate, by an analysis of the actual procedure, the transcendental-logical conditions of the historic methods of positive legal knowledge.

31.   Just as the nature of law, and of the community which it constitutes, stands most clearly revealed when its very existence is threatened, so the significance of the basic norm emerges most clearly when the legal order undergoes not legal change, but revolution or substitution. In an hitherto monarchic State a number of men attempt to overthrow by force the legitimate monarchic government and to set up a republican form in its place. If in this they are successful, if, that is, the old government ceases and the new begins to be effective, in that the behaviour of the men and women, for whom the order claims to be valid, conforms in the main no longer to the old but to the new order, then this latter is operated as a legal order, the acts

which it performs are declared legal, the conditions which it proscribes, illegal. A new basic norm is presupposed—no longer that which delegated legislative authority to the monarch, but one which delegates such authority to the revolutionary government. Had the attempt been a failure, had the new order, that is, remained ineffective, in that behaviour did not conform to it, then the acts of the new government become not constitutional but criminal (high treason), not legislation but delict, and this on the ground of the validity of the old order, which presupposed a basic norm delegating legislative power to the monarch.

If we ask what, then, determines the content of the basic norm, we find, on analysing judicial decisions back to their first premiss, the following answer: The content of the basic norm is determined by the condition of fact out of which the order emerges, given that to the order there corresponds, amongst the human beings to whom it refers, a substantial measure of actual behaviour.

This gives us the content of a positive legal norm. (It is not, of course, a norm of a State's legal order, but a norm of international law, which, as a legal order superior to that of the individual States, legally determines their sphere of jurisdiction.) * * *

KELSEN, PRINCIPLES OF INTERNATIONAL LAW 6 (1ST ED. 1952) *

3.   Legal Norm and Rule of Law: The "Ought"

A norm prescribes or permits a certain human behavior. A set of norms which form for some reason or another a unit we call a normative order. The law is a normative order, and since legal norms provide for coercive acts as sanctions, the law is a coercive order.

The statements by which the science of law describes its object, the law, as a system of legal norms are statements to the effect that under certain conditions (among which the delict plays an essential part) a certain consequence, namely a sanction, ought to take place. These statements are called rules of law in contradistinction to legal norms, described by the rules of law. Legal norms are issued by legal authorities, rules of law are statements made by the legal science, which is not a legal authority and hence not competent to issue legal norms prescribing or permitting human behavior.

The connection established by a legal norm between the delict as condition and the sanction as consequence, is not a relation between cause and effect, such as is indicated in the statement: If a metallic body is heated, it expands. This statement is a so-called law of nature. By the laws of nature natural science describes its object, nature, just as legal science describes its object, the law, by rules of law. In the rule of law the connection between condition and consequence is characterized by the term "ought," in order to emphasize that the rule of law has not the meaning of a law of nature. It does not express the idea of a necessary or probable connection between one fact and another. Its meaning is not: if a delict occurs, a sanction will—necessarily or probably—take place; but: if a delict is committed, a sanction ought to be applied, even if it is actually not applied. By the formula "ought to be applied" nothing else is expressed but the idea that if the delict is committed the application of the sanction is legal. The statement that a sanction ought to be applied if a delict has been committed does not necessarily mean that a certain individual is legally obliged to apply a sanction. He may be only authorized to apply the sanction. Whether the application of the sanction provided for by the law is or is not the content of an obligation is a question different from the question as to the meaning of the connection between condition and consequence in the rule of law.

DeVISSCHER, THEORY AND REALITY IN PUBLIC INTERNATIONAL LAW 88, 365 (1957).*

Between the political fact and the law, the philosophers and jurists have always assigned capital importance to a conception of which, to tell the truth, neither group has taken great pains to establish the foundations or define the limits. This conception, more than any other, has led them to hasty conclusions or left them wandering in nebulous speculations. Belief in a community wider and higher than the political units into which men are divided certainly meets a demand of reason. But, though postulated by the law, does this demand correspond to historical reality? Or is it only an aspiration still too ill defined and too limited in its incidence to impose the idea of law and to find embodiment in institutions?

The classical doctrine of the law of nations rests on the postulate of an international society which orders and subordinates sovereignties for the common good of humanity. Such an image, as a social datum, can however be confirmed only by the habitual methods of observing and tabulating experience. Between political organizations historically constructed on foundations of national individualism, on the one side, and on the other an idea of order which presents itself as the ideal synthesis of human solidarities, thought, stimulated by moral aspirations and by a need for unity, can conceive a scale of values arranged in a desirable hierarchy. It cannot from a postulated harmony proceed to the conclusion of a social community. As for taking this as achieved because it would be socially good to have it so, this is a type of argument which, though common in displays of oratory, is nonetheless devoid of scientific value. Of these reasonings, as of all those built upon the primacy of the Civitas Maxima or the

* Translated by P. E. Corbett (copyright ⓒ 1957 by Princeton University Press). Reprinted with the permission of the translator and the Princeton University Press.

rationally necessary interdependence of society and law, it may be said that they take as proven precisely what requires proof: namely the existence of a sense of community and the willingness of particular collectivities to keep their conduct in conformity with the higher good of a universal community.

Every society rests at once upon material and upon moral factors. It is the resultant of solidarities active enough to call for an organization of power and sufficiently conscious of a common good to engender the idea of law and the sense of obligation.

* * *

The hour is not one for doctrinal generalizations moving in the rhythm of a transcendental logic, or for brilliant systematizations in which intellectual ingenuity often counts for more than respect for the facts. It is rather one that challenges us to recognize the limits which in our day the dependence of international law on the historical forms of power distribution sets to its effectiveness, and to seek in the human ends of power the moderating principle that may develop aspirations to international collaboration. Every renewed recognition of the foundations of power stimulates a renewal of values; every return to the realities holds promise of effectiveness.

In the same spirit, the individualistic distribution of power among nations has appeared to us to be, if not the sole, at least the primary cause of the present deficiencies of international law. In fact, every attempt to organize international relations is an attempt to redistribute power, and there can be no doubt that this is the way of progress. Some forms of federalism can certainly provide the framework. But among these attempts it is essential to distinguish those for which a spontaneous process of integration ensures a firm foundation and a mission of order and peace from those which owe their inspiration to a political conjuncture or simply to deductions of the systematizing spirit. Federalism, as a new form of power distribution in international relations, must reckon with the social laws that govern all transformations of power. It must reckon with time, which has no respect for what is done without its aid. No more than any other mode of organization has it any value in itself. Partial federations, especially those which it is proposed to create from the ground up, in the very heart of a generalized political tension, without adequate spiritual affinities or independent economic and military resources, are liable to be nothing more than instruments of the antagonisms that divide the peoples.

A redistribution of power has no moral and universal significance save in the safeguards that it offers to order and peace. To be a force for order in a system of peace, it must proceed from solidarities profoundly enough felt to generate new disciplines. It must above all be inspired by ends broader and higher than those which have traditionally guided the political action of national sovereignties.

FRIEDMANN, THE REALITY OF INTERNATIONAL
LAW—A REAPPRAISAL

10 Columbia Journal of Transnational Law 46, 47 (1971).*

A second approach, far more prevalent in the theory and practice of contemporary states, is that of limited respect for the "live and let live" rules of international law as an appropriate guide to the conduct of nations, subject to the overriding national interests of states. The most articulate contemporary proponent of this view is former Secretary of State Dean Acheson who, in a debate on the rights and wrongs of the Cuban missile crisis of October 1962, asserted that matters of national survival were entirely beyond the reach of international law. This view has been expressed and applied, with varying degrees or emphasis, by most statesmen of our time, among whom are President Kennedy, Premier Khrushchev and Chancellor Adenauer. It is certainly held by the present leaders of Israel, a state which has since its birth in 1948 constantly fought for its survival among hostile neighbors and which has since 1967 openly asserted the paramountcy of what it considers to be conditions of survival over rules of international law, including resolutions passed by the United Nations.

We may consider as an extension of this doctrine of the paramountcy of national interest the now increasingly important assertion of hegemonical spheres of influence of certain major powers. The most important and open assertion of such a hegemonical claim is the statement made by President Johnson in May of 1965 that the United States could not and would not tolerate another communist government in the Western Hemisphere. An even more blatant application of this doctrine of hegemonical supremacy was the military occupation of Czechoslovakia by its ally, the Soviet Union, in August 1968, because of the alleged deviation of the incumbent Government of Czechoslovakia from socialism. In both cases the paramount power not only itself defined the nature and seriousness of the deviation, but it also presumed to act on behalf of other states—in the case of the Dominican intervention, the American states, and in the case of the occupation of Czechoslovakia, the "fraternal" countries of the East European bloc.

The extent to which mutual acquiescence by the great powers in the paramount spheres of influence of another great power (notwithstanding the many specific assertions of "sovereign equality" in the United Nations Charter and in successive resolutions of the United Nations) has become part of an emerging international law, superimposed upon and perhaps displacing the customary law of nations, has been the subject of some debate. This debate has continued since the Soviet intervention in Hungary and the Cuban missile crisis. It has been suggested that the precarious understanding between the United States and the Soviet Union not to interfere in each other's

* Reprinted by permission of the Columbia Journal of Transnational Law.

"sphere of influence" may point towards the development of a new theory of international obligation, taking its place beside the established sources of international law. It is part of the contemporary doctrine of international law that there is an increasing variety of international law sources of unequal strength and that the principal traditional sources, custom and treaty, are now widely held to have been supplemented by declaratory resolutions of the United Nations. Nevertheless, it is impossible to reconcile both the negative aspect of hegemonical reciprocity, i. e., forbearance to intervene in the actions of another power within its accepted sphere of influence, and the positive aspects, i. e., the claim of a superpower to intervene unilaterally in the affairs of a more or less determined number of "sovereign" states, with the basic structure of international law.

If accepted or acquiesced in, it clearly indicates the emergence of two types of international legal order: one prevailing for the great majority of states, and based upon the theory of "sovereign equality" of all states, big or small, and another ensuring certain unilateral privileges and powers of intervention to a small number of superpowers. Ultimately, one or the other must prevail. Some contemporary developments, notably the increasing importance of the combination of capital power and advanced technology exemplified in the exploration of the seabed and of outer space, point toward the increasing supremacy of a small number of powers, possibly ending in the Orwellian world of 1984.

A third approach is sometimes intermingled with the second. We may term it the use of international law as rhetorical argument. The open assertion of the supremacy of national interest over the restraints of international law, or of hegemonical power, is disguised by patently spurious legal justification. From the perspective of the "reality" of international law, the only comfort in this approach lies in the fact that the actor state deems it necessary to seek to justify its action in terms of international law. * * *

     * * *

The three approaches mentioned above all imply, to a greater or lesser degree, the subordination of the restraints imposed by the norms of international law to freedom of national action. A fourth and opposed approach is a genuine belief in the supremacy of international legal order over national sovereignty. Lip service paid to this philosophy far exceeds its application in contemporary affairs. The ideal of supremacy of international over national law, at least in the application of force, was a basic conception of both the League of Nations Covenant and the United Nations Charter. It was believed in by the principal intellectual godfather of the League of Nations, President Wilson, even though he failed to persuade his own country to join that organization. A number of twentieth century statesmen, such as Britain's Sir Robert Cecil and France's Aristide Briand, may be counted among the supporters of this conception. Among its theoretical supporters we may count such authorities as the late Sir Hersch Lauterpacht, particularly in his earlier work, or the well-known treatise of Clark and Sohn, World Peace through World Law. The great majority of not only statesmen, politicians and ordinary laymen, but also of the theorists of international law, either reject this approach or accept it only with major reservations. It is therefore particularly important to underline that, in the contemporary setting, the postulate of the supremacy of international over national law may be based on two different kinds of motivation: either the ideal of the brotherhood of all men, an essentially religious or humanistic ideology; or the gradual subordination of national to international legal authority as a matter of self-interest and survival. It is this latter approach that is gaining increasing importance in the light of contemporary developments, and to which we will devote some observations later in this article.

1 O'CONNELL, INTERNATIONAL LAW 38 (2D ED. 1970) *

The Theory of the Relationship: Monism and Dualism

Almost every case in a municipal court in which a rule of international law is asserted to govern the decision raises the problem of the relationship of international law and municipal law; and in many cases before international tribunals it must also be disposed of when deciding the jurisdictional competence of a State to affect alien interests through its own internal legal order.

There are four possible attitudes towards the question:

(a) That international law has primacy over municipal law in both international and municipal decisions. This is the *monist* theory.

(b) That international law has primacy over municipal law in international decisions, and municipal law has primacy over international law in municipal decisions. This is the *dualist* theory.

(c) That municipal law has primacy over international law in both international and municipal decisions. This is a species of monism in reverse.

(d) That there should be no supposition of conflict between international law and municipal law.

Each of these four attitudes will be examined in turn.

(a) Monism

The monist position is an emanation of Kantian philosophy which favours a unitary conception of law. According to this view, since the capacities of States derive from the idea of law, the jurisdiction to exercise these capacities is granted by the law. It follows that the law to which jurisdictional reference must be made is independent of sovereignty and determinative of its limits. If a State exceeds the

* Reprinted with the permission of O'Connell and Stevens & Sons, Ltd., London.

limits, its acts are invalid. This argument concedes to international law a broader and more fundamental competence than to municipal law. However, it tends to sidestep the point made by the dualists, namely, that a municipal court may be instructed to apply municipal law and not international law, and hence has no jurisdiction (using the term as descriptive of the capacity in municipal law to decide a case) to declare the relevant municipal law invalid. Hence, the characterisation of the jurisdictional excess as "invalid," or even merely "illegal" (if there is any difference between the terms), is of no meaning internally within the municipal law of the acting State. To this objection, the monist has only one answer, that this conflict of duties, owing to a defect in organisation, has been wrongly resolved.

* * *

(b) Dualism

The dualist position is associated with Hegelianism and has governed the judicial attitudes of States where this philosophy has prevailed. The common starting point is the proposition that law is an act of sovereign will, municipal law being differentiated from international law in that it is a manifestation of this will internally directed, as distinct from participation in a collective act of will by which the sovereign undertakes obligations with respect to other sovereigns. This results in a dualism of legal origin, of subjects and of subject matters. International law and municipal law are two quite different spheres of legal action, and theoretically there should be no point of conflict between them. Municipal law addresses itself to the subjects of sovereigns, international law to the sovereigns themselves. If the sovereign by an act of municipal law exceeds his competence in international law it does not follow that municipal law is void; it merely follows that the sovereign has violated international law. Anzilotti has explained the relationship between the dualist thesis and the alleged incapacity of the individual in international law as follows:

> A rule of international law is by its very nature absolutely unable to bind individuals, i. e., to confer upon them rights and duties. It is created by the collective will of States with the view of regulating their mutual relations; obviously it cannot therefore refer to an altogether different sphere of relations. If several States were to attempt the creation of rules regulating private relations, such an attempt, by the very nature of things, would not be a rule of international law, but a rule of uniform municipal law common to several States.

(c) Inverted monism

The theory that municipal law is in its nature superior to international law has never found favour in international tribunals, and is no more than an abstract possibility. It is associated with Bergbohm, whose almost pathological resentment against natural law led to an exaggerated emphasis on the State will. Unlike Austin, who would deny even the term "law" to international law and thereby avoid a potential collision of two systems, Bergbohm allows for international law as a manifestation of the "auto limitation" of the sovereign will. The State is superior to and antecedent to the international community, and remains the only law-making entity. Unlike Triepel, who would distinguish the State will as internally manifested from the State will as externally manifested, Bergbohm allows for only one manifestation, and international law is thus a derivation from municipal law.

(d) The theory of harmonisation

According to this view, neither the monist nor the dualist position can be accepted as sound. Each attempts to provide an answer, derived from a single theoretical premise, to two quite different questions. The first question is whether international law is "law" in the same sense as municipal law, i. e., whether both systems are concordant expressions of a unique metaphysical reality. The second question is whether a given tribunal is required by its constitution to apply a rule of international law or municipal law, or vice versa, or authorised to accord primacy to the one over the other. The resemblance between the two questions is only apparent; the lack of jurisdiction in a given tribunal to accord primacy to international law in the event of a conflict between it and municipal law has no relevance to the question whether municipal law does or does not derive its competence from the same basic juridical reality as international law. In some federal systems of law, a State court may be required to apply state legislation which a federal court would declare unconstitutional. The norms of reference are different but the systems are concordant.

The starting point in any legal order is man himself, considered in relation to his fellow man. Law, it has often been said, is life, and life is law. The individual does not live his life exclusively in the legal order of the State any more than he lives it exclusively in the international order. He falls within both jurisdictions because his life is lived in both. Here again, the comparison with a federal system is instructive. It follows that a monistic solution to the problem of the relationship of international law and municipal law fails because it would treat the one system as a derivation of the other, ignoring the physical, metaphysical and social realities which in fact detach them. The world has not yet reached that state of organisation where there is only one civitas maxima delegating specific jurisdiction to regional administrations.

But a dualist solution is equally deficient because it ignores the all-prevailing reality of the universum of human experience. States are the formal instruments of will for the crystallisation of law, but the impulse to the law derives from human behaviour and has a human goal. Positive international law is not pure whim, but an expression of needs and convictions. If it were otherwise, international law and municipal law would be competitive regimes ill-suited to the solution of human problems. The correct position is that international law and municipal law are concordant bodies of doctrine, each autonomous in the sense that it is directed to a specific, and, to some extent, an exclusive area of human conduct, but harmonious in that in their totality the several rules aim at a basic human good.

1 O'CONNELL, INTERNATIONAL LAW 21 (2D ED. 1970) *

It is incorrect to speak of treaties as "sources" of international law. They are no more than contracts between the parties, and their significance as legal acts derives from the existence of rules of customary law by which their validity and their binding quality is determined, and according to which they are interpreted. In discussing the formation of international law, however, treaties are not without significance. They might be either evidence of a customary rule or the stimulus to one. This led Bluntschli, following Bergbohm, to distinguish treaties which are mere contracts from "law-making" treaties. The distinction is inapt because it can never be the treaty which makes law, but a custom which adopts the treaty as the rule of law.

* * *

* * * [T]he role of the multilateral treaty in the making of customary law is not to be underestimated. The moral persuasiveness of the rules, and the political pressure underlying their acceptance, may be such that their translation from conventional to customary law is immediate, or almost so. The suitability of the rules for general recognition in the existing stage of legal development is the vital point in determining whether the translation has actually occurred. The Kellogg-Briand Pact of Paris, 1928, which contained a renunciation of war as an instrument of policy was treated by the War Crimes Tribunals as laying down a rule of international law concerning the illegality of aggressive war. The provisions of the United Nations Charter, which permit of organisational action even with respect to non-members, and certain of the provisions of the Statute of the International Court of Justice, have this dynamic effect on the making of law.

Obviously the more States subscribe to a treaty, and the more its provisions reflect the juridical conscience of mankind, the more will it be a stimulus to the creation of law. * * *

OLIVER, CONTEMPORARY PROBLEMS OF TREATY LAW

88 Recueil des Cours, Hague Academy of International Law
421, 422, 433 (1955).

Traditional international law is, tragically at a very low level of effective application in today's world, and its development along traditional lines is not currently promising. For most areas develop-

---

* Reprinted with the permission of O'Connell and Stevens & Sons, Ltd., London.

ment through codification has not come, despite dedicated and scholarly efforts over the years. The settlement of international disputes through the effective utilization of the judicial process has actually lost ground. Meanwhile, legal scholarship has tended more and more to detach itself from reality by (a) excluding from legal science the whole activity of relative valuation; or (b) by devoting meticulous attention to the study of a customary international public law which actually has developed very little, or (c) by claiming for legal methods a degree of effectiveness which legal institutions and the men of the law actually cannot supply.

While these discouraging things have been happening something else has been taking place: I suggest that the real international law of the present, and possibly of the very considerable future, may, * * * be found relatively unnoticed in the underbrush of international agreements, of foreign office practice, of national judicial and administrative actions, and of the ways of life of international organizations.

* * *

Although scholars in international law do not always face up to them, the facts are that international law grows mainly by international agreements; that international law is put into effect principally by foreign offices and by national courts, rather than by international tribunals; and that treaties very seldom, in contemporary times, at least, find their enforcement through international judicial organs.

Under this condition of international society it seems clear that national inhibitions on the negotiation of international agreements and national disinclinations to enforce treaties through municipal tribunals would have very direct and important effects, not only on the conduct of foreign relations, but also upon the viability of international law itself.

KAPLAN AND KATZENBACH, THE POLITICAL FOUNDATIONS OF INTERNATIONAL LAW 5 (1961) *

No one can observe the international political system without being aware of the fact that order does exist, and that this order is related in important ways to formal and authoritative rules, that is, to a body of law and to a process of law-government. These rules are sustained by the genuine interests which nations have in restraining certain forms of international conduct, even though these constraints must apply to their own conduct as well as to that of other states. To understand the substance and limits of such constraining rules, it is necessary to examine the interests which support them in the international system, the means by which they are made effective, and the functions they perform. Only in this way is it possible to predict the areas in which rules operate, the limits of rules as effective constraints, and the factors which underlie normative change. * * *

International Law as "Law"

Sometimes international law is viewed as a rather strange breed of law to which the term "law" is applied only by courtesy if at all. A number of great legal philosophers—Hobbes, Pufendorf, Bentham, and Austin are examples—have all doubted the legal character of international law, and the charges and counter charges which pervade the international community today seem to provide empirical support for their view. Clearly some definitions of law would exclude international law. Disputes, for example, are not routinely decided by an international judiciary, and there exists no coercive agency of formal international status which can effectively enforce the law. Rules do not emanate from any single "sovereign." Indeed, the legal order is not primarily vertical, or hierarchical, as it normally is in domestic government. Rather it is structured horizontally, composed predominantly of formally equal centers of legal authority called "states." We have only the beginnings of supranational authority in the United Nations and in various regional organizations.

It is possible, of course, to define law in such a way as to require a hierarchical structure. Austin did this in his theory that rules become authoritative and binding because they are sovereign commands. If law is defined in this way, then it is accurate to say that there is little in the international community.

          * * *

Now, in spite of the differences in terminology and the fact that a critic may get considerable political mileage from invoking the accusation that international law has been flaunted, processes in the international and domestic arenas are in some respects comparable. The particular decision disposes of the case and enters into the body of available precedent, whether that decision is persuasive or not. The focus of critical attention is to undercut its status as a norm to be invoked by others in similar circumstances, and it is to this end that some continue to call it a violation of international law. The more arbitrary it can be made to appear, the more radical the innovation, the more it can be related to selfish objectives of a particular state, and the more it offends widely shared and deeply felt values, the less persuasive it will be as precedent for others.

We cannot ignore the fact that in this process the same official may combine legislative and adjudicative functions, with emphasis, indeed, upon the former. Although national officials talk as if they were concerned only with what the law is, they are in fact equally concerned with promoting rules for the future which support policies they favor. The range of legislative creativity is limited by the interstitial nature of disputes, by the need to state principles that are widely acceptable and that are unobjectionable if invoked by others in like circumstances, and by the political cost of too flagrant a disregard of the expectations of other states based on past practices. In the absence of developed supranational legislative institutions, rules are prescribed, amended, adjusted, and applied by a time-consuming process of agreement or by unilateral state decisions. As a result rules are often quite fluid until formalized in treaties, and are subjected to political strain in their interpretation and application. Considerations of policy, customarily denominated "political," which would be largely irrelevant in predicting decision by a domestic court because clearly beyond its function, may well be relevant, often controlling, when we examine invocations of law in the international process.

But to say this is not to concede the naive criticisms which plague intelligent discussion about international law. Often it is said that since a state may decide for itself what constitutes international law, how it should be interpreted, and how it should be applied to a fact situation, it can decide cases arbitrarily. Obviously this argument is but a rephrasing of the thought that an independent judiciary is essential to impartial decision, and, hence, to law. If this argument is meant to imply that states do in fact act without regard to international prescriptions, it is descriptively inaccurate. If it implies that they are "free" to do so, it is wrong on both theoretical and practical grounds. If it implies that upon occasion, and particularly in times of crisis, states act without regard to what is generally accepted as controlling doctrine, it is quite right.

This argument is close cousin to the old saw that the Constitution means what the Supreme Court says it means—a formulation that, without qualification, would imply judicial autocracy. It ignores the institutional framework in which the Supreme Court sits, works, and decides. Similarly, each state has a stake in preserving the general structure of international law—the existence of a system of order effected through compliance with recognized norms—even though particular norms may be distasteful to a particular state. Each state will seek to influence and change those norms which it dislikes, since there is always temptation to evade adverse consequences in particular fact situations. However, the general interest in preserving the system is a force both for self-limitation as a means of inducing others to a similar response, and for the use of a variety of political pressures when others overstep the bounds of what is tolerable. Quite a bit has to be at stake, and a state has to be quite sure of its ability to "get away with it," before it will overtly violate norms which are generally accepted. Radical innovation which offends other decision makers may be worth it, but such innovations have political costs as well as profits.

Another appeal of the enforcement argument relates to the uncertainty, or flexibility, of the legal norms themselves, and to the degree to which different formulations and applications legitimately can be put forward. As we have noted, debate (in the absence of adjudication by an impartial judiciary) tends to be carried on in terms of accusations about non-compliance with the law. If, of course, one accepts as correct one's own formulation, that rule, so interpreted and applied, is not always adhered to by others. This fact creates the illusion of either no law or no enforcement of the law. A limited choice of rules and a limited discretion in their interpretation is, however, a far cry from no rules at all. Most of us would like to have the rule as we interpret and apply it enforced internationally, though we might be more sceptical of a norm formulated and enforced by others. Few of our domestic political leaders are enthusiasts for world government, though they are loud critics of weak international law enforcement.

Doubts about a law-system which lacks judge and sheriff have, we think misleadingly, been frequently expressed as a theory of international law which describes it as a "voluntary" system based on the "consent" of "sovereign" states. It does not require much insight into law-politics to see a parallel between this theory and the consent theory of domestic government. Whatever the moral appeal of the consent theory at both levels (it represents a dislike for coercion), states "consent" to international prescriptions in the same sense that individuals "consent" to existing laws. They recognize the general need for a system of order, they regard the bulk of existing regulation as either desirable or at least tolerable, and they accept what remains because they have to—because they lack the ability to change it. The more intolerable a regulation is, the more pressure there is to seek a change by any means possible.

The point is not, of course, that legal institutions in the international community are adequate to contemporary affairs. Obviously they are not. But these institutions, such as they are, exist and contribute to international order. They will continue until some political combination has the capability to create new institutions more consonant with order and, we can at least hope, with a decent regard for human values. This creative process is presently taking place, on both a universal scale (the United Nations complex) and, perhaps more successfully, in a variety of regional and functional organizations such as NATO and the European Communities.

The authors recognize the merits of criticisms that distinguished observers such as George Kennan have made regarding too great a reliance upon legal processes. American foreign policy has often been formulated without sufficient attention to the role of force and of national interests. We do not wish to encourage naiveté of the sort he describes as "legal idealism," a reliance upon abstract rules that are institutionally unsupported. We concede that nations often do act in partisan ways in support of immediate political objectives. But we contend that much of international conduct is doctrinally consonant with normative standards, even though inconsistent with particular immediate interests, and that long-term self-interest can and does provide political support for internationally lawful conduct.

TUNKIN, FORTY YEARS OF CO–EXISTENCE AND INTERNATIONAL LAW

Soviet Yearbook of International Law 1958, at 42 (Moscow, 1959).

Bourgeois jurisprudence usually regards agreement between states as the result of the "concurrence of wills" of these states, expressing their "common will".

But applied to contemporary general international law this concept is invalid. Agreement, as a form of creating rules of contemporary international law, is the result of the coordination of wills of different states, which in fact are the wills of their ruling classes (in a socialist country the will of the people).

Coordination of wills of states refers both to the contents of a particular rule and to its recognition as a rule of international law.

This coordination of wills of the states in the process of creating a norm of general international law does not signify their merging into some kind of "common will" or "single will". These wills cannot fuse because their class natures, expressed in the aims and tasks of the states concerned, are different and even contradictory (the wills of socialist and capitalist states), they are, however, coordinated and aimed at establishing a definite rule as a norm of law. A norm of general international law is an expression not of a "single will", but of "coordinated wills", i. e., wills equally directed towards a definite aim-recognition of the given rule as a norm of international law.

Agreement presupposes that the wills of states are not only "coordinated" in relation to recognition of the given rule, but are also mutually conditioned. Agreement between states includes "interconditionality" of wills, the substance of which is that the assent of one state to recognize a particular rule as a norm of international law is conditional on analogous assent by the other state. "Interconditionality" is the thread which links the wills of different states in the process of shaping or extending the sphere of operation of a norm of international law.

The norms of general international law, then, express the "coordinated and mutually conditioned wills" of the states belonging to two co-existing social systems.

General international law reflects not only community of interests, as claimed by bourgeois international lawyers, but also the contradictions between them; not only co-operation, but also a struggle. The less, therefore, can we, in contemporary conditions, regard agreement which is a method of establishing norms of general international law, as an expression of ideological identity of the countries of the two systems.

Norms of contemporary general international law, developing in conditions of co-existence of states belonging to two diametrically different economic systems, cannot be socialist, since agreement on this basis is impossible between the socialist and the capitalist countries. The generally accepted rules are aimed at realizing the democratic aims of regulating relations between states in the interests of ensuring world peace and furthering relations between them on the basis of mutual benefit and equality.

From what has been said it would be possible to define contemporary general international law as the aggregate of rules created by agreement between states, regulating their relations in the process of struggle and co-operation in the direction of ensuring peaceful co-existence, expressing the wills of the ruling classes of these states; the compliance with these norms being ensured, whenever necessary, by the states applying enforcement measures individually or collectively.

Marxist-Leninist theory shows that law does not arise as a result of the identity of human nature, ideology, etc., that it arose historically as a result of the division of society into classes and the appearance of irreconcilable class contradictions. The point made by many bourgeois scholars that without some kind of identity between people law in general and international law in particular would be impossible, is simply a generality and explains nothing, signifying merely that without a definite identity between people human society and, of course, law, would be impossible.

International law, like national law, is a product of class society. Its explanation and its basis should be sought not in "human nature", in the idea of justice, and so on. Its general character as a category of the superstructure is determined by the economic structure of society, by the laws of its development. One should bear in mind, of course, that the influence of these laws, determining the basic features of international law, passes through a complex pattern of other influences. Marxist-Leninist theory takes life in all its complexity.

The economic structure determines the main features of the superstructure in general and of international law as a part of the superstructure in particular. But international law is influenced also by the other parts of the superstructure, politics, national law, philosophy, morals, etc. Here we have a complicated interplay of varying phenomena in which international law, being subjected to the influence of the economic structure and of the other parts of the superstructure, itself influences these other parts of the superstructure and the economic structure of society.

* * *

The rules of international law being borne in the process of struggle and co-operation between states, are the result of the clash and co-ordination of the wills of the ruling classes of different states. They are created by sovereign states. The wills of the ruling classes in the different countries, which clash in the process of creating these rules, are juridically equal. But it goes without saying that in moulding international law the actual influence exerted by these wills is not at all identical. It depends on the rôle played by the particular state in international relations and on the nature of the principles which it advances. Contemporary international law develops under the ever-growing influence of the socialist states and the other states pursuing the policy of peaceful co-existence in international relations, under the influence exerted by all the forces of peace.

* * *

As a result of the struggle waged by all the progressive forces, and primarily by the Soviet Union and the other socialist states, there have arisen in international law such important universally recognized principles as the principle of prohibition of the use of force in international relations (the principle of non-aggression), the principle of self-determination of nations, non-interference in internal affairs, equality, and others.

At the same time we see the continued development and strengthening of the old democratic principles and rules: respect for state sovereignty, non-interference in internal affairs, equality, and others.

The process of establishing new progressive principles and norms of international law is continuing. Vital significance should be attached to the formation of international-law rules concerning reduction of armaments and banning atomic and hydrogen weapons—use of which should be recognized as contrary to law in view of the generally recognized principles of international law—the efforts to secure a generally recognized definition of aggression, universal recognition of the rules banning war propaganda, etc.

* * *

However, since contemporary general international law is the aggregate of rules created by agreement between the states of the two systems it can be used as an instrument of one foreign policy of these states. The rules of international law express the coordinated wills of the ruling classes of states and are instruments of their policy.

This, of course, does not mean that international law can be an instrument of any policy. Its rules can be used as an instrument of the policy only in the framework of the contents of these norms, i. e., in the framework of agreement between states, which have brought those norms into being.

The "positions-of-strength" policy pursued by the imperialist powers, and the "cold war" which is the outcome of this policy, have, undoubtedly, diminished the rôle of international law in international relations since the end of the Second World War.

In these circumstances, we find in bourgeois international-law literature nowadays not a few pessimistic assessments concerning the importance of international law in international relations.

Particularly widespread at present in bourgeois international-law literature is the view that international law in its present state is embryonic, primitive law, and that only the establishment of a "world state" or the greatest possible approximation to it can make international law "real" law.

Were we to accept this view the prospects for international law would be gloomy indeed, since the idea of establishing a "world state", a "world government", and so on, as things are today, is not realistic—it is out of tune with the laws of social development in our times.

Concepts of world government in present conditions are not only utopian, they are reactionary. From these concepts it is but a step to affirming the hopelessness of any attempt to consolidate and develop general international law, to recognition of the rule of force in international relations.

Enhancing the rôle of international law in ensuring peaceful co-existence should be sought not by establishing a world state and abolishing the state sovereignty of the countries, by creating a new international law, etc., but primarily by consolidating, developing and consistently observing the generally accepted principles and norms of the international law now in operation, which to a large degree is inscribed in the Charter of the United Nations.

The basic condition for the effectiveness of contemporary general international law is a recognition by all states of the situation when capitalist and socialist states exist side by side, and rejection of any attempt to change this situation by force. Contemporary general international law, which regulates interstate relations for the purpose of ensuring peaceful cooperation between them is, by virtue of this, objectively aimed against the policy of force and against arbitrary international action. And precisely for this peace-loving forces have every opportunity to use general international law in the struggle for peace.

McDOUGAL, INTERNATIONAL LAW, POWER AND POLICY: A CONTEMPORARY CONCEPTION

Academie de Droit International, 82 Recueil des Cours 137 (1953).

The Tasks of a Policy-Oriented Jurisprudence (Philosophy-Science of Law) in Our Time

* * *

2. The great challenge to students of international law today, in this context of world social and power processes and growing threat to freedom, is, * * * to extend their aspirations beyond tra-

ditional exercises in technical formulae for determining what conduct is lawful and what unlawful to the much more urgent task of determining and recommending that international law, of the many possible systems of international law, which is best designed to promote a free world society. The dilemma that confronts us in the world today offers alternatives not so much between non-law, or naked force, and law, as between different kinds of law, a law promoting human indignity or a law promoting human dignity. In this dilemma, it is the over-riding moral responsibility of legal scholars, as the appropriate skilled specialists of society, to identify or invent and to recommend the prescriptions, organizations, and decisions that favor a law of human dignity.

To meet this challenge legal scholars will require a comprehensive guiding theory and intellectual techniques adequate to perform certain specific functions. These functions the author and a colleague have elsewhere characterized as the elements of a "policy-oriented" approach to the study of law. We emphasize policy purposes because we do not believe that a jurisprudence which purports to be "scientific" only is adequate to the crisis of our time. Though it is imperative that a scholar should seek to minimize the degree to which his preferences distort the accuracy of his observation of events, a creative jurisprudence requires not only the ways of thinking and procedures of observation commonly called scientific but also other integrated and interrelated methods of thought and observation. In briefest summary, the various functions indispensable to a policy-oriented approach to the study of international law and to the choice of an international law appropriate to a free world society may be indicated as follows:

(1) The clarification of goal values and the detailed relation of the flow of particular decisions that constitute the world power process to such goal values.

(2) The description of trends in decision, in terms of effects upon values, and the identification in the greatest degree possible of the variables, predispositional and environmental, that affect particular decisions.

(3) The critical projection of trends into the future, on the basis of historical and scientific knowledge, in attempt to predict what future decisions are likely to be.

(4) The appraisal of decisions in terms of their compatibility with goal values and the invention and evaluation of new alternatives of policy—prescriptions and institutions—designed for the better securing of such goal values.

3. Each of these multiple functions of a creative jurisprudence —preferential, descriptive-scientific, predictive, and inventive—has been a principal focus or objective of varying conceptions of law in the past and each function is today performed, by legal scholars and

others, consciously and unconsciously, with varying degrees of effectiveness. The enduring significance of many of the great classical writers upon international law is due in measure to the effectiveness with which, by a judicious commingling of positivistic and natural law approaches, they were able to perform all these functions for their time. It may be questioned, however, whether our contemporary theory about international law, taken in the large and without disparagement of the many brilliant individual contributions, is adequate to meet the challenge that confronts us.

*   *   *

The Inadequacies of Contemporary Theory About International Law

It is no new thought that contemporary theory about international law exhibits certain deep confusions about its appropriate subject-matter and the relationship of that subject-matter to the social and power processes by which men seek a free, peaceful, and abundant world society. For our immediate purposes these confusions may perhaps be most conveniently outlined in terms of over-emphasis on technical rules, unrelated to policies, as factors in guiding and shaping decisions, of over-emphasis on naked power as a factor in decision, of failure to achieve comprehensive description of the participants in the world power process, and of failure to achieve comprehensive description of the techniques of policy formulation and application employed by such participants. We may consider each of these types of confusion in turn.

I.   Overemphasis on Technical Rules, Unrelated to Policies, as Factors in Guiding and Shaping Decisions

The most fundamental obscurity in contemporary theory about international law secretes itself in over-emphasis, by most writers and many decision-makers, upon the potentialities of technical "legal" rules, unrelated to policies, as factors and instruments in the guiding and shaping of decisions. This over-emphasis begins in the very definition of the subject-matter of international law as a system of rules. Despite many differences, and even internecine fights, as to justifications—in terms of natural law, consent of states, religion, metaphysics, and so on—for particular systems of rules and for particular rules within systems, most observers today agree upon this basic type of definition.

*   *   *

The ambiguity inherent in this type of statement has been characterized by the writer and a colleague as "normative-ambiguity".

*   *   *

For demonstration with respect to customary rules we offer in exhibit the case of Bernstein v. Van Heyghen Frères S.A. The facts in this important case were as follows:

The plaintiff, Bernstein, a German national of Jewish faith, had been imprisoned in 1937 by "Nazi officials" and, by threats of bodily and other harm, had been compelled to transfer a ship he owned to a Nazi designee. This designee then transferred the ship to the defendant Belgian Corporation which took, it was alleged, with knowledge of the coercion practiced upon Bernstein. During the war the ship was sunk and the proceeds of insurance, substantially in excess of what the defendant paid for the ship, were put upon deposit in a New York bank. Bernstein, having escaped to the United States, brought suit in federal court for conversion and sought to attach the insurance proceeds. The United States Circuit Court of Appeals affirmed a district court in quashing the attachment and dismissing the complaint. Speaking for the majority of the Court, Judge Learned Hand, one of our greatest judges, referred to what he regarded as appropriate prior decisions and extracted a rule "that a court of the forum will not undertake to pass upon the validity under the municipal law of another state of the acts of officials of that state, purporting to act as such". Though he noted a certain inconsistency between his decision and the practices of our military government in occupied Germany, Judge Hand could find no clear executive view in our government which would permit him to reach another decision. Referring to the same prior decisions, Judge Clark dissented. He thought that the earlier precedents did "not deal with, or even appear to visualize, the situation where our executive acts later to repudiate the recognition which has been granted and to declare the acts of that nation as wrongful and void, to be wiped out by a tremendous war effort and by acts of retribution at the war's end". He added: "Many things have happened since the days when Nazi Germany was the recognized government of German territory—so many and so important that we have no precedent to govern the case. In short, a new one must be formulated."

* * *

It is, fortunately, becoming increasingly recognized that "law" and "policy" are not distinct and that every application of general rules, customary or conventional or however derived, to specific cases in fact requires the making of policy choices. From the perspective of a scientific observer, it is obvious that the behavior of decision-makers in the world power process is influenced by many variables, environmental and predispositional, other than legal rules, and that technical legal rules, divorced from the content of the policy perspectives of decision-makers and the groups with which they identify, are not competent to coerce or predict decisions or to prescribe what decisions ought to be or even adequately to describe what decisions have been. This impotence of technical legal rules has seldom been better stated than by Professor Kelsen: [a reiteration of his "Pure Theory" doctrine, see p. 1174].

* * *

It should perhaps be added that we recognize that we draw from Professor Kelsen's observation a conclusion different from that drawn by Professor Kelsen himself. Professor Kelsen considers it a "veritable usurpation of competence" for "jurists" to attempt "to determine the social ends to be attained" because "no matter how profound may be one's understanding of what the law is, this cannot cast light on what, because it is 'just', socially good, must be the content of law". "This question," he insists, "is not juridical but specifically political. It is the domain par excellence of the politician". Where, with deference, we differ from Professor Kelsen is in this insistence that the task of the jurist, the peculiarly legal function, must stop when the jurist outlines for decision-makers the various alternatives that the legal forms afford. Our suggestion is that, if an international law of human dignity is to be achieved, the jurist, as a responsible interpreter of the policy commitments embodied in legal prescriptions and procedures and as a skilled specialist with peculiarly intimate opportunity to observe such prescriptions and procedures in action, must extend his role beyond mere inquiry into and advice about legal syntactics, or the logical interrelations among legal propositions, to the further tasks of inquiry into and advice about the possible effects upon overall community values of the various alternatives that the legal forms afford.

II.   Over-emphasis on Naked Power as a Factor in Decision

At the opposite extreme from over-emphasis on technical rules, is an attitude increasingly common today which underestimates the role of rules, and of legal processes in general, and over-emphasizes the importance of naked power. This attitude is sometimes referred to as the "pure theory of power" as contrasted with the "pure theory of law". In many of the manifestations of this attitude it seems to be assumed, though the assumption is not always made explicit, that the detailed application of legal rules is always a function of the immediate power interests, of a mere calculation of momentary expediencies without regard to long-term community interests of the decision-maker and that legal rules—however clearly related to community policies, however sustained by balancing of power, and however sanctioned—are in some unchangeable nature of things irretrievably powerless to restrain the lawless behavior of absolutely and permanently sovereign nation-states.

* * *

It is submitted that all the contemporary manifestations of the "pure power" theory * * * both profoundly misconceive law and power and greatly underestimate both the role that law presently plays in the world power process and the role that, with a more effective balancing of power, it could be made to play in promoting and

preserving the values of a free, peaceful, and abundant world society.
*   *   *

III.   Failure to Achieve Comprehensive Description of the Participants in the World Power Process

It is common knowledge that in recent years the participants in the world power process have undergone and are continuing to undergo tremendous transformations. The traditional, territorially organized bodies politic, known as "nation-states", are, on the one hand, being dwarfed by the emergence of huge new bi-polarized and other regional groupings and, on the other hand, being challenged by the rise of a host of new and powerful functional organizations— including international governmental organizations, transnational political parties, transnational pressure groups, and transnational private associations. Contemporary theory about international law, obsessed by a technical conception of the "subjects of international law", continues, however, greatly to over-estimate the role of the "nation-state" and to underestimate the role of all these other new participants.
*   *   *

IV.   Failure to Achieve Comprehensive Description of the Techniques of Policy Formulation and Application in the World Power Process

The most casual observation of the flow of decisions in the world arena today reveals that policies are being formulated, recommended, prescribed, and reformulated and represcribed in multiplied thousands of agreements, conferences, resolutions, declarations, codifications, and customary practices of foreign office and other officials as well as by judicial and arbitral decision and that policies are being applied, appraised and terminated, in countless informal interactions in international and national arenas of all kinds. In much of the technical literature on international law, however, one still finds an over-concentration on "the court" as the principal instrument of law in world affairs and a supporting assumption that the principal function of a court, with its "given" rules, is the maintenance of opposition to change *   *   *.

The inadequacies of contemporary theory about international law add up, accordingly, to failure effectively to perform the various functions indicated above as indispensable to a policy-oriented approach to the study of international law.

The question now is what framework of inquiry might permit the more effective performance of these functions and, in particular, assist the legal scholar in his distinctive task of clarifying the policies implicit in past and proposed systems of international law. It is reasonably obvious that such a framework must offer a comprehensive way of talking about the world social and power processes in which decisions occur, rational criteria for identifying the decisions regarded as law, and an organization of studies for examining the flow of specific decisions which will facilitate both the testing of specific decisions for compatibility with the goal values of a free society and scientific study of the variables which in fact affect decision. Many different systems of inquiry might of course be devised for achieving these purposes. The framework we propose seeks both a way of outlining the total context of world social and power processes and a way of keeping specific decisions constantly at the focus of attention, however various the participants, the arenas of interaction, the base values invoked, the instruments of policy applied, or outcomes achieved in any particular context. It must be recognized, however, that no intellectual tools can be devised which will cut the "big, blooming, buzzing confusion" which is the world about us with final and dogmatic precision. What we are attempting to do is, almost literally, slowly to turn a globe or sphere (the context of the world social and power processes) for the purpose of spotlighting, investigating, and relating to total context now one set of decisions, with all their goals and conditioning variables, and then another set. The performance of this task must inevitably be marked by over-laps, gaps, and imprecisions.

* * *

The comprehensive framework of theory that we propose for describing the world social process is indicated in skeltonized form in Chart I, which is set out below [1].

1.

Chart I
Community Process

People
  with   power
  perspectives   respect
    identifications   using base values   enlightenment through institutions
    demands   wealth
    expectations   well-being
                            rectitude
                            skill
                            affection

myth   doctrine
        formula (legal rules)
        miranda

                                unprocessed
       organizational routines   on resources land   to shape and distribute
           government   processed   scope values
technique   party   land
           pressure groups   facilities
           private associations   human energy
       non-organizational
power
respect   people
enlightenment   among   with
wealth   perspectives
well-being   identifications
rectitude   demands
skill   expectations
affection

The most general formulation upon which this Chart is based is: *people* strive to maximize *values* by applying *institutions* to *resources.*[2]

With respect to *people*, we would emphasize that the most relevant description must include not merely their numbers, spatial distribution, physical characteristics, value and institutional positions and so on, but also their perspectives (subjectivities, predispositions) —their demands for values, their identifications with others, and their factual expectations (beliefs) about past and future.

By the term *values*, we refer to major categories of desired events. For purposes of the present comprehensive analysis we recommend as convenient the following eight categories: power, respect, enlightenment, wealth, well-being, skill, affection, and rectitude. In brief, preliminary definition, *power* may be taken to refer to participation in the making of important decisions (decisions involving severe deprivations); *respect*, to access to other values on the basis of merit, without discrimination on grounds irrelevant to capacity; *enlightenment*, to access to the knowledge on which rational choice depends; *wealth*, to control over economic goods and services; *well-being*, to the enjoyment of physical and psychic health; *skill*, to proficiency in the exercise of latent talent; *affection* to the enjoyment of congenial human relations; and *rectitude*, to the sharing of common standards of responsibility.

The term *institutions* is used to refer to the pattern of practices by which values are shaped and shared. Such patterns include, as may be seen from the Chart, both myth and technique, or both rules and operations.

Resources include the physical objects and materials and human energy that are employed in the shaping and sharing of values and their significance obviously varies greatly from value to value and context to context.

The postulate that people strive to maximize their values is introduced as a dynamic principle to account for individual and group choices. It is a postulate that has proved most fruitful in many branches of psychological and social science investigation.

Keeping in mind this brief explanation of terms and major postulate, we may now read Chart I as formulating a description of community or social process in terms of people, with varying perspectives, in varying situations, employing base values, by practices (myth and technique), to effect a redistribution among people of certain demanded or "scope" values. In any particular study of specific value processes, the people and their perspectives, the situations in which they demand values, the base values they employ, the

---

2. More detailed expositions of the general mode of analysis we recommend may be found in Lasswell and Kaplan, Power and Society (1950); Lasswell, Power and Personality (1948) and The World Revolution of our Time (1951); Lerner and Lasswell (eds.) The Policy Sciences (1951); Lasswell, Leites and Associates, Language of Politics (1949).

practices by which they shape and share values, and the effects they obtain upon the distribution of values may be described in as much detail as the materials permit or as the particular problem of the investigator requires.

It may be emphasized that any particular value may be either employed as a means or sought as an end, may be either a base value or a scope value. The total world social process may, indeed, be usefully conceived as a series of interrelated value processes: a power process, a respect process, an enlightenment process, a wealth process, a well-being process, a skill process, an affection process, and a rectitude process. Any given interaction may be identified by examining in detail the demands and expectations of the people in the situation.

It is because of the interrelation of value processes, the point may bear further emphasis, that rational inquiry by jurists cannot be confined exclusively to power processes. Though we will presently recommend a conception of law in terms of a form of power (including both myth and technique, rules and operations), any realistic study of power processes requires the relation of such processes to the other value processes. The events which give rise to controversies and result in the invocation of power decisions occur, as already indicated, in every value process; power decisions may be in fact affected by considerations of any or all the other values; and, finally, such decisions may in turn affect any one or all of the values. In more abstract statement, the world process affects each of the other value processes and the other value processes in turn affect the world power process and each other. The jurist who would concern himself with causes and effects, conditions and consequences, must be prepared to extend his inquiries to the totality of value processes.

   *   *   *

Part VII

THE USE OF FORCE IN THE INTERNATIONAL SYSTEM

Throughout most of the life of the world's present state system, states have been regarded by international law as being permitted to use almost all of their advantages, political, economic and military, in pursuit of their national interests. Although minor military incursions on the territory of a neighboring state might be considered unlawful (unless justified, possibly, as an act of "reprisal" in response to some unlawful act of the neighbor), if the military actor chose to make "war" [a] upon its neighbor that state of affairs was not considered a violation of international law. Two qualifications must be made to this assertion, however. A state could, of course, be bound by treaty not to make war on a particular state. And as seen in Chapter 10, by international custom and conventions, states at war with each other were bound to wage it more or less humanely; that is, although the fact of war could not be prevented by law, it was hoped that the manner of waging it could be regulated.

In this Part, we are concerned with modern efforts to outlaw war and other uses of military force. We shall also explore the extent to which international law seeks as well to control the way in which states pursue their national interests through forcing their will on other states by non-military means.

When states are forbidden to pursue their national interests by the use of armed force, an urgent need arises for other authorized sources of regulated force in the international system. In this Part, we examine the extent to which the United Nations and regional organizations may use force for lawful ends when individual nation states or groups of states allied with each other are forbidden to use force in pursuit of their national interests.

a. In international jurisprudence in recent centuries, "war" has been a word of art. In popular usage it has meant the overt use of military force against another state. In law, however, it meant a legal relationship existing between states, created by intention of those states and generally but not always involving the use of armed force. Whether this legal relationship could be created (or lawfully created) without a "declaration of war" was a question entangled in inconsistent state practice and international convention. See, generally, Starke, An Introduction to International Law, Chapter 16 (5th ed., 1963).

Chapter 19

THE USE OF FORCE BY STATES

SECTION A. EVOLUTION OF LAW AGAINST USE OF FORCE BY STATES

The League of Nations. The Covenant of the League of Nations did not outlaw war as such. Instead, it sought to obligate states to resort to methods of peaceful settlement; in turn, members of the League agreed under certain circumstances not to resort to war. See in particular the following articles of the covenant: Article 12 ("* * * they agree in no case to resort to war until three months after the award by the arbitrators or the report by the Council."); Article 13 ("The Members of the League agree that they will carry out in full good faith any award that may be rendered, and that they will not resort to war against a Member of the League which complies therewith."); Article 15 ("If a report by the Council is unanimously agreed to by the Members thereof other than the representatives of one or more of the parties to the dispute, the Members of the League agree that they will not go to war with any party to the dispute which complies with the recommendations of the report.")

These qualified commitments against waging war should be contrasted to the language of the Peace Pact of Paris and of Article 2(4) of the United Nations Charter, set forth hereafter. Also to be contrasted with Article 2(4) of the charter is Article 10 of the Covenant, in which members of the League undertook to "respect and preserve as against external aggression the territorial integrity and existing political independence of all members of the League." Was this article also a backhanded commitment not to commit such aggression?

The mechanisms for enforcing the ambiguous and qualified obligations not to wage war were contained in Article 10 of the Covenant ("* * * the Council shall advise upon the means by which this obligation shall be fulfilled") and in Article 16 (the provisions for collective measures by the members of the League in the event a member of the League should "resort to war in disregard of its covenants under Articles 12, 13 or 15").

As is well known, the United States did not become a member of the League of Nations. The Covenant of the League was an integral part of the Treaty of Versailles. When it was submitted to the Senate for its advice and consent, Senator Henry Cabot Lodge led the Senate to the adoption of a number of reservations, notably one to Article X, to the effect that the United States would not assume an obligation to preserve the territorial integrity or political independence of any country unless "in any particular case the Congress, which, under the Constitution, has the sole power to declare war or authorize the employment of the military or naval forces of the United States, shall by act or joint resolution so provide." Stone (ed.), Wilson and the League of Nations 98 (1967). President Wilson refused to accept the Lodge reservations. As a result, the treaty (with the covenant) was rejected by the Senate. Analyses of the rejection of the League from a variety of points of view are published in the Stone symposium.

As for the effect of the Covenant on the unilateral use of force by states and the efforts of the League to restrain that force, it can only be stated that the results were dismal.

_____

MORGENTHAU, POLITICS AMONG NATIONS 290 (4TH ED., 1967) *

* * * Collective measures of enforcement under Article 16 were applied in only one of the five cases in which undoubtedly a member of the League resorted to war in violation of the Covenant. With regard to the Sino-Japanese conflict that started in 1931, the Assembly of the League of Nations found unanimously that "without any declaration of war, part of the Chinese territory has been forcibly seized and occupied by the Japanese troops," and that far-flung hostilities, initiated by Japan, had taken place between troops of the Chinese and Japanese governments. Yet the Assembly found also that Japan had not resorted to war in violation of the Covenant and that, therefore, Article 16 did not apply.

In 1934, during the Chaco War of 1932–35, when Paraguay continued hostilities against Bolivia in violation of the Covenant, many members of the League limited the arms embargo, originally imposed upon both belligerents, to Paraguay. This was a discriminatory measure falling far short of the spirit and the letter of the first paragraph of Article 16. When Japan, which by then had resigned from the League, invaded China in 1937, the Assembly found that Japan had violated the Nine Power Treaty of 1922 and the Briand-Kellogg Pact, that Article 16 was applicable, and that the members of the League had the right to take enforcement measures individually under that provision. No such measures were ever taken. When the Soviet Union went to war with Finland in 1939, it was expelled from the League by virtue of Article 16, paragraph 4, but no collective action of enforcement was taken against it.

In contrast to these cases, the Assembly found in 1935 that the invasion of Ethiopia by Italy constituted resort to war within the meaning and in violation of the Covenant and that, therefore, Article 16, paragraph 1, was to apply. In consequence, collective economic sanctions against Italy were decided upon and applied. Yet the two

* Reprinted with the permission of Alfred A. Knopf, Inc., New York.

measures, provided for by Article 16, paragraph 1, that offered the best chance of making international law prevail under the circumstances and that in all probability would have compelled Italy to desist from its attack upon Ethiopia—namely, an embargo on oil shipments to Italy and the closure of the Suez Canal—were not taken. "However," as Sir H. Lauterpacht puts it, "although the sanctions of Article 16, paragraph 1, were formally put into operation and although an elaborate machinery was set up with a view to their successive and gradual enforcement, the nature of the action taken was such as to suggest that the repressive measures were being adopted as a manifestation of moral reprobation rather than as an effective means of coercion."

One can, therefore, sum up the attempts at establishing a centralized system of law enforcement under Article 16 of the Covenant by saying that in most of the cases that would have justified the application of sanctions, sanctions were not applied at all. In the sole case in which they were applied, they were applied in such an ineffective fashion as virtually to assure both their failure and the success of the recalcitrant state.

TRAVAUX–PREPARATOIRES FOR THE PEACE PACT OF PARIS (THE KELLOGG–BRIAND PACT)

[1928] 1 Foreign Relations of the United States 32 (1942).

French Draft of Treaty for the Condemnation and Renunciation of War as an Instrument of National Policy

The President of the German Empire, the President of the United States of America, the President of the French Republic, His Majesty the King of England, Ireland and the British Dominions, Emperor of India, His Majesty the King of Italy, His Majesty the Emperor of Japan:

Equally desirous not only of perpetuating the happy relations of peace and friendship now existing among their peoples, but also of avoiding the danger of war between all other nations in the world,

Having agreed to consecrate in a solemn act their most formal and most definite resolution to condemn war as an instrument of national policy and to renounce it in favor of a peaceful settlement of international conflicts,

Expressing, finally, the hope that all the other nations of the world will be willing to join in this humane effort to bring about the association of the civilized peoples in a common renunciation of war as an instrument of national policy, have decided to conclude a treaty and to that end have designated as their respective plenipotentiaries:

The President of the German Empire:
The President of the United States of America:
The President of the French Republic:

His Majesty the King of Great Britain, Ireland and the British Dominions, Emperor of India:

His Majesty the King of Italy:

His Majesty the Emperor of Japan:

who, after exchanging their full powers found to be in good and due form have agreed on the following provisions:

Article One

The High Contracting Parties without any intention to infringe upon the exercise of their rights of legitimate self-defense within the framework of existing treaties, particularly when the violation of certain of the provisions of such treaties constitutes a hostile act, solemnly declare that they condemn recourse to war and renounce it as an instrument of national policy; that is to say, as an instrument of individual, spontaneous and independent political action taken on their own initiative and not action in respect of which they might become involved through the obligation of a treaty such as the covenant of the League of Nations or any other treaty registered with the League of Nations. They undertake on these conditions not to attack or invade one another.

[handwritten margin note: UNILATERAL NOT COLLECTIVE DEFENSE]

Article Two

The settlement or solution of all disputes or conflicts of whatever nature or origin which might arise among the High Contracting Parties or between any two of them shall never be sought on either side except by pacific methods.

Article Three

In case one of the High Contracting Parties should contravene this treaty, the other Contracting Powers would ipso facto be released with respect to that Party from their obligations under this treaty.

[handwritten margin note: RELEASE CLAUSE]

Article Four

The provisions of this treaty in no wise affect the rights and obligations of the Contracting Parties resulting from prior international agreements to which they are parties.

Article Five

The present treaty will be offered for the accession of all Powers and will have no binding force until it has been generally accepted unless the signatory Powers in accord with those that may accede hereto shall agree to decide that it shall come into effect regardless of certain abstentions.

Article Six

The present treaty shall be ratified.

The ratifications shall be deposited at * * *; within three months from the date of the deposit of the ratifications it shall be communicated by the Government of * * * to all the Powers with an invitation to accede.

* * *

The Secretary of State to the Ambassador in France (Herrick)

WASHINGTON, April 21, 1928—6 p. m.

117. The French draft of the anti-war treaty seems entirely unacceptable, but you will please avoid any discussion of matter awaiting receipt of full advice on our position which you will receive by cable early in coming week.

KELLOGG

The Secretary of State to the Ambassador in France (Herrick)

WASHINGTON, April 23, 1928—5 p. m.

* * * In its present form the French draft treaty is wholly unacceptable to the United States since it cannot in any respect be regarded as an effective instrument for the promotion of world peace. It emphasizes war, not peace, and seems in effect to be a justification rather than a renunciation of the use of armed force. The United States will sign no treaty of the nature now under discussion which cannot reasonably be expected to lessen the danger of an outbreak of war and thus promote the cause of world peace. * * *

There seem to be six major considerations which the French Government has emphasized in its correspondence and in its draft treaty, namely, that the treaty must not (1) impair the right of legitimate self-defense; (2) violate the Covenant of the League of Nations; (3) violate the treaties of Locarno; (4) violate certain unspecified treaties guaranteeing neutrality; (5) bind the parties in respect of a state breaking the treaty; (6) come into effect until accepted by all or substantially all of the Powers of the world. The views of the United States on these six points are as follows:

(1) Self-defense. There is nothing in the American draft of an anti-war treaty which restricts or impairs in any way the right of self-defense. That right is inherent in every sovereign state and is implicit in every treaty. Every nation is free at all times and regardless of treaty provisions to defend its territory from attack or invasion and it alone is competent to decide whether circumstances require recourse to war in self-defense. If it has a good case, the world will applaud and not condemn its action. Express recognition by treaty of this inalienable right, however, gives rise to the same difficulty encountered in any effort to define aggression. It is the identical question approached from the other side. Inasmuch as no treaty provision can add to the natural right of self-defense, it is not in the interest of peace that a treaty should stipulate a juristic conception of self-defense since it is far too easy for the unscrupulous to mold events to accord with an agreed definition.

(2) The League Covenant. The Covenant imposes no affirmative primary obligation to go to war. The obligation, if any, is secondary and attaches only when deliberately accepted by a state. Article ten of the Covenant has, for example, been interpreted by a resolution submitted to the Fourth Assembly but not

formally adopted owing to one adverse vote to mean that "it is for the constitutional authorities of each member to decide, in reference to the obligation of preserving the independence and the integrity of the territory of members, in what degree the member is bound to assure the execution of this obligation by employment of its military forces." There is, in my opinion, no necessary inconsistency between the covenant and the idea of an unqualified renunciation of war. The covenant can, it is true, be construed as authorizing war in certain circumstances but it is an authorization and not a positive requirement. The German Government, moreover, which is a member of the League of Nations, does not regard itself as barred thereby from becoming a party to the form of anti-war treaty which the United States has proposed.

(3) The Treaties of Locarno. If the parties to the treaties of Locarno are under any positive obligation to go to war, such obligation certainly would not attach until one of the parties has resorted to war in violation of its solemn pledges thereunder. It is therefore obvious that if all the parties to the Locarno treaties become parties to the multilateral anti-war treaty proposed by the United States, there would be a double assurance that the Locarno treaties would not be violated by recourse to arms. In such event it would follow that resort to war by any state in violation of the Locarno treaties would also be a breach of the multilateral anti-war treaty and the other parties to the anti-war treaty would thus as a matter of law be automatically released from their obligations thereunder and free to fulfil their Locarno commitments. The United States is entirely willing that all parties to the Locarno treaties should become parties to its proposed anti-war treaty either through signature in the first instance or by immediate accession to the treaty as soon as it comes into force in the manner provided in Article III of the American draft, and it will offer no objection when and if such a suggestion is made.

(4) Treaties of neutrality. The United States is not informed as to the precise treaties which France has in mind and cannot therefore discuss their provisions. It is not unreasonable to suppose, however, that the relations between France and the states whose neutrality she has guaranteed are sufficiently close and intimate to make it possible for France to persuade such states to adhere seasonably to the anti-war treaty proposed by the United States. If this were done no party to the anti-war treaty could attack the neutralized states without violating the treaty and thereby automatically freeing France and the other Powers in respect of the treaty-breaking state from the obligations of the anti-war treaty. If the neutralized states were attacked by a state not a party to the anti-war treaty, the latter treaty would of course have no bearing and France would be as

free to act under the treaties guaranteeing neutrality as if she were not a party to the anti-war treaty. It is difficult to perceive, therefore, how treaties guaranteeing neutrality can be regarded as necessarily preventing the conclusion by France or any other power of a multilateral treaty for the renunciation of war.

(5) Relations with a treaty-breaking state. As indicated above, there can be no question as a matter of law that violation of a multilateral anti-war treaty through resort to war by one party thereto would automatically release the other parties from their obligations to the treaty-breaking state. Any express recognition of this principle of law is wholly unnecessary.

(6) Universality. From the beginning it has been the hope of the United States that its proposed multilateral anti-war treaty should be world-wide in its application, and appropriate provision therefor was made in the draft submitted to the other Governments on April 13. From a practical standpoint it is clearly preferable, however, not to postpone the coming into force of an anti-war treaty until all the nations of the world can agree upon the text of such a treaty and cause it to be ratified. For one reason or another a state so situated as to be no menace to the peace of the world might obstruct agreement or delay ratification in such manner as to render abortive the efforts of all the other Powers. It is highly improbable, moreover, that a form of treaty acceptable to the British, French, German, Italian and Japanese Governments as well as to the United States would not be equally acceptable to most, if not all, of the other Powers of the world. Even were this not the case, however, the coming into force among the above-named six Powers of an effective anti-war treaty and their observance thereof would be a practical guaranty against a second world war. This in itself would be a tremendous service to humanity and the United States is not willing to jeopardize the practical success of the proposal which it has made by conditioning the coming into force of the treaty upon prior universal or almost universal acceptance.

In the foregoing paragraphs of this telegram the position of the Government of the United States is fully and clearly set forth; you are authorized to use any or all of the above exposition, at your discretion, in discussing at the Foreign Office the question of a multilateral treaty for the renunciation of war. You may even seek an opportunity, if you think it desirable, to present in the appropriate quarter views as outlined above. I earnestly hope that sooner or later there may develop out of the discussions which have been initiated among the six powers an acceptable and effective form of treaty for renunciation of war. The important thing is to get peoples and governments to thinking in terms of peace, and I cannot refrain from belief that once the initial inertia is overcome a rapid spread of the treaty's sphere of influence will occur.

Of course I realize that the political problems of Europe are more difficult in some respects than are those of the Americans, and it may be that considerations put forward by France will find more general support than I expect. Under these circumstances and in order to prevent a complete failure of the negotiations—an outcome which in my opinion would be a tremendous disappointment to mankind— I would be willing to have included in treaty a provision recording express understanding that should any party to the treaty become involved in war, then the other parties shall be released, ipso facto, from their obligations under the treaty so far as regards the belligerent party. A provision of that nature would satisfy every legitimate requirement of the League of Nations, the treaties of Locarno and any normal treaty guaranteeing neutrality without compromising the fundamental purpose of the anti-war treaty, and would also satisfy any lingering doubts in any quarter on the question of self-defense. Neither the Covenant of the League of Nations, nor the Locarno treaties, nor neutrality treaties or emergencies requiring belligerent acts of self-defense obligate any state to resort to war until a prior act of war has been committed by an offending state. The perpetration of that act would release automatically, under such a clause, the innocent parties to the anti-war treaty and would leave them free to carry out their commitments under the League or Locarno or any others.

At this time I do not wish you suggest inclusion of any such qualifying clause or to make any reference to it in your discussions in any way, but I should be pleased to have you feel out the general situation and to telegraph full report.

KELLOGG

GENERAL TREATY FOR RENUNCIATION OF WAR AS AN INSTRUMENT OF NATIONAL POLICY OF AUGUST 27, 1928

46 Stat. 2343, 94 L.N.T.S. 59 (1929).

Article I

The High Contracting Parties solemnly declare in the names of their respective peoples that they condemn recourse to war for the solution of international controversies, and renounce it as an instrument of national policy in their relations with one another.

Article II

The High Contracting Parties agree that the settlement or solution of all disputes or conflicts of whatever nature or of whatever origin they may be, which may arise among them, shall never be sought except by pacific means.

UNITED STATES TREATIES IN FORCE, JANUARY 1, 1972

Renunciation of War

Treaty providing for the renunciation of war as an instrument of national policy. Signed at Paris August 27, 1928; entered into force for the United States July 24, 1929.

46 Stat. 2343; TS 796; 2 Bevans 732; 94 LNTS 57.

States which are parties:

Afghanistan	Iraq
Albania	Ireland
Australia	Italy
Austria	Japan
Barbados	Latvia
Belgium	Liberia
Brazil	Lithuania
Bulgaria	Luxembourg
Canada	Mexico
Chile	Netherlands
China	New Zealand
Colombia	Nicaragua
Costa Rica	Norway
Cuba	Panama
Czechoslovakia	Paraguay
Denmark	Peru
Dominican Republic	Poland, including
Ecuador	Free City of Danzig
Egypt	Portugal
Estonia	Romania
Ethiopia	Saudi Arabia
Finland	South Africa
France	Spain
Germany	Sweden
Greece	Switzerland
Guatemala	Thailand
Haiti	Turkey
Honduras	Union of Soviet
Hungary	Socialist Reps.
Iceland	United Kingdom
India	United States
Iran	Venezuela
	Yugoslavia

---

1. *Parties during World War II.* The Department of State's compilation of Treaties in Force on December 31, 1941 lists all of the above states except Austria and Barbados as parties to the Pact of

Paris (subject to a Special Note disclaiming the department's having passed upon the effect of war on any of the treaties in the compilation).

2. *Why was the Pact of Paris a futile bar to war?* Even before the outbreak of World War II, armed conflict had been carried on by Japan in China, by Germany, Italy and the USSR in Spain, and by Italy in Ethiopia.

BROWN, UNDECLARED WARS

33 American Journal of International Law 538, 540 (1939).

We see, therefore, in the light of theory and practice, that the problem of the undeclared war remains largely an academic one which involves considerations more ethical than legal. And this is true also of the self-denying declaration embodied in the General Treaty of 1928 for the Renunciation of War, generally entitled the Kellogg Pact. This agreement, while purporting to renounce the use of war, really consecrated the vague and dangerous right of self-defence. The various signatories explicitly reserved the right to resort to war and to judge for themselves "whether circumstances require recourse to war in self-defence." Within four years of the signing of this Pact occurred three breaches of the Pact, namely, the aggression by Russia against China in 1929, the occupation of Manchuria by Japan in 1931, and the invasion of Colombia by Peru in 1932. The more recent instances of warlike acts by Japan, Germany, and Italy are too vividly in mind to require comment. It is necessary, however, to stress the lamentable and unforeseen consequence of the Kellogg Pact in encouraging aggressor nations hypocritically to avoid any formal declaration of war in order to elude the constraints of this pious declaration.

Still another most unexpected inducement to avoid a formal declaration of war, as revealed in the case of the conflict now going on between Japan and China, has been the natural desire to escape the disabilities of recent neutrality legislation of the United States, whereby the shipment of arms and munitions of war to belligerents is automatically forbidden. The question presents itself whether, in the absence of a formal declaration of war by either side, it should not be incumbent on neutral nations to brush all legal niceties aside and openly acknowledge a state of war where the laws of war and neutrality should apply. Nations intent on peace and determined to uphold the reign of law have a solemn duty to avoid any implied connivance in the evasion of international obligations. Neutrality is not merely to conserve national interests, but also to preserve an impartial rôle which may enable a nation to affirm with vigor the responsibilities and rights of peoples under international law.

The situation is certainly a most unhappy one. It is stultifying to discover that an idealistic agreement such as the Kellogg Pact, and neutrality legislation conceived for a generous purpose, should actually conduce to the fiction of the undeclared war. * * *

CHARTER OF THE UNITED NATIONS

Article 2

The Organization and its Members, in pursuit of the Purposes stated in Article 1, shall act in accordance with the following Principles.

* * *

4. All Members shall refrain in their international relations from the threat or use of force against the territorial integrity or political independence of any state, or in any other manner inconsistent with the Purposes of the United Nations.

* * *

Article 39

The Security Council shall determine the existence of any threat to the peace, breach of the peace, or act of aggression and shall make recommendations, or decide what measures shall be taken in accordance with Articles 41 and 42, to maintain or restore international peace and security.

Article 41

The Security Council may decide what measures not involving the use of armed forces are to be employed to give effect to its decisions, and it may call upon the Members of the United Nations to apply such measures. These may include complete or partial interruption of economic relations and of rail, sea, air, postal, telegraphic, radio, and other means of communication, and the severance of diplomatic relations.

Article 42

Should the Security Council consider that measures provided for in Article 41 would be inadequate or have proved to be inadequate, it may take such action by air, sea, or land forces as may be necessary to maintain or restore international peace and security. Such action may include demonstrations, blockade, and other operations by air, sea, or land forces of Members of the United Nations.

Article 51

Nothing in the present Charter shall impair the inherent right of individual or collective self-defence if an armed attack occurs against a Member of the United Nations, until the Security Council has taken measures necessary to maintain international peace and security. Measures taken by Members in the exercise of this right of self-defence shall be immediately reported to the Security Council and shall not in any way affect the authority and responsibility of the Security Council under the present Charter to take at any time such action as it deems necessary in order to maintain or restore international peace and security.

"Intervention" in relation to the force prohibition of the Charter. The term "intervention" has factual, political and legal connotations. Common to all three meanings, in the context of international affairs, is the series of overriding or dominant influences of one state upon the will or capabilities of another state, particularly as to events and conditions in the latter. In the history of Latin-American relations prior to the coming into being of the United Nations and the Organization of American States, the opposition by Latin America to the penchant of the United States to land the Marines "to protect American lives and property," and for other purposes viewed as good by the United States, coalesced into a "principle of non-intervention." While some writers of that period contended that this principle was one of general international law, others viewed it as a political principle without legal content that ought eventually to be stated as a rule of international law. Since the creation of the United Nations, legal discourse has, with increased frequency, engaged the term. Does it now have legal meaning; if so, what is its scope?

The Charter of the United Nations does not apply the term in describing the rights and duties of states with respect to the employment of physical force. As seen, Article 2(4) forbids the use of force directed against "territorial integrity or political independence of any state, or in any manner inconsistent with the Purposes of the United Nations." The existence of an act of "aggression" (not intervention), if found by the Security Council, triggers certain permissible United Nations responses, but even aggression is not in terms forbidden to states. It is from Article 2(7) of the Charter of the United Nations that emanations have emerged forbidding intervention by states although, in its terms, that provision is directed toward the organization rather than its members: "Nothing contained in the present Charter shall authorize the United Nations to intervene in matters which are essentially within the domestic jurisdiction of any state * * *." This provision is buttressed in the Charter by broadly stated principles: "self-determination of peoples," Article 1(2); "sovereign equality" of states, Article 2(1).

By the twenty-fifth year of the United Nations, the General Assembly was able, in its Declaration of Principles of International Law Concerning Friendly Relations and Co-operation Among States in

Accordance with the Charter of the United Nations,[a] to proclaim the following:

> "The principle concerning the duty not to intervene in matters within the domestic jurisdiction of any State, in accordance with the Charter."

In elucidation of this principle, the assembly declared: "No State or group of States has the right to intervene directly or indirectly, for any reason whatever in the internal or external affairs of any other State." And further: "Every State has an inalienable right to choose its political, economic, social and cultural systems, without interference in any form by another State."

Consider the following polar situations: (1) State A crosses the border into State B to conquer and annex that state. There is no doubt that Article 2(4) has been violated; the event would probably not be described by such a gentle term as "intervention."

(2) State A provides military aid to the government of State B at its request; that government is under threat from elements in its own country. Is State A using force against State B's "political independence"; i. e., is this an Article 2(4) violation? How do you define the "state" whose political independence is endangered? Surely not the established government; possibly the dissidents; or the people of the state as whole? If the latter, does Article 2(4) mean that they are free to (literally) fight their way to a resolution of diverse political goals without outside contributions of men and arms to any side in the fray? If that conclusion is not readily deducible from Article 2(4), has the emerging positive law of intervention and non-intervention brought the law to that point? Or does intervention by states remain, as it once was, a means of describing an international relations political objective?

Comparable problems of determining whether intervention is a term of legal significance or of political rhetoric arise in connection with attempts to exert pressure on the will of a state by means other than military, e. g., economic. See p. 1266.

---

a. The complete text of the declaration is set forth in the Documentary Supplement.

SECTION B. THE PROBLEM OF SELF-DEFENSE

1. MISSILES IN CUBA [a]

THE SOVIET THREAT TO THE AMERICAS, ADDRESS
BY PRESIDENT KENNEDY

47 United States Department of State Bulletin 715 (1962).

*   *   *

Neither the United States of America nor the world community of nations can tolerate deliberate deception and offensive threats on the part of any nation, large or small. We no longer live in a world where only the actual firing of weapons represents a sufficient challenge to a nation's security to constitute maximum peril. Nuclear weapons are so destructive and ballistic missiles are so swift that any substantially increased possibility of their use or any sudden change in their deployment may well be regarded as a definite threat to peace.

[margin annotation: INCREASED THREAT]

For many years both the Soviet Union and the United States, recognizing this fact, have deployed strategic nuclear weapons with great care, never upsetting the precarious status quo which insured that these weapons would not be used in the absence of some vital challenge. Our own strategic missiles have never been transferred to the territory of any other nation under a cloak of secrecy and deception; and our history, unlike that of the Soviets since the end of World War II, demonstrates that we have no desire to dominate or conquer any other nation or impose our system upon its people. Nevertheless, American citizens have become adjusted to living daily on the bull's eye of Soviet missiles located inside the U.S.S.R. or in submarines.

In that sense missiles in Cuba add to an already clear and present danger—although it should be noted the nations of Latin America have never previously been subjected to a potential nuclear threat.

*   *   *

Acting, therefore, in the defense of our own security and of the entire Western Hemisphere, and under the authority entrusted to me by the Constitution as endorsed by the resolution of the Congress, I have directed that the following initial steps be taken immediately:

First: To halt this offensive buildup, a strict quarantine on all offensive military equipment under shipment to Cuba is being initiated. All ships of any kind bound for Cuba from whatever nation

---

a. For an analysis of the political context of the Cuban missile crisis, see p. 97.

SHIPPING
QUARANTINE

or port will, if found to contain cargoes of offensive weapons, be turned back. This quarantine will be extended, if needed, to other types of cargo and carriers. We are not at this time, however, denying the necessities of life as the Soviets attempted to do in their Berlin blockade of 1948.

Second: I have directed the continued and increased close surveillance of Cuba and its military buildup. The Foreign Ministers of the OAS [Organization of American States] in their communique of October 3 rejected secrecy on such matters in this hemisphere. Should these offensive military preparations continue, thus increasing the threat to the hemisphere, further action will be justified. I have directed the Armed Forces to prepare for any eventualities; and I trust that, in the interest of both the Cuban people and the Soviet technicians at the sites, the hazards to all concerned of continuing this threat will be recognized.

Third: It shall be the policy of this nation to regard any nuclear missile launched from Cuba against any nation in the Western Hemisphere as an attack by the Soviet Union on the United States, requiring a full retaliatory response upon the Soviet Union.

Fourth: As a necessary military precaution I have reinforced our base at Guantanamo, evacuated today the dependents of our personnel there, and ordered additional military units to be on a standby alert basis.

Fifth: We are calling tonight for an immediate meeting of the Organ of Consultation, under the Organization of American States, to consider this threat to hemispheric security and to invoke articles 6 and 8 of the Rio Treaty in support of all necessary action. The United Nations Charter allows for regional security arrangements—and the nations of this hemisphere decided long ago against the military presence of outside powers. Our other allies around the world have also been alerted.

Sixth: Under the Charter of the United Nations, we are asking tonight that an emergency meeting of the Security Council be convoked without delay to take action against this latest Soviet threat to world peace. Our resolution will call for the prompt dismantling and withdrawal of all offensive weapons in Cuba, under the supervision of U.N. observers, before the quarantine can be lifted.

Seventh and finally: I call upon Chairman Khrushchev to halt and eliminate this clandestine, reckless, and provocative threat to world peace and to stable relations between our two nations. * * *

This nation is prepared to present its case against the Soviet threat to peace, and our own proposals for a peaceful world, at any time and in any forum—in the OAS, in the United Nations, or in any other meeting that could be useful—without limiting our freedom of action.

* * *

INTER-AMERICAN TREATY OF RECIPROCAL ASSISTANCE OF SEPT. 2, 1947

62 Stat. 1681, 21 U.N.T.S. 77.

Article 6. If the inviolability or the integrity of the territory or the sovereignty or political independence of any American State should be affected by an aggression which is not an armed attack or by an extra-continental or intra-continental conflict, or by any other fact or situation that might endanger the peace of America, the Organ of Consultation shall meet immediately in order to agree on the measures which must be taken in case of aggression to assist the victim of the aggression or, in any case, the measures which should be taken for the common defense and for the maintenance of the peace and security of the Continent.

Article 7. In the case of a conflict between two or more American States, without prejudice to the right of self-defense in conformity with Article 51 of the Charter of the United Nations, the High Contracting Parties, meeting in consultation shall call upon the contending States to suspend hostilities and restore matters to the statu quo ante bellum, and shall take in addition all other necessary measures to reestablish or maintain inter-American peace and security and for the solution of the conflict by peaceful means. The rejection of the pacifying action will be considered in the determination of the aggressor and in the application of the measures which the consultative meeting may agree upon.

Article 8. For the purposes of this Treaty, the measures on which the Organ of Consultation may agree will comprise one or more of the following: recall of chiefs of diplomatic missions; breaking of diplomatic relations; breaking of consular relations; partial or complete interruption of economic relations or of rail, sea, air, postal, telegraphic, telephonic, and radiotelephonic or radiotelegraphic communications; and use of armed force.

Article 9. In addition to other acts which the Organ of Consultation may characterize as aggression, the following shall be considered as such:

a. Unprovoked armed attack by a State against the territory, the people, or the land, sea, or air forces of another State;

b. Invasion, by the armed forces of a State, of the territory of an American State, through the trespassing of boundaries demarcated in accordance with a treaty, judicial decision, or arbitral award, or, in the absence of frontiers thus demarcated, invasion affecting a region which is under the effective jurisdiction of another State.

CHARTER OF THE ORGANIZATION OF AMERICAN STATES

2 U.S.T. 2394, 119 U.N.T.S. 3.ª

Article 15.   No State or group of States has the right to intervene, directly or indirectly, for any reason whatever, in the internal or external affairs of any other State.   The foregoing principle prohibits not only armed force but also any other form of interference or attempted threat against the personality of the State or against its political, economic and cultural elements.

Article 16.   No State may use or encourage the use of coercive measures of an economic or political character in order to force the sovereign will of another State and obtain from it advantages of any kind.

Article 17.   The territory of a State is inviolable; it may not be the object, even temporarily, of military occupation or of other measures of force taken by another State, directly or indirectly, on any grounds whatever.   No territorial acquisitions or special advantages obtained either by force or by other means of coercion shall be recognized.

Article 18.   The American States bind themselves in their international relations not to have recourse to the use of force, except in the case of self-defense in accordance with existing treaties or in fulfillment thereof.

Article 19.   Measures adopted for the maintenance of peace and security in accordance with existing treaties do not constitute a violation of the principles set forth in Articles 15 and 17.

RESOLUTION OF COUNCIL OF THE ORGANIZATION OF AMERICAN STATES, MEETING AS THE PROVISIONAL ORGAN OF CONSULTATION, OCTOBER 23, 1962

47 United States Department of State Bulletin 722 (1962).

Whereas,

The Inter-American Treaty of Reciprocal Assistance of 1947 (Rio Treaty) recognizes the obligation of the American Republics to "provide for effective reciprocal assistance to meet armed attacks against any American state and in order to deal with threats of aggression against any of them,"

* * *

a.   Subsequent to the time the Cuban missile crisis occurred, the Charter of the OAS was revised (Protocol of Buenos Aires, February 27, 1967, 21 UST 607).   Articles 15 through 19 were renumbered 18 through 22 in the revision.

The Council of the Organization of American States, Meeting as the Provisional Organ of Consultation, Resolves:

1.   To call for the immediate dismantling and withdrawal from Cuba of all missiles and other weapons with any offensive capability;

2.   To recommend that the member states, in accordance with Article 6 and 8 of the Inter-American Treaty of Reciprocal Assistance, take all measures, individually and collectively, including the use of armed force, which they may deem necessary to ensure that the Government of Cuba cannot continue to receive from the Sino-Soviet powers military material and related supplies which may threaten the peace and security of the Continent and to prevent the missiles in Cuba with offensive capability from ever becoming an active threat to the peace and security of the Continent;

3.   To inform the Security Council of the United Nations of this resolution in accordance with Article 54 of the Charter of the United Nations and to express the hope that the Security Council will, in accordance with the draft resolution introduced by the United States, dispatch United Nations observers to Cuba at the earliest moment;

4.   To continue to serve provisionally as Organ of Consultation and to request the Member States to keep the Organ of Consultation duly informed of measures taken by them in accordance with paragraph two of this resolution.

UNITED STATES PROCLAMATION

INTERDICTION OF THE DELIVERY OF OFFENSIVE WEAPONS TO CUBA

47 United States Department of State Bulletin 717 (1962).

Whereas the peace of the world and the security of the United States and of all American States are endangered by reason of the establishment by the Sino-Soviet powers of an offensive military capability in Cuba, including bases for ballistic missiles with a potential range covering most of North and South America;

Whereas by a Joint Resolution passed by the Congress of the United States and approved on October 3, 1962, it was declared that the United States is determined to prevent by whatever means may be necessary, including the use of arms, the Marxist-Leninist regime in Cuba from extending, by force or the threat of force, its aggressive or subversive activities to any part of this hemisphere, and to prevent in Cuba the creation or use of an externally supported military capability endangering the security of the United States; and

Whereas the Organ of Consultation of the American Republics meeting in Washington on October 23, 1962, recommended that the Member States, in accordance with Articles 6 and 8 of the Inter-American Treaty of Reciprocal Assistance, take all measures, individually and collectively, including the use of armed force, which they may deem necessary to ensure that the Government of Cuba cannot continue to receive from the Sino-Soviet powers military material and related supplies which may threaten the peace and security of the Continent and to prevent the missiles in Cuba with offensive capability from ever becoming an active threat to the peace and security of the Continent:

Now, Therefore, I, John F. Kennedy, President of the United States of America, acting under and by virtue of the authority conferred upon me by the Constitution and statutes of the United States, in accordance with the aforementioned resolutions of the United States Congress and of the Organ of Consultation of the American Republics, and to defend the security of the United States, do hereby proclaim that the forces under my command are ordered, beginning at 2:00 p. m. Greenwich time October 24, 1962, to interdict, subject to the instructions herein contained, the delivery of offensive weapons and associated materiel to Cuba.

For the purposes of this Proclamation, the following are declared to be prohibited materiel:

Surface-to-surface missiles; bomber aircraft; bombs, air-to-surface rockets and guided missiles; warheads for any of the above weapons; mechanical or electronic equipment to support or operate the above items; and any other classes of materiel hereafter designated by the Secretary of Defense for the purpose of effectuating this Proclamation.

To enforce this order, the Secretary of Defense shall take appropriate measures to prevent the delivery of prohibited materiel to Cuba, employing the land, sea and air forces of the United States in cooperation with any forces that may be made available by other American States.

The Secretary of Defense may make such regulations and issue such directives as he deems necessary to ensure the effectiveness of this order, including the designation, within a reasonable distance of Cuba, of prohibited or restricted zones and of prescribed routes.

Any vessel or craft which may be proceeding toward Cuba may be intercepted and may be directed to identify itself, its cargo, equipment and stores and its ports of call, to stop, to lie to, to submit to visit and search, or to proceed as directed. Any vessel or craft which fails or refuses to respond to or comply with directions shall be subject to being taken into custody. Any vessel or craft which it is believed is en route to Cuba and may be carrying prohibited materiel or may itself constitute such materiel shall, wherever possible, be directed to proceed to another destination of its own choice and shall be taken into custody if it fails or refuses to obey such directions. All vessels or craft taken into custody shall be sent into a port of the United States for appropriate disposition.

In carrying out this order, force shall not be used except in case of failure or refusal to comply with directions, or with regulations or directives of the Secretary of Defense issued hereunder, after reasonable efforts have been made to communicate them to the vessel or craft, or in case of self-defense. In any case, force shall be used only to the extent necessary.

[The Proclamation was signed by President Kennedy at 7:06 P.M., October 23, 1962.]

KENNEDY, THIRTEEN DAYS (1969) *

[Robert Kennedy, Attorney General and brother of the President, participated in the White House discussions of the committee that advised the President on the handling of the Cuban missile crisis. Some of his observations about legal aspects of the handling of the crisis are set out below.]

    * * *

Finally, we agreed on a procedure by which we felt we could give some intelligent recommendations to the President. We knew that time was running out and that delay was not possible. We split into groups to write up our respective recommendations, beginning with an outline of the President's speech to the nation and the whole course of action thereafter, trying to anticipate all possible contingencies and setting forth recommendations as to how to react to them.

In the early afternoon, we exchanged papers, each group dissected and criticized the other, and then the papers were returned to the original group to develop further answers. Gradually from all this came the outline of definitive plans. For the group that advocated the blockade, it was an outline of the legal basis for our action, an agenda for a meeting of the Organization of American States, recommendations for the role of the United Nations, the military procedures for stopping ships, and, finally, the circumstances under which military force might be used. For the group that advocated immediate military action, it was an outline of the areas to be attacked, a defense of our position in the United Nations, suggestions as to how

* Reprinted with the permission of W. W.
Norton & Company, Inc., New York.

to obtain support from Latin American countries, and a proposed communication to Khrushchev to convince him of the inadvisability of moving militarily against us in the Caribbean, Berlin, or elsewhere in the world.　(at 44–45).

*　*　*

The President made his decision that afternoon in favor of the blockade.　There was one final meeting the next morning, with General Walter C. Sweeney, Jr., Commander in Chief of the Tactical Air Command, who told the President that even a major surprise air attack could not be certain of destroying all the missile sites and nuclear weapons in Cuba.　That ended the small, lingering doubt that might still have remained in his mind.　It had worried him that a blockade would not remove the missiles—now it was clear that an attack could not accomplish that task completely, either.

The strongest argument against the all-out military attack, and one no one could answer to his satisfaction, was that a surprise attack would erode if not destroy the moral position of the United States throughout the world.　(at 48–49).

*　*　*

The diplomatic effort was of great significance.　We were able to establish a firm legal foundation for our action under the OAS Charter, and our position around the world was greatly strengthened when the Organization of American States unanimously supported the recommendation for a quarantine.　Thus the Soviet Union and Cuba faced the united action of the whole Western Hemisphere.　(at 51).

*　*　*

The next day, Tuesday, was the important meeting of the OAS previously mentioned.　It was anticipated that we might have difficulty obtaining the two thirds vote of support necessary for the ordering of a quarantine.　But the Latin American countries, demonstrating a unique sense of unity, unanimously supported the recommendations of the United States.　In fact, a number contributed men, supplies, and ships during the several weeks that followed.　(at 57).

*　*　*

It was the vote of the Organization of American States that gave a legal basis for the quarantine.　Their willingness to follow the leadership of the United States was a heavy and unexpected blow to Khrushchev.　It had a major psychological and practical effect on the Russians and changed our position from that of an outlaw acting in violation of international law into a country acting in accordance with twenty allies legally protecting their position.　(at 121).

CHAYES, THE LEGAL CASE FOR U. S. ACTION ON CUBA

47 United States Department of State Bulletin 763, 764 (1962).

* * * The quarantine action involves a use of force and must be squared with this principle.

The promise not to use force is not absolute. One qualification comes readily to mind. Article 51 affirms that nothing in the charter, including article 2(4), impairs "the inherent right of individual or collective self-defense if an armed attack occurs." The quarantine action was designed to deal with an imminent threat to our security. But the President in his speech did not invoke article 51 or the right of self-defense. And the OAS acted not under article 3, covering cases of armed attack, but under article 6, covering threats to the peace other than armed attack.

Self-defense, however, is not the only justifiable use of force under the charter. Obviously, the United Nations itself could sanction the use of force to deal with a threat to the peace. So it did in Korea and in the Congo. We accept use of force in these instances as legitimate for two reasons. First, all the members have constituted the United Nations for these purposes. In signing the charter they have assented to its powers and procedures. Second, the political processes by which the U.N. makes a decision to use force give some assurance that the decision will not be rashly taken.

I submit that the same two factors legitimize use of force in accordance with the OAS resolution dealing with a threat to the peace in the hemisphere. The significance of assent is attested by the fact that, though Cuba is now and has been for some time the object of sanctions and hostility from the OAS and has been suspended from participation in its agencies, she has remained a party to the treaties and a member of the inter-American system, as, in a like case, did the Dominican Republic. The significance of the political processes in the Organization is attested by the fact that, despite the disproportion of power between the United States and its neighbors to the south, it was not until the danger was clear and present that the necessary majority could be mustered to sanction use of armed force. But when that time came, the vote was unanimous.

Some have asked whether we should not first have gone to the Security Council before taking other action to meet the Soviet threat in Cuba. And I suppose that in the original conception of the United Nations, it was thought that the Security Council would be the agency for dealing with situations of this kind. However, the drafters of the charter demonstrated their wisdom by making Security Council responsibility for dealing with threats to the peace "primary" and not "exclusive." For events since 1945 have demonstrated that the Security Council, like our own electoral college, was not a viable institution. The veto has made it substantially useless in keeping the peace.

The withering away of the Security Council has led to a search for alternative peacekeeping institutions. In the United Nations itself the General Assembly and the Secretary-General have filled the void. Regional organizations are another obvious candidate.

MEEKER, DEFENSIVE QUARANTINE AND THE LAW

57 American Journal of International Law 515, 523 (1963).

Charter Limitation on the "Threat or Use of Force"

Before leaving the Charter of the United Nations it is relevant also to consider Article 2, paragraph 4, which provides:

> All Members shall refrain in their international relations from the threat or use of force against the territorial integrity or political independence of any state, or in any other manner inconsistent with the Purposes of the United Nations.

It was recognized that the defensive quarantine was dependent, ultimately, upon the use of naval forces for its effectiveness. Accordingly, there was acknowledged to be a threat, and potentially a use, of armed force. However, it did not follow that this must contravene Article 2, paragraph 4.

In considering the obligations imposed on Members by that article, it should be noted that not all threats or uses of force are prohibited; only those which are inconsistent with the purposes of the United Nations are covered by Article 2, paragraph 4. The presence of the word "other" in the concluding clause of the paragraph makes this clear. Even assuming that the measures taken could be considered to impinge upon the territorial integrity or political independence of some state or states, they would not be contrary to Article 2, paragraph 4, as long as they were not inconsistent with the purposes of the United Nations. The defensive quarantine, as indicated earlier, was considered to be in accordance with Chapter VIII of the Charter.

It is clear that collective action for peace and security which the Security Council may take under Chapter VII does not contravene Article 2, paragraph 4. It is also clear that individual or collective self-defense against armed attack, in accordance with Article 51, does not violate the Charter. Here it may be noted that the United States, in adopting the defensive quarantine of Cuba, did not seek to justify it as a measure required to meet an "armed attack" within the meaning of Article 51. Nor did the United States seek to sustain its action on the ground that Article 51 is not an all-inclusive statement of the right of self-defense and that the quarantine was a measure of self-defense open to any country to take individually for its own defense in a case other than "armed attack." Indeed, as shown by President Kennedy's television address of October 22 and by other statements of the Government, reliance was not placed on either contention, and the United States took no position on either of these issues.

The quarantine was based on a collective judgment and recommendation of the American Republics made under the Rio Treaty. It was considered not to contravene Article 2, paragraph 4, because it was a measure adopted by a regional organization in conformity with the provisions of Chapter VIII of the Charter.[a] The purposes of the Organization and its activities were considered to be consistent with the purposes and principles of the United Nations as provided in Article 52. This being the case, the quarantine would no more violate Article 2, paragraph 4, than measures voted by the Council under Chapter VII, by the General Assembly under Articles 10 and 11, or taken by United Nations Members in conformity with Article 51.

Finally, in relation to the Charter limitation on threat or use of force, it should be noted that the quarantine itself was a carefully limited measure proportionate to the threat and designed solely to prevent any further build-up of strategic missile bases in Cuba.

---

2. REVOLT IN THE DOMINICAN REPUBLIC

MEEKER, THE DOMINICAN SITUATION IN THE PERSPECTIVE OF INTERNATIONAL LAW

53 United States Department of State Bulletin 60 (1965).

* * *

The revolt that began on April 24 arose out of an unstable political situation in the Dominican Republic. The government headed by Donald Reid Cabral did not have a popular mandate. It was trying to deal with an unsatisfactory economic situation which it had inherited. The government's efforts to correct the economic situation were reasonably effective, but because of that fact they did increase the political strain.

Some senior military officers who had been removed from key positions in a reform program carried out by the Reid government were obviously unhappy with that government. At the same time, junior military officers were complaining that the military reforms

a. At p. 522, the author addresses the question of the conformity of the action of the regional organization to Article 53(1) of the Charter: "But no enforcement action shall be taken under regional arrangements or by regional agencies without the authorization of the Security Council * * *".

were not broad enough and that the government was acting too slowly in implementing them.

The Dominican Revolutionary Party was seeking to restore to power former President Juan Bosch, who had been deposed in September 1963.

From these elements there arose a loose association which set off the April 24 revolution.

The next day Reid Cabral resigned and went into hiding. Rebels seized the national palace, and a leader of the Dominican Revolutionary Party was installed as provisional president. For a time the rebels appeared to be making headway. Then, on April 26, elements of the armed forces began to move against rebel-held areas of Santo Domingo. They conducted air attacks on the city.

Meanwhile, large quantities of arms were distributed by the rebels to civilians, and disorder grew rapidly. Repeated efforts by the United States Embassy to bring about a cease-fire between the opposing factions were unsuccessful. In the course of April 26 a large number of American citizens had assembled at a hotel west of Santo Domingo, seeking safety and assistance in being evacuated.

April 27 saw a complete breakdown of law and order. The rebel provisional president of only 2 days abandoned his office and took asylum in a Latin American embassy.

During the course of April 28 the antirebel forces lost their momentum after earlier progress against the rebels. The situation in Santo Domingo became increasingly confused. The breakdown in public order resulted in indiscriminate shooting on a rising scale. The police were no longer effective. Armed mobs were terrorizing the city, firing on homes and other buildings, including the United States and other embassies.

During this period the activities of Communist leaders in organizing mobs and in directing their wanton forays increased markedly. With the withdrawal of a number of moderate political leaders from the rebel movement, it appeared that the Communists were in a fair way to take it over.

Late in the afternoon of April 28 the antirebel military and police authorities informed the United States Embassy that they could no longer provide any assurance for the safety of American lives.

This, then, was the situation on the Wednesday afternoon before President Johnson ordered the landing of Marines to the west of the city of Santo Domingo.

* * * We landed troops in the Dominican Republic in order to preserve the lives of foreign nationals—nationals of the United States and many other countries. We continued our military presence in the Dominican Republic for the additional purpose of preserving the capacity of the OAS to function in the manner intended by the

OAS Charter—to achieve peace and justice through securing a cease-fire and through reestablishing orderly political processes within which Dominicans could choose their own government, free from outside interference.

* * *

In the context of Cuba, only a few miles away, and of the announced drive of the Communists to expand their control in this hemisphere, external threat to the Dominican Republic was by no means fancified. The threat of a Communist takeover had to be viewed as very real.

Here was the very kind of threat which the Latin American foreign ministers had in mind when they declared at Punta del Este in January 1962:

> The principles of communism are incompatible with the principles of the Inter-American system. * * * (and) adherence by any member of the Organization of American States to Marxism-Leninism is incompatible with the inter-American system and the alignment of such a government with the communist bloc breaks the unity and solidarity of the hemisphere.

This meeting of foreign ministers therefore urged:

> * * * the member states to take those steps that they may consider appropriate for their individual or collective self-defense, and to cooperate, as may be necessary or desirable, to strengthen their capacity to counteract threats or acts of aggression, subversion, or other dangers to peace and security resulting from the continued intervention in this hemisphere of Sino-Soviet powers, in accordance with the obligations established in treaties and agreements such as the Charter of the Organization of American States and the Inter-American Treaty of Reciprocal Assistance.

---

3. DEFENSE OF SOCIALISM IN CZECHOSLOVAKIA

KOVALEV, SOVEREIGNTY AND INTERNATIONAL DUTIES OF SOCIALIST COUNTRIES

Reprinted from Pravda
The New York Times, Sept. 27, 1968, Sec. 1, at 3, col. 1.*

[In 1968, military forces of the USSR and other Warsaw Pact countries entered Czechoslovakia; the displacement of the existing "liberal" Communist government followed.]

In connection with the events in Czechoslovakia, the question of the correlation and interdependence of the national interests of the socialist countries and their international duties acquire particular topical and acute importance.

The measures taken by the Soviet Union, jointly with other socialist countries, in defending the socialist gains of the Czechoslovak people are of great significance for strengthening the socialist community, which is the main achievement of the international working class.

We cannot ignore the assertions, held in some places, that the actions of the five socialist countries run counter to the Marxist-Leninist principle of sovereignty and the rights of nations to self-determination.

Abstract Approach Seen

The groundlessness of such reasoning consists primarily in that it is based on an abstract, nonclass approach to the question of sovereignty and the rights of nations to self-determination.

The peoples of the socialist countries and Communist parties certainly do have and should have freedom for determining the ways of advance of their respective countries.

However, none of their decisions should damage either socialism in their country or the fundamental interests of other socialist countries, and the whole working class movement, which is working for socialism.

This means that each Communist party is responsible not only to its own people, but also to all the socialist countries, to the entire Communist movement. Whoever forgets this, in stressing only the independence of the Communist party, becomes one-sided. He deviates from his international duty.

One-Sidedness Opposed

Marxist dialectics are opposed to one-sidedness. They demand that each phenomenon be examined concretely, in general connection with other phenomena, with other processes.

Just as, in Lenin's words, a man living in a society cannot be free from the society, one or another socialist state, staying in a system of other states composing the socialist community, cannot be free from the common interests of that community.

The sovereignty of each socialist country cannot be opposed to the interests of the world of socialism, of the world revolutionary movement. Lenin demanded that all Communists fight against small-nation narrow-mindedness, seclusion and isolation, consider the whole and the general, subordinate the particular to the general interest.

The socialist states respect the democratic norms of international law. They have proved this more than once in practice, by coming out resolutely against the attempts of imperialism to violate the sovereignty and independence of nations.

It is from these same positions that they reject the leftist, adventurist conception of "exporting revolution," of "bringing happiness" to other peoples.

However, from a Marxist point of view, the norms of law, including the norms of mutual relations of the socialist countries, cannot be interpreted narrowly, formally, and in isolation from the general context of class struggle in the modern world. The socialist countries resolutely come out against the exporting and importing of counter-revolution.

Opposing Systems Stressed

Each Communist party is free to apply the basic principles of Marxism-Leninism and of socialism in its country, but it cannot depart from these principles assuming, naturally, that it remains a Communist party.

Concretely, this means, first of all, that, in its activity, each Communist party cannot but take into account such a decisive fact of our time as the struggle between two opposing social systems—capitalism and socialism.

This is an objective struggle, a fact not depending on the will of the people, and stipulated by the world's being split into two opposite social systems. Lenin said: "Each man must choose between joining our side or the other side. Any attempt to avoid taking sides in this issue must end in fiasco."

It has got to be emphasized that when a socialist country seems to adopt a "non-affiliated" stand, it retains its national independence, in effect, precisely because of the might of the socialist community, and above all the Soviet Union as a central force, which also includes the might of its armed forces. The weakening of any of the links in the world system of socialism directly affects all the socialist countries, which cannot look indifferently upon this.

NATO Threat Seen

The antisocialist elements in Czechoslovakia actually covered up the demand for so-called neutrality and Czechoslovakia's withdrawal from the socialist community with talking about the right of nations to self-determination.

However, the implementation of such "self-determination," in other words, Czechoslovakia's detachment from the socialist community, would have come into conflict with its own vital interests and would have been detrimental to the other socialist states.

Such "self-determination," as a result of which NATO troops would have been able to come up to the Soviet border, while the community of European socialist countries would have been split, in effect encroaches upon the vital interests of the peoples of these countries and conflicts, as the very root of it, with the right of these people to socialist self-determination.

Discharging their internationalist duty toward the fraternal peoples of Czechoslovakia and defending their own socialist gains, the U.S.S.R. and the other socialist states had to act decisively and they did act against the antisocialist forces in Czechoslovakia.

Gomulka Is Quoted

Comrade W. Gomulka, First Secretary of the Central Committee of the Polish United Workers party, commented figuratively on this score when he said:

"We tell those friends and comrades of ours in the other countries who think they are upholding the righteous cause of socialism and the sovereignty of the peoples by condemning and protesting against the entry of our troops into Czechoslovakia: When the enemy mines our house, the community of socialist states, with dynamite, it is our patriotic, national and international duty to obstruct this by using the means that are necessary."

People who "disapprove" of the actions of the allied socialist states are ignoring the decisive fact that these countries are defending the interests of all of world socialism, of the entire world revolutionary movement.

The system of socialism exists in concrete form in some countries, which have their own definite state boundaries; this system is developing according to the specific conditions of each country. Furthermore, nobody interferes in the concrete measures taken to improve the socialist system in the different socialist countries.

However, the picture changes fundamentally when a danger arises to socialism itself in a particular country. As a social system, world socialism is the common gain of the working people of all lands; it is indivisible and its defense is the common cause of all Communists and all progressives in the world, in the first place, the working folk of the socialist Countries.

"Rightist" Aim Described

The Bratislava statement of the Communist and Workers' parties says of socialist gains that "support, consolidation and defense of these gains, won at the price of heroic effort and the self-sacrifice of each people, represents a common international duty and obligation for all the socialist countries."

What the right-wing anti-socialist forces set out to achieve in recent months in Czechoslovakia did not refer to the specific features of socialist development or the application of the principle of Marxism-Leninism to the concrete conditions obtaining in that country, but constituted encroachment on the foundations of socialism, on the basic principles of Marxism-Leninism.

This is the nuance that people who have fallen for the hypocritical nonsense of the antisocialist and revisionist elements still cannot understand. Under the guise of "democratization" these elements were little by little shaking the socialist state, seeking to demoralize the Communist party and befog the minds of the masses, stealthily hatching a counterrevolutionary coup, and they were not duly rebuffed inside the country.

Could Not Stand Aside

Naturally the Communists of the fraternal countries could not allow the socialist states to be inactive in the name of an abstractly understood sovereignty, when they saw that the country stood in peril of antisocialist degeneration.

The actions in Czechoslovakia of the five allied socialist countries accords also with the vital interests of the people of the country themselves.

Socialism, by delivering a nation from the shackles of an exploiting regime, insures the solution of the fundamental problems of the national development of any country that has embarked upon the socialist road. On the other hand, by encroaching upon the mainstays of socialism, the counterrevolutionary elements in Czechoslovakia undermined the very foundations of the country's independence and sovereignty.

Formal observance of the freedom of self-determination of a nation in the concrete situation that arose in Czechoslovakia would mean freedom of "self-determination" not of the popular masses, the working people, but of their enemies.

The antisocialist path, "neutrality", to which the Czechoslovak people were pushed would bring it to the loss of its national independence.

World imperialism, on its part, supported the antisocialist forces in Czechoslovakia, tried to export counterrevolution to that country in this way.

The help to the working people of Czechoslovakia by other socialist countries, which prevented the export of counterrevolution from abroad, constitutes the actual sovereignty of the Czechoslovak socialist republic against those who would like to deprive it from its sovereignty and give up the country to imperialism.

Political Means Exhausted

The fraternal Communist parties of the socialist countries were for a long time taking measures, with maximum self-restraint and patience, to help the Czechoslovak people with political means to stop the onslaught of antisocialist forces in Czechoslovakia. And only when all such measures were exhausted did they bring armed forces into the country.

The soldiers of the allied socialist countries now in Czechoslovakia proved by their actions indeed that they have no other tasks than the tasks of defending socialist gains in that country.

They do not interfere in the internal affairs of the country, are fighting for the principle of self-determination of the peoples of Czechoslovakia not in words but in deeds, are fighting for their inalienable right to think out profoundly and decide their fate themselves, without intimidation on the part of counterrevolutionaries, without revisionists and nationalist demagogy.

Class Approach to Law

Those who speak about the "illegal actions" of the allied socialist countries in Czechoslovakia forget that in a class society there is not and there cannot be non-class laws.

Laws and legal norms are subjected to the laws of the class struggle, the laws of social development. These laws are clearly formulated in Marxist-Leninist teaching, in the documents jointly adopted by the Communist and Workers' parties.

Formally juridical reasoning must not overshadow a class approach to the matter. One who does it, thus losing the only correct class criterion in assessing legal norms, begins to measure events with a yardstick of bourgeois law.

Such an approach to the question of sovereignty means that, for example, the progressive forces of the world would not be able to come out against the revival of neo-Nazism in the Federal Republic of Germany, against the actions of butchers Franco and Salazar, against reactionary arbitrary actions of "black colonels" in Greece, because this is "the internal affair" of "sovereign" states.

Vietnam Example Cited

It is characteristic that both the Saigon puppets and their American protectors also regard the notion of sovereignty as prohibiting support for the struggle of progressive forces.

They proclaim at every crossroads that the socialist countries, which are rendering help to the Vietnamese people in their struggle for independence and freedom, are violating the sovereignty of Vietnam. Genuine revolutionaries, being internationalists, cannot but support progressive forces in all countries in their just struggle for national and social liberation.

The interests of the socialist community and of the whole revolutionary movement, the interests of socialism in Czechoslovakia demand complete exposure and political isolation of the reactionary forces in that country, consolidation of the working people and consistent implementation of the Moscow agreement between the Soviet and Czechoslovak leaders.

There is no doubt that the actions of the five allied socialist countries in Czechoslovakia directed to the defense of the vital interests of the socialist community, that the sovereignty of socialist Czechoslovakia first and foremost, will be increasingly supported by all those who have the interest of the present revolutionary movement, of peace and security of peoples, of democracy and socialism at heart.

---

4. THE CLAIM OF COLLECTIVE SELF–DEFENSE IN SOUTH VIETNAM

THE LEGALITY OF UNITED STATES PARTICIPATION IN THE DEFENSE OF VIET–NAM, MEMORANDUM PREPARED BY THE LEGAL ADVISER OF THE DEPARTMENT OF STATE

54 United States Department of State Bulletin 474 (1966).a

March 4, 1966

1. The United States and South Viet-Nam Have the Right Under International Law to Participate in the Collective Defense of South Viet-Nam Against Armed Attack.

In response to requests from the Government of South Viet-Nam, the United States has been assisting that country in defending itself against armed attack from the Communist North. This attack has taken the forms of externally supported subversion, clandestine supply of arms, infiltration of armed personnel, and most recently the sending of regular units of the North Vietnamese army into the South.

International law has long recognized the right of individual and collective self-defense against armed attack. South Viet-Nam and the United States are engaging in such collective defense consistently with international law and with United States obligations under the United Nations Charter.

A. South Viet-Nam Is Being Subjected to Armed Attack by Communist North Viet-Nam

The Geneva accords of 1954 established a demarcation line between North Viet-Nam and South Viet-Nam. They provided for withdrawals of military forces into the respective zones north and south of this line. The accords prohibited the use of either zone for the resumption of hostilities or to "further an aggressive policy."

During the 5 years following the Geneva conference of 1954, the Hanoi regime developed a covert political-military organization in South Viet-Nam based on Communist cadres it had ordered to stay

---

a. In the text appearing in the Bulletin there are two types of footnotes: those which appeared in the original of the memorandum and those which were added when it was published in the Bulletin. When the footnotes are of the first type, they are specifically identified thus: [Footnote in original].

in the South, contrary to the provisions of the Geneva accords. The activities of this covert organization were directed toward the kidnaping and assassination of civilian officials—acts of terrorism that were perpetrated in increasing numbers.

In the 3-year period from 1959 to 1961, the North Viet-Nam regime infiltrated an estimated 10,000 men into the South. It is estimated that 13,000 additional personnel were infiltrated in 1962, and, by the end of 1964, North Viet-Nam may well have moved over 40,-000 armed and unarmed guerrillas into South Viet-Nam.

The International Control Commission reported in 1962 the findings of its Legal Committee:

> * * * there is evidence to show that arms, armed and unarmed personnel, munitions and other supplies have been sent from the Zone in the North to the Zone in the South with the objective of supporting, organizing and carrying out hostile activities, including armed attacks, directed against the Armed Forces and Administration of the Zone in the South.

> * * * there is evidence that the PAVN [People's Army of Viet Nam] has allowed the Zone in the North to be used for inciting, encouraging and supporting hostile activities in the Zone in the South, aimed at the overthrow of the Administration in the South.

Beginning in 1964, the Communists apparently exhausted their reservoir of Southerners who had gone North. Since then the greater number of men infiltrated into the South have been native-born North Vietnamese. Most recently, Hanoi has begun to infiltrate elements of the North Vietnamese army in increasingly larger numbers. Today, there is evidence that nine regiments of regular North Vietnamese forces are fighting in organized units in the South.

In the guerrilla war in Viet-Nam, the external aggression from the North is the critical military element of the insurgency, although it is unacknowledged by North Viet-Nam. In these circumstances, an "armed attack" is not as easily fixed by date and hour as in the case of traditional warfare. However, the infiltration of thousands of armed men clearly constitutes an "armed attack" under any reasonable definition. There may be some question as to the exact date at which North Viet-Nam's aggression grew into an "armed attack," but there can be no doubt that it had occurred before February 1965.

B.   International Law Recognizes the Right of Individual and Collective Self-Defense Against Armed Attack

International law has traditionally recognized the right of self-defense against armed attack. This proposition has been asserted by writers on international law through the several centuries in which the modern law of nations has developed. The proposition has been acted on numerous times by governments throughout modern history.

Today the principle of self-defense against armed attack is universally recognized and accepted.

The Charter of the United Nations, concluded at the end of World War II, imposed an important limitation on the use of force by United Nations members. Article 2, paragraph 4, provides:

> All Members shall refrain in their international relations from the threat or use of force against the territorial integrity or political independence of any state, or in any other manner inconsistent with the Purposes of the United Nations.

In addition, the charter embodied a system of international peacekeeping through the organs of the United Nations. Article 24 summarizes these structural arrangements in stating that the United Nations members:

> * * * confer on the Security Council primary responsibility for the maintenance of international peace and security, and agree that in carrying out its duties under this responsibility the Security Council acts on their behalf.

However, the charter expressly states in article 51 that the remaining provisions of the charter—including the limitation of article 2, paragraph 4 and the creation of United Nations machinery to keep the peace—in no way diminish the inherent right of self-defense against armed attack. Article 51 provides:

> Nothing in the present Charter shall impair the inherent right of individual or collective self-defense if an armed attack occurs against a Member of the United Nations, until the Security Council has taken the measures necessary to maintain international peace and security. Measures taken by Members in the exercise of this right of self-defense shall be immediately reported to the Security Council and shall not in any way affect the authority and responsibility of the Security Council under the present Charter to take at any time such action as it deems necessary in order to maintain or restore international peace and security.

Thus, article 51 restates and preserves, for member states in the situations covered by the article, a long-recognized principle of international law. The article is a "saving clause" designed to make clear that no other provision in the charter shall be interpreted to impair the inherent right of self-defense referred to in article 51.

Three principal objections have been raised against the availability of the right of individual and collective self-defense in the case of Viet-Nam: (1) that this right applies only in the case of an armed attack on a United Nations member; (2) that it does not apply in the case of South Viet-Nam because the latter is not an independent sovereign state; and (3) that collective self-defense may be undertaken only by a regional organization operating under chapter VIII of the United Nations Charter. These objections will now be considered in turn.

C. The Right of Individual and Collective Self-Defense Applies in the Case of South Viet-Nam Whether or Not That Country Is a Member of the United Nations

1. South Viet-Nam enjoys the right of self-defense

The argument that the right of self-defense is available only to members of the United Nations mistakes the nature of the right of self-defense and the relationship of the United Nations Charter to international law in this respect. As already shown, the right of self-defense against armed attack is an inherent right under international law. The right is not conferred by the charter, and, indeed, article 51 expressly recognizes that the right is inherent.

The charter nowhere contains any provision designed to deprive nonmembers of the right of self-defense against armed attack.[3] Article 2, paragraph 6, does charge the United Nations with responsibility for insuring that nonmember states act in accordance with United Nations "Principles so far as may be necessary for the maintenance of international peace and security." Protection against aggression and self-defense against armed attack are important elements in the whole charter scheme for the maintenance of international peace and security. To deprive nonmembers of their inherent right of self-defense would not accord with the principles of the organization, but would instead be prejudicial to the maintenance of peace. Thus article 2, paragraph 6—and, indeed, the rest of the charter—should certainly not be construed to nullify or diminish the inherent defensive rights of nonmembers.

2. The United States has the right to assist in the defense of South Viet-Nam although the latter is not a United Nations member

The cooperation of two or more international entities in the defense of one or both against armed attack is generally referred to as collective self-defense. United States participation in the defense of South Viet-Nam at the latter's request is an example of collective self-defense.

The United States is entitled to exercise the right of individual or collective self-defense against armed attack, as that right exists in

3. While nonmembers, such as South Viet-Nam, have not formally undertaken the obligations of the United Nations Charter as their own treaty obligations, it should be recognized that much of the substantive law of the charter has become part of the general law of nations through a very wide acceptance by nations the world over. This is particularly true of the charter provisions bearing on the use of force. Moreover, in the case of South Viet-Nam, the South Vietnamese Government has expressed its ability and willingness to abide by the charter, in applying for United Nations membership. Thus it seems entirely appropriate to appraise the actions of South Viet-Nam in relation to the legal standards set forth in the United Nations Charter. [Footnote in original.]

international law, subject only to treaty limitations and obligations undertaken by this country.

It has been urged that the United States has no right to participate in the collective defense of South Viet-Nam because article 51 of the United Nations Charter speaks only of the situation "if an armed attack occurs *against a Member of the United Nations*." This argument is without substance.

In the first place, article 51 does not impose restrictions or cut down the otherwise available rights of United Nations members. By its own terms, the article preserves an inherent right. It is, therefore, necessary to look elsewhere in the charter for any obligation of members restricting their participation in collective defense of an entity that is not a United Nations member.

Article 2, paragraph 4, is the principal provision of the charter imposing limitations on the use of force by members. It states that they:

> * * * shall refrain in their international relations from the threat or use of force against the territorial integrity or political independence of any state, or in any other manner inconsistent with the Purposes of the United Nations.

Action taken in defense against armed attack cannot be characterized as falling within this proscription. The record of the San Francisco conference makes clear that article 2, paragraph 4 was not intended to restrict the right of self-defense against armed attack.[4]

One will search in vain for any other provision in the charter that would preclude United States participation in the collective defense of a nonmember. The fact that article 51 refers only to armed attack "against a Member of the United Nations" implies no intention to preclude members from participating in the defense of nonmembers. Any such result would have seriously detrimental consequences for international peace and security and would be inconsistent with the purposes of the United Nations as they are set forth in article 1 of the charter. The right of members to participate in the defense of nonmembers is upheld by leading authorities on international law.[6]

D. The Right of Individual and Collective Self-Defense Applies Whether or Not South Viet-Nam Is Regarded as an Independent Sovereign State

1.   South Viet-Nam enjoys the right of self-defense

It has been asserted that the conflict in Viet-Nam is "civil strife" in which foreign intervention is forbidden. Those who make this as-

---

4.   See 6 UNCIO Documents 459. [Footnote in original.]

6.   Bowett, Self-Defense in International Law, 193–195 (1958); Goodhart, "The North Atlantic Treaty of 1949," 79 Recueil Des Cours, 183, 202–204 (1951,

vol. II), quoted in 5 Whiteman's Digest of International Law, 1067–1068 (1965); Kelsen, The Law of the United Nations, 793 (1950); see Stone, Aggression and World Order, 44 (1958). [Footnote in original.]

sertion have gone so far as to compare Ho Chi Minh's actions in Viet-Nam with the efforts of President Lincoln to preserve the Union during the American Civil War. Any such characterization is an entire fiction disregarding the actual situation in Viet-Nam. The Hanoi regime is anything but the legitimate government of a unified country in which the South is rebelling against lawful national authority.

The Geneva accords of 1954 provided for a division of Viet-Nam into two zones at the 17th parallel. Although this line of demarcation was intended to be temporary, it was established by international agreement, which specifically forbade aggression by one zone against the other.

The Republic of Viet-Nam in the South has been recognized as a separate international entity by approximately 60 governments the world over. It has been admitted as a member of a number of the specialized agencies of the United Nations. The United Nations General Assembly in 1957 voted to recommend South Viet-Nam for membership in the organization, and its admission was frustrated only by the veto of the Soviet Union in the Security Council.

In any event there is no warrant for the suggestion that one zone of a temporarily divided state—whether it be Germany, Korea, or Viet-Nam—can be legally overrun by armed forces from the other zone, crossing the internationally recognized line of demarcation between the two. Any such doctrine would subvert the international agreement establishing the line of demarcation, and would pose grave dangers to international peace.

The action of the United Nations in the Korean conflict of 1950 clearly established the principle that there is no greater license for one zone of a temporarily divided state to attack the other zone than there is for one state to attack another state. South Viet-Nam has the same right that South Korea had to defend itself and to organize collective defense against an armed attack from the North. A resolution of the Security Council dated June 25, 1950, noted "with grave concern the armed attack upon the Republic of Korea by forces from North Korea," and determined "that this action constitutes a breach of the peace."

2. The United States is entitled to participate in the collective defense of South Viet-Nam whether or not the latter is regarded as an independent sovereign state

As stated earlier, South Viet-Nam has been recognized as a separate international entity by approximately 60 governments. It has been admitted to membership in a number of the United Nations specialized agencies and has been excluded from the United Nations Organization only by the Soviet veto.

There is nothing in the charter to suggest that United Nations members are precluded from participating in the defense of a recognized international entity against armed attack merely because the entity may lack some of the attributes of an independent sovereign state. Any such result would have a destructive effect on the stability of international engagements such as the Geneva accords of 1954 and on internationally agreed lines of demarcation. Such a result, far from being in accord with the charter and the purposes of the United Nations, would undermine them and would create new dangers to international peace and security.

E.   The United Nations Charter Does Not Limit the Right of Self-Defense to Regional Organizations

Some have argued that collective self-defense may be undertaken only by a regional arrangement or agency operating under chapter VIII of the United Nations Charter. Such an assertion ignores the structure of the charter and the practice followed in the more than 20 years since the founding of the United Nations.

The basic proposition that rights of self-defense are not impaired by the charter—as expressly stated in article 51—is not conditioned by any charter provision limiting the application of this proposition to collective defense by a regional arrangement or agency. The structure of the charter reinforces this conclusion. Article 51 appears in chapter VII of the charter, entitled "Action With Respect to Threats to the Peace, Breaches of the Peace, and Acts of Aggression," whereas chapter VIII, entitled "Regional Arrangements," begins with article 52 and embraces the two following articles. The records of the San Francisco conference show that article 51 was deliberately placed in chapter VII rather than chapter VIII, "where it would only have a bearing on the regional system." [7]

Under article 51, the right of self-defense is available against any armed attack, whether or not the country attacked is a member of a regional arrangement and regardless of the source of the attack. Chapter VIII, on the other hand, deals with relations among members of a regional arrangement or agency, and authorizes regional action as appropriate for dealing with "local disputes." This distinction has been recognized ever since the founding of the United Nations in 1945.

For example, the North Atlantic Treaty has operated as a collective security arrangement, designed to take common measures in preparation against the eventuality of an armed attack for which collective defense under article 51 would be required. Similarly, the Southeast Asia Treaty Organization was designed as a collective defense arrangement under article 51. Secretary of State Dulles emphasized this in his testimony before the Senate Foreign Relations Committee in 1954.

By contrast, article 1 of the Charter of Bogotá (1948), establishing the Organization of American States, expressly declares that the

---

7.   17 UNCIO Documents 288.   [Footnote in orginal.]

organization is a regional agency within the United Nations. Indeed, chapter VIII of the United Nations Charter was included primarily to take account of the functioning of the inter-American system.

In sum, there is no basis in the United Nations Charter for contending that the right of self-defense against armed attack is limited to collective defense by a regional organization.

F. The United States Has Fulfilled Its Obligations to the United Nations

A further argument has been made that the members of the United Nations have conferred on United Nations organs—and, in particular, on the Security Council—exclusive power to act against aggression. Again, the express language of article 51 contradicts that assertion. A victim of armed attack is not required to forgo individual or collective defense of its territory until such time as the United Nations organizes collective action and takes appropriate measures. To the contrary, article 51 clearly states that the right of self-defense may be exercised "until the Security Council has taken the measures necessary to maintain international peace and security." [8]

As indicated earlier, article 51 is not literally applicable to the Viet-Nam situation since South Viet-Nam is not a member. However, reasoning by analogy from article 51 and adopting its provisions as an appropriate guide for the conduct of members in a case like Viet-Nam, one can only conclude that United States actions are fully in accord with this country's obligations as a member of the United Nations.

Article 51 requires that:

> Measures taken by Members in the exercise of this right of self-defense shall be immediately reported to the Security Council and shall not in any way affect the authority and responsibility of the Security Council under the present Charter to take at any time such action as it deems necessary in order to maintain or restore international peace and security.

The United States has reported to the Security Council on measures it has taken in countering the Communist aggression in Viet-Nam. In August 1964 the United States asked the Council to consider the situation created by North Vietnamese attacks on United States destroyers in the Tonkin Gulf. The Council thereafter met to debate the question, but adopted no resolutions. Twice in February 1965

8. An argument has been made by some that the United States, by joining in the collective defense of South Viet-Nam, has violated the peaceful settlement obligation of article 33 in the charter. This argument overlooks the obvious proposition that a victim of armed aggression is not required to sustain the attack undefended while efforts are made to find a political solution with the aggressor. Article 51 of the charter illustrates this by making perfectly clear that the inherent right of self-defense is impaired by "Nothing in the present Charter," including the provisions of article 33. [Footnote in original.]

the United States sent additional reports to the Security Council on the conflict in Viet-Nam and on the additional measures taken by the United States in the collective defense of South Viet-Nam. In January 1966 the United States formally submitted the Viet-Nam question to the Security Council for its consideration and introduced a draft resolution calling for discussions looking toward a peaceful settlement on the basis of the Geneva accords.

At no time has the Council taken any action to restore peace and security in Southeast Asia. The Council has not expressed criticism of United States actions. Indeed, since the United States submission of January 1966, members of the Council have been notably reluctant to proceed with any consideration of the Viet-Nam question.

The conclusion is clear that the United States has in no way acted to interfere with United Nations consideration of the conflict in Viet-Nam. On the contrary, the United States has requested United Nations consideration, and the Council has not seen fit to act.

G. International Law Does Not Require a Declaration of War as a Condition Precedent To Taking Measures of Self-Defense Against Armed Attack

The existence or absence of a formal declaration of war is not a factor in determining whether an international use of force is lawful as a matter of international law. The United Nations Charter's restrictions focus on the manner and purpose of its use and not on any formalities of announcement.

It should also be noted that a formal declaration of war would not place any obligations on either side in the conflict by which that side would not be bound in any event. The rules of international law concerning the conduct of hostilities in an international armed conflict apply regardless of any declaration of war.

H. Summary

The analysis set forth above shows that South Viet-Nam has the right in present circumstances to defend itself against armed attack from the North and to organize a collective self-defense with the participation of others. In response to requests from South Viet-Nam, the United States has been participating in that defense, both through military action within South Viet-Nam and actions taken directly against the aggressor in North Viet-Nam. This participation by the United States is in conformity with international law and is consistent with our obligations under the Charter of the United Nations.

*   *   *

III. Actions by the United States and South Viet-Nam are Justified Under the Geneva Accords of 1954

A. Description of the Accords

The Geneva accords of 1954 established the date and hour for a cease-fire in Viet-Nam, drew a "provisional military demarcation line" with a demilitarized zone on both sides, and required an exchange of prisoners and the phased regroupment of Viet Minh forces from the south to the north and of French Union forces from the north to the south. The introduction into Viet-Nam of troop reinforcements and new military equipment (except for replacement and repair) was prohibited. The armed forces of each party were required to respect the demilitarized zone and the territory of the other zone. The adherence of either zone to any military alliance, and the use of either zone for the resumption of hostilities or to "further an aggressive policy," were prohibited. The International Control Commission was established, composed of India, Canada and Poland, with India as chairman. The task of the Commission was to supervise the proper execution of the provisions of the cease-fire agreement. General elections that would result in reunification were required to be held in July 1956 under the supervision of the ICC.

B.   North Viet-Nam Violated the Accords From the Beginning

From the very beginning, the North Vietnamese violated the 1954 Geneva accords. Communist military forces and supplies were left in the South in violation of the accords. Other Communist guerrillas were moved north for further training and then were infiltrated into the South in violation of the accords.

C.   The Introduction of United States Military Personnel and Equipment Was Justified

The accords prohibited the reinforcement of foreign military forces in Viet-Nam and the introduction of new military equipment, but they allowed replacement of existing military personnel and equipment. Prior to late 1961 South Viet-Nam had received considerable military equipment and supplies from the United States, and the United States had gradually enlarged its Military Assistance Advisory Group to slightly less than 900 men. These actions were reported to the ICC and were justified as replacements for equipment in Viet-Nam in 1954 and for French training and advisory personnel who had been withdrawn after 1954.

As the Communist aggression intensified during 1961, with increased infiltration and a marked stepping up of Communist terrorism in the South, the United States found it necessary in late 1961 to increase substantially the numbers of our military personnel and the amounts and types of equipment introduced by this country into South Viet-Nam. These increases were justified by the international law principle that a material breach of an agreement by one party entitles the other at least to withhold compliance with an equivalent, corresponding, or related provision until the defaulting party is prepared to honor its obligations.

In accordance with this principle, the systematic violation of the Geneva accords by North Viet-Nam justified South Viet-Nam in suspending compliance with the provision controlling entry of foreign military personnel and military equipment.

D.   South Viet-Nam Was Justified in Refusing To Implement the Election Provisions of the Geneva Accords

The Geneva accords contemplated the reunification of the two parts of Viet-Nam. They contained a provision for general elections to be held in July 1956 in order to obtain a "free expression of the national will." The accords stated that "consultations will be held on this subject between the competent representative authorities of the two zones from 20 July 1955 onwards."

There may be some question whether South Viet-Nam was bound by these election provisions. As indicated earlier, South Viet-Nam did not sign the cease-fire agreement of 1954, nor did it adhere to the Final Declaration of the Geneva conference. The South Vietnamese Government at that time gave notice of its objection in particular to the election provisions of the accords.

However, even on the premise that these provisions were binding on South Viet-Nam, the South Vietnamese Government's failure to engage in consultations in 1955, with a view to holding elections in 1956, involved no breach of obligation. The conditions in North Viet-Nam during that period were such as to make impossible any free and meaningful expression of popular will.

Some of the facts about conditions in the North were admitted even by the Communist leadership in Hanoi. General Giap, currently Defense Minister of North Viet-Nam, in addressing the Tenth Congress of the North Vietnamese Communist Party in October 1956, publicly acknowledged that the Communist leaders were running a police state where executions, terror, and torture were commonplace. A nationwide election in these circumstances would have been a travesty. No one in the North would have dared to vote except as directed. With a substantial majority of the Vietnamese people living north of the 17th parallel, such an election would have meant turning the country over to the Communists without regard to the will of the people. The South Vietnamese Government realized these facts and quite properly took the position that consultations for elections in 1956 as contemplated by the accords would be a useless formality.[23]

[Portions of the memorandum have been omitted: the argument that the United States had undertaken commitments to assist South Viet-Nam and the discussion of the constitutional authority of the President of the United States to commit forces to South Viet-Nam.]

---

23.   In any event, if North Viet-Nam considered there had been a breach of obligation by the South, its remedies lay in discussion with Saigon, perhaps in an appeal to the co-chairman of the Geneva conference, or in a reconvening of the conference to consider the situation. Under international law, North Viet-Nam had no right to use force outside its own zone in order to secure its political objectives. [Footnote in original.]

WRIGHT, LEGAL ASPECTS OF THE VIET–NAM SITUATION

60 American Journal of International Law 750, 755 (1966).a

* * *

The legal issues, clarification of which might contribute to a judgment of the validity of the diverse images of the Viet-Nam situation, may be stated as follows:

1.   Are the hostilities between North and South Viet-Nam international hostilities or civil strife, i.e., is Viet-Nam two states or one?

2.   Was the requirement for an election in 1956 dependent on the development of conditions assuring that the election would be free and fair?

3.   Was the requirement concerning elections in the resolutions of the Geneva Conference such an integral part of the Cease-Fire Agreement between France and the Democratic Republic of Viet-Nam (Ho Chi Minh) as to permit suspension of the cease-fire when the elections were frustrated?

4.   If it is assumed that the cease-fire line continued in operation, was North Viet-Nam guilty of "armed attacks" upon South Viet-Nam justifying the United States bombing attacks north of the cease-fire line, which began in February, 1965, as measures of "collective self-defense"?

* * *

1.   The evidence suggests that Viet-Nam is one state and that the hostilities of Ho Chi Minh's government against the Saigon Government would be civil strife within its domestic jurisdiction unless forbidden by the cease-fire Agreement.

During the hostilities between the "Democratic Republic of Viet-Nam" under Ho Chi Minh and France, supporting the "Republic of Viet-Nam" under Bao Dai from 1946 to 1954 and during the Geneva Conference, both sides regarded Viet-Nam as one state, the legal issue being whether it was an independent state or a "Free State" within the French Community. When the hostilities ended with French defeat, large areas of the south were occupied by Ho Chi Minh's forces, the Viet-Minh, and areas in the north by forces of France and Bao Dai. The Cease-Fire Agreement of 1954 signed by representatives of France and the Democratic Republic of Viet-Nam provided for the withdrawal of these forces across the cease-fire line, substantially the 17th parallel, and very explicitly declared that this line was not an international boundary but a "provisional military demarcation line" and that the territories at each side were not states but "zones." The final resolutions of the Conference declared that "the independence, unity and territorial integrity" of Viet-Nam should be respected, and

a.   This article is reprinted at p. 271 in a symposium entitled The Vietnam   War and International Law (R. Falk, ed., 1968).

provided that elections "shall" be held in July, 1956, to determine the government of Viet-Nam.   These resolutions did not constitute a formal treaty and were not signed by any of the delegates.   They were, however, accepted by all of the delegates except those of the United States and Bao Dai's Republic of Viet-Nam, both of whom made statements "noted" by the Conference.   In regard to the reservation by Bao Dai's representative, the Chairman at the final session of the Conference, Anthony Eden, said:

> We can not now amend our final act, which is the statement of the Conference as a whole, but the Declaration of the Representative of the State of Vietnam will be taken note of.

It seems clear that the Conference recognized Viet-Nam as one state and provided that it should be united by one government in 1956.

After the Geneva Conference and frustration of a four-year effort by Ho Chi Minh to have the elections held, the Southern Zone, now under Ngo Dinh Diem, supported by the United States, declared itself independent and was recognized by some governments, placed under the protection of SEATO, and permitted to represent Viet-Nam in some international organizations, but it was not admitted to the United Nations.   Ho Chi Minh, the Communist states and many unaligned states, including India, did not accept this situation.   In 1956, Diem began to be actively resisted by the Viet-Cong, the name given to the Viet-Minh in the Southern Zone, and after 1958 Ho Chi Minh's government began to assist it by infiltrations of men and supplies from the Northern Zone.   Diem's government, although supported by United States economic, educational and military aid, was not able to eliminate the Viet-Cong, which in 1960 organized the "South Vietnam National Liberation Front" in control of much of the Southern Zone outside of the major cities.   Diem became increasingly dictatorial and unpopular and was assassinated on November 1, 1963.   The succession of unstable governments which have followed him have never controlled half of the territory of South Viet-Nam.

South Viet-Nam was clearly regarded as part of Viet-Nam before 1954 and as a "zone" of that state separated by a temporary cease-fire line by the Geneva Conference, and it seems not to have acquired sufficient governmental authority, stability, public support, or recognition to become an independent state under international law since then.   Consequently, apart from the Cease-Fire Agreement and American intervention, hostilities in Viet-Nam should be regarded as civil strife.

2.   Diem and the United States have contended that it was understood at Geneva that the election called for by the resolutions could not be held until conditions assured that the election would be free and fair.   It is true that the resolution referred to "free general elec-

tions by secret ballot" and that General Bedell Smith, reserving for the United States on the Resolutions, said:

> In the case of nations now divided against their will, we shall continue to seek to achieve unity through free elections super- vised by the United Nations to insure that they are conducted fairly.

The conditions in Viet-Nam which might impair the freedom and fairness of elections were, however well known to the members of the Geneva Conference when they provided categorically for the holding of elections in July, 1956, for their supervision by the International Control Commission, and for consultations to prepare for them be- ginning on July 20, 1955. The delay of two years was "in order to ensure that sufficient progress in the restoration of peace has been made, and that all the necessary conditions obtain for free expression of the national will." These political provisions resulted from com- promises between the Western and Communist states represented at Geneva. They were believed necessary to achieve agreement and peace in Southeast Asia. Failure to observe their precise terms would, there- fore, jeopardize the entire agreement, as subsequent events demon- strated.

It would appear, therefore, that Ho Chi Minh was entitled to re- gard the holding of elections in July, 1956, as obligatory on the par- ties to the Cease-Fire Agreement, including France and its successor in South Viet-Nam, Diem. The premature withdrawal from Viet- Nam of the French, who were considered responsible for preparing for the elections in the Southern Zone has been criticized, but the government of the Southern Zone clearly succeeded to this respon- sibility. General responsibility for carrying out the political provi- sions of the Geneva Conference lay with the "Co-Chairmen (Britain and the Soviet Union) and the Geneva Powers" as indicated by the In- ternational Control Commission in its tenth report in 1960.

3. The evidence suggests that the provisions concerning elec- tions in the final resolutions of the Geneva Conference were consid- ered essential elements in the Cease-Fire Agreement. This agree- ment, therefore, became suspendable when the elections were frustrat- ed by one of the parties and the other party, Ho Chi Minh, was free to consider his obligation to respect the cease-fire line suspended and to continue his long effort to unify Viet-Nam by force.

There can be little doubt but that Ho Chi Minh regarded the Geneva resolutions as a part of the settlement to which he agreed. Military unification of Viet-Nam was within his grasp after the de- feat of France at Dien Bien Phu if external aggression, especially by the United States, could be avoided. It is incredible that he would have agreed to the cease-fire, even though he desired it, in the hope that it would prevent such intervention, unless he was convinced that unification would shortly be effected by the peaceful method of elections. A study of the diplomacy at Geneva suggests that the principal Powers except the United States were more interested in peace than in ideologies, and recognized that the political provisions of the settlement, which would probably result in a national Communist Viet-Nam, were the price of peace, and were therefore no less important than the military provisions.

The Department of State's legal brief emphasizes the principle of international law that

> A material breach of an agreement by one party entitles the other at least to withhold compliance with an equivalent, corresponding, or related provision until the defaulting party is prepared to honor its obligations.[29]

The brief used this principle to justify its escalation of hostilities in response to North Vietnamese infiltration contrary to the cease-fire requirements, but the principle seems more in point to permit North Viet-Nam to regard the obligation to respect the cease-fire line as suspended after the provision for terminating this temporary line in 1956 was frustrated by the refusal of South Viet-Nam to co-operate in carrying out the election. Not only was the provision for elections a major factor in inducing Ho Chi Minh to accept the temporary cease-fire, but it is expressly mentioned in the Cease-Fire Agreement, which provides:

> Pending the general elections which will bring about the unification of Viet-Nam, the conduct of civil administration in each regrouping zone shall be in the hands of the party whose forces are to be regrouped there in virtue of the present Agreement.

This provision of the Cease-Fire Agreement could only be interpreted by reference to the conference resolutions which provided:

> The Conference recognises that the essential purpose of the Agreement relating to Viet-Nam is to settle military questions with a view to ending hostilities and that the military demarcation line is provisional and should not in any way be interpreted as constituting a political or territorial boundary. The Conference expresses its conviction that the execution of the provisions set out in the present declaration and in the Agreement on the cessation of hostilities creates the necessary basis for the achievement in the near future of a political settlement in Viet-Nam.

> The Conference declares that, so far as Viet-Nam is concerned, the settlement of political problems, effected on the basis of respect for the principles of independence, unity and territorial integrity, shall permit the Vietnamese people to enjoy the fundamental freedoms, guaranteed by democratic institutions established as a result of free general elections by secret ballot. In order to ensure that sufficient progress in the restoration of peace has been made, and that all the necessary conditions obtain for free expression of the national will, general elections shall be

held in July 1956, under the supervision of an international commission composed of representatives of the member states of the International Supervisory Commission, referred to in the Agreement on the cessation of hostilities. Consultations will be held on this subject between the competent representative authorities of the two zones from 20th July, 1955, onwards.

Although the Government of the Republic of Viet-Nam (Bao Dai) was not a party to these agreements, France was, and the Diem government established in the Southern Zone as successor to France was bound by them. Its failure to carry out the provisions, which were regarded as the essence of the agreement by the "Democratic Republic of Viet-Nam" (Ho Chi Minh), would relieve the latter of the obligation to respect the cease-fire line and would entitle it to continue its interrupted effort to unify Viet-Nam by force.

The resistance to this effort by the Saigon Government, therefore, constituted "civil strife" within the domestic jurisdiction of Viet-Nam, and American intervention involving the use of armed force against the Viet-Cong in the south and the bombing of installations in the north was a violation of traditional international law forbidding intervention in the domestic jurisdiction of another state and prohibited even to the United Nations, unless the situation constituted a threat to or breach of the peace entitling it to take measures to restore international peace and security.

There is no doubt but that breach of a valid cease-fire line constitutes a violation of international law, as does violation of an international boundary. This was held in the Korean situation of 1950, as noted by the State Department's legal brief. This brief does not discuss the question of whether the cease-fire line in Viet-Nam became suspendable after frustration of the conditions which induced its acceptance by one of the parties, nor is this question discussed by the International Control Commission, which continued to examine alleged violations of the Cease-Fire Agreement up to 1965, thus suggesting that it continued to operate and to bind the parties. The Control Commission's responsibility was, however, limited to supervising the execution of the military provisions of the Geneva Agreement and did not extend to judging the effect on these provisions of non-fulfillment of the political settlement reached at Geneva. It did, however, recognize the importance of fulfillment of these provisions and the responsibility of the Geneva Powers in the matter. In its tenth report in 1960 the Commission said:

> During the period under report, there has been no progress in regard to the political settlement envisaged in the Final Declaration. The parties have not held consultations with a view to holding free nation-wide elections leading to the reunification of Vietnam and thereby facilitating early fulfillment of the tasks assigned to the Commission and the termination of its activities.

The Commission is confident that this important problem is engaging the attention of the Co-Chairmen and the Geneva Powers and that they will take whatever measures they deem necessary to resolve it.

The United States legal brief dismisses the contention that the hostilities were civil strife, by characterizing any analogy to the American Civil War as:

an entire fiction disregarding the actual situation in Viet-Nam. The Hanoi regime is anything but the legitimate government of a unified country in which the South is rebelling against lawful national authority.

There are undoubtedly differences in the two cases but there are also similarities. The issue of civil strife in America in 1861 and in Viet-Nam in 1965 was whether the Declaration of Independence of the United States of July 4, 1776, and the Declaration of Independence of the Democratic Republic of Viet-Nam of September 2, 1945, closely resembling it, contemplated in each case a unified state as held by Lincoln and Ho Chi Minh, or permitted secession as held by Jefferson Davis and Diem. There is no doubt that a "unified country" did not exist in the United States during the period when the Confederate States of America occupied the South or in Viet-Nam when the Republic of Viet-Nam (Diem) occupied much of the southern half of that country. It is true the analogy is imperfect because the United States was a unified country for many years before 1861 and Viet-Nam has been in almost continuous strife with France or South Viet-Nam since its Declaration of Independence. Furthermore South Viet-Nam has received more recognition as a state than did the Confederate States. Nevertheless the position of Ho in regard to the legal unity of Viet-Nam is similar to that of Lincoln in regard to the United States, and the position of the United States in Viet-Nam is similar to that which Great Britain would have had if it had intervened in behalf of the Confederacy as it threatened to do in 1861, giving rise to diplomatic notes by Secretary of State Seward and a resolution by Congress indicating that such a move would be an unfriendly act.

Giving full consideration to the military and political provisions of the Geneva settlement, it would appear that the cease-fire had lapsed by 1958 and the situation had become one of civil strife in which outside states were forbidden by international law to intervene even on the invitation of one side.

4. Even if the cease-fire line remained legally effective, North Viet-Nam could not be accused of "aggression" against South Viet-Nam unless it had launched an unjustifiable "armed attack" upon the latter prior to the United States bombing raids across that line in February, 1965. The basic American argument to justify these raids was that they were acts of "collective self-defense" permitted by Article

51 of the United Nations Charter. The meaning of this article has been controversial.

It is true that traditional international law permitted military action in self-defense if there were an "instant and overwhelming necessity permitting no moment for deliberation," i. e., if hostile forces were about to attack. It seems clear, however, that the San Francisco Conference, by limiting self-defense to cases of "armed attack," intended to eliminate all preventive or pre-emptive action in order to maintain to the utmost the basic obligation of Members of the United Nations to "refrain in their international relations from the threat or use of force."

Furthermore it is clear that "armed attack" implies military action. Consequently military defensive action is not permissible under the Charter in response to economic, psychological, or other forms of subversion or intervention not involving military coercion. There can be no doubt but that bodies of armed "volunteers" crossing a frontier or cease-fire line, such as the Chinese in the Korean hostilities of 1950, or ostensibly private "military expeditions" or "armed bands" leaving one country for the purpose of attacking another, as the Cuban refugees in the Bay of Pigs affair of 1961, constitute, if of considerable magnitude, an "armed attack."

Finally an "armed attack" which constitutes a legitimate act of self-defense against an illegal "armed attack" cannot justify subsequent attacks by the aggressor.

According to the International Control Commission there were frequent violations of the Cease-Fire Agreement after 1957. In that and subsequent years it noted violations by the Southern Zone by permitting the establishment of United States military personnel and aircraft in its area and by entering into a de facto military alliance with SEATO and the United States. The United States legal memorandum sought to justify these actions by asserting that "from the very beginning, the North Vietnamese violated the 1954 Geneva accords" by leaving Communist military forces and supplies in the South and infiltrating Communist guerrillas from the North to the South. The Control Commission's report of June, 1955, however, indicated that both sides were satisfied with the manner in which withdrawals and transfers required by the agreement were effected. The United States brief asserted that 23,000 men were infiltrated from the North to the South from 1957 to 1962, and the Control Commission noted charges of such infiltration during this period, but not until 1962 did it assess the allegations and the evidence to support them. On that date it submitted a Special Report which called attention to the "rapid deterioration of the situation," and quoted a report of its legal committee, with the Polish member dissenting:

* * * in specific instances there is evidence to show that armed and unarmed personnel, arms, munitions and other sup-

plies have been sent from the Zone in the North to the Zone in the South with the objective of supporting, organizing and carrying out hostile activities, including armed attacks, directed against the Armed Forces and administration of the Zone in the South.   These acts are in violation of Articles 10, 19, 24, and 27 of the Agreement on the Cessation of Hostilities in Vietnam. * * *   there is evidence to show that the PAV (Peoples Army of Vietnam) has allowed the Zone in the North to be used for inciting, encouraging, and supporting hostile activities in the Zone in the South, aimed at the overthrow of the Administration in the South.   The use of the Zone in the North for such activities is in violation of Articles 19, 24, and 27 of the Agreement on the Cessation of Hostilities in Vietnam.

In the same report the Control Commission concluded that South Viet-Nam had violated Articles 16 and 17 of the Geneva Agreement by receiving military aid from the United States and Article 19 by making a de facto military alliance with that country.

In a Special Report of 1965 the Control Commission noted a joint communiqué of February 7, 1965, from the acting Premier of South Viet-Nam and the United States Ambassador announcing military action against military installations in North Viet-Nam in response to aggression by North Viet-Nam forces against Pleiku and Tuy Hoa; and also a communiqué of February 8, 1965, from the North Vietnamese mission protesting the bombing in North Viet-Nam on February 7 by air forces of "the United States imperialists."   The Commission commented without concurrence of the Canadian member: "These documents point to the seriousness of the situation and indicate violations of the Geneva Agreement."

There seems to be no evidence that organized contingents of the North Vietnamese army crossed the cease-fire line until after the United States bombing attacks began in February, 1965.   Whether infiltrations before that date were of sufficient magnitude to constitute "armed attacks" and whether they could be justified as defense measures against the military activities of South Viet-Nam and the United States in violation of the Geneva agreements is controversial.   The Department of State's legal brief of March 4, 1966, says:

In these circumstances an "armed attack" is not as easily fixed by date and hour as in the case of traditional warfare.   However, the infiltration of thousands of armed men clearly constitutes an "armed attack" under any reasonable definition.   There may be some question as to the exact date at which North Viet-Nam's aggression grew into an "armed attack," but there can be no doubt that it had occurred before February 1965.

The reports of the Control Commission indicating gradual increase in violations of the Geneva cease-fire by both sides after 1958 do not permit of a clear judgment on which side began "armed attacks." The problem is in any case irrelevant if the cease-fire line had become ineffective because of the frustration of the elections and United States intervention, as suggested above. There is no evidence of any action by North Viet-Nam which could be regarded as an armed attack upon the South prior to 1958, after Ho Chi Minh had engaged in four years of fruitless effort to carry out the resolutions of the Geneva Conference. In these circumstances Ho Chi Minh's action in support of the Viet-Cong did not constitute aggression or armed attack in international relations but civil strife within the domestic jurisdiction of Viet-Nam, similar to the action of the North against the South in the American Civil War. Whether called "intervention," "reprisals" or "collective defense," the United States response by bombings in North Viet-Nam, which began in February, 1965, violated international law, the United Nations Charter, and the Geneva Agreement, if the latter were in effect.

* * *

Question. Article 51 of the Charter of the United Nations contemplates that a state can use force in individual or collective self-defense only until action is taken by the Security Council. The design of the Charter apparently envisioned only temporary self-defense measures. But there has been fighting in Vietnam for almost as many years as the United Nations has existed. Why did the Security Council not take action in this case? See p. 1303.

SECTION C. CHALLENGES TO THE PROHIBITION OF THE USE OF FORCE

1. "POLICE ACTION" AND ARTICLE 2(4) OF THE CHARTER: SUEZ (1956)

President Nasser of Egypt nationalized the Universal Suez Canal Company in July, 1956. British and French concern over this assumption of control over access to oil from the Middle East was intense. Higgins concludes that "Secret arrangements were proceeded with for an Anglo-French 'police' action following an Israeli attack upon Egypt. * * * There now seems ample evidence that a highly secret meeting took place at Sèvres on 23 October between the French, British, and Israelis, when plans for the Israeli attack, and the ensuing 'police action' were co-ordinated, and formally agreed upon. The United States was not informed." Higgins, United Nations Peacekeeping, 1946–1967, I. The Middle East 225 (1969).

On October 23, Israel attacked Egyptian fedayeen (Palestine army) bases in Sinai and advanced toward the Suez Canal. Britain and France served ultimatums on Israel and Egypt to cease hostilities and withdraw from the canal. When Egypt rejected the ultimatum, British and French aircraft launched attacks on Egyptian air bases and troops from both countries entered Egyptian territory at Port Said, from the air and from the sea. A draft resolution calling upon Israel and Egypt to cease fire and calling upon all members to refrain from the use of force in any manner inconsistent with the purposes of the United Nations was vetoed by Britain and France in the Security Council and the matter was brought before the General Assembly at an emergency meeting.[a] The United Kingdom representative (Sir Pierson Dixon) gave the following explanation of the action of his country and France (Gen.Ass.Off.Rec., 1st Emergency Special Sess., 1956 Plenary, p. 5):

> 69.   From all the information at our disposal, we had reason to judge that a major clash, whose consequences would have been incalculable, between Israel and its Arab neighbours was more imminent than at any time since the signing of the armistice agreements in 1949. The sudden Israel mobilization and incursion into Egypt made it imperative to take very speedy and effective measures to prevent a war between Israel and Egypt which could only lead to a general conflagration throughout the Middle East and which would, in its train, have involved prolonged disruption of free passage through the Suez Canal, the canal which is of such vital interest to so many nations.

> * * *

> 74.   With regret, I say that the Security Council, in our opinion, could have provided no effective remedy in time.

> 75.   I need not here go into the reasons why those provisions of the Charter which were designed to provide the Council with a military arm have remained in abeyance. It is well known that it is because a permanent member of the Security Council, by a persistent misuse of the veto, has seen fit to thwart the intentions of the Charter. The result has been that the world has not been able to rely on the United Nations for the collective security which the Organization was designed to provide. Least of all, in view of the intransigence of the parties and the cynical misuse of its veto power by the Soviet Union, could we expect swift and effective action from the United Nations in an emergency in the Middle East.

> 76.   It is hard to say these things, but I fear they are true. It is precisely because of this unhappy limitation in the effective

a.   The General Assembly's subsequent
establishment of a peacekeeping force
(UNEF) is discussed in Chapter 20.

powers of the Security Council to deal with such an emergency that the United Kingdom and French Governments were compelled to intervene at once, as they were fortunately in a position to do.

77.   It was through no wish of ours that a situation arose in which we were compelled to act independently of the United Nations.   Indeed, as soon as the news of the Israel action reached us here in New York, in the afternoon of 29 October, I took immediate steps, with the representatives of the United States and France, to make it clear that the Council should be seized of this situation at once.

78.   We did not, however, consider that the course of action proposed by the United States, without consultation with Her Majesty's Government, could effectively achieve the twin objectives of separating the belligerents at once and of safeguarding free passage through the Canal.

79.   It was in these circumstances that we were obliged to cast our negative votes in the Security Council.   The action which we and the French Government have taken is essentially of a temporary character, and, I repeat it, designed to deal with a unique emergency.   Our intervention was swift because the emergency brooked no delay.   It has been drastic because drastic action was evidently required.   It is an emergency police action.   The situation is not dissimilar to that which obtained at the time of the North Korean invasion.   On that occasion the Member of the United Nations which had forces on hand and was in a position to intervene at once courageously did so.   By a happy chance —and I mean the absence of the Soviet representative from the Security Council on that occasion—the Council was able to endorse the United States action.   The same fortunate chance was not ours.   I cannot, however, believe that the United States would not, in any case, have acted, and rightly so, in the circumstances.

*   *   *

99.   Let me, at this stage, towards the end of my speech, briefly restate the objectives of the Anglo-French intervention. The overriding purposes are: the safeguarding of the Suez Canal and the restoration of peaceful conditions in the Middle East. Let me say with all the emphasis at my command that neither we nor the French Government have any desire whatever that the military action which we have taken should be more than temporary in its duration.   It will be terminated as soon as the emergency is over.   It is our intention that our action to protect the Canal, to terminate hostilities and to separate the combatants should be as short as possible in duration.

100.   The action taken by my Government and by the Government of France has been called an act of aggression against

Egypt. This is a charge which we emphatically deny. There is much debate about what constitutes aggression, but it is certainly not true to say that every armed action constitutes aggression. Every action must clearly be judged in the light of the circumstances in which it has taken place and the motives which have prompted it.

101. The action of France and the United Kingdom is not aggression. We do not seek the domination of Egypt or of any part of Egyptian territory. Our purpose is peaceful, not warlike. Our aim is to re-establish the rule of law, not to violate it; to protect, and not to destroy. What we have undertaken is a temporary police action necessitated by the turn of events in the Middle East and occasioned by the imperative need not only to protect the vital interests of my own and many other countries, but also to take immediate measures for the restoration of order.

102. Our action is in no way aimed at the sovereignty of Egypt, and still less at its territorial integrity. It is not of our choice that the police action which we have been obliged to take is occurring on Egyptian territory. We have taken the only action which we could clearly see would be effective in holding the belligerents apart and which would give us a chance to re-establish peace in the area. By entering the Suez Canal area, we would only be seeking to protect a vital waterway, and it is also the only practicable line of division between the combatants.

---

2.   THE SIX DAY WAR: ANTICIPATORY SELF–DEFENSE?

THE SIX DAY WAR

IV U.N. Monthly Chronicle, July 1967, p. 8.

Meeting of June 5

Following the outbreak of hostilities in the Middle East, the Security Council met in emergency session.

The Council had a letter from the representative of the United Arab Republic which stated that Israel had "committed a treacherous premeditated aggression" against his country that morning, launching attacks in the Gaza Strip, Sinai, and several airports in Cairo, the Suez Canal area, and other localities. Preliminary reports, it was stated, indicated that 23 Israeli planes had been shot down and several pilots captured. The letter went on to say that the United Arab Republic, "in repelling this aggression * * * had decided to defend itself by all means in accordance with Article 51 of the Charter of the United Nations".

The Secretary-General, U Thant, in his statement, said the United Nations had no means of ascertaining how the hostilities began.

Reports coming in from the parties were conflicting, but all agreed that there was serious military action on land and in the air at a number of points which was spreading. The United Nations Emergency Force (UNEF), which was in the process of withdrawal, was no longer on the Line. Information from the UNEF Commander, General Indar Jit Rikhye, therefore, was necessarily general. He gave the Council the information he had received, including the report that three UNEF soldiers in the Indian contingent were killed and an undetermined number wounded when Israeli aircraft strafed a UNEF convoy. The authorities of the United Arab Republic reported large-scale air raids throughout the country, including Cairo, but Israel denied that Cairo had been raided. The authorities of the United Arab Republic also reported an Israeli attack on El Quiseima in Sinai and stated that its artillery in Gaza had started firing at Israel-controlled territory. General Odd Bull, Chief of Staff of the United Nations Truce Supervision Organization in Palestine (UNTSO), reported firing in Jerusalem. At his request, Israel and Jordan had accepted a cease-fire. Overflights by Syrian jet fighters and air battles over the Syrian-Israeli Armistice Line were reported.

The Secretary-General went on to say that the Israeli representative at ISMAC had informed the UNTSO officer at Tiberias that Israel considered itself at war with Syria. ISMAC reported that the Damascus airport had been attacked. The Secretary-General said that UNTSO headquarters had been occupied by Jordanian soldiers. Israeli troops, following heavy firing, had driven out the Jordanian soldiers and, ordering General Bull and his staff out of Government House, escorted them into Israel. The Secretary-General had requested Israel to restore the compound to exclusive United Nations control.

The Secretary-General also reported that Damascus airport and other locations in Syria were said to be under intermittent air attack, and that Israel claimed that Megiddo, Ailabum and a locality south of Akko had been attacked from the air. Firing was still going on in Jerusalem, and he supported the idea of declaring it an open city in order to protect its irreplaceable religious places.

Gopalaswami Parthasarathi (India) asked the Council to condemn Israel for the "wanton, irresponsible and brutal action" in which Indian soldiers were killed.

Mr. Rafael (Israel) told the Council that fighting had broken out on Israel's frontiers and that the Israeli Defence Forces were repelling the Egyptian Army and Air Force. He said that, in the early morning hours, Egyptian armoured columns had moved in an offensive thrust against Israel's borders and Egyptian planes had taken off from airfields in Sinai and struck out towards Israel. Egyptian artillery in the Gaza Strip had shelled the villages of Kissufim, Nahal-Oz and Ein Hashelosha in Israel. Israeli forces had engaged the Egyptians in the air and on land, and fighting continued.

Mr. Rafael said he was bringing this development to the attention of the Council in accordance with Article 51 of the Charter. The Israeli Minister of Defence, he added, had stated that Israel had no desire for conquest; it was simply defending itself.

Mohamed Awad El Kony (United Arab Republic) said the attack on his country was so widespread that it had to be premeditated. The United Arab Republic, he said, had no choice but to defend itself in accordance with Article 51 of the Charter, and it would continue to do so. He asked that the Council condemn the aggression.

* * *

[At a subsequent meeting of the Security Council, the spokesman for Israel delivered the following explanation of Israel's military action. Security Council, Off.Rec. 1358th Meeting, 13 June 1967, S/PV. 1358, at p. 20].

198. Let us look again at the events which preceded the outbreak of fighting on 5 June. On 18 May, the Government of the United Arab Republic demanded the eviction of the United Nations Emergency Force which was deployed along the Gaza Strip and the Sinai desert and at Sharm el Sheikh at the entrance to the Gulf of Aqaba, and on that day UNEF ceased to exist. Was this an act which promoted peace? Was this an act which demonstrated peaceful intent? It was not; it was preparation for aggression. The Emergency Force had to be gotten out of the way so that the aggression on Israel could be prepared and mounted.

199. On 23 May, the United Arab Republic declared that the Strait of Tiran would be closed to Israel shipping and to ships of other nations carrying what were described as strategic goods, that is to say, anything which the United Arab Republic chose to define as strategic goods, to Israel's southernmost port of Eilat. Was this act of blockade a peaceful act? Did this re-imposition of the blockade demonstrate peaceful intent? It did not. This was a clear act of hostility and the exercise of an internationally rejected claim to belligerency. A blockade is a classical act of war.

200. During this time, that is, the last week of May, Egypt started a massive build-up of forces in the Sinai desert. Some 80,000 men were assembled, with hundreds of assault aircraft, a thousand tanks. These huge forces were deployed in an offensive position along the Sinai frontier with Israel, along the Gaza Strip and at the approaches to Eilat. The deployment of these forces was accompanied by a mounting crescendo of warlike propaganda from Cairo. A holy war was proclaimed by the religious authorities in the Egyptian capital, and the Egyptian people were urged to march forward in a jehad to destroy Israel. The Egyptian President naturally was foremost

in inciting his people for the coming war. This is what he said before the Central Council of Arab Trade Unions on 26 May 1967:

> The Arab people want to fight. We have been waiting for the suitable day when we shall be completely ready, since if we enter a battle with Israel we should be confident of victory and should take strong measures. We do not speak idly. We have lately felt that our strength is sufficient and that if we enter into battle with Israel we shall, with God's help, be victorious. Therefore, we have now decided to take real steps. The battle will be a full-scale one, and our basic aim will be to destroy Israel.

201. What were we in Israel and what was the Security Council expected to make of these words? A call for peace, or a call for war?

202. On 30 May, President Nasser signed a military agreement with King Hussein of Jordan, and Jordan began to mobilize. On 4 June, a similar agreement was signed with Iraq, and Iraqi detachments began arriving in Jordan and in Egypt. Was this evidence of peaceful intent? Were these agreements in keeping with the Charter of the United Nations? Were these aggressive movements of troops in accordance with solemn agreements which Egypt and Jordan had entered into with Israel in 1949 with the object of preventing all hostile acts and serving as a transition to permanent peace? They were clear evidence of a preparation for aggression.

203. While these military moves were going on in Egypt, Jordan and Iraq, Syria had also mobilized its forces to the last man, and 50,000 troops were poised aggressively on the heights which overlook Israel. We were surrounded. The armed ring was closed. All that the Arab forces were waiting for was the signal to start.

204. That signal was given on 5 June, when Egyptian planes in accordance with the plans contained in battle order 6/67 of Air Force and Air Defence Headquarters of the Eastern Area in Sinai, dated 26 May 1967, took off for their assigned targets in Israel, while at the same time an artillery barrage on Israel farming villages was opened from the Gaza Strip. Shortly afterwards, Jordan guns sited amid the holy places of the Holy City of Jerusalem started shelling the Israel capital, causing heavy casualties, and the Syrian artillery joined the devil's chorus in the north. The aggression had begun.

205. This is the record; this is what happened. Israel was designated to be the helpless victim of a massive assault. In accordance with its rights under Article 51 of the United Nations Charter, the victim defended itself, alone and successfully.

---

1. *Territorial control.* Israel's success in the Six Day War resulted in her military occupation of substantial territory: Sinai, the

Gaza Strip, parts of Jerusalem, portions of Jordan on the West Bank of the Jordan River and the Syrian Golan Heights.

2. *Questions.* Was Israel's military action lawful under the Charter? Article 51 preserves "the inherent right of individual * * * self-defense if an armed attack occurs * * *". Was Israel's response to an attack that occurred or against a much greater threatened attack? Was Israel acting in "anticipatory" self-defense? Is such action lawful under the Charter?

3. *Views of certain writers.* Writing before there had been major tests of the meaning of the Charter, Stone observed in discussing Article 51: "Major troop concentrations on the border would presumably warrant anticipatory use of force * * *" Stone, Legal Controls of International Conflict 244, n. 8 (1954).

Following the Cuban missile crisis and prior to the events in the Middle East in 1967, the publicists in the United States were deeply divided on anticipatory self-defense, at least as an abstract concept.

Wright:

> Finally it has been argued that the quarantine and the O.A. S. resolution were justified as measures of "individual or collective self-defense" permitted by Article 51 of the Charter. It is suggested that the term "armed attack," which alone justified such defense without prior United Nations authority, must be interpreted to include a serious threat of armed attack.[53] Reference has been made to the statement by Secretary of State Webster in the Caroline case, generally accepted prior to the Charter, that military defensive action was permissible in case of "an instant and overwhelming necessity," thus creating a limited right of preventive action; that such a construction is necessary in the nuclear age because to delay defensive action until an actual nuclear attack would be suicidal, and that the Charter supports this construction by forbidding "threat" as well as "use" of force in Article 2, paragraph 4.

> These arguments are not convincing. It appears that the Charter intended to limit the traditional right of defense by states to actual armed attack, even though it forbade "threat of force" and authorized the Security Council to intervene to stop "threats to the peace." Professor, now Judge, Philip Jessup wrote in 1948:

> > This restriction in Article 51 very definitely narrows the freedom of action which states had under international law. A case could be made out for self-defense in the traditional law where the injury was threatened but no attack had yet taken place. Under the Charter, alarming military prepara-

---

53. The United States has not used this argument officially * * *.

tions by a neighboring state would justify a resort to the Security Council, but would not justify resort to anticipatory force by the state which believed itself threatened.[54]

The obligation of states to refrain from threats to the peace under Article 2, paragraph 4, and the competence of the United Nations to take action in case of a threat to the peace under Article 39, were not intended to give a unilateral right of military self-defense in case of such threats. For that reason, self-defense against "threats" was excluded in Article 51, and states were explicitly obliged to submit disputes or situations which they think threaten peace, to the United Nations and to refrain from unilateral use of force. * * * The Cuban Quarantine, 57 Am.J.Int'l L. 546, 559 (1963).

McDougal:

The more important limitations imposed by the general community upon this customary right of self-defense have been, in conformity with the overriding policy it serves of minimizing coercion and violence across state lines, those of necessity and proportionality. The conditions of necessity required to be shown by the target state have never, however, been restricted to "actual armed attack"; imminence of attack of such high degree as to preclude effective resort by the intended victim to non-violent modalities of response has always been regarded as sufficient justification, and it is now generally recognized that a determination of imminence requires an appraisal of the total impact of an initiating state's coercive activities upon the target state's expectations about the costs of preserving its territorial integrity and political independence. Even the highly restrictive language of Secretary of State Webster in the Caroline case, specifying a "necessity of self defense, instant, overwhelming, leaving no choice of means and no moment for deliberation," did not require "actual armed attack," [4] and the understanding is now widespread that a test formulated in the previous century for a controversy between two friendly states is hardly relevant to contemporary controversies, involving high expectations of violence, between nuclear-armed protagonists. The requirement of proportionality, in further expression of the policy of minimizing coercion, stipulates that the responding use of the military instrument by the target state be limited in intensity and magnitude to what is

54. Philip Jessup, A Modern Law of Nations 166 (New York, Macmillan, After an exhaustive discussion of "The Use of Force in Self-Defence," Ian Brownlie concludes that "the beginning of an armed attack is a condition precedent for resort to force in self-defence." 37 Brit.Yr.Bk. of Int.Law 266 (1962). * * *

4. Mr. Webster to Mr. Fox, April 24, 1841, in 29 British and Foreign State Papers 1129, 1138 (1840–41). See also Jennings, "The Caroline and McLeod Cases," 32 A.J.I.L. 82 (1938).

reasonably necessary promptly to secure the permissible objectives of self-defense under the established conditions of necessity.

   * * *

   * * * The apparent purpose of the inept language of Article 51, commonly ascribed to the late Senator Vandenburg, was only that of accommodating regional organizations, as specifically envisioned for the inter-American system by the Act of Chapultepec, with the more comprehensive centralized system of collective security projected by the Charter. Similarly, nothing in the "plain and natural meaning" of the words of the Charter requires an interpretation that Article 51 restricts the customary right of self-defense. The proponents of such an interpretation substitute for the words "if an armed attack occurs" the very different words "if, and only if, an armed attack occurs." The Soviet-Cuban Quarantine and Self-Defense, 57 Am.J.Int'l L. 597, 598 (1963).

Henkin:

   * * * While there have been few challenges to Article 2, recurring crises, we have noted, have evoked suggestions for broader readings of the exception of Article 51. One that has been strongly urged is that in the day of nuclear weapons and the ever-present possibility of sudden devastation, nations cannot wait for an armed attack to occur. At least, it is urged, the Charter must now be read to permit "anticipatory self-defense"— the right to act in self-defense in anticipation of attack.

The argument has specious appeal, but is fundamentally unpersuasive. If the Charter originally permitted force in self-defense only if an armed attack occurs, today's weapons hardly argue for extending the exception. The original reasons for barring "anticipatory self-defense" in regard to "old-fashioned war" apply even more to the new war. The logic of the deterrent and the balance of terror does not suggest that nations should be encouraged to preventive or even pre-emptive attack. The exception of Article 51 was limited to the situation "if an armed attack occurs," which is comparatively clear, objective, easy to prove, difficult to misinterpret or fabricate. To permit anticipation may virtually destroy the rule against the use of force, leaving it to every nation to claim anticipation and unlease the fury. Nations will not be prevented or deterred by the fear that later— if there is anyone left to judge—someone may determine that there had in fact been no threat of armed attack legitimately anticipated.

Proponents of anticipatory self-defense raise the specter of the all-out nuclear attack and of the obvious need to anticipate it. In fact, of course, for determining what the Charter means or should mean, the major nuclear attack and the pre-emptive strike are not the relevant concerns. A nation planning all-out attack will not be deterred by the Charter, though it may well talk "anticipatory self-defense" in its justification. Nor does one prescribe rules for the nation threatened with such an attack. If a nation is satisfied that another is about to obliterate it, it will not wait. But it has to make that decision on its own awesome responsibility. Anticipation in that case may have to be practiced; it need not be preached. The Charter need not make a principle of it; the law need not authorize or encourage it. But surely that extreme hypothetical case, beyond the realm of law, should not be used to justify new rules for situations that do not involve the impending mortal thrust. "Anticipatory self-defense" as a rule of law has meaning only in less extreme cases. There, anticipatory self-defense, it should be clear, becomes easily a euphemism for "preventive war." The United Nations Charter in the beginning did not authorize it. Attempts later, in relation to Suez and Sinai, to read the Charter as permitting anticipatory self-defense, were rejected. Nothing since, least of all the new weapons, suggests that international society would be better if the Charter were changed or read to authorize it. Force, Intervention and Neutrality in Contemporary International Law, Proceedings, Am.Soc.Int'l L. 147, 150 (1963).

4. *Possible special factors to the Israeli case.* Are the following observations relevant to an appraisal of the lawfulness of the Israeli military action in the Six Day War?

It will be recalled that ever since 1948, the year of Israel's accession to statehood, the Arab states, including Lebanon, have regarded themselves as being in a state of war with her. This state of war has never been officially terminated; on the contrary, the Arab states have on numerous occasions asserted its continuing existence in seeking to justify various anti-Israel measures taken by them (such as the blocking of the Suez Canal and the Tiran Strait to Israeli navigation). Blum, The Beirut Raid and the International Double Standard, 64 Am.J.Int'l L. 73, 77 (1970). The author further states:

  * * * One of the most disturbing aspects of the Middle East conflict—disturbing as much to the cause of "world order" as to the cause of Israel—is the fact that on no single occasion over the past fifteen years has Israel been able to get satisfaction from the political organs of the United Nations on her complaints against neighboring Arab states. The Soviet veto that has been made available to the Arabs, to block any decision by the Security Council which the latter regarded as unfavorable to them, ensured that such a decision, even if it received the requisite number of votes in the Council, would not be adopted. This fact was naturally taken into account by other members of the Security Council

more favorably disposed to Israel, and largely conditioned the very tone and formulation of many a watered-down draft resolution concerning Israeli complaints, since it was realized that the submission of a draft resolution giving satisfaction to Israel was bound to become an exercise in futility. This pattern, in turn, led to a growing conviction in Israel, which United Nations practice never effectively disproved, that it was difficult, if not impossible, for her rights to be recognized by the United Nations. (at 98)

---

3. SUPPORT FOR ANTI–COLONIAL FORCES

UNITED NATIONS, GENERAL ASSEMBLY RESOLUTION ADOPTED NOVEMBER 2, 1972

A/Res/2908 (XXVII).

The General Assembly,

Recalling the Declaration on the Granting of Independence to Colonial Countries and Peoples, contained in its resolution 1514 (XV) of 14 December 1960, and the programme of action for the full implementation of the Declaration, contained in its resolution 2621(XXV) of 12 October 1970,

Recalling all its previous resolutions concerning the implementation of the Declaration, in particular resolution 2878 (XXVI) of 20 December 1971,

Deeply concerned that twelve years after the adoption of the Declaration many Territories are still under colonial and alien domination and that millions of oppressed persons live under conditions of ruthless and blatant colonialist and racialist repression,

Deeply deploring the continued refusal of the colonial Powers, especially Portugal and South Africa, to implement the Declaration and other relevant resolutions on decolonization, particularly those relating to the Territories under Portuguese domination, Namibia and Southern Rhodesia,

Strongly deploring the policies of those States which, in defiance of the relevant resolutions of the Security Council, the General Assembly and the Special Committee on the Situation with regard to the Implementation of the Declaration on the Granting of Independence to Colonial Countries and Peoples, continue to co-operate with the Governments of Portugal and South Africa and with the illegal racist minority régime in Southern Rhodesia,

Deeply disturbed at the intransigent attitude of certain administering Powers which, despite the repeated appeals addressed to them by the General Assembly and the Special Committee, persist in their refusal to co-operate with the Special Committee in the discharge of the mandate entrusted to it by the General Assembly,

Reaffirming its view that racial discrimination in colonial Territories can be eradicated fully and with the greatest speed by the faithful and complete implementation of the Declaration,

*   *   *

1.   Reaffirms its resolutions 1514(XV) and 2621(XXV) and all other resolutions on decolonization, and calls upon the administering Powers, in accordance with those resolutions, to take all the necessary steps to enable the dependent peoples of the Territories concerned to exercise fully and without further delay their inalienable right to self-determination and independence;

5.   Reaffirms that the continuation of colonialism in all its forms and manifestations—including racism, apartheid and activities of foreign economic and other interests which exploit colonial peoples, as well as the waging of colonial wars to suppress the national liberation movements of the colonial Territories in Africa—is incompatible with the Charter of the United Nations, the Universal Declaration of Human Rights and the Declaration on the Granting of Independence to Colonial Countries and Peoples and poses a threat to international peace and security;

6.   Reaffirms its recognition of the legitimacy of the struggle of the colonial peoples and peoples under alien domination to exercise their right to self-determination and independence by all the necessary means at their disposal, and notes with satisfaction the progress made by the national liberation movements of the colonial Territories, particularly in Africa, both through their struggle and through reconstruction programmes, towards the national independence of their countries;

7.   Condemns the policies, pursued by certain colonial Powers in the Territories under their domination, of imposing non-representative régimes and arbitrary constitutions, strengthening the position of foreign economic and other interests, misleading world public opinion and encouraging the systematic influx of foreign immigrants while evicting, displacing and transferring the indigenous inhabitants to other areas, and calls upon those Powers to desist forthwith from such policies;

8.   Urges all States and the specialized agencies and other organizations within the United Nations system to provide moral and material assistance to all peoples struggling for their freedom and independence in the colonial Territories and to those living under alien domination—in particular to the national liberation movements of the Territories in Africa—in consultation, as appropriate, with the Organization of African Unity;

9.   Requests all States, directly and through their action in the specialized agencies and other organizations within the United Nations

system, to withhold or continue to withhold assistance of any kind from the Governments of Portugal and South Africa and from the illegal racist minority régime in Southern Rhodesia until they renounce their policy of colonial domination and racial discrimination;

* * *

---

1. *Vote on the resolution.* The foregoing resolution, sponsored by 55 Powers, was adopted by a roll-call of 99 in favor to 5 against (France, Portugal, South Africa, United Kingdom, United States), with 23 abstentions (Australia, Austria, Belgium, Brazil, Canada, Costa Rica, Denmark, El Salvador, Fiji, Finland, Guatemala, Iceland, Ireland, Italy, Japan, Luxembourg, Malawi, Netherlands, New Zealand, Norway, Spain, Sweden, Uruguay). Equatorial Guinea, Gambia, Nicaragua, Pakistan and Paraguay were absent. IX U. N. Monthly Chronicle, Dec. 1972, p. 28.

2. *Legal basis for assistance to national liberation movements.* The text of the Declaration on the Granting of Independence to Colonial Countries and Peoples, referred to in the resolution, is in the Documentary Supplement.

Among the states explaining their vote on Resolution 2908 was Colombia.

> The representative of Colombia said that his country had always respected moral and political principles and had acted in accordance with them. It believed that all peoples had the right to self-determination and had the right to throw off the colonial yoke in order to guide their destinies. Accordingly, his delegation would vote for the 55-Power draft resolution. However, his delegation considered it essential to observe that it understood the words "by all the necessary means at their disposal" in the text to be means authorized by international law and in accordance with the rules of civilization. It believed that the provision on withholding assistance should be observed in accordance with resolutions adopted by the General Assembly. IX U.N. Monthly Chronicle, Dec. 1972, pp. 28, 55.

Is military assistance included in the "assistance" that states are urged by the General Assembly to provide to liberation movements? Would the provision of such military assistance be consistent with the commitments in Article 2(4) of the Charter? Or is there an exception from Article 2(4)'s prohibition in the case of "wars of liberation" being waged against a colonial state by people in the colony? Does Article 1(2) of the Charter, referring to "self-determination of peoples" supply an answer to the question?

3. *Self-determination and the use of force.* How far is a state justified in using its military force in support of "peoples" seeking

their "self-determination?" Could France lawfully provide military force to aid Quebec separatists in Canada? Could Western Europeans lawfully do the same with respect to Lithuanians, Latvians and Estonians in the USSR? How do you distinguish these cases from European colonialism in Africa? Is it relevant that the Portuguese constitution provides that "The Overseas Provinces, as an integral part of the Portuguese State, are united as between themselves and with Metropolitan Portugal?" III Peaslee, Constitutions of Nations 755 (3rd ed. 1968).

SECTION D.   USE OF STATE COERCION SHORT OF MILITARY FORCE

Is non-military coercion subject to the law? Is a state free to impose its will on that of another so long as it refrains from the grosser violations of state personality that are encompassed in physical, military force? Does Article 2(4) of the charter proscribe only military force, or also coercions of different types? Is there an emerging law of non-intervention (or a developing body of general international law) that embraces such a proscription? For example, is an economically strong state guilty of illegal conduct if it uses its economic power to seek to force another state to do what it wishes: (a) as to internal non-economic matters, such as establishing honest and democratic governments; (b) as to alignment among power blocs in international relations; (c) as to economic conduct (i) of the same sort as that of the denial practiced by the powerful state (e. g., trade denial as a pressure for change in the trading policy of the pressured state) or (ii) of a different sort (e. g., denial of economic development assistance to induce settlement of a nationalization claim)?

CHARTER OF THE ORGANIZATION OF AMERICAN STATES

119 U.N.T.S. 3; 2 UST 2394; as amended February 27, 1967, 21 UST 607.

Article 19.   No State may use or encourage the use of coercive measures of an economic or political character in order to force the sovereign will of another State and obtain from it advantages of any kind.

JOVA, A REVIEW OF THE PROGRESS AND PROBLEMS OF THE ORGANIZATION OF AMERICAN STATES

65 United States Department of State Bulletin, 284, 287 (1971).

* * *

An uncomfortable departure in our OAS affairs occurred in January of this year when Ecuador accused the United States of violating article 19 of the OAS Charter, which prohibits "use of coercive measures of an economic or political character in order to force the sovereign will of another State." Our dispute with Ecuador arose over the right of American vessels to fish off the coast of that country, in waters which Ecuador claims lie within its maritime sovereignty but which we maintain are high seas. After Ecuador had seized 14 American tuna boats in less than 2 weeks, the United States applied section 3(b) of the Foreign Military Sales Act suspending such sales to that country.

On the assertion that the United States move violated charter article 19, Ecuador called for a Meeting of Consultation of OAS Foreign Ministers, who happened to be in Washington anyway for the special General Assembly session. In their concurrent meeting on this new issue, there were severe criticisms of the United States laws which allegedly apply economic sanctions and impinge upon other nations' sovereignty. For its part, the United States defended its duty to protect the legitimate rights of its citizens in international waters. The outcome, however, was a resolution supported by both Ecuador and the United States, which merely stated the positions of the two disputing parties and called upon them to resolve their differences in accordance with charter principles and "abstain from the use of any kind of measure that may affect the sovereignty" of another state. This in itself involved a constructive effort on both sides to calm the situation, although the basic issue continues.

While the OAS action hardly constituted an indictment of the United States in its dispute with Ecuador, the implications of the issue for the future are of concern to us should there be future applications of U. S. legislation that might be deemed by OAS members to be "coercive" and in violation of charter article 19.

ANNEX TO UNITED NATIONS GENERAL ASSEMBLY RESOLUTION 2625 (XXV), OF OCTOBER, 24, 1970

U.N. Gen. Ass. Off. Rec. Annexes, 25th Sess.,
Supp. No. 28 (A/8028), pp. 122, 123.

Declaration on Principles of International Law Concerning Friendly Relations and Co-operation Among States in Accordance with the Charter of the United Nations

*   *   *

The principle concerning the duty not to intervene in matters within the domestic jurisdiction of any State, in accordance with the Charter

No State or group of States has the right to intervene, directly or indirectly, for any reason whatever, in the internal or external affairs of any other State. Consequently, armed intervention and all other forms of interference or attempted threats against the personality of the State or against its political, economic and cultural elements, are in violation of international law.

No State may use or encourage the use of economic, political or any other type of measures to coerce another State in order to obtain from it the subordination of the exercise of its sovereign rights and to secure from it advantages of any kind. Also, no State shall organize, assist, foment, finance, incite or tolerate subversive, terrorist or armed activities directed towards the violent overthrow of the régime of another State, or interfere in civil strife in another State.

The use of force to deprive peoples of their national identity constitutes a violation of their inalienable rights and of the principle of non-intervention.

Every State has an inalienable right to choose its political, economic, social and cultural systems, without interference in any form by another State.

Nothing in the foregoing paragraphs shall be construed as affecting the relevant provisions of the Charter relating to the maintenance of international peace and security.

*   *   *

Chapter 20

THE USE OF FORCE BY THE UNITED NATIONS

LETTER FROM EDWARD R. STETTINIUS, SECRETARY OF STATE OF THE UNITED STATES, TO PRESIDENT HARRY TRUMAN

13 United States Department of State Bulletin 77, 80 (1945).

Summary of Report on Results of San Francisco Conference

* * *

It will be the duty of the Security Council, supported by the pledged participation, and backed by military contingents to be made available by the member states, to use its great prestige to bring about by peaceful means the adjustment or the settlement of international disputes. Should these means fail, it is its duty, as it has the power, to take whatever measures are necessary, including measures of force, to suppress acts of aggression or other breaches of the peace. It will be the duty of the Security Council, in other words, to make good the commitment of the United Nations to maintain international peace and security, turning that lofty purpose into practice. To that end the Council will be given the use and the support of diplomatic, economic and military tools and weapons in the control of the United Nations.

* * *

---

1. *The "Grand Design"*. As we have seen, the Charter of the United Nations forbade the use of force by states (Article 2(4)), save in the limited area of self-defense (Article 51). A near monopoly of force was reposed in the Security Council, under Chapter VII,[a] in which the Council was empowered to respond to the dramatic conditions of Article 39 ("any threat to the peace, breach of the peace, or act of aggression") by resort to the powerful measures of Articles 41 and 42, including armed forces at its disposal under the terms of Article 43, especially "immediately available national air-force contingents" (Article 45).

It was a vision of many in 1945 that the air borne strike forces of the United Nations Security Council would range forth, on call, to restrain and control anyone who dared disturb the peace that World War II had painfully produced.

---

a. The monopoly was recognized also in Chapter VIII, in which Article 53 required Security Council authoriza- tion for enforcement action under regional arrangements.

2. *What went wrong?* The Charter was grounded in a belief and a hope: the belief that only with the cooperation of the great powers could the United Nations succeed, and the hope that because they had cooperated in war they would continue to do so during the peace (hence, the "veto"). That cooperation was not forthcoming. An immediate effect of the fragmentation of great power policy was the failure of the powers to make the agreements called for in Article 43; the council thus did not have at its disposal the forces projected at the United Nation's founding. See Sohn, Basic Documents of the United Nations 89 (2nd ed. rev'd, 1968), especially Note at 98, detailing the United States and Soviet disagreements with respect to the size relationships of the various force contributions to be made by the permanent members of the force.

Indeed, in the one case in which the Security Council has acted in anything like the classic case of aggressive invasion envisioned at the founding (the case of Korea), the council was able to act only because the Soviet Union was not present to prevent its acting. See p. 739.

A further factor of significance in the appraisal of the Charter provisions for dealing with threats to the peace is the fact that world tensions have taken new shapes since the days of World War II. The disintegration of old empires and the rise of the self-consciousness of formerly subject peoples and races have brought new demands on the organs of the United Nations, e. g., with respect to the question of apartheid.

3. *Scope of the chapter.* This chapter is concerned with two principal themes that have become significant because of the foregoing political factors. First is the question of the ways in which the United Nations has sought to accommodate, politically and legally, to the failure of the Security Council force monopoly to operate as designed. Second is the development of the power of the United Nations to use force to assist the drive of subject peoples toward self determination.

SECTION A. UNITING FOR PEACE

When North Korean troops crossed the 38th parallel into South Korea (the Republic of Korea) in June, 1950, the Security Council of the United Nations was able immediately to adopt resolutions responding to this event. The council determined there had been a breach of the peace; it recommended that members of the United Nations furnish assistance to the Republic of Korea and that such assistance take the form of military forces available to a unified command under the United States and authorized to use the United Nations flag.

The Soviet Union's representative was not present in meetings of the council from January 1950 until August of that year. The foregoing resolutions in the Security Council dealing with the Korean case were adopted without veto.

After the representative of the USSR returned to the meetings of the Security Council, the General Assembly was urged by a group of states acting under the leadership of the United States to assert its own authority in cases in which the security council failed to act because of the veto. The "Uniting for Peace Resolution" was the form in which that assertion was cast. Resolution 337(V) follows.

UNITING FOR PEACE, RESOLUTION 377(V)

U.N. Gen. Ass. Off. Rec., 5th Sess., Supp. No. 20 (A/1775), p. 10.

The General Assembly,

Recognizing that the first two stated Purposes of the United Nations are:

To maintain international peace and security, and to that end: to take effective collective measures for the prevention and removal of threats to the peace, and for the suppression of acts of aggression or other breaches of the peace, and to bring about by peaceful means, and in conformity with the principles of justice and international law, adjustment or settlement of international disputes or situations which might lead to a breach of the peace, and

To develop friendly relations among nations based on respect for the principle of equal rights and self-determination of peoples, and to take other appropriate measures to strengthen universal peace,

Reaffirming that it remains the primary duty of all Members of the United Nations, when involved in an international dispute, to seek settlement of such a dispute by peaceful means through the procedures laid down in Chapter VI of the Charter, and recalling the successful achievements of the United Nations in this regard on a number of previous occasions,

Finding that international tension exists on a dangerous scale,

Recalling its resolution 290(IV) entitled "Essentials of peace", which states that disregard of the Principles of the Charter of the United Nations is primarily responsible for the continuance of international tension, and desiring to contribute further to the objectives of that resolution,

Reaffirming the importance of the exercise by the Security Council of its primary responsibility for the maintenance of international peace and security, and the duty of the permanent members to seek unanimity and to exercise restraint in the use of the veto,

Reaffirming that the initiative in negotiating the agreements for armed forces provided for in Article 43 of the Charter belongs to the Security Council, and desiring to ensure that, pending the conclusion of such agreements, the United Nations has at its disposal means for maintaining international peace and security,

Conscious that failure of the Security Council to discharge its responsibilities on behalf of all the Member States, particularly those responsibilities referred to in the two preceding paragraphs, does not relieve Member States of their obligations or the United Nations of its responsibility under the Charter to maintain international peace and security,

Recognizing in particular that such failure does not deprive the General Assembly of its rights or relieve it of its responsibilities under the Charter in regard to the maintenance of international peace and security,

Recognizing that discharge by the General Assembly of its responsibilities in these respects calls for possibilities of observation which would ascertain the facts and expose aggressors; for the existence of armed forces which could be used collectively; and for the possibility of timely recommendation by the General Assembly to Members of the United Nations for collective action which, to be effective, should be prompt,

A

1. Resolves that if the Security Council, because of lack of unanimity of the permanent members, fails to exercise its primary responsibility for the maintenance of international peace and security in any case where there "appears to be a threat" to the peace, breach of the peace, or act of aggression, the General Assembly shall consider the matter immediately with a view to making appropriate recommendations to Members for collective measures, including in the case of a breach of the peace or act of aggression the use of armed force when necessary, to maintain or restore international peace and security. If not in session at the time, the General Assembly may meet in emergency special session within twenty-four hours of the request therefor. Such emergency special session shall be called if requested by the Security Council on the vote of any seven Members, or by a majority of the Members of the United Nations;

2. Adopts for this purpose the amendments to its rules of procedure set forth in the annex to the present resolution;

B

3. Establishes a Peace Observation Commission which, for the calendar years 1951 and 1952, shall be composed of fourteen Members, namely: China, Colombia, Czechoslovakia, France, India, Iraq,

Israel, New Zealand, Pakistan, Sweden, the Union of Soviet Socialist Republics, the United Kingdom of Great Britain and Northern Ireland, the United States of America and Uruguay, and which could observe and report on the situation in any area where there exists international tension the continuance of which is likely to endanger the maintenance of international peace and security. Upon the invitation or with the consent of the State into whose territory the Commission would go, the General Assembly, or the Interim Committee when the Assembly is not in session, may utilize the Commission if the Security Council is not exercising the functions assigned to it by the Charter with respect to the matter in question. Decisions to utilize the Commission shall be made on the affirmative vote of two-thirds of the Members present and voting. The Security Council may also utilize the Commission in accordance with its authority under the Charter;

4. Decides that the Commission shall have authority in its discretion to appoint sub-commissions and to utilize the services of observers to assist it in the performance of its functions;

5. Recommends to all governments and authorities that they co-operate with the Commission and assist it in the performance of its functions;

6. Requests the Secretary-General to provide the necessary staff and facilities, utilizing, where directed by the Commission, the United Nations Panel of Field Observers envisaged in General Assembly resolution 297B(IV);

C

7. Invites each Member of the United Nations to survey its resources in order to determine the nature and scope of the assistance it may be in a position to render in support of any recommendations of the Security Council or of the General Assembly for the restoration of international peace and security;

8. Recommends to the States Members of the United Nations that each Member maintain within its national armed forces elements so trained, organized and equipped that they could promptly be made available, in accordance with its constitutional processes, for service as a United Nations unit or units, upon recommendation by the Security Council or the General Assembly, without prejudice to the use of such elements in exercise of the right of individual or collective self-defence recognized in Article 51 of the Charter;

9. Invites the Members of the United Nations to inform the Collective Measures Committee provided for in paragraph 11 as soon as possible of the measures taken in implementation of the preceding paragraph;

10. Requests the Secretary-General to appoint, with the approval of the Committee provided for in paragraph 11, a panel of mili-

tary experts who could be made available, on request, to Member
States wishing to obtain technical advice regarding the organization,
training, and equipment for prompt service as United Nations units
of the elements referred to in paragraph 8;

D

VI .   11.   Establishes a Collective Measures Committee consisting of
fourteen Members, namely: Australia, Belgium, Brazil, Burma,
Canada, Egypt, France, Mexico, Philippines, Turkey, the United
Kingdom of Great Britain and Northern Ireland, the United States
of America, Venezuela and Yugoslavia, and directs the Committee, in
consultation with the Secretary-General and with such Member States
as the Committee finds appropriate, to study and make a report to the
Security Council and the General Assembly, not later than 1 September 1951, on methods, including those in section C of the present
resolution, which might be used to maintain and strengthen international peace and security in accordance with the Purposes and Principles of the Charter, taking account of collective self-defence and
regional arrangements (Articles 51 and 52 of the Charter);

12.   Recommends to all Members States that they cooperate with
the Committee and assist it in the performance of its functions;

13.   Requests the Secretary-General to furnish the staff and facilities necessary for the effective accomplishment of the purposes
set forth in sections C and D of the present resolution;

E

14.   Is fully conscious that, in adopting the proposals set forth
above, enduring peace will not be secured solely by collective security arrangements against breaches of international peace and acts
of aggression, but that a genuine and lasting peace depends also upon
the observance of all the Principles and Purposes established in
the Charter of the United Nations, upon the implementation of the
resolutions of the Security Council, the General Assembly and other
principal organs of the United Nations intended to achieve the maintenance of international peace and security, and especially upon respect for and observance of human rights and fundamental freedoms
for all and on the establishment and maintenance of conditions of
economic and social well-being in all countries; and accordingly

15.   Urges Member States to respect fully, and to intensify, joint
action, in co-operation with the United Nations, to develop and stimulate universal respect for and observance of human rights and fundamental freedoms, and to intensify individual and collective efforts
to achieve conditions of economic stability and social progress, particularly through the development of under-developed countries and
areas.

*   *   *

Authority under the Charter of the United Nations. A major argument that the United Nations General Assembly does not have the authority under the Charter to exercise the power it has asserted in operative paragraph 1 of the Uniting for Peace Resolution is that Article 11(2) of the charter provides: "Any such question on which *action* is necessary shall be referred to the Security Council by the General Assembly either before or after discussion." (Emphasis supplied.) How do you appraise this argument?

SECTION B. THE UNITED NATIONS EMERGENCY FORCE IN EGYPT

SEYERSTED, UNITED NATIONS FORCES IN THE LAW OF PEACE AND WAR 46 (1966)

[As recounted at p. 1252, in October 1956, Egypt was attacked first by Israel and thereafter by France and the United Kingdom, the latter two states purporting to be carrying on a "police action" to quell the Israeli-Egyptian fighting. The Security Council of the United Nations was called into session and a draft resolution calling for a cease-fire was vetoed by France and the United Kingdom.]

* * * The Security Council, being unable to act because of French and United Kingdom negative votes, called an emergency special session of the General Assembly, as provided in the Uniting for Peace Resolution, "in order to make appropriate recommendations". The Assembly adopted on 2 November 1956 Resolution 997 (ES-I) urging the parties to agree to an immediate cease-fire (par. 1) and promptly to "withdraw all forces behind the armistice lines, to desist from raids across the armistice lines into neighbouring territory and to observe scrupulously the provisions of the armistice agreements" (par. 2). The resolution also urged, generally, that "steps be taken to reopen the Suez Canal and restore secure freedom of navigation" (par. 4).

On the following day the Secretary-General reported to the Assembly that France and the United Kingdom had declared themselves willing to stop military action if, inter alia, both the Egyptian and the Israeli Governments agreed to accept a United Nations Force to keep the peace; and if the United Nations decided to constitute and maintain such a Force until an Arab-Israeli peace settlement was reached and until satisfactory arrangements had been agreed in regard to the Suez Canal, both agreements to be guaranteed by the United Nations.

By Resolutions 998 (ES-I) of 4 November, 1000 (ES-I) of 5 November and 1001 (ES-I) of 7 November 1956 the General Assembly thereupon without a negative vote established an emergency international United Nations Force—later referred to as the United Nations Emergency Force (UNEF). The purpose, organization, status, functioning and financing of the Force were defined (a) in the Assembly's resolutions of 5 and 7 November 1956, (b) in the Second and Final Report of the Secretary-General on the Plan for an Emergency International United Nations Force approved by General Assembly Resolution 1001; (c) in a number of subsequent General Assembly resolutions; (d) in an "Aide-memoire on the Basis for Presence and Functioning of UNEF in Egypt", approved by Egypt and the General Assembly in November 1956; (e) in another agreement concluded by the Secretary-General with Egypt on 8 February 1957 concerning the status of UNEF in Egypt; (f) in the "Regulations for the United Nations Emergency Force" enacted by the Secretary-General on 20 February 1957; and lastly, (g) in a letter dated 21 June 1957 from the Secretary-General to the States providing contingents. This letter of 21 June 1957 refers to or reproduces as annexes most of the documents cited above and constitutes, together with the replies of each "participating" State, the basic agreements between these States and the United Nations.

* * *

The Force is equipped with normal regimental weapons and with means of transportation and reconnaissance—including motor vehicles and aircraft—but not with heavy arms. The troops have a right to fire in self-defence. They are never to take the initiative in the use of arms, but may respond with force to an armed attack upon them, including attempts to use force to make them withdraw from positions which they occupy under orders from the Commander. It has been said that UNEF serves by being present and by acting as a plate-glass window—not capable of withstanding assault but nevertheless a lightly armed barrier that all see and tend to respect.

As we have seen, in Korea the United Nations had entrusted to one of its Member States the task of organizing the Force and directing its operations, and the Collective Measures Committee had also recommended this system for military action under the Uniting for Peace Resolution. In the case of UNEF, however, the Organization chose itself to assume these functions. The General Assembly appointed a *Commander* of the Force—as a regular United Nations official, responsible to the Organization and fully independent of the policies of any one nation—to organize the Force "in consultation with the Secretary-General as regards size and composition". He was entrusted with full command authority and operational responsibility for the performance of the functions assigned to the Force by the United Nations and for the deployment and assignment of troops placed at the disposal of the Force, though he was to exercise this authority and responsibility "in consultation with the Secretary-General".

* * *

The Force is a subsidiary organ of the United Nations and in particular of the General Assembly, and it enjoys the status, privileges and immunities of the Organization in accordance with the Convention on the Privileges and Immunities of the United Nations. This applies also to the property, funds and assets of "participating" Governments used in the host State. The Commander and the staff detailed from the United Nations Secretariat to serve with him are entitled to privileges and immunities under the Convention as officials of the United Nations; the military members of the UNEF Command are entitled to privileges and immunities as experts on mission for the United Nations. Personnel recruited locally enjoy only immunity in respect of official acts as provided in § 18(a) of the Convention, which is the most basic immunity of an international official. Members of national contingents are not covered by the Convention on the Privileges and Immunities of the United Nations, but are accorded largely corresponding privileges and immunities, including immunity in respect of official acts, in Egypt under the Status Agreement with that country. All members of the Force are entitled to the legal protection of the United Nations as agents of the Organization.

* * *

UNITED NATIONS GENERAL ASSEMBLY RESOLUTIONS ESTABLISHING THE EMERGENCY FORCE (UNEF)

U.N. Gen. Ass. Off. Rec., 1st Emergency Special Sess. (1956), Annexes, p. 33.

On 2 November 1956, at its 562nd plenary meeting, the General Assembly adopted the draft resolution submitted by the United States of America. (A/3256). For the final text, see resolution 997 (ES–I) below.

On 4 November 1956, at its 563rd plenary meeting, the General Assembly adopted the draft resolution submitted by Canada (A/3276) and the draft resolution submitted by Afghanistan, Burma, Ceylon, Ethiopia, India, Indonesia, Iran, Iraq, Jordan, Lebanon, Liberia, Libya, Nepal, Pakistan, Philippines, Saudi Arabia, Syria, Thailand and Yemen (A/3275). For the final text, see resolutions 998 (ES–I) and 999 (ES–I) respectively, below.

On 5 November 1956, at its 565th plenary meeting, the General Assembly adopted the draft resolution submitted by Canada, Colombia and Norway (A/3290). For the final text, see resolution 1000 (ES–I) below.

On 7 November 1956, at its 567th plenary meeting, the General Assembly adopted the draft resolution submitted by Argentina, Burma, Ceylon, Denmark, Ecuador, Ethiopia and Sweden (A/3308) as amended verbally, and the draft resolution submitted by Afghanistan, Burma, Ceylon, Ethiopia, India, Indonesia, Iran, Iraq, Jordan, Lebanon, Liberia, Libya, Nepal, Pakistan, Philippines, Saudi Arabia, Syria,

Thailand and Yemen (A/3309). For the final text, see resolutions 1001 (ES–I) and 1002 (ES–I) respectively, below.

On 10 November 1956, at its 572nd plenary meeting, the General Assembly adopted the draft resolution submitted by the United States of America (A/3329) as amended verbally. For the final text, see resolution 1003 (ES–I) below.

Resolution 997 (ES–I)

[Document A/RES/390]

The General Assembly,

Noting the disregard on many occasions by parties to the Israel-Arab armistice agreements of 1949 of the terms of such agreements, and that the armed forces of Israel have penetrated deeply into Egyptian territory in violation of the General Armistice Agreement between Egypt and Israel of 24 February 1949,

Noting that armed forces of France and the United Kingdom of Great Britain and Northern Ireland are conducting military operations against Egyptian territory,

Noting that traffic through the Suez Canal is now interrupted to the serious prejudice of many nations,

Expressing its grave concern over these developments,

1. Urges as a matter of priority that all parties now involved in hostilities in the area agree to an immediate cease-fire and, as part thereof, halt the movement of military forces and arms into the area;

2. Urges the parties to the armistice agreements promptly to withdraw all forces behind the armistice lines, to desist from raids across the armistice lines into neighbouring territory, and to observe scrupulously the provisions of the armistice agreements;

3. Recommends that all Member States refrain from introducing military goods in the area of hostilities and in general refrain from any acts which would delay or prevent the implementation of the present resolution;

4. Urges that, upon the cease-fire being effective steps be taken to reopen the Suez Canal and restore secure freedom of navigation;

5. Requests the Secretary-General to observe and report promptly on the compliance with the present resolution to the Security Council and to the General Assembly, for such further action as they may deem appropriate in accordance with the Charter;

6. Decides to remain in emergency session pending compliance with the present resolution.

Resolution 998 (ES–I)

[Document A/RES/391]

The General Assembly,

Bearing in mind the urgent necessity of facilitating compliance with its resolution 997 (ES–I) of 2 November 1956,

Requests, as a matter of priority, the Secretary-General to submit to it within forty-eight hours a plan for the setting up, with the consent of the nations concerned, of an emergency international United Nations Force to secure and supervise the cessation of hostilities in accordance with all the terms of the aforementioned resolution.

Resolution 999 (ES–I)

[Document A/RES/392]

The General Assembly,

Noting with regret that not all the parties concerned have yet agreed to comply with the provisions of its resolution 997 (ES–I) of 2 November 1956,

Noting the special priority given in that resolution to an immediate cease-fire and, as part thereof, to the halting of the movement of military forces and arms into the area,

Noting further that the resolution urged the parties to the armistice agreements promptly to withdraw all forces behind the armistice lines, to desist from raids across the armistice lines into neighbouring territory, and to observe scrupulously the provisions of the armistice agreements,

1.   Reaffirms its resolution 997 (ES–I) and once again calls upon the parties immediately to comply with the provisions of the said resolution;

2.   Authorizes the Secretary-General immediately to arrange with the parties concerned for the implementation of the cease-fire and the halting of the movement of military forces and arms into the area, and requests him to report compliance forthwith and, in any case, not later than twelve hours from the time of adoption of the present resolution;

3.   Requests the Secretary-General, with the assistance of the Chief of Staff and the members of the United Nations Truce Supervision Organization, to obtain compliance of the withdrawal of all forces behind the armistice lines;

4.   Decides to meet again immediately on receipt of the Secretary-General's report referred to in paragraph 2 of the present resolution.

Resolution 1000 (ES–I)

[Document A/RES/394]

The General Assembly,

Having requested the Secretary-General, in its resolution 998 (ES–I) of 4 November 1956, to submit to it a plan for an emergency international United Nations Force, for the purposes stated,

Noting with satisfaction the first report of the Secretary-General on the plan (A/3289), and having in mind particularly paragraph 4 of that report,

1. Establishes a United Nations Command for an emergency international Force to secure and supervise the cessation of hostilities in accordance with all the terms of General Assembly resolution, 997 (ES–I) of 2 November 1956;

2. Appoints, on an emergency basis, the Chief of Staff of the United Nations Truce Supervision Organization, Major-General E. L. M. Burns, as Chief of the Command;

3. Authorizes the Chief of the Command immediately to recruit, from the observer corps of the United Nations Truce Supervision Organization, a limited number of officers who shall be nationals of countries other than those having permanent membership in the Security Council, and further authorizes him, in consultation with the Secretary-General, to undertake the recruitment directly, from various Member States other than the permanent members of the Security Council, of the additional number of officers needed;

4. Invites the Secretary-General to take such administrative measures as may be necessary for the prompt execution of the actions envisaged in the present resolution.

Resolution 1001 (ES–I)

[Document A/RES/395]

The General Assembly,

Recalling its resolution 997 (ES–I) of 2 November 1956 concerning the cease-fire, withdrawal of troops and other matters related to the military operations in Egyptian territory, as well as its resolution 998 (ES–I) of 4 November 1956 concerning the request to the Secretary-General to submit a plan for an emergency international United Nations Force,

Having established by its resolution 1000 (ES–I) of 5 November 1956 a United Nations Command for an emergency international Force, having appointed the Chief of Staff of the United Nations Truce Supervision Organization as Chief of the Command with authorization to him to begin the recruitment of officers for the Command, and having invited the Secretary-General to take the administrative measures necessary for the prompt execution of that resolution.

Noting with appreciation the second and final report of the Secretary-General (A/3302) on the plan for an emergency international United Nations Force as requested in General Assembly resolution 998 (ES–I), and having examined that plan,

1.   Expresses its approval of the guiding principles for the organization and functioning of the emergency international United Nations Force as expounded in paragraphs 6 to 9 of the Secretary-General's report;

2.   Concurs in the definition of the functions of the Force as stated in paragraph 12 of the Secretary-General's report;

3.   Invites the Secretary-General to continue discussions with Governments of Member States concerning offers of participation in the Force, toward the objective of its balanced composition;

4.   Requests the Chief of the Command, in consultation with the Secretary-General as regards size and composition, to proceed forthwith with the full organization of the Force;

5.   Approves provisionally the basic rule concerning the financing of the Force laid down in paragraph 15 of the Secretary-General's report;

6.   Establishes an Advisory Committee composed of one representative from each of the following countries: Brazil, Canada, Ceylon, Colombia, India, Norway and Pakistan, and requests this Committee, whose Chairman shall be the Secretary-General, to undertake the development of those aspects of the planning for the Force and its operation not already dealt with by the General Assembly and which do not fall within the area of the direct responsibility of the Chief of the Command;

7.   Authorizes the Secretary-General to issue all regulations and instructions which may be essential to the effective functioning of the Force, following consultation with the Committee aforementioned, and to take all other necessary administrative and executive action;

8.   Determines that, following the fulfilment of the immediate responsibilities defined for it in operative paragraphs 6 and 7 above, the Advisory Committee shall continue to assist the Secretary-General in the responsibilities falling to him under the present and other relevant resolutions;

9.   Decides that the Advisory Committee, in the performance of its duties, shall be empowered to request, through the usual procedures, the convening of the General Assembly and to report to the Assembly whenever matters arise which, in its opinion, are of such urgency and importance as to require consideration by the General Assembly itself;

10.   Requests all Member States to afford assistance as necessary to the United Nations Command in the performance of its functioning, including arrangements for passage to and from the area involved.

Resolution 1002 (ES–I)

[Document A/RES/396]

The General Assembly,

Recalling its resolution 997 (ES–I) of 2 November 1956, 998 (ES–I) and 999 (ES–I) of 4 November 1956 and 1000 (ES–I) of 5 November 1956, adopted by overwhelming majorities,

Noting in particular that the General Assembly, by its resolution 1000 (ES–I), established a United Nations Command for an emergency international Force to secure and supervise the cessation of hostilities in accordance with all the terms of its resolution 997 (ES–I),

1.   Reaffirms the above-mentioned resolutions;

2.   Calls once again upon Israel immediately to withdraw all its forces behind the armistice lines established by the General Armistice Agreement between Egypt and Israel of 24 February 1949,

3.   Calls once again upon the United Kingdom and France immediately to withdraw all their forces from Egyptian territory, consistently with the above-mentioned resolutions;

4.   Urges the Secretary-General to communicate the present resolution to the parties concerned, and requests him promptly to report to the General Assembly on the compliance with this resolution.

Resolution 1003 (ES–I)

[Document A/RES/400]

The General Assembly

1.   Decides to place on the provisional agenda of its eleventh regular session, as a matter of priority, the question on the agenda of its first emergency special session;

2.   Refers to its eleventh regular session, for consideration, the records of the meetings and the documents of its first emergency special session;

3.   Decides that, notwithstanding paragraph 1 above, the first emergency special session may continue to consider the question, if necessary, prior to the eleventh regular session of the Assembly.

----

1.   *Legal basis for the United Nations Emergency Force.*   In establishing the Emergency Force, did the General Assembly of the

United Nations avail itself of all of the power it had asserted in the Uniting for Peace Resolution? The force was not physically located on Israeli territory. Could it have lawfully entered Israeli territory to perform its function as a "plate-glass window" without the consent of the Government of Israel?

2.   *Withdrawal of the Emergency Force.* At the request of the Government of the United Arab Republic (Egypt), the Secretary-General of the United Nations (U Thant) withdrew the Emergency Force from the territory of the Republic in May and June, 1967. (See the account of the Six Day War of June 1967 at p. 1255.) The action of the Secretary-General of the United Nations in acceding to this request at that particular point of time was highly controversial. WHY? He explained his action in detail in a report to the United Nations. Gen. Ass. Off. Rec., 5th Emergency Spec. Sess. (1967), Annexes (A/6730/Add. 3), p. 9.

SECTION C. THE UNITED NATIONS IN THE CONGO

SEYERSTED, UNITED NATIONS FORCES IN THE LAW
OF PEACE AND WAR 60 (1966)

* * *

Shortly after the accession to independence of the Republic of the Congo on 30 June 1960, some units of the Congolese forces mutinied against their Belgian officers and committed acts of violence against members of the European population, in particular Belgians. The Belgian Government, acting against the wish of the Congolese Government, sent troops in order to maintain or restore order. This gave rise to bitterness and panic among the African population and to a new flight of Europeans and the consequent breakdown of many public services and important economic enterprises. In this situation the President and the Prime Minister of the Congo, by telegrams of 12 and 13 July 1960, requested the urgent dispatch of a United Nations Force composed of military units from neutral countries in order to protect Congolese territory against what they termed the Belgian "act of aggression".

On 14 July the Security Council, at the request of the Secretary-General and without a dissenting vote, adopted a resolution calling upon Belgium to withdraw its troops and authorizing the Secretary-General

to take the necessary steps, in consultation with the Government of the Republic of the Congo, to provide the Government with such military assistance, as may be necessary, until, through the efforts of the Congolese Government with the technical assistance of the United Nations, the national security forces may be able, in the opinion of the Government, to meet fully their tasks.

The vote was 8–0–3. China, France and the United Kingdom abstained because they could not support Belgian troop withdrawal before the United Nations Force had taken over; they did, however, support the dispatch of the United Nations Force.

* * *

Despite its greater size and heavier tasks, the United Nations Force in the Congo was constituted on a much more modest formal basis than the UNEF. In view of the urgency of the matter and the difficulties involved in reaching agreement among its members, the Security Council did not lay down in its resolutions even the basic principles on which the Force should be organized, as the General Assembly had done in the case of UNEF. The organization of the Force, including the appointment of its Supreme Commander, was thus left to the Secretary-General, who, however, made detailed reports to the Council. In September 1960, when the Security Council was unable to agree on what action to take after the split between President Kasa-Vubu and Prime Minister Lumumba, the matter was referred to the General Assembly under the Uniting for Peace Resolution. However, the resolutions of the General Assembly did not concern themselves directly with the Force, except for the budgetary aspects.

* * *

The costs of the Force were covered by the United Nations in essentially the same manner as those of UNEF. In 1961 the expenses of ONUC averaged approximately $10 million per month, of which about 83 per cent were for direct expenses and about 17 per cent were for reimbursement to the Governments providing contingents. The budgets for 62–63 were of the same order. The sums were assessed upon Member States after deduction for voluntary contributions and for waiver of reimbursement by States providing airlift services. The General Assembly had expressly decided that the expenses were "expenses of the Organization" subject to legally binding assessment of Member States under Article 17 of the Charter, but that they were nevertheless to be kept separate as being essentially different in nature from the expenses under the regular budget. However, some Members refused to accept this decision and to pay the corresponding amounts assessed upon them in respect of UNEF and ONUC. Consequently, the General Assembly, by its Resolution 1731 (XVI), decided to submit the question to the International Court of Justice for an advisory opinion.[a]

* * *

a. The advisory opinion of the International Court of Justice is set forth at p. 1290.

The Congo Force had to perform a number of tasks throughout a vast territory in order to fulfil its mandate to assist in the maintenance of law and order and the protection of life and property, to prevent foreign intervention in the form of men, arms or military supplies, and to prevent civil war. Apart from a number of civilian activities, like maintenance of essential services, mediation and persuasion, the Force performed, inter alia, the following functions: patrolling areas threatened by disorders, establishing and guarding United Nations protected areas where people in danger of arbitrary arrest or other persecution could take refuge; guarding and defending the residences of Congolese political leaders and diplomatic representatives of foreign States to protect them against arbitrary arrest or violence; guarding government buildings; guarding, isolating and neutralizing the meeting place of the Congolese Parliament and ensuring the free passage through the Congo of its members; guarding, and in emergencies temporarily closing, ports and airfields to secure the supplies to and the movements of the United Nations Force and to prevent Congolese troop movements or external aid to the opposing sides in the civil war; arrest and eviction of foreign military personnel or mercenaries; disarming civilians and military groups which have broken loose from their commanders; rescuing civilians, wounded and dead out of areas affected by civil war. Last, but not least, the functions included occupying, patrolling and if necessary defending areas threatened by armed invasion, and establishing, guarding and defending road blocks or neutral zones between opposing Congolese forces, or removing road blocks or other obstacles and opposition to the United Nations movements and operations created by local military units; guarding and defending United Nations personnel and positions.

These and other activities could not avoid interfering with the plans of the various central and provincial authorities in the Congo * * *.

Less violent, but more extensive military operations took place during the final phase of the United Nations action in Katanga in December 1962 and January 1963. After a six-day period of unanswered firing on United Nations positions and incidents involving seizure and detention of members of the United Nations Force by the Katangese gendarmerie, the United Nations on 28 December launched its final action against the forces of the provincial Katangese government. The United Nations Force first cleared the Katangese road blocks in Elisabethville and seized the key positions in that city. Subsequently, it advanced towards and occupied other cities in southern Katanga. This action cost 10 killed and 77 wounded on the United Nations side and nearly as many civilian casualties. One of the actions carried out during this phase—the advance on and occupation of Jadotville, which was carried out by the commanders in the field without consultation with headquarters at New York and

Leopoldville—was termed by the Officer-in-Charge of the United Nations operation in the Congo as "the first experience of a strictly United Nations armed force under United Nations command with combat conditions in the field". By 21 January 1963 the United Nations Force had under control all important centres hitherto held by the Katangese, the Katangese airforce had been eliminated and the Katangese gendarmerie as an organised fighting force had ceased to exist. M. Tschombe ended the seccessionist activities and officials and security forces of the Central Government could gradually move into the Province, although these forces were, during the first period, placed under United Nations command (as a Congolese contingent of the United Nations Force).

This ended the major United Nations military operations in the Congo. The Force remained in the country for another year-and-a-half, but it was gradually reduced in strength, not merely because of the restoration of national unity, but also because of the lack of funds. The last United Nations troops left the Congo in the summer of 1964.

* * *

UNITED NATIONS SECURITY COUNCIL RESOLUTIONS ESTABLISHING THE OPERATIONS IN THE CONGO (ONUC)

Resolutions and Decisions of the Security Council 1960.

U.N. Sec. Council Off. Rec., 15th Year, p. 5.

143 (1960). Resolution of 14 July 1960

[S/4387]

The Security Council,

Considering the report of the Secretary-General on a request for United Nations action in relation to the Republic of the Congo,

Considering the request for military assistance addressed to the Secretary-General by the President and the Prime Minister of the Republic of the Congo,

1. Calls upon the Government of Belgium to withdraw its troops from the territory of the Republic of the Congo;

2. Decides to authorize the Secretary-General to take the necessary steps, in consultation with the Government of the Republic of the Congo, to provide the Government with such military assistance as may be necessary until, through the efforts of the Congolese Government with the technical assistance of the United Nations, the national security forces may be able, in the opinion of the Government, to meet fully their tasks;

3. Requests the Secretary-General to report to the Security Council as appropriate.

> Adopted at the 873rd meeting by 8 votes to none, with 3 abstentions (China, France, United Kingdom of Great Britain and Northern Ireland).

145 (1960). Resolution of 22 July 1960

[S/4405]

The Security Council,

Having considered the first report of the Secretary-General on the implementation of Security Council resolution 143 (1960) of 14 July 1960,

Appreciating the work of the Secretary-General and the support so readily and so speedily given to him by all Member States invited by him to give assistance,

Noting that, as stated by the Secretary-General, the arrival of the troops of the United Nations Force in Leopoldville has already had a salutary effect,

Recognizing that an urgent need still exists to continue and to increase such efforts,

Considering that the complete restoration of law and order in the Republic of the Congo would effectively contribute to the maintenance of international peace and security,

Recognizing that the Security Council recommended the admission of the Republic of the Congo to membership in the United Nations as a unit,

1. Calls upon the Government of Belgium to implement speedily Security Council resolution 143 (1960) on the withdrawal of its troops and authorizes the Secretary-General to take all necessary action to this effect;

2. Requests all states to refrain from any action which might tend to impede the restoration of law and order and the exercise by the Government of the Congo of its authority and also to refrain from any action which might undermine the territorial integrity and the political independence of the Republic of the Congo;

3. Commends the Secretary-General for the prompt action he has taken to carry out resolution 143 (1960) and for his first report;

4. Invites the specialized agencies of the United Nations to render to the Secretary-General such assistance as he may require;

5. Requests the Secretary-General to report further to the Security Council as appropriate.

> Adopted unanimously at the 879th meeting.

146 (1960). Resolution of 9 August 1960

[S/4426]

The Security Council,

Recalling its resolution 145 (1960) of 22 July 1960, inter alia calling upon the Government of Belgium to implement speedily Security Council resolution 143 (1960) of 14 July 1960 on the withdrawal of its troops and authorizing the Secretary-General to take all necessary action to this effect,

Having noted the second report of the Secretary-General on the implementation of the aforesaid two resolutions and his statement before the Council,

Having considered the statements made by the representatives of Belgium and the Republic of the Congo to the Council at this meeting,

Noting with satisfaction the progress made by the United Nations in carrying out the Security Council resolutions in respect of the territory of the Republic of the Congo other than the province of Katanga,

Noting however that the United Nations had been prevented from implementing the aforesaid resolutions in the province of Katanga although it was ready, and in fact attempted, to do so,

Recognizing that the withdrawal of Belgian troops from the province of Katanga will be a positive contribution to and essential for the proper implementation of the Council's resolutions,

1. Confirms the authority given to the Secretary-General by Security Council resolutions 143 (1960) and 145 (1960) and requests him to continue to carry out the responsibility placed on him thereby;

2. Calls upon the Government of Belgium to withdraw immediately its troops from the province of Katanga under speedy modalities determined by the Secretary-General and to assist in every possible way the implementation of the Council's resolutions;

3. Declares that the entry of the United Nations Force into the province of Katanga is necessary for the full implementation of the present resolution;

4. Reaffirms that the United Nations Force in the Congo will not be a party to or in any way intervene in or be used to influence the outcome of any internal conflict, constitutional or otherwise;

5. Calls upon all Member States, in accordance with Articles 25 and 49 of the Charter of the United Nations, to accept and carry out the decisions of the Security Council and to afford mutual assistance in carrying out measures decided upon by the Council;

6. Requests the Secretary-General to implement the present resolution and to report further to the Security Council as appropriate.

> Adopted at the 886th meeting by 9 votes to none, with 2 abstentions (France, Italy).

157 (1960). Resolution of 17 September 1960

[S/4526]

The Security Council,

Having considered the item on its agenda as contained in document S/Agenda/906,

Taking into account that the lack of unanimity of its permanent members at the 906th meeting of the Security Council has prevented it from exercising its primary responsibility for the maintenance of international peace and security,

Decides to call an emergency special session of the General Assembly, as provided in General Assembly resolution 377A(V) of 3 November 1950, in order to make appropriate recommendations.

> Adopted at the 906th meeting by 8 votes to 2 (Poland, Union of Soviet Socialist Republics), with 1 abstention (France).

---

1. *Legal basis for the United Nations operations in the Congo.* The Congolese action was authorized by the Security Council of the United Nations. Was the legality of the Congolese action more firmly based on the Charter than the Emergency Force in the Middle East (which, as seen above, was authorized by the General Assembly)? Did the council act pursuant to Article 39? If so, what was the requisite "threat to the peace, breach of the peace, or act of aggression?" Was it the sending of troops by Belgium to maintain and restore order? The council never made a finding to that effect.

Can the council's action be grounded on the request of the Congolese government for aid? What is the Charter basis for the council's response to such a request?

2. *Analysis of the legal basis for peacekeeping forces by the International Court of Justice.* The legal basis for both the Emergency Force and the Congolese operations was the subject of analysis by the International Court in the Certain Expenses case, which follows. The court was asked for an advisory opinion because certain members of the United Nations refused to pay amounts assessed

against them as "expenses of the Organization" (Article 17). The members refusing claimed that the Middle East and Congolese operations did not qualify as such "expenses." The case was significant because of its financial implications, since Article 19 of the Charter prescribes a loss of the right to vote in the General Assembly in the case of certain financial delinquencies on the part of a member. But the advisory opinion of the court is also significant because of its analysis of the "constitutional" powers of the United Nations and its organs to employ or authorize military force.

CERTAIN EXPENSES OF THE UNITED NATIONS (ADVISORY OPINION)

International Court of Justice, 1962.
[1962] I.C.J.Rep. 151.

[The General Assembly of the United Nations requested an advisory opinion by Resolution 1731 (XVI), adopted on December 20, 1961. The request is paraphrased as follows. Designations, by number and date, of specific resolutions adopted by the Security Council and the General Assembly have been omitted from the paraphrase.]

The General Assembly,

Recognizing its need for authoritative legal guidance as to obligations of Member States under the Charter of the United Nations in the matter of financing the United Nations operations in the Congo and in the Middle East,

Decides to submit the following question to the International Court of Justice for an advisory opinion:

Do the expenditures authorized in General Assembly resolutions relating to the United Nations operations in the Congo and the expenditures authorized in General Assembly resolutions relating to the operations of the United Nations Emergency Force constitute "expenses of the Organization" within the meaning of Article 17, paragraph 2, of the Charter of the United Nations?

* * *

The question on which the Court is asked to give its opinion is whether certain expenditures which were authorized by the General Assembly to cover the costs of the United Nations operations in the Congo (hereinafter referred to as ONUC) and of the operations of the United Nations Emergency Force in the Middle East (hereinafter referred to as UNEF), "constitute 'expenses of the Organization' within the meaning of Article 17, paragraph 2, of the Charter of the United Nations".

* * *

The text of Article 17 is in part as follows:

"1. The General Assembly shall consider and approve the budget of the Organization.

2. The expenses of the Organization shall be borne by the Members as apportioned by the General Assembly."

* * *

It is perhaps the simple identification of "expenses" with the items included in a budget, which has led certain arguments to link the interpretation of the word "expenses" in paragraph 2 of Article 17, with the word "budget" in paragraph 1 of that Article; in both cases, it is contended, the qualifying adjective "regular" or "administrative" should be understood to be implied. Since no such qualification is expressed in the text of the Charter, it could be read in, only if such qualification must necessarily be implied from the provisions of the Charter considered as a whole, or from some particular provision thereof which makes it unavoidable to do so in order to give effect to the Charter.

In the first place, concerning the word "budget" in paragraph 1 of Article 17, it is clear that the existence of the distinction between "administrative budgets" and "operational budgets" was not absent from the minds of the drafters of the Charter, nor from the consciousness of the Organization even in the early days of its history. In drafting Article 17, the drafters found it suitable to provide in paragraph 1 that "The General Assembly shall consider and approve the budget of the Organization". But in dealing with the function of the General Assembly in relation to the specialized agencies, they provided in paragraph 3 that the General Assembly "shall examine the administrative budgets of such specialized agencies". If it had been intended that paragraph 1 should be limited to the administrative budget of the United Nations organization itself, the word "administrative" would have been inserted in paragraph 1 as it was in paragraph 3.

* * *

Actually, the practice of the Organization is entirely consistent with the plain meaning of the text. The budget of the Organization has from the outset included items which would not fall within any of the definitions of "administrative budget" which have been advanced in this connection. Thus, for example, prior to the establishment of, and now in addition to, the "Expanded Programme of Technical Assistance" and the "Special Fund", both of which are nourished by voluntary contributions, the annual budget of the Organization contains provision for funds for technical assistance; in the budget for the financial year 1962, the sum of $6,400,000 is included for the technical programmes of economic development, social activities, human rights activities, public administration and narcotic drugs control.

* * *

It is a consistent practice of the General Assembly to include in the annual budget resolutions, provision for expenses relating to the maintenance of international peace and security. Annually, since 1947, the General Assembly has made anticipatory provision for "unforeseen and extraordinary expenses" arising in relation to the "maintenance of peace and security".

* * *

These annual resolutions on unforeseen and extraordinary expenses were adopted without a dissenting vote in every year from 1947 through 1959, except for 1952, 1953 and 1954, when the adverse votes are attributable to the fact that the resolution included the specification of a controversial item—United Nations Korean war decorations.

* * *

In the light of what has been stated, the Court concludes that there is no justification for reading into the text of Article 17, paragraph 1, any limiting or qualifying word before the word "budget".

Turning to paragraph 2 of Article 17, the Court observes that, on its face, the term "expenses of the Organization" means all the expenses and not just certain types of expenses which might be referred to as "regular expenses". * * *

Passing from the text of Article 17 to its place in the general structure and scheme of the Charter, the Court will consider whether in that broad context one finds any basis for implying a limitation upon the budgetary authority of the General Assembly which in turn might limit the meaning of "expenses" in paragraph 2 of that Article.

The general purposes of Article 17 are the vesting of control over the finances of the Organization, and the levying of apportioned amounts of the expenses of the Organization in order to enable it to carry out the functions of the Organization as a whole acting through its principal organs and such subsidiary organs as may be established under the authority of Article 22 or Article 29.

Article 17 is the only article in the Charter which refers to budgetary authority or to the power to apportion expenses, or otherwise to raise revenue, except for Articles 33 and 35, paragraph 3, of the Statute of the Court which have no bearing on the point here under discussion. Nevertheless, it has been argued before the Court that one type of expenses, namely those resulting from operations for the maintenance of international peace and security, are not "expenses of the Organization" within the meaning of Article 17, paragraph 2, of the Charter, inasmuch as they fall to be dealt with exclusively by the Security Council, and more especially through agreements negotiated in accordance with Article 43 of the Charter.

The argument rests in part upon the view that when the maintenance of international peace and security is involved, it is only the Security Council which is authorized to decide on any action relative thereto. It is argued further that since the General Assembly's power is limited to discussing, considering, studying and recommending, it cannot impose an obligation to pay the expenses which result from the implementation of its recommendations. This argument leads to an examination of the respective functions of the General Assembly and of the Security Council under the Charter, particularly with respect to the maintenance of international peace and security.

Article 24 of the Charter provides:

> In order to ensure prompt and effective action by the United Nations, its Members confer on the Security Council primary responsibility for the maintenance of international peace and security. * * *

The responsibility conferred is "primary", not exclusive. This primary responsibility is conferred upon the Security Council, as stated in Article 24, "in order to ensure prompt and effective action". To this end, it is the Security Council which is given a power to impose an explicit obligation of compliance if for example it issues an order or command to an aggressor under Chapter VII. It is only the Security Council which can require enforcement by coercive action against an aggressor.

The Charter makes it abundantly clear, however, that the General Assembly is also to be concerned with international peace and security. Article 14 authorizes the General Assembly to "recommend measures for the peaceful adjustment of any situation, regardless of origin, which it deems likely to impair the general welfare or friendly relations among nations, including situations resulting from a violation of the provisions of the present Charter setting forth the purposes and principles of the United Nations". The word "measures" implies some kind of action, and the only limitation which Article 14 imposes on the General Assembly is the restriction found in Article 12, namely, that the Assembly should not recommend measures while the Security Council is dealing with the same matter unless the Council requests it to do so. Thus while it is the Security Council which, exclusively, may order coercive action, the functions and powers conferred by the Charter on the General Assembly are not confined to discussion, consideration, the initiation of studies and the making of recommendations; they are not merely hortatory.

* * *

The argument supporting a limitation on the budgetary authority of the General Assembly with respect to the maintenance of international peace and security relies especially on the reference to "action" in the last sentence of Article 11, paragraph 2. * * *

The Court considers that the kind of action referred to in Article 11, paragraph 2, is coercive or enforcement action. This paragraph, which applies not merely to general questions relating to peace and security, but also to specific cases brought before the General

Assembly by a State under Article 35, in its first sentence empowers the General Assembly, by means of recommendations to States or to the Security Council, or to both, to organize peace-keeping operations, at the request, or with the consent, of the States concerned. This power of the General Assembly is a special power which in no way derogates from its general powers under Article 10 or Article 14, except as limited by the last sentence of Article 11, paragraph 2. This last sentence says that when "action" is necessary the General Assembly shall refer the question to the Security Council. The word "action" must mean such action as is solely within the province of the Security Council. It cannot refer to recommendations which the Security Council might make, as for instance under Article 38, because the General Assembly under Article 11 has a comparable power. The "action" which is solely within the province of the Security Council is that which is indicated by the title of Chapter VII of the Charter, namely "Action with respect to threats to the peace, breaches of the peace, and acts of aggression". If the word "action" in Article 11, paragraph 2, were interpreted to mean that the General Assembly could make recommendations only of a general character affecting peace and security in the abstract, and not in relation to specific cases, the paragraph would not have provided that the General Assembly may make recommendations on questions brought before it by States or by the Security Council. Accordingly, the last sentence of Article 11, paragraph 2, has no application where the necessary action is not enforcement action.

The practice of the Organization throughout its history bears out the foregoing elucidation of the term "action" in the last sentence of Article 11, paragraph 2. * * *

The Court accordingly finds that the argument which seeks, by reference to Article 11, paragraph 2, to limit the budgetary authority of the General Assembly in respect of the maintenance of international peace and security, is unfounded.

It has further been argued before the Court that Article 43 of the Charter constitutes a particular rule, a lex specialis, which derogates from the general rule in Article 17, whenever an expenditure for the maintenance of international peace and security is involved. Article 43 provides that Members shall negotiate agreements with the Security Council on its initiative, * * *

The argument is that such agreements were intended to include specifications concerning the allocation of costs of such enforcement actions as might be taken by direction of the Security Council, and that it is only the Security Council which has the authority to arrange for meeting such costs.

With reference to this argument, the Court will state at the outset that, for reasons fully expounded later in this Opinion, the operations known as UNEF and ONUC were not enforcement actions within the compass of Chapter VII of the Charter and that therefore Article 43 could not have any applicability to the cases with which the Court is here concerned. However, even if Article 43 were applicable, the Court could not accept this interpretation of its text for the following reasons.

There is nothing in the text of Article 43 which would limit the discretion of the Security Council in negotiating such agreements. It cannot be assumed that in every such agreement the Security Council would insist, or that any Member State would be bound to agree, that such State would bear the entire cost of the "assistance" which it would make available including, for example, transport of forces to the point of operation, complete logistical maintenance in the field, supplies, arms and ammunition, etc. If, during negotiations under the terms of Article 43 a Member State would be entitled (as it would be) to insist, and the Security Council would be entitled (as it would be) to agree, that some part of the expense should be borne by the Organization, then such expense would form part of the expenses of the Organization and would fall to be apportioned by the General Assembly under Article 17. It is difficult to see how it could have been contemplated that all potential expenses could be envisaged in such agreements concluded perhaps long in advance. * * *

Moreover, an argument which insists that all measures taken for the maintenance of international peace and security must be financed through agreements concluded under Article 43, would seem to exclude the possibility that the Security Council might act under some other Article of the Charter. The Court cannot accept so limited a view of the powers of the Security Council under the Charter. It cannot be said that the Charter has left the Security Council impotent in the face of an emergency situation when agreements under Article 43 have not been concluded.

         *   *   *

The Court has considered the general problem of the interpretation of Article 17, paragraph 2, * * * In determining whether the actual expenditures authorized constitute "expenses of the Organization within the meaning of Article 17, paragraph 2, of the Charter", the Court agrees that such expenditures must be tested by their relationship to the purposes of the United Nations in the sense that if an expenditure were made for a purpose which is not one of the purposes of the United Nations, it could not be considered an "expense of the Organization".

The purposes of the United Nations are set forth in Article 1 of the Charter. The first two purposes as stated in paragraphs 1 and 2, may be summarily described as pointing to the goal of international peace and security and friendly relations. The third purpose is the achievement of economic, social, cultural and humanitarian goals and respect for human rights. The fourth and last purpose is: "To be a center for harmonizing the actions of nations in the attainment of these common ends."

The primary place ascribed to international peace and security is natural, since the fulfilment of the other purposes will be dependent upon the attainment of that basic condition. These purposes are broad indeed, but neither they nor the powers conferred to effectuate them are unlimited. Save as they have entrusted the Organization with the attainment of these common ends, the Member States retain their freedom of action. But when the Organization takes action which warrants the assertion that it was appropriate for the fulfilment of one of the stated purposes of the United Nations, the presumption is that such action is not ultra vires the Organization.

If it is agreed that the action in question is within the scope of the functions of the Organization but it is alleged that it has been initiated or carried out in a manner not in conformity with the division of functions among the several organs which the Charter prescribes, one moves to the internal plane, to the internal structure of the Organization. If the action was taken by the wrong organ, it was irregular as a matter of that internal structure, but this would not necessarily mean that the expense incurred was not an expense of the Organization. Both national and international law contemplate cases in which the body corporate or politic may be bound, as to third parties, by an ultra vires act of an agent.

In the legal systems of States, there is often some procedure for determining the validity of even a legislative or governmental act, but no analogous procedure is to be found in the structure of the United Nations. Proposals made during the drafting of the Charter to place the ultimate authority to interpret the Charter in the International Court of Justice were not accepted; the opinion which the Court is in course of rendering is an advisory opinion. As anticipated in 1945, therefore, each organ must, in the first place at least, determine its own jurisdiction. If the Security Council, for example, adopts a resolution purportedly for the maintenance of international peace and security and if, in accordance with a mandate or authorization in such resolution, the Secretary-General incurs financial obligations, these amounts must be presumed to constitute "expenses of the Organization".

* * *

The expenditures enumerated in the request for an advisory opinion may conveniently be examined first with reference to UNEF and then to ONUC. In each case, attention will be paid first to the operations and then to the financing of the operations.

In considering the operations in the Middle East, the Court must analyze the functions of UNEF as set forth in resolutions of the General Assembly. Resolution 998 (ES–I) of 4 November 1956 requested the Secretary-General to submit a plan "for the setting up, with the consent of the nations concerned, of an emergency international United Nations Force to secure and supervise the cessation of hostilities in accordance with all the terms of" the General Assembly's previous resolution 997 (ES–I) of 2 November 1956. The verb "secure" as applied to such matters as halting the movement of military forces and arms into the area and the conclusion of a cease-fire, might suggest measures of enforcement, were it not that the Force was to be set up "with the consent of the nations concerned".

In his first report on the plan for an emergency international Force the Secretary-General used the language of resolution 998 (ES–I) in submitting his proposals. The same terms are used in General Assembly resolution 1000 (ES–I) of 5 November in which operative paragraph 1 reads:

> Establishes a United Nations Command for an emergency international Force to secure and supervise the cessation of hostilities in accordance with all the terms of General Assembly resolution 997 (ES–I) of 2 November 1956.

This resolution was adopted without a dissenting vote. In his second and final report on the plan for an emergency international Force of 6 November, the Secretary-General, in paragraphs 9 and 10 stated:

> While the General Assembly is enabled to establish the Force with the consent of those parties which contribute units to the Force, it could not request the Force to be stationed or operate on the territory of a given country without the consent of the Government of that country. This does not exclude the possibility that the Security Council could use such a Force within the wider margins provided under Chapter VII of the United Nations Charter. I would not for the present consider it necessary to elaborate this point further, since no use of the Force under Chapter VII, with the rights in relation to Member States that this would entail, has been envisaged.

> 10. The point just made permits the conclusion that the setting up of the Force should not be guided by the needs which would have existed had the measure been considered as part of an enforcement action directed against a Member country. There is an obvious difference between establishing the Force in order to secure the cessation of hostilities, with a withdrawal of forces, and establishing such a Force with a view to enforcing a withdrawal of forces.

Paragraph 12 of the Report is particularly important because in resolution 1001 (ES–I) the General Assembly, again without a dissenting vote, "Concurs in the definition of the functions of the Force as stated in paragraph 12 of the Secretary-General's report". Paragraph 12 reads in part as follows:

> the functions of the United Nations Force would be, when a cease-fire is being established, to enter Egyptian territory with

the consent of the Egyptian Government, in order to help maintain quiet during and after the withdrawal of non-Egyptian troops, and to secure compliance with the other terms established in the resolution of 2 November 1956. The Force obviously should have no rights other than those necessary for the execution of its functions, in co-operation with local authorities. It would be more than an observers' corps, but in no way a military force temporarily controlling the territory in which it is stationed; nor, moreover, should the Force have military functions exceeding those necessary to secure peaceful conditions on the assumption that the parties to the conflict take all necessary steps for compliance with the recommendations of the General Assembly.

It is not possible to find in this description of the functions of UNEF, as outlined by the Secretary-General and concurred in by the General Assembly without a dissenting vote, any evidence that the Force was to be used for purposes of enforcement. Nor can such evidence be found in the subsequent operations of the Force, operations which did not exceed the scope of the functions ascribed to it.

It could not therefore have been patent on the face of the resolution that the establishment of UNEF was in effect "enforcement action" under Chapter VII which, in accordance with the Charter, could be authorized only by the Security Council.

On the other hand, it is apparent that the operations were undertaken to fulfil a prime purpose of the United Nations, that is, to promote and to maintain a peaceful settlement of the situation. This being true, the Secretary-General properly exercised the authority given him to incur financial obligations of the Organization and expenses resulting from such obligations must be considered "expenses of the Organization within the meaning of Article 17, paragraph 2".

Apropos what has already been said about the meaning of the word "action" in Article 11 of the Charter, attention may be called to the fact that resolution 997 (ES–I), which is chronologically the first of the resolutions concerning the operations in the Middle East mentioned in the request for the advisory opinion, provides in paragraph 5:

Requests the Secretary-General to observe and report promptly on the compliance with the present resolution to the Security Council *and* to the General Assembly, for such further *action as they may deem appropriate in accordance with the Charter.*

The italicized words reveal an understanding that either of the two organs might take "action" in the premises. Actually, as one knows, the "action" was taken by the General Assembly in adopting two days later without a dissenting vote, resolution 998 (ES–I) and, also without a dissenting vote, within another three days, resolutions 1000 (ES–I) and 1001 (ES–I), all providing for UNEF.

The Court notes that these "actions" may be considered "measures" recommended under Article 14, rather than "action" recommended under Article 11. The powers of the General Assembly stated in Article 14 are not made subject to the provisions of Article 11, but only of Article 12. Furthermore, as the Court has already noted, the word "measures" implies some kind of action. So far as concerns the nature of the situations in the Middle East in 1956, they could be described as "likely to impair   .   .   .   friendly relations among nations", just as well as they could be considered to involve "the maintenance of international peace and security". Since the resolutions of the General Assembly in question do not mention upon which article they are based, and since the language used in most of them might imply reference to either Article 14 or Article 11, it cannot be excluded that they were based upon the former rather than the latter article.

The financing of UNEF presented perplexing problems and the debates on these problems have even led to the view that the General Assembly never, either directly or indirectly, regarded the expenses of UNEF as "expenses of the Organization within the meaning of Article 17, paragraph 2, of the Charter". With this interpretation the Court cannot agree.   *   *   *

The Court concludes that, from year to year, the expenses of UNEF have been treated by the General Assembly as expenses of the Organization within the meaning of Article 17, paragraph 2, of the Charter.

*   *   *

The operations in the Congo were initially authorized by the Security Council in the resolution of 14 July 1960 which was adopted without a dissenting vote. The resolution, in the light of the appeal from the Government of the Congo, the report of the Secretary-General and the debate in the Security Council, was clearly adopted with a view to maintaining international peace and security. However, it is argued that that resolution has been implemented, in violation of provisions of the Charter inasmuch as under the Charter it is the *usurpation of power?* Security Council that determines which States are to participate in carrying out decisions involving the maintenance of international peace and security, whereas in the case of the Congo the Secretary-General himself determined which States were to participate with their armed forces or otherwise.

By paragraph 2 of the resolution of 14 July 1960 the Security Council *"Decides* to authorize the Secretary-General to take the necessary steps, in consultation with the Government of the Republic of the Congo, to provide the Government with such military assistance as may be necessary". Paragraph 3 requested the Secretary-General "to report to the Security Council as appropriate". The Secretary-General made his first report on 18 July and in it informed the Se-

curity Council which States he had asked to contribute forces or ma-
tériel, which ones had complied, the size of the units which had already arrived in the Congo (a total of some 3,500 troops), and some
detail about further units expected.

On 22 July the Security Council by unanimous vote adopted a
further resolution in which the preamble states that it had considered
this report of the Secretary-General and appreciated "the work of the
Secretary-General and the support so readily and so speedily given to
him by all Member States invited by him to give assistance". In operative paragraph 3, the Security Council "*Commends* the Secretary-
General for the prompt action he has taken to carry out resolution
S/4387 of the Security Council, and for his first report".

On 9 August the Security Council adopted a further resolution
without a dissenting vote in which it took note of the second report
and of an oral statement of the Secretary-General and in operative
paragraph 1: "*Confirms* the authority given to the Secretary-General
by the Security Council resolutions of 14 July and 22 July 1960 and
requests him to continue to carry out the responsibility placed on him
thereby". This emphatic ratification is further supported by operative paragraphs 5 and 6 by which all Member States were called upon
"to afford mutual assistance" and the Secretary-General was requested "to implement this resolution and to report further to the Council
as appropriate".

The Security Council resolutions of 14 July, 22 July and 9 August
1960 were noted by the General Assembly in its resolution 1474 (ES–
IV) of 20 September, adopted without a dissenting vote, in which it
"fully supports" these resolutions. Again without a dissenting vote,
on 21 February 1961 the Security Council reaffirmed its three previous resolutions "and the General Assembly resolution 1474 (ES–IV)
of 20 September 1960" and reminded "all States of their obligations
under these resolutions".

Again without a dissenting vote on 24 November 1961 the Securi-
ity Council, once more recalling the previous resolutions, reaffirmed
"the policies and purposes of the United Nations with respect to the
Congo (Leopoldville) as set out" in those resolutions. Operative
paragraphs 4 and 5 of this resolution renew the authority to the Secretary-General to continue the activities in the Congo.

In the light of such a record of reiterated consideration, confirmation, approval and ratification by the Security Council and by
the General Assembly of the actions of the Secretary-General in implementing the resolution of 14 July 1960, it is impossible to reach
the conclusion that the operations in question usurped or impinged
upon the prerogatives conferred by the Charter on the Security Council. The Charter does not forbid the Security Council to act through
instruments of its own choice: under Article 29 it "may establish
such subsidiary organs as it deems necessary for the performance

of its functions"; under Article 98 it may entrust "other functions" to the Secretary-General.

It is not necessary for the Court to express an opinion as to which article or articles of the Charter were the basis for the resolutions of the Security Council, but it can be said that the operations of ONUC did not include a use of armed force against a State which the Security Council, under Article 39, determined to have committed an act of aggression or to have breached the peace. The armed forces which were utilized in the Congo were not authorized to take military action against any State. The operation did not involve "preventive or enforcement measures" against any State under Chapter VII and therefore did not constitute "action" as that term is used in Article 11.

For the reasons stated, financial obligations which, in accordance with the clear and reiterated authority of both the Security Council and the General Assembly, the Secretary-General incurred on behalf of the United Nations, constitute obligations of the Organization for which the General Assembly was entitled to make provision under the authority of Article 17.

* * *

At the outset of this opinion, the Court pointed out that the text of Article 17, paragraph 2, of the Charter could lead to the simple conclusion that "the expenses of the Organization" are the amounts paid out to defray the costs of carrying out the purposes of the Organization. It was further indicated that the Court would examine the resolutions authorizing the expenditures referred to in the request for the advisory opinion in order to ascertain whether they were incurred with that end in view. The Court has made such an examination and finds that they were so incurred. The Court has also analyzed the principal arguments which have been advanced against the conclusion that the expenditures in question should be considered as "expenses of the Organization within the meaning of Article 17, paragraph 2, of the Charter of the United Nations", and has found that these arguments are unfounded. Consequently, the Court arrives at the conclusion that the question submitted to it in General Assembly resolution 1731 (XVI) must be answered in the affirmative.

For these reasons, THE COURT IS OF OPINION, by nine votes to five,

that the expenditures authorized in General Assembly resolutions 1583 (XV) and 1590 (XV) of 20 December 1960, 1595 (XV) of 3 April 1961, 1619 (XV) of 21 April 1961 and 1633 (XVI) of 30 October 1961 relating to the United Nations operations in the Congo undertaken in pursuance of the Security Council resolutions of 14 July, 22 July and 9 August 1960 and 21 February and 24 November 1961, and General Assembly resolutions 1474 (ES–IV) of 20 September 1960 and 1599 (XV), 1600 (XV) and 1601 (XV) of 15 April 1961, and the expenditures authorized in General Assembly resolutions 1122 (XI) of 26 November 1956, 1089 (XI) of 21 December 1956, 1090 (XI) of 27 February 1957, 1151 (XII) of 22 November 1957, 1204 (XII) of 13 December 1957, 1337 (XIII) of 13 December 1958, 1441 (XIV) of 5 December 1959 and 1575 (XV) of 20 December 1960 relating to the operations of the United Nations Emergency Force undertaken in pursuance of General Assembly resolutions 997 (ES–I) of 2 November 1956, 998 (ES–I) and 999 (ES–I) of 4 November 1956, 1000 (ES–I) of 5 November 1956, 1001 (ES–I) of 7 November 1956, 1121 (XI) of 24 November 1956 and 1263 (XIII) of 14 November 1958, constitute "expenses of the Organization" within the meaning of Article 17, paragraph 2, of the Charter of the United Nations.

[A declaration, separate opinions and dissenting opinions omitted.]

---

1. *Aftermath of Certain Expenses case.* Although the General Assembly of the United Nations subsequently adopted a resolution in which it accepted the advisory opinion of the International Court of Justice, members that had refused to recognize peacekeeping expenses as "expenses of the organization" (principally France and the Soviet Union) continued to refuse to accept the court's interpretation of the charter and became in arrears in their payments to the United Nations. The United States determined to force the issue of Article 19, entailing the loss of vote by those members. When the assembly met for the Nineteenth Session in December, 1964, it was decided to avoid an immediate clash on the issue and the assembly proceeded to do such business as it could without taking any formal votes. This working arrangement was almost shattered by Albania, however, which forced a formal vote over the question of returning to a normal voting procedure. The significance of this vote was brushed aside by being denominated "procedural," so as to avoid a sharp declaration that the delinquents had lost the right to have their votes counted.

Shortly before the opening of the next session of the assembly, the United States took the position that it would not press for the application of the vote deprivation provisions of Article 19 but that it would reserve its position on the law. The assembly thus returned, in the fall of 1965, to its normal voting procedures, with no member deprived of a vote for failing to pay UNEF or ONUC assessments.

Years of continuing consideration of the problem in the United Nations have not resulted in a resolution of the constitutional issue of financing peacekeeping, except through practice.

2. *Financing peacekeeping in Cyprus.* In contrast to the effort to impose peacekeeping costs throughout the membership of the United Nations, as in UNEF and ONUC, is the Cyprus experience. When the

Security Council authorized the establishment of a peacekeeping force for Cyprus in 1964, it recommended that all costs pertaining to the force should be met "in a manner to be agreed upon by them, by the Governments providing the contingents and by the Government of Cyprus."   The Secretary-General of the United Nations was also authorized to accept voluntary contributions.   Res. 186 (1964), Resolutions and Decisions of the Security Council 1964, Security Council Off. Rec. 19th year, p. 2.   Successsive extensions of the stationing of the force have continued through December 1972; the Cyprus account was then reported by the Secretary-General to have a deficit in excess of $13 million.   X U.N. Monthly Chronicle, Jan. 1973, p. 13.

SECTION D.   THE UNITED NATIONS FAILURE TO ACT IN VIETNAM

A UNITED STATES INITIATIVE TO BRING THE VIETNAM QUESTION TO THE UNITED NATIONS

III U.N. Monthly Chronicle, March 1966, p. 3.

The Security Council, which was convened on February 1 at the request of the United States, the following day decided to inscribe on its agenda the question of Viet-Nam.   This decision was taken at the Council's third meeting on February 2 by a vote of 9 in favour (Argentina, China, Japan, Jordan, Netherlands, New Zealand, United Kingdom, United States, Uruguay) to 2 against (Bulgaria, U.S.S.R.), with 4 abstentions (France, Mali, Nigeria, Uganda).   Following the adoption of the agenda, the Council, as suggested by its President, Akira Matsui (Japan), adjourned indefinitely for private, informal consultations on the most appropriate and effective way of conducting the debate on the item.

United States Request

The United States asked that the Council be convened to consider the question of Viet-Nam   *   *   *

The United States also submitted a draft resolution that would have the Council: call for immediate discussions without preconditions among the appropriate interested governments to arrange a conference looking towards the application of the Geneva Accords of 1954 and 1962 and the establishment of a durable peace in South East Asia; recommend that the first order of business of such a conference be arrangements for a cessation of hostilities under effective supervision; offer to assist in achieving the purposes of this resolution by all appropriate means, including the provision of arbitrators or mediators; call on all concerned to co-operate fully in the implementation of the resolution; and request the Secretary-General to assist as appropriate in the implementation of the resolution.

Council's Debate

Arthur J. Goldberg (United States) said the request for a Council meeting to consider the problem of Viet-Nam signalled a new dimension in the peace offensive in which the United States was engaged and which it was determined to continue.

U.S. INVOLVEMENT PREDICATED ON NV VIOLATION OF GENEVA ACCORDS

The role of the United States in Viet-Nam had been based from the beginning on the indisputable fact that North Viet-Nam had consciously and flagrantly violated the provisions of the Geneva Agreements, particularly Article 19 of the Agreement on the cessation of hostilities, wherein North Viet-Nam was enjoined to ensure that its territory would "not be used for the resumption of hostilities or to further an aggressive policy". Despite that written pledge, North Viet-Nam, aided by Peiping, had led, equipped and sustained the fighting in the South.

While the United States remained determined to resist that aggression, Mr. Goldberg continued, it had never lost sight of the need for a peaceful settlement. That was its mission in the Council now.

His Government had repeatedly sought and encouraged others to seek a formula that would move the conflict to the conference table. It had made repeated appeals for whatever help the United Nations, collectively or individually, through any of its organs, including its Secretary-General, might be able to provide in bringing about unconditional discussions and negotiations for an acceptable formula to restore peace in Viet-Nam. It had undertaken a brief pause in the aerial attacks against military targets in North Viet-Nam in mid-May and made the purpose of its action known to the North Vietnamese. But neither Hanoi nor Peiping had made any sign that they shared the desire to move the problem to the conference table. Nevertheless, the United States had persevered in its quest for peace.

Some had urged that a longer suspension of the bombing of military targets in North Viet-Nam might create an atmosphere conducive to negotiations. Respect for that opinion led the United States to suspend the bombing again on December 24 for more than five weeks, thus more than honouring the counsel received.

The suspension, Mr. Goldberg emphasized, was undertaken against the background of Hanoi's unyielding intransigence towards every peace move for more than a year and with no assurance whatsoever that it would bring peace or negotiations closer.

The United States explained these objectives by means of an unprecedented diplomatic offensive—through consultations with His Holiness the Pope, who as a great spiritual leader had manifested deep concern about the peace of the world; by sending six special Presidential envoys to 34 capitals to confer with Chiefs of State or Heads of

Government; and through personal communications from President Johnson to the Heads of Government of many more.

The United States had informed Hanoi of the suspension and advised them that their reciprocation, through a serious contribution towards peace, would favourably affect the possibility of a further extension of the suspension of the bombing.

Hanoi had made no positive response. * * * President Ho Chi Minh interpreted the United States' search for a negotiated solution as an excuse for war and he laid down three preconditions which must be accepted before he would even begin negotiations.

These preconditions were: that the United States accept the four-point stand of the Democratic Republic of Viet-Nam Government and prove this by actual deeds; that it end all bombing and other war acts against the Democratic Republic of Viet-Nam uncondition- ally; and—a new precondition—that it recognize the National Front for the Liberation of South Viet-Nam as the sole and genuine repre- sentative of the South Vietnamese people.

In exchange, President Ho Chi Minh offered absolutely nothing— no let-up in war acts on his side; and no willingness to negotiate or even to talk quietly through diplomatic channels with a view to bring- ing about negotiations.

By rejecting the United States offer to continue suspension of the bombings, if there were a reciprocal response from North Viet-Nam, President Ho Chi Minh and other North Vietnamese leaders had assumed full responsibility for the resumption of the bombing.

   * * *

The United States had not brought the question of Viet-Nam to the Council earlier because many Council members had said that such action would interfere with the peace initiatives under way and would not contribute to a peaceful solution. The United States had honoured that advice. But now that President Ho Chi Minh had closed the door to one avenue, the United States had come to explore another.

Nikolai Fedorenko (U.S.S.R.) said his delegation objected to con- vening the Council to discuss the question of Viet-Nam and was op- posed to including the item in the agenda. His Government support- ed the just position of the Government of the Democratic Republic of Viet-Nam that the question be settled within the framework of the Geneva Accords.

The United States proposal that the Council consider the ques- tion of Viet-Nam was merely a diversionary tactic to cover—through talks on a so-called settlement—the Pentagon's plans for expanding the war.

The Government of the United States had renewed its barbaric air raids on the Democratic Republic of Viet-Nam and at the same time called for an urgent session of the Council.

The statement of the representative of the United States, which greatly distorted the true situation, was further confirmation that Washington had not yet begun to think of a genuine settlement and was staging a propaganda show.

The United States, which was intensifying its aggression, increasing its troops, expanding its intervention and earmarking fabulous sums for aggression in Viet-Nam, was not looking for peace. It had rejected the just and well-founded plan of the Democratic Republic of Viet-Nam and the National Liberation Front of South Viet-Nam for a political settlement. It was unwilling to revert to strict compliance with the Geneva Accords of 1954. It refused to recognize that the problem of Viet-Nam could be solved only with the participation of the National Liberation Front, which was the only genuine representative of the people of South Viet-Nam.

The United States was continuing its flagrant interference in the domestic affairs of Viet-Nam. It had set up the puppet Saigon régime and, with its interventionist forces, was trying to throttle the struggle of the people of South Viet-Nam for freedom and independence. Acting from a position of force, it spoke in threats and ultimatums which could not but provoke indignation. Resumption of the bombings was a manifestation of that policy of force and of threats.

* * *

Roger Seydoux (France) said his delegation could not support the request to inscribe the question of Viet-Nam on the Council's agenda. The United Nations, where only one of the principal parties involved in the conflict—the United States—was represented, was not the proper framework for achieving a peaceful solution. Even if the Council should request the other parties to appear before it, discussions would not be held on an equal footing. A debate in the Council might result only in a useless confrontation, confusion and, in the absence of a real discussion, in misunderstanding. A solution could be achieved only through negotiations based upon the principles of the Geneva Accords.

Sori Coulibaly (Mali) said a discussion in the Security Council should be undertaken with an eye to effectiveness, usefulness and the possibility of arriving at decisions acceptable to the parties concerned and to those affected by the decisions. These conditions did not exist.

Only one of the parties concerned had expressed the wish to have the United Nations discuss the question; the others, which were not members of the Organization, had explicitly stated their preference for a discussion within the framework of the Geneva Agreements and the Commissions they provided for. He agreed with the view that the Geneva Agreements and Commissions were the most appropriate framework for reopening the question.

Resuming the bombing and convening the Council simultaneously did not seem to him to be good strategy for finding a lasting solution to a tragedy which might well become a tragedy for all mankind.

Since the parties suffering most cruelly from the conflict were opposed to any discussion of the question in the United Nations, a debate in the Council would serve no useful purpose. Moreover, the Council's interventions, if they were to be effective, must be timely and made under conditions assuring complete success.

* * *

Apollo K. Kironde (Uganda) said the United States should have brought the matter to the Council long before it became so deeply involved in Viet-Nam and long before it began the bombings. His delegation welcomed the United States draft resolution, which indicated that the United States was trying to repair its mistake in by-passing the Council. The Security Council, however, could reach the right decision only by hearing direct evidence from the four parties concerned.

The representative of Uganda then suggested that, as the Council had already had a useful exchange of views on the subject, the President conclude the debate, summarizing it and bringing out the points of agreement and disagreement. The Council could then meet at some future date, perhaps in a different venue. It might be better to refer the matter to the Geneva venue.

* * *

Mateo Marqués-Sere (Uruguay) favoured adoption of the agenda. He said that once the Council had decided to deal with the question, there would be nothing to prevent members from proposing that it be dealt with in some other body and under some other mandate.

J. G. de Beus (Netherlands) said his delegation, while aware of the difficulties involved, would vote for the inclusion of the item in the agenda.

The fact that some of the countries concerned were not members of the United Nations was no reason to object to a discussion; rather, it was a good reason to invite all concerned to participate in a discussion.

Basically, his delegation could agree with the statement that the problem should be solved in the context of the Geneva Conference of 1954. However, that was no reason to object to the proposed discussion in the Council; the purpose of the proposal was not to resolve the question in the United Nations, but to arrange for a preconference looking towards the application of the Geneva Accords of 1954 and 1962.

Undoubtedly, one could imagine more favourable circumstances for the Council to undertake a debate on Viet-Nam. But that was no reason for not holding a debate now. If events were allowed to run their course, further escalation of the war seemed inevitable.

* * *

Mr. Goldberg (United States) said the representatives of France, Mali, Uganda, the Soviet Union and Bulgaria had pointed out that the Geneva Conference, at which all parties to the conflict were represented, remained the appropriate body to deal with the question of Viet-Nam. The United States had no quarrel with that contention. The first of the 14 points of United States policy on Viet-Nam stated that "the Geneva Agreements of 1954 and 1962 are an adequate basis for peace in South East Asia".

The purpose of the draft resolution was to assist in the reconvening of the Geneva Conference. The choice before the Council was not whether to deal with the problem in the Council or in Geneva, but whether to deal with it at all. The door to Geneva was, at least for the time being, closed. The question to be decided was: would the door to the United Nations also be closed?

Some members had pointed out that several of the parties to the conflict were not members of the United Nations and, therefore, not in a position to present their case. Others, however, had pointed out that the Charter provided that any state which was not a member of the United Nations, if it was a party to a dispute under consideration by the Council, should be invited to participate, without vote, in the discussion. Moreover, Article 2, paragraph 6 of the Charter said: "The Organization shall ensure that states which are not members of the United Nations act in accordance with these principles so far as may be necessary for the maintenance of international peace and security." The United Nations had dealt and presumably would deal again with matters in which members or non-members had refused to participate.

One of his colleagues had suggested that the Council should not attempt to deal with the problem unless it was certain of success. The Council had not been inhibited in the past from dealing with threats to the peace because it could not be assured of success; indeed, it could hardly expect to have any such assurances in advance. What credit or prestige could the Council hope to have if it refused even to attempt to carry out its Charter obligations?

The United States did not expect the Council to solve the problem of Viet-Nam, with or without the other parties to the conflict, but only to lend its tremendous weight and prestige by calling for "immediate discussions without preconditions * * * among the appropriate interested governments to arrange a conference looking towards the application of the Geneva Accords of 1954 and 1962". The United States request to the Council was no different from the appeal of the non-aligned countries. It asked only that the Council offer its assistance in bringing about peace in South East Asia, perhaps through the provision of arbitrators or mediators, as His Holiness, the Pope, had suggested, or through other appropriate means.

*   *   *

At the request of Waleed M. Sadi (Jordan) the President then postponed the voting until the following afternoon.

When the Council reconvened on February 2, the representative of Jordan said that, while his Government agreed that there were reasons to warrant the belief that a discussion of the Vietnamese question in the United Nations would be useless, it was perhaps equally valid to believe that such a debate would not be harmful. Therefore, his delegation would vote for the adoption of the agenda.

Mr. Fedorenko (U.S.S.R.) reiterated his delegation's objection to including the question in the agenda. He said that the problem should be resolved within the framework of the Geneva Accords with the participation of all the parties concerned, and with the adoption of the programme of the Democratic Republic of Viet-Nam and the National Liberation Front of South Viet-Nam regarding a political settlement. He stressed the fact that the United States in 1954 had given its solemn promise to refrain from violating the Geneva Accords by threats or use of force. He read a passage from President Ho Chi Minh's message which said that the United States, if it really respected the Agreements and truly wanted peace, must withdraw all its troops, as well as those of its satellites, from South Viet-Nam and engage in direct negotiations with the National Liberation Front as the sole representative of the people of South Viet-Nam.

The Soviet representative then read into the record a message from the National Liberation Front stating that the Security Council had no right to take decisions on matters involving South Viet-Nam and that, as far as the National Liberation Front was concerned, all its resolutions on Viet-Nam would be null and void. The statement stressed that the only just way to achieve a peaceful settlement was through the withdrawal of United States troops and those of its satellites and the liquidation of all United States military bases in South Viet-Nam so that the Vietnamese people could settle their own domestic affairs.

* * *

Letter from President of Security Council

The President of the Security Council, Akira Matsui (Japan), on February 26 transmitted to the Secretary-General the text of a letter which he had sent to members of the Council that day. In his letter, Mr. Matsui said that, while there had been a useful exchange of views during the informal consultations held among Council members after the adjournment, some serious differences remained unresolved, principally regarding the wisdom of having the Council consider the problem of Viet-Nam at this time. A number of members felt that the Council might find some way to contribute towards a solution of the problem, but others took the view that consideration in the Council would not be useful at present. Some, adhering to their positions when the adoption of the provisional agenda was discussed on February 1 and 2, had chosen not to participate in the consultations.

These differences in views, Mr. Matsui continued, made it impossible for him to report agreement on a precise course of action which the Council might follow. They had also given rise to a general feeling that it would be inopportune for the Council to hold further debate at this time and that a report by the President in the form of a letter, rather than a statement at a formal meeting of the Council, would be the most appropriate step.

Mr. Matsui observed that the feeling among many Council members during the proceedings of February 1 and 2 and the resulting consultations might be summarized as follows:

1. There was general grave concern and growing anxiety over the continued hostilities in Viet-Nam and a strong desire for the early cessation of hostilities and a peaceful solution of the problem;

2. There appeared to be a feeling that the termination of the conflict in Viet-Nam should be sought through negotiation in an appropriate forum in order to work out the implementation of the Geneva Accords.

It was his understanding, Mr. Matsui said in concluding, that the Council, having decided on February 2 to place on its agenda the item contained in the letter of January 31 from the Permanent Representative of the United States, remained seized of the problem of Viet-Nam.

Letter from Permanent Representative of France

In a reply to the letter of February 26 from the President of the Security Council, Roger Seydoux, the Permanent Representative of France to the United Nations, stated on February 28 that, in the opinion of his delegation, no conclusion should be put forward regarding the feeling of the Council or of any of its members on the question of Viet-Nam since there had been no discussion of the matter in the Council and informal and private consultations clearly could not take the place of such discussions. Moreover, it had been the constant position of his Government over the years that the discussion of the affairs of Viet-Nam in the Council would do nothing to bring a peaceful solution any closer.

* * *

III U.N. Monthly Chronicle, April 1966, p. 9.

Communications

* * *

In a letter dated March 1, the Permanent Representative of the Soviet Union, Nikolai Fedorenko, said that the attempt made in Mr. Matsui's letter to sum up the general feeling of Council members on the question of Viet-Nam could not fail to arouse strong objections. Mr. Matsui had no right to send such a letter, as the Council had not instructed its President to make a statement. He had gone beyond the limits of his competence and had violated the Council's rules of procedure and its established practice.

Many members, considering that the matter should be settled under the Geneva Agreements of 1954, had objected to having the item on Viet-Nam included in the Council's agenda. As a result of disagreement among its members, the Council had held no discussion on the substance of the question of Viet-Nam. Nevertheless, the President, exceeding his powers, had attempted to determine unofficially the consensus regarding a possible Council decision. Despite the objections which the representatives of a number of Council members, including some permanent members, had expressed to such illegal action, and although some representatives had refused outright to participate in consultations on the question, the President had seen fit to send his letter.

Those irresponsible actions by the President could be regarded only as a blatant attempt to support the manoeuvre of the United States which, by raising the question of Viet-Nam in the Council, was trying to conceal its steps to expand the aggressive war in South East Asia.

The Permanent Mission of the USSR to the United Nations considered it necessary to stress that the statement by the President of the Security Council was illegal, had no legal force, and could be regarded only as the opinion of the representative of Japan.

*   *   *

---

1. _Delay_ of Security Council consideration of the Vietnam question. The foregoing approach to the Security Council was made years after the United States was actively engaged in conflict in Vietnam. Did the United States violate any of its Charter obligations by failing to bring the matter formally to the Security Council before January, 1966? Was the Security Council precluded from considering the question because of the failure of the United States to request it to take action at an earlier date?

2. *Legal aspects of the failure of the Security Council to deal with the Vietnam question.* Beyond the political motivation of the USSR to block the peace initiative of the United States at the very moment of a resumption of bombing there were the legal arguments against the Security Council's consideration of the Vietnam question. Were those arguments merely political in legal dress or did they have legal substance under the Charter?

Prior approaches to the Security Council by the United States had been by way of reporting actions taken in claimed self-defense in response to particular attacks. In August, 1964, the council met at the request of the United States to hear and discuss a United States report on the Tonkin Gulf events; action by the council was neither sought nor taken. Letters of report were sent to the council by the United States from time to time. See, e. g., 52 United States Department of State Bulletin 240 (1965) (letter from Ambassador Stevenson reporting that the Viet Cong had made attacks on airfields, barracks and villages in South Vietnam and that, in self-defensive response, the United States had made aerial attacks on North Vietnamese staging areas).

SECTION E. USE OF UNITED NATIONS AUTHORITY NOT INVOLVING MILITARY FORCE

---

1. SOUTH AFRICA: APARTHEID

The racial situation in South Africa has concerned the United Nations since its founding. Numerous resolutions directed toward the abolition of the system of racial separation (apartheid) in that country produced no discernible effect. See, for example, the General Assembly resolution and debate at p. 608. In 1963, the members of the Security Council apparently decided that persuasion and exhortation were insufficient means to correct at least one aspect of that country's policies. Resolution 181 (1963) was adopted to establish an arms embargo. A glimpse is afforded hereafter of the successive endeavors of the United Nations to deal with the apartheid question.

SECURITY COUNCIL RESOLUTION 181 (1963) OF AUGUST 7, 1963

Resolutions and Decisions of the Security Council 1963.

U.N. Sec. Council Off. Rec. 18th year, p. 7.

The Security Council,

Having considered the question of race conflict in South Africa resulting from the policies of apartheid of the Government of the Republic of South Africa, as submitted by the thirty-two African Member States,

Recalling its resolution 134 (1960) of 1 April 1960,

Taking into account that world public opinion has been reflected in General Assembly resolution 1761(XVII) of 6 November 1962, and particularly in its paragraphs 4 and 8,

Noting with appreciation the interim reports adopted on 6 May and 16 July 1963 by the Special Committee on the Policies of apartheid of the Government of the Republic of South Africa,

Noting with concern the recent arms build-up by the Government of South Africa, some of which arms are being used in furtherance of that Government's racial policies,

Regretting that some States are indirectly providing encouragement in various ways to the Government of South Africa to perpetuate, by force, its policy of apartheid,

Regretting the failure of the Government of South Africa to accept the invitation of the Security Council to delegate a representative to appear before it,

Being convinced that the situation in South Africa is seriously disturbing international peace and security,

1.   Strongly deprecates the policies of South Africa in its perpetuation of racial discrimination as being inconsistent with the principles contained in the Charter of the United Nations and contrary to its obligations as a Member of the United Nations;

2.   Calls upon the Government of South Africa to abandon the policies of apartheid and discrimination, as called for in Security Council resolution 134 (1960), and to liberate all persons imprisoned, interned or subjected to other restrictions for having opposed the policy of apartheid;

3.   Solemnly calls upon all States to cease forthwith the sale and shipment of arms, ammunition of all types and military vehicles to South Africa;

4.   Requests the Secretary-General to keep the situation in South Africa under observation and to report to the Security Council by 30 October 1963.

> Adopted at the 1056th meeting by 9 votes to none, with 2 abstentions (France, United Kingdom of Great Britain and Northern Ireland).

EXTRACTS FROM DEBATE ON THE ARMS EMBARGO RESOLUTION

U.N. Sec. Council Off. Rec., Plenary Meeting 1056, August 7, 1963.

3.   Mr. Fedorenko (Union of Soviet Socialist Republics) (translated from Russian): In the course of the Security Council's debate we have heard a number of deeply interesting and cogent speeches by representatives of the African continent, which revealed to the full

the tragic situation of the many millions of people of African and Asian origin in the Republic of South Africa who are subjected by Verwoerd's criminal régime to savage racial discrimination, persecution and oppression.

4. It is quite clear that the Security Council is faced with a dangerous situation which is a source of serious international tension and constitutes a threat to peace and security not limited to the continent of Africa.

    * * *

5. The Soviet delegation considered and still considers that the Security Council should condemn the racist régime of South Africa in the strongest possible terms for its most flagrant violation of the elementary rights of the people and its flouting of United Nations decisions and institute immediate economic, political and other sanctions against the Republic of South Africa. It is precisely by this means that the South African racists can be forced to change their criminal and barbaric policies. It has long been time to pass from exhortation and persuasion, from the exercise of mere "moral influence" on the South African racists, as is proposed by the Western Powers, to positive action and decisive measures.

6. As regards the draft resolution submitted to the Security Council by the representatives of Ghana, Morocco and the Philippines [S/5384] it represents, as has already been noted, the very least that the Security Council should do in the present circumstances in order to put a stop to the wild excesses of racism in South Africa and eradicate a hotbed of international tension.

7. Confirmation of this is to be found also in the speech by the representative of Ghana, Mr. Quaison-Sackey, who remarked [1054th meeting] when introducing the draft resolution that "In fact, world opinion expects the Council to take measures which are far more stern than the present draft resolution would ask the Council to take". The same point was also made by the Ministers for Foreign Affairs of Sierra Leone and Tunisia, Mr. Karefa-Smart and Mr. Mongi Slim.

8. However, since the African countries have found it possible to confine themselves at this stage to the measures contained in the draft resolution by Ghana, Morocco and the Philippines, the Soviet delegation will support this draft and will vote for it. Needless to say, in so doing, the Soviet Union has not abandoned its deep conviction of the need to adopt more radical measures against the racist régime in the Republic of South Africa.

    * * *

23. Mr. Yost (United States of America): My Government is able to support this resolution because it reflects the attitude of the United States toward the racial policies of the Republic of South Africa. We particularly appreciate the co-operation of the sponsors of the resolution which has facilitated our desire to vote in favour of

it. We have, over a period of years, expressed our strong disapproval of the policy of racial discrimination being pursued in South Africa contrary to the obligations of the Republic's Government under Articles 55 and 56 of the Charter. Thus we wholeheartedly endorse the appeal to South Africa to abandon these policies and to liberate those persons who have been imprisoned, interned or subjected to other restrictions merely because they are opposed to the policy of apartheid. My delegation also supports the request that all Member States cease forthwith the sale and shipment of arms, ammunition and military vehicles. As you will recall, Ambassador Stevenson announced in this chamber [1052nd meeting] that the United States Government had taken another important step demonstrating its concern at the continued lack of progress in ending racial discrimination in South Africa, by voluntarily deciding to end the sale of all military equipment to the Government of South Africa by the end of this year.

* * *

26. With respect to the eighth preambular paragraph of the resolution, I wish to emphasize that the United States is most gratified that the sponsors have seen fit to change their original formulation from "is seriously endangering international peace and security" to "is seriously disturbing international peace and security". In making this change they clearly recognize that a number of Council members are not prepared to agree that the situation in South Africa is one which now calls for the kind of action appropriate in cases of threats to the peace or breaches of the peace under Chapter VII of the United Nations Charter. As members of the Council are aware, Chapter VII does not speak in terms of disturbances of the peace, even serious ones, but only of actual threats to the peace or breaches of the peace or acts of aggression. The resolution's preambular reference to disturbing the peace thus refers to those underlying elements of this certainly serious situation which, if continued, are likely to endanger the maintenance of international peace and security. This is quite different from finding a fully matured threat to, or breach of, the peace in the present situation. There are in this troubled world many disturbances of international peace and security, but even in those parts of the world where there is now sporadic fighting on international frontiers, this Organization has wisely been cautious about invoking the powers of the Security Council under Chapter VII.

27. The change in wording to which I have referred has been of the greatest importance in determining the decision of the United States to vote for this resolution; in fact, it was a decisive factor. I might add that the fact that operative paragraphs 2 and 3 of the resolution as adopted call upon Member States to take certain action, does not of course give these paragraphs a mandatory character.

28. The words "call upon" are found in Chapter VI as well as Chapter VII of the Charter. They have been repeatedly employed

by the General Assembly as well as by the Security Council and in the customary practice of the United Nations they do not carry mandatory force.

REPORT OF THE SPECIAL COMMITTEE ON THE POLICIES OF APARTHEID OF THE GOVERNMENT OF THE REPUBLIC OF SOUTH AFRICA (JUNE 17, 1965) [a]

U.N. Gen. Ass. Off. Rec., Annexes, 20th Sess.,
Agenda Item 36, A/5932, p. 2, at p. 4.

* * *

18. The Special Committee reaffirms its deep conviction that the situation in the Republic of South Africa constitutes a serious threat to the peace in terms of Article 39 of the Charter and that mandatory measures under Chapter VII of the Charter are the only effective peaceful means to resolve the situation.

19. The General Assembly and the Security Council have recognized that the racial policies pursued by the Government of the Republic of South Africa are contrary to the fundamental principles and purposes of the United Nations, to its obligations as a Member State and to the provisions of the Universal Declaration of Human Rights, and that they have caused international friction and are seriously disturbing the maintenance of international peace and security.

20. In the five years since the Security Council first had the question under consideration, in the aftermath of the massacre of peaceful demonstrators at Sharpeville, the South African defence budget has increased more than five times. Thousands of opponents of apartheid and leaders of non-White organizations have been imprisoned, executed, forced into exile or restricted by arbitrary banishments, bans or house arrest orders. Non-White organizations have been declared unlawful or prevented from normal activity by imprisonment or banning of leaders and other forms of harassment. Peaceful means for protesting racial discrimination and for securing an end to such discrimination have been progressively eliminated. Opponents of apartheid and supporters of non-White organizations have been obliged to resort to clandestine means and violence in order to secure their just demands. Ruthless repressive measures may have succeeded in controlling resistance temporarily from time to time, but they only add to tension and bitterness and increase the danger of violent conflict.

21. A violent conflict in South Africa, as the Special Committee has warned repeatedly, cannot but have the most serious internation-

---

a. Members of the Special Committee were Algeria, Costa Rica, Ghana, Guinea, Haiti, Hungary, Malaysia, Nepal, Nigeria, the Philippines and Somalia.

al repercussions. It is likely to involve not only the States of Asia and Africa which have proclaimed solidarity with the oppressed people of South Africa and in particular the African States which consider the military build-up in South Africa a menace to their security, but it must inevitably involve all countries of the world. In this connexion, the Special Committee expresses its grave concern over the increasing collaboration of racist minority and colonial Governments of Southern Africa to prevent the emergence of non-racial, democratic societies, and to the serious danger that the policies and activities of these Governments may provoke racial conflicts which would affect race relations all over the world.

22. The Special Committee, therefore, considers that refusal to recognize the serious threat to the peace presented by the present situation in the Republic of South Africa, and refusal to take timely and decisive mandatory action, must inevitably lead to the threat assuming even more alarming proportions and erupting into violent conflict. Moreover, the reluctance to take effective action, after repeated defiance of resolutions of the General Assembly and the Security Council by the South African Government, would weaken the authority, prestige and effectiveness of the United Nations.

* * *

UNITED NATIONS GENERAL ASSEMBLY RESOLUTION 2054 (XX) OF DECEMBER 15, 1965

U.N.Gen.Ass.Off.Rec., 20th Sess., Supp. No. 14 (A/6014), p. 16.

The General Assembly,

Recalling its resolutions on the policies of apartheid of the Government of the Republic of South Africa,

Having considered the reports of the Special Committee on the Policies of apartheid of the Government of the Republic of South Africa,[a]

* * *

Gravely concerned at the aggravation of the explosive situation in the Republic of South Africa as a result of the continued implementation of the policies of apartheid by the Government of South Africa in violation of its obligations under the Charter of the United Nations and in defiance of the resolutions of the Security Council and the General Assembly,

Profoundly disturbed at the fact that the policies and actions of the Government of South Africa are thus aggravating the situation in neighbouring territories in southern Africa,

a. The immediately preceding report, p. 1316.

Noting the measures taken by Member States in pursuance of the resolutions of the General Assembly and the Security Council,

Having studied the notes, annexed to the Special Committee's report of 17 June 1965, on the build-up of military and police forces in the Republic of South Africa and on recent investments by foreign-owned corporations in that country,

Considering that prompt and effective international action is imperative in order to avert the grave danger of a violent racial conflict in Africa, which would inevitably have grave repercussions throughout the world,

Recalling its resolution 1761 (XVII) of 6 November 1962 recommending the application of economic and diplomatic sanctions against South Africa,

1. Urgently appeals to the major trading partners of the Republic of South Africa to cease their increasing economic collaboration with the Government of South Africa, which encourages that Government to defy world opinion and to accelerate the implementation of the policies of apartheid;

* * *

4. Condemns the Government of South Africa for its refusal to comply with the resolutions of the Security Council and the General Assembly and its continued implementation of the policies of apartheid;

5. Firmly supports all those who are opposing the policies of apartheid and particularly those who are combating such policies in South Africa;

6. Draws the attention of the Security Council to the fact that the situation in South Africa constitutes a threat to international peace and security, that action under Chapter VII of the Charter is essential in order to solve the problem of apartheid and that universally applied economic sanctions are the only means of achieving a peaceful solution;

7. Deplores the actions of those States which, through political, economic and military collaboration with the Government of South Africa, are encouraging it to persist in its racial policies;

8. Again requests all States to comply fully with all the resolutions of the Security Council on this question and to halt forthwith the sale and delivery to South Africa of arms, ammunition of all types, military vehicles, and equipment and materials intended for their manufacture and maintenance;

* * *

[Adopted by a vote of 80 in favor to 2 against (South Africa and Portugal), with 16 abstentions (Australia, Austria, Belgium, Canada, Finland, France, Iceland, Ireland, Italy, Japan, Luxembourg, Netherlands, New Zealand, Norway, United Kingdom and United States).]

EXTRACTS FROM DEBATE ON GENERAL ASSEMBLY
RESOLUTION 2054 (XX)

U.N. Gen. Ass. Off. Rec., 20th Sess., Plenary Meeting 1396, December 15, 1965.

25.   Mr. Achkar (Guinea) (translated from French):

*   *   *

28.   We certainly have no illusions about the action which the General Assembly has just taken, because we have also noted the abstentions and reservations of the principal trading partners of South Africa, who bear a special responsibility in this question.   However, we sincerely hope that these trading partners will have plenty of time to think over the views and positions of the great majority of Member States, so as to revise their own attitude in the future— we hope, the near future—and enable the Security Council, which will soon take up the question of apartheid, to offer us positive action and no longer mere speeches of inoperative and misleading resolutions.

*   *   *

35.   Not content with constantly acting against the principles of the Charter, this régime has also turned the white minority into a secret army, like the OAS in Algeria, and is preparing to launch a suicidal attack with the sole aim of preserving its domination based on racial factors and ill-acquired and exorbitant privileges.   The policies of this régime are not merely a threat to peace in southern Africa; they could equally well set ablaze a racial war which would destroy any hope of international co-operation and world peace.   The South African régime is waging a campaign in which we, who are seeking to put an end to racism, are accused of merely coveting the riches of South Africa and cherishing the hope of completely eliminating its white population.

36.   May I recall here that the independent States of Africa are much too occupied with the need to rid their peoples of the sad heritage of colonialism, to develop their own wealth and to build up their nations, to have any thoughts of expansionist adventures.   They have no time for that.   However, we are ready to make every possible sacrifice to end the humiliation to which the South African people are being subjected and to end the exploitation of South Africa by foreign interests, which pull the strings of the puppets in the police Government of Verwoerd, for they are the puppets of these interests, and the puppets of the Government which are using this country as a source of unlawful profits.

*   *   *

41.   We cannot state too often that, if the Security Council does not help us in this task by taking coercive decisions, it will have encouraged recourse to the only remaining solution to this problem of

apartheid, in other words, violence and war between the races in South Africa. If the Security Council encourages that and makes it possible, then neither the Security Council nor the Organization will survive.

* * *

51. Mr. O'Hara (United States of America): I have asked for the floor to explain briefly the position of the United States on the votes taken today.

52. In the vote in the Special Political Committee on draft resolution A [A/6159, para. 17], the United States voted against paragraph 6 thereof. We appreciated having the opportunity to vote separately on this paragraph, and we voted against it because, as I said in the Committee, the United States does not believe that the situation in South Africa, deplorable as it is, constitutes at this time a threat to international peace and security within the meaning of Chapter VII. Accordingly, we do not consider a recommendation for coercive action appropriate under, or authorized by, the Charter.

53. Despite the vote we cast on operative paragraph 6, the United States abstained on the draft resolution as a whole. There are a number of provisions, particularly in its operative section, in addition to operative paragraph 6, to which we do not wholly subscribe. We nevertheless abstained, first, because we believe that the policies of apartheid present significant dangers to the continent of Africa and to the world community, and secondly, because apartheid is a policy which is totally repugnant to the concepts on which this Organization is founded and on which our own nation is based.

54. With these considerations in mind, we felt that we could not oppose this resolution which, despite provisions which we could not support, expresses this attitude unequivocally.

* * *

56. Mr. Jakobson (Finland): My delegation fully shares the concern expressed in the resolution that we have voted upon today over the situation created by the continued implementation by the South African Government of the policy of apartheid and by its refusal to heed the numerous resolutions condemning this policy adopted over the past years by both the Security Council and the General Assembly. We also share the conviction that the United Nations must not fail in its effort to put an end to the system of apartheid as well as to other forms of discrimination, indeed to all violations of human rights. * * * We do believe, however, that in dealing with the problem of apartheid, as with any other issue, we must adhere to the principles and procedures laid down by the Charter. It is quite clear to my delegation that, according to the Charter, it is the Security Council and only the Security Council that shall determine the existence of any threat to the peace or decide upon such measures as sanctions. The resolution now passed, in our view,

exceeds the competence of the General Assembly by attempting to determine the fact of the existence of a threat to international peace and security, as well as by prejudging the choice of the means to be employed for solving that problem. For this reason, my delegation was unable to support the resolution.

SECURITY COUNCIL RESOLUTION 282 (1970) OF JULY 23, 1970

Resolutions and Decisions of the Security Council 1970.

U.N. Sec. Council Off. Rec., 25th Year, p. 12.

The Security Council,

Having considered the question of race conflict in South Africa, resulting from the policies of apartheid of the Government of the Republic of South Africa, as submitted by forty Member States,

Reiterating its condemnation of the evil and abhorrent policies of apartheid and the measures being taken by the Government of South Africa to enforce and extend those policies beyond its borders,

Recognizing the legitimacy of the struggle of the oppressed people of South Africa in pursuance of their human and political rights as set forth in the Charter of the United Nations and the Universal Declaration of Human Rights,

Gravely concerned by the persistent refusal of the Government of South Africa to abandon its racist policies and to abide by the resolutions of the Security Council and the General Assembly on this question and others relating to southern Africa,

Gravely concerned by the situation arising from violations of the arms embargo called for in its resolutions 181 (1963) of 7 August 1963, 182 (1963) of 4 December 1963 and 191 (1964) of 18 June 1964,

Convinced of the need to strengthen the arms embargo called for in the above resolutions,

Convinced further that the situation resulting from the continued application of the policies of apartheid and the constant build-up of the South African military and police forces, made possible by the continued acquisition of arms, military vehicles and other equipment and of spare parts for military equipment from a number of Member States and by local manufacture of arms and ammunition under licences granted by some Member States, constitutes a potential threat to international peace and security,

Recognizing that the extensive arms build-up of the military forces of South Africa poses a real threat to the security and sovereignty of independent African States opposed to the racial policies of the Government of South Africa, in particular the neighboring States,

1.　Reiterates its total opposition to the policies of apartheid of the Government of the Republic of South Africa;

2.　Reaffirms its resolutions 181 (1963), 182 (1963) and 191 (1964);

3.　Condemns the violations of the arms embargo called for in resolutions 181 (1963), 182 (1963) and 191 (1964);

4.　Calls upon all States to strengthen the arms embargo

(a) By implementing fully the arms embargo against South Africa unconditionally and without reservations whatsoever;

(b) By withholding the supply of all vehicles and equipment for use of the armed forces and paramilitary organizations of South Africa;

(c) By ceasing the supply of spare parts for all vehicles and military equipment used by the armed forces and paramilitary organizations of South Africa;

(d) By revoking all licences and military patents granted to the South African Government or to South African companies for the manufacture of arms and ammunition, aircraft and naval craft or other military vehicles and by refraining from further granting such licences and patents;

(e) By prohibiting investment in, or technical assistance for, the manufacture of arms and ammunition, aircraft, naval craft, or other military vehicles;

(f) By ceasing provision of military training for members of the South African armed forces and all other forms of military cooperation with South Africa;

(g) By undertaking the appropriate action to give effect to the above measures;

5.　Requests the Secretary-General to follow closely the implementation of the present resolution and report to the Security Council from time to time;

6.　Calls upon all States to observe strictly the arms embargo against South Africa and to assist effectively in the implementation of the present resolution.

> Adopted at the 1549th meeting by 12 votes to none, with 3 abstentions (France, United Kingdom of Great Britain and Northern Ireland, United States of America).

EXTRACT FROM REPORT OF THE SPECIAL COMMITTEE ON APARTHEID TO THE GENERAL ASSEMBLY AND THE SECURITY COUNCIL, AUGUST 23, 1972

IX U.N. Monthly Chronicle, November 1972, p. 20.

The report of the Special Committee on Apartheid to the General Assembly and the Security Council, dated 23 August, reviewed the work of the Committee during the year, described the activities of intergovernmental and non-governmental organizations in the campaign against apartheid, and contained a series of conclusions and recommendations. Among the conclusions were the following:

After 20 years of United Nations debate, the international community had not compelled South Africa to abide by the numerous resolutions adopted by the General Assembly and the Security Council on the abolition of apartheid. There had been an aggravation of the situation in the whole of southern Africa resulting from the aggressive expansionist policies without which apartheid could not prosper and survive. Repressive measures by the South African Government had been intensified, and opposition to apartheid had increased all over the country. Implementation of the Bantustan scheme was being relentlessly pursued, with the aim of uprooting the indigenous inhabitants and dispossessing them of their land. The situation continued to be explosive and carry in it the seeds of violent conflict, posing a grave threat to international peace and security. Failing meaningful negotiations between the South African régime and the true representatives of the African people, the Special Committee remained firmly convinced that economic and other sanctions were the only alternatives to force and the most effective means of persuading South Africa to respond to international public opinion.

*   *   *

UNITED NATIONS GENERAL ASSEMBLY RESOLUTION 2923E (XXVII) OF NOVEMBER 15, 1972

IX U.N. Monthly Chronicle, December 1972, p. 56.

Resolution 2923E (XXVII) said the General Assembly was strongly convinced that the United Nations had a vital interest in securing the speedy elimination of apartheid; it was gravely concerned about the explosive situation in South Africa and in southern Africa as a whole resulting from the inhuman and aggressive policies of apartheid pursued by the Government of South Africa, a situation constituting a threat to international peace and security; it had noted that the Security Council had decided to examine as a matter of urgency methods of resolving the present situation arising out of the policies of apartheid of the Government of South Africa; it reaffirmed the inalienable right of the people of South Africa to self-determination and freedom; and it was alarmed at the forcible removal of the African people from their rightful homes to the so-called "Bantustans".

* * *

The resolution again called upon all Governments to implement fully the arms embargo against South Africa; reaffirmed its conviction that economic and other sanctions constituted one of the essential means of achieving a peaceful solution of the grave situation in South Africa; requested the Security Council to consider urgently the situation in South Africa with a view to adopting such effective measures under Chapter VII of the Charter; and firmly supported the efforts of all those engaged in the struggle inside South Africa against apartheid.

* * *

The resolution was adopted by a roll-call vote of 100 in favour to 4 against (Portugal, South Africa, United Kingdom, United States), with 21 abstentions (Australia, Austria, Belgium, Canada, Denmark, Finland, France, Greece, Guatemala, Ireland, Israel, Italy, Japan, Luxembourg, Malawi, Netherlands, New Zealand, Norway, Spain, Sweden, Uruguay).

---

2. SOUTHERN RHODESIA

Although Southern Rhodesia was largely a self-governing territory rather than strictly a colony in the British system, it was not fully independent up until the 1960's. Because it was governed by a white majority, the United Kingdom was unwilling to grant it independence until satisfactory constitutional arrangements were arrived at in Rhodesia to provide improvements in the political powers of the black majority. Negotiations between the British and the governing regime in Southern Rhodesia having failed, Southern Rhodesia declared its independence on November 11, 1965 (an act referred to as Unilateral Declaration of Independence or UDI).

A series of resolutions in the Security Council of the United Nations condemned UDI, called on the United Kingdom to quell the rebellion and even specifically called on the United Kingdom to prevent, by force if necessary, the delivery of oil by tankers destined for Rhodesia. Security Council Resolutions 216 and 217 [a] (1965) of November 12, 1965 and 221 [b] (1966) of April 9, 1966. "Selective" sanctions were

a. Resolution and Decisions of the Security Council 1965. U.N.Sec. Council Off.Rec., 20th Year, p. 8.

b. Resolutions and Decisions of the Security Council 1966. U.N.Sec. Council Off.Rec., 21st Year, p. 5.

voted by the council in Resolution 232ᶜ (1966) of December 16, 1966. Stating that it was acting "in accordance with Articles 39 and 41 of the United Nations Charter", the council determined "that the present situation in Southern Rhodesia constitutes a threat to international peace and security." The council thereupon decided that all States Members of the United Nations shall prevent:

(a) the import into their territories of asbestos, iron ore, chrome, pig-iron, sugar, tobacco, copper, meat and meat products and hides, skins and leather originating in Southern Rhodesia and exported therefrom after the date of this resolution;

(b) any activities by their nationals or in their territories which promote or are calculated to promote the export of their commodities from Southern Rhodesia and any dealings by their nationals or in their territories in any of these commodities originating in Southern Rhodesia and exported therefrom after the date of this resolution, including in particular any transfer of funds to Southern Rhodesia for the purposes of such activities or dealings.

These measures having failed, the council adopted more comprehensive sanctions two years later.

SECURITY COUNCIL RESOLUTION 253 (1968)
OF MAY 29, 1968

Resolutions and Decisions of the Security Council 1968
U.N. Sec. Council Off. Rec., 23rd year, p. 5.

The Security Council,

Recalling and reaffirming its resolutions 216 (1965) of 12 November 1965, 217 (1965) of 20 November 1965, 221 (1966) of 9 April 1966, and 232 (1966) of 16 December 1966,

Taking note of resolution 2262 (XXII) adopted by the General Assembly on 3 November 1967,

Noting with great concern that the measures taken so far have failed to bring the rebellion in Southern Rhodesia to an end,

Reaffirming that, to the extent not superseded in this resolution, the measures provided for in resolutions 217 (1965) of 20 November 1965 and 232 (1966) of 16 December 1966, as well as those initiated by Member States in implementation of those resolutions, shall continue in effect,

Gravely concerned that the measures taken by the Security Council have not been complied with by all States and that some States,

c. Resolutions and Decisions of the
Security Council 1966.   U.N.Sec.
Council Off.Rec., 21st Year, p. 7.

contrary to resolution 232 (1966) of the Security Council and to their obligations under Article 25 of the Charter of the United Nations, have failed to prevent trade with the illegal régime in Southern Rhodesia,

Condemning the recent inhuman executions carried out by the illegal régime in Southern Rhodesia which have flagrantly affronted the conscience of mankind and have been universally condemned,

Affirming the primary responsibility of the Government of the United Kingdom to enable the people of Southern Rhodesia to achieve self-determination and independence, and in particular their responsibility for dealing with the prevailing situation,

Recognizing the legitimacy of the struggle of the people of Southern Rhodesia to secure the enjoyment of their rights as set forth in the Charter of the United Nations and in conformity with the objectives of General Assembly resolution 1514 (XV) of 14 December 1960,

Reaffirming its determination that the present situation in Southern Rhodesia constitutes a threat to international peace and security,

Acting under Chapter VII of the Charter of the United Nations,

1.   Condemns all measures of political repression, including arrests, detentions, trials and executions which violate fundamental freedoms and rights of the people of Southern Rhodesia, and calls upon the Government of the United Kingdom to take all possible measures to put an end to such actions;

2.   Calls upon the United Kingdom as the administering Power in the discharge of its responsibility to take urgently all effective measures to bring to an end the rebellion in Southern Rhodesia, and enable the people to secure the enjoyment of their rights as set forth in the Charter of the United Nations and in conformity with the objectives of General Assembly resolution 1514 (XV);

3.   Decides that, in furtherance of the objective of ending the rebellion, all States Members of the United Nations shall prevent:

(a) The import into their territories of all commodities and products originating in Southern Rhodesia and exported therefrom after the date of this resolution (whether or not the commodities or products are for consumption or processing in their territories, whether or not they are imported in bond and whether or not any special legal status with respect to the import of goods is enjoyed by the port or other place where they are imported or stored);

(b) Any activities by their nationals or in their territories which would promote or are calculated to promote the export of any commodities or products from Southern Rhodesia; and any dealings by their nationals or in their territories in any commodities or products originating in Southern Rhodesia and exported therefrom after the date of this resolution, including in particular any transfer of funds to Southern Rhodesia for the purposes of such activities or dealings;

(c) The shipment in vessels or aircraft of their registration or under charter to their nationals, or the carriage (whether or not, in bond) by land transport facilities across their territories of any commodities or products originating in Southern Rhodesia and exported therefrom after the date of this resolution;

(d) The sale or supply by their nationals or from their territories of any commodities or products (whether or not originating in their territories, but not including supplies intended strictly for medical purposes, educational equipment and material for use in schools and other educational institutions, publications, news material and, in special humanitarian circumstances, food-stuffs) to any person or body in Southern Rhodesia or to any other person or body for the purposes of any business carried on in or operated from Southern Rhodesia, and any activities, by their nationals or in their territories which promote or are calculated to promote such sale or supply;

(e) The shipment in vessels or aircraft of their registration, or under charter to their nationals, or the carriage (whether or not in bond) by land transport facilities across their territories of any such commodities or products which are consigned to any person or body in Southern Rhodesia, or to any other person or body for the purposes of any business carried on in or operated from Southern Rhodesia;

4. Decides that all States Members of the United Nations shall not make available to the illegal régime in Southern Rhodesia or to any commercial, industrial or public utility undertaking, including tourist enterprises, in Southern Rhodesia any funds for investment or any other financial or economic resources and shall prevent their nationals and any persons within their territories from making available to the régime or to any such undertaking any such funds or resources and from remitting any other funds to persons or bodies within Southern Rhodesia, except payments exclusively for pensions or for strictly medical, humanitarian or educational purposes or for the provision of news material and in special humanitarian circumstances, food-stuffs;

5. Decides that all States Members of the United Nations shall:

(a) Prevent the entry into their territories, save on exceptional humanitarian grounds, of any person travelling on a Southern Rhodesian passport, regardless of its date of issue, or on a purported passport issued by or on behalf of the illegal régime in Southern Rhodesia;

(b) Take all possible measures to prevent the entry into their territories of persons whom they have reason to believe to be ordinarily resident in Southern Rhodesia and whom they have reason to believe to have furthered or encouraged, or to be likely to further or encourage, the unlawful actions of the illegal régime in Southern Rhodesia or any activities which are calculated to evade any measure decided upon in this resolution or resolution 232 (1966) of 16 December 1966;

6.   Decides that all States Members of the United Nations shall prevent airline companies constituted in their territories and aircraft of their registration or under charter to their nationals from operating to or from Southern Rhodesia and from linking up with any airline company constituted or aircraft registered in Southern Rhodesia;

7.   Decides that all States Members of the United Nations shall give effect to the decisions set out in operative paragraphs 3, 4, 5 and 6 of this resolution notwithstanding any contract entered into or licence granted before the date of this resolution;

8.   Calls upon all States Members of the United Nations or of the specialized agencies to take all possible measures to prevent activities by their nationals and persons in their territories promoting, assisting or encouraging emigration to Southern Rhodesia, with a view to stopping such emigration;

9.   Requests all States Members of the United Nations or of the specialized agencies to take all possible further action under Article 41 of the Charter to deal with the situation in Southern Rhodesia, not excluding any of the measures provided in that Article;

10.   Emphasizes the need for the withdrawal of all consular and trade representation in Southern Rhodesia, in addition to the provisions of operative paragraph 6 of resolution 217 (1965);

11.   Calls upon all States Members of the United Nations to carry out these decisions of the Security Council in accordance with Article 25 of the Charter of the United Nations and reminds them that failure or refusal by any one of them to do so would constitute a violation of that Article;

12.   Deplores the attitude of States that have not complied with their obligations under Article 25 of the Charter, and censures in particular those States which have persisted in trading with the illegal régime in defiance of the resolutions of the Security Council, and which have given active assistance to the régime;

13.   Urges all States Members of the United Nations to render moral and material assistance to the people of Southern Rhodesia in their struggle to achieve their freedom and independence;

14.   Urges, having regard to the principles stated in Article 2 of the Charter of the United Nations, States not Members of the United Nations to act in accordance with the provisions of the present resolution;

15.   Requests States Members of the United Nations, the United Nations Organization, the specialized agencies, and other interna-

tional organizations in the United Nations system to extend assistance to Zambia as a matter of priority with a view to helping it solve such special economic problems as it may be confronted with arising from the carrying out of these decisions of the Security Council;

16.   Calls upon all States Members of the United Nations, and in particular those with primary responsibility under the Charter for the maintenance of international peace and security, to assist effectively in the implementation of the measures called for by the present resolution;

17.   Considers that the United Kingdom as the administering Power should ensure that no settlement is reached without taking into account the views of the people of Southern Rhodesia, and in particular the political parties favouring majority rule, and that it is acceptable to the people of Southern Rhodesia as a whole;

18.   Calls upon all States Members of the United Nations or of the specialized agencies to report to the Secretary-General by 1 August 1968 on measures taken to implement the present resolution;

19.   Requests the Secretary-General to report to the Security Council on the progress of the implementation of this resolution, the first report to be made not later than 1 September 1968;

20.   Decides to establish, in accordance with rule 28 of the provisional rules of procedure of the Security Council, a committee of the Security Council to undertake the following tasks and to report to it with its observations:

(a) To examine such reports on the implementation of the present resolution as are submitted by the Secretary-General;

(b) To seek from any States Members of the United Nations or of the specialized agencies such further information regarding the trade of that State (including information regarding the commodities and products exempted from the prohibition contained in operative paragraph 3(d) above) or regarding any activities by any nationals of that State or in its territories that may constitute an evasion of the measures decided upon in this resolution as it may consider necessary for the proper discharge of its duty to report to the Security Council;

21.   Requests the United Kingdom, as the administering Power, to give maximum assistance to the committee, and to provide the committee with any information which it may receive in order that the measures envisaged in this resolution and resolution 232 (1966) may be rendered fully effective;

22.   Calls upon all States Members of the United Nations, or of the specialized agencies, as well as the specialized agencies themselves, to supply such further information as may be sought by the Committee in pursuance of this resolution;

23.   Decides to maintain this item on its agenda for further action as appropriate in the light of developments.

Adopted unanimously at the 1428th meeting.

UNITED STATES EXTENDS PROGRAM BANNING TRADE WITH SOUTHERN RHODESIA

59 United States Department of State Bulletin 199 (1968).

The President on July 29 signed an Executive order implementing United Nations Security Council Resolution No. 253 of May 29, 1968, which extends the program of mandatory economic sanctions against Southern Rhodesia.

The President acted under the United Nations Participation Act of 1945, as amended. Section 5 of the act empowers the President to implement Security Council decisions adopted pursuant to article 41 of the United Nations Charter.

In its Resolution No. 253, the Security Council unanimously decided that all member states shall extend the earlier prohibitions on imports from and exports to Southern Rhodesia to cover all commodities and products except exports to Southern Rhodesia of publications, news material, and articles needed for medical, educational, and humanitarian purposes. The resolution also obligates each member state to prohibit any activities promoting or calculated to promote such imports and exports, the carriage of such articles in ships and aircraft of its registry or under charter to its nationals, and transfers to Southern Rhodesia of funds and other financial or economic resources other than pensions, payments for news material, and transfers for medical, educational, and humanitarian purposes. Finally, the resolution decides that member states shall prevent their air carriers and aircraft of their registry or under charter to their nationals from operating to Southern Rhodesia or coordinating operations with airline companies constituted in or aircraft registered in Southern Rhodesia.

This Executive order prohibits these activities covered by the resolution, including transactions involving commodities and products exported from Southern Rhodesia after May 29 (the date of the resolution). The order delegates to the Secretaries of Commerce, the Treasury, and Transportation authority to promulgate regulations necessary to carry out the prohibitions. The Secretary of Commerce on July 16 acted under authority of the Export Control Act to impose the further restrictions on exports to Southern Rhodesia called for by the resolution. The further regulations required under the Executive order will be issued shortly and will be effective July 29. The prohibitions of Executive Order No. 11322 of January 5, 1967, implementing Security Council Resolution No. 232 of December 16, 1966, continue in effect.

It is a criminal offense to engage in the prohibited activities. Provision will be made in the regulations to deal with cases of undue hardship arising from transactions commenced before the date of the order.

In Resolution No. 253 the Security Council also decided that member states shall prevent the entry into their territory of persons traveling on Southern Rhodesian passports and take all possible measures to prevent the entry of individuals ordinarily resident in Southern Rhodesia who are likely to further or encourage the illegal regime or evade the economic sanctions. The Departments of State and Justice are implementing these provisions under the Immigration and Nationality Act.

The mandatory sanctions imposed by the Security Council's resolution of May 29 supplement the selective mandatory sanctions imposed in December 1966 and the earlier voluntary measures taken by a large majority of the members of the United Nations in response to the Council's appeal of November 20, 1965, just after the Smith regime in Southern Rhodesia had unilaterally declared its independence, that economic relations with Southern Rhodesia be broken. The United States is fully supporting the Security Council resolutions.

UNITED STATES DISCUSSES ENFORCEMENT OF SANCTIONS AGAINST RHODESIA

66 United States Department of State Bulletin 490 (1972).

[Statement by Ambassador Phillips, United States Representative in United Nations Security Council, February 28, 1972.]

The United States Government, both inside and outside of the U. N., has supported the right of self-determination and has opposed the odious practice of racial discrimination.

From the inception, the United States has voted for Security Council decisions imposing mandatory economic sanctions against the rebel regime in Rhodesia. I submit that the United States has been second to none in the vigorous enforcement of these sanctions. The effectiveness of the action of my government is documented in the reports of the Sanctions Committee.

Members of the Council are aware of a special situation affecting the United States enforcement of the sanctions on Rhodesia. I refer, of course, to the so-called Byrd provision of the military procurement bill, the provisions of which I am certain are well known to all around this table.

The considerations leading to the enactment into law of the Byrd provision emerged clearly in the statements and testimony on the legislation in our Congress. Among these was the concern of Congressmen that while the United States was becoming dependent on a single high-priced source of chrome ore, Rhodesian ore was being exported in quantity to other countries. Since the United States was scrupulously observing the sanctions, U. S. executive officials found it impossible to offer any persuasive refutation of this conclusion. The Congress felt that for compelling reasons of national security the United States should not be placed in a distinctly disadvantageous position with regard to the importation of strategic commodities.

It is an inescapable fact of life that this legislation, having been duly enacted according to our constitutional processes, is now the law of the land. However, as Ambassador Bush made clear both at Addis and in later statements in various African countries he was privileged to visit, the United States remains interested in seeing that sanctions work. I reaffirm that we stand ready to assist the Sanctions Committee in its efforts, and we pledge that we will continue our full participation in its activities.

However, Mr. President, we also believe that this Council should face squarely the true nature of the problem confronting the U. N. concerning the effectiveness of the sanctions program.

The United States continues to be committed to the sanctions program voted in Security Council Resolution 253 of 1968, but we also believe that the enforcement of these sanctions by other countries is patently inadequate. It seems to us that countries that are open with information about their imports are at a disadvantage vis-a-vis countries that are not open with such information. To put it more bluntly, there are widespread violations of the sanctions which are not being brought to light, while the light is being focused on relatively unimportant exceptions to the application of sanctions in the case of my country. Others have during this debate alluded to this aspect of the sanctions program.

Let us be blunt about the nature of the problem. The sanctions are not going to work if there is a double standard about compliance with them. There are countries around this very table that have consistently voted for the sanctions and that say they favor strengthening the machinery, yet which may be violators of the program.

The first and essential step is to acknowledge that sanctions, while they have had a measurable effect on the Rhodesian economy, have not been working very well with respect to a number of Rhodesian exports for a long period of time. Rhodesian exports continue at levels which appear to approximate, and in some cases exceed, presanctions levels. This can be explained only by a widespread pattern of violation of or indifference to the requirements of the sanctions effort.

There have been alleged violations which concern at least nine countries sitting in this Council, including most of the permanent members. In fairness both to the countries against which the allegations have been made and to the countries which have tried scrupulously to adhere to the sanctions, these allegations should be investigated.

The fourth report of the Sanctions Committee established that Rhodesian indirect exports to world markets through third countries rose from $8 million in 1966 to $215 million in 1970. It is common knowledge that in the last few years Rhodesia has been able to export the bulk of its mineral output. These exports must go somewhere—and they did not go to the United States.

It is notable that the fourth report of the Sanctions Committee points out that exports of chrome ore from South Africa to some major industrial countries more than doubled and in one case rose more than 10 times within the past 4 years. Many of the importing countries are members of this Security Council, and it is most difficult to escape the presumption that much of this increased purchase of ore did come from Rhodesia. As members of the Council are aware, we have been unable to obtain general agreement that where there is reasonable question as to the origin of imported minerals, those minerals be subject to the effective chemical tests that are available. And, as you know, only the United Kingdom, the United States, and Denmark have actually taken steps to prosecute firms found to be in violation of sanctions.

Mr. President, in 1965 Rhodesia exported $67 million in strategic materials.

All indications are that Rhodesia's exports of strategic commodities in 1970 were as high as or higher than the 1965 exports, and none of those commodities were imported into the United States. Somebody bought these goods. Somebody has been buying them each year since sanctions went into effect. And it was not the United States, which has scrupulously enforced the sanctions program. In short, the United States has not been the problem.

As a result of our recent legislation, the United States no longer prohibits the importation of strategic commodities from Rhodesia. But let us keep this in perspective. Prior to sanctions, however, United States imports of those commodities amounted to less than 2 percent of Rhodesia's total presanctions exports. The United States continues, therefore, to enforce scrupulously the embargo on commodities which constitute 98 percent of Rhodesia's presanctions exports. The Byrd provision therefore is only a very small part of the problem, and the United States is prepared to report all exceptions under it. In 1968, 1969, 1970, and 1971, all indications are that Rhodesian exports of strategic commodities were as high or higher than they were in 1965. In these 4 years, the United States took only one lot, which had been paid for before sanctions. That one lot represented 6 percent of 1 year's production of only one commodity and less than one-half of 1 percent of Rhodesia's total exports through third countries. I say again, the United States has not been the problem.

My government therefore suggests that this Council ask the Sanctions Committee to request from governments periodic reports on the importation of strategic minerals from all sources. The list of minerals should show worldwide trade in all those key commodities which are also produced in Rhodesia. The reports should also indicate sources of origin for each item or commodity. Reports of this nature should greatly assist the Sanctions Committee to obtain a fuller picture of on-going trade with Rhodesia. We could envisage that in case of questionable shipments, the committee would be able to request and obtain samples of such shipments and subject those samples to chemical analysis to determine their origin. My government would be prepared to cooperate fully in this effort.

* * *

DIGGS v. SHULTZ, SECRETARY OF TREASURY

United States Court of Appeals, District of Columbia, 1972.
470 F.2d 461.

McGOWAN, CIRCUIT JUDGE: This is an appeal from the dismissal by the District Court of a complaint seeking declaratory and injunctive relief in respect of the importation of metallurgical chromite from Southern Rhodesia. The gravamen of this action was an asserted conflict between (1) the official authorization of such importation by the United States, and (2) the treaty obligations of the United States under the United Nations Charter. Plaintiff-appellants sought summary judgment, as did defendant-appellees alternatively to a motion to dismiss for failure to state a claim upon which relief could be given.

The District Court's ruling for appellees was grounded primarily upon lack of standing, but it encompassed as well a concept of the nonjusticiability of the issues raised. Although we believe there was standing upon the part of at least some of the appellants to pursue thier cause of action judicially, we think that cause is not one in respect of which relief can be granted. Accordingly, we affirm the judgment of dismissal.

I

In 1966 the Security Council of the United Nations, with the affirmative vote of the United States, adopted Resolution 232 directing that all member states impose an embargo on trade with Southern Rhodesia—a step which was reaffirmed and enlarged in 1968. In compliance with this resolution, the President of the United States issued Executive Orders 11322 and 11419, 22 U.S.C. § 287c, establishing criminal sanctions for violation of the embargo. In 1971, however, Congress adopted the so-called Byrd Amendment to the Strategic and

Critical Materials Stock Piling Act, 50 U.S.C. § 98–98h, which provides in part:

Sec. 10. Notwithstanding any other provision of law * * * the President may not prohibit or regulate the importation into the United States of any material determined to be strategic and critical pursuant to the provisions of this Act, if such material is the product of any foreign country or area not listed as a Communist-dominated country or area * * * for so long as the importation into the United States of material of that kind which is the product of such Communist-dominated countries or areas is not prohibited by any provision of law.

Since Southern Rhodesia is not a Communist-controlled country, and inasmuch as the United States imports from Communist countries substantial quantities of metallurgical chromite and other materials available from Rhodesia, the Byrd Amendment contemplated the resumption of trade by this country with Southern Rhodesia. By direction of the President, the Office of Foreign Assets Control issued to the corporate appellees in this case a General License authorizing the importation of various materials from Southern Rhodesia, and they began importation.

Alleging that the Byrd Amendment did not and could not authorize issuance of such a license contrary to this country's treaty obligations, appellants sought to enjoin further importation, to require official seizure, and to restrain use, of materials already imported under the General License, and to declare the General License null and void.

II

The question of standing turns first on whether the party seeking relief has alleged a sufficient personal interest in the controversy to insure concrete adverseness in the presentation of the issues. Data Processing Service v. Camp, 397 U.S. 150, 152, 90 S.Ct. 827 (1969); Baker v. Carr, 369 U.S. 186, 204, 82 S.Ct. 691 (1962). Appellants allege various personal injuries, and we agree with the District Court that these allegations amply provide the injury in fact element of the standing requirement.[1]

Another requirement of standing is that the complainant be within the zone of interests sought to be protected by the law in question.

---

1. We adopt the District Court's identification of those plaintiffs who meet the injury in fact requirement. Appellants M'Gabe and Zimbabive complain they are unable to return to their homeland, Rhodesia. Appellants Diggs, Conyers, Rangel, Stokes and Franck all alleged that they have been refused entry into Rhodesia; and the American Committee on Africa complains that its chairman has also been denied entry. The Council for Christian Social Action of the United Church of Christ alleges its missionaries have been arrested and deported from Rhodesia. Appellant Vidal asserts injury because sale of one of his books is banned in Rhodesia. None of the other plaintiffs have standing; and it is not contended in this court that they have.

Data Processing Service v. Camp, 397 U.S. 150, 153, 90 S.Ct. 827 (1969). United Nations Security Council Resolution 232 was—and is—an attempt by means of concerted international pressure to turn the Rhodesian Government away from the course of action which has resulted in the adverse circumstances experienced by appellants. They are unquestionably within the reach of its purpose and among its intended beneficiaries.

Finally, the concept of standing has been characterized as contemplating that there be a "logical nexus between the status asserted and the claim sought to be adjudicated," in order to insure that the litigant is the proper party to represent the interests involved. Flast v. Cohen, 392 U.S. 83, 102, 88 S.Ct. 1942, 1953 (1967).[2] The District Court found the causal relationship of appellants' claims to the challenged actions too attenuated to constitute such a nexus. That finding rested largely on the conclusion that appellants' quarrel was really with the Rhodesian Government rather than with appellees. But that view fails to focus on the exact nature of the grievance appearing in the complaint.

Appellants, along with many other persons, have suffered, and continue to suffer, tangible injuries at the hands of Southern Rhodesia. In an attempt to terminate the policies giving rise to those wrongs, the United Nations, with the United States as an assenting member, established the embargo. The precise injury of which appellants complain in this law suit is allegedly illegal present action by the United States which tends to limit the effectiveness of the embargo and thereby to deprive appellants of its potential benefits. That quarrel is directly and immediately with this government, and not with Southern Rhodesia.

Appellees suggest that the prospects of significant relief by means of the embargo are so slight that this relationship of intended benefit is too tenuous to support standing. But this strikes us as tantamount to saying that because the performance of the United Nations is not always equal to its promise, the commitments of a member may be disregarded without having to respond in court to a charge of treaty violation. It may be that the particular economic sanctions invoked against Southern Rhodesia in this instance will fall short of their goal, and that appellants will ultimately reap no benefit from them. But, to persons situated as are appellants, United Nations action constitutes the only hope; and they are personally aggrieved and injured by the dereliction of any member state which weakens the capacity of the world organization to make its policies meaningful.

2. It is far from clear that this formulation adds anything of substance to the two requirements just discussed. It states a proposition that can well be thought to be related to the merits of a claim rather than to the existence of standing to press it. The District Court, with some support in Supreme Court language, chose to pursue the question as an aspect of standing, although the rationale followed by it is relevant to its dismissal for failure to state a claim warranting relief.

Of course it is true that appellants' plight stems initially from acts done by Southern Rhodesia, and that their primary quarrel is with it. But this does not foreclose the existence of a judicially cognizable dispute between appellants, on the one hand, and appellees, on the other, who are said to be acting in derogation of the solemn treaty obligation of the United States to adhere to the embargo for so long as it is in being.[3]

III

The District Court, in its comments to the effect that non-justiciability would necessitate dismissal of the complaint even if standing be found, reasoned as follows: It is settled constitutional doctrine that Congress may nullify, in whole or in part, a treaty commitment. Congress, by the Byrd Amendment in 1971, acted to abrogate one aspect of our treaty obligations under the U. N. Charter, that is to say, our continued participation in the economic sanctions taken against Southern Rhodesia. The considerations underlying that step by Congress present issues of political policy which courts do not inquire into. Thus, appellants' quarrel is with Congress, and it is a cause which can be pursued only at the polls and not in the courts.

In this court appellants do not seriously contest the first of these propositions, namely, the constitutional power of Congress to set treaty obligations at naught.[4] They seek, rather, to show that, in the Byrd Amendment, Congress did not really intend to compel the Executive to end United States observance of the Security Council's sanctions, and that, therefore, it is the Executive which is, without the essential shield of Congressional dispensation, violating a treaty engagement of this country. Appellants point out in this regard that the Byrd Amendment does not in terms require importation from Southern Rhodesia, but leaves open two alternative courses of action. The statute says the President may not ban importation from Rhodesia

3. The passage of the Byrd Amendment was the subject of widespread notice and comment within the United Nations, resulting in the reaffirmation by the Security Council on February 8, 1972 of the sanctions against Southern Rhodesia. The resolution to this end declared that any legislation passed by any member state "with a view to permitting, directly or indirectly, the importation from Southern Rhodesia of any commodity falling within the scope of obligations imposed (by the 1968 resolution), including chrome ore, would undermine sanctions and would be contrary to the obligations of States."

4. Moser v. United States, 341 U.S. 41, 45, 71 S.Ct. 553 (1951); Clark v. Allen, 331 U.S. 503, 508–9, 67 S.Ct. 1431 (1947); Pigeon River Co. v. Cox, 291 U.S. 138, 160, 54 S.Ct. 361 (1934); Edge v. Robertson, 112 U.S. 580, 597, 5 S.Ct. 247 (1884).

Although appellants concede that Congress has the power to override treaty obligations (Appellants' Br. at 23), they contend that our commitment to the U.N. has more force than an ordinary treaty. Appellants argue on the basis of their interpretation of the U.N. Charter that Congress could override Resolution 232 only by withdrawing from the U.N. entirely. There is, however, no evidence that this country's membership in that organization was intended to be on the all-or-nothing basis suggested by appellants.

of materials classified as critical and strategic unless importation from Communist countries is also prohibited. Instead of permitting resumption of trade with Rhodesia, the President, so it is said, could (1) have banned importation of these materials from Communist nations as well as from Rhodesia, or (2) have taken steps to have these materials declassified, thereby taking them in either case out of the scope of the Byrd Amendment.

Citing the canon of construction that a statute should, if possible, be construed in a manner consistent with treaty obligations, appellants argue that the Byrd Amendment, although discretionary on its face, should be construed to compel the President to take one or the other of these two steps as a means of escape from the necessity of breaching the U. N. Charter. But these alternatives raise questions of foreign policy and national defense as sensitive as those involved in the decision to honor or abrogate our treaty obligations.[5] To attempt to decide whether the President chose properly among the three alternatives confronting him "would be not to decide a judicial controversy, but to assume a position of authority over the governmental acts of another and co-equal department, an authority which plainly we do not possess." Frothingham v. Mellon, 262 U.S. 447, 489, 43 S.Ct. 597, 601 (1923).

We think that there can be no blinking the purpose and effect of the Byrd Amendment. It was to detach this country from the U. N. boycott of Southern Rhodesia in blatant disregard of our treaty undertakings. The legislative record shows that no member of Congress voting on the measure was under any doubt about what was involved then; and no amount of statutory interpretation now can make the Byrd Amendment other than what it was as presented to the Congress, namely, a measure which would make—and was intended to make— the United States a certain treaty violator. The so-called options given to the President are, in reality, not options at all. In any event, they are in neither case alternatives which are appropriately to be forced upon him by a court.[6]

5. Russia supplied 60 per cent of our metallurgical chromite in 1970 while the embargo was being observed by the United States, S.Rep.No.92–359, 92d Cong., 1st Sess., 121 (1971), and a decision to discontinue importation would be a serious step in a very delicate area. Similarly, the decision to remove certain materials from the critical and strategic list should be done in a manner consistent with the objectives of that act. 50 U.S.C.A. § 98. Appellants' view would require reclassification of materials without regard to whether they continue to be critical to national defense. Appellants argue that the apparent surplus in the stockpile indicates the materials are no longer critical. This confuses two distinct functions under the act. One is classification of materials as strategic or critical in order to encourage their development in this country and to avoid dangerous dependency upon other nations. The other is the acquisition of certain quantites of these materials to be stockpiled for use in an emergency. A surplus in the stockpile at a given moment does not mean that it is no longer necessary to be concerned about the dependency of this country on outside sources for the materials in question.

6. The Supreme Court in Baker v. Carr was at pains to point out that the so-

Under our constitutional scheme, Congress can denounce treaties if it sees fit to do so, and there is nothing the other branches of government can do about it. We consider that this is precisely what Congress has done in this case; and therefore the District Court was correct to the extent that it found the complaint to state no tenable claim in law.

Affirmed.

WILBUR K. MILLER, SENIOR CIRCUIT JUDGE, concurs in the result.

Questions. Ambassador Phillips and the Court of Appeals assume without question that the United States is legally bound internationally to comply with the Security Council's directive to apply economic sanctions. Is it clear that the Security Council's directive is lawful under the Charter? The council purported to act under Articles 39 and 41. What was the factual basis for the finding that the "present situation in Southern Rhodesia constitutes a threat to international peace and security?" [a] Or is that question irrelevant? That is, can the following be said to be the law of the Charter? Once the Security Council has found under Article 39 that there is a threat to the peace it has the power to require member states to take whatever actions it deems appropriate under Article 41 and member states are obligated to comply with its directive by reason of Article 25, since the council's findings of fact under Article 39 are conclusive.

SECURITY COUNCIL RESOLUTION 320 (1972), OF SEPTEMBER 29, 1972

IX U.N. Monthly Chronicle, October 1972, p. 29.

The Security Council,

Recalling its resolution 253 (1968) of 29 May 1968 and subsequent resolutions in which all States are required to implement and make effective the economic, political and other sanctions against

called "political question doctrine" is an aspect of the separation of powers prescribed by the Federal Constitution; and that, in the intra-federal context, it continues to have meaningful vitality to restrain interference by one branch of the federal establishment with concerns committed to another. The case before us is a classic one for the careful appraisal by a court of the consequences of an exercise of jurisdiction it may technically be thought to have.

a. Compare Fenwick, When is There a Threat to the Peace?—Rhodesia, 61 Am.J.Int'l L. 753 (1967), with McDougal and Reisman, Rhodesia and the United Nations: The Lawfulness of International Concern, 62 Am.J. Int'l L. 1 (1968).

Southern Rhodesia (Zimbabwe) decided upon by the Council in furtherance of the objective of ending the rebellion in that territory,

Taking into account its resolutions 314 (1972) of 28 February 1972 and 318 (1972) of 28 July 1972 concerning the co-operation and obligations of States and the measures necessary to ensure the scrupulous observance and strict implementation of sanctions,

Deeply concerned that, despite their obligations under Article 25 of the Charter, several States continue to violate sanctions covertly and overtly in contravention of the provisions of resolution 253 (1968),

Gravely concerned about the detrimental consequences which violations could cause to the effectiveness of sanctions and, in the wider sense, to the authority of the Council,

Deeply concerned by the report of the United States that it has authorized the importation of chrome ore and other minerals from Southern Rhodesia (Zimbabwe),

Condemning the refusal of South Africa and Portugal to co-operate with the United Nations in the observance and implementation of sanctions against Southern Rhodesia (Zimbabwe),

1.   Reaffirms its decision that sanctions against Southern Rhodesia (Zimbabwe) shall remain fully in force until the aims and objectives set out in resolution 253 (1968) are completely achieved;

2.   Calls upon all States to implement fully all Security Council resolutions establishing sanctions against Southern Rhodesia (Zimbabwe) in accordance with Article 25 and Article 2(6) of the Charter;

3.   Urges the United States to co-operate fully with the United Nations in the effective implementation of sanctions;

4.   Requests the Security Council Committee established in pursuance of resolution 253 (1968) concerning the Question of Southern Rhodesia to undertake, as a matter of urgency, consideration of the type of action which could be taken in view of the open and persistent refusal of South Africa and Portugal to implement sanctions against the illegal régime in Southern Rhodesia (Zimbabwe) and to report to the Council not later than 31 January 1973;

5.   Further requests the Committee to examine and submit a report to the Security Council not later than 31 January 1973 on all proposals and suggestions made at the 1663rd to 1666th meetings of the Council for extending the scope and improving the effectiveness of sanctions against Southern Rhodesia (Zimbabwe).

––––––––

3.   NAMIBIA (SOUTH WEST AFRICA)

At the conclusion of the First World War, the Covenant of the League of Nations provided, Article 22, for the establishment of a system of Mandates, whereby advanced nations would be entrusted with the tutelage of colonies and territories formerly belonging to defeated Germany and the Turkish Empire. The Covenant adopted "the principle that the well-being and development of such peoples form a sacred trust of civilization."

The allies agreed to confer a Mandate for German South West Africa upon "His Britannic Majesty to be exercised on his behalf by the Government of the Union of South Africa to administer the territory   *   *   *."   Under the terms of the Mandate, as defined by the Council of the League, "The Mandatory shall promote to the utmost the material and moral well-being and the social progress of the inhabitants of the territory   *   *   *."   League of Nations, Off. Jour., 2nd year No. 1, 89 (1921). In addition, the Mandatory was required to make an annual report to the council indicating the measures taken to carry out its obligations under the terms of the Mandate.

Upon the demise of the League at the founding of the United Nations, a new system of trusteeships was established under Chapter XII of the charter. All states upon whom Mandates had been conferred, except South Africa, made agreements bringing the Mandates into the trusteeship system. The United Nations took the position that it had the legal right to assume the supervisory powers over the Mandate that had previously been exercised by the League; South Africa countered that it had no responsibility to the United Nations. A series of advisory opinions by the International Court of Justice defined the relationship between the United Nations and South Africa with respect to the Mandate; in 1966, a contentious case testing South Africa's performance of its obligations under the Mandate was dismissed by the International Court of Justice for what may be called "lack of standing" by the states initiating the proceeding, Liberia and Ethiopia.

The General Assembly's Resolution 2145 in October 1966 moved the question of South West Africa to a new level of discourse. The assembly's resolution was followed in 1970 by a Security Council resolution designed to put teeth into the assembly's prior action.

GENERAL ASSEMBLY RESOLUTION 2145 (XXI) OF OCTOBER 27, 1966

U.N. Gen. Ass. Off. Rec., 21st Sess., Supp. No. 16 (A/6316), p. 2.[a]

The General Assembly,

Reaffirming the inalienable right of the people of South West Africa to freedom and independence in accordance with the Charter of the United Nations, General Assembly resolution 1514 (XV) of 14

a.   The footnotes in the text are those of the original.

December 1960 and earlier Assembly resolutions concerning the Mandated Territory of South West Africa,

Recalling the advisory opinion of the International Court of Justice of 11 July 1950,[7] accepted by the General Assembly in its resolution 449 A (V) of 13 December 1950, and the advisory opinions of 7 June 1955 [8] and 1 June 1956 [9] as well as the judgment of 21 December 1962,[10] which have established the fact that South Africa continues to have obligations under the Mandate which was entrusted to it on 17 December 1920 and that the United Nations as the successor to the League of Nations has supervisory powers in respect of South West Africa,

Gravely concerned at the situation in the Mandated Territory, which has seriously deteriorated following the judgment of the International Court of Justice of 18 July 1966,[11]

Having studied the reports of the various committees which had been established to exercise the supervisory functions of the United Nations over the administration of the Mandated Territory of South West Africa,

Convinced that the administration of the Mandated Territory by South Africa has been conducted in a manner contrary to the Mandate, the Charter of the United Nations and the Universal Declaration of Human Rights,

Reaffirming its resolution 2074 (XX) of 17 December 1965, in particular paragraph 4 thereof which condemned the policies of apartheid and racial discrimination practised by the Government of South Africa in South West Africa as constituting a crime against humanity,

Emphasizing that the problem of South West Africa is an issue falling within the terms of General Assembly resolution 1514 (XV),

Considering that all the efforts of the United Nations to induce the Government of South Africa to fulfil its obligations in respect of the administration of the Mandated Territory and to ensure the well-being and security of the indigenous inhabitants have been of no avail,

Mindful of the obligations of the United Nations towards the people of South West Africa,

7. International status of South West Africa, Advisory Opinion: I.C.J. Reports 1950, p. 128.

8. South West Africa—Voting procedure, Advisory Opinion of June 7th, 1955: I.C.J. Reports 1955, p. 67.

9. Admissibility of hearings of petitioners by the Committee on South West Africa, Advisory Opinion of June 1st, 1956: I.C.J. Reports 1956, p. 23.

10. South West Africa Cases (Ethiopia v. South Africa; Liberia v. South Africa), Preliminary Objections, Judgment of 21 December 1962: I.C.J. Reports 1962, p. 319.

11. South West Africa, Second Phase, Judgment, I.C.J. Reports 1966, p. 6.

Noting with deep concern the explosive situation which exists in the southern region of Africa,

Affirming its right to take appropriate action in the matter, including the right to revert to itself the administration of the Mandated Territory,

1. Reaffirms that the provisions of General Assembly resolution 1514 (XV) are fully applicable to the people of the Mandated Territory of South West Africa and that, therefore, the people of South West Africa have the inalienable right to self-determination, freedom and independence in accordance with the Charter of the United Nations;

2. Reaffirms further that South West Africa is a territory having international status and that it shall maintain this status until it achieves independence;

3. Declares that South Africa has failed to fulfil its obligations in respect of the administration of the Mandated Territory and to ensure the moral and material well-being and security of the indigenous inhabitants of South West Africa and has, in fact, disavowed the Mandate;

4. Decides that the Mandate conferred upon His Britannic Majesty to be exercised on his behalf by the Government of the Union of South Africa is therefore terminated, that South Africa has no other right to administer the Territory and that henceforth South West Africa comes under the direct responsibility of the United Nations;

5. Resolves that in these circumstances the United Nations must discharge those responsibilities with respect to South West Africa;

6. Establishes an Ad Hoc Committee for South West Africa—composed of fourteen Member States to be designated by the President of the General Assembly—to recommend practical means by which South West Africa should be administered, so as to enable the people of the Territory to exercise the right of self-determination and to achieve independence, and to report to the General Assembly at a special session as soon as possible and in any event not later than April 1967;

7. Calls upon the Government of South Africa forthwith to refrain and desist from any action, constitutional, administrative, political or otherwise, which will in any manner whatsoever alter or tend to alter the present international status of South West Africa;

8. Calls the attention of the Security Council to the present resolution;

9. Requests all States to extend their whole-hearted co-operation and to render assistance in the implementation of the present resolution;

10. Requests the Secretary-General to provide all the assistance necessary to implement the present resolution and to enable the Ad Hoc Committee for South West Africa to perform its duties.

SECURITY COUNCIL RESOLUTION 276 (1970) OF JANUARY 30, 1970

Resolutions and Decisions of the Security Council 1970.

U.N. Sec. Council Off. Rec., 25th year, p. 1.

The Security Council,

Reaffirming the inalienable right of the people of Namibia to freedom and independence recognized in General Assembly resolution 1514 (XV) of 14 December 1960,

Reaffirming General Assembly resolution 2145 (XXI) of 27 October 1966, by which the United Nations decided that the Mandate for South West Africa was terminated and assumed direct responsibility for the Territory until its independence,

Reaffirming Security Council resolution 264 (1969) of 20 March 1969 in which the Council recognized the termination of the Mandate and called upon the Government of South Africa to withdraw immediately its administration from the Territory,

Reaffirming that the extension and enforcement of South African laws in the Territory together with the continued detentions, trials and subsequent sentencing of Namibians by the Government of South Africa constitute illegal acts and flagrant violations of the rights of the Namibians concerned, the Universal Declaration of Human Rights and the international status of the Territory, now under direct United Nations responsibility,

Recalling Security Council resolution 269 (1969) of 12 August 1969,

1. Strongly condemns the refusal of the Government of South Africa to comply with the resolutions of the General Assembly and Security Council pertaining to Namibia;

2. Declares that the continued presence of the South African authorities in Namibia is illegal and that consequently all acts taken by the Government of South Africa on behalf of or concerning Namibia after the termination of the Mandate are illegal and invalid;

3. Declares further that the defiant attitude of the Government of South Africa towards the Council's decisions undermines the authority of the United Nations;

4. Considers that the continued occupation of Namibia by the Government of South Africa in defiance of the relevant United Na-

tions resolutions and of the Charter of the United Nations has grave consequences for the rights and interests of the people of Namibia;

5. Calls upon all States, particularly those which have economic and other interests in Namibia, to refrain from any dealings with the Government of South Africa which are inconsistent with paragraph 2 of the present resolution;

6. Decides to establish, in accordance with rule 28 of its provisional rules of procedure, an Ad Hoc Sub-Committee of the Council to study, in consultation with the Secretary-General, ways and means by which the relevant resolutions of the Council, including the present resolution, can be effectively implemented in accordance with the appropriate provisions of the Charter, in the light of the flagrant refusal of South Africa to withdraw from Namibia, and to submit its recommendations by 30 April 1970;

7. Requests all States, as well as the specialized agencies and other relevant organs of the United Nations, to give the Sub-Committee all the information and other assistance it may require in pursuance of the present resolution;

8. Further requests the Secretary-General to give every assistance to the Sub-Committee in the performance of its task;

9. Decides to resume consideration of the question of Namibia as soon as the recommendations of the Sub-Committee have been made available.

> Adopted at the 1529th meeting by 13 votes to none, with 2 abstentions (France, United Kingdom of Great Britain and Northern Ireland).

ADVISORY OPINION ON THE CONTINUED PRESENCE OF SOUTH AFRICA IN NAMIBIA (SOUTH WEST AFRICA) [a]

International Court of Justice, 1971.

[1971] I.C.J.Rep. 16

[The Security Council of the United Nations submitted the following question to the International Court of Justice for an advisory opinion:

"What are the legal consequences for States of the continued presence of South Africa in Namibia, notwithstanding Security Council resolution 276 (1970)?"

The International Court of Justice reviewed the history of the Mandate and its own prior advisory opinions. It concluded that the

a. The full name of the case is: Legal Consequences for States of the Continued Presence of South Africa in Namibia (South West Africa), notwithstanding Security Council Resolution 276 (1970), Advisory Opinion.

Mandate had survived the demise of the League, that South Africa's obligations continued unimpaired and that the General Assembly of the United Nations had the authority to exercise the supervisory functions formerly exercised by the Council of the League. In its summary of the events preceding the request for the advisory opinion, the court took note of South Africa's claim of a right to annex South West Africa.]

82. * * * In the present proceedings the representative of South Africa maintained on 15 March 1971:

> * * * if it is accepted that the Mandate has lapsed, the South African Government would have the right to administer the Territory by reason of a combination of factors, being (a) its original conquest; (b) its long occupation; (c) the continuation of the sacred trust basis agreed upon in 1920; and, finally (d) because its administration is to the benefit of the inhabitants of the Territory and is desired by them. In these circumstances the South African Government cannot accept that any State or organization can have a better title to the Territory.

83. These claims of title, which apart from other considerations are inadmissible in regard to a mandated territory, lead by South Africa's own admission to a situation which vitiates the object and purpose of the Mandate. Their significance in the context of the sacred trust has best been revealed by a statement made by the representative of South Africa in the present proceedings on 15 March 1971: "it is the view of the South African Government that no legal provision prevents its annexing South West Africa." As the Court pointed out in its Advisory Opinion on the International Status of South-West Africa, "the principle of non-annexation" was "considered to be of paramount importance" when the future of South West Africa and other territories was the subject of decision after the First World War (I.C.J. Reports 1950, p. 131). What was in consequence excluded by Article 22 of the League Covenant is even less acceptable today.

84. Where the United Nations is concerned, the records show that, throughout a period of twenty years, the General Assembly, by virtue of the powers vested in it by the Charter, called upon the South African Government to perform its obligations arising out of the Mandate. On 9 February 1946 the General Assembly, by resolution 9 (I), invited all States administering territories held under mandate to submit trusteeship agreements. All, with the exception of South Africa, responded by placing the respective territories under the trusteeship system or offering them independence. The General Assembly further made a special recommendation to this effect in resolution 65(I) of 14 December 1946; on 1 November 1947, in resolution 141(II), it "urged" the Government of the Union of South Africa to propose a trusteeship agreement; by resolution 227(III) of 26 No-

vember 1948 it maintained its earlier recommendations. A year later, in resolution 337(IV) of 6 December 1949, it expressed "regret that the Government of the Union of South Africa has withdrawn its previous undertaking to submit reports on its administration of the Territory of South West Africa for the information of the United Nations", reiterated its previous resolutions and invited South Africa "to resume the submission of such reports to the General Assembly". At the same time, in resolution 338(IV), it addressed specific questions concerning the international status of South West Africa to this Court. In 1950, by resolution 449(V) of 13 December, it accepted the resultant Advisory Opinion and urged the Government of the Union of South Africa "to take the necessary steps to give effect to the Opinion of the International Court of Justice". By the same resolution, it established a committee "to confer with the Union of South Africa concerning the procedural measures necessary for implementing the Advisory Opinion * * *". In the course of the ensuing negotiations South Africa continued to maintain that neither the United Nations nor any other international organization had succeeded to the supervisory functions of the League. The Committee, for its part, presented a proposal closely following the terms of the Mandate and providing for implementation "through the United Nations by a procedure as nearly as possible analogous to that which existed under the League of Nations, thus providing terms no more extensive or onerous than those which existed before". This procedure would have involved the submission by South Africa of reports to a General Assembly committee, which would further set up a special commission to take over the functions of the Permanent Mandates Commission. Thus the United Nations, which undoubtedly conducted the negotiations in good faith, did not insist on the conclusion of a trusteeship agreement; it suggested a system of supervision which "should not exceed that which applied under the Mandates System * * *". These proposals were rejected by South Africa, which refused to accept the principle of the supervision of its administration of the Territory by the United Nations.

85. Further fruitless negotiations were held from 1952 to 1959. In total, negotiations extended over a period of thirteen years, from 1946 to 1959. In practice the actual length of negotiations is no test of whether the possibilities of agreement have been exhausted; it may be sufficient to show that an early deadlock was reached and that one side adamantly refused compromise. In the case of Namibia (South West Africa) this stage had patently been reached long before the United Nations finally abandoned its efforts to reach agreement. Even so, for so long as South Africa was the mandatory Power the way was still open for it to seek an arrangement. But that chapter came to an end with the termination of the Mandate.

86. To complete this brief summary of the events preceding the present request for advisory opinion, it must be recalled that in 1955

and 1956 the Court gave at the request of the General Assembly two further advisory opinions on matters concerning the Territory. Eventually the General Assembly adopted resolution 2145 (XXI) on the termination of the Mandate for South West Africa. Subsequently the Security Council adopted resolution 276 (1970), which declared the continued presence of South Africa in Namibia to be illegal and called upon States to act accordingly.

87. The Government of France in its written statement and the Government of South Africa throughout the present proceedings have raised the objection that the General Assembly, in adopting resolution 2145 (XXI), acted ultra vires.

* * *

90. As indicated earlier, with the entry into force of the Charter of the United Nations a relationship was established between all Members of the United Nations on the one side, and each mandatory Power on the other. The mandatory Powers while retaining their mandates assumed, under Article 80 of the Charter, vis-à-vis all United Nations Members, the obligation to keep intact and preserve, until trusteeship agreements were executed the rights of other States and of the peoples of mandated territories, which resulted from the existing mandate agreements and related instruments, such as Article 22 of the Covenant and the League Council's resolution of 31 January 1923 concerning petitions. The mandatory Powers also bound themselves to exercise their functions of administration in conformity with the relevant obligations emanating from the United Nations Charter, which member States have undertaken to fulfil in good faith in all their international relations.

91. One of the fundamental principles governing the international relationship thus established is that a party which disowns or does not fulfil its own obligations cannot be recognized as retaining the rights which it claims to derive from the relationship.

92. The terms of the preamble and operative part of resolution 2145 (XXI) leave no doubt as to the character of the resolution. In the preamble the General Assembly declares itself "Convinced that the administration of the Mandated Territory by South Africa has been conducted in a manner contrary" to the two basic international instruments directly imposing obligations upon South Africa, the Mandate and the Charter of the United Nations, as well as to the Universal Declaration of Human Rights. In another paragraph of the preamble the conclusion is reached that, after having insisted with no avail upon performance for more than twenty years, the moment has arrived for the General Assembly to exercise the right to treat such violation as a ground for termination.

93. In paragraph 3 of the operative part of the resolution the General Assembly "*Declares* that South Africa has failed to fulfil its obligations in respect of the administration of the Mandated Territory

and to ensure the moral and material well-being and security of the indigenous inhabitants of South West Africa and has, in fact, disavowed the Mandate". In paragraph 4 the decision is reached, as a consequence of the previous declaration "that the Mandate conferred upon His Britannic Majesty to be exercised on his behalf by the Government of the Union of South Africa is *therefore* terminated * * *". (Emphasis added.) It is this part of the resolution which is relevant in the present proceedings.

94. In examining this action of the General Assembly it is appropriate to have regard to the general principles of international law regulating termination of a treaty relationship on account of breach. For even if the mandate is viewed as having the character of an institution, as is maintained, it depends on those international agreements which created the system and regulated its application. As the Court indicated in 1962 "this Mandate, like practically all other similar Mandates" was "a special type of instrument composite in nature and instituting a novel international régime. It incorporates a definite agreement * * *" (I.C.J. Reports 1962, p. 331). The Court stated conclusively in that Judgment that the Mandate "* * * in fact and in law, is an international agreement having the character of a treaty or convention" (I.C.J. Reports 1962, p. 330). The rules laid down by the Vienna Convention on the Law of Treaties concerning termination of a treaty relationship on account of breach (adopted without a dissenting vote) may in many respects be considered as a codification of existing customary law on the subject. In the light of these rules, only a material breach of a treaty justifies termination, such breach being defined as:

    (a) a repudiation of the treaty not sanctioned by the present Convention; or

    (b) the violation of a provision essential to the accomplishment of the object or purpose of the treaty (Art. 60, para. 3).

95. General Assembly resolution 2145 (XXI) determines that both forms of material breach had occurred in this case. By stressing that South Africa "has, in fact, disavowed the Mandate", the General Assembly declared in fact that it had repudiated it. The resolution in question is therefore to be viewed as the exercise of the right to terminate a relationship in case of a deliberate and persistent violation of obligations which destroys the very object and purpose of that relationship.

* * *

100. The revocability of a mandate was envisaged by the first proposal which was made concerning a mandates system:

    "In case of any flagrant and prolonged abuse of this trust the population concerned should be able to appeal for redress to the League, who should in a proper case assert its authority to the full, even to the extent of removing the mandate and entrusting it to some other State if necessary." (J. C. Smuts, The League of Nations: A Practical Suggestion, 1918, pp. 21–22.)

Although this proposal referred to different territories, the principle remains the same. The possibility of revocation in the event of gross violation of the mandate was subsequently confirmed by authorities on international law and members of the Permanent Mandates Commission who interpreted and applied the mandates system under the League of Nations.

* * *

103. The Court is unable to appreciate the view that the General Assembly acted unilaterally as party and judge in its own cause. In the 1966 Judgment in the South West Africa cases, referred to above, it was found that the function to call for the due execution of the relevant provisions of the mandate instruments appertained to the League acting as an entity through its appropriate organs. The right of the League "in the pursuit of its collective, institutional activity, to require the due performance of the Mandate in discharge of the 'sacred trust'", was specifically recognized (ibid., p. 29). Having regard to this finding, the United Nations as a successor to the League, acting through its competent organs, must be seen above all as the supervisory institution, competent to pronounce, in that capacity, on the conduct of the mandatory with respect to its international obligations, and competent to act accordingly.

104. It is argued on behalf of South Africa that the consideration set forth in paragraph 3 of resolution 2145 (XXI) of the General Assembly, relating to the failure of South Africa to fulfil its obligations in respect of the administration of the mandated territory, called for a detailed factual investigation before the General Assembly could adopt resolution 2145 (XXI) or the Court pronounce upon its validity. The failure of South Africa to comply with the obligation to submit to supervision and to render reports, an essential part of the Mandate, cannot be disputed in the light of determinations made by this Court on more occasions than one. In relying on these, as on other findings of the Court in previous proceedings concerning South West Africa, the Court adheres to its own jurisprudence.

105. General Assembly resolution 2145 (XXI), after declaring the termination of the Mandate, added in operative paragraph 4 "that South Africa has no other right to administer the Territory". This part of the resolution has been objected to as deciding a transfer of territory. That in fact is not so. The pronouncement made by the General Assembly is based on a conclusion, referred to earlier, reached by the Court in 1950:

> "The authority which the Union Government exercises over the Territory is based on the Mandate. If the Mandate lapsed, as the Union Government contends, the latter's authority would equally have lapsed." (I.C.J. Reports 1950, p. 133.)

This was confirmed by the Court in its Judgment of 21 December 1962 in the South West Africa cases (Ethiopia v. South Africa; Liberia v. South Africa) (I.C.J. Reports 1962, p. 333). Relying on these decisions of the Court, the General Assembly declared that the Mandate having been terminated "South Africa has no other right to administer the Territory". This is not a finding on facts, but the formulation of a legal situation. For it would not be correct to assume that, because the General Assembly is in principle vested with recommendatory powers, it is debarred from adopting, in specific cases within the framework of its competence, resolutions which make determinations or have operative design.

106. By resolution 2145 (XXI) the General Assembly terminated the Mandate. However, lacking the necessary powers to ensure the withdrawal of South Africa from the Territory, it enlisted the cooperation of the Security Council by calling the latter's attention to the resolution, thus acting in accordance with Article 11, paragraph 2, of the Charter.

107. The Security Council responded to the call of the General Assembly. It "took note" of General Assembly resolution 2145 (XXI) in the preamble of its resolution 245 (1968); it took it "into account" in resolution 246 (1968); in resolutions 264 (1969) and 269 (1969) it adopted certain measures directed towards the implementation of General Assembly resolution 2145 (XXI) and, finally, in resolution 276 (1970), it reaffirmed resolution 264 (1969) and recalled resolution 269 (1969).

108. Resolution 276 (1970) of the Security Council, specifically mentioned in the text of the request, is the one essential for the purposes of the present advisory opinion. Before analysing it, however, it is necessary to refer briefly to resolutions 264 (1969) and 269 (1969), since these two resolutions have, together with resolution 276 (1970), a combined and a cumulative effect. Resolution 264 (1969), in paragraph 3 of its operative part, calls upon South Africa to withdraw its administration from Namibia immediately. Resolution 269 (1969), in view of South Africa's lack of compliance, after recalling the obligations of Members under Article 25 of the Charter, calls upon the Government of South Africa, in paragraph 5 of its operative part, "to withdraw its administration from the territory immediately and in any case before 4 October 1969". The preamble of resolution 276 (1970) reaffirms General Assembly resolution 2145 (XXI) and espouses it, by referring to the decision, not merely of the General Assembly, but of the United Nations "that the Mandate of South-West Africa was terminated". In the operative part, after condemning the non-compliance by South Africa with General Assembly and Security Council resolutions pertaining to Namibia, the Security Council declares, in paragraph 2, that "the continued presence of the South African authorities in Namibia is illegal" and that consequently all acts taken by the Government of South Africa "on behalf of or concerning

Namibia after the termination of the Mandate are illegal and invalid". In paragraph 5 the Security Council "Calls upon all States, particularly those which have economic and other interests in Namibia, to refrain from any dealings with the Government of South Africa which are inconsistent with operative paragraph 2 of this resolution".

109. It emerges from the communications bringing the matter to the Security Council's attention, from the discussions held and particularly from the text of the resolutions themselves, that the Security Council, when it adopted these resolutions, was acting in the exercise of what it deemed to be its primary responsibility, the maintenance of peace and security, which, under the Charter, embraces situations which might lead to a breach of the peace. (Art. 1, para. 1.) In the preamble of resolution 264 (1969) the Security Council was "Mindful of the grave consequences of South Africa's continued occupation of Namibia" and in paragraph 4 of that resolution it declared "that the actions of the Government of South Africa designed to destroy the national unity and territorial integrity of Namibia through the establishment of Bantustans are contrary to the provisions of the United Nations Charter". In operative paragraph 3 of resolution 269 (1969) the Security Council decided "that the continued occupation of the territory of Namibia by the South African authorities constitutes an aggressive encroachment on the authority of the United Nations * * *". In operative paragraph 3 of resolution 276 (1970) the Security Council declared further "that the defiant attitude of the Government of South Africa towards the Council's decisions undermines the authority of the United Nations".

110. As to the legal basis of the resolution, Article 24 of the Charter vests in the Security Council the necessary authority to take action such as that taken in the present case. The reference in paragraph 2 of this Article to specific powers of the Security Council under certain chapters of the Charter does not exclude the existence of general powers to discharge the responsibilities conferred in paragraph 1. Reference may be made in this respect to the Secretary-General's Statement, presented to the Security Council on 10 January 1947, to the effect that "the powers of the Council under Article 24 are not restricted to the specific grants of authority contained in Chapters VI, VII, VIII and XII * * * the Members of the United Nations have conferred upon the Security Council powers commensurate with its responsibility for the maintenance of peace and security. The only limitations are the fundamental principles and purposes found in Chapter I of the Charter."

111. As to the effect to be attributed to the declaration contained in paragraph 2 of resolution 276 (1970), the Court considers that the qualification of a situation as illegal does not by itself put an end to it. It can only be the first, necessary step in an endeavour to bring the illegal situation to an end.

112.   It would be an untenable interpretation to maintain that, once such a declaration had been made by the Security Council under Article 24 of the Charter, on behalf of all member States, those Members would be free to act in disregard of such illegality or even to recognize violations of law resulting from it.   When confronted with such an internationally unlawful situation, Members of the United Nations would be expected to act in consequence of the declaration made on their behalf.   The question therefore arises as to the effect of this decision of the Security Council for States Members of the United Nations in accordance with Article 25 of the Charter.

113.   It has been contended that Article 25 of the Charter applies only to enforcement measures adopted under Chapter VII of the Charter.   It is not possible to find in the Charter any support for this view.   Article 25 is not confined to decisions in regard to enforcement action but applies to "the decisions of the Security Council" adopted in accordance with the Charter.   Moreover, that Article is placed, not in Chapter VII, but immediately after Article 24 in that part of the Charter which deals with the functions and powers of the Security Council.   If Article 25 had reference solely to decisions of the Security Council concerning enforcement action under Articles 41 and 42 of the Charter, that is to say, if it were only such decisions which had binding effect, then Article 25 would be superfluous, since this effect is secured by Articles 48 and 49 of the Charter.

114.   It has also been contended that the relevant Security Council resolutions are couched in exhortatory rather than mandatory language and that, therefore, they do not purport to impose any legal duty on any State nor to affect legally any right of any State.   The language of a resolution of the Security Council should be carefully analysed before a conclusion can be made as to its binding effect.   In view of the nature of the powers under Article 25, the question whether they have been in fact exercised is to be determined in each case, having regard to the terms of the resolution to be interpreted, the discussions leading to it, the Charter provisions invoked and, in general, all circumstances that might assist in determining the legal consequences of the resolution of the Security Council.

115.   Applying these tests, the Court recalls that in the preamble of resolution 269 (1969), the Security Council was *"Mindful* of its responsibility to take necessary action to secure strict compliance with the obligations entered into by States Members of the United Nations under the provisions of Article 25 of the Charter of the United Nations".   The Court has therefore reached the conclusion that the decisions made by the Security Council in paragraphs 2 and 5 of resolutions 276 (1970), as related to paragraph 3 of resolution 264 (1969) and paragraph 5 of resolution 269 (1969), were adopted in conformity with the purposes and principles of the Charter and in accordance with its Articles 24 and 25.   The decisions are consequently binding on

all States Members of the United Nations, which are thus under obligation to accept and carry them out.

116. In pronouncing upon the binding nature of the Security Council decisions in question, the Court would recall the following passage in its Advisory Opinion of 11 April 1949 on Reparation for Injuries Suffered in the Service of the United Nations:

> The Charter has not been content to make the Organization created by it merely a centre 'for harmonizing the actions of nations in the attainment of these common ends' (Article 1, para. 4). It has equipped that centre with organs, and has given it special tasks. It has defined the position of the Members in relation to the Organization by requiring them to give it every assistance in any action undertaken by it (Article 2, para. 5), and to accept and carry out the decisions of the Security Council. (I.C.J. Reports 1949, p. 178.)

Thus when the Security Council adopts a decision under Article 25 in accordance with the Charter, it is for member States to comply with that decision, including those members of the Security Council which voted against it and those Members of the United Nations who are not members of the Council. To hold otherwise would be to deprive this principal organ of its essential functions and powers under the Charter.

117. Having reached these conclusions, the Court will now address itself to the legal consequences arising for States from the continued presence of South Africa in Namibia, notwithstanding Security Council resolution 276 (1970). A binding determination made by a competent organ of the United Nations to the effect that a situation is illegal cannot remain without consequence. Once the Court is faced with such a situation, it would be failing in the discharge of its judicial functions if it did not declare that there is an obligation, especially upon Members of the United Nations, to bring that situation to an end. As this Court has held, referring to one of its decisions declaring a situation as contrary to a rule of international law: "This decision entails a legal consequence, namely that of putting an end to an illegal situation" (I.C.J. Reports 1951, p. 82).

118. South Africa, being responsible for having created and maintained a situation which the Court has found to have been validly declared illegal, has the obligation to put an end to it. It is therefore under obligation to withdraw its administration from the Territory of Namibia. By maintaining the present illegal situation, and occupying the Territory without title, South Africa incurs international responsibilities arising from a continuing violation of an international obligation. It also remains accountable for any violations of its international obligations, or of the rights of the people of Namibia. The fact that South Africa no longer has any title to administer the Territory does not release it from its obligations and responsibilities under

international law towards other States in respect of the exercise of its powers in relation to this Territory. Physical control of a territory, and not sovereignty or legitimacy of title, is the basis of State liability for acts affecting other States.

119.   The member States of the United Nations are, for the reasons given in paragraph 115 above, under obligation to recognize the illegality and invalidity of South Africa's continued presence in Namibia. They are also under obligation to refrain from lending any support or any form of assistance to South Africa with reference to its occupation of Namibia, subject to paragraph 125 below.

120.   The precise determination of the acts permitted or allowed —what measures are available and practicable, which of them should be selected, what scope they should be given and by whom they should be applied—is a matter which lies within the competence of the appropriate political organs of the United Nations acting within their authority under the Charter. Thus it is for the Security Council to determine any further measures consequent upon the decisions already taken by it on the question of Namibia. In this context the Court notes that at the same meeting of the Security Council in which the request for advisory opinion was made, the Security Council also adopted resolution 283 (1970) which defined some of the steps to be taken. The Court has not been called upon to advise on the legal effects of that resolution.

121.   The Court will in consequence confine itself to giving advice on those dealings with the Government of South Africa which, under the Charter of the United Nations and general international law, should be considered as inconsistent with the declaration of illegality and invalidity made in paragraph 2 of resolution 276 (1970), because they may imply a recognition that South Africa's presence in Namibia is legal.

122.   For the reasons given above, and subject to the observations contained in paragraph 125 below, member States are under obligation to abstain from entering into treaty relations with South Africa in all cases in which the Government of South Africa purports to act on behalf of or concerning Namibia. With respect to existing bilateral treaties, member States must abstain from invoking or applying those treaties or provisions of treaties concluded by South Africa on behalf of or concerning Namibia which involve active intergovernmental cooperation. With respect to multilateral treaties, however, the same rule cannot be applied to certain general conventions such as those of a humanitarian character, the non-performance of which may adversely affect the people of Namibia. It will be for the competent international organs to take specific measures in this respect.

123.   Member States, in compliance with the duty of non-recognition imposed by paragraphs 2 and 5 of resolution 276 (1970), are under obligation to abstain from sending diplomatic or special missions to South Africa including in their jurisdiction the Territory of

Namibia, to abstain from sending consular agents to Namibia, and to withdraw any such agents already there. They should also make it clear to the South African authorities that the maintenance of diplomatic or consular relations with South Africa does not imply any recognition of its authority with regard to Namibia.

124. The restraints which are implicit in the non-recognition of South Africa's presence in Namibia and the explicit provisions of paragraph 5 of resolution 276 (1970) impose upon member States the obligation to abstain from entering into economic and other forms of relationship or dealings with South Africa on behalf of or concerning Namibia which may entrench its authority over the Territory.

125. In general, the non-recognition of South Africa's administration of the Territory should not result in depriving the people of Namibia of any advantages derived from international co-operation. In particular, while official acts performed by the Government of South Africa on behalf of or concerning Namibia after the termination of the Mandate are illegal and invalid, this invalidity cannot be extended to those acts, such as, for instance, the registration of births, deaths and marriages, the effects of which can be ignored only to the detriment of the inhabitants of the Territory.

126. As to non-member States, although not bound by Articles 24 and 25 of the Charter, they have been called upon in paragraphs 2 and 5 of resolution 276 (1970) to give assistance in the action which has been taken by the United Nations with regard to Namibia. In the view of the Court, the termination of the Mandate and the declaration of the illegality of South Africa's presence in Namibia are opposable to all States in the sense of barring erga omnes the legality of a situation which is maintained in violation of international law: in particular, no State which enters into relations with South Africa concerning Namibia may expect the United Nations or its Members to recognize the the validity or effects of such relationship, or of the consequences thereof. The Mandate having been terminated by decision of the international organization in which the supervisory authority over its administration was vested, and South Africa's continued presence in Namibia having been declared illegal, it is for non-member States to act in accordance with those decisions.

127. As to the general consequences resulting from the illegal presence of South Africa in Namibia, all States should bear in mind that the injured entity is a people which must look to the international community for assistance in its progress towards the goals for which the sacred trust was instituted.[a]

*   *   *

132. The Government of South Africa also submitted a request that a plebiscite should be held in the Territory of Namibia under the

a. Paragraphs 128 through 131 of the opinion are set forth at p. 619 in the context of the United Nations Charter obligations respecting human rights.

joint supervision of the Court and the Government of South Africa (para. 16 above). This proposal was presented in connection with the request to submit additional factual evidence and as a means of bringing evidence before the Court. The Court having concluded that no further evidence was required, that the Mandate was validly terminated and that in consequence South Africa's presence in Namibia is illegal and its acts on behalf of or concerning Namibia are illegal and invalid, it follows that it cannot entertain this proposal.

*   *   *

133.   For these reasons,

THE COURT IS OF OPINION, in reply to the question:

"What are the legal consequences for States of the continued presence of South Africa in Namibia, notwithstanding Security Council resolution 276 (1970)?"

by 13 votes to 2,

(1) that, the continued presence of South Africa in Namibia being illegal, South Africa is under obligation to withdraw its administration from Namibia immediately and thus put an end to its occupation of the Territory;

by 11 votes to 4,

(2) that States Members of the United Nations are under obligation to recognize the illegality of South Africa's presence in Namibia and the invalidity of its acts on behalf of or concerning Namibia, and to refrain from any acts and in particular any dealings with the Government of South Africa implying recognition of the legality of, or lending support or assistance to, such presence and administration;

(3) that it is incumbent upon States which are not Members of the United Nations to give assistance, within the scope of subparagraph (2) above, in the action which has been taken by the United Nations with regard to Namibia.

[A declaration and separate and dissenting opinions omitted.]

---

1.   *Security Council action.* By Resolution 301 (1971) of October 20, 1971 [Resolutions and Decisions of the Security Council, 1971, Sec. Council Off. Rec., 26th year p. 7], the Security Council took note "with appreciation" of the advisory opinion and stated that it agreed

with its opinion as expressed in paragraph 133. It called upon South
Africa to withdraw from the Territory of Namibia and further:

    11. Calls upon all States, in the discharge of their responsi-
bilities towards the people of Namibia and subject to the exceptions set forth in paragraphs 122 and 125 of the advisory opinion
of 21 June 1971:

    (a) To abstain from entering into treaty relations with
South Africa in all cases in which the Government of South
Africa purports to act on behalf of or concerning Namibia;

    (b) To abstain from invoking or applying those treaties or
provisions of treaties concluded by South Africa on behalf of
or concerning Namibia which involve active intergovernmental
co-operation;

    (c) To review their bilateral treaties with South Africa in
order to ensure that they are not inconsistent with paragraphs 5
and 6 above;

    (d) To abstain from sending diplomatic or special missions
to South Africa that include the Territory of Namibia in their
jurisdiction;

    (e) To abstain from sending consular agents to Namibia
and to withdraw any such agents already there;

    (f) To abstain from entering into economic and other forms
of relationship or dealings with South Africa on behalf of or
concerning Namibia which may entrench its authority over the
Territory;

    12. Declares that franchises, rights, titles or contracts re-
lating to Namibia granted to individuals or companies by South
Africa after the adoption of the General Assembly resolution 2145
(XXI) are not subject to protection or espousal by their States
against claims of a future lawful Government of Namibia
* * *.

The resolution was adopted by a vote of 13 to none, with France
and the United Kingdom abstaining.

The South African position has remained unchanged.

    2. *Legal basis for actions by the General Assembly and the Se-
curity Council of the United Nations.* Was the action of the assembly
in terminating the Mandate legislative in character or can it be explained as merely the act of a party to an agreement declaring that, in
its opinion, the agreement has been terminated by the other party's
breach?

Is the court's view, in paragraphs 109, 110, 113 and 115, of the
power of the Security Council to make legally binding decisions jus-

tified by the Charter? If the Security Council is not limited to making binding decisions only in Chapter VII cases involving breaches of the peace, what are the limits now? Must it be acting in the "maintenance of international peace and security," under the first paragraph of Article 24? Or is it limited only by the "fundamental principles and purposes found in Chapter 1 of the Charter"? See paragraph 110 of the court's opinion. If such an expansive reading is possible, then the limits are (a) formal, i. e., the existence of the veto, and (b) practical, i. e., the unwillingness of the council to exercise force to enforce even its legally binding resolutions.

Do you view an expanded interpretation of the Security Council's power to render binding decisions a desirable development? Would your view be the same if your country was not a permanent member of the Security Council?

*

INDEX

END OF VOLUME